Dictionary of the Literature of the Iberian Peninsula

Dictionary of the Literature of the Iberian Peninsula

L–Z

EDITED BY
Germán Bleiberg, Maureen Ihrie, and Janet Pérez

GREENWOOD PRESS
Westport, Connecticut • London

Publisher's Note: This reference work was initiated with the distinguished scholar Germán Bleiberg, but due to his ill health (and subsequent death), Maureen Ihrie took over its editorial direction, later bringing in a colleague, Janet Pérez. As publisher of this volume, we wish to acknowledge our profound appreciation of the extraordinary effort Dr. Ihrie put into this project. Without her dedication, this project would never have seen print.

Library of Congress Cataloging-in-Publication Data

Dictionary of the literature of the Iberian peninsula / edited by
Germán Bleiberg, Maureen Ihrie, and Janet Pérez.
p. cm.
Includes bibliographical references.
1. Spain—Literatures—Dictionaries. 2. Spain—Literatures—Bio-bibliography—Dictionaries. 3. Portugal—Literatures—Dictionaries. 4. Portugal—Literatures—Bio-bibliography—Dictionaries. I. Bleiberg, Germán. II. Ihrie, Maureen. III. Pérez, Janet.
PN849.S6D54 1993
860′.03—dc20 90–2755
ISBN 0–313–21302–X (set : alk. paper)
ISBN 0–313–28731–7 (v. 1 : lib. bdg. : alk. paper)
ISBN 0–313–28732–5 (v. 2 : alk. paper)

British Library Cataloguing in Publication Data is available.

Library of Congress Catalog Card Number: 90–2755
ISBN: 0–313–21302–X (set)
ISBN: 0–313–28731–7 (vol. 1)
ISBN: 0–313–28732–5 (vol. 2)

First published in 1993

Greenwood Press, 88 Post Road West, Westport, CT 06881
An imprint of Greenwood Publishing Group, Inc.

Printed in the United States of America

The paper used in this book complies with the Permanent Paper Standard issued by the National Information Standards Organization (Z39.48–1984).

10 9 8 7 6 5 4 3 2 1

The editors would like to dedicate the dictionary to the memory of Germán Bleiberg, whose life and work enriched us all so very much.

Contents

Contributors

Samuel Amell
Ohio State U

Joseph R. Arboleda
Lafayette College

Samuel G. Armistead
U of California, Davis

Pamela Bacarisse
U of Pittsburgh

Emilie Bergmann
U of California, Berkeley

Maryellen Bieder
Indiana U

Frieda H. Blackwell
Howard Payne U

Germán Bleiberg
(deceased) SUNY Albany

Peter Bly
Queen's U

Carole Bradford
Bowling Green State U

Mary Lee Bretz
Rutgers U

James F. Brown
Isidore Newman School

Donald C. Buck
Auburn U

Israel Burshatin
Haverford College

Rosario Cambria
Baldwin-Wallace College

Anthony J. Cárdenas
U of New Mexico

Manuela Renata Valente de Carvalho
Vanderbilt U

C. Maurice Cherry
Furman U

Victoria Codina-Espurz
U of Pittsburgh

Deborah Compte
Trenton State College

Porter Conerly
(*no affiliation*)

Joanna Courteau
Iowa State U

Betty Jean Craige
U of Georgia

Sydney Cravens
Texas Tech U

Anne Cruz
U of California, Irvine

Eugene Del Vecchio
U of Maine

Angelo DiSalvo
Indiana State U

Brian Dutton
U of Wisconsin

Cristina Enríquez
U of Minnesota

Frances Bell Exum
Winthrop College

William Ferguson
Clark U

Elisa Fernández Cambria
Cleveland State U

Dario Fernández-Morera
Northwestern U

Joseph A. Feustle
U of Toledo

Peter Fothergill-Payne
U of Calgary

E. Inman Fox
Northwestern U

Natércia Fraga
(No affiliation)

David Frier
U of Glasgow

Carolyn Galerstein
U of Texas at Dallas (recently deceased)

Salvador García Castañeda
Ohio State U

David Thatcher Gies
U of Virginia

Joan Gilabert
U of Arizona

Judith Ginsberg
(no affiliation)

Richard Glenn
U of Alabama

Alan A. González
North Carolina State U (emeritus)

Luis F. González-Cruz
Pennsylvania State U

Luis T. González-del-Valle
U of Colorado

James Ray Green
Boston U

Patricia Grieve
Columbia U

Reginetta Haboucha
Herbert H. Lehman College

Martha T. Halsey
Pennsylvania State U

Russell G. Hamilton
Vanderbilt U

Andrea Warren Hamos
Assumption College

David K. Herzberger
U of Connecticut

Elizabeth T. Howe
Tufts U

James Iffland
Boston U

Maureen Ihrie
Kansas State U

Estelle Irizarry
Georgetown U

Salvador Jiménez Fajardo
SUNY Binghamton

Roberta Johnson
U of Kansas

Harold G. Jones
Syracuse U

Margaret E. W. Jones
U of Kentucky

Theodore L. Kassier
U of Alaska, Anchorage

Charles King
U of Colorado

Edmund L. King
Princeton U (emeritus)

Willard F. King
Bryn Mawr College

Kathleen L. Kirk
(no affiliation)

Robert Kirsner
U of Miami

Kathleen Kish
U of North Carolina

Dennis Klein
U of South Dakota

Robert R. Krueger
U of Northern Iowa

Joy Buckles Landeira
(no affiliation)

Ricardo Landeira
U of Colorado

Catherine Larson
Indiana U

Robert E. Lewis
Simon's Rock of Bard College

Margarita Lezcano
Eckerd College

Gabriel Lovett
Wellesley College (emeritus)

Drosoula Lytra
City College CUNY

G. Grant MacCurdy
California State U

Ann L. MacKenzie
Liverpool University

Linda Maier
Wake Forest U

Howard Mancing
Purdue U

Robert Manteiga
U of Rhode Island

Kathleen March
U of Maine

Fernando J. B. Martiñho
(no affiliation)

Luis Martul Tobío
(no affiliation)

Carmen Chaves McClendon
U of Georgia

Douglas McKay
U of Colorado at Colorado Springs

Kathleen McNerney
West Virginia U

Isabel McSpadden
Texas Tech U

Hector Medina
Rhode Island College

Maria Rosa Menocal
Yale U

Martha Miller
U of North Carolina at Charlotte

Stephen Miller
Texas A. and M. U

Harold K. Moon
Brigham Young U

Eunice D. Myers
Wichita State U

Eric Naylor
U of the South

Esther Nelson
California State U at Northridge

Colbert Nepaulsingh
SUNY Albany

Geraldine Nichols
U of Florida

D. J. O'Connor
U of New Orleans, Lakefront

Patricia W. O'Connor
U of Cincinnati

Fernando Operé
U of Virginia

Nelson Orringer
U of Connecticut

José Ortega
U of Wisconsin, Parkside

Marie-Sol Ortolá
U of Connecticut

María Teresa Pajares
U of Georgia

Gilbert Paolini
Tulane U

Carlos J. Pereira
(no affiliation)

Genaro J. Pérez
U of Texas at Permian Basin

Janet Pérez
Texas Tech U

Daniel Pires
U of East Asia

Peter L. Podol
Lock Haven U

Phoebe Porter Medina
U of New Hampshire

Kay Pritchett
U of Arkansas

Helen H. Reed
Syracuse U

Elizabeth Rhodes
Boston College

Laura Rivkin-Golden
U of Colorado, Boulder

Nicholas Round
U of Glasgow

Anna Sánchez Rue
(no affiliation)

Pilar Sáenz
George Washington U

María A. Salgado
U of North Carolina

Jana Sandarg
Augusta College

Robert Sandarg
Paine College

Veronica Sauter
(no affiliation)

Raymond Sayers
Queens College CUNY

Stacey Schlau
West Chester U

Kessel Schwartz
U of Miami

Sara Schyfter
SUNY Albany

Isabel Segura
(no affiliation)

Dennis P. Seniff
Michigan State U (deceased)

Leopoldo Serrão
(no affiliation)

Nina Shecktor
Kutztown U

George Shipley
U of Washington

Jaime H. da Silva
U de Puerto Rico

Lucy Sponsler
U of New Orleans

María Stycos
Cornell U

Catherine Swietlicki
U of Wisconsin, Madison

Robert ter Horst
U of Rochester

Currie K. Thompson
Gettysburg College

Leslie P. Turano
Girton College

John Turner
Bowdoin College

Noël M. Valis
Johns Hopkins U

John E. Varey
Editor, Tamesis Books Ltd.

Louise O. Vasvari
SUNY Stony Brook

Gloria Feiman Waldman
York College, CUNY

Merry Wheaton
(no affiliation)

John Wilcox
U of Illinois, Urbana-Champaign

Victoria Wolff Unruh
U of Kansas

Frederick G. Williams
U of California, Santa Barbara

Phyllis Zatlin
Rutgers U

Marielena Zelaya Kolker
(no affiliation)

Preface

The goal of this reference work, which was begun in the late 1970s, is to acquaint a wider audience with the rich history of literary achievements in the Iberian Peninsula. It is a sad fact that the contributions of Iberian-born writers continue to be largely unknown territory for most European and American readers. The *Dictionary of the Literature of the Iberian Peninsula* is intended to ease access to such writers and movements. We have defined literature in a broad sense, to include historical, religious, cultural, and philosophical writings as well as prose, poetry, and drama. Entries on selected literary movements, styles, and literatures have been included, as have a limited number of definitions pertinent to literary or cultural terms.

The point of departure for the present work and a guide in determining format was the classic *Diccionario de literatura española* by Germán Bleiberg and Julián Marías. Many changes were made in coverage, however, particularly the exclusion of Spanish-American writers and foreign-born Hispanists of this century. Major emphases in new entries are writers in other languages of the peninsula (in addition to Spanish) and updated coverage to better represent authors of the second half of the twentieth century, including many who have become recognized as important only in the last two decades. While all major entries have been reworked, and many entries are entirely new, others, especially those on lesser figures, are based largely on former editions of the Bleiberg and Marías *Diccionario*.

The present *Dictionary* generally includes literature from the tenth century to the mid–1980s. With a very few exceptions, it is limited to writers born in the Iberian Peninsula. Unlike similar reference works, this one includes representatives from all major peninsular literatures: Catalan, Galician, Portuguese, and Spanish. Where contributors have been available for the lesser vernacular languages, we have included their entries, but systematic coverage of these languages has not been possible. Some literatures are covered less comprehensively than we would have wished, but what is included constitutes a solid advance in presenting otherwise generally underrepresented literatures—Portuguese, Catalan, and Gallego—in an English-oriented work. The *Dictionary* also devotes more attention to writings by traditionally neglected or forgotten female authors, especially those of the twentieth century. Consistent, broad-based coverage has been our general goal, but by no means is this dictionary to be considered comprehensive or all-inclusive. Ultimately, constrictions of time and space and a shortage of willing contributors became determining factors in delimiting content. Many entries originally commissioned were not done by those who had agreed to do them, with the result that some had to be done very late and hastily by the editors to prevent exclusion. And, as one might expect, there are inevitable sins of omission and commission on our part.

The *Dictionary* has been compiled to appeal to users ranging from English-speaking nonspecialists to scholars of Iberian literature. To address needs of the former group, virtually all literary titles have been followed in the text with either a published translation or a literal rendering of the original, and an effort has been made to list existing English translations of works in the Bibliography. To ensure the *Dictionary*'s value to specialists, virtually all major entries have been composed by noted scholars and are complemented by bibliographies of primary texts and selected critical studies, as well as the earlier-mentioned translations. The citations are as complete as possible. Because the limitations imposed by the formats of all dictionaries and reference works necessarily exclude anything other than selected bibliography, we have emphasized items on the basis of accessibility and representativeness wherever choices were made.

More than 140 experts contributed their labor and expertise to this work, and we are proud of the caliber of scholars who joined together to compile it. Although many individuals made numerous and significant contributions to the Spanish section of the *Dictionary*, they compose a group too large to mention individually. We do wish to mention those authors who contributed to literatures not covered in the original *Diccionario*: Joan Gilabert, for many Catalan entries, Peter Fothergill-Payne, for coverage of Portuguese literature, Kathleen McNerney, for contributions of Catalan and Galician female writers, and Kathleen March, for many Galician entries. Gratitude is also due to Sara Schyfter for her assistance in launching the project. We thank all of the contributors for their help, and many others who eased our work by suggesting likely contributors, editing the manuscript, typing, and so forth. We would also like to thank various institutions for their support: Union College granted a summer stipend to help support research of minor entries; Lafayette College awarded funds for typing, research assistance for one semester, and much interlibrary loan and photocopying support; the Graduate School of Texas Tech University subvened substantial duplication and mailing expenses; Kansas State University granted funds to process the copyedited manuscript and to prepare the *Dictionary*'s index. We also thank Greenwood Press for its patient commitment to this task.

GENERAL FORMAT OF ENTRIES

1. Biographical entries first give the person's name, in inverted order with the last name capitalized, followed by any pseudonym, dates and places of birth

and death—or active period—and then a short phrase identifying the person and/or field of activity. If the author is better known under a pseudonym, the pseudonym will come before the real name in the entry. Important "less-preferred" names, pseudonym or real, will be cross-referenced to the main entry. Punctuation is consistent with the following example:

> **CLARÍN,** pseudonym of Leopoldo Alas (1852, Zamora–1909, Oviedo), critic and novelist.

Although diacritical marks are not customarily placed on capitalized letters, they are here indicated in names and words at the beginning of each entry in order to assist in pronunciation.

2. If the entry is the title of a work or name of an institution, it is followed by a translation to English, pertinent dates as appropriate, and a brief explanation. For example:

> ***MISERIA DE OMNE, Libro de*** (Book of Man's Misery), anonymous mid- to late-fourteenth-c. narrative poem.

or

> ***MESTER DE CLERECÍA*** (Craft of Clerks or Clerics), a medieval form of verse.

3. Within the main text of each entry, titles authored by the subject of the entry are followed by a translation to English placed within parentheses. Where possible, publication, or sometimes composition, dates are indicated immediately *before* the translation to English. If a published English translation of a work has been found, that title is given, underlined, and followed by the date of publication. If no published translation has been located, a literal rendering of the original is given without italics (or, in the case of poems, without quotations). Titles of journals, newspapers, and so forth, in an entry are not generally translated, unless they are pertinent to the subject. The entry of a translated work appears as follows:

> ***SU ÚNICO HIJO*** (1891; *His Only Son*, 1980).

An untranslated work is listed according to the following example:

> ***LA PALABRA EN LA REALIDAD*** (1963; The Word in Reality).

When titles are names of people, places, or characters, they generally are not translated unless a published translation exists. Quotes are translated.

4. Most entries conclude with a three-part bibliography. Section A lists main primary texts or additional titles not discussed in the body of the entry. Section B contains translations to English of any primary texts. Section C indicates

pertinent critical studies in any language but emphasizing English where available. Sections A and B are arranged alphabetically by titles and followed by editor, translator, and so forth. Section C is arranged alphabetically by author. Where extensive bibliography exists, we have had to be selective for reasons of space. We have attempted to make citations complete, but here, too, explanation is in order. The long period of time (more than a decade) required for completion of this task has meant that some entries done early in the process are not entirely up to the moment bibliographically. Although on-line computer searches on each entry might theoretically have remedied some of this, the editors had no funds available for this endeavor. The time elapsed since original submission of certain entries has also meant in the cases of some contemporary writers that significant recent events (major awards, death of author, etc.) may not be indicated. For obvious reasons, we could not rectify all such problems.

5. The English alphabetical order has been followed; thus, CH and LL are not treated as separate letters but are interfiled appropriately.

6. Regarding the names of religious figures, custom exercises a strong role in determining whether a writer such as San Juan de la Cruz, Sta. Teresa de Jesús, or Fray Luis de León is indexed by his or her first or last name. In general, we have followed Spanish usage and employed cross-referencing to guide readers.

7. Cross-referencing has been indicated with asterisks. If a person, topic, or such, that appears as a main entry elsewhere in the *Dictionary* is mentioned in an article, at the first incidence of the term an asterisk is placed immediately before the part of the name or title under which it is entered. If there are other complementary subjects or titles not mentioned in the text of a particular entry, they will be listed at the end of the entry's text. For example:

> ***CABALLERO DEL CISNE, Leyenda del*** (Legend of the Knight of the Swan), a tale which first appeared in Germany and then in other countries. . . . The legend, closely allied with the French epic, appeared in Spain in the pseudo-history *La gran *conquista del Ultramar* (c. 1300; The Great Conquest of the Holy Land).

In a few cases plural forms of an entry have been asterisked, although the entry is entered in its singular form.

8. Entry authorship is indicated at the conclusion of each article. When no author is indicated, the responsibility is that of the editors.

Abbreviations

abr.	abridged, abridgment
anon.	anonymous
bibliog.	bibliography, bibliographic
bio.	biography
c.	century, circa
cf.	*confer*, compare
ch.	chapter(s)
comp.	compiled, compiler
cont.	continued
d.	deceased
e.g.	*exempli gratia*, for example
ed.	editor, edited by, edition
et al.	*et alii*, and others
facs.	facsimile
ff.	following
fl.	flourished
i.e.	*id est*, that is
il.	illustrated, illustrated by
intro.	introduction
l., ll.	line, lines
lges.	languages
lit.	literature
ms., mss.	manuscript, manuscripts
n.	note(s)
n.d.	no date
n.p.	no place of publication, no publisher, no pages

P	Press
pref.	preface
prol.	prologue
pseud.	pseudonym
pub.	publication, published
repub.	republished
rev.	revised, revised by, revision
rpt.	reprint
sel.	selected by, selection
ss.	following
st.	stanza
supp.	supplement
tr.	translated by
U	University
UNESCO	United Nations Educational, Scientific and Cultural Organization
UP	University Press
vol(s).	volume(s)

JOURNALS, PUBLISHERS, AND SERIES

BAE	Biblioteca de Autores Españoles
BBMP	*Boletín de la Biblioteca Menéndez Pelayo*
BH	*Bulletin Hispanique*
BHS	*Bulletin of Hispanic Studies*
BRAE	*Boletín de la Real Academia Española*
BRAH	*Boletín de la Real Academia de Historia*
BSS	*Bulletin of Spanish Studies*
CH	*Cuadernos Hispanoamericanos*
CSIC	Consejo Superior de Investigaciones Científicas
DA	*Dissertation Abstracts*
DAI	*Dissertation Abstracts International*
EDHASA	Editora y Distribuidora Hispano Americana, S.A.
HR	*Hispanic Review*
HSMS	Hispanic Seminar of Medieval Studies
JHP	*Journal of Hispanic Philology*
JSS:TC	*Journal of Spanish Studies: Twentieth Century*
KRQ	*Kentucky Romance Quarterly*
MLN	*Modern Language Notes*

MLR	*Modern Language Review*
MLS	*Modern Language Studies*
NBAE	Nueva Biblioteca de Autores Españoles
NRFH	*Nueva Revista de Filología Hispánica*
PUF	Presses Universitaires de France
RABM	Revista de Archivos, Bibliotecas y Museos
RAE	Real Academia Española
RAH	Real Academia de la Historia
RCEH	*Revista Canadiense de Estudios Hispánicos*
REH	*Revista de Estudios Hispánicos*
RFE	*Revista de Filología Española*
RFH	*Revista de Filología Hispánica*
RH	*Revue Hispanique*
RHM	*Revista Hispánica Moderna*
RN	*Romance Notes*
RO	Revista de Occidente
RPH	*Romance Philology*
RR	*Romance Review*
SBE	Sociedad de Bibliófilos Españoles
SUNY	State University of New York
TLS	*Times Literary Supplement*
TWAS	Twayne's World Authors Series
UNAM	Universidad Nacional Autónoma de México
UCLA	University of California, Los Angeles
UNCSRLL	University of North Carolina Series in Romance Languages and Literatures
YFS	*Yale French Studies*

L

LABORDA MEDIR, Clemencia (1908, Lérida–1980, Madrid), Spanish poet and playwright. Although born in a province of Catalonia, she grew up mainly in Castile. She was not a university graduate, but largely self-taught, reading especially poets she admired such as *Jiménez and *García Lorca. Although most of her poetry treats traditional themes—religion, love, family—she also wrote civil and occasional poetry, and lived long enough to include the space age and man's reaching the moon among her later subjects. Laborda's theater was essentially Catholic in inspiration, and includes *La sacristía* (1957; The Sacristy), her first play staged in Madrid in 1953, which treats the expiation of a crime of passion. For a number of other plays, no information is available beyond the titles: *Aniversario de bodas* (Wedding Anniversary), *Don Juan en la niebla* (Don Juan in the Fog), *En media hora de sueño* (In a Half Hour of Dreaming), *Fachada a la calle* (Facade Overlooking the Street), *Laura y el ángel* (Laura and the Angel) and *Una familia ideal* (An Ideal Family), reportedly inspired by *Pride and Prejudice*. Laborda also authored a number of novels, mentioned by titles only in *Women Writers of Spain*: *Historia de una niña* (Story of a Girl), and *El sobrino* (The Nephew). Her first book of poetry, religious in inspiration and classical in form, *Jardines bajo la lluvia* (1943; Gardens beneath the Rain), was well received critically. Among her other poetic works are *Caudal* (n.d.; Treasury), *Ciudad de soledades* (1948; City of Solitudes); *Retorno a la provincia* (1961; Return to the Province), *Niños y jardines* (n.d.; Children and Gardens), and *Tiempo del hombre, tiempo de Dios* (1972; Man's Time, God's Time).

BIBLIOGRAPHY

Primary Texts

Jardines bajo la lluvia. Madrid: Aguado, 1943.
Retorno a la provincia. Caracas: Lírica Hispana, 1961.
La sacristía. Madrid: Escelicer, 1957.

Criticism

Galerstein, C. L., and K. McNerney. *Women Writers of Spain*. Westport, CT: Greenwood, 1986.

Janet Pérez

LACACI, María Elvira (192?, El Ferrol, Galicia–), Spanish poet. Lacaci began publishing at the time she moved to Madrid in 1952, when the dominant mode in Spanish literature, poetry included, was social realism. Although she was grouped with the social poets during the 1950s, much of her poetry is concerned with religious themes, the search for God, and presence of the deity in everyday life. That part of her poetry which seemingly coincides with the aims of so-called critical realism (veiled denunciation of the Franco regime) consists largely of descriptions of social outcasts, victims of socio-economic injustice, poverty and pain. The devoutly Christian tone of the poetic persona contrasts with the impassiveness or subdued irony of many other "social" poets, although they coincide in defending human rights, in feelings of solidarity with humanity at large, and sympathy for the poor and downtrodden. Lacaci's first published collection, *Humana voz* (1957; Human Voice), contains thirty-eight poems and presents many urban scenes from mass transport to movie theaters, accentuating the collectivity yet stressing the presence of a protective, benevolent divinity. *Sonido de Dios* (1962; The Sound of God) deals with various aspects of the poetic persona's relationship with God, from search to encounter and moments of illumination. *Al este de la ciudad* (1963; To the East of the City), Lacaci's longest work, is more or less equally divided between works of religious inspiration and expressions of sympathy for the unfortunate and suffering.

BIBLIOGRAPHY

Primary Texts

Al este de la ciudad. Barcelona: Flors, 1963.
Humana voz. Madrid: Rialp, 1957.
Sonido de Dios. Madrid: Rialp, 1962.

Criticism

Cano, José Luis. *Poesía española contemporánea: Generaciones de posguerra*. Madrid: Guadarrama, 1974. 181–88.

Janet Pérez

LACASA, Cristina (1929, Tarrasca–), Spanish poet and short story writer. A very lyrical, personal and independent poet, she has worked largely in isolation from poetic groups and movements, although occasionally approaching some of the "testimonial" themes of the so-called mid-century generation; however, her testimony is individual, personal rather than collective, and much more positive in tone. *La voz oculta* (1953; The Occult Voice), autobiographical and post-Romantic, echoes *Bécquer in its concern with the themes of love and poetry. *Los brazos en estela* (1958; Arms in the Wake) is a hopeful celebration of life whose point of departure is childhood memories, the present dreams, and the future, a hope of fulfillment. *Un resplandor que no perdonó la noche* (1961; A Fiery Glow Which Did Not Pardon the Night) is concerned with the joys and sorrows of life, treated from a fresh and optimistic perspective. One of Lacasa's most autobiographical and confessional works is *Con el sudor alzado* (1964; With Sweat Raised), with emphasis upon her life's ambitions and failures. *Poemas de la muerte y de la vida* (1966; Poems of Death and of Life) is one of the high points of Lacasa's production, an inward-turning meditation upon the eternal poetic themes of love, life and death. Her following work is profoundly pacifistic, *Encender los olivos como lámparas* (1969; To Light the Olive Branches like Lamps), expressing her opposition to violence, war and brutality. Other poetry collections include *Ha llegado la hora* (1971; The Hour Has Arrived), *Opalos del instante* (1982; Opals of the Instant), *En un plural designio* (1983; In a Plural Design), and *Ramas de la esperanza (Poemas ecológicos)* (1984; Branches of Hope [Ecological Poems]). Lacasa's short story collections are *Jinetes sin caballo* (1979; Riders without a Horse) and *Los caballos sin bridas* (1981; Horses without Reins).

BIBLIOGRAPHY

Primary Texts

En un plural designio. Carboneras, Cuenca: El Toro de Barro, 1983.
Encender los olivos como lámparas. Madrid: Agora, 1969.
Jinetes sin caballo. Barcelona: Ambito Literario, 1979.
Opalos del instante. Madrid: Rialp (Adonais), 1982.
Poemas de la muerte y de la vida. Lérida: Diputación Provincial, 1966.

Janet Pérez

LAFFÓN, Rafael (1900, Seville–1978, Seville), poet, with euphuistic tendencies, derived from *Modernism. His writing gradually became more humane and simple. His works, some of which have been translated to French, Italian, and Belgian, include *Cráter* (1921; Crater), *Signo más* (1927; Plus Sign), *Identidad* (1934; Identity), *Romances y madrigales* (1944; Ballads and Madrigals), *Vigilia del jazmín* (1952; Vigil of Jasmine), *La rama ingrata* (1959; The Ungrateful Branch), and *La cicatriz y el reino* (1964; The Scar and the Kingdom). In 1958 he was awarded a National Literature Prize.

BIBLIOGRAPHY

Primary Texts

La cicatriz y el reino. Seville: Muestra, 1964.
Identidad. Madrid: Literatura, 1934.
La rama ingrata. Sel., prol. F. López Estrada. Madrid: Agora, 1959.

Signo más. Seville: Mediodía, 1927.
Vigilia del jazmín. Valencia: Alfonso el magnánimo, 1952.

Isabel McSpadden

LAFORET, Carmen (1921, Barcelona–), Spanish novelist and short story writer. One of the first promising new writers to appear after the Spanish Civil War, she won the first Nadal Prize with *Nada* (1944; *Andrea*, 1964) when only twenty-three. This autobiographically structured novel re-creates the story of a young woman from the Canary Islands who comes to post-war Barcelona to live with relatives and attend the U in the immediate post-war years (as did the author herself). The dirty, over-crowded, run-down house crammed with unpleasant or eccentric relatives, and Andrea's own hunger and frustration, contrast sharply with the lives of more fortunate classmates. An unexpected family tragedy precipitates her leaving for Madrid to begin anew. The elements of violence, despair, solitude, alienation and psychological abnormalities found in this work (which once contributed to its being classed as *tremendista*) are also present in *La isla y los demonios* (1952; The Island and the Demons), set in the Canary Islands and constituting something of a prelude for *Nada*, although the characters are not the same. Laforet's third novel, *La mujer nueva* (1956; The New Woman), is the result of a religious experience, and reaffirms essential Catholic spiritual and moral values. Featuring an older feminine protagonist, it portrays via flashbacks some twenty years of the woman's life from freedom bordering on license during the Republic, to the restrictions placed on women by the Franco regime, a contrast complicated by a civil marriage (no longer recognized). *La insolación* (1963; Sunstroke) was announced as the first of a trilogy, but subsequent volumes have yet to appear.

Laforet is well known for her short stories and novels, in which she masterfully condenses the best features of the more extensive works. *La muerta* (1952; The Dead Woman) and *La llamada* (1954; The Call) are short fiction collections containing some of the best of Laforet. *Paralelo 35* (1967; The 35th Parallel) comprises commentaries on Laforet's trip to the United States, and interests mainly for revelation of her likes and dislikes. She has written essentially nothing since, excepting a few newspaper articles. *La niña y otros relatos* (1970; The Girl and Other Tales) is a collection of stories previously published in other collections.

Best known for her portrayal of women and adolescents, Laforet excels in psychological characterization. Themes of hunger, poverty, solitude, alienation, the need for love, the nurturing character of woman, moral dilemmas, and rites of passage are constant elements in her works. Basically realistic, the exaggerations or distorted emphasis in her descriptive passages reinforce the psychological perspective by externalizing via style the options or emotions of the protagonists.

BIBLIOGRAPHY

Primary Texts

Nada. Barcelona: Destino, 1945. 25th ed., 1979.
Novelas I. 12th ed. Barcelona: Planeta, "Clásicos Contemporáneos," 1977. Contains all of Laforet's fiction to date.

English Translation

Andrea. Tr. Charles F. Payne. New York: Vantage, 1964.

Criticism

Decoster, Cyrus C. "Carmen Laforet: A Tentative Evaluation." *Hispania* 40 (1957): 187–91.
El Saffar, Ruth. "Structural and Thematic Tactics of Suppression in Carmen Laforet's *Nada*." *Symposium* 28 (1974): 119–29.
Galerstein, Carolyn. "Carmen Laforet and the Spanish Spinster." *Revista de Estudios Hispánicos* 11 (1977): 303–15.
Johnson, Roberta. *Carmen Laforet*. Boston: G. K. Hall, 1981.
Jones, Margaret E. W. "Dialectical Movement as Feminist Technique in the Works of Carmen Laforet." In *Studies in Honor of Gerald E. Wade*. Madrid: Jose Porrúa Turanzas, 1979. 109–20.
Ullman, Pierre L. "The Moral Structure of Carmen Laforet's Novels." In *The Vision Obscured: Perceptions of Some Twentieth Century Catholic Novelists*. New York: Fordham UP, 1970. 201–19.

Margaret E.W. Jones

LAFUENTE, Modesto (1806, Rabanal de los Caballeros, Palencia–1866, Madrid), costumbrista (*Romanticism), essayist, reformer and teacher. After studying for the priesthood, he launched a literary and political career, discovering his métier in a mildly satirical, jocose prose style that portrayed political foibles of his day. The *Periódico Satírico de Política y Costumbres* (1837–44; Satirical Newspaper of Politics and Mores), also known as *Capilladas* (The Monk's Cowl), published under the pseudonym Fray Gerundio, exposes political intrigues and poverty. Better known today as a minor genre writer, in his *Teatro social del siglo XIX* (1846; Nineteenth-century Social Theater) he analyzes social structures within the ideology of reformism, while in *Viaje aerostático de Fray Gerundio y Tirabeque* (1847; Brother Gerundio's and Tirabeque's Aerostatic Journey) the protagonists contrast aspects of Spanish life. He also authored the *Revista Europea* (1848; European Journal) and *Viajes de Fray Gerundio por Francia, Bélgica, Holanda y orillas del Rhin* (1843; Brother Gerundio's Journeys through France, Belgium, Holland, and the Banks of the Rhine). Elected to a chair at the Academy of History, he wrote *Historia general de España* (1850–59; A General History of Spain), which evinces a lucid prose style.

BIBLIOGRAPHY

Primary Texts

Fray Gerundio. Periódico Satírico de Política y Costumbres. 2nd ed. 15 vols. Madrid: Mellado, 1839–44.
Historia general de España. Madrid: Mellado, 1859.
Teatro social del siglo XIX. 2 vols. Madrid: Mellado, 1846.
Viaje aerostático de Fray Gerundio y Tirabeque. Madrid: Mellado, 1847.

Criticism

Alonso Cabeza, María D. "Costumbrismo y realismo social." *Revista de Literatura* 44.88 (July-Dec. 1982): 69–96.
Baquero Goyanes, Mariano. *Perspectivismo y contraste*. Madrid: Gredos, 1963.
Ferreras, J. Ignacio. *Introducción a una Sociología de la novela española del siglo XIX*. Madrid: Taurus, 1973.
Montesinos, José F. *Costumbrismo y novela*. Madrid: Castalia, 1960.

Eugene Del Vecchio

LAFUENTE FERRARI, Enrique (1898, Madrid–1985, Madrid) professor of art, archivist. He is the author of the most complete documented historical manual on Spanish painting, the *Breve historia de la pintura española* (1934; Brief History of Spanish Painting). He has also contributed numerous studies on specific aspects of art, such as *Goya en las colecciones madrileñas* (2nd ed., 1983; Goya in the Madrid Collections), and studies which explore the relationship between art and literature, such as *Los retratos de Lope de Vega* (1935; Lope de Vega's Portraits), *Ortega y las artes visuales* (1970; Ortega and the Visual Arts), and *La novela ejemplar de los retratos de Cervantes* (1948; The Exemplary Novel of Cervantes's Portraits).

BIBLIOGRAPHY

Primary Texts

Goya en las colecciones madrileñas. 2nd rev. ed. Madrid: Amigos del Museo del Prado, 1983.
Ortega y las artes visuales. Madrid: RO, 1970.
Los retratos de Lope de Vega. Madrid: Helénica, 1935.

English Translations

The Frescos in San Antonio de la Florida in Madrid. Tr. Stuart Gilbert. New York: Skira, 1955.
Goya, Complete Etchings, Aquatints and Lithographs. Tr. R. Rudorff. London: Thames and Hudson, 1962.
Velázquez; Biographical and Critical Study. Tr. from French version by J. Emmons. Lausanne: Skira, 1960.

Isabel McSpadden

LAGOS, Concha, pseudonym Gutiérrez Torrero, Concepción (1909, Córdoba–), Spanish poet. During the 1950s, Lagos became involved in Madrid literary circles, associating with poets Gerardo *Diego, José *García Nieto, José *Hierro and Jorge *Campos, and founding the magazine *Cuadernos de Agora* (1956–64), which she directed for a time. Her Andalusian background is evident in cultivation of the Andalusian tradition of personal poetry, and she uses predominantly traditional or classical themes and meters, although some popular metrical forms and occasional free verse appear. In her later works, a more philosophical manner appears, with metaphysical concerns, mystical and religious meditations, transcendental prophecies, and transformations of one age or epoch into another. Early works were *La soledad de siempre* (1958; Everlasting Solitude), of existential inspiration; *Agua de Dios* (1958; Water from God), on the theme of childhood, and first part of a trilogy including *Arroyo claro* (1958; Clear Stream), whose water imagery symbolizes potential transformation, and *Canciones desde la barca* (1962; Boat Songs), which comprises sailing ballads. *Luna de enero* (1961; January Moon) treats a passionate, renounced love; and *Tema fundamental* (1961; Fundamental Theme) explores religious or spiritual growth with an abundance of musical or sensory imagery. *Campo abierto* (1959; Open Country) is dedicated to poems on eleven poets of the Generation of 1950 and to an exploration of the nature of poetry. Peculiar to Lagos's poetry is the mixture of metaphysical preoccupation and speculation with an existential concern for man's daily existence, human solitude, anguish and doubt. Problems of religious faith, hope and despair appear in *Los anales* (1966; Annals), while *Diario de un hombre* (1970; A Man's Diary) treats humankind, with man's defects and existential solitude.

Lagos has also written prose works, including *Al sur del recuerdo* (1955; To the South of Memory), a short novel presenting fragments of childhood memories of the writer's early life in Andalusia, and *El pantano (del diario de una mujer)* (1954; The Swamp [from a Woman's Diary]), likewise a series of fragments, whose first-person narrator, a woman from Andalusia, is affected by the necessity of residing on Spain's swampy northern coast.

Recent works include *Teoría de la inseguridad* (1980; Theory of Insecurity), developing the metaphor of life as an ocean voyage guided by faith in a harmonious universe; *La paloma* (1982; The Dove), another collection of songs; and *Elegías para un álbum* (1982; Elegies for an Album), a nostalgic vision of intersecting time planes using the metaphor of photographs from a family album.

BIBLIOGRAPHY

Primary Texts

Antología 1954–1976/Concha Lagos. Esplugas de Llobregat: Plaza y Janés, 1976.
La aventura. Madrid: Alfaguara, 1973.
El corazón cansado. Madrid: Agora, 1957.
El cerco. Madrid: Alfaguara, 1971.
Fragmentos en espiral desde el pozo. Sevilla: Aldebaran, 1974.

Janet Pérez

LAGUNA, Andrés (1499, Segovia–1560, Segovia), physician, Erasmist, humanist. A cosmopolitan man, he studied at the Universities of Salamanca and Paris, taught at the U of Alcalá, and received an honorary degree from the U of Bologna. Physician to Charles V and to Pope Julius III, he traveled throughout Europe. Laguna wrote and translated many medical treatises; most notable is his excellent illustrated commentary of Dioscorides (first c. A.D.), the *Pedazio Dioscorides Anazarbeo* (1555; Pedanius Dioscorides of Anazarbos). He also translated two dialogues by Lucian (''Ocypus'' and ''Tragopodagra'') into Latin, accompanied by his translation of Aristotle's *De mundo* in 1538; and translated Cicero's *Catiline Orationes* into Spanish (1557). In 1543, he published a *Discurso sobre Europa* (Discourse on Europe), with a Latin text, which discusses the Turks.

Most recently, Marcel Bataillon revived Laguna's memory by declaring him author of the *Viaje de Turquía,* a satirical, Erasmist, pre-picaresque dialogue which follows the adventures of Pedro de Urdemalas, a Spanish captive in Turkey. This attribution has been contested by some critics who feel Cristóbal de *Villalón to be the author. Nevertheless, Laguna occupies an eminent position among Spanish thinkers and humanists. *See also* Erasmism; Humanism.

BIBLIOGRAPHY

Primary Texts

Annotationes in Galeni interpretes. Lugduni: Rouillium, 1553.
La ''Materia médica'' de Dioscórides; transmisión medieval y renacentista. Barcelona: Emporium, 1953. Vol. 4.
Viaje de Turquía. In NBAE 2.
Viaje de Turquía. Madrid: Cátedra, 1980.

English Translation

Commentary on articular disease, dedicated to His Holiness Pope Julius III. Tr. R. Burbank. In *Journal of Bone and Joint Surgery* (July 1927): n.p.

Criticism

Bataillon, M. *Erasmo y España.* Mexico City: Fondo de cultura económica, 1950.
Ortolá, Marisol. *Un estudio del 'Viaje de Turquía' Autobiografía o ficción.* London: Tamesis, 1983.

LAIGLESIA, Álvaro de (1922, San Sebastián–1981, Manchester, England), journalist, humorist. As long-time director of the weekly *La Codorniz*, Laiglesia first won fame as a comic writer in the *tremendismo* movement. He has published more than thirty novels and collections of short stories, all in a comic vein. All have been most popular, going into as many as twenty editions, with three or four printings in the first year of publication. Among his more popular works, published by Planeta, are *La mosca en mi sopa* (1944; The Fly in My Soup), *El baúl de los cadáveres* (1948; The Corpses' Trunks), *La gallina de los huevos de plomo* (1950; The Hen Who Laid Lead Eggs), *Todos los ombligos son redondos* (1955; All Bellybuttons Are Round), *Se busca rey en buen estado* (1968; Sought, King in Good Condition), and *Morir con las medias puestas* (1980; Dying with Your Stockings On). He also contributed to the ''Maestros de humor'' (Masters of Humor) series by Plaza y Janés. Laiglesia's fiction is characterized by a humorous, agile style, and often ironically satirizes social mores. Many works incorporate unconventional subject matter ranging from the life hereafter to Spain's tourist industry. Also a dramatist, in 1946, with Miguel *Mihura, he staged *El caso de la mujer asesinadita* (The Case of the Slightly Murderous Woman), an off-beat murder mystery hailed by critics for its originality. He and Claudio de la *Torre produced the farce *Los sombreros de dos picos* (1948; Two Pointed Hats), which, its authors claimed, took aim at the chaos of modern society. With Janos Voszany, he wrote the comedies *El drama de la familia invisible* (1949; The Drama of the Invisible Family), whose lead characters never appear onstage, and *El escándalo del alma desnuda* (1950; The Scandal of the Naked Soul), a social satire. Critics labeled these plays as amusing and entertaining with great popular appeal, but lacking in transcendental value. Laiglesia's years on *La Codorniz* are chronicled in *''La Codorniz'' sin jaula. Datos para la historia de una revista* (1981; ''The Quail'' without a Cage. Facts for the History of a Magazine). Laiglesia's works, lively and funny, have been written for mass consumption, and have not received critical study.

BIBLIOGRAPHY

Primary Texts

El caso de la mujer asesinadita. Madrid: Alfil, 1955.
''La Codorniz'' sin jaula. Barcelona: Planeta, 1981.
Con amor y sin verguenza. Barcelona: Planeta, 1970.
La gallina de los huevos de plomo. 9th ed. Barcelona: Planeta, 1972.
Todos los ombligos son redondos. Barcelona: Planeta, 1982.

Frieda H. Blackwell

LAÍN ENTRALGO, Pedro (1908, Urrea de Gaén, Teruel–), physician, philosopher, professor of history of medicine, essayist and educator. A member of the Academies of Medicine and of the Language, Laín abandoned his serious research during the 1950s to become rector of the U of Madrid (1951–56), eventually resigning to return to his investigations of the doctor-patient relationship. The contemporary historian J. L. Abellán has divided Laín's production into three stages, the first (1941–56) marked by concern for Spanish history; the second (1957–76) dominated by interest in anthropology; and the third (1977 to the present) evincing a return to history in a more general sense. Such divisions, however, are far from absolute, although Laín himself has suggested a tripartite scheme for his own evolution. Philosophically, Laín falls within the general tradition of Christian metaphysics, and has been influenced by Dilthey, Scheler, and Heidegger, as well as by the Spanish thinker Zubiri (both mentor and friend). In the 1930s and 1940s, Laín stayed close to Catholic dogma, which provided a bulwark in uncertain times, later moving in the direction of Christian existential thought, with special concern for the problem of the Other. During the 1950s, his earlier studies of Freud developed into a preoccupation with psychosomatic psychology and illness, and Laín adopted the view that sickness is less a biological condition than a meaningful, personal response created by the sufferer to a problematic life situation. Interest in the existential Other over several decades leads to a deep and long-lasting preoccupation with love and its variants (friendship, neighborliness, charity, goodwill and philanthropy), evinced in a series of works from the 1960s and 1970s dealing with the relationship between doctor and patient, and with friendship.

Characteristic and significant works include *Medicina e historia* (1941; Medicine and History), *Estudios de la historia de la medicina y de antropología médica* (1943; Studies on the History of Medicine and Medical Anthropology), *La antropología en la obra de Fray Luis de Granada* (1943; Anthropology in the Work of Fray Luis de Granada), *Sobre la cultura española* (1953; On Spanish Culture), *Menéndez Pelayo* (1944); *La generación del noventa y ocho* (1945; The Generation of 1898), *Introducción histórica a la patología psicosomática* (1950; Historical Introduction to Psychosomatic Pathology), *Reflexiones sobre la vida espiritual de España* (1953; Reflections on Spiritual Life in Spain), *La espera y la esperanza* (1954; Waiting and Hoping), *La curación por la palabra en la Antigüedad clásica* (1958; Curing by the Word in Classic Antiquity), *Ocio y trabajo* (1960; Leisure and Work), *Teoría y realidad del otro* (1961; Theory and Reality of the Other), *Panorama de la ciencia moderna* (1962; Panorama of Modern Science), *Marañón y el enfermo* (1962; [Dr.] Marañón and the Patient), *El problema de la Universidad* (1967; Problems of the University), *Una y diversa España* (1968; Spain One and Many), and *La medicina hipocrática* (1970; Hippocratic Medicine). Among the most significant of the foregoing are *La espera y la esperanza* and *Teoría y realidad del otro*.

The latter work constitutes something of a philosophical introduction to *La relación médico-enfermo* (1964; The Doctor-Patient Relationship), revised as *El médico y el enfermo* (1969; The Doctor and the Patient), which is studied as a form of love or medical friendship. *Sobre la amistad* (1971; On Friendship) expands upon this theme, attempts to define the meaning of friendship, and examines the varieties of love, from love of individuals to love of nature and love of God. However, in later years, Laín continues to be interested in the problems of Spanish history, as seen in *Ejercicios de comprensión* (1959; Exercises in Understanding), the above-mentioned *Una y diversa España*, in *A qué llamamos España* (1971; That Which We Call Spain), and *En este país* (1986; In This Country). Among the volumes devoted to the history of medicine are *La historia clínica. Historia y teoría del relato patográfico* (1950; Clinical History. Theory and History of the Pathographic Story), the above-mentioned *Introducción histórica al estudio de la Patología psicosomática*, and his seven-volume *Historia universal de la Medicina* (Universal History of Medicine), which began appearing in 1971. Laín has also written a number of literary works, mostly unpublished.

BIBLIOGRAPHY

Primary Texts

Antropología médica para clínicos. Barcelona: Salvat, 1984.
Descargo de conciencia (1930–1960). Barcelona: Barral, 1976. Memoirs.

Enfermedad y pecado. Barcelona: Toray, 1961.
La medicina actual. 2nd ed. Barcelona: Orbis, 1986.
Mysterium doloris. Hacia una teología cristiana de la enfermedad. Madrid: Publicaciones de la Universidad Internacional Menéndez Pelayo, 1955.

Criticism

Abellán, José Luis. "Laín, filósofo de la cultura española." *CH* 446–47 (Aug.–Sept. 1987): 421–56.
Gracia Guillén, Diego. "Conversación con Pedro Laín Entralgo." *CH* 400 (1983): 11–32. Interview.
Orringer, Nelson. "Faith, Hope and Love: Stages of Laín Entralgo's Scientific Evolution." *Letras Peninsulares* 1.2 (Fall 1988): 133–50.
Soler Puigorial, P. *El hombre, ser indigente. El pensamiento antropológico de Pedro Laín Entralgo*. Madrid: Guadarrama, 1966.

Janet Pérez

LAMPILLAS, Francisco Javier. *See* Llampillas, Francisco Javier

LANZA, Silverio, pseudonym of Juan Bautista Amorós (1856, Madrid–1912, Getafe, Madrid), novelist, short story writer and aphorist. Apparently the only child of aristocratic parents, Amorós first left home to be a sailor. Upon the death of his mother (his father had died when Amorós was a small child), he returned to Madrid. He later married and then, withdrawing from court life, moved to Getafe and there led a rather reclusive existence till his death. His works were never popular during his life, but he did maintain ties with several contemporary writers such as *Sawa and, later, *Gómez de la Serna, and attended **tertulias*. *Azorín considered him a precursor of the *Generation of 1898 and praised his vivid dialogue and his psychological and analytical approach to depicting contemporary society and its flaws. His best works include *Ni en la vida, ni en la muerte* (1890; Neither in Life Nor in Death), a denunciation of political bossism for which he was sued; *Artuña* (1893), an ambitious two-volume work which dissects the contemporary woman in Spain; and *Para mis amigos* (1892; For My Friends), an ironic, sometimes lugubrious collection of short stories.

BIBLIOGRAPHY

Primary Texts

Artuña. 2 vols. Madrid: Cao y Val, 1893.
Ni en la vida, ni en la muerte. Madrid: Escolar, 1981.
Obra selecta. Ed. Luis Granjel. Madrid: Alfaguara, 1966. Contains preliminary study and bibliography.
Páginas escogidas e inéditas. Ed. Ramón Gómez de la Serna. Madrid: Biblioteca Nueva, 1918.
Para mis amigos. Madrid: n.p., 1892.

Criticism

See *Obra selecta*, ed. Granjel.

Eugene Del Vecchio

LARANJEIRA, Manuel Fernandes (1877, Vergada–1912, Espinho), Portuguese essayist and poet. He graduated in medicine from the U of Porto in 1904, completing his qualifications with a thesis entitled *A Doença de Santidade* (1907; The Holiness Syndrome) on the psychopathology of religious mysticism. As a student he had been active as a drama critic and was much taken with the works of Dostoyevski, Ibsen and Schopenhauer. He had always tended toward depression, a condition made worse by syphilis and compounded by the state of medical knowledge in his time, which all led to his suicide in 1912. His more general pessimism about the human condition and character is reflected in nearly all his writing, much of which he refrained from publishing and often destroyed during his bouts of depression. He was, however, influential through his professional writing, and his lecture on João de Deus's reading primer, which was published as *A 'Cartilha Maternal' e a Fisiologia* (1909; The "Mother's Primer" and Physiology); through his contacts with João de *Barros, Teixeira de *Pascoaes, António *Patrício, and Miguel de *Unamuno and through his teaching at the Universidade Livre in Porto. The only other work published during his lifetime was a collection of poetry titled *Comigo* (1911; Talking to Myself).

His political views are recorded in a series of articles originally published in *O Norte*, an anti-royalist paper, in December-January 1907–8 and republished as *O Pessimismo Nacional* (1955; Portuguese Pessimism). His letters to the friends listed above were also published posthumously and help document his state of mind, as does the diary he kept during 1908 and 1909 published as *Diário Intimo* (1957; Personal Diary).

BIBLIOGRAPHY

Primary Texts

A Doença de Santidade. Porto: n.p., 1907.
A 'Cartilha Maternal' e a Fisiologia. Porto: Porto Médico, 1909.
Comigo. Coimbra: F. França, 1911.
Cartas. Pref. Miguel de Unamumo. Lisbon: Portugália, 1944.
Pessimismo Nacional. Lisbon: Contraponto, 1955.
Diário Intimo. Ed. Alberto Serpa. Lisbon: Portugália, 1957.

Criticism

Maia, João. 'Manuel Laranjeira.' *Brotéria* 65 (1957): 197–99 and 68 (1959): 566–67.
Morejón, J. G. "Unamuno & Manuel Laranjeira." *Annali del Instituto Orientale di Napoli—Sezione Romanza* 6 (1964): 21–42.
Serrão, Joel. *Temas Oitocentistas II*. Lisbon: n.p., 1962.

Peter Fothergill-Payne

LAREDO, Bernardino de (1482, Seville–1540, Seville), physician, Franciscan, writer. Of a well-to-do family, he received his M.D. from the U of Seville, and then in 1510 entered a Franciscan convent near Seville. Continuing his interest in medicine, he published a book of advice for the care and treatment of invalids and common ills titled *Metáfora de medicina y cirujía* (1522; Explanation of Medicine and Surgery). Also his is the important mystical treatise *Subida del Monte Sión* (1535; *The Ascent of Mount Scion*, 1952). Written about 1529 and published anonymously, it influenced Sta. *Teresa early in her career. *See also* Mysticism.

BIBLIOGRAPHY

Primary Texts

Metáfora de medicina. Seville: Varela, 1522.

Subida del Monte Sión. In *Místicos franciscanos españoles*. Ed. J. F. Gomis. 3 vols. Madrid: Nebrija, 1948–49. Vol. 2.

English Translation

The Ascent of Mount Scion. Tr., ed., intro. E. Allison Peers. New York: Harper, 1952. Tr. of Book 3.

Criticism

Peers, E. Allison. *Studies of the Spanish Mystics*. 3 vols. London: Sheldon, 1930. 2: 41–76.

LARRA, Luis Mariano de (1830, Madrid–1901, Madrid), prolific dramatist. Son of Mariano José de *Larra, he wrote comedies of manners, **zarzuelas*, and theater in the *costumbrismo* vein. *Pérez Escrich, who collaborated with Larra on the *zarzuela La guerra santa* (1979 performance; The Holy War), accused Larra of plagiarizing Pérez Escrich's *El cura de aldea* in Larra's *La oración de la tarde* (1858; Afternoon Prayer), but Larra was acquitted by a literary tribunal. *See also* Romanticism.

BIBLIOGRAPHY

Primary Texts

Many plays in the Spanish Plays collection.

LARRA, Mariano José de (1809, Madrid–1837, Madrid), journalist and critic; also known as Fígaro (taken from a play by Beaumarchais), El Duende (The Goblin) and El Pobrecito Hablador (The Poor Chatterer)—both taken from titles of periodicals that he founded, as well as Andrés Niporesas and Ramón Arriala (an anagram of his own name): he is most widely known, however, by his own name and as Fígaro. His father, a physician who had been a Bonaparte collaborator, had to flee Spain after the Napoleonic War in 1813, taking his family with him to France. Mariano studied in Bordeaux and Paris and in 1818, when Ferdinand VII granted amnesty to political emigrés like Dr. Larra, the family returned to Spain. There is speculation that the youngster had forgotten his native language by then and that upon repatriation he had to relearn it. He was enrolled in the Escuela Pía de San Antón (humanities, mathematics and Spanish grammar), where, in his leisure hours, he translated passages from the French and the classics. In 1822 his family moved to Navarra for one year; when they returned to Madrid, Mariano resumed his studies at the Colegio Imperial de la Compañía de Jesús; the following year he joined his father in Valladolid, where he undertook the study of law. Before establishing permanent residence in Madrid, he studied law in Valencia, then in Madrid, where he settled into literary activity in 1827. There he became part of the Parnasillo, a regular meeting of the literati, and he began writing. He soon founded two journals that were both short-lived: *El Duende Satírico del Día* (1828; The Satirical Goblin of The Day) and *El Pobrecito Hablador* (1823–33; The Poor Chatterer). Soon afterwards he became the drama critic for *La Revista Española*, in which he adopted the pen name Fígaro; thereafter he became a columnist for *El Español*, *El Mundo* and *El Observador*. Larra was a brilliant socio-political satirist and a ruthless, perceptive drama critic. He also had political ambitions (he was elected a deputy to Cortes for Avila in 1836 but never filled the post because of political upheaval). In 1829 he married Josefina Wetoret y Martínez (known as Pepita Martínez), by whom he had three children (their only son became a mediocre writer and critic; one daughter became a woman of unconventional morals and the other one vanished into middle-class anonymity after marrying her first cousin). Larra's marriage was a disaster, aggravated by rumors of Pepita's infidelity and his own passionate affair with Dolores Armijo, the wife of a bureaucrat named Cambronero. When she decided to terminate the affair and join her husband in the Philippines, where he had been assigned, she sought a meeting with Larra on February 13, 1837, in his home. In the course of their interview, she stuck to her irrevocable decision and demanded that he return compromising letters that she had written him earlier. After much pleading he surrendered the letters and within minutes of her departure he shot himself in the head; when his six-year-old daughter entered her father's study later that day she discovered her father's body. (Dolores Armijo drowned in a storm that sank the ship she had taken to join her husband.) The tragedy of Larra's death and his funeral set the stage for one of the most dramatic discoveries in Spanish literary history: an unknown, grief-stricken, pale youth stepped forth at Larra's graveside to read his personal elegy to the fallen writer; he almost fainted into the grave but was saved just in time. His name was José *Zorrilla (1817–93).

Larra cultivated undistinguished verse, a historical play, *Macías*, and a historical novel, *El doncel de Don Enrique el Doliente* (The Page of Don Enrique, the Invalid), both based on the same topic (and published in the same year, 1834); in order to earn a living he translated many plays from French into Spanish. Larra's genius, however, was intellectual rather than creative, and it is his essays that have engaged scholars without interruption for over a century. They appeared in journals of the day and he collected and published their first edition in *Fígaro, Colección de artículos dramáticos, literarios, políticos y de costumbres* (1835–37; Fígaro, Collected Essays on Drama, Literature, Politics and Manners). Traditionally, Larra's essays are classified in the manner the author himself designated in his edition; however, it is somewhat inaccurate to do so because they all satirize social customs, politics, politicians and Romantic literature and drama of the period. He normally relies on double entendre and abundant dialogue; some of the essays on manners reflect personal problems and convictions (*El casarse pronto y mal*, An Early, Bad Marriage, for example). His drama criticism is striking because although Larra was himself a Romantic (indeed, often dubbed the greatest of Spanish Romantics), he was able to penetrate the vulgarity, superficiality and ostentation of many of his Spanish and foreign contemporaries and to attack the insensitive, bombastic, shallow interpretations of widely acclaimed performers. Larra's review of Dumas's *Antony*, to which he devoted two articles in *El Español* (June 23 and 25, 1835), is representative of these essays: in it he mercilessly ridicules plot, characters and interpretations. Politically, Larra was a liberal who resented the lingering, suffocating regimes of the first third of the century. He believed in the freedoms of the French Revolution and he upheld intellectual independence, political freedom, truth and morality. *Día de difuntos de 1836, Fígaro en el cementerio* (All Soul's Day, 1836; Fígaro in the Cemetery) is an indictment of the hypocrisy, *censorship and intellectual restrictions that afflicted Spain. In the essay he conceives Madrid as a graveyard; the government buildings as tombstones that identify the remains of truth, justice, freedom, morality, etc. At the end of the essay the author looks into his own heart, also a tombstone with an inscription: "Here lies hope." Larra stuns the reader time and again with his socio-political invectives. Other writers of the period, to be sure, wrote essays on manners, but Larra distinguished himself from Ramón de *Mesonero Romanos (1803–82) and Serafín *Estébanez Calderón (1799–1867) by his bitterness and despair. Their essays are little more than amusing accounts of daily life, but Larra goes far beyond that with his underlying cry for reflection, overhaul and new direction for his country. His spirit is akin to earlier writers', such as José *Cadalso (1741–82), in some of whose *Cartas marruecas* (1789; Moroccan Letters) popular Spanish values are questioned and criticized. Larra certainly is related to the writers of the *Generation of 1898, who hailed him as their immediate precursor and overall spiritual leader. They recognized in him their own profound concern for Spain and their determination to save it from self-destruction. Larra's popularity is limited almost exclusively to intellectuals and scholars, but he is widely taught in schools and universities. *See also* Essay; Romanticism.

BIBLIOGRAPHY

Primary Texts

Artículos de costumbres. Ed. J. R. Lomba y Pedraja. Clásicos Castellanos 45. 19th ed. Madrid: Espasa-Calpe, 1975.

Artículos de crítica literaria y artística. Ed. J. R. Lomba y Pedraja. Clásicos Castellanos 52. 7th ed. Madrid: Espasa-Calpe, 1975.

Artículos políticos y sociales. Ed. J. R. Lomba y Pedraja. Clásicos Castellanos 77. 6th ed. Madrid: Espasa-Calpe, 1972.

Artículos sociales, políticos y de crítica literaria. Ed. J. Cano Ballesta. Madrid: Alhambra, 1982.

Artículos varios. Ed. E. Correa Calderón. Madrid: Castalia, 1976.
Fígaro. Colección de artículos. Madrid: Repullés, 1835–37.
Obras. In BAE 127–30.
Obras selectas. Ed. J. Johnson. Gerona: Bosch, 1973.
Las palabras. Artículos y ensayos. Ed. J. L. Varela. Madrid: Espasa-Calpe, 1982.

English Translations

"Don Cándido Buena's Ambitious Son." In *Masterpieces of Spanish Humor*. Ed. I. Goldberg. Kansas: Haldeman-Julius, 1926.
Quitting Business. Tr. K. C. Kaufman. In *Poet Lore* (Boston) 30 (1924): n.p.
Selected Essays. Ed. C. B. Bourland. Boston: Ginn, 1932.

Criticism

Bellini, G. *Larra e il suo tempo*. Milan: Goliardica, 1967.
Benítez, R., ed. *Mariano José de Larra*. Madrid: Taurus, 1979. Reproduces documents and articles previously published in diverse journals.
Brent, A. "Larra's Dramatic Works." *RN* 8 (1967): 207–12.
Burgos, C. *Fígaro (Revelaciones, "ella" descubierta, epistolario inédito)*. Madrid: Alrededor del Mundo, 1919.
Casalduero, J. "La sensualidad en el romanticismo: sobre el *Macías*." In *Estudios sobre el teatro español*. Madrid: Gredos, 1967. 219–31.
Escobar, J. *Los orígenes de la obra de Larra*. Madrid: Prensa Española, 1973.
———. "Un episodio biográfico de Larra, crítico teatral, en la temporada de 1834." *NRFH* 25 (1976): 45–72.
Gies, D. T. "Larra and Mendizábal: A Writer's Response to Government." *Cithara* 12 (1973): 74–90.
Hespelt, H. "The Translated Dramas of Larra and Their French Originals." *Hispania* 15 (1932): 117–34.
Kirkpatrick, S. *Larra: el inextricable laberinto de un romántico liberal*. Madrid: Gredos, 1977.
Ruiz Otín, D. *Política y sociedad en el vocabulario de Larra*. Madrid: Centro de Estudios Constitucionales, 1983.
Sánchez Estevan, I. *"Fígaro": Ensayo biográfico*. Madrid: Hernando, 1934.
Tarr, F. C. "Larra's *Duende Satírico del Día*." *Modern Philology* 26 (1928): 31–45.
Ullman, P. *Mariano de Larra and Spanish Political Rhetoric*. Madison: U of Wisconsin P, 1971.
Umbral, F. *Larra. Anatomía de un dandy*. Madrid: Alfaguara, 1965.
Varela, J. L. *Larra y España*. Madrid: Espasa-Calpe, 1983.

Joseph R. Arboleda

LARREA, Juan (1895, Bilbao–), Spanish poet, essayist, critic. Educated as a librarian and archaeologist, he began his professional career at the National Historical Archives in Madrid, simultaneously publishing poetry in literary magazines including *Cervantes* and *Grecia*, associated with the vanguard of the era. In 1926 he renounced his career to settle in Paris, where he joined the circle of literary and artistic surrealists. Most of his poetry written during the Paris years was composed in French, subsequently translated to Spanish for publication in little magazines such as *Carmen* and *Litoral*. After 1932, however, Larrea ceased for many decades his poetic activity. Following the close of the Spanish Civil War, Larrea went into exile in Mexico, collaborating with *España peregrina* and *Cuadernos americanos*, perhaps the most significant exile periodicals, with numerous articles on history, art, literature and archaeology, as well as some visionary philosophical essays, *Rendición del espíritu* (1943; Rendition of the Spirit), published in Mexico. His archaeological background led to a special interest in pre-Colombian cultures, and he received a number of grants from Guggenheim and other philanthropic organizations for research on the Saint James myth, living in New York from 1949 to 1956, after which he settled for some two decades in Argentina.

Originally identified with the "creationist" school founded by Vicente Huidobro and typified by the early poetry of Jorge Luis Borges, Larrea cultivated an original form of metaphor found in works of the same period of Vicente *Aleixandre, Rafael *Alberti, and Gerardo *Diego, the latter being the translator of Larrea's French poems to Spanish. His collected poems were on the verge of being published in Spain when the Civil War erupted, with the result that Larrea remained essentially unknown in Spain and most of Europe for some three decades. The Italian scholar Vittorio Bodini, in *I surrealisti spagnoli* (1963; The Spanish Surrealists), termed Larrea the father of Spanish surrealism and in subsequent years published bilingual editions of his collected poems in Italian-French and Italian-Spanish versions under the title *Versión celeste* (1969). In the post-Franco period, Larrea has returned to Spain and is becoming increasingly well known, although his work to date remains but little studied.

BIBLIOGRAPHY

Primary Texts

César Vallejo y el surrealismo. Madrid: n.p., 1977.

Oscuro dominio. Mexico: n.p., 1934.

Rubén Darío y la nueva cultura americana. Valencia: Pre-Textos, 1987.

English Translation

A Tooth for a Tooth: Selected Poems of Juan Larrea (1925–1932). Tr. David Bary. Lanham, MD: UP of America, 1987.

Criticism

Aullón de Haro, Pedro. "Introducción a la poesía de Juan Larrea." *Anales de Literatura Española* 3 (1984): 47–64.

Bary, David. *Larrea, poesía y transfiguración*. Madrid: n.p., 1976.

———. *Nuevos estudios sobre Huidobro y Larrea*. Valencia: Pre-Textos, 1984.

———. *Lo que va de siglo*. Valencia: Pretextos, 1987. 83–90.

Gurney, Robert. "Larrea's Poetic Odyssey." *What's Past Is Prologue: A Collection of Essays in Honour of L. J. Woodward*. Ed. Bernard Bentley et al. Edinburgh: Scottish Academic P, 1984. 70–81.

Janet Pérez

LAVERDE Y RUIZ, Gumersindo (1840, Santander–1890, Madrid), poet, essayist and teacher. His poetry combines a certain mysterious, lyric subjectivity with an excessively rhetorical form. *La luna y el lirio* (1859; The

Moon and the Lily), a ballad which narrates a lover's story, is replete with the standard romantic vocabulary of nights, dawns, and flowers, and vaguely echoes the legendary Ossian; *Paz y misterio* (1859; Tranquility and Mystery) is predominantly of a fantastic tone and suggests *Bécquer's ineffability. As a mentor and close friend of Marcelino *Menéndez y Pelayo, he influenced the younger man's projects. Don Marcelino eulogizes Laverde in *Horacio en España*. In *Ensayos críticos sobre filosofía, literatura, e instrucción pública españolas* (1868; Critical Essays on Spanish Philosophy, Literature and Public Education), Laverde vigorously defends orthodox Christian values in the face of Krausist reformist ideas. He died prematurely of a prolonged nervous affliction. *See also* Krausism.

BIBLIOGRAPHY

Primary Texts

Ensayos críticos sobre filosofía, literatura, e instrucción pública españolas. Lugo: Soto Freire, 1868.

Epistolario de Laverde Ruiz y Menéndez Pelayo 1874–1890. Ed. Ignacio Aguilera. 2 vols. Santander: Publicaciones de la Excma. Diputación Provincial de Santander, 1967.

Selección y estudio de J. M. Cossío. Santander: Librería Moderna, 1951.

Criticism

Arribans Arranz, Filemón. "Laverde en la Universidad de Valladolid." *BBMP* 37 (1961): 185–93.

Cossío, J. M. de. "Don Gumersindo de Laverde y Ruiz, poeta montañéz." *BRAE* 8 (1931): 731–71.

Eugene Del Vecchio

LAYNEZ, Pedro (1538–42?, Madrid–1584, Madrid), poet. Laynez was enthusiastically praised by contemporaries such as Lope de *Vega, close friend *Cervantes, etc., but later readers have been less admiring of his verse. His writing follows Italianate tradition. *See also* Italian literary influences.

BIBLIOGRAPHY

Primary Texts

Obras. Ed., study. J. de Entrambasaguas. 2 vols. Madrid: CSIC, 1951.

Poesías. Ed., prol. A. Marín Ocete. Granada: U of Granada, 1950.

LAZARILLOS, a group of *picaresque works, the first of which gave illustrious birth to the genre. The *Lazarillo de Tormes* is the shortened title of a book which narrates the life of a character whose name is given to the novel itself. The complete title is *La vida de Lazarillo de Tormes y de sus fortunas y adversidades* (1554; *The Life of Lazarillo de Tormes: His Fortunes and Adversities*, 1962). The protagonist writes to "vuestra merced" (Your Worship), narrating his story as if it were an autobiography.

The oldest known editions are from 1554, and the fact that they were published in Burgos, Alcalá de Henares and Antwerp the same year adds bibliographical problems to other unsolved difficulties such as anonymity of the author, date of composition, ideological intention and message.

In the seventeenth c., two attributions were proposed for the anonymity dilemma. Father José de *Sigüenza suggested Juan de Ortega, and Valerius Andreas proposed Diego *Hurtado de Mendoza in his 1607 *Catalogus Clarorum Hispaniae Scriptorum*. This last authorship was questioned and then refuted by the French scholar Morel-Fatio in 1886. More recently, other names have been put forward. Francisco Márquez Villanueva reaffirmed the attribution to Sebastián de *Horozco, which had been proposed by José María Asensio. Julio *Cejador also retained Asensio's suggestion, based on the fact that in Horozco's *Cancionero,* Lazarillo appears with the blind beggar in an episode reminiscent of the final episode of *Tratado* 2. Germán *Bleiberg suggested the name of *Garcilaso de la Vega in a paper presented at Oxford during the annual meeting of British Hispanists (March 1980), and Francisco Rico wondered whether it could not have been the work of a poet. The authorship problem remains unsolved and poses the question of ideological intentions. Some critics feel the *Lazarillo* was written by a heterodox, or even a Lutheran, whose purpose was to attack the Catholic church, or by an Erasmist thinker with satirical intentions (as suggested by Morel-Fatio). For Américo *Castro, it is the work of a **converso*. Others, such as Marcel Bataillon, see the short novel as a literary tour de force founded on folklore and with no specific ideological intention, that is, the author wanted to write a comical novel based on facetious sources.

The 1554 *Lazarillo* is devoted to the portrayal of human poverty and to a satirical representation of certain human types such as lascivious and stingy priests and pretentious yet hungry hidalgos. The protagonist is a poor human being—a pícaro—who writes a selective autobiography in order to present to "vuestra merced" the history of the "caso" (case, or matter), mentioned as such in the prologue and unveiled in the last *Tratado*. It concerns his wife's adulterous relationship with an archpriest, his last master. To clarify the case, Lázaro proposes an autobiography, chronologically reported and written as a confession. He uses the narration to explain the story of his economic success and achieved prosperity, beginning with his miserable birth on the banks of a river.

The work is divided into seven *Tratados* (treatises) of varying length, following the prologue in which Lázaro identifies himself as the writer of his life and explains his reasons for doing so. Each *Tratado* is devoted to specific moments of the protagonist's social growth. The first one deals with Lázaro's genealogy: the parents and the mother's lover have names, and they belong to specific social groups which are thereby identified and classified for the purpose of the narration. This *Tratado* presents the blind beggar who adopts Lázaro as his son and awakens him to distrust and the hardships of life. It ends as Lázaro shows he has understood his master's teachings. The second *Tratado* tells of his relationship with the priest of Maqueda, in which the themes of hunger (Lázaro's) and avarice (the priest's) dominate. The third *Tratado* continues the theme of hunger through presentation of the starving hidalgo who prefers to eat thanks to Lázaro's abilities, rather than earn his own living.

The fourth, fifth and sixth *Tratados* portray a decaying society built on corruption and deceit, as Lázaro learns how to depend on his personal skills in order to become autonomous and achieve a certain economic independence. The seventh, final *Tratado* culminates in the recounting of Lázaro's social success, paralleled to Charles V's triumphant arrival at Toledo.

The *Lazarillo* was forbidden by the *Inquisition in 1559, and in 1574 there appeared a revised version, titled *Lazarillo castigado* (Lazarillo Chastised), in which the fourth and fifth *Tratados* were eliminated and irreverent references to the Church and its dignitaries censored.

The work soon met fame outside Spain. Several translations appeared in French (1560, 1561, 1594, 1598), English (1576, 1586, etc.), German (1617, 1627), and Dutch (Antwerp, 1579). Foreign editions were also printed in Antwerp (1555, Guillermo Simon, editor; 1595, Plantin), in Bergamo (1597), and in Milan (1587).

Critical bibliography on the original *Lazarillo* is extensive; recent contributions are listed in the bibliography. *See also* Erasmism.

BIBLIOGRAPHY

Primary Texts

Lazarillo de Tormes. Ed. F. Rico. Barcelona: Planeta, 1976.

La vida de Lazarillo de Tormes. Ed. E. W. Hesse and H. F. Williams. Intro. Américo Castro. Madison: U of Wisconsin P, 1948. 2nd ed., 1961.

English Translation

The Life of Lazarillo de Tormes: His Fortunes and Adversities. Tr. W. S. Merwin. Intro. L. C. de Morelos. Garden City, NY: Doubleday, 1962.

Criticism

Fiore, R. L. *Lazarillo de Tormes*. TWAS 714. Boston: Twayne, 1984.

Guillén, Claudio. "Los silencios de *Lázaro de Tormes*." *Insula* 42.490 (September 1987): 21, 23–24.

Márquez Villanueva, Francisco. "Sebastián de Horozco y el Lazarillo de Tormes." *RFE* (1957): n.p.

Santoyo, Julio César. *Ediciones y traducciones del "Lazarillo de Tormes" (1568–1977)*. Vitoria: Colegio Universitario de Alava, 1978.

Weiner, Jack. "Las interpolaciones en el *Lazarillo de Tormes* (Alcalá de Henares, 1554) con énfasis especial sobre las del ciego." *Hispano* 29 (Sept. 1985): 15–21.

La vida de Lazarillo. Part Two.

A year after publication of the *Lazarillo*, there appeared an anonymous continuation, or second part, published in Antwerp, in 1555, by the printer Martin Nucio. The author of this continuation picks up Lázaro's new adventures exactly where they had been left in the seventh *Tratado*, repeating the last words of the text: "en este tiempo estaba en mi prosperidad, y en la cumbre de toda buena fortuna'' (at this moment, I was prosperous, and at the summit of all good fortune). From there on, the author elaborates a new set of adventures told by the protagonist, giving the impression that he will expand upon the model set by the first *Lazarillo*. Lázaro's adventures, however, are of a totally different nature. The marvelous and the extraordinary create the ambience against which historical events are recaptured and interpreted (wars against the infidel), and society is criticized. Satirical effects in the narration are obtained through deplacement of reality in a new sphere, the bottom of the sea. Political conspiracies are observed and analyzed through the actions of the fish among whom Lázaro lives.

Led by cupidity and encouraged by his wife and the archpriest, Lázaro—who now serves a new master, a knight of the Order of St. James—becomes a soldier and navigates to Algiers where he hopes to become rich. A shipwreck delays his plans, and he is forced to enter the kingdom of the fish. There, he becomes a tuna. Next, he begins a new career in the army. As captain of the king's army, and faithful servant, he experiences ingratitude, indifference and cruelty, which incite him to meditate and compare similar earthly sentiments. The aristocratic servant suffers at the court of earthly kings. After marrying the king's concubine (an elevated reflection of his earthly experience), he becomes a lord. His adventures under the sea end when, given the task of leading the female tuna to their place of ovulation, he is caught by fishermen. Back on land, he becomes a freak, and is exhibited as a circus wonder. After reincorporating his human shape, he is brought to the U of Salamanca, where his knowledge and wisdom are matched with that of the best scholars of the institution. As in *The Golden Ass*, which was translated to Spanish in 1543, or in *Pitagoras the Cock*, the author uses the theme of transformation to review social, political and human vices.

This continuation, reprinted in Milan in 1587 and 1615, and in Spain only in 1844, has been scorned by critics, who emphasize its lack of artistic value. As a result, very little has been written about it.

BIBLIOGRAPHY

Primary Texts

La vida de Lazarillo . . . Aumentada con dos segundas partes anónimas. Madrid: Castelló y Omar y Soler, 1844–45.

Los tres Lazarillos. Ed. J. M. Solà-Solé. Barcelona: Puvill 1987—. Vol. 1.

Criticism

Aubrun, Charles. ''La Dispute de l'Eau et du Vin.'' *BH* 58 (1958): 453–56.

Brownlee, Marina Scordilis. ''Generic Expansion and Generic Subversion: The Two Continuations of the *Lazarillo de Tormes*.'' *Philological Quarterly* 66.3 (1982): n.p.

Stephen, Maximo Saludo. *Misteriosas Andanzas Atunescas de Lazarillo de Tormes*. San Sebastián: n.p., 1959.

Williams, R. H. ''Notes on the Anonymous Continuation of the *Lazarillo de Tormes*.'' *Romanic Review* 16 (1925): 223–35.

The continuation of *La vida de Lazarillo* by Juan de Luna.

Dissatisfied with the lack of verisimilitude of the anonymous continuation, Juan de Luna rewrote the *Lazarillo* (Paris, 1620). The author eliminated the metamorphosis of Lázaro and all the episodes depicting Lázaro's life under the sea among the tuna. The parabolic and allegorical representation of contemporary circumstances is lost in Luna's version of the *Lazarillo*. The tuna disappear as a social group; the themes of descent, resurrection, and reincarnation are ignored; the protagonist's pilgrimage is totally terrestrial. His adventures once more incorporate urban centers. Lázaro is stereotyped into a pícaro, who here is a useless human being who prefers to be ridiculed rather than lose the advantages of his idle existence. In search of a new master who will offer him an easy life, he is constantly taken advantage of, mocked, beaten and denigrated. Luna's Lázaro is grotesque, absurd and repulsive. The text comprises a series of farcical situations in which Lázaro is the accepting victim; ultimately, he becomes a disembodied parody of the social/literary type, the pícaro. Through this comical parody, Luna violently attacks certain human behaviors. To be sure, he portrays an inhuman world dominated by cruelty, indifference and cupidity.

BIBLIOGRAPHY

Primary Text

Segunda parte de la vida de Lazarillo de Tormes. Ed., prol. J. L. Laurenti. Clásicos Castellanos 215. Madrid: Espasa-Calpe, 1979.

English Translations

The pursuit of the historie of Lazarillo. . . . Tr. T. Walkley. London: Hawkins, 1631. Microfilm of 3rd ed., tr. D. Rowland. London: Leahe, 1639, in Huntington Library, Ann Arbor, MI.

The Life of Lazarillo . . . with sequel by Juan de Luna. Tr. R. S. Rudder and C. Criado de Rodríguez-Puértolas. New York: Ungar, 1971.

Criticism

Cossío, J. M. de. "Las continuaciones del *Lazarillo de Tormes*." *RFE* 25 (1941): 514–23.

Laurenti, J. L. *La vida de Lazarillo de Tormes. Estudio crítico de la segunda parte de Juan de Luna*. Mexico: Andrea, 1965.

———. "El nuevo mundo social de la segunda parte de *La vida de Lazarillo de Tormes* de Juan de Luna (1620)." *BBMP* 47 (1971): n.p.

Solà-Solé, J. M. *Los tres Lazarillos*. Barcelona: Puvill, 1987—.

Marie-Sol Ortolá

LEDESMA, Alonso de (1562?, Segovia–1633, Segovia), poet. With the exception of several years of schooling in Alcalá, Ledesma spent his entire life in Segovia, becoming one of its most illustrious citizens and active participants in the literary life there and beyond. Considered the first *conceptista* poet, he was lauded by *Cervantes in the *Viaje del Parnaso,* by Lope de *Vega in the *Laurel de Apolo*, by *Gracián y Morales in the *Agudeza y arte de ingenio*, to name only a few. His first published work, *Conceptos espirituales* (1600; Spiritual Concepts), underwent many editions in his life alone. Later titles include *Juegos de Nochebuena* (1611; Christmas Eve Entertainments)—which is **a lo divino* re-workings of old folksongs and tunes, *Romancero y monstruo imaginado* (1615; Ballad Book and Imaginary Monster), and *Epigramas y hieroglíficos a la vida de Cristo*... (1625; Epigrams and Hieroglyphics on the Life of Christ...). Virtually all of his early poetry was religious, but in later years profane verses became more prominent. The dominant theme still was explanation of dogma and moral edification, however. *See also Conceptismo.*

BIBLIOGRAPHY

Primary Texts

Conceptos espirituales y morales. 3 vols. Madrid: CSIC, 1969.
Epigramas y hieroglíficos. Madrid: J. Gonzàlez, 1625.
Juegos de Nochebuena. In BAE 35.
Romancero y monstruo imaginado. Barcelona: Cormellas, 1616.

Criticism

d'Or, M. *Vida y poesía de Alonso de Ledesma.* Pamplona: U of Navarra, 1974.
Smieja, F. "Alonso de Ledesma y la 'Segunda parte del Romancero General' de 1615." *Hispanófila* 4 (1960): 15–19.
———. "Ledesma y su poesía a lo divino." *Estudios segovianos* 15 (1963): 323–48.

LEDESMA MIRANDA, Ramón (1901, Madrid–1963, Madrid), poet. He wrote two books of poems: *La faz iluminada* (1928; The Illumined Face) and *Treinta poemas de transición* (1928; Thirty Poems of Transition). His early works exhibit the influence of Rubén Darío, but later writing evolves into a more dense poetry in the style of *Unamuno. Ledesma Miranda has also written novels, novelettes and short stories. Among his novels are *Antes del mediodía* (1930; Before Noon), *Agonía y tres novelas más* (1931; Anguish and Three Novels), *Evocación de Laura Estébanez* (1933; Evocation of Laura Estébanez). *Saturno y sus hijos* (1934; Saturn and His Children) and *Viejos personajes* (1936; Old Characters) are collections of novelettes. He achieved his greatest success with the novel *La casa de la fama* (1950; The House of Fame), winning the National Prize for Literature in 1951.

BIBLIOGRAPHY

Primary Texts

La casa de la fama. 2nd ed. Madrid: Nebrija, 1951.
Evocación de Laura Estébanez. Madrid: Gráfica Universal, 1933.
Historias de medio siglo. Madrid: Nacional, 1965. Articles from newspapers over the years.
Saturno y sus hijos. Madrid: n.p., 1934.

Isabel McSpadden

LEDO ANDIÓN, Margarita (1951, Castro de Rei, Lugo–), Galician poet and prose writer. A graduate of the School of Journalism of Barcelona, Ledo Andión collaborated in such magazines as *Cambio 16* and *Ciudadano* until, for political reasons, she was forced to move to Porto, Portugal, where she was lecturer of Galician. On her return to Galicia she founded and directed the weekly *A nosa terra* (Our Land).

BIBLIOGRAPHY

Primary Texts

O corvo érguese cedo. Monforte: n.p., 1973. Poetry.
Mamá-Fe. La Coruña: Xerais, 1983. Short stories.
Parolar cun eu, cun intre, cun inseuto. Monforte: n.p., 1970. Poetry.
Trasalba ou Violeta e o Militar Morto. La Coruña: Xerais, 1985. Novel.

Kathleen March

LEIVA Y RAMÍREZ DE AVELLANO, Francisco de (1630, Málaga–1676, Málaga), dramatist. One of many minor dramatists of the *Calderón school, Leiva wrote some fifteen plays in a variety of *comedia* styles. He used historical themes in two works: *Marco Antonio y Cleopatra* and *La mayor constancia de Mucio Scévola* (The Superior Steadfastness of Mucius Scaevola), based on the legendary Roman hero. Among his most popular plays were the religious drama *Nuestra Señora de la Victoria y restauración de Málaga* (Our Lady of Victory and the Liberation of Málaga) and the comedy of manners *Cuando no se aguarda y Príncipe tonto* (When One Is Impatient and the Foolish Prince). The latter is considered one of the best plays of its type from the period. Leiva's intrigue play *El socorro de los mantos* (Succour Provided by Cloaks) was written under the pseudonym Carlos de Avellano. Most of Leiva's works were published either in pamphlet form or in the numerous collections of plays which appeared in the last quarter of the seventeenth c.

BIBLIOGRAPHY

Primary Texts

Selected plays in BAE 47.

Criticism

Díaz de Escobar, N. *Francisco de Leyba y Ramírez de Avellano*. Málaga: Zembrana, 1899.

Donald C. Buck

LENA, Pero Rodríguez de. *See* Rodríguez de Lena, Pero

LEÓN, Luis de (1527 or 1528, Belmonte [Cuenca]–1591, Madrigal de las Altas Torres [Avila]), poet, exegete, theologian, professor. Scion of a family (of remote Jewish ancestry) distinguished in the practice and study of law, Luis professed in the Augustinian order (1544), trained for theological scholarship under Melchor *Cano and Domingo de *Soto at Salamanca, and with Cipriano de Huerga in Alcalá, and also in Toledo, and won his first of several Salamanca chairs, the ordinarily Dominican chair of St. Thomas, in 1561. A figure greatly esteemed and resented throughout his career, Fray Luis quickly worked his way to the center of Salamanca's highly charged field of partisan doctrinal dispute. There his brilliant and fervent humanistic dedication to the Hebrew and Greek textual foundations of Christianity provoked extreme reactions from conservative Scholastics, principally Dominican defenders of the Vulgate's authority. In 1572 several of these, led by León de Castro and Bartolomé de Medina, conspired to denounce Fray Luis and two colleagues to the *Inquisition, which arrested them. Fray Luis's prolonged and eloquent defense of his orthodox faith exhibited a keen legal mind, a want of tact, and an excess of combativeness. In solitary confinement and deprived of the sacrament for nearly five years, Fray Luis transformed his agony into a number of extensive prose and intensive poetic documents for which he is now regarded as Spain's foremost Christian humanist; seldom if ever was Inquisitorial persecution met so productively and countered by comparable spiritual and intellectual fortitude. Virtually exonerated and released from his Valladolid cell in December 1576, Fray Luis was warmly received by his Salamanca students and colleagues; an apocryphal story true to his embattled character claims that Fray Luis began his new term by dismissing the disruptive efforts of his tormenters: "Dicebamus hesterna die" (As we were saying yesterday . . .). Subsequently winning competitive chairs in moral philosophy and in biblical studies, Fray Luis began to publish his Latin and Spanish writings, prefacing each volume with an emblem (derived from Horace) defiantly alluding to his regeneration after torment: a severely pruned oak tree vigorously budding anew. In 1582 he was denounced to the Inquisition again, for his energetic efforts to counter the Dominican understanding of free will; he was absolved two years later. He devoted his last years to work on behalf of his university and his order, political skirmishing, writing and publication, and the editing of the works of Santa *Teresa de Jesús, of whom he was the first biographer.

Late in life Fray Luis gathered and edited his scattered poems and dedicated them to his friend and protector, don Pedro Portocarrero; this autograph ms. was lost; the poems were published in 1631, by Francisco de *Quevedo, from an imperfect copy. Modern editors generally recognize twenty-three authentic original poems and dispute the status of several others. Along with his own poems the poet collected his Scriptural translations, from Psalms, Job, and Proverbs, and rich evidence of his enthusiasm for classical and Italian learning, including translations from Petrarch and Bembo; Euripides and Pindar; two dozen of Horace's odes (highly esteemed by his colleague Francisco *Sánchez de las Brozas, and since), Virgil's *Eclogues* and parts of the *Georgics*.

The example of *Garcilaso de la Vega decisively influenced Fray Luis's choice of an appropriate stanza for his Castilian odes; sixteen of the original poems are constructed of *liras* (hendecasyllables and heptasyllables arranged *aBabB*), modeled after Garcilaso's "Canción V." In two Pindaric odes, adopting a public and heroic voice to celebrate familiar episodes of national myth, Fray Luis memorializes the traitor King Roderick ("Folgaba el Rey Rodrigo," King Roderick was taking his pleasure) and his miraculous opposite number, the liberator and Patron Saint James ("Las selvas conmoviera," I would stir the forests). Most of the poems, however, are Horatian: an intimate voice develops rational arguments in a sinuous succession of *liras*, finely controlled (partly by the delicate play of punctuation and enjambment) and yet heated by accumulated interjections ("¡Qué descansada vida!," How restful the life; "¡Oh, ya seguro puerto!," O safe refuge), interrogatives ("¿Cuándo será que pueda?," When will I fly from here?; "¿Y dejas, Pastor santo?," Holy Shepherd, do you leave?), imperatives ("No te engañe el dorado," Let the golden vase not deceive you; "Huid, contentos, de mi triste pecho," Happiness, flee my saddened breast), apostrophes, and, especially, binary oppositions. When arranged horizontally, these systematic antitheses counterpoise deliverance, represented in the forms of pastoral and cultivated nature, against bondage to urban vanities and rash values symbolized by maritime commerce, most memorably in Ode 1, "La vida retirada," The Secluded Life, a de-ironized formulation of Horace's *Beatus ille*:

¿Qué presta a mi contento,
si soy del vano dedo señalado;
si, en busca deste viento,
ando desalentado,
con ansias vivas, con moral cuidado?

¡Oh monte, oh fuente, oh río!
¡Oh secreto seguro, deleitoso!
roto casi el navio,
a vuestro almo reposo
huyo de aqueste mar tempestuoso.

(What good does it avail me / when I am praised by the vain, / if searching for their empty wind / I exhaust my spirit / in anxious, mortal pursuits? // O mountain, o fount, o river! / O secret refuge of delight! / my ship nearly broken apart / to your cherished peace / I flee this stormy sea.)

More frequently vertical arrangements and transcendental symbolism predominate: on a conventional Christian Neoplatonic (Ptolemaic) cosmic model Fray Luis displays supernatural light, harmony, mathematical regularity, and love, over against our sublunary shadowed world of *mundanal ruido*, unpredictable change, and pain:

Cuando contemplo el cielo
de innumerables luces adornado,
y miro hacia el suelo
de noche rodeado,
en sueño y en olvido sepultado,
el amor, y la pena
despiertan en mi pecho un ansia ardiente;
despiden larga vena
los ojos hechos fuente,
Loarte, y digo al fin con voz doliente:

'Morada de grandeza,
templo de claridad y hermosura,
el alma, que a tu alteza
nació, ¿qué desventura
la tiene en esta cárcel baja, escura?'

(When I study the heavens / adorned with innumerable lights, / and look back toward the earth / surrounded by night, / buried in sleep and forgetfulness, // love, and pain, / awaken in my breast a burning desire; / my eyes, become a spring, / let flow their stream, / Loarte, and finally my sad voice speaks: // "Dwelling-place of grandeur, / temple of light and beauty, / my soul, which on your heights / was born, what misadventure / holds it in this low, dark cell?")

[from Ode 8]

At least nine of the poems date from the time of the poet's own incarceration or recall it (none more appropriately than Ode 23, which begins: "Aquí la envidia y mentira / me tuvieron encerrado," Here envy and lies / held me locked away); the chronology of most of the rest is disputed. If the spiritual pulse of all these poems is ardently Christian, the imagination shaping them is habitually syncretistic; scarcely a stanza goes unenriched by a refined admixture of the poet's classical and biblical learning.

Among Fray Luis's didactic writings in Spanish, four stand out. The earliest, undertaken c. 1561, was a translation from Hebrew, with commentary, of the Song of Songs. The excellence of the work earned it considerable circulation in unauthorized copies; the imprudence of the undertaking, in contravention of the church's prohibition against translating Scripture into the vernacular, gave the poet's detractors evidence for their denunciation eleven years later. Following his imprisonment, Fray Luis published his commentary in Latin translation (1582); the Spanish version did not appear until 1798. *La perfecta casada* (1583; The Perfect Wife), still widely read, glosses the wisdom of Proverbs 31 and in its spirit counsels the wife to observe a practical, prudent, moderate, cooperative regime, subordinate to the husband's and respectful of social and biblical authority and convention.

De los nombres de Cristo (1583; On the Names of Christ) is Fray Luis's prose masterpiece and a remarkable work. Begun, at least, in prison, its three books in 500 pages combine, in elegantly crafted Ciceronian periods, generous measures of imaginative wish fulfillment with learned scriptural exegesis, soaring rhapsodies to the forms of nature, and scarcely concealed denunciations of the ignorance and treachery of the author's calumniators. Within a country retreat comfortably removed from the city three friends—a theologian, a scholar and a poet, apparently refractions of Fray Luis himself—engage in two days of humane colloquy incidentally framed by the author to parody the Inquisition's procedures: the youngest interlocutor uncovers a ms. on which the oldest had written words of uncertain significance; the latter is pressed to account for his act. The words are *Pimpollo* (Branch), *Faces de Dios* (Countenance of God),

Camino (Way), *Pastor* (Shepherd), *Monte* (Mount), *Padre del siglo futuro* (Everlasting Father), *Brazo de Dios* (Arm of the Lord), *Rey de Dios* (God's King), *Príncipe de Paz* (Prince of Peace), *Esposo* (Spouse), *Hijo de Dios* (Son of God), *Amado* (Beloved), *Jesús*, and *Cordero* (Lamb). Their Old Testament meanings are seen to prefigure New Testament truths and the person of Christ, which confirm and fulfill their significance. At one moment of pause in the graceful unfolding of these rich figurations, a lovely songbird nearby, attacked viciously by two crows, falls from its perch and drowns, apparently. But after a time the three disconsolate onlookers find reason to celebrate: the bird reappears out of the water, its song resounds, it flies higher than ever, safe in the company of its kind. (In his poems as well Fray Luis occasionally symbolized his two principal enemies in animal forms, and in one prison ode he cries: "del vuelo las alas he quebrado" I have broken the wings of my flight.)

Exposición del Libro de Job (Exposition of the Book of Job) is Fray Luis's longest work in length, 650 pages, and duration of his involvement, from before 1572 to 1591. To his literal translation ("conservando, cuanto es posible, el sentido latino y el aire hebreo," preserving the Latin meaning and Hebrew tone) he appends extensive commentary, at points achingly personal, and a second translation in *terza rima* ("pretendiendo por esta manera aficionar algunos al conocimiento de la Sagrada Escritura," seeking in this way to engage readers' interest in knowing Sacred Scripture). Clearly the circumstances of his imprisonment greatly fortified the poet-exegete's identification with that other isolated, mistreated, defiant, faithful—and ultimately vindicated—reasoner who had cried in his own dark hour

> "¡Apiadadvos, apiadadvos de mi, vos mis amigos, porque mano de Dios tocó en mi! ¿Por qué me perseguís como Dios, y de mi carne no vos hartades? ¡Quién me diese agora, y fuesen escriptas mis palabras! ¡Quién diese en libro, y fuesen esculpidas! ¡Con péndola de fierro y plomo, para siempre en peña fuesen tajadas! Yo conozco que mi Redentor vive, y que a la postre sobre polvo me levantaré."
>
> (Fray Luis's literal translation of Job 19:21–25: Have pity on me, have pity on me, you my friends, for the hand of God has touched me! Why do you, like God, pursue me, and why are you not satisfied with my flesh? Oh that my words were written! Oh that they were inscribed in a book! Oh that with a pen of iron and lead they were graven in rock for ever! I know that my Redeemer lives, and at the last he will raise me up upon the earth.)

Fray Luis's vigorous and malleable vernacular and the eclipse of Latin as the language of intellectual discourse have obscured the biblical commentaries and theological treatises (*De incarnatione* [On the Incarnation], *De fide* [On Faith], *De spe* [On Hope], *De charitate* [On Charity]) that won the learned professor the admiration of his students and peers. Since Fray Luis's forceful personality imprinted evidence of his mind, temperament, and values, and the accidents of his experience, on all his writings, the under-studied Latin documents invite the attention of today's scholarly students. All of the serene surfaces under which

Fray Luis's spiritual and emotional tensions are barely contained call still for the kind of understanding that Fray Luis urged on his Latinist poet friend Juan de Grial:

> El tiempo nos convida
> a los estudios nobles, y la fama,
> Grial, a la subida
> del sacro monte llama,
> do no podrá subir la postrer llama;
> alarga el bien guiado
> paso y la cuesta vence y solo gana
> la cumbre del collado
> y, do más pura mana
> la fuente, satisfaz tu ardiente gana;
> . . . que yo, de un torbellino
> traidor acometido y derrocado
> del medio del camino
> al hondo, el plectro amado
> y del vuelo las alas he quebrado

(The season invites us / to noble pursuits, and fame, / Grial, to scale / the sacred mount calls us, / where the final flame cannot mount; // stretch out your well-measured / pace and conquer the slope and win alone / the summit of the hill / and, where the fount flows most pure / satisfy your ardent thirst; // . . . for I, by a traitorous / whirlwind overcome and hurled down / from midway on my path / to the depths, have broken / my beloved lyre and the wings on which I soared)

(from Ode II)

See also Escuela Salmantina; Humanism; Renaissance; Siglo de Oro.

BIBLIOGRAPHY

Primary Texts

De los nombres de Cristo. Ed. Cristóbal Cuevas García. Madrid: Cátedra, 1977.

Magistri Luysii Legionensis agustiniani Divinorum Librorum primi apud Salmanticenses interpretis Opera nunc primum ex mss. ejusdem omnibus PP. Augustiniensium studio edita. 7 vols. Salamanca: n.p., 1891–95.

Obras completas castellanas. Ed. P. Félix García, O.S.A. 2 vols. Madrid: Biblioteca de Autores Castellanos, 1967.

Poesías. Ed. Oreste Macrí. Barcelona: Crítica, 1982.

Poesías: poesías originales, traducciones clásicas, traducciones sagradas. Ed. P. Angel Custodio Vega. Barcelona: Planeta, 1970.

English Translations

The Unknown Light: The Poems of Fray Luis de León. Tr. Willis Barnstone. Albany: State U of New York P, 1979.

Criticism

Alonso, Dámaso. *Poesía española: ensayo de métodos y límites estilísticos*. Madrid: Gredos, 1950.

Bell, Aubrey F. G. *Luis de León: A Study of the Spanish Renaissance*. Oxford: Clarendon, 1925.

Durán, Manuel. *Luis de León*. TWAS 136. New York: Twayne, 1971.

Guy, Alain. *La Pensée de Fray Luis de León: contribution à l'étude de la philosophie espagnole au XVIe siècle*. Limoges: Vrin, 1943.

Rivers, Elías R. *Luis de León. The Original Poems: Critical Guides to Spanish Texts*. London: Grant and Cutler, 1983.

Salvá, Miguel, and Pedro Sainz de Baranda, eds. *Colección de documentos inéditos para la historia de España: Proceso original que la Inquisición de Valladolid hizo al Maestro Fr. Luis de León, religioso del orden de S. Agustín*. Vols. 10–11. Madrid, 1847; rpt. Vaduz: Kraus Reprint, 1964.

George Shipley

LEÓN, María Teresa (1904, Logroño–), Spanish novelist, journalist, translator and essayist. An early feminist and vanguardist, she married the poet Rafael *Alberti, and with him collaborated in revolutionary activities and in defense of the Republic during the Spanish Civil War. She also worked with Antonio *Machado and the National Council for the Theater during this same period and campaigned in support of workers and the poor. At war's end, she and Alberti went into exile in France and then Argentina, remaining for almost a quarter-century. During the 1960s they moved to Rome and with the transition to democracy under the monarchy finally returned to Spain. León's work varies from early vanguardist and experimental prose, to stories motivated largely by ideological activism, to memoirs of war and exile and historically grounded fiction written for children. *La bella del mal amor* (1930; The Beauty Wrongly Loved) is an early collection of short stories on rural and traditional themes, redolent of medieval balladry, as is *Rosa-Fría, patinadora de la luna* (1934; Cold Rosa, Skater of the Moon), another story collection with an admixture of fantasy and lyricism. By contrast, *Cuentos de la España actual* (1937; Tales of Present-Day Spain) is ideologically committed and combative, a group of realistic and sometimes naturalistic tales of class struggle, social violence and hatred intended to propagate Marxist doctrines. *Contra viento y marea* (1941; Against Wind and High Water) is a novel presenting life as a struggle against enormous odds, inspired by experiences during the Civil War. *Morirás lejos* (1942; You'll Die Far Away), another short story collection, treats war and exile, including Mexican myths encountered during a brief stay in that country. *Las peregrinaciones de Teresa* (1950; Teresa's Pilgrimage) contains nine stories exploring feminine psychology, linked together by the symbolic character of Teresa. In *Juego limpio* (1959; Playing Fair), León presents the fictional memoirs of Friar Camilo, who leaves the monastery because of the Civil War. *Memoria de la melancolía* (1970; Memoir of Melancholy) is a testimonial of exile, while *La historia tiene la palabra* (1977; Historia Will Have the Last Word) is a kind of war memoir recounting efforts (in which León and Alberti took part) to save national artistic treasures during the Civil War. *Una estrella roja* (1979; A Red Star) is one of the most important and accessible of León's works, a short story anthology incorporating the earlier *Cuentos de la España actual*, *Morirás lejos*, and *Fábulas del tiempo amargo* (1962; Fables of the Bitter Time) in which the writer begins to transcend political activism and return to literary concerns.

BIBLIOGRAPHY

Primary Text

Una estrella roja. Prol. Joaquín Marco. Madrid: Espasa-Calpe, 1979.

Criticism

Pérez, Janet. *Contemporary Women Writers of Spain*. Boston: Hall, 1988. 45–49.

Janet Pérez

LEÓN, Ricardo (1877, Barcelona–1943, Torrelodones, Madrid), poet, novelist and academician in 1915. He is a representative of the exaltation of Hispanic tradition and religious feeling. Although he has two books of poems, *Lira de bronce* (1901; Bronze Lyre) and *Alivio de caminantes* (1911; Walker's Relief), he is better known as a novelist. *Casta de hidalgos* (1908; *A Son of The Hidalgos*, 1921), the first novel to give him success, was followed by *Comedia sentimental* (1909; Sentimental Comedy), a story of disillusioned love. *Alcalá de los Zeguíes* (1909) deals with the Andalusian "caciques" (political bosses); *El amor de los amores* (1910; *The Wisdom of Sorrow*, 1951) tries to create a "divine" Don Quixote, giving preference to mystic love over human love; *Los centauros* (1912; The Centaurs) portrays the picaresque atmosphere in our c. He has also written philosophical dialogues: *La escuela de sofista* (1910; School of Sophists) and *Los caballeros de la Cruz* (1916; The Knights of the Cross). León composed historial narrations on war subjects: *Europa trágica* (1917–18; Tragic Europe), *Las siete vidas de Tomás Portolés* (1931; The Seven Lives of Tomás Portolés), *Rojo y gualda* (1932; Red and Yellow) and *Bajo el yugo de los bárbaros* (1931; Under the Barbarian Yoke). The last two works were inspired by episodes of Spain's political life after the Second Republic. *Cristo en los infiernos* (1943; Christ in Hell) relates scenes of the period preceding the Spanish Civil War. Other novels are *Amor de caridad* (1922; Charity), *Humos de rey* (1923; Kingly Airs), *El hombre nuevo* (1927; The New Man), *Los trabajadores de la muerte* (1927; Workers of Death), *Jauja* (1928; Utopia) and *Las niñas de mis ojos* (1929; The Apples of My Eyes). His prose, rich in words, has been described as "brilliant"; nevertheless he sometimes falls into the trap of a versified cadence.

BIBLIOGRAPHY

Primary Texts

Colección de obras completas. 2nd ed. 2 vols. Madrid: Biblioteca Nueva, 1952–56.

English Translations

A Son of the Hidalgos. Tr. Catalina Páez. Garden City, NY: Doubleday, 1921.

The Wisdom of Sorrow. Tr. Philip H. Riley and Hubert J. Tunney. Notre Dame, IN: Ave Maria, 1951.

Criticism

Asín Palacios, Miguel. "Necrología." In *BRAE* 24 (1945): n.p.

Martínez, Eduardo Juliá. "Biografía de Ricardo León." *Cuadernos de Literatura Contemporánea* 11–12 (1943): 367–76.

Isabel McSpadden

LEÓN MARCHANTE, Manuel (between 1620 and 1627, Pastrana, Guadalajara–1680, Alcalá de Henares, Madrid), poet, dramatist, author of *entremeses*. His many poems are of little literary merit, but his *entremeses* exhibit talent. His *Obras poéticas póstumas* (1722; Posthumous Poetic Works) includes several plays worthy of mention, such as *No hay amar como fingir* (There's No Loving Like Pretending) and *La Virgen de la Salceda* (The Virgin of Salceda). León Marchante also carried on an amatory correspondence with a cousin who entered a convent; the correspondence has been preserved.

BIBLIOGRAPHY

Primary Texts

El gato y la montera, sainete nuevo. . . . In Spanish Plays 465.

"La picaresca." Ed. R. Foulché-Delbosc. In *RH* 38 (1916): 532–612. Correspondence.

Obras poéticas póstumas. Madrid: Barrio, 1722–33.

La Virgen de la Salceda. Madrid: Sanz, 1754.

Criticism

García-López, J. C. *Biblioteca de escritores de la provincia de Guadalajara*. Madrid: Rivadeneyra, 1899.

Méndez Plancarte, A. *León Marchante, jilguerillo del Niño Dios*. Mexico City: Abside, 1948.

LERA, Ángel María de (1912, Vitoria–1986, Madrid), Spanish novelist and journalist. Lera studied humanities in the Seminary of Vitoria and law at the U of Granada. During the years of the Second Republic (1931–36), he served as a socialist military administrator, for which he was condemned to death by the victorious Falangists, spending several years in prison under a death sentence before it was commuted to life in prison. After twenty years as a political prisoner, he was released in one of the Franco government "amnesties" and at first lived with great difficulty, with a series of odd jobs. Subsequently, he began to write for newspapers and magazines and was fortunate in that many of his novels were adapted as movies in the United States, including *Los clarines del miedo* (1958; Trumpets of Fear), which deals with bullfighting, and *La boda* (1959; The Wedding). His considerable popular success also led to numerous translations in England, Canada, the United States, France, Italy, Germany, Sweden, Finland, Hungary, Czechoslovakia, Poland, Romania, and Russia.

Lera received a number of significant literary prizes, including the Galdós Prize, and another of the *Academia Española for his novel, *Tierra para morir* (1964; Land to Die), which treats the problem of emigration and migrant workers in Spain, a theme expanded in *Hemos perdido el sol* (1963; We've Lost the

Sun); and the Planeta Prize for *Las últimas banderas* (1967; The Last Flags), which is significant as being the first novel published within Franco Spain with a pro-Republican perspective and written by an ex-Republican (it describes the fall of Madrid in the Civil War and the way the retreating Loyalists rolled up their flags before leaving the city). This novel is the first of a tetralogy on the war, comprising in addition *Los que perdimos* (1970; We Who Lost [the War]); *La noche sin riberas* (1976; Night without Shores); and *Oscuro amanecer* (1977; Dark Dawn), all with a considerable autobiographical basis. Most of the characters are, as was Lera, Loyalists, prisoners, dreamers obsessed with the recovery of freedom, who discover that liberty is illusory outside the prison walls, as their individuality and identity are menaced by a dehumanized "mass" society: in the prison, they were at least numbers, while at large, they are nobody. Another novel, belonging to this period but not forming part of the tetralogy, is *Se vende un hombre* (1973; Man for Sale), which received a prize from the *Ateneo of Seville. Among his volumes of journalistic reporting are *Mi viaje alrededor de la locura* (1972; My Voyage around Insanity), *Con la maleta al hombro* (1965; With My Suitcase on My Back), *Por los caminos de la medicina rural* (1966; Along the Roads of Rural Medicine), and *Los fanáticos* (1969; Fanatics).

BIBLIOGRAPHY

Primary Texts

Mi viaje alrededor de la locura. Barcelona: Planeta, 1972.
Los olvidados. Madrid: Aguilar, 1957.
Oscuro amanecer. Barcelona: Argos, 1977.
Los que perdimos. Barcelona: Planeta, 1974.
Trampa. Madrid: Aguilar, 1962.

Criticism

Listerman, Mary Sue. *Ángel María de Lera*. TWAS 652. Boston: Twayne, 1982.

Janet Pérez

LETRILLA, a type of poem. Lines of the *letrilla* are usually short (eight syllables or less), often include a refrain, and treat topics in a light, graceful fashion. They may be amorous, satiric, or religious in subject. This type of poem existed in the fourteenth c., but the term did not appear until later. Francisco *Martínez de la Rosa compared the *letrilla* to Cupid, with his grace, charm, and ability to slip away lightly.

LEVERONI, Rosa (1910, Barcelona–1985, Barcelona), poet, translator and librarian. Her poetry expresses the excitement, pain and joy of love in a thoughtful and circumspect tone. She shows influence of Noucentisme in her striving for the formal perfection of classicism, and of several Catalan poets whose work she studied. She uses elements of nature to explain her inner self and sometimes classic imagery to describe her feelings and experiences. She worked as a librarian at the Universitat Autònoma until 1939 and is known for her research on Ausiàs

*March. Carles *Riba and Salvador *Espriu encouraged her, and both celebrated her as an excellent poet in introductions to her books. She also contributed to the journals *Ariel* and *Poesia* and translated T. S. Eliot but produced no creative works after 1952. There are two collections of her work: *Poesia* (1981; Poetry) with a prologue by Maria Aurèlia *Capmany; and *Presència i record* (1952; Presence and Memory) with a prologue by Salvador Espriu. She won a prize in the Jocs Florals of 1956 celebrated at Cambridge, England. *See also* Juegos.

BIBLIOGRAPHY

Primary Texts

Epigrames i cançons. Barcelona: Gili, 1938.
Poesia. Barcelona: Edicions 62, 1981.
Presència i record. Barcelona: Ossa Menor, 1952.

Kathleen McNerney

LEYENDA NEGRA, La. *See* Black Legend

LEYVA, José (1938, Seville–), novelist. Leyva's first novels, written during the 1960s decline of post-war neo-realism, had to wait a decade for publication when the "New Novel" had gained some critical acceptance. The experimental, vanguard nature of Leyva's work and its difficulty for readers has meant a dearth of attention from the critical establishment, except for the Biblioteca Breve Prize awarded *La circuncisión del Señor Solo* (The Circumcision of Mr. Alone) in 1972. Other novels to date are *Leitmotiv* (1972), *Heautontimoroumenos* (1973; The Self-Tormentor), *La primavera de los murciélagos* (1974; Springtime of the Bats), and *La calle de los árboles dormidos* (1974; The Street of Sleeping Trees). Leyva conceives all these as parts of a super-novel entitled "Menos Uno" (Minus One) which would include paintings and other artistic creations in addition to the text and would have to be "read" in a museum or art gallery.

Leitmotiv, conceived as an homage to Kafka, portrays situations and events reminiscent of the absurd world of the Austrian writer, with continuously changing environment and characters never what they seem to be. *La circuncisión del Señor Solo* underscores man's alienation via a hallucinatory sequence of events in a country governed by a cabala of priests who force men to be circumcised. The novel is structured as a dialogue between protagonist and reader (or possibly himself) in which he speaks of his fear, pain and suffering. *Heautontimoroumenos*, probably Leyva's most hermetic work, combines print and paintings, with experimental typography tracing visual patters which combine with the drawings that Leyva terms "iconograms" to produce an extraordinary spectacle. The narrative consciousness is a man in a catatonic state, suffering extreme schizophrenia since his personality has split into hundreds of individuals, not merely two or three. *La calle de los árboles dormidos* contains 349 numbered fragments, including 26 announcements following newspaper format. These fragments, of varying length (with the smallest only two words), portray the lives of newspaper workers and the news covered. The narrative intends to give the public instant and simultaneous access to the news via a combination of printed and electronic media. Because of its continuity of action and a relatively closed ending, this is the most conventional of Leyva's novels to date. *La primavera de los murciélagos*, the least studied of Leyva's novels, is a literary labyrinth enclosing an irrational, chaotic fictional universe, at once grotesque, absurd and satiric. Nicolás Babel, presumptive protagonist, serves to link otherwise disparate episodes, acting as narrative consciousness and the "reader's guide" through infernal regions surrealistically reminiscent of earth. The protagonist's last name transparently symbolizes the confusion and misunderstanding which inform his life and predominate throughout the novel, whose characters collectively evoke Brueghel's paintings. Lacking conventional plot and logical sequence or linear temporality, the novel is what Umberto Eco would classify an open work, without a definitive ending, requiring active readers who can collaborate to supply meaning and overcome the lack of transitions, logic, sequentiality, authorial interpretation and clarification.

BIBLIOGRAPHY

Primary Texts

La circuncisión del Señor Solo. Barcelona: Seix Barral, 1972.
Europa. Madrid: Mondadori, 1988.
Heautontimoroumenos. Madrid: Betancor, 1973.
Leitmotiv. Barcelona: Seix Barral, 1972.
La primavera de los murciélagos. Barcelona: Seix Barral, 1974.

Criticism

Díaz, Janet W. "Origins, Aesthetics and the *nueva novela española*." *Hispania* 59:1 (March 1976): 109–17.
Joly, Monique, Ignacio Soldevila, and Juan Tena. *Panorama du Roman Espagnol Contemporain (1939–1975)*. Montpellier: Centre d'Etudes Sociocritiques U.E.R. II, Université Paul Valéry, 1984.
Pérez, Genaro. *La novelística de J. Leyva*. Madrid: Porrúa, 1985.
Soldevila Durante, Ignacio. *La novela desde 1936*. Madrid: Alhambra, 1980.

Genaro J. Pérez

LIBERTINO, Clemente. *See* Mello, Francisco

LIBRO DE DICHOS DE SABIOS ET PHILOSOPHOS. *See Dichos de Sabios et Philosophos, Libro de*

LIMA, Angelo de (1872, Oporto–1921, Lisbon), poet of the Portuguese Modernist movement, who spent the last twenty years of his life in Rilhafoles, the Lisbon mental hospital. This gave critics hostile to the group the opportunity to describe its journal *Orpheu* (1915; Orpheus), in the second issue of which the first significant collection of Angelo de Lima's poetry was published, in phrases such as "madhouse literature." In fact, though, it is true to say that they were shocked and irritated by all the contributions, not just his, and nowadays his work does not seem unduly bizarre, nor is it at all obvious that it is the product of a deranged mind.

Medical records have brought to light the unhealthy family background of the poet, alleging that his grandfather was a murderer, and revealing that his father, who achieved a certain fame as a poet himself, died insane; Angelo and a sister were the only survivors of nine children, and four of these died from meningitis, which he claimed to suffer from in later years.

After expulsion from the Lisbon Military College, he attended classes at the Fine Arts Academy in Oporto, then joined the army, where his drunkenness, absenteeism and anti-social behavior caused him many problems. On his return from a short spell in Mozambique, he took up art classes again and became for a brief period the art editor of *A Geraçao Nova* (The New Generation). However, it was not long before his unacceptable behavior caused him to be interned in a psychiatric hospital for four years. Two years after his release, he caused uproar in a Lisbon theater and was admitted to Rilhafoles, this time definitively. He was reported to be prey to a persecution complex, aural hallucinations and "overexcitement." It was also alleged that he had attempted sexual relations with his sister. Many of his accompanying physical complaints were attributed to alcoholism, and he was labeled a "degenerate"; his condition was diagnosed as "moral insanity." It was also claimed that his artistic talents had been exaggerated by his friends.

In fact, some of the forty-three poems that make up his oeuvre have a value unconnected with the abnormal circumstances of his life and have been admired by critics and poets alike. One example is the sonnet "Pára-me de repente o Pensamento," sometimes called "Tédio" (My Thoughts Suddenly Stop; Tedium), which was described by Fernando *Pessoa in 1935 as "extraordinary," and "one of the best ever written in Portuguese." Although this particular poem explicitly treats his insanity, Angelo de Lima also produced several equally impressive pieces that do not. Worth mentioning is an effective version of "Un peu de musique" (A little music) by Victor Hugo.

Like his contemporaries in Portugal, he can be judged as largely post-symbolist, with a strong vein of decadentism running through some of the poems, but there is also a distinctive and, in that period, disturbing element of discontinuity which never, however, lapses into incoherence. Others, of course, were consciously eschewing traditional form at the time and indulging in the verbal dislocation that arises from spontaneous self-expression, soon to come under the heading of surrealism; while it would be absurd to classify Angelo de Lima a precursor of this movement, it might be claimed that at least some of its characteristics came naturally to him because of his tragic condition.

Little scholarly work has been published on Lima's poetry. The bibliography is almost entirely made up of biographical articles, often short and published in newspapers, which mostly deal with the poet's insanity.

BIBLIOGRAPHY

Primary Texts

Poesias Completas. Ed., intro. F. Guimaraes. Oporto: Inova, 1971.

Pamela Bacarisse

LIÑÁN DE RIAZA, Pedro (1557?, Toledo–1607, Madrid), poet. One of the younger sons of a noble family, he studied in Salamanca and later became secretary to the Marquis of Camarasa. He also served as a soldier in the Royal Guard of Philip III, and at the end of his life he was chaplain of a church in Torrijos.

Liñán de Riaza is mentioned by Lope de *Vega and Agustín de *Rojas as an author of *comedias*; however, none of his works for the theater has survived. *Cervantes, Lope and *Gracián y Morales highly praised his verse, but subsequent generations have forgotten him. Some of his poems were included in the *Romancero general* (1600) and in Pedro *Espinosa's *Flores de poetas ilustres* (1605; Anthology of Illustrious Poets). In the nineteenth c., his poetry was collected and published under the title *Rimas* (1876; Rhymes), but the editor erroneously attributed a number of poems to him. He wrote in both traditional and Italianate meters. According to Julian Fitz Randolph, "In Italianate genres and in most of his compositions in traditional Spanish verse form, he is generally conservative yet very diversified. As a *romancista,* he appears to represent the transition from a previous generation to the group responsible for the triumph of the highly innovative *romancero nuevo.*" (Randolph, J. F. "*Vida* y obra de Liñán de Riaza." *DAI* 31 (9, 10) 1971: 5420-A.) *See also* Italian Literary Influences.

BIBLIOGRAPHY

Primary Text

Rimas. Zaragoza: Hospicio provincial, 1876.

Criticism

Randolph, J. F. "Vida y obra de Liñán de Riaza." Diss., U of California, Berkeley, 1970.

Hector Medina

LIÑÁN Y VERDUGO, Antonio de (c. 1560, Vera de Rey, Cuenca–?, ?), supposed author of *Guía y avisos de forasteros que vienen a la corte* (1620; Guide and Admonition to Strangers Coming to the Court), a didactic work with *picaresque elements, sometimes labeled *novela cortés* (courtly novel or novel of manners) or an early precursor of *costumbrismo* (*Romanticism). The work's episodic structure, loosely bound by a moralizing frame-tale, is composed of a series of anecdotes illustrating the dangers of life in seventeenth-c. Madrid, told in lively, colloquial language to a young man, don Diego, by a scholar, the *Maestro*, and by a seasoned courtier, don Antonio, familiar with the varieties of deceit to be encountered in that milieu. The work draws on Boccaccian as well as picaresque narrative sources for its anecdotes and offers a detailed picture of customs, pastimes, occupations, neighborhoods, and popular language in Madrid.

Jean Sarrailh (1919) suggested that clues to Liñán's identity and origins were included in comments made by a character in the novel, the scholarly *Maestro*. In the absence of extratextual documents concerning Liñán y Verdugo's existence, Manuel Fernández Nieto (1973) rejects Sarrailh's meticulously researched biographical hypotheses and brings new evidence to bear on Zarco Cuevas's belief (1929) that the *Guía's* author might be the Mercedarian friar Alonso *Remón, author of the *Vida del Caballero de Gracia* (1620; Life of the Knight of Grace), *Entretenimiento y juegos honestos* (1623; Pastimes and Honest Games) and *La casa de la razón y el desengaño* (1625; The House of Reason and Disillusion).

BIBLIOGRAPHY

Primary Text

Guía y avisos de forasteros, a donde se les enseña a huir de los peligros que ay en la vida de Corte, y debaxo de nouelas morales, y exemplares escarmientos, se les auisa, y aduierte de como acudiran a sus negocios cuerdamente. Madrid: Viuda de Alonso Martín, 1620.

Criticism

Fernández Nieto, M. "Nuevos datos sobre autores de novela cortesana." *RABM* 76.2 (1973): 423–37.

Sarrailh, Jean. "Algunos datos acerca de don Antonio Liñán y Verdugo, autor de la *Guía y avisos de forasteros*, 1620." *RFE* 6 (1919): 346–63.

Zarco Cuevas, J. "¿Quién fue el verdadero autor de la *Guía y avisos de forasteros* impresa en Madrid en el año 1620?" *BRAE* 16 (1929): 185 ff.

Emilie Bergmann

LINARES, Luisa-María (1915, Madrid–), principally a novelist. Linares developed her powers of observation in the course of extensive travel as a child with her father, dramatist Luis Linares Becerra, and began writing stories at age eight. She began publishing novels at age twenty-four with *En poder de Barba Azul* (1939; Held by Blue Beard), a work which she also assisted in adapting for successful stage and film versions. She also assisted in the adaptations for stage and screen versions of *Doce lunas de miel* (1944; Twelve Honeymoons) and *Un marido a precio fijo* (1955; Fixed Price for a Husband). Among the best-known of her many (more than thirty) novels, all of which feature women protagonists, are *Sólo volaré contigo* (1956; I'll Only Fly with You), *Salomé la magnífica* (1957; Salome, the Magnificent), *Casi siempre te adoro* (1960; I Almost Always Adore You), *Mis cien últimos amores* (1963; My Last Hundred Loves), *Juan a las ocho, Pablo a las diez* (1965; *Web of Fear*, 1979), *De noche soy indiscreta* (1965; At Night, I'm Indiscreet). With their adventure-loving heroines, uncomplicated plots, witty dialoque, exotic settings, and happy endings, these novels have enjoyed wide popularity, particularly among upper middle-class women. All of Linares's novels have been made into movies, most have been translated into other languages (French, German, English, Dutch, Finnish, Swedish, etc.) and adapted for stage, film and television in various countries outside of Spain (principally France, Argentina and Italy). One of her novels was selected as the "Book of the Month" in Vienna (*Cada día tiene su secreto* [Each Day Has Its Secret]), and she has collaborated on many internationally known journals, such as *Elle*, *Marie Claire*, *Constanze*, *Freundin*, *Bunte Illustrierte*, *Beatijs*, *Grazia*, and *Woman's Own*.

BIBLIOGRAPHY

Primary Texts

En poder de Barba Azul. Barcelona: Juventud, 1982.
Un marido a precio fijo. Barcelona: Juventud, 1979.
Mis cien últimos amores. Barcelona: Juventud, 1963.
Juan a las ocho, Pablo a las diez. Barcelona: Juventud, 1977.
De noche soy indiscreta. Barcelona: Juventud, 1965.

English Translations

Web of Fear (*Juan a las ocho, Pablo a las diez*). Ontario: Mistic Books, 1979.
Fatal Legacy (*No digas lo que hice ayer*). Ontario: Mistic Books, 1979.

Patricia W. O'Connor

LINARES RIVAS, Manuel (1867, Santiago de Compostela–1938, Galicia), politician, judge, congressman, playwright. A follower of *Benavente, many of his plays were bourgeois and satirical in tone with a didactic intent. His plays appealed to the average viewer—he sometimes borders on vulgarity. *Mal año de lobos* (1927; Bad Year for Wolves) and *Todo Madrid lo sabía* (1931; All Madrid Knew It) are two of his best works. He wrote the theatrical adaptation of *Pérez Lugín's *La casa de la Troya* (The House of Troy) and *Currito de la Cruz* (1923).

BIBLIOGRAPHY

Primary Texts

Obras completas. 15 vols. Madrid: Biblioteca Hispania, 1913–21.
Obras escogidas. Madrid: Aguilar, 1947.
Mis mejores cuentos. Madrid: Prensa popular, 1921.

Isabel McSpadden

LISANDRO Y ROSELIA, Tragicomedia de (1542; Tragicomedy of Lisander and Roselia), one of the six principal sequels to the **Celestina*. Generally considered the best of such imitations, although all are profoundly different from their model, it has been attributed to a Sancho de Muñón. María Rosa Lida de Malkiel has studied in depth the *Celestina* and its relation to continuations and to a wide body of subsequent literature.

BIBLIOGRAPHY

Primary Text

Tragicomedia de Lisandro y Roselia. Madrid: Rivadeneyra, 1872.

Criticism

Lida de Malkiel, María Rosa. *La originalidad artística de la "Celestina."* 2nd ed. Buenos Aires: Editorial universitaria de Buenos Aires, 1970.

LISBOA, António Maria (1928, Lisbon–1953, Lisbon), Portuguese poet, member of the surrealist group of Lisbon associated with Mario *Cesariny de Vasconcelos. Lisboa authored *Ossóptico* (1952) and *Erro Próprio*, a lecture-manifest (1962; Personal Error), *Isso-Ontem-Único* (1953); *A Verticalidade e a Chave* (1956; Verticality and the Key), and *Poesia* (1962; Poetry), a partial anthology. Certain titles and many individual poems incorporate a very personal, experimental language, filled with word fragments and neologisms. This increasingly hermetic form of expression is used especially in poems dealing with love and the ephemeral, but is not fully developed. Other poems have a demythologizing intent. Lisboa was also associated with Alexandre *O'Neill, but perhaps because of his early death, is considered inferior to the latter.

BIBLIOGRAPHY

Primary Texts

Erro Próprio. Lisbon: Guimaraes, 1962.
Poesia. Lisbon: Guimaraes, 1962.
A Verticalidade e a Chave. Lisbon: Contraponto, 1956.

LISBOA, Irene do Céu Vieira (1892, Lisbon–1958, Lisbon), Portuguese prose fiction writer. Lisboa published numerous pedagogical works under the pseudonym of Manuel Soares, and her first literary works were published under another masculine pseudonym, João Falcó, due to the prevailing lack of tolerance for women writers and the complications which she risked in her personal and professional life. *Contarelos* (1926) and several volumes of meditations and impressions in poetic prose or free verse were attributed to Falcó: *Solidão* (1936); *Um dia e outro dia* (1936; One Day and Another), and *Outono, havias de vir* (1937; Autumn, You'd Have to See). These volumes, expressing the anguish of profound isolation, are not fiction in the usual sense, given a certain documentary or autobiographical content. *Começa uma vida* (1940; A Life Begins), *Voltar atrás para quê?* (1940; Why Turn Back?) and the series of scenes involving Adelina in *Esta Cidade!* (1942; This City) all possess a lively narrative interest and certain novelistic qualities, although they are essentially direct observations of common types and episodes of popular daily life in Lisbon and the mountains. Lisboa's work is infused with the desolation of an intelligent and cultured woman confined to the backward milieu of the petit-bourgeois Portugal of her day. Her writings present the co-existence of simple people, servants, office and construction workers, and others of the lower class, whose problems, attitudes and feelings are faithfully recorded in a transparent style which incorporates the language of the streets, especially as seen in the series of three "notebooks," *A Pena* (1940; Sorrow). *Apontamento*s (1943; Appointments), *O*

Pouco e o Muito (1956; A Little and a Lot), *Título qualquer serve* (1958; Any Title Will Do), and *Crónicas da Serra* (1960; Mountain Chronicles) belong to the neo-realist literature of social criticism prevailing in Spain during much of the 1950s and 1960s.

BIBLIOGRAPHY

Primary Texts

Apontamentos. Lisbon: Gráfica Lisbonense, 1943.
Começa uma vida. Lisbon: Seara Nova, 1940.
Esta cidade! Lisbon: Gráfica Lisbonense, 1942.
Solidão. 2nd ed. Lisbon: Portugália, 1965.
Título qualquer serve. Lisbon: Portugália, 1958.

Janet Pérez

LISTA Y ARAGÓN, Alberto (1775, Seville–1848, Seville), poet, dramatist, critic and educator. Considered the best of the *Escuela sevillana (School of Seville) poets, Lista was a major figure of the Spanish Enlightenment and a considerable influence on the developing Romantic movement. He overcame several health problems in early childhood and a modest economic background to excel at the U in Seville, where he studied philosophy, theology and mathematics. Although Lista entered the priesthood in 1803, he preferred to dedicate his life to literature, education and the liberal cause, to which he devoted much of his creative energies. This commitment to political, religious and social reform caused several internal and external conflicts for Lista. Although a priest, he joined a Masonic lodge for a time and throughout his life was a major contributor to the liberal press in Spain. He was exiled for a brief period by the absolutist government of Ferdinand VII; on the other hand, Lista was accused of being a collaborator with the French occupation forces in Seville. However, Lista made his most lasting contribution to the intellectual development of Spain as a teacher. He held several teaching posts, most notably as professor of mathematics, history and humanities at the Colegio de San Mateo in Madrid, and he culminated his educational career as dean of philosophy at the U of Seville. During the absolutist repression of higher education during the 1820s, Lista continued to give private lessons in his own home. His pupils included many of the future intellectual, governmental and literary leaders of Spain during the nineteenth c., among them General León y Navarrete, Ventura de la *Vega, *Espronceda, Agustín *Durán, *Bécquer and *Amador de los Ríos.

Lista's poetry exhibits a predominantly classic orientation, with certain "pre-romantic" tendencies. As in *Cadalso, one can find a quasi-Romantic stance, utilizing a more personal, even autobiographical viewpoint, and realistic (as opposed to idealized) descriptions of nature, as in his poem *La cabāna* (The Cottage). In general, however, Lista looked to such authors as Horace and the

Spanish *Renaissance classicists as his models. His religious poetry shows influences of Fray Luis de *León, as in the ode *A la muerte de Cristo* (On the Death of Jesus), and of San *Juan de la Cruz, in *El canto del esposo* (The Husband's Canticle). Fernando de *Herrera's spirit pervades much of Lista's poetry, particularly in its imagery and tone. His poem *La bondad natural al hombre* (The Bountifulness of Nature to Man) recalls the attitudes of Rousseau, and both *Jovellanos and *Meléndez Valdés exerted considerable influence on Lista in his didactic poetry. Lista even produced a free-verse adaptation of Pope's *Dunciad* under the title *El imperio de la estupidez* (The Empire of Stupidity). He tried his hand at drama with *El enfermo de aprensión* (Sick from Apprehension) and produced a translation of Marie-Joseph de Chénier's *Charles IX* as *La escuela de los reyes o Carlos IX* (The School for Kings or Charles IX). Lista was known more as a drama critic than as a dramatist, however, and his impact on Spanish *theater can be seen in his numerous periodical essays, in which he championed the efforts of Leandro Fernández de *Moratín, and in his series of lectures for the *Ateneo in Madrid, *Literatura dramática* (1836; Dramatic Literature). In 1844 Lista published a collection of his *Ensayos literarios y críticos* (Literary and Critical Essays) which displays his substantial breadth of knowledge and insightful critical acumen. Although Lista's fame rests more on his educational and critical work rather than literary output, the influence of his literary background on his life and works in general was widespread. He himself expressed his philosophy of writing in terms of his literary heritage: "pensar como *Rioja y decir como *Calderón" (think like Rioja and write like Calderón).

BIBLIOGRAPHY

Primary Texts

Selected works in BAE 67.

Poesías inéditas de don Alberto Lista. Ed. J. María de Cossío. Madrid: Sociedad de Menéndez y Pelayo, 1927.

Criticism

Clarke, D. C. "On the Versification of Alberto Lista." *RR* 43 (1952): 109–16.

Cossío, J. M. "Don Alberto Lista, crítico teatral de *El Censor*." *BRAE* 17 (1930–31): 396–422.

Jover, J. M. "Alberto Lista y el romanticismo español." *Arbor* 73 (1952): 127–36.

Juretschke, H. "Alberto Lista, representante del régimen liberal." *Arbor* 67–68 (1951): 389–407.

———. *Vida, obra y pensamiento de Alberto Lista.* Madrid: CSIC, 1951.

Medford, J. C. J. "Alberto Lista and the Romantic Movement in Spain." *BSS* 16 (1939): 84–103.

Fernando Operé

LISUARTE DE GRECIA (Lisuarte of Greece), a chivalric novel of the **Amadís de Gaula* cycle. The deeds and fortunes of Lisuarte, grandson to Amadís, first appeared in 1514 with the full title *El séptimo libro de Amadís. En el cual se trata de los grandes fechos de armas de Lisuarte de Grecia, fijo de Esplandián* *y de Perión de Gaula* (The Seventh Amadís Book. In Which Are Treated the Great Feats of Arms of Lisuarte of Greece, Son of Esplandián, and Perión of Gaul). Feliciano de *Silva is credited with authorship of this weak member of the *Amadís* series. *See also* Caballerías, Libros de.

BIBLIOGRAPHY

Primary Text

El séptimo libro. . . . Estela: Anvers, 1564.

Criticism

Umbert, W. *Studien zu den letzen Büchern des Amadis romans.* Halle: n.p., 1923.

Patricia Grieve

LLAGUNO Y AMIROLA, Eugenio de (?, Vitoria–1799, Madrid), neoclassical erudite, politician, editor. Of various noteworthy editions he supervised, his edition of Pero *López de Ayala's works is particularly outstanding. An original work is *Noticias de los arquitectos y arquitectura de España desde su Restauración* (1829; Information on Spanish Architects and Architecture since the Restoration), a storehouse of data for the history of architecture in Spain.

BIBLIOGRAPHY

Primary Text

Noticias de los arquitectos. . . . Madrid: Imprenta Real, 1829.

Criticism

Apraiz, R. de. ''El ilustre alavés don Eugenio de Llaguno y Amirola: su vida, su obra.'' *Boletín de la Real Academia vascongada* 4 (1948): 53–95.

LLAMPILLAS, Francisco Javier (1731, Mataró–1810, Sesti, Italy), critic and literary historian. Father Llampillas (or Lampillas) belonged to the Jesuit order. He taught rhetoric in Barcelona, and after the expulsion of the Jesuits from Spain in 1767, Llampillas became professor of theology in Ferrara, Italy. Llampillas encountered considerable anti-Spanish sentiment among the Italian *literati* during his exile there. Three critics in particular, Tiraboschi, Bettinelli and Signorelli, found Spanish literature to be abstruse as well as a decadent, corrupting influence on Italian literature. Llampillas's patriotic feelings prompted him to correct their erroneous evaluations with his six-volume *Saggio storico-apologetico della Letteratura Spagnola* (1778–81; Historical-Apologetical Essay on Spanish Literature). Both Tiraboschi and Bettinelli responded to Llampillas who, in turn, published their works along with his counter-response as the seventh volume of his essays (Rome, 1781). Llampillas's nationalistic stance was immediately popular in Spain and his entire series was soon translated into Spanish by Josefa *Amar y Borbón, under the title *Ensayo histórico-apologético de la literatura española contra las opiniones preocupadas de algunos escritores modernos italianos* (1782–89; Historical Apologetical Essay on Spanish Literature against the Prejudiced Opinions of Some Modern Italian Critics). The series as a whole constitutes a well-reasoned, if rather polemical, defense of Spanish prose, poetry and theater, from Roman times to the *Siglo de Oro. Llampillas, for example, argued in favor of *Góngora's poetry by pointing out that the convoluted, baroque style of Góngora was a general trend in early seventeenth-c. European literature and not limited solely to Spanish poets. Llampillas was particularly vociferous in his defense of Spain's national *theater against the rigid precepts of neo-classic theories, and favorably compares *Calderón's works to Italian opera. *See also* Italian Literary Influences.

BIBLIOGRAPHY

Primary Text

Ensayo histórico apologético.... Tr. J. Amar y Borbón. 2nd ed. 7 vols. Madrid: Marín, 1789.

Criticism

Menéndez Pelayo, M. *Historia de las ideas estéticas.* Madrid: CSIC, 1944. 3: 350–55.

Rossi, G. C. "Calderón en la crítica española del siglo XVIII." In *Estudios sobre las letras en el siglo de oro.* Madrid: Gredos, 1967. 71–76.

Donald C. Buck

LLANOS, Valentín de (1795, Valladolid–1885, Madrid), novelist. After studies in Valladolid, Llanos traveled in Europe, and in the winter of 1820–21 he became acquainted with John Keats in Rome. Once in London, where he went into voluntary exile, he met and married Fanny Keats, the poet's sister. After Ferdinand VII's death, Llanos and his family returned to Spain. He became secretary to Minister Mendizábal (1835), represented Valladolid in the 1836–37 legislature, was an alderman at the Madrid Town Hall (1840), served as Spanish consul in Gibraltar (1840–43), and then, being of independent means, he retired from public life. Llanos wrote a historical novel, *Don Esteban; or Memoirs of a Spaniard written by himself* (1825), and the following year published *Sandoval; or the Freemason* (1825), another historical novel, and *Don Esteban's* reprint. Llanos also authored the "memoirs" of General Van Halen, *Narrative of Don Juan Van Halen's imprisonment...* (1827), and various other pieces. Chronologically, Llanos was the first Spanish Romantic author to write a historical novel with a Spanish theme. He wrote in English because his novels, in which he defended his own Liberal creed, were intended to promote the Liberal cause among English readers. *See also* Romanticism.

BIBLIOGRAPHY

Primary Texts

Don Esteban; or, Memoirs of a Spaniard written by himself. 3 vols. London: Colburn, 1825.

Sandoval; or the Freemason. 3 vols. London: Colburn, 1826.

Narrative of Don Juan Van Halen's imprisonment in the dungeons of the Inquisition at Madrid. 2 vols. London: Colburn, 1827.

Criticism

Edgcumbe, F. *Letters of Fanny Brawne to Fanny Keats*. London: Oxford UP, 1936.
Llorens, V. *Liberales y Románticos. Una emigración española en Inglaterra. (1836–1844)*. Madrid: Castalia, 1968.

Salvador García Castañeda

LLANTOS, Libro de los (Book of Tears), apocryphal work. *Pellicer de Ossau fabricated and attributed it as title to octaves supposedly composed by Diego de *San Pedro. The attribution was a hoax, as was his attribution of a *Libro de las* **querellas* to *Alphonse X the Wise.

LLORENTE, Teodor (1836, Valencia–1911, Valencia), poet and translator. Bilingual in Catalan and Spanish, he used both languages in his work. Early compositions eulogized his native land and its ideals. In *La nova Era* (about 1860; The New Age), he sang the triumph of the Cross; in *Als Poetes de Catalunya* (about 1860; To Catalan Poets), he supported increasing Catalan-Valencian ties while deploring separatist tendencies. His writings take a more romantic and imaginative tone in *Llibret de versos* (1884–85; Book of Poems) and in *Nou llibret de versos* (1902; New Book of Poems), which are mainly *costumbrista* descriptions of scenes from Valencian life, as in the composition titled *La barraca* (The Cabin). Llorente also translated Romantic authors such as Goethe (*Faust*), Byron, Heine (*Buch der Lieder*), and Victor Hugo into Spanish verse. *See also* Romanticism.

BIBLIOGRAPHY

Primary Texts

Llibret de versos. Valencia: Llorente, 1885.
Nou Llibret de versos. Valencia: Domenech, 1909.
Poesies valencianes. 5th ed. Valencia: Domenech, 1936.

Criticism

Masreira, A. *Teodor Llorente*. Barcelona: n.p., 1905.
Navarro Reveter, Juan. *Teodor Llorente, su vida y sus obras*. Barcelona: Granada, 1910.

Eugene Del Vecchio

LLOVET, Enrique (1918, Málaga–), writer, diplomat, theater critic and chronicler. He contributes articles to the daily *ABC*, using the pen name Marco Polo. He has also published poems, *Donaires de la piedra y el agua* (1941; Charms of Stone and Water); a novel titled *Elizondo* (1945); *Lo que no sabemos del teatro* (1967; What We Don't Know about the Theater), *España viva* (1967; Spain Live), and *Magia y milagro de la poesía popular* (1956; Magic and Miracle of Popular Poetry).

BIBLIOGRAPHY

Primary Texts

España viva. Madrid: Aguado, 1967.
Magia y milagro de la poesía popular. Madrid: n.p., 1956.

Isabel McSpadden

LLULL, Ramon (c. 1232, Mallorca–1315, ?), prose writer and poet. Llull was one of the most prolific writers of the Middle Ages (*Edad Media, Literatura de la) and a polyglot whose writings enjoyed an immense popularity throughout Europe during and beyond his own time. In his youth he filled various positions under Jaume I the Conqueror and led a rather dissipated life. At the age of thirty he experienced a spiritual crisis and changed radically. Breaking his family ties (a wife and two children), he began to travel throughout the ancient world and fought tirelessly for the conversion of infidels. To that effect he founded in Mallorca an institute of Oriental languages in order to facilitate the conversion of Jews and Moslems. We have evidence of Llull residing at various times in Paris, Vienna (where he attended the famous Council), Tunis, and many other cities. He suddenly vanished after 1315 and is believed to have died a martyr in Tunis.

Llull's colossal literary production can be divided according to the language in which he wrote: Arabic, Catalan or Latin. He wrote philosophical or theological treatises in Latin and Catalan, thus being the first European to use a Romance language in writing philosophy. All critics agree that his *Llibre d'Evast e d'Aloma e de Blanquerna* (1285/1295; *Book of Evast, Aloma and Blanquerna*, 1926), composed in five parts symbolizing the five wounds of Christ, is his most outstanding work in Catalan. In this work Llull gives a faithful representation of the society of his day, contrasting it to the perfect, ideal society which he imagines. It is a true novel of great originality for its time and one of the first written in a Romance language. The *Llibre d'Amic e Amat* (Book of the Lover and Beloved), the most sublime example of Llull's poetic prose, is in fact a part of *Blanquerna*. It is a masterpiece of mystical literature recounting the search of the *amic*—the "lover," symbolically, the Christian—for his *amat*—the "beloved," God or Jesus Christ. Llull's originality consists in having revised the concepts and expressions of love in troubadour poetry into sacred form. It anticipates San *Juan de la Cruz, although Llull shows greater originality by not following so strictly the biblical "Song of Songs."

The theme of love is also present in *Arbre de Filosofia d'Amor* (1298; *Tree of Love*, 1926), composed of 365 versicles (the days of the year) but in a more formal philosophical or theological content, showing clear influences of Arabic literature (i.e., *mysticism).

Other important prose works include *Llibre de contemplació* (*The Art of Contemplation*, 1925), in which he combines scholastic philosophy and popular stories, many of them autobiographical. The book ends with an acid criticism of contemporary society. *Félix o Libre de meravelles* (1289; The Book of Marvels) is the story of Felix, who travels throughout the ancient known world admiring the beauties of nature. In a rather interesting section of the book, *Llibre de les besties* (Book of Animals), the most metaphysical problems of human beings are discussed by animals. *Llibre d'orde de cavayleria* (Book of the Chivalric Order) is a didactic work in which a hermit instructs a squire in how to become a proper knight. It was prefaced by the *Llibre del gentil e los tres savis* (The Book of the Gentile and the Three Wise Men) in which a Christian, a Moslem and a Jew try to convert a pagan in a friendly, free competition. It should be pointed out that the *Llibre d'orde de Cavayleria* was imitated in Castilian by Don *Juan Manuel.

Most of Llull's early poetry, written in the troubadour style, has been lost, but some of his later poems have been preserved. The most valuable is the "Cant de Ramon" (1300; Song of Ramon) and "Lo desconhort" (1295/1305; The Disconsolation). The first is a sort of index to the ambitions and failures of Llull who in spite of everything managed to remain faithful to his ideal. "Lo desconhort," written in monorhymed alexandrine verse, is a long, meditative lament in which, in a long dialogue with a hermit, the poet analyzes his failure to achieve some of his evangelistic aims. Like Saint Thomas, Llull rejected Averroistic philosophy—an attitude shared by a large number of Arabs and Jews alike—but whereas St. Thomas though that philosophy and theology can arrive at truth by separate ways and without contradicting each other, Llull believed that, starting from universally held religious values, Christian dogma could be demonstrated rationally. Llull, often called the "Doctor Il·luminat" (Enlightened Doctor), is also the precursor of modern symbolic logic. *See also* Catalan Literature.

BIBLIOGRAPHY

Primary Texts

Desconhort. N.p.: Anales du'Midi, 1939.

Llibre d'Amic e d'Amat.—Llibre d'Ave Maria. Barcelona: Els Nostres Classics, 1927.

Llibre d'Evast e Blanquerna. Barcelona: Els Nostres Clàssics, 1935.

Llibre de maravelles. 4 vols. Barcelona: Els Nostres Clàssics, 1931–34.

Obras literarias. Castilian ed., by M. Batllorí and M. Caldentey. Madrid: Editorial Católica, 1948.

Ramon Llull: Obres. 20 vols. Palma: Institut d'Estudis Catalans, 1901–50.

English Translations

The Art of Contemplation. Tr. E. A. Peers. London: Society for Promoting Christian Knowledge, 1925.

Blanquerna. Tr. E. A. Peers. London: Burns, Oates and Washbourne, 1926.

The Book of the Beasts. Tr. E. A. Peers. London: Burns, Oates and Washbourne, 1927.

Selected Works of Ramon Llull (1232–1316). Ed. and tr. A. Bonner. Lawrenceville, NJ: Princeton UP, 1985.

The Tree of Love. Tr. E. A. Peers. London: Society for Promoting Christian Knowledge, 1926.

Criticism

Batllorí, P. M. *Ramon Llull en el mon del seu temps*. Barcelona: Dalmau, 1960.

Butlletí de la Societat Catalana d'Estudis Històrics. Vol 2. Barcelona: n.p., 1953.

Carreras Artau, T., and J. Carreras Artau. *Historia de la filosofía española: Filosofía cristiana de los siglos XIII y XIV*. Madrid: Real academia de ciencias exactas, 1939.

Cruz Hernández, M. *El pensamiento de Ramon Llull*. Madrid: Fundación Juan March, 1977.

Llinarès, A. *Raymond Llulle*. Paris: Presses Universitaires, 1953.

Miscel·lània Lul·liana. 2 vols. Mallorca: Miramar, 1952–55.

Molas, J. *El sentiment del dolor en la poesia de Ramon Llull*. In *Homenatge a Carles Riba*. Barcelona: Janes, 1954. 242–53.

———. "La poesía de Ramon Llull i l'amor cortès." *Studia Monographica et Recensiones* 14 (1955): 43–55.

Platzeck, E. F. *Raimund Lull. seine Werke, die Grundlagen seines Denkens*. 2 vols. Dusseldorf: Schwann, 1962–64.

Pring-Mill, R. *El microcosmos l·lulià*. Palma de Mallorca: Moll, 1961.

Tusquets, J. *Ramón Lull, pedagogo de la cristiandad*. Madrid: CSIC, 1954.

Joan Gilabert

LOA (praise), theatrical term. In general, it refers to a short panegyric (about five minutes duration), usually in verse, executed by one or two actors, speaking directly to the audience, before the start of a play. The underlying purpose of the *loa* was one of transition: to gain the attention of the public, secure their silence, and cultivate their interest and goodwill with respect to what they were to see onstage. Comparable to the Greek and Latin prologues, the Spanish *loa*, often called *introito* the first half of the sixteenth c., grows in popularity through the 1500s, reaching its peak around 1610–20. Many surviving *loas* are anonymous; known authors of note include Lope de *Rueda and Agustín de *Rojas.

BIBLIOGRAPHY

Primary Text

Colección de entremeses, loas, bailes, jácaras y mojigangas desde fines del siglo XVI hasta mediados del XVII. Ed. E. Cotarelo y Mori. In NBAE 17 & 18.

Criticism

Flecniakoska, J.-L. *La loa*. Madrid: Mateu-Cromo, 1975.

LOBO, Eugenio Gerardo (1679, Cuerva, Toledo–1750, Barcelona), soldier, poet. He defended Philip V in the War of Succession (1701–14) and participated in the siege of Lérida and the reconquest of Orán (1732), where he was seriously wounded. Nicknamed "el capitán coplero" (Captain Verse), he exercised many forms of verse. The *Rasgo épico* . . . (Epic Piece . . .) recounts the battle at Orán in 1,700 octaves; the verse satire *Exhortación políticocristiana a la Nación Española* (Political-Christian Exhortation to the Spanish Nation) bemoans the current state of the nation, and sorely provoked the king. His jocose verse was quite popular, but his sonnets, **décimas*, and *romances* (**romancero*) comprise the finest part of his poetry. Lobo also composed two plays, *El más justo rey de Grecia* (The Most Just King of Greece), and *Los mártyres de Toledo* (The

Martyrs of Toledo). Lobo's poetry was collected as *Selva de las musas* (1717; The Muses' Forest), *Obras poéticas* (1724?; Poetic Works), and *Obras poéticas y líricas* (1738; Poetic and Lyric Works).

BIBLIOGRAPHY

Primary Texts

Poesías. In BAE 61.

LOBÓN DE SALAZAR, Francisco (eighteenth c.), priest. Father *Isla used the name of this priest, without permission, to publish part one of his *Historia del famoso predicador Fr. Gerundio de Campazas*... (1758; History of the Famous Preacher Friar Gerundio de Campazas...).

LOFRASO, Antonio de (1530, Sardinia–1590, ?), writer. He wrote and published in Barcelona a weak *pastoral novel titled *Los diez libros de fortuna de amor* (1573; Ten Books on Love's Fortune) and was immortalized by *Cervantes's ironic comment in the *Quijote* (1.6) that the work was the most charming and senseless piece ever seen. In the eighteenth c., a Spanish teacher in England took Cervantes literally, unfortunately, and, thinking he was rendering enormous service to the cause of Spanish letters, arranged for publication of a second edition.

BIBLIOGRAPHY

Primary Texts

Los diez libros de fortuna de amor. Barcelona: Malo, 1573.
Los diez libros de fortuna de amor. Ed. P. de Pineda. 2 vols. London: Chapel, 1740.

LOMAS CANTORAL, Jerónimo de (fl. 1578, Valladolid–?), poet. Most of his verse follows Italian models such as Petrarch, *Sannazaro, Bembo, etc. *Cervantes praised him in the *Canto de Calíope*. *See also* Italian literary influences.

BIBLIOGRAPHY

Primary Text

Obras. Madrid: Cosin, 1578.

Criticism

Covarse, E. Segura. "Don Jerónimo de Lomas Cantoral." *Revista de Literatura* 3 (1952): 39–75.

LÓPEZ ALARCÓN, Enrique (1881, ?–1948, America), poet, newspaper editor. A post–Rubén Darío poet of great vigor, he published *Constelaciones* (Constellations). He composed outstanding sonnets, such as "Soy español" (I am Spanish), which exalts Spanish character. As a successful playwright, he collaborated often with Ramón de Godoy, Cristóbal de *Castro and others on such works. López Alarcón also wrote an eyewitness account of military conflict, titled *Melilla, 1909. Diario de la guerra.* (1913; Melilla, 1909. War Diary).

BIBLIOGRAPHY

Primary Texts

Constelaciones. Málaga: Zambrana, 1906.
Gerineldo. With Cristóbal de Castro. In Spanish Plays Collection, vol. 377.
Melilla, 1909. Diario de la guerra. Madrid: Alvarez, 1913.

Isabel McSpadden

LÓPEZ ANGLADA, Luis (1919, Ceuta–), military officer and poet. His first poems are linked to the group Espadaña from León. With Fernando González, he took part in founding *Halcón.* Some of his books are *Indicios de la rosa* (1945; Signs of the Rose), *Al par de tu sendero* (1946; By Your Path), *Destino de la espada* (1947; Destiny of the Sword), *La vida conquistada (1948–51)* (1952; Conquered Life), *Ayer han florecido los papeles donde escribí tu nombre* (1964; Yesterday the Papers Where I Wrote Your Name Blossomed), and most recently, *Memorial de antiguos vientos* (1986; Notebook of Ancient Winds). In 1961 he received the National Literature Prize.

BIBLIOGRAPHY

Primary Texts

Al par de tu sendero. Valladolid: n.p., 1946.
Antología. Pref. Gerardo Diego. Madrid: Oriens, 1962.
Ayer han florecido los papeles donde escribí tu nombre. Gandía: Ayuntamiento, 1964.
Memorial de antiguos vientos. Toledo: Ayuntamiento, 1986.
La vida conquistada (1948–51). Madrid: Rialp, 1952.

Isabel McSpadden

LÓPEZ BARRIOS, Francisco (1945, Granada–), novelist and journalist. He studied political science and information in Madrid. López Barrios founded the literary supplement of *Diario de Granada* and was the editor of *Cuadernos de la Penibética.* He has collaborated in *Triunfo, La Calle, Gaceta del Arte,* etc.

With M. J. Huguerty he wrote a fictionalized essay *Murieron para vivir* (1983; They Died to Live), dealing with the manifestations of Islamic mysticism in contemporary Spain. The novel *Dicen que Ramón Ardales ha cruzado el Rubicón* (1976; They Say that Ramón Ardales Has Crossed the Rubicon) is a testimony to the traumatic consequences of Franco's repression in his generation. In the same vein, *Alguna vez, más tarde y para siempre* (1984; Sometimes, Later, and Forever) focuses on the moral, psychological and political effects of the Spanish Civil War. López Barrios's prose is characterized by stylistic exactness and the skillful use of narrative time.

He is also author of *La nueva canción en castellano* (1976; The New Castilian Song); *Balada de la toma de Smara* (1976; Ballad of the Conquest of Smarna), a poetic text on the Sahara war, and a vanguard theatrical piece, ''Boeing, Boeing, Elena,'' performed in Madrid in 1970.

BIBLIOGRAPHY

Primary Texts

Alguna vez, más tarde y para siempre. Barcelona: Noguer, 1984.
Murieron para vivir. Barcelona: Argos-Vergara, 1983.
Dicen que Ramón Ardales ha cruzado el Rubicón. Madrid: Akal, 1976.
Balada de la toma de Smara. Velez-Málaga: Sur, 1976.

Criticism

Ortega, José. ''*Alguna vez, más tarde y para siempre* de López Barrios.'' *Ideal* (Granada) December 8, 1984: 4.

José Ortega

LÓPEZ DE AYALA, Adelardo (1829, Guadalcanal, Seville–1879, Madrid), playwright, poet, critic, politician and orator. As a liberal politician, he drew up the manifesto for the September Revolution of 1868. He was minister during the provisional government of Amadeus (1870–73), and later he supported Cánovas's preparations for the Restoration and became president of the Congress. In 1870 he became a member of the Academy of Language. Though he wrote poetry and a novel (*Gustavo,* published posthumously), he is best known for his dramatic works. Along with *Tamayo y Baus, López de Ayala represents the post-romantic realistic tendency in Spanish *theater. His first works reveal the influence of *Calderón de la Barca; historical plays of this first period are *Un hombre de estado* (1851; A Statesman), about the life and tragic death of Rodrigo Calderón, and *Rioja* (1854), which deals with the Sevillan poet of that name. During his second period he wrote comedies of manners which portray the urban atmosphere of the moment and satirize manners and conventions of contemporary society. A moralizing intent filters through the drawing room dialogues of these works. Best known of this period are *El tejado de vidrio* (1856; The Glass Roof), which illustrates how licentiousness can backfire on he who practices it; *El tanto por ciento* (1863; The Percentage), which condemns materialism; *El nuevo don Juan* (1863; The Modern Don Juan), which attacks the Spanish archetype (unlike the Romantics who admired the rebellious nature of *Don Juan); and *Consuelo* (1878; Consolation), which illustrates how personal unhappiness may result from placing materialistic selfishness above love. As a whole, López de Ayala criticizes the positivistic spirit of the age as he defends love and marriage. His dramatic works reveal sharp psychological observation and comprise a meticulous description of contemporary society. He is a master of scenic technique and a refined, careful versifier.

BIBLIOGRAPHY

Primary Texts

Obras. 7 vols. Madrid: Pérez Dubrull, 1881–85.
Obras completas. Ed. J. M. Castro y Calvo. 3 vols. In BAE 180–82.

Criticism

Artigas, M. "Carta inédita de López de Ayala, a propósito de *Un hombre de estado.*" *BBMP* (1919): n.p.

Coughlin, E. V. *Adelardo López de Ayala*. TWAS 466. Boston: Twayne, 1977.

Oteyza, L. de. *López de Ayala o el figurón político-literario*. Madrid: Espasa-Calpe, 1932.

Serrano Sanz, M. "Cartas de algunos literatos a Arrieta, Chapí y Adelardo López de Ayala." *BRAE* 19 (1932): 118–34 and 362–87.

Phoebe Porter Medina

LÓPEZ DE AYALA, Ignacio (1747, Grazalema–1789, Tarifa), neo-classical dramatist, poet, and historian. Little is known of Ayala's life before 1771, when he was named professor of poetics at the newly secularized Reales Estudios de San Isidro in Madrid. Ill health forced him to retire from his teaching duties in 1773, but following the death of his replacement Nicolás Fernández de *Moratín in 1780, Ayala returned to his post. As a faithful member of the famous *tertulia* at the San Sebastián Inn in the early 1770s, Ayala directed his literary activities toward that group's neo-classical ends. He composed his best-known tragedy, *Numancia destruida* (1775; Numancia Destroyed), and read it to his friends at the inn. He read there another tragedy, *Habides* (date unknown), as well as short biographical sketches of famous Spaniards from a collection he had hoped to publish with the title *Plutarco español* (Spanish Plutarch). His work as a historian, which included *Historia de Federico el Grande* (1767; History of Frederick the Great) and *Historia de Gibraltar* (1782; *History of Gibraltar*, 1845), earned him election to the Royal Academy of History. He was also an active member in the Academy of San Fernando and the Royal Economic Society of Madrid. Ayala served on numerous governmental and literary commissions, translated several books from French and Latin, composed topical poems in Spanish and Latin, and wrote two dissertations on astronomy. He enjoyed the respect of Spain's leading politicians and intellectuals for his dedication to the humanities, socio-economic problems, and scientific concerns.

BIBLIOGRAPHY

Primary Texts

Numancia destruida. Ed. R. F. Sebold. Salamanca: Anaya, 1971.

Habides. Ed. E. V. Coughlin. Barcelona: Hispam, 1974.

English Translation

History of Gibraltar. Tr. J. Beel. London: Pickering, 1845.

David Thatcher Gies

LÓPEZ DE AYALA, Pero (1332, Vitoria–1407, Calahorra), historian, translator and poet. During the turbulent lifetime of Pero López de Ayala, which embraces both the Black Death and the Great Schism, Castile was ruled by five kings and one regent: *Alphonse XI, Henry II, John I, Henry III, and Ferdinand of Antequera, regent for the Infant John II. Ayala wrote chronicles for the reigns of four of these rulers whom he served—all except Alphonse XI and John II; he died before completing the chronicle about the reign of Henry III. Peter I has come to be called "el Cruel" (The Cruel One) partly because of how Ayala's chronicle depicts him. He left Peter's service and joined the forces of Henry of Trastámara and was captured by the English troops of the Black Prince at the battle of Nájera (1367) where Henry was defeated. Shortly after the battle of Aljubarrota (1385), Ayala was imprisoned in Portugal for more than a year. He was ambassador at the French court of Charles VI and was also influential in negotiating an agreement with the British House of Lancaster; he was appointed chancellor of Castile in 1399. With Ayala, therefore, we are confronted by a writer with substantial European experience, something that cannot be said for most Castilian writers before him. From the literary point of view his imprisonment and, to a certain extent, his desertion of Peter I are felicitous occurrences because they forced him to put on paper things that might not otherwise have been written. In addition to being a chronicler, Ayala was also a translator and a poet. His *Libro de la caza de las aves* (Book of Bird Hunting) is a translation and augmentation of a Portuguese work on falconry by Pero Menino; he also translated portions of the work of Livy, Gregory the Great, Isidore of Seville, Boethius, and Boccaccio. Ayala is best known for a long work (more than 2,000 stanzas, most of them in **cuaderna vía*) which has come to be called the *Rimado de Palacio*. The title is explained by the fact that a long section of the work is devoted to a rhymed satire of contemporary court and palace customs. The *Rimado* treats mainly six topics: (1) formulaic confession where the author tells how he has sinned in terms of the commandments, the seven deadly sins, the corporal and spiritual works of mercy, the five senses, and the virtues and vices. It is worth noting that this form of writing was also used by the *Arcipreste de Hita before Ayala, and by the *Arcipreste de Talavera after him; (2) satire of palace society; (3) concern over the Great Schism in the Catholic Church; (4) a sermon on the Book of Job based on the *Magna Moralia* of Gregory the Great; (5) the principles of good government based partly on the *De regimine principum* of Egidius Romanus; and (6) short *zejelesque* lyrical songs mainly in praise of the Virgin Mary. If Ayala intended that there be any artistic connections between these sections of his work, his design is apocalyptic. In its apocalyptic state the work seems to reflect the turbulence of the times during which it was composed. There are, in every part of it, passages of appealing lyric quality and intense concern for humankind. *See also Cronicas*; Edad Media, Literatura de la.

BIBLIOGRAPHY

Primary Texts

"Libro de Poemas" o "Rimado de Palacio." Ed. M. García. 2 vols. Madrid: Gredos, 1978.

Libro rimado de palacio. Ed. J. Joset. Madrid: Alhambra, 1978.

Criticism

García de Andóin, F. *El Canciller Ayala: su obra y su tiempo*. Vitoria: Obra Cultural de la Caja de Ahorros Municipal de la Ciudad de Vitoria, 1976.

Mirrer-Singer, L. *The Language of Evaluation: A Sociolinguistic Approach to the Story of Pedro el Cruel in Ballad-Chronicle*. Philadelphia: Benjamins, 1986.

Colbert Nepaulsingh

LÓPEZ DE AYALA Y MOLERO, Ángeles (1856, Seville–c. 1910, Barcelona?), journalist, novelist, playwright. Because Ángeles was still a child when her mother died, her father sent her to a convent in Osuna (Seville) for two years. When she returned home, her family noted Angeles's interest in literature and commanded her education to a preceptor. She debuted in Seville, 1880, with a comedy, *Lo que conviene a un marido* (What Is Good for a Husband). After marrying and moving to Madrid and then to Barcelona, she began a life of intense social and political activity. A freethinker and holder of republican ideas, she founded journals such as *El Progreso* (1906–9) and *El Libertador*—a journal of the freethinkers—and represented freethinking Catalan women in several international meetings. She was indicted seven times for her beliefs, and three times went to prison. She founded the Sociedad Progresiva Femenina and El Nivel Rojo, a layman organization similar to the Red Cross.

She wrote plays, novels and poetry, although her poems, published separately in journals and magazines, were never collected. Because of her unconventional social and political ideas, histories of literature have ignored her. Thus, proper appreciation and objective evaluation of her writing have yet to be achieved.

BIBLIOGRAPHY

Primary Texts

Abismos. Madrid: n.p., 1896.

Absurdos socialas. Barcelona: n.p., 1899.

De tal siembra tal cosecha. Barcelona; n.p., 1899. (Presented in Barcelona, Circo's Theater, May 14, 1899.)

Justicia. In *El Progreso* [Madrid] (1899).

Los terremotos de Andalucía o Justicia de Dios. Madrid: Tipología de los huérfanos, 1887. Novel.

El triunfo de la virtud. Seville; n.p., 1881. (Prizewinner in a Sevillan contest to commemorate the second centenary of Calderón de la Barca.)

Criticism

Cejador y Frauca, Julio. *Historia de la lengua y literatura castellana*. 14 vols. Madrid: Espasa-Calpe, 1960.

Ferreras, Juan Ignacio. *Catálogo de novelas y novelistas españoles del s. XIX*. Madrid: Cátedra, 1979.

Méndez Bejarano, M. *Diccionario de escritores, maestros y oradores naturales de Sevilla*. Seville: Tipología Girones, 1922.

Cristina Enríquez

LÓPEZ DE GÓMARA, Francisco (1511, Gómara, Soria–1559, Soria), historian of the conquest and colonization of the New World. López de Gómara studied Latin and classical literature with the humanist Pedro de Rúa in Soria before taking ecclesiastical orders and traveling to Italy, where he probably lived for nearly a decade. In 1541 he accompanied an expeditionary force against Algiers, led by the Emperor Charles V, and met Hernán *Cortés, whom he served as secretary and chaplain until the death of the latter in 1546. He subsequently remained in the employ of Cortés's son until his own death in 1559.

Gómara's first history, the *Crónica de los Barbarrojas* (1853; Chronicle of the Redbeards), which recounts the career of two Moorish corsairs, evidences the classical erudition and incisive style which are the hallmarks of his later writings. He is best known for his two-part *Historia general de las Indias* and *Historia de la conquista de México* (1552; *General History of the Indies* and *History of the Conquest of Mexico*, 1964). This widely read but controversial work was banned by royal decree in 1553, possibly due to the influential opposition of Bartolomé de las *Casas, who attacked Gómara's essentially negative view of the American Indians and his close personal ties to Cortés. Bernal *Díaz del Castillo, in his own history, states that because Gómara witnessed none of the events which he narrated, he was led into numerous factual errors by the sources on which he depended. He also accuses Gómara of overlooking the merits of the captains and common soldiers who participated in the Conquest of Mexico in his desire to underscore the heroic role of Cortés. Recent studies have tended to defend Gómara from the charges of his critics, although it cannot be disputed that the *Conquest of Mexico*, commissioned by Cortés and paid for by his son, is an unquestionably partisan history.

In his critical use of classical writers, his emphasis on the role of the individual in the making of history, his fascination with the marvels of the New World, and his enthusiastic portrayal of the achievements of Spanish conquerors and explorers, Gómara reflects a number of tendencies in *Renaissance historical writing. Agreeing with Lluís *Vives that history should concern itself only with truly great and significant events, he avoids the inclusion of detail which would obscure the larger outlines of the historical narrative. In spite of his humanistic orientation, however, he goes beyond the accepted historiographical precepts of his day in an effort to portray adequately the realities of the New World. Gómara's description of the American Indians, read and used by Montaigne and the Italian adventurer and historian Girolamo Benzoni, is considered to have played a part in the formation of the *Black Legend of Spanish atrocities in the New World. His highly personal style, concise, humorous, and ironic, has been unanimously praised by critics as a model of Spanish prose.

Toward the end of his life, Gómara wrote a schematic and quite possibly unfinished history of the reign of Charles V, the *Anales del emperador Carlos V* (*Annals of the Emperor Charles V*, 1912).

BIBLIOGRAPHY

Primary Texts

Annals of the Emperor Charles V. Ed. Roger Bigelow Merriman. Oxford: Clarendon, 1912. Spanish text, pp. 159–72.

Crónica de los Barbarrojas. In *Memorial histórico español*. Madrid: Real Academia de la Historia, 1853. 327–439.
Historia de la conquista de México. Ed. Jorge Gurría Lacroix. Caracas: Biblioteca Ayacucho, 1979.
Historia general de las Indias y vida de Hernán Cortés. Ed. Jorge Gurría Lacroix. Caracas: Biblioteca Ayacucho, 1979.

English Translations

Annals of the Emperor Charles V. Ed. Roger Bigelow Merriman. Oxford: Clarendon, 1912. English text, pp. 1–158.
Cortés: The Life of the Conqueror by His Secretary, Francisco López de Gómara. Tr. and ed. Lesley Byrd Simpson. Berkeley: U of California P, 1964.

Criticism

Esteve Barba, Francisco. *Historiografía indiana*. Madrid: Gredos, 1964. 94–102.
Fueter, Eduard. *Geschichte der Neureren Historiographie*. 1st ed., 1911. Munich and Berlin: R. Olderbourg, 1936. 299–300.
Iglesia, Ramón. *Cronistas e historiadores de la conquista de México: el ciclo de Hernán Cortés*. Mexico: El Colegio de México, 1944. 97–215.
Lewis, Robert E. "El testamento de Francisco López de Gómara y otros documentos tocantes a su vida y obra." *Revista de Indias* 173 (Jan.-June 1984): 61–79.
———. "The Humanistic Historiography of Francisco López de Gómara (1511–1550)." Diss., U of Texas at Austin, 1983.

Robert E. Lewis

LÓPEZ DE HOYOS, Juan (?, Madrid–1583, Madrid), teacher, priest. *Cervantes was his student, and López de Hoyos referred to him as his most beloved disciple. Subsequent criticism considers López de Hoyos to have been an Erasmian who influenced Cervantes considerably. He published three homage collections: *Relación de la muerte . . . del . . . Príncipe Don Carlos* (1568; Account of the Death . . . of . . . Prince Charles); *Historia de la enfermedad . . . de la Sereníssima Reyna . . . Isabel de Valois* (1569; History of the Illness . . . of Her Most Serene Highness . . . Isabel of Valois); and *Real apparato y sumptuoso recibimiento [de] . . . d. Ana de Austria* (1572; Royal Ceremony and Sumptuous Reception of . . . Doña Ana of Austria). Four poems by Cervantes appear in the *Historia*. *See also* Erasmism.

BIBLIOGRAPHY

Primary Texts

Historia de la enfermedad. . . . Madrid: Pierres Cosin, 1569.
Relación de la muerte. . . . Madrid: Pierres Cosin, 1568.

Criticism

Pérez Mínguez, F. *El maestro López de Hoyos*. Madrid: Hernández, 1916.

LÓPEZ DE PALACIOS RUBIOS, Juan. *See* Palacios Rubios, Juan López de

LÓPEZ DE SEDANO, Juan José (1729, Villoslada, Logroño–1801, Madrid), literary critic, editor. Through the patronage of *Esquilache, Sedano became an official of the Royal Library in the rare books and special collections division. This position allowed him to travel extensively throughout Spain and to write about archaeological inscriptions. Sedano is remembered primarily through his nine-volume anthology, *Parnaso español; Colección de poesías escogidas de los más célebres poetas castellanos* (1768–78; Spanish Parnassus, Collection of Poetry Chosen from the Most Famous Spanish Poets), a work which has been discredited for its many critical errors although it was the most extensive anthology published at its time. Aligning himself with classical reformers, Sedano translated from Molière and Goldoni and wrote a few original plays such as *Jahel* (1763), which included a long preface containing Sedano's views on the *theater. His participation in literary polemics is documented through his *El Belianís Literario* (1765; The Literary Belianis), published under the pseudonym Patricio Bueno de Castilla (Good Castilian Countryman), and *Coloquios de la espina* (1785; Colloquia of the Thorn), under the pseudonym Juan María Chevero y Eslava de Ronda.

BIBLIOGRAPHY

Primary Text

Parnaso español; Colección de poesías escogidas de los más célebres poetas castellanos. Madrid: Sancha, 1768–78.

Criticism

Alborg, J. L. *Historia de la literatura española.* Madrid: Gredos, 1975.

Cox, M. *Eighteenth Century Spanish Literature.* TWAS 526. Boston: Twayne, 1979.

Carmen Chaves McClendon

LÓPEZ DE ÚBEDA, Francisco (155?, Toledo–?, Madrid), writer and physician. The putative author of *El libro de entretenimiento de La Pícara Justina* (1605; *The Life of Justina, the Country Jilt*, 1707) was a court doctor in the entourage of Philip III; he also played the role of buffoon and amused the courtiers with his burlesque wit. A native of Toledo, probably from a **converso* family and of Andalusian ancestry, he was well-versed in the classics, the Scriptures, emblematic literature, and Spanish *picaresque prose. He was also familiar with the literary tradition of the court jesters, typified by the *Crónica Burlesca del Emperador Carlos V* (1529; Burlesque Chronicle of the Emperor Charles V) by Francesillo de *Zúñiga, to whose maliciously ironic sense of humor his own bears a striking resemblance.

The confusion surrounding his authorship began only nine years after the publication of *La Pícara Justina* with *Cervantes's supposed allusion to his ecclesiastical garb in *Viaje del Parnaso*. The misinterpretation was initiated by the eighteenth-c. bibliographer Nicholás *Antonio when he suggested that López de Ubeda was but a pseudonym for a Dominican friar, Andrés *Pérez, the true author of the book. Other scholars perpetrated this mistake, persisting even in the face of new biographical data presented by C. *Pérez Pastor in 1895 that documented the actual historical existence of a doctor from Toledo, Francisco López de Ubeda. Pérez Pastor recorded the names of his parents, Luis López de Ubeda and Doña María de Contreras, and also the dowry agreement between their son and Jerónima de Loaisa, whom he married in Madrid in 1590.

A reassessment of the biographical data, some enigmatic passages of the text, and the dedicatory letter to Don Rodrigo Calderón, a powerful courtier, led Marcel Bataillon to insist on the authorship of López de Ubeda and to formulate a reinterpretation of the text, traditionally both maligned and misunderstood. *La Pícara Justina* is not the work of a priest, a bad writer trying to produce a realistic picaresque novel, but rather the tour de force of a court physician and satirist. Written to entertain an aristocratic audience, it commemorates the journey undertaken by Philip III's court in 1602 to León, a small, cold, primitive city that could not have pleased those accustomed to luxury—hence the burlesque treatment of its architecture, inhabitants, and customs. The text is in part a *roman à clef* with numerous subtle, ironic references to contemporary people and events. López de Ubeda is a malevolently witty linguistic virtuoso with an enormous repertoire of rhetorical figures of speech and thought. *La Pícara Justina* is a mine of riddles, wordplays, jokes, caricatures, literary parodies, and social satire, a testimony to the prodigious imagination of its author.

The structure of *La Pícara Justina* is that of a picaresque novel, a pseudo-autobiography and open-ended series of episodic adventures, that appears to parody *Alemán's *Guzmán de Alfarache*. The originality of the work lies in its comic intention. It is also the first picaresque novel with a female protagonist, yet may be interpreted as misogynistic due to the *converso* anti-heroine's loquacity, capriciousness, malice, and vanity.

As Bataillon has pointed out, it was not uncustomary for Golden Age court doctors to function in a dual capacity, practicing both medicine and buffoonery; that is, they provided cures for both body and spirit. López de Ubeda was acquainted with Oliva *Sabuco de Nante's medical treatise, *Filosofía de la Naturaleza del Hombre* (1587; Philosophy of the Nature of Man), which recognizes the therapeutic value of humor. Though some jokes in *La Pícara Justina* may still be lost on the modern reader, the identification of the author, his reading public, and their social and historical context has led to an appreciation of the text's risqué humor, linguistic playfulness, and parodic intent. Further textual analyses and source studies may unravel remaining mysteries of this enigmatic entertainment. *See also* Siglo de Oro.

BIBLIOGRAPHY

Primary Texts

La Pícara Justina. Ed. Bruno Damiani. Madrid: Porrúa, 1982.

La Pícara Justina. Ed. Antonio Rey Hazas. Madrid: Nacional, 1977.

English Translation

The Life of Justina. The Country Jilt. The Spanish Libertines. Tr. Captain John Stevens. London: Samuel Bunchley, 1707.

Criticism

Bataillon, Marcel. *Pícaros y Picaresca: La Pícara Justina*. Madrid: Taurus, 1969.
Damiani, Bruno. *Francisco López de Ubeda*. TWAS 431. New York: Twayne, 1974.
Foulché-Delbosc, Raymond. "L'auteur de la Pícara Justina." *RH* 10 (1903): 236–41.
Parker, Alexander. *Literature and the Delinquent. The Picaresque Novel in Spain and Europe 1599-1753*. Edinburgh, Scotland: Edinburgh UP, 1967. Chap. 2.
Pérez Pastor, Cristóbal. *La Imprenta en Medina del Campo*. Madrid: Sucesores de Rivadeneyra, 1875.
Rico, Francisco. *The Picaresque Novel and Point of View*. Tr. Charles Davis with Harry Sieber. Cambridge: Cambridge UP, 1983. Chap. 3.

Helen H. Reed

LÓPEZ DE VILLALOBOS, Francisco (1473?, Zamora–1549, ?), distinguished physician, poet and translator. A Jewish *converso, he studied at the U of Salamanca and later became the physician for the Duke of Alba (1507), Ferdinand the Catholic (1509) and Charles V (1519–39). He wrote a considerable number of medical and literary works. *El sumario de la medicina* (1498; The Summary of Medicine) is a medical poem in which the author tries to popularize medicine. It is perhaps the first didactic medical poem in Spanish literature. His *Tratado sobre las pestíferas bubas* (1498; Treatise on the Pestiferous Buboes), included in *El sumario*, is one of the first studies done on syphilis. In *Los ocho problemas* (1543; The Eight Problems) he humorously criticizes the customs and vices of his day. López had a reputation as a very funny man who liked to mock. For many his most praiseworthy performance is *Las tres grandes* (1544; The Three Big Ones), namely talkiness, obstinacy and laughter. His frolicsome humor and strokes of wit shine here. He also completed an elegant translation of Plautus's *Amphitruo*, which is considered to be the first Spanish adaptation for the theater of a Latin comedy; wrote *Glosa de los dos primeros libros de Plinio* (1543; Gloss of the First Works by Pliny), which caused a famous polemic with Hernán *Núñez; and left an important collection of letters in Spanish and Latin, and a celebrated poem, "Venga ya la dulce muerte" (Let Sweet Death Come to Me), which is accompanied by an explanatory prose commentary. *See also* Humanism; Renaissance.

BIBLIOGRAPHY

Primary Texts

Los problemas de Villalobos. In BAE 36.
Algunas obras del doctor Francisco López de Villalobos. Madrid: Ginesta, 1886.
El sumario de la medicina, con un tratado sobre las pestíferas bubas. Intro. E. García del Real. Madrid: Cosano, 1948.

English Translation

The Medical Works of Francisco López de Villalobos. Commentary, bio. G. Gaskoin. London: Churchill, 1870.

Hector Medina

LÓPEZ DE YANGÜAS, Hernán (1487?, Yangüas, Soria–?), humanist, writer, playwright, proverb collector. His various works share a clear didactic intent; this goal, and other structural and thematic features, link López de Yangüas more to medieval than to *Renaissance traditions. He is author of one of the oldest *autos sacramentales* (**auto*), the *Farsa sacramental en coplas* (c. 1518?; Sacramental Farce in Verse); unfortunately, only fragments of the original have survived. He also published a **refranero* titled *Las 50 preguntas vivas con otras tantas respuestas* (1543?; Fifty Lively Questions with Corresponding Answers) and a *Triunfo de locura* (1521; Triumph of Insanity), which shows the influence of Erasmus's *Praise of Folly* and/or Sebastian Brandt's *Stultifera navis*. Dramatic writings by López de Yangüas include the allegorical *Farsa del mundo y moral* (1524; Farce of the World and Moral)—which demonstrates how man must not let his appetite be ruled by worldly things; the *Egloga de la Natividad* (n.d.; Nativity Eclogue)—a dialogue between four shepherds explaining the nativity which recalls the work of Juan del *Encina; and the *Diálogo del mosquito* (1521; Dialogue of the Mosquito)—which is a pessimistic, Lucianesque conversation between a man and a mosquito, with the same lesson as the *Farsa del mundo y moral*.

BIBLIOGRAPHY

Primary Texts

Cuatro obras. Ed. A. Pérez y Gómez. Cieza: La fonte que mana y corre, 1960. Facs.
Diálogo del mosquito. Barcelona: Pro-Libris, 1951. Facs. of 1521 ed.
Obras dramáticas. Ed., study F. González Ollé. Clásicos Castellanos 162. Madrid: Espasa-Calpe, 1967.

LÓPEZ GARCÍA, Bernardo (1838, Jaén–1870, Madrid), poet. He is remembered for one poem, *Al dos de mayo* (On May Second), a ringing, vigorous account of Spanish resistance to Napoleon's entry into Madrid in 1808. The rest of his work has not held up well to the test of time.

BIBLIOGRAPHY

Primary Texts

Poesías. 2nd ed. Madrid: Fernando Fe, 1882.

LÓPEZ IBOR, Juan José (1906, Sollana, Valencia–), Spanish essayist. A psychiatrist who taught legal medicine in several universities between 1932 and 1945, López Ibor has produced several non-technical, popular volumes related to aspects of his profession: *El español y su complejo de inferioridad* (1951; The Spaniard and the Spanish Inferiority Complex); *La aventura humana* (1965; The Human Adventure); *Rebeldes* (1965; Rebels); and *Las neurosis* (1966; The

Neuroses). As the holder of a chair of psychiatry in Madrid, he has also published many professional articles and treatises. *See also* Essay.

LÓPEZ MOZO, Jerónimo (1942, Madrid–), Spanish dramatist and critic. He began to write in the 1960s when the neo-realist "social theater" was still alive and has occasionally written realistic works. More often, López Mozo uses formal aspects of Brecht's distancing techniques, sometimes in combination with intense dramatism. A favorite technique is historical transposition, using one historical reality as a transparent "mirror" of a contemporary parallel or analogue; another is demythification. López Mozo's theater is anti-bourgeois, experimental and revulsive. His first piece, written in 1964, is *Los novios o la teoría de los números combinatorios* (Sweethearts, or the Theory of Combinatory Numbers), produced by a non-professional group in 1965. Other early works which likewise failed to find a commercial producer include *Los sedientos* (1965; The Thirsty), *La renuncia* (1966; Renunciation), *Moncho y Mimi* (Moncho and Mimi) and *Collage Occidental*, both from 1967. Other works dating from this period are *Blanco en quince tiempos* (1967; White in Fifteen Movements), *Negro en quince tiempos* (1967; Black in Fifteen Movements), *El retorno* (1968; The Return), and *Crap, fábrica de municiones* (1968; The Crap Munitions Factory).

Guernica (1969), inspired in part by Picasso's famous painting, offers a poetic-dramatic re-creation of the bombing of this Basque village in the guise of a "happening" (one of four by this author). *Anarquía 36* (1971), "documentary" theater, dramatizes an investigation of the role of the anarchists in the Spanish Civil War. *El Fernando* (1972) and *El retablo de La Lozana* (1977) belong to contemporary historical theater of a special sort. *El Fernando*, a work of a collective nature, uses the format of the traditional farce as vehicle for a ferocious satire of the absolute monarch Ferdinand VII. Francisco *Delicado's Golden Age *picaresque novel, *La lozana andaluza*, is adapted by López Mozo in *El retablo de La Lozana*, without wishing to use the adventures of the female picaro to parallel present situations but rather to portray the impact of the Renaissance upon medieval civilization. *Parece cosa de brujas* (It Seems Like Witchcraft), an absurd, Brechtian farce written in collaboration with Luis Matilla, employs historical transposition to study the exploitation of fear as a repressive mechanism for the retention of power. López Mozo, together with others of his generation, frequently employs absurdist elements (in the style of Beckett), at times in combination with such traditional Spanish ingredients as the *esperpento*, following *Valle-Inclán, or the grotesque and pantomime, as in *El testamento* (1966; *The Will*, 1976). Among his best achievements is *Matadero solemne* (1969; Solemn Slaughterhouse), which is among his most Brechtian works. *See also* Contemporary Spanish Theater.

BIBLIOGRAPHY

Primary Texts

"A propósito de *Matadero solemne*." *Primer acto* 122 (June 1970): 63–64.
Maniquí (1970). In *El Urogallo* (Madrid) 7: 1971.
Tiempos muertos (Cinco obras breves). Madrid: La Avispa, 1985.

English Translation

"The Will." In *New Generation Spanish Drama*. Ed. George E. Wellwarth. Montreal: Engendra Press, 1976.

Criticism

Ruiz Ramón, Francisco. "Introducción al teatro de López Mozo." *Estreno* 1.1 (1975): 14–18.

Saabach, Mario. "Aportaciones para una introducción al teatro de Jerónimo López Mozo." *Pipirijaina. Textos* 6 (1978?): 2–9.

Janet Pérez

LÓPEZ PACHECO, Jesús (1930, Madrid–), poet and novelist. A professor of Spanish literature at the U of Western Ontario, he continues to be, with only two novels, one of the clearest voices of the social novel. *Central eléctrica* (1958; The Power Station), a Nadal Prize finalist, abounds in epic qualities. The collective struggle portrayed in the construction of a dam and power station transcends the national scope, for it is ultimately the struggle of man against nature. The novel is imbued with a lyrical prose which is both precise and suggestive. *La hoja de parra* (1973; The Fig Leaf) is exemplary of the so-called novel of demythification. In his critical assessment of contemporary Spanish society, reflected in the lives of two newlyweds, the author employs a variety of narrative techniques, combining realism and fantasy, and demonstrates an acute awareness of his linguistic resources. *Lucha por la respiración* (1980; Fighting for Air) is a collection of his short stories. He has published several volumes of poetry.

BIBLIOGRAPHY

Primary Texts

Algunos aspectos del orden público en el momento actual de la histeria de España. Mexico: Era, 1970.

Canciones del amor prohibido. Barcelona: Literaturasa, 1961.

Central Eléctrica. Barcelona: Destino, 1970.

Dejad crecer este silencio. Madrid: Rialp, 1953.

La hoja de parra. Barcelona: Bruguera, 1977.

Lucha por la respiración. Barcelona: Destino, 1980.

Mi corazón se llama Cudillero. Mieres, Spain: El Ventanal, 1961.

Pongo la mano sobre España. Rome: Rapporti Europei, 1961.

Criticism

Gil Casado, Pablo. *La novela social española*. 2nd ed. Barcelona: Seix Barral, 1973.

Porter Conerly

LÒPEZ-PICÓ, Josep Maria (1886, Barcelona–1959, Barcelona), Catalan poet, editor, publisher. An exceptionally prolific lyricist, Lòpez-Picó published more than thirty volumes of poetry, beginning around the end of the first decade of this c. and producing one or more a year up to the end of the Civil War; thereafter, the Franco regime's outlawing of the vernacular languages and attempts to suppress Catalan culture altered the rhythm of productivity of Lòpez-Picó's declining years. Important early works are *Intermetzzo galant* (1910; Gallant Intermezzo), *Torment froment* (1910; Trembling Torment), *Poems de port* (1911; Poems of the Harbor), and *Epigrammata* (1911). Lòpez-Picó is an outstanding creator of poetic images, of home, landscape, and emotions, and was influenced by symbolist and modernist currents in his formative years. His great popularity resulted in a number of followers, of decadentist and symbolist and frequently hermetic tendencies. Lòpez-Picó was one of the leaders of Catalan poetry around World War I and helped to found the *Almanac de la Poesia* in 1912, a sort of annual or yearbook of poetry. In 1915 he joined with Joaquim Folguera to found the bi-monthly *Rivista*, aesthetic mouthpiece of his generation. He contributed to many other Catalan journals, *Quaderns de poesia*, *Vell i nou*, *Quaderns d'estudi*, *Empori*, etc. Other significant collections are *Amor, Senyor* (1913; Love, Lord); *Espectacles i mitologia* (1913; Spectacles and Mythology); *L'ofrena* (1916; The Offering); *Paraules* (1916; Words); *L'oci de la paraula* (1927; The Leisure of the Word). Purity of language and the utmost precision possible in images are aims of Lòpez-Picó's poetry, reflections of his relationship to symbolism, which have resulted in his poetry's being considered cold, a quality which may limit its durability over time. *See also* Catalan Literature.

Janet Pérez

LÓPEZ PINCIANO, Alonso (c. 1547, Valladolid–c. 1627, Valladolid), physician, poet, and humanist. Best known as "el Pinciano," the surname he selected to honor his native city of Valladolid (Lat. "Pintia"), he was the personal physician to the Infanta María, sister of Philip II and widow of Maximilian II. In addition to translating works by Hippocrates and Thucydides, he composed *El Pelayo* (1605), an epic poem in twenty cantos concerning the initial phase of the Reconquest of Spain from the Moors. His major contribution, however, is his *Philosophia antigua poética* (1596; Compendium of Ancient Philosophy), an epistolary work, which gave him the opportunity to communicate his own poetic theory through commentaries on the classical philosophers, most notably Aristotle. The content shows the author to be well versed in contemporary Italian letters as well as in ancient philosophy, and the dialogue form of the thirteen letters clearly owes its influence to Plato. Among other things, the *Philosophía* contains an attack on the dramatic innovations present in Lope de *Vega's dramatic school by one who strove to preserve classical precepts. *See also* Aristotelianism; Italian literary influences.

BIBLIOGRAPHY

Primary Text

Philosophia antigua poética. Ed. A. Carballo. 3 vols. Biblioteca de Antiguos Libros Hispánicos 19–21. Madrid: CSIC, 1953.

English Translation

Philosophía antigua poética. Tr. Richard Aarre Impola. "The *Philosophía antigua poética* of Alonso López Pinciano Translated with an Introduction and Annotations." Diss., Columbia U, 1972.

Criticism

Clements, Robert J. "López Pinciano's *Philosophia antigua poetica* and the Spanish Contributions to Renaissance Literary Theory: A Review Article." *HR* 23 (1955): 48–55.

Fradejas Lebrero, José. "Los cuentos de Alonso López Pinciano." *Revista de Literatura* 12 (1957): xxiii-xxiv and 111–12.

Shepard, Sanford. *El Pinciano y las teorías literarias del Siglo de Oro*. 2nd ed. Madrid: Gredos, 1970.

C. Maurice Cherry

LÓPEZ PINILLOS, José (1875, Seville–1922, Madrid), journalist, novelist, playwright. He wrote under the pseudonym Parmeno. Among his novels are *La sangre de Cristo* (1907; Christ's Blood), *Doña Mesalina* (1910), *Las águilas* (1911; The Eagles), *Frente al mar* (1914; By the Sea), *Ojo por ojo* (1915; An Eye for an Eye), and *El luchador* (1916; The Fighter). His works are characterized by violent realism, somber settings and characters, and a crude vocabulary with many archaisms. His theater is showy and harsh; the best known plays by him are *Esclavitud* (1918; Slavery) and *Embrujamiento* (1922; Bewitchment).

BIBLIOGRAPHY

Primary Texts

Las águilas. Madrid: Renacimiento, 1911.
Embrujamiento. Madrid: Pueyo, 1923.
Esclavitud. Madrid: Pueyo, 1919.
La sangre de Cristo. Madrid: Biblioteca nueva, 1907.

Isabel McSpadden

LÓPEZ RUBIO, José (1903, Motril, Granada–1988?, Madrid), Spanish playwright, screenplay writer and translator-adaptor. Educated first in a private school run by French nuns and then in an Augustinian school in Madrid, López Rubio was interested in the theater from early adolescence, both as author and performer. His literary career began with articles and stories in Madrid periodicals and editorial work for a humor magazine. An incipient collaborator with *Jardiel Poncela, he attended the *tertulias* of Ramón *Gómez de la Serna during the 1920s, and later wrote a pair of comedies in collaboration with Edgar Neville, during a period when he published his first fiction, *Cuentos inverosímiles* (1924; Tales without Verisimilitude), and a novel, *Roque Six* (1929). His first two productions were plays written with Eduardo Ugartein 1929–30, *De la noche a la mañana* (From Night to Morning) and *La casa de naipes* (House of Cards). A long association with the movies dates from this time, as he first worked under contract to MGM in the States (1930) and then writing screenplays for Fox Films in Spain. He spent the years 1932–35 in Hollywood, and then in 1936 his incipient directing career in Spain was cut short by the Civil War; he spent the years 1937–39 in the United States and Mexico. Between 1940 and 1949, he worked in film production in Spain, beginning to write once more for the theater. The première of *Alberto* (1949) marked a significant date for post-war Spanish theater as well as for López Rubio, who began turning out plays with regularity, including two in 1950 and three in 1951: *Celos del aire* (literally, Jealous of the Air; translated by Holt as "In August We Play the Pyrenees"), awarded the *Academia Española's Fastenrath Prize; *Estoy pensando en ti* (I'm Thinking of You); *Veinte y cuarenta* (Twenty and Forty); *Una madeja de lana azul celeste* (A Skein of Sky Blue Wool); and *Cena de Navidad* (Christmas Dinner). *El remedio en la memoria* (1952; Remedy in Memory) was followed by three productions in 1954: *La venda en los ojos* (Blindfold), *Cuenta nueva* (New Account), and *La otra orilla* (The Other Shore). One of López Rubio's most successful works, *La venda en los ojos*, received the National Prize for Theater, the Alvarez Quintero Prize, and the Maria Rolland Prize for Drama. It was followed by a musical comedy, *El caballero de Barajas* (1955; The Gentleman from Barajas), and two 1956 productions, *Un trono para Cristy* (A Throne for Cristy) and *La novia del espacio* (Space Sweetheart).

Departing from his successful comedy format, López Rubio turned for the first time to tragedy in 1958 with *Las manos son inocentes* (The Hands Are Innocent). He returned to comedy for his next work, *Diana está comunicando* (1960; Diana's on the Phone), followed by *Esta noche, tampoco* (1961; Not Tonight, Either). He began to travel frequently, visiting Scandinavia and Brazil, then traveling to Latin America and once more to the United States, where he lectured and presented seminars in several colleges and universities. His prolific output declined, although *Nunca es tarde* (It's Never Too Late) premiered in 1964 and *Veneno activo* (Active Poison) in 1971; in 1968–69, he resided in El Escorial and wrote a series for television entitled *Al filo de lo imposible* (On the Verge of the Impossible). Another significant critical success came with *El corazón en la mano* (1972; With Heart in Hand), which garnered his second National Prize for Drama and another prize awarded by the newspaper *El Alcázar*. In 1976, he began a series of teledramas entitled *Mujeres insólitas* (Extraordinary Women) based on the biographies of famous historical women. His final years were plagued by ill health. *See also* Contemporary Spanish Theater.

BIBLIOGRAPHY

Primary Text

Teatro selecto de José López Rubio. Prol. Alfredo Marquerie. Madrid: Escelicer, 1969.

English Translation

The Blindfold. Tr. Marion Holt. In *The Modern Spanish Stage: Four Plays*. Ed. Marion Holt. New York: Hill and Wang, 1970.

Criticism

Holt, Marion Peter. *The Contemporary Spanish Theater (1949–1972)*. Boston: Twayne, 1975. 34–51.

———. *José López Rubio* (in English). Boston: Twayne, 1980.
———. Intr. to *La venda en los ojos*. New York: Appleton-Century-Crofts, 1966.
Torrente Ballester, Gonzalo. *Teatro español contemporáneo*. Madrid: Guadarrama, 1957. 288–300.

Janet Pérez

LÓPEZ SALINAS, Armando (1925, Madrid–), Spanish novelist. Of a working-class family, López Salinas was one of many future writers whose childhood was shattered by the Spanish Civil War and who, as a result, came to literature with a heightened political and social consciousness. He belongs to the so-called Mid-Century Generation of critical neo-realists. After the war, his time was divided between school and a variety of odd jobs to help his family; he worked as a housepainter, a traveling salesman, and administrative trainee. In 1945, he enrolled in a vocational school where he studied industrial engineering and was trained as a draftsman, after which his income improved and he was able to indulge his interest in literature. His fiction is inspired to a considerable degree by his own experience of life's difficulties and the average citizen's economic struggles. His first literary success came when he won the Acento Prize for a story collection, *Aquel abril* (ca. 1955; That April). His first novel, *La mina* (1959; The Mine), was a finalist for the then-prestigious Nadal Prize and (perhaps because of its political impact) was subsequently translated into French, Italian, Russian, Czech and Polish. His second novel, *Año tras año* (1960; Year after Year), even more openly critical of the Franco regime, was not publishable in Spain, although it won a prize from the exiled Spanish publishers, Editorial Ruedo Ibérico in Paris, and was a finalist for the Formentor International Novel Prize.

One of the ways in which Spanish writers during the late 1950s and early 1960s attempted to circumvent the censors and yet communicate a critical message was via ''travel books'' involving visits to some of the country's poorest and most backward regions, and López Salinas contributed to this genre with *Caminando por las Hurdes* (in collaboration with Antonio *Ferres, 1960; Walking through Hurdes Province) and *Viaje al país gallego* (in collaboration with Javier Alfaya, 1967; Trip to the Galician Country), both focusing upon the severest economic problems. Other works include a novel, *Por el río abajo* (in collaboration with the novelist Alfonso *Grosso, 1966; Down the River); another work of fiction, *Estampas madrileñas* (1965; Portraits of Madrid), and a piece written for children's theater, *El pincel mágico* (1967; The Magic Paintbrush).

Janet Pérez

LÓPEZ SILVA, José (1860, Madrid–1925, Buenos Aires), poet. In 1883 he became a contributor to *Madrid cómico*. His poetry is descriptive, with great local flavor; much of it is now forgotten. Representative volumes include *Migajas* (1898; Crumbs), *Los barrios bajos* (1894; Slums), *La gente de pueblo* (1908; Provincial People), etc. Also a playwright who collaborated with Ricardo de la

*Vega, Julio Pellicer and others, he composed several works for the *género chico*. Best known is his script for the musical comedy *La Revoltosa* (1897; The Rebellious Lady), written in collaboration with *Fernández Shaw, and with music by Chapí. In all his works, López Silva exhibits a *costumbrista* bent, and influence of his friend Ricardo de la Vega. Although criticized by *Cejador y Frauca, he was praised by Juan de *Valera (*Ecos argentinos*, 1901). *See also* Romanticism.

BIBLIOGRAPHY

Primary Texts

Los barrios bajos. 8th ed. Madrid: Fe, 1911.
Migajas. 4th ed. Madrid: Fe, 1911.
Sainetes madrileños. With C. Fernández Shaw. Madrid: Renacimiento, 1911.

LÓPEZ SOLER, Ramón (1806, Barcelona–1836, Madrid), poet, journalist, novelist and translator. After dropping out of law school, he worked most of his adult life as a journalist; in 1832 he worked for Madrid's *Revista española* (Spanish Journal), in 1833 for Barcelona's *El Vapor* (The Steamboat), and finally, in 1836, as editor for Madrid's *El Español* (The Spaniard). Earlier he co-founded *El Europeo* (1823–24; The European), a magazine that introduced the norms of European *Romanticism to Spain. He is best known as one of the first adaptors of historical novels. In his rendition of Scott's *Ivanhoe*, titled *Los bandos de Castilla o El caballero del cisne* (1830; The Factions of Castile or The Knight of the Swan), he evokes the reign of John II of Castile and his ill-fated minister, Don Alvaro de Luna. Under the pen name Gregorio Pérez de Miranda, he published *Kar-Osman. Memorias de la casa de Silva* (1832; Kar-Osman. Memoirs of Silva House), which is Byronic in inspiration and portrays the heroine's affair with the Greek chief of a rebellion against the Turks; *Jaime ''el barbudo''* (1832; James the Bearded); *El primogénito de Alburquerque* (1833; The Firstborn of Alburquerque); and *La Catedral de Sevilla* (1834; The Cathedral of Seville), which imitates Hugo's *Notre Dame de Paris* with the action displaced to Seville during the reign of Peter the Cruel. Among his translations figure *Causas secretas y anécdotas curiosas concernientes a la insurrección de Polonia* (1831; Secret Causes and Curious Anecdotes Concerning the Polish Insurrection). Today López Soler is considered a precursor of the Spanish historical novel, which culminates with *Espronceda, Mariano José de *Larra and Enrique *Gil y Carrasco, and as someone who acclimatized some of the more salient aspects of European Romanticism to Spanish soil.

BIBLIOGRAPHY

Primary Texts

Los bandos de Castilla. Madrid: Aguilar, 1963.
La catedral de Sevilla. Madrid: Repullés, 1934.
Jaime ''el Barbudo.'' Barcelona: n.p., 1932.

Kar-Osman. Memorias de la casa de Silva. Barcelona: Bergnes, 1932.
El primogénito de Alburquerque. Madrid: Repullés, 1934.

Criticism

Peers, E. Allison. *Historia del movimiento romántico español*. 2nd ed. Madrid: Gredos, 1973.
Picoche, Jean Louis. "Ramón López Soler, plagiaire et précurseur." *BH* 82 (1980): 81–93.

Eugene Del Vecchio

LÓPEZ ÚBEDA, Juan (?, Toledo–after 1596, ?), religious poet. He published a collection of poems by himself and other poets, titled *Vergel de flores divinas* (1582; Garden of Divine Flowers)—the second edition of the *Vergel* (1588) contained poetry by Luis de *León. He also published a *Cancionero general de la doctrina cristiana* (1579; General Songbook of Christian Doctrine)—a collection of **a lo divino* poetry for popular use, and four dramatic works, also religious in nature.

BIBLIOGRAPHY

Primary Texts

Poesías. In BAE 35.
Cancionero general de la doctrina cristiana. Alcalá: Ramírez, 1586.
Vergel de flores. Alcalá: Gracián, 1588.

LÓPEZ-VALDEMORO Y DE QUESADA, Juan Gualberto (1855, Málaga–1935, Madrid), Count of las Navas, prose author. The librarian of the Royal Palace, and professor of paleography at the Central U, he became a member of the *Academia Española in 1924. Some of his short stories appear in *La docena del fraile* (1886; Monk's Dozen). He collaborated with Juan de *Valera, *Thebussem and *Campillo on a short story collection titled *Cuentos y chascarrillos andaluces* (Andalusian Stories and Tales) and authored several articles in the volumes of *Historia y viajes* (History and Travels) and *Cosas de España* (Things of Spain). A principal contributor to the monumental Enciclopedia Espasa, he also wrote *El espectáculo más nacional* (1899; The Most Indigenous Sport), on bullfighting.

BIBLIOGRAPHY

Primary Texts

El espectáculo más nacional. Madrid: Rivadeneyra, 1900.
La docena del fraile. Madrid: Ducazcal, 1895.
Obras incompletas de el conde de las Navas. Madrid: Católica, 1929. (*Cuentos y chascarrillos andaluces*.)

Isabel McSpadden

LORENZO, Pedro de (1917, Casas de Don Antonio, Cáceres–), Extremaduran journalist and novelist. A precocious child, Pedro de Lorenzo began writing at the age of eight. During the Civil War he served as a war correspondent for the

Falangists, and from 1939 to 1941 he studied law at the U of Salamanca. The following year, at age twenty-five, he was named director of *El Diario Vasco* (The Basque Daily) in San Sebastián. By 1943 he was back in Madrid, where he was a founder of the magazine *Garcilaso* and where his name became associated with the poetry movement known as Juventud Creadora (Creative Youth), a group of young poets whose self-declared patriotism and adherence to the *Renaissance arms-and-letters ideal of *Garcilaso de la Vega were soon to be criticized for their superficiality. During this period he published his first novel, *La quinta soledad* (1943; The Fifth Solitude); a collection of essays, . . . *Y al oeste, Portugal* (1946; . . . And to the West, Portugal); and another novel, *La sal perdida* (1947; Lost Salt).

Lorenzo's preferred masters were Juan Ramón *Jiménez, *Azorín, and Gabriel *Miró. The latter two have played an instrumental role in the development of his style, which is pure and concise, yet polished and lyrical. Rafael Gómez López-Egea has remarked that stylistically Lorenzo has a calling toward perfection, a perfection made up of balance and proportion.

In 1952 he published the novel *Una conciencia de alquiler* (A Rented Conscience), inaugurating his cycle "Los descontentos," which focuses on postwar Spain. Besides numerous other novels and essays, he is the author of travel books such as *Imagen de España: Extremadura* (1968; *Extremadura*, 1968) and a very important memoir of sorts entitled *Los cuadernos de un joven creador* (1971; A Young Creator's Notebooks). He has served as professor of style in the Journalism School of Madrid and as a director of the newspaper *ABC*.

BIBLIOGRAPHY

Primary Texts

Una conciencia de alquiler. Madrid: Artes Gráficas, 1952.
Los cuadernos de un joven creador. Madrid: Gredos, 1971.
La quinta soledad. Madrid: Garcilaso, 1943.
La sal perdida. Madrid: Nacional, 1947.
. . . *Y al oeste, Portugal*. Madrid: Nacional, 1946.

English Translations

Extremadura. Tr. Selma Margaretten. Madrid: Clave, 1968.

Criticism

Castelo, Santiago. *Pedro de Lorenzo*. Madrid: EPESA, 1973.
de la Concha, Víctor. *La poesía española de posguerra: Teoría e historia de sus movimientos*. Madrid: Prensa Española, 1973.
Gómez López-Egea, Rafael. "La narrativa de evocación en Pedro de Lorenzo." *Arbor* 341 (May 1974): 123–29.
———. "Vida y estilo en Pedro de Lorenzo." *Arbor* 338 (Feb. 1974): 111–16.

James F. Brown

LOZANO, Cristóbal (1609, Hellín, Albacete–1667, Toledo), novelist, essayist, poet and playwright. Doctor of theology and a man of great culture, he held several ecclesiastical appointments until he died as chaplain of the New Kings of Toledo. Lozano was a prolific writer. His works include numerous poems, six *comedias*, one *auto sacramental* (**auto*), three religious treatises and a considerable number of historical, religious and legendary novels and short stories. His poetry and his dramatic productions, which are embodied in his prose works, have little merit. His only religious treatise that has survived is *El buen pastor* (1641; The Good Shepherd). He is mainly remembered for his historical, religious and legendary narratives. His most famous works are the trilogy formed by *David perseguido* (1652, 1659, 1661 [in three volumes]; The Persecution of David), *El Rey Penitente; David arrepentido* (1656; The Penitent King; David Repentant) and *El Gran Hijo de David más perseguido* (1663, 1665, 1673 [in three parts]; The Persecution of David's Son), ascetic works on the character of King David; *Reyes Nuevos de Toledo* (1667; The New Kings of Toledo), where the author, who was attached to the metropolitan cathedral of Toledo and, with *Calderón, served in the chapel set apart for the burial of the New Kings, gives an account of the construction of the chapel, and the adventures of the kings who sleep under its altars; *Soledades de la vida y desengaños del mundo* (1658; Solitudes of Life and Disillusions of the World), a collection of didactic short stories that influenced the Romantic writers. One of his short stories relates the legend of Lisardo, the student that witnessed his own funeral. This story influenced *Espronceda in *El estudiante de Salamanca* (1837; The Student from Salamanca). Lozano also furnished *Zorrilla with suggestions for many of his plays. *See also* Asceticism.

BIBLIOGRAPHY

Primary Texts

Historias y leyendas. Ed., prol. Joaquín de Entrambasaguas. Madrid: Espasa-Calpe, 1955.
Soledades de la vida y desengaños del mundo. Madrid: B. López, 1812.

Criticism

Entrambasaguas y Peña, Joaquín de. *El doctor Cristóbal Lozano*. Madrid: RABM, 1927.

Hector Medina

LUCA DE TENA, Juan Ignacio (1897, Madrid–1975, Madrid) Marquis of Luca de Tena, playwright. Son of the founder of the Madrid daily *ABC*, he directed the newspaper from 1929 to 1939 and worked as a journalist. His plays include *¿Quién soy yo?* (Who am I?), which won the Piquer Prize in 1935; *De lo pintado a lo vivo* (1944; From the Painted to the Real), *Espuma de mar* (Sea Froth), etc. He has written several scripts for **zarzuelas* (*El huésped del sevillano* [1933; The Guest of the Sevillano]) and some historical plays based on the Restoration period (*¿Dónde vas, Alfonso XII?* [1952; Where Are You Going, Alphonse XII?] and *¿Dónde vas, triste de ti?* ([1959; Where Are You Going, You Poor Thing?]). In 1946 he became a member of the *Academia Española.

BIBLIOGRAPHY

Primary Texts

¿Dónde vas, Alfonso XII? Madrid: Alfil, 1952.

El huésped del sevillano. Madrid: n.p., 1933.
¿Quién soy yo? Madrid: Alfil, 1953.

Isabel McSpadden

LUCA DE TENA, TORCUATO (1923, Madrid–), journalist, novelist, dramatist. Son of dramatist Juan Ignacio, Marquis of *Luca de Tena, and grandson of the newspaper *ABC*'s founder Torcuato, this writer has followed the family tradition. After studying law, Luca de Tena became a correspondant for *ABC*, traveling to several countries. His first literary effort, the modest book of verses *Espuma, nube, viento* (1945; Foam, Cloud, Wind), was followed by the journalistic chronicle *El Londres de la postguerra* (1948; Postwar London), meriting a Larragoiti Journalism Award. His first novel, *La otra vida del Capitán Contreras* (1953; *The Second Life of Captain Contreras*, 1960), detailing a seventeenth-c. soldier's disillusioning resurrection in the twentieth c., was followed by *La edad prohibida* (1955; The Forbidden Age), memoirs of adolescence, which received the National Literary Award and the Malaga-Costa del Sol Award (1960), and by *La mujer del otro* (1961; The Wife of Another), a novel of adultery, winner of the Planeta Award. *La brújula loca* (1964; The Crazy Compass) and *Pepa Niebla* (1970; Pepa Niebla), which present psychological profiles of a child during the Civil War and a schizophrenic, respectively, are more mature works. More recent novels, published by Planeta, include *Cartas de más allá* (1978; Letters from Beyond), *Los renglones torcidos de Dios* (1979; God's Twisted Pages), *Escritos en las olas* (1979; Written on the Waves) and *Los hijos de la lluvia (a.C.)* (1985; Children of the Rain). Although receiving scant critical attention, perhaps due to adherence to traditional novelistic forms, and accusations of superficiality, these works have been popular, going into multiple editions. Like his father, Luca de Tena has written drama, beginning with *La otra vida del Capitán Contreras* (1967), an adaptation of his novel, done in collaboration with his father. *Hay una luz sobre la cama* (1975; *There's a Light over the Bed*, thesis, U of Virginia, 1979), whose protagonist appeared in *Pepa Niebla*, was first staged in Madrid in 1969, followed by *El triunfador* (1975; The Victor), staged in 1971, *Una visita inmoral* (1975; An Immoral Visit) and *El extraño mundo de Nacho Larranga* (1979; Nacho Larranga's Strange World). Several nonfiction works have come from Luca de Tena's journalistic work. Collaboration with Capt. Teodoro Palacios, held in Russian prison camps for eleven years, produced *Embajador en el infierno* (1955; Ambassador in Hell), recipient of both the National and Army Literary awards. Results of historical investigations appeared in *Los mil y un descubrimientos de América* (1968; The Thousand and One Discoveries of America) and in *Yo, Juan Domingo Perón* (1976; I, Juan Domingo Peron), an autobiography. Since 1962, Luca de Tena has been editor of *ABC*.

BIBLIOGRAPHY

Primary Texts

La brújula loca. Barcelona: Planeta, 1976.
Embajador en el infierno. Barcelona: Planeta, 1969.

Escrito en las olas. Barcelona: Planeta, 1969.
La fábrica de sueños. Barcelona: Planeta, 1978.
El futuro fue ayer. Barcelona: Planeta, 1987.
Los hijos de la lluvia (a. C.). Barcelona: Planeta, 1985.
La otra vida del Capitán Contreras. Barcelona: Destino, 1957.
Los renglones torcidos de Dios. Barcelona: Planeta, 1984.
Señor ex ministro. Barcelona: Planeta, 1977.
Yo, Juan Domingo Perón. Barcelona: Planeta, 1976.

English Translation

Another Man's Wife. Tr. J. Marks. New York: Knopf, 1965.
The Second Life of Captain Contreras. Tr. and ed. B. Conrad. Boston: Houghton Mifflin, 1960.

Frieda H. Blackwell

LUCENA, Juan de (fifteenth c., Castile–Burgos), prose writer. One of the few facts known about him is that he was John II's foreign ambassador and his private counselor. Lucena is best known, however, for the didactic prose dialogue *Libro de vida beata* (1483; On a Happy Life). The *Vida beata* was written between 1452 and 1453, judging from the historical allusions it contains. The interlocutors of the dialogue are important figures of the reign of John II, such as Iñigo de Mendoza, the Marquis of *Santillana, Alonso de *Cartagena, Bishop of Burgos, and Juan de *Mena. This suggests the likelihood that Lucena was acquainted with all three, which in turn reinforces Lucena's importance in the court of King John.

The dialogue is simply written, with erudite references avoided; the lively conversation adeptly reveals the personality of each speaker. In essence, the book is a philosophical treatise on the forms of happiness. In conformity with the religious spirit of the age, it is determined at the end that true happiness consists in loving and serving God. Many scholars believe that the *Vida beata* is an imitation of Boethius's *De consolatione*.

BIBLIOGRAPHY

Primary Text

Aquí comiença un tratado en estilo breve, en sentencia no sólo largo mas hondo e prolijo el qual ha nombre vita beata. Zamora: Centenera, 1483.

Criticism

Lapesa, R. "Sobre Juan de Lucena: escritos suyos mal conocidos inéditos." In *De la Edad Media a nuestros días*. Madrid: Gredos, 1967. 23–44.
Morreale, M. "Tratado de Juan de Lucena sobre la felicidad." *NRFH* 20 (1955): 1–21.

Angelo DiSalvo

LUCEÑO, Tomás (1844, Madrid–1931, Madrid), lawyer, playwright. He is considered the founder of the *zarzuela genre. Aside from *zarzuela* scripts, he wrote various *sainetes (short farces), such as *Cuadros al fresco* (1892; Outdoor Pictures), *Fiesta nacional* (1882; National Holiday), *Las recomendaciones* (1892;

Recommendations), etc. Some of his *sainetes* are accompanied by music of Barbieri, Chapí, Chueca, Bretón, Vives, and others. His plays are found throughout the Spanish Plays Collection.

Isabel McSpadden

LUIS, Leopoldo de (1918, Córdoba–), lyrical poet. The intimate poetry of *Alba del hijo* (1946; Dawn of the Son) is followed by transcendent lyric in *Teatro real* (1957; Royal Theater). Other books by Luis are *Huésped de un tiempo sombrío* (1948; Guest of a Somber Time), *Los imposibles pájaros* (1949; Impossible Birds), *Los horizontes* (1957; Horizons), *Elegía en otoño* (1952; Elegy in Autumn), *El padre* (1954; The Father), and *El extraño* (1955; The Stranger). He has also published an extensive *Antología de la poesía social española contemporánea* (1965; Anthology of Contemporary Spanish Social Poetry) and most recently, the following titles: *Con los cinco sentidos* (1970; With All Five Senses), *Del temor y de la miseria* (1985; On Fear and Misery) and *Reflexiones sobre mi poesía* (1985; Reflections on My Poetry). With Jorge Urritia, he also edited the poetry of Miguel *Hernández.

BIBLIOGRAPHY

Primary Texts

Con los cinco sentidos. Zaragoza: Javalambre, 1970.
Del temor y de la miseria. Madrid: Orígenes, 1985.
Obra poética completa/Miguel Hernández. Intro., study, and notes. Madrid: Alianza, 1982.
Poesía 1946–1968. Barcelona: Plaza y Janés, 1968.
Reflexiones sobre mi poesía. Madrid: Universidad Autónoma, 1985.

Isabel McSpadden

LUJÁN, Pedro de (fl. 1546, ?–1571, ?), writer. Of Jewish lineage, he served the viceroy of Aragón, Juan Claros de Guzmán. Luján wrote one of the continuations to the *Amadís* series. Titled *Don Silves de la Selva* (1546; Sir Silves of the Forest), his is one of the better sequels, although it did not meet with popular success. As the twelfth volume, it closes the *Amadís* cycle. Luján also penned a very interesting moralistic work, the *Coloquios matrimoniales* (1571; Colloquies on Marriage). *See also* Caballerías, Libros de.

BIBLIOGRAPHY

Primary Texts

Coloquios matrimoniales. Madrid: Atlas, 1943.
Don Silves de la Selva. Seville: Dominico d'Robertis, 1546.

LUJÁN DE SAYAVEDRA, Mateo. Pseudonym used by Juan *Martí for his apocryphal continuation to Mateo *Alemán's *Guzmán de Alfarache*.

LULL, Ramón. *See* Llull, Ramón

LUNA, Álvaro de (1390?, Cañete–1453, Valladolid), politician, writer and poet. This powerful favorite of John II of Castile effectively ruled the kingdom for many years. His attempts to strengthen the central monarchy created many enemies, such as the Marquis of *Santillana, among the nobility. He also had many supporters; Juan de *Mena extolled him in the *Laberinto de fortuna*, for example. Luna accumulated enormous wealth, but suffered a spectacular fall from favor and was beheaded.

He wrote poems of the troubadour style. In his prose work *Libro de las claras y virtuosas mujeres* (1446; Book of Famous and Virtuous Women), he takes the female side in the anti-/ pro-feminist polemic of the fifteenth c. The work consists of three parts: in the first there are figures of the Old Testament (Sarah, Esther); in the second, women of classical antiquity (Lucrecia, Dido); and in the third, Christian heroines (St. Ann, St. Mary of Egypt).

Luna did not write the *Crónica de don Álvaro de Luna* (1546; Chronicle of Álvaro de Luna), a sympathetic history which covers almost the entire reign of John II. Its author was probably his former servant Gonzalo Chacón the elder.

BIBLIOGRAPHY

Primary Text

Libro de las claras e virtuosas mujeres. Ed. M. Castillo. Madrid-Toledo: Menor, 1909.

O'Callaghan, J. F. *A History of Medieval Spain*. Ithaca: Cornell UP, 1975.

Siló, C. *Don Alvaro de Luna y su tiempo*. Madrid: Espasa-Calpe, 1940.

Eric Naylor

LUNA, José Carlos de (1890, ?–1966, ?), poet. Andalusian subjects served as his inspiration. His more successful works include *El Cristo de los gitanos* (1932; The Christ of the Gypsies), *La taberna de los reyes* (1933; The Tavern of the Kings), and *El Café de Chinitas* (1940).

BIBLIOGRAPHY

Primary Texts

Gitanos de la Bética. Madrid: Publicaciones Españolas, 1951.

La mar y los barcos. Madrid: Nacional, 1950.

Obras completas. 4 vols. Madrid: Escelicer, 1942-?.

Isabel McSpadden

LUZÁN CLARAMUNT DE SUELVES Y GUERRA, Ignacio (1702, Zaragoza–1754, Madrid), literary theorist, writer. Educated in Italy, Luzán was greatly influenced by Vico's ideal on aesthetics and, upon returning to Spain in 1733, began working on his most important contribution, *Poética o reglas de la poesía en general y de sus principales especies* (1737; Poetics or Rules on Poetry in General and on Its Principal Kinds). Inspiration for the *Poética* came from the French, Boileau and Father Le Bossu, the Italian Muratori, and the commentaries of Aristotle. It is divided into four books: (1) Origin, Progress and Essence of Poetry; (2) Profit and Pleasure from Poetry; (3) Dramatic Poetry; and (4) Epic Poetry. Throughout the Poetics, Luzán seeks to establish the place of poetic writing, whether it be lyric, dramatic or epic, within the context of the rules of nature. Nature and natural law, therefore, establish the basis for creative inspiration. Cited often merely for the establishment of the neo-classical dramatic unities, the Poetics must be considered one of the greatest influences in the development and evolution of Spanish lyricism. Luzán was a member of the Royal Academy of Letters, the Academy of History, and the Academy of San Fernando. In 1747, he served as secretary of the Spanish embassy in Paris—a duty that inspired his writing of *Memorias de Paris* (1751; Essay on Paris), in which he discusses the cultural and intellectual life of the neighboring country. During the final years of his life, he occupied many political posts, such as member of the Council on Finances, member of the Business Development Committee, and Treasurer of the Royal Library. *See also* Aristotelianism.

BIBLIOGRAPHY

Primary Text

La poética o reglas de la poesía en general y de sus principales especies. Barcelona: Labor, 1977.

Criticism

Cid de Sirgado, I. M. *Afrancesados y neoclásicos.* Madrid: Cultura Hispánica, 1973.

Jones, T. B., and B. B. Nicol. *Neoclassical Dramatic Criticism, 1560–1770.* Cambridge: Cambridge UP, 1976.

Makawiecka, G. *Luzán y su "Poética."* Barcelona: Planeta, 1973.

Sebold, R. P. *El rapto de la mente.* Madrid: Prensa Espanõla, 1970.

Carmen Chaves McClendon

***LYSANDRO Y ROSELIA*, Tragicomedia de.** *See Lisandro y Roselia*

M

MACHADO, Antonio (1848, Santiago de Compostela–1892, Seville), folklorist. Father of Antonio and Manuel *Machado, he may also be considered the pioneer father of folklore studies in Spain. Representative titles are listed in the bibliography.

BIBLIOGRAPHY

Primary Texts

Antología de su prosa. 3 vols. Madrid: Cuadernos para el diálogo, 1972.

Cantes flamencos. 2nd ed. Colección Austral 745. Buenos Aires: Espasa-Calpe, 1947.

Cantos populares españoles, recogidos, ordenados e ilustrados. Ed. F. Rodríguez Marín. 5 vols. Madrid: Atlas, 1951?

Folklore español. Biblioteca de las tradiciones populares españolas. 11 vols. Seville: Alvarez, 1883–86.

MACHADO, Manuel (1874, Seville–1947, Madrid), older brother of Antonio *Machado Ruiz, he held the degree of master of philosophy and letters and was a librarian, newspaper writer, critic, playwright, and lyric poet. He was elected to the *Academia Española in 1938.

Works

Poetry: *Alma* (1900; Soul); *Alma, Museo, Los cantares* (1907; Soul. Museum. The Songs), *Caprichos* (1905; Caprices), *La fiesta nacional* (1906; The National Holiday), *El mal poema* (1909; The Bad Poem), *Apolo* (1910; Apollo), *Cante hondo* (1912; Flamenco Singing), *Canciones y dedicatorias* (1915; Songs and Dedications), *Sevilla y otros poemas* (1919; Seville and Other Poems), *Ars moriendi* (1922; The Art of Dying), *Phoenix* (1935), *Horas de oro* (1938; Golden Hours). Prose: *La guerra literaria* (1913; The Literary War), *Un año de teatro* (1918; A Year of Theater), *Estampas sevillanas* (1949; Prints of Seville). Theater works (most in collaboration with Antonio Machado): *Desdichas de la fortuna, o Julianillo Valcárcel* (1926; The Misfortunes of Fortune or Julianillo Valcárcel), *Juan de Mañara* (1927; Juan de Mañara), *Las adelfas* (1928; The Oleanders),

La Lola se va a los puertos (1930; Lola Goes Off to Sea), *La prima Fernanda* (1931; Cousin Fernanda), *La duquesa de Benamejí* (1932; The Dutchess of Benamejí), *El pilar de la victoria* (1945; The Pillar of Victory), *El hombre que murió en la guerra* (1947; The Man Who Died in the War).

Manuel Machado was not a prolific poet; yet, of the Machado brothers, he was initially the more famous. Today, though this fame has diminished, his poetry is considered one of the best examples of literary *Modernism in Spain. Sensuality, epicurism, humor, melancholy, and a fatalism inherited from the Arab conquerers of Spain, are its constant notes. Like his melancholic gardens, Machado's modernism is more reminiscent of the young Juan Ramón *Jiménez, Gregorio *Martínez Sierra, Ramón del *Valle-Inclán and Francisco *Villaespesa than of the so-called father of the movement, Rubén Darío. Machado's poem ''El Reino Interior'' (The Inner Kingdom), the title of a famous poem of introspection by Darío, reminds the reader more of the epicurean Darío of ''Autumnal'' (Autumn) than of the one who was torn by inner anguish.

Machado's first autobiographical poem of *Alma* tells us that he has the ''spikenard soul of the Spanish Arab'' (''Adelfos,'' [Oleanders]). The fatalism and melancholy of that traditional blood line blend in Machado with a rich vein of French poetry, elegant, amoral, vivacious and sincere, coming from Paul Verlaine, the Parnassian and the symbolist poets. Seville, where Machado was born, and Paris, where he frequently visited and worked, starting in 1899 with a job as a translator for the Garnier Brothers, are the geographic centers of his poetry.

Caprichos, with themes of gallantry and erotic love, shows the influence of Verlaine. The poem ''Abel'' shares an interest in the Cain and Abel theme with other writers of the literary *Generation of 1898, and with Manuel's brother Antonio, though the emphasis here is more on artistic values than on moral issues. *La fiesta nacional* deals with the bullfights and gives ample evidence of Machado's powerful ability to paint with words. He is considered at his best when creating poetic pictures such as these. *Museo* reaches back into Spain's past with portraits of the famous in Spanish history or literature such as Minaya-Fáñez and the *Cid of the *Poema de mio Cid*; the poet Gonzalo de *Berceo; Don Carnal of Juan Ruiz, the *Arcipreste de Hita's *Libro de Buen Amor*. The poems of *Cante hondo* deal with the Andalusian folklore of flamenco ballads. For his use of this theme, some critics consider Manuel Machado to be a forerunner of Federico *García Lorca and Rafael *Alberti. *Horas de oro* marked a significant departure from the sensual and the chic in favor of religious poetry deeply rooted in Spanish Catholicism.

In the mid 1920s, Manuel worked with his brother and fellow poet Antonio on modern adaptations of plays from the Golden Age of Spanish literature. The works of playwrights such as *Tirso de Molina and Lope de *Vega were chosen for updating. The two also wrote a tragi-comedy and, in 1927, brought out an adaptation of the *Don Juan theme in *Juan de Mañara*, a theme quite popular with their contemporaries in Spain. Their best and most successful play was the 1930 *La Lola se va a los puertos*, based on the folklore of the *cante hondo* flamenco songs.

BIBLIOGRAPHY

Primary Texts

Bibliografía machadiana: bibliografía para un centenario. Ed. M. Carrión Gútiez. Madrid: Ministerio de Educación y Ciencia, 1976.

Obras completas de Manuel y Antonio Machado. Madrid: Biblioteca Nueva, 1978.

English Translations

Several poems. Tr. Anthony Edkins. In *Poet Lore* 66 (1971): 295–96.

See also *The Literature of Spain in English Translation*. Ed. R. Rudder. New York: Ungar, 1975. 504–6.

Criticism

Alonso, Dámaso. "Ligereza y gravedad en la poesía de Manuel Machado." *Poetas españoles contemporáneos*. Madrid: Gredos, 1958. 50–102.

Brotherston, Gordon. *Manuel Machado. A Revaluation*. Cambridge: Cambridge UP, 1968.

Diego, Gerardo. *Manuel Machado, poeta*. Madrid: Nacional, 1974.

Joseph A. Feustle

MACHADO RUIZ, Antonio (1875, Seville–1939, Collioure, France), Spanish poet and playwright. A younger brother of Manuel *Machado, with whom he later collaborated on several plays, Antonio came from a prominent, once-wealthy family of liberal professional background. His paternal grandfather was a former governor of the province of Seville, and his father, a pioneer in the field of Spanish folklore, was an authority on Andalusian flamenco song and folk poetry. In 1885, when his grandfather was appointed to a professorship at the Central U in Madrid, the family moved there, and the two future writers were educated at the intellectually decisive Institución Libre de Enseñanza, the famous liberal Free Institute which formed most of Spain's important thinkers, writers and artists of the first half of this century.

Declining family fortunes and the death of Machado's father in 1893 meant that Antonio could not attend the university; in 1899, he accepted a job as a translator in Paris, together with Manuel. The turn-of-the-century years in Europe's intellectual capital were stimulating and provided contact with important aesthetic currents and literary figures, a contact which Machado maintained through periodical subscriptions and book purchases throughout the rest of his life. He began writing poetry around 1899 but published nothing before 1901, when his first poems appeared in the journal *Electra*, followed by his first book, *Soledades* (1902; Solitudes), dated 1903. This collection is much influenced by the *modernismo* movement and Machado's discovery of the Nicaraguan poet Rubén Darío around the end of the century. Machado's early poems are his most self-consciously aesthetic creations, motivated by formal considerations and the "art for art's sake" credo, and exhibit Parnassian influences later left behind as the poet moved away from *modernista* formalism and stylized motifs to increasingly personal, ethical and philosophical preoccupations. Machado soon published a much amplified edition of his first volume, subsequently entitled

Soledades, galerías y otros poemas (1907; Solitudes, Galleries and Other Poems).

Machado's first book was well received, and in 1904, some of his poems appeared in what was then the country's premier poetry magazine, *Helios*, directed by Juan Ramón *Jiménez. This same journal published an open letter to Machado from *Unamuno, who would be an important spiritual and intellectual influence for most of the rest of the poet's life; Unamuno's well-known opposition to *modernismo* led to his urging Machado to abandon aestheticism and French influences, advice which seems to have been been taken to heart, as Machado began to move away from his until-then bohemian existence and to become increasingly serious and imbued with feeling, in contrast to the often cold Parnassian and modernist verse. In 1906, Machado began seriously to prepare himself for the teaching profession, successfully taking the *oposiciones* (public oral examinations) in 1907 and receiving a post in the provincial Castilian capital of Soria. The Sorian highlands have been immortalized in Machado's *Campos de Castilla* (1912; Fields of Castile), and in Soria he met his teenage bride, Leonor, whom he married in 1909.

In 1911, Machado received a government grant to study in Paris with the philosopher Henri Bergson, whose notions of time and intuition were of special interest to the poet. After a few months in Paris, Leonor suffered a severe hemorrhage (a symptom of advanced tuberculosis), and they returned to Soria for her final months; she died in 1912, and he could no longer bear the area without her. He requested and received a transfer to Baeza, on the border between Castile and Andalusia. His depression was severe, and he thought of suicide, eventually turning to philosophy for a rationale for living. He began studying during the summers at the U of Madrid, preparing himself for doctoral examinations in philosophy, which he finally passed in 1918, with a prestigious group of examiners, including the leading philosopher, *Ortega y Gasset. The first incomplete edition of his complete poems appeared in 1917, as well as *Páginas escogidas* (Selected Pages). Both his tragic loss of Leonor and the melancholy, monotonous time in Baeza (1912–19) inspired some of Machado's most memorable poems.

In 1919, the poet secured a vacant post in Segovia, and once again moved to Castile, this time to a historic and traditional town not far from Madrid, which allowed him to visit the capital on weekends and indulge his first passion, the theater. Through social contacts, he became increasingly involved in popular movements, some inspired by the Russian Revolution, and also came under the influence of Tolstoy. *Nuevas canciones* (1924; New Songs) reflects both experiences of the time in Baeza and some of the new philosophical and ideological currents to which the poet was exposed in Segovia. Proximity to Madrid allowed him to establish relationships with the new groups of poets, those who would form the *Generation of 1927. *De un cancionero apócrifo* (1926; From an Apocryphal Songbook), incorporating new philosophical poems and an aphoristic manner, is essentially the last collection of poetry published under the poet's own name (later verse is attributed to his mask or alter ego, Juan de Mairena). Also around 1926, he met his second great love, the woman identified in his poems as Guiomar, Pilar Valderrama. His passionate but apparently platonic and largely one-sided autumnal love affair with this minor poet was eventually ended by the outbreak of the Civil War, although apparently by then they had begun to drift apart.

Machado's years in Segovia are important for another reason, as this is the period of his theatrical collaboration with his brother, Manuel. *Julianillo Valcárcel* (1926), a Golden Age drama, was their first effort. For several years thereafter, they produced at least one new play each season, their major success being *La Lola se va a los puertos* (1929; Lola Goes to the Ports); their last theatrical production came after Antonio's death, when *El hombre que murió en la guerra* (1941; The Man Who Died in the War) was staged in Madrid, thanks primarily to the conservative politics of Manuel. Most of their plays are not especially innovative; they might be classified as vaguely folkloric.

The first part of *Juan de Mairena* (published in book form in 1936) appeared in 1934 and marks Machado's last important philosophical poetry and prose collection; his life thereafter would be devoted largely to activities in support of the Republican cause in the Civil War, war articles published in *Hora de España* and even propaganda, in spite of his age and infirmities. Both the poet and his aged mother, with whom he had lived for much of the time after Leonor's death, were forced into exile at the war's close, the hardships of the exodus march costing the lives of both almost as soon as they crossed the border into France near the Mediterranean village of Collioure, where Machado was buried in Feburary of 1939. For more than fifteen years after the war, the Franco regime considered his name anathema, discouraging or prohibiting editions of his works and critical tributes or studies. By the twentieth anniversary of his death, the atmosphere had begun to improve, and there were homage observances in Collioure, Segovia, the Sorbonne and Madrid. Not until after the death of Franco, however, did the Spanish government officially recognize Machado as one of the "glories" of Spanish poetry and dedicate a statue in his memory.

Machado is unquestionably one of the greatest Spanish poets of this or any century and, together with Unamuno and Juan Ramón Jiménez, a most significant influence on succeeding generations of poets in Spain. His most characteristic poetry is simple, unassuming, almost prosaic (like the poet himself), yet imbued with a quiet nobility and depth of feeling unparalleled in any of his compatriots. Although Machado handles rhyme and rhythm with competent artistry in his early collections, it is in the subtly cadenced, unrhymed lines of *Campos de Castilla* that he reaches his greatest heights of power. He strove consciously to produce a modernized counterpart of the medieval **romancero* (ballad-books) in "La tierra de Alvargonzález" and yet was able to anticipate ideas of Heidegger and the existentialists in pieces from *Juan de Mairena*. Aspects of symbolism and impressionism remain in his mature style, but the complexity of his symbols is belied by the accessibility of his style and lexicon, never abstruse no matter how great the psychological profundity. Like his own favorite poet, Jorge *Manrique, Machado cultivated the eternal themes of the world's great poetry, with simplicity, power, and unmistakable originality.

BIBLIOGRAPHY

Primary Texts

Los complementarios y otras obras póstumas. Buenos Aires: n.p., 1957.

La guerra. Madrid: n.p., 1937.

Poesías completas. Buenos Aires: Losada, 1943; numerous later editions.

Obras completas de Manuel y Antonio Machado. Madrid: Plenitud, 1947; 4th ed., 1957.

Obras, poesía y prosa. Buenos Aires: Losada, 1964.

English Translation

Eighty Poems of Antonio Machado. Tr. Willis Barnstone. New York: Las Américas, 1959.

Criticism

Cobb, Carl. *Antonio Machado*. New York: Twayne, 1971.

Cobos, Pablo A. *Humor y pensamiento en la metafísica poética de Antonio Machado*. Madrid: Insula, 1963.

Gullón, Ricardo. *Las galerías secretas de Antonio Machado*. Madrid: Taurus, 1958.

McVan, Alice Jane. *Antonio Machado*. New York: Hispanic Society, 1959.

Peers, E. Allison. *Antonio Machado*. Oxford: Clarendon, 1940.

Sánchez Barbudo, Antonio. *Estudios sobre Unamuno y Machado*. Madrid: Guadarrama, 1959.

———. *Los poemas de Antonio Machado*. Barcelona: Lumen, 1967.

MACÍAS, El Enamorado (Macías, the Lover), fifteenth-c. Galician troubadour. His poems are found in the *Cancionero de *Baena* and other collections. Of even greater interest are the legends Macías himself inspired: in one, upon having written poetry to a married woman he loved, the enraged husband had him imprisoned and then killed him there with a lance; in another, when Macías knelt to kiss the ground where his beloved had walked, he was assassinated. Subsequent centuries have seized on the figure of Macías for artistic inspiration: Mariano José de *Larra composed *El doncel de don Enrique el Doliente* (1834; Henry the Sorrowful and Macías); *Bances Candamo wrote *El español más amante y desgraciado Macías* (n.d.; The Best and Most Unfortunate Spanish Lover Macías); and Lope de *Vega penned *Porfiar hasta morir* (To Persist Until Death). *See also* Gallic Portuguese Poetry.

MACÍAS PICAVEA, Ricardo (1847, Santoña, Santander–1899, Valladolid), novelist, reformer, teacher. Active in politics, he wrote newspaper articles in defense of democratic ideals. His concerns anticipated those of the *Generation of 1898. His best known work, *La instrucción pública en España y sus reformas* (1882; Public Education in Spain and Its Reform), he studies Spain's educational problems. *El problema nacional: hechos, causas y remedios* (1891; The National Problem: Events, Causes and Solutions) considers different aspects of Spanish life with a reformist aim. His regional novel, *Tierra de campos* (1892; Land of Fields), is a realistically sympathetic description of rural scenes and people. Macías Picavea also was a professor at the Instituto de Valladolid.

BIBLIOGRAPHY

Primary Texts

La instrucción pública en España y sus reformas. Madrid: Suárez, 1882.
El problema nacional: hechos, causas y remedios. Madrid: Suárez, 1899.
La tierra de campos. Madrid: Suárez, 1897.

Criticism

Caudet, F. "Un olvidado antecedente temático y tonal del 98: *La tierra de campos*, de R. Macías Picavea, 'Novela-epopeya' de Castilla." *REH* (University, Alabama) 6 (1972): 327–33.

Eugene Del Vecchio

MADARIAGA, Salvador de (1886, La Coruña–1978, Locarno, Switzerland), historian, diplomat, essayist, novelist and poet of Basque origin. Following secondary education and engineering school in Paris, Madariaga worked in his profession for a short time in Spain. Then he went to London, where he was an editor for the *Times* and wrote articles about World War I that were subsequently collected and published in Spain as *La guerra desde Londres* (1917; The War from London). During the aftermath of the war he published in English a book which set the course of a lifelong devotion to cross-cultural study and dialogue: *Shelley and Calderón and Other Essays on English and Spanish Poetry* (1920). And in 1921 he entered the more immediately political arena when he took an executive staff position with the League of Nations; in 1926 he became head of the section on disarmament (see his 1929 book *Disarmament*). During this period his work established his reputation as being one of the few students of international problems whose thinking demonstrated a good balance between idealism and intelligence. At the same time Madariaga continued publishing on Spanish and English literary and cultural topics (e.g., *Guía del lector del Quijote [Ensayo psicológico sobre el Quijote]*—1926, English tr. 1961 as *Don Quixote; Englishmen, Frenchmen, Spaniards*—1928) and accepted in 1928 the chair of Spanish literature at Oxford U. He went to work on the first edition of *Spain* (1930). Herein he began to formulate and subsequently revise his vision of his country in light of its most recent history, especially the creation of the Republic, the Civil War, Franco's victory and post-war developments. In his personal life the establishment of the Republic in 1931 signified renewed political and diplomatic activity for Madariaga: first as Spanish ambassador to the United States and then to France. Subsequently he was named national delegate to the League of Nations, and, in 1934, minister of education for the Republican government. With the outbreak of the Civil War Madariaga fled Spain and resumed his post at Oxford. His best-known works of political science and history began to appear: *Anarchy or Hierarchy* (1937; Spanish ed. 1935), *Christopher Columbus* (1939), *Hernán*

Cortés (1941 in Spanish, 1942 in English), *Cuadro histórico de las Indias* (1945; Historical Situation of the Indies), and, to cut short a very long list of titles, *The Rise of the Spanish American Empire* (1947; Spanish ed. 1956). During these years, as well as before and afterwards, Madariaga published several volumes of poetry and at least twelve novels, with *Romances de ciego* (1922; Blind Man's Ballads), *El corazón de piedra verde* (1942; The Heart of Green Stone) and *El semental negro* (1961; The Black Stud) being among the most valued today. In 1967 he published *Memorias de un federalista* (Memoirs of a Federalist), an autobiographical piece which covers briefly his life from his birth until the mid 1970s. A longer autobiography, *Morning without Noon. Memoirs* (*Memorias. Amanecer sin mediodía*), appeared in English and Spanish editions in 1974, but stresses only the years 1921–36. Having spent more than half of a long life abroad, Madariaga returned to Spain for a visit in 1976 following the death of Franco and was received into the *Academia Española forty years after his election to it. Perhaps the best introduction to his person and work may be found in the essays collected by César Antonio Molina under the titled *Salvador de Madariaga* (1986).

Stephen Miller

MADERA, Asunción (1901, Las Palmas, Grand Canary–), Spanish journalist and poet writing under the name of Chona Madera. Her poetry collections include the following: *El volcano silencio* (1944, 1947; The Volcano Silence); *Mi presencia más clara* (1956; My Clearest Presence); *Las estancias vacías* (1961; The Empty Rooms); *La voz que me desvela* (1965; The Voice That Wakens Me); *Los contados instantes* (1967; Counted Instants); *Continuada señal* (1970; Continued Signal); and *Mi otra palabra* (1977; My Other Word).

BIBLIOGRAPHY

Primary Texts

Los contados instantes. Las Palmas: n.p., 1967.
Mi otra palabra. Málaga: Guadalhorce, 1977.
El volcano silencio. Las Palmas: n.p., 1944.
La voz que me desvela. Las Palmas: n.p., 1965.

Janet Pérez

MADRID, Alonso de (fl. 1521, Madrid?–?,?), Franciscan mystic, religious author. Only his birthplace seems certain. In 1521, his *Arte para servir a Dios* (Art of Serving God), was published; St. *Teresa praised its clarity and usefulness in the early stages of mental prayer. J. Christiaens has verified existence of seventy-one editions—thirty-six Spanish, eleven Latin, nine French, nine Italian, and six Dutch. Later critics term it a "jewel of mystic literature." Alonso de Madrid also is credited with the *Espejo de ilustres personas* (1542; Mirror of Illustrious Persons), which offers instructions for conduct of a Christian life to those "in the public eye," as they have a great responsibility to be an example to others. *See also* Mysticism.

BIBLIOGRAPHY

Primary Text

Obras. In NBAE 16.

English Translation

"On Patience" and "Four Prayers." In *The Spirit of the Spanish Mystics*. Ed. K. Pond. London: Burns and Oates, 1958. 75–79. From the *Arte para servir a Dios*.

Criticism

Christiaens, J. "Alonso de Madrid: contribution à sa biographie et à l'histoire de ses écrits." *Les Lettres Romanes* 9 (1955): 251–68 and 439–62.

Guillaume, A. P. "Un précurseur de la Réforme catholique, Alonso de Madrid." *Revue d'Histoire Eclésiastique* 25 (1929): n.p.

MADRID, Francisco de (?–?) soldier, secretary to King John, and then to Ferdinand and Isabel. Madrid wrote a short, allegorical play in verse titled *Egloga* (c. 1495; Eclogue). Written in octaves of **arte mayor*, it is a political propaganda piece which discusses the French invasion in Italy by Charles VII of France, painting him as most bellicose, and then calling for peace.

BIBLIOGRAPHY

Primary Text

Égloga. Ed., intro. J. E. Gillet. In *HR* 11 (1943): 275–303.

MADRIGAL, Alfonso de (1400?, Madrigal de la Sierra, Avila–1455, Bonilla de la Sierra, Avila), prolific religious writer, Bishop of Avila. Nicknamed El Tostado after his father, Alonso Tostado, he began to teach law, theology and philosophy at the U of Salamanca in 1433. Questions regarding the orthodoxy of some material provoked the enmity of Cardinal Torquemada, and Madrigal fled, or was summoned, to Rome and there condemned for heresy. He recanted all errors. King John II requested his return to Spain, first as royal chancellor in 1444, then, in 1449, Madrigal became Bishop of Avila.

The quantity of Madrigal's writings literally inspired a proverb: "escribir más que el Tostado" (to write more than Tostado). The first edition of his *Opera omnia* (1507–31, Venice; Complete Works), numbered twenty volumes. He wrote commentaries of Old Testament books and the Gospels, explanations of the Mass and Confession, etc. A few memorable titles are *Libro de las paradoxas* (Book of Paradoxes) and *Tratado de como al ome es necesario amar* (Treatise on How Man Needs to Love). He also translated *Seneca's *Medea* into Spanish. He is buried in the Avila Cathedral.

BIBLIOGRAPHY

Primary Texts

Cuestiones de filosofía moral. In BAE 65.

Opera omnia. Ed. R. Bovosius. Venice: n.p., 1569. Rpt. 1728.

"Tratado . . . de como . . . amar." In *Opúsculos de los siglos XIV á XVI*. Madrid: Sociedad de Bibliófilos españoles, 1892. 219–44.

MAEZTU, María de (1882, Vitoria–1947, Buenos Aires), prose writer. She studied in Salamanca with *Unamuno, in Madrid with *Ortega, in Marlburg with Cohen and Natorp. A specialist in pedagogy, she taught and lectured in Spain, Europe, and America. In 1915 she founded the Residencia de Señoritas (Young Women's Residence). In 1936, she moved to Buenos Aires and remained there until her death. Aside from articles and essays, she published *Historia de la cultura europea* (1941; History of European Culture) and a twentieth-c. anthology of Spanish prose writers, accurately and vividly compiled and annotated.

BIBLIOGRAPHY

Primary Texts

Antología, siglo XX. 4th ed. Buenos Aires: Espasa-Calpe, 1952.
Historia de la cultura europea. Buenos Aires and Barcelona: Juventud, 1941.

Isabel McSpadden

MAEZTU, Ramiro de (1874, Vitoria–1936, Madrid), journalist and essayist. The son of an English mother and a Cuban-born Basque father, Maeztu was born into comfortable circumstances. However, when he was a young man a series of financial reverses left the family ruined and forced his father to sail for Cuba in hopes of salvaging what he could of their land holdings. Young Ramiro soon joined him and spent several years on the island, where he learned firsthand of the colonists' hatred for Spain. Back in Bilbao in 1895, he wrote for a local newspaper, *El Porvenir Vascongado*, and earned considerable reputation because of his knowledge of the Caribbean situation. After military service he went to Madrid and continued writing for journals and newspapers. His first collection of essays, *Hacia otra España* (1899; Toward Another Spain), appeared the year after the disastrous war with the United States.

In 1905 Maeztu left Spain for London, where he was to live for fourteen years as foreign correspondent for several Spanish-language newspapers. There, he married and his only child, a son, was born. During these years he traveled extensively through the Continent and became convinced of his homeland's backwardness in comparison with other West European nations. But his admiration for Anglo-Saxon culture diminished greatly during World War I, which he witnessed as a British war correspondent, as he saw the suffering and death that the Germanic nations inflicted on each other. The war was also at least partially responsible for a reawakening of his dormant Catholicism, whose tenets were to be central to his later thought.

Back in Spain in 1919, he became a columnist for the Madrid newspaper *El Sol*. By this time he was well known in England, Spain, and Latin America as well. Maeztu's only visit to the United States came in the summer of 1925, when he served as guest lecturer at Middlebury College in Vermont. During the 1920s he became increasingly reactionary. His support of Primo de Rivera's government earned him an ambassadorship to Argentina from 1927 until the fall of the dictator in 1930. In Spain once more, he founded a society called Acción

Española (Spanish Action) and a journal by the same name. This publication espoused his fascist ideology (Maeztu, however, condemned the racist policies of Nazi Germany) and his concept of Hispanism, an idea which dominated his later years.

He was elected representative to the Spanish Parliament in 1934 from the province of Guipúzcoa and in 1935 was inducted into the *Academia Española. As the nation moved toward the brink of civil war, Maeztu refused to take refuge in France and was arrested by Republican militiamen in July 1936. He was executed three months later, on October 29.

It has been estimated that Maeztu wrote over 13,000 essays and articles, and from these he compiled several major books which illustrate the evolution of his thought. His experiences in Cuba gave rise to *Hacia otra España*, the work which most closely identifies him with the *Generation of 1898. Like other early writings of this generation, it laments Spain's deplorable state and seeks to analyze the causes of the nation's decay, including the nineteenth-c. colonial wars which drained its manpower and finances. Maeztu, in searching for a new Spain, based his hopes on an economic revival and the "Europeanization" of the country. This rebellious and anti-traditionalist attitude changed during his stay in London and is due in part to the spiritual crisis which reaffirmed his Catholicism. His 1916 book *Authority, Liberty and Function in the Light of War*, published with some revisions three years later in Spanish under the title *La crisis del humanismo* (1919; The Crisis of Humanism), established his conservative, traditional personality. The book draws heavily from Catholic doctrine and the concept of sacrifice inherent in Christian thought.

His most purely literary publication is *Don Quijote, Don Juan y la Celestina* (1925; Don Quijote, Don Juan and Celestina), in which these three most famous characters of Spanish literature are held to represent love, power, and wisdom, respectively. Maeztu seeks to demonstrate the interdependence of these three qualities and maintains that they are symbolic of the character and spirit of the Spanish people.

A renewed interest in the positive aspects of Spain's past and his stay in Buenos Aires, where he became cognizant of his nation's role in the founding of a new Spanish-American culture, were two of the foundation stones for Maeztu's idea of Hispanism, to which he devoted his later years. The concept is explained in *Defensa de la Hispanidad* (1934; In Defense of Hispanism), a book which represents a total about-face from his earliest writings. Now, instead of rejecting traditional Spanish values, Maeztu praises them as the source of three hundred years of peace and stability during Spain's zenith. A return to greatness will require a return to tradition. The author envisions an alliance of all the Hispanic nations based on the common language, religion, and values they share.

Maeztu's place in Spanish letters is problematic. While his ultra-conservatism makes him generally unpopular today, it should be remembered that he was one of the premier members of the Generation of 1898, and his impassioned prose reflects a concern for Spain's future that is the hallmark of twentieth-c. Spanish thought. *See also* Essay.

BIBLIOGRAPHY

Primary Texts

Artículos periodísticos (1897–1905). Ed. E. Inman Fox. Madrid: Castalia, 1975.
La crisis del humanismo. Barcelona: Minerva, 1919.
Defensa de la Hispanidad. Madrid: Fax, 1934.
Don Quijote, Don Juan y la Celestina. Madrid: Espasa-Calpe, 1925.
Hacia otra España. Bilbao: Biblioteca Vascongada de Fermín Herrán, 1899.
Obra. Ed. Vicente Marrero. Madrid: Nacional, 1974. Includes his most important works.

English Translation

Authority, Liberty and Function in the Light of War. London: Allen and Unwin, 1916.

Criticism

Blanco Aguinaga, Carlos. *Juventud del 98*. Madrid: Siglo Veintiuno, 1970.
Fox, E. Inman. ''Una bibliografía anotada del periodismo de Ramiro de Maeztu y Whitney (1897–1904).'' *CH* 291 (Sept. 1974): 528–81.
Landeira, Ricardo. *Ramiro de Maeztu*. Boston: Twayne, 1978. In English.
Marrero, Vicente. *Maeztu*. Madrid: Rialp, 1955.
Nozick, Martin. ''An Examination of Ramiro de Maeztu.'' *PMLA* 69 (Sept. 1954): 719–40.
Rocamora, Pedro. ''Ramiro de Maeztu y la Generación del 98.'' *Arbor* 341 (May 1974): 7–22.

James F. Brown

MAL LARA, Juan de (1524, Seville–1571, Seville), distinguished humanist, essayist, poet and playwright. A pupil of Hernán *Núñez and Francisco Escobar, he opened in Seville the renowned Escuela de Humanidades y Gramática (School of Humanities and Grammar), which was frequented by many key figures of the city's cultural life: Diego *Girón (who succeeded Mal Lara as the school's director), Francisco de *Medina, Francisco de *Pacheco, and Fernando de *Herrera. Mal Lara's most important book is *La Philosophía vulgar* (1568; Philosophy of the Common People), a collection of a thousand proverbs, all classified and each with its expository essay, in imitation of Erasmus. The book can still be read with pleasure, both for the style and for the unusual historical anecdotes with which it abounds. He also wrote plays and other works as well as poetry. No plays survive. An admirable poet in Spanish and Latin, his best known work of poetry is *La hermosa Psyche* (Beautiful Psyche). Other important works by Mal Lara are *In Aphtonii Progymnasmata Scholia* (1567; On the Early Training Commentary of Aphtonius), where he puts forward the teachings of Escobar; *Recibimiento que hizo Sevilla al rey Felipe II* (1570; Philip II's Reception in Seville) and *Descripción de la galera real de Don Juan de Austria* (Description of Juan of Austria's Royal Gallery). *See also* Erasmism; Humanism; Renaissance.

BIBLIOGRAPHY

Primary Texts

Filosofía vulgar. Ed. A. Vilanova. Barcelona: n.p., 1958.

El libro quinto de la "Psyche". Ed. M. Gasparini. Salamanca: Colegio Trilingüe de la Universidad, 1947.

Recibimiento que hizo Sevilla al rey Felipe II. Seville: Sociedad de Bibliófilos Andaluces, 1882.

Criticism

Gasparini, Mario. *Juan de Mal Lara*. Firenze: La Nuova Italia, 1943.

Sánchez y Escribano, F. *Juan de Mal Lara: su vida y su obra*. New York: Hispanic Institute, 1941.

Melczer, William. "Juan de Mal Lara et l'école humaniste de Seville." In *L'Humanisme dans les lettres espagnoles*. Ed. Agustín Redondo. Paris: Vrin, 1979.

Hector Medina

MALDONADO DE GUEVARA, Francisco (1891, Salamanca–1985, ?), professor, literary scholar. Professor of Spanish language and literature at the Universities of Murcia, Oviedo, Valladolid and Salamanca, and up until his retirement, at the U of Madrid, he published numerous studies over a variety of subjects: Fray Luis de *León, *Gracián y Morales, *Cervantes, **Lazarillo de Tormes*, emblematic literature, etc. His great erudition and knowledge of several languages allowed him to establish original parallels, such as his interpretation of the *Don Juan legend. A collection of his essays was published under the title *Cinco salvaciones* (1953; Five Salvations). Maldonado also founded the prestigious Cervantine journal *Anales cervantinos* in 1951 and directed it until 1960, when he became honorary director.

BIBLIOGRAPHY

Primary Texts

Cinco salvaciones. Madrid: RO, 1953.

Interpretación del Lazarillo de Tormes. Madrid: Bermejo, 1957.

Sydney Cravens

MALDONADO DE GUEVARA Y OCAMPO, Luis (1860, Salamanca–1926, Madrid), prose author. Father of Francisco *Maldonado de Guevara, he was also a university professor. Noted as an author of narratives on rural customs, using peasant dialects, as in *Las querellas del ciego de Robliza* (1894; The Complaints of the Blind Man of Robliza), his major work is the short story collection *Del campo y de la ciudad* (1903; Of the Country and of the City). Maldonado met with some success in the theater with his play *La montaraza de Olmedo* (The Mountain Girl from Olmedo).

BIBLIOGRAPHY

Primary Text

Del campo y de la ciudad. 2nd ed. Salamanca: Calatrava, 1932.

Sydney Cravens

MALÓN DE CHAIDE, Pedro (c. 1530, Cascante, Navarra– 1589, Barcelona), Augustinian monk, translator of Old Testament texts and writer of ascetical, religious literature. His importance resides in the publication of the influential ascetical and biographical narrative *La conversión de la Magdalena* (Barcelona, 1588; *Lines from the Conversion of the Magdalene*, n.d.). In the prologue Malón de Chaide claims to have composed this book in the vulgar tongue to offer the reading public an alternative to the popular romances of chivalry (*caballerías) and to the *pastoral literature in vogue. Malón de Chaide was one of several religious writers who favored the use of Castilian over Latin so that their writings could be more accessible to the lay readers.

Malón de Chaide divides the *Conversión* into three parts corresponding to the three phases of Mary Magdalen's life: sinner, penitent and state of grace. He follows the ascetical process which leads the repentant sinner to the state of perfection. In other words, he transforms this process into a literary creation that will be spiritually edifying as well as holding the reader's interest (enseñar deleitando). The *Conversión* made an important contribution to the development of Castilian prose. In addition, A. A. Parker suggests that it had a direct influence on Mateo *Alemán's *Guzmán de Alfarache*. *See also* Ascetical literature.

BIBLIOGRAPHY

Primary Text

La conversión de la Magdalena. Ed. Félix García. *Clásicos Castellanos*, vol. 1. Madrid: Espasa-Calpe, 1930.

English Translation

Lines from the Conversion of the Magdalene. Tr. Thomas Walsh. N.p.: n.p., n. d.

Criticism

Monasterio, Ignacio, O.S.A. *Místicos agustinos españoles.* 2nd. ed. 2 vols. El Escorial: Agustiniana, 1929.

Parker, A. A. *Literature and the Delinquent.* Edinburgh: Edinburgh UP, 1977.

Angelo DiSalvo

MALUQUER I GONZÁLEZ, Concepció (1918, Salas–), poet and novelist. Though born in the Pyrenees, she has lived most of her life in Barcelona and makes the city a theme of some works. She won the Premi ciutat de Barcelona prize with her long poem *La creu dels vents* (1959; The Crossroads of the Winds), a dialogue between the city and the four cardinal winds. Another long poem, *La ciutat y les hores* (1960; The City and the Hours), a finalist for the same prize, presents the twenty-four hours of the day personified by twenty-four female characters. Later books are novels which depict characters of the upper classes bored by the monotony of their lives, notably *Parèntesi* (1962; Parenthesis) and *¿Que s'ha fet d'en Pere Cots*? (1966; What Happened to Pere Cots?). Her long novels contain rich observations of contemporary phenomena that affect the life of Catalans, namely, tourism and immigration.

BIBLIOGRAPHY

Primary Texts

Aigua térbola. Andorra: Alfaguara, 1967.
La ciutat y les hores. Barcelona: Moderna, 1960.
La creu dels vents. Barcelona: Moderna, 1959.
Dues cases. Barcelona: Arimany, 1960.
Gent del nord. Barcelona: Club, 1971.
Gent del Sud. Barcelona: Club, 1964.
Parèntesi. Barcelona: Alberti, 1962.
¿Que s'ha fet d'en Pere Cots? Andorra: Alfaguara, 1966.

Kathleen McNerney

MANRIQUE, Gómez (1412, Amusco, Palencia–c. 1491, Toledo), poet and playwright. Personal modesty made him consider himself more a soldier than a poet. He had, in fact, an active military and political career as a *corregidor* (royal representative) in Ávila and Toledo. An enemy of the powerful Alvaro de Luna, the king's *privado* (favorite), he was later a strong supporter of Isabel and Ferdinand, to whom he dedicated his long poem *Regimiento de príncipes* (1482; A Princes' Guide), a book of advice on how best to rule. Almost half of his poems belong to the courtly, Galaico-Provençal poetic tradition. These are beautifully ornamented compositions that demonstrate a technical virtuosity as good as that of the best poets of his time. The *Batalla de amores* (Battle of Love) stands out as a skillful presentation of the progress of love rendered in images rooted in his military experience. But it is in the didactic and moralistic poetry where his highly refined art is seen at its best: he displays an elegant and sober style enhanced by a rich lexicon and generous classical allusions in, for example, the *Exclamación y querella de la gobernación* (Exclamation and Complaints Concerning Government) and the previously mentioned *Regimiento*. The *Coplas para el señor Diego de Ávila* (Stanzas for Diego de Ávila), usually acknowledged as the best poetic piece of his oeuvre, set in many ways the tone for his nephew Jorge's *Coplas a la muerte de su padre*. Utilizing a highly moral and serious tone, he discusses topics typical of the contemporary intellectual climate such as worldly vanity and the transitory condition of all things human. Noteworthy but somewhat exaggerated in its praise is the elegiac *Planto* (Lament) on the death of his uncle, the Marquis of *Santillana in which Gómez Manrique celebrates both his martial and his humanistic qualities. Manrique's minor compositions include poems of consolation, others praising the Virgin and a few burlesque pieces. There is little consensus among the critics concerning the merit of Manrique's attempts at drama. One should remember, however, that the unpretentious *Representación del Nacimiento de Nuestro Señor (The Birth of*

Our Lord, 1964) and the very short *[Lamentaciones] fechas para la Semana Santa* (Laments for Holy Week) are the only indications of the existence of a Castilian drama between the **Auto de los Reyes Magos* and the plays of Juan del *Encina. *See also* Gallic Portuguese Poetry; Humanism; Renaissance.

BIBLIOGRAPHY

Primary Texts

Cancionero castellano del siglo XV. Ed. R. Foulché-Delbosc. NBAE 19 and 22.

Los Manriques, poetas del siglo XV. Ed. Joaquín de Entrambasaguas. Zaragoza-Madrid: Ebro, 1966.

English Translation

The Birth of Our Lord. Tr. R. O'Brien. In *Early Spanish Plays*. Ed. R. O'Brien. New York: Las Americas, 1964.

Criticism

Clarke, Dorothy. *Morphology of Fifteenth-Century Castilian Verse*. Pittsburgh: Duquesnes UP, 1964.

Scholberg, K. R. *Introducción a la poesía de Gómez Manrique*. Madison, WI: HSMS, 1984.

Sieber, Harry. ''Dramatic Symmetry in Gómez Manrique's *La Representación del Nacimiento de Nuestro Señor*.'' *HR* 33 (1965): 118–35.

María Teresa Pajares

MANRIQUE, Jorge (1440, Paredes de Nava–1479, castle of Garci Muñoz, Calatrava), soldier, poet. Of illustrious lineage, Grand Master of the Order of Santiago, nephew to Gómez *Manrique, he supported the reign of Prince Alphonse, and later, of Isabel and Ferdinand. He left about fifty lyric compositions, which may be grouped into three categories: (1) courtly love verse—the largest group by far; (2) satiric poems—three pieces, each aimed at a different woman; and (3) moral poetry. This final category holds the jewel of his work—the *Coplas a la muerte de su padre don Rodrigo* (*Coplas*, 1919). This eloquent commemoration of his father's death was written in 1476 and published for the first time eighteen years later. The forty octosyllabic stanzas, with **pie quebrado* rhyme, soberly and eloquently collect the themes and spirit of the waning Middle Ages: fleeting time, the brevity of human life and little value of earthly things, fortune, and death, the great equalizer. Also present, arrestingly fused to the abovementioned concerns, are various aspects of *Renaissance thought: the comparison of present virtue with that of classical heroes, the pride and honor of a well-conducted life, and the earthly fame which accompanies the eternal reward for such a life. Despite the use of many familiar topics, and even clichés, the poem is striking in its freshness and quiet force, secured by the perfection of its style. It continues to engage readers today, more than five hundred years later. Manrique died in battle three years after he wrote the *Coplas*. *See also* Edad Media, Literatura de la; Humanism.

BIBLIOGRAPHY

Primary Texts

Coplas a la muerte de su padre. Ed. C. Díaz Castañón. Madrid: Castalia, 1984.
Obras completas. Prol. J. García López. Barcelona: Montaner y Simón, 1942.
Poesía. Ed., intro. J. M. Alda Tesán. Madrid: Cátedra, 1976.

English Translation

Coplas de Jorge Manrique, with Henry Wadsworth Longfellow's Rendering. Oxford: Blackwell, 1919.

Criticism

Gilman, S. "Tres retratos de la muerte en las *Coplas* de Jorge Manrique." *NRFH* 12 (1959): 305–24.
Salinas, P. *Jorge Manrique o tradición y originalidad*. 2nd ed. Barcelona: Seix Barral, 1981.
Serrano de Haro, A. *Personalidad y destino de Jorge Manrique*. 2nd ed. Madrid: Gredos, 1975.

MANTERO, Manuel (1930, Seville–), poet, novelist, critic, currently residing in Athens, Georgia. Mantero received his licenciate degree from the U of Seville in 1953, and his doctorate from the U of Salamanca in 1957, after which he taught at the Universities of Seville and Madrid before coming to the United States; in 1969 he went to Western Michigan U for four years and afterwards to the U of Georgia, holding in 1988 the position of research professor of Spanish literature there.

Manuel Mantero started publishing his poems in the 1950s in the little magazines of Andalusia, where he became known as one of a generation of Andalusian poets of that decade. Although he has always maintained an independence from any group, he continues to be discussed as part of that generation. He published his first book, *Mínimas del ciprés y los labios* (1958; Little Bits of the Cypress and the Lips) at age twenty-seven, published the prize-winning *Misa solemne* (1966; Solemn Mass) at age thirty-six, and then left Spain to live and teach in the United States.

For his poetry Mantero has received several awards: the National Literature Prize for *Tiempo del hombre* (1960; Man's Time), which, as he says, represents the daily life of an individual in Madrid; the Pensión de Literatura from the March Foundation (1964); the *Academia Española's Fastenrath Prize for *Misa solemne*, which he modeled on the Catholic Mass; and the U of Georgia Albert Christ-Janer Award (1981) for his life's work.

Mantero has published numerous other books, including *Poesía: 1958–1971* (1972; Poetry: 1958–1971); a novel, *Estiércol de león* (1980; Lion Leavings); and two books of criticism, of which the most recent is *Poetas españoles de posguerra* (1985; Spanish Postwar Poets), as well as editions, anthologies and essays.

BIBLIOGRAPHY

Primary Texts

Estiércol de león. Barcelona: Plaza y Janés, 1980.
Mínimas del ciprés y los labios. Cadiz: Alcaraván, 1958.
Misa solemne. Madrid: Nacional, 1966.
Poesía: 1958–1971. Barcelona: Plaza y Janés, 1972.
Poetas españoles de posguerra. Madrid: Espasa-Calpe, 1985.
Tiempo del hombre. Madrid: Agora, 1960.

English Translation

Manuel Mantero: New Songs for the Ruins of Spain. Sel., tr. Betty Jean Craige. Lewisburg: Bucknell UP, 1986.

Criticism

Cano, José Luis. "La poesía de Manuel Mantero." In *Poesía española contemporánea. Las generaciones de posguerra.* Madrid: Guadarrama, 1974.
Debicki, Andrew P. "Manuel Mantero." In *Poetry of Discovery.* Lexington: UP of Kentucky, 1982.
Hernández, Antonio. "Manuel Mantero." In *La poética del 50.* Madrid: Zero-Zyx, 1978.
Josia, Vincenzo. "Manuel Mantero." In *Poeti Sivigliani di Oggi.* Rome: Opere Nuove, 1966.
Ruiz Copete, Juan de Dios. "Manuel Mantero o la poesía de la observación profunda." In *Poetas de Sevilla.* Seville: Caja de Ahorros Provincial, 1971.

Betty Jean Craige

MÀNTUA, Cecília A. *See* Alonso i Manant, Cecilia

MANUEL MARÍA (TEIXEIRA FERNÁNDEZ) (1930, Outeiro de Rei, Lugo–), Galician poet. Known by his given names, Manuel María studied in Lugo, where he frequented the *tertulia* of Pimentel, *Fole, and Anxel Johán. He did not complete his studies at the U of Santiago, and in Monforte de Lemos became a court employee while directing the poetry collection Xistral. He is the contemporary Galician poet who has been awarded the greatest number of recognitions for his writing and has the most extensive list of publications. He is also a dramatist, author of essays, and narrator. His poems have appeared in numerous journals of Galicia, Spain, and other countries.

Manuel María is a figure of socio-historical significance, for he published the first work in Galician after the Civil War. In the early work there are vestiges of the Imagist school of the 1920s, which did not preclude vigorous existentialist creations. At times it resembles neo-romanticism as well as popular realism. Although religious themes are not absent from Manuel María's poetry, he is known for his social realism and criticism of unjust conditions in Galician society. Through satire and criticism, the author holds up such values as love, nature, and patriotism. *See also* Galician Literature.

BIBLIOGRAPHY

Primary Texts

Advento. Buenos Aires: Galicia, 1954.
Aldraxe contra a xistra. Geneva: E Roi Xordo, 1973.
Canciós do lusco ó fusco. Monforte de Lemos: Xistral, 1970.
Cantos rodados pra alleados e colonizados. Pontevedra: Xistral, 1976.
Catavento de neutrós domesticados. Lugo: Alvarellos, 1979.
O libro das Baladas. Santiago: Follas Novas, 1978.
Mar Maior. Vigo: Galaxia, 1963.
Morrendo a cada intre. Lugo: La Voz de la Verdad, 1952.
Odas nun tempo de paz e de ledicia. Porto: Razão Actual, 1972.
Poemas ó Outono. Madrid: Agrupación Cultural Galega "Lostrego," 1977.
Poemas pra construir unha patria. Edicións Ceibe da Asamblea Nacional–Popular Galega, 1977.
Proba documental. Monforte de Lemos: Xistral, 1968.
As rúas do vento ceibe. La Coruña: Asociación Socio-Pedagóxica Galega, 1979.
Terra Chá. 1st ed. Lugo: Celta, 1954. 3rd ed., 1972.
Versos do lume e o vagalume. Orense: Galiza Editora, 1982.
Versos pra cantar en feiras e romaxes. Montevideo: Patronato da Cultura Galega, 1969.

Criticism

Costa Clavell, Javier. *Literatura gallega actual*. Madrid: Nacional, 1959.
Oliveira Guerra. "O poeta Manuel María." *Céltica* (Porto) 2 (1960): n.p.
Tudela, Mariano. "La poesía gallega de Manuel María." *CH* 68–69 (1956): n.p.
Vázquez Cuesta, Pilar. "Literatura Gallega." In *Historia de las literaturas hispánicas no castellanas*. Madrid: Taurus, 1980.

Kathleen March

MARAGALL, Joan (1860, Barcelona–1911, Barcelona), poet, journalist, thinker, essayist and translator. Scion of an industrial family, he was educated in Barcelona. In 1884 he graduated from law school at the U of Barcelona. After a brief and intermittent period as a lawyer he became a journalist for the *Diario de Barcelona* (Barcelona Daily News), writing in Castilian; he wrote in Catalan for a variety of other publications. His first poems are dated from 1878; from then on he continued writing poetry until his death. He married Clara Noble in 1891; they had thirteen children. Today he is widely considered a giant of Catalan poetry whose influence extends beyond time and literary movements.

Maragall was also a man of action, deeply involved in Catalan politics, culture, and the events of his time. A deeply devoted Christian, he did not hesitate to criticize the traditional church or the established social order. He understood that the durability of the Catalan nation would only be made possible when its leaders (i.e., writers) embraced the convictions of all classes and ideologies. In this respect, his essays on Barcelona are exemplary, especially those dealing with the riots of the Setmana Tràgica (Tragic Week of 1909). Aside from its intrinsic literary value, Maragall's work is still appealing to younger generations of Catalans because of his noble spirit, his great passion for truth, and his Christian ecumenical charity.

Although many critics tie Maragall to the flowering of the literary movement called *Modernisme* (*Modernism), the fact is that his powerful artistic character goes beyond it and defies classification. More intensely than other great writers of the Renaixença (Catalan Renaissance of the nineteenth c.), Maragall felt the influence of other writers and thinkers, in particular the German Romantics. His translations of Goethe, Novalis and Hölderlin are in themselves poetic masterpieces.

Maragall's contributions to modern Catalan lexicon are immense. One could easily say that modern Catalan poetic language exists only after his poetry. A man of clear and great historical vision, he was equally fascinated by language. He thought that beauty is better achieved by direct simplicity, and true emotions should not degenerate into melodramatic words. Above all, he believed that true poetry is the result of absolute sincerity, in accordance with his theory of the "paraula viva" (the living word). One could detect in his theories the influence of the best German Romantics such as Goethe and Hölderlin but Maragall goes beyond them, affirming that poetic expressions written at the moment of inspiration are in direct and tragic conflict with his deepest creative purpose. His technique at times may give the impression of being simple or even careless, reminiscent of the creative instant; but he wrote, nonetheless, poetry that showed a tremendous force and beauty of a language born and nurtured for the uses of ordinary life. Maragall's favorite themes are love and nature. His best poems are serene on the surface but reveal a great inner passion for life. Like Nietzsche, he loves nature and exalts life, but always within the framework of ecumenical Christianity. His best known poem, "Cant espiritual" (Spiritual Song), reveals, however, the distilled, sensuous and classical Mediterranean longing for both the world and eternal life, both beauty and spirit: "Més enllà veig el cel i les estrelles, / i encara allí voldria esserhi hom" (Beyond I see the sky and stars, / and even there I wish to be a man).

Others of his best poems are "El Compte Arnau" (Count Arnau), "Joan Serrallonga," "La vaca cega" (The Blind Cow), "Goigs a la Verge de Núria" (Rapture to the Virgin of Nuria) and the beautiful "Nausica" based on the episode of the *Odyssey* in which the hero on his return to Ithaca falls in love with the princess Nausica. The best collections of his poetry are *Poesies* (1895; Poems), *Les disperses* (1904; Dispersed), *Enllà* (1906; Beyond), *Seqüències* (1911; Sequences) and, of course, his version of *Himnes homèrics* (1911; Homeric Hymns).

Maragall was a friend and correspondent of several members of the *Generation of 1898, especially *Unamuno, who admired his integrity, loved his poetry and translated "La vaca cega" into Castilian. *See also* Catalan literature.

BIBLIOGRAPHY

Primary Texts

Obres completes. 2 vols. Barcelona: Selecta, 1981.

Criticism

Benet, Josep. *Maragall i la setmana tràgica.* Barcelona: Institut d'Estudis Catalans, 1963.
Carner, Josep. Prologue to vol. 1 of *Obres completes.*
Corredor, Josep M. *Joan Maragall.* Barcelona: Aedos, 1960.
d'Ors, Eugeni. *Estilos de pensar . . . Juan Maragall.* Madrid: Epesa, 1944.
Serra d'or 11 (1962). Issue dedicated to Joan Maragall.
Terry, Arthur. *La poesía de Juan Maragall.* Barcelona: Barcino, 1963.

Joan Gilabert

MARAÑÓN, Gregorio (1887, Madrid–1960, Madrid), nonfiction author, doctor of great prestige and professor of endocrinology (his scientific specialty for which he was world known), academician in the Academies of Medicine, Sciences, Language and History. Besides his clinical activity and medical publications, he wrote works combining his scientific knowledge and an interest in social and historical issues: *Tres ensayos sobre la vida sexual* (1926; Three Essays on Sexuality), *Gordos y flacos* (Fat and Thin People), *Amor, conveniencia y eugenesia* (1931; Love, Convenience, and Eugenics), *Amiel* (1932), *Las ideas biológicas del padre Feijoo* (1934; Father Feijoo's Biological Ideas), and *Ensayo biológico sobre Enrique IV de Castilla y su tiempo* (1934; Biological Essay on Henry IV of Castile and His Time). Marañón also wrote a series of historical-biographical works which benefit from his scientific background: *Raíz y decoro de España* (1933; Root and Decorum of Spain), *Vocación y ética* (1935; Vocation and Ethics), *Vida e historia* (Life and History), *Crónica y gesto de la libertad* (Chronicle and Gesture of Liberty), *Tiberio* (*Tiberius. A Study in Resentment,* 1956), *Tiempo viejo y tiempo nuevo* (Old Time and New Time), *Don Juan, elogio y nostalgia de Toledo* (Praise and Nostalgia of Toledo), *Ensayos liberales* (Liberal Essays), *Cajal, su tiempo y el nuestro* (1947; Cajal, His Time and Ours), *El Greco y Toledo* (1957), *Los tres Vélez* (1960; The Three Velezes) and his two great historical interpretations— *El conde-duque de Olivares (La pasión de mandar)* (The Count-Duke Olivares [The Passion to Rule]) of 1936 and *Antonio Pérez* (1947; *Antonio Perez*, 1954).

The volume and value of Marañón's scientific and historical works should not conceal his literary importance. His prose is easy, persuasive and stimulating. Essays by him possess vivid evocation and an ability to animate lives, as in *Antonio Pérez*. His prose boasts life, spontaneity, artistic quality, and a capacity to sympathize with remote lives and epochs; thus his considerable erudition does not obscure effective historical comprehension in the reader.

BIBLIOGRAPHY

Primary Texts

Obras completas. Ed. A. Juderías. 10 vols. Madrid: Espasa-Calpe, 1966–72.

English Translations

Antonio Perez: Spanish Traitor. Tr. C. D. Ley. London: Hollis and Carter, 1954; New York: Roy, 1955.

Tiberius. A Study in Resentment. Tr. W. B. Wells. London: Hollis and Carter, 1956.

Criticism

Cortes, Guillermo. *Algo sobre Gregorio Marañón.* San Salvador: Ahora, 1978.

Gómez Santos, Marino. *Vida de Gregorio Marañón.* Madrid: Taurus, 1971.

Keller, Gary. *The Significance and Impact of Gregorio Marañón: Literary Criticism, Biographies and Historiography.* New York: Bilingual P, 1977.

Isabel McSpadden

MARAVALL, José Antonio (1911, Játiva, Valencia–), literary scholar. Professor at the U of Madrid, he directed the Casa de España (House of Spain) in Paris and is author of noteworthy essays on various subjects related to literature. His work *El humanismo de las armas en Don Quijote* (1948; The Humanism of Arms in Don Quijote) has a foreword by *Menéndez Pidal. He has published an extensive, well-documented study, *El concepto de España en la Edad Media* (1955; The Concept of Spain in the Middle Ages), and *Teoría del saber histórico* (1958; Theory of Historical Knowledge). Maravall produced his best works, filled with critical sagacity and excellent philosophical and literary taste, in the decade of 1959–1969: *Ortega en nuestra situación* (1959; Ortega in Our Situation); *Carlos V y el pensamiento político del Renacimiento* (1960; Charles V and Political Thought of the Renaissance); *Menéndez Pidal y la historia del pensamiento* (1960; Menéndez Pidal and the History of Thought); *Las Comunidades de Castilla, una primera revolución moderna* (1963; The Peoples' Uprising in Castile, a First Modern Revolution); *El mundo social de "La Celestina"* (1964; The Social World of "La Celestina"), which received the European Writers' Prize; *Antiguos y modernos, La idea de progreso en el desarrollo inicial de una sociedad* (1966; Ancients and Moderns, The Idea of Progress in the Initial Development of a Society); and *Estado moderno y mentalidad social. Siglos XV a XVII* (1972; The Modern State and Social Mentality. Fifteenth to Seventeenth Centuries).

He has collaborated with the prestigious journals *Revista de Occidente, Cruz y Raya* and *El Sol*, and after the Civil War he has continued to collaborate with the most prestigious publications. Director of *Cuadernos Hispanoamericanos*, a member of the Royal Academy of History, he is an associate professor at the U of Paris.

BIBLIOGRAPHY

Primary Texts

Antiguos y modernos, La idea de progreso en el desarrollo inicial de una sociedad. Madrid: Sociedad de Estudios y Publicaciones, 1966.

La cultura del barroco: análisis de una estructura histórica. Esplugas de Llobregat: Ariel, 1975.

El humanismo de las armas en Don Quijote. Madrid: Instituto de Estudios Políticos, 1948.

El mundo social de "La Celestina." Madrid: Gredos, 1964.

English Translations

Dictatorship and Political Dissent; Workers and Students in Franco's Spain. New York: St. Martin's, 1979.

Culture of the Baroque. Tr. T. Cochran. Minneapolis: U of Minnesota, 1986.

Isabel McSpadden

MARÇAL I SERRA, Maria-Mercè (1952, Ivars d'Urgell–), poet and teacher. She studied philology at the U of Barcelona, where she now resides, and is professor of Catalan language and literature at the Institut Rubió i Ors in Sant Boi de Llobregat. She participated in the founding of the Llibres del Mall collection in 1973 and in 1976 won the Carles Riba prize for her first book of poetry, *Cau de llunes* (1977; Moons' lair). The poems are divided into four thematic parts: the first and last sections, in very different styles, are love poems; in the last part the poet uses popular traditions which render very musical poetry. The second part is nourished by her socio-political attitude, and the third by her feminist commitment. In her second book, *Bruixa de dol* (1979; Witches in Mourning), the author finds her own voice while recovering some Catalan literary traditions. Images of witches and fairies pervade this erotic and feminist poetry. In *Sal oberta* (1982; Open Salt) she again insists on speaking in her own voice, from her own experience, from the point of view of a woman. *Terra de mai* (1982; Neverland) is a collection of fifteen sestinas, in which she very successfully uses the medieval form for poetry with modern preoccupations and imagery. While following the six-line, six-stanza verse form with a closing tercet, the language and rhythm flow gracefully in this often sensual poetry. She has published poetry in various journals, and some of her lyrics have been sung by Marina Rossell, Ramon *Muntaner, Maria del Mar Bonet, and other bards of the Nova Canço. An insightful literary critic as well, she is responsible for the selection and a long introduction to the work of Clementina *Arderiu in *Contraclaror: Antologia Poetica* (Barcelona: laSal, 1985).

BIBLIOGRAPHY

Primary Texts

Bruixa de dol. Barcelona: Mall, 1979.

Sal oberta. Barcelona: Mall, 1982.

La germana, l'estrangera. Barcelona: Mall, 1985.

Terra de Mai. Valencia: El cingle, 1982.

Cau de llunes. Barcelona: Aymà, 1977.

English Translations

Selections from *Bruixa de dol*, tr. by Kathleen McNerney, are in a special issue of *Seneca Review* on Catalan poetry, 16.1 (May 1986): n.p.

Kathleen McNerney

MARCELA DE SAN FÉLIX, Sor (1605, Toledo–1688, Madrid), poet and dramatist. Unjustly best known through her father Lope de *Vega's poem to her profession in the convent of the Discalced Trinitarians in Madrid at age sixteen, Sor

Marcela was an excellent playwright and poet in her own right. As a nun, she mitigated the effects of being a "natural" daughter and claimed her legitimacy as Lope's literary inheritor. Sor Marcela accomplished her best writing when she allegorized the ideals of religious life, when she was daringly humorous about convent domesticity, and when she depicted her encounters with self through solitude.

Her extant work is contained in two mss. held by the convent in which she lived and wrote. One is a 585-page collection of six allegorical plays and thirty-eight poems by Sor Marcela; the other, a compendium of nuns' lives, contains a brief biography by the same author. At the behest of a confessor, according to the convent chronicle, she burned the other four or five collections of her plays and poetry. As a curious but not uncommon act of obedience, she also seems to have written and destroyed pages about her own life. Those writings that remain nevertheless reveal the wide range of her literary vocabulary, which encompasses the rarefied idealism of refined religiosity and the conversational colloquialism of mundane existence.

While Sor Marcela's mystical poems lyricize her quest for spiritual perfection through asceticism, her **loas* and plays—entertainment with a pedagogical purpose—capture the flavor and vocabulary of conversation in Madrid during those years. Popular theater techniques and popular language thus revitalized religious ideas and elements of mystic literature. Sor Marcela's poems elaborate an aesthetic of asceticism; in the very experience of meeting God's spirit in oneself lies the wellspring of true eloquence. Her work proves she could be solemn, silly, didactic, narrative, amorous, ascetic, sacred and profane. Her style ranged from colloquial, to rhetorical, to flowery artifice, to the hauntingly lyrical. In short, Sor Marcela de San Félix lived up to the literary lineage she sometimes mocked but never forgot.

BIBLIOGRAPHY

Primary Texts

"En uso de Sor Marcela de San Félix." Ms. Madrid: Convent of the Descalzas Trinitarias, n.d.

"Noticias de la Vida de la Madre Sor Catalina de San José. Religiosa Trinitaria Descalza." In *Fundación del Convento de la Santísima Trinidad, de Madrid, y noticia de las religiosas que en el han florecido. . . .* Ms. Convent of the Descalzas Trinitarias, 1762.

Several plays and poems. In BAE 270.

English Translations

See Arenal and Schlau, below.

Criticism

Arenal, E., and S. Schlau. "Not Only a Famous Writer's Daughter: Recording the Drama of Female Religious Life." In *Untold Sisters: Hispanic Nuns in Their Own Works.* Albuquerque: U of New Mexico P, 1989. Contains selections with translations.

Barbeito Carneiro, M. I. "La ingeniosa provisora Sor Marcela de Vega." *Cuadernos bibliográficos* 44 (1982), separate issue.

Castro, A. and H. A. Rennert. *Vida de Lope de Vega (1562–1635)*. Salamanca, Madrid: Anaya, 1968.
Laca, J. R. *Lope de Vega: Parientes, amigos y "trastos viejos."* Madrid: Deral, 1967.

Stacey Schlau

MARCH, Ausiàs (c. 1397, Gandia–1459, Valencia), poet and member of the Catalan nobility noted for its dedication to the arts. As a military officer of the Catalan armies in the Mediterranean, he traveled widely in the classical world, especially Italy. His first marriage was to Isabel de Martorell, sister of Joanot *Martorell, the principal author of *Tirant lo Blanc*. He left four illegitimate children. His poetic work (128 poems with a total of 1,000 verses) is of the utmost importance to the Castilian poets of the *Siglo de Oro (*Quevedo, Francisco *Sánchez de las Brozas, etc.). Immensely popular on the Iberian Peninsula, his poetry was repeatedly published in Castilian and Catalan during the fifteenth c. It is platonic love poetry dedicated to Lady Teresa, until *Cants de mort* (Songs of death), in which the poet describes the pain he feels for the death of his lovers. "Cant espiritual" (Spiritual Song) is perhaps his best known poem and the most difficult, for he deals with the themes of evil, good, the limitations of man, the theory of love, etc. His best known characteristic is the "bella eloqüença" poetry based on images rather than on metaphors. He uses the Catalan of Valencia without any trace of Provençalisms. His major sources, besides the classics, are the *Suma* by St. Thomas and *Ethics* by Aristotle, but one can also find traces of medieval masters, especially Ramon *Llull. He is credited with introducing the new Italian lyric into the Iberian Peninsula. *See also* Aristotelianism; Catalan Literature; Italian Literary Influences.

BIBLIOGRAPHY

Primary Texts

Antologia poèticalAusiàs March. Valencia: Tres i Quatre, 1979.
Obra poéticalAusiàs March, Sel. and tr. Pere Gimferrer. Madrid: Alfaguara, 1978.
Obra poética completa. Ed., intro., notes Rafael Ferreres. 2 vols. Madrid: Castalia, 1979.
Obras. Tr. Jorge de Montemayor. Madrid: CSIC, Instituto "Nicolás Antonio," 1947.
Les Obres. Critical ed. Amadeu Pagès. Barcelona: Institut d'Estudis Catalans, 1912–14.
Traducciones castellanas de Ausias March en la edad de oro. Ed. Martín de Riquer. Barcelona: Instituto Español de Estudios Mediterráneos, 1946.

English Translations

Selected poemslAusiàs March. Ed. and tr. Arthur Terry. Edinburgh: UP, 1976.

Criticism

Fuster, J. *Obres completes*, vol I. Barcelona: Edicions 62, 1968.
Girolano, C. di. "Ausiàs March and the Troubadour Poetic Code." *Catalan Studies*. Volume in memory of Josephine de Boer. Barcelona: Hispam, 1977.
McNerney, Kathleen. *The Influence of Ausiàs March on Early Golden Age Castilian Poetry*. Amsterdam: Rodopi, 1982.
Pagès, Amadeu. *Auzias March et ses prédécesseurs*. Paris: Champion, 1912.

———. *Commentaire des poésies d'Auzias March.* Paris: Champion, 1925.
Ramirez i Molas, P. *La poesía de Auzias March.* Basel: Geigy, 1970.

Joan Gilabert

MARCH, Susana (1918, Barcelona–), poet and novelist. She began to write poetry at an early age, publishing *Rutas* (1938; Itineraries) at the age of twenty, followed by *Ardiente voz* (1948; The Fervent Voice), *El viento* (1951; The Wind), *La tristeza* (1953; Sadness)—which won her honorable mention in the prestigious Adonais competition—and *Esta mujer que soy* (1959; The Woman I Am). In 1966, an anthology of her poems was published, *Poemas. Antología* [1938–59], followed by *Los poemas del hijo* (1970; Poems about My Son). Susana March also published a collection of short stories, *Narraciones* (1945; Narrations), and five novels, the best known ones being *Niña* (1949; Nina), and *Algo muere cada día* (1955; Something Dies Within Us Every Day), translated into French as *Les ruines et les jours* (1960).

March's poems and novels are characterized by the centrality of the feminine speaker or character. Both the poems and the novels sensitively treat themes such as a woman's love for a man, for her children, or for her mother. While *Niña* focuses on a woman's passionate love for a man, *Algo muere cada día* presents a more complete account of a woman's life. Illuminating for the insights we gain into the lives of ordinary people living in Barcelona during the Spanish Civil War, the novel's greatest merit lies in its revealing and convincing portrayal of a modern woman's concerns. Encompassing the main stages of life, *Algo muere cada día* allows the reader to follow the development of the central character María from early childhood and youth to maturity. Old age is presented only indirectly through María's relationship with her mother. It is to be hoped that March will yet offer us a full study of a woman confronting old age and her own inevitable end, particularly since a chronological correlation can be drawn between March's novelistic characters and her own age.

Narrated in the first person, like Carmen *Laforet's *Nada*, this novel presents all events from the point of view of the protagonist. María, who grows up in Barcelona in the years leading up to the Spanish Civil War, marries, has three children, becomes a poet and a successful writer, and eventually the family's breadwinner. Yet, in spite of her independence of spirit and economic self-sufficiency, she feels that her spiritual yearnings are either ignored or silenced in her intimate relationships with men. María's most loving relationship is with her mother. A parallel can again be drawn with Laforet's *Nada* where the young heroine Andrea's most lasting friendship is with another woman, the supportive Ena. The cherished relationship between mother and daughter is also highlighted in March's poetry, in poems such as "Mi madre y yo" (My Mother and I, in *La tristeza*) or "La madre" (Mother, in *Esta mujer que soy*). Maternal love for a son is treated in numerous poems but in none more poignantly than in "Mi hijo ha crecido este verano" (My Son Has Grown This Summer, in *La tristeza*).

March explores a variety of attitudes toward men through the female characters in her novels and the feminine speakers in her poetry. *Niña* studies a woman's passion that survives her lover's weakness and eventual death, while *Algo muere cada día* traces the erosion of love. "A un hombre" (To a Man, in *Esta mujer que soy*) expresses a desire for mutual understanding and true friendship to relieve the existential anguish that both women and men suffer.

Susana March was born in the same year as Gloria *Fuertes and is equally difficult to place in any literary generation. Although not as daring in the use of language as Fuertes, March has written some of her most effective poems using colloquial language and alluding to scenes from everyday life. Like Fuertes, March also expresses a critical view of the place assigned women by society. "Una señora" (A Lady, from *Una mujer que soy*) is a good example of the use of ordinary language and humor to convey a critical perspective. The poem begins: "Hay cosas / que no puede decir una señora" (There are things that a lady may not say). Because the right to one's own voice is under discussion, this poem could be regarded as a statement on the complexities faced by a writer, complexities that arise out of her identity as a woman in a society where her behavior is subject to taboos. The ambiguity of a woman's ability to express her true self is conveyed through paradoxical language where she screams but her scream is silent.

A prolific writer, Susana March has collaborated with *Fernández de la Reguera, her husband, on several historic novels set in the twentieth century. Between 1963 and 1972 nine were published by Editorial Planeta in a series titled Episodios Nacionales Contemporáneos.

BIBLIOGRAPHY

Primary Texts

Algo muere cada día. Barcelona: Bruguera, 1973.

Niña. Barcelona: Planeta, 1955.

Poemas: Antología [1938–59]. Santander: La Isla de los Ratones, 1966.

Los poemas del hijo. Santander: Bedia, 1970.

La tristeza. Madrid: Rialp, 1953.

English Translations

"Long, Long Ago" and "Threshold." Tr. H. W. Patterson. In *Antología Bilingüe (Español-Inglés) de la Poesía Española Moderna*. Madrid: Cultura Hišpanica, 1965.

Les ruines et les jours. Tr. Annie Brousseau. Paris: Gallimard, 1960.

Criticism

M., A. "Poemas de Susana March." *Papeles de Son Armadans* (Mallorca) 44 (1967): 125–28.

María Stycos

MARCHANTE, Manuel León. *See* León Marchante, Manuel

MARCHENA RUIZ DE CUETO, José (1768, Utrera–1821, Madrid), translator, topical writer, hoaxer, poet. An impassioned supporter of Voltaire and the French Revolution, he translated works of Voltaire, Molière, Montesquieu, and

Rousseau into Spanish and served as secretary to Generals Moreau and Morat, under Napoleon. His literary hoaxes include a supposed unknown fragment of Petronius's *Satyricon*, and some poetry by Catullus. The best of his own verse is his "A Cristo crucificado" (To the Crucified Christ), not to be confused with the anonymous *"Soneto a Cristo crucuficado," written during the *Siglo de Oro.

BIBLIOGRAPHY

Primary Texts

Obras literarias de don José Marchena. Ed., study M. Menéndez y Pelayo. 2 vols. Seville: Rasco, 1892–96.

Poesías. In BAE 67.

English Translation

The Satyricon of Petronius Arbiter . . . with the forgeries of Nodot and Marchena. Tr. W. C. Firebaugh. New York: Boni and Liverwright, 1922.

MARCO, Concha de (1916, Madrid?–), Spanish poet, short story writer, essayist and translator. Marco was trained in the natural sciences, but is known primarily for her poetry, including *Diario de la mañana* (1967; Morning Newspaper), which reads like the daily paper; with headlines and such sections as crossword puzzles, syndicated columns and the like. The poems are inspired by incidents of the type reported in newspapers of the day. *Veinticinco años de poesía femenina española* (1969; Twenty-Five Years of Spanish Feminine Poetry) is an anthology, apparently the fruit of the same interest in women's writing which produced *La mujer española del Romanticismo: estudios biográficos* (1969; The Spanish Woman during Romanticism: Biographical Studies). *Acta de identificación* (1969; Certificate of Identity) contains poems with a historical basis which somehow relate to contemporary problems. *Congreso en Maldoror* (1970; Convention in Maldoror) alludes ironically to the terminology and proceedings of an academic convention with titles such as "Research Paper," "Discussion," and "Refutation." Her collection *Tarot* (1973) received the Critics' Prize.

BIBLIOGRAPHY

Primary Texts

Hora 0.5. Santander: La Isla de los Ratones, 1966.

La mujer. Leon: Everest, 1969.

Una noche de invierno. Madrid: Rialp (Adonais), 1974.

Janet Pérez

MARGARITA LA TORNERA, Leyenda de (Legend of Margarita La Tornera). The literary trajectory of this widespread medieval poetic theme began with *Alphonse X (Cantiga 94) although antecedents can be found in Cesáreo de Heisterbach and Gautier de Coincy. Margarita, a nun in charge of her convent's treasury, falls in love with a young man and flees the convent to be with him.

Prior to her departure she deposits her keys at the Virgin's altar and prays for the divine protection of Our Lady. The Virgin Mary then takes on the appearance of the nun and carries out the duties that had been hers. When Margarita becomes disillusioned with her lover and goes back contritely to the convent, she attempts to return to her tasks only to find that her absence has not even been noticed. It is then that she realizes the favor which the Virgin Mary has done for her. In literature this legend has been touched on in Spain by *Montalvo, Lope de *Vega (*La buena guarda*), *Avellaneda, Luis *Vélez de Guevara (*La Abadesa del cielo)*, *Rosete Niño, and *Zorrilla as well as by Nodier and Maeterlinck abroad. The nineteenth-c. Spanish composer Ruperto Chapí wrote an opera with this title.

BIBLIOGRAPHY

Primary Text

Cotarelo, Armando. *Una cantiga célebre del Rey Sabio*. Madrid: A. Marzo, 1904.

Lucy Sponsler

MARÍA DE SAN ALBERTO, Sor (1568, Valladolid–1640, Valladolid), poet, playwright, archivist. With her sister *Cecilia del Nacimiento, María de San Alberto was educated by their mother in the classical subjects generally available only to men and inherited both her artistic and her musical ability. After María de San Alberto professed, St. *Teresa de Jesús became a particularly significant influence in her spiritual and artistic life. In the convent, protected by her brothers' high positions in the church hierarchy, she achieved fame as a poet, painter and leader. Active as a scribe and three times mother superior, she also entered poetry contests, wrote plays for her sisters' edification and entertainment, and recounted mystical experiences in her notebooks. Her work remains largely unpublished; it includes an entire ms. of poems dedicated to Sta. Teresa, a book-length *Vida de la venerable hermana Estefanía de los Apóstoles* (1618; Life of the Venerable Sister Stephanie of the Apostles), music written to accompany one of her plays, and Christian poems written in the dialect of Spain's African slaves. María de San Alberto's verse is at its best when she achieves an eclectic balance between the forms of her intellectual upbringing and popular language.

BIBLIOGRAPHY

Primary Texts

Various unpublished mss. Valladolid: Convent of the Carmelitas Descalzas de la Concepción.

Criticism

Alonso Cortés, B. *Dos monjas vallisoletanas poetisas*. Thesis, U of Madrid, 1941.

Anon. "Vida de la madre María de San Alberto y de la madre Cecilia del Nacimiento." Ms. Valladolid: Convent of the Carmelitas Descalzas de la Concepción, n.d.

Arenal, E., and S. Schlau. "Two Sisters among the Sisters: Intellectual Servants, Ecclesiastic Upper Crust." *Untold Sisters: Hispanic Nuns in Their Own Works*. Albuquerque: U of New Mexico P, 1989. Contains selections and English translations.

Rodríguez, J. L., and J. Urrea. *Santa Teresa en Valladolid y Medina del Campo*. Valladolid: Caja de Ahorros Popular de Valladolid, 1982.

Stacey Schlau

MARÍA DE SAN JOSÉ, Sor (?, Ávila–1603, Cuerva), poet and narrative writer. Admired by Sta. *Teresa for her intellectual and literary gifts, María de San José became one of Sta. Teresa's protégées, and one of the saint's most consistent correspondents. As mother superior of the Discalced Carmelite convent in Seville, she became embroiled in the conflicts surrounding the new order. After Teresa's death, she went to Portugal and founded a convent. There, she wrote a narration of the persecution titled "Fundación del Convento de Carmelitas Descalzas en Sevilla, y persecuciones que padecieron hasta la época de la muerte de Santa Teresa" (n.d.; The Discalced Carmelite Convent of Seville's Foundation, and the Persecutions Suffered Therein until the Time of St. Teresa's Death). The other prose work for which she is best known is a biography of Sta. Teresa, written in *pastoral form and titled "Libro de recreaciones" (n.d.; Book of Recreations); it contains a defense of learning in women and a condemnation of male clerics who oppose it. According to Serrano y Sanz, her prose is clear and elegant, without affectation, and her poems worthy of praise.

BIBLIOGRAPHY

Primary Texts

Escritos espirituales. Ed., notes Simeón de la Sagrada Familia. Rome: Postulación General OCD, 1979.

"Fundación del Convento de Carmelitas. . . . " Ms. Madrid: National Library.

"Libro de recreaciones." Ms. Madrid: National Library.

"Redondillas exhortando a las Carmelitas Descalzas a conservar las Constituciones de Santa Teresa." Ms. Madrid: National Library.

Criticism

Arenal, E., and S. Schlau. "More Than One Teresa. A Movement of Religious Women." *Untold Sisters: Hispanic Nuns in Their Own Works*. Albuquerque: U of New Mexico P, 1989.

Serrano y Sanz, M. *Apuntes hacia una biblioteca de escritoras españolas*. In BAE 270.

Stacey Schlau

MARÍA EGIPCIACA, Vida de Santa (Life of St. Mary of Egypt), anonymous religious poem. Composed in the late thirteenth or early fourteenth c., the 1,451-line poem narrates the life of St. Mary of Egypt. Born around 354 AD, she led a sinful youth, then traveled to Jerusalem out of curiosity, converted, then lived in the wilderness for forty-seven years as penance. The legend was very popular in medieval Spain (*see* Edad Media); this particular poem has charming descriptions of the young Mary and the various stages of her life. *See also* Hagiography.

BIBLIOGRAPHY

Primary Text

Vida de Sta. María Egipciaca. In BAE 57.

MARIANA, Juan de (winter 1535–36, Talavera de la Reina–1624, Toledo), political, religious and historical writer. After *Gracián y Morales, he is the most important Jesuit writer of seventeenth-c. Spain. He entered the order in 1544 and in 1561 was ordained in Rome. For about the next thirteen years, he taught at various colleges in Italy, Sicily and then Paris. The five years in Paris were ones of great political turmoil and surely influenced Mariana's later writing. In 1574 he returned to Toledo, where he stayed until death. After he was appointed examiner of candidates for the clergy in 1579, this and sundry minor duties in the order replaced his earlier teaching career. As well as contributing to an edition of St. Isidore's works, and editing the 1586 **Indice*, he began to write. In 1592 the initial version of his most significant work appeared, the *Historiae de rebus Hispaniae* (*General History of Spain,* 1699). To the initial twenty books, five more were added in 1595, and the final edition of thirty books appeared in 1606. A Spanish translation of the original Latin was printed in 1601. An ornate, eloquent, elegantly narrated work, it covers Spanish history up to the Catholic monarchs. It merited five editions in twenty-two years and became the standard Spanish history text both in and outside of Spain for the next two hundred years.

Other writings brought problems to Mariana, many of which converged in the years 1609–10. In 1609 Mariana published an essay titled "De monetae mutatione" (On Alterations in the Currency) in his *Tractatus septem* (Seven Treatises). The treatise, which actually had appeared earlier in another work, attacks the recent debasement of the Spanish coin. The republication so angered Philip II's advisers, they arranged for Mariana's apprehension on charges of doctrinal shortcomings. It appears that during the search through his belongings they found another ms., in Spanish rather than Latin, titled Discurso de las enfermedades de la Compañía de Jesús (written before 1606; Discourse on the Errors Incident to the Governance of the Society of Jesus), which caused great distress among the members of the order. Mariana was taken to Madrid for trial and detainment. While there, Henry IV of France was assassinated (1610), and a book by Mariana, written for Philip II and titled *De rege et regis institutione* (1599; *The King and the Education of the King*, 1948), was held accountable, for it discusses, among other things, the justifiability of tyrranicide. Despite the fact that the assassain denied knowing of the treatise, Mariana's work was publicly denounced and burned.

Sometime before 1611, Mariana was exonerated of wrongdoing, lightly reprimanded, and allowed to return to the order in Toledo. He dedicated his remaining years to biblical investigations, publishing *Scholia* to both Old and New Testaments in 1619. In 1623, Philip IV named him a royal chronicler, and he died in February of the following year.

BIBLIOGRAPHY

Primary Texts

De rege et regis institutione. Mainz: Lipp, 1609.

Del rey y de la institución. . . . Madrid: Sociedad Literaria y Tipográfica, 1845.

Discurso de las enfermedades de la Compañía de Jesús. Ed. E. Berriobero y Herrán. Madrid: Mundo Latino, 1931.

Historia general. . . . Valencia: Monfort, 1783–96.

Obras. In BAE 30 and 31.

English Translations

The General History of Spain. . . . Tr. J. Stevens. London: Sare, Saunders and Bennett, 1699.

The King and the Education of the King. Tr. from Latin. Washington, DC: County Dollar P, 1948.

The Political Economy of Juan de Mariana. By J. Laures. New York: Fordham UP, 1928.

Criticism

Cirot, Georges. *Études sur l'Historiographie espagnole: Mariana historien*. Bordeaux; Féret, 1905.

Lewy, G. *Constitutionalism and Statecraft during the Golden Age of Spain. A Study of the Political Philosophy of Juan de Mariana*. Geneva: Droz, 1960.

Macedo de Steffans, D. ''La doctrina del tiranicidio: Juan de Salisbury (1115–80) y Juan de Mariana (1535–1624).'' *Anales de historia antigua y medieval* 35 (1959): 123–33.

Norris, F. I. ''Mariana and the Classical Tradition of Statecraft.'' *KRQ* 24 (1977): 389–97.

Soons, Alan. *Juan de Mariana*. TWAS 654. Boston: Twayne, 1982.

Maureen Ihrie

MARÍAS, Julián (1914, Valladolid–), philosopher and essayist. A vital force in contemporary thought, Marías combines the Spanish intellectual tradition with immense personal creativity. The favored disciple of *Ortega y Gasset, with whom he founded the Instituto de Humanidades (Humanist Institute) in 1948, Marías is the central figure in the Escuela de Madrid (School of Madrid). A member of the *Academia Española and a frequent contributor to the daily press, Marías is an incisive interpreter of current events. He has lectured throughout Spain and Latin America and has been visiting professor at Harvard, UCLA, Yale, Indiana U, the U of Oklahoma and Wellesley College.

Major works include *Historia de la filosofía* (1941; *History of Philosophy*, 1967); *La Filosofía del Padre Gratry* (1941; The Philosophy of Father Gratry); *Miguel de Unamuno* (1943; *Miguel de Unamuno*, 1966); *El Tema del hombre* (1943; The Human Theme), an anthology; *San Anselmo y el insensato* (1944; Saint Anselm and the Insensate); *Introducción a la filosofía* (1947; *Reason and Life: The Introduction to Philosophy*, 1975); *Filosofía española actual: Unamuno, Ortega, Morente, Zubiri* (1949; Contemporary Spanish Philosophy); *Ortega y la idea de la razón vital* (1949; Ortega and the Idea of Vital Reason); *El Método histórico de las generaciones* (1949; *Generations: A Historical Method*, 1970); *Ortega y tres antípodas* (1950; Ortega and Three Antipodes); *La Escolástica en su mundo y en nuestro* (1951; Scholasticism in Its World and Ours); *Aquí y ahora* (1952; Here and Now); *La Filosofía en sus textos* (1953; Philosophical

Texts), an anthology; *Idea de la metafísica* (1954; The Idea of Metaphysics); *Biografía de la filosofía* (1954; *A Biography of Philosophy*, 1984); *Ensayos de teoría* (1954; Essays in Theory); *La Estructura social* (1955; *The Structure of Society*, 1986); *El Intelectual y su mundo* (1956; The Intellectual and His World), essays; *La Escuela de Madrid* (1959; The School of Madrid).

Among later works are *Ortega: Circunstancia y vocación* (1960; *José Ortega y Gasset: Circumstance and Vocation*, 1970); *Ortega ante Goethe* (1961; Ortega and Goethe); *Imagen de la India* (1961; Image of India); *Los Españoles* (1962; The Spanish); *Los Estados Unidos en escorzo* (1964) and *Análisis de los Estados Unidos* (1968), combined in translation as *America in the Fifties and Sixties* (1972); *Meditaciones sobre la sociedad española* (1966; Meditations on Spanish Society); *Consideración de Cataluña* (1966; Considerations of Catalonia); *Nuestra Andalucía* (1966; Our Andalusia); *Israel: Una resurrección* (1968; Israel: A Resurrection); *Antropología metafísica* (1970; *Metaphysical Anthropology*, 1971); *Acerca de Ortega* (1971; About Ortega), essays; *La Justicia social y otras justicias* (1974; Social and Other Justices). *La España real* (1976; The Real Spain) is the first part of a trilogy on Spanish social conditions. Subsequent volumes include *La Devolución de España* (1977; Spain Restored to Itself) and *España en nuestras manos* (1978; Spain in Our Hands).

Recent works are *Problemas del cristianismo* (1979; The Problems of Christianity); *La Mujer en el siglo XX* (1980; Women in the Twentieth Century); *Breve tratado de la ilusión* (1984; Brief Treatise on Illusion); *España inteligible* (1985; Intelligible Spain); and *Cara y cruz de la electrónica* (1985; The Two Sides of Electronics), which studies the benefits and dangers of computers. The *Obras completas* currently consists of eight volumes.

BIBLIOGRAPHY

Primary Texts

Antropología metafísica. Madrid: RO, 1983.
Historia de la filosofía. Madrid. RO, 1980.
Introducción a la filosofía. Madrid: RO, 1981.
Miguel de Unamuno. Madrid: Espasa-Calpe, 1980.
Ortega: Circunstancia y vocación. Madrid: RO, 1966.

English Translations

History of Philosophy. Tr. Stanley Applebaum and Clarence C. Strowbridge. New York: Dover, 1967.
José Ortega y Gasset: Circumstance and Vocation. Tr. Frances M. López-Morillas. Norman: U. of Oklahoma P, 1970.
Metaphysical Anthropology. Tr. Frances M. López-Morillas. University Park: Pennsylvania State UP, 1971.
Miguel de Unamuno. Tr. Frances M. López-Morillas. Cambridge: Harvard UP, 1966.
Reason and Life: The Introduction to Philosophy. Tr. Kenneth S. Reid and Edward Sarmiento. Westport, CT: Greenwood, 1975.

Criticism

Agua, Juan del, et al. *Homenaje a Julián Marías*. Madrid: Espasa-Calpe, 1985.
Bleznick, Donald W. "A Conversation with Julián Marías." *Hispania* 69 (1986): 594–96.
Donoso, Antón. *Julián Marías*. TWAS 642. Boston: Hall, 1982.
Raley, Harold C. *Responsible Vision: The Philosophy of Julián Marías*. Clear Creek, IN: American Hispanist, 1980.
Soler Planas, Juan. *El Pensamiento de Julián Marías*. Madrid: RO, 1973.
Zancarano, P. A. "Julián Marías on the Empirical Structure of Human Life and Its Sexuate Condition." *International Philosophical Quarterly* 23 (1983): 425–40.

Robert Sandarg

MARICHAL, Juan (1922, Sta. Cruz de Tenerife, Canary Islands–), professor, scholar. The Civil War interrupted his studies, but he continued them in France, Morocco, Mexico—where he studied with Gaos, Xirau, Recaséns-Siches and Bosch-Gimpera—and Princeton, where he obtained his doctorate in 1949 with a dissertation on *Feijoo, directed by Américo *Castro. Currently he is a professor of Romance language and literature at Harvard. Marichal has studied the Spanish *essay and its ideological ramifications, from the *Renaissance to *Ortega and his generation. Besides essays which have appeared both in American and European journals, he has written an excellent book on the subject, *La voluntad del estilo* (1957; The Will of Style). Marichal also prepared the posthumous editions of poetry, theater and prose of Pedro *Salinas, his father-in-law. He directed the outstanding edition of Manuel *Azaña's *Obras completas* (1966–68; Complete Works), adding excellent forewords to the four volumes of the collection. He has also published a volume titled *El nuevo pensamiento político español* (1966; The New Spanish Political Thought).

BIBLIOGRAPHY

Primary Texts

Cuatro fases de la historia intelectual latinoamericana. Madrid: Juan March, 1978.
El nuevo pensamiento político español. Mexico: n.p., 1966.
Teoría e historia del ensayismo hispánico. Madrid: Alianza, 1984. Rev. ed. of *La voluntad del estilo*.

Isabel McSpadden

MARICHALAR, Antonio (1893, Logroño–1973, Madrid), Marquis of Montesa, distinguished art and literature critic, historian and biographer. He began writing for the daily *Lunes del Imparcial*, then collaborated assiduously on *Revista de Occidente* and the *Criterion* from their founding. He has written for journals throughout Europe and the Americas; important essays are those dedicated to Santayana, Joyce, Valéry, Claudel, Virginia Woolf, and Chesterton. Outstanding studies include those on Pascal, Descartes, Corneille, *Garcilaso de la Vega, *Góngora, *Boscán and *Espronceda. His book *Riesgo y ventura del duque de Osuna* (1930; *The Perils and Fortune of the Duke of Osuna*, 1932) has gone through many editions. In 1933 he published a volume of essays titled *Mentira desnuda* (The Naked Lie). In the 1940s he specialized in the history of the sixteenth c. with studies of Savonarola, Philip of Bourgogne and Dr. Velasco. For Boscán's centenary (1942) he published an edition of *El cortesano* (The Courtier). Later publications are *Tres figuras del XVI* (1945; Three Figures of the Sixteenth Century), *Las cadenas del duque de Alba* (1947; The Chains of the Duke of Alba), *Un poeta navarro del XVII* (1947; A Navarrese Poet of the Seventeenth Century), and the excellent biography *Julián Romero* (1952).

BIBLIOGRAPHY

Primary Texts

Julián Romero. Madrid: Espasa-Calpe, 1952.
Mentira desnuda. 1st ed. Madrid: Espasa-Calpe, 1933.
Riesgo y ventura del duque de Osuna. 3rd ed. Buenos Aires: Espasa-Calpe Argentina, 1945.

English Translations

The Perils and Fortune of the Duke of Osuna. Tr. H. de Onís. Philadelphia: Lippincott, 1932.

Sydney Cravens

MARÍN, Diego (1914, Ciudad Real–), scholar. Professor at the U of Toronto, he has edited some of Mariano José de *Larra's works (1948) and written a book on Spain, *La vida española* (1955; Spanish Life), and a history of Spanish civilization. Also his is the important study *Poesía española. Estudios y textos (siglo XV-XX)* (1958; Spanish Poetry, Studies and Texts [Fifteenth-Twentieth Century]). Marín translated to English *Ortega's *Meditaciones del Quijote* and updated Angel del Río's *Historia de la literatura española*. More recent is his *Poesía paisajística española* (1976; Spanish Landscape Poetry).

BIBLIOGRAPHY

Primary Texts

Poesía española. Estudios y textos (siglo XV-XX). Rev. ed. Madrid: Castalia, 1971.
Poesía paisajística española. London: Tamesis, 1976.
La vida española. Rev. ed. New York: Appleton-Century-Crofts, 1955.

English Translation

The Civilization of Spain. Tr. E. Rugg. Toronto: U of Toronto P, 1969.

Isabel McSpadden

MARINEO SÍCULO, Lucio (1444?, Vizzina, Sicily–c. 1533, Spain), professor, chronicler, most influential in disseminating *Renaissance culture in Spain. Of a common family, his correspondence indicates he did not learn to read until age twenty-five. After teaching Greek and Latin in Palermo, Italy, from c. 1479 to 1484, he traveled to Spain and taught Latin for twelve years at the U of

Salamanca, where *Nebrija also lectured. In 1496, Ferdinand and Isabel summoned him to court to teach Latin to priests, young nobility and royalty. Named a chronicler by Ferdinand, and later royal chaplain (1505), he was entrusted with various missions by the monarchs. His letters attest to his intimate contact with the court for some thirty-seven years.

All his writing was in Latin. His first work was an encomium of the geography and people of Spain, *De Hispaniae laudibus* (c. 1492; Praise of Spain). His historical writings are collected under the title *De rebus Hispaniae memorabilibus* (1530; Memorable Events of Spain). His correspondence, *Epistolarum* . . . (1514; Letters), perhaps holds the greatest interest, for the detailed information on university life and on the events he personally witnessed during his years at the court. *See also* Humanism; Universities.

BIBLIOGRAPHY

Primary Texts

Epistolario. Tr., ed. P. Verrua. Genoa: Alighieri, 1940.
Vida y hechos de los Reyes Católicos. Madrid: Atlas, 1943.

English Translations

See Lynn, in Criticism.

Criticism

Lynn, C. *A College Professor of the Renaissance. Lucio Marineo Siculo among the Spanish Humanists*. Chicago: U of Chicago, 1937. Includes translations of many letters, and excerpts.

Maureen Ihrie

MARIÑO CAROU, María (1918, Noia, La Coruña–1967, O Courel), Galician poet. Often associated with the Galician poet U. Novoneyra, Mariño Carou is the author of one of the most personal, intimate poetries written in the post-war period. Her themes tend to center on the mountain and its surrounding area, with a desire to see herself transformed into nature. There is a tragic sense with mysterious uneasiness which may be compared to Rosalía de *Castro. The mystical experience which Mariño Carou conveys is one which leads to self-annihilation, although in her unpublished *Verba que comenza* (The Word That Begins), there is a desire to surround herself with concrete items. It is possible to detect an interest in popular expression and content. *See also* Galician Literature.

BIBLIOGRAPHY

Primary Texts

Palabra no tempo. Lugo: n.p., 1963.
Verba que comenza. (unpublished)

Criticism

Fernández Teixeiro, Manuel María. ''María Mariño.'' *El Progreso* (Lugo) Jan. 1964.
López Casanova, Arcadio. ''A palabra alcendida de María Mariño.'' *Grial* 3 (1964): n.p.

Méndez Ferrín, Xosé Luis. "A poesía de María Mariño." *La Noche* (Santiago), Feb.-March 1965.
Novoneyra, Uxío. "Apología póstuma." *La voz de Galicia* (La Coruña) July 11, 1967.
Trabazo, L. "María Mariño." *La Voz de Galicia* Jan. 1964.

Kathleen March

MÁRMOL, Manuel María de (1776, Seville–1840, Seville), chaplain, orator, poet. His neo-classical verses, which belong to the *Escuela sevillana tradition, are collected in *Romancero* (1834; Ballad Book). Mármol also wrote a *pastoral play, *Los amantes generosos* (The Generous Lovers).

BIBLIOGRAPHY

Primary Texts

Los amantes generosos. Seville: Hidalgo, 1806.
Colección de epigramas. Huelva: Garrido, 1828.
Colección de poesías diversas. Huelva: Garrido, 1828.
Intervalos de mi enfermedad. Seville: Aragón, 1816.
Romancero. 2 vols. Seville: Hidalgo, 1834.

MÁRMOL CARVAJAL, Luis (1520?, Granada–1600, ?), chronicler. He served as a soldier and fought in Tunisia (1535) when still quite young. He then spent more than twenty years in Africa, where he served in numerous military campaigns and lived in captivity a number of times. Mármol wrote *Descripción general de Africa* (vols. 1 and 2, 1573, vol. 3, 1599; General Description of Africa) and his most known work, *Historia de la rebelión y castigo de los moriscos del reino de Granada* (1600; History of the Revolt and Punishment of the Moors from Granada), in which, as opposed to *Hurtado de Mendoza, he defended the politics of his government.

BIBLIOGRAPHY

Primary Texts

Historia de la rebelión y castigo de los moriscos del reino de Granada. In *Historiadores de sucesos particulares*. *BAE* 21.
Descripción general de Africa. Madrid: Instituto de Estudios Africanos del Patronato Diego Saavedra Fajardo del CSIC, 1953.

Hector Medina

MARQUERÍE, Alfredo (1907, Mahón, Menorca–1974, Minglanilla, Cuenca), journalist, poet, biographer, novelist, essayist and press correspondent, traveling extensively. Well known for his theater reviews in *ABC* and *Pueblo*, he wrote many works about the theater, such as *Cuando cae el telón* (1951; When the Curtain Falls) and *Cómicos* (1952; Comics). He published his first poetry works in Segovia: *Rosas líricas* (1923; Lyrical Roses), *Veintitrés poemas* (1927; Twenty-Three Poems) and *Reloj* (1934; The Clock). Novels by Marquerie include *Cuatro pisos y la portería* (1940; Four Floors and the Lobby) and *Una vida estúpida* (1934; A Stupid Life). He died in a car accident.

BIBLIOGRAPHY

Primary Texts

Alfonso Paso y su teatro. Madrid: Escelicer, 1960.
Cien anécdotas de teatro. Madrid: Pizarro, 1958.
Personas y personajes; memorias informales. Prol. S. Gasch. Barcelona: Dopesa, 1971.
Veinte años de teatro en España. Madrid: Nacional, 1959.

Isabel McSpadden

MÁRQUEZ, Juan (1564, Madrid–1621, Salamanca), religious and political writer. Few biographical facts exist about this Augustinian theologian and writer of religious and political works. However, a few religious treatises that he wrote are preserved. In addition, he was the author of several plays which have never been published. Certain references to him made by contemporary writers indicate he was also a great preacher. His most important work is a political treatise on the education of a Christian ruler. Márquez apparently takes the typically Spanish point of view, which opposes Machiavelli's ideas, in his *El governador cristiano* (1612; The Christian Ruler). Nevertheless, it is quite apparent that Márquez knew the Italian's work. The subtitle of *El governador cristiano* establishes Moses and Joshua as models for the ideal Christian ruler. It is interesting that Márquez's models should be two Old Testament figures and not Christ or Spanish rulers such as Ferdinand, Philip II or Charles I. Another of his works is a religious treatise called *Los dos estados de la Espiritual Hierusalem: sobre los Psalmos CXXV y CXXXVI* (Medina del Campo, 1603; The Two States of the Heavenly Jerusalem: On Psalms 125 and 136). Márquez also composed a historical work tracing the origins of the Augustinian order.

BIBLIOGRAPHY

Primary Texts

El governador cristiano. Deducido de las vidas de Moysén y Iosue. Príncipes de Dios. Salamanca: Cea y Tesa, 1612.
Los dos estados de la Espiritual Hierusalem: sobre los Psalmos CXXV y CXXXVI. Medina del Campo: Lasso, 1603.
Origen de los Frayles Ermitanos de la Orden de San Agustín y su verdadera institución antes del gran Concilio Lateranense. Salamanca: Antonio Ramírez, Viuda, 1618.

Criticism

Monasterio, Ignacio. "Estudios criticos sobre el M° Fray Juan Márquez." *Ciudad de Dios* 14 (1887): 744–53, 801–12; 15 (1888): 33–46, 112–23, 157–69, 246–57, 304–13, 380–88, 437–51; 16: 15–24, 159–70; 18: 37–45, 158–67, 293–304, 440–53, 524–33.
Pérez Pastor, Cristóbal. "Documentos para la biografía de Fr. Juan Márquez." *Bibliografía madrileña*. Madrid: Huérfanos, 1907. 3: 282–84.
Santiago Vela, G. de. *Ensayo de una biblioteca de la Orden de San Agustín*. Madrid: Asilo de Huérfanos, 1920. 5: 174–231.

Simón Díaz, José. *Manual de bibliografía de la literatura española*. Madrid: Gredos, 1980. 414–15.

Angelo DiSalvo

MARQUINA, Eduardo (1879, Barcelona–1946, New York), poet, playwright, novelist. He died in America while fulfilling a diplomatic mission. He collaborated with several journals and newspapers and was a member of the *Academia Española. Within *modernism, he represents a poetic voice inspired almost always by national traditions, lending a noble patriotism to his verse. Gómez Baquero wrote of him: ''[he is a] civil poet, poet of ideas, poet of honest and profound love, a love whose garlands embellish the familiar altar, the themes of his poetry are robust and virile. His inspiration is not solitary nor does it lock itself in the interior abodes, rather it looks on the spectacle the world offers and it accompanies with its vibration the figures and scenes that parade through the stage of the human drama.'' His is a love of the country, of the *Siglo de Oro, of the House of Austria's empire. His sensitivity perceives intimate touches of nature's beauty. He adds to his lyrical emotion a vigorous epic resonance, both in his poetry and in his theater. In his theater, Marquina strived for renovation; typical titles reveal preferred themes: *Las hijas del Cid* (1908; The Cid's Daughters); *Doña María la Brava* (1909; Maria the Brave); *En Flandes se ha puesto el sol* (1910; The Sun Has Set in Flanders), perhaps his best drama; *El gran capitán* (1916; The Great Captain); *La ermita, la fuente y el río* (1927; The Hermitage, the Fountain and the River); and *Teresa de Jesús* (1933). Comedies include *Cuando florezcan los rosales* (1914; When the Rose Bushes Bloom) and *El camino de la felicidad* (1929; The Way to Happiness), and he has also written scripts for **zarzuelas*. His poetry volumes include *Odas* (1900; Odes), *Las vendimias* (1901; Grape Harvest), and *Canciones del momento* (1910; Songs for the Moment). His quality as a ''civil poet'' can be appreciated in *Tierras de España* (1914; Lands of Spain). As a novelist he wrote *La caravana* (1907; The Caravan), *Almas anónimas* (1908; Anonymous Souls), and *Maternidad* (1917; Maternity). In the Buenos Aires magazine *Caras y Caretas* he published autobiographical memories titled ''Yo y los días'' (Me and the Days) in 1937 and 1938.

BIBLIOGRAPHY

Primary Texts

Obras completas. Madrid: Aguilar, 1946.

Criticism

Montero Alonso, José. *Vida de Eduardo Marquina*. Madrid: Nacional, 1965.

Pemán, José María. ''Necrología.'' In *BRAE* 25 (1946): n.p.

Juliá, E. ''Eduardo Marquina, poeta lírico y dramático.'' In *Cuadernos de literatura contemporánea* (Madrid) 3/4 (1942): n.p. Includes bibliography.

Isabel McSpadden

MARRERO SUÁREZ, Vicente (1922, Arucas, Grand Canary–), essayist. He is author of *Picasso y el toro* (1951; *Picasso and the Bull*, 1956) and *El poder entrañable* (1952; Intimate Power). He expresses his ideological disagreement with liberalism in *Maeztu* (1955), *La guerra de España y el trust de los cerebros* (1961; The Spanish War and the Brain Trust), and *La consolidación política: teoría de una posibilidad española* (1964; Political Consolidation: Theory of a Spanish Possibility). He also founded and for ten years directed the magazine *Punta Europa*.

BIBLIOGRAPHY

Primary Texts

El Cristo de Unamuno. Madrid: Rialp, 1960.
La guerra de España y el trust de los cerebros. Madrid: Punta Europa, 1961.
Historia de una amistad. Madrid: Magisterio Español, 1971.

English Translation

Picasso and the Bull. Tr. A. Kerrigan. Chicago: Regnery, 1956.

Isabel McSpadden

MARSÉ, Juan (1933, Barcelona–), Spanish novelist and journalist. Orphaned by the Civil War, Marsé spent his formative years in the impoverished environment of post-war Barcelona. Economic difficulties prevented him from completing his secondary education and forced him to seek employment at age thirteen. His fiction reveals an intimate acquaintance with working-class Barcelona and an exceptional intellectual sophistication, which is surprising in light of his scant formal education. Possibly a major portion of his self-education took place in Paris, where he lived for two years following the publication of his first novel.

Marsé acquired stature as a writer with his third novel, *Ultimas tardes con Teresa* (1966; My Last Evenings with Teresa), which received the Biblioteca Breve Prize sponsored by Seix Barral publishing company. Favorably received by critics, who considered it an important step beyond Luis *Martín Santos's "dialectical realism," this work was, nevertheless, declared a flawed masterpiece by Peruvian novelist Mario Vargas Llosa, one of the panelists who awarded the Biblioteca Breve Prize. Its sequel, *La oscura historia de la prima Montse* (1970; The Murky Story about Cousin Montse), which inspired a film by the same title, is a more polished piece. Both works narrate the exploits of a social misfit protagonist, and both focus ironically on the contradictions of contemporary Barcelona class structure.

Si te dicen que caí (1973; *The Fallen*, 1979), which received the Premio Internacional de Novela "México," is generally recognized as Marsé's most accomplished work. An extremely complex narrative which ultimately defeats all attempts to naturalize it, this novel nevertheless presents a convincing and moving account of life in post-war Barcelona. It has much in common with the many other self-referential texts produced in Spain in the same decade. It also exemplifies a deep preoccupation with intertextuality by building a complex series of covert references to a Falangist hymn (quoted in the title) into its narrative structure.

Despite critics' enthusiastic reception of this novel, Marsé appears to have become convinced that the work's complexity made it inaccessible to the public he wished to reach. In any case, his next three novels make fewer demands of their readers. It would be misleading to regard these works as simple or traditionally realistic narratives, however. All three reward a probing reading, which reveals a fundamental preoccupation—reminiscent of *Si te dicen que caí*—with the nature of reality and our perception of it. The first of these three novels, *La muchacha de las bragas de oro* (1978; *Golden Girl*, 1981), was made into a film which, because of its prurient nature, probably contributed significantly to critics' reluctance to take the novel seriously and to their delay in perceiving its fundamental dimension as an investigation of the textual and tenuous nature of knowledge. *Un día volveré* (1982; The Return) was better received, as was *Ronda del Guinardó* (1984; The Guinardó Round). Both novels continue to probe the themes of textuality and the tenuous character of knowledge, and both record the misery and deprivation of post-war Barcelona, which has provided the background for much of Marsé's best writing.

Currently in his fifties and convalescing from surgery, Marsé occupies a somewhat ambiguous position in the Spanish literary world. Although his work has been circulated more widely and translated more extensively than that of most other contemporary Spanish novelists, his reputation appears to have been damaged by his lapse into prurience in *La muchacha de las bragas de oro*, and some suggest that his Barcelona background has limited his appeal to Spanish critics. Only time will determine his ultimate stature as a novelist.

BIBLIOGRAPHY

Primary Texts

Un día volveré. Barcelona: Plaza y Janés, 1982.
La muchacha de las bragas de oro. Barcelona: Planeta, 1978.
La oscura historia de la prima Montse. Barcelona: Seix Barral, 1970.
Ronda del Guinardó. Barcelona: Seix Barral, 1984.
Si te dicen que caí. Ed. William M. Sherzer. Madrid: Cátedra, 1982.
Ultimas tardes con Teresa. Barcelona: Seix Barral, 1970.

English Translations

The Fallen. Tr. Helen R. Lane. Boston: Little, Brown, 1979.
Golden Girl. Tr. Helen R. Lane. Boston: Little, Brown, 1981.

Criticism

Garvey, Diane I. "Juan Marsé's *Si te dicen que caí*: The Self-reflexive Text and the Question of Referentiality." *MLN* 95 (1980): 376–87.

Levine, Linda Gould. "*Si te dicen que caí*: un calidoscopio verbal." *JSS:TC* 7 (1979): 309–27.

Magini González, Shirley. "*Ultimas tardes con Teresa*: culminación y destrucción del realismo social en la novelística española." *Anales de Narrativa Española Contemporánea* 5 (1980): 13–26.

Montenegro, Nivia. "El juego intertextual de *Si te dicen que caí*." *Revista Canadiense de Estudios Hispánicos* 5 (1981): 145–55.

Nichols, Geraldine Cleary. "Dialectical Realism and Beyond: *Ultimas tardes con Teresa.*" *JSS:TC* 3 (1975): 163–74.
Sherzer, William M. *Juan Marsé: entre la ironía y la dialéctica.* Madrid: Fundamentos, 1982.
Thompson, Currie K. "A Question of (Id)entity: the Reification of Desire in Juan Marsé's *La muchacha de las bragas de oro.*" *Symposium* 39 (1985): 61–73.

Currie K. Thompson

MARTÍ, Juan (1570?, Valencia–1604, ?), writer of the false second part of the *picaresque novel *Guzmán de Alfarache*. Very little is known of Martí. He was from Valencia, and it is believed that he became a lawyer and perhaps a professor of law there. The second part of the *Guzmán de Alfarache* (1602) was published under the pseudonym Mateo Luján de Sayavedra, and although the critic *Foulché-Delbosc has expressed doubts, most scholars agree that the author was Juan Martí. The novel merits interest for the historical information it records and for its literary value. Martí exaggerates the use of moral discourse, however, which interferes with appreciation of other qualities of the novel. This work has been judged primarily on the fact that it was presented as something it was not, a continuation of Mateo *Alemán's *Guzmán de Alfarache*, rather than on its own literary merits.

BIBLIOGRAPHY

Primary Text

Guzmán de Alfarache. Ed. M. Rivadeneyra. BAE 3.

Nina Shecktor

MARTÍN DE CÓRDOBA. *See* Córdoba, Martín Alonso de

MARTÍN DESCALZO, José Luis (1930, Madridejos, Toledo–), Spanish novelist. What makes Martín Descalzo relatively unusual among the novelists of his generation is that he is a Roman Catholic priest (he was ordained in Rome in 1953). He began his literary activities in the poetry magazine *Estría*, part of a young movement of priests who were also writers. In 1952, he won the Insula Poetry Prize for his "Siete sonetos del alba" (Seven Sonnets of Dawn), which are part of the book *Fábulas con Dios al fondo* (Fables with God in the Depths). *Diálogos de cuatro muertos* (Dialogues of Four Dead Persons) won the Naranco Prize for novelettes. In 1955, he published *Un cura se confiesa* (A Priest Confesses), and in 1956, he won the prestigious Nadal Prize with his first attempt at a long novel, *La frontera de Dios* (The Border of God). Despite Spain's being a Catholic country, it has not had in modern times a tradition of Catholic novels, due perhaps to the intransigence of the church hierarchy within the peninsula. Thus, Martín Descalzo's fiction stands apart from other novels and tales of the period, resembling more the neo-Catholic novel of other countries than anything Spanish, except for his incorporation of a serene, tragic Castilian vision. Martín Descalzo is a very prolific writer, who has produced a large number of works intended to provide moral, spiritual and ethical guidance through the medium of fiction, as in *El hombre que no sabía pecar* (1961; The Man Who Didn't Know How to Sin). Martín Descalzo attempted the theater with *La hoguera feliz* (1962; The Fortunate Bonfire). He has been classed with the so-called Metaphysical Group under the aegis of critic and novelist Manuel García Viñó, which includes many writers of "social" fiction, neo-realists of a more or less documentary bent who aspire to some transcendence through the incorporation of art, religion, philosophical issues or other values in place of the social (and implicitly political) criticism which characterizes the works of other writers of the critical realist school.

Janet Pérez

MARTÍN GAITE, Carmen (1925, Salamanca–), novelist and essayist, earned her doctorate in Romance philology at the U of Madrid. In 1950, she married Rafael *Sánchez Ferlosio, novelist and philologist; the marriage ended after several years in separation. Her first literary recognition came with *El balneario* (1945; The Spa), a collection of brief fiction comprising the title novelette and seven short shories which exhibit a characteristic preoccupation with time and the rhythm and events of daily life. "The Spa" is a strange, Kafkaesque nightmare in which a disturbed woman and her alienated husband visit a curative spring and he is apparently drowned. It is ultimately revealed as a dream by a bored, middle-aged spinster whose life is so dull she longs for the anguished dream situation. *Entre visillos* (1957; Between the Blinds) established Martín Gaite's reputation, winning the prestigious Nadal Prize. This novel employs the motif of the *visillos* (jalousies covering the windows of most Spanish buildings), a symbol of entrapment or imprisonment for the feminine figures whose lives unfold behind them and who view the world from between the blinds. This symbolism intensifies the monotony of the life of several girls in a provincial town, all frustrated, limited and bound by convention, not allowed to study or pursue a career. The only working girl (an ostracized casino singer) longs for marriage, while matrimony is portrayed as overly idealized and disappointing. *Las ataduras* (1960; Bonds) is a collection of seven tales, the title novelette and half a dozen shorter pieces, insinuating further feminist concerns. In "Bonds," a provincial girl who dares to be different and undertake university studies ends much like the companions she scorned, for she elopes with a French intellectual to Paris, and although he spurns marriage, she finds herself nonetheless condemned to maternity and domesticity. *Ritmo lento* (1962; Slow Motion), a personal favorite of the author, portrays an inert and passive character, unable to adapt to the society in which he lives. His extreme aboulia leads finally to confinement in a sanatorium, whence he contemplates life during most of the narrative. The title suggests that his vital rhythm is out of tempo with that of society at large; he is the achronic individual.

Martín Gaite became interested in history early in the 1960s, resulting in several works of historical investigation, including *El proceso de Macanaz* (1970;

The Trial of Macanaz), the historical biography of a tragic political career, and *Usos amorosos del dieciocho en España* (1973; Customs of Love in Eighteenth-Century Spain), a study of relationships between the sexes, of frequently feminist bent. Other non-fiction works include an anthology of poetry in Gallego, and *La búsqueda de interlocutor y otras búsquedas* (1975; The Search for an Interlocutor and Other Searches), a collection of essays previously published over a decade in various periodicals. Their common theme is the need for a mirror or listener, the need of dialogue, the existential Other. The idea of the interlocutor or conversation as basic to storytelling is developed in a book-length essay, *El cuento de nunca acabar* (1983; The Never-Ending Tale), completed when Martín Gaite was writer-in-residence at the U of Virginia.

Retahilas (1974; Extended Skeins), another long, morose novel in *tempo lento*, retrospective and introspective, continues and furthers the writer's interest in the feminine condition and her obsession with passing time, time the destroyer. Written in the form of a night-long conversation between Eulalia, a mature woman, and her young nephew as they await the death of the former's grandmother, it is stylistically elaborate and linguistically innovative, figuring among major critical successes of the novelist. Martín Gaite's most recent works include *Fragmentos de interior* (1978; Glimpses inside a House), which again exemplifies her concern with daily life via the portrait of a middle-class Madrid family (emotionally and professionally frustrated parents, rebellious adolescents, romantically disillusioned maid), and *El cuarto de atrás* (1978; *The Back Room*, 1983), a hybrid blend of mystery novel, memoirs and reflections on problems of the novelist's art. During a night of insomnia, the writer narrator (a *persona* of the novelist) receives a strange visitor, an enigmatic man in black with supernatural or diabolic characteristics. Their conversation, combining the magical and the absurd with childhood recollections, dreams and reflections on love, provides a key to Martín Gaite's intellectual history, literary evolution and artistic values. Availability in English translation provides an intimate glimpse of one of the two or three most important women novelists presently writing in Spanish.

BIBLIOGRAPHY

Primary Texts

A rachas. Ed. Jesús Munarriz. Madrid: Peralta, 1976. Poems.
El balneario. Madrid: Afrodisio Aguado, 1945. Title novella plus short stories.
El castillo de las tres murallas. Barcelona: Lumen, 1981. Novel for children.
Cuentos completos. Madrid: Alianza, 1978.

English Translation

The Back Room. Tr. Helen R. Lane. New York: Columbia UP, 1983.

Criticism

Bellver, Catherine G. "War as Rite of Passage in *El cuarto de atrás*." *Letras Femeninas* 12.1–2 (1986): 69–77.

Brown, Joan Lipman. "*El balneario* by Carmen Martín Gaite: Conceptual Aesthetics and 'L'étrange pure.' " *JSS:TC* 6.3 (1978): 163–74.

———. "*Tiempo de silencio* and *Ritmo lento*: Pioneers of the New Social Novel in Spain." *HR* 50.1 (1982): 61–73.
———. *Secrets from the Back Room: The Fiction of Carmen Martín Gaite*. University, MS: Romance Monographs, 1987.
Chittenden, Jean S. "*El cuarto de atrás* as Autobiography." *Letras Femeninas* 12.1–2 (1986): 78–84.
Servodidio, Mirella, ed. *From Fiction to Metafiction: Essays in Honor of Carmen Martín-Gaite*. Lincoln, NE: Society of Spanish and Spanish American Studies, 1983.

Janet Pérez

MARTÍN RECUERDA, José (1922, Granada–), Spanish playwright and director. Already well-known for his award-winning productions as director of the University Theater of Granada, which carried his adaptations of the Spanish classics to towns and villages throughout Andalusia, Recuerda won the Lope de Vega Prize for 1958 for his drama *El teatrito de don Ramón* (1969; Don Ramón's Small Theater). The latter drama and his plays composed in the 1950s and 1960s—*La llanura* (1977; The Plain), *Las salvajes en Puente San Gil* (1963; The Savages in Puente San Gil), and *Como las secas cañas del camino* (1966; Like the Dry Stalks along the Way)—portray victims of the cruelty, hypocrisy, and repression he finds in the towns and villages of southern Spain.

Recuerda's later historical dramas portray popular figures of Granada who are, likewise, victims: Mariana Pineda of *Las arrecogías del Beaterio de Santa María Egipciaca* (1974; *The Inmates of the Convent of St. Mary Egyptian*, 1985) and Juan de Dios of *El engañao* (1981; The Man Who was Deceived). The former drama, which opened shortly after the end of government *censorship of the theater in Spain, had one of the most successful runs of any play in the nation's post–Civil War period and brought Recuerda considerable acclaim. Both historical plays are Baroque spectacles of song and dance, intimate poetry and savage violence. They evince Recuerda's concept of theater-as-festival. His recent *Carnaval de un reino* (1981; Carnival of a Kingdom), which opened in 1984, is set in Castile and deals with the possible youth of Fernando de *Rojas's famous characters, *Celestina. It completes Recuerda's trilogy of history plays.

Recuerda's theater has its roots in the poetic tragedies of *García Lorca and the *esperpentos*, or savage, subversive farces, of *Valle-Inclán, Spain's precursor of the theater of cruelty. Like the former poet and playwright, Recuerda excels in the creation of female characters: the chorus girls of *Las salvajes*, Mariana Pineda and her sister prisoners in *Las arrecogías*, as well as Juana la Loca and the prostitutes of *El engañao*. All are women of great vitality who rebel against the political repression to which they are subjected. Since 1971, Recuerda has been professor and director of the Juan del Enzina Theater Chair at the U of Salamanca. He has also taught and lectured at various universities in the United States. *See also* Contemporary Spanish Theater.

BIBLIOGRAPHY

Primary Texts

Carnaval de un reino. Las ilusiones de las hermanas viajeras. Murcia: Godoy, 1981.
La Cicatriz. In *Canente. Revista Literaria* (Málaga) 7 (no date): 81–110.

El engañao. Caballos desbocaos. Ed. Martha T. Halsey and Angel Cobo. Madrid: Cátedra, 1981.
La llanura. El Cristo. Granada: Don Quijote, 1982.
Las salvajes en Puente San Gil. Las arrecogías del Beaterio de Santa María Egipciaca. Ed. Francisco Ruiz Ramón. Madrid: Cátedra, 1977.
La Trotski. In *Primer Acto* 207 (Jan.-Feb. 1985): 57–96.
El teatrito de don Ramón. Como las secas cañas del camino. Ed. Gerardo Velázquez Cueto. Barcelona: Plaza y Janés, 1984.

English Translation

The Inmates of the Convent of St. Mary Egyptian. Adapted and tr. Robert Lima. In *Drama Contemporary: Spain.* Ed. Marion Holt. New York: Performing Arts Journal Edition, 1985.

Criticism

Halsey, Martha T. "The Violent Dramas of Martín Recuerda." *Hispanófila* 70 (October 1980): 71–93.
Holt, Marion. "José Martín Recuerda." In *The Contemporary Spanish Theater (1949–1972).* Boston: Twayne, 1975. 150–53.
Monleón, José. "Martín Recuerda o la otra Andalucía." In *Teatro.* By José Martín Recuerda. Madrid: Taurus, 1969. 9–21.
Oliva, César. "José Martín Recuerda." In *Cuatro dramaturgos "realistas" en la escena de hoy.* Murcia: n.p., 1978. 115–49.
Weingarten, Barry. "José Martín Recuerda's *Como las secas cañas del camino* and the Rural Drama." *HR* 51 4 (Autumn 1983): 435–48.

Martha T. Halsey

MARTÍN SANTOS, Luis (1924, Larache, Morocco–1964, San Sebastián); Spanish novelist and essayist. The son of a military officer, Martín Santos was born in North Africa, but moved with his family to San Sebastián in 1929. He studied medicine, specializing in psychiatry, and during the last years of his life, he was director of the Sanatorio Psiquiátrico of San Sebastián. Literarily, Martín Santos was independent and original, a friend of Juan *Benet and of *Sánchez Ferlosio. He was imprisoned by the Franco regime as a political dissident and died in an automobile accident shortly before his fortieth birthday, reportedly leaving up to five unpublished novels (much of his work ran afoul of the censors).

Martín Santos published a number of psychiatric treatises and essays which combined his avid interest in existential philosophy with his professional specialization, including *Dilthey, Jaspers y la comprensión del enfermo mental* (1955; Dilthey, Jaspers, and Understanding the Mentally Ill), and *Libertad, temporalidad y transferencia en el psicoanálisis existencial* (1964; Freedom, Temporality, and Transference in Existential Psychoanalysis). *Tiempo de silencio* (1962; *Time of Silence*, 1974), one of the most significant novels of the postwar period in Spain, may be credited with sounding the death knell of the neorealist "social" novel and serving as the prototype of the "new" novel of the late 1960s and the 1970s. Although fully in sympathy with the political dissent and critical intent of the "social" novelists, Martín Santos believed that their methods were impoverishing Spanish literature through over-simplification and at the same time failing to achieve their aims. As a psychiatrist and an existentialist, he objected to dualistic portraits of society in which the poor appeared as uniformly virtuous victims, the rich as evil with no redeeming features. In *Time of Silence*, he employs a method which he christened "dialectical realism" that exposes the human complexities and shortcomings of all characters, regardless of class, while making clear the role of socio-economic factors. It is a rich and dense novel, employing such techniques as the Joycean interior monologue (then unknown in Spain, although Martín Santos had read Joyce in English and possibly in French translations). His experiments with shifting narrative perspective, highly innovative use of language and imaginative syntax had a tremendous impact on Spanish writers of the next two decades.

Time of Silence is also an indictment of the backwardness of science and research in Spain, a scathing exposé of the stagnation of the academic hierarchy and of shallowness and artificiality in the intelligentsia, presented via the misadventures of Pedro, a young doctor, attempting to carry on cancer research in Madrid. High mortality rates in his expensive laboratory mice lead him eventually to seek replacements in a shantytown built over a city dump at the edge of town, allowing presentation of the lowest dregs of Spanish society, later contrasted with the indolent aristocracy Pedro encounters in intellectual soirées, and juxtaposed with the trivial mentalities of the lower-middle-class habitués of his inexpensive boardinghouse. Naively, Pedro is lured into performing an illegal abortion, and with similar naïveté he is roped into engagement with his landlady's daughter. These episodes end badly, with the patient dying and Pedro's fiancée being murdered in retaliation, while he is first jailed and later banned from the research institute, his promising career shattered. The "time of silence" of the title alludes to the futility of protest under the regime, to muzzling of dissent by the *censorship, and to widespread apathy and indifference or fear in the Spanish populace, most of whom were unwilling to take a stand or speak out.

Apólogos y otras prosas inéditas (1970; Apologues and Other Unpublished Prose) is a miscellaneous collection containing stories, articles, short and long apologues, and the prologue to an unpublished novel entitled *Tiempo de destrucción* (1975; Time of Destruction [only fragments were published]). Initial expectations of post-Franco publication of the several novels allegedly left unpublished at the death of Martín Santos have gone unfulfilled, and the two posthumous titles have added little either to the understanding of Martín Santos or to his stature. *Time of Silence* remains one of the two or three most important novels published under Franco and has been the subject of numerous studies.

BIBLIOGRAPHY

Criticism

Anderson, Robert. "*Tiempo de silencio:* Myth and Social Reality." Diss., St. Louis U, 1973.

Curley, Thomas. "Man Lost in Madrid." *New York Times Book Review*, November 29, 1974: 57.

Díaz, Janet W. ''Luis Martín-Santos and the Contemporary Spanish Novel.'' *Hispania* 51 (1968): 232–38.
Eoff, Sherman, and José Schraibman. ''Dos novelas del absurdo: *L'étranger* y *Tiempo de silencio*.'' *Papeles de Son Armadans* 56 (1970): 213–41.
Palley, Julian. ''The Periplus of Don Pedro.'' *BHS* 48 (1971): 239–54.
Rey, Alfonso. *Construcción y sentido de ''Tiempo de silencio*.'' Madrid: Porrúa, 1977.
Seale, Mary. ''Hangman and Victim: An Analysis of Martín-Santos' *Tiempo de silencio*.'' *Hispanófila* 44 (1972): 45–52.

Janet Pérez

MARTÍN-VIVALDI, Elena (1907, Granada–), poet. She studied philosophy and letters at the U of Granada and worked as a librarian in Seville, Huelva and Granada. Her poetic career was influenced by the sixteenth-c. bucolic and Petrarchan poet *Garcilaso and by Juan Ramón *Jiménez. Her first books of verse include *Escalera de luna* (1945; Moon Staircase) and *Diario incompleto de abril* (written in 1947 and published in 1971; April's Incomplete Diary). The emotional intensity of love becomes solitude and suffering in *El alma desvelada* (1953; The Awakened Soul), *Materia de esperanza* (1968; A Matter of Hope), and *Cumplida soledad. 1953–1976* (1976; Perfect Solitude).

Durante este tiempo 1965–1972 (1972; During This Time) constitutes one of the best of Martín-Vivaldi's poetic collections, not only for the variety of themes treated, but also for the technical brilliance of the verses. In one of her last books of verse, *Nocturnos* (1981; Nocturnes), the poet returns to the motif of solitude.

In general, Martín-Vivaldi's poetry exhibits a poetic lyricism rooted in deep feeling and emotion. She resorts to the concise use of traditional and free verse with plain and precise language.

BIBLIOGRAPHY

Primary Texts

El alma desvelada. Madrid: Insula, 1953.
Arco de desenlace. Granada: ''Veleta al Sur,'' 1963.
Cumplida soledad. Granada: ''Veleta al Sur,'' 1958.
Nocturnos. Granada: Don Quijote, 1981.
Tiempo a la orilla. Poesía 1942–1984. Granada: ''Silene,'' 1985.

Criticism

Gallego Morell, A. Prologue to *Los árboles presento*. Granada: U of Granada, 1977.
Gutiérrez, José. *Manual de nostalgias*. Granada: ''Silene,'' 1982.
Molina Campos, E. ''Introducción a la poesía de Elena Martín Vivaldi.'' In *Tiempo a la orilla*.

José Ortega

MARTÍNEZ BALLESTEROS, Antonio (1929, Toledo–), playwright and director. A member of the so-called underground theater, he has continued to work in his native city and has seen his work performed primarily abroad, especially in the United States. His finest works are generally considered to be the two collections of four one-act farces entitled respectively *Farsas contemporáneas* (1969; Contemporary Farces) and *Retablo en tiempo presente* (1969–70; Contemporary Altarpieces). The former won the Guipúzcoa Prize for 1969, and the latter was awarded the Palencia Prize for 1970. These clever social satires combine humor and dramatic conflict quite efficaciously. *Los esclavos* (The Slaves), one of the *Farsas contemporáneas*, was performed in a Madrid cabaret theater in 1970 by a first-rate professional company. *Los placeres de la egregia dama* (1975; The Pleasures of the Exemplary Lady) received its world premiere at the State U of New York at Binghamton in 1976. That full-length drama converts sexual impotence into a dramatic metaphor that both explains and characterizes the true nature of the tyrant obsessed with power. Martínez Ballesteros founded a theater group named Pigmalión in Toledo in 1966 and has directed that company ever since its inception. He brought the group to the symposium in honor of the tenth anniversary of the journal *Estreno* held at the U of Cincinnati in April 1985, where they performed a collective farce based on a sketch by the playwright entitled *Los comediantes* (The Comic Actors). His work in Toledo as a director appears to represent the major thrust of his creative energies at the present time. *See also* Contemporary Spanish Theater.

BIBLIOGRAPHY

Primary Texts

Contemporary Spanish Theater. Ed. Patricia O'Connor and Anthony Pasquariello. New York: Scribner's Sons, 1980. Contains both *La distancia* and *Los esclavos*.

Farsas contemporáneas. Madrid: Escelicer, 1970.

Los placeres de la egregia dama. In *Estreno* 1.3 (Fall 1975).

Teatro difícil. Madrid: Escelicer, 1971. Contains *Retablo en tiempo presente*.

English Translations

The Position. Tr. Robert Lima. In *Modern International Drama* 4.2 (Spring 1971).

The Straw Men. Tr. Leon Lyday. In *Modern International Drama* 3.1 (Fall 1969).

Criticism

Pérez-Stansfield, María Pilar. *Teatro español de posguerra*. Madrid: José Porrúa Turanzas, 1983.

Ruiz Ramón, Francisco. *Historia del teatro español siglo XX*. Madrid: Cátedra, 1977.

Wellwarth, George. *Spanish Underground Drama*. University Park: Pennsylvania State UP, 1972.

Peter L. Podol

MARTÍNEZ CACHERO, José María (1924, Oviedo–), literary scholar, professor. An expert on *Azorín, he has also published studies on *Clarín, *Bécquer, *Jovellanos, Flórez Estrada, *Menéndez Pelayo, etc. He has prepared for publication the material for the final four volumes of *Escritores y artistas asturianos* (Asturian Writers and Artists), after the death of its author, Constantino *Suárez.

BIBLIOGRAPHY

Primary Text

La novela española entre 1936 y 1980: historia de una aventura. Madrid: Castalia, 1985.

Isabel McSpadden

MARTÍNEZ DE LA ROSA, Francisco (1787, Granada–1862, Madrid), dramatist, diplomat and politician. Martínez de la Rosa embodies many of the conflicting literary and political currents that dominated Spain in the first half of the nineteenth c. Fiercely patriotic, he opposed the French invasion of 1808 and traveled to England to enlist aid, where he published a fiery newspaper piece, "La revolución actual en España" (1808; The Present Revolution in Spain). On his return to Spain he became an elected member of the famous Cortes de Cádiz (Parliament) and there he supported the astonishing Constitution of 1812. The return of Ferdinand VII in 1814 put an end to Spain's liberal dreams, and Martínez de la Rosa was imprisoned and sentenced to death, but when Riego's 1820 uprising offered the promise of a new constitutional regime, Martínez de la Rosa returned to government service. By now his views had become more moderate, but again the dreams were shattered by the repressions of 1823 and the resurrection of Ferdinand, a specter which haunted Spain until the king's death in 1833.

Martínez de la Rosa spent his years of exile, 1823–31, in France, where he could freely discuss his political ideas. His literary thoughts flourished as well, and his clever mind quickly endeared him to the literary groups in the French capital. He had, after all, at the age of eighteen, been named professor of philosophy at the U of Granada, and his early readings had included large doses of European social, political and literary thought. His first collection of *Obras literarias* (1827–30; Literary Works) was published in Paris. Martínez's intelligence and moderate political views attracted the attention of the Queen Regent María Cristina, who called upon him to serve as head of the government in 1834. His two major successes of that year were the promulgation of the Royal Statute and the Spanish premiere of a play he had written in Paris, *La conjuración de Venecia* (1834; The Venice Conspiracy), considered to be one of the first Spanish Romantic plays because of its rebellious hero, tragic love story, cases of mistaken identities, and rejection of social tyranny. It is Martínez de la Rosa's best and most remembered literary achievement. With the exception of a pair of political tracts and a historical novel written later—*El espíritu del siglo* (1835; The Spirit of the Century), *Bosquejo de la política de España* (1855; Outline of Spanish Politics), *Doña Isabel de Solís, Reina de Granada* (1837; Isabel de Solís, Queen of Granada)— *La conjuración* represents the final point of the author's writing career.

A transition from neo-classicism to *Romanticism is clearly evident in his works. He followed the classical mode of tragedy in *La viuda de Padilla* (1814; Padilla's Widow), in *Moraima* (1818), and in the Sophoclean *Edipo* (1829; Oedipus), while experimenting with the neo-classical comedy in *Lo que puede* *un empleo* (1820; What a Job Can Do) and *La niña en casa y la madre en la máscara* (1821; The Girl at Home and the Mother at the Masked Ball). His theories of literature were recounted in *Poética* (1827; Poetics), a work which underlines his belief, both politically and aesthetically, that the *justo medio* (the moderate middle ground) is the best way to achieve one's desired goals. He suppressed that belief, if only temporarily, when he wrote, in French in 1830, the rebellious historical drama *Aben Humeya* (translated into Spanish in 1836) and *La conjuración.* His poetry, from the earliest odes (1800–1805) and the *Elegía a la muerte de la duquesa de Frías* (1811; Elegy on the Death of the Duchess of Frías), through his collection of lyrical *Poesías* (1833; Poetry), tends toward neo-classical forms and *pastoral themes. Other works of his include a collection of political epigrams, *El cementerio de Momo* (1804?; The Cemetery of Momo) and a biography of *Hernán Pérez del Pulgar* (1834), plus some minor dramas.

After 1834, Martínez's literary output declined but his prestige rose. He was named director of the *Academia Española in 1839, but when María Cristina was forced into a three-year exile in Paris (1840–43), Martínez de la Rosa joined her. The Moderate party's return to power in 1844 boosted Martínez's fortunes once again. He was appointed ambassador to Paris and to Rome, named president of the Council of State, and repeatedly returned to the Congress. As elder statesman he continued to take active interest in his country's politics. He died in 1862. *See also* Romanticism.

BIBLIOGRAPHY

Primary Texts

Obras. Ed. Carlos Seco Serrano. Madrid: Atlas, 1962.

Obras dramáticas. Ed. Jean Sarrailh. Madrid: Espasa-Calpe, 1964.

Criticism

Avrett, R. "A Brief Examination into the Historical Background of Martínez de la Rosa's *La conjuración de Venecia.*" *RR* 21 (1930): 132–37.

Geraldi, Robert. "Francisco Martínez de la Rosa: Literary Atrophy or Creative Sagacity?" *Hispanófila* 27 (1983): 11–19.

Herrero, Javier. "Terror y literatura: ilustración, revolución y los orígenes del movimiento romántico." *La literatura española de la Ilustración: Homenaje a Carlos III.* Madrid: Universidad Complutense, 1988. 131–53.

Mayberry, Nancy, and Robert Mayberry. *Francisco Martínez de la Rosa.* Boston: Hall, 1988.

McGaha, Michael. "The Romanticism of *La conjuración de Venecia.*" *KRQ* 20 (1973): 235–42.

Sarrailh, Jean. *Un homme d'Etat espagnol: Martínez de la Rosa.* Bordeaux: Feret, 1930.

Torres, David. "Las comedias moratinianas de Martínez de la Rosa." *CH* 339 (1978): 492–502.

David Thatcher Gies

MARTÍNEZ DE MENESES, Antonio (1608, Toledo–after 1650, ?), playwright. Virtually nothing is known of his life. He collaborated with many contemporaries, such as *Cáncer y Velasco (*El arca de Noé* [Noah's Ark]), *Moreto,

*Belmonte Bermúdez (*El príncipe perseguido* [The Pursued Prince]), *Matos Fragoso, Juan de *Zabaleta, etc. Most popular was his *El tercero de su afrenta* (Procurer of His Own Dishonor). His works fall within the *Calderón school of drama. *See also* Theater in Spain.

BIBLIOGRAPHY

Primary Texts

Various plays. In *Colección general de comedias escogidas del teatro antiguo español.* 33 vols. Madrid: Ortega, 1826–34.

El tercero de su afrenta. In BAE 47.

MARTÍNEZ DE PISÓN, Ignacio (1960, Zaragoza–), Spanish novelist and short-story writer. Despite a degree in Spanish and Italian philology, Martínez de Pisón is devoted almost completely to writing, doing sporadic teaching and translating. His short novel, *La ternura del dragón* (1984; The Tenderness of the Dragon) revolves around a seriously-ill adolescent, bedridden in his grandparents' house, and the process whereby his happy fantasy world slowly turns threatening and nightmarish. *Alguien te observa en secreto* (1985; Someone is Secretly Observing You) is a short-story collection in which quotidian reality is transformed via imagination and perversity. Most of the characters are deviants, alienated, or suffer neuroses, which increases the ambiguity already inherent in the manner of narration. *Antofagasta* (1987) and *La última isla desierta* (The Last Desert Island) are two novelettes published together under the title of the first. *Antofagasta* effects another incursion into mental sadism (already seen in stories of *Alguien te observa*) as appearances of normality are maintained while highly refined and subtle humiliations are effected. The protagonist, a ghost writer for well-known political figures, is able to carry out their dirty work only by taking refuge in an internal paradise, "Antofagasta." *La última isla desierta* investigates the relationships of chance and fate, suggesting that what seems accidental is merely a disguised causality. The three characters on the island imagine they are exercising free will because they are ignorant of the inscrutable superior power which imposes their decisions. Martínez de Pisón is considered one of the most important "New Narrators" of Spain.

Janet Pérez

MARTÍNEZ I CIVERA, Empar Beatriu, also known as Beatriu Civera (1914, Valencia–), novelist, journalist and fashion designer. As a child, she wrote "comedies" which she, her sister, and other friends presented. Educated in a nuns' school, she considered life in the convent at one time, but married instead. She edited the periodical *La Voz Valenciana* during the Civil War and was later chosen as secretary-general of the literary journal *Lo Rat Penat*, the first woman to hold that position. As writers who have had an impact on her work, she names Zola, *Unamuno, Pío *Baroja, Sartre and de Beauvoir. She has won various literary prizes, including the Víctor Català Prize for *Vides alienes* (1975; Alien lives).

BIBLIOGRAPHY

Primary Texts

La crida indefugible. N.p.: n.p., 1969.
Una dona com una altra. Valencia: Sicània, 1959.
Entre el cel i la terra. Valencia: Sicània, 1956.
Vides alienes. Barcelona: Selecta, 1975.

Kathleen McNerney

MARTÍNEZ-MARINA, Francisco (1754, Oviedo–1833, Zaragoza), law historian, economist, political writer. He was a canon at the collegiate church of San Isidro in Madrid, librarian and rector of the U of Alcalá, and director of the Royal Academy of History. Politically a reformist, he sought to reconcile the revolutionary and traditional ideals at the turn of the nineteenth c., for which he was censored by the moribund *Inquisition. His best work was the *Ensayo histórico-crítico sobre la antigua legislación castellana* (1808; A Historical-Critical Essay on Ancient Castilian Legislation), an organic study of private and public law from Visigothic times to *Alphonse the Wise's *Siete Partidas*. The *Teoría de las cortes de León y Castilla* (1813; Theory of the Courts of Leon and Castile) and the *Juicio crítico de la Novísima Recopilación* (1820; Critical Judgment on the Newest Code of Law) lack the method and scientific rigor of the *Essay*. He also wrote an *Ensayo histórico-crítico sobre el origen y progreso de las lenguas, señaladamente el romance castellano* (1805; A Historical-Critical Essay on the Origin and Development of Languages, Especially the Castilian Language), a pioneering work that contains an important study of Arabic words in Spanish.

BIBLIOGRAPHY

Primary Texts

Ensayo histórico-crítico sobre la antigua legislación castellana. Madrid: Sociedad literaria y tipográfica, 1845.
Ensayo histórico-crítico sobre el origen y progreso de las lenguas. . . . Madrid: Collado, 1813.

Eugene Del Vecchio

MARTÍNEZ MEDIERO, Manuel (1939, ?–), playwright. The holder of a master of arts degree in economics, he initially made his reputation through the prizes he won in competitions rather than as a result of staged productions of his plays. He received the Sitges Prize for *El último gallinero* (1969; The Last Chicken Coop) and the National University Prize for *Espectáculo siglo XX* (1970; Twentieth-Century Spectacle). Extravagant farce, satire and political allegory were established as the primary components of the work of this "underground dramatist." His theater of cruelty of 1970 included the grim and powerful farce *El convidado* (The Guest), a one-act drama which has received a number of performances in New York City and at various universities in the United States, and *Las planchadoras* (The Ironers), which received the Akoy Prize in 1971.

The latter was produced commercially in Madrid in 1978. During the final years of the Franco dictatorship, Martínez Mediero became the first and only one of the so-called underground playwrights to achieve commercial success on the stages of Madrid. *El bebé furioso* (1974; The Furious Baby) ran for more than 250 performances in 1974, and *Las hermanas de Búfalo Bill* (1972; The Sisters of Buffalo Bill) exceeded 555 the following year. The latter dealt with the theme of power in considering the continuing influence of Francoism on the Spanish people. After the death of the dictator, Martínez Mediero began to explore new themes inspired by Spain's altered situation. His most significant works, however, sought to illuminate the present through the depiction and demythification of Spain's historical past. *Juana del amor hermoso* (1982; Juana of the Beautiful Love) enjoyed a run of over 200 performances in 1983. The play questions the insanity of Juana La Loca while concomitantly contrasting the liberal views and *joie de vivre* of the "mad queen" with the rigid morality of her mother, Isabel of Castile. In his most recent work staged, *Papá Borgia* (1985; Papa Borgia), Martínez Mediero turns once again to the era of Isabel, utilizing contemporary colloquialisms to produce striking anachronisms in the satirical mode that has characterized his entire career as a dramatist. *See also* Contemporary Spanish Theater.

BIBLIOGRAPHY

Primary Texts

Las bragas perdidas en el tenedero y *Juana del amor hermoso*. Madrid: Fundamentos, 1982.

Espectáculo siglo XX. Madrid: Escelicer, 1971.

Las hermanas de Búfalo Bill. Madrid: Fundamentos, 1980.

Teatro antropofágico. Madrid: Fundamentos, 1978.

Teatro de la libertad. Badajoz: "Esquina Viva," 1978.

Criticism

Pérez-Stansfield, María Pilar. *Teatro español de posguerra*. Madrid: José Porrúa Turanzas, 1983.

Ruiz Ramón, Francisco. *Historia del teatro español siglo XX*. Madrid: Cátedra, 1977.

Wellwarth, George. *Spanish Underground Drama*. University Park: Pennsylvania State UP, 1972.

Peter L. Podol

MARTÍNEZ-MENCHÉN, Antonio (1930, Linares, Jaén–), novelist, short story writer, and essayist. He studied law in Madrid, where he has worked for the civil service since 1960. Some of his literary essays have been collected in *Del desengaño literario* (1970; Of Literary Disillusion). He has also written sociological criticism.

In Martínez-Menchén's first novel, *Cinco variaciones* (1963; Five Variations), the anonymous characters are detached from the outside world and search within themselves for a way to overcome their isolation. Emotional experiences, revealed by interior monologues, are the only resource left to them in questioning an alienated and fragmented world. In *Las tapias* (1969; The Walls), the social barriers that separate the characters from the exterior world are so insurmountable that their alienation, as in the fiction of Kafka, becomes pathological. The impersonal and shadowy characters of *Inquisidores* (1977; Inquisitors) escape the cruelty and solitude of society by exercising their private fantasy and imagination. Childhood memories of the Civil War and the psychological effects of a repressive post-war society characterize the eleven stories of this volume. Linguistic precision and imaginative, meticulous treatment of alienated man are the most noteworthy features of his prose. *Pro Patria Mori* (1980; In Defense of Fatherland) is a novel written in the form of a diary kept by the main character. It documents the effects of fascist repression on the generation of Spaniards who were children during that conflict. The style is precise, direct, and structured as a pseudo-dialogue with a counterpoint technique that connects the death of the real father with the agony of the ''terrible father,'' symbolized by Franco. *La caja china* (1985; The Chinese Box) is a short novel with Kafkaesque overtones in which the character/victim conducts a monologue in search of his identity under the political-cultural oppression of Franco.

BIBLIOGRAPHY

Primary Texts

La caja china. Diputación Provincial de Jaén, 1985.
Cinco variaciones. Barcelona: Seix Barral, 1963.
Inquisidores. Madrid: Zero Zyx, 1977.
Pro Patria Mori. Madrid: Legasa, 1980.
Las tapias. Barcelona: Seix Barral, 1969.

Criticism

Ortega, José. *Antonio Ferres y Martínez Menchén, novelistas de la soledad*. Caracas: Universidad A. Bello, 1973.

José Ortega

MARTÍNEZ MONROY, José (1837, Cartagena–1861, Cartagena), poet. An early death put an end to the great promise of this Romantic poet, as seen in such poems as ''La victoria de Tetuán'' (The Victory of Tetuan), ''Al telégrafo eléctrico'' (To the Electric Telegraph), and ''Lo que dice mi madre'' (What My Mother Says). *See also* Romanticism.

BIBLIOGRAPHY

Primary Texts

Poesías. Madrid: Rivadeneyra, 1864.
El poeta Monroy. Ed., sel. J. Rodríguez Cánovas. Cartagena: Athenas, 1967. Biography and selections.

MARTÍNEZ MURGUÍA, Manuel (1833, Frexel-Arteixo, Coruña–1923, La Coruña), literary critic, important historian. In his early years in Santiago, Murguía became part of the poetic circles of Galician provincialism, his vocation for literature and history took root, and his ideological orientation was also defined. In 1853 he left for Madrid and soon began collaborating in the most prestigious newspapers and magazines there. The major part of his writing was published in newspapers. In Madrid he met the poet Rosalía de *Castro; they wed in 1858. From this date on his life is almost entirely linked to Galicia. In direct relation to the ongoing nationalistic resurgence, Murguía studied history, becoming one of the fundamental theoreticians of Galician nationalism's rebirth, and directed his research to the demonstration of Galicia's existence as a nation. After 1885 he participated very actively in the defense of Galician regionalism through articles and speeches. In 1890 he was elected president of the Asociación Regionalista Gallega (Galician Regional Association), the first autonomous Galician political party. From then on he is linked more strongly to political struggles and comes to be president of the Liga Gallega (Galician League), successor to the Asociación Regionalista Gallega. In 1896 his polemics in defense of Galician with Juan *Valera and *Pardo Bazán were widely publicized. Ten years later Murguía was named the first president of the Real Academia Gallega (Royal Galician Academy) and from that point on until his death he abandoned politics and devoted his efforts exclusively to historical research. Before his death in 1923, he saw the rise of Galician nationalism. In this manner, his life spanned the entire trajectory of the appearance and consolidation of the independence movement in Galicia. *See also* Galician Literature.

BIBLIOGRAPHY

Primary Texts

Antología gallega. Vigo: Compañel, 1862.
El arte en Santiago durante el siglo XVIII. Madrid: Fé, 1884.
Desde el cielo. Madrid: Artística Española, 1910.
Diccionario de escritores gallegos. Vigo: Compañel, 1862.
Don Diego Gelmírez. La Coruña: Carré, 1898.
En prosa. La Coruña: Carré, 1895.
Galicia. Barcelona: D. Cortezo, 1888.
Historia de Galicia. La Coruña: Carré, 18??.
Los precursores. La Coruña: Latorre y Martínez, 1885.
Los trovadores gallegos. La Coruña: Ferrer, 1905.

Criticism

Beramendi, J. G. "La Galicia de Murguía." In *Galicia*. By M. Murguía. Vigo: Xerais, 1982.
Fraguas Fraguas, Antonio. *Manuel Murguía: o patriarca*. Vigo: Grafsina, 1979.
García Acuña, José. "Murguía, poeta." *Boletín de la Real Academia Gallega* 21 (1933): 173–79.
García Pereiro, María Carmen. "Teoría da lingua gallega en Murguia." *Grial* 61 (1978): 363–66.
Risco, Vicente. "Murguía." *Arquivos do Seminario de Estudos Galegos* 6 (1933): vii-xlvi.

Varela, José Luis. *Poesía y restauración cultural de Galicia en el siglo XIX*. Madrid: Gredos, 1958.

Luis Martul Tobío

MARTÍNEZ OLMEDILLA, Augusto (1880, Madrid–1965, Madrid), prolific novelist and short story writer. *Memorias de un afrancesado* (1904; Memoirs of a French Sympathizer) describes the customs of Madrid. His novels are realistic, and sometimes crude; some of them are thesis works. Among them are *Los hijos* (1912; Sons), *Siempreviva* (1913; Everlasting), *La ley de Malthus* (1913; Malthus's Law) and *El plano inclinado* (1914; The Inclined Plane). He has also written some plays, such as *La estatua de nieve* (The Snow Statue) and *El despertar de Fausto* (The Awakening of Faust). His book on Madrid's theaters, *Los teatros de Madrid* (Madrid's Theaters), is also important.

BIBLIOGRAPHY

Primary Texts

El final de Tosca; la novela de una gran cantante. 2nd ed. Madrid: Reus, 1952.
Los hijos. Madrid: Alrededor del Mundo, 1912.
La ley de Malthus. 2nd ed. Madrid: Saez, 1933.
Los teatros de Madrid, anecdotario de la farándula madrileña. Madrid: n.p., 1948.

Isabel McSpadden

MARTÍNEZ SIERRA, Gregorio (1881, Madrid–1947, Madrid) and **MARTÍNEZ SIERRA, María** (née María de la O Lejárraga, 1874, San Millán de la Cogolla, Spain–1974, Buenos Aires, Argentina), principally playwrights. Gregorio and María collaborated on essays, poems, novels, short stories, and newspaper articles as well as the many (more than fifty) plays for which they are principally famous. *El poema del trabajo* (1898; Labor's Poem), allegorical prose poems in praise of work, was published two years before their marriage. Other early works, written in the modernistic style, included *Diálogos fantásticos* (1899; Fantastic Dialogues), *Flores de escarcha* (1900; Frost Flowers), and *Teatro de ensueño* (1905; Dream Theater). They also collaborated on novels: *Tú eres la paz* (1906; You Are Peace) and *La humilde verdad* (1905; The Humble Truth). The early works, set most often in rural Spain, demonstrate strong admiration for the simple, natural life and tend to present moral lessons through parables. In approximately 1910, Gregorio and María, realizing that their interest lay more in people than in landscape, began writing for theater and eventually produced over fifty plays, most of which featured strong, practical, maternal women characters. Most of the plays, unlike the preceding narrative works, were set in Madrid. Among the best known are *Canción de cuna* (1911; *Cradle Song*, 1923), *Primavera en otoño* (1911; Autumn Spring), *El reino de Dios* (1915; *The Kingdom of God*, 1929), *Sueño de una noche de agosto* (1918; *The Romantic Young Lady*, 1929), *Seamos felices* (1929; Let's Be Happy), *Triángulo* (1930; *Take Two from One*, 1931). In 1931, Gregorio went to Hollywood to supervise filming of some of his plays and to write movie scripts for MGM and Paramount

Pictures. María remained in Spain and was elected Socialist *diputada* (representative) to the *Cortes* (Parliament). With the outbreak of the Spanish Civil War (1936), Gregorio moved to Buenos Aires and returned in 1946 only a few weeks before his death. María, who remained in Nice (France) during and after the war, died in Buenos Aires six months shy of her 100th birthday. *See also* Contemporary Spanish Theater.

BIBLIOGRAPHY

Primary Texts

Amanecer. Madrid: Velasco, 1914.

Canción de cuna. Madrid: Velasco, 1911.

Feminismo, feminidad, españolismo. Madrid: Clásica Española, 1916.

El reino de Dios. Madrid: Pueyo, 1916.

English Translations

Cradle Song and Other Plays. Tr. John Garret Underhill. New York: Dutton, 1931. Also includes *The Lover* (*El enamorado*), *Love Magic* (*Hechizo de amor*), *Poor John* (*El pobrecito Juan*), and *Madame Pepita*.

Divine Treasure (*Juventud, divino tesoro*). Tr. George Portnoff. Boston: Meador, 1936.

Holy Night (*Navidad*). Tr. Philip Hereford, New York: Dutton, 1928.

The Kingdom of God and Other Plays. Tr. Helen and Harley Granville-Barker. New York: Dutton, 1929. Also includes *Two Shepherds* (*Los pastores*), *Wife of a Famous Man* (*La mujer del héroe*), and *The Romantic Young Lady* (*Sueño de una noche de agosto*).

Take Two from One (*Triángulo*). Tr. Helen and Harley Granville-Barker. London: Siedgwick and Jackson, 1931.

Criticism

Goldsborough Serrat, Andrés. *Imagen humana y literaria de Gregorio Martínez Sierra*. Madrid: Gráficos Cóndor, 1965.

Gullón, Ricardo. *Relaciones amistosas y literarias entre Juan Ramón Jiménez y los Martínez Sierra*. Río Piedras: Ediciones de la Torre, 1961.

Martínez Sierra, María. *Gregorio y yo*. México: Biografías Gandesa, 1953.

O'Connor, Patricia W. *Gregorio and María Martínez Sierra*. TWAS 412. Boston: Twayne, 1977.

Patricia W. O'Connor

MARTÍNEZ SILÍCEO, Juan (1486, ?–1557, ?), priest, professor. He was born Martínez Guijarro, but Latinized his second surname. After studies in Rome and Paris, he rose to the position of cardinal in the Roman church. He also taught philosophy at the U of Salamanca and instructed the future Philip II. Martínez Silíceo composed extensive commentaries to Aristotle's works, books on calculus, arithmetic, etc. *See also* Aristotelianism; Humanism; Renaissance; Siglo de Oro.

MARTÍNEZ VILLERGAS, Juan (1816, Gomeznarro, Valladolid–1894, Zamora), satirical poet, critic and journalist. An exalted Republican, Villergas led an active life engaged in politics, directing papers, and writing biting satires against contemporary politicians, military men and writers. He was frequently prosecuted, and Narváez, whom he seriously insulted, kept him in jail for seven months. He was exiled in Paris (1852), traveled to Argentina, Mexico and Peru and several times to Cuba, where he founded the newspaper *El moro Muza* (Muza, the Moor) against the Cuban independentists. A feared satirist and critic, he was most popular among the masses. He wrote three novels after the manner of Eugène Sue, *Los misterios de Madrid* (1844–45; The Mysteries of Madrid), *La vida en el chaleco* (1859; Life in the Waistcoat) and *Los Espadachines* (1869; The Swordsmen); several satirical poems like *El baile de las brujas* (1843; The Witches' Dance), against Regent Espartero, or *Patifiesto* (1854), against Queen María Cristina; a sharp and passionate *Juicio crítico de los poetas españoles contemporáneos* (1854; Critical Judgment of Contemporary Spanish Poets); and the famous *Sarmenticidio* (Sarmenticide), in which he attacked the Argentinian Domingo F. Sarmiento for his anti-Spanish attitude; among many other writings. Villergas started newspapers wherever he went and in Madrid, with his co-religionaries *Ayguals de Izco and Ribot y Fontseré, created *El tío Camorra* (1847; Uncle Trouble), *Don Circunstancias* (1848; Mr. Circumstances), *La Risa* (1843–44; Laughter) and *El dómine Lucas* (1844–46; Master Lucas).

BIBLIOGRAPHY

Primary Texts

El baile de las brujas. Madrid: Panorama Español, 1843.

Los espadachines. Novela. 2 vols. Madrid: Victoria, 1869.

Juicio crítico de los poetas españoles contemporáneos. Paris: Rosa y Bouret, 1854.

Sarmenticidio, o a mal sarmiento, buena podadera. Paris: Agencia General de la Librería Española y Estranjera, 1853.

La vida en el chaleco. Novela original de costumbres no menos originales. La Habana: El Iris, 1859.

Criticism

Alonso Cortés, Narcisco. *Juan Martínez Villergas. Bosquejo biográfico crítico*. 2nd ed. Valladolid-La Habana: Viuda de Montero, 1913.

Barrantes, Vicente. "Villergas y su tiempo." *La España Moderna*, 67 (1894): 53–69

García Casteñeda, Salvador. "El satírico Villergas y sus andanzas hispanoamericanas." *Anuario de Letras* (Mexico) 10 (1972): 133–151.

———. "Juan Martínez Villergas y un cuadro de Esquivel." *REH* 7 (1973): 179–92.

Salvador García Castañeda

MÁRTIR DE ANGLERÍA, Pedro (c. 1457, Arona, Italy–1526, Granada), humanist, chronicler. Of a noble but not wealthy family, educated in Milan, Pedro Mártir first arrived in Spain in 1487 as part of the entourage of Count Tendilla. After participating in the final moments of the Reconquest, in 1492 he took religious orders. In 1501 he became chaplain to Queen Isabel. Over the years, he discharged various responsibilities for the monarchs, including humanistic instruction of young nobles such as Iñigo de *Mendoza, Alonso de Silva, etc. In 1520, Charles I appointed him chronicler of the Indies. Mártir de

Anglería is remembered for two publications. One, titled *Opus epistolarum* (1530; Epistolary Works), contains 813 letters written by Anglería to various contemporaries over the course of thirty-seven years. They comprise a history of the most important events in Spain from 1488 to 1525. Even more important is the *Decadas de orbe novo* (written 1493–1525; *The Eight Decades of Peter Martyr*, 1912). Although the first Decade appeared in 1511, the first complete edition was published in 1530. Covering the years 1493–1525 and following the model of Livy, it is the first historical account of the discovery of the New World and contains cultural and horticultural information as well as political and military data. Mártir also wrote a summary of his journey to Babylonia undertaken in 1502 for King Ferdinand, titled *Legatio Babyloni*. *See also* Humanism; Renaissance; Siglo de Oro.

BIBLIOGRAPHY

Primary Texts

Cartas de Pedro Mártir sobre las comunidades. Tr. José de la Canal. Escorial: Real Monasterio, 1945. Selections.

Decadas de orbe novo. Alcalá: Eguía, 1530.

Décadas del Nuevo Mundo. Tr. to Spanish J. Torres Asensio. Buenos Aires: Bajel, 1944.

Legatio. Seville: Cromberger, 1511.

"Pedro Mártir de Anglería, Epistolario, Estudio y Traducción." Spanish tr., study López de Toro. In *Documentos inéditos para la historia de España*. Vols. 9–12. Madrid: n.p., 1953.

English Translation

The Eight Decades of Peter Martyr. Tr., notes, intro. F. A. MacNutt. New York and London: Putnam's, 1912.

Criticism

O'Gorman, E. *Cuatro historiadores de Indias, siglo XVI: Pedro Mártir de Anglería, Gonzalo Fernández de Oviedo y Valdéz, Bartolomé de las Casas, Joseph de Acosta*. Mexico: Secretaria de Educación Pública, 1972.

Olmedillas de Pereiras, María. *Pedro Mártir de Anglería y la mentalidad exoticista*. Madrid: Gredos, 1974.

Salas, Alberto Mario. *Tres cronistas de Indias: Pedro Mártir de Anglería, Gonzalo Ferñandez de Oviedo, fray Bartolomé de las Casas*. Mexico: Fondo de Cultura Económica, 1959.

MÁRTIR RIZO, Juan Pablo (1593, Madrid–1642, Madrid), poet, essayist and translator. Perhaps the grandson of Pedro *Mártir de Anglería, he was married for a short time but later became a priest. He helped Pedro de *Torres Rámila to write his *Spongia* (1617), a violent attack against Lope de *Vega. He played an important role in the bitter aesthetic controversy between Lope and the neoclassicists over dramatic principles. His most important works are *Historia de Cuenca* (1629; History of Cuenca), *Norte de príncipes* (1626; Guide for Princes), *Defensa de la verdad que escribió don Francisco de Quevedo y Villegas* (1630?; Defense of the Truth Written by don Francisco de Quevedo), and *Historia trágica* *de la vida y muerte del duque de Virón* (1629; The Tragic History of the Life and Death of the Duke of Virón), which was the source for *Pérez de Montalbán's play, *El mariscal de Virón* (1635; The Marshal of Virón). Besides his poetry and translations of Latin and French authors, he wrote biographies on *Seneca and Maecenas. *See also* Siglo de Oro; Theater in Spain.

BIBLIOGRAPHY

Primary Texts

Historia trágica de la vida y muerte del duque de Virón. Barcelona: n.p., 1629.

Defensa de la verdad que escribió don Francisco de Quevedo y Villegas. Madrid: n.p., 1630?

Historia de Cuenca. Madrid: n.p., 1629.

Norte de príncipes y Vida de Rómulo. Ed., study, notes José Antonio Maravall. Madrid: Instituto de estudios políticos, 1945.

Hector Medina

MARTORELL, Joanot (1413/15, Gandia–1468, Valencia), novelist. Scion of an aristocratic family, he was knighted as a very young man, and one of his sisters married the poet Ausiàs *March. Martorell took part in a chivalric duel (against Joan de Montpalau) in defense of another sister and as a knight and feudal lord participated in other disputes. He also spent some time in London (1438–39) where he says he learned English (the transcription of English names attests to this) and became familiar with the main British sources of his *Tirant lo Blanch*: *Historia regnum Britanniae* (1135) by Geofrey of Monmouth and *Travels of Sir John Mandeville* by Jean d'Outremeuse.

Tirant lo Blanch begins with the knight's arrival in England, where he is knighted and wins several duels with famous knights. He later defends the Island of Rhodes against the Turks, conducting warfare more in the manner of modern strategy than the individual effort of a traditional knight. In the face of the threat to the Byzantine Empire from the Turks, Tirant succors Byzantium and wins the day. This fact recalls the famous expedition of the Almogàvers (Catalan mercenary troops commanded by the legendary Roger de Flor). Tirant and Carmesina, the daughter of the emperor, fall in love and several erotic scenes follow. Later adventures and wars take place in Africa, where Tirant is at the service of several kings. Finally, the hero dies peacefully in his bedroom and Carmesina follows him to the grave.

*Cervantes's Don Quixote has a great collection of chivalric novels in his library, and according to the judgment of the priest, *Tirant lo Blanch* is one of the novels worth preserving for posterity and therefore it is not burned. Obviously the ironic and realistic nature of *Tirant* pleased Cervantes. However, the realism is only partial. The geographical and most of the historical settings are fictitious, though Roger de Flor's expedition to the Levant and the siege of Rhodes are indisputable facts. Moreover, truly incredible elements are extremely rare, and the amorous intrigues of the novel reflect Boccaccian influence. The episodes based on historical facts have autobiographical elements and reveal influences of *Muntaner and *Llull. As in *Don Quixote*, realism of the court scenes contrasts with the idealistic character of the rest of the novel. It is even questionable whether the risqué tone of some of the scenes was the author's real aesthetic intention. Some passages clearly show that the hero of *Tirant*, like Don Quixote, does not feel at home in his era and symbolizes the anachronistic chivalric dreams and the crisis of values so typical of the fifteenth c. Dámaso *Alonso considers *Tirant lo Blanch* the best European novel of the fifteenth c., and David Rosenthal, the recent English translator of Martorell's work, believes it a classic of Western literature.

Finally, it must be pointed out that *Tirant* was revised by Martí Joan de *Galba (d. 1490), and though we do not know the true extent of Galba's contribution to the novel, Joan Coromines believes that most of the work was written by Martorell. Perhaps only the part of the novel dealing with North Africa was written by Galba. Besides the above-mentioned English sources we may add *La tragèdia de Lancelot* (The Tragedy of Lancelot) by Lluis Gras, *Historia de Jacob Xalabín* (The Story of Jacob Xalabín), *La Vita nuova* (New Life) by Dante, the Latin letters by Petrarch, the works of Boccaccio, *La Crònica* (The Chronicle) by Muntaner, the writings of the siege of Rhodes by Frances de Flor i Jacme de Vilasegut and the Anglo-Normand poem *Guy de Warwick*. *See also* Caballerías, Libros de; Catalan Literature; Italian Literary Influences.

BIBLIOGRAPHY

Primary Text

Tirant lo Blanch. Annotated ed. by Martín de Riquer. Barcelona: Edicions 62, 1983.

English Translation

Tirant lo Blanch. Tr. David H. Rosenthal. New York: Schocken, 1984.

Criticism

Alonso, Dámaso. "*Tirant lo Blanch*, novela moderna." In *Primavera temprana de la literatura europea*. Madrid: Guadarrama, 1961.

D'Olwer, Lluís Nicolau. "Sobre les fonts catalanes del *Tirant lo Blanch*." *Revista de Bibliografia catalana*, 8 (1905): 5–37.

Entwistle, W. J. "*Tirant lo Blanch* and the Social Order of the End of the 15th Century." *Estudis Romànics*, 2 (1949–50): 149–64.

Gili y Gaya, Samuel. "Noves recerques sobre *Tirant lo Blanch*." *Estudis Romànics* 1 (1947–48): 135–47.

McNerney, Kathleen. *"Tirant lo Blanc" Revisited: A Critical Study*. Medieval and Renaissance Monograph Series 4. Detroit: Michigan Consortium for Medieval and Early Modern Studies, 1983.

Pierce, Frank. "The Role of Sex in the *Tirant lo Blanch*." *Estudis Romànics* 10 (1962): 291–300.

Riquer, Martín de. *Caballeros andantes españoles*. Madrid: Espasa-Calpe, 1967.

Thomas, Henry. *Spanish and Portuguese Romances of Chivalry*. Cambridge: Cambridge UP, 1920.

Vaeth, Joseph. *"Tirant lo Blanch," a Study of Its Authorship, Principal Sources and Historical Settings*. New York: Columbia UP, 1918.

Joan Gilabert

MARURI, Julio (1920, Santander–), poet. Related to the group of *Hierro and José Luis *Hidalgo, he was a founder of the magazine *Proel*. In 1947 he received second prize for his poetry book *Los años* (The Years). In 1950 he entered the Carmelite order, taking the name Fray Casto del Niño Jesús. In 1956, Vicente *Aleixandre wrote a poem-foreword for Maruri's *Obra poética*, and in 1957 his *Antología poética* received the National Literature Prize.

BIBLIOGRAPHY

Primary Texts

Los años. Madrid: n.p., 1947.
Antología. Torrelavega: Cantalapiedra, 1957.

Isabel McSpadden

MASDÉU, Juan Francisco (1744, Palermo–1817, Valencia), historian, poet. A member of the Jesuit order, with their expulsion from Spain in 1767 he moved to Italy. There, he published a twenty-volume *Historia crítica de España* (1783–1807; Critical History of Spain), a work so thorough it only covers events to the eleventh c. Its impressive erudition is marred by an excessive desire to discount all legend, which leads him to question the historical existence of the *Cid. The work provoked some controversy. Masdéu also wrote poetry, books on Italian and Spanish poetics, and a *Religión española* (written c. 1816; Spanish Religion).

BIBLIOGRAPHY

Primary Texts

Arte poética fácil. Valencia: Burguete, 1801.
Arte poética italiana. . . . Parma: Stamperia nazionale, 1803.
Historia crítica de España. . . . 20 vols. Madrid: Sancha, 1783–1807.
Religión española. Gerona: Revista de ciencias históricas, 1881.

MASOLIVER, Liberata (1911, Barcelona–), Spanish novelist who has written primarily on the theme of the Civil War and on religious themes. She began in the mid–1950s writing serial jungle adventure novels: *Efún* (1955), *Selva negra, selva verde* (1959; Black Jungle, Green Jungle), and *La mujer del colonial* (1962; The Colonist's Wife), most of them involving a conflict between flesh and spirit. A more realistic work from this period is *Los Galiano* (1957; The Galianos), set in Barcelona in the mid–1950s, a critique of growing materialism, sexual license, fads and fashions, and the loss of spiritual values in an urban bourgeois ambient. The writer's first historical novel based on the Civil War, *Barcelona en llamas* (1961; Barcelona in Flames), depicts daily life in wartime Barcelona from the perspective of a female Nationalist sympathizer imprisoned by the

Republican militia. *Maestro albañil* (1963; Master Bricklayer) presents the life of a working-class couple and the machinations of the husband to obtain the baby his wife is unable to have. *Pecan los buenos* (1964; The Good Sin) is a variation on the same theme, as a self-sacrificing wife obsessed with maternity turns to her husband's best friend after learning that the husband is sterile because of his affairs and venereal disease. *Un camino llega a la cumbre* (1966; A Road Reaches the Summit) relates a difficult spiritual journey after the protagonist is raped. The summer vacations of wealthy Catalans on the Costa Brava are depicted in *Casino veraniego* (1968; Summer Casino), while *Hombre de paz* (1969; Man of Peace) returns to war-torn Barcelona to present the moral and emotional conflicts of a pro-Republican surgeon. *Dios con nosotros* (1970; God Is with Us) and *Estés donde estés* (1972; Wherever You May Be) are both religious novels.

BIBLIOGRAPHY

Primary Texts

Barcelona en llamas. Barcelona: Barna, 1961.
Un camino llega a la cumbre. Barcelona: Peñíscola, 1966.
Casino veraniego. Barcelona: Peñíscola, 1968.
Maestro albañil. Barcelona: Peñíscola, 1963.
La mujer del colonial. Barcelona: Barna, 1962.
Pecan los buenos. Barcelona: Peñíscola, 1964.

Janet Pérez

MASPONS I LABROS, María del Pilar, also known as Maria de Bell-lloc (1841, Barcelona–1907, ?), folklorist, novelist and journalist. Her verses are emotional and simple, sometimes with religious themes, written in a natural style and popular tone with a facility of expression. She won prizes in the Jocs Florals (*Juegos) in 1875 and 1880. She gathered and wrote down many popular legends and published collections of them, such as *Elisabeth de Mur* (1880), *Llegendes Catalanes* (1881; Catalan Legends) and *Montseny* (1890). She also wrote a historical novel, *Vigatans i botiflers* (1878; The Boys from Vic), about the loss of Catalan rights and the deaths of the fighters for the independence of the country during the wars of succession. She contributed to various Catalan periodicals such as *La Renaixença*, *Lo Gay Saber*, *La Ilustració Catalana*, *La Veu de Montserrat* and *La Veu de Catalunya*. She was the sister of Francesc Maspons and was married to F. Pelay Briz. *See also* Catalan literature.

BIBLIOGRAPHY

Primary Texts

Elisabeth de Mur. Barcelona: Novel • la Catalana, 1924.
Lectura Popular. Barcelona: Ilustració Catalana, 1879. 33–64
Llegendes Catalanes. Barcelona: Tipografia Espanyola, 1881.
Montseny. Barcelona: Biblioteca de la Tomasa, 1890.

Salabrugas: Poesies Catalanas. Barcelona: la Renaixença, 1874.
Vigatans i botiflers. Barcelona: Joan Roca, 1878.

Kathleen McNerney

MASSANÉS DE GONZÁLEZ, María Josepa (1811, Tarragona–1887, ?), Catalan poet with a firm scholarly training. Her father, a military man, was forced into exile in 1827, where he remained until 1832. Besides Catalan and Castilian, Massanés mastered Italian and French. She wrote her first literary compositions at age twelve. This early work, addressed to her father, already reveals her natural dispositions for literature. Massanés first published her poems in several newspapers, *El Vapor, El Guardia Nacional, La religión;* later they were collected in a volume called *Poesías* (1841; Poems). Her work also appeared in foreign newspapers such as the *Noticiero de Ambos Mundos* from North America. In the prologue of *Poesías,* the author criticizes male discrimination against the intellectual work of women. This volume was followed by *Flores marchitas* (1850; Wilted Flowers), a compilation of poems which are largely personal addresses. In 1840, together with other Catalan poets, Massanés was sought out to write for the *Album* which was presented to the monarchs of Spain during their visit to Barcelona. A few years later, Massanés wrote, in Catalan, and published her well-known poem ''La roja barretina catalana'' (1860; The Red Catalan Cap), on the occasion of the arrival at Barcelona of the victorious Catalan volunteers from the African War. One of her most significant and far-reaching poems is ''El beso maternal'' (The Maternal Kiss), which evokes filial respect. (The New York State government had it translated for use in the school system.) Her poem ''Creurer es viurer'' (Believing Is Living) was awarded a prize in the Jocs Florals (*Juegos), the renowned Catalan poetry competition of Barcelona, in 1864. In prose, Massanés wrote *Importancia de la perfecció dels brodats* (1881; The Importance of Perfection in Needlework), an opening celebration speech for the Gimpera sisters' needlework exhibition in 1881. The speech calls for regeneration of the crumbling Spanish industry and its protection from foreign competition. *Poesies* (1908; Poems) is her last compilation of verse and was published posthumously. Massanés was a member of the Academia de las Buenas Letras (Fine Arts Academy). Before dying, she submitted all her work to the Biblioteca Museo Balaguer. Her poetry, brilliant in style, boasts rich imagery, strong moral principle, tranquility, and love for humanity.

BIBLIOGRAPHY

Primary Texts

Flores marchitas. Barcelona: A. Brusi, 1850.
Importancia de la perfecció dels brodats. Barcelona: Renaixença, 1881.
Poesías. Barcelona: Rubió, 1841.
Poesies. Barcelona: Ilustració Catalana, 1908.

Respirall. Barcelona: Estampa Peninsular, 1879. This compilation is also included in *Rimas*.
Rimas. Barcelona: Roca, 1879.

Victoria Codina-Espurz

MATEO, Lope (1898, Salamanca–1970, Valladolid), journalist, poet. His poetry is traditional, inspired in Castile, and tends toward a heroic mood. His first book, *Ráfagas de la selva* (1922; Flashes from the Forest), collects earlier writings. *Madre Castilla* (1943; Mother Castile) received a prize in Milenario de Castilla. He collaborated in several newspapers and wrote a biography of Isabella of Castile. *El sendero enamorado* (1951; The Beloved Path) is prose, *Hablo contigo, España* (1966; I'm Talking with You, Spain) is poetry.

BIBLIOGRAPHY

Primary Texts

Hablo contigo, España. Madrid: Nacional, 1966.
El sendero enamorado. Madrid: Publicaciones Españolas, 1951.

Isabel McSpadden

MATEO LUJÁN DE SAYAVEDRA. *See* Martí, Juan

MATHEU I SADO, Roser (1892, Barcelona–), poet and biographer. Daughter of the poet Francesc Matheu, she grew up in a social and familial climate very favorable to her creativity. She won several prizes at the Jocs Florals (*Juegos). The physical and emotional trauma of the Civil War influenced her work, but her books are still characterized by a great tenderness and humanism. She also wrote biographies of important Catalan women, such as the writer and feminist, Dolors *Monserdà de Macià.

BIBLIOGRAPHY

Primary Texts

Cançons de Setembre. Barcelona: La Revista, 1936.
La Carena. Barcelona: Altes, 1933.
Poemes a la filla. Barcelona: Altes, 1949.
Poemes de la fam. Barcelona: Barcino, 1952.
Quatre dones catalanes. Barcelona: Fundació Salvador Vives Casajuana, 1972.

Criticism

Manent, Albert. "Roser Matheu: entre la cultura del vuit-cents i la del nou-cents." *Serra d'Or* (March 1983): 23–29.

Kathleen McNerney

MATOS FRAGOSO, Juan de (1608?, Alvito, Portugal–1689?, Madrid), lyric poet and dramatist. After studying in Evora, he spent most of his life in Madrid. His first known composition is a sonnet lamenting the death of *Pérez Montalbán. Matos Fragoso wrote plays in collaboration with *Moreto, *Cáncer y Velasco, and *Diamante and also reworked others' themes within the structure of Calderonian drama, to which cycle he belongs. Examples of this work include *La venganza en el despeño y tirano de Navarra* (Revenge in the Fall and Tyrant of Navarre) and *El sabio en su retiro y villano en su rincón* (The Scholar in His Retreat and the Peasant in His Haven), where echoes of Lope de *Vega and of *Rojas Zorrilla's *García del Castañar* abound. Noteworthy religious works are *El Job de las mujeres* (The Women's Job), *Santa Isabel, reina de Hungría* (St. Elizabeth, Queen of Hungary) and *San Félix de Cantalicio y San Gil de Portugal*—written with Cáncer and Moreto. *El yerro del entendido* (The Wise Man's Error) repeats the story of *Cervantes's *El curioso impertinente. El marido de su madre* (His Mother's Husband) explores the atmosphere of incest in the life and legend of St. Gregory. Matos also composed many historical dramas and dramas of intrigue. One of the latter, titled *Riesgos y alivios de un manto* (Risks and Comforts of a Cape) boasts superb versification.

Despite their dependence on earlier works, Matos Fragoso's plays do exhibit fine plot development and are of a high lyric quality. Some of his plays left a lasting mark on the taste and literature of his day and subsequent eras, such as his *Traidor contra su sangre* (Traitor to His Own Blood), which inspired the Duque de *Rivas's *El moro expósito* (The Foundling Moor). Matos Fragoso also wrote many **entremeses* and various lyric works such as *Fábula burlesca de Apolo y Leucotoe* (1652; Burlesque Story of Apollo and Leucothea), and the *Fábula de Eco y Narciso* (1655; Story of Echo and Narcissus). *See also* Theater in Spain.

BIBLIOGRAPHY

Primary Texts

BAE 47 contains 6 plays.

El ingrato agradecido. Ed. H. C. Heaton. New York: Hispanic Society, 1926.

Spanish Drama of the Golden Age: A Catalogue of the Comedia Collection of the University of Pennsylvania Libraries. New Haven, CT: Research Publications, 1971.

Frances Bell Exum

MATURANA DE GUTIÉRREZ, Vicenta (1793, Cádiz–1856, Alcalá de Henares, Madrid), novelist and poet. Her life was not an easy one. The daughter of a high army officer, at age four she moved with her family to Madrid and was educated there. Her father died during the Independency War, and soon after, her mother also died. The queen was her protector, so she was named keeper of the queen's wardrobe. In 1820, she married a Carlist officer who died on the battlefield in 1830. After the Carlists lost the war she moved with her children to France, struggling to survive. She returned to Spain in 1850. In 1825 her first novel, *Teodoro o el huérfano agradecido* (Teodoro or the Grateful Orphan) was published anonymously; in 1829 a second one, *Sofía y Enrique* appeared, followed by *Amar después de la muerte* (Love after Death). The introduction to *Sofía y Enrique* states that "she does not want to encourage such an exclusive desire for reading among women readers that would cause them to forget their duties as wives and mothers,'' but soon after she invites women to cultivate their talents and become rivals of the famous French female writers. She also wrote excellent poetry, *Ensayos poéticos de* . . . (1828; Poetic Exercises of . . .) and *Poesías* (1859; Poems). Her poetry embraces a wide range of topics and uses many different meters. According to Serrano Sanz, ''she had an exuberant fantasy and a remarkable lyrical sense and her poems . . . lack any kind of conventionalism.''

BIBLIOGRAPHY

Primary Texts

Ensayos poéticos. Madrid: Vergés, 1828. Also, Paris: Lecointa y Lasserra, 1841. Also, Madrid: Aguado, 1856.

Poesías. Madrid: Aguado, 1859.

Sofía y Enrique. 2 vols. Madrid: Villalpando, 1829.

Teodoro o el huérfano agradecido. Madrid: Verges, 1825.

Criticism

Díaz Plaja, Guillermo. *Historia general de las literatures hispánicas*. 6 vols. Barcelona: n.p., 1949–57.

Ferreras, J. I. *Los orígenes de la novela decimonónica 1800–1830*. Madrid: Taurus, 1973.

Serrano Sanz, Manuel. *Apuntes para una biblioteca de escritoras españolas desde el año 1401 al 1833*. Madrid: Sucesores de Rivadeneyra, 1905.

Women Writers of Spain. An Annotated Bio-Bibliography. Eds. Carolyn Galerstein and Kathleen McNerney. Westport, CT: Greenwood, 1986.

Cristina Enríquez

MATUTE, Ana Mariá (1926, Barcelona–), Spanish novelist and short story writer. Matute belongs to the Mid-Century Generation of novelists, so dubbed because of the publication of their first works around 1950, a group characterized from their viewing social, political and moral issues from the perspective of critical realism. While basically realistic, Matute's prose is heavily overlaid with lyrical elements and powerful metaphors and employs devices such as interior monologue and stream of consciousness more often found in modernist and experimental fiction. Her first novel, *Los Abel* (1948; The Abel Family), updates the Cain-Abel theme, as does her masterful short novel, *Fiesta al noroeste* (1952; Celebration in the Northwest [Cemetery]), winner of the Café Gijón Prize. The Cain-Abel archetype (conflict between brothers) appears in various forms in most of Matute's novels as a symbol of the Spanish Civil War, which also divided families and produced fratricidal encounters. Other constant themes of her work are betrayal, solitude, unhappiness, alienation, hypocrisy, rites of passage, time, and the re-creation of various mythical and biblical themes. Most of her books focus upon children or adolescents who must cross the threshold into adulthood willy-nilly, with all that this rite of passage implies. *Los hijos muertos* (1958; The Dead Children) won the significant Critics' Prize. Like *En esta tierra* (1955; In This Land—originally titled *Las luciérnagas* [The Fireflies], censored and rewritten), *Los hijos muertos* is an attempt to understand some of the forces in conflict in the Spanish Civil War and to analyze the loss of ideals, of youth and hope that the war entailed.

Matute's trilogy, "Los mercaderes" (The Moneychangers), is structured upon a basic assumption of the division of humanity in two groups, the preponderant "mercaderes" for whom everything has its price, and the few "heroes" who are willing to sacrifice everything in the name of an ideal. The conflict between materialism and idealism, another basic constant of Matute's fiction, appears even in her children's literature. The three novels of the trilogy are thematically related and have a few common characters, but can be read independently as there are no connections between the plots. *Primera memoria* (1959; First Memoirs), winner of the Nadal Prize, is cast as the retrospective diary of Matia, who looks backward from an adult perspective upon her cowardly betrayal of her friend Manuel when both were adolescents living in one of the Balearic Islands. Told against the background of the distant battles of the Civil War, with the encounters between juvenile gangs in the foreground, the novel provides a kind of Civil War in miniature at the same time that it symbolically evokes Peter's denial of Christ (the biblical allusion is a favorite device of Matute, whose readers—with their common religious training—could be counted upon to perceive the parallels). *Los soldados lloran de noche* (1964; The Soldiers Cry in the Night) concentrates upon Manuel, omitting most of the major characters of the first part of the trilogy. Released after imprisonment for a crime he did not commit because he has inherited a fortune he morally abhors, Manuel decides to adopt the already lost cause of a communist organizer, Jeza, and carry out his mission to the mainland in the closing weeks of the Republic's resistance to the Franco army, a suicidal voyage somewhat redeemed by its aura of pure, hopeless idealism. *La trampa* (1969; The Trap) returns to Matia some three decades later to reconstruct the bitter story of the narrator-protagonist's frustrated life, her inability (and that of other characters) to escape life's "traps," and the final defeat of idealism. Employing multiple perspectives, this most disillusioned of Matute's novels portrays the existential inauthenticity of each narrative consciousness and analyzes the way in which human weaknesses may trap each one, disguising personal revenge as "necessary" political assassination, lust as charity, and exploitation as tradition.

In *La torre vigía* (1971; The Watchtower), Matute combines the ambient of the novels of chivalry with a first-person narration and her enduring socio-political concerns with experimental novelistic techniques to present a unique and somewhat disconcerting tale set in the tenth century somewhere in Central Europe. Themes of the knightly quest and chivalric honor or idealism are juxtaposed to sordid poverty, fanatic superstitions and prejudice, and sexual depravity and violence which ultimately lead the young hero (like Manuel of the trilogy) to opt for suicidal purity rather than a life of war, oppression and loss of ideals. A similar work (to be set also in the tenth century) was announced several times with the title "Olvidado Rey Gudú" (Forgotten King Gudu), but it has never appeared. Matute's deteriorating health makes it unlikely that this novel will ever be published.

Matute is well known for various collections of short studies treating similar subjects: the unusual, lyrical and sometimes grotesque vignettes of *Los niños tontos* (1957; The Stupid Children), the backwardness and poverty of rural areas depicted in *Historias de la Artámila* (1961; Stories of Artamila), the focus upon children and adolescents caught in the cycle of poverty and despair in the more varied tales of *El tiempo* (1957; Time). She has also written several books for children of various ages and takes pride in her prizes won for juvenile fiction, for example, *El polizón del "Ulises"* (1965; The Cabin Boy of the *Ulysses*).

BIBLIOGRAPHY

Primary Texts

A la mitad del camino. Barcelona: Rocas, 1961.
Algunos muchachos. Barcelona: Destino, 1968.
Obra completa. 5 vols. Barcelona: Destino, 1976.
Pequeño teatro. Barcelona: Planeta, 1954.
El río. Barcelona: Argos, 1963.
Tres y un sueño. Barcelona: Destino, 1961.

English Translations

Awakening, tr. James Mason (London: Hutchinson, 1963), and *School of the Sun*, tr. Elaine Kerrigan (New York: Pantheon Books, 1963), are British and American renderings of *Primera memoria*.

Criticism

Brown, Joan L. "Unidad y diversidad en *Los mercaderes*, de Ana María Matute." In *Novelistas femeninas de la postguerra española*. Ed. Janet Pérez. Madrid: Porrúa, 1983. 19–32.
Díaz, Janet. *Ana Mariá Matute*. New York: Twayne, 1971.
Doyle, Michael Scott. "*Sólo un pie descalzo*." *Latin America in Books* 7.2 (July 1984): 24–25.
El Saffar, Ruth. "En busca de Edén: Consideraciones sobre la obra de Ana María Matute." *Revista Iberoamericana* 47.116–17 (July-December 1981): 223–31.
Jones, Margaret E. W. "Religious Motifs and Biblical Allusions in the Works of Ana María Matute." *Hispania* 51.3 (September 1968): 416–23.
———. *The World of Ana María Matute*. Lexington: U of Kentucky P, 1970.
Thomas, Michael D. "The Rite of Initiation in Matute's *Primera memoria*," *KRQ* 25.2 (1978): 153–64.

Margaret E. W. Jones

MAURA, Antonio (1853, Palma de Mallorca–1925, Torrelodones), politician, jurist and orator. He came to Madrid in 1868 in the middle of the revolution. At first he was a member of the Liberal party, but later on he became a Conservative and a leader of that party, after his famous speech in which he claimed that the revolution should originate at the top. Maura was justly proud of his oratorical skills. *Azorín stated in *Parlamentarismo español* that Maura was "an artist conscientious and reflective about elocution and gesture, he is flexible, delicate and knows how to emphasize . . . and how to be ironical and energetic."

Maura's entrance speech to the *Academia Española was titled *La oratoria como género literario* (Oratory as a Literary Genre).

BIBLIOGRAPHY

Criticism

Castillo, J. R. *Antonio Maura: Treinta y cinco años de vida pública.* Madrid: n.p., 1953.
Catalá y Gávila. *Antonio Maura. Ideario político.* Madrid: n.p., 1953.
Pérez Delgado, R. *Antonio Maura.* Madrid: Tebas, 1974.
Sanz Aguero, Marcos. *Antonio Maura.* Madrid: Círculo de Amigos de la Historia, 1976.

Isabel McSpadden

MAURA, Honorio (1886, Madrid–1936, Madrid), Spanish dramatist. An aristocrat educated in Switzerland and Germany as well as Spain, Maura traveled through South America before deciding, upon his return to Spain, to devote himself to the theater. As a political conservative, he was a victim of the social unrest and class-motivated assassinations around the time of the outbreak of the Civil War in 1936. As a dramatist, his strong point is his skillful handling of language, dialogue and situations. With refinement and occasional elegant irony, he treats the world of the aristocracy, sometimes somewhat frivolously, sometimes with a slight moralizing intent. His works are basically intended only as entertainment, and he succeeded in maintaining the interest and patronage of the theater-going public. Better works include *Cuento de hadas* (Fairy Tale), *El balcón de la felicidad* (The Balcony of Happiness), *Hay que ser modernos* (It's Necessary to be Modern), *La noche loca* (Crazy Night), *La condesita y su bailarín* (The Little Countess and Her Dancer), *Como la hiedra al tronco* (Like Ivy on the Tree Trunk), and *¡Me lo daba el corazón!* (My Heart Told Me So!). He collaborated with Gregorio *Martínez Sierra on *Mary la insoportable* (Unbearable Mary), *Susana tiene un secreto* (Susan Has a Secret), and *Julieta compra un hijo* (Julie Buys a Son).

MAURA Y HERRERA, Julia (1910, Madrid–1970, Madrid), Spanish dramatist. Maura belonged to a distinguished, aristocratic family; her grandfather had served Alfonso XII as prime minister, while her father, the Duke of Maura, was a well-known historian and writer, and her uncle Honorio, a dramatist. Julia Maura has the distinction of being the most frequently produced female playwright in post-war Spain, with eighteen comedies on the stage in slightly over two decades. Her works are usually traditional in technique and fairly conservative in ideology, dealing with stock themes such as honor and public opinion. Characters are usually drawn from the upper class and often treated with sentimentality. Her plays include *La mentira del silencio* (1944; The Lie of Silence), *Siempre* (1952; Always), *Chocolate a la española* (1953; Chocolate, Spanish Style), *La eterna doña Juana* (1954: The Eternal Lady Juana), *La riada* (1956; The Torrent), and *Jaque a la juventud* (1965; Checkmate to Youth). This final work seems to indicate a change of direction to a new and more contemporary focus and an emphasis upon the new materialism and changing morality in Spain.

BIBLIOGRAPHY

Primary Texts

Estos son mis artículos. Madrid: Aguilar, 1953.
Historias crueles. Madrid: Aguilar, 1964.
Jaque a la juventud. Madrid: Alfil, 1965.

Criticism

O'Connor, Patricia W. "¿Quiénes son las dramaturgas contemporáneas, y qué han escrito?" *Estreno* 10.2 (1984): 9–12.
Patterson, Mamie Salva. *La mujer-víctima en el teatro de autoras españolas del siglo XX*. Diss., U of Kentucky, 1979.

Janet Pérez

MAURI, Juan María (1772, Málaga–1845, Paris), poet. Educated abroad, he was an *afrancesado* (French sympathizer) in the War of Independence. Subsequently, he emigrated to France. His original poetry holds merit, and his translations of Spanish poetry into French, found in *Espagne poétique* (1826–27; Poetic Spain), are inspired.

BIBLIOGRAPHY

Primary Texts

Espagne poétique. Paris: Mongie, 1826–27.
Poesías. In BAE 29 and 67.

MAYÁNS Y SISCAR, Gregorio (1699, Oliva, Valencia–1781, Valencia), literary critic and scholar. Trained in law in Valencia and Salamanca, Mayáns y Siscar was an official in the Royal Library from 1733 to 1739 before returning to his native Oliva, where he maintained an active correspondence with most contemporary literary figures. He is one of the best examples of eighteenth-c. erudition through meticulous scholarship, care for detail and insatiable desire to reform through critical thought. He dedicated most of his attention to the study and editing of the major *Siglo de Oro writers: *Oración en alabanza de las obras de D. Saavedra Fajardo* (1725; Oration in Praise of the Works of Saavedra Fajardo), later also included in his *Ensayos oratorios* (1739; Oratory Essays); *Orígenes de la lengua española* (1737; Origins of the Spanish Language), in which Juan de *Valdés's *Diálogo de la lengua* (Dialogue of Language) first appeared. Mayáns y Siscar edited *Nebrija's *Reglas de Ortografía* (1735 and 1765; Orthography Rules) and *Organum Rhetoricum* (1774; Rhetoric) and published *Obras y traducciones poéticas de Fr. Luis de León* (1761; Works and Poetic Translations of Fr. Luis de León). In 1737, as a prologue to his edition of the *Quijote*, Mayáns wrote *Vida de Miguel de Cervantes* (Life of Miguel de *Cervantes), which was the first biography of the Spanish master. Mayáns's extensive work on the literary production of Lluís *Vives was published posthumously by his brother, Juan Antonio, in eight volumes (1782–90). Besides studying the Spanish masters, Mayáns published some original work: *Oración* *que exhorta a seguir la verdadera idea de la elocuencia española* (1727; Exhortation of the True Spanish Eloquence); *El orador Christiano* (1737; The Christian Orator); *Retórica* (1757; Rhetoric); and *Gramática latina* (1768; Latin Grammar). His copious amount of correspondence is beginning to come to light through the publications from the city of Oliva. In his literary polemics, Mayáns used, among others, the pseudonyms Justo Vindicio, Plácido Veranio, Aulo Amnes, Miguel Sánchez, Gerónimo Grayas, and Vigilancio Cosmolitano. His autobiography in Latin, *Gregorii Mayansii, Generosi Valentini, Vita* (1756; The Life of the Generous Valencian, Gregorio Mayáns), provides a view of the eighteenth-c. intellectual life and its participants.

BIBLIOGRAPHY

Primary Texts

Gregorii Mayansii, Generosi Valentini, Vita. Valencia: Ayuntamiento de Oliva, 1974.
Mayáns y Burriel. Valencia: Ayuntamiento de Oliva, 1973.
Mayáns y Marti. Valencia: Ayuntamiento de Oliva, 1975.
Mayáns y Los Médicos. Valencia: Ayuntamiento de Oliva, 1972.
Mayáns y Nebot. Valencia: Ayuntamiento de Oliva, 1975.
Vida de Miguel de Cervantes. Madrid: Clásicos Castellanos, 1972.

Criticism

Gutiérrez, Jesús. "Dos décadas de estudios mayansianos." *Dieciocho* 5 (1982): 187–92.
Mestre, Antonio. *Ilustración y reforma de la Iglesia. Pensamiento Político-religioso de Don Gregorio Mayáns y Siscar (1699–1781).* Valencia: Ayuntamiento de Oliva, 1968.
———. *Historia, fueros y actitudes políticas. Mayáns y la historiografía del XVIII.* Valencia: Ayuntamiento de Oliva, 1970.
———. "El descubrimiento de Fr. Luis de León en el siglo XVIII." *BH* 83 (1981): 5–64.

Carmen Chaves McClendon

MAYORAL DÍAZ, Marina (1942, Mondoñedo, Lugo–), Galician and Castilian critic, novelist and short story writer. Mayoral teaches Spanish literature at Madrid's Universidad Complutense and is considered an authority on the poetry of Rosalía de *Castro, although she has also published critical works on textual analysis and (in collaboration with her husband Andrés Amorós and the dramatist Francisco Nieva) theatrical analysis. Her novels reflect the Galician ambient with its atmosphere of legend, folklore, superstition and mystery, but also treat the conflict between this atmosphere and current trends, whether introduced by returning Galicians who have lived elsewhere or suffered by those Galicians who leave the region to reside in Madrid or other more modern areas. Her first novel, *Cándida otra vez* (1979; Candida Again), is set at approximately the time of composition, during the period of transition from the Franco era to the new democratic regime. Mayoral explores the ambivalence with which supposedly liberal "opposition" intellectuals experience the passing of the old regime, whose disappearance leaves them without a cause. Historical and political change are interwoven with cultural modifications, with an implied warning that not all that is new is good, and that caution should be exercised before sacrificing all tradition in the name of progress. Providing the narrative interest is a mystery related to the name and character of the protagonist. Mayoral employs the mystery-story format and structure in several of her subsequent works. *Al otro lado* (1981; On the Other Side) depicts several members of an extended Galician clan living in Madrid, where much of the closeness and communication of the past have been lost, and the younger generation falls prey to contemporary dangers including drugs, homosexuality, isolation, crime, depression and suicide. The title alludes to the world ''beyond'' the visible one, including areas of spiritual experience, precognition, extra-sensory perception, déjà vu, and beyond death. *La única libertad* (1982; The Only Freedom) is a semi-gothic tale set in a crumbling rural manor in which the terminally ill protagonist attempts to write the history of La Braña, the family home, and in so doing, to assert her own identity vis-à-vis the ancestral past, thereby establishing a kind of existential liberty within her limited situation.

Contra muerte y amor (1985; Against Love and Death) is Mayoral's fourth novel, three intertwined stories of love and separation, set once again in the north of Spain, in a semi-rural area torn between old ways and new. The protagonist is a ''modern'' woman, a television journalist, whose father is a retired boxer living in a Cantabrian fishing village. The novel is realistic in style, symbolic in intent, depicting not only the conflict between past and present, but the endless succession of seasons, of generations, of death and renewal via the trials and triumphs of specific individuals.

BIBLIOGRAPHY

Primary Texts

Cándida otra vez. Barcelona: Pozanco, 1979.
Contra muerte y amor. Madrid: Cátedra, 1985.
La única libertad. Madrid: Cátedra, 1982.

Janet Pérez

MEDINA, Francisco de (1544–1615?,?), professor, poet. He taught Latin at the U of Osuna. A member of the *Escuela sevillana, he composed the prologue to Fernando de *Herrera's *Anotaciones a Garcilaso* (1580; Annotations to Garcilaso); it is actually a poetic manifesto for Herrera. Most of Medina's work is translation of Latin authors. He did write an ''Oda a Garcilaso'' (Ode to Garcilaso).

BIBLIOGRAPHY

Primary Text

Obras de Garci Lasso de la Vega con anotaciones de Francisco de Herrera. . . . Seville: n.p., 1580.

MEDINA, Pedro de (1493, Medina Sidonia–1567, Seville), cosmographer, astronomer, moralist, and chronicler. As tutor in the ducal house of Medina Sidonia, Medina had access to the library and traveled in the entourage of Alfonso de Guzmán, both of which afforded him both theoretical and practical knowledge in cosmography. His scientific writings are based on the Ptolemaic system and, hence, are a repository of traditional ideas on the universe. He officially embarked on his career as a cosmographer in 1538 with his *Libro de cosmographía* (Book of Cosmography). Dedicated to the emperor, it earned him a pilot's license, yet he was not appointed in the Casa de Contratación, the crown's agent for expeditions to the Indies. His *Arte de Navegar* (1545; Art of Navigation), with numerous editions in French, Italian, German, Dutch, and English, was dedicated to Prince Philip to further his petition as royal cosmographer. Of a different nature is his *Libro de grandezas y cosas memorables de España* (1548; Grandeurs and Memorable Things of Spain), a travelogue and guide to Spain and Portugal. In the midst of his disputes and rivalries with officials in the Casa de Contratación, he wrote his *Libro de la verdad* (1555; Book on Truth). The *Suma de cosmographía* is a digest of his Art of Navigation; its clear and simple presentation would indicate that it was directed to the layman rather than the professional. Oddly enough, it was never printed, which, according to some, was due to the recent circulation of the theories of Copernicus. Medina never realized his aspirations to the Casa de Contratación, yet he remained active in the conferences of the Royal Council of the Indies. His last work was the *Crónica de los Duques de Medina Sidonia* (1561; Chronicle of the Dukes of Medina Sidonia). *See also* Catechetical Literature; Humanism; Renaissance; Siglo de Oro.

BIBLIOGRAPHY

Primary Texts

Crónica de los Duques de Medina Sidonia. Colección de documentos inéditos para la historia de España, vol. 39. Madrid: n.p., 1861.

Libro de cosmographía. A Navigator's Universe. The Libro de Cosmographía of 1538. Facs. ed. Tr. Ursula Lamb. Chicago: U of Chicago P, 1972.

Obras de Pedro de Medina. Ed. Angel González Palencia. Madrid: Clásicos Españoles, 1944. (Includes the *Libro de las grandezas* and the *Libro de la verdad*.)

Suma de cosmographía. Ed. Juan Fernández Jiménez. Valencia: Albatrós, 1980.

English Translation

See *A Navigator's Universe*, Primary Texts.

Criticism

Fernández Jiménez, Juan. "La obra de Pedro de Medina (ensayo bibliográfico)." *Archivo Hispalense* 180 (1976): 113–28.

Lamb, Ursula. "The Cosmographies of Pedro de Medina." *Homenaje a Rodríguez Moñino*. Madrid: Castalia, 1966.

Toro Ruiz, Luis. "Notas biográficas de Pedro de Medina." *REH* (Madrid) 2 (1936): 31–38.
See also Lamb and Fernández Jiménez, Primary Texts.

Porter Conerly

MEDINILLA, Baltasar Elisio de (1585, Toledo–1620, Toledo), poet of the school of Lope de *Vega. He was assassinated by one Jerónimo de Andrada y Rivadeneyra. He wrote *a lo divino* verse, a narrative poem inspired by his country home titled *Descripción de Buenavista* (Description of Buenavista), and a *Discurso sobre el remedio de las cosas de Toledo* (1617; Discourse on the Remedy of Matters in Toledo). His *Limpia concepción de la Virgen Señora Nuestra* (1617; Immaculate Conception of Our Lady the Virgin) is a theological religious poem in octaves.

BIBLIOGRAPHY

Primary Text

Limpia concepción de la Virgen Señora Nuestra. Madrid: Martín, 1617.

Criticism

San Román y Fernández, F. de B. de. *Elisio de Medinilla y su personalidad literaria.* Toledo: Peláez, 1921.

MEDIO, Dolores (1914, Oviedo–), Spanish novelist, winner of several prestigious literary prizes. Her work is relatively traditional and with many conventional aspects of nineteenth-c. novelists. Medio's best novels to date include *Funcionario público* (1956; Public Servant), *El pez sigue flotando* (1959; The Fish Continues Afloat), *Diario de una maestra* (1961; A Teacher's Diary), and the trilogy *Los que vamos a pie* (1963; We, Pedestrians).

Funcionario público, set in Madrid, describes the monotonous existence of Pablo Marín, a telegraph operator in the Spanish capital. His mediocre, empty life acquires new meaning when he finds papers belonging to Natalie Blay and sets out to locate her. This unknown woman becomes the symbol of all the things he wants but will not obtain. The novel portrays vividly the myriad of problems encountered by Spaniards after the Civil War: lack of housing, shortage of everything from food to bathrooms, numerous economic problems, and exploitation of the middle and lower classes.

El pez sigue flotando introduces several characters living in the same Madrid apartment house. The short chapters portray slices of life, allowing the author to experiment with point of view. The well-done collage effect facilitates social criticism, as the author describes the social and economic conditions of the tenants who are, to an extent, a microcosm of the Spanish nation.

Diario de una maestra, an autobiographical work, reflects the author's teaching experience in Nava (a small Asturian town near Oviedo), a position she lost because her teaching methodology was too revolutionary. A third-person narrative is utilized, notwithstanding the title, lending a more objective perspective to the townspeople's negative response to the innovative teacher.

BIBLIOGRAPHY

Primary Texts

Bibiana. Madrid: Bullón, 1963.
Diario de una maestra. Barcelona: Destino, 1961.
El fabuloso imperio de Juan sin tierra. Barcelona: Plaza y Janés, 1981.
Farsa de verano. Madrid: Espasa Calpe, 1973.
Funcionario público. Barcelona: Destino, 1956.
Nosotros, los Rivero. Barcelona: Destino, 1953.
La otra circunstancia. Barcelona: Destino, 1972.
El pez sigue flotando. Barcelona: Destino, 1959.

Criticism

Díaz, Janet. "Three New Works by Dolores Medio." *Romance Notes* 11.2 (Winter 1969): 244–50.
Jones, Margaret E. W. *Dolores Medio*. New York: Twayne, 1974. In English.

Genaro J. Pérez

MEDRANO, Francisco de (1570, Seville–1607, Seville), poet. Of a comfortable background, he joined the Society of Jesus in 1584, but left the order in 1602. His extant poetry includes fifty-two sonnets and thirty-four odes. Dámaso *Alonso has called Medrano the finest translator of Latin poetry into Castilian after Luis de *León.

BIBLIOGRAPHY

Primary Text

Vida y obra de Medrano. Ed., study D. Alonso and (vol. 2 only) S. Reckert. 2 vols. Madrid: CSIC, 1948, 1958.

Criticism

See Primary Text, Alonso.

MELÉNDEZ VALDÉS, Juan, pseudonym Batilo (1754, Ribera del Fresno, Extremadura–1817, Montpellier), poet. It is Batilo who best expressed the strains of lyrical sensuality so characteristic of eighteenth-c. poets. His delicate use of language and refined aestheticism have earned him a high place in the canon of Spanish poetry, and his deep commitment to progress and reform makes him an outstanding figure in the period known as the Enlightenment.

Meléndez spent his first thirteen years in Extremadura in the humble family dwelling before being sent off to Madrid in 1767 to study philosophy with some Dominican friars under the guidance of an uncle. In Madrid he began to compose verses. By all accounts he was a bright, tender, peaceful, kind, and talented adolescent, qualities he developed further during his studies at the famous Reales Estudios de San Isidro, whose professors formed the core of neo-classical Madrid. Meléndez was encouraged to proceed to the U, so in 1772 he went to Salamanca to continue his study of the classics and to take up a new interest, law. By his own statement, his readings were not particularly structured, but they were broad, and he built a solid base of knowledge which he would draw upon time and again throughout his career. In 1773, as a second-year student, he met José *Cadalso, the soldier-poet recently transferred to Salamanca with his regiment. Cadalso, at thirty-two, seemed an odd companion for the young Meléndez, but their mutual passion for poetry sealed a friendship which was both close and productive. Cadalso's worldliness, charm, and knowledge of literature fascinated Meléndez, who in turn brought a quick mind, a sensitive demeanor, and a thirst for knowledge to the relationship. Meléndez's intellectual development continued through contact with local poets (Father Diego *González, José *Iglesias de la Casa, etc.) who came to be known as the Salamancan School (*Escuelo Salmantina). In 1775 Meléndez received his university degree.

Soon thereafter, Meléndez suffered a physical collapse from which it took him months to recover, but in that same year—1776—a second important friendship (this one with *Jovellanos) began and was carried on exclusively through correspondence until the two met in person five years later. Jovellanos served him as spiritual and moral tutor, encouraging him to apply his talents to worthy projects and to avoid wallowing in emotional excess (a very real danger: Meléndez was deeply affected by the death of his father in 1774 and devastated emotionally by the death of his brother, to whom he was very close, in 1777). He decided on a university career. Soon he was teaching law and humanities at Salamanca while continuing to develop his skills as a poet. He entered the poetry competition announced by the *Academia Española in 1779 and his entry, "Batilo. Égloga en alabanza de la vida del campo" (Batilo. Eclogue in Praise of Country Life), won first prize when the results were announced in March 1780. The poem was subsequently published by the academy. The following year Meléndez won another competition—this time for a professorship in classical languages in Salamanca—and he was invited to Madrid (where he could finally meet Jovellanos) to read a poem at the prestigious Fine Arts Academy of San Fernando. His composition, "A la gloria de las artes" (To the Glory of the Arts) increased his rapidly rising fame as a poet. In 1782 he married, and in early 1783 he was awarded his doctor of law degree from Salamanca. Slowly he became involved in University affairs, working actively on projects designed to improve the quality of services offered by the school, but his work enmeshed him in intramural political squabbles. His work as a writer continued, although a play, *Las bodas de Camacho el rico* (1785; The Wedding of the Wealthy Camacho), while highly regarded by his academic friends, was a dismal failure when staged in Madrid.

The first volume of Meléndez's poetry was published in 1785, and it achieved immediate success. Meléndez was credited with bringing about nothing less than a renaissance in Spanish poetry. Further poems followed, although, surprisingly, his output declined. Tired of teaching and even more so of the internecine fighting at the University, he accepted a position as magistrate in Zaragoza and moved there in 1789. There his enlightened sense of progress, justice and humanity was amply demonstrated in his excellent work, and his reputation as a brilliant and sensitive jurist grew. He moved to Valladolid in 1791 where he advanced his views and worked on several projects (he edited an encyclopedic journal, for example, but it was never published because of problems with censors). His verses became more openly philosophical and even political, as Meléndez aligned himself more and more with Manuel Godoy, the powerful prime minister whose later downfall would have a serious impact on Meléndez's life. But for now, Meléndez's career was on the rise. In 1797 he published a new three-volume collection of *Poesías* (Poems) and in that same year moved to Madrid to take up residence as district attorney. The *Poems* gained him a position in the Academia Española.

Meléndez's high status in Madrid was short-lived. The political intrigues which forced Jovellanos out of the capital in 1798 affected those closely associated with him as well (Meléndez visited Jovellanos twice a day); in August, Meléndez was relieved of his duties and sent to Medina del Campo, where he did charitable work until 1801, when he was once again moved, this time to Zamora. He did not understand the reasons for this harsh treatment until months later, at which time he wrote a defense and an explanation of the episode (it had to do with trumped-up charges involving some of his friends), achieved vindication, and was reinstated in his job. Political times were still difficult, though, so in 1802 he decided to return to Salamanca, where he spent the next six years quietly organizing his huge library.

The Napoleonic invasion of 1808 changed Meléndez's life, as it changed those of all contemporary intellectuals. His patriotic call-to-arms, "Alarma española" (1808; Spanish Alarm), betrayed his initial opposition to the French. This opposition became a forced and grudging silence, but it gradually developed into a sincere respect for José, the "intruder king," whose government promised to institute precisely those reforms so coveted by Meléndez and his enlightened peers. Meléndez became a member of José I's Council of State in 1809, a seeming capitulation to the enemy which severely strained his relations with his friends Jovellanos and *Quintana, both of whom had chosen to oppose the new regime rather than to collaborate with it. Meléndez's participation in the government (he was named to several other posts) unfairly earned him a reputation as a traitorous "afrancesado." To the contrary, he was a brilliant, enlightened, reform-minded individual who wished progress for his country. Ferdinand VII, of course, banished both liberal patriots and enlightened collaborators when he returned to power in 1813, and Meléndez was forced into exile in France. He knew, as he crossed the border, that he would never see his homeland again. After several years of ill health, forced moves, and severe economic straits, he died in Montpellier in 1817.

Meléndez Valdés was an avid reader, a disciple of Spanish poets and European philosophers. He was a sensitive poet who elevated Spanish verse to its highest level since the *Siglo de Oro. His poems are on the one hand graceful, charming, seductive, and witty—as in the cycles of odes called "La paloma de Filis" (Phyllis's Dove), "Los besos de amor" (Kisses of Love) and "Galatea o la ilusión del canto'' (Galatea, or Song's Illusion)—and on the other, thoughtful, philosophical, and frequently infused with the spirit of melancholic desolation so characteristic of *Romanticism. Sebold has identified Meléndez's term ''fastidio universal'' (universal weariness) from ''A Jovino: el melancólico'' (1794; To Jovino: The Melancholic) as the first true expression in Spanish of Romantic *angst*. Meléndez, called ''sweet Batilo'' by friends and critics, has long been accused of being a languorous and weak poet, whose excessive use of diminutives and delicate love themes indicates a flaccid nature. This characterization distorts the real Meléndez, a survivor and a solid thinker, a serious man who chose to express himself poetically in simple, clear terms. His prose essays, *Discursos forenses* (published in 1821; Forensic Discourses), reveal his total commitment to the advancement of Spain's social, legal and philosophical institutions. His lifelong goal was to drag Spain out of the lethargy and backwardness it suffered. His poems and legal writings served this end, and even his most erotic poems carry his readers toward nature, virtue, harmony and order (Horaces's *utile dulci*, a concept avidly defended by the neo-classicists). The great variety of his writings, his superb poetic control, and the forceful expression of his three major themes (as identified by Polt)—nature, philosophy, patriotism—make him the greatest poet of his generation.

BIBLIOGRAPHY

Primary Texts

Obras en verso. Ed. J.H.R. Polt and Jorge Demerson. 2 vols. Oviedo: Centro de Estudios del Siglo XVIII, 1981–83.

Poesías. Ed. Pedro Salinas. Madrid: La Lectura, 1925.

Poesías. Ed. Emilio Palacios. Madrid: Alhambra, 1979.

Poesías selectas. Ed. John H. R. Polt and Georges Demerson. Madrid: Castalia, 1981.

Criticism

Cox, R. Merritt. *Juan Meléndez Valdés*. TWAS 302. New York: Twayne, 1974.

Demerson, Georges. *Don Juan Meléndez Valdés y su tiempo*. Madrid: Taurus, 1971.

Forcione, Alban. ''Meléndez Valdés and the *Essay on Man*.'' *HR* 34 (1966): 291–306.

Froldi, Rinaldo. *Un poeta illuminista: Meléndez Valdés*. Milan: Cisalpino, 1967.

Polt, John H. R. *Batilo*. Oviedo: Centro de Estudios del Siglo XVIII, 1987.

Polt, John H. R. ''La imitación anacreóntica en Meléndez Valdés.'' *HR* 47 (1979): 193–206.

Sebold, Russell P. ''Sobre el nombre español del dolor romántico.'' In *El rapto de la mente*. Madrid: Prensa Española, 1970. 123–37.

David Thatcher Gies

MELLO, Francisco Manuel de (1609, Lisbon–1666, Lisbon), talented bilingual moralist, prose and poetry writer, historian. His was a tumultuous life. He served Spain as a soldier in Flanders and at one point was imprisoned because of the rebellion of Portugal, which at that time was part of Spain. Later, he was exiled to Brazil, in part for amorous complications, but after five years was pardoned, and returned to Portugal to fulfill various sensitive diplomatic missions. He wrote in Portuguese and Spanish. Mello's collection of poetry, *Obras métricas* (1665; Metrical Works), uses the pseudonym Melodino and follows the **culturanismo* style of *Góngora. Divided into three sections, the first and third are in Spanish, while the second is in Portuguese. Of more interest is *Hospital de las letras* (1657; Hospital of Letters), which contains some of the best literary criticism of the day.

Mello's work on the Catalan rebellion, published under the pseudonym Clemente Libertino, is *Historia de los movimientos, y separación de Cataluña* (1645; History of the Movements and Separation of Cataluna). Its topic is the first year of the war, 1640. Literary aesthetics prevail over historical accuracy, however, for Mello strives to produce certain reactions in his public; images and metaphors are used quite effectively to this end.

Mello also composed two amusing *picaresque works: *Relogios falantes* (n.d.; The Talking Clocks) and *Escritorio avarento* (n.d.; The Miserly Study). *Cartas familiares* (Personal Letters) comprises twenty years of correspondence and shows his prose at its best. Mello also penned a rather pejorative piece titled *Carta de guía de casados* (1651; The Government of a Wife), which was popular in its day.

BIBLIOGRAPHY

Primary Texts

Cartas familiares. 2nd ed. Ed M. Rodrigues Lapa. Lisbon: Sá de Costa, 1942.

Historia de los movimientos, separación y guerra de Cataluña. Ed. Joan Estruch. Barcelona: Fontamara, 1982.

Hospital das letras; apólogo dialogal quarto (ano de 1657). Lisbon: Ibis, 1960.

English Translation

The Government of a Wife. Tr. J. Stevens. London: J. Towson and R. Knaplock, 1697.

Relics of Melodino. Tr. E. Lawson. London: Baldwin, Cradock and Joy, 1815.

Criticism

Ferreira, J. *Don Francisco Manoel de Melo escreveu a "Arte de furtar."* Oporto: D Barreira, Livraria Simões Lopes, 1945.

Prestage, E. *Don Francisco Manoel de Mello*. Oxford: Oxford UP, Humphrey Milford, 1922.

Nina Shecktor

MELO, Francisco Manuel de. *See* Mello, Francisco Manuel de

MELODINO. *See* Mello, Francisco Manuel de

MENA, Juan de (1411, Córdoba–1456, Torrelaguna), poet. The few facts known with some certainty about the life of Juan de Mena are the dates and places of his birth and death and his holding the honorary title of Veinticuatro (alderman) of his native city of Córdoba and later also that of official chronicler and secretary of Latin letters to John II. On the basis of equivocal family documents and the pessimistic tone of his writings—a supposed characteristic of Christian convert intellectuals—it has been widely conjectured that Mena was of Jewish blood. Although no record exists of his schooling, it is probable that he began his studies in Córdoba and later attended the U of Salamanca. He almost certainly spent several years in Florence in the retinue of a Spanish cardinal, where he had ample opportunity to become acquainted with Italian literature. After his return to Spain, Mena wrote his major work, the *Laberinto* (1444; The Labyrinth of Fortune), dedicated to his patron, John II. The title of the work may be a daring metaphor meant to represent John II's strife-torn Castile, but as a book title it can also mean ''Compendium'' or ''Thesaurus.'' At court he seems to have maintained a friendship both with don Alvaro de *Luna, who figures prominently in the *Laberinto* as a political ideal, and with the Marquis of *Santillana, to whom Mena had dedicated his earlier *Coronación* (1438; Coronation). In spite of Mena's apparent success at court and regular stipends received from the king, it seems that he may have died in poverty because tradition has it that his friend Santillana had to pay for his tomb.

In the nineteenth and well into the present c. it had become commonplace to extoll Mena primarily for his *Laberinto* and to dismiss, ignore, and even ridicule his prose as pedantic. The two known prose works on which this judgment was based were the *Comentario* (1439; Commentary) to his allegorical poem, *Coronación*, and the *Ilíada* (*Iliad*), or *Omero romanzado* (c. 1442; Homer in the Romance Tongue), a condensed translation of the Latin *Ilias latina*, itself an extremely lengthy compendium of the Homeric legend. An extensive seminal study by María Rosa Lida de Malkiel as well as the publication of various hitherto unknown minor prose works only recently attributed to Mena—*Memorias de algunos linajes* (Origins of Certain Lineages), *Tratado de amor* (Treatise on Love), *Tratado de duque* (Treatise on the Title of Duke)—have made possible a re-evaluation of Mena's work, showing that both in his prose and in his poetry he employed three different styles, didactic, narrative and ornamental, each of which he manipulated to his given artistic purpose. The Commentary to the *Coronación*, for example, alternates didactic and narrative passages, while the brief *Tratado de duque*, a panegyric to the duke of Medina Sidonia, is wholly ornamental. Two further prose attributions to Mena have won little favor: although Mena did possess the official title of chronicler to the king, no portion of the *Crónica de Juan II* can be attributed to him with any degree of certainty; further, although the majority of modern critics tend to favor the dual-authorship theory of *La *Celestina*, there has appeared no defense of Mena as the author of Act I, even though Fernando de *Rojas mentions him in his Prologue along with Rodrigo *Cota as one of the possible authors.

Besides the *Laberinto* and the *Coronación*, Mena's poetic production includes courtly love poetry and verses on political and moral themes, many of which were collected in the **Cancionero* collections of the time. Two particularly interesting love poems are the ''Claro oscuro'' (Clear Obscure) and ''Al hijo muy claro de Hiperión'' (To the Illustrious Son of Hiperion), in which there is both a semantic and a metrical duality, with an alternation between ''obscure'' fourteen-syllable *arte mayor* stanzas full of classical allusions and ''clear'' lyrical octosyllabic stanzas. The political poems include satires and various short poems of circumstance; in them Mena extolls don Alvaro de Luna, King John II and other nobles, many of whom reappear in the *Laberinto*. Among the poems of a moral tone attributed to Mena are ''Dezir sobre la justicia'' (Poem about Justice) and ''El Razonamiento con la Muerte'' (Reasoning with Death), both of which are imbued with a pessimistic tone and reflections on death.

The *Coronación*, or *Calamicleos*, written in fifty-one double five-lined stanzas known as *quintillas*, is a panegyric to the Marquis of Santillana. It is a rather hermetic allegory in the form of a double vision. The poet, losing his way in search of Parnassus, is first forced to contemplate the pains of Hell before he reaches Mount Parnassus, where he witnesses the coronation of the marquis. As its alternate title indicates, the poem has a secondary purpose, the denunciation of the evils and evildoers of the society of his day. Mena makes obvious his intent of ''reprehending vices'' through the glorious example of the life of Santillana.

The lengthiest and also the most complex of Mena's creations is his masterwork, the *Laberinto*, which is also known as *Las Trescientas* for the 300 stanzas in which it is written. As the earlier *Coronación*, the *Laberinto* is also locked into the medieval framework of an allegorical vision. Here the poet, with the aid of the device of the three wheels of Fortune, representing Past, Present and Future Time, parades forth a long series of historical and mythological figures. The principal intent of the work is political and moral: to incite the king, to whom it is dedicated, to put an end to the civil wars plaguing the kingdom and to realize the great destiny of Spain. Interwoven into the overall epic-narrative structure of the work are numerous didactic and ornamental digressions. The *Laberinto* is the culmination of a whole genre of allegorical didactic works of moral intent which abounded in the fifteenth c. The allegory of Fortune, which serves to unite the work, was so frequently employed throughout the Middle Ages that it would be impossible to trace its exact antecedents in Mena's work. The most obvious source is the *Divine Comedy*, which had been translated into Spanish by Enrique de *Villena in 1427. Other possible influences are Boccaccio's *Amorosa visione* and the lengthy French tradition of Fortune literature, which began in the thirteenth c. with the *Roman de la Rose*. Whatever his sources, Mena adds a note of originality in fusing the wheel of Fortune and that other great medieval commonplace, Death, thus creating his three wheels of Time, each with its seven concentric circles representing the planets.

Although both the *Laberinto* and the *Coronación* give ample evidence that Mena knew and admired Dante, it is probable that he nevertheless did not seek to imitate him directly, because not even Dante would have received from Mena the respect accorded to classical authors. The favorite authors cited throughout

Mena's work are both medieval authors writing in Latin, such as Boethius and Saint Isidore, and classical authors like Virgil, Lucan (Mena's fellow-citizen of Córdoba), *Seneca and Ovid. Mena's classical readings have left their trace throughout his work. For example, several notable episodes in the *Laberinto* are inspired by the Odyssey, by Ovid's *Ars Amatoria*, or by Lucan's *Farsalia*, while in others Mena makes use of a technique of compound imitation, combining two different sources, such as in the fusion of a scene from Virgil's *Georgics* with Lucan's imitation of it.

In the fifteenth c. the fourteen-syllable *arte mayor* replaced the **cuaderna vía* of the previous two centuries as the new "learned" verse form, reaching its culmination in the middle of the century with Mena and the Marquis of Santillana. In the *Laberinto* Mena utilizes the *arte mayor* in its two most frequent rhyme schemes, the "embraced" *abba acca* and the "alternating" *abab bcbc*. The artistic triumph achieved by this verse through the enduring popularity of the *Laberinto* allowed it to continue unopposed as the dominant poetic form well into the next century, until the introduction from Italy of the *octava real* (*octavas) and the *silva*.

María Rosa Lida de Malkiel has characterized Juan de Mena as the representative artist of the Spanish pre-Renaissance, qualifying him as "belatedly medieval" seen from the vantage point of Italian humanism while at the same time "prematurely modern" when considered within the Spanish historical framework. Characteristic of this duality in his work are the diffusion of rhetorical features and frequent archaisms, which coexist with the most daring neologisms. By far the most constant and pervasive rhetorical device used by Mena is amplification, interpreted in the medieval manner, as artifice of dilation and ornamentation. In its simplest forms it appears as various figures of repetition (e.g., anaphora, epanalepsis, chiasmus) and enumeration. Of particular interest are the frequent pairs of synonyms in which the first member is a neologism, while the second is its more commonly used gloss ("muy rubicunda o muy colorada"; very rubicund or very rosy). Another form of amplification, the etymological perifrasis (" . . . Fenicia la bella / dicha del fénix"; Phoenecia the Beautiful / said of the phoenix), exemplifies Mena's constant philological preoccupation, most evident in the *Coronación* and in the *Tratado de duque*.

Mena, sensitive to the inadequacy of the Spanish of his day for translating the great works of classical literature, undertook a conscious effort to create a new poetic language which would be capable of being elevated to the level of Latin. The most pervasive feature of this linguistic renovation is a constant syntactical Latinization, which not uncommonly renders very difficult the understanding of many passages. Among the most recurrent are appositions, exclamatory and interrogative relative clauses, and especially the abuse of absolute constructions and the frequent placing of the verb in sentence-final position, even in prose works. The apostrophe, a variant of the rhetorical interjection, is the single most outstanding syntactical device employed in the *Laberinto* and determines its total structure, inasmuch as the whole work is conceived as one lengthy apostrophe to the king. On the lexical level the Latinization is most startling in the often tight accumulation of neologisms (''quando amor es ficto, vaniloco, pigro''; when love is feigned, boastful, reluctant) which appear side by side with a wide variety of straggling archaisms (*cedo*, *vido*, *nol*: *doy*, *vio*, *no le*, in modern Spanish). Less apparent by their form and therefore much more deceptive are the semantic neologisms which look outwardly like popular words but are used by Mena with a deliberately obscure Latin meaning which did not survive in the modern language (*dañado*, not harmed but condemned, as in its Latin etymon *Damnatus*). It is likely that Mena's strong Latinization of both syntax and lexicon, which makes much of his work so obscure, is due not only to stylistic considerations but is also a deliberate attempt to exclude those readers who are not sufficiently cultured to understand ''learned'' poetry.

Mena's work, especially the *Laberinto* and the *Razonamiento con la Muerte*, was admired and imitated by many of his contemporaries, including Juan de Montoro, Santillana and *Gómez Manrique, and he continued to influence Spanish and even Portuguese learned poets—and, more surprisingly, prose writers—through the seventeenth c. The *Laberinto* was also parodied in an extremely obscene erotic poem, the *Caragicomedia*, dating from the early sixteenth c.

The *Laberinto* was first annotated in the classical edition (1499, 1505) of Hernán *Núñez, more commonly known as El Comendador griego, and again in 1582 by Francisco *Sánchez de las Brozas, El Brocense, editor also of the poetry of *Garcilaso de la Vega. *See also* Italian Literary Influences.

BIBLIOGRAPHY

Primary Texts

La Coronación. Ed. Feliciano Delgado León. Córdoba: Publicaciones del Monte de Piedad y Caja de Ahorros de Córdoba, 1978. Contains only excerpts from the *Commentary*.

La Coronación. Ed. A. Pérez Gómez. Cieza: n.p., 1964. Facs. of fifteenth-c. edition (Toulouse? 1489?); contains full *Commentary*.

La Ylíada en romance. Ed. Martín de Riquer. Selecciones Bibliófilos 3. Barcelona: SADAG, 1949. Facs. of 1519 edition.

Laberinto de Fortuna. Ed. Louise O. Vasvari. Madrid: Alhambra, 1976.

Obras menores. Ed. Miguel Angel Pérez Prieto. Madrid: Alhambra, 1979.

Tratado de amor. Ed. M. L. Gutiérrez-Arraus. Madrid: Alcalá, 1975.

Tratado sobre el título de duque. Ed. Louise O. Vasvari. London: Tamesis, 1976.

Criticism

Clarke, D. C. *Juan de Mena's ''Laberinto de Fortuna'': Classic Epic and ''Mester de Clerecía.''* Romance Monographs 5. University, MS: Romance Monographs, 1973.

Deyermond, A.''Structure and Style as Instruments of Propaganda in Juan de Mena's *Laberinto de Fortuna*.'' In *Proceedings of the Patristic, Medieval, and Renaissance Conference, 5, 1980*. 1983, 159–67.

Lida de Malkiel, María Rosa. *Juan de Mena, poeta del prerrenacimiento español*. Mexico City: Colegio de México, 1984.

Louise O. Vasvari

MENDOZA, Bernardino de (1540?, Guadalajara–1604, Madrid), diplomat, historian, poet. His valuable *Comentarios de lo sucedido en las guerras de los Países Bajos desde el año 1567 hasta el de 1577* (1591, in French, 1592 in Spanish; Commentary of Events in the Wars with the Low Countries from 1567 to 1577) provides firsthand testimony of the conflict there. In 1578 he became ambassador to England. His poetry, *Odas a la conversión de un pecador* (Odes to a Sinner's Conversion), was edited in 1779 by *Cerdá y Rico. Extremely knowledgeable is his treatise *Theoría y práctica de la guerra* (1595; *Theorique and practise of warre,* 1597).

BIBLIOGRAPHY

Primary Texts

Comentarios. In BAE 28.

Odas a la conversión de un pecador arrepentido. In *Poesías espirituales*. Ed. Cerdá y Rico. Madrid: Sotos, 1789.

Theórica y práctica de la guerra. Antwerp: Plantiniana, 1596.

English Translation

Theorique and practise of warre. Tr. E. Hoby. London: n.p., 1597.

Criticism

Morel-Fatio, A. "Don Bernardino de Mendoza." In *Etudes sur l'Espagne*. Paris: Bouillon, 1925. 4: 373–490.

MENDOZA, Eduardo (1943, Barcelona–), novelist. Born and raised in Barcelona, he moved to New York in 1973 and lived and worked there as a translator until 1982. He has authored four novels. *La verdad sobre el caso Savolta* (1975; The Truth about the Savolta Affair) was a great success, both among public and critics, and received the Premio de la Crítica (Critics' Award) in 1976. It marked a new direction in the Spanish novel, a rupture with the vanguard and experimental novel popular in the sixties and seventies, rendering plot and story their original value. His two subsequent novels, *El misterio de la cripta embrujada* (1979; The Mystery of the Enchanted Crypt) and *El laberinto de las aceitunas* (1982; The Olive Labyrinth), are parodies of the hard-boiled detective novel. With these two novels, set in present-day Barcelona, Mendoza, through a mixed structure of detective novel and parody, has achieved great success among the public. His most recent novel, *La ciudad de los prodigios* (1986; The Prodigious City, tr. as *The City of Marvels*, 1988), returns to the theme and setting of his first one. In it, Mendoza re-creates a period of the past through documentation rather than personal experience: the years between the two World Fairs in Barcelona (1888 and 1929). Mendoza's work can be divided into two parts: one of less importance whose humor and the use of a popular genre have earned him commercial success; the other consisting of his two major works, *La verdad sobre el caso Savolta* and *La ciudad de los prodigios*, which offer the reader a complete and detailed picture of Barcelona during the first decades of the twentieth c.

BIBLIOGRAPHY

Primary Texts

La ciudad de los prodigios. Barcelona: Seix Barral, 1986.
El laberinto de las aceitunas. Barcelona: Seix Barral, 1983.
El misterio de la cripta embrujada. Barcelona: Seix Barral, 1983.
La verdad sobre el caso Savolta. Barcelona: Seix Barral, 1983.

English Translation

The City of Marvels. Tr. B. Molloy. San Diego: Harcourt Brace Jovanovich, 1988.

Criticism

Martínez Cachero, José María. *La novela española entre 1936 y 1980.* Madrid: Castalia, 1985.
Soldevila Durante, Ignacio. *La novela desde 1936.* Madrid: Alhambra, 1980.

Samuel Amell

MENDOZA, Íñigo de (fifteenth c., ?–?,?), religious poet. Biographical data concerning this Franciscan is scarce. The reign of Ferdinand and Isabel saw a shift from the more courtly type of poetry to a more popular one, and Fray Íñigo de Mendoza was one of the important composers of popular religious poetry. He is most remembered for a long composition written in *quintillas dobles* (double five-line stanzas) and called *Vita Christi* (1482; The Life of Christ). The work also incorporates many popular poems and rustic dialogues between shepherds. Perhaps because of his unreformed ways, contemporary writers made negative references about Mendoza; even if the remarks about his character were true, they do not detract from his religious poetry. The *Vita Christi* was intended to encompass the entire life of Jesus, but the poem ends abruptly with the slaughter of the innocents. The rustic simplicity and vigor so common to Franciscan poetry characterize this work. Moral and political digressions, **coplas*, **villancicos himnos* and *romances* in praise of the Child Jesus and the Virgin Mary add further to its length. Menéndez y Pelayo suggests the influence of contemporary poets such as Juan de *Mena and the *Coplas de *Mingo Revulgo*, which would mean that Mendoza wrote poems **a lo divino*. Rodríguez-Puértolas reveals a well-developed, almost combative political stance behind Mendoza's presentation of historical figures, his attacks on power, criticism of the excesses of nobility, etc. *See also* Humanism; Renaissance.

BIBLIOGRAPHY

Primary Texts

Cancionero. Toledo: Vázquez, 1486.
Cancionero. Zaragoza: Hurus de Constancia, 1492–95.

Fray Iñigo de Mendoza y sus "Coplas de Vita Christi." Ed. J. Rodríguez-Puértolas. Madrid: Gredos, 1968.

Criticism

Amador de los Ríos, J. *Historia de la literatura española.* Madrid: Gredos, 1969. 7: 238–46.

Menéndez y Pelayo, M. *Historia de la poesía española en la Edad Media.* In *Obras completas.* Vol. 6. Madrid: Suárez, 1916.

See also Rodríguez-Puértolas, in Primary Texts.

Angelo DiSalvo

MENDOZA DE VIVES, María (1819, Ardales, Málaga–1894, Barcelona), poet, novelist. From a well-to-do family (her father was a physician), by 1839–40 she had already collaborated with regularity in Malagan publications such as *El Guadalorce* and *La Alhambra.* Married in 1841, she moved first to Catalonia, and then, in 1863, to Manila (the Philippines) where her husband had been appointed attorney-general. Widowed in 1865, she returned to Spain, settling in Barcelona. She published two books of poems, *Poesías y leyendas* (n.d.; Poems and Legends) and *Flores de Otoño* (1879; Autumnal Flowers), but many other compositions appeared separately in periodicals. Two of them were prize-winners in literary contests (Gerona, 1875, and Madrid, 1878). Her verse shows a preference for Oriental, biblical and popular legends. Her Andalusian origins clearly influenced her treatment of language and selection of topics. This influence surfaces in her fiction as well. From 1862 until her death she published seven novels. *Preferencias de un padre* (1867; Preferences of a Father) was translated into Catalan. *Las barras de plata* (The Silver Bars), whose Spanish edition appeared in 1877, first appeared in French in 1866. Some of her novels were published as serials in the *Diario de Barcelona.*

BIBLIOGRAPHY

Primary Texts

El alma de una madre. Quien mal anda mal acaba. Barcelona: Manera, 1862.

Las barras de plata. Barcelona: Manera, 1887.

Flores de otoño. Barcelona: Barcelonesa, 1879.

Poesías y leyendas. Barcelona: Manero, n.d.

La Pubilla Ferraró. Biblioteca para todos, vols. 1 and 2. Barcelona: Manero, 1887.

Criticism

Cejador y Frauca, Julio. *Historia de la lengua y literatura castellana.* 14 vols. Madrid: Tipología de Archivos, 1915–22.

Ferreras, J. I. *Catálogo de novelas y novelistas españoles del s. XIX.* Madrid: Cátedra, 1979.

Cristina Enríquez

MENDOZA Y BOBADILLA, Cardinal Archbishop Francisco de. *See Tizón de la nobleza de España.*

MENÉNDEZ PIDAL, Ramón (1869, La Coruña–1968, Madrid), Spanish critic and literary historian. Menéndez Pidal studied at the U of Madrid, where he was a disciple of *Menéndez Pelayo and became distinguished for his erudition and work in literary history while still quite young. Official recognition came in 1893 when the *Academia Española awarded a prize for his work on the *Poema del Cid* (published in book form a few years later). His first important book was *La leyenda de los infantes de Lara* (1896; The Legend of the Princes of Lara), an exhaustive study of the origins of the legend and its transmission through the centuries. This investigation was significant as the author's first investigation of primitive Castilian epic poetry (then almost completely unknown) which Menéndez Pidal would subsequently explain quite exhaustively. In the *Crónicas generales de España (Catálogo de la Real Biblioteca)* (c. 1898; General Chronicles of Spain [Catalog of the Royal Library]), the first systematic study of Spanish historiography was undertaken. In 1899, Menéndez Pidal obtained the chair of Romance philology at the U of Madrid, which he held until his retirement in 1939. Here, too, he was a significant force for renovation, and he produced a large number of disciples who have since constituted Spain's main body of historico-literary scholars.

He was elected to the Academia Española in 1902 and in 1904 published the first of many successively improved editions of his *Manual de gramática histórica española* (Manual of Historical Spanish Grammar), the first clear exposition of the phonetic and morphological principles in the evolution of Spanish. This work became the basis for the formal study of linguistics in Spain, and most systematic investigation since then has been inspired by it and other works of Menéndez Pidal. The publication of his *Cantar de Mío Cid; texto, gramática y vocabulario* (1908–12; The Poem of Lord Cid; Text, Grammar and Vocabulary) established him in the forefront of Romance philologists in the world, thanks to his rigorous discussion of paleographic and linguistic details and his clarity of articulation and exposition. This work, together with the author's studies of early epic poetry and the chronicles, made him an authority on the Middle Ages. A series of university lectures presented in Baltimore in 1909 was published in French (translation by H. Mérimée) with the title, *L'Epopée castillane à travers la Littérature espagnole* (1910; The Castilian Epic in Spanish Literature), tracing the persistent presence of the epic tradition throughout history, while another series of lectures given at Columbia U was published under the title *El romancero español* (Spanish Ballad Collections).

Establishment of the Junta para Ampliación de Estudios (1907; Junta for Broader Studies) and of the Center for Historical Studies in Spain provided an opportunity for Menéndez Pidal to extend his influence. He founded the *Revista de Filología Española* in 1914, bringing into it a number of his disciples, and soon established it as the best journal of its kind. His prestige attracted numerous foreign collaborators. In various collections of the Center for Historical Studies he also published important essays, one of the most important being *Poesía juglaresca y juglares* (1924; Minstrels and Minstrel Poetry). Possibly his masterpiece is *Orígenes del español* (1926; The Origins of the Spanish Language), an epoch-making text in Romance linguistics; no other modern language has been so precisely studied in its pre-literary period. Years of prolonged investigation of the chronicles and the origins of Spanish epic poetry culminated in another major work, *La España del Cid* (1929; The Cid's Spain), an evaluation of the exact historical significance of the Castilian "national" hero, a study combining minute knowledge of historical documents and broad critical vision of major historical problems and events, which has served to modify prior notions of the Middle Ages. Menéndez Pidal was elected director of the Royal Spanish Academy in 1925, a post he held until 1939, and resumed in 1947. He received honorary doctorates from many foreign universities, including Toulouse, Hamburg, Oxford, Tubinga, Paris, Louvaine and Brussels. Although semi-retired after he resigned his chair in 1939, he continued to work, revising, perfecting and reprinting earlier works, and completing three long-awaited major studies: *Historia de la Lengua Española* (History of the Spanish Language), *Historia de la Epopeya* (History of Epic Poetry), and *Romancero general* (General Ballad Collection). Late in life, he made significant contributions to the study of origins of the French epic (*La Chanson de Roland* [1959]) and published several volumes of the *Romancero Hispánico* (1953; Hispanic Ballad Collection). His studies in other areas included the analysis of the **kharjas* (lyric poetry of the Mozárabes in Spain), and study of the historiography of Spain's colonies in the New World, with a work on Fr. Bartolomé de las Casas (1963).

BIBLIOGRAPHY

Criticism

Hess, Steven. *Ramón Menéndez Pidal*. TWAS 651. Boston: Twayne, 1982.

MENÉNDEZ Y PELAYO, Enrique (1861, Santander–1921, Santander), Cantabrian writer. Brother of Marcelino. After studying medicine, he dedicated himself to writing poetry, fiction and plays in which stylistic and moral concerns dominate. See his *Memorias de uno a quien no sucedió nada* (1922; Memoirs of One to Whom Nothing Ever Happened) and Gerardo *Diego's introduction and selection of his works: *Enrique Menéndez-Pelayo*.

BIBLIOGRAPHY

Primary Text

Enrique Menéndez-Pelayo. Sel., intro. G. Diego. Santander: Librería Moderna, 1951.

Stephen Miller

MENÉNDEZ Y PELAYO, Marcelino (1856, Santander–1912, Santander), Cantabrian critic, historian and theoretician of literature and culture. He was the youngest major figure of the Generation of 1868 and the foremost academic of his time. His great teacher was Manuel *Milà i Fontanals, an initiator of the integration of nineteenth-c. Spanish scholarship into the currents of the latest theories and techniques of German aesthetics, Romance philology and comparative literature.

As happened with other members of the Generation of 1868, the period between his death and the present saw his reputation suffer at the hands of different ideological and generational imperatives. In consequence, the Sociedad Menéndez Pelayo of Santander published in 1983 a collection of papers bearing the title of Ciriaco Morón Arroyo's contribution, "Menéndez Pelayo: hacia una nueva imagen" (Menéndez Pelayo: Toward a New Image). Therein is controverted the widespread, yet unsubstantiated allegation of Menéndez y Pelayo's being an erudite, unoriginal writer whose close-minded Catholicism and narrow nationalism led to the exclusion of a salutary European dimension in Spanish intellectual life.

To refute that view and to explain better the real burden of Menéndez y Pelayo's labors, Morón Arroyo identifies and explicates the two fundamental "axioms" upon which the former based his work: the *Renaissance tradition of Spanish humanism, and the concept of "history as a work of art." Against what has often been alleged Menéndez y Pelayo not only should not be identified with the Thomistic scholasticism which dominated post–Civil War official Spain, but, to the contrary, should be recognized as its intellectual opposite. *Nebrija, *Vives, Alfonso and Juan de *Valdés, Luis de *Léon and *Arias Montano form his tradition of thought which was eradicated from Spanish universities by scholasticism. In discussing Vives in his collection of essays *La ciencia española* (1882; Spanish Science), Menéndez y Pelayo emphasized the humanist's reliance on "empirical observation, the historical sense which sees the data itself, not as a function of preconceived systems." As regards the second axiom, it is the attempt to arrive at a synthetic understanding of the work, author, ideology or period being studied. Rather than produce series of partial, analytic works, the ideal of Menéndez y Pelayo was to undertake the kinds of broad investigations which gave rise to the following titles: *Historia de los heterodoxos españoles* (1880–82; The History of the Heterodox Spaniards), *Historia de las ideas estéticas en España* (1883–84; The History of Aesthetic Ideas in Spain), *Antología de poetas líricos castellanos* (1890–1908; Anthology of Castilian Lyric Poets), and *Orígenes de la novela española* (1905–10; Origins of the Spanish Novel). Moreover, to this list should be added extensive studies of the history of poetry in Latin America, studies to accompany his multi-volume, Royal Academy editions of the works of Lope de *Vega and *Calderón, the presence of Horace in Spanish literature, and a *Bibliografía hispanolatina clásica* (A Bibliography of Classical Hispano-Latin Literature), upon which he labored for many years.

During his lifetime Menéndez y Pelayo was an extremely well-known and well-connected figure in literary, university and intellectual circles. His correspondence shows that he was in frequent contact with the likes of *Pérez Galdós, *Pereda and *Clarín. His polemics with such leading representatives of *Krausism as Salmerón and F. *Giner de los Ríos demonstrated his divergence from the primarily doctrinal nature of their enterprise, but also attached to him the stigma of opposing, in Giner, the founder of the alternative body of higher education called the Institución Libre de Enseñanza. Menéndez y Pelayo, as Morón Arroyo points out, did have an unfortunate relationship with education. Although he was a professor at the U of Madrid from 1878 to 1898, he gave up his chair in order to become director of the *Biblioteca Nacional (National Library). In so doing he signaled his disdain for both official and alternative universities as places where knowledge is created and relegated them to the lesser function of transmitting the work done by those who only researched and wrote. His chief disciple, *Menéndez Pidal, followed his example and may therefore share with him the responsibility for the comparatively slight importance given to teaching in Spanish universities. On the other hand, though, he did establish the very high standards of scholarship which characterize the best literary and general philological investigation in Spain until today. Furthermore, he must be credited with extending these same standards to historical studies during his time as director of the Royal Academy of History.

Much of Menéndez y Pelayo's vast output still maintains a respectable place in current academic discussion of the many topics and figures he studied. Yet Morón Arroyo argues that the narrowly focused consultation of specific works may lead to a false image of the larger significance of Menéndez y Pelayo's labor: the example of and call to the constantly renewed "reflection on the roots and substance of what is Spanish" as the starting point for the pursuit of knowledge in all fields.

His writings are collected in the *Edición nacional de las obras completas de Menéndez Pelayo*. The collection of his letters, a very important primary source of information about him and the leading cultural questions and figures of the day, is being published; arranged in chronological order, the seven volumes published through 1986 bring the correspondence from June 1868 to June 1886, under the editorial supervision of Manuel Revuelta Sañudo. Finally, it should be noted that Menéndez y Pelayo's vast library and collection of mss. constitute a research library of the first class for those interested in any of the themes he studied; it is installed in his family home in Santander and open to the public as the Biblioteca Menéndez Pelayo.

BIBLIOGRAPHY

Primary Texts

Edición nacional de las obras completas de Menéndez Pelayo. Santander: CSIC, 1940–57.

Epistolario de Menéndez Pelayo. Ed. M. Revuelta Sañudo. Madrid: Fundación Universitaria Española, 1982- . 7 vols. as of 1986.

Criticism

Alonso, Dámaso. *Menéndez Pelayo, crítico literario*. Madrid: "Mater et Magistra," 1962.

Artigas, Manuel. *La vida y la obra de Menéndez Pelayo*. Zaragoza: n.p., 1939.

Laín Entralgo, Pedro. *Menéndez Pelayo. Historia de sus problemas intelectuales*. Madrid: Instituto de Estudios Políticos, 1944.

Menéndez Pelayo. Hacia una nueva imagen. Santander: Sociedad Menéndez Pelayo, 1983.
Saínz Rodríguez, Pedro. *Menéndez Pelayo, ese desconocido.* Madrid: Fundación Universitaria Española, 1975.
Sanemeterio, Modesto. *Menéndez Pelayo. Su época y obra literaria.* Madrid: "Mater et Magistra," 1962.

Stephen Miller

MESA, Cristóbal de (c. 1562, Zafra–1633, Madrid), poet, humanist, and priest. Despite his erudition and skill as a writer, Cristóbal de Mesa was never accorded the recognition he deserved during his lifetime, probably because of the ease with which he alienated others. While a student at the U of Salamanca, he came under the influence of the eminent humanist Francisco *Sánchez el Brocense, who significantly affected his future course. Mesa never completed his studies at Salamanca, but moved to Seville, where he met Fernando de *Herrera and others in his literary circle. Upon his ordination to the priesthood, Mesa became chaplain to the Count of Castelar and spent five years in Italy, where he became a friend of Torquato Tasso and was greatly attracted to the Italian school. When he returned to Spain, he became a member of the Academia Salvaje, formed close ties to *Cervantes, and developed a distaste for Lope de *Vega, despite the latter's esteem for Mesa's poetry. His first major work was *Las Navas de Tolosa* (1594), a heroic poem in thirty cantos. A far less plodding treatment of Spanish history was his *La restauración de España* (1607; The Restoration of Spain), a poem in royal octaves which celebrates Pelayo's victory over the Moors at Covadonga. He later composed a religious epic poem, *El Patrón de España* (1612; The Patron Saint of Spain), which renders an account of the transfer of the remains of St. James to Spain. Mesa is also remembered for his precise translations of Virgil's *Aeneid* (1615), *Eclogues* (1618) and *Georgics* (1618). *See also* Humanism; Italian Literary Influences; Siglo de Oro.

BIBLIOGRAPHY

Primary Texts

"Églogas." Ed. J. López de Sedano. In *Parnaso español.* Madrid: Ibarra, 1768. vol. 1.
Epístolas. Ed. Antonio Rodríguez Moñino. *El Criticón* 2 (1935): 39–50.

Criticism

Beall, Chandler B. "Cristóbal de Mesa and Tasso's *Rime.*" *MLN* 60 (1945): 469–72.
Caravaggi, Giovanni. "Torquato Tasso e Cristóbal de Mesa." *Studi Tassiani* 20 (1970): 46–85.
López Prudencio, J. "Valores olvidados, Cristóbal de Mesa." *Revista del Centro de Estudios Extremeños* 16 (1942): 165–78.
Pfandl, Ludwig. *Historia de la literatura nacional española en la Edad de Oro.* Barcelona: Gili, 1952.

Rodríguez Moñino, Antonio. *Cristóbal de Mesa: Estudio bibliográfico (1562–1633)*. Badajoz: Diputación Provincial, 1951.

C. Maurice Cherry

MESA, Enrique de (1878, Madrid–1929, Madrid), Spanish poet whose life was spent near his birthplace. His works show medieval influence, especially that of the *Arcipreste de Hita and the **cancioneros*. His poetic collections, most of them brief, include *Tierra y alma* (1906; Land and Soul), *Cancionero castellano* (1911; Castilian Songbook), *El silencio de la cartuja* (1916; The Silence of the Carthusian Monastery—recipient of the Royal Spanish Academy's Fastenrath Prize), and *La posada y el camino* (1928; The Inn and the Road). These were collected in a volume of *Obras completas* (Complete Works) in 1930, which also included the prose texts *Flor pagana* (1915; Pagan Flower), *Tragicomedia* (1910), and *Apostillas a la escena* (1929; Approaches to the Stage), representing part of his activity as a theater critic. Mesa also worked as a journalist. His poetry is often folkloric in inspiration, or filled with somewhat conventional landscapes and ruralist motifs, but many of his lyric compositions are well wrought.

BIBLIOGRAPHY

Poesías completas. 3rd ed. Buenos Aires and Mexico: Espasa-Calpe, 1944.

Janet Pérez

MESONERO ROMANOS, Ramón de (1803, Madrid–1882, Madrid), *costumbrista* author and man of letters. The second of five children born to a comfortable banking family, in his early years he witnessed the turbulence and upheaval of the Napoleonic invasion and other social-economic crises. These early memories surely contributed to Mesonero's conscious efforts later in life to avoid turmoil and dissent, to seek "the middle road" and constructive avenues of action and to avoid the wrath of political repression. Mesonero's father died when Ramón was only sixteen, leaving him in control of the family estate. The business was sold a few years later, allowing the family to live from the income of the sale and that of various rental properties. Ramón seems to have been largely self-educated, as there is no indication of any formal training past high school.

Mesonero's first published work was a collection of short articles and sketches, *Mis ratos perdidos o ligero bosquejo de Madrid en 1820 y 1821* (1822; My Free Time or A Quick Outline of Madrid in 1820 and 1821); it met with an enthusiastic response, though the author later spurned it as an immature piece. During the 1820s, also marked by political strife in Spain, he continued to write articles, to cultivate his passion for the theater, and to collect material for the *Manual de Madrid* (1831; A Madrid Manual). Baroque theater was his favorite, despite his neo-classical tastes. Mesonero composed five adaptations of Baroque Golden Age classics during this decade, and also translated to Spanish a French play by Mazeres, and wrote one original work, *La señora de protección y escuela de pretendientes* (n.d.; The Influence Peddler and Her School for Position Seekers).

It was censored (*see* Censorship). Mesonero later transformed it into an excellent prose piece, *Pretender por alto* (To Start at the Top), which was included in *Escenas Matritenses* (1842; Madrid Scenes). Although he composed no other plays, he continued to write critical articles on theater and edited various theatrical works for the *Biblioteca de Autores Españoles (BAE).

In the late 1820s Mesonero began participating in several literary groups. These associations matured and flowered over the years and later gave birth to such illustrious societies as the *Ateneo Ciéntifico. Throughout the years, he was a key participant.

After a decade of gathering materials, Mesonero composed his first major work, the *Manual de Madrid. Descripción de la corte y de la villa* (1831; A Madrid Manual. Description of the Court and the Town). This fourteen-chapter guide provides the history, biographies, town layout, information on monuments, etc.; it was very successful. A second edition was printed in 1833, and another in 1835, with an important Apéndice (Appendix) added in which Mesonero suggests various sorts of urban reform (inspired by travel to cities in England and France in 1833 and 1834). Some of these reforms were enacted almost immediately; others were brought to fruition later, through efforts of Mesonero. In these years he emerges as a dedicated civic leader.

The year 1835 also marks the appearance of the *Panorama matritense* (Madrid Panorama), a three-volume work which is his first acknowledged collection of *costumbrista* articles. In these short sketches or essays of manners Mesonero describes, in mildly satirical, realistic fashion, scenes from daily Madrid life. The following year, he founded the illustrious literary magazine *El Semanario Pintoresco Español* (The Picturesque Spanish Weekly), which became a major organ of dissemination of *costumbrismo* for him and other contributors such as Eugenio de *Ochoa, Juan *Hartzenbusch, José *Zorrilla, *Gil y Zárate, and many others. Mesonero's use of the pseudonym El curioso parlante (The Curious Chatterbox) appeared at this time.

In 1842, Mesonero collected all his sketches and articles, including the *Panorama matritense* (but not *Mis ratos perdidos*), and published them with the title *Escenas matritenses* (1842; Scenes of Madrid). This is the cornerstone of his opus, and it was enormously successful. Mesonero's *costumbrismo* affected a humorous tone, facile style and disinterested pose which endeared him to his bourgeois audience. Conspicuously absent is the mordant tone and caustic wit of Mariano José de *Larra, who commented "retrata más que pinta" (he "copies" more than he describes). Some of the best sketches are "El día de toros" (After the Bullfight), "Antes, ahora y después" (Before, Now, and Later), "Costumbres literarias" (Literary Customs), "El romanticismo y los románticos" (Romanticism and the Romantics), and "El barbero de Madrid" (The Madrid Barber). His final *costumbrista* effort was *Tipos, grupos y bocetos de cuadros de costumbres* (1843–62; Types, Groups and Outlines of Costumbrista Sketches).

Other works by Mesonero evoke the same general outlook and tone. *Recuerdos* *de viaje por Francia y Bélgica en 1840 y 1841* (1841; Memoirs of a Journey through France and Belgium in 1840 and 1841) is a witty travelogue; *El antiguo Madrid* (1861; Old Madrid) is strictly architectural; *Memorias de un setentón* (1880; Memoirs of a Septuagenarian) is an unacknowledged masterpiece of the genre. Among his critical activity one can point out *Tirso de Molina, Cuentos, fábulas, descripciones, diálogos, máximas y apotegmas, epigramas y dichos agudos escogidos en sus obras* (1848; Tirso de Molina, Stories, Fables, Descriptions, Dialogues, Maxims, Epigrams and Clever Sayings from His Works), his activities as a member of the *Academia Española, to which he was elected in 1847, and his earlier mentioned work for the BAE. *See also* Romanticism.

BIBLIOGRAPHY

Primary Texts

Escenas matritenses. Panorama Matritense, escenas matritenses, tipos y caracteres. Ed. Sáinz de Robles. 2nd ed. Madrid: Aguilar, 1957.
Manual de Madrid. Descripción de la corte y de la villa. Madrid: Burgos, 1831.
Memorias de un setentón. Ed. J. Julio Perlado. 2 vols. Madrid: Publicaciones españolas, 1961.
Obras de don Ramón de Mesonero Romanos. Ed. C. Seco Serrano. BAE 199–203.
Recuerdos de viaje por Francia y Bélgica en 1840 y 1841. Madrid: Burgos, 1841.
Trabajos no coleccionados. Ed. Sons of author. 2 vols. Madrid: Hernández, 1903–5.

English Translations

"After the Bull Fight." Tr. anon. In *The Humor of Spain.* Ed. S. M. Taylor. London: Scott, 1894.
"The Nearsighted Lover." Tr. J. Pasmantier. In *An Anthology of Spanish Literature in English Translation.* New York: Ungar, 1958.
"The Short-Sighted Lover." Tr. W. E. Colford. In *Classic Tales from Modern Spain.* Great Neck, NY: Barron's, 1964.

Criticism

Cotarelo y Mori, E. "Elogio biográfico de Don Ramón de Mesonero Romanos." *BRAE* 12 (1925): 155–91, 309–43, 433–69.
Curry, R. A. *Ramón de Mesonero Romanos.* TWAS 385. Boston: Twayne, 1976.
Montesinos, J. F. *Costumbrismo y novela.* Madrid: Castalia, 1960.
Romero, F. *Mesonero Romanos: activista del madrileñismo.* Madrid: Instituto de Estudios Madrileños, 1968.
Sebold, R. "Comedia clásica y novela moderna en las *Escenas matritenses* de Mesonero Romanos." *BH* 83 (July-December, 1981): 331–37.

Eugene Del Vecchio and Maureen Ihrie

MESTER DE CLERECÍA (craft of clerks or clerics), a medieval form of verse. The term *clerecía* refers not only to men of the cloth but essentially to any man of learning. Willis (1956) points out the very scholastic implications as well as others conveyed by the term as it is found in the *Libro de *Alexandre*. This same text, as Deyermond points out, serves as a source for the division of poetry of this period into epic by minstrels and **cuaderna vía* by clerics.

Mester traygo fermoso, no es de joglaria
mester es sen pecado, ca es de clereçia
fablar curso rimado por la cuaderna uia
a sylabas contadas, que es grant maestria.

(An art I bring, it is not that of minstrels, / it is an art without defect, because it is for clerics / to speak with metered rhyme in the fourfold way / with counted syllables, which is a great ability.)

Cuaderna vía is a meter with fourteen-syllable lines (alexandrines), with caesura in the middle, full rhyme, monorhymed quatrains, *aaaa, bbbb*, etc.

Facts do not bear out these assumptions. Gonzalo de *Berceo, a *cuaderna vía* poet par excellence, refers to himself as a *joglar* (minstrel) on more than one occasion. In the *Milagros de Nuestra Señora*, as recompense for his poetry he requests the typical ministrel's fare, ''a good glass of wine.'' Other evidence in the *Libro de Alexandre* refers favorably to the ministrel's craft as well. The cleric's disdain toward the minstrel is mythical.

Although there is significantly less metrical irregularity in the *cuaderna vía* than is found in extant epic poems, *mester de clerecía* poetry does become decidedly more irregular as it progresses. Clarke-Shadi emphasizes that this poetic mode is not a genre; consequently, we find that the *Poema de *Fernán González* is an epic poem written in the clerkly craft.

The *mester de clerecía* poetry, that is, ''learned'' poetry, didactic or at least informative, entertaining and stylistically refined, often involving reworkings of pieces (some fictional) from other languages, had always been chameleonic and constantly metamorphosed in form as well as content, and continued to be so long after the writing of the *Rimado de palacio* [of *López de Ayala]. The only major change in the *mester de clerecía* at the end of the fourteenth c. was the substitution of the *copla de *arte mayor* for the *cuaderna vía*, principal but not exclusive metric form employed by the *clerecía* poets in the thirteenth and fourteenth centuries. (Clarke-Shadi 62)

Other works under this heading include Berceo's *El duelo de la Virgen*, *Los himnos, Los loores de Nuestra Señora*, *Los signos del juicio final, Vida de San Millán, Vida de Sta. Oria, Vida de Sto. Domingo, Martirio de San Lorenzo* and *Sacrificio de la Misa*. Perhaps the earliest of *cuaderna vía* poems (the question is still debated) is the *Libro de Alexandre*, a kind of *speculum principis*. Contending with it for the first spot is the *Libro de Apolonio*. As one moves into the fourteenth c., one finds the *Vida de San *Ildefonso*, the *Libro de *miseria de omne* (sixteen instead of fourteen syllables per line), and the *Proverbios de Salamón*. Also in this meter, although with some irregularity, are most of the poems found in the *Libro de buen amor* by the *Arcipreste de Hita. Although manifesting substantial differences in meter, one can also include the *Poema de *Alfonso Onceno,* the *Coplas de Yoçef*, and the *Poema de *Yúçuf*. Returning to a more regular meter, we find the last significant *cuaderna vía* poem, Pero López de Ayala's *Rimado de palacio*. Finally, in this craft we can also include Juan de *Mena's *Laberinto de fortuna*, as Clarke-Shadi observes, "The fact which seems to have escaped notice, that the *Laberinto de Fortuna* is also one of the finest examples of the medieval *mester de clerecía* (which is not a genre), does not in any way detract from its epic nature" (62). *See also* Edad Media, Literatura de la.

BIBLIOGRAPHY

Primary Texts

Beneficiado de Ubeda. Vida de San Ildefonso. Ed. M. Alvar Ezquerra. Bogota: Instituto Caro y Cuervo, 1975.

"Coplas de Yoçef. A Medieval Spanish Poem in Hebrew Characters. Ed. I. González Llubera. Cambridge: Cambridge UP, 1935.

"El libro de Alexandre": Texts of the Paris and the Madrid Manuscripts. Ed. R. S. Willis. Princeton: Princeton UP; Paris: Presses Universitaires, 1934.

Libro de Apolonio Ed. M. Alvar. 3 vols. Madrid: Castalia, 1976.

[Libro de miseria]. Translation and Poetization in the Quaderna Vía. Study and Edition of the Libro de miseria d'omne. Ed., study J.E. Connolly. Madison: HSMS, 1987.

Obras completas de Gonzalo de Berceo. Ed. B. Dutton. 5 vols. London: Tamesis, 1967–80.

Poema de Alfonso XI. Ed. Yo ten Cate. Madrid: CSIC, 1956.

Poema de Fernán González. Ed. A. Zamora Vicente. Clásicos Castellanos 128. 2nd ed. Madrid: Espasa-Calpe, 1963.

"Poema de Yúçuf," materiales para su estudio. Ed. R. Menéndez Pidal. Granada: U of Granada, 1952.

"Proverbios de Salamón." Ed. C. E. Kany. In *Homenaje a Menéndez Pidal.* Madrid: Hernando, 1925. 1: 269–85.

Rimado de palacio. Ed. K. Adams. Salamanca: Anaya, 1971.

[Sem Tob] San Tob de Carrión. "Proverbios morales." Ed. I. González Llubera. Cambridge: Cambridge UP, 1947.

Vida de Santo Domingo de Silos. Ed. B. Dutton. London: Tamesis, 1978.

Criticism

Baldwin, S. "Narrative Technique in Gonzalo de Berceo." *KRQ* 23 (1976): 17–28.

Cirot, G. "Inventaire estimatif du *mester de clerecía.*" *BH* 48 (1946): 193–209.

———. "Sur le *mester de clerecía.*" *BH* 44 (1942): 5–16.

Clarke [Shadi], D. C. *Juan de Mena's "Laberinto de fortuna." Classic Epic and "Mester de clerecía."* Romance Monographs 5. University, MS: Romance Monographs, 1973.

Davis, G. "The Debt of the *Poema de Alfonso* to the *Libro de Alexandre.*" *HR* 15 (1947): 436–52.

Deyermond, A. D. "Mester es sen pecado." *Romanische Forschungen* 77 (1965): 111–16.

González Llubera, I. "The Text and Language of Santob de Carrión's *Proverbios morales.*" *HR* 8 (1940): 113–24.

Gybbon-Monypenny, G. B. "The Spanish *mester de clerecía* and Its Intended Public:

Concerning the Validity as Evidence of Passages of Direct Address." In *Medieval Miscellany Presented to Eugène Vinaver*. Manchester: n.p., 1965. 230–44.

Lida de Malkiel, M. R. "La leyenda de Alejandro en la literatura medieval." *RPH* 15 (1961–62): 311–18.

———. "Datos para la leyenda de Alejandro en la literatura medieval." *RPH* 15 (1961–62): 412–23.

López Estrada, F. "Notas sobre el poema clerical de la Vida de San Ildefonso." In *Etudes de philologie romane et d'histoire littéraire offerts a Jules Horrent à l'occasion de son soixantième anniversaire*. Tournai: Gedit, n.d. 255–66.

Marchand, J. W. "Gonzalo de Berceo's *De los signos que aparesçeran ante del juiçio.*" *HR* 45 (1977): 283–95.

Orduna, G. "La estructura del *Duelo de la Virgen* y la cántica *Eya Velar.*" *Humanitas* (Tucumán) 10 (1958): 75–104.

Perry, T. A. "The Present State of Shem Tov Studies." *La Corónica* 7 (1978): 34–38.

Willis, R. S. "*Mester de clerecía.* A Definition of the *Libro de Alexandre.*" *RPH* 10 (1956–57): 212–24.

Anthony J. Cárdenas

MESTER DE JUGLARÍA (craft of minstrels). This craft, office, or duty consists of, as is commonly held, a narrative verse form, supposedly used by poets who recited epic poetry in the eleventh and twelfth centuries. It is a form whose standard line-length is irregular, generally sixteen syllables long, but which can fluctuate anywhere from ten to twenty syllables. The lines are divided into hemistiches separated by caesura. Rhyme is assonant. Poems written according to this craft are the **Cantar de Mio Cid* (1972; *Poem of the Cid*, 1975) and other epic poems. Poems of this craft are often contrasted with those of the **mester de clerecía* (craft of clerks). This dichotomy is not altogether watertight. *Juglares* (minstrels) were once thought to voice anonymously the poetry of the masses. As the poem passed from mouth to mouth a minstrel intervened at some point to jot it down. Further investigation has produced evidence to suggest that authors of these poems (or redactors, if one insists) were quite learned, professional men, not at all the kind one normally associates with the term *minstrel*.

Besides the *Cantar de Mio Cid* and the *Mocedades de Rodrigo* (Youthful Exploits of Rogrigo), both incomplete, the third epic poem, a mere fragment, is the **Roncesvalles*. Other epics written in this craft must be reconstructed from the chronicles, for example, *Alphonse X's *Estoria de Espanna* (c. 1270; *History of Spain*). The best example is the recovery of the epic of the *Siete Infantes de Lara* (The Seven Young Nobles of Lara [see *Infantes de Lara, Leyenda de los*]). Because the *Estoria de Espanna* used it, including it as history, one can reconstruct actual lines of the epic poem from within the prose text. Such is the first major piece of scholarship offered by the great medieval scholar Ramón *Menéndez Pidal, in his *La leyenda de los infantes de Lara*. Other epics recovered from other chronicles are *Rodrigo el Godo* (Roderic the Goth), *Bernardo del Carpio*, and the *Cerco de Zamora* (Siege of Zamora). *See also* Edad Media, Literatura de la.

BIBLIOGRAPHY

Primary Texts

Castillo, Rosa, ed. *Leyendas épicas españolas*. Ed. Rosa Castillo. Odres Nuevos 3. Valencia: Castilla, 1956.

Deyermond, A. D. *Epic Poetry and the Clergy: Studies on the "Mocedades de Rodrigo."* London: Tamesis, 1968.

Menéndez Pidal, Ramón. *Floresta de leyendas heroicas españolas: Rodrigo el último godo*. vol. 1: *La Edad Media*. Madrid: Clásicos Castellanos, 1925.

———. *La leyenda de los Infantes de Lara*. Madrid: Hijos de Ducazcal, 1896; 2nd ed., Madrid: Hernando, 1934.

———. *Reliquias de la poesía épica española*. Madrid: Espasa-Calpe, 1951.

Reig [Salva], Carola. *El Cantar de Sancho II y Cerco de Zamora*. RFE, Anejo 37. Madrid: CSIC, 1947.

Smith, Colin, ed. *Poema de mio Cid*. Oxford: Clarendon, 1972.

English Translation

The Poem of the Cid. Tr. Rita Hamilton and Janet Perry. Intro., notes Ian Michael. New York: Barnes and Noble, 1975.

Criticism

Anderson, J. O. "The 'Letter of Death' Motif in *La leyenda de los Siete Infantes de Lara*." *Hispania* 13 (1930): 315–18.

Bowra, C. M. *Heroic Poetry*. 1952; rpt. London: Macmillan, 1964.

Catalán Menéndez-Pidal, Diego. "Crónicas generales y cantares de gesta. El *Mio Cid* de Alfonso X y del pseudo Ben-Alfaray." *HR* 31 (1963): 195–215 and 291–306.

Chasca, Edmund de. *El arte juglaresco en el "Cantar de mio Cid."* Madrid: Gredos, 1967. [2nd ed. of *Estructura y forma en el. "Poema de mio Cid."*]

Cummins, J. G. "The Chronicle Texts of the Legend of the *Infantes de Lara*." *BHS* 53 (1976): 101–16.

Deyermond, A. D. *"Mio Cid" Studies*. London: Tamesis, 1977.

———. "The Singer of Tales and Mediaeval Spanish Epic." *BHS* 42 (1965): 1–8.

Entwistle, W. J. "The *Cantar de Gesta* of Bernardo del Carpio." *MLR* 23 (1928): 432–52.

Harvey, L. P. "The Metrical Irregularity of the *Cantar de Mio Cid*." *BHS* 40 (1963): 137–43

Krappe, A. H. *"The Cantar de los Infantes de Lara* and the Chanson de Roland." *Neuphilologische Mitteilungen* 25 (1924): 15–24.

Menéndez Pidal, Ramón. *Poesía juglaresca y orígenes de las literaturas románicas. Problemas de historia literaria y cultural*. 6th ed. of *Poesía juglaresca y juglares*. Madrid: Instituto de Estudios Políticos, 1957.

———. "Un nuevo cantar de gesta español del siglo XIII." *RFE* 4 (1917): 105–204.

Singleton, M. "The Two Techniques of the *Poema de Mio Cid*. An Interpretative Essay." *RPH* 5 (1951–52): 222–27.

Webber, Ruth House. "The Diction of the Roncesvalles Fragment." In *Homenajes a Rodríguez Moñino*. Madrid: Castalia, 1966. 2: 311–21.

Anthony J. Cárdenas

METGE, Bernat (1343?, Barcelona–1413, ?), prose writer, translator and humanist of the Catalan pre-Renaissance. Metge was a cosmopolitan intellectual and political figure who traveled widely throughout the Western world and served as secretary of state to King Martí l'Humà. He married twice and sired five illegitimate children. His poetry does not have the importance of his prose writing. *Llibre de Fortune e Prudencia* (1381; Book of Fortune and Prudence) is an allegoric poem of Provençal influence; *Ovid enamorat* (Ovid in Love) is a translation of the second volume of the pseudo-Ovidian text *De vetula*; and *Historia de Valter e Griselda* (Story of Walter and Griselda) is a Catalanized translation of the Latin version of Petrarch—as such it is the first translation of Petrarch in the Iberian Peninsula. *Lo somni* (1399; The Dream), his major work, consists of four volumes which treat a great variety of themes. In this sort of daily-life chronicle of two Catalan kings, Joan I and Martí l'Humà, Metge presents himself as an Epicurean master finally converted to the immortality of the soul. With this book Metge becomes the foremost example of Catalan pre-Renaissance, because of his direct knowledge of several classical authors, his very strong Italian inspiration (Boccaccio, Petrarch), his intellectual curiosity and his skeptical, rationalist spirit. *See also* Catalan literature; Italian literary influences.

BIBLIOGRAPHY

Primary Texts

Lo somni. Ed. J. M. Casacuberta. Barcelona: Barcino, 1959.

Obras. Ed. M. de Riquer. Barcelona: U of Barcelona, 1959. (Critical ed., intro., and documentation.)

Obres menors. Ed. M. Olivar. Barcelona: Atenes, 1927.

Obra completa. Eds. L. Badia and X. Lamuela. Barcelona: Selecta, 1975.

Criticism

Casella, M. "*El Somni* de B. M. e i primi influssi italiani nella letteratura catalana." *Archivum Romanicum* 3 (1919): 145–205.

d'Owler, N. "Les Obres de B. M." In *Paisatges de la nostra història*. Barcelona: n.p., 1929.

Par, A. "Sintaxi Catalana segons los escrits en prosa de B. M." *Beihefte zur Zeitschrift für Romanische Philologie* 66 (1923): n.p.

Riquer, M. de. "Notes sobre B. M." *Estudis Universitaris Catalans* 18 (1933): 329–444.

Soldevila, F. "Documents relativs a Bernat Metge." *Estudis Universitaris Catalans* 6 (1912): 46–58 and 199–210.

Joan Gilabert

MEXÍA, Hernán (fl. late fifteenth c., Jaén–Jaén?), poet, alderman of Jaén. His ten extant poems are largely satiric, although some treat the theme of love. Most famous is *Los defectos de las condiciones de las mujeres* (Defects of Women's Conditions), which recalls comments on the same theme by the *Arcipreste de Talavera in the *Corbacho*.

BIBLIOGRAPHY

Primary Text

Poesías. In NBAE 19.

MEXÍA, Pero (1497, Seville–1551, Seville), distinguished scholar and humanist. This learned gentleman, famous throughout Europe for his scholarly achievements, studied first in his native city and later in Salamanca. He held important positions, including that of chronicler of the emperor (from 1548, following the death of Fray Antonio de *Guevara). He corresponded in Latin with Erasmus, Lluiś *Vives and Ginés de *Sepúlveda; a partisan of Erasmus, he was also an avowed anti-Lutheran.

His abundant and varied work is typical of the *Renaissance. The *Silva de varia lección* (Seville, 1540; *Forest or Collection of Histories*, 1571) is a rich collection of anecdotes, histories, miracles, and miscellaneous observations, written in a style that seems to prefigure the journalism of later centuries. The work enjoyed an extraordinary success; in the sixteenth c. alone it went through seventeen editions and it was also translated into Italian (1542), French (1552), and English (1571). It is thought to be the inspiration for Christopher Marlowe's *Tamburlaine*. The *Silva* shows the influence of Gellius's *Attic Nights*; other sources are Athenaeus's *Banquet of the Sophists*, Pliny's *Natural History*, Valerius Maximus, and Macrobius's *Saturnalia*.

Mexía's other works were equally successful; the *Historia imperial y cesárea* (Seville, 1545; *The Historie of all the Romane Emperors* . . . , 1604), an attempt at a universal vision of history which recounts the lives of the Caesars and their supposed continuation until Maximilian I of Austria; and the *Diálogos o coloquios* (Seville, 1547; Dialogues or Colloquys), some on scientific topics such as astronomy, others that deal with contemporary customs and beliefs. The dialogue form that Mexía uses here was much in fashion at the beginning of the sixteenth c. As soon as he became the new imperial chronicler, Mexía began his ambitious *Historia del Emperador Carlos V* (History of the Emperor Charles V), a work left unfinished at its author's death. The narrative of the *Historia* ends in 1530, year of the imperial coronation at Bologna. Prudencio de *Sandoval and the later chroniclers—often without giving proper credit—drew heavily on this work of Mexía's, both in substance and in technique; the book is characterized by a fluent and polished style, as well as a scrupulous care in the use of sources. Especially noteworthy is the author's treatment of the War of the Comunidades (1520–21) and the Sack of Rome (1527). *See also* Erasmism; Humanism.

BIBLIOGRAPHY

Primary Texts

Diálogos o coloquios. Ed. and study, M. M. Mulroney. Iowa City: U of Iowa, 1930.

Historia del Emperador Carlos V. Ed. and study J. de Mata Carriazos. Madrid: Espasa-Calpe, 1945.

"Rarezas bibliográficas: la collección de ediciones y traducciones del sevillano Pedro Mejía (1496–1552) en la biblioteca de la Universidad de Illinois." Ed. A. Porqueras Mayo and J. Laurenti. *Archivo Hispalense* 57 (1974): 121–38.

Silva de varia lección. Ed. Justo García Soriano. 2 vols. Madrid: Sociedad de bibliófilos españoles, 1933–34.

English Translations

Silva de varia lección. In *Palace of Pleasure*. Tr. William Painter. London, 1566–67; modern edition: New York: AMS P, 1967.

See also ''Rarezas bibliográficas'' in Primary Texts.

Criticism

Castro Díaz, Antonio. *Los ''Coloquios'' de Pedro Mexía: un género, una obra y un humanista sevillano del siglo XVI*. Seville: Excma. Diputación Provincial, 1977.

Costes, René. ''Pedro Mexía, chroniste de Charles-Quint.'' *BH* 22 (1920): 1–36, 256–68; 23 (1921): 95–110.

Menéndez y Pelayo, M. ''El magnífico caballero Pedro Mexía'' [1874]. In *Estudios y discursos de crítica histórica y literaria*. Madrid: CSIC, 1941. 2: 25–38.

Meseguer, J. ''Sobre el erasmismo de Pedro Mexía, cronista de Carlos V.'' In *Archivo Iberoamericano* 7 (1947): 394–413.

Michelena, Janet. ''The Source of Christopher Marlowe's *Tamburlaine*.'' In *Rackham Literary Studies* 3 (1972); 123–28.

William Ferguson

MEY, Sebastián (1586?, Valencia–1641?, Valencia), fabulist. Part of the famous Mey family of publishers, he wrote a collection of fifty-seven fables and anecdotes titled *Fabulario de cuentos antiguos y nuevos* (1613?; Collected Fables, Ancient and New). Many are translations of classical, Oriental and Italian stories; each ends with a moral written in couplet.

BIBLIOGRAPHY

Primary Texts

Cuentos viejos de la vieja España. Ed. F. C. Sáinz de Robles. Madrid: Aguilar, 1949. Contains eight from Mey's collection.

Fabulario. In NBAE 21.

MIDDLE AGES. *See* Edad Media, Literatura de la

MIEZA, Carmen Farrés de (1931, Barcelona–1976, Barcelona), novelist. She published only two novels, both based on her experience as the daughter of an expatriate. Although she remained in Spain after the Civil War and completed her training as a teacher, in 1954 she joined her father who had fled to Mexico immediately after the war. *La imposible canción* (1962; The Impossible Song) portrays the lives of Catalonian exiles living in Mexico City but dreaming of a return to the homeland, a hope they realize can never be fulfilled. *Una mañana cualquiera* (1965; Any Tomorrow; Premio Urriza) studies the complex relationships between a late adolescent who comes from Spain to Mexico to visit her exiled father and his ignorant lower-class Mexican wife. The father, a doctor, represents the bitterness, desolation and solitude of exile, but the daughter expects to become a citizen of the world. After her return to Spain, Mieza established a publishing firm, Ediciones Marte. She also published several short stories, one of which won the 1960 story contest in El Correo Catalán of Barcelona; *Bar-*

celona, Tarragona, Lérida, Gerona (1966), a travel book, no. 7 in the Rutas de España (Routes of Spain) series; and *La mujer del español* (1977; The Spaniard's Wife), a collection of interviews.

BIBLIOGRAPHY

Primary Texts

Barcelona, Tarragona, Lérida, Gerona. Madrid: Publicaciones Españolas, 1966.
La imposible canción. Barcelona: Brugera, 1962.
Una mañana cualquiera. Lérida: Prisma, 1965.
La mujer del español. Barcelona: Marte, 1977.

Criticism

Galerstein, C. "Spanish Women Novelists and Younger-Generation Writers in Exile and Return: Outsiders or Insiders." In *European Writers in Exile in Latin Amerca.* Ed. H. H. Moeller. Heidelberg: Winter, 1983. 137–48.
———. "The Second Generation in Exile." *Papers on Language and Literature* 21.2 (Spring 1985): 220–28.

Carolyn Galerstein

MIGUÉIS, José Rodrigues (1901, Lisbon–1980, New York), Portuguese novelist and short story writer. After obtaining a law degree from the U of Lisbon, Miguéis studied in Brussels (1935), but spent most of his life in New York thereafter, excepting visits to Portugal and a year in Brazil. He became a member of the Seara Nova literary and political group in 1922 and published his novella *Páscoa feliz* (1932; Happy Easter) a decade later. The psychological and social subtleties of this work caused it to be seen as a major work, although in some ways it is little different from models of nineteenth-c. realism, with the addition of the discovery of Dostoyevski (the narrator-protagonist, Renato Lima, has been seen as an illustration of Dostoyevski's idea of free will). He represents a proto-existentialist exploration of problems of responsibility, authenticity, free will and awareness. Another novella, *Léah* (1940), was first published as a serial, then collected in volume form in 1958 as *Léah e outras histórias* (Leah and Other Stories). *Léah* abounds in familiar social problems, from the protagonist's genteel poverty, to other economic issues, and such psycho-social problems as adjustment to a foreign culture, the homesickness of the emigrant, problems of the worker compounded by problems of culture and aloneness. Hailed as a masterwork of neo-realism, *Léah* is a love story, wherein love is first brought about by common poverty and then later frustrated by it. *Onde a noite se acaba* (1946; Where the Night Ends) is a story collection, as are *Gente de terceira classe* (1962; Third-Class People), *Comércio com o inimigo* (1973; Business with the Enemy) and *As harmonias do "Canelão"* (1974; Canelão's Harmonies), all of exceptional quality. *Uma aventura inquietante* (1958; A Worrisome Adventure) employs the format of the detective story to convey a moral message; *Um homem sorri à morte-com meia cara* (1959; One Smiles at Death with Only One Side of One's Face) has an autobiographical basis in a serious illness—a massive cerebral infection—suffered by the writer. Also somewhat autobiographical in its evocations of the author's youth in Lisbon is *A escola do paraíso* (1960; School of Paradise). One of the most discussed works of Miguéis is *Nikalai! Nikalai!* (2nd ed., 1982), which presents the misadventures of White Russian exiles or emigrés in Belgium, where they live very badly and long for Russia. The work is narrated by a secret service agent, actually a double agent who switches his loyalty, suffers identity and language problems, and indulges in a kind of metanarrative game concerning who is the author, what is fact and what is fantasy. Published with the same work is *A múmia* (The Mummy), a tale of frustrated love, set in Portugal. *O milagre segundo Salomé* (1974; The Miracle, According to Salome) is a two-volume novel, ironically alluding to the Fatima apparitions, in the course of a lengthy sentimental romance featuring a country girl who finds wealth in the city.

BIBLIOGRAPHY

Primary Texts

É proibido apontar. Lisbon: Estúdios Cor, 1964.
O pão não cai do céu (serial publication 1975–76); book, Lisbon: Estampa, 1981.
Reflexões dum burguês. Lisbon: Estampa, 1974.

English Translations

Steerage and Other Stories. Providence, RI: Gávea-Brown, 1983.
Lisbon in Manhattan. Providence, RI: Gávea-Brown, 1984.

Criticism

Lopes, Oscar. "O pessoal e o social no obra de Miguéis." in *Cinco personalidades literarias*. Oporto: Divulgacão, 1961. 49–84.
Kerr, John A., Jr. *Miguéis—to the Seventh Decade*. University, MS: Romance Monographs, 1977.

Janet Pérez

MIHURA SANTOS, Miguel (1905, Madrid–1977, Madrid), author of twenty-three full-length plays. Mihura established his reputation as a pioneer in the development of a new articulation of sophisticated dramatic humor between 1936 and 1944. During this period he co-authored three plays of a startling avant-garde flavor (collaborating with Joaquín *Calvo Sotelo, Tono, and Alvaro de *Laiglesia) and promoted the bizarre humor of *La Ametralladora* and *La Codorniz*, popular weekly magazines he founded in 1936 and 1941, respectively. The abstract satire, colloquial nonsense, and extravagant dialogue that he cultivated in these periodicals carried over into the writing of his first and most notable comedy of single authorship, *Tres sombreros de copa* (1952; Three Top Hats). This play climaxed an exciting era of exploration with unconventional dramatic structure unfettered by concessions to public demands. The work is still considered Mihura's finest contribution to the Spanish theater: it is rich in human worth, refined humor, and its exaltation of the importance of freedom from constricting habit and boredom. Over the next sixteen years, Mihura staged nineteen plays of varying artistic merits. They range from shallow farces of intrigue, such as *Melocotón en almíbar* (1958; Peaches and Syrup), to works of solid construction in which parody, satire, and caricature are infused with an engaging character development and a tender yet profound sense of humanity. The outstanding plays of this period include *Mi adorado Juan* (1956; My Beloved Juan), *Maribel y la extraña familia* (1959; Maribel and the Strange Family), and *La bella Dorotea* (1963; Lovely Dorotea). Mihura's outstanding contribution to early twentieth-c. Spanish drama is a smiling, indulgent acceptance of reality and an awareness that, although human predicaments are often insurmountable, ideals and illusions must be cultivated as worthwhile adornments of the human spirit. His writings affirm that individuals can acquire positive values through self-liberation from social conformity and enervating routine.

BIBLIOGRAPHY

Primary Texts

Obras completas. Barcelona: AHR, 1962. Thirteen plays and three prose writings.

Criticism

McKay, Douglas. *Miguel Mihura*. TWAS 436. Boston: Twayne, 1977.

Douglas McKay

MILÀ I FONTANALS, Manuel (1818, Vilafranca del Penedès–1884, Vilafranca del Penedès), philologist, literary critic and historian, literary theorist, translator and poet. Educated in Barcelona, he studied the classics, mathematics, philosophy, modern languages and jurisprudence. Himself a disciple of distinguished professors (R. Martí d'Eixalà, Joaquim Roig and Dr. Quintana), he also left equally famous pupils (*Rubió i Ors, *Piferrer, *Menéndez Pelayo and others). Married in 1845, he devoted his entire life to research and teaching.

A true polyglot, he is considered one of the founding fathers of modern humanistic research on the Iberian Peninsula. He started as a Romantic and was a regular contributor to the review *El Vapor*, where in 1836 he published the first and perhaps best, even today, critical essay on European *Romanticism in general and on Catalan Romanticism in particular, "Clásicos y Románticos" (Classics and Romantics). From then on his publications in Romantic magazines (*El Vapor*, *El propagador de la libertad* and *El Guardia nacional* among others) were prodigious: dozens of articles and poems appear, inspired mostly by Byron, Lamartine and Chateaubriand. Then an ardent follower of liberal Romanticism, he crystallized his view of literature in *Estudios literarios* (1838; Literary Studies). But in 1839 he published the famous panegyric to Walter Scott's historical novel *Moral literaria—Contraste entre la escuela escéptica y Walter Scott* (Literary Morality—A Contrast between the Skeptical School and Walter Scott), becoming thus a defender of traditional Romanticism. Between 1838 and 1844, he spent large periods of time in the Bibliothèque National of Paris studying Provençal poetry, codices and medieval manuscripts; this study resulted in the *Compendio de arte poética* (1844; Compendium of Poetic Art). In 1853 he published one of his most important works, *Observaciones sobre la poesía* *popular* (Observations on Popular Poetry), in which he expounded the development of traditional Catalan poetry, which, according to Milà, is the result of the evolution of aesthetic feeling and tradition. In 1882 he reiterated this thesis in another book, *Romancerillo catalán* (Catalan Popular Songs), accompanying his commentaries with a collection of 550 songs. This second period of his life (1840–84), especially until 1861, is without doubt his most productive. Articles appeared by the dozens, and he even took part, as a poet, in the Jocs Florals (**Juegos*) of 1859. His second most important work also appeared, the *Estética* (1857–69; Aesthetics), in which he tries to introduce into the Iberian Peninsula the North European schools of thought: the Scottish school of psychology, Hegel, Kant, etc. In 1861 he produced his third masterpiece, *De los trobadores en España* (On the Troubadours of Spain) and in 1874, *De la poesía heroico-popular castellana* (The Castilian Heroic-Popular Poetry) in which he advanced the thesis that the **Romancero* (popular poetry) is in fact a branch of the Castilian epic.

As a poet Milà was equally prolific. Although he wrote in Castilian and Catalan, almost all critics agree upon the superiority of Milà's Catalan compositions. Poems like "La font de Melior" (The Fountain of Melior), included in the volume *Los trobadors nous* (1858; The New Troubadours), "Un temple antic" (1879; An Old Church) and "La cançó del Pros Bernat" (1867; The Song of Pros Bernat) are among the best produced by Catalan Romanticism. But for Milà, Romanticism is essentially a historical literary movement, more archaeological and retrospective than anything else. Despite his rather conservative view of literature, he left an extraordinary imprint on the Renaixença of Catalan letters, and in the later years of his life he became more militant regarding the "Catalan question." In many ways Milà brilliantly takes up the broken tradition of Catalan humanistic scholarship. One still marvels at his excellent translations of Horace, Dante, Shakespeare, W. Scott, Schlegel, Manzoni and many others. *See also* Catalan literature.

BIBLIOGRAPHY

Primary Texts

La cançó del Pros Bernat. Ed. R. D'Abadal. Vic: n.p., 1947.

Epistolari d'en Milà i Fontanals. Collected and annotated by N. d'Olwer. Barcelona: Biblioteca Filològica de l'Institut de la Llengua Catalana, 1922.

Obres Catalanes. Ed. G. Gili. Barcelona: n.p., 1908.

Obras completas. Ed. Marcelino Menéndez Pelayo. 8 vols. Barcelona: Verdaguer, 1886–96.

Criticism

Jorba, J. Prologue. To *Teoria romàntica*. By M. Milà i Fontanals. Barcelona: Ediciones 62, 1977.

Juretschke, Hans. "Alemania en la obra de Milà y Fontanals." *Boletín de la Real Academia de Buenas Letras de Barcelona* 35 (1972–73): 5–67.

Menéndez Pelayo, Marcelino. "El Dr. D. Manuel Milà i Fontanals, semblanza literaria." In *Estudios de crítica literaria*. Buenos Aires: Glem, 1942.

Roig i Roqué, Josep. *Bibliografia d'en Manuel Milà i Fontanals*. Barcelona: Librería Religiosa, 1913.
Rubió i Lluch, A. *Manuel Milà i Fontanals, Notes biogràfiques i crítiques*. Barcelona: Asociacio Protectora de l'ensenyanza catalana, 1918.

Joan Gilabert

MILLÁN ASTRAY, Pilar (1892, Madrid–1949, Madrid), Spanish novelist and dramatist. Millán Astray belonged to a conservative, upper-class family closely linked to the military establishment and the Franco uprising (her brother was a general), which led to her imprisonment by leftists during the Civil War. During the 1920s and 1930s when most of her works were written, Millán was unusual in being one of very few women in Spain—especially in the theater—to write under her own name. Considerable popular success notwithstanding, her works are conservative and conventional, with few values beyond simple entertainment. She wrote a number of children's books, including *El ogro* (1921; The Ogre), and a volume of memoirs which detail her prison experience: *Cautivas; 32 meses en las prisiones rojas* (1940; Captives; 32 months in Red Prisons). Theatrical genres cultivated vary from the melodrama to comedy, drama and **sainete* (a brief, humorous, satirical work with lower-class characters). *Sainetes* include *Los amores de la Nati* (1931; Nati's Love Affairs), *Las ilusiones de la Patro* (1925; Patro's Illusions), *Mademoiselle Naná* (1928) and *La tonta del bote* (1925), all of which tend to view the aspirations of working girls and servants with a certain condescending paternalism. Longer comedies include *Al rugir el león* (1923; When the Lion Roars), *Ruth la Israelita* (1923; Ruth the Israelite), *El paso de las hortensias* (1924; The Passage of Hortensias), *La Galana* (1926; The Elegant One), *Pancho Robles* (1926), *Magda la Tirana* (1926; The Tyrant Magda), *Adán y Eva* (1929; Adam and Eve), *El millonario y la bailarina* (1931; The Millionaire and the Dancing Girl), *La casa de la bruja* (1932; The Witch's House), and *La condesa Maribel* (1942; Countess Marybelle). Among her novels are *La llave de oro* (1921; The Golden Key) and *Las dos estrellas* (1928; The Two Stars).

BIBLIOGRAPHY

Primary Texts

El juramento de la primorosa. Madrid: Velasco, 1924.
Teatro, 1923–1942. Madrid: E. de Miguel, 1942.

Janet Pérez

MIÑANO, Sebastián (1779, Becerril de Campos–1845, Bayonne, France?), *costumbrista* and historian. A cleric, he attained the rank of cardinal. Owing to his French sympathies, he lived in Paris between 1814 and 1816. As a writer for the Madrid newspaper *El Censor*, he contributed the *Cartas de Don Justo Balanza* (Don Just Balance's Letters) and the *Cartas del Madrileño* (Letters from a Madrid Native). These are all satirical *cuadros de costumbres*, filled with caustic, ironic criticism. His *Cartas del pobrecito holgazán* (1820; Letters from a Poor Little Idler) and the *Lamentos políticos del pobrecito holgazán* (Political Complaints from a Poor Little Idler) constitute the first nineteenth-c. *costumbrista* essays, wherein he attacks the absolutist regime and satirizes sundry Spanish customs. Highly popular when written, these *cuadros* served as a model to later practitioners of the genre. Miñano also wrote *Histoire de la révolution d'Espagne de 1820 à 1823. Par un espagnol témoin oculaire* (1824; History of the Revolution in Spain during 1820–23 by an Eyewitness) and a *Diccionario geográfico-estadístico de España y Portugal* (1826–29; A Geographic and Statistical Dictionary of Spain and Portugal), for which Fermín *Caballero took him to task. He was also a member of the Royal Academy of History. *See also* Academia; Romanticism.

BIBLIOGRAPHY

Primary Texts

Cartas del Madrileño. Madrid: Amarita, 1821.
Cartas del pobrecito holgazán. Valencia: Domingo y Mompié, 1820.
Diccionario geográfico-estadístico de España y Portugal. 11 vols. Madrid: Peralta, 1826–29.
Histoire de la révolution d'Espagne de 1820 à 1823. Par un espagnol témoin oculaire. Paris: Dentu, 1824.
Lamentos políticos del pobrecito holgazán. Madrid: Ciencia Nueva, 1968.

Criticism

Aguilera, Ignacio. "Cartas de D. Sebastián de Miñano y Bedoya." *BBMP* 47 (1971): 391–445.
Ochoa, Eugenio de. *Apuntes para una biblioteca de españoles contemporáneos.* 2 vols. Paris: Baudry, 1840.

Eugene Del Vecchio

MINGO REVULGO, Coplas de (Mingo Revulgo's Verses), fifteenth-c. poem. Cast as a dialogue between two shepherds, Mingo Revulgo and Gil Arrebato, this satirical poem presents a trenchant critique of fifteenth-c. Spanish affairs. As representative of the people, Mingo Revulgo blames the king (Henry IV) and his favorite (Beltrán de la Cueva) for ruling badly and offers his own norms for effective government. Gil Arrebato, representing the nobility, counters that the people are also to be held accountable. The poem consists of thirty-two nine-line stanzas, a *redondilla,* and a *quintilla*. Soberly elegant in style, its satirical impact is heightened by careful argumentation. Probably written around 1460, this poem was glossed by Hernando del *Pulgar, whose praise of it was so glowing that the historian Juan de *Mariana attributed it to Pulgar in Book 23, Chapter 17 of his *Historia general de España* (1601). Of particular interest to scholars of Spanish theater is the influence the poem had on early Spanish dramatists, especially Juan del *Encina.

BIBLIOGRAPHY

Primary Text

Coplas de Mingo Revulgo, glosadas por Hernando del Pulgar. Intro. Federico Síanz de Robles. Madrid: Espasa-Calpe, 1972. (Facs. of original 1545 Seville ed.)

Criticism

Ciceri, Marcella. ''La tradizione manoscritta delle *Coplas de Mingo Revulgo,*'' *Quaderni di Lingue e Letterature* 1 (1976): 191–201.

Rodríguez-Puértolas, Julio ''Sobre el autor de las *Coplas de Mingo Revulgo.*'' In *Homenaje a Rodríguez Moñino, II.* Madrid: Castalia, 1966. 131–42.

Stern, Charlotte. ''The *Coplas de Mingo Revulgo* and the Early Spanish Drama.'' *HR* 44 (1976): 311–32.

James Ray Green

MIR, Miguel (1841, Palma de Mallorca–1912, Madrid), prose author. He joined the Jesuit order in 1857 but left in 1891, later penning two criticisms of the society: *Los jesuitas de puertas adentro* (1896; The Jesuits from Inside) and *Historia interna documentada de la Compañía de Jesús* (1913; Documented Internal History of the Society of Jesus)—the latter was translated to French. His thorough editions and literary studies include *Sta. Teresa de Jesús; su vida, su espíritu, sus fundaciones* (1912; St. Teresa; Her Life, Her Spirit, Her Foundations), *Bartolomé Leonardo de Argensola* (1891), and two editions for the NBAE, titled *Oradores clásicos españoles* (1906; Spanish Classical Orators) and *Escritores místicos españoles* (1911; Spanish Mystic Writers).

BIBLIOGRAPHY

Primary Texts

Escritores místicos españoles. NBAE 16.

Historia interna documentada de la Compañía de Jesús. Madrid: Ratés, 1913.

Los jesuitas de puertas adentro. Barcelona: Tasso, 1896.

Oradores clásicos españoles. NBAE 1.

Sta. Teresa de Jesús; su vida, su espíritu, sus fundaciones. Madrid: Ratés, 1912.

MIRA DE AMESCUA, Antonio (1574, Guadix–1644, Granada), playwright and poet. Illegitimate son of Melchor de Amescua y Mira, descendant of the Conquistadores, and Beatriz de Torres Heredia, he studied law and theology at the Colegio Imperial de San Miguel in Granada. In 1602 he met Lope de *Vega in Granada and the same year dedicated a sonnet to him. In 1609 he was appointed by Philip II chaplain of the Royal Chapel, and in 1610 the Count of Lemos took him in his service to Naples. Later he was appointed chaplain of Ferdinand, son of Philip II. After a bitter inquiry about his illegitimacy, he retired to Guadix.

Mira de Amescua was a baroque writer from his first poem ''España, que en tiempo de Rodrigo'' (1605; Spain in the Time of Rodrigo). ''Canción a una mudanza'' (Song to a Change) was published in 1654 in the collection *Poesías varias* (Selected Poems). His *Acteón y Diana* is a mythological fable in fifty-eight octaves.

He cultivated all theatrical genres, and much of his theater may be considered lyric. Many critics consider him a transitional author, because while the accumulation of sensational incidents, complicated plot, and mixture of tragic and comic in his plays link Mira to the Lope cycle, his baroque style resembles that of *Calderón.

His dramatic production may be classified into five categories: (1) *auto sacramental* (*auto). These perhaps are the best of his pieces. More than the symbolic aspect, Mira emphasized simplicity and humanism. Among the best known are *La jura del príncipe* (The Prince's Oath), *La fe de Hungría* (The Faith of Hungary), *Las pruebas de Cristo* (The Trials of Christ), and *La Santa Inquisición* (The Holy Inquisition). (2) Religious. Some are biblical, like *El arpa de David* (David's Harp) and *El clavo de Jael* (Jael's Nail). Among the religious pieces dealing with saints we find Mira's masterpiece, *El esclavo del demonio* (1612; The Devil's Slave). This play, based on the legend of the Friar Gil de Santarén who sold his soul to the devil but later was converted, was inspired by the *Primera parte de la historia general de Santo Domingo y su orden de predicadores* (1584; First Part of the General History of Saint Domingo and His Order of Preachers), written by Hernando del *Castillo. Some scenes were modeled on *El mágico prodigioso* (The Prodigious Magician) and *La devoción de la cruz* (The Devotion of the Cross), both written by Calderón. (3) Mythological. *Hero y Leandro*, *Polifemo y Circe*. (4) National history and legend. *El conde Alarcos* (Count Alarcos), *La adversa fortuna de Don Álvaro de Luna* (The Misfortune of Alvaro de Luna), *Ruy López de Ávalos*. (5) Intrigue. *La casa del tahur* (The Gambler's House), *La fénix de Salamanca* (The Phoenix of Salamanca), *Galán, valiente y discreto* (Gallant, Brave and Discreet), etc. *See also* Theater in Spain.

BIBLIOGRAPHY

"Canción real a una mudanza." In *Spanish Poetry of the Golden Age*. Ed. M. Buchanan. Toronto: Toronto UP, 1942. 90–93.

La adversa fortuna de Don Álvaro de Luna. Ed. Luigi di Filippo. Florence: Felice le Monnier, 1966.

La casa del tahur. Ed. V. G. Williamsen. Madrid: Castalia, 1973.

El esclavo del demonio. Ed. J. A. Castañeda. Madrid: Cátedra, 1980.

Galán, valiente y discreto. Ed. F. W. Forbes. Madrid: Playor, 1973.

No hay dicha ni desdicha hasta la muerte. Ed. V. G. Williamsen. Columbia: U of Missouri P, 1970.

Criticism

Castañeda, J. A. *Mira de Amescua*. TWAS 449. Boston: Twayne, 1977.

Cotarelo y Mori, E. *Mira de Amescua y su teatro*. Madrid: RABM, 1931.

Gallego Morell, A "La poesía lírica de Mira de Amescua y bibliografía del escritor." *BRAE* 64 (1984): 333–61.

Fucilla, J. G. "Mira de Amescua's *El esclavo del demonio* in Italy." In *Aspetti e problemi delle letterature iberiche: Studi offerti a Franco Meregallo*. Ed. G. Bellini. Rome: Bulzoni, 1981. 171–82.

Williamsen-Ceron, A. "The Comic Function of Two Mothers: Belisa and Angela." *Bulletin of the Comediantes* 36.2 (1984): 167–74.

Wilson, E. M. "*La próspera fortuna de Don Alvaro de Luna*: An Outstanding Work by Mira de Amescua." *BHS* 33 (1956): 25–36.

Hector Medina

MIRALLES, Josep. *See* Domènech i Escuté de Cañellas, Maria

MIRALLES GRANCHA, Alberto (1940, Barcelona–), Spanish playwright and director. Miralles grew up in post-war Spain during the oppressive Franco era which first outlawed and then systematically discriminated against the vernacular languages and cultures, including that of Catalunya, where he lived. He obtained his degree in Romance philology from the U of Barcelona and participated in early renovation of the theater outside Madrid through his founding of the theatrical Grupo Cátaro in 1967, as well as his activity as a professor in Barcelona's Institute of the Theater. He first came to attention as a director of works of the European vanguard (such as Peter Weiss's *Marat-Sade*) in the late 1960s, then won the Guipúzcoa Prize in 1968 for his *Catarocolón*, which appeared in print in 1975, winning a prize of the *Academia Española as the best theatrical text published that year. Production of the same work by Grupo Cátaro in 1968 also won the National Sitges Prize for Theater. In 1977, Miralles published *Teatro español actual: una alternativa social* (Current Spanish Theater: A Social Alternative), an analysis of the intellectual climate of his generation. He has continued to be active as a member of the National Dramatic Center, directed by Adolfo Marsillach, and as director of two children's theater groups, La Trepa in Barcelona and Trabalenguas in Madrid, as well as teaching acting, improvisation and directing in Madrid and Barcelona, and developing his own theatrical style. *See also* Contemporary Spanish Theater.

Janet Pérez

MIRANDA, Luis de (c. 1500, Plasencia–c. 1572, ?), presbyter, poet, dramatist. He journeyed to what is now Paraguay in 1535 and became involved in politics there. His *Romance elegíaco* (c. 1537; Elegiac Ballad) recounts in quatrains the conquest of the Plate River; it is one of the first poems about Paraguay. Miranda's popular seven-act play *Comedia pródiga* (1554, Seville; Prodigal Play) combines a biblical story with Celestinesque elements (*Celestina). It is the first play written in Asunción, Paraguay.

BIBLIOGRAPHY

Primary Texts

Comedia pródiga. Valencia: Amparo, 1953. Facs.

Romance. Versiones paleográfica y moderna. Intro. J. Torre Revello. Buenos Aires: Coni, 1952.

MIRÓ, Gabriel (1879, Alicante–1930, Madrid), Levantine novelist. Born in the Mediterranean city of Alicante, which was to be inextricably linked to his writings, Miró grew up in a middle-class environment as the son of an engineer. From age seven to twelve he was a student at the Jesuit school of Santo Domingo in Orihuela, and these years were to have a decisive influence on both his personality and his literature. By his own admission, it was an unhappy time which left him with a propensity toward melancholy and a certain pessimism. Of delicate health, the young Miró spent many a day in the school's infirmary, through whose windows he had ample opportunity to contemplate the world of nature. Thus, his illnesses had at least one positive effect, which was to instill in him a fascination with, and an abiding interest in, the landscape of Spain's eastern coast.

He showed an early talent for painting and received instruction and encouragement from his uncle, the artist Lorenzo Casanova. Miró said that he probably would have been a painter rather than a novelist had it not been for his uncle's premature death. Although he studied law at the Universities of Valencia and Granada, he was to spend his non-literary career principally in various bureaucratic positions in Alicante, Barcelona, and Madrid. The publication of his first book, *La mujer de Ojeda* (1901; The Woman from Ojeda), occurred the same year as his marriage to Clemencia Maignon, daughter of the French consul in Alicante. In 1914 the couple moved to Barcelona, where Miró became friends with the musician Oscar Esplá. Six years later he relocated to Madrid, where he lived until his death, of peritonitis, in 1930.

Although his most productive years coincided chronologically with the *Generation of 1898, ideologically he had little in common with it. Whereas the men of 1898 drew inspiration from the arid, stark Castilian landscape, Miró preferred the soft, lyrical tones of his native region. As a whole his works also reveal a remarkable paucity of ideas when compared to the other great prose writers of his day. To be sure, Miró was aware of Spain's backwardness and the human consequences of a corrupt provincial environment, but his novels do not present the problematic Spain that characterized much of the Generation of 1898. For that reason, and also because of the sentimental, erotic flavor of his early work, he is sometimes criticized as a superficial neo-romantic. In reality, as Angel del Río has pointed out, he assimilated some 1898 tendencies (including protagonists with abulia and a pessimistic outlook) and the musical, poetic style of modernism to create his own personal reality of sentiments and sensations.

Miró's style is at times both pleasing and frustratingly difficult. His highly lyrical prose is rich in sensory imagery and he had few equals as a master of the language. The pace of his books, however, can be quite labored; in fact, he has been compared to *Azorín in this respect. Also like Azorín is his minute attention to detail. In *A Literary History of Spain*, G. G. Brown has commented on this aspect of his writing: "Miró's art is to select the details that most of us would miss, and then to dwell on them so that they divulge their full and exact significance. In his best writing he builds these details into patterns of general significance which makes serious and penetrating statements about the human condition."

His novelistic production was fairly extensive. After *La mujer de Ojeda* (which the author himself repudiated and refused to have re-issued), the next important work was *La novela de mi amigo* (1908; The Novel of My Friend), the story of a failed artist who commits suicide. It has been described as a typical Miró novel for its lyricism, its feeling for nature, a Romantic protagonist and the bohemian-decadent atmosphere in which it takes place. The same year Miró published *Nómada* (1908; Nomad), which won an award from *El Cuento Semanal* (Weekly Fiction), a publication directed by the novelist Eduardo Zamacois.

Many of his novels were short, anecdotal pieces which tend to be forgotten by critics today. Among them, however, were three works whose protagonist, Sigüenza, is seen as Miró's alter ego and his most memorable character. These books were *Del vivir* (1904; On Living), *Libro de Sigüenza* (1917; *Libro de Sigüenza*, 1935), and *Años y leguas* (1928; Years and Leagues).

Miró's first long novel was *Las cerezas del cementerio* (1910; The Cherries in the Cemetery), a romantic and erotic book which inaugurated his mature period. It relates the story of Félix Valdivia, an abulic, decadent type, and his love for Beatriz, whose daughter harbors a secret love for Félix. The action takes place against the backdrop of the sensual Levantine landscape, often a trademark of Miró's prose. *El abuelo del rey* (1915; The King's Grandfather) recounts the lives of three generations of a provincial family and was viewed as a technical advance because the author eliminated much of the decadent tendencies of his earlier works. His most important novels were *Nuestro Padre San Daniel* (1921; *Our Father San Daniel*, 1930) and its sequel, *El obispo leproso* (1926; The Leprous Bishop). Both are set in the fictional town of Oleza (Orihuela), a typical backward village in rural Spain.

His novels have been criticized by some as superficial, excessively descriptive, too sentimental, and lacking in character and plot development. Yet in spite of these objections his place in twentieth-c. Spanish literature would be assured if only for his genius in manipulating the language, for in this area he was an artist and poet of the first rank.

BIBLIOGRAPHY

Primary Texts

El abuelo del rey. Barcelona: Ibérica, 1915.
Años y leguas. Buenos Aires: Losada, 1958.
Las cerezas del cementerio. Barcelona: Domenech, 1910.
Del vivir. Alicante: Esplá, 1904.
Libro de Sigüenza. Barcelona: Domenech, 1917.
La mujer de Ojeda. Alicante: Carratalá, 1901.
Nómada. Madrid: "El Cuento Semanal," no. 62, 1908.
La novela de mi amigo. Alicante: Esplá, 1908.
Nuestro Padre San Daniel. Madrid: Atenea, 1921.

El obispo leproso. Madrid: Biblioteca Nueva, 1926.
Obras completas. 4th ed. Madrid: Biblioteca Nueva, 1961.

English Translations

Figures of the Passion of Our Lord. Tr. C. J. Hogarth. New York: Knopf, 1925.
Our Father San Daniel. Tr. Charlotte Remfry-Kidd. London: Benn, 1930.
Libro de Sigüenza. Tr. W. Wilson. New York: Norton, 1935. English tr. of fragments.

Criticism

Barbero, Teresa. *Gabriel Miró*. Madrid: EPESA, 1974.
Brown, G. G. "The Biblical Allusions in Gabriel Miró's Oleza Novels." *MLR* 70 (1975): 786–94.
———. *A Literary History of Spain: The Twentieth Century*. New York: Barnes and Noble, 1972.
Landeira, Ricardo, ed. *Critical Essays on Gabriel Miró*. Lincoln, NE: Society of Spanish and Spanish American Studies, 1979.
López Landeira, Richard. *An Annotated Bibliography of Gabriel Miró (1900–1978)*. Manhattan, KS: Society of Spanish and Spanish American Studies, 1978.
Nora, Eugenio G. de. *La novela española contemporánea (1898–1927)*. 2nd ed. Madrid: Gredos, 1963.
Ramos, Vicente. *El mundo de Gabriel Miró*. 2nd ed. Madrid: Gredos, 1970.
Vidal, R. *Gabriel Miró: Le style, les moyens d'expression*. Bordeaux: Féret, 1964.

James F. Brown

MISERIA DE OMNE, Libro de (Book of Man's Misery), anonymous mid-to-late-fourteenth-c. narrative poem. Written in *mester de clerecía*, it is an adaptation of Innocent III's somber treatise *De contemptu mundi* and does include some original, satiric additions and glosses.

BIBLIOGRAPHY

Primary Text

Libro de miseria de omne. Ed., study M. Artigas. 2 vols. *BBMP* (1919–20): n.p.

MISTERIO DE ELCHE (*Mystery of Elche*, 1964), anonymous medieval miracle play. Written in Catalan c. 1492, it narrates the Passing and the Assumption of the Virgin Mary. Contemporary references to the discovery of the New World and the forced conversion of the Jews are included, and there is musical accompaniment. Even in the twentieth c. the work has been performed in Elche each August.

BIBLIOGRAPHY

Primary Texts

"Auto lírico-religioso en dos actos representados todos los años en. . . ." In *Boletín de la Sociedad Española de Excursiones*. N.p.: n.p., 1896.
La festa d'Elche, ou Le drame lyrique liturgique espagnole. Le trépas et l'assomption de la Vierge. Ed. F. Pedrell. Paris: Schola, 1906.

English Translation

Mystery of Elche. Tr. W. Starkie. In *Eight Spanish Plays of the Golden Age*. New Year: Modern Library, 1964.

Criticism

Mitjana, R. "El Misterio de Elche." In *Discantes y contrapuntos*. Valencia: Sempere, 1905.

MODERN SPANISH NOVEL. After the *Generation of 1898, no specific literary movement emerged with the same coherence until after the Civil War. However, the more traditional tendency continues in the works of Gabriel *Miró, whose novels are visual pictures with minimal plot, heavily laden with metaphor and sensory appeal (*Nuestro Padre San Daniel* [1921; *Our Father San Daniel*, 1930] and *El obispo leproso* [1926; The Leprous Bishop]). Concha *Espina's more realistic novels and penchant for women characters reflect the daily life in the provinces: *La esfinge Maragata* (1914; Mariflor) is set in León; *El metal de los muertos* (1920; The Metal of the Dead) describes worker-capitalist problems in the mining industry to reveal a more social concern. Ricardo *León's advocacy of traditional values is evident in *Casta de hidalgos* (1908; *A Son of the Hidalgos*, 1921).

A more experimental group of novelists also followed the Generation of 1898 but differed from them in a more consciously intellectual stance, a more cosmopolitan and universal orientation, philosophical interests and a taste for literary experimentation. The leading novelist of the period is Ramón *Pérez de Ayala (also associated with the *novecentista* group), who writes in classical style, applying philosophical and metaphysical considerations to his plots. *Belarmino y Apolonio* (1921; *Belarmina and Apolonio*, 1971) deals with *perspectivismo* (relativity) on artistic, philosophical and personal levels; *Tigre Juan* (1926; *Tiger Juan*, 1933) and its sequel *El curandero de su honra* (1926; *The Healer of His Honor*, 1933) humanize *Don Juan and the Spanish honor code. More experimental avant-garde novelists of the period would include Ramón *Gómez de la Serna, whose virtuosity with the *greguería* spills into his novels: subtle humor, metaphor, fragmentation of reality are elements in *El doctor inverosímil* (1921; The Improbable Doctor); Benjamín *Jarnés's virtuosity of style is apparent in works like *Locura y muerte de nadie* (1929; Madness and Death of Nobody).

A brief interest in social realism was truncated by the Civil War. Among this group would be included Ramón *Sender's early works (*Siete domingos rojos* [1932; *Seven Red Sundays*, 1936] or *Mr. Witt en el cantón* [1935; *Mr. Witt among the Rebels*, 1937]) and Joaquín *Arderíus's *Campesinos* (1931; Peasants).

The Civil War (1936–39) severed the continuity of literary tradition on several counts: the immediate necessity of recovery, depressed economic conditions, the demise or exile of established writers who could have provided leadership (*García Lorca, *Valle-Inclán, Antonio *Machado, *Unamuno, Max *Aub, Ramón Sender, etc.), the imposition of strict *censorship, and a general atmosphere of suspicion and distrust encouraged literature that skirted serious literary or social issues in favor of pleasant entertainment.

In the decade following the Civil War, the Spanish novel turned to the past for inspiration, continuing the realistic-naturalistic-*costumbrista* tradition of the nineteenth c., unbroken via the ever-popular novels of *Pérez Galdós. Twentieth-c. interpretations did not tamper substantially with hallowed techniques. Traditional post-war realism takes a demographic approach to a social or physical reality, sketching a rich and varied background of human life against which a character (generally of the middle class) acts out a personal drama while simultaneously representing a class or type. An interest in environmental and family influences enriches the plot with detailed accounts of social interaction and descriptions of people, places, home, and work. The omniscient author provides a moral or ethical overlay; possibly theses have universal implications. Both historical and contemporary periods are used as settings. Ignacio *Agustí's _Mariona Rebull_ (1944) was one of the best-sellers of this type. It describes the social ambitions and marriage of Joaquín Ríus, played against the social background and labor unrest of fin de siècle life in Barcelona. History and personal drama are skillfully merged, much in the manner of Pérez Galdós's _Episodios nacionales_. Other examples of traditional realism are José María *Gironella's _Los cipreses creen en Dios_ (1953; _The Cypresses Believe in God_, 1954), a poignant chronicle of events leading up to the Civil War; Elena *Quiroga's _La sangre_ (1952; Blood), in which a chestnut tree narrates a Galician family history; Dolores *Medio's Nadal-winner _Nosotros los Rivero_ (1953; We Riveros), describing Oviedo before the Second Republic; or Miguel *Delibes's _Mi idolatrado hijo Sisí_ (1953; My Idolized Son Sisí), a story of how egotism can destroy all it touches. Juan Antonio de *Zunzunegui, one of the most prolific writers in the traditional vein, is well known for novels such as _La vida como es_ (1954; Life As It Is), an ambitious cross-section of Madrid life, including the structured society of the underworld; _Esta oscura desbandada_ (1952; This Dark Disbandment) chronicles the depressing conditions of post-war Madrid.

Modern *picaresque narrative, influenced by its traditional models, _costumbrismo_ and the less orthodox realism of Pío *Baroja, also made an appearance. The "scandalous" _Lola, espejo oscuro_ (1950; Lola, In a Glass Darkly), by Darío *Fernández Flórez, presents the memoirs of a high-class prostitute; _Nuevas andanzas y desventuras de Lazarillo de Tormes_ (1944; New Sallies and Misfortunes of Lazarillo de Tormes) is Camilo José *Cela's loosely constructed "novel" which antedates the travel literature so popular during the 1950s and 1960s (Cela's own _Viaje a la Alcarria_ [1948; _Journey to the Alcarria Region_, 1964]; Juan *Goytisolo's _Campos de Níjar_ [1960: Fields of Nihar]). _Industrias y andanzas de Alfanhuí_ (1951; Tricks and Sallies of Alfanhui), by Rafael *Sánchez Ferlosio, changes the focus of the usual crude realism of the original with lyrical and fantastic elements.

One of the first variations of realism, _tremendismo_, was so named because of the "tremendous" impression created by the accumulation of truculence, mental and physical violence, gruesome details, anguish and alienation. Although such exaggerated realism was not unknown in Spanish literature (compare the picaresque, the more clinical *naturalism, the _esperpentos_ of Valle-Inclán), _tremendismo_ adds to this a consciously social and existential note. The first contemporary version is Camilo José Cela's *La familia de Pascual Duarte* (1942; *The Family of Pascual Duarte*, 1964), memoirs of a man sentenced to die for an unspecified crime. Consistently mistreated by family and society, Pascual reveals a life filled with violence, cruelty, rape, death and finally matricide. Carmen *Laforet's *Nada* (1944; *Andrea*, 1964) won the first Nadal novel prize in 1944. It is another *tremendista* work about a girl who comes to Barcelona after the Civil War to live with her eccentric relatives and attend the university. Tension, anxiety, unhappiness, hostility, poverty, and the accumulation of strange, disquieting details accompany the psychological study of a young woman's growth to maturity.

The most extensive variant of realism cultivated in the post-war period is the social novel (also known as "critical realism" or "testimonial novel"). The writer who wished to air injustices of any type—social, economic, religious, etc.—was frustrated by a censorship which still carefully monitored criticism. This tension, coupled with an increasing cinematic influence which disclosed the possibilities of visual commentaries via techniques like montage, sequencing, fleeting vignettes, etc., fostered a style in which the author progressively withdrew from visibility, ceding his traditional role as authority figure. The social novel thus approached journalistic technique in its presentation of "objective facts" which could state the case without necessity of commentary or explanation. Author manipulation entered mainly in the arrangement, juxtaposition or disproportionate focus on facts presented. Somewhat less panoramic than traditional realism, the social novel takes a socially critical stance missing from the earlier movement. Characters are drawn from the lower or lower-middle classes, the individual standing as both group representative and individual personality. Detailed descriptions of work conditions, home life, local customs and dialect accompany the plot. Subjects cover a wide range: the civil servant and post-war housing shortage (Dolores Medio, *Funcionario público* [1955; Public Servant]); relocation in Spain (*La piqueta* [1959; The Pick Ax], by Antonio *Ferres); life in the mines (*La mina* [1960; The Mine] by Armando *López Salinas); viniculture and socio-economic problems in Andalusia (José Manuel *Caballero Bonald's *Dos días de setiembre* [1961; Two Days in September]); worker emigration (*Hemos perdido el sol* [1963; We Have Lost the Sun], by Angel María de *Lera); the effects of and attitude toward technical progress in a small village (Jesús *López Pacheco's *Central eléctrico* [1956; Powerhouse]); the monotony of village life (*Los bravos* [1954; The Wild Ones], by Jesús *Fernández-Santos); criticism of bourgeois values (*Encerrados con un solo juguete* [1960; Closed Up with Only One Toy], by Juan *Marsé).

Cela's *La colmena* (1953; *The Hive,* 1953) was another major literary event in which multiple protagonists (over 200) appear in brief fragmented episodes in post-war Madrid. The final impression is one of hopeless, depressing conditions: selfishness, egotism, lack of human understanding are prevalent; hunger and sex are the primary motivations. The social message of the work is apparent through the material presented; no commentary is necessary, and the multiple characters discourage close identification with a single viewpoint. Other episodic approaches to the novel are found in Luis *Romero's *La noria* (1952; The Waterwheel); Dolores Medio's *La pez sigue flotando* (1959; The Fish Stays Afloat) or Luis *Goytisolo's *Las mismas palabras* (1963; The Same Words), although none of these reaches the diffuseness of character and fragmentary nature of *The Hive*. This technique is also referred to as *unanimismo* because of the single location used as focal point for diverse characters.

The progressive disappearance of the author culminates in the objectivist novel. Loosely connected with the French "New Novel," the *novela objetivista* differs stylistically from the other realistic movements in the deliberate elimination of the usual authorial commentary, manipulation of plot via sequential or chronological shifts, coincidence, or literary devices such as metaphor, accumulation, and lyrical passages. Instead, the reader is confronted with a wealth of seemingly unrelated information from which must be sifted out what is important, if anything. Such a phenomenological approach to literature avoids psychological studies, commentaries, or "theses," since the only "truth" available is what appears on the surface, just as in real life. Rafael Sánchez Ferlosio's *El Jarama* (1955; *The One Day of the Week*, 1962) presents a group of Madrid youth who spend a day at a beach on the Jarama River. Conversations and interactions within the group as well as with other groups provide a skeletal plot; a tragic accident at the end of the work does not add appreciably to the dramatic action. So "objective" was this work that the author was accused of having transcribed a tape of the conversations which form the major portion of the novel. The facts speak for themselves: a lack of commitment to anything, a refusal to admire ideals, a certain vacuousness, and the obvious generation gap characterize this young group. Juan *García Hortelano's *Nuevas amistades* (1959; New Friendships) and *Tormenta de verano* (1961; *Summer Storm*, 1962) both attack the emptiness of the middle-class life with the *objetivista* technique.

Less "objectively" oriented, but still faithful to the critical intent of the social novel, is a group which allows a much more personal note to enter the work. The critical stance and realistic point of departure are unchanged, but this variation—critical realism, subjective realism, *realismo de denuncia* are a few of its names—internalizes the experience, broadening the issues to include psychological reactions, and accords increasing importance to the prose style and technique as message as well as medium: metaphor, interior monologue, stream of consciousness, less precision of detail, and fragmentation of time or logic return the author to a place of prominence. The rich content of many of these novels may suggest mythical models, cyclical time schemes, rites of passage, etc. Complacency and hypocrisy of the middle class receive sharp censure as innocence is crushed, idealism ridiculed and egotism and cynicism prevail. Ana María *Matute's *Los hijos muertos* (1958; *The Lost Children*, 1965) applies the above themes to the Civil War and its aftereffects; her 1959 Nadal Winner *Primera memoria* (1959; *School of the Sun*, 1959) modernizes the timeless betrayal of Christ, reenacted by adolescents. Like Matute's works, several of the early novels of Juan Goytisolo describe precocious children or adolescents, victims of the system, who assume adult awareness too early. *Juegos de manos* (1954; *The Young Assassins*, 1959) describes a group of well-to-do bourgeois youths who rebel against the status quo; *Duelo en el Paraíso* (1958; *Children of Chaos*, 1958) has been compared thematically to Golding's *Lord of the Flies*. Miguel Delibe's *El camino* (1950; *The Path*, 1961) follows a young boy's memories of his childhood as he prepares to leave his rural home for school in the city.

Many authors of this period use basic realism as a point of departure for various technical or thematic concerns. Elena Quiroga's later works offer psychological emphasis: *Tristura* (1960; Sadness) describes the reactions of a young girl; *Presente profundo* (1973; Profound Present) tells of conflicting points of view and lifestyles of two suicides. Ramón *Hernández's novels range from studies of individual behavior and group interaction (*Palabras en el muro* [1969; Words on the Wall]) to the alienation of today's youth (*Algo está ocurriendo aquí* [1976; Something Is Happening Here]). Miguel Delibes's *Cinco horas con Mario* (1966; Five Hours With Mario) and Elena *Soriano's works (for example, *Espejismos* [1955; Mirages]) use a psychological approach as a point of departure for special concerns. Ana María *Moix's *Julia* (1969) and *Walter, ¿por qué te fuiste?* (1973; Walter, Why Did You Leave?) explore shifting dimensions of reality via a search into the past. The intellectual or metaphysical symbolic novelists form a more cohesive group which, in their deliberate expansion of technique and ideology, react to the social novel (Carlos *Rojas, Andrés *Bosch, Manuel García Viñó). *Torrente Ballester's early works, such as his trilogy *Los gozos y las sombras* (1957–62; Joys and Shadows), reveal an interest in issues that transcend the traditional form in which it is presented. Francisco *García Pavón's *Las hermanas coloradas* (1970; The Red-headed Sisters) is one part of a popular detective series. Francisco *Umbral's chronicle-like treatment of Madrid life, seen in his various *Diarios*, differs from the focus in his novels (*Las ninfas* [The Nymphs] won the Nadal prize in 1975) which explore human relationships, often emotional or sexual attachments. Alvaro *Cunqueiro's *realismo mágico* (magical realism) foreshadows elements of the new novel (*Un hombre que se parece a Orestes* [1969; A Man Who Looks Like Orestes]). More experimental techniques overlaid the basic realism in the late 1960s such as Matute's *La torre vigía* (1971; The Watchtower), Delibes's *Parábola del náufrago* (1969; *The Hedge*, 1983) or Juan Marsé's *Ultimas tardes con Teresa* (1965; Last Afternoons with Teresa). These works foreshadow the new novel which emerged in the 1970s, but are still within the bounds of realism with critical intentions.

Luis *Martín Santos's *Tiempo de silencio* (1962; *Time of Silence*, 1964) marked a turning point from the realistic, social novel to a new approach to literature. Pedro has ambitions of making a breakthrough in cancer research; his works, friends, and other activities bring him in contact with all walks of society in Madrid. One by one, his personal and professional dreams fail, and he returns to the provinces to be reintegrated into the mediocre life there. *Tiempo de silencio* combines select elements from the earlier social novel—realism of situation, specific time and place, critical stance concerning social and national conditions. Added to this is an overlay of rich, baroque style: complex sentences, neologisms, borrowings from other languages and disciplines (anthropology, sociology, medicine, biology, art, among others), stream of consciouness, parody, irony, satire, sarcasm, abrupt changes in tone, all of which emphasize the author's increasing importance and jolts the reader from a passive role. The dialectical realism ascribed to the author combines elements from the social world as well as the individual, moving from simple description to dynamic action. Martín Santos's psychiatric training also enhances the intellectual dimensions of the work: existential psychoanalysis and the idea of the "project" (a step toward the necessity for self-definition) give serious consideration to the role of the individual in contemporary society. Martín Santos's untimely death in 1964 robbed Spanish literature of a strong leader.

During the late years of the 1960s, a new literary orientation was competing with the realistic novel. Denominated the "new novel," or the *contraola* (counterwave), it enjoys a wider international context because of the influence of the Spanish American New Novel, the French New Novel, and important figures like Joyce and Faulkner. The new novel forgoes realism of situation for an interest in experimentalism in all aspects of literature. Traditional literary conventions are ignored, the role of the author-reader-character often blurred. Deliberate confusion is created in the fragmentation of and/or overlapping of characters, places, time periods, etc. This requires greater concentration and even participation of the reader, now from a more select, intellectual group. A renewed interest in the "problem of Spain" becomes universalized into an attack on all branches of tradition and social convention, including language. Plot takes second place to process, which is the subject of many of these works, with language elevated from a medium to the object. The influence of baroque literature both in language (**culteranismo*) and perspective (**conceptismo*) is evident, and the efforts to raise language to a place of pre-eminence include freeing it from its traditional boundaries: this includes disregard for conventional punctuation, difficult vocabulary, complex structure, borrowings from other languages and sources such as newspapers, other literary works, popular slogans, etc. Juan *Benet's complex novels about a mythical place called Región (*Volverás a Región* [1968; *Return to Región*, 1985]) antedate the movement by several years, but are a most representative sample. Many established writers have moved from the more realistic approach to this type of literature: Camilo José Cela's antinovel *Oficio de tinieblas, 5* (1973; Office of Darkness, 5); Juan Goytisolo's bitter, demythologizing trilogy *Señas de identidad* (1966; Marks of Identity), *Reivindicación del conde don Julián* (1970; The Claim of Count Julian) and *Juan sin tierra* (1975; *Juan the Landless*, 1977); Gonzalo Torrente Ballester's *Saga/fuga de j.b.* (1972; Saga/Flight of j.b.) or *Fragmentos de apocalipsis* (1977; Fragments of Apocalypse); Luis Goytisolo's later works (*Recuento* [1973; Recounting]); Caballero Bonald's *Agata ojo de gato* (1974; Cat's Eye Agate).

Among the emergent group of younger writers are José María Vaz de Soto (*Fabian* [1977]), J. *Leyva (*La circunsición del señor solo* [1972; The Circumcision of Mr. Solo]), M. *Antolín Rato (*Cuando 900 mil Mach aprox.* [1975; When 900 Thousand Mach Approaches]), José María *Guelbenzu (*La noche in casa* [1977; Evening at Home]), a list that is far from exhaustive.

A final note must include those novelists who left Spain after the Civil War and continued to write. Among the best known are Ramón J. Sender (*Crónica del alba* [1942; *Chronicle of Dawn*, 1944] *Mosén Millán* [1953]); Francisco *Ayala (*Muertes de perro* [1958; *Death As A Way of Life*, 1964]; *El fondo del vaso* [1962; The Bottom of the Glass]); Max Aub (*Campo cerrado* [1943; Closed Field]; *Campo abierto* [1951; Open Field]).

BIBLIOGRAPHY

Criticism

Buckley, Ramón. *Problemas formales de la novela contemporánea*. 2nd ed. Barcelona: Península, 1973.

Corrales Egea, José. *La novela española actual*. Madrid: Cuadernos para el Diálogo, 1971.

Gil Casado, Pablo. *La novela social española (1942–1973)*. Barcelona: Seix Barral, 1973.

Guillermo, Edenia, and Juana Amelia Hernández. *La novelística española de los sesenta*. New York: Torres, 1971.

Nora, Eugenio G. de. *La novela española contemporánea*. 2nd ed. 3 vols. Madrid: Gredos, 1963–70.

Sobejano, Gonzalo. *Novela española de nuestro tiempo*. 2nd ed. Madrid: Prensa Española, 1975.

Yerro, Tomás. *Aspectos técnicos y estructurales de la novela española actual*. Pamplona: Universidad de Navarra, 1977.

Margaret E. W. Jones

MODERNISM. A term first used to describe the literary movement which is conventionally dated as beginning with the publication of *Azul* (Blue) by the Nicaraguan poet Rubén Darío in 1888, and which reached its fullest development around 1910 in the pages of the Mexican poet Amado Nervo's *La Revista Moderna* (The Modern Review). It was inspired by French Symbolism and Parnassianism. With greater frequency, though, the term is coming to designate the broad cultural change found in Federico de Onís's classic description of Modernism: "the universal crisis of letters and the spirit which initiates around 1885 the dissolution of the nineteenth century"; it "manifested itself gradually in art, science, religion, politics and all other aspects of life, and possessed, therefore, all the characteristics of a profound historical change which continues today" (p. xv).

In Spain Modernism represents the questioning of the concept of progress, and the bourgeois-dominated structure of society, art and thought. Its pre-history may be most clearly seen in the evolution of the work of Benito *Pérez Galdós and Leopoldo Alas (*Clarin). These two writers are usually associated with the novel and the criticism of Realism/*Naturalism. But this designation overlooks what may be called the pre-modernist elements in their critical and creative writings from the late 1880s onwards and perpetuates the misunderstanding of their work produced by the intergenerational rivalry with the members and disciples of the *Generation of 1898.

For Galdós and Alas the cultural crisis leading to Modernism takes the form of focusing their novels, stories and plays less and less on the observation and artistic re-creation of the typical persons, places, situations and conflicts of Spanish national life. Already in his 1882 review of Galdós's *El amigo Manso* (Our Friend Manso), Alas signals his preference for the psychological study of an introspective character out of step with his society; moreover, he contrasts this approach to the novel with what is more typical of Galdós during the 1870s and early 1880s, that is, the presentation of "the external world, social phenomena." In the 1895 prologue to his collection of short stories titled *Cuentos morales* (Moral Stories), Alas recurs to this opposition as he explains both the title of his new book and, in effect, a significant emphasis of his and Galdós's literary creations from the late 1880s onwards. He says the stories are "moral" because his attention is directed to "the phenomena of free behavior, to the psychology of intentional actions." Rather than stress "the description of the exterior world" and the "moving narration of historical, social vicissitudes," Alas seeks "interior man, his thought, his feelings, his will."

In his entry speech of 1897 to the *Academia Española Galdós explained the reasons for this change of emphasis. Between the beginning of his literary career in the 1860s and its creative height in the mid–1880s, Galdós believed that the Spanish middle class, with all its vices and virtues, was the moving force of a society evolving toward a more prosperous and just order. And he thought it incumbent for the writer to give literary form to this great collective social undertaking.

Literature of that kind operated on the principle of *castigat ridendo*, holding a mirror up to society in order that it see and judge itself, but without the novelist exercising the moralist's role of praise and condemnation. During the 1880s Galdós began to judge Spanish society differently. What he had seen as a socially and economically progressive middle class, he came to view as a corrupt, self-interested bourgeoisie and lost interest in depicting it.

Convinced that novels of the realist-naturalist type were socially ineffectual and perhaps even irrelevant, Galdós's novels followed increasingly the path of interiorizaton first stressed by Alas in the 1882 book review mentioned above. And in the 1897 speech Galdós stated that the change which all observed in society between the 1860s and the 1880s was producing the need for new literary forms, but that those forms had not yet appeared. He ended by voicing the conviction that "human ingenuity lives in all surroundings, and that it sends forth its flowers in the gay porticoes of splendid architecture as well as among sad and desolate ruins."

From this perspective, then, Spanish Modernism as a manifestation of fundamental cultural upheaval is a lack of faith in the past and present of national life; as a literary movement it is the individualistic search, by those who have lost that faith, for the "flowers," the new forms, which Galdós asserts will rise from the cultural and literary dissolution of the nineteenth c. pointed to by Onís. It comprehends both the radical questioning of national and personal reality engaged in by the Generation of 1898 as well as *Ortega and his group's stress on modernizing Spain through greater integration with the rest of Europe. It reveals itself in creative works such as *Azorín's *La voluntad* (1902; Will Power), Pío *Baroja's *Camino de perfección* (1902; The Path of Perfection), and Galdós's *El caballero encantado* (1909; The Enchanted Man), and essays such as *Ganivet's *Idearium español* (1897; *Spain: An Interpretation*, 1946), *Unamuno's *La vida de Don Quijote y Sancho Panza* (1905; *The Life of Don Quixote*, 1927) and *El sentimiento trágico de la vida* (1912; *The Tragic Sense of Life*, 1958), and Ortega's *El tema de nuestro tiempo* (1923; *The Modern Theme*, 1931).

In the more traditional, literary context the following are high points of Spanish Modernism: Azorín's simple poetic prose; *Valle-Inclán's romanticized decadent Bradomín and his times in the *Sonatas* (1902–5), the stories of "lost souls, goblins and robbers" collected in *Jardín umbrío* (1903; The Garden of Shadows), and the millennarian history of *Flor de santidad* (1904; The Flower of Saintliness); and the earlier verse of Antonio *Machado and Juan Ramón *Jiménez. The poetry of Salvador *Rueda, Manuel *Machado, *Villaespesa, the earlier Valle-Inclán, Cristóbal de *Castro and *Martínez Sierra is also representative.

Although Modernism as a literary movement lost its greatest force before 1920, the modernist search for beauty, independent of concerns which were at once larger and more prosaic, was continued by the vanguard writers of prose guided by the principles formulated in Ortega's *La deshumanización del arte* (1925; *The Dehumanization of Art*, 1948). Meanwhile the poets of the *Generation of 1927 continued to pursue beauty–without losing sight of those larger concerns, albeit in a highly poeticized way.

With the onslaught of the Spanish Civil War (1936–39), its aftermath of political repression and economic hardship, and the attendant deaths of Unamuno, Valle-Inclán and A. Machado, and the exile of Jiménez, Spanish Modernism lost any remaining identity as a literary movement. It continued, nevertheless, as a fundamental inspiration for cultural examination and renewal.

Even though the thick volume *Modernism (1890–1930)* has not an article on Spanish or South American Modernism, it provides a valuable overview of the movement's literary and broad cultural dimensions in England, most of Europe, and the United States consonant with the thrust of this presentation.

BIBLIOGRAPHY

Primary Text

De Onís, Federico. *Antología de la poesia española e hispanoamericana*. Madrid: Hernando, 1934.

Criticism

Estudios críticos sobre el modernismo. Ed. H. Castillo. Madrid: Gredos, 1968.
Gullón, Ricardo. *Direcciones del modernismo*. Madrid: Gredos, 1963.
Bradbury, M. and J. McFarlane, Eds. *Modernism (1890–1930)*. Atlantic Highlands, NJ: Humanities P, 1978.
El modernismo. Ed. L. Litvak, Madrid: Taurus, 1975.

Stephen Miller

MOIX, Ana María (1947, Barcelona–), novelist, short story writer, poet, journalist, essayist and translator. Moix studied Letras (liberal arts, especially literature) at the U of Barcelona. Younger sister of Terenci *Moix, a well-known novelist in Castilian and Catalan, she began her career writing a sort of free-form poetry, filled with images, techniques, words, and characters inspired by the mass media. On the basis of her first two books of poetry, *Baladas del dulce Jim* (1969; Sweet Jim's Ballads) and *Call me Stone* (1969 [only the title is in English]), she was included in José María *Castellet's *Nueve novísimos* (1970; Nine of the Newest), a polemical but widely read anthology of nine poets typifying the "new" Spanish poetry as Castellet defined it: a "poetry of rupture" vis-á-vis its antecedent, the committed and aesthetically flat social poetry of the 1950s and 1960s. Unlike her fellow nominees to that anthology, however, Moix soon turned away from poetry; *No time for flowers* (1971 [only the title is in English]), a series of prose poems with a definite narrative thread, is the last book of poetry she has published to date. Long out of print, the three books of verse have been collected and republished as *A imagen y semejanza* (1983; In the Image and Likeness).

Her first novel, *Julia* (1970), has been called autobiographical; certainly the world portrayed—that of the Catalan bourgeoisie in the decades immediately following the Spanish Civil War—is the world Moix grew up in. Some characters and events are likewise inspired by her life, but the extent of their literary elaboration makes them fictional rather than real creatures. The novel is a relentless psychological whodunit, narrated as the interior monologue of the disturbed and intermittently suicidal young protagonist, Julia. It traces the causes of her will to die back to her upbringing in the repressive, decadent, and contradictory atmosphere of Francoist Barcelona. A number of stories in *Ese chico pelirrojo a quien veo cada día* (1971; That Red-headed Boy I See Every Day) continue the exploration of that environment, and of the progressive warping of the young and vulnerable by their elders and the social system they represented. Her second novel, *Walter, ¿por qué te fuiste?* (1973; Walter, Why Did You Leave?), probes the same issues; part of Julia's family again serves as paradigm for the Catalan bourgeoisie, a social and ethnic group in profound crisis. *Walter* is an ambitious and self-conscious novel, with several narrative voices, a complex time frame, and an unexpected admixture of fantasy. After *Walter*, Moix turned away from (adult) fiction for twelve years. *Las virtudes peligrosas* (1985; The Dangerous Virtues), a collection of novellas, marks her return.

Other works published by Moix are *24 × 24* (1972)—twenty-four interviews of well-known Hispanic intellectuals, originally published in the newspaper *Tele-exprés. La maravillosa colina de las edades primitivas* (1976; The Marvelous Hill of Ancient Times) is a retelling for children of Egyptian legends; *Mi libro de . . . los Robots* (1985; My Book of Robots) is another book for children. *María Girona: una pintura en llibertat* (1977; María Girona: Painting in Freedom) consists of two essays on the contemporary Catalan artist María Girona—one is written by J. M. Castellet, and the other by Moix. Entitled "El món poètic de María Girona" (The Poetic World of María Girona), this essay is Moix's debut in Catalan.

Finally, Moix has done a great deal of translation, from French to Castilian (S. Beckett's *Malone meurt*, *Textes pour rien*, *Comme c'est*; M. Leiris's *Gran fuit de niège*; M. Duras's *L'amant*; L. Aragon's *Le Libertinage*), and from Catalan to Castilian (M. *Rodoreda's *Quanta, quanta guerra*; M. *Pessarodona's *Berlin Suite* and *Poèmes 1969–1981*; she also wrote a prologue for the latter).

BIBLIOGRAPHY

Primary Texts

A imagen y semejanza. Barcelona: Lumen, 1983.

Ese chico pelirrojo a quien veo cada día. Barcelona: Lumen, 1971.

Julia. Barcelona: Seix Barral, 1970.

La maravillosa colina de las edades primitivas. Barcelona: Lumen, 1976.

María Girona: una pintura en llibertat. Barcelona: Edicions 62, 1977.

Mi libro de . . . los Robots. Barcelona: Bruguera, 1985.

24 × 24. Barcelona: Península, 1972.

Las virtudes peligrosas. Barcelona: Plaza and Janés, 1985.

Walter, ¿por qué te fuiste? Barcelona; Seix Barral, 1973.

Criticism

Jones, Margaret E. W. "Ana María Moix: Literary Structures and the Enigmatic Nature of Reality." *JSS:TC* 4 (1976): 105–11.

Martín, Salustiano. "*Walter, ¿por qué te fuiste?*" *Reseña* 69 (1973): 11–14.

Nichols, Geraldine Cleary. "*Julia*: 'This is the way the world ends. . . .' " *Novelistas femeninas de la postguerra española*. Ed. Janet W. Pérez. Madrid: Porrúa Turanzas, 1983. 113–24.

———. "Mitja poma, mitja taronja: Génesis y destino literarios de la catalana contemporánea." *Anthropos* 60–61 (1986): 113–23. Moix is one of seven authors considered.

Schyfter, Sara E. "Rites Without Passage: The Adolescent World of Ana María Moix's *Julia*." *The Analysis of Literary Texts: Current Trends in Methodology*. Ypsilanti, MI: Bilingual Press, 1980. 41–50.

Thomas, Michael D. "El desdoblamiento psíquico como factor dinámico en *Julia*, de Ana María Moix." In *Novelistas femeninas de la postguerra española*. Ed. Janet W. Pérez. Madrid: Porrúa, 1983. 125–34.

Geraldine Nichols

MOIX, Terenci (1943, Barcelona–), literary name of Ramon Moix i Messeguer, internationally known contemporary Catalan novelist. Thematically, Moix demythifies all values of contemporary society: sexual mores, political ideologies, the educational system of the consumer society, mass media, etc. Stylistically, his prose is ornate, elaborate and signals a radical break with the neorealistic and the socially conscious novel of post-war literature. His success is not limited to the general public for throughout his relatively short career he has amassed almost every literary prize devoted to Catalan narrative. A professional writer, Moix is a frequent free-lance writer in the most influential magazines and newspapers of Catalonia: *Tele-exprés*, *El Correo Catalán*, *Destino*, *Serra d'Or*, etc. He has shown a strong interest in writing for and revitalizing the Catalan theater and has also translated and produced foreign plays for the stage and television; his versions of Oscar Wilde's *Salomé* (1978) and Shakespeare's *Hamlet* (1979) have been widely acclaimed. His literary production is, in many ways, free of the traumas and taboos of the generations of Catalan writers marked by the Civil War. The very titles of his books are symbolic of the kind of literature he creates.

Novels: *La torre dels vicis capitals* (1968; The Tower of the Capital Sins), Víctor Català Prize; *Onades sobre una roca deserta* (1969; Waves over a Deserted Rock), Josep Plà prize; *El día que va morir Marilyn Monroe* (1969; The Day When Marilyn Monroe Died), Serra d'Or Prize of criticism; *Món mascle* (1971; Masculine World); and *Sadístic, esperpèntic i àdhuc metafísic* (1976; Sadistic, Deformed and Even Metaphysical), Joan Estelrich Prize.

Collection of short stories: *L'imperi sodomita i altres històries herètiques* (1976; The Sodomite Empire and Other Heretical Stories).

Essays: *Los "comics," arte para el consumo y formas "pop"* (1968; The Comics, Art of Consumerism and Pop Forms); *Hollywood Stories* (1970); *El sadismo de nuestra infancia* (1970; The Sadism of Our Childhood); *Sólo para amantes de mitos* (1972; Only for Lovers of Myths).

Travel books: *Terenci del Nil o viatge sentimental a Egipte* (1971; Terenci of the Nile or a Sentimental Journey to Egypt); *Terenci a U.S.A.* (Terenci in the U.S.A.).

BIBLIOGRAPHY

Primary Texts

Amami Alfredo. Barcelona: Plaza y Janés, 1984.

Los "comics." Barcelona: Sinera, 1968.

El día que va morir Marilyn. Barcelona: Edicions 62, 1969.

Melodrama, o, La increada conciencia de la raza. Barcelona: Lumen, 1974.

Mundo macho. Prol. P. Gimferrer. Barcelona: Anma, 1971. Spanish tr. of *Món mascle*.

No digas que fue un sueño. Barcelona: Planeta, 1986.

Terenci del Nilo: viaje sentimental a Egipto. Barcelona: Plaza y Janés, 1983. Spanish tr.

La torre de los vicios capitales. Spanish tr. J. E. Lahosa. Barcelona: Seix Barral, 1972.

Criticism

Graells, J. G., and Oriol Pi de Cabanyes. *La generació literaria dels 70*. Barcelona: n.p., 1971.

Molas, Joaquim. "La novel·la oberta de Terenci Moix." In *Lectures Crítiques*. Barcelona: n.p., 1975.

Joan Gilabert

MOJIGANGA, a theatrical term. The word is derived from *bojiganga*, found in the *Viaje entretenido* of Agustín de *Rojas Villandrando, and in the *Quijote* (2.11), as noted by critics *Clemencín and *Cotarelo. Shergold suggests a possible connection with the Flemish word *Ommegang*, which means a parade of floats. The term was first used to describe a public carnival celebration in which individuals dressed in unusual costumes, wore animal masks, played musical instruments and engaged in mumming. In the seventeenth c. it is applied to a separate brief comic interlude on the order of a *sainete* or an *entremés*. Shergold describes a *mojiganga* produced in 1637 thus: "It included cardinals who gave blessings and pronounced absolutions, and indecent farces performed on the town rubbish carts. Probably it was intended as a parody of the triumphal cars of the other festivities, or even of the *carros* of the *auto sacramental* [*auto]. Other burlesque masquerades included one of kitchen boys and other servants, riding on mules and carrying the instruments of their work, and another of the King's huntsmen, in different liveries and ridiculous disguises." (288)

BIBLIOGRAPHY

Primary Texts

Entremeses, loas, bailes, jácaras y mojigangas de fines del siglo XVI a mediados del XVII. Ed. E. Cotarelo y Mori. NBAE 17 and 18.

Criticism

Shergold, N. D. *A History of the Spanish Stage*. Oxford: Clarendon, 1967.

Frances Bell Exum

MOLINA, Luis de (1535, Cuenca–1600, Madrid), philosopher and theologian. A Jesuit theologian who taught philosophy at the U of Coimbra and theology at Evora. He later taught moral philosophy at Madrid the year that he died. Subsequent to the years that he left his duties as professor, he devoted himself to writing theological and moral-political works. His most important theological treatise was to become the center of numerous theological debates which involved both the Jesuit and Dominican orders. The treatise was called *Concordia liberi arbitrii cum gratiae donis, divina praescientia, providentia, praedestinatione et reprobatione* (Lisbon, 1588; Harmony between Free Will and Divine Grace). In this most significant work Molina attempts to reconcile the problem of free will, efficacious (saving) grace and God's foreknowledge of the individual's cooperation with that grace. This doctrine is called *scientia media* (middle knowledge). It implies God's knowing beforehand that the individual will indeed cooperate with His grace in order to save himself. In other words, the power of this grace is efficacious in that it will bring about the individual's salvation. However, Molina maintains that this efficacious grace does not, nor can it, interfere with a person's free will. The *Concordia* is in effect a compromise between the proponents of complete free will and those who teach that God's grace is more important than free will: predestination. In his *De justitia et jure* (Cuenca, 1592–1600; On Justice and Law) Molina demonstrates that he is not only a theologian but also a moralist and economist. Truly, he is one of the great Spanish thinkers of that time. *See also* Báñez, Domingo; Congruismo; Molinismo.

BIBLIOGRAPHY

Primary Texts

Concordia liberi arbitrii cum gratiae donis, divina praescentia, providentia, praedestinatione et reprobatione. Lisbon: Hispani y Arenas, 1588. In Biblioteca Nacional in Madrid. An *Appendix ad Concordiam* was also published at Lisbon in 1589.

De justitia et jure. 6 vols. Mainz: n.p., 1607–9.

Los seis libros de la justicia y el derecho. Tr. Manuel Fraga Iribarne. Madrid: Cosano, 1941.

English Translation

Extracts on Politics and Government. In *Justice, Tract II*. Ed. George A. Moore. Chevy Chase, MD: Country Dollar, 1951.

Criticism

Pereña, Vicente L. "Circunstancia histórica y derecho de gentes de Luis de Molina." *Revista Española de Derecho Internacional* 10 (1957): 137–49.

Queralt, A. "El fin natural en Luis de Molina." *Estudios Eclesiásticos* 34 (1960): 177–216.

Rabeneck, J. "De vita et scriptis Ludovici Molina." *Archivum Historium Societas Iesu* 19 (1950): 75–145.

Smith, Gerard. *Freedom in Molina*. Chicago: Loyola UP, 1966.

Angelo DiSalvo

MOLINISMO (Molinism), a theological teaching set forth in Luis de *Molina's treatise called *Concordia arbitrii cum gratiae donis* (Lisbon, 1588: Harmony between Free Will and Divine Grace). St. Augustine developed a doctrine of grace, free will and predestination that has through the centuries spawned numerous debates in Western Europe. Molina takes a middle-of-the-road approach with his concept of *scientia media* (middle knowledge) which preserves the individual's free will in choosing good over evil and thus gaining salvation. Molina explains that God has foreknowledge that the individual will be saved, having cooperated with His freely given grace. The fact that God's efficacious (saving) grace assists the individual in choosing to do good does not interefere with the person's free will. Molina places more emphasis on free will than the Dominicans represented by Domingo *Báñez who place greater emphasis on the power of God's grace. *See also* Congruismo.

BIBLIOGRAPHY

Criticism

The Catholic Encyclopedia. New York: McGraw-Hill, 1967. 9: 1010–11.

Angelo DiSalvo

MOLINOS, Miguel de (1628, Muniesa, Aragón–1692, Rome), one of the most controversial religious figures of his day. He is best known for his religious work *Guía espiritual* (Rome, 1676; *Spiritual Guide*, 1699). Molinos studied at Coimbra and received a degree in theology. After spending some time in Valencia, he settled in Rome where he became very popular as a spiritual director. When the *Spiritual Guide* first appeared, it was received with acclaim and its contents were found to conform to Catholic dogma. Indeed, the work is saturated with references to the Bible, the church fathers and the eminent teachers of the church including Thomas Aquinas and St. *Teresa de Avila.

However, opposition to his mystical doctrine put forth in this work soon appeared in certain Jesuit circles that defended a more disciplined and meditative approach. On July 18, 1685, Molinos was arrested and subjected to an intense investigation by the *Inquisition. He was condemned to ten years imprisonment where he was to pray and do penance for the rest of his life. Molinos's disavowal of the Ignatian method of spiritual exercises probably was partially responsible for his demise.

The Spiritual Guide sets forth his method of contemplation. He distinguishes between the meditative process and contemplation. He writes that contemplation is achieved not in an active way, but through a total abandonment to the will and operation of God. In other words, the individual, once having purified the soul through penitence and meditation, no longer needs to act, think or even desire when it reaches contemplation. The soul now becomes quiet and completely passive in order to allow God to take charge. The theological problem in Molinos's exposition is that the individual's will is obliterated. Thus, works, spiritual exercises, pilgrimages, acts of penance, homage to saints and even Masses are deemed unnecessary. However, we must keep in mind that Molinos reminds the reader that the meditative stage precedes contemplation. In the meditative stage the sensible acts of devotion are considered proper and necessary. *See also* Ignacio de Loyola, San; Molinosismo; Mysticism.

BIBLIOGRAPHY

Primary Texts

Guía espiritual que desembarca al alma y la conduce por el interior campo para alcanzar la perfecta contemplación y el rico tesoro de la interior paz. Rome: Miguel Hércules, 1675.

Guía espiritual. Ed. José Ignacio Tellechea Idígoras. Madrid: Fundación Universitaria Española, 1975.

English Translations

The Spiritual Guide Which Disentangles the Soul and Brings It by the Inward Way to the Getting of Perfect Contemplation and the Rich Treasure of Internal Peace. Tr. from Italian. Venice: n.p., 1688.

The Spiritual Guide. Tr. Kathleen Lyttelton. 4th ed. London: Methuen, 1920.

Criticism

Bigelow, John. *Molinos the Quietist.* New York: Scribner, 1882.

Dudon, P. *Le quiétiste espagnol Michel Molinos. (1628–1696).* Paris-Lille: A. Taffin, 1921.

Entrambasaguas, Joaquín de. *Miguel de Molinos.* Madrid: Aguilar, 1935.

Fernández Alonso, J. "Una bibliografía inédita de Miguel de Molinos." *Anthología Annua* 12 (1964): 293–321.

Rey, Asensio. "Carácter ideológico y literario del quietismo de Miguel de Molinos en su *Guía espiritual.*" Diss., New York U, 1974.

Angelo DiSalvo

MOLINOSISMO (Molinosism), a system of religious contemplation. This term is not to be confused with *Molinismo, which is the doctrine developed by Luis de *Molina. Molinosismo is a system of contemplation developed by Miguel de *Molinos in his *Guía espiritual* (Rome, 1675; *Spiritual Guide*, 1699). This method of contemplation has as its goal the purification of the soul by the individual's disentangling himself from all earthly affairs. This is accomplished through an inward way which will ultimately lead to perfect contemplation and complete internal peace: quietism. Molinos perceives the soul as the abode of God; thus it must be kept clean and pure. The soul cannot involve itself with the concerns and desires of the world. According to Molinos, the individual will attain this state of perfection in two stages: meditation and contemplation. In the first stage the individual may employ reason to ponder the truths of the Catholic religion. This more active stage is equivalent to the meditative and illuminative stages of the *vía mistica*. However, once the soul ceases to struggle and desire, it no longer needs to reason since it has reached the stage of perfect contemplation in silence and repose (quiet). Now, in a most passive state, the soul will receive the divine light of truth undisturbed and oblivious to the material world. Having reached this stage, the soul becomes indifferent to everything that is not God, including the Sacraments, the Mass and other manifestations of sensible devotion. Molinos and his doctrine were condemned by the *Inquisition on September 3, 1687. *See also* Mysticism.

BIBLIOGRAPHY

Criticism

The Catholic Encyclopedia. New York: McGraw-Hill, 1967. 9: 1013–114.

Angelo DiSalvo

MOLÍNS, Marqués de, pseudonym of Mariano Roca de Togores (1812, Albacete–1889, Lequeitia, Vizcaya), dramatist and poet. He held various political and diplomatic positions during his life and succeeded *Rivas in the direction of the *Academia Española* (1865). His dramatic works obtained a modicum of success. *Doña María de Molina* (1837; Doña María of Molina) is a five-act prose and verse historical drama set in the time of Sancho IV; *La espada de un caballero* (1831; A Nobleman's Sword) is a two-act verse drama about the Duke of Alba staged in 1846. His *Obras poéticas* (1857) show an eclectic poetic style that fluctuates between classicism and *Romanticism. A friend of Mariano José de *Larra, he accompanied him on his last walk the morning of his suicide and wrote *El último paseo de Fígaro* (1837; Fígaro's Last Stroll).

BIBLIOGRAPHY

Primary Texts

Doña María de Molina. Madrid: Repullés, 1837.
La espada de un caballero. Madrid: Repullés, 1846.
Obras completas. Madrid: Tello, 1881.
Obras poéticas. Madrid: Tejado, 1857.

Criticism

Bretón de los Herreros, Manuel. *Estudio crítico*. Madrid: La España Moderna, n.d.
Gallego, A. *El Marqués de Molíns. Su vida y sus obras*. Albacete: Comercial, 1912.

Eugene Del Vecchio

MOLL I CASASNOVAS, Francesc de Borja (1903, Ciudadela, Menorca–), Balearic philologist and linguist, editor and publisher. Originally planning for the priesthood, Moll studied for eight years in the Seminary of Ciudadela, receiving intensive preparation in Romance philology and linguistics, so that in 1921 at the age of only eighteen he began working with the eminent Catalan philologist Antoni M. Alcovar on the *Diccionari-català-valencià-balear* (1962; Dictionary of Catalan, Valencian and Balearic [Dialects]), a task not completed until more than forty years later. Just prior to the death of his mentor Alcovar (1932), Moll published *Ortografia Mallorquina segons les normes de l'Institut* (Mallorcan Orthography According to Institute Rules), an important stabilizing and standardizing force in the language. Other contributions to his vernacular are the *Vocabulario Mallorquí-castellà* (1965; a kind of bilingual dictionary of Mallorcan and [Castilian] Spanish); *Gramàtica catalana referida especialmente a les Illes Balears* (1968; Catalan Grammar Referring Especially to the Balearic Isles); and *Els llinatges catalans (Catalunya, Pais Valencià, Illes Balears)* (1959; Catalan Names [Catalonia, Valencia and the Balearic Islands]). He produced an important historical grammar of Catalan (1952), initiated the cultural foundation Obra Cultural Balear, founded the journal *Les Illes d'Or* (in 1934); and edited another magazine, *Raixa*, which during the 1950s expanded into a publishing enterprise. He also founded a series, "Els treballs y els dies" (1963; Works and Days), and was co-author of a linguistic atlas of the Iberian Peninsula.

MONARDES, Nicolás (c. 1493, Seville–1588, Seville), physician, medical writer. In 1533 he received his medical degree from the U of Alcalá. Monardes wrote various treatises—the first appeared in 1539—but his international reputation stems from the *Dos libros, el uno que trata de las cosas que traen de Nuestras Indias . . .* (1569; tr. as *Joyfull newes out of the newe founde worlde*, 1925), followed by a second part in 1571, and a combined edition of parts one and two, published in 1574, with woodcuts. They describe in detail the plants, minerals and other substances—tobacco, coca, sasparilla, bezaar stone, resins, peppers, etc.—arriving in Seville (the port of entry for all Spanish ships) from the New World. He describes each carefully and indicates their real and purported medical properties and uses. The works were quickly translated into Italian, French, English, and Latin, disseminating Monardes's name to physicians throughout Europe.

BIBLIOGRAPHY

Primary Text

Primera y Segunda y Tercera Partes De la Historia Medicinal. Seville: Díaz, 1580.

English Translation

Joyfull newes of the newe founde worlde. 2 vols. Tr. J. Frampton. Intro. S. Gaselee. London: Constable; New York: Knopf, 1925.

Criticism

Pereira, C. *El Dr. Monardes, sus libros y su museo. BBMP* (Oct. 1922): n.p.

Maureen Ihrie

MONCADA, Francisco de (1586, Valencia–1635, Goch, Flanders), politician, naval officer, historical author. He served as ambassador to Germany, governor in Milan, and handled a variety of important missions for Philip IV. His major work is a literary chronicle which recounts the military exploits of fourteenth-c. mercenaries who fought their way around the Mediterranean. Titled *Expedición de catalanes y aragoneses contra turcos y griegos* (1623; *The Catalan Chronicle of Francisco de Moncada*, 1975), it is a vivid, dramatic account of heroism in the Antilles, about 75,000 words long. It inspired *García Gutiérrez's later *Venganza catalana* (1864; Catalan Revenge). Moncada also wrote a *Vida de Boecio* (1642; Life of Boethius), which was published seven years after Moncada perished in battle.

BIBLIOGRAPHY

Primary Texts

Empresas y victorias. Ed. Foulché-Delbosc. *RH* 45 (1919): 349–509.

Expedición de catalanes y. . . . Ed. S. Gil y Gaya. Clásicos Castellanos 54. Madrid: Espasa-Calpe, 1954.

English Translation

The Catalan Chronicle of Francisco de Moncada. Tr., intro. F. Hernández. Ed. J. M. Sharp. El Paso: Texas Western P, 1975.

Nina Shecktor

MONCAYO, Juan de (c. 1600, Zaragoza–after 1656, ?), poet. Of noble birth, he served in the court of Philip IV. When not on official business, he resided in Zaragoza (although he made rather frequent trips to Madrid) and was active in literary circles there. His *Rimas* (Rhymes) first appeared in 1636; a second edition, with various additions, deletions and modifications, was published in 1652. His great admiration for *Góngora determined in large part the vocabulary and style of Moncayo's verse. Although he does not reach the excellence of his model, Moncayo's poetry is certainly a worthy contribution to seventeenth-c. letters. *See also* Culturanismo.

BIBLIOGRAPHY

Primary Texts

Rimas. Ed., intro. A. Egido. Clásicos Castellanos 209. Madrid: Espasa-Calpe, 1976.

Criticism

Arco, Ricardo del. "El poeta aragonés Juan de Moncayo, Marqués de San Felices." *BRAE* 30 (1950): 23–46 and 223–55.

MONDÉJAR, Gaspar . . . Marqués de. *See* Ibáñez de Segovia, Gaspar

MONDRAGÓN, Jerónimo de (fl. 1598, ?), humanist, jurisconsult in Zaragoza, author. The little that is known of his life is contained in his book, the *Censura de la locura humana y excelencias de ella* (1598; Censure of Human Folly and Its Excellences). In it Mondragón argues that the truly insane are regarded as of sound mind in this world, while sane men are held to be crazy. He includes all manner of unusual anecdotes to support this thesis, which was clearly derived from Erasmus's *In Praise of Folly*. The *Censura* occupies an important place as a late manifestation of *Erasmism in *Siglo de Oro Spain. Mondragón also composed an *Arte para componer metro castellano* (1593; Art of Composing Castilian Verse), which is now lost.

BIBLIOGRAPHY

Primary Text

Censura de la locura humana y excelencias de ella. Ed., prol., A. Vilanova. Barcelona: n.p., 1953.

MONGUÍO, Luis (1908, Tarragona–), diplomat, teacher, critic. After receiving his law degree from the U of Madrid (1928), he became a member of the Spanish Diplomatic and Consular Service (1930–39). After the Civil War, Monguío emigrated to the United States, and in 1944 he was naturalized. He then served with the Military Intelligence Service of the US Army (1944–46), before assuming his first college teaching position, at Mills College (1946–57). He subsequently has taught at Berkeley, Bennington College, and SUNY Albany and has been honored by a variety of institutions. He is the author of well over a hundred articles and several books, on both Spanish and Spanish American writers—selected representative studies include *La poesía postmodernista peruana* (1954; Post-Modernist Peruvian Poetry), *Don José Joaquín de Mora y el Perú del Ochocientos* (1967; Don José Joaquín de Mora and Peru of the 1800s), and *Poesías de Don Felipe Pardo y Aliaga* (1973; Poetry of Don Felipe Pardo Aliaga).

BIBLIOGRAPHY

Primary Texts

César Vallejo. New York: Hispanic Institute, 1952. 2nd ed., Lima: Perú Nuevo, 1960.

La poesía postmodernista peruana. Berkeley: U of California P; Mexico: Fondo de Cultura Económica, 1954.

Estudios sobre literatura hispanoamericana y española. Mexico: De Andrea–Studium, 1958.

Sobre un escritor elogiado por Cervantes. Berkeley: U of California Publications in Modern Philology, 1960.

Don José Joaquín de Mora y el Perú del Ochocientos. Berkeley: U of California P; Madrid: Castalia, 1967.

Notas y estudios sobre literatura peruana y americana. Mexico: Nuevo Mundo, 1972.

Poesías de Don Felipe Pardo y Aliaga. Intro, ed. notes and indexes. Berkeley: U of California Publications in Modern Philology, 1973.

Robert Kirsner

MONLAU, Pedro Felipe (1808, Barcelona–1871, Madrid), physician, encyclopedic erudite. His range of expertise and writings spanned philosophy, archaeology, literature, philology, physiology, psychology, medicine, and politics. He taught many of these subjects at the university level. Monlau's efforts at theater failed, but his *Diccionario etimológico de la lengua castellana* (1856; Etymological Dictionary of the Spanish Language) is still valuable. Monlau's most significant achievement was probably the introduction of hygiene as a medical concern into Spain. He wrote on public health, hygiene in the workplace, and even on hygiene in marital relationships.

BIBLIOGRAPHY

Primary Texts

Diccionario etimológico de la lengua castellana. Prol. A. Herrero Mayor. 2nd ed. Buenos Aires: Ateneo, 1944.

Higiene del matrimonio. Paris: Garnier, 1928.

Higiene industrial. In *Condiciones de vida y trabajo obrero en España a mediados del siglo XIX*. Ed., study A. Jutglar. Barcelona: Anthropos, 1984.

Nociones de higiene doméstica. . . . 3rd ed. Madrid: Rivadeneyra, 1867.

Maureen Ihrie

MONROY Y SILVA, Cristóbal de (1612, Alcalá de Guadaira, Seville–1649, Alcalá de Guadaira), poet, historical writer, dramatist. He attended the U of Seville briefly, and then the U of Salamanca, before returning to his birthplace. Active in local politics, he may have been named alderman in perpetuity of his hometown in 1639. He died there of the plague at age thirty-seven, cutting short a promising dramatic career.

Monroy wrote at least thirty-eight works, including a history of Troy (1641), a history of his birthplace, the poem *Canción real de la vida de San Pablo* (1631–32?; Splendid Song of St. Paul's Life), some thirty-one plays and two shorter dramatic pieces. Not all has survived, for Monroy evidently burned his mss., leaving only copies preserved by friends. His plays belong to the school of Lope de *Vega; they span a wide range of topics and seem to have been well received.

BIBLIOGRAPHY

Primary Texts

Dos comedias inéditas de don Cristóbal de Monroy y Silva. Ed., study M. R. Bem Barroca. Chapel Hill, NC: Hispanófila, 1976.

Fuenteovejuna (Dos comedias). Lope de Vega and Cristóbal de Monroy. Ed. F. López Estrada. Clásicos Castalia 10. Madrid: Castalia, 1969.

Criticism

Bem Barroca, M. R. "Vida y obra de Don Cristóbal de Monroy y Silva." Diss., U of Seville, 1967.

Nina Shecktor

MONSERDÀ DE MACIÀ, Dolors (1845, Barcelona–1919, Barcelona), poet, novelist, journalist and essayist. Reared in a well-read family with many social and literary contacts, she first published poetry and articles on social issues in Castilian. She wrote two early plays, one in Castilian and one in Catalan; both were performed at the Teatre Romea in the 1870s. She wrote a third play much later, published posthumously, having refrained from writing for the theater for many years because of her husband's disapproval. Nevertheless, Monserdà can be considered a major figure in early Catalan feminism, as she composed numerous essays on the condition of women, particularly working women. Like her Galician counterpart, Emilia *Pardo Bazán, she was particularly interested in advocating better education for women; like her counterparts in other countries, she was an abolitionist and well aware of the feminist movements in other places. In 1877, she began to write poetry in Catalan, later contributing short narrations and novels to the Renaixença literary movement, often featuring a female narrator and strong women characters. She continued to publish on social issues affecting women, often depicting the everyday lives of ordinary women. As a writer, she helped move fiction by women into a realist vein through the portrayal of contemporary social conditions. She believed women had a right to a career, but that they should choose between that and marriage; however, in her own case she seems to have combined the two. She married Eusebi Macià in 1865 and had four children, two of whom survived; she never stopped writing. Her poetry won many prizes, and she collaborated in such journals as *La Llar*, *Modas y Labors*, and *Or y Grana*. *See also* Catalan Literature.

BIBLIOGRAPHY

Primary Texts

Amor mana; comèdia en tres actes. In *La Quitèria*, 3rd ed. Barcelona: Políglota, 1930. 223–73.

Del Món. 2 vols. Barcelona: L'Avenc, 1908. Rpt. in one vol., ed. Isabel Segura. Barcelona: laSal, 1983.

La fabricanta; novela de costums barcelonines (1860–1875). Illus. Enrich Monserdà. Barcelona: Biblioteca de Francesch Puig, 1904. Rpt., ed. Roser Matheu. Barcelona: Selecta, 1972.
La familia Asparó; novels de costums del nostre temps. Barcelona: La Renaixença, 1900.
Maria Gloria, novel. la de costums barcelonines. Barcelona: Llibrería Parera, 1917.
No sempre la culpa es d'ella. Barcelona: n.p., 1917.
Poesies. Barcelona: Ilustració Catalana, 1911.
Poesies catalanes. Barcelona: La Renaixença, 1888.
Sembrad y cojeréis, comedia en tres actos y en verso. Barcelona: Jaime Jepús, 1874.

Criticism

Borrell Felip, Núria. *Pedagogia social de Dolors Monserdà de Macià.* Licenciate Thesis, U of Barcelona, n.d.
Matheu, Roser. *Quatre dones catalanes.* Barcelona: Fundació Salvador Vives Casajuana, 1972.
Segura, Isabel. Introduction to the reprint of *Del Món.* Barcelona: laSal, 1983. 9–33.

Kathleen McNerney

MONTALVO, Garci Ordóñez [or Rodríguez] de (c. 1440, ?–before 1505, ?), alderman of Medina del Campo, author. In 1508 in Zaragoza, there appeared the four-book **Amadís de Gaula*, illustrious parent of the genre of chivalric novels. Earlier versions of the work existed—as early as 1345 to 1350, but have not survived. The 1508 edition is divided into four books; the first three were edited and restyled by Montalvo and finished around 1492, the fourth was redone almost fully by him around that time, and he most probably also composed a book five, the *Sergas de Esplandián* (Esplandian's Deeds), whose first extant edition is dated 1510. It is the first and best of many, many sequels to the cycle. *See also* Caballerías, Libros de.

BIBLIOGRAPHY

Primary Texts

Place, E. B. "Fictional Evolution: The Old French *Romances* and the Primitive *Amadís* Reworked by Montalvo." *PMLA* 71.3 (1956): 521–29.

MONTEIRO, Adolfo Vítor Casais (1908, Porto–1972, São Paulo), poet, critic, essayist, editor, novelist. Adolfo Casais Monteiro was born July 4, 1908, in Portugal's second largest city, and there received his early education, including a licenciatura degree from the city's Faculty of Letters in 1933. The following year he graduated from the Normal School at the U of Coimbra, began his teaching career in Porto, published his second volume of poems and married fellow writer Alice Gomes.

About this time, forces began to exert themselves on the young couple, which would dramatically mark them both personally and literarily. It was the beginning of the fascist fervor which would grip the government of Portugal and of many European countries, leading directly to the Spanish Civil War, and subsequently to World War II. Their opposition to the government led to the loss of his job in 1937 and to the first of repeated arrests and imprisonment for both of them. Casais Monteiro's poetic production, which had begun with a published volume in 1929, focused almost exclusively on the political conflicts, the loss of liberty, censorship, and the great anxiety which the turbulent decades of the 1930s and 1940s produced. One particularly poignant work of this era is entitled *Canto da Nossa Agonia* (1942; Song of our Agony). Thinking that with the Allied victory over fascism, Portugal's government would change, Casais Monteiro wrote *Europa* (1946), his sixth volume of poetry, an evocation to the devastated continent and an appeal for Portugal to rejoin Europe and take her rightful place among the civilized nations of the world. But the next decade proved to be just as repressive and difficult, since Salazar had not relinquished his hold. In 1954, seeking a freer intellectual atmosphere where he could develop his ideas unhampered by censorship and the ever-present threat of arrest, Casais Monteiro decided to leave Portugal for Brazil. By then he had published eight of his nine volumes of poetry, his only novel, and half of his sixteen volumes of essays.

In Brazil, Casais Monteiro became one of the leading voices raised in opposition to the Salazar regime. He also published assiduously in newspapers and journals on various literary and artistic themes, becoming a respected critic. He entered Brazil's intellectual and academic life, serving on the faculties of various noted institutions, and after 1962, as professor of literary theory at the U of São Paulo, Araraquara campus. In 1969, he accepted an invitation as visiting professor of Portuguese at the U of Wisconsin, Madison, and obtained the publication of his complete poetic works in Portugal. In poor health the last years of his life, he died while yet in exile in Brazil, in 1972.

In addition to his anguished poetry and satirical essays, Casais Monteiro had played a major role in Portuguese letters as an editor of several important journals, among them *presença*, where from 1931 to 1940—when it ceased publication—he was continually helping to shape the intellectual thought of his countrymen by bringing to its readers quality works by the leading writers of the nation. It was young editor Casais Monteiro who wrote Fernando *Pessoa and from him received and published the now celebrated letter in which the poet described, among other things, the appearance of the heteronyms. Casais Monteiro, more than anyone else, is justly credited with bringing Fernando Pessoa's significance as Portugal's leading modern poet to the attention of readers and critics alike.

Casais Monteiro's themes reflect not only his democratic spirit, but show his concern for man's isolation. Often mordant, he cultivated the short poem, with varied and uneven rhythms, reflective of the turbulent times his life spanned. His essays, always quick-witted and satirical, became more reflective and studied with time, especially after he moved to Brazil where, as a university professor, he could dedicate more energy and thought to his labors. Always quick to grasp what was really of worth and what was not, he was nevertheless pained by the contradictory and perplexing forces at work in the world. Although his poetry is filled with negative images, he strives to combat them as he reaches for light, understanding and tolerance.

Whether writing introductions to works by other authors, or in-depth studies of such noted writers as Fernando Pessoa, Manuel Bandeira and Ribeiro Couto (to name three), Casais Monteiro consistently sought the essential truth. Even though this no-nonsense, iconoclastic attitude earned for him the scorn of mediocre minds, it brought him the gratitude of an entire generation of writers who might otherwise have never learned the truth in the government-controlled society that characterized Portugal before 1974.

BIBLIOGRAPHY

Primary Texts

Fernando Pessoa, Poesia. Rio de Janeiro: Coleção ''Nossos Clássicos,'' Livraria Agir, 1957.

Manuel Bandeira, estudo da sua obra poética, seguido de uma antologia. 2nd ed. Rio de Janeiro: ''Cadernos de Cultura,'' Ministério da Educação e Cultura, 1958.

A Palavra essencial, estudos sobre a poesia. São Paulo: Companhia Editora Nacional, Editora da Universidade de São Paulo, 1965.

A Poesia da ''presença,'' estudo e antologia. Rio de Janeiro: Ministério da Educação e Cultura, Serviço de Documentação, 1959. 2nd ed. Lisbon: Moraes, 1972.

See also Criticism.

Criticism

Adolfo Casais Monteiro. Poetry selections by João Rui de Sousa, studies by António Ramos Rosa, E. M. de Melo e Castro and João Rui de Sousa. Lisbon: Assírio and Alvim, 1973.

''O Poeta Casais Monteiro.'' In Adolfo Casais Monteiro, *Poesias Escolhidas.* Salvador [Bahia]: Imprensa Oficial da Bahia Salvador, 1960.

presença, folha de arte e crítica. Commemorative publication on the occasion of the fiftieth anniversary of its founding, coordinated by João Gaspar Simões, with studies by him, David Mourão-Ferreira, Fernando Guimarães, and Luís Amaro. Lisbon: Secretaria de Estado da Cultura, 1977.

Saraiva, António José, & Óscar Lopes. *História da Literatura Portuguesa.* 10th ed. Porto: Porto, 1978.

Sena, Jorge de. *Régio, Casais, a ''presença'' e outros afins.* Porto: Brasília, 1977.

Frederick G. Williams

MONTEMAYOR, Jorge de (1520?, Montemôr-o-velho–1561, Piamonte), poet and prose writer. He achieved international fame as author of *Los siete libros de la Diana* (1559?; *The Seven Books of the Diana*, 1968), a *pastoral romance in prose and verse. Recent acknowledgment of his popularity as a poet and his early interest in religious literature has widened critical perspective with respect to Montemayor in particular and the pastoral genre in general.

Almost nothing is known about Montemayor's life. He used as his last name the Spanish adaptation of the town in Portugal where he was probably born. His refusal to reveal details of his familial origins perhaps indicates illegitimacy or a **converso* background, or both. Lack of illustrious name and title did not hinder his association with the imperial family in the cosmopolitan style of a popular courtier during most of his short adult life.

Montemayor began his writing career as an author of religious prose and poetry, establishing his interest in spirituality at an early age. In 1548, his *Exposición moral sobre el psalmo 86* (Ethical Exegesis of Psalm 86) was published at Alcalá. By 1550, some of his devotional poetry had appeared in anthologies of religious verse.

From 1548 to 1552, Montemayor was a singer in the chapels of Princesses María and Juana in Spain. He accompanied Juana to Portugal in 1552 and worked for her there until 1554. That year, his collection of secular and religious poetry entitled *Obras* (Works) was published in Antwerp. The secular poems are of a **cancionero* style expressing traditional love complaints. The two long eclogues included indicate Montemayor's interest in human spirituality and reveal his talent to individualize characters successfully through presentation of their emotional lives only. The religious verse forms the larger part of the *Obras* and includes numerous long, dogmatic poems, some of which were republished in his 1558 *Segundo cancionero spiritual* (Second Spiritual Song Book) in Antwerp. The Valdés **Indice* of 1559 prohibited his religious works; he was, after all, a layman whose spiritual writings seem to have been influenced by illuminist ideas.

Montemayor's *Segundo cancionero* (Second Song Book) of secular poems was published as the twin volume to his religious *Segundo cancionero spiritual* (Second Spiritual Song Book) in 1558. His growing interest in long, novelistic pastoral works is evident in the 1558 volume, which includes "La historia de Alcida y Silvano" (The Story of Alcida and Silvano), a charming love story in verse (not published since 1795); two more eclogues appearing with the two published in 1554; and numerous shorter poems. The third eclogue is an important precursor of the *Diana*; it foresees the romance in elements of character, plot, and structure. The *Segundo cancionero* was published with minor variations and great success under the title of *Cancionero* (Song Book), reprinted seven times between 1562 and 1588. In 1560, Montemayor's translation of Ausiàs *March's *Cantos de amor* (Love Songs) was published in Valencia, the culmination of his long interest in the Catalan poet whose verse he imitated frequently.

The *Diana*, probably first published in 1559, captured perfectly the imagination of sixteenth-c. Europe with its polished conversations, interpolated stories, mythological references, and dogmatic passages of the popular philosophy of love, all written in a highly rhythmic prose punctuated with lyric poetry. Juxtaposition of Neoplatonic idealism in love and the realities of human emotions which belie love's perfection allows Montemayor to acknowledge the supreme value of eternal, pure love (translating passages directly from León *Hebreo's 1535 *Dialoghi d'amore*) and simultaneously narrate stories of love's incessant change. He brought new life to a literary tradition begun in classical times by casting into prose as well as poetry the interwoven (sometimes bizarre) plots, related against the static pastoral backdrop. The *Diana*'s lovers endure emotional trials the way epic and chivalric heroes suffered for honor and glory, and thus the book indicates a new awareness of man's inner being, considering personal happiness to be as valid as social and economic prosperity. (The delightful story of Abindarráez, el *Abencerraje, was added to the *Diana* after 1561 and is not Montemayor's work.)

Montemayor's untimely death, supposedly in a love feud in Italy, 1561, added intrigue to his already romantic and mysterious reputation and reinforced the attractions of his popular romance. The *Diana* was published twenty-six times in Spanish before 1600 and was translated into French (1582), English (1598), and German (1619). It inspired several continuations and initiated the vogue of the pastoral romance, which lasted through the seventeenth c. *See also* Platonism; Renaissance.

BIBLIOGRAPHY

Primary Texts

El cancionero del poeta George de Montemayor. Ed. Ángel González Palencia. Madrid: Sociedad de Bibliófilos Españoles, 1932.

La Diana. Ed. Franciso López Estrada. 4th ed. Madrid: Espasa-Calpe, 1967.

La Diana. Ed. Enrique Moreno Báez. 2nd ed. Madrid: RAE, 1981.

English Translation

Critical Edition of Montemayor's Diana and Gil Polo's Enamoured Diana. Oxford: Clarendon, 1968.

Criticism

Avalle-Arce, Juan Bautista. *La novela pastoril española*. 2nd ed. Madrid: Istmo, 1975.

Correa, Gustavo. "El templo de la Diana en la novela de Jorge de Montemayor." *Thesaurus* 16 (1961): 59–76.

Darbord, Michel. *La poésie religieuse espagnole des Rois Catholiques à Phillippe II*. Paris: Centre de Recherches de l'Institut d'Etudes Hispaniques, 1965.

López Estrada, Francisco. "La exposición moral sobre el salmo 86 de Jorge de Montemayor." *Revista de Bibliografía Nacional* 5 (1944): 499–525.

———. *Los libros de pastores en la literatura española*. Madrid: Gredos, 1974.

Perry, Anthony T. "Ideal Love and Human Reality in Montemayor's La Diana." *PMLA* 84 (1969): 227–34.

Elizabeth Rhodes

MONTENGÓN Y PARET, Pedro de (1745, Alicante–1824, Naples), novelist and poet. Still a novice in the Jesuit order when Charles III decreed the expulsion of the Jesuits from Spain (1767), he went to Italy, living in Ferrara and Genoa. Two years later he left the order and married. Montengón then returned to Spain for two years, was expelled again for political reasons, and left for Naples, where he remained until his death.

He lived under the influences of two artistic worlds, Spain and Italy, in a period of transition from the neo-classicism of Charles III's reign to an incipient *Romanticism. These two influences are evident even in his first poetry, published in three volumes in Ferrara, titled *Odas* (1778–79; Odes), with the pseudonym Filipatro. Italian and Spanish influences also co-exist in his translation into Spanish of four tragedies of Sophocles (1820), and the epic poem *Fingal* (tr.

1800), by Ossian. Montengón's free-style translations abound with Italianisms, and there are even some Gallicisms.

His best work is narrative. It was Montengón who introduced to Spain genres then popular in France, such as the philosophical and pedagogical novel, and the so-called historical-philosophical novel. His principal work, *Eusebio* (1786–88), is a four-volume novel clearly influenced by Rousseau's *Émile,* which had appeared in 1762. Set in the United States, *Eusebio* has a complicated, involved plot and focuses on love and tragedy. Despite the declaration of Catholicism in the prologue, *Eusebio* is an exaltation of the religion of nature. The *Inquisition prohibited circulation of the first two volumes, thus Montengón was forced to rewrite them. A new edition was published in 1807.

Other works of Montengón include *Antenor* (1778), and *El Rodrigo. Romance Epico* (1793; Roderick. Epic Ballad). The latter suffers from a stilted, poetic prose. *El Mirtilo o los pastores trashumantes* (1795; Mirtilo, or the Nomadic Shepherds) is a *pastoral work, which attests to the revival of interest in the genre at that time. *See also* Italian Literary Influences.

BIBLIOGRAPHY

Primary Texts

El Antenor. Madrid: Sancha, 1788.
Eusebio. Madrid: Villamil, 1836.
El Mirtilo, o los pastores trashumantes. Madrid: Sancha, 1795.
Odas de D. Pedro Montengón. Madrid: Sancha, 1794.
La pérdida de Espana reparada por el Rei Pelayo: Poema épico. Naples: Presso, 1820.
El Rodrigo. Poema épico. Madrid: Sancha, 1793.

Criticism

Alarcos Llorach, E. ''Montengón, el Hamlet y nuestra literatura del Siglo de Oro.'' *Castilla* 1 (1940–41): 157–60.
———. ''El senequismo de Montengón.'' *Castilla* 1 (1940–41): 149–56.
Catena, E. ''Noticia bibliográfica sobre las obras de Don Pedro Montengón y Paret.'' In *Homenaje a la memoria de Rodríguez Moñino*. Madrid: Castalia 1975. 195–204.
Fabbri, M. *Un aspetto dell'illuminismo spagnuolo: l'opera letteraria di Pedro Montengón*. Pisa: Libreria Goliardica, 1972.
García Sáez, S. *Montengón, un prerromántico de la Ilustración*. Alicante: Caja de Ahorros Provincial, 1974.

Fernando Operé

MONTERO, Isaac (1925?, Madrid?–), Spanish novelist. Montero is one of the more obscure members of the Mid-Century Generation of critical neo-realists or ''social novelists,'' due to difficulties early in his career with the Franco *censorship which resulted in mutilations, prohibitions, and confiscations of his works. He won the Sésamo Prize for brief fiction in 1957 (a largely symbolic distinction) with a short story collection. *Una cuestión privada* (1962; A Private Matter), a short novel, was drastically cut by the censors. *Al final de la primavera* (1963; At the End of Springtime), another novelette, was followed by his first long novel, *Alrededor de un día de abril* (1966; Around about a Day in April), published at the author's expense after having been censored, and promptly confiscated by the regime. For some six years, Montero refrained from publishing, and then in 1972 appeared *Los días de amor, guerra y omnipotencia de David el callado* (The Days of Love, War and Omnipotence of David the Silent), a hallucinatory, mad, fabulous love story enlightened by insights from psychiatry and the world of culture in a fatalistic, deadly context. The same year of 1972 saw the appearance of the first volume of his *Documentos secretos* (Secret Documents; vol. 2, 1974; vol. 3, 1978), a series of three tomes which contain long short stories or novelettes. His fiction up to this time is described by the author himself as falling within the realistic, ''testimonial'' vein of critical intent, but usually incorporating an intellectual content not commonly found in the ''social'' novel, a much more personal narrative voice, and occasional objects or events of dubious, anomalous or marvelous nature not typical of this school. In addition to a clear moralizing intent, Montero exhibits a variety of influences, beginning with *Cervantes and the *picaresque novel, up to the post-war French *nouveau roman* and detective fiction.

Arte real (1979; Royal Art) marked a turning point in Montero's work, being based upon a type of police investigation of what should have been the perfect crime, treated parodically through a complex, Baroque *reductio ad absurdum*. *Pájaro en una tormenta* (1984; Bird in a Storm) belongs within the same thematic nucleus, insofar as it too treats a policeman's investigation of a crime during the early years of democracy in post-Franco Spain. On another level, it deals with the corruption of police ''inherited'' from the former regime and is more an investigation of the individual policeman as well as of the more generalized force, of its political activity, infighting and power struggles, and hidden sins reaching back to the Civil War and early post-war era. In this aspect, it is typical of Montero's art which, even in his apparently simpler early ''social'' realism, always concealed a kind of moral or ethical investigation beneath the superficial ''surface'' narrative.

Janet Pérez

MONTERO, Rosa (1951, Madrid–), Spanish journalist and novels. Montero is a well-known feminist and has dealt repeatedly with women's issues in both her newspaper articles and novels, as well as in radio and television journalism. She has been closely involved with media in Spain since the beginning of the 1970s and is one of the most highly visible women writers. Published collections of interviews include *España para ti para siempre* (1976; Spain for You Forever) and *Cinco años de País* (1982; Five Years of ''Country''—referring both to Spain and the name of the newspaper with which she is associated). *Crónica del desamor* (1979; Chronicle of Falling out of Love), her first novel, is told as an autobiographical narrative, but explores collective feminist issues: relationships between women and between the sexes, homosexuality, the generation gap, contraception and abortion, and the problems Spanish women face in the job market. *La función Delta* (1981; Function Delta) is structured as two diaries, one of youth, the other of age, written by the same woman. The counterpoint between the two diaries may be considered an experiment in narrative technique; it functions not only to contrast youth and age, illusion and reality, sexual ''power'' and the loss thereof, but to explore other problems facing professional women in Spain which make success almost as much to be feared as failure. The ''youthful'' diary's focus is upon a single week in the dying woman's life when, at the age of thirty, she directed her first movie; the present tense of the narrative, in which she is a terminally ill sexagenarian, confronts mortality, aging, and the question of friendship versus love in the context of the war between the sexes. *Te trataré como a una reina* (1983; I'll Treat You Like a Queen) is set in Barcelona's infamous red-light district, the Barrio Chino, with its sleazy nightclubs, brothels, and pervasive drugs. The characters by and large share an unbearable existential isolation and desperate desire to escape their situations, an illusion symbolized by the neon sign of the false paradise of the Tropicana bar.

BIBLIOGRAPHY

Primary Texts

Amado amo. Madrid: Debate, 1988.
Crónica del desamor. Madrid: Debate, 1984.
La función Delta. Madrid: Debate, 1981.
Te trataré como a una reina. Barcelona: Seix Barral, 1983.

Janet Pérez

MONTES, Eugenio (1897, Orense–), Spanish and Galician poet, journalist and essayist. Montes first became known as a member of the poetic vanguard of the late 1920s and early 1930s, although he is more widely known for his newspaper articles, usually philosophical meditations on historical or cultural events written in a neo-Baroque style with many conceits. His most noteworthy titles include *El viajero y su sombra* (1940; The Traveler and His Shadow), *Melodía italiana* (1944; Italian Melody), *Elegías europeas* (1948; European Elegies) and *La estrella y la estela* (1953; The Star and the Wake [in the Water]), the last being an example of his characteristic wordplay. He was elected to the *Academia Española.

MONTESER, Francisco Antonio de (c. 1602, Alameda, Seville–1668, Madrid), burlesque, satiric playwright. Married to actress Manuela de Escamilla, he wrote a celebrated burlesque version of Lope de *Vega's tragic love story *El caballero de Olmedo*. With Antonio de *Solís and Diego de Silva he also composed a burlesque *Restauración de España* (Spain's Restoration). **Entremeses* such as ''Los locos'' (The Crazies) and ''La hidalga'' (The Noblewoman) comprise the best of his writing.

BIBLIOGRAPHY

Primary Texts

El caballero de Olmedo. In BAE 49.

Several *entremeses.* In *Colección de entremeses. . . .* Ed. E. Cotarelo y Mori. In NBAE 17–18.

Frances Bell Exum

MONTESINO, Ambrosio (?, Huete–1512, Madrid), Franciscan monk, translator, preacher to the royal family, and poet. He contributed greatly to the popular religious poetry written during the reign of Catholic monarchs. Said to be Isabel's favorite poet, he was an integral part of her court and rose to be Bishop of Sarda (Albania). One of his most significant contributions to Spanish religious literature was the translation into Spanish of the Carthusian Landolph of Saxony's *Vita Christi* (Life of Christ). This translation was to become most valuable in the development of vernacular religious prose. The translation was Juan de *Avila's favorite book and was also highly recommended by St. *Teresa to her community of nuns. The translation was carried out as a result of a royal decree, and Cardinal *Cisneros covered the costs of having it published at his own printshop.

Notwithstanding the significance of this translation, Montesino's claim to fame in his own day was through his religious poetry. As with so many Franciscan poets, he was influenced by popular Castilian poetry: *villancicos*, *coplas* and *romances* (*Romancero*). His poems were inspired by events in the life of Christ and the Virgin Mary instead of by theological precepts or hagiographic themes. His poetical works are collected in his *Cancionero* (Toledo, 1508; Songbook) revealing the possible influence of medieval Franciscan poets such as Jacopone da Todi (1236–1306). Montesino, in addition, wrote the "Meditaciones de San Augustín" (Meditations of St. Augustine) and a *Breviario de la Inmaculada Concepción* (1508; Breviary of the Immaculate Conception).

BIBLIOGRAPHY

Primary Texts

Breviario de la Inmaculada Concepción de la Virgen Nuestra Señora. Toledo: n.p., 1508.

Cancionero de diversas obras de nuevo trobadas todas. Toledo, 1508. In *Romancero y Cancionero sagrados.* BAE 35.

Epístolas y evangelios por todo el año. Toledo: n.p., 1512. (In British Museum)

Vita Christi, Cartuxano romançado por Fray Ambrosio Montesino. 4 vols. Alcalá: Stanislao de Polonia, 1502–3. (In British Museum)

English Translation

Song of the Virgin on the Flight into Egypt. New York: Mill House, 1951.

Angelo DiSalvo

MONTESINOS, José Fernández. *See* Fernández Montesinos, José

MONTIANO Y LUYANDO, Agustín de (1697, Valladolid–1764, Madrid), dramatist, literary critic. One of the founders—and the first director—of the Royal Academy of History, member of many other academies (*Academia). His criticism and literary output follow neo-classical tastes. His most important work is the *Discurso sobre las tragedias españolas* (1750–53; Discourse on Spanish Tragedies), which argues that Spanish dramatists conformed to classical precepts in composing tragedy, and generally ignores much of the drama of the *Siglo de Oro. The *Discursos* included two original plays by Montiano, *Virginia* and *Ataulpho*, both neo-classical tragedies. Montiano also wrote a political piece, the *Cotejo de la conducta de Su Majestad con la del rey británico* (n.d.; Comparison of His Majesty's Conduct with That of the British King). Nicolás Fernández de *Moratín was Montiano's protegé.

BIBLIOGRAPHY

Primary Text

Discurso sobre las tragedias españolas. 2 vols. Madrid: Mercurio, 1750–53.

Criticism

Uhagón y Guardamino, F. R., ed. *Don Agustín de Montiano y Luyando....* Madrid: RABM, 1926.

MONTORIOL I PUIG, Carme (1893, Barcelona–1966, ?), playwright, poet, novelist and translator. After dedicating her early years to music, she came into contact with letters by translating Shakespeare, Pirandello and Baring into Catalan. She was most successful as a playwright, though the controversial subject matter she chose caused a scandal among some critics and sectors of the public. *L'abisme* (1933; The Abyss) deals with a complex mother-daughter relationship which demythifies the traditional view of motherhood; *L'huracà* (1935; The Hurricane) is about the incestuous relationship between a mother and her son. She also wrote about familial relationships in her novel *Teresa o la vida amorosa d'una dona* (1932; Teresa, or the Love Life of a Woman), in which a woman separates from her husband and begins a new life with work playing the role as liberator of women since it means economic independence. Her literary career did not begin until she was thirty-seven, a period which coincided with the liberties of the Second Republic. She participated in women's associations and was president of the Lyceum Club. She never wrote again after the Civil War, for the political situation created by the Franco dictatorship prohibited Catalan and confined women to their homes.

BIBLIOGRAPHY

Primary Texts

L'abisme. Barcelona: Llibreria Millà, 1933. Republished with *L'huracà*. Barcelona: laSal, 1983.
Avarícia. Barcelona: Llibreria Millà, 1936.
Diumenge de Juliol. Barcelona: La Rosa dels Vents, 1936.
L'huracà. Barcelona: Millà, 1935. Republished with *L'abisme*. Barcelona: laSal, 1983.
Teresa o la vida amorosa d'una dona. Barcelona: Llibreria Catalònia, 1932.

Criticism

Fransitorra, Albina. Prologue to *L'abisme*; *L'huracà*. Barcelona: laSal, 1983. 11–24.

Isabel Segura

MONTORO, Antón de (1404, Montoro, Córdoba–1480?, Seville?), tailor and used-clothes dealer, satiric poet. Nicknamed "el ropero de Córdoba" (Córdoba's Clothier), when anti-Semitic riots erupted in Córdoba in 1473, he fled to Seville, remaining there. The strongest, and largest, verse type of Montoro is jocose and burlesque; some of his barbs provoked literary altercations with fellow poets. *See also* Converso.

BIBLIOGRAPHY

Primary Texts

Cancionero de Antón de Montoro. Ed., prol. E. Cotarelo. Madrid: Perales y Martínez, 1900.

MONTOYA, Luis (c. 1490, Belmonte, Cuenca–1569, Lisbon?), religious writer. The only biographical fact that we have about Luis Montoya is that he was an Augustinian monk who was prior in Lisbon for eleven years and master of novices for the same monastery. He is known in history for being the confessor of King Sebastian of Portugal. His contribution to Spanish religious literature consists of several devotional and meditative treatises. These represent an inner and affective religiosity common to the Augustinian writers. Written in the vernacular, the first one is called *Meditaciones de la Pasión* (Medina de Campo, 1534; Meditations on the Passion). This meditative work has been published in some of the works of St. Francis Borja. Montoya was ordained at the Augustinian monastery in Salamanca in 1515. *See also* Asceticism.

BIBLIOGRAPHY

Primary Texts

Meditaciones de la Pasión para las siete horas canónicas. Medina del Campo: P. Tovans, 1534.

Obras de los que aman a Dios. Lisbon: Juan de Barreyra, 1560.

Vida de Jesús dulcíssimo y amabalíssimo unigénito hijo de Dios y dela sacratíssima Virgen María Señora Nuestra. Lisbon: M. Borges, 1565.

Angelo DiSalvo

MOR DE FUENTES, José (1762, Monzón, Huesca–1848, Monzón), engineer, writer. Much of his life he lived in Zaragoza. Aside from translations of Horace, Tacitus, Salustius, Rousseau, Edward Gibson and Goethe, he published original poetry, plays and novels. Finest is his autobiographical work, *Bosquejillo de la vida y escritos de Don José Mor de Fuentes, delineado por él mismo* (1836; Brief Outline of the Life and Writings of José Mor de Fuentes, By Himself), which boasts a lively, direct style and was praised by *Azorín. Also autobiographical is *La Serafina* (1797; Serafina), which contains vivid recollections of events and places in Zaragoza and merited several editions.

BIBLIOGRAPHY

Primary Texts

José Mor de Fuentes; bosquejillo de su vida y escritos. Madrid: Atlas, 1943.
La Serafina. Ed., intro. I. M. Gil. Zaragoza: U of Zaragoza, 1959.

MORA, José Joaquín de (1783, Cádiz–1864, Madrid), man of letters and politician. He taught law at the U of Granada, then fought against the French in the Spanish War of Independence, was taken prisoner and interned in France. Back in Spain, and together with his friend *Alcalá Galiano, he opposed Nicolás *Böhl de Faber in the famous "querella calderoniana" (Dispute on Calderón). In it, the former defended neo-classicism versus Böhl, who represented the ideas of German Romanticism and thus sponsored a revival of the Spanish national literature, mainly of Calderón's dramas. In Madrid, Mora directed or contributed to newspapers like *Crónica Científica y Literaria* (1817; Scientific and Literary Chronicle) and *Correo General de Madrid* (1820–21; General Courier of Madrid). His liberal ideas forced him into exile in London; he was extraordinarily active there. He composed numerous translations of historical, political and literary works, among them the first translation of *Ivanhoe* (1825) into Spanish. One of the most outstanding personalities among the emigrés, he created the newspapers *Museo Universal de Ciencias y Artes* (1824–26; Universal Museum of Sciences and Arts) and *Correo Literario y Político de Londres* (The London Literary and Political Courier). He also edited several literary almanacs entitled *No me olvides* (Forget Me Not) from 1824 to 1827. From that time, until 1843, he lived in and traveled through several of the new Spanish American republics. There he taught, held important official posts, started newspapers, and, in Buenos Aires, directed the *Gaceta de Buenos Aires* (The Buenos Aires Gazette). Although Mora began as a neo-classic, he later evolved toward a more eclectic position between neo-classicism and *Romanticism. He published *Poesías* (1826, 1836; Poetry), *Cuadros de Historia de los árabes* (1826; Scenes from the History of the Arabs), and *Leyendas españolas* (1840; Spanish Legends).

BIBLIOGRAPHY

Primary Texts

Compendio de las vidas de los filósofos antiguos. Paris: Librería de Cormon y Blanc, 1825.
De la libertad del comercio. Sevilla: Establecimiento Tipográfico, 1843.
Ensayo sobre las preocupaciones. Madrid: F. Denné, 1823.
Leyendas españolas. London: C. y H. Senior, 1840.
Meditaciones poéticas. London: R. Ackermann, 1826.

Criticism

Alborg, Juan Luis. *Historia de la literatura española.* Madrid: Gredos, 1980. 4: 73–80 and 93–100.

Amunátegui, Miguel Luis. *Don José Joaquín de Mora*. Santiago de Chile: Nacional, 1888.

Monguío, Luis. "Don José Joaquín de Mora en Buenos Aires en 1827." *RHM* 31 (1965): 303–28.

———. *Don José Joaquín de Mora y el Perú del Ochocientos*. Berkeley and Los Angeles: U of California P, 1967.

Pitollet, Camille. *La querelle calderonienne de Johan Nikolas Böhl von Faber et José Joaquín de Mora, reconstituée d'après les documents originaux*. Paris: F. Alcan, 1909.

Salvador García Castañeda

MORAES, Francisco (1500?, Braganza, Portugal–1572, Evora, Portugal), novelist. Secretary to the Portuguese ambassador in Paris, he wrote an excellent chivalric novel of the **Palmerín* cycle which appeared in a Spanish translation by Luis *Hurtado twenty years before the original Portuguese edition, *Palmeirim da Inglaterra* (1567; Palmerin of England), appeared. A popular work, it was rapidly translated into French (1553), Italian (1553) and English (1602). *See also* Caballerías, Libros de.

BIBLIOGRAPHY

Primary Texts

Palmeirim de Inglaterra. Ed. M. Rodrigues Lapa. Lisbon: n.p., 1941. (Portuguese)

Palmerín de Inglaterra. In NBAE 11. (Spanish)

English Translation

Palmerin of England. Tr. A. Munday. 4 vols. London: Longman, 1807. Abridged.

MORALES, Ambrosio de (1513, León?–1591, ?), historian. At one time professor at Alcalá, Morales was a key figure in the development of modern Spanish historical investigation based on direct observation and access to source materials. He is one of the first historians writing in Spain to use non-literary materials to obtain more accurate facts. Employing this very modern method of historical research, he wrote a continuation of the all-encompassing *Corónica general de España* initiated by Florián de *Ocampo at Zamora in 1544. Morales composed *Las antigüedades de las ciudades de España* (Alcalá, 1575; Antiquities of Spanish Cities), basing his documentation on inscriptions, records and coins he personally saw in his travels. This more exacting concept of historical investigation qualifies him as a founder of modern Spanish historiography.

BIBLIOGRAPHY

Primary Texts

Las antigüedades de las ciudades de España que van nombradas en la Corónica con la averiguación de sus sitios y nombres antiguos. Alcalá: Íñiguez de Lequerica, 1575.

Apologia de Ambrosio de Morales con una información al Consejo del Rey nuestro Señor, hecha por su orden y mandamiento en defensa de los Anales de Gerónymo Zurita. Zaragoza: Lanaja, 1610.

La corónica general de España que continuava Ambrosio Morales. Prossiguiendo adelante de los cinco Libros que el M° Florián de Ocampo dexó escritos. 2 vols. Alcalá: Iñiguez de Lequerica, 1574–77.

Opúsculos castellanos cuyos originales se conservan inéditos en la Biblioteca del Escorial. Ed. F. Valerio Cifuentes. 3 vols. Madrid: Cano, 1793.

Viaje de Ambrosio de Morales por orden del rey D. Phelipe II a los reynos de León y Galicia, y principado de Asturias. Ed. Fr. H. Flórez. Madrid: A. Marín, 1765.

Angelo DiSalvo

MORALES, Tomás (1885, Moya, Gran Canaria–1921, Las Palmas), Spanish poet. Morales studied medicine in Cádiz and Madrid and from 1911 onward devoted himself to the pursuit of this profession in the Canary Islands. Many themes of his rich, varied and brilliant post-modernist poetry are drawn from his medical experience. Morales has been very influential upon subsequent poets of the Canaries, who have frequently imitated his treatment of intimate emotions and childhood memories. Among his most vigorous poems are those devoted to the sea, with their evocative music and occasional neo-Baroque grandiosity. Important collections are *Poemas de la gloria, del amor y del mar* (1908; Poems of Love, Glory, and the Sea); and in two volumes, *Las rosas de Hércules* (vol. 2, 1919; vol. 1, 1922; The Roses of Hercules). Counted among the disciples of Morales are such island poets as Fernando *González, Claudio de la *Torre, Angel Johan, Agustín Millares, José María Millares, Ventura Doreste and Pedro Lezcano. *See also* Modernism.

MORATÍN, Leandro Fernández de, pseudonym Inarco Celenio (1760, Madrid–1828, Paris), neo-classical dramatist and poet. Leandro was the son of the famous neo-classicist Nicolás Fernández de *Moratín, and while their aesthetic concerns were very similar (Leandro was educated by his father), Leandro surpassed Nicolás in both artistic style and popularity. Due to an early battle with smallpox which left him scarred and timid, Leandro turned to books for the pleasures he did not find in other children or children's games. His voluminous reading helped him to develop a deep love for literature. It also gave him a strong belief that literature was a moral guide to man's behavior and, as such, that it needed to be studied, refined, and, in the case of Spanish literature, reformed.

His first poetic endeavor was the pseudonymous epic ''La toma de Granada'' (1779; The Seige of Granada), which he wrote for a competition sponsored by the *Academia Española. José María *Vaca de Guzmán, the man who one year earlier had defeated Nicolás in a similar competition, won the prize, but Leandro felt proud of his achievement—and even more so when he received his father's sincere (and infrequently granted) praise. Similar results occurred in 1782 when Leandro entered another academy competition (although this time he triumphed alone; Nicolás had died in May 1780). Highest honors went to Juan Pablo *Forner this time, but Leandro's poem, ''Lección poética'' (1782; A Poetic Lesson), once again won second prize, and the budding poet was beginning to gain a reputation in literary circles as a bright and talented young man. His skills grew as he frequented the *tertulia* of his friend Father *Estala, and the promise he had earlier demonstrated was fulfilled in 1785 when he published a critical (and heavily emended) edition of his father's poem "Las naves de Cortés destruidas" (Cortés's Ships Destroyed).

Leandro penned his first play, *El viejo y la niña* (1786; The Old Man and the Girl), but opposition from both ecclesiastical authorities and the capital's acting companies prevented it from being produced at this time. When the Count of Cabarrús was dispatched by the government of Charles III to Paris in a diplomatic post, he asked his friend Gaspar Melchor de *Jovellanos to recommend someone to accompany him as secretary. Jovellanos named Leandro; in 1787 he was off to Paris for a successful, if short, tour of duty. Impressed with the French capital, he enjoyed his numerous contacts with that city's literary elite. Cabarrús fell from power within a year, and Leandro, who had by then penned a musical play, *El barón* (1787; The Baron), returned to Spain. Moratín's stern opinion of the contemporary literary scene in his country was revealed in his hugely successful didactic poem, "La derrota de los pedantes" (1789; The Defeat of the Pedants), a biting satire that denounced what he perceived as a veritable plague of terrible poetry.

With Manual Godoy's rapid rise to power in 1790 Moratín's fortunes changed. He secured protection, employment, and powerful friends. *El viejo y la niña* was triumphantly staged at last. Two years later a hilarious new play, *La comedia nueva o el Café* (1792; The New Comedy or the Café) opened at the Príncipe Theater to cheers from Moratín's supporters and screams of protest from his enemies—some of whom saw themselves depicted in this attack on the pedantic (and in Leandro's neo-classical view) idiotic plays currently seen on Madrid's stages. Shortly thereafter Moratín began a journey through Europe in order to establish contacts, deepen his knowledge of literature, and broaden his historical perspective. But Paris in September 1792 was not the joyous place it had been a few years before; Moratín witnessed some of the hideous excesses of the Reign of Terror and quickly booked passage to the safer surroundings of London. There he took refuge in the study of English literature, producing a translation of *Hamlet* (published in Madrid in 1798). By 1793 he was on his way back across Europe to Italy, where he lived and studied until his return to Spain late in 1796.

His good friend, Juan Antonio Melón, interceded on his behalf with Godoy to secure Moratín a position as secretary of the interpretation of languages, a post which granted him moderate prestige, sufficient salary, and freedom to pursue his literary interests. When the government began to study theatrical reform Moratín was placed on a commission to research the matter, and eventually he was named director of theaters. He wrote more plays: in 1801 he finished his famous *El sí de las niñas* (*The Maiden's Consent*, 1962), although it was not staged yet; in 1803 he produced a reworking of *El barón*; and in 1804 another comedy, *La mojigata* (The Pious Deceiver), received its Madrid premiere. His plays followed the neo-classical rules of drama, observing the unities, maintaining decorum and verisimilitude, ridiculing vice, exaggeration, hypocrisy, and stupidity, and provided models of good behavior which he hoped his audiences would emulate. Moratín's dominant passion was the theater (he never married), and his exquisite taste made him one of the most respected arbiters of Spanish neo-classical literature.

Moratín constantly rewrote his plays and poems, polishing his style and language in order to achieve that delicate balance between inspiration and artistic perfection which the neo-classicists so ardently sought. His greatest success was the premiere on January 24, 1806, of *El sí de las niñas*, a play which, while hissed by his obstreperous enemies, was enormously popular in its various stagings and printed versions. Still, his enemies enjoyed the last word by later orchestrating a suppression of some of the play's parts by the *Inquisition. Moratín never wrote for the theater again. He did continue to collect data for an encyclopedic *Orígenes del teatro español* (The Origins of Spanish Drama), published posthumously.

The tumultuous events of 1808 affected Moratín tragically. Viewed as an *afrancesado* (French sympathizer) because of his contacts with Godoy and the French government of José Bonaparte, Moratín suffered recriminations, economic hardship, and physical discomfort, but he survived with dignity. His literary interests never abated, and in 1812 he even managed to stage *La escuela de los maridos* (1812; The School for Husbands), an adaptation of Molière's *L'Ecole des maris*, just before his forced emigration from Madrid. Ill, weak, and demoralized, Moratín traveled to Valencia, where he wrote articles on literature for the local newspaper. Soon he was forced to flee once again, this time to Barcelona. His fortunes improved somewhat in 1814 when King Ferdinand VII ordered his confiscated goods returned to him and his adaptation of Molière's *Le médecin malgré lui* was staged in Barcelona as *El médico a palos* (1814; The Doctor in Spite of Himself). Still, his life was extremely difficult. In 1817 he emigrated to Paris, staying with his friend Melón. When Riego caused a change in government in Spain in 1820, an amnesty was declared and Moratín returned to Barcelona. There he prepared a valuable collection of his father's *Obras póstumas* (1821; Posthumous Works), enjoyed the company of old friends, attended theatrical productions, and relished being back "home." This homecoming was not to last. In 1821 a plague of yellow fever forced Moratín once again to begin a journey of exile. He traveled to Bordeaux to live with Manuel *Silvela, an intimate friend. In France, Moratín found the comfortable family life he had so long sought. He worked on his *Orígenes del teatro español*, oversaw the Paris publication of his three-volume *Obras dramáticas y líricas* (1825; Dramatic and Lyric Works), and moved with the Silvela family to Paris when Silvela's business interests took him away from Bordeaux. Moratín died in Paris in 1828; in 1853 his remains were returned to Madrid.

Following his death, his fame increased rapidly with the publication of a four-volume *Obras* (1830–31; Works) by the Royal Academy of History, which contained the first printed edition of the *Orígenes*. The *Biblioteca de Autores Españoles published the *Obras de D. Nicolás y D. Leandro Fernández de Moratín* (1846; Works of D. Nicolás and D. Leandro Fernández de Moratín), and additional material appeared in a three-volume *Obras póstumas* (1867–68; Posthumous Works). Moratín left a voluminous correspondence, a valuable diary, and interesting travel notes. He is remembered as Spain's most accomplished neo-classical author. *See also* Theater in Spain.

BIBLIOGRAPHY

Primary Texts

El barón. El sí de las niñas. Ed. Manuel Camarero Gea. Barcelona: Plaza y Janés, 1984.

La comedia nueva. El sí de las niñas. Ed. John Dowling and René Andioc. Madrid: Castalia, 1969.

Diario (mayo 1780-marzo 1808). Ed. René Andioc and Mirielle Andioc. Madrid: Castalia, 1968.

Epistolario. Ed. René Andioc. Madrid: Castalia, 1973.

Obras. 4 vols. Madrid: Aguado, 1830–31.

Obras de D. Nicolás y D. Leandro Fernández de Moratín. Madrid: Rivadeneyra, 1846.

Obras póstumas. 3 vols. Madrid: Rivadeneyra, 1867–68.

Teatro completo. Ed. Manuel Fernández Nieto. Madrid: Nacional, 1977.

English Translations

The Baron. Tr. Fanny Holcroft. In *Theatrical Review* 2 (London, 1805).

The Maiden's Consent. Tr. Harriet de Onís. New York: Barron's, 1962.

Criticism

Andioc, René. "Sobre Goya y Moratín hijo." *HR* 50 (1982): 119–32.

———. *Teatro y sociedad en el Madrid del siglo XVIII*. Madrid: Fundación Juan March–Castalia, 1976.

Cabañas, Pablo. "Moratín y la reforma del teatro de su tiempo." *Revista de Bibliografiía Nacional* 5 (1944): 63–102.

Casalduero, Joaquín. "Forma y sentido de *El sí de las niñas*." *NRFH* 11 (1957): 36–56.

Coloquio internacional sobre Leandro Fernández de Moratín. Albano Terme: Piovan, 1980.

Dowling, John. "The Inquisition Appraises *El sí de las niñas*." *Hispania* 22 (1961): 237–44.

———. *Leandro Fernández de Moratín*. TWAS 149. Boston: Twayne, 1971.

Glendinning, Nigel. "Rito y verdad en el teatro de Moratín." *Insula* 161 (1960): 6, 15.

———. "Moratín y el derecho." *Papeles de Son Armandans* 47 (1967): 123–48.

Helman, Edith. "Goya, Moratín y el teatro." *Jovellanos y Goya*. Madrid: Taurus, 1970. 257–71.

Marías, Julián. "Moratín y la originalidad del siglo XVIII español." *Homenaje a José Manuel Blecua*. Madrid: Gredos, 1983. 415–21.

Ruiz Morcuende, Federico. *Vocabulario de don Leandro Fernández de Moratín*. Madrid: RAE, 1945.

Sebold, Russell P. ''Historia clínica de Clara: *La mojigata* de Moratín.'' *Estudios ofrecidos a E. Alarcos Llorach*. Oviedo: Universidad de Oviedo, 1977. 2: 447–68.

David Thatcher Gies

MORATÍN, Nicolás Fernández de, pseudonym Flumisbo Thermodonciaco (1737, Madrid–1780, Madrid), neo-classical critic, poet and dramatist. Educated by the royal family, the Jesuits, and the law professors at the U of Valladolid, Moratín developed a keen sense of literature and a need to ''reform'' Spanish letters.

His first comedy, *La petimetra* (1762; The Petimetra), followed the neo-classical rules of art but remained unproduced, as did his tragedies *Lucrecia* (1763) and *Guzmán el Bueno* (1777; Guzmán the Brave). Another comedy, *La defensa de Melilla* (1775; The Defense of Melilla), has since been lost. Only *Hormesinda* (1770) made it to the stage (with José *Cadalso's girlfriend, María Ignacia Ibáñez, in the lead role), and while it is widely regarded as one of the high points of neo-classical drama, it met with only limited financial and critical success.

Moratín was more influential as a critic of literature and as a poet. His three essays, *Desengaños al teatro español* (1762–63; Reproaches to the Spanish Theater), increased the volume of anti-Calderón complaints voiced earlier in José *Clavijo y Fajardo's *El Pensador* and helped contribute to the 1765 ban on *Calderón's *autos sacramentales* (**auto*). Moratín was not opposed to *Siglo de Oro theater per se, but he did strenuously object to what he perceived as that period's harmful moral lessons and disregard for the demands of aesthetic reason, as well as his own century's abysmally low standards of theatrical oratory and presentation. In several verse satires, published in his ten-installment periodical, *El Poeta* (1764–66; The Poet), he trenchantly called into question such values. However, other poems in this first collection revealed a considerably less reformist and angry mood. In many Anacreontic odes, he celebrated the joys of life and love with young Dorisa, a singer-actress thought to be Francisca Ladvenant (and not, by the way, his wife). This collection offered a wide metrical and thematic variety, for along with the satires and odes it contained heroic ballads, sonnets, *silvas*, elegies, epigrams, and a **décima*. *El Poeta* established Moratín as the leading poet of his generation.

Other poems followed. The didactic and erudite *Diana o el arte de la caza* (1765; Diana or The Art of the Hunt) combined the two basic elements of his artistic creed: proper (neo-classical) form and proper (instructive) content. Equally didactic but considerably less proper was his scandalously amusing poem *El arte de las putas* (1771?; The Whores' Art), which circulated only in ms. among his friends, was prohibited by the *Inquisition in 1777, and only published privately in 1898 and 1977. For the first poetry competition of the *Academia Española he produced a good epic poem, ''Las naves de Cortés destruidas'' (1778; Cortés's Ships Destroyed), but lost the prize to José María *Vaca de Guzmán. In these same years, the final years of his tragically short life, he was known as "El cantor de las doncellas" (The Singer of the Maidens) for the eclogues and tercets he wrote in celebration of the annual festivities at the schools for girls run by the Sociedad Económica Matritense.

One of Moratín's enduring passions was the popular bullfight. A prose *Carta histórica sobre el origen y progresos de la fiesta de toros en España* (1777; Historical Letter Concerning the Origin and Advances of the Bullfight in Spain) followed his very successful poem "La fiesta de toros en Madrid" (1772?; Bullfight Festival in Madrid), considered by many to be the best poem written in eighteenth-c. Spain. He also wrote a classical ode on the subject, "Oda a Pedro Romero, torero insigne" (Ode to Pedro Romero, Remarkable Bullfighter), and made it one of the four topics of discussion permitted at his influential **tertulia* at the Fonda de San Sebastián in the early 1770s, where the leading figures of neo-classical Madrid gathered to share ideas, critique each other's works, and read selections from works-in-progress. The other topics permitted to the participants—José Cadalso, Tomás de *Iriarte, Ignacio *López de Ayala, Pietro Napoli Signorelli, among others—were theater, poetry, and "loves." Another important forum for the diffusion of Moratín's ideas was his chair in poetics at the prestigious Imperial College in Madrid, a position which he inherited in 1773 from an infirm Ayala and which he held until his own death at the age of forty-two in 1780.

Many of Moratín's poems remained unpublished until 1821, when his son, Leandro, brought out an *Obras póstumas* (Posthumous Works), although serious questions remain about the extent to which Leandro rewrote much of his father's material. That edition contained a useful biographical study of Nicolás, reprinted in 1846 in the BAE edition of the *Obras de D. Nicolás y D. Leandro Fernández de Moratín* (Works of Nicolás and Leandro Fernández de Moratín).

BIBLIOGRAPHY

Primary Texts

El arte de las putas. Ed. Manuel Fernández Nieto. Madrid: Siro, 1977.
Obras póstumas. Ed. Leandro Fernández de Moratín. Barcelona: Viuda de Roca, 1821.
Obras de D. Nicolás y de D. Leandro Fernández de Moratín. Madrid Rivadeneyra, 1846.
La petimetra. Ed. J. Cañas Murillo. Cáceres: Universidad de Extremadura, 1989.

Criticism

Dowling, John. "The Taurine Works of Nicolás Fernández de Moratín." *South Central Bulletin* 22 (1962): 31–34.
———. "El texto primitivo de 'Las naves de Cortés destruidas.' " *BRAE* 57 (1977): 431–83.
Gies, David T. *Nicolás Fernández de Moratín*. TWAS 558. Boston: Twayne, 1979.
Helman, Edith. "The Elder Moratín and Goya." *HR* 23 (1955): 219–30.
Lázaro Carreter, Fernando. "La transmisión textual de 'Fiesta de toros en Madrid.' " *Clavileño* 4 (1953): 33–38.
Revista de Literatura 42 (1980). Monograph dedicated to Moratín.

Simón Díaz, José. ''Nicolás Fernández de Moratín, opositor a cátedras.'' *RFE* 28 (1944): 154–76.

David Thatcher Gies

MORENO VILLA, José (1887, Málaga–1955, Mexico), poet, painter, translator, and critic. In his autobiography *Vida en claro* (Mexico, 1944; Life in Its True Light) Moreno establishes his own chronology and interprets the meaning of his own life. Born in Málaga, he studied with the Jesuits but completed his education in Germany (1904–8). While in Germany he studied chemistry, but he learned even more intently about art and literature; of the German poets his favorites were Goethe, Schiller, and Heine. Upon his return to Spain, he moved to Madrid, abandoned chemistry, and lived at the Residencia de Estudiantes, where he became involved with the Fine Arts Center. He wrote poetry, had several exhibitions of his own paintings, and published the review *Arquitectura* (Architecture). The Civil War forced him to leave Spain and to take refuge in Mexico, where he lived until his death in 1955.

In his first book of poems, *Garba* (1913), Moreno Villa acknowledged his masters: Darío, Antonio *Machado, and *Jiménez. He became a poet of transition moving from *modernism toward the later ''isms.'' His use of the Andalusian **copla* and of the gypsy theme foreshadowed *García Lorca's work. His next volume, *El pasajero* (1914; Traveler), an abstract book, full of anguish and spiritual longings, was followed by the more human and passionate poetry of *Evoluciones* (1918; Evolutions), *Florilegio* (1920; Selections), and *Colección* (1924; Collection). His next books, *Jacinta, la Pelirroja* (1929; Jacinta, the Red-haired) and the *Carambas* series (1931; Good Gracious!) contain many of the disparate elements and the dissolution of forms associated with surrealism. *Puentes que no acaban* (1931; Bridges That Do Not End) and *Salón sin muros* (1936; Room without Walls) are representative of several styles and metrical forms. The books published in Mexico, *Puerta severa* (1941; Severe Door) and *La noche del verbo* (1942; The Night of the Word), abandoned experimentation to return to more human and even religious themes. In 1949 he published an anthology that included almost all his poetic works, *La música que llevaba (1913–1947)* (The Music I Carried). His last book appeared posthumously, *Voz en vuelo a su cuna* (Málaga, 1961; Voice in Flight toward Its Cradle).

Several of Moreno Villa's books mix poetry and prose, but he also wrote prose works such as *Patrañas* (1921; Fabulous Stories) and the short stories of *Pruebas de Nueva York* (1924; Evidence of New York). He edited several **pasos* of Lope de *Rueda and wrote one original play, *La comedia de un tímido* (1924; The Play of a Timid Man). He also wrote several essays dealing with Spanish and Mexican art: *Doce manos mexicanas* (1941; Twelve Mexican Hands), *La escultura colonial mexicana* (1942; Mexican Colonial Sculpture), *Lo mexicano en las artes plásticas* (1948; Mexicanness in the Plastic Arts), and *Los autores como actores* (1951; Authors as Actors).

BIBLIOGRAPHY

Primary Texts

Cornucopia de México. 3rd ed. Mexico: Sep/Setentas, 1976.
Doce manos mexicanas. Mexico: Loera y Chávez, 1941.
Florilegio. Sel., prol. P. Henríquez Ureña. San José de Costa Rica: Monge, 1920.
Voz en vuelo a su cuna. Mexico: Ecuador 0°0′0″, 1961.

Criticism

Chandler, Richard E., and Kessel Schwartz. *A New History of Spanish Literature*. Baton Rouge: U of Louisiana P, 1961. 377–79.
Cirré, J. F. *La poesía de José Moreno Villa*. Madrid: Insula, 1963.
Izquierdo, Luis. "Los tres movimientos de la poética de José Moreno Villa (y una antología mínima)." *Nueva Estafeta* 21–22 (1980): 76–94.

María A. Salgado

MORETO, Agustín (1618, Madrid–1669, Toledo), playwright and poet. He is considered by most critics the greatest of *Calderón's disciples. A son of well-to-do Italian parents, he studied logic and physics at the U of Alcalá de Henares, where he graduated as licentiate in 1639. He then took minor orders, held a benefice in Toledo and later moved back to Madrid. He became a priest and in 1657 was chaplain to Cardinal Archbishop Baltasar de Moscoso, who subsequently put him in charge of the Hermandad del Refugio, an organization for the relief of the poor in Toledo.

Moreto was very popular with the court and the public. A careful craftsman, he valued perfection of form more than originality of plot. Many of his plays recast or adapt earlier dramas. Nevertheless, he did not simply rework earlier dramas in a mechanical manner, but rather studied the sources carefully, selected suitable elements, and rejected unnecessary complication. He excelled at creating very good plays out of weak ones. Gongoristic tendencies do not encumber Moreto's dramatic poetry; his language is direct and straightforward, and he almost always wrote sharp, balanced verse. He tended to construct plots carefully, emphasizing structure and combining subplot with main plot, or double plots of equal importance, in a skillfully controlled, meaningful manner. He also handles emotion and character portrayal adeptly.

The exact number of Moreto's plays whose texts have been preserved remains unresolved. Specialists now generally agree that we have thirty-three plays written by him alone, nineteen collaborations and six of doubtful authenticity. He also wrote **loas*, **jácaras*, **mojigangas*, and **entremeses*. His *entremeses* rank with the best of the genre. His plays include *comedias de salón*, *comedias de capa y espada*, *comedias* of character and customs, historical plays and dramas on biblical subjects and lives of saints. Moreto's greatest masterpiece is *El desdén con el desdén* (1654; Disdain Conquered by Disdain), which is considered the best drawing-room comedy of the seventeenth c. The plot is simple and ordered with consummate skill. Diana, heiress to the county of Barcelona, mocks at marriage: her father surrounds her with the neighboring gallants, among whom is Carlos, Count of Urgel. Carlos wins her love feigning disdain. The setting of the play is elegant, the dialogue sparkling and unaffected, and as Leonard Mades in the revised edition cited in the bibliography, points out, "The twists and turns of the love game are worked out with the height of finesse, and the humor bristles." Around twenty *comedias* have been proposed as sources for this play, which also served as the inspiration for a number of adaptations: Molière's *La Princesse d'Élide* (1664), Carlo Gozzi's *La Principessa filosofa, o sia il controveleno* and others (Marivaux, Tauro and Lesage). His other masterpiece, *El lindo don Diego* (1662; Don Diego the Dandy), is a *comedia de capa y espada*, which can also be called a *comedia de figurón*, a type of play in which a farce is developed from a rather grotesque caricature of the protagonist. The play is essentially a comic exposé of a conceited and ridiculous dandy. Moreto is clearly indebted to Guillén de *Castro's *El Narciso en su opinión* (1625; Narcissus to Himself), but the adaptation is clearly superior to the source.

Moreto wrote several other plays worthy of note. Among the *comedias de capa y espada* are *No puede ser* (1660; It Can't Be), *El parecido en la corte* (n.d.; The Likeness at Court), and *La confusión de un jardín* (1681; The Confusion of a Garden). His best religious play is *San Franco de Sena* (1652; St. Franco of Sena), an illustration of the adage that "the best sinners make the best saints." Other religious plays are *La vida de San Alejo* (1658; The Life of St. Alejo), *La cena del rey Baltasar* (1648?; King Balthazar's Feast) and *Caer para levantar* (1662; Falling in Order to Arise). His best historical plays are *El valiente justiciero* (1657; The Valiant Justice-Maker), *La fuerza de la ley* (1654; The Strength of the Law), *Antíoco y Seleuco* (1654), *Los jueces de Castilla* (1654; The Magistrates of Castile) and *Cómo se vengan los nobles* (1668; How Nobles Avenge Themselves). *See also* Theater in Spain.

BIBLIOGRAPHY

Primary Texts

Comedias escogidas. Ed. Luis Fernández-Guerra y Orbe. BAE 39.

El desdén con el desdén. In *Diez Comedias del Siglo de Oro*. Ed. José Martel and Hymen Alpern. Rev. Leonard Mades. New York: Harper and Row, 1968.

El lindo don Diego (published with Guillén de Castro's *El Narciso en su opinión*). Ed., intro. A. V. Ebersole. Madrid: Taurus, 1968.

Criticism

Casa, Frank P. *The Dramatic Craftmanship of Moreto*. Cambridge: Harvard UP, 1966.

Castañeda, James A. *Agustín Moreto*. TWAS 308. New York: Twayne, 1974.

Kennedy, Ruth Lee. *The Dramatic Art of Moreto*. Philadelphia: n.p., 1932.

Hector Medina

MORISCO, a major religious and cultural group in *Siglo de Oro Spain. The term refers to Moors who have professed conversion to Christianity. They became a rather powerful sector of society, and the sincerity of their profession was felt to be dubious, thus they were expelled from Spain by Philip III in 1609. An estimated 500,000 were forced to leave Spain. *See also Converso*; *Mozárabe; Mudéjar*.

BIBLIOGRAPHY

Criticism

Castro, A. *The Structure of Spanish History*. Tr. E. King. Princeton: Princeton UP, 1954.
Chejne, A. G. *Islam and the West. The Moriscos*. Albany, NY: SUNY P, 1983.
Domínguez Ortiz, A., and B. Vincent. *Historia de los moriscos*. Madrid: RO, 1978.
García-Arenal, M. *Los moriscos*. Madrid: Nacional, 1975.
Longá, P. *Vida religiosa de los moriscos*. Madrid: Maestra, 1915.

MOSQUERA DE FIGUEROA, Cristóbal (1547?, Seville–1610, Ecija), poet, historical author. He studied at the U of Salamanca and the U of Osuna, obtaining a degree in canon law in 1575. An esteemed member of the *Escuela sevillana, he wrote the prologue to Fernando de *Herrera's *Relación de la guerra de Chipre* . . . (1572) and one to *Mal Lara's *La Galera Real*. His poetry, sacred and profane, exhibits dignity and decorum—and the clear influence of *Garcilaso de la Vega, Herrera and Luis de *León. He also wrote the informative historical account *Comentario en breve compendio de disciplina militar* . . . (1596; Commentary of Military Discipline in Brief Outline) based on what he witnessed in the Azores.

BIBLIOGRAPHY

Primary Texts

Comentario en breve compendio. . . . Madrid: Sánchez, 1596.
Obras. Ed., prol. G. Díaz Plaja. Madrid: RAE, 1955.

Criticism

Montoto, S. "Mosquera de Figueroa." *HR* 9 (1941): 298–300.

MOURA, Vasco (Navarro da) Graça (1942, Porto–), Portuguese poet, essayist, translator. A lawyer with a degree from the U of Lisbon's School of Law, he was secretary of social order of the IV Provisional Government, resulting from the 1974 Carnation Revolution, and secretary of returnees (from the former Portuguese African colonies) in the VI Provisional Government. Also director of the state radio-television network, he is currently director of O Oiro do Dia publisher's poetry series out of Porto.

An erudite continuer of Porto liberalism in the national intelligentsia, his earlier poetry of the 1960s anticipated the fall of the decadent Salazarist regime. Moura is prolific in poetry and scholarly literary criticism. His essays particularly contribute cultural-historical Euro-Portuguese background to such topics as the erotic in national poetry as in *David Mourão-Ferreira ou a mestria de Eros* (1978; David Mourão-Ferreira or the Mastery of Eros), or the expressly *European* quality of Portuguese literature, especially in Camonean tradition and canon (*Camões e a divina proporção* [1985; Camões and the Divine Proportion], for which he received the 1986 Jacinto do Prado Coelho Essay Prize from the Portuguese Center of the International Association of Literary Critics).

Moura's poetry of the 1970s and 1980s establishes his virtuosity and craft and twines its themes and interrogations along the two lines of the pursuit of eros and the meditations of an erudite melancholy. In 1978, he renders fifty of Shakespeare's less known sonnets in a non-literal, popular Portuguese. His poetic reflections on post-revolutionary Portuguese life of the late 1970s matures into distant, ironic comment in the 1980s. In his autobiographic 1981 ''poema-tempo/ time poem,'' he ironically confronts love with the language-reality problem, with eros losing in spirit, where the beloved becomes ''uma literalidade obtida / an obtained literality'' and ''a revolução tornou-se uma pirueta sobre o / real canceroso//the revolution has turned into a pirouette spinning on top of / the real cancer.'' Enigma becomes Moura's next poetic preoccupation—*Nó cego, o regresso* (1982; Love-Knot, the Return)—where such questions as ''Como meter o mundo / num poema?//How does the world fit in a poem?'' go unanswered. Reiterative memory predominates next where Moura's intuitive vision simplifies into logic and *naturalism (e.g., Escherian transformations) and memory exoticizes past and distant places—*A Sombra das figuras* (1985; The Shadow of the Figures)—where the melancholy intellect laments that ''o poema / é um beco sem saída//the poem [= poetry] / is a dead end street.''

BIBLIOGRAPHY

Primary Texts

Camões e a divina proporção. Lisbon: Author's ed., 1985.
O Mês de Dezembro e outros poemas. Porto: n.p., 1976.
Nó cego, o regresso. Porto: O Oiro do Dia, 1982.
Os Rostos comunicantes. Lisbon: Author's ed., 1984.

Robert R. Krueger

MOZÁRABE, a cultural-religious group in central and southern Spain. *Mozárabes* were Christian Spaniards living in Moorish-controlled territory during the Reconquest (c. 718–1492). Over the years, this group developed a distinct dialect; they are also the source for **aljamía* literature. *See also Converso*; *Morisco; Mudéjar*.

MUDÉJAR, a cultural and religious group. The term denoted Muslims living in Christian-controlled lands during the Reconquest (c. 718–1492) who did not convert to Christianity. The mudéjares, segregated as were the **conversos*, developed a distinctive style of art and architecture which blended Christian motifs and Arab ornamentation (thirteenth through sixteenth centuries). *See also Morisco; Mozárabe*.

MÚGICA, Rafael. *See* Celaya, Gabriel

MUÑIZ HIGUERA, Carlos (1927, Madrid–), dramatist. After earning a law degree from the Universidad Central in Madrid, Muñiz worked in the Ministry of the Treasury, an experience with bureaucracy which left its mark in several of his plays. In 1955 his *Telarañas* (Cobwebs), a play about loneliness and alienation which employs both expressionistic and realistic techniques, had its premiere; it was unsuccessful with both audiences and critics. In the same year, however, his drama *El grillo* (1958; The Cricket), a work of social criticism in which the economic plight of an office worker who never receives a promotion and whose complaints resemble the crickets' unheeded song, was awarded the Premio Nacional de Cámara y Ensayo award. It met with considerable success when it was produced in 1957 as part of a government program designed to encourage new playwrights. Although his *El precio de los sueños* (1965; The Price of Dreams) was awarded the Carlos Arniches Drama Prize in 1958, it was never produced. Like the earlier works it depicts rather passive and apathetic characters in an oppressed economic situation, yet here these provincial middle-class characters rather foolishly try to keep up appearances instead of realistically confronting their financial situation. *El tintero* (1961; The Inkwell) depicts in neo-expressionistic style the fruitless struggle of a humble office worker, Crock, to survive the brutal dehumanization of a mechanized, bureaucratic "system" which ritualistically triumphs with the suicide of the protagonist, and the absurd condemnation to the gallows of his only friend. Neither the one act *Un solo de saxofón* (1969; A Saxophone Solo), written in 1961, nor *Las viejas difíciles* (1967; The Difficult Old Ladies), written in 1961–62, has been staged. Both works present individuals who must either acquiesce to the dehumanization, moral intransigence, and reactionary values of the dominant system, or face destruction at its hands.

Government *censorship and the unwillingness of producers to take risks with controversial works were influential in Muñiz's virtual abandonment of the theater in the 1960s; he wrote for radio and television and then turned to the practice of law. In 1972, after five years of research, he wrote the historical work *La tragicomedia del serenísimo Príncipe Don Carlos* (1974; Tragicomedy of the Most Serene Prince Don Carlos), which was initially banned by censors and not staged until 1980. Critics have seen the influence of Ramón del *Valle-Inclán's grotesque genre, the *esperpento* as well as the epic theater of Bertolt Brecht and the documentary theater of Peter Weiss in this play based on the sixteenth-c. Spanish monarch Philip II and his son Don Carlos. Extensive historical footnotes testify to the author's desire to rectify contemporary views of the father and son and their tormented relationship. *See also* Contemporary Spanish Theater.

BIBLIOGRAPHY

Primary Texts

El caballo del caballero. Primer Acto 5 (April 1965): n.p.

Carlos Muñiz: El tintero, Un solo de saxofón, Las viejas difíciles. Ed. José Monleón. Madrid: Taurus, 1969.

El grillo. Madrid: Arión, 1958.
El precio de los sueños. Madrid: Alfil, 1965.
La Tragicomedia del serenísimo Príncipe Don Carlos. Madrid: Edicusa, 1974.

Criticism

Borras, Angelo. "Sound, Music and Symbolism in Carlos Muñiz's Theatre." *RN* 12 (1970): 31–35.
Cramsie, Hilde F. *Teatro y censura en la España franquista: Sastre, Muñiz y Ruibal*. New York: Lang, 1984.
Donahue, Francis. "Carlos Muñiz and the Expressionist Imagination." *RN* 15 (1973): 230–33.
Oliva, César. *Cuatro dramaturgos realistas en la escena de hoy: sus contradicciones estéticas*. Murcia: U of Murcia, 1978.
Zeller, Loren. "La evolución técnica y temática en el teatro de Carlos Muñiz." *Estreno* 2.2 (1976): 41–49.

Judith Ginsberg

MUÑÓN, Sancho de. *See Lisandro y Roselia, Tragicomedia de*

MUÑOZ, Juan Bautista (1745, Museros, Valencia–1799, Seville), Dominican, historian. Commissioned by the king to compose a history of the discovery and conquest of the New World, he wrote the *Historia del Nuevo Mundo* (1793; History of the New World), which covers events to 1500 and is still an excellent source for the early years of the discovery. At his sudden, unexpected death, he left behind an invaluable 166-volume collection of documents about the New World. Called the Muñoz collection, it is now housed in the Royal Academy of History in Madrid.

BIBLIOGRAPHY

Primary Texts

"Cargos hechos por el Señor D. Juan Bautista Muñoz contra el Abate Filibero de Parri Palma." In *Las polémicas de Juan Bautista Muñoz*. Ed., study C. W. de Onís. Madrid: Porrúa Turanzas, 1984.
Catálago de la colección de don Juan Bautista Muñoz. 3 vols. Madrid: RAH, 1954–56.
Historia del nuevo mundo. Madrid: Ibarra, 1793.
Puerto Rico en los manuscritos de don Juan Bautista Muñoz. Ed., study V. Murga Sanz. Río Piedras: U of Puerto Rico, 1960.
Sto. Domingo en los manuscritos de Juan Bautista Muñoz. Ed., notes R. Marte. Sto. Domingo: Fundación García Arévalo, 1981.

English Translation

The history of the new world. . . . Tr. anon. London: G. G. and J. Robinson, 1797.

MUÑOZ PABÓN, Juan Francisco (1866, Hinojos, Huelva–1920, Seville), Spanish poet and novelist. His lyric compositions appear principally in two collections, *Menudencias épicas* (1897; Epic Minutiae) and *Romancero del Niño de Nazaret* (1899; Ballad-Book of the Child of Nazareth). His novels are essentially *costumbrista*, that is, word-paintings of the regional customs, language, culture, food, dress, songs and dance of specific areas of Spain, and in the case of Muñoz Pabón, of Andalusia. His moralizing tendency and Christian preoccupations are frequently noticeable, in spite of his skill in imitating popular speech. Both his style and themes have been compared with those of Father Luis *Coloma. His most popular novels are *Justa y Rufina* (1900), *La Millona* (1902), *Temple de acero* (Nerves of Steel), and *Juegos florales* (1906; Floral Games), a novel treating regional poetry competitions, in which he inserted numerous poems.

MUÑOZ ROJAS, José Antonio (1909, Antequera, Málaga–), Spanish poet, critic and short story writer. Although he received a law degree, he served as a lecturer in Spanish at Cambridge. While still very young, he distinguished himself as a poet of the emerging generation with his first book, *Versos de retorno* (1929; Verses of Return). *Ardiente jinete* (1934; Burning Horseman) won a prize in a national literature contest. His writing was interrupted by the Civil War, but continued his poetic output after the conflict with *Sonetos de amor por un autor indiferente* (1942; Love Sonnets by an Indifferent Author) and *Abril en el alma* (1943; April in My Soul). Among his fiction are the story collections *Historias de familia* (1946; Family Histories) and *Las cosas del campo* (1951; Things of the Countryside). *Cantos a Rosa* (1955; Songs to Rosa) is another poetry collection, while *Las musarañas* (1957; Cobwebs) contains poetic prose fiction.

MUÑOZ SECA, Pedro (1881, Puerto de Santa María–1936, Madrid), Spanish dramatist. Muñoz Seca was a prolific author of comedies, often following the tradition of the **género chico* (one-act plays, usually of a satiric nature) or the so-called *astracán* (hilarious theatrical works based upon puns, plays on words or ideas, and absurd situations). He frequently parodied Spanish classical theater or neo-classic tragedies, or satirized public figures and politicians of his day. His humor could be biting and sarcastic, although his use of language was exceptionally clever. *La venganza de don Mendo*, a verse parody of a well-known tragic drama, is considered his best comedy. During the period of the Republic (1931–36), he began to produce political satires of an anti-Republican bent, including *La oca* (The Seal), *Anacleto se divorcia* (Anacleto Gets a Divorce), *La voz de su amo* (His Master's Voice), and *Jabalí* (The Wild Boar). He was killed in Madrid during the early months of the Civil War.

Primary

Obras completas. 6 vols. Madrid: Rivadeneyra, 1946–48.

MUNTANER, Ramon (1265, Peralada–1336, Eivissa), best known chronicler of *Catalan literature. Born to a wealthy and powerful family, he intermingled with royalty and nobility from his early youth. In 1285 when he was twenty years old the Muntaners' castle, Peralada, was burned and destroyed, and all material possessions were lost. Young Ramon left Catalonia and joined the troops of Roger de Lluria, with whom he took part in the conquest of the island of Menorca (1286–87). After 1300 Muntaner served in the Italian wars and finally in 1302 became an administrator, diplomat and military leader of the legendary Roger de Flor, participating with the mercenary Almogàvers in numerous campaigns in the Orient (Galliopolis, Negropontus, Thebes, etc.). In 1315, accompanying Jaume II, the infant future king of Mallorca, he returned to Catalonia to occupy several important posts in the bureaucracy of the Catalan Empire. He died while serving as mayor of Eivissa in 1336.

Muntaner is best known as the author of *La Crònica* (The Chronicle). It deals with the expedition to the East at the zenith of Catalan dominance in the Mediterranean. After the war with Sicily, members of the expedition—the Almogàvers—entered the service of the Byzantine emperor Andronicus, providing the shock troops that battled the Turks. The Catalans and Aragonese won important victories until the assassination of their commander Roger de Flor, after which they unleashed a violent vengeance. In a series of lightning campaigns utilizing the modern concept of ''Blitzkrieg,'' the Almogàvers founded the duchies of Athens and Neopatria. Numbering only about 6,000, they took over an empire of several millions of inhabitants, successfully fighting against the French, Genoese, and Venetians as well. The epic hero of these incredible but true exploits is the figure of Roger de Flor. The main sources of Muntaner's epic are the Franco-Germanic epic tradition (Roland, Arthurian tales, Tristan, Lancelot) and the techniques of the jongleurs. On one occasion he even retells a fable by Aesop. In short, in spite of the title, Muntaner adopts an epic tone and exaggerates in order to exalt ''lo bell catalanesc'' (the beautiful Catalan language) and the politics and military exploits of the country he so dearly loves. His enthusiasm is boundless and often he seems to be at a loss for words ''¿què us dire?'' (what can I say?). This deeply personal touch and the plasticity of the narration are unique among similar epic narrations of his times. Since its first printed edition in 1558 it has been translated, partially or in its entirety, into Castilian, Italian, French, German and English. Joanot *Martorell took it as one of his most important sources of inspiration for *Tirant lo Blanch*. Finally, it must be pointed out that *La Crònica* plays a similar role as *El *Cid* (*The Cid*) in Castilian or *La Chançon de Roland* (*The Song of Roland*) in French, in Catalan literature and national consciousness.

BIBLIOGRAPHY

Primary Texts

Los almogávares en Bizancio, crónica medieval. Valencia: Prometeo, 1900.

Crònica. In *Les quatre grans cròniques*. Ed. F. Soldevila. Barcelona: Selecta, 1971.

Pàgines escollides de Muntaner. Ed. R. d'Alòs-Muner. Barcelona: Barcino, 1936.

English Translation

The Chronicle of Muntaner. Tr. Lady Goodenough. Nendeln, Liechtenstein: Kraus Reprint, 1967.

Criticism

Keighley, R. G. "Muntaner and the Catalan Grand Company." *Revista Canadiense de Estudios Hispánicos* 4 (1979): 37–53.

Montoliu, Manuel de. *Les quatre grans cròniques*. Barcelona: Alpha, 1959.

Olwer, Lluís Nicolau d'. *L'esperit català en nostra història*. Barcelona: n.p., 1929. 127–51.

———. "La crònica de Ramon Muntaner. Filiació dels seus textos." *Homenatge a A. Rubió i Lluch*. Barcelona: n.p., 1936. 1: 69–76.

Riba, Carles. "En Ramon Muntaner, home d'imperi." *Obres Completes,* vol. 2: *Assaigs crítics*. Barcelona: Selecta, 1967. 321–24.

Sobré, Josep Miquel. *L'èpica de la realitat. L'escriptura de Ramon Muntaner i Bernat Desclot*. Barcelona: Curial Edicions Catalanes, 1978.

Joan Gilabert

MURIÀ I ROMANI, Anna (1904, Barcelona–), journalist, political activist and novelist. She studied at the Institut de Cultura i Biblioteca Popular de la Dona Catalana in 1927, the first of her extensive collaborations in the many publications of the time. She was very active politically from 1930 to 1939, including membership on the central committee of the Estat Català during the war. Her novels involve various relationships and point to the importance of economic independence for women. *Joana Mas* (1933; Joana Mas) contrasts two women; one married a man much older than herself and quite well off; the other is single and independent, but has a very unstable sentimental life. *Res no és veritat, Alícia* (1984; Nothing Is True, Alícia) presents us with a complex web of relationships, focusing on one between a brother and sister. Her major opus, *Aquest serà el principi* (1986; This Will Be the Beginning), is a complex work with no narrator; all characters speak for themselves. It is divided into three historical periods: the proclamation of the Second Republic and the Civil War, exile and a return to Catalonia. While no one character represents the author, all of them form a part of her life. She left Barcelona for France in 1939; there she met Augustí *Bartra, poet, whom she married and with whom she went into exile. They traveled to the Dominican Republic, Cuba and Mexico before returning to Catalonia in 1970. Murià also wrote children's books and studies of the poetry of her husband.

BIBLIOGRAPHY

Primary Texts

Aquest serà el principi. Barcelona: laSal, 1986.

Joana Mas. Barcelona: Llibreria Catalònia, 1933.

La Peixera. Barcelona: GSEC, 1938.

Res no és veritat, Alícia. Barcelona: Antonio Picazo, 1984.

Criticism

A special issue of *Mirall de glaç: Quadern de literatura* (Terrassa) was dedicated to Murià in the spring of 1982.

Isabel Segura

MURILLO, Enrique (1944, Barcelona–), Spanish novelist, poet and essayist. Murillo studied journalism and literature in Barcelona and resided for an extended period in London. Since 1973 he has worked as a translator for several publishers, rendering into Spanish British and American classics from Coleridge to Ezra Pound, Truman Capote, Djuna Barnes and others (including Nabokov). A movie and theater critic, he has also written a book-length essay on the literary theory of *Modernism and published a volume of poetry, *Las dimensiones saciadas* (1979; The Satiated Dimensions) praised by Leopoldo María *Panero for its meticulous care. His first narrative collection, *El secreto del arte* (1984; The Secret of Art) links together several tales in an investigation of the diffuse frontiers separating the world of normalcy from that of madness, with a psychological complexity and ambiguity reminiscent of Henry James and a style which reminded Spanish critics of Conrad. *El centro del mundo* (1988; The Center of the World) is a novel about the search for truth, as the protagonist tries to unravel the mystery of a friend's death, not in detective fashion, but a protracted meditation during a night of insomnia as he struggles with seemingly contradictory causes and motives which leave him with an insoluble ethical dilemma.

Janet Pérez

MYSTICISM (from the Greek μυστικος [mystikos] meaning secret or hidden knowledge). A religious experience in which a direct union, fusion or marriage takes place between the soul and God. The mystics teach that this union requires an extraordinary (sanctifying) grace which is not granted to the ordinary person. As a consequence, few have attained this state. In Spain, mystical literature took on diverse forms and modes of expression during the *Siglo de Oro. There are writers such as Fray Juan de los *Angeles who wrote about the mystical process without necessarily having experienced union. The Augustinian Alonso de *Orozco was one of the first in Spain to describe the mystical way, although he avoided writing about his own mystical unions for reasons of personal humility. The two greatest Spanish mystics, St. John of the Cross (*Juan de la Cruz) and St. Teresa of Ávila, did indeed thoroughly write about both the process and their respective experiences, producing works that are the highest expression of mystical literature in Western Europe. However, each possessed a unique individual approach, since St. Teresa employed the language of Castilian rusticity and St. John used a more intellectual language. In spite of the different literary styles and intellectual approaches, in classical Spanish mysticism the soul is moved to attain union with the Divine Essence in an active way through the affections (love) instead of through theological speculation or as a result of contemplating the created world.

Spanish mysticism includes the three stages that comprise the mystical way (*vía mística*): purgative, illuminative and unitive. It shares the first two with *ascetical literature. Within the purgative stage the individual rids his soul of everything that does not pertain to God. This stage or phase of the mystical process is likened to the dark night or to the abysmal nothingness in which one loses desire for everything (*sequedad*), even spiritual things. This purgation of the soul predisposes it to receive the divine light within the illuminative stage (phase). Once the soul's understanding has been illuminated, it is now prepared to seek union in the unitive stage. The three stages of the mystical way correspond to the three parts of the soul: memory, intellect (understanding) and will.

The mystics, inspired by the *Canticle of Canticles*, associate this mystical union with marriage, which becomes the consummate union of love, a total fusion of the soul with God. It is important to note that in the case of the Spanish mystics, the soul participates in the life of the Trinity without losing its own identity. The soul's will remains active when union is ultimately achieved, for the soul is never felt to be absorbed into the All, losing its own essence in the process. In other words, classical Spanish mysticism, even though it has incorporated certain Platonic elements, is never deistic or pantheistic.

Mysticism has had a long and illustrious history bequeathing to the Spanish mystics a wealth of images, symbols and models. From the *Canticle of Canticles* the mystics have established the relationship between the soul (Bride) and God (Bridegroom). The sixth-c. tract *Mystical Theology* by the Pseudo-Dionysus contributed abundantly to the development of western mysticism. Johannes Tauler of Strasbourg (1300–1361) and the Flemish Jan van Ruysbroeck (1293–1381) proffered a number of symbols and images as well as terminology. From the latter, St. John of the Cross drew images such as the unnamable abyss, nothingness or what is referred to as the negative way. Within the medieval Hispanic context, Ramon *Llull (d. 1315) influenced subsequent Spanish mysticism with the corpus of his works, but most especially with *El llibre d'Amic e Amat* (Palma de Mallorca, 1904; *The Book of the Lover and the Beloved*, 1945). St. Bernard of Clairvaux, St. Francis of Assisi and St. Bonaventure, as part of the enduring Augustinian-Franciscan religious tradition, taught the mystics to reach God by looking inward and loving profoundly. Reformed Franciscans such as Francisco de *Osuna and San Pedro de *Alcántara were sources of guidance and became inspirations for St. Teresa. Indeed, the Christian-Platonism which informed the reform movements in Spain paved the way for the great mystical expression of the Golden Age.

Sacred Scripture and ecclesiastical history posited such models as the marriage between Jahweh and Israel, Mary as the Bride of Christ and Christ in his relationship to the Mystical Body (the church). Spanish mysticism incorporated other symbols in order to enhance the rendering into human language of the unitive stage. St. Teresa in her *Interior Castle* (1946) and St. John of the Cross in the *Ascent to Mt. Carmel* (1889), *Dark Night of the Soul* (1891) and *Spiritual Canticle* (1919) express in the most sublime language the experiences leading up to and subsequent to mystical union. In this mystical literature one will come across recurring images, one of which is the dark night (*noche oscura*), which is the spiritual disvesting (*desnudez*) of every thought or feeling that does not apply to God. The fountain (*fonte-fuente*, or *noria*, a type of well) signifies the source of God's love which may be found in the deepest or innermost part of the soul (*hondón*). The image of the castle (*castillo interior*) with its multiple chambers symbolizes the soul into which the individual must enter to seek God and subsequent union therein. The individual must withdraw into himself (*recogerse*) in order to make the ascent to God in a seemingly contradictory process. The flame (*llama viva*) is a metaphor which conjures up the all-consuming love that fills the soul before it is united to God. The wound or transfixing (*transverberación*) is effected by God's piercing love for the soul and is here likened to a lover who longs for his beloved. The hunt (*caza*) is associated with the search for God and hence the sheep (*pastorcito*) represents Christ. The butterfly (*mariposa*) conjures up the image of the soul rising to God.

A number of these images reveal the soul's active participation in the mystical process of the Spanish mystics. In classical Spanish mysticism the union is also accompanied by ecstasies and visions; however, the mystics continuously warn their readers of the dangers inherent in these spiritual phenomena. St. Teresa's transverberations imply a sensual transposition brought about by God's wounding love. Yet, the mystic's abandonment is always considered to be short-lived. The Spanish mystics maintain that union is a unique privilege which is freely granted to a few at limited intervals. They insist that one's obligations and duties must not be shunned. In effect, this is a more practical stance since the individual must never lose sight of his place in the Christian community of which he is a part. The mystic is not to consider himself as being above sin, nor can he avoid his responsibilities to peers. It is important to note that the Spanish mystics are also ascetics and a good portion of their writings could fall under the category of ascetical literature since both processes are interrelated. *Ascent to Mt. Carmel* and *Dark Night of the Soul* are essentially ascetical in nature because they describe the purgative and illuminative stages of the *vía mística*. The mystic must also practice all of the Christian virtues in the spiritual exercises leading up to union. It is precisely on this point that the Spanish Illuminists were judged to be heretical since they abandoned their responsibilities, believing themselves to be above sin and beyond the fallen condition of humanity. *See also* Alumbrados; Platonism.

BIBLIOGRAPHY

Primary Texts

Lull, Ramón. *El libro del Amigo y del Amado*. Madrid: Aguilar, 1940.
Juan de la Cruz, San. *Obras completas*. Editorial de Espiritualidad, 1980.

Teresa de Jesús, Santa. *Obras completas*. 2nd ed. Madrid: Editorial de Espiritualidad, 1976.

English Translations

Lull, Ramón. *The Book of the Lover and the Beloved*. New York: Macmillan, 1945.

St. John of the Cross. *The Complete Works of St. John of the Cross, Doctor of the Church*. Tr. E. Allison Peers. New rev. ed. London: Burns, Oates and Washburne, 1953.

St. Theresa of Avila. *The Complete Works of St. Teresa of Jesus*. Tr. E. Allison Peers. New York: Sheed and Ward, 1950.

Criticism

Bayer, R. "Les Thèmes du Néoplatonisme et la mystique espagnole de la Renaissance." *Hommage à Ernest Martinenche*. Paris: D'Artney, 1939. 59–74.

Cilveti, Angel L. *Introducción a la mística española*. Madrid: Cátedra, 1974.

Domínguez Berrueta, J. *Filosofía mística española*. Madrid: CSIC, 1947.

Green, Otis H. "The Historical Problem of Castilian Mysticism." *HR* 6 (1938): 93–103.

Groult, Pedro. *Místicos de los Países Bajos y la literatura española del Siglo de Oro*. Tr. Rodrigo Molina. Madrid: Universitaria Española, 1976.

Hatzfeld, Helmut. *Estudios literarios sobre la mística española*. Madrid: Gredos, 1955.

———. "The Influence of Ramón Lull and Jan van Ruysbroeck on the Language of the Spanish Mystics." *Tradito* 6 (1946): 337–97.

Molina, Rodrigo. "Antecedentes medievales de la mística española." *Papeles de Son Armadans* 59 (1970): 229–50. (Includes Bernard of Clairvaux, Bonaventure and Lull.)

Peers, Edgar A. *Studies of the Spanish Mystics*. 3 vols. London: Methuen, 1927–60.

Sáinz Rodríguez, Pedro. *Introducción a la historia de la literatura mística en España*. Madrid: Voluntad, 1927.

Sánchiz Alventosa, J. *La escuela mística alemana y sus relaciones con nuestros místicos del Siglo de Oro*. Madrid: Verdad y Vida, 1940.

Angelo DiSalvo

N

NADA, Sor (seventeenth c., Andalusia?–?), nun, religious writer. Her true identity remains a mystery. Under the name Sor Nada (Sister Nothing), she wrote several pieces on the Soul, and its conversations with Jesus. All mss. are found in the *Biblioteca Nacional.

BIBLIOGRAPHY

Criticism

Galerstein, Carolyn, and Kathleen McNerney. *Women Writers of Spain*. Westport, CT: Greenwood, 1986.

NAMORA, Fernando (1919, Condeixa-a-Nova, Coimbra–), Portuguese novelist and poet. Namora received the degree of doctor of medicine from the ancient U of Coimbra, subsequently working as a young country doctor in the hinterlands, treating peasants, miners, and mountaineers. He moved to Lisbon's Cancer Institute in 1950, remaining there until 1965, when he abandoned medicine definitively for literature. His first poems appeared while he was in medical school: *Terra* (1941; Earth) would later become part of a larger collection of socially oriented poetry entitled *Novo Cancioneiro* (New Songbook). *Fogo na noite escura* (1943; Fire in the Dark of Night), a neo-realist novel of social problems and psychological analysis, brought him to the attention of the reading public. Medical work among the poor supplies much of the narrative content of subsequent works of fiction, including *Casa da malta* (1945; House of Tramps), in which the socio-critical content increases; *Minas de San Francisco* (1946; St. Francis Mines), in which his fiction becomes still more combative; and the prose series, *Retalhos da vida de um médico* (vol. 1, 1949; *Mountain Doctor*, n.d.; vol. 2, 1963; Fragments of the Life of a Doctor). During the 1950s Namora's fiction, like that of coetaneous counterparts in Spain, aimed at combating socio-economic ills by using literature as a weapon. This attitude is evident in *A noite e a madrugada* (1950; The Night and the Dawn), *O trigo e o joio* (1954; *Fields of Fate*, 1970), and to a lesser extent, the poetry collection *As frias madrugadas*

(1959; The Cold Dawns). His writing in the 1960s began to become more subjective and meditative, as is evident in *Domingo à tarde* (1961; Sunday Afternoon) and *Os clandestinos* (1972; The Clandestine [Activists]), whose hero's secret love affairs lighten the burden of his underground political activities. Contemporary society, progress, and technology—both positive and negative aspects of life in the late twentieth c.—appear in *Marketing* (1969), a satire of some of the less desirable facets of modern technological development, as well as in *Os adoradores do sol* (1971; The Sun Worshippers), and *Estamos no vento* (1974; Winds of Change), an exhortation to youth. *A nave de pedra* (1975; The Ship of Stone) is autobiography.

BIBLIOGRAPHY

Primary Texts

Cidade solitaria. 2nd ed. Lisbon: Arcádia, 1959.
Mar de sargaços. N.p.: n.p., 1940.
Relêvos. N.p.: n.p., 1937.
As sete partidas do mundo. 2nd ed. Lisbon: Arcádia, 1958.
Um sino na montanha. Lisbon: Europa-America, 1968.

English Translations

Fields of Fate. Tr. D. Ball. NY: Crown, 1970.
Mountain Doctor. Tr. D. Ball. London: Kimber, 1956.

Criticism

Rogers, W. G. "Fields of Fate." *New York Times Book Review.* March 22, 1970; 38.
Simões, João Gaspar. *Critica.* Lisbon: Delfos, 1969. 3: 99–101.
Vasconcelos, Taborda de. *Fernando Namora.* Lisbon: Arcádia, 1972.

Janet Pérez

ÑAQUE, a type of acting troupe of the *Siglo de Oro. The term designated a troupe of two actors who would travel from village to town performing short skits and plays, usually playing the tambourine, etc. *See also* Compañía.

NASARRE, Blas Antonio (1689, Alquézar, Huesca–1751, Madrid), scholar and literary critic who proclaimed that Alonso F. de *Avellaneda's *Don Quijote* was superior to that of *Cervantes. A professor of law in Zaragoza and a church dignitary in Lugo, he moved to Madrid to serve as librarian to the king and became a member of the *Academia Española. Highly regarded as an excellent scholar and literary authority, Nasarre edited and wrote the prologue for the edition of Cervantes's plays which appeared in 1749. He criticized Spanish classical theater using Cervantes as his example. Many opposed these judgments, and in 1750, Tomás de Zavaleta published *Discurso crítico* (Critical Discourse), in which he explains his opposition to Nasarre. It has been said that the publication of this work contributed to Nasarre's death.

Nina Shecktor

NATAS, Francisco de las (sixteenth c., ?–?), priest, playwright. He wrote a *Comedia Claudiana* (1536; Play of Claudio), now lost, and the surviving *Comedia Tidea* (1550; Play of Tideo). A recasting of the **Celestina,* the *Comedia Tidea* departs from its model in offering a happy resolution. The language is surprisingly vulgar at times, so much so that it was listed in the **Indice* of 1559 and that of 1583.

BIBLIOGRAPHY

Primary Text

Comedia Tidea. Ed. U. Cronan. In *Teatro español del siglo XVI.* Bibliófilos madrileños 10. Madrid: Suárez, 1913.

NATIONAL LIBRARY. *See* Biblioteca Nacional

NATURALISM, a nineteenth-c. literary movement, mainly in the novel and theater, whose principal exponent and theorist was the French writer Émile Zola. Greatly influenced by Claude Bernard's *Introduction à l'étude de la médecine expérimentale* (1865; *Introduction to the Study of Experimental Medicine*, 1949), Zola claimed that the Naturalist was an anatomist of the flesh and soul, a doctor of moral sciences, who applied the experimental methodology of modern medicine to the analysis of human behavior, discovering its causes and explaining its consequences, according to the two fundamental principles of physical environment and heredity. In this bleak, narrowly based search for the total truth about life, the Naturalist rejected the imagination of the Romantic and expanded the Realist's ideal of objective observation. More precisely, in the novel Naturalism led to the cultivation of the free, indirect style and the selection of low-class characters and settings as subject matter. Topics like sexual relationships and psychic disorders were now treated with much more frankness. The repercussions of French Naturalism on Spanish letters after the first translation of a Zola novel in 1880 were inevitable, very significant and apparent in three areas.

First, Naturalism became the subject of a heated public debate when the novelist Emilia *Pardo Bazán collected a series of articles under the title *La cuestión palpitante* (1882–83; The Burning Question) with a prologue by another novelist, Leopoldo Alas (*Clarín). Although the series was generally interpreted as a defense of Zola's movement (his treatises were not translated into Spanish until the 1890s), it was, in fact, an attempt to accommodate the new style within Spain's traditional brand of realism (dating from the *Siglo de Oro *picaresque novel) and moral values. By also claiming an essential place for imagination in the novel and criticizing Zola's excessively scientific method, Pardo Bazán not only incurred the disavowal of the French leader, but anticipated some of the arguments put forward by her most formidable opponent in the polemic, the novelist Juan *Valera, who, in his *Apuntes sobre el nuevo arte de escribir novelas* (1887; Notes on the New Art of Writing Novels), protested that literature could never concern itself with the scientific search for truth; it was only meant to give pleasure and entertainment. Other, more narrow-minded conservative critics fulminated against the pornography and political subversiveness of Naturalism. By 1887, however, the polemic had abated, with what victory there was going to Pardo Bazán and her supporters.

Second, a number of public events in 1882 and 1883 were designed by Alas and other young members of the Gall Club in Madrid to promote the cause of Naturalism in Spain. A literary journal, *Arte y letras* (Art and Letters), was launched for a brief period; debates took place in Madrid's prestigious literary club, the *Ateneo; and a public banquet was held in honor of the leading novelist of the period, Benito *Pérez Galdós.

Third, the most important novels of the period 1880–87 incorporated a number of Naturalist features: lengthy descriptions of low-class areas and activities, subtle analyses of the perturbed mental states of the characters and the use of the free, indirect style. However, neither Galdós, Alas, nor Pardo Bazán was ever as audaciously explicit as Zola in the treatment of sexual matters or in the support of social and political reform. Furthermore, none of them could accept that heredity and environment were the exclusive determinants of human behavior. All three emphasized the power of the individual human spirit to overcome those two strong forces, especially after 1887, when the works of Tolstoy and Dostoyevski became known in Spain. Nonetheless, without the influence of Zola's Naturalism it is doubtful whether the three masterpieces by Galdós, Alas and Pardo Bazán respectively in this decade would have been written: *Fortunata y Jacinta* (1886–87; *Fortunata and Jacinta*, 1973); *La regenta* (1884–85; *La regenta*, 1984); and *Los Pazos de Ulloa* (1886; *The Son of the Bondwoman*, 1908). Only minor writers like Eduardo López Bago, Felipe *Trigo, Jacinto Octavio *Picón, Alejandro *Sawa, and later, Vicente *Blasco Ibáñez, adhered strictly to Zola's prescriptions for the Naturalist novel.

In the theater, adaptations of Zola's novels, especially *Thérèse Raquin* (1867; *Thérèse Raquin*, 1955), were frequent in the 1880s. Eugenio *Sellés's *Las esculturas de carne* (1883; The Sculptures of the Flesh) was the principal Spanish Naturalist play.

In short, as the critic Angel del Río noted, Spanish Naturalism was, by comparison with its French progenitor, "imprecise, accommodating and diluted."

BIBLIOGRAPHY

Primary Texts

Pardo Bazán, Emilia. *La cuestión palpitante*. In *Obras completas*. Ed. Harry L. Kirby, Jr. Madrid: Aguilar, 1973. 3: 574–660.

Valera, Juan. *Apuntes sobre el nuevo arte de escribir novelas*. Madrid: Tello, 1905.

Zola, Émile. *Le Naturalisme au théâtre*. In *Oeuvres complètes*. Ed. Henri Mitterand. Paris: Cercle du Livre Précieux, 1968. 11: 265–557.

———. *Le Roman expérimental*. In *Oeuvres complètes*. Ed. Henri Mitterand. Paris: Cercle du Livre Précieux, 1968. 12: 1143–1414.

———. *Les Romanciers naturalistes*. In *Oeuvres complètes*. Ed. Henri Mitterand. Paris: Cercle du Livre Précieux, 1968. 11: 15–262.

English Translations

Zola, Émile. *The Experimental Novel and Other Essays*. Tr. B. M. Sherman. New York: Cassell, 1932.

Criticism

Barroso, Fernando J. *El naturalismo en la Pardo Bazán*. Madrid: Playor, 1973.

Brown, Donald Fowler. *The Catholic Naturalism of Pardo Bazán*. UNCSRLL 28. 2nd ed. 1957; rpt. Chapel Hill: U of North Carolina P, 1971.

López Jiménez, Luis. *El naturalismo y España: Valera frente a Zola*. Madrid: Alhambra, 1977.

Medina, Jeremy. *Spanish Realism: The Theory and Practice of a Concept in the Nineteenth Century*. Madrid: Porrúa, 1979.

Pattison, Walter T. *El naturalismo español: historia externa de un movimiento literario*. Madrid: Gredos, 1965.

Peter Bly

NAVAGGIERO, Andrea (1483, Venice–1529, Blois, France), humanist scholar, diplomat, and poet. As Venetian ambassador to the court of Charles V in Granada, he met Juan *Boscán in 1526, persuading him to experiment with Italianate metrical forms, thereby opening the period of classical Spanish lyric poetry. Boscán's widow published his works as well as those of his friend, *Garcilaso de la Vega, in *Las obras de Boscán y algunas de Garcilaso de la Vega, repartidas en quatro libros* (1543; The Works of Boscán and Some of Garcilaso de la Vega, Divided into Four Books). Navaggiero was, consequently, directly instrumental in popularizing in Spain the Petrarchan sonnet (those in the *itálico modo* of the Marquis of Santillana were still unpublished at the time), the *ottava rima* of Ariosto, and the *terza rima* of Dante. Leaving Spain in 1528, Navaggiero went to the court of Francis I in Blois, where he died the following year.

Proof of his interest in Spanish life and customs is Navaggiero's *Il viaggio fatto in Spagna* (1563; The Trip Made through Spain), an objective work that would influence later Spanish chroniclers, notably Jerónimo de *Zurita and the *Argensola brothers. A friend and collaborator of the printer Aldus Manutius, he published a series of valuable editions of the works of Virgil, Terence, Lucretius, Ovid, Horace, and Cicero. His own Latin *carmina*, notably the *Lusus*, contain echoes of Virgil and other classical poets. *See also* Humanism; Italian Literary Influences; Renaissance.

BIBLIOGRAPHY

Primary Texts

Carmina quinque illustrium poetarum Petri Bembi, Andreae Naugerii, Balthassaris Castillionii, Joannis Casae, et Angeli Politiani, additis Jacobi Sadoleti. . . . Bergamo: P. Candelotti, 1753.

Lusus. [Latin text of Navaggiero's with French translation by Du Bellay and Ronsard.] Haarlem: J. Enschedé en Zonen, 1947.

Opera omnia. Eds. Jo. Antonio J.U.D. and Cayetano Vulpiis. Patavii: J. Cominus Vulpiorum, 1718.

Orationes duae, carmina que nonnulla. Venice: n.p., 1530.

Il viaggio fatto in Spagna, et in Francia. Venice: D. Farri, 1563. A new edition was published by G. M. Malvezzi and Jac. Bernardi (Pinerolo, 1871). The most recent Spanish translation is *Viaje por España, 1524–1526.* Madrid: Turner, 1983.

English Translation

"Funeral Oration [by Andrea Navaggiero], Delivered at Venice, on the Death of the Doge Leonardo Loredano." Tr. Chas. Kelsall. *Pamphleteer* (London) 12 (1818): [187]–229.

Criticism

Alonso Gamo, José María. *Viaje a España del magnífico señor Andrés Navagero (1524–1526).* . . . Tr. and preliminary study. Valencia: Castalia, 1951.

Fabié, Antonio María. *Viajes por España de Jorge de Einghen . . . y de Andrés Navajero.* Tr. with intro. Madrid: F. Fé, 1879.

López de Meneses, A. "Andrés Navagero, traductor de Gonzalo Fernández de Oviedo." *Revista de Indias* (Madrid) 18 (1958): 73–126.

Dennis P. Seniff

NAVARRETE, Martín Fernández de. *See* Fernández de Navarrete, Martín

NAVARRO TOMÁS, Tomás (1884, Albacete–1979, Massachusetts), editor and phoneticist. A disciple and collaborator of Ramón *Menéndez Pidal, he served as director of the phonetics laboratory of the Centro de Estudios Históricos (Center for Historical Studies) and in the Cuerpo de Archiveros (Archivists Corps). He taught at Columbia U for many years.

His scholarly work includes critical editions of *Garcilaso de la Vega and Saint *Teresa and studies of Spanish dialectology. His first articles on phonetics, published in the *Revista de Filología Española*, introduced the methodology for this area of research in Spain. His widely known *Manual de pronunciación española* (1932; Manual of Spanish Pronunciation) established his authority in the field and led, in 1935, to his election to the *Academia Española. His acceptance speech into the Academy, on the Castilian accent, continued his earlier work on Spanish phonetics. He later published *El español en Puerto Rico* (1948; Spanish in Puerto Rico), the first linguistic geography of a Spanish American nation. His *Métrica española* (Spanish Metrics) first appeared in 1956, and was revised three years later under the title *El arte del verso* (1959; The Art of Verse). The results of his research conducted before 1936 in the archives of various towns in the Spanish province of Huesca are found in his *Documentos lingüísticos del Alto Aragón* (1957; Linguistic Documents of Upper Aragon). *Atlas lingüístico de la península ibérica* (1962; Linguistic Atlas of the Iberian Peninsula) appeared in 1962. Navarro Tomás was a notable pedagogue with many disciples in Spain and the Americas and is generally considered the founder of modern Hispanic phonetics.

BIBLIOGRAPHY

Primary Texts

Arte del verso. Mexico: Compañía General de Ediciones, 1959.

Documentos lingüísticos del Alto Aragón. Syracuse, NY: Syracuse UP, 1957.

El español en Puerto Rico: contribución a la geografía lingüística hispanoamericana. Río Piedras: U de Puerto Rico, 1948.

Estudios de fonología española. Syracuse, NY: Syracuse UP, 1946.

Manual de pronunciación española. 4th ed. Madrid: RFE, 1932.

English Translation

Studies in Spanish Phonology. Tr. Richard D. Abraham. Coral Gables, FL: U of Miami P, 1968.

Judith Ginsberg

NAVARRO VILLOSLADA, Francisco (1818, Viana, Navarre–1895, Viana), novelist, journalist and dramatist. After studying philosophy and theology in Santiago and law in Madrid, he became a parliamentary deputy and a senator. He belonged to the traditionalist party, supported Ferdinand VII's brother, don Carlos, and defended the Catholic ideal. As a journalist, he founded a number of periodicals such as *El Arpa del creyente*, *El Padre Cobos* and *El pensamiento español*. He defended his conservative ideas against those who attacked him in aggressive articles. He also wrote historical novels during a period when this genre had become obsolete. Most outstanding were *Doña Urraca de Castilla* (1849), *Doña Blanca de Navarra* (1874) and *Amaya; O Los vascos en el siglo VIII* (1877; Amaya; or the Basques in the Eighth C.). *Doña Urraca* deals with the battles which took place in Galicia between doña Urraca and the bishop Gelmírez in the twelfth c. In this novel, the medieval world is re-created and historical figures mix naturally with fictional ones. *Doña Blanca* deals with the Prince of Viana's sister, married to Henry IV of Castille, and it takes place in the fifteenth c. It is Navarro Villoslada's most successful work; it immediately achieved four editions, has been translated into English and Portuguese, and in this century has come out in a half dozen editions. *Amaya* takes place in the eighth c. and tells the story of the fusion of the Basques and the Visigoths in Christianity and of their battles against the Muslim invaders, the reconquest and re-population of Castile.

BIBLIOGRAPHY

Primary Texts

Obras completas. Intro. Juan Nep. Goy. Madrid: Fax, 1947.

English Translation

Doña Blanca of Navarre; An Historical Romance. New York: T. L. Magagnos, 1854.

Criticism

Alborg, Juan Luis. *Historia de la literatura española.* Vol. 4: *El Romanticismo.* Madrid: Gredos, 1980. 691–92.

Cornish, Beatrice Q. ''A Contribution to the Study of the Historical Novels of Francisco Navarro Villoslada.'' In *Homenaje a C. Echegaray.* San Sebastian: n.p., 1928. 199–234.

Ferreras, Juan Ignacio. *El triunfo del liberalismo y de la novela histórica; 1830–1870.* Madrid: Taurus, 1976. 176–77.

Peers, Allison. *A History of the Romantic Movement in Spain.* 2 vols. Cambridge: Cambridge UP, 1940.

Simón Díaz, José. ''Para la biografía de Navarro Villoslada.'' *Homenaje a Van Praag.* Amsterdam: Boekdrukkerij V/H Gebr Hoitsema, 1956. 117–22.

Phoebe Porter Medina

NAVAS, Juan Gualberto López Valdemoro y de Quesada, Conde de. *See* López-Valdemoro y de Quesada, Juan Gualberto

NEBRIJA, Elio Antonio de (c. 1442, Lebrija, Seville–1522, Alcalá de Henares), *Renaissance lexicographer, grammarian, and classicist. Antonio Martínez de Cala, also known as Martínez de Jarava, preferred as his surname Lebrija, the name of his birthplace, or Nebrija, a variation of Nebrissa, its Latin equivalent. After studying at the U of Salamanca with such renowned scholars as Pascual Aranda and Pedro de Osma, he went to Bologna at the age of nineteen to pursue studies at the Colegio de San Clemente in both the sciences and the humanities, particularly in the field of classical philology. Upon returning to Spain in 1473, he accepted a post under Alfonso de Fonseca, the archbishop of Seville. Two years later he was offered a professorship in rhetoric and grammar at the U of Salamanca, where during the years 1475–86 and 1509–13 he waged a campaign to secure for Latin a place at the core of the humanistic tradition. Of his many accomplishments, in fact, Nebrija appears to have been proudest of his role as patriarch of classical studies in Renaissance Spain, especially in light of the considerable resistance he faced from students and faculty of the university. Despite the demands imposed by his teaching and prolific scholarship, he found time during his years in Salamanca to marry Isabel de Solís and to rear six sons and a daughter.

In 1490 he was appointed royal historian; and in 1513 he accepted a position at Cardinal *Cisneros's new university in Alcalá de Henares, where he taught logic and classics until his death. Nebrija's fame as the one most instrumental in transporting the culture of the Italian Renaissance to Spain spread throughout Europe, and he was offered several positions outside of his homeland. He preferred, however, to remain in Spain, where he could foster the growth of humanistic inquiry in several disciplines.

In Salamanca he completed his first major work, the *Introductiones latinae*

(1481; An Introduction to Latin), which became the quintessential Latin grammar in Spain. Drawn heavily from the classical grammars of the fourth c., the *Introductiones* was so successful that it had to be reprinted several times. It was translated into Spanish by Nebrija at the specific request of Queen Isabel and was for nearly two centuries employed in its Latin versions in Italy and France. Nebrija further displayed his expertise as a Latinist with publication of the *Interpretatio dictionum ex sermone latino in hispaniensem* (1492; Latin-Spanish Dictionary) and its companion work, *Interpretación de las palabras castellanas en lengua latina* (c. 1495; A Spanish-Latin Dictionary). The importance of this contribution was overshadowed to some degree by the appearance of the *Gramática de la lengua castellana* (1492; Grammar of the Castilian Language), which Nebrija dedicated to Queen Isabel and which earned distinction as the first grammar of a modern European language. That such a dedicated classicist would devote considerable energy to the analysis of a vulgar tongue lent respectability to the modern languages. Nebrija envisioned an inextricable bond between the language of Spain and her empire, and in his famous prologue to the *Gramática* he explained that he was motivated to compile it both because of the inherent values of Castilian and through the necessity of preparing a manual for use in instructing those who would fall under Spanish rule in the conquest of the New World. So systematic was his treatment of Castilian phonology, syntax, etymology, morphology, and orthography that his work remained in use in Spain as late as the nineteenth c. and became the model for grammars of other languages.

Nebrija's works included numerous studies in philosophy, law, rhetoric, theology, botany, archaeology, classical literature, and history, the most celebrated of the latter being his *Antigüedades de España* (1499; Spanish Antiquities), in which he examined the archaeological richness of his country. Among his later works were *De liberis educandis* (1509; On the Education of Children), a handbook for the proper instruction of youth, which reflected the advice of many classical thinkers, and the *Reglas de orthographía* (1517; Norms of Castilian Orthography), a product of his long-term advocacy of spelling reform. In addition to his individual projects was his major role as editor of the vulgate portions of Cardinal Cisneros's *Biblia poliglota complutense* (1514–17; Polyglot *Bible of Alcalá de Henares). *See also* Humanism; Italian Literary Influences; Universities.

BIBLIOGRAPHY

Primary Texts

Diccionario latino-español (Salamanca, 1492). Intro. Germán Colón and Amadeu-J. Soberanas. Barcelona: Puvill, 1979. Facs.

Gramática de la lengua castellana. Ed. Antonio Quilis. Madrid: Nacional, 1980.

Introductiones latinae. Ed. E. Bustos. Salamanca UP, 1981. Facs.

Reglas de orthographía en la lengua castellana. Ed. Antonio Quilis. Bogotá: Instituto Caro y Cuervo, 1977.

Vocabulario de romance en latín: Transcripción crítica de la edición revisada por el autor (Seville, 1516). Intro. Gerald J. Macdonald. Madrid: Castalia, 1973.

Criticism

Fernández-Sevilla, Julio. "Un maestro preferido: Elio Antonio de Nebrija." *Thesaurus* 29 (1974): 1–33.

Nebrija y la introducción del Renacimiento en España. Actas de la III Academia Literaria Renacentista. Ed. Victor García de la Concha. Salamanca: U of Salamanca, Academia Literaria Renacentista, 1983.

Olmedo, P. Félix G. *Nebrija en Salamanca (1475–1513)*. Madrid: Nacional, 1944.

RFE 29 (1945): Homage issue devoted to Nebrija and his times.

Rico, Francisco. *Nebrija frente a los bárbaros: El canon de gramáticos nefastos en las polémicas del humanismo*. Salamanca: U of Salamanca, 1978.

Tate, R. B. "Nebrija, historiador." *BHS* 34 (1957): 125–46.

C. Maurice Cherry

NEIRA DE MOSQUERA, Antonio (1818, Santiaga de Compostela–1853, Santiago de Compostela), journalist, prose author. His difficult personality provoked many enemies. Aside from journalistic pieces, he wrote a short story, "Don Suero de Toledo" (n.d.; Don Suero of Toledo), which he subsequently expanded under the title *La marquesa de Camba y Rodeiro* (n.d.; The Marchionesse of Camba y Rodeiro). *Las ferias de Madrid* (1845; Madrid Holidays) is a satiric collection of *costumbrismo*-style essays. *See also* Romanticism.

BIBLIOGRAPHY

Primary Texts

Las ferias de Madrid. Madrid: Almarabu, 1984. Facs.

Monografías de Santiago. Ed., study B. Varela Jácome. Santiago de Compostela: Bibliófilos Gallegos, 1950.

NEIRA VILAS, Xosé (1928, Gres, Pontevedra–), prose author. Raised in the country, Neira Vilas studied marketing and emigrated to Argentina. In Buenos Aires he discovered Galician culture and in 1953 organized the group Mocedades Galeguistas (Galician Youth). In 1961 he moved to Cuba and eight years later was one of the founders of the Instituto de Literatura y Lingüistica (Institute of Literature and Linguistics). After a long absence, he returned to Galicia in 1972, after which he has maintained closer contact. Although he has practiced many genres, he is best known for his prose writing. *See also* Galician Literature.

BIBLIOGRAPHY

Primary Texts

Aqueles anos de Moncho. Madrid: n.p., 1975. (novel)

O cabaliño de buxo. Lugo: Castro, 1971.

Camiño bretemoso. Vigo: n.p., 1967. (novel)

Castelao en Cuba. Sada, La Coruña: 1983. (document)

Doce canciós galegas. Buenos Aires: n.p., 1958.

Galegos no golfo de México. Sada, La Coruña: 1980. (essay)

Historias de emigrantes. Montevideo: n.p., 1968. (short stories)

Lar. Madrid: n.p., 1973. (short stories)

Memorias dun neno labrego. Buenos Aires: n.p., 1961. (novel)
A prensa galega de Cuba. Sada, La Coruña: n.p., 1985.
Querido Tomás. Sada, La Coruña: n.p., 1980. (novel)
Remuiño de sombras. Vigo: Castrelos, 1973. (narrative)
Xente no rodicio. Vigo: Galaxia 1965. (short stories)

Criticism

Alonso Montero, Xesús. "Neira Vilas e as súas memorias." *Realismo y conciencia crítica en la literatura gallega*. Madrid: Ciencia Nueva, 196?
Lorenzo Rivas, Pilar. *Contribución ao estudo da novela de protagonista infantil e xuvenil na literatura galega contemporánea*. La Coruña: n.p., 1981.
Losada, Basilio. "Camiño bretemoso." *Grial* (December 1967): n.p.
———. "A muller de ferro." *Grial* (1970): 28.
Lucas, María. *La visión de Galicia en Xosé Neira Vilas*. Sada, La Coruña: Castro, 1977.
Martul Tobío, Luis. "Xosé Neira Vilas." *Gran Enciclopedia Gallega*. Santiago-Gijón: Silverio Cañada, 1974 ss.

Luis Martul Tobío

NELKEN Y MAUSBERGER, Margarita (1896, Madrid–1968, Mexico), Spanish essayist, novelist, art critic and politician. Nelken studied painting, literature, music and sociology, and became deeply involved in politics in the years before the Civil War. Under the Second Republic (1931–36), she was a representative of the Socialist Workers party in the Cortes Constituyentes (Congress), and joined the Communist party during the Civil War, but later left it in exile. She was a major feminist, and in addition to her two novels, she wrote a number of books for or about women, besides publications on politics and art. Her novels are *La aventura de Roma* (1923; The Roman Adventure) and *La trampa del arenal* (1923; Sand Trap). *La condición de la mujer en España* (1922?; The Condition of Women in Spain) is a significant early analysis of many types of women's problems, ranging from prostitution to maternity, lack of legal empowerment, working conditions and domestic circumstances. *Las escritoras españolas* (1930; Spanish Women Writers) was a pioneering attempt to combat the widespread notion that there were no women writers in Spain. *Por qué hicimos la Revolución* (1936?; Why We Made a Revolution) is dedicated to leftist comrades who fell in the October 1934 revolution, and provides a history of Spanish workers and workers' movements. *La mujer ante las cortes constituyentes* (1931; Woman before the Parliament) attempts to educate women concerning newly acquired political rights and responsibilities. Many other works have to do with art: *Tres tipos de Virgen: Fray Angélico, Rafael, Alonso Cano* (1929; Three Types of Virgins: Fra Angélico, Raphael, Alonso Cano), *Historia del hombre que tuvo el mundo en la mano, Johann Wolfgang von Goethe* (1943; History of the Man Who Had the World in His Hand, J. W. von Goethe), *Escultura mexicana contemporánea* (1951; Contemporary Mexican Sculpture), *Carlos Orozco Romero* (1959), *Carlos Mérida* (1961), *El expresionismo en la plástica mexicana de hoy* (1964; Expressionism in Mexican Plastic Arts Today), and *Un mundo etéreo: La pintura de Lucinda Urrusti* (1976; An Ethereal World: The Paintings of Lucinda Urrusti).

BIBLIOGRAPHY

Primary Text

Primer frente. Mexico: Angel Chapero, 1944.

Janet Pérez

NIEREMBERG, Juan Eusebio (c. 1595, Madrid–1658, Madrid), Jesuit professor, ascetic writer, theologian. His German parents came to Madrid in the service of Charles V's daughter, Maria of Austria. Nieremberg studied in Madrid, at the U of Alcalá and at the U of Salamanca. In 1614, he entered the Society of Jesus, much to his father's dismay. Nieremberg composed no fewer than seventy-three works in his life, some of which were widely translated. Early works of note include *Vida divina y camino real para la perfección* (1633; Divine Life and Royal Road to Perfection), and *Aprecio y estima de la divina gracia* (1638; Value and Esteem of Divine Grace). His most famous work is *De la diferencia entre lo temporal y lo eterno, crisol de desengaños* (1640; *A Treatise on the difference betwixt the temporal and eternal,* 1672); it is a baroque philosophical study which contrasts the two realms with a wealth of historical and literary references. What some consider his finest writing appeared in 1641: *De la hermosura de Dios y su Amabilidad* (On God's Beauty and His Lovableness). It attempts to harmonize classical authorities with the Christian world. Nieremberg also wrote biographies of St. *Ignacio de Loyola (1631) and St. Francis Borgia (1644), among others. In 1656 he completed the best Spanish translation of the day of Thomas à Kempis's *Imitation of Christ*. His letters preserve fascinating material about contemporary life in Spain. *See also* Catechetical Literature.

BIBLIOGRAPHY

Primary Texts

Aprecio y estima de la divina gracia. Madrid: Apostolado, 1947.
Epistolario. Ed. N. Alonso Cortés. Clásicos Castellanos 30. Madrid: Espasa-Calpe, 1945.
Imitación de Cristo. Madrid: Haler-Blasco de Garay, 1936.
Obras escogidas. In BAE 103 and 104 (1957).
Obras espirituales. Madrid: Gómez Fuentenebro, 1890–92.

English Translation

A treatise on the difference betwixt the temporal and eternal. Tr. V. Mullineaux. London: n.p., 1672.

Angelo DiSalvo

NIETO, Ramón (1934, La Coruña–), Spanish novelist and short story writer. Although Nieto obtained a law degree from the U of Madrid (where he also studied literature), there is no indication that he ever practiced the legal profession. Raised in the difficult, early post-war years when the Franco dictatorship was most oppressive, he turned to literature in the 1950s, beginning under the influence of the social realists and objectivists, practitioners of a critical neo-realism or neo-naturalism of political intent. His first short stories appeared in various periodicals and were gathered in book form under the title *La tierra* (1957; Land, or Earth). *Los desterrados* (1958; The Exiles) is also a short story collection; *La fiebre* (1960; Fever) is a novel, as are *El sol amargo* (1961; The Bitter Sun), *La patria y el pan* (1962; The Fatherland and Bread), *La cala* (1963; The Cove) and *Vía muerta* (1964; Dead Way), all written under the general rubric of ''objective'' realism. *La cala*, for example, illustrates what may be termed the ''rebellion of objects,'' as a man visiting an island (presumably one of the Baleares) for the day picks up a rope lying in the road without knowing why, and later is unable to resist using it to strangle a girl he encounters.

Nieto has occupied top editorial positions in a number of important Spanish publishing firms, and for some five years, he was publications director for UNESCO, in Paris. After a decade of silence, he published a major new novel, *La señorita* (1974), an abstract political allegory which also represents an experiment with four simultaneous narrative planes corresponding to four social groups or classes, each with its own peculiar rhetoric (most noteworthy is the Falangist rhetoric of the regime, although other interest groups are similarly parodied). *La señorita* is among his most polemic works, but was accorded a generally favorable critical reception. Another long silence intervened before the appearance of *Los monjes* (1984; The Monks), another symbolic novel, and his most mature accomplishment to date. The ''monks'' have lost their function in this world; incarcerated in a decrepit monastery with their daily routines, their lives are little more than mechanical dreams until the disturbing appearance of a new and unexpected element, Carmela, who completely transforms their tranquil dozing. Love and humor, tenderness and death are interwoven in an irreverent, provocative novel of rich imagination and language of extraordinary beauty.

Janet Pérez

NIFO, Francisco Mariano (1719, Alcáñiz–1803, Madrid), translator, journalist. He preferred to spell his surname Nipho. A positivist and encyclopedist, although the quality of his writing is not high, his publications and translations, and role as prolific disseminator of facts, opinions and ideas make him a pioneer of the modern newspaper writer. His most lasting work is the *Caxón de sastre literario* (n.d.; Literary Hodge Podge), a seven-volume compilation of classical excerpts and lyric poetry. Nifo defended the *auto sacramental* (**auto*) against attacks by *Clavijo y Fajardo.

BIBLIOGRAPHY

Primary Texts

Caxón de sastre literario. Madrid: Escribano, 1781–82.

La nación española defendida de los insultos del Pensador y sus secuaces. Madrid: Ramírez, 1764.

Criticism

Enciso Recio, L. *Nipho y el periodismo español del siglo XVIII*. Valladolid: U of Valladolid, 1956.
Entrambasaguas, J. de. "Algunas notas relativas a D. Francisco Mariano Nifo." *RFE* 28 (1944): 357–77.
Guinard, P. J. "Un journaliste espagnole du XVIIIe siècle." *BH* 59 (1957): 263–83.

NIÑO, Crónica de don Pero. *See* Díez de Gámez, Gutierre

NIPHO, Francisco Mariano. *See* Nifo, Francisco Mariano

NOCEDAL, Cándido (1821, La Coruña–1885, Madrid), journalist, orator, of the literati. A newspaper columnist, he made his name famous as "El padre Cobos" (Father Cobos). On December 16, 1867, he founded the Catholic newspaper *La Constancia* (Steadfastness), which ran until September 28, 1868. His speeches as academician at the Spanish and Moral and Political Sciences academies were dedicated to the defense of Spanish Catholic unity, to the death of Aparisi y Guijarro and, upon his admission to the academy, to the contemporary Spanish novel. He also prefaced *Jovellanos's works for the *Biblioteca de Autores Españoles.

BIBLIOGRAPHY

Primary Texts

"Antonio Aparisi y Guijarro. Discurso necrológico escrito para la Academia Española." *Academia Española* 4 (1873): 179–240.
Compendio de la historia de España desde Ataulfo hasta nuestros días. Madrid: Burgos, 1841.
Gaspar Melchor de Jovellanos. Obras publicadas e inéditas. Madrid: Hernando, 1933.
Vida de Jovellanos. Madrid: Rivadeneyra, 1865.

Eugene Del Vecchio

NOCEDAL Y ROMEA, Ramón (1848, Madrid–1907, Madrid), journalist, dramatist, political activist. Son of Cándido *Nocedal and nephew of actor Julián *Romea, he was director of the Catholic paper *El Siglo Futuro*, founded by his father. His plays, written with the pseudonym Un *Ingenio de Esta Corte, include *La Carmañola* (1869; The Carmagnole) and *El juez de su causa* (1868; Judge of His Case). A member of the extreme political right, he led the political movement of traditionalism called *integrismo*, which opposed liberal ideology in any form.

BIBLIOGRAPHY

Primary Texts

La Carmañola. Madrid: Rodríguez, 1869. Rpt. Louisville, KY: Falls City Microcards, 1960.
Causa célebre. Discurso . . . sobre la masonería. Quito: Prensa Católica, 1925.
Obras. 10 vols. Madrid: Fortanet, 1907–28.

Ramón Nocedal y Romea. Ed. J. de Carlos Gómez-Rudulfo. Madrid: Tradicionalista, 1952. Anthology.

NOEL, Eugenio, pseudonym of Eugenio Muñoz Diáz (1885, Madrid–1936, Barcelona), short story writer, novelist and rabid anti-bullfighting campaigner. In the era known as the Golden Age of Bullfighting, when the matador "demigods" Joselito and Juan Belmonte dominated most Spaniards' minds, Eugenio Noel took it upon himself to be the social conscience of Spain. In books of essays, in the daily press and in hundreds of lectures throughout Spain and Hispanic America, he excoriated bullfighting, flamenco music and dance, and other "lowly" customs which he felt contributed to the degeneration of Spain. This execratory attitude is evident in works such as the anthology *Escritos antitaurinos* (1967; Articles against Bullfighting), a compilation of a number of early pieces, and in *Pan y toros* (probably 1912; Bread and Bulls).

Being of nature rebellious, obsessive, exaggerated and bohemian in his manner of dress, way of being and literary style (picturesque details of which are superbly described in his autobiographical, posthumous work in two volumes, *Diario íntimo; la novela de la vida de un hombre* (1962, 1968; Intimate Diary; the Novel of a Man's Life), he had to struggle to make a living as a writer. Many of his short stories were dashed off quickly, to be published individually in weekly series such as La Novela Corta (The Short Novel), merely to sustain himself and his family. The collection entitled *El "allegretto" de la sinfonía VII* (1918; The "Allegretto" of the Seventh Symphony) contains four stories (or short novels) originally published individually, which are an excellent example of Noel's ability to paint authentic characters and emotions with a masterful use of language.

While Noel's literary production included some forty short stories, he wrote only one full-length novel, *Las siete Cucas* (1927; The Seven Cucas). Here we find some of the best and also the worst of Noel's fictional prose: successful analysis of the changing psychology of the main characters; excellent portrayal of the stultifying atmosphere of a backward Castilian town; use of a richly varied, flexible and authentic linguistic style which, unfortunately, also serves to paralyze the narration and lead the reader into a fragmented multitude of unnecessary quotes and pedantic digressions within the minefield of his confused ideology.

BIBLIOGRAPHY

Primary Texts

El "allegretto" de la sinfonía VII. Madrid: Espasa-Calpe, 1976.

Diario íntimo; La novela de la vida de un hombre. 2 vols. Madrid: Taurus, 1962, 1968.

Escritos antitaurinos. Madrid: Taurus, 1967.

Pan y toros. Valencia: Sempere, n.d. [1912].

Las siete Cucas. 2nd ed. Madrid: Taurus, 1970.

Criticism

Azorín. *Los valores literarios*. 2nd ed. Buenos Aires: Losada, 1957.

Caba, Pedro. *Eugenio Noel. Novela de la vida de un hombre intenso*. Valencia: America, 1949.

Cambria, Rosario. *Los toros: tema polémico en el ensayo español del siglo XX*. Madrid: Gredos, 1974.
González Ruano, César, and Francisco Carmona Nenclares. *Nuestros contemporáneos: Eugenio Noel*. Madrid: Renacimiento, 1927.
Prado, Angeles. *La literatura del casticismo*. Madrid: Moneda y Crédito, 1973.

Rosario Cambria

NOGALES, José (1860?, Aracena, Huelva–1908, Seville), journalist, novelist. After studying law in Seville, he became a journalist in Madrid, but later returned to southern Spain. A talented storyteller, his articles, short stories and novels reflect Andalusian culture and themes.

BIBLIOGRAPHY

Primary Texts

Mariquita León. Barcelona: Maucci, 1901.
. . . *Tipos y costumbres*. Barcelona: Vanguardia, 1900.
Las tres cosas del Tío Juan. Madrid: n.p., 1916.

NOLA, Ruperto (fifteenth c., Cataluña–?), author of a cookbook. Principal chef to one of the Ferdinands who ruled Naples, Nola composed a cookbook in Catalan (1520) which he later translated into Spanish with the title *Libro de cocina . . . de muchos potajes y salsas y guisados* (Logroño, 1525; Cookbook of Many Vegetables, Sauces and Stews).

BIBLIOGRAPHY

Primary Text

Libro de guisados. Ed. and study D. Pérez. Madrid: iberoamericana, 1929.

Frances Bell Exum

NOMBELA, Julio (1836, Madrid–1919, Madrid), Spanish journalist, playwright and novelist. Born in the heyday of *Romanticism, Nombela came to maturity in the era of realism, and lived through *naturalism, *modernism, and a number of lesser movements. He was a prolific writer whose complete works (1914) fill twenty-two volumes. He was involved in Carlist politics in the late nineteenth c. and was well known for his contributions to newspapers and periodicals. From 1856 to 1858, he was director of *El Diario Español*, where his first novels were published in serial form. Most of these are lacking in enduring literary value; examples are *El amor propio* (Self-Love), *La mujer muerta en vida* (1861; The Living Dead Woman), *La pasión de una reina* (1862; A Queen's Passion), *El coche del diablo* (1863; The Devil's Stagecoach); *El primer millón* (1867; The First Million); *La mujer de los siete maridos* (1867; The Woman With Seven Husbands); and *El vil metal* (1876; Vile Metal). A tireless writer, he treated numerous and widely diverse themes, as seen in a few representative titles: *Historia de la Música* (1860; History of Music); *Crónica de la provincia de Navarra* (1868; Chronicle of the Province of Navarre); *Retratos a la pluma*

(Pen Portraits) and, near the end of his life, *Intimidades y recuerdos* (1909–12; Intimacies and Recollections), a series of memoirs which may be most significant for his details of the life of the poet, Gustavo Adolfo *Bécquer, a personal friend.

BIBLIOGRAPHY

Primary Texts

Obras literarias, 22 vols. Madrid: n.p., 1905–14

NORA, Eugenio G[arcía] de (1923, Zacos, León–), Spanish poet and critic. Nora obtained a degree in philosophy and letters, and has served for many years as a professor of Spanish in Bern (Switzerland). He was among the founders of and early contributors to the poetry review *Espadaña*, one of the most important to appear in the early post-war years, distinguished by its position of dissent from the "Garcilasista" poetry (anachronistic pastoral imitations of the Renaissance poet *Garcilaso de la Vega) promulgated by the regime. His first poetry collections include *Cantos al destino* (1945; Songs to Destiny), *Amor prometido* (1946; Promised Love); and *Contemplación del tiempo* (1947; Contemplation of Time), the last distinguished as runner-up for the Adonais Prize, one of the most prestigious awards for poetry in Spain. In 1953, he won the important Boscán Prize for *España, pasión de vida* (1954; Spain, Passion of Life), and published another book, *Siempre* (1953; Always). His poetry as a whole is characterized by a spirit of non-conformity, not strident, but quite visible. Ironically, perhaps, Nora is better known for his work as a critic and literary historian, in particular his three-volume study, *La novela española contemporánea* (1958; 1962, 1976; The Contemporary Spanish Novel).

NOROÑA, Conde de (1760, Castellón de la Plana–1815, Madrid), poet. Gaspar María de Nava Álvarez de Noroña, a career military man and a member of the Spanish diplomatic service, is a poet of minor literary significance who wrote Anacreontic poetry in the fashion of *Meléndez Valdés. He is best known today for his *Poesías Asiáticas* (Oriental Poetry) published posthumously in 1833, which contains versions and translations of English and Latin Oriental poetry. Of note is that fact that Noroña's translations reflect a strong reaction against French taste in manners, customs, and language.

BIBLIOGRAPHY

Primary Texts

"Noroña's 'Poesías Asiáticas.' " By J. Fitzmaurice-Kelly. *RH* 18 (1908): 439–67.

Criticism

Martínez, E. Juliá. "Un escritor castellonense visto por Menéndez y Pelayo." *Boletín de le Sociedad Castellonense de Cultura* 33 (1957): 316–35; and 34 (1958): 8–23.

Polt, John H. R. *Poesía del siglo XVIII*. Madrid: Castalia, 1975.

Carmen Chaves McClendon

NOVO Y COLSON, Pedro (1846, Cádiz–1931, Madrid), Spanish dramatist. A professional naval officer, Novo was also a disciple of José *Echegaray, and his dramas sometimes echoed the same post-romantic effects, tending to sentimentality and melodrama in their worst moments, although he was also able to produce comedies, works in the vein of the *sainete* and *zarzuela*. His naval background may be perceived in his historical drama *Vasco Núñez de Balboa* (1878), based on the life and achievements of the discoverer of the Pacific. In the same year, another drama, *La manta del caballo* (Horse Blanket), was produced. Novo was not above parodying his own titles, and in 1884 produced the drama *Corazón de hombre* (Heart of a Man) as well as the comedy, *Hombre de corazón* (A Man of Heart). *Todo por ella* (1890; Everything for Her) approaches the musical comedy, and another comedy of the period is *Un archimillonario* (1886; A Multimillionaire). *La bofetada* (1890; The Buffeting), a prose drama, was his greatest popular success, treating enduring human problems without excessive effects or sentimentality. He also produced prose fiction with a nautical background, *Un marino del siglo XIX o Paseo científico por el Océano* (1871; A Nineteenth-C. Sailor, or Scientific Tour of the Ocean).

NOVOA, Matías de (1576?, Toledo–1652, Toledo), prose author. The Duke of Lerma arranged for Novoa to enter the service of Philip III when he was still a prince, and Novoa later served Philip IV. Novoa subsequently composed his *Memorias* (Memoirs), which remained in ms. form until the nineteenth c. They preserve an intimate, sincere personal view of the rule of these two kings; there also is a very favorable presentation of the Duke of Lerma throughout.

BIBLIOGRAPHY

Primary Text

Memorias de Matías de Novoa . . . Primera parte . . . y Segunda parte. Prol. Cánovas del Castillo. 6 vols. Madrid: Ginesta, 1875 and 1877–78.

NOVOA SANTOS, Roberto (1885, La Coruña–1933, Santiago de Campostela), Spanish essayist. A professor of medical pathology in the Universities of Madrid and Santiago, he was a prestigious lecturer on the relationships between medicine and philosophy and medicine and literature. In addition to many works in his professional specialization, he authored such titles as *El instinto de la muerte* (1927; The Instinct toward Death); *La mujer, nuestro sexto sentido y otros esbozos* (1928; Woman, Our Sixth Sense, and Other Sketches); and *Patografía de Santa Teresa de Jesús* (1932; Pathograph of Saint Theresa).

NÚÑEZ, Hernán (1475?, Valladolid–1553, Salamanca), professor, classicist, erudite. He studied in Bologna, Italy, from 1490 to 1498. Nicknamed El Pinciano (Pincia was the original name of Valladolid), and El comendador griego (The Greek Commander), he participated in preparation of the *Bible of Alcalá. Professor of rhetoric at Alcalá, and of Greek at Salamanca, he prepared critical editions of works by Pliny (1544 and 1582), *Seneca (1519 and 1536), and Pomponius Mela (1542). These were used throughout Europe. Núñez also compiled a popular proverb collection, *Refranes, o proverbios en romance* (1555; Sayings, or Proverbs in Spanish). *See also* Humanism; *Refranero*; Renaissance.

BIBLIOGRAPHY

Primary Text

Refranero español. Intro., sel. F. C. Sáinz de Robles. 2nd ed. Madrid: Aguilar, 1950.

NÚÑEZ ALONSO, Alejandro (1905, Gijón–), Spanish novelist. Núñez Alonso lived for a time in Mexico, perhaps as an exile in the immediate post-war years, where he apparently published a first novel entitled *Konco* (n.d.). *La gota de mercurio* (1953; The Drop of Mercury) was a finalist for the important Nadal Prize, and *Segunda agonía* (1955; Second Death-Throes), an intense, dramatic, and obsessively erotic novel, with touches of existentialism and a protagonist who suffers almost equally from irresistible temptations and unavoidable scruples of conscience, received favorable critical notice. These novels, like *Tu presencia en el tiempo* (1955; Your Presence in Time), may be termed contemporary; after this point, Núñez Alonso turned almost exclusively to the cultivation of historical fiction, in the style of the Hollywood spectacular. *El lazo de púrpura* (1956; The Purple Tie), re-creating the world of the Tribe of Judah at the beginning of the Christian era, was favorably reviewed, and brought recognition to the novelist as a scrupulous and methodical re-creator of archaeological settings. This work is the first volume of a novelistic pentad, also comprising *El hombre de Damasco* (1958; The Man from Damascus), which re-creates customs, institutions and historical events of the Roman Empire and details the conversion of St. Paul; *El denario de plata* (1959; The Silver Coin), tracing the fortunes of the silver pieces paid to Judas and painting neighborhoods in the Rome of the Caesars; *La piedra y el César* (1960; The Stone and Caesar), re-creating the years of the Apostolate of St. Peter in Rome and the installation of the primitive Christian church there, against the background of the conflicts between paganism and the nascent new religion; and *Las columnas de fuego* (1961; Columns of Fire), in which the novelist traces the evangelization of Spain by the apostle, reconstructs *Tarraco* (the prototypical Tarragona) and *Cesaraugusta* (Roman Zaragoza), as well as portraying the burning of Rome, the persecution of Christians, and various histories of martyrdom, including St. Peter and St. Paul. Throughout the pentad, the character of Benasur de Judea serves as a witness and a unifying narrative perspective or consciousness to events of the first fifty years of the Christian era, culminating with the eruption of Vesuvius and the destruction of Pompeii. *Gloria en subasta* (1965; Glory Auctioned) won for Núñez Alonso the significant and prestigious Critics' Prize.

Janet Pérez

NÚÑEZ CABEZA DE VACA, Álvar (1490, Jerez de la Frontera–1559, Seville), adventurer, governor of Paraguay. Grandson of the conqueror of the Canary Islands, he accompanied Pánfilo de Narváez to Florida in 1527. Only he and three other men survived the trip. Cabeza de Vaca wandered between the Gulfs of Mexico and California for nine years, often a captive of Indians. In 1537, he published an account of these years, the *Naufragios y relación de* *la Jornada que hizo a la Florida . . .* (*Adventures in the Unknown Interior of America*, 1962). Subsequently Cabeza de Vaca was named governor of Paraguay (1540–45); the *Comentarios* (1554; Commentaries), penned by his secretary, Pedro de Hernández, with Cabeza de Vaca's assistance, record events of his years as governor.

BIBLIOGRAPHY

Primary Texts

Comentarios. In BAE 22.
Naufragios y Comentarios; con dos cartas. Madrid: Calpe, 1922.
Relación de los naufragios y Comentarios. . . . Madrid: Suárez, 1906. Rpt. of 1555 ed.

English Translation

Cabeza de Vaca's Adventures in the Unknown Interior of America. Notes, tr. C. Covey. New York: Collier, 1961.

NÚÑEZ DE ARCE, Gaspar (1834, Valladolid–1903, Madrid), poet, playwright and politician. He held various political offices: civil governor of Barcelona, overseas deputy and minister. However, due to his liberal, progressive ideas, he was first jailed, and then exiled under Narváez. In 1874, he became a member of the *Academia Española. His dramatic works include *Deudas de la honra* (1863; Debts of Honor), *Quien debe paga* (1867; He Who Owes, Pays), *Justicia providencial* (1872; Providential Justice), and *El haz de leña* (1872; The Bundle of Kindling), generally considered to be his best play. It is a somewhat melodramatic work which deals with the relationship between Philip II and his son, Charles. Eventually, Núñez de Arce ceased writing for the theater in order to dedicate himself to poetry. His poetry may be divided into three groups. First, his collection of poems, *Gritos del combate* (1875; War Cries), treats moral, political and religious conflicts of the period. Some of the poems in this collection are "A Darwin," "A Voltaire," "La Duda" (Doubt), "Tristezas" (Sadness), and "El miserere" with a romantic theme. He also wrote several long narrative poems such as "Raimundo Lulio" (1875), about the great medieval writer; "El Vértigo" (1879; Vertigo) about the theme of remorse; "La selva oscura" (1879; The Dark Forest), an allegorical poem inspired by Dante; "La última lamentación de Lord Byron" (1879; The Last Sorrow of Lord Byron), a realistic meditation on the English poet; and "La visión de Fray Martín" (1880; Friar Martin's Vision), in which Luther's spiritual battles are described. Later on, Núñez de Arce wrote sentimental narrative poems such as "Un idilio" (1884; An Idyll), "La pesca" (1884; Fishing), and "Maruja" (1886). These later poems dwell on the description of atmosphere. His grandiloquent style and the sentimentalism of his later poetry link his work to romantic poetry. Nevertheless, much of his verse deals with contemporary problems and his didactic intentions also connect him to literary currents of the moments. Like *Quintana and *García Tassara, he wrote poetry to serve civic and social purposes. The themes of the necessity and dangers of liberty, and the conflict between faith and doubt often appear in his poems. Frequently he upbraids the social evils of the period and lashes out against contemporary society. Núñez de Arce was always very careful with the form of his poems; their rhythmic verses achieve moments of virtuosity. His diction is sonorous and highly expressive but somewhat declamatory for modern tastes.

BIBLIOGRAPHY

Primary Texts

El haz de leña. Madrid: Vesco, 1916.
Miscelánea literaria, cuentos, artículos, relaciones y versos. Barcelona: Maucci, 1900.
Poesías completas. Ed. Ramón Villasuso. Buenos Aires: Sopena Argentina, 1944.

Criticism

Cossío, José María de. "El poeta Núñez de Arce." *BBMP* 30 (1959): 31–81.
Knowlton, John Frederick. "Gaspar Núñez de Arce: His Poetry and the Critics." DA 26 (1965): 4662. U of Oregon.
———. "Two Epistles: Núñez de Arce and Jovellanos." *RN* 7 (1966): 130–33.
Menéndez y Pelayo, Marcelino. "Don Gaspar Núñez de Arce." *Estudios y discursos de crítica histórica y literaria*. Vol. 4. Madrid: CSIC, 1941.
Romo Arreguí, Josefina. *Vida, poesía y estilo de don Gaspar Núñez de Arce*. Madrid: CSIC, 1946.

Phoebe Porter Medina

NÚÑEZ DE REINOSO, Alonso (1492?, Guadalajara–?, Italy?), novelist in exile, known for one completed work, *La historia de los amores de Clareo y Florisea, y de los trabajos de la sin ventura Isea, natural de la ciudad de Efesa* (1552; Story of the Love of Clareo and Florisea, and of the Travails of the Unfortunate Isea, from the City of Ephesus). Knowledge of the life of Núñez de Reinoso is limited to facts which can be deduced from his work. His birth date and date and place of death are not known, and there is little information available about his youth. C. Rose argues that he left Spain because he was a **converso*, and she divides his life into three phases corresponding to the countries in which he lived: Spain, Portugal and Italy.

His extant work was published in Venice by the Giolito Press, a publishing house which had had several of its books confiscated by the *Inquisition and many of its members indicted or imprisoned. *Clareo y Florisea* was not published in Spain until the nineteenth c., thus most of the author's contemporaries were unaware of the work. Set within a *pastoral framework, it has one narrator, Isea, and is divided into two parts. The first part recounts the problems of Clareo and Florisea and is in part an adaptation of Achilles Tatius's *Clitophon and Leucippe*. The second part, which tells of Isea's own personal suffering, is original and follows the pattern of a chivalric tale. Isea's mood is always one of melancholy, yet she prefers her self-imposed exile to the possibility of forgetting her past suffering. C. Rose discerns many themes and styles common to literature of *conversos*: pastoral prose, melancholy tone, adverse fortune, etc.

BIBLIOGRAPHY

Primary Text

Historia de los amores. . . . In *Novelistas anteriores a Cervantes*, BAE 3.

Criticism

Rose, Constance H. *Alonso Núñez de Reinoso: The Lament of a Sixteenth-Century Exile.* Rutherford: Fairleigh Dickinson UP, 1971.

Nina Shecktor

OBREGÓN, Antonio de (1910, Madrid–), Spanish poet, journalist, novelist. Obregón began early, during the late 1920s and early 1930s, as a collaborator of *La Gaceta Literaria* and *Ortega y Gasset's intellectually prestigious *Revista de Occidente*. His poetry and prose poems appear in *El campo, la ciudad, el cielo* (1929; The Country, The City, and Heaven). He published a number of novels, including *Efectos navales* (1931; Naval Effects) and *Hermes en la vía pública* (1934; Hermes on the Public Thoroughfare). He had a certain reputation as a literary critic, and also produced a number of screenplays.

OCAMPO, Florián de (1495?, Zamora–1558?, Zamora), royal historian. A student of *Nebrija at the U of Alcalá, he rose to become court historian for Charles V. He was also named canon of the Zamora Cathedral in 1547. Ocampo is most remembered for his editions of earlier histories. Most successful was *Las cuatro partes enteras de la crónica de España* (1541; The Four Complete Parts of the Chronicle of Spain) of *Alphonse X the Wise. An original work is his *Los cuatro libros primeros de la crónica general de España* (1543; The First Four Books of the General Chronicle of Spain). An unfinished project, it narrated the history of the world up to the Romans, liberally mixing legends, anecdotes and curiosities with fact under the guise of joining classical ideas with those of the House of Austria.

BIBLIOGRAPHY

Primary Texts

Corónica general de España. 10 vols. Madrid: Cano, 1791–92.
Los cuatro libros primeros. . . . Zamora: n.p., 1543.

Criticism

Bataillon, M. "Sur Florián de Ocampo." *BH* 25 (1923): 33–58.
Cotarelo, E. "Varias noticias acerca de Florián de Ocampo." *BRAE* 13 (1926): 259–68.

OCAÑA, Francisco de (fifteenth c., ?–?), religious poet. He penned a collection of popular songs titled *Cancionero para cantar la noche de Navidad y las fiestas de Pascua* (1603; Songbook for Singing on Christmas Night and for Easter Celebrations).

BIBLIOGRAPHY

Primary Texts

Cancionero para cantar. . . . Alcalá: n.p., 1603. Rpt. with prol. by A. Pérez Gómez. Valencia: ''la fonte que mana y corre,'' 1957.

BAE 35 contains two songs.

Criticism

Millares Carlo, A. ''Notas biobibliográficas sobre Fray Gonzalo de Ocaña, escritor del siglo XV.'' In *Homenaje a Fernando Antonio Martínez*. . . . Bogotá: Caro y Cuervo, 1979. 510–32.

OCHOA Y MONTEL, Eugenio de (1815, Lezo, Guipúzcoa–1872, Madrid), editor, journalist, translator, and all-around man of letters. Ochoa was the illegitimate son of a well-known abbot who enabled him to study with Alberto *Lista in Madrid and later to study art in Paris, where he lived from 1828 to 1834. Unable to continue a career in painting due to his defective vision, Ochoa returned to Madrid to serve on the editorial board of the *Gaceta de Madrid* (Madrid Gazette) and shortly afterwards, with his brother-in-law Francisco de Madrazo began the influential literary magazine *El Artista* (65 nos., 1835–36; The Artist), dedicated to the glorification of Spanish arts and letters. In its pages, Ochoa steadfastly defended *Romanticism and derogatorily termed neo-classical literature ''clasiquista''; he contributed critical commentaries on history, the novel, poetry, and theater and was widely regarded as one of the most perspicacious critics of his time.

Ochoa's outstanding translations of such authors as Dumas, Hugo, Sand, and Soulié helped spread French Romanticism to Spain, and in 1837, he returned to Paris, where he stayed until 1844. In Paris, Ochoa discovered a ms. of the *Cancionero de *Baena*, which had been presumed lost, and contributed to a new edition of it in 1851. He also compiled a useful *Catálogo razonado de manuscritos españoles existentes en la Biblioteca Real de Paris* (1844; Organized Catalog of Spanish Manuscripts Available in the Royal Library of Paris). In 1838, the Parisian editor Baudry offered Ochoa the direction of the sixty-volume series ''Colección de los mejores autores españoles antiguos y modernos'' (Collection of the Best Spanish Authors, Both Ancient and Modern). His series of *Tesoros* (Treasures) of masterpieces of Spanish ballads, lyric poetry, mystics, and narrative prose helped make previously unfamiliar texts accessible to the average reader. And his editions of such authors as *Gil y Zárate, *Hartzenbusch, the Marqués de *Santillana, and *Quevedo contributed to the general revival of interest in a national literature.

Although Ochoa failed to produce truly first-rate original work, he did attempt several genres. Two plays premiered in 1835, *Incertidumbre y amor* (Uncertainty and Love) and *Un día del año 1823* (One Day in the Year 1823), and he published a historical novel based on the conflict between Philip II and his son Charles, *El auto de fe, 1568* (1837), and the first volume of a trilogy entitled *Los guerrilleros* (1855; The Partisans) in a journal. His poetry, ranging in style from neoclassic to Romantic, is collected in *Ecos del alma* (1841; Echoes from the Soul).

In addition to his literary pursuits, Ochoa was elected to the *Academia Española, held administrative posts in several government ministries, and served as a representative in the Spanish Parliament. He died in 1872 at the age of fifty-seven.

BIBLIOGRAPHY

Primary Texts

El auto de fe, 1568. 3 vols. Madrid: Sancha, 1837.

Catálogo razonado de los manuscritos españoles existentes en la Biblioteca Real de París, seguido de un suplemento que contiene los de las otras tres bibliotecas públicas (del Arsenal, de Santa Genoveva y Mazarina). Paris: Imprenta Real, 1844.

Ecos del alma. Paris: Librería De Rosa, 1841.

Rimas inéditas de Don Íñigo López de Mendoza, marqués de Santillana, de Fernán Pérez de Guzmán y de otros poetas del siglo XV. Paris: Fain y Thunot, 1844.

Tesoro de los romanceros y cancioneros españoles, históricos, caballerescos, moriscos y otros. Paris: Baudry, 1838.

Criticism

Alborg, Juan Luis. *Historia de la literatura española*. vol. 4. Madrid: Gredos, 1980.

Peers, E. Allison. *A History of the Romantic Movement in Spain*. 2 vols. Cambridge: Cambridge UP, 1940.

Randolph, Donald Allen. *Eugenio de Ochoa y el Romanticismo español*. U of California Publications in Modern Philology, vol. 75. Berkeley: U of California P, 1966.

Shaw, Donald L. *A Literary History of Spain: The Nineteenth Century*. London: Benn, 1972.

Linda Maier

OCTAVAS (octaves), a form of poetry. *Octavas* are eight-line stanzas of poetry, of which there are three main subtypes: (1) *Octavas de arte mayor* are stanzas of eight twelve-syllable **arte mayor* lines (middle caesura and two accented syllables in each hemistich). The number of syllables varies because it is a rhythmic rather than syllabic form. Juan de *Mena is the most famous practitioner of *octavas de arte mayor*. (2) *octavas reales* (royal octaves) are an epic form of verse derived from Italian epic poetry and first adapted to Spanish by Juan *Boscán. They are stanzas of eight eleven-syllable lines, rhyming *abababcc*. *Ercilla's *La Araucana* was written in *octavas reales*. The form has also been employed in some lyric poetry. (3) *Octavillas* (little octaves), also called *octavas de *arte menor,* are eight-line stanzas written with lines of eight syllables or less.

OJEDA, Pino (1930, El Palmar de Teror, Gran Canaria, Canary Islands); Spanish poet. A leading representative of the Canary Islands school of poets, she founded and directed the poetry review *Alisio*, and published several collections of poems, including *Niebla del sueño* (n.d.; The Mist of Dreams), *Como el fruto en el árbol* (1954; Like Fruit on the Tree), a runner-up for the important Adonais Prize for poetry; and *La piedra sobre la colina* (1964; The Stone on the Hill). She is not a prolific lyricist, and her works are punctuated by long silences, a decade between *Como el fruto en el árbol* and *La piedra sobre la colina*, and more than twenty years between the latter and her next (and presently her latest) book, *El alba en la espalda* (1987; Dawn on My Shoulder). This most recent collection treats many of poetry's timeless, universal themes; death (especially as encountered in daily life); time, the destroyer; absence; memory; as well as shadowy figures, both familiar and unknown.

Janet Pérez

OLAVIDE, Pablo de (1725, Lima, Peru–1803, Baeza), distinguished public figure, translator, writer. Olavide was raised in Lima, receiving a degree in theology in 1740, and a doctorate in civil and canon law a year later, when he was sixteen. He subsequently occupied several public positions. In 1746, after the severe earthquake in Lima, in which both his parents and one of two sisters perished, Olavide was named director of the committee to supervise reconstruction and proper handling of valuables recovered in the process. Subsequently, charges of mishandling were filed, and in 1750 Olavide journeyed to Spain in this regard, was arrested, briefly incarcerated and fined. In 1755 he married a wealthy Spanish noblewoman twenty years his senior. Ferdinand VI pardoned Olavide in 1757, but restricted his return to public office for ten years. During this time Olavide made many trips to Paris, where he quickly became an intimate of Voltaire, Diderot, and other members of the reigning intelligentsia. A friend of *Jovellanos, he was denounced to the *Inquisition for "lack of religion," tried and found guilty in 1778. He fled to France, there suffering the horrors of a revolution, including imprisonment. By this time, the courage of his ideas in the face of repeated political persecutions had made Olavide a larger than life symbol for like-minded European intellectuals, and the subject of poems, a novel, and other works. Upon returning to Spain in 1798, by then a convert to Catholicism, he began to write religious poems and paraphrases of the Psalms, and published a work probably begun while in prison in France: *El evangelio en triunfo* (1798; The Triumph of the Gospel). It narrates the religious conversion of a skeptic, and enjoyed many editions in Spanish, French, Italian and Russian. Estuardo Núñez's ground-breaking work has documented how, of various novels in mss. form at Olavide's death, seven mss. were brought from Spain to the United States and published in 1828 by one Cayetano Lanuza, who emigrated from Spain to New York City for political reasons, and edited these novels of Olavide for the Hispanic community there.

BIBLIOGRAPHY

Primary Texts

El evangelio en triunfo. 4 vols. Mexico: Navarro, 1852.

Obras dramáticas desconocidas. Ed. E. Núñez. Lima: Biblioteca Nacional del Perú, 1971.

Obras selectas. Ed. E. Núñez. Lima: Banco de Crédito del Perú, 1987. Prol., previously unknown works, complete biblio.

Poemas cristianos. . . . Lima: Moreno, 1902.

Criticism

Castañeda, V. ''Relación del auto de fe contra don Pablo de Olavide.'' In *RABM* 20 (1916): 93–111.

Defourneaux, M. *Pablo de Olavide, ou l'Afrancesado*. Paris: PUF, 1959.

Núñez, E. *El nuevo Olavide*. Lima: Villanueva, 1971.

See also *Obras selectas* in Primary Texts.

Maureen Ihrie

OLID, Juan de (fifteenth c., ?–?), servant and secretary to constable Miguel Lucas de Iranzo, Olid was once thought to be a possible author of the *Hechos del condestable don Miguel Lucas de Iranzo (crónica del siglo XV)* (written c. 1473–74; Deeds of the Constable Don Miguel Lucas de Iranzo [Fifteenth-Century Chronicle]). The work has also been attributed to Diego Gámez, another servant of Iranzo, and to Pedro de *Escavias (by far the most likely possibility).

BIBLIOGRAPHY

Primary Text

Hechos del condestable don Miguel Lucas de Iranzo (crónica del siglo XV). Ed. and study, J. de Mata Carriazo. Madrid: Espasa-Calpe, 1940.

OLIVEIRA, Carlos de (1921, Belém, Brazil–1981, Lisbon), Portuguese poet and novelist. A member of the *Novo Cancioneiro* (New Ballad Book) group, Carlos de Oliveira was the only one to continue writing verse as well as prose. His work has its roots in the region of Gândara, whose environment is one of privation and anguish. The folkloric content is combined with both elegiac and protesting tones, a social-psychological portrait of reality. Oliveira was a member of the neo-realist movement which began to form in the second half of the 1930s. All his poetry was published under fascism, which left its mark in a sense of threatening as well as a profound historical sensitivity. His prose is a close-up view of the immensely unjust conditions in modern Portugal, a society whose organization comes close to being absurd by the very co-existence of such inequalities today.

BIBLIOGRAPHY

Primary Texts

Uma Abelha na Chuva. Coimbra: Coimbra Editora, 1953.

Alcateia. Coimbra: Coimbra Editora, 1944.

O Aprendiz de Feiticeiro. Lisbon: Dom Quixote, 1971.
Cantata. Lisbon: Iniciativas Editoriais, 1960.
Casa na Duna. Coimbra: Coimbra Editora, 1943.
Colheita Perdida. Coimbra: Colecçao Galo, 1948.
Descida aos Infernos. Porto: Cadernos das Nove Musas, 1949.
Entre Duas Memórias. Lisbon: Dom Quixote, 1971.
Finisterra. Lisbon: Sá da Costa, 1978.
Mae Pobre. Coimbra: Coimbra Editora, 1945.
Micropaisagem. Lisbon: Dom Quixote, 1968.
Pastoral. Lisbon: Sá da Costa, 1977.
Pequenos Burgueses. Coimbra: Coimbra Editora, 1948.
Poesias. Lisbon: Portugália, 1962.
Sobre o Lado Esquerdo. Lisbon: Iniciativas Editoriais, 1968.
Terra de Harmonia. Lisbon: Centro Bibliográfico, 1950.
Trabalho Poético. 2 vols. Lisbon: Sá da Costa, 1976.
Turismo. Coimbra: Novo Cancioneiro, 1942.

Kathleen March

OLIVER, Federico (1873, Chipiona, Cádiz–1956, Madrid), Spanish dramatist. Married to the famous actress Carmen Cobena, Oliver first gained notice with his drama *La muralla* (1898; The Wall). He has written works which are realistic with a dose of social satire, such as *Los pistoleros* (1931; The Gun-Toters), and a detective or mystery comedy, *Han matado a don Juan* (1929; They've Killed Don Juan). He composed librettos for the **zarzuela*, including *Las hilanderas* (The Spinning Women), and he did a dramatic adaptation of the novel of Alberto Insua, *El negro que tenía el alma blanca* (1930; The Negro Who Had a White Soul). *Los cómicos de la legua* (1925; The Comedians of the League) is considered his masterpiece.

OLIVER, Maria-Antònia (1946, Manacor, Mallorca–), novelist, television screenwriter, translator and journalist. She has distinguished herself as a creator of fantasy, delving with mastery into her magical island heritage as a source for much of her fiction. She moved to Barcelona to pursue university studies, but quickly opted for a full-time writing career. Her occasional newspaper columns and book reviews as well as her translations from French and English complement her writing style. Oliver's work often shows a bipolar structure; her first, *Cròniques d'un mig estiu* (1970; Chronicles of Half a Summer), is a coming-of-age novel of an adolescent boy with a background of the destruction of Mallorca by the tourist invasion. *Cròniques de la molt anomenada ciutat de Montcarrà* (1972; Chronicles of the Oft-named City of Montcarrà) uses the fantastic Mallorcan "rondalles" (tales) to address the same theme, this time with a family chronicle as counterpoint. Beginning with a rhyming fairy-tale motif, *El Vaixell d'iràs i no tornaràs* (1976; The Ship That Never Returned), moves back and forth from an elaborate and magical tale of adventures to philosophical monologues by a strong woman who solves difficult problems in solidarity with a few friends who dare to question authority. In the prologue to her two published screenplays, Oliver describes her transition from writing fiction, a solitary occupation, to writing for television, a necessarily collaborative work. The prologue to her collection of short stories, *Figues d'un altre paner* (1979; A Horse of a Different Color), is also very important in studying the progression of her work over time, as she herself explains some of the evolutionary processes. In *Punt d'arròs* (1979; Knit—Purl) she acknowledges her debt to Virginia Woolf, some of whose work she translated, while she addresses a myriad of feminist issues, capturing the monotony of the routines and repetitions of daily life with the image of the "padrina" constantly knitting. Her two most recent novels, written simultaneously, underscore her feminist point of view in very different ways. *Estudi en lila* (1985; Study in Lilac) is a detective story dealing with the problem of rape and its aftermath; *Crineres de foc* (1985; Manes of Fire) interweaves two interrelated stories, exploring the need for self-identification in women and in peoples. Oliver's one somewhat autobiographical piece is the novella *Coordenades espai-temps per guardar-hi les ensaimades* (1975; Time-Space Coordinates for Keeping the Pastries). Oliver is married to writer Jaume *Fuster; they live in Barcelona and sometimes Ger, La Cerdanya.

BIBLIOGRAPHY

Primary Texts

Coordenades espai-temps per guardar-hi les ensaimades. Barcelona: Pòrtic, 1975.
Crineres de foc. Barcelona: Laia, 1985.
Cròniques de la molt anomenada ciutat de Montcarrà. Barcelona: Edicions 62, 1972.
Cròniques d'un mig estiu. Barcelona: Club Editor, 1970.
Estudi en lila. Barcelona: Magrana, 1985.
Figues d'un altre paner. Palma de Mallorca: Moll, 1979.
Punt d'arròs. Barcelona: Galba, 1979.
El vaixell d'iràs i no tornaràs. Barcelona: Laia, 1976.
Vegetal i Muller qui cerca espill. Barcelona: La llar del llibre, 1982.

Kathleen McNerney

OLIVER BELMÁS, Antonio (1903, Cartagena–1968, Madrid), Spanish poet and essayist. A member of the *Generation of 1927, Oliver was married to the poet and novelist Carmen *Conde. His poetry collections include *Mástil* (1927; Main Mast); *Tiempo cenital* (1931?; Time at the Zenith); *Elegía a Gabriel Miró* (1935; Elegy for Gabriel Miró); *Libro de loas* (1947; Book of Loas [dramatic pieces in praise of the Virgin Mary]); *Loas arquitectónicas* (1951; Architectural Loas); and an elegy dedicated to the bullfighter Manolete. His essays were published under the pseudonym Andrés Caballero, as in the case of *De Cervantes a la poesía* (1944; From Cervantes to Poetry). As a professor of literature at the U of Madrid in the years after the Civil War, he was in charge of the Rubén Darío Seminar, and in 1960 published *Este otro Rubén Darío* (This Other Rubén

Darío) as well as an edition of Darío's *Cantos de Vida y Esperanza* (1963; Songs of Life and Hope).

OLIVEROS DE CASTILLA Y ARTÚS DALGARBE (Oliveros of Castilla and Arthur Dalgarbe), anonymous fifteenth-c. novel of chivalry. It is a 1499 translation of a French work first published in 1482, which itself was a translation of the original English work. Two ancient themes run through the work: that of perfect friendship, and the heroic sacrifices and feats it inspires, and that of the "grateful deceased." The latter stems from the legal custom of refusing a coffin to those in debt. In this work, the hero Oliveros receives help at various critical moments from a corpse whose debts Oliveros had settled, thus allowing the deceased a coffin. The same theme is found in *Calderón's *El mejor amigo, el muerto* (The Best Friend, The Dead Man) and in Lope de *Vega's *Don Juan de Castro o hacer bien a los muertos* (Don Juan de Castro or Doing Good for the Dead).

BIBLIOGRAPHY

Primary Texts

La Historia de los nobles cavalleros Oliveros de Castilla y Artús Dalgarbe. New York: Hispanic Society, 1902. Facs.

See also NBAE 11.

OLLER I MORAGAS, Narcís (1846, Valls–1930, Barcelona), novelist, short story writer, playwright and translator. Born into a well-to-do family, he lost his father when he was two years old, and grew up in the home of his uncle who had a well-stocked library from which young Oller read avidly. Oller himself confessed in his memoirs that he read at an early age, and was therefore influenced by Rousseau, Voltaire, Lamartine, B. de Sant Pierre, E. Sue, Dumas, Victor Hugo, *Espronceda, *Pastor Díaz, and the Greek and Catalan classics. Thus, the future father of the modern Catalan novel, like his forefathers of the time of Charlemagne, draws a very strong influence from France. In his youth, Oller was a liberal and a "demòcrata convençut" (a convinced democrat), but after the political excesses of the Revolution of 1868 and the following republican years, he became a moderate conservative. He studied law, married and spent the rest of his long life as a satisfied and good Catalan bourgeois. His life, like that of his much admired Émile Zola, was not spectacular, but his literary contribution to the renaissance of the Catalan novel is monumental. Unlike other nineteenth-c. European novelists, Oller did not have an immediate narrative tradition to draw upon nor even a stable language to work with, and yet his enormous narrative talent and tireless persistence allowed him to become a giant of the nineteenth-c. European novel. He was a friend and correspondent of the many major writers of nineteenth-c. Spain and France: *Pérez-Galdós, *Clarín, *Pereda, Juan *Valera, *Pardo Bazán, Marcelino *Menéndez y Pelayo, the Goncourt brothers, Daudet and Émile Zola. The latter even wrote a prologue to the French translation of Oller's first important novel, *La papallona* (1882; The

Butterfly), praising him and calling him a literary brother (''J'envoie a Narcis Oller, non l'encouragement d'un précurseur, mais la poignée de main d'un frére''). Nonetheless, in only one short novel, *L'Escanyapobres* (1884; The Miser), does Oller follow the deterministic principles of his friend Zola. The rest of his major works are in the realistic tradition of Galdós and Balzac and, like them, Oller tried to fictionalize the history of his time. The chronicle of the evolution of the modern industrial revolution properly begins with the transformation of a rural village into a mercantile and mining city in *L'Escanyapobres*, follows with the decadence of an aristocratic family—the Galcerans—in *Vilaniu* (1885), reaches its vital zenith with the triumph and fall of the financial world of Gil Foix in the three volumes of *La febre d'or* (1890–92; Gold Fever), and ends with *Pilar Prim* (1906), stylistically and structurally his best novel, which narrates the daily life of the already established bourgeoisie of twentieth-c. Catalonia. After 1906 the modernists criticized him rather acidly, and he became increasingly isolated and bitter, writing only occasionally and mostly short stories: *Rurals i urbanes* (1916; Rural and Urban Stories), *Al llapis i a la ploma* (1918; With the Pencil and the Pen), and perhaps his best work, in aesthetic terms, *Memòries Literàries* (Literary Memoirs), published posthumously in 1962. Like *Verdaguer in poetry and *Guimerà in theater, Oller is the central figure of the narrative genre of modern *Catalan literature. During the last two decades of the nineteenth c. his work was widely acclaimed by critics—Sardà and Ixart in Catalonia, Menéndez Pelayo and Clarín in Castile, Albert Savine and Pavlovsky in France. After being ignored by scholars for a good number of years, Oller's work is again studied and appreciated by a growing number of researchers in several countries.

Other minor works include *Croquis del natural* (1878; Sketches from Nature), *Sor Sanxa* (1879); *Isabel de Galceràn* (1880); *Notes de color* (1883; Notes in Color); *La bogeria* (1897; Madness).

BIBLIOGRAPHY

Primary Texts

''Una amistad literaria: La correspondencia epistolar entre Galdós y Narciso Oller.'' Ed. W. H. Shoemaker. *Boletín de la Real Academia de Buenas Letras* 25 (1963–64): 248–306.

''Epistolari de Jose Ixart a Narcís Oller.'' Ed. Joan Oller i Rabassa. *La Revista* (January-June 1936): n.p.

Memòries Literàries: història del meus llibres. Prol. Gaziel. Barcelona: Aedos, 1962.

Obres Completes. Intro. Manuel de Montoliu and epilogue, Maurici Serrahima. Barcelona: Selecta, 1948.

Criticism

Beser, Sergi. ''La novel·la d'un personatge sense novel·la: el Josep Rodon de Narcís Oller.'' *Serra d'Or* (Sept. 1967): 213–18.

Gilabert, Joan. ''*La febre d'or* de Narcís Oller i *Miau* de Galdós: dues visions de la

realitat social a l'Espanya del segle XIX.'' *Estudis de llengua, literatura i cultura catalanes*. Montserrat: Publicacions de l'Abadia de Montserrat, 1979. 241–54.
———. *Narcís Oller*. Barcelona: Marte, 1977.
Triadu, Joan. *Narcís Oller*. Barcelona: Barcino, 1955.
Yates, A. ''The creation of Narcís Oller's *La febre d'or*.'' *BHS* 52 (1975): 55–57.

Joan Gilabert

OLMO, Lauro (1922, Barco de Valderroas, Orense–), Spanish playwright, short story writer, novelist, poet, and adapter. Before turning to the theater, Olmo published several poetry and short story collections as well as two novels. *Doce cuentos y uno más* (1956; Twelve Stories and One More) won the Leopoldo Alas Award and *Golfos de bien* (1968; Good Good-for-nothings) has become a classic. His novel *Ayer: 27 de octubre* (1958; Yesterday: October 27), was runner-up for the Nadal Award. In his dramas Olmo has adopted the Spanish tradition of the **entremés* and **sainete*, brief sketches of everyday life and customs, to give popular form to a radically critical vision of Spanish society. Plays such as *La camisa* (1962; *The Shirt*, 1981) and *English Spoken* (1968) represent a genuinely popular theater directed to the working class and dealing with its problems. The former play, which deals with the emigration of Spain's unemployed to work in the more industrialized countries of Europe, received an array of awards that included the Valle-Inclán for 1961, the Larra Award for 1961–62, the National Theater Award for 1963, and the Alvarez Quintero Prize of the *Academia Española in 1963. It has been widely performed outside of Spain. *English Spoken* deals with the problems of Spaniards returning from abroad.

La pechuga de la sardina (1963; The Breast of the Sardine) treats sexual repression and other problems of Spanish women in the 1960s; *El cuerpo* (1966; The Body), which parodies machismo, represents a veiled attack on fascism. In the collection of short plays on the press and the management of the news, *El cuarto poder* (1984; The Fourth Estate), which Olmo calls a ''tragicomic kaleidoscope,'' the farsical and expressionistic elements present to a limited extent in the earlier plays come to the forefront, together with mime, grand guignol, and an invitation to the spectators to become active participants.

Olmo has recently created a series of popular musicals based on characters and episodes from *Arniches's *sainetes*: *Del Madrid castizo I* and *II* (From Authentic Madrid I and II). These popular ''fiestas'' portraying life in old Madrid, as well as Olmo's adaptations of individual *sainetes* and **zarzuelas* or operettas, have been staged each summer, starting in 1978, in Madrid's open-air theater, La Corrala.

His recent play, *Pablo Iglesias* (1984), dramatizes the life of the founder of Spain's Socialist party, spanning some sixty years of history. Passages from Iglesias's own articles and speeches are utilized, as are music and poetry. With his wife, Pilar *Enciso, Olmo has also written several plays for children, of which *Asamblea general* (1965; General Assembly), which is based on a fable of La Fontaine, has become a classic. It has won an award from Spain's Royal Academy. *See also* Contemporary Spanish Theater.

BIBLIOGRAPHY

Primary Texts

La camisa. El cuarto poder. Ed. Angel Berenguer. Madrid: Cátedra, 1984.

La camisa. English Spoken. José García. Madrid: Espasa-Calpe, 1981.

Golfos de bien. Barcelona: Plaza y Janés, 1980.

Mare vostrum. La señorita Elvira. La Coruña: Ediciós do Castro, 1982.

Pablo Iglesias. La Coruña: Ediciós do Castro, 1984.

La pechuga de la sardina. Mare vostrum. La señorita Elvira. Ed. José Martín Recuerda. Barcelona: Plaza y Janés, 1986.

English Translation

The Shirt (*La camisa*). In *Plays of Protest from the Franco Era*. Tr., intro. Patricia W. O'Connor. Madrid: Sociedad General Española de Librería, 1981. 103–74.

Criticism

Ariza, A. K., and I. F. Ariza. Introduction. In *La camisa*. By Lauro Olmo. Oxford: Pergamon, 1976. 1–18.

Doménech, Ricardo. ''El teatro de Lauro Olmo.'' *CH* 229 (1969): 161–72.

Halsey, Martha T. ''The Political *Sainetes* of Lauro Olmo.'' *Hispanófila* 66 (1978): 67–86.

Monleón, José. ''Lauro Olmo o la denuncia cordial.'' In *Teatro*. By Lauro Olmo. Madrid: Taurus, 1970. 9–47.

Oliva, César. ''Lauro Olmo.'' In *Cuatro dramaturgos realistas en la escena de hoy*. Murcia: n.p., 1978. 45–76.

Martha T. Halsey

OLONA, Luis de (1823, Málaga–1863, Barcelona), theater impresario, librettist, playwright. Before becoming a dramatist, he studied law. Extremely popular in his day, Olona contributed greatly to the revival of the **zarzuela* with works such as *El duende* (1851; The Sprite), *El secreto de la reina* (n.d.; The Queen's Secret), which was translated from a French work by Rosier y de Leuvin, and *Buenas noches, señor don Simón* (n.d.; Goodnight, Mr. Simon). His plays include *Cástor y Pólux* (n.d.; Castor and Pollux), *Los misterios de Madrid* (n.d.; Madrid's Mysteries) and *El memorialista* (n.d.; The Memorialist). Olona collaborated with his brother José—also a prolific writer of *zarzuelas*—on some works.

BIBLIOGRAPHY

Primary Texts

El duende. Madrid: Omana, 1851. Microprint. Louisville, Ky.: Falls City Microcards, 1963.

El memorialista. 3rd ed. Madrid: Montoya, 1885. Microprint. Louisville, Ky.: Falls City Microcards, 1962.

El secreto de la reina. Madrid: Castillo, 1852.

OÑA, Pedro de (155?, Burgos–1626, Gaeta, Venezuela), Mercedarian religious writer, erudite. Philip III appointed him bishop of Venezuela in 1602. Aside from several works in Latin, Oña wrote the ascetic piece *Postrimerías del hombre*

(1603; Man's Final Stages), which discusses sin and death in clear language and simple style. *See also* Ascetical Literature.

BIBLIOGRAPHY

Primary Text

Primera parte de las postrimerías del hombre. Madrid: Sánchez, 1603.

O'NEILL (de Bulhões), Alexandre (Manuel Vahia de Castro) (1924, Lisbon–), poet, critic, fiction writer. Moving beyond his enthusiasm for the *Movimento Surrealista*, O'Neill, in his 1951 *Tempo de Fantasmas* (Time of Ghosts), plotted a more existential course, swinging between acidic irreverence for the establishment and lyrical abandon, as in *Abandono Vigiado* (1960; Guarded Abandon), a grotesque game of biting irony and cryptic wordplay. O'Neill withdraws with time, and, abandoning now the surrealistic fantastics, between *Ombro na obreira* (1969; With Shoulder at the Door Post) and *Entre a cortina e a vidraça* (1972; Between the Curtain and the Windowpane), his poetry becomes more circumstantial, neo-realistically tangible, if humoristically ironic toward the quotidian. O'Neill, a publicity technician, also organizes anthologies including Portuguese, Brazilian and U.S. poets.

BIBLIOGRAPHY

Primary Texts

As Andorinhas não tem restaurante [crônicas]. Lisbon: n.p., 1970. Fiction.
Poesias Completas (1951–1981). Lisbon: Casa da Moeda, 1982.
O Princípio de utopia. Lisbon: Moraes, 1986.

English Translations

Six poems. In *Contemporary Portuguese Poetry: An Anthology in English.* Sel. Helder Macedo and E. M. de Melo e Castro. Manchester: Carcanet, 1978.

Criticism

Ferreira, António Mega. "O'Neill: 'Não me vejo como poeta satírico.' " *Jornal de Letras, Artes & Ideias* (Lisbon) 4.112 (Aug. 28—Sept. 3, 1984): 5–6.
Padrão, Maria da Glória. "O'Neill, ou o diabo na desconstrução." *Jornal de Letras, Artes & Ideias* (Lisbon) 3.76 (Dec. 20–26, 1983): 3.

Robert R. Krueger

ORGANYÀ. *See* Homilies d'Organyà.

OROZCO, Beato Alonso de (1500, Oropesa–1591, Madrid), Augustinian mystic, preacher to Charles V, confessor to Princess Doña Juana, writer of ascetical and mystical works and saints' lives. A prolific writer, Orozco espoused an inner spirituality and abhorred the false miracles then prevalent in his society. Although enough evidence exists that he had mystical experiences, Orozco did not describe them in his writings, considering them to be very personal. However, he was one of the first religious writers in Spain to detail the mystical process (*vía mística*). In both his *Vergel de oración y monte de contemplación* (Seville, 1544;

Garden of Prayer and Mount of Contemplation) and *El memorial de amor santo* (Seville, 1545; Memorial of Holy Love), the reader is able to follow the spiritual path which leads to contemplation of God. Another important work is the *Libro de la suavidad de Dios* (Salamanca, 1576; Book of the Gentle Sweetness of God). Orozco also contributed to Marian devotional literature with the two works *Las siete palabras de la Virgen* (Valladolid, 1556; The Seven Words of the Virgin) and the *Tratado de la corona de Nuestra Señora* (Madrid, 1588; Treatise of the Crown of Our Lady). Orozco composed "vidas de santos" (lives of saints) one of which was the *Historia de la Reina Sabá* (Salamanca, 1565; Story of the Queen of Sheba), wife of King Solomon. *See also* Ascetical Literature; Hagiography; Mysticism.

BIBLIOGRAPHY

Primary Texts

Historia de la Reina Sabá. Manila: Amigos del país, 1883.
Obras. Madrid: Venerable Siervo de Dios Fray Alonso de Orozco, 1746.

Criticism

Allison Peers, Edgar. *Studies of the Spanish Mystics.* vol. 2. London: Sheldon, 1930.
Monasterio, Ignacio, O.S.A. *Místicos agustinos españoles.* 2nd ed. 2 vols. El Escorial: Agustiniana, 1929.
Santiago Vela, Gregorio. "Orozco (Bto. Alonso de)." *Ensayo de una biblioteca de la Orden de San Agustín* 6 (1922): 96–169.

Angelo DiSalvo

OROZCO, Juan de (?, Toledo–1608, Guadix), religious writer. Son of the poet Sebastián de Orozco and brother of the lexicographer Sebastián de *Covarrubias, he probably studied in Salamanca. He rose in the church to become bishop of Agrigento (Sicily) and then of Guadix. At one point, questions regarding some of his publications forced him to journey to Rome and vindicate himself, which he did.

Orozco is essentially a moralist. The *Tratado de la verdadera y falsa profecía* (1588; Treatise on True and False Prophecy) rejects astrology as a source of knowledge. His principal work, *Las emblemas morales* (1589; Moral Emblems), enjoyed four editions and was translated to Latin; it clearly explains the theory and use of emblems, and includes one hundred emblems. Orozco's *Doctrina de príncipes enseñado por el Sto. Job* (1605; Doctrine of Princes Taught by St. Job) influenced *Saavedra Fajardo. *Consuelo de afligidos* (1605; Consolation for the Afflicted) is also worthy of mention.

BIBLIOGRAPHY

Primary Texts

Doctrina de príncipes. . . . Valladolid: Sancha, 1605.
Emblemas morales. 3rd ed. Segovia: Juan de la Cuesta, 1589.
Tratado de la verdadera y falsa profecía. Segovia: Juan de la Cuesta, 1588.

ORRIOLS, Maria Dolors (1914, Vic–), novelist. She studied music and art, before deciding to devote herself to literature. Thereafter she contributed stories and articles to Catalan magazines, often publishing clandestinely following the Civil War. Several of her short stories won prizes. After a long lapse, she began writing again in the 1980s.

BIBLIOGRAPHY

Primary Texts

Calvacades. Barcelona: Aymà, 1949.
Contradansa. Barcelona: Pòrtic, 1982.
Cop de porta. Barcelona: Pòrtic, 1980.
Petjades sota l'aigua. Vic: Eumo, 1984.
Reflexos. Barcelona: Juris, 1951.
Retorn a la Vall. Barcelona: Juris, 1950.

Kathleen McNerney

ORS, Eugenio d' (1881, Barcelona–1954, Villanova i Geltru, Barcelona), Catalan essayist, philosopher, art critic, novelist and, to a lesser degree, playwright. A considerable part of his work was first published in journals and newspapers, having thus immediate dissemination. His journalistic contribution, the Glossary (1907–49), embraces his literary production in its entirety. Born of a Cuban mother and a Catalan father, he spent the first half of his life mostly in his native Catalonia, where he was closely linked to the Renaissance of Catalan letters of the turn of the c., being very much part and mentor of Novecentism. After his breakup with the Mancomunitat he abandoned his native Catalonia, stopped publishing in Catalan, and from then on he only wrote in Castilian, some in French and occasionally in Italian. He studied in Spain, France and Switzerland, lectured widely in Europe and America, and held public positions in Barcelona, Burgos and Madrid. His work is well known in Spain and France, also in Italy.

Themes

Although there are variations during different periods of his literary life, nevertheless d'Ors's interest in culture in a very broad sense remains as a constant throughout. The Glossary is a reflection of d'Ors's enormous curiosity and wealth of knowledge, for there is room in it for philosophy, art, politics, literature, science, current events, even the minutiae of everyday happenings. Through his alert observations of even the most minute events, he reflects "the throbbing of times." The glosses, the seminal work of d'Ors, are an unceasing flow that commences at the very beginning of his literary career and stretches to the very last day of his life. His philosophy of man who works and plays is part of a dualistic system of values such as Classicism versus Baroque, Rome versus Babel, monarchy versus anarchy. All these concepts are part of a gigantic system for the interpretation of culture, denominated by d'Ors's Science of Culture. At the heart of his figurative thought is the concept of correlation between forms and ideas. Such a notion is already present in his conceptualized figure of Ben

Plantada, an idealization of "catalanidad," who also embodies the characteristics of Classicism. This figurative thought in turn permeates his theory of Science of Culture and is at the heart of his art criticism. *Tres horas en el Museo del Prado* (1922; *Three Hours in the Prado Museum*, 1954) incorporates his concepts of morphology and techtonics in the analysis of works of art. The same method is applied when analyzing Goya, Picasso, Zabaleta, Poussin, El Greco, Cezanne. Most of his novels correspond to the Catalan period of his literary production. However his posthumous *Lidia de Cadaques* (1954) is in itself a compendium as well as an attempt at a reconciliation with his native Catalonia. All his fictions are of an intellectual character reflecting the dualistic values that embody his theory of Science of Culture.

Style

D'Ors's prose is highly artistic although it suffers from some artificiality. In spite of his constant advocation of and striving toward Classicism, his style has a clear Baroque affinity and certain obscurity in its terminology. There are felicitous institutions and formulas with the intent of a definition that have become coined phrases: "all that is not tradition, is plagiarism," "the anecdotic as opposed to the categorical," "the auscultation of the throbbing of times." His style is highly original, incorporating some terminology of his own: anecdote purporting picturesqueness as opposed to category meaning profundity; the angel is what is truly unknown to man; the eon as an idea with a biography; the gloss as a daily injection of culture in the chores of everyday life; the love of definition as the drafting of a profile. His work abounds in metaphors, some acute: "*Quevedo is a crosseyed Dante," some amusing: "*Espronceda is a piano played only with a finger. *Bécquer, an accordion played by an angel. *Zorrilla is obviously a pianola." His numerous writings attest to the immense curiosity of their author, as well as to his originality in terminology. *See also* Essay.

BIBLIOGRAPHY

Primary Texts

A great deal of his literary production comes from the Glossary, published in Catalan as:
Glosari 1906–1910. Barcelona: Selecta, 1950.
Then continued in Castilian as:
Novísimo Glosario. Madrid: Aguilar, 1946.
Nuevo Glosario. 3 vols. Madrid: Aguilar, 1947–49.
Major Philosophical Works:
De la amistad y del diálogo. Madrid: Residencia de Estudiantes, 1914.
La ciencia de la cultura. Madrid: Rialp, 1964.
La filosofía del hombre que trabaja y que juega. Barcelona: Antonio López, 1914.
La muerte de Isidro Nonell. Spanish tr. E. Díez Canedo. Madrid: Suárez, 1905.
El secreto de la filosofía. Barcelona: Iberia, 1947.
Art criticism:
Lo Barroco. Madrid: Aguilar, 1964.
La ben plantada. Prol. Enric Jardi. Barcelona: Selecta, 1980. Catalan ed.

Goya. Picasso. Zabaleta. Madrid: Aguilar, 1964.
Gualba, la de mil voces. Barcelona: Planeta, 1981.
Mis salones. Itinerario del arte moderno en España. Madrid: Aguilar, 1945.
Oceanografía del tedio. Barcelona: Tusquets, 1981.
Sije. Barcelona: Planeta, 1982.
Tres horas en el Museo del Prado. Madrid: Aguilar, 1957.
La verdadera historia de Lidia de Cadaques. Barcelona: Planeta, 1982.
Drama:
Guillermo Tell. Study, R. Gibert. Madrid: Magisterio Español, 1971.
Prometeu encadenat. Prol. E. Jardi. Barcelona: Edicions 62, 1980. In Catalan.

English Translations

Pablo Picasso. Tr. W. H. Wells. New York: Weyhe, 1936.
Paul Cezanne. Tr. W. H. Wells. New York: Weyhe, 1930.
Three Hours in the Prado Museum. Tr. J. Forrester. Barcelona: PLD, 1954.

Criticism

Aguilera Cerni, Vicente. *Ortega y d'Ors en la cultura artística española*. Madrid: Ciencia Nueva, 1966.
Amorós, Andrés. *Eugenio d'Ors, crítico literario*. Madrid: Prensa Española, 1971.
Aranguren, José Luis. *La filosofía de Eugenio d'Ors*. 2nd ed. Madrid: Espasa-Calpe, 1981.
Jardi Cassani, Enric. *Eugeni d'Ors*. Barcelona: Ayma, 1967.
Macrí, Oreste. "La historiografía del barroco literario." *Thesaurus* 15 (1960): 1–70.
Manach, Jorge. "Santayana y d'Ors." *Cuadernos Americanos* (Sept.-Oct. 1955): 77–101.
"Recuerdo homenaje a Eugenio d'Ors." *Insula* 109 (Madrid) Oct. 15, 1954.
Sáenz, Pilar. *The Life and Works of Eugenio d'Ors*. Michigan: International Book, 1983.
———. "Morfología y Tectónica: Principio de estética orsiana." *Papeles de Son Armadans* 135 (June 1967): 237–62.

Pilar Sáenz

ORTEGA MUNILLA, José (1856, Cárdenas, Cuba–1922, Madrid), Spanish newspaper editor and novelist. It is important and ironic to note that this writer is the father of the philosopher *Ortega y Gasset. This is because the latter is one of the Spanish intellectuals most responsible for the oblivion and opprobrium into which the cultural work of his father and his cohorts in the realist/naturalist movement— *Pérez Galdós, *Clarín, *Pardo Bazán, etc.—fell during most of the first half of the twentieth c. in Spain, and in which, among certain circles, it remains still. For Ortega Munilla, along with the rest of the Generation of 1868, was instrumental in creating a high level of humanistic culture which the political corruption, ineptitude and disasters of the period occluded for subsequent generations—particularly in the eyes of Ortega y Gasset, for whom veritably all aspects of national political, social and aesthetic life in the second half of the nineteenth c. merited disdain.

Within the context of literary and general cultural history, Ortega Munilla's most important and fruitful labor was as editor of *Los Lunes de El Imparcial*

(The Mondays of The Impartial) between 1879 and 1906. This literary supplement to a leading Madrid daily of the period became an exceedingly significant forum for publication of a weekly review of national life written by Ortega Munilla, and stories, parts of novels, reviews and essays by and about Galdós, *Pereda, Clarín, Pardo Bazán, Juan *Valera, Marcelino *Menéndez y Pelayo, Jacinto Octavio *Picón, Ortega Munilla himself, and for at least two writers of the *Generation of 1898: *Valle-Inclán and *Azorín. That this labor has not received more recognition is doubly ironic when the analogous labor of Ortega y Gasset as founder and editor of the outstanding journal *Revista de Occidente* is widely recognized and praised.

A better-studied aspect of Ortega Munilla's activities is as author of prose fiction; Ferreras offers a three-part classification of it: *La cigarra* (1879; The Cicada), *Lucio Tréllez* (1879) and *Sor Lucila* (1880; Sister Lucila) constitute, in something approaching the manner of *Fernán Caballero, the three "sentimental novels." The properly realist fiction was written under the acknowledged influence of Galdós and includes *Don Juan Solo* (1880; Don Juan Alone), *El tren directo* (1880; The Express Train), *El fondo del tonel* (1881; The Bottom of the Barrel), *Panza-al-trote* (1883; The Freeloader), *Orgía del hambre* (1884; The Orgy of Hunger), *Cleopatra Pérez* (1884), and *Idilio lúgubre* (1887; Gloomy Idyll). The last group is described as the fiction "of the decadence and end of realism": *La viva y la muerta* (1895; Stepmother and Deadmother), *Frateretto: cuento de oro y amores* (1914; Frateretto: A Story of Gold and Love), *El paño pardo* (1914; Earth-brown Corduroy), *Estrazilla* (1917), and *La Señorita de la Cisniega* (1918; The Mistress of Cisniega). Two novels of his middle period, *Don Juan Solo* and *Cleopatra Pérez*, are considered his best; they fall into the general Galdosian category of Madrilenian novels of manners.

Finally it should be mentioned that Ortega Munilla did act as a representative to parliament during his period of most intense literary activity, and that he was admitted into the *Academia Española in 1902. *See also* Naturalism.

BIBLIOGRAPHY

Primary Texts

La cigarra. 3rd ed. Seville: Alvarez, 1882.

Cleopatra Pérez. Ed., intro. Juan Ignacio Ferreras. Madrid: Cátedra, 1976.

Don Juan solo. Madrid: Sanz Calleja, 1919.

Estrazilla. Madrid: Velasco, 1918. Rpt. Louisville, KY: Falls City Microcards, 1971.

Viñetas del sardinero. Madrid: Alvarez, 1918.

Criticism

Schmidt, Ruth. "José Ortega Munilla: Friend, Critic and Disciple of Galdós." *Anales Galdosianos* 6 (1971): 107–11.

———. *Ortega Munilla y sus novelas*. Madrid: RO, 1973.

Stephen Miller

ORTEGA Y FRÍAS, Ramón (1825, Granada–1883, Madrid), novelist and historian. Of the 150 novels that Ortega wrote, only a few have been kept. Among the best are *El Diablo en Palacio* (1857; The Devil in the Palace); *El* *peluquero del Rey* (1860; The King's Barber); *Rostros blancos y conciencias negras* (1865; White Faces and Black Consciences), etc. Ortega was an imitator of *Fernández y González and, like him, he cultivated the historical and custom novel with simplistic, truculent themes and superficial dialogue.

BIBLIOGRAPHY

Primary Texts

La casa de Tócame-Roque o un crimen misterioso. Madrid: Castro, 1877.
Cervantes. Madrid: Mariano C. y Gómez Editor, 1859.
El diablo en Palacio. Madrid: Gracia y Orga, 1957–58.
Guzmán el Bueno. Madrid: Ediciones Siglo XX, 1952.

Criticism

Cuenca, Francisco. *Biblioteca de Autores Andaluces* (Havana) 5.1 (1921): 264–65.

José Ortega

ORTEGA Y GASSET, José (1883, Madrid–1955, Madrid), philosopher, journalist, educator, statesman, and scion of two powerful families of publishers. Ortega received his education in Málaga and in the Universities of Deusto and Madrid. Dissatisfied with the prospect of a career in journalism, despite his lifelong gift for metaphor and rhythmic prose, he pursued post-doctoral studies in Germany from 1905 to 1907. At Leipzig he studied philology, and at Berlin the philosophy of life of Georg Simmel, before discovering the discipline he craved at Marburg-an-Lahn under the neo-Kantians Hermann Cohen and Paul Natorp. After obtaining the chair of metaphysics at the U of Madrid, where he succeeded the Krausist Nicolás Salmerón, he returned to Marburg for most of 1911. In 1914 he published his first book, *Meditaciones del Quijote* (*Meditations on Quixote*, 1984), essays of circumstance with philosophical underpinnings; and he founded a short-lived party of intellectuals, the League of Political Education. Among the various journals he initiated, the *Revista de Occidente* (1923–36) had the greatest impact on Spanish culture, into which it introduced contemporary European philosophy, aesthetics, science, and historiography. In 1929 Ortega resigned his university chair in protest against the military dictator Miguel Primo de Rivera, and in 1930 published his best-known work *La rebelión de las masas* (*The Revolt of the Masses*, 1985) with its veiled criticism of his adversary. When the Second Spanish Republic was declared in 1931, Ortega, Ramón *Pérez de Ayala, and Gregorio *Marañón founded the Movement at the Service of the Republic, a party modeled after the League of 1914, though also favoring liberal socialism and regional home-rule. As elected representative of León to the Spanish Parliament, Ortega quickly wearied of the extremism he found on the Left and the Right, left politics in 1933, and went into self-imposed exile in 1936, shortly before the outbreak of civil war. He sought refuge in France, the Netherlands, Argentina, and Portugal before returning to Spain in 1945. In 1948, in collaboration with his faithful former student Julián *Marías, he founded the Institute of Humanities, a research center with no ties to the

Franco regime. From 1950 until his death, feeling ill at ease in Spain, Ortega lectured when possible in Germany, Switzerland, even once in the United States. He left behind in Spain and Latin America a number of students deserving of recognition in the history of philosophy, and the most notable have been Xavier *Zubiri and Juan David *García Bacca.

His *Obras completas* (Complete Works), from his first journal article (1902) to his last posthumous lecture (1954), fill twelve volumes of over 500 pages each in the *Revista de Occidente* edition, although the collection is by no means "complete." The variety of themes he cultivated, mainly epistemological, historical, aesthetic, and political, but not excluding cultural anthropology, travel literature, biography, psychology, and fashion, attests to his openness to the greatest intellectual stimuli of his times. He wished to be remembered as the philosopher of "vital reason," whose doctrine he condensed into the phrase, "I am myself and my circumstance." In other words, I as a living being am a self-aware dialogue with my concrete surroundings, a gamut of possibilities in which my reason helps me affirm myself. In mature works (1929–54), Ortega asserted (1) my life is the "radical reality," the reality in which all other realities appear to me as in a framework; (2) my life is awareness of a task to perform, a problem of self-authentication; (3) my task consists of deciding among specific possibilities for selfhood; and (4) the latitude for choice among these possibilities defines my personal freedom, whereas their finiteness in number corresponds to the fatality in my existence.

These four basic principles gradually emerged out of Ortega's readings and original syntheses of Nietzsche, Simmel, Cohen, Natorp, Husserl, Heidegger, and Dilthey. From Nietzsche and Simmel he learned that the study of man as such could become the focus of philosophy, and that self-surmounting life was the proper frame of reference for such an examination. Cohen gave Ortega a will to system and the idea of life, the self-conscious task or problem of seeking identity. The subtle exchange of ideas between the neo-Kantian psychologist Natorp and the phenomenologist Husserl—an exchange published in their works—permanently affected Ortega's thought. Natorp first brought Husserl to Ortega's attention in 1912. Husserl, in turn, shook Ortega's faith in physico-mathematical logic, the basis of Natorp's psychology and of all Marburg neo-Kantianism. Yet Natorp cautioned Ortega against Husserl's excessive confidence in mental reflection for obtaining knowledge. Aware of this overconfidence as reflected in Husserl's *Ideas* (1913), Ortega found more convincing Husserl's *Logical Investigations* (1900, 1901) and his "Philosophy of Rigorous Science" (1910–11), stressing the cognitive value of direct, unmediated intuition of experience. The phrase "I am myself and my circumstance" contains echoes of Husserl's *Ideas*, modified to exclude Husserl's overestimation of reflection and to stress the naturalness and immediacy of true knowledge. The term *circumstance* also contains a patriotic nuance: Ortega philosophizes to revitalize Spain with conceptual discipline, the lesson of Cohen. In Husserl's 1927 *Yearbook* of phenomenological research, Ortega read Heidegger's *Being and Time*, from which he culled an order for his four main tenets along with most of the content of the third and fourth. He also derived from Heidegger a new appreciation of Wilhelm Dilthey, and from Dilthey came Ortega's life-centered lexicon of his mature writings.

In vain Ortega's more conservative students attribute to him a system, when in fact he wrote no clear and complete chain of principles applicable to all reality. Instead, like Simmel, Dilthey, and Max Scheler, his thought always stayed in flux. He did, however, evolve a method, which he would call "vital reason." This is a three-step process for overcoming obstacles to personal identity. First I experience a person, object, or activity as a problem, disorienting me. Next I submit my problem to phenomenological reduction, a means for defining it. Finally I narrate the historical causes of the phenomenon so defined to discover an orientation with respect to it. Problem-posing, influenced by Cohen, became a permanent feature of Ortega's essays as of 1910; Husserl's phenomenological reduction, as of 1913; and Dilthey's historical narrative, as of 1933.

Cohen taught Ortega that individual life is an identity problem, with the principles of culture—especially of physico-mathematical logic—as a plausible solution. Cohen subordinated life to logical culture; but in the 1910 essay "Adam in Paradise," Ortega subordinated all culture to life, the identity problem. Henceforth he usually began his essays by posing problems of personal identity, to be solved with discursive and descriptive reason. The contents of the problems varied with the authors Ortega was reading at the time: mainly Marburg neo-Kantians until 1913; chiefly phenomenologists and phenomenological psychologists until 1929; primarily Dilthey, his students, and his followers until 1954. The problems increased in intensity and universality over Ortega's forty-five years of philosophizing. In *Meditaciones del Quijote*, he queried, What is Spain, the other half of his person? He offered no complete response until *España invertebrada* (1921; *Invertebrate Spain*, 1937), where the question received a more concrete historical formulation: Why Basque and Catalan separatism? Ortega answered with a synthesis of all Spanish history, its ills and suggested remedies. In *El tema de nuestro tiempo* (1923; *The Modern Theme*, 1961), a more speculative work, he inquired, Why has his generation failed to recognize its historical mission, the subordination of culture to life? In *La rebelión de las masas*, he asked, Why throughout Europe crowds throng public places historically reserved for the select few, among them himself? World crisis led to the Spanish Civil War of 1936 and to World War II. After having seen both from afar, Ortega in his sociology course *Man and People* (1949–50) raised the question, What is society? Lack of a clear answer, he felt, had produced global hostilities. In sum, Ortega's greatest gift to civilization may well be his trenchant verbalization of some of the most serious issues facing the twentieth century.

To reach solutions, Ortega applied Husserl's phenomenological reduction to the terms of the problems. First, he suspended current forejudgments to arrive at a self-evident generalization about the problem. Next he analyzed the generalization by pruning away everything inessential to understanding the problem.

Finally he gathered the essentials into a direct definition, whose aspects he enumerated and described. For instance, *The Dehumanization of Art* (1925) and *The Revolt of the Masses*, Ortega's best-known books, apply phenomenological reduction to specific historical problems. Both works address historical anomalies: in 1925, the unprecedented unpopularity of contemporary art; in 1930, as noted, the unusual thronging of once-exclusive public places. Next Ortega sets aside received forejudgments—in 1925, the impression that the unpopularity of the new art will subside; in 1930, the view that the ubiquitous mobbing in Europe has to do with political change.

In his writing on dehumanized art, Ortega argues that the new aesthetics seem to differ from all the old in lying beyond the masses' grasp. Avant-garde art seeks to offer the purest aesthetic enjoyment. To clarify, Ortega imitates Husserl in rising from particulars to a self-evident generalization—here, a notion of aesthetic enjoyment as disinterested contemplation of the aesthetic object as a fiction. The purer the enjoyment, the more artists stress the fiction, and the less they encourage participation in the artistic content, the "human" element. Among artists who seem to Ortega to carry this "dehumanization" to an extreme, he mentions the composers Debussy and Stravinsky, the playwright Pirandello, and (analytical) cubist painters and poets. Unmediated intuition of all this "dehumanized" art, detached from further presuppositions, enables Ortega to define it with seven general characteristics. The most general, "dehumanization," gives the book its title; and most of the work consists of the description, one by one, of the other tendencies enumerated.

The Revolt of the Masses has a parallel structure. It phenomenologically analyzes early twentieth-c. public life in many areas of culture. With political forejudgments placed in abeyance, Ortega asserts what for him is a self-evident generalization: that human society is a dynamic unit of intellectual and moral elites and masses. To capture the essence of today's masses, who govern public life, Ortega distinguishes them from every related phenomenon: masses of the past and elites of every age. The masses of the present are as irresponsible as the masses of the past, but enjoy and exercise social powers formerly attributable only to especially qualified individuals, men who make great self-demands, who strive for excellence in all fields of endeavor, regardless of their social classes. Most of Ortega's book consists of a phenomenological description of today's mass-man in revolt against his moral and mental superior. To be sure, Ortega's description contains positive aspects of the rebellion: the rise of the level of history, the adventure of living in an insecure time, the increase of possibilities for self-realization. But negative aspects far outnumber positive ones: the masses today show aggressiveness in public affairs, anti-liberalism, lack of historical sense, excessive specialization, unhealthy dependence on the state, and historical disorientation, for which only a "United States of Europe" can provide the cure.

No work written by Ortega after 1913 escapes the impact of Husserl's phenomenological method. Yet as of 1932 Ortega modifies that method under Dilthey's influence: after posing his problem for study and suspending common forejudgments about it, Ortega begins to make a self-evident generalization in Dilthey's terms about human life. Further, having reduced that generalization to the essence of the experience under study, Ortega narrates its history by taking into account, as Dilthey does, the shifting structure of human beliefs (in Dilthey, *Weltanschauungen*). Ortega's most concise and densest work, *Historia como sistema* (1935; *Toward a Philosophy of History,* 1961), displays how Dilthey's ''historical reason'' complements Husserl's phenomenological method in Ortega's thought. Here Ortega poses, as usual, a specific problem: natural science, once the substitute for religious faith, has today lost its self-confidence. Contemporary man feels disoriented. In what can he place his trust to guide him through the universe? To the same question, Husserl offers as an answer his phenomenological method, while Dilthey proposes the adoption of his historical reason. *History as a System*, however, justifies synthesizing Husserl and Dilthey. Ortega calls the synthesis ''vital and historical reason.''

Man, writes Ortega, has lost faith in the natural sciences because they have failed to discover his essence. To orient his readers, Ortega tries to accomplish with his method what the natural sciences have not. Following Husserl's practice, he suspends forejudgments: in this case, the presupposition, made by natural and human sciences alike, that man has a nature, an eternal, unchanging substance, capable of being studied by the (natural) scientific method. Phenomenological reduction leads Ortega to conclude that man is neither his ''nature,'' nor his body, nor his psyche, but his life. Having arrived at the essence of man, Ortega enumerates aspects of that essence: human life is a problematical task of self-creation in view of finite possibilities, which constrain the individual to choose among them while limited by his past, never repeatable. What determines his choice is the structure of his beliefs, as Dilthey maintains. Ortega narrates the series of basic beliefs which have generated Western man. The narrative purports to prove the thesis of *Historia como sistema*: that man is by definition his own life, systematically knowable for the historian. First, relates Ortega, man believed in God, lost that faith, came to believe in nature, grew disenchanted, and now has nothing left but the process of his own disillusionment, the science of which is history. This science is worthy of ending the Western crisis of belief in rational thought, because history, as distinguished from other sciences, tells man what he is: the pathway of his own experiences. Historical reason, learned by Ortega in Dilthey, prevails in the essays of the 1940s and 50s, mostly biographical essays on Velásquez, Goya, and Goethe, analyzed from the standpoint of vocation, historical circumstance, and underlying systems of beliefs.

Within this period Ortega wrote his highly acclaimed posthumous work, *La idea de principio en Leibniz y la evolución de la teoría deductiva* (1947–50; *The Idea of Principle in Leibniz and the Evolution of Deductive Theory*, 1971). The longest, richest, and most technical writing to have flowed from Ortega's pen, this unfinished book is his subtle response to his critics. In his final years, he deplored the indifference of German readers to his works and their accolades of

Heidegger. At the same time, between 1941 and 1949, Jesuit neo-Thomists of Franco Spain and Mexico attacked Ortega's style of thinking. Behind the glittering metaphors, reflecting sensualism and relativism, his detractors discovered no stable principles, no terminological rigor, no solid, systematic structure. Ortega therefore prepared a posthumous reply which would turn the barbs of his adversaries against themselves. Not even Heidegger would escape. The tricentennial of Leibniz's birth (1946) would form the situational pretext. With terminological rigor unseen elsewhere in his books, Ortega took for his point of departure Heidegger's 1929 essay "On the Essence of Ground" ("Vom Wesen des Grundes"), concerning the idea of principle in Leibniz, Aristotle, and Kant. Heidegger, however much he contributed to Ortega's greatest book, had made no historical analysis of the first principles. But Dilthey had, enabling Ortega to criticize Aristotle and the Schoolmen for their lack of veracity, imprecision, inconsistency, and the sensualism of their logic. He extended his critique to their ontology—the basis of his neo-Thomistic foes' logic and ontology. Finally, he argued the derivative, mediated character of Heidegger's ontology, child of Scholasticism. In terms of rigor, rejection of sensualism, and love of first principles, Ortega divided philosophy into two camps, one headed by Plato, the other by Aristotle. In Plato's camp, that of "principled" philosophers, Ortega situated Descartes, Leibniz, Husserl, and himself; while in the enemy's camp, that of Aristotle, he placed Euclid, the Stoics, the Schoolmen, Kierkegaard, *Unamuno, contemporary neo-Thomists, and Heidegger.

Leaving aside the accuracy of Ortega's critique, how justified is his apology of his own mental style? His most memorable metaphors (for example, life as a problem, life as a sport) have German sources (H. Cohen and M. Scheler, respectively) whose rejection of sensualism is a matter of historical record. Ortega himself claims to rely on the evidence of phenomenological intuition, contemplation of essences, which include sensory data, but also concepts and signs as well. An orange, the color orange, a circle, and a polygon of infinite sides are all capable of being intuited as Ortega understands this form of mental perception. For Ortega, just as for the Munich phenomenologist Alexander Pfander, metaphor serves as a means or instrument for expressing newly discovered intuitions, which otherwise would remain unexpressed. How could the metaphor "the depths of the soul" be improved to convey a reality undoubtedly experienced by any individual with sentiments? In translating tropes and doctrines received outside Spain, Ortega does for Spanish philosophy what *modernistas* like Darío, *Valle-Inclán, the *Machado brothers, and Juan Ramón *Jiménez do for Spanish poetry. All revitalize local culture by opening it to stimuli from without.

Moreover, when embedding in his prose whole families of related metaphors, each pertaining to some aspect of a given doctrine or its analogue, Ortega simply continues the tradition of the Spanish Krausists and of Unamuno. The dazzle of a metaphor, of course, sometimes obfuscates Ortega's meaning; but the same occurs in other metaphorical thinkers like Plato, Hegel, Nietzsche, and Husserl. Metaphor replaces rigid terminology in Ortega's writing for a pedagogical reason:

he can thereby lure his readers to philosophy in a country like Spain without a sustained secular philosophical tradition. His prose, musical, and figures, lends itself to memorization. The metaphors (for instance, life as the radical reality) do denote stable principles of human existence in Ortega's thought as of 1929. The principles, few in number, form the building-blocks of a philosophical method, without, however, attaining the universality of a system. Here as in other respects, Ortega identifies with Plato, also methodical, though lacking a system. Ortega can claim a place in Western literature as one of the greatest prose writers of the twentieth c. and as a philosopher of transition between early Husserlian phenomenology and Heidegger's ontology of existence. Although he does not achieve the radical grasp of problems that Heidegger does (for Ortega misreads metaphysics into Heidegger), the Madrid philosopher shows greater breadth and attention to current issues.

In the Spanish-speaking world, he deserves recognition for having invented a philosophical vocabulary which has passed in many cases into the common language. Moreover, he has decisively influenced Spanish and Latin America essay writing in style and content. Through him, Spain and Latin America have come into contact with contemporary European culture, especially ideas derived from German-speaking countries. Ortega has affected liberal political thinking in his own nation and abroad. Finally, he has made philosophy accessible and even fascinating to vast numbers of readers. *See also* Essay; Krausism.

BIBLIOGRAPHY

Primary Texts

La deshumanización del arte y otros ensayos. 11th ed. Madrid: RO, 1976.
La deshumanización del arte y otros ensayos. Madrid: Espasa-Calpe, 1987.
Ensayos sobre la "Generación del 98" y otros escritores españoles contemporáneos. Madrid: RO, 1981.
Epistolario completo Ortega-Unamuno. Madrid: el Arquero, 1987.
España invertebrada. Madrid: RO, 1951.
Espíritu de la letra. Madrid: Cátedra, 1985.
Meditaciones del Quijote. Madrid: Cátedra, 1984.
Meditaciones sobre la literatura y el arte. Madrid: Castalia, 1987.
Sobre la razón histórica. Madrid: RO, 1979.
Obras completas. 12 vols. Madrid: Alianza/RO, 1983.

English Translations

The Dehumanization of Art, and Other Essays on Art, Culture and Literature. Princeton: Princeton UP, 1968.
Historical Reason. Tr. P. Silver. New York: Norton, 1984.
The Idea of Principle in Leibniz and the Evolution of Deductive Theory. Tr. M. Adams. New York: Norton, 1971.
Meditations on Hunting. Tr. H. B. Wescott. New York: Scribner, 1972. Tr. of a prologue to *Veinte años de caza mayor* by E. Figueroa y Alonso Martínez.
The Modern Theme. Tr. J. Cleugh. New York: Harper, 1961.
On Love; Aspects of a Single Theme. Tr. T. Talbot. New York: Meridian, 1957.
Phenomenology and Art. Tr., intro. P. Silver. New York: Norton, 1975.

Psychological Investigations. Tr. J. García-Gómez. New York: Norton, 1987.
The Revolt of the Masses. Tr., notes, intro. A. Kerrigan. Ed. K. Moore. Foreword S. Bellow. Notre Dame, IN: U of Notre Dame P, 1985.
Toward a Philosophy of History. Tr. H. Weyl. New York: Norton, 1961.

Criticism

Cerezo Galán, P. *La voluntad de aventura. Aproximamiento crítico al pensamiento de Ortega y Gasset*. Barcelona: Ariel, 1984.
Orringer, N. R. *Ortega y sus fuentes germánicas*. Madrid: n.p., 1979.
———. "Ortega y Gasset's Critique of Method." *Comparative Criticism* 6 (1984): 135–54.
———. "La crítica a Aristóteles de Ortega, y sus fuentes." In *Ortega, hoy*. Ed. M. Durán. Vera Cruz, NM: n.p., 1985. 173–223.
Ouimette, V. *José Ortega y Gasset*. Boston: n.p., 1982.

Nelson Orringer

ORTÍZ, Agustín (sixteenth c., Aragón–?), playwright. He composed a work inspired by the **Celestina* titled *Radiana* (1534). The five acts are written in **pie quebrado*; the influence of Gil *Vicente is also apparent.

BIBLIOGRAPHY

Primary Text

The "Comedia Radiana" of Agustín Ortíz. Intro., notes R. E. House. Chicago: n.p., 1910.

ORTIZ, Lourdes (1943, Madrid–), novelist, playwright, children's tales writer, essayist, translator and professor of art history at the Royal Superior School of Dramatic Art in Madrid. Though she has been successful in various genres, she is best known as a novelist. Her first novel, *Luz de la memoria* (1976; Light of Memory), forms part of the period of transition of the 1970s when novels mostly dealt with the past in an autobiographical and dialogue form. With *Picadura mortal* (1979; Fatal Bite) she essayed the detective genre. The novel *En días como éstos* (1981; On Days Like These) deals with contemporary problems and the crisis of values in society. In *Urraca* (1982; Urraca) she re-creates a memorable portrait of Urraca as the queen who writes a historical-political chronicle of ambition and power, while Urraca the woman meditates about life and death and recalls the passionate encounters of her life from the loneliness of her cell where she is kept a prisoner. *Arcángeles* (1986; Archangels) is a novel of initiation of the protagonist, as seen through a series of scenarios in the labyrinth of life of present-day Madrid.

Ortiz is one of the most representative writers who experiments with novelistic forms but who always maintains her individual voice through the command of the word, be that virile or lyrical, poetic or metaphorical, to fit the context. Her abundant and varied cultural references bear witness to her vast cultural background and her multifaceted personality.

BIBLIOGRAPHY

Primary Texts

Novels

Arcángeles. Barcelona: Plaza y Janés, 1986.
En días como éstos. Madrid: Akal, 1981.
Luz de la memoria. Madrid: Akal, 1979.
Picadura mortal. Madrid: Sedmay, 1979.
Urraca. Madrid: Puntual, 1982.

Short Stories - Theater

Los motivos de Circe. Madrid: Dragón, 1988.

Theater

Las murallas de Jericó. Madrid: Hyperión, 1980.

Essays

Communicación Crítica. Co-authored with Pablo del Río. Madrid: Pablo del Río, 1978.
Rimbaud. Barcelona: Dopesa, 1979.
Larra: Escritos Políticos. Madrid: Ciencia Nueva, 1967. Annotated.

Children's Tales

La caja de lo que pudo ser. Madrid: Altea, 1981.
Los viajeros del futuro. Madrid: Santillana, 1982.

Criticism

Aparicio, Mara. "Urraca." *Nueva Estafeta* 48–49 (Nov.-Dec. 1982): n.p.
Azancot, Leopoldo. "Arcángeles." *ABC* (Supplement) May 17, 1986.
Blanco Villa, Luis. "Un personaje perdido en la ciudad." *Ya* May 21, 1986.
Mateo Diez, Luis. "El poder, el amor y la muerte." *Guía del Ocio* (Oct. 1982).
Morales Villena, Gregorio. "Lourdes Ortiz y Alvaro Pombo: opera quinta." *Insula* 480 (1986).
Sobejano, Gonzalo. "Ante la novela de los años setenta." *Insula* 396–97 (Nov.-Dec. 1979): 1, 22.
Suñen, Luis. "Bajar a los infiernos." *El País* 23 (Oct. 1986).
Tebar, Juan. "Novela criminal española de la transición." *Insula* 464–65 (July-Aug. 1985).

Drosoula Lytra

ORTIZ DE ZÚÑIGA Y DEL ALGARVE, Diego (1633, Seville–1680, Seville), historian, genealogist. Author of the learned *Anales esclesiásticos y seculares de la ciudad de Sevilla* (1677; Ecclesiastic and Secular Annals of the City of Seville), which covers the years 1246 to 1671. He also wrote *Discurso genealógico de los Ortizes de Sevilla* (1670; Genealogical Discourse on the Ortiz Family of Seville), which traces his own lineage, and the *Posteridad ilustre de Juan de Céspedes* (n.d.; Illustrious Posterity of Juan de Céspedes).

BIBLIOGRAPHY

Primary Texts

Anales eclesiásticos. Ed. A. M. Espinosa. 5 vols. Madrid: Imprenta Real, 1795–96.
Discurso genealógico. . . . Ed. Pérez de Guzmán. 2nd ed. Madrid: Ciudad lineal, 1929.
Posteridad ilustre de Juan de Céspedes. Madrid: n.p., 1954. Facs.

OSÓRIO DE CASTRO, António Gabriel Maranca (1933, Setúbal–), contemporary Portuguese poet. By training and profession a lawyer, Osório appears late on the literary scene with his self-published book of poems *A Raiz Afectuosa* (1972; The Caring Root) and with *A Mitologia Fadista* (1974; The Fado's Mythology), a collection of essays which appeared originally in two opposition journals, *O Tempo e o Modo* and *Seara Nova,* during the Salazar-Caetano dictatorship.

The bulk of his work, however, is post-Revolution and silent about that event. In spite of this, his verse is profoundly marked by a reaction not to its political or socio-economic consequences, but rather to its vitriolic usurpation of the word by demagogues. It is also characterized by a quietist faith in the poet as an artisan who forges poetry's prime matter, the word. Each volume explores set themes. Family and death permeate *Ignorância da Morte* (1978; Ignorance of Death). Love is the concern of *Lugar do Amor* (1981; Love's Locus). Spirituality and ethics are treated in *Décima Aurora* (1982; The Tenth Dawn), which contains both verse and prose poems and is influenced by Chinese culture. And, in *Adão, Eva e o Mais* (1983; Adam, Eve and All Else), Osório considers the role of myth, especially those of Creation and Resurrection.

Osório stands out as one of the most important voices in Portuguese poetry since *Pessoa.

BIBLIOGRAPHY

Primary Texts

Adão, Eva e o Mais. Lisbon: Nacional, 1983.
Décima Aurora. Lisbon: Na Regra do Jogo, 1982.
A Ignorância da Morte. Lisbon: Presença, 1982.
O Lugar do Amor. Lisbon: Moraes, 1985.
A Mitologia Fadista. Lisbon: Horizonte, 1974.
A Raiz Afectuosa. Oporto: Gota de Agua, 1984.

Criticism

Lisboa, Eugénio. ''Um Inventário Escrupuloso sobre a Poesia de António Osório.'' *Colóquio* 72 (n.d.): 77–81.

Jaime H. da Silva

OSUNA, Francisco de (1492, Osuna–c. 1541, Seville ?), religious writer and mystic. A reformed Franciscan (Franciscan of the Strict Observance), writer of ascetical-mystical literature, spiritual teacher of St. *Teresa of Avila, he is the most important Spanish mystic after St. John of the Cross (*Juan de la Cruz) and St. Teresa. From 1520 to 1560 Osuna was the most widely read of Spain's religious writers, and to some extent, he influenced every mystical writer between 1572 and 1650. He developed a method of prayer and meditation referred to as *recogimiento*. Educated at Alcalá, he later formed part of a group of religious reformers who gathered at the castle of Don Diego López Pacheco, Marquis of Escalona, which included Juan de *Valdés as well as several **alumbrados*.

However, it was his contact with one of the Franciscan retreat houses (*re-*

colectorios), Nuestra Señora de la Salceda, which brought him into contact with the meditative process of *recogimiento* (withdrawal). The author of a six-volume *Abecedario espiritual* (Spiritual Alphabet), Osuna developed an affective spirituality, common to the Franciscans, whereby the soul of the individual in prayer retreats within itself by means of love, which activates the will without the assistance of intellectual speculation. In the meditative process established by Osuna, the individual not only lifts his soul toward God, but also withdraws (*recoger*) within himself, gathering (*recogiendo*) all of his spiritual resources. Osuna utilized the medieval alphabet in his six *Abecedarios*, composing a series of distichs corresponding to each letter. The introductory distich contains a religious thought which is followed by an extensive commentary (*glosa*). For example, the *Tercer abecedario espiritual (Third Spiritual Alphabet*, 1948) contains twenty-three *tratados* or religious tracts with each one preceded by an introductory distich. It is in this *Third Spiritual Alphabet* that Osuna developed the meditative process of *recogimiento*, which can be rendered as both a spiritual withdrawal and a gathering in of the religious forces of the soul. *See also* Ascetical Literature; Erasmism; Mysticism.

BIBLIOGRAPHY

Primary Texts

Ley de amor o quarta parte del Abecedario espiritual. Burgos: Juan de Junta, 1536. (The 1544 edition published in Burgos had a profound impact on the spiritual development of St. Teresa.)

Norte de estados. Burgos: Juan de Junta, 1541.

Tercera parte del libro llamado Abecedario espiritual. Escritores místicos. Madrid: n.p., 1911. 1:319–587.

English Translation

The Third Spiritual Alphabet. Tr. a Benedictine of Stanbrook. Westminster, MD: Newman, 1948.

Criticism

Dobbins, Dunstan. *Franciscan Mysticism*. New York: Wagner, 1927.

Ros, Fidèle. *Un Maître de Sainte Therese. Le père François d'Osuna. Sa vie, son oeuvre, sa doctrine spirituelle*. Paris: Gabriel Beauchesne, 1936.

Angelo DiSalvo

OTAOLA, Simón (1907, San Sebastián, Guipúzcoa–1980, Mexico City, Mexico), novelist. Otaola, a Basque, received his education and lived in Madrid from age ten. As an adult he was active in the labor movement and held a position of leadership in the Oil Workers Union of Spain (CAMPSA). During the Spanish Civil War he fought on the Madrid front and later became the political delegate (*comisario*) of an army division in the Lérida and Ebro fronts. In 1939, after the defeat of the Spanish Republic, he joined the massive exile to Mexico, where he lived until his death. He made his living primarily in advertising for the Mexican movie industry, but he also participated in many other intellectual pursuits. His literary work mingles chronicle and fiction, usually on the theme of life in the Spanish exiled community. His books, published in Mexico, are *Unos hombres* (1950: A Few Men), *La librería de Arana* (1953; Arana's Bookstore), *Los tordos en el pirul* (1953; Spotted Horses at Pirul), *El lugar ese . . .* (1957; That Place . . .), *El Cortejo* (1963; The Mourners), and *Tiempo de recordar* (1978; Time to Remember). *La librería de Arana* and *El Cortejo* are his best known works; the former relates the gatherings and activities of the refugees in their first decade or so of exile. The protagonist is another Spanish writer and intellectual, José Ramón Arana, whose bookselling business was really ambulatory: it consisted of the books he could carry himself from customer to customer. The story is told with agility and ease, and it conveys a sense of optimism, good humor and great communal intellectual ferment. *El Cortejo*, thirteen years later, deals with the wake and funeral of a member of the group, an event which brings together the bulk of the *transterrado* community; the tone is now one of sadness and imminent dispersion. Although lip service was still being paid to the hope of return to a democratic Spain, for most the prospect of death in exile and a progressively evident assimilation to Mexico had become a reality. *El Cortejo* is a *roman à clef* where many of the *transterrados* are identifiable. Above all, it is an elegiac evocation of the shared experience of the Spanish diaspora. Otaola is also a sensitive observer of Mexican rural life. *Los tordos en el pirul* is a masterful portrait of a small town in central Mexico. San Felipe Torres Mochas, the town, presently impoverished, but still alive in its traditions and recollections of prosperity, dates back to the sixteenth c. Otaola conveys its folkways, without the trappings of tourist-oriented folklore, in a limpid prose full of affection and empathy. It is a valuable document of a provincial Mexico that is rapidly disappearing. *Tiempo de recordar* narrates a journey to Veracruz, the landing site of most of the exiles, in an effort to recapture the already distant odyssey of 1939, but the past proves irretrievable. Otaola writes about events that are laden with nostalgia, and through all his books there is a sense of impending evanescence, but his mastery of irony and his irreverent sense of humor give his narrative tension and energy and steer it clear of the dangers of sentimentality.

BIBLIOGRAPHY

Primary Texts

El Cortejo. Mexico: Mortiz, 1963.
La librería de Arana. Mexico: n.p., 1953.
El lugar ese. . . . Mexico: Los Presentes, 1957.
Los tordos en el pirul. Mexico: Aquelarre, 1953.
Unos hombres. Mexico: Corzo, 1950.

Criticism

Marra-López, José Ramón. *Narrativa española fuera de España. 1939–1961*. Madrid: Guadarrama, 1964.

Zelaya Kolker, Marielena. *Visiones americanas de los escritores transterrados españoles de 1939*. Madrid: Instituto de Cooperación Iberoamericana, 1985.

Marielena Zelaya Kolker

OTERO, Blas de (1916, Bilbao–1979, Bilbao), Spanish poet. Together with Gabriel *Celaya, Otero was considered a leader of the "social poets" of the 1950s and 1960s, although Otero's existential and metaphysical concerns are greater than those of Celaya and the social poets generally (Eugenio de *Nora, Victoriano *Crémer, José *Hierro, *Caballero Bonald, *López Pacheco, Angela *Figuera, Gloria *Fuertes, José Agustín *Goytisolo, José Angel *Valente, and others). Otero was probably the greatest poet of the group, but he was not fully a "social" poet, for his concerns transcended the more narrow political criticism infusing the movement as a whole, and he did not limit the function of poetry (as Celaya once did) to changing society. Otero is very much in the tradition of *Unamuno and Antonio *Machado, and greatly admired the latter, writing a number of poems which consciously allude to this master. His *Cántico espiritual* (1942; Spiritual Canticle) echoes the doubt and anguish characteristic of Unamuno, although expressed more indirectly—concealing the existential content in emotion—due to the Franco *censorship. Even so, a number of his works could not be published in Spain, including *En castellano* (In Plain Words), finally published in France as *Parler clair* in 1959; and others were published in Puerto Rico and Paris respectively: *Esto no es un libro* (1963; This Is Not a Book) and *Que trata de España* (1964; This Tells of Spain).

Although other works were published by Otero before *Angel fieramente humano* (1950; Savagely Human Angel), this was the first one to attract public attention. From the beginning, Otero's was a strong, technically perfect lyric voice, combining Machado's restraint with Unamuno's desire to provoke and engage the conscience of his readers. While the social elements which emerged in his poetry from this point onward made it less abstract, with more emphasis on the concrete, physical circumstances of the contemporary world and of twentieth-c. man, Otero continued to seek answers to ultimate mysteries and did not abandon his ethical quest in favor of either political commitment or social ideologies. *Redoble de conciencia* (1951; Drumroll of Conscience) makes clear the underlying ethical inspiration of his social beliefs. *Pido la paz y la palabra* (1955; I Ask for Peace and My Turn to Speak) shows increased identification with the social poetry movement inasmuch as the poet now concentrates more specifically on contemporary Spain and the plight of its citizens. Human suffering and social injustice are more than political issues for him, however, and his personal indignation is deeply felt, not merely an ideological pose. *Ancia* (1958) uses the first syllable of *Angel* and the last of *conciencia*, combining and reordering the contents of *Angel fieramente humano* and *Redoble de conciencia*, and adding a few more poems. Most of his books written after this point tend to reiterate essentially the same ideas. *Hacia la inmensa mayoría* (1962; For the Vast Majority) collects and reprints Otero's first four books, while *Expresión y reunión* (1969; Expression and Reunion) brings together all of Otero's books (1941–69), including those published outside Spain. Later works are *Mientras* (1970; Meanwhile), *Historias fingidas y verdaderas* (1970; Feigned and True Stories)—which has the peculiarity of being written in prose—and *Escrito para* (1974; Written for). Otero conceived of poetry as communication, and consequently utilized as clear a language as feasible, often colloquial or idiomatic, with straightforward syntax and relatively few rhetorical figures, with repetition being his most important lyric device. Metrics become more irregular in his last books, but notwithstanding their simplicity, his poems are all the products of painstaking and careful reiteration.

BIBLIOGRAPHY

Primary Texts

Expresión y reunión. Madrid: Alianza, 1981.
Verso y prosa. Madrid: Cátedra, 1976.

Criticism

Alarcos Llorach, Emilio. *La poesía de Blas de Otero*. 2nd ed. Salamanca: Anaya, 1973.
Daydí-Tolson, Santiago. "The Preeminence of Blas de Otero." *The Post–Civil War Spanish Social Poets*. Boston: G. K. Hall, 1983.
Semprún Donahue, Moraima de. *Blas de Otero en su poesía*. Chapel Hill: U of North Carolina P, 1977.

Janet Pérez

OTERO PEDRAYO, Ramón (1888, Orense–1976, Orense), Galician writer, orator, professor. In the village of Trasalba, from which he was never truly separated, Ramón Otero Pedrayo sustained a close relationship with nature and daily rural customs. This environment is present in much of his fiction, and is often felt through the conflict of patriarchy with modernization. An avid reader and prolific writer, Otero Pedrayo studied in Santiago and Madrid, becoming a professor of geography and history. In 1929 he became a member of the Royal Galician Academy. From 1931 to 1933, he was a representative for the Partido Nacionalista Republicano (Republican Nationalist party), and his pro-Galician activities resulted in his being persecuted by Franco's regime. Past president of the important Seminario de Estudos Galegos (Galician Studies Seminar), don Ramón maintained constant contact with the Galician intellectual world, and his contribution to modern culture is unequaled in quantity. He was awarded the Premio Galicia of the Fundación Juan March (1962) and the Premio of the Diputación Provincial de Orense for his study of Father *Feijoo.

Otero Pedrayo's writing is vast, in themes and quantity, but its basic focus is always Galicia. In addition to textbooks, he wrote novels, short stories, poetry, essays (including travel narratives and literary criticism), drama, and numerous historical studies. Not directly political, his promotion of his native land and literature, particularly during the difficult post–Civil War period, is nevertheless politically significant. When he retired, in 1958, his last class open to the public was given in the then-censored Galician, his preferred language. A member of the Grupo Nós (We Group), fundamental for the comprehension and diffusion of today's Galician culture, Otero Pedrayo wrote what Vicente *Risco called its autobiography in the novel *Arredor de sí* (1926; Around Oneself). In general, his creative prose is realistic, although its detailed descriptions of the rural world resemble *costumbrismo*. However, the author was less interested in static portraits than in the portrayal of historical changes among the classes of Galician society, caught as they were between maintaining an identity rooted in a distant past of injustice and poverty, and a future which threatened to undermine those very roots. One result of his analyses is the elaboration of a theory of nature (*Teoría da paisaxe*), part of an overall metaphysics of Galician identity. Today there is a Fundación Otero Pedrayo which awards an annual prize for service to Galician culture. *See also* Galician Literature.

BIBLIOGRAPHY

Primary Texts

Arredor de sí. 2nd ed. Vigo: Galaxia, 1970.
Bocarribeira: Poemas para leer e queimar. Madrid: n.p., 1958.
Os camiños da vida. Santiago: n.p., 1928.
Ensayo histórico sobre la cultura gallega. Santiago: n.p., 1933. (Published in Galician in Vigo, Galaxia, 1982.)
Entre a vendima e a castañeira. Vigo: Galaxia, 1957.
Galicia, una cultura de Occidente. León: n.p., 1976.
O libro dos amigos. Buenos Aires: n.p., 1953.
Pantelas, home libre. La Corũna, 1925.
Pelerinaxes. I. Santiago. Nós, 1929.
Parladoiro. Vigo: n.p., 1973.
Síntesis histórica do século XVIII en Galicia. Vigo: Galaxia, 1969.
Teatro de máscaras. Orense: n.p., 1975.
Rosalía. Vigo, 1985.

English Translation

Santiago de Compostela. Tr. D. MacDermott. 2nd ed. Barcelona: Noguer, 1958.

Criticism

Carballo Calero, Ricardo. "Otero Pedrayo: Unha visión de Galicia." *Grial* 56 (1977): n.p.
Cardeñoso, Severino, comp. *Nuestro amigo Ramón Otero Pedrayo*. Vigo: n.p., 1979.
Casares, Carlos. *Otero Pedrayo*. Vigo: Galaxia, 1981.
March, Kathleen N. "La conflictividad lingüistica en *Arredor de sí* de Ramón Otero Pedrayo." *Cuadernos de Estudios Gallegos* 34.99 (1983): n.p.
Pedrosa Rúa, Cristina. "Sobre *Arredor de sí* de Otero Pedrayo." *Grial* 35 (1972): 100–108.
Rodrigues Lapa, M. "Otero Pedrayo e o problema da língua." *Grial* 55 (1977): n.p.

Kathleen March

OUDIN, César (?, ?–1625, ?), French polyglot, grammarian, Hispanophile. Royal translator for the king of France (for German, Italian, Flemish and Spanish), his major publications include a Spanish grammar (1606?), his translation of the *Quijote* (1614), and the *Tesoro de las dos lenguas francesa y española* (1607; Thesaurus of French and Spanish Languages). He also published a *Refranes o proverbios castellanos traducidos al francés* (1605; Spanish Sayings or Proverbs Translated to French).

BIBLIOGRAPHY

Primary Texts

Refranes o proverbios castellanos traducidos al francés. Paris: Sommaville, 1659.

Tesoro de las dos lenguas francesa y española. Paris: Hispano-Americanas, 1968. Facs. of 1675 ed.

Le valeureux don Quijote de la Mancha. 3rd ed. Paris: Fouet, 1620.

English Translation

A grammar Spanish and Englishe . . . Composed in French by Caesar Oudin . . . Englished . . . by I. Wadsworth. London: Haviland, 1622.

Criticism

Morel Fatio, A. *Ambrosio de Salazar et L'étude de l'espagnol en France sous Louis XIII*. Paris: Picard; Toulouse: Privat, 1900.

P

PACHECO, Francisco de (1535, Jerez de la Frontera–1599, Seville), humanist, Latinist, canon of the Cathedral of Seville. Although only fragments of his literary activities survive, Pacheco's peers unanimously extolled his erudition. In addition to a distinguished career within the church, Pacheco was a major force in the intellectual and cultural life of Seville; his home came to serve as the gathering place, or *Academia, for scholars and literati of the city. When his nephew, of the same name, was orphaned, Pacheco took him in and supervised his education, exposing him to the finest and latest humanistic influences of the day. Pacheco the uncle was also praised by contemporaries for his poetry, both in Latin and Spanish. *See also*, Humanism; Pacheco, Francisco de (b. 1564).

BIBLIOGRAPHY

Criticism

Brown, Jonathan. *Images and Ideas in Seventeenth-Century Spanish Painting*. Princeton: Princeton UP, 1978.

PACHECO, Francisco de (1564, Sanlúcar de Barrameda–1654?, Seville?), painter, poet, art theorist. Nephew of Francisco de *Pacheco (1535–1599), father-in-law to famed painter Diego Velázquez de Silva, Pacheco spent formative years at his uncle's home in Seville, meeting virtually all the cultural leaders of the city there. Trips to Madrid and Toledo expanded his circle of contacts further. In 1599 he published the *Libro de descripciones de verdaderos retratos de ilustres y memorables varones* (Descriptive Book of True Portraits of Illustrious and Memorable Gentlemen), a biographic, bibliographic and pictorial description of the most important members of late sixteenth- and early seventeenth-c. culture in Seville. The first edition of Fernando de *Herrera's poetry was published by Pacheco in 1619. In 1638 he wrote, and in 1649 published, his main theoretical work, *Arte de la pintura* (The Art of Painting), which gives a historical overview of past art theories, especially Italian, discusses some Spanish painters, and offers his own theories on painting. Pacheco also left some poetry which clearly belongs to the **escuela sevillana* tradition.

BIBLIOGRAPHY

Primary Texts

Arte de la pintura. Ed. F. J. Sánchez Cantón. 2 vols. Madrid: Valencia de Don Juan, 1956.

Fernando de Herrera y la escuela sevillana. Ed. G. Chiappini. Madrid: Taurus, 1985. 36–38 and 175–81.

Libro de . . . retratos. Ed. E. de Asensio y Toledo. Seville: Tarascó, 1886.

Poesías. In BAE 32.

Criticism

See Chiappini, ed. *Fernando de Herrera*, in Primary Texts.

PAÇO D'ARCOS, Joaquim Belford Correia da Silva (1908, Lisbon–1979, Lisbon), Portuguese novelist and playwright. The second son of a noble family of diplomats. His elder brother Henrique (Anrique) Paço d'Arcos was also a writer though achieving lesser fame. His childhood and youth were spent overseas, first in Angola, then Macao and Mozambique according to the various colonial governorships held by his father. This way of life continued during his early adult life, during which time he was his father's private secretary. He then emigrated for a time, first to Brazil, where he worked as a businessman and journalist, moving thereafter to France. The latter part of his active career was spent with the Portuguese Ministry of External Affairs as chief of the Press Relations Office. He was also for a time president of the Portuguese Society of Authors.

A onetime pupil of Camilo *Pessanha, he became a prolific writer. Initially, the novel and short story attracted his attention, though he turned progressively to writing for the theater and critical essays. There is also one volume of poetry, *Poemas Imperfeitos* (1952; Imperfect Poems), but it played no great part in his literary development.

His novels and short stories divide into three phases, the first being largely autobiographical and set in Africa and the Orient. Such are *Herói Derradeiro* (1932; The Last Hero), *Amores e Viagens de Pedro Manuel* (1935; Pedro Manuel's Loves and Travels) and *Diário de um Emigrante* (1936; Diary of an Emigrant). The second period sees novels analyzing the various levels of life among the Lisbon bourgeoisie between the two World Wars. They carry the generic title of "Crónica da Vida Lisboeta" (Chronicle of Lisbon Life) and have a Balzacian touch to them. They are *Ana Paula* (1938), *Ansiedade* (1940; Anxiety) and *O Caminho da Culpa* (1944; The Road to Shame). The third and last phase is more cosmopolitan in background, as witness the short stories *A Neve Sobre o Mar* (1942; Snow on the Sea) and *O Navio dos Mortos* (1952; Ship of the Dead) and the novel *Tons Verdes em Fundo Obscuro* (1946; Shades of Green on a Dark Background), which take their inspiration from a world at war and Portugal's uneasy neutrality.

His plays conform on the whole to the second two phases of his prose writing. He wrote a number of essays on the art of the novelist and on current affairs.

He was awarded the Eça de Queiroz Prize in 1936 for *Diário de um Emigrante* and the Fialho de Almeida Prize in 1942 for *A Neve Sobre o Mar*.

BIBLIOGRAPHY

Primary Texts

Crónica da Vida Lisboeta. Ed. António Soares Amora et al. Rio de Janeiro: José Aguilar, 1974.
Teatro I. Lisbon: Guimarães, n.d. [1965].
O Crime Inútil. Lisbon: Guimarães, 1984.

Criticism

Cruz, Duarte Ivo. *O Teatro de Joaquim Paço d'Arcos*. Braga: Cruz, 1965.
Malpique, Manuel da Cruz. *Joaquim Paço d'Arcos, O Homem e a Obra*. (Lisbon) *Ocidente* 52 (1962). Special Issue devoted to Paço d'Arcos.

Peter Fothergill-Payne

PADILLA, Juan de (1468, Seville–1522?, Seville), poet. Juan de Padilla was a member of the Carthusian monastic order (Santa María de las Cuevas, in Seville), and for that reason is often referred to as *El Cartujano*. He is one of the last practitioners of the Dantesque allegorical tradition in Spain, as well as the last Spanish poet to compose in *coplas de *arte mayor*.

Padilla's long heroic poem, *Laberinto del Marqués de Cádiz* (1493; Labyrinth of the Marquis of Cádiz), as well as some mythological fables written in his youth, have unfortunately been lost. His most important extant works are the *Retablo de la vida de Cristo* (Seville, 1513, Altarpiece of the Life of Christ) and *Los doce triunfos de los doce Apóstoles* (Seville, 1521; The Twelve Triumphs of the Twelve Apostles). Padilla's mode of expression is more Dantesque than Juan de *Mena's (cf. the latter's *Trescientas*), although in the historical episodes he is Mena's inferior; Mena's influence on him seems to have been principally in the area of Latinate syntax and diction, in the use (or abuse) of which devices he often outstrips his model. *See also* Italian Literary Influences.

BIBLIOGRAPHY

Primary Texts

Los doce triunfos de los doce Apóstoles; fragments of the *Retablo de la vida de Cristo*. In *Cancionero castellano del siglo XI*. Ed. R. Foulché-Delbosc. Madrid: Bailly-Ballière, 1915. 1: 288–449.
Los doce triunfos de los doce Apóstoles. vol. 1. Ed. Enzo N. Guardini. Florence: Istituto Ispánico, 1975.

Criticism

De Vries, H. *Materia mirable: Estudio de la composición numérico-simbólica en las dos obras contemplativas de Juan de Padilla, el Cartujano*. Groningen: Offsetdrukkerij, 1972.
Gimeno Casalduero, J. "Castilla en *Los doce triunfos* del Cartujano." *HR* 39 (1971): 357–77.
———. "Sobre El Cartujano y sus críticos." *HR* 29 (1961): 1–14.

Herrero García, M. "Nota al Cartujano." *Revue Internationale des Études Basques* 15 (1924): 589.

Tarré, J. "*El retablo de la vida de Cristo* compuesto por el Cartujano de Sevilla." *Archivum Historicum Societatis Iesu* (Rome) 25 (1956): 243–53.

William Ferguson

PADILLA, Pedro de (?, Linares–c. 1599, ?), poet. According to Lope de *Vega in the *Laurel de Apolo*, Pedro de Padilla was born in Linares. He entered the Carmelite order in Madrid in 1585; we know that he was still alive in 1599, since he approved Lope's *Isidro* in that year.

He was attacked by Prete Jacopín (Juan Fernández de Velasco, Condestable de Castilla) in the latter's bitter *Observaciones* on Fernando de *Herrera's edition of *Garcilaso de la Vega. But Padilla was held in high esteem as a poet by other contemporaries, including Lope and *Cervantes. The latter wrote a number of laudatory verses for Padilla's books. These include the following titles: *Tesoro de varias poesías* (Madrid, 1580; Treasury of Poems); *Romancero* (1583; Ballad Book); *Jardín espiritual* (1585; Spiritual Garden), and *Grandezas y excelencias de la Virgen Señora Nuestra* (1581; Greatness and Excellence of the Virgin Mary). The *Tesoro* comprises the first part of his poems; the second part is the collection entitled *Eglogas pastoriles* (Sevilla, 1582; Pastoral Eclogues).

Pedro de Padilla's poetry is very much of his time, without any distinguishing characteristics that would make it remarkable among the works of his contemporaries. But his verse is eminently respectable, and at times achieves a high level of poetic expression. He is also known for his translations, including *La verdadera historia, y admirable suceso del segundo cerco de Diu, estando don Juan Mazcarenhas por capitán y gobernador* (Alcalá, 1597: History of the Second Siege of Diu under don Juan Mazcarenhas; tr. from the Portuguese of Jerónimo Corterreal), and the *Monarchia de Christo* (Valladolid, 1590; The Reign of Christ).

BIBLIOGRAPHY

Primary Texts

Romancero de Pedro de Padilla. Sociedad de Bibliófilos Españoles 19. Madrid: Ginesta, 1880.

Selected poems in BAE 35.

Criticism

Bajona Oliveras, I. "La amistad de Cervantes con Pedro de Padilla." *Anales Cervantinos* 5 (1955–56): 231–41.

Fucilla, J. G. "Le dernier poème de Pedro de Padilla." *BH* 57 (1955): 133–36.

———. "Pedro de Padilla and the Current of the Italian. Quattrocentist Preciosity in Spain." *Philological Quarterly* (Iowa) 9 (1930): 225–38.

Pérez Gómez, Antonio. "*El Jardín espiritual* de Pedro de Padilla: peculiaridades bibliográficas." In *Homage to John M. Hill*. Ed. Walter Poesse. Bloomington: Indiana UP, 1965. 59–63.

Rodríguez Marín, Francisco. ''Documentos sobre fray Pedro de Padilla.'' *BRAE* 5 (1918): 313.

William Ferguson

PADRÓN, Justo Jorge (1943, Las Palmas, Canary Islands–), Spanish poet and critic. Padrón studied law and liberal arts at the U of Barcelona, continuing in Paris, Stockholm and Oslo (where he became familiar with Scandinavian poets and poetry). He now lives in Madrid, where he founded and edits the international journal *Equivalences*. He has served as general secretary of the Spanish PEN Club since 1983, is a corresponding member of several academies (including the Mallarmé Academy of Paris, the International Pontzen Academy of Naples, the North American Academy of the Spanish Language, and the World Academy of Arts and Culture). A founding member of the European Poetry Festival held in Leuven (Belgium), he also belongs to the International Committee of the World Congresses of Poets.

Padrón's poetry has received considerable recognition in the form of translations into twenty-seven languages, and twenty international prizes, including the International Grand Prize of the Swedish Academy (1972), the Fastenrath Prize of the *Academia Española (1977), the Biennial Award of the Swedish Writers' Association (1977), the Brussels Gold Medal of French Culture (1981), Gustavo Adolfo Bécquer Medal of Honor (1984), and Zeus Cultural Award (Athens, 1985). His books of poetry include *Los oscuros fuegos* (1971; Dark Fires); *Mar de la noche* (1973; Sea of the Night); *Los círculos del infierno* (1976; The Circles of Hell); *El abedul en llamas* (1978; The Birch Tree in Flames); *Otesnita* (1979); *La visita del mar* (1984; The Sea's Visit); *Los dones de la tierra* (1984; The Gifts of Earth); *Sólo muere la mano que te escribe* (1988; Only the Hand That Writes You Dies).

Padrón belongs to a group of younger Spanish poets including Antonio *Colinas and Jaime Silas. Although Padrón is at times a neo-Romantic like Colinas, his work seldom evinces the distancing of the culturists, recalling instead the introspective, meditative lyrics of Francisco *Brines (to whom Padrón dedicated his second book). Destructive aspects of time are a major concern of Padrón's poetry, which covers the gamut from hope to desolation, from the obsession with death's grimness to hope of salvation, or refuge in eroticism or in nature. *Los oscuros fuegos* is the poet's farewell to youth, expressing a sense of failure or defeat in contending with time and hostile reality and looking ahead to the hallucinatory imagery of *Los círculos del infierno*, in which the poetic identity becomes fog, smoke, insubstantiality. This third book abounds in negative images of the human condition, beset by a sense of existential void, monotony and regimentation. The oppressive effects of bureaucratic and military regulation are another theme. Uncertainty as to the nature of reality, the border between dreams, hallucinations and imagination on the one hand and ''true'' reality on the other, appears in *Mar de la noche*. *El abedul en llamas*, by contrast, expresses a certain innocence, as the idyllic nature of Scandinavia contributes to healing the poet's wounded spirit, as he attempts to escape from his own darker self and find light and rebirth in the beauty of earth and cosmos. *Otesnita*, inspired by a brief love affair, contrasts impossible ideal tenderness with loss and disappointment, beauty and delight with despair. *La visita del mar* reiterates two major thematic nuclei, the sense of wonder and delight at nature, and man's existential fear and doubt upon contemplating the inevitable reality of death. *Los dones de la tierra* centers around the four basic elements—earth, air, fire, and water—as a lyric escape from personal and metaphysical uncertainty, but the poet returns to metaphysical preoccupation in *Sólo muere la mano que te escribe*, a collection suffused with memory, with sensual love poems, and a vision of cosmic reality as a place beyond death.

BIBLIOGRAPHY

English Translations

On the Cutting Edge. Selected Poems, tr. Louis Bourne. London: Forest Books, 1989.

Janet Pérez

PÁEZ DE CASTRO, Juan (1515?, Quer, Guadalajara–1570, Quer), humanist, scholar. Fluent in Greek, Latin, Italian, Hebrew and Arabic, a student of math, history and law, he participated in many cultural activities of the day and counted among his friends Juan de *Vergara, Ambrosio de *Morales, Diego *Hurtado de Mendoza, Florián de *Ocampo, etc. It was his idea to establish a library which would serve as repository for all types of knowledge and scholarship. He presented his plan, which included advice on how to acquire mss. and books, and the physical plan of the building, to Philip II. Páez de Castro also left behind an interesting body of correspondence. *See also* Humanism; Renaissance.

BIBLIOGRAPHY

Primary Text

Juan Páez de Castro. N.p.: n.p., n.d.

Criticism

García López, J. C. *Biblioteca de escritores de la provincia de Guadalajara*. Madrid: Rivadeneyra, 1899.

PÁEZ DE RIBERA, Ruy (late fourteenth c., Seville?–after 1424, ?), poet. His fourteen extant pieces are found in the *Cancionero de *Baena*. Titles such as "Destierro e la Pobreza" (Exile and Poverty), "Proceso que ovieron en uno la Dolencia e la Vejez" (Trial Which Ocurred between Ailment and Age) are felt to be based on personal experiences, but almost no other information about Páez de Ribera has been found.

BIBLIOGRAPHY

Primary Texts

Cancionero de Baena. Ed. José María Azáceta. 3 vols. Madrid: CSIC, 1966.
"Proceso entre la soberbia e la mesura." See Place, in Criticism.

Criticism

Place, E. B. "More about Ruy Páez de Ribera." *HR* 14 (1946): 22–37.

PALACIO, Manuel del (1831, Lérida–1906, Madrid), journalist and political satirist. The son of a soldier, he spent his childhood living in various regions of Spain. In 1861 he became a member of the famous literary group *La Cuerda* in Granada. He collaborated on most of the periodicals of his day: as editor of *La Discusión* (1868), *El Regulador* (1859) and *El Pueblo* (1860); as founder of the satirical paper *Gil Blas* (1864–70); and as director of *Nosotros* (1858–59), *El Mosquito* (1864–69), *El Comercio* (1860) and *El Pensador Ilustrado* (1866). Palacio was exiled to Puerto Rico in 1867, shortly before the September Revolution, for his political activities. With the victory of the revolution, he returned to Spain and held various administrative posts with the Ministry of State: secretary of the Spanish embassy in Florence, Spanish representative in Uruguay, director of the library archives of the Ministry of State. He became a member of the *Academia Española in 1892. *Clarín called him "half a poet" when saying that in Spain there were only two and a half poets, *Campoamor, *Núñez de Arce and Manuel del Palacio. Palacio responded with the pamphlet *Clarín entre dos platos* (1889; Clarín on a Silver Platter).

He cultivated political satire in prose and verse. Collaborating with Luis Rivera, he collected humorous stories of other writers in *Museo Cómico o Tesoro de los chistes, cuentos y fábulas* (1863; Comedy Museum, or Treasury of Jokes, Stories and Fables); the following year they wrote *Cabezas y calabazas* (1864; Heads and Pumpkins), a series of caricatures of well-known writers, artists and politicians. Years later, Palacio published *Páginas sueltas* (1901; Loose Pages), a collection of articles and poems written for different periodicals. The miscellaneous nature of his work is reflected in the titles *Doce reales de prosa y algunos versos gratis* (1864; Twelve Cents Worth of Prose and Some Verses for Free) and *Fruta verde* (1881; Unripe Fruit). Political essays of an anecdotal nature are collected in *De Tetuán a Valencia, haciendo noche en Miraflores* (1865; From Tetuan to Valencia, Sleeping Over in Miraflores). Palacio's principal poetic works are collected in the following volumes: *Cien sonetos políticos, filosóficos, biográficos, amorosos, tristes y alegres* (1870: One Hundred Political, Philosophical, Biographical, Amorous, Sad and Happy Sonnets), *Letra menuda* (1877; Small Handwriting), *Melodías íntimas* (1884; Intimate Melodies) and *Chispas* (1894; Sparks). In *Veladas de otoño* (1884; Autumn Evenings) he collected traditional legends in the style of *Zorrilla. Juan *Valera considered Palacio's legends to be superior to those of Zorrilla. Valera also admired the elegance, purity, and skill of Palacio's verse. Palacio is best known for the wit and irony of his satirical poems such as "Los envidiosos" (The Envious Ones). As one of the principal sonnet writers of the nineteenth c., he used the form to caricature well-known figures of the day. Palacio also composed serious sonnets on philosophical ideas and the theme of love. An excellent versifier, his language is simple and straightforward, despite constant wordplay.

BIBLIOGRAPHY

Primary Texts

Poesías escogidas. Ed. J. O. Picón. Madrid: RABM, 1916.
Cabezas y calabazas. Madrid: Guijarro, 1864.
Chispas. Madrid: Delgado, 1894.
Cien sonetos políticos, filosóficos. . . . Madrid: Fortanet, 1870.
De Tetuán a Valencia, haciendo noche en Miraflores. Madrid: Centro General de Administración, 1865.

Criticism

Sánchez, L., and J. Cascales. *Antología de la Cuerda granadina*. Mexico: M. León Sánchez, 1928.
Sandoval, M. De. "Manuel del Palacio." *BRAE* 18 (1931): 691–711.
Robles, J. "Notas sobre Manuel del Palacio." *MLN* 44 (1928): 43–69.

Phoebe Porter Medina

PALACIO VALDÉS, Armando (1853, Entralgo, Asturias–1938, Madrid), novelist. Palacio Valdés, like his good friend Leopoldo Alas (*Clarín) and the younger Ramón Pérez de Ayala, is closely identified with Asturias, its settings, people, and especially its sense of humor, somewhat akin to Dickens's. Raised in Avilés, he later studied in Oviedo and received his law degree from the U of Madrid. He has written engagingly of his childhood and youth in *La novela de un novelista* (1921; The Novel of a Novelist). His early days reflect the exuberant, liberal times of the Revolution of 1868. He was later to retreat somewhat from this youthful position, fervently embracing Mother Church in his mature years. Evidence of a critical and even biting view of Spanish society, literature, and religion is visible in his early efforts at criticism, in his contributions to the journal *Revista Europea*—most, but not all, later published as *Los oradores del Ateneo* (1878; Orators of the Atheneum), *Los novelistas españoles* (1878; Spanish Novelists), and *Nuevo viaje al Parnaso* (1879; New Expedition to Parnassus)—and the volume, *La literatura en 1881* (1882; Literature in 1881, written in collaboration with Leopoldo Alas). On José María de *Pereda's death in 1906, he was elected to his place in the *Academia Española, but he did not deliver his acceptance speech until December 1920. He died during the final bitter moments of the Spanish Civil War, having outlived his times and his fellow novelists of the Generation of 1868.

Palacio Valdés's first novel, *El señorito Octavio*, appeared in 1881 and was subtitled a "novel without transcendence." It is a curious, uneven blend of melodrama, passion, and character satire. It is not until his second and more popular novel, *Marta y María* (1883; *Martha and Mary*, 1886), that the Asturian writer finds his literary stride in the sharp character analysis he applied to the two women. This novel, like most of his work, is regional—Asturian—in setting and character. Other Asturian scenarios are found in *José* (1885; *José*, 1961), an absorbing love story among fisherfolk, *El idilio de un enfermo* (1884; Idyll of a Sick Man), *El cuarto poder* (1888; *The Fourth Estate*, 1901), on the power of the press, *La fe* (1892; *Faith*, 1892), on false mysticism (already touched on in *Marta y María*) and the adulterous priest figure, *El maestrante* (1893; *The Grandee*, 1894), and *La aldea perdida* (1903; The Lost Village), a nostalgic evocation of a pre-industrial Asturias and its destruction by modern-day progress. ''Yes! I too was born and lived in Arcadia,'' writes Palacio Valdés in the ''Invocation'' to this last-named novel: like his autobiographical writings, this work provides us with a key to one of Palacio Valdés's essential, underlying myths—the association between childhood and the (lost) paradise of his native Asturias. Two novels set principally in Madrid—*Riverita* (1886) and *Maximina* (1887; *Maximina*, 1888)—are also autobiographical in tone and story, reflecting the author's first, bittersweet marriage with Luisa Maximina Prendes Busto (1883–85). For Miguel de *Unamuno, *Maximina* was one of those rare, moving novels which remained engraved in his memory. *La espuma* (1891; *Froth*, 1891) is another novel of the capital, dealing mainly with the upper class; while the delightful *La hermana San Sulpicio* (1889; *Sister Saint Sulpice*, 1890), his most popular piece of fiction, is set in Andalusia. Other novels include *La alegría del capitán Ribot* (1899; *The Joy of Captain Ribot*, 1900), *Los majos de Cádiz* (1896; The Dandies of Cádiz), *La hija de Natalia* (1924; Natalie's Daughter), and *Santa Rogelia* (1926; Saint Rogelia). *Tristán o el pesimismo* (1906; *Tristan,* 1925), an interesting psychological study, remained one of Palacio Valdés's personal favorites (see ed. by M. Baquero Goyanes, 1971). He also published short story collections, memoirs, a historical essay, *El gobierno de las mujeres* (1931; Government by Women), and another on World War I, *La guerra injusta* (1917; The Unjust War).

Palacio Valdés practiced a form of moderate realism in his fiction, shying away in general from the extremes of idealism and naturalism. The result: pleasant novels of manners for the most part, in which he excelled in character analysis—particularly secondary, flat types—and the creation of setting. His style—clear, natural, gently humorous—reflects his desire to please his middle-class readership, to transmit the image of a warm and kindly narrator, who regrettably at times falls into sticky sentimentality. There are, however, exceptions to this good-humored, albeit cautious, optimism, exceptions such as his first novel, *Marta y María*, *Tristán*, and so on, which show the writer to be quite the reverse of a smiling Pangloss, even indulging in a certain morbid curiosity for the unhealthy and unnatural in his characters. Many of his novels are structured round the idea of contrast, or dualism (*El señorito Octavio*, *Marta y María*, *José*, *Tristán*, etc.). Palacio Valdés was an enormously popular writer, not only in Spain but abroad as well, as the numerous translations—especially into English—demonstrate. D. L. Shaw attributes this popularity to Palacio Valdés's refusal to follow through with the fictional difficulties, psychological and otherwise, he created: ''he knew how to construct a strong fictional situation, but lacked the tough-mindedness to work it out'' (*A Literary History of Spain. The Nineteenth Century*, 1972). Not a deep writer, he isn't extraordinary like Clarín and Galdós, but he certainly is worthwhile, if accepted on his own—circumscribed—terms.

BIBLIOGRAPHY

Primary Texts

Obras completas. 19 vols. Madrid: Suárez, 1894–1919; 24 vols. Madrid: Suárez, 1908–27; 2 vols. Madrid: Aguilar, 1935.

Tristan o el pesimismo. Ed. M. Baquero Goyanes. Madrid: Narcea, 1971.

English Translations

Faith. Tr. I. F. Hapgood. New York: Cassell, 1892.

The Fourth Estate. Tr. R. Challice. New York: Brentano's, 1901.

Froth. Tr. C. Bell. London: Heinemann, 1891.

The Grandee. Tr. R. Challice. London: Heinemann, 1894.

José. Tr. H. de Onís. New York: Barron's, 1961.

The Joy of Captain Ribot. Tr. M. C. Smith. London: World Fiction Library, 1923.

Martha and Mary. Tr. W. H. Bishop. In *Library of the World's Best Literature.* Ed. C. D. Warner. New York: Warner, 1917. Excerpt.

Maximina. Tr. N. H. Dole. New York/Boston: Crowell, 1888.

Sister Saint Sulpice. Tr. N. H. Dole. New York: Crowell, 1925.

Tristan. Tr. J. B. Reid. Boston: Four Seas, 1925.

Criticism

Boletín del Instituto de Estudios Asturianos (1953). Homage volume.

Cruz Rueda, A. *Armando Palacio Valdés. Su vida y su obra.* 2nd ed. Granada: Prieto, 1938.

Gómez-Ferrer Morant, G. "Armando Palacio Valdés en la transición del XIX al XX." *Revista de la Universidad Complutense de Madrid* 28.116 (1979): 231–60.

Pascual Rodríguez, M. *Armando Palacio Valdés. Teoría y práctica novelística.* Madrid: Sociedad General Española de Librería, 1976.

Roca Franquesa, J. M. *Palacio Valdés: técnica novelística y credo estético.* Oviedo: Instituto de Estudios Asturianos, 1951.

Shaw, D. L. *A Literary History of Spain.* New York: Barnes and Noble, 1972.

Valis, N. M. "Palacio Valdes' First Novel." *RN* 20.3 (1980): n.p.

Noël M. Valis

PALACIOS-RUBIOS, Juan López de (1450?, Palacios Rubios, Salamanca–1525?, ?), distinguished jurist, adviser to the monarchy for twenty years. He studied and taught at the U of Salamanca, and was also a professor at the U of Valladolid. As royal adviser, he played a key role in the political and theological debate over the Indians in the New World, and influenced Spanish policy in the New World, as seen in his *Libellus de insulis oceanis* (written c. 1512–14; Book on the Oceanic Islands). His last extant work is the *El tratado del esfuerzo bélico heroico* (1524; Treatise on Heroic Martial Deeds), which praises valor. *See also* Black Legend.

BIBLIOGRAPHY

Primary Texts

De las islas del Mar Océano. . . . Intro. S. Závala. Tr., notes, bibliog. A. Millares Carlo. Mexico: Fondo de Cultura Económica, 1954.

Tratado del esfuerzo bélico heroico. Madrid: RO, 1941.

Criticism

Bullón, E. *Un colaborador de los Reyes Católicos. El Doctor Palacios Rubios y sus Obras.* Madrid: Suárez, 1927.

See also Závala's introduction and Millares Carlo's notes to *De las islas del Mar Océano,* in Primary Texts.

PALAFOX Y MENDOZA, Juan (1600, Fitero, Navarre–1659, Osma), bishop, prose writer. An illegitimate child of a distinguished Aragonese family, he studied in Salamanca, was ordained, and in 1610 arrived in Mexico as bishop of Puebla. He held this position for thirty-nine years, and was an active supporter of education and culture, as well as religious matters. In 1649 he returned to Spain and there held the position of Bishop of Osma until his death.

Palafox left some 565 pieces in his corpus of writing, and covered many subjects: religious, biographical, historical, political, moral and literary. His *Tratados mejicanos* (writings from 1649 to 1659; Mexican Treatises) are a compilation of valuable historical information. *Año espiritual* (1656; *The Spiritual Year,* 1693) reveals sincere religious spirit. *Vida interior* (1687; Inner Life) is his own very interesting spiritual autobiography.

BIBLIOGRAPHY

Primary Texts

Año espiritual. Brussels: Foppens, 1662.

Libro de las virtudes del indio. Mexico: Secretaria de Educación Pública, 1950.

Obras. 13 vols. Madrid: Ramírez, 1742.

Tratados mejicanos. Study by F. Sánchez Castaner. In BAE 217–18.

Varón de deseos: que se declaran. . . . Madrid: Cano, 1786.

Vida interior. In *Virtudes del indio.* Madrid: Minuesa, 1893.

English Translation

Christmas nights' entertainments. Tr. Kelly. N.p.: Piet, 1871.

The History of the Conquest of China by the Tartars. N.p.: Deep and Deep, 1978.

The Spiritual year: or Devout contemplations, digested into distinct arguments for every month in the year. . . . London: S. Smith, 1693.

Criticism

García, Genaro. *Don Juan de Palafox y Mendoza.* Mexico: Bouret, 1918.

Porqueras-Mayo, A. "La colección Palafox: Fondos raros en la Universidad de Illinois." *XVII Congreso del Instituto Internacional de Literatura Iberoamericana.* 3 vols. Madrid: Centro Iberoamericano, 1978. 1:311–326.

Sánchez-Castaner, F. "Don Juan de Palafox, escritor barroco hispanoamericano." *XVII Congreso del Instituto Internacional de Literatura Iberoamericana.* 3 vols. Madrid: Centro Iberoamericano, 1978. 1:297–309.

———. "La obra literaria de Juan de Palafox y Mendoza, escritor hispanoamericano." *Actas del Tercer Congreso Internacional de Hispanistas.* Mexico: Colegio de Mēxico, 1970.

PALAU, Bartolomé (c. 1525, Burbáguena, Teruel–?, ?), Aragonese priest and early dramatist. Very little is known of Palau's personal history other than that he studied at the U of Salamanca. His earliest known work is the *Farsa llamada Custodia del hombre* (1547; Corpus Christi Play), an allegorical piece composed of five acts of **pie quebrado* verse for the annual Corpus Christi festival. His six-act *Historia de la gloriosa Santa Orosia* (c. 1550; Life of Saint Orosia) is significant primarily because it appears to have been the first Spanish drama to derive subject matter from national history. Because he was Aragonese, Palau was familiar with traditional versions of the saint's life, and he blended these with popular accounts concerning Count Julian, King Rodrigo, La Cava, and the fall of Visigothic power in Spain. *La farsa llamada salamantina* (1552; Salamancan Farce), a *picaresque work in five acts with ten-line strophes of *pie quebrado*, was apparently produced for students at the University. Palau's *Victoria Christi* (1569; The Victory of Christ) was so successful that it was printed a minimum of nine times. An Easter play in six parts apparently borrowed from one of Gil *Vicente's works, it details the redemption of the world through Christ's birth against a background of Old and New Testament traditions. *See also* Theater in Spain.

BIBLIOGRAPHY

Primary Texts

Farsa llamada Custodia del hombre. Ed. Léo Rouanet. In "Bartolomé Palau y sus obras: *Farsa llamada Custodia del hombre*." *Archivo de Investigaciones Históricas* 1 (1911): 267–303, 357–90, 535–64; 2 (1911): 93–154.

La farsa llamada salamantina. Ed. Alfred Morel-Fatio. In "La *Farsa llamada Salamantina* de Bartolomé Palau." *BH* 2 (1900): 237–304.

Victoria Christi (1670 ed.). Spanish Drama of the Golden Age; microfilm reel 80. New Haven: Research Publications, 1972.

Criticism

Crawford, James P. Wickersham. *Spanish Drama before Lope de Vega*. Rev. ed. Philadelphia: U of Pennsylvania P, 1967.

House, Ralph E. "Sources of Bartolomé Palau's *Farsa Salamantina*." *RR* 4 (1913): 311–22.

See also Morel-Fatio, *La farsa llamada salamantina*, in Primary Texts.

C. Maurice Cherry

PALAU, Melchor (1843, Mataró–1910, Madrid), lawyer, poet, philologist and critic. Most of his poetry—in Catalan as well as in Spanish—falls into one of two categories: (1) scientific, with poems like "A la Imprenta" (To Printing), "A la Geología" (To Geology), or "Al polo ártico" (To the Arctic Pole), found in *Verdades poéticas* (1879; Poetic Truths); and (2) popular verse, as in *Cantares* (1878; Songs) and *Nuevos Cantares* (1890; New Songs). As a philologist he compiled a *Diccionario de catalanismos* (n.d.; Dictionary of Catalanisms). He was admitted to the *Academia Española in 1908.

BIBLIOGRAPHY

Primary Texts

Acontecimientos literarios: impresiones y notas bibliográficas, 1895. Madrid: Huérfanos del Sagrado Corazón de Jesús, 1896.

Cantares populares y literarios. Barcelona: Montaner y Simón, 1900.

Poesies catalanes. Barcelona: L'Avenç, 1906.

Verdades poéticas. 6th ed. Barcelona: Granada, 1908.

PALENCIA, Alfonso Fernández de (1423, Osma, Soria–1492, ?), chronicler, essayist and translator. Relative of Alonso de *Cartagena, he had a solid humanistic background. When he was seventeen, he went to Italy, where he studied and figured among the relatives of Cardinal Bessarion and the disciples of the Greek humanist Jorge de Trebisonda. He returned to Spain in 1453 and later succeeded Juan de *Mena as Latin secretary and chronicler to Henry IV. Later on Palencia would change to the side of the king's younger brother, Alfonso, and play an important role in the negotiations to arrange the marriage of Isabel and Ferdinand.

Palencia wrote copiously; some of his works are lost. His most important books are *Batalla campal entre los lobos y los perros* (1457?; Pitched Battle between Wolves and Dogs), an allegorical work full of allusions to events and historical characters at the time of Henry IV; his critical and yet patriotic *Perfección del triunfo militar* (1459; Perfection of the Military Triumph), where he vaunts his countrymen as among the best fighting men in Europe; and *Gesta hispaniensia ex annalibus suorum dierum colligentis* (1477), also known as *Décadas* (Decades), a chronicle of the disturbed and corrupt reign of Henry IV (1454–74). The book has been translated into Spanish with the title of *Crónica de Enrique IV* (1904–12; Chronicle of Henry IV). Palencia preceded *Nebrija with the earliest Spanish-Latin dictionary, *Universal vocabulario* (1491; Universal Vocabulary), and also elegantly translated works of Plutarch and Flavius Josephus. *See also* Humanism.

BIBLIOGRAPHY

Primary Texts

Crónica de Enrique IV. Tr. A. Paz y Mélia. *Colección de escritores castellanos*. Vols. 126, 127, 130 and 134. Madrid: Revista de archivos, 1904–12.

Gesta hispaniensia ex annalibus suorum dierum colligentis. Madrid: Academia de la Historia, 1835.

Dos tratados de Alfonso Palencia [Batalla campal entre los lobos y los perros and *Perfección del triunfo militar*]. Intro. Antonio María Fabié. Madrid: Durán, 1876.

Criticism

Hill, John M. *Alfonso de Palencia: Universal vocabulario. Registro de voces españolas internas*. Madrid: RAE, 1957.

Tate, R. B. "*El tratado de la perfección del triunfo militar de Alfonso de Palencia* (1459): La villa de discreción y la arquitectura humanista." In *Essays on Narrative Fiction*

in the Iberian Peninsula in Honour of Frank Pierce. Ed. R. B. Tate. Oxford: Dolphin, 1982. 163–73.
———. "Political Allegory in Fifteenth-Century Spain: A Study of the *Batalla campal de los perros contra los lobos* by Alfonso de Palencia (1423–92)." *Journal of Hispanic Philology* 1 (1977): 169–86.

Hector Medina

PALENCIA, Ceferino (1860, Fuente de Pedro Naharro, Cuenca–1928, Madrid), Spanish dramatist. He was married to the celebrated actress Maria Tubau, who was a magnificent interpreter of his works. As head of the theatrical company, Palencia traveled throughout the Americas with his wife, and upon her death, he assumed her position as professor of declamation at the Conservatory of Dramatic Art (1915). His more important works are *El cura de San Antonio* (n.d.; The Priest of San Antonio), *Cariños que matan* (1882; Deadly Affections); *El guardián de la casa* (1883; The Keeper of the House); *La charra* (1884; The Horsewoman), and *Currita Albornoz* (1897), based upon a character from the novel *Pequeñeces* (Picayune Things) by Father *Coloma, also adapted for the stage by Palencia; and *Pepita Tudó* (1901). He is remembered as a facile versifier and able observer of types and settings of his epoch, although he tends to moralize, somewhat in the fashion of Adelardo *López de Ayala.

PALLARÉS, Pilar (1957, Culleredo, La Coruña–), Galician poet. A secondary school teacher of Galician language and literature, Pallarés belongs to a younger generation of writers in the national language who are less socially oriented than those immediately preceding. More intimistic and carefully constructed, her poetry has benefited from readings of writers in other languages. A recipient of several literary awards, Pallarés has published poetry in several Galician journals. The post-Franco environment has rapidly seen the increase in Galician consciousness as evidenced by the author's choice of this language in which to write. Pallarés may be included among the growing group of feminist Galician writers. *See also* Galician Literature.

BIBLIOGRAPHY

Primary Texts

Entre lusco e fusco. Sada, La Coruña: Ediciós do Castro, 1980.
Sétima soidade. El Ferrol: Sociedade de Cultura Valle-Inclán, 1984.

Kathleen March

PALMA, El Bachiller Alonso (fifteenth c., Toledo?–?), historical author. Palma composed a history of Castile titled *Divina retribución sobre la caída de España en tiempo del noble rey Don Juan I* (Divine Retribution for the Fall of Spain in the Era of Don Juan I). This work covers the period from 1385, when the Castilians lost the battle of Aljubarrota, to 1478, date of the victory of Ferdinand and Isabel at Toro. This victory is viewed by the author as divine revenge or compensation for the loss suffered by Juan I. The ms. is preserved in the Escorial.

BIBLIOGRAPHY

Primary Text

Divina retribución sobre la caída de España en tiempo del noble Rey Juan el Primero. Ed. J. M. Escudero de la Peña. Madrid: Tello, 1879.

Lucy Sponsler

PALMA, Luis de la (1560, Toledo–1641, Madrid), Jesuit preacher, professor and ascetic writer. He taught at the U of Murcia, was a famed preacher, but published only at the behest of a superior in his order. Several works were published posthumously. His two most distinguished contributions to the corpus of Golden Age *ascetical literature are *Historia de la sagrada pasión* (1624; *The History of the Sacred Passion,* 1872) and *Camino espiritual de la manera que le enseña el bienaventurado padre San Ignacio* (1629; *A treatise on the particular examen of conscience, according to the method of St. Ignatius,* 1873).

BIBLIOGRAPHY

Primary Texts

Obras completas. In BAE 144, 145, and 160.

Obras: Historia de la sagrada pasión. Camino espiritual. Práctica y breve declaración del camino espiritual. Ed., study F. X. Rodríguez-Molero. Madrid: Católica, 1967.

English Translations

The History of the Sacred Passion. Tr., and rev. ed. H. J. Coleridge. London: Burns and Oates, 1889.

A treatise on the particular examen of conscience, according to the method of St. Ignatius. London: Burns and Oates, 1873.

Criticism

Rodríguez Molero, F. X. "Mística y estilo de la 'Historia de la Santa [sic] Pasión' del Padre la Palma." *Revista de Espiritualidad* 3 (1944): 295–331.

***PALMERÍN* Romances.** The *Palmerín* romances constitute one of the most important cycles of Castilian romances of chivalry, second only to the *Amadís* series. The first text, *Palmerín de Olivia* (1511), set in Constantinople, presents an account of the adventures of Palmerín and Polinarda. Hardly an unimaginative imitation of **Amadís de Gaula* as some critics have suggested, it is a romance rich in adventure and original in characterization. *Primaleón* (1516) continues the story line with the adventures of Primaleón and Polendos, sons of Palmerín and Polinarda, and adds another notable character, Don Duardos, prince of England, who inspired Gil *Vicente's play *Don Duardos*. Subsequent generations of the *Palmerín* family appear in *Platir* (1533), *Flotir* (1554, actually an Italian work, supposedly translated from the Spanish), and most significantly, *Palmerín de Inglaterra* (1547; *Palmerin of England*, 1807). The Toledan version, Luis *Hurtado de Toledo's translation of the 1544 Portuguese original by Francisco *Morães (1500?–1572), received *Cervantes's praise, as it, along with the

Amadís, was saved from the flames in the famous scrutiny of Don Quijote's library. *Palmerín de Inglaterra* contains few innovative techniques, but its plot is carefully structured and its style and characterization are exceptional. This work marks the end of the *Palmerín* cycle in Spain, though in Portugal there are other continuations of the *Palmerín de Inglaterra*. *See also* Caballerías, Libros de.

BIBLIOGRAPHY

Primary Texts

Libro del muy esforzado caballero Palmerín de Inglaterra. By Francisco de Morães. Ed. A. Bonilla y San Martín. NBAE 11. Madrid: NBAE, 1908.

Palmerín de Inglaterra. Ed. Luis Alberto de Cuenca. Madrid: Miraguano, 1979.

Palmerín de Olivia. Ed. Giuseppe Di Stefano. Vol. 1 of *Studi sul ''Palmerin de Olivia.''* Pisa: Università di Pisa, 1966.

English Translation

Palmerin of England. Tr. Anthony Munday. London: Longman, 1807.

Criticism

Eisenberg, Daniel. *Castilian Romances of Chivalry in the Sixteenth Century*. London: Grant and Cutler, 1979. (An indispensable bibliography.)

Mancini, Guido. ''Introducción al *Palmerín de Olivia*.'' In *Dos estudios de literatura española*. Barcelona: Planeta, 1969. 7–202 (A Spanish translation of vol. 2 of the *Studi sul ''Palmerin de Olivia.''* Pisa: Università di Pisa, 1966.)

Patchell, Mary. *The Palmerin Romances in Elizabethan Prose Fiction*. New York: Columbia UP, 1947.

Saggi e ricerche. Vol. 3 of *Studi sul ''Palmerín de Olivia.''* Pisa: Università di Pisa, 1966.

Thomas, Henry. *Spanish and Portuguese Romances of Chivalry*. Cambridge, England: Cambridge UP, 1920. rpt. New York: Kraus, 1969.

James Ray Green and Patricia Grieve

PALMIRENO, Juan Lorenzo (1514?, Alcáñiz, Teruel–1580, Valencia), professor, humanist. Palmireno was a classics professor at the Universities of Zaragoza and Valencia; his numerous Latin-Spanish vocabularies, geared to ease student mastery of Latin, attest to the enthusiasm he brought to his profession. Such titles include *Vocabulario del humanista* (1569; The Humanist's Vocabulary) and *El vocabulario de medidas y monedas* (1563; Vocabulary of Measures and Money). Of great interest is his *Rhetorica* (1546 and 1565; Rhetoric), as it contains various fragments of university school plays which were used for pedagogical purposes. *See also* Humanism; Universities.

BIBLIOGRAPHY

Primary Texts

El latino de repente. Barcelona: Cormellas, 1615.

Rhetorice prolegomena. Valencia: Mey, 1564.

Vocabulario del humanista. Barcelona: Malo, 1575.

Criticism

Gallego, A. "La risa en el teatro escolar de Juan Lorenzo Palmireno." In *Risa y sociedad en el teatro español del Siglo de Oro.* Paris: Centre Nat. de la Recherche Scientifique, 1980. 187–94.

———. "Juan Lorenzo Palmireno. Contribution à l'histoire de l'Université de Valencia." Diss., Toulouse, 1980.

Lynn, Caro. "Juan Lorenzo Palmireno, Spanish Humanist." *Hispania* 12 (1929): 243–58.

PÀMIES I BERTRAN, Teresa (1919, Balaguer, Lleida–), essayist and novelist. Exiled after the Spanish Civil War, she returned to Catalonia in 1971. She has lived in Mexico (where she studied journalism at the Universidad Femenina), Czechoslovakia, and France. She has written essays in the most prestigious magazines and newspapers of Spain: *Serra d'or*, *Oriflama*, *Canigò*, *Presència*, *Cuadernos para el Diálogo*, *Triunfo*, *Miundo Diaro*, and *Avui*.

Her fictional work deals mainly with the personal testimony of important moments of the history of Spain and Catalonia: civil war, exile, clandestinity, etc. This "documentary literature" constitutes most of her fictional world, sometimes in the form of "memories" or in other cases in books so structured. She is also one of the most important and original theoreticians of feminism in Marxist thought.

Major Works: *La filla del pres* (1967; The Convict's Daughter), *Va ploure tot el dia* (1974; It's Going to Rain All Day), *Quan érem capitans* (1974; When We Were Captains), *Quan érem refugiats* (1975; When We Were Refugees), *Dona de pres* (1975; The Convict's Woman), *Si vas a París, Papà . . .* (1975; If You Go to Paris, Daddy), *Amor clandestí* (1976; Secret Love), *Maig de les dones* (1976; May of the Women), *Records de guerra i d'exili* (1976; Memories of War and Exile), *Memòria dels morts* (1981; Memory of the Dead), *Opinió de dona* (1983; A Woman's Opinion), *Una española llamada Dolores Ibárruri (La Pasionaria)* (1976; A Spaniard Called Dolores Ibarruri [La Pasionaria]), *Romanticismo militante* (1976; Militant Romanticism), and together with her father, Tomàs Pàmies, *Testament a Praga* (1970; Testament in Prague).

She has been awarded many literary honors, among them the Premi Joan Estelrich, the Premi President Companys dels Jocs Florals de 1967, and the Premi Josep Pla.

BIBLIOGRAPHY

Primary Texts

Una española llamada Dolores Ibárruri (La Pasionaria). Barcelona: Martínez Roca, 1976.

Maig de les dones. Barcelona: Laia, 1976.

Quan érem capitans. Barcelona: Dopesa, 1974.

Records de guerra i d'exili. Barcelona: Dopesa, 1976.

Romanticismo militante. Barcelona: Galba, 1976.

Criticism

Riera Llorca, Vicenç. "La crònica novel·lesca de Teresa Pàmies." *Serra d'Or* (May 1977): 325–27.

Servià, J. M. *Catalunya, Tres generacions*. Barcelona: n.p., 1975. 133–51.

Joan Gilabert

PAMPHILUS DE AMORE, Latin play. Also called *Liber Pamphili*, it is a twelfth- or thirteenth-c. humanistic comedy that appears to derive from Ovid and Terence, but is clearly not the work of either author. The drama's importance for Spanish letters results from its influence on the fourteenth-c. author, Juan Ruiz, *Arcipreste de Hita, who paraphrased *Pamphilus* in the doña Endrina and don Melón episode of *Libro de buen amor*, stanzas 555–865.

BIBLIOGRAPHY

Primary Text

Una comedia latina del siglo XII: el "Liber Panphili" reproducción de un manuscrito in edito y versión castellana. Ed. A. Bonilla y San Martín. Madrid: Fortanet, 1917.

English Translation

Libro de buen amor. Ed., with intro. and English paraphrase, by R. S. Willis. Princeton: Princeton UP, 1972.

Patricia Grieve

PANERO, Juan (1908, Astorga–1937, Astorga). One of the poets of the *Generation of 1936, also known as the Escorial group, of which his brother Leopoldo was a member, Juan Panero participated in the revival of classical and religious themes. His poetry shows a deep appreciation for simple, everyday reality and also for divine and human love. His stylistic preference is for classical, well-structured verse and longer meters, sometimes interspersed with shorter lines. In 1936, the year before his death, he published his only book of poems, *Cantos del ofrecimiento* (Songs of Offering). Some of his poetry was also collected posthumously in the magazine *Escorial* and the weekly supplement *Sí* of *Arriba*. Luis *Rosales wrote a memorial to his friend Juan in *La casa encendida* (1949).

BIBLIOGRAPHY

Primary Text

Cantos del ofrecimiento. Madrid: "Colección Héroe," 1936.

Criticism

Cano Ballesta, Juan. *La poesía española entre pureza y revolución (1930–1936)*. Madrid: Gredos, 1972.

Kay Pritchett

PANERO, Leopoldo María (1948, Madrid–), poet and critic. Included in J. M. Castellet's *Nueve novísimos poetas españoles* (1970; Nine Very New Spanish Poets), he is associated with the *novísimo* generation of Spanish poets. His poetry is often surrealistic and tends to emphasize the darker side of human experience. He has published eight volumes of poetry: *Por el camino de Swann* (1968; By Swann's Way), *Así se fundó Carnaby Street* (1970; That's How They Founded Carnaby Street), *Teoría* (1973; Theory), *Narciso* (1979; Narcissus), *Last River Together* (1980), *El que no ve* (1980; He Who Doesn't See), *Dióscuros* (1982; Darkgods), and *El último hombre* (1984; The Last Man). He is also the author of two volumes of short fiction, *En lugar del hijo* (1977; In the Son's Place) and *Dos relatos y una perversión* (1984; Two Stories and a Perversion). He has translated works by Lewis Carroll and E. Leard and written prologues to works by Sade and Dylan Thomas.

BIBLIOGRAPHY

Primary Texts

Así se fundó Carnaby Street. Barcelona: Llibres de Sinera, 1970.
Dióscuros. Madrid: Ayuso, 1982.
El que no ve. Madrid: Banda de Moebius, 1980.
Teoría. Barcelona: Lumen, 1973.
El último hombre. Madrid: Pluma Rota, Ed. Libertarias, 1984.

Criticism

Cobo, E. "La destrucción como supervivencia en Leopoldo María Panero." *CH* 332 (1978): 313–16.
Gimferrer, Pere. "Tres heterodoxos." In *30 años de literatura en España*. Barcelona: Kairós, 1971.
Miró, Emilio. "Así se fundó Carnaby Street." *Insula* 288 (1970): n.p.
———. "La poesía última de Leopoldo María Panero y José Ramón Ripoll." *Insula* 456–57 (1984): 17.
Saavecha, J. "Centelleos en la gama quisquilla de la alharaca cotidiana: *Last river together*." *Pueblo* (Madrid) June 28, 1980.

Kay Pritchett

PANERO TORBADO, Leopoldo (1909, Astorga, León–1962, Madrid), poet and critic. A member of the first post-war generation of poets; many of his poems praise traditional and religious values and strive for a balance between concept and expression. He was singled out by Dámaso *Alonso as the most authentically emotional poet of his time. A resemblance has been noted between his verse and that of the English Romantic poets, several of whom he translated into Spanish. His early compositions appeared in literary journals, such as *Haz*, *Escorial* and *Fantasía*. His collections include *Versos del Guadarrama, 1930–1939* (1939; Verses of the Guadarrama), *La estancia vacía* (1944; The Empty Room), *Escrito a cada instante* (1949; Continuously Written), and *Canto personal. Carta perdida a Pablo Neruda* (1953; Personal Chant. Lost Letter to Pablo Neruda). He also edited *Antología de la poesía hispanoamericana* (1944; Anthology of Spanish American Poetry). He received the Fastenrath Prize in 1949 and the National Prize for Literature in 1950. His collected poetry was published posthumously in 1973, with a prologue and annotations by Juan Luis Panero.

BIBLIOGRAPHY

Primary Texts

Antología. Madrid: Plaza y Janés, 1977.

Canto personal. Carta perdida a Pablo Neruda. Madrid: Cultura Hispánica, 1956.

Obras completas. Ed. J. L. Panero. 2 vols. Madrid: Nacional, 1973.

English Translations

''Como en los perros'' (Just as in Dogs), ''Como la hiedra'' (Just as the Ivy), and ''Hasta mañana'' (Until Tomorrow). In *Antología bilingüe (español-inglés) de la poesía española moderna*. Tr. Helen Wohl Patterson. Madrid: Cultura Hispánica, 1965.

Poems in *Recent Poetry of Spain*. Tr. Louis Hammer and Sara Schyfter. Old Chatham, NY: Sachem Press, 1983. 38–47.

Criticism

Aller, César. *La poesía de Leopoldo Panero*. Pamplona: Eunsa, 1976.

Connolly, Eileen. *Leopoldo Panero: la poesía de la esperanza*. Madrid: Gredos, 1969.

García Nieto, J. *La poesía de Leopoldo Panero*. Madrid: Nacional, 1963.

Homenaje a Leopoldo Panero. *CH* 187–88 (1965).

Ruiz-Fornells, Enrique. ''Religión y dedicación mística en la poesía de Leopoldo Panero.'' In *Santa Teresa y la literatura mística hispánica*. Ed. Manuel Criado de Val. Madrid: EDI–6, 1984. 757–67.

Kay Pritchett

PANES, Antonio (1625, Granada?–1676, ?), Franciscan mystic. He wrote *Escala mística* (1675; Ladder of Mysticism) and *Estímulo de amor divino* (n.d.; Stimulus of Divine Love), a collection of religious poems. *See also* Mysticism.

BIBLIOGRAPHY

Primary Texts

Escala mística, y estímulo de amor divino. Valencia: Conejos, 1743.

PARAVICINO Y ARTEAGA, Hortensio Félix (1580, Madrid–1633, Madrid), orator, preacher. After studies with the Jesuits and at the Universities of Alcalá and Salamanca, he joined the Trinitarian order in 1600. His legendary oratorical skills were cited by Lope de *Vega, and parodied by *Calderón. Upon his death, the order collected and published over one hundred of his extant sermons in collections such as *Obras póstumas divinas y humanas* (1641; Posthumous Works, Divine and Human), and *Oraciones evangélicas o discursos panegíricos y morales* (1638; Evangelical Prayers or Panegyric and Moral Discourses). The sermons boast a dense, baroque style, replete with antitheses, hyperbaton, etc., well before *Góngora, and were very popular. Included in the 1650 edition of the *Obras póstumas* is a play, *Gridonia o cielo de amor vengado* (Gridonia Or Love's Heaven Avenged), and a **loa*.

BIBLIOGRAPHY

Primary Texts

Obras póstumas. . . . Alcalá: Fernández, 1650.
Oraciones evangélicas. Madrid: Quiñones, 1641.
Páginas escogidas. Ed., sel., prol. L. Santa María. Barcelona: Caralt, 1943.

Criticism

Alarcos, E. "Los sermones de Paravicino." *RFE* 24 (1937): 162–97 and 249–319.
Herrero García, M. *Sermonario clásico . . . con un ensayo sobre la oratoria sagrada*. Madrid: Escelicer, 1941.

PARDO BAZÁN, Emilia (1852, La Coruña–1921, Madrid), novelist, short story writer and critic. An only child of aristocratic parents, she was indulged and encouraged to read and study on her own. Her favorite childhood readings included the *Quijote,* Homer's *Iliad* and the Bible; she also read books of history, romantic novels, La Fontaine's *Fables* and Racine. She overcame the educational obstacles of the nineteenth-c. Spanish woman by virtually educating herself. During her adolescence, she read works of the Krausists and German philosophers; she studied Italian, and learned English by reading Shakespeare. At the age of sixteen she married José Quiroga and soon thereafter moved to Madrid, where she received an award for her essay on the eighteenth-c. Spanish essayist Father *Feijoo, titled "Ensayo crítico de las obras del padre Feijoo" (1878; Critical Essay on the Works of Father Feijoo). Stimulated by scientific readings, she published a series of fourteen articles on popular science in the *Revista Compostelana* in 1878, and the following year she published two more articles on Darwinism, Dante and Milton in *La Ciencia Cristiana*. In 1881, Francisco *Giner de los Ríos, an important Krausist, printed her only book of poetry, *Jaime* (James), a small collection of verses written for her son.

In spite of these early attempts at erudition, Pardo Bazán is best known for her fiction, which was to become her principal means of expression. Her first novel, *Pascual López* (1879), combines the realistic autobiography of a medical student and a fantastic tale of alchemy. Walter Pattison has persuasively argued that in this first novel, Pardo Bazán satirizes romantic novels of terror. This first work contains both Cervantine and *picaresque elements.

Pardo Bazán is generally recognized as the initiator of *Naturalism in Spain, and in the prologue to her second novel, *Un viaje de novios* (1881; *A Wedding Trip*, 1891), she discusses the French Naturalist school's theory of the novel as a social-psychological study which reflects reality. She expresses dislike of the Naturalists' pessimism and preference for crude subject matter. This novel about a mismatched marriage cannot be considered Naturalistic.

In 1883, Pardo Bazán published a series of articles that had appeared in *La Epoca* (1882–83) in book form under the title *La cuestión palpitante* (The Burning Question). It had a tremendous impact on the Spanish literary scene. In the book, she discusses Naturalism and contrasts it to Spanish realism, which she prefers because it "offers a more ample, complete and perfect theory than

Naturalism.'' In her view, Spanish realism encompasses both the material and spiritual sides of man, and both the tragic and the humorous aspects of reality. She also discusses the history of the novel in France (Flaubert, the Goncourts, Daudet and Zola), and the English and Spanish novel. Although Pardo Bazán truly advocates a compromise between the Naturalist and Idealist positions, she was passionately attacked as an apologist for the Naturalist school.

Her next novel, *La tribuna* (1882; The Woman Speechmaker), may be considered a Naturalistic work. Based on Pardo Bazán's observation and documentation of the workers in a tobacco factory in La Coruña, it tells the tale of a woman cigarette maker who becomes a political leader and demands rights for her fellow workers. Pardo Bazán describes in detail the popular atmosphere and speech of these workers in La Coruña; indeed, it is the first Spanish novel to deal compassionately with the plight of the worker.

El cisne de Vilamorta (*The Swan of Vilamorta*, 1891) appeared in 1884. It is a realistic novel that portrays the clash between romantic aspirations and harsh reality.

In 1886, Pardo Bazán published her best-known work, *Los pazos de Ulloa (The Son of the Bondswoman*, 1908), which was greatly praised by contemporary and later critics. This novel traces the decline and decadence of an aristocratic rural Galician family. The isolation in which this country gentry live eventually brutalizes them. Just as nature takes over the decaying manor house, natural instincts and passions rule human relationships in the novel. In the end, all attempts of the young priest Julian to bring order, morality and civilization to the life of the manor are foiled by the chaotic forces of nature. The Naturalistic theme of the deterministic force of the environment is complemented by detailed renderings of crude and violent scenes. Its sequel, *La madre naturaleza* (1887; Mother Nature), narrates the incestuous love between a brother and sister unaware of their sibling relationship. Sensuous descriptions of the lush Galician countryside serve as the natural setting for the amorous relationship between the two lovers. As in *Los pazos de Ulloa*, Galician rural types, language and customs abound. Again, nature predominates over social rules and taboos; the animal and sexual sides of man are stronger than the civilized side.

Insolación (1889; *Midsummer Madness*, 1907) imparts a similar message, although the tone of this short novel is more frivolous. The protagonist is a young widow who succumbs to the summer heat and the charms of an Andalusian dandy. An aristocratic lady, she is caught between her sense of social decorum and her natural, amorous instincts; the latter prevail and the novel concludes with a happy marriage. The tone of the other short novel that appeared in 1889, *Morriña* (*Homesickness*, 1891), is sad and nostalgic. The novel centers around the hopeless love of a young Galician maid who works for a family in Madrid. She is used by the capricious son of the household, then left and forgotten by him. In despair, she commits suicide. As in *Insolación*, woman is depicted as victim to man and her own sexual nature, but here the result is tragic.

Pardo Bazán's next two novels, *Una cristiana* (1890; *Secret of the Yew Tree, or A Christian Woman,* 1891) and *La prueba* (1891; The Test), present religious, moral and social duty as more powerful than natural inclination. These two closely integrated novels hold the protagonist up as a model of the perfect Christian woman. Married to a man she does not love, she fulfills her wifely duty of caring for him as he dies of leprosy. She eventually manages to overcome the repugnance she feels for him, and grows to love him. She denies her love to another, younger man and suffers even more; yet the denial of amorous instincts and the faithful loyalty to her husband imbue her with moral superiority.

Doña Milagros (1894) and *Memorias de un solterón* (1896; Memories of a Bachelor) are also closely integrated works; they examine domestic problems and the position of women in Spanish society. Both present a family with many daughters and focus on the intellectual and social limitations forced on women. By far the most interesting character is Feíta, an intelligent, modern woman who struggles to break out of the limiting female role, educate herself and earn her own living as governess and tutor so that she will not need to depend upon men. Many autobiographical elements can be found in this character.

La piedra angular (1891; *The Angular Stone,* 1892) treats capital punishment, which doña Emilia opposed. Her next four novels—*El saludo de las brujas* (1897; The Witches' Greeting), *El tesoro de Gastón* (1897; Gaston's Treasure), *El niño de Guzmán* (1898; Guzman's Child) and *Misterio* (1905; *The Mystery of the Lost Dauphin*, 1906)—are escapist novels, less successful artistically than her former works.

Pardo Bazán's last three novels—*La quimera* (1905; The Chimera), *La sirena negra* (1908; The Black Siren) and *Dulce dueño* (1911; Sweet Master)—mark a new orientation in her writing. All three novels use realistic elements mixed with idealistic and symbolistic components to tell tales of spiritual evolution in the protagonists. All end in their conversion to Christianity. *La quimera* centers on a young artist's search for an aesthetic ideal which he eventually finds in Van Eyck's "Divine Lamb." The protagonist's journey of intellectual and aesthetic discovery appears to parallel doña Emilia's own artistic evolution. In the end, the protagonist undergoes a religious conversion but dies before he can paint his masterpiece. *La sirena negra* is a psychological study of a fin de siècle decadent obsessed with thoughts of death and the void. As in *La quimera*, Pardo Bazán gives this novel a religious solution as the protagonist finally embraces Christianity to fill the emptiness in his perverse, decadent soul. *Dulce dueño* tells the story of a female protagonist who, in imitation of her patron saint, Catherine of Alexandria, rejects human love and marriage in favor of a mystical union with Christ. The autobiographical form of this novel creates some ambiguity as to Pardo Bazán's stance: the protagonist claims to be a saint and yet the reader discovers in the final chapter that she is writing her memoirs from an insane asylum.

For its quantity and quality, Pardo Bazán was never surpassed as a writer of short stories, many of which she collected in a series of eight volumes. Her short fiction is comprised of a wide range of subjects; she wrote love stories, tragic and humorous stories, fantastic tales, patriotic and historical stories, religious tales and stories of saints, narratives of rural Galician life, animal fables, allegorical tales, horror stories and psychological tales. She also wrote twenty short novels and seven dramatic works, but her drama never proved to be very successful.

Besides *La cuestión palpitante*, Pardo Bazán's critical writings include *La revolución y la novela en Rusia* (1887; *Russia, Its People and Its Literature*, 1890), *La literatura francesa moderna* (3 vols., 1910, 1912, 1914; Modern French Literature), and *El lirismo en la poesía francesa* (1926; Lyricism in French Poetry), a collection of her university lectures, published posthumously. Pardo Bazán's contributions to journalistic literature are also impressive. From 1891 to 1893 she wrote and published her own magazine, *El nuevo teatro crítico*, which contained stories, historical and biographical sketches, essays and literary reviews. Among the many periodicals to which she contributed essays and stories are *ABC de Madrid*, *Blanco y Negro*, *La Época*, *La Esfera*, *La España Moderna*, *La Ilustración artística*, *La Lectura* and *El Liberal*. *See also* Galician Literature.

BIBLIOGRAPHY

Primary Texts

Obras completas. Vols. 1 and 2. Study, notes by F. C. Saínz de Robles. 3rd ed. Madrid: Aguilar, 1973.

Obras completas. Vol. 3. Intro., notes by Harry L. Kirby, Jr. Madrid: Aguilar, 1973.

English Translations

The Angular Stone. Tr. Mary J. Serrano. New York: Casell, 1892.

Midsummer Madness. Tr. Amparo Loring. Boston: C. M. Clark, 1907.

Morriña (Homesickness). Tr. Mary J. Serrano. New York: Casell, 1891.

The Mystery of the Lost Dauphin (Louis XVII). Tr. Annabel Hord Seeger. New York and London: Funk and Wagnalls, 1906.

Russia, Its People and Its Literature. Tr. Fanny Hale Gardiner. Chicago: A. C. McClurg, 1890.

Secret of the Yew Tree, or A Christian Woman. Tr. Mary Springer. New York: Mershon, 1900.

Shattered Hope; or, The Swan of Vilamorta. Tr. Mary J. Serrano. New York: Mershon, 1900.

The Son of the Bondswoman. Tr. Ethel Harriet Hearn. New York: Lane, 1908.

A Wedding Trip. Tr. Mary J. Serrano. New York: Casell, 1891.

Criticism

Baquero Goyanes, Mariano. *Emilia Pardo Bazán*. Madrid: Publicaciones españolas, 1971.

Barroso, Fernando J. *El naturalismo en la Pardo Bazán*. Madrid: Colección Plaza Mayor Scholar, 1973.

Bravo-Villasante, Carmen. *Vida y obra de Emilia Pardo Bazán*. Madrid: RO, 1962.

Brown, Donald F. *The Catholic Naturalism of Pardo Bazán*. UNCSRLL 28. Chapel Hill: U of North Carolina P, 1971.

Clemessy, Nelly. *Emilia Pardo Bazán, Romancière (La Critique, La Théorie, La Practique)*. Vols. 1, 2. Paris: Centre de Recherches Hispaniques, 1973.

Feal Deibe, Carlos. "La voz femenina en *Los pazos de Ulloa.*" *Hispania* 70.2 (May 1987): 214–221.

González López, Emilio. *Emilia Pardo Bazán: Novelista de Galicia*. New York: Hispanic Institute, 1944.

Hemingway, Maurice. *Emilia Pardo Bazán: The Making of a Novelist*. Cambridge: Cambridge UP, 1983.

———. "Pardo Bazán and the Rival Claims of Religion and Art." *BHS* 66.3 (July 1989): 241–50.

Henn, David. *The Early Pardo Bazán: Theme and Narrative Technique in the Novels of 1879–89*. Liverpool: Cairns, 1988.

Osborne, Robert E. *Emilia Pardo Bazán: Su vida y sus obras*. Mexico: Gutenberg, 1964.

Porter, Phoebe. "The *Femme Fatale*: Emilia Pardo Bazán's Portrayal of Evil and Fascinating Women." In *LA CHISPA '87: Selected Proceedings*. Ed. Gilbert Paolini. New Orleans: Tulane U, 1987.

Valera Jácome, Benito. *Estructuras novelísticas de Emilia Pardo Bazán*. Santiago de Compostela: Cuadernos de Estudios Gallegos, 1973.

Whitacker, Daniel S. "*La quimera* of Emilia Pardo Bazán: The Pre-Raphaelite Factor in the Regeneration of a Decadent Dandy." *Hispania* 70.4 (Dec. 1987): 746–51.

Phoebe Porter Medina

PARTINUPLES, el libro del esforzado caballero Conde Partinuples, que fue emperador de Constantinopla (The Book of the Brave Knight Count Partonopeus, who was Emperor of Constantinople), novel. First published in 1513 (Alcalá), this translation of a twelfth-c. French work, *Partinopeus de Blois,* has enjoyed great popularity over the years. It narrates the myth of Psyche, changing the sex of the protagonist.

BIBLIOGRAPHY

Primary Text

El conde Partinuples. Ed., prol., I. B. Anzoátegui. Colección Austral 418. Buenos Aires: Espasa-Calpe Argentina, 1944.

English Translation

Partonopeu de Blois; a French romance of the 12th Century. Ed. J. Gilden. Villanova, PA: Villanova UP, 1967.

Criticism

Seidenspinner-Núñez, D. "Symmetry of Form and Emblematic Design in *El conde Partinuples.*" *KRQ* 30.1 (1983): 61–76.

Smith, R. T. "The *Partinuples, conde de Bles*: A Bibliographical and Critical Study of the Earliest Known Edition, Its Sources and Later Structural Modifications." *DAI* 38 (1978): 4872A.

PASAMAR, Pilar Paz (1933, Jerez de la Frontera–), Spanish poet. Pasamar's family moved to Madrid at the close of the Civil War and there she was educated, although she returned frequently to Andalusia, and has lived in Cádiz since her marriage (1957), being associated for geographic reasons with the Andalusian School of poets. *Mara* (1951), her first collection published when she was only eighteen, was highly praised by Juan Ramón *Jiménez. The major concern is metaphysical, a search for God completely unrelated to immediate surroundings and cultural circumstances. Pasamar's dialogue with the deity and with poetry itself sets her apart from her generation, the "mid-century" or "social" poets, characterized by neo-realist, critical works of implicit political intent. *Los buenos días* (1954; The Good Days), continuing the metaphysical quest for ultrasensory essence, resembles the thematics of Juan Ramón Jiménez in *Dios deseado y deseante*, as well as recalling the Spanish mystic tradition. *Ablativo Amor* (1956; Ablative Love) and *Del abreviado mar* (1957; About the Abbreviated Sea) follow similar conceptions of poetic language, although the first consists of sonnets and the second exhibits much freer form, evoking the syncopated expression of the internal monologue. In the existential inspiration of *Ablativo Amor*, the quest for a silent God intensifies, while *Del abreviado mar* presents meditations on life and God in the maritime language familiar to the poet. *La soledad, contigo* (1960; Solitude, with You) continues the quest for God in quotidian minutia, the daily life of the poet's domestic world, now melancholic and sentimental, as she seeks the transcendent beyond the laurel, parsley and saffron in her kitchen cabinets. Despite its pantheistic spirit, this is an unmistakably feminine book, dominated by maternal concerns and domestic tasks, a woman's satisfactions and frustrations. In 1964, Pasamar published a book-length essay, *Poesía femenina de lo cotidiano* (Feminine Poetry of Everyday Things).

Violencia inmóvil (1967; Motionless Violence) is the most anguished collection to date, probing life's mysteries and ultimate meaning, contrasting quotidian world perceptions with "intellectual" vision, concreteness and ambiguity, clarity and indefiniteness. Images here are drawn from literary intertexts, and the book forms a single uninterrupted discourse, rather than individual poems. A fifteen-year hiatus intervenes before the next collection, *La torre de Babel y otros asuntos* (1982; The Tower of Babel and Other Matters), a compilation of largely unrelated poems previously unpublished, lacking the thematic unity of earlier collections. *La alacena* (1985; The Kitchen Cabinet), an anthology, contains selections from all of Pasamar's published collections, as well as an excerpt from a forthcoming one, *Orario* (which plays on homophones and the connotation of timetable versus prayer time).

Janet Pérez

PASAMONTE, Jerónimo de (c. 1555, Aragon–after 1604, ?), soldier, author of an autobiography. His life story, *Vida y trabajos de Jerónimo de Pasamonte* (1603; Life and Misfortunes of Jerónimo de Pasamonte), is a lively *picaresque narration of his troubles as a child, journey to Italy, participation in the battle of Lepanto (1571) and the battle of Tunis (1573), his subsequent eighteen years as captive of the Moors (1574–92), various escape attempts, and peripatetic life, still fraught with misfortune, after being freed. Certain parallels have been cited between Pasamonte's *Vida* and the character Ginés de Pasamonte of *Cervantes's *Quijote*. Certainly it is possible that Cervantes had read the ms. of Pasamonte's work; it is also true that Cervantes participated in the battle of Lepanto, and was in Moorish captivity at the same time.

BIBLIOGRAPHY

Primary Text

Vida y trabajos de Jerónimo de Pasamonte. Ed. Foulché-Delbosc. *RH* 55 (1922): 311–446. Also in BAE 90.

Criticism

Kattan, O. "Algunos paralelos entre Gerónimo de Pasamonte y Ginesillo en el *Quijote*." *CH* 244 (1970): 190–206.

PASCOAES, Teixeira de, pseudonym of Joaquim Pereira Teixeira de Vasconcelos (1877, São João de Gatão [near Amarante]–1952, São João de Gatão), Portuguese poet and thinker. The son of a relatively wealthy family, Pascoaes spent an idyllic youth in the countryside of the Upper Douro near Amarante. His schooling and university years were both unprofitable experiences and after a short career in law, in which he had graduated in 1901 from the U of Coimbra, he returned to the family estate and lived out his life as a local worthy. While in practice in Porto he was active in the Renascença Portuguesa movement and became the principal theoretician of Saudosismo. Through his activity in the group he came into close contact with Leonardo *Coimbra, Raúl *Brandão and Afonso Lopes *Vieira. Later, through his poetry, he came into contact with Miguel de *Unamuno. From 1912 to 1916 he was literary editor of *A Águia*, the Renascença movement's journal which he had helped to found in 1910.

From his earliest youth he had been writing poetry and had published several collections during his student years but it is rather as a propagandist for Saudosismo, the central doctrine of the Renascença movement, that he is best remembered. He published *O Espírito Lusitano e o Saudosimo* (1912; The Portuguese Spirit and Saudosismo); *O Gênio Português—na sua Expressão Filosófica, Poética e Religiosa* (1913; The Portuguese Genius in Its Philosophical Poetic and Religious Manifestations); *A Era Lusíada* (1914; The Lusitanian Age), and what was perhaps his most thorough working out of his position, *Arte de Ser Português* (1915; The Art of Being Portuguese).

Politically, his position is one of Romantic traditionalism keen to reject foreign and "ungodly" influences and to foster the traditional "folk" values that he claims the people have drawn from their native soil and traditional way of life. His argument for, and development of, his position has much in common with other intuitive right-leaning theoreticians of his time elsewhere in Europe and particularly with Barrés and Bernanos in France and of both the French Action Française and French-Canadian Action Nationale movements.

BIBLIOGRAPHY

Primary Texts

Obras Completas. Ed. J. do Prado Coelho. 11 vols. Lisbon: Livraria Bertrand, n.d. [1965].

Criticism

Margarido, Alfredo. *Teixeira de Pascoaes*. Lisbon: Arcádia, 1961.

Prado Coelho, Jacinto do. *A Poesia de Teixeira de Pascoaes*. Coimbra: Atlántida, 1945.

———. Introduction to *Obras Completas*. vol. 1. (see above)

Régio, José. "Introduction à Teixeira de Pascoaes." *Bulletin des Études Portugaises* 16 (1952): 187–98.

Peter Fothergill-Payne

PASO, Alfonso (1926, Madrid–1978, Madrid), dramatist. This prolific playwright chronicled everyday life in post-war Spain. Son of *sainetero* Antonio Paso and actress Juana Gil Andrés, he formed the vanguard theatrical group Arte Nuevo (New Art) while still a university student but became increasingly conservative in later years. Paso displayed a natural dramatic facility in many genres—comedy, tragedy, social satire and farce—but his theater has more breadth than depth. Although he enjoyed greater commercial than critical success, *Los Pobrecitos* (1957; The Poor Little Ones) received the Carlos Arniches Prize in 1957, while *El Cielo dentro de casa* (1957; *Blue Heaven*, 1962) garnered the National Theater Award in 1957.

Early works are *Veneno para mi marido* (1953; Poison for My Husband); *Cuarenta y ocho horas de felicidad* (1956; Forty-Eight Hours of Bliss); *Usted puede ser asesino* (1958; You Can Be a Killer); *El Canto de la cigarra* (1958; *Song of the Grasshopper*, 1968), a Broadway hit in 1968; *La Eternidad se pasa pronto* (1959; Eternity Passes Quickly); *Receta para un crimen* (1959; *Recipe For a Crime*, 1962); and *Cena de matrimonios* (1959; Dinner for Married Couples).

Between 1960 and 1962 Paso wrote no less than thirty-two plays, including *La Boda de la chica* (1960; The Girl's Wedding); *Cosas de papá y mamá* (1960; *Oh, Mama! No, Papa!*, 1962); *Preguntan por Julio César* (1960; They're Calling for Julius Caesar); *Aurelia y sus hombres* (1961; Aurelia and Her Men), National Theatre Award in 1961; *Vamos a contar mentiras* (1961; Let's Tell Lies); *Rebelde* (1962; The Rebel); *Judith* (1962); *El Mejor mozo de España* (1962; The Finest Lad in Spain), a day in the life of Lope de Vega; and *Las que tienen que servir* (1962; Those Who Must Serve), which had over six hundred performances.

Subsequent works include *La Corbata* (1963; The Necktie); *Prefiero España* (1964; I Prefer Spain); *La Oficina* (1965; The Office); *Este Cura* (1966; This Priest); *En el Escorial, cariño mío* (1968; In the Escorial, My Dear); *Nerón-Paso* (1969; Nero-Paso), in which Paso played the role of Nero; *La Noche de verdad* (1970; The Night of Truth); *Mentiras entre hombre y mujer* (1970; Lies between Men and Women); *Juan Jubilado* (1971; Juan Retired). Paso authored two novels, *¡Sólo diecisiete años!* (1969; Only Seventeen) and *Cálida Josefina* (1973; Sweet Josephine). *See also* Contemporary Spanish Theater.

BIBLIOGRAPHY

Primary Texts

Mathías, Julio, ed. *Teatro Selecto*. Madrid: EPESA, 1971.

English Translations

Blue Heaven. Tr. R. Denham. New York: Dramatists Play Service, 1962.
Oh, Mama! No, Papa! Tr. R. Denham. New York: Dramatists Play Service, 1962.
Recipe for a Crime. Tr. R. Denham. New York: Dramatists Play Service, 1962.
Song of the Grasshopper. Tr. W. Layton and A. Penon. New York: n.p., 1967.

Criticism

Marquerie, Alfredo. *Alfonso Paso y su teatro*. Madrid: Escelicer, 1960.
Mathías, Julio. *Alfonso Paso*. Madrid: EPESA, 1971.
Urmeneta, Fermín de. "Alfonso Paso o el teatro caricaturesco." *Revista de Ideas Estéticas* 35 (1977): 239–45.

Robert Sandarg

PASO HONROSO, Libro del (Book of the Pass of Arms), notarial account of a chivalric feat. First set down in 1588 by Pedro Rodríguez de Lena, the *Libro* attests that Suero de Quiñones, accompanied by nine fellow knights, successfully defended for one month (July 10-August 9, 1434) the pass at the bridge of San Marcos of Órbigo against all challengers. Sixty-eight knights responded to the challenge, and 700 matches were held. The competition was initiated to demonstrate Suero's courtly devotion to his lady, and provides posterity with a persuasive example of how novels of chivalry do have a basis in reality. There are several extant versions, not all by Rodríguez de Lena, none of which is complete. *See also* Caballerías, Libros de.

BIBLIOGRAPHY

Primary Text

Espadas, Juan. "El paso honroso de Suero de Quiñones: Edición crítica y estudio preliminar." *DAI* 39 (1979): 6158A U Pennsylvania.

Criticism

Espadas, Juan. "Pedro Rodríguez de Lena y su papel en el *Libro del passo honroso*." *La Corónica: Spanish Medieval Language and Literature Journal and Newsletter*. 10.2 (Spring 1982): 179–85.
Labandeira Fernández, Amancio. *El passo honroso de Suero de Quiñones*. Madrid: Fundación Univ. Española, 1977.

Veronica Sauter

PASO Y CANO, Manuel (1864, Granada–1901, Madrid), playwright, poet and journalist. He studied letters at Granada and collaborated in *El Defensor de Granada* and other publications from Madrid. He is the author of several plays: *Después del combate* (1890; After the Fight), an adaptation of a drama by Almeida Garret; *Curro Vargas* (1900), a lyric drama; *La cortijera* (1900; The Farm Lady), etc.

Sensualism and pessimism characterize his verses that were collected in *Poesías* (1900; Poetry) and *Nieblas* (1902; Mists). The best poem of this latter volume is "El canto a la Alhambra" (Song to the Alhambra).

BIBLIOGRAPHY

Primary Texts

Nieblas. Madrid: Sociedad de Autores Españoles, 1902.
Poesías. Madrid: Marzo, 1900.

Criticism

Arco y Molinero, Angel del. ''Tres ingenios granadinos: Baltasar Martínez Durán, Manuel Paso y Cano y Angel Ganivet.'' *Alhambra* 19 (1916): 422 et passim.

José Ortega

PASOS, a theatrical term. Lope de *Rueda gave this name to his short, comic farces; they contain all the features of what is subsequently called the **entremés*.

PASTOR DÍAZ, Nicomedes (1811, Vivero, Lugo–1863, Madrid), rector of the U of Madrid, journalist, essayist, orator and politician. His melancholy, somber poetry belongs to *Romanticism, as seen in *Poesías* (1840; Poems), with such themes as night, loneliness, and unhappy fate. He also wrote novels, literary criticism, and articles on various topics. His autobiographical novel, *De Villahermosa a la China, coloquios íntimos* (1858; From Villahermosa to China, Intimate Colloquies), was harshly judged. Pastor Díaz also supervised publication of a nine-volume *Galería de españoles célebres contemporáneos* (1841–64; Gallery of Famous Contemporary Spaniards), and edited the works of Gertrudis *Gómez de Avellaneda and the Duke of *Rivas.

BIBLIOGRAPHY

Primary Texts

Obras. Ed. Castro y Calvo. BAE 227, 228, 241.

Criticism

Rodríguez González, F. *Pastor Díaz en la poesía y en la literatura gallega*. La Coruña: Real Academia Gallega, 1923.
del Valle Mori, J. *Pastor Díaz: Su vida y sus obras*. Havana: n.p., 1911.

PASTORAL, adjective applied to a type of prose narrative usually interspersed with verse depicting bucolic life. The pastoral romance flourished in Spain during the middle of the sixteenth c. Its most immediate models were Italian; however, an independent tradition of pastoral elements in poetry and drama was well established in Spanish literature. The Galician *vaqueiras* and **pastorelas*; the *serranillas* (mountain songs) of the Marqués de *Santillana; the rustic interludes and eclogues of the Spanish dramatists Juan del *Encina, Lucas *Fernández, and Gil *Vicente; and the bucolic compositions of *Garcilaso de la Vega all express the lyric, erotic, and dramatic sentiments that are customarily associated with pastoral literature. It is not until 1549, the year in which the first Spanish translation of Sannazaro's *Arcadia* was published, that one can properly speak of the ''pastoral romance'' in Spain. The pastoral ideal popularized in this genre was nurtured by the *Renaissance interest in Neoplatonic philosophy and the

Arcadian myth. The writers of the Spanish *Siglo de Oro quickly embraced the genre and produced numerous works which further distinguished the tradition. The characteristic features of pastoral romance are shepherds who are no more than a pretext to mask real personages and who appear not as humble villagers, but refined and learned courtiers in pastoral disguise; an artificial and idealized natural setting; a complicated plot focusing on the amatory sentiments of the characters and usually containing numerous improbable incidents; and a prose narrative with intercalated lyrics. *Montemayor, Gil *Polo, *Cervantes, *Gálvez de Montalvo, and Lope de *Vega all experimented with the genre, and each composed a pastoral romance. *See also* Italian Literary Influences.

BIBLIOGRAPHY

Criticism

Avalle-Arce, Juan Bautista. *La novela pastoril española.* Madrid: Istmo, 1959; 2nd ed., 1974.

Gerhardt, Mia. *La Pastorale.* Assen: Van Goreum, 1950.

López Estrada, Francisco. *Los libros de pastores en la literatura española.* Madrid: Gredos, 1974.

Poggioli, Renato. *The Oaten Flute.* Cambridge, MA: Harvard UP, 1975.

Solé-Leris, Amadeu. *The Spanish Pastoral Novel.* TWAS 575. Boston: Twayne, 1980.

Deborah Compte

PASTORELA, a musical composition of lyrical narration, with variable verse structure. It relates the meeting of the poet knight with a shepherd or shepherdess, in a manner similar to that of the *chansons de rencontre*. In the *exordium* the knight appears passing through a pleasant setting, with frequent use of the motifs of horseback riding, springtime, and *locus amoenus*. A prelude to the *debate*, the meeting too has a characteristic lexicon of certain verbs plus the description of a maiden. The true nucleus of the *pastorela* is the *debate* or *disputa* between knight and shepherdess. The former may be interested or not, and according to his feelings, may offer numerous arguments in favor of the young woman's acceptance of his advances. There are, however, French and Galician *pastorelas* in which no seduction occurs, but rather the knight listens, from his hiding place, to the shepherdess's song of love for another. In other cases, the knight participates in a rural dance or lovers' encounter, or debates with a shepherd the sufferings of each which are caused by a disdainful lover.

For her part, the shepherdess may accept or reject the knight's advances, on her own accord or with the help of others. Some poems conclude either with the knight's boasting of his seductive ability, or with a burlesque-type finale. *Menéndez Pidal terms the ending of the disinterested *pastorelas* fragmentary, for they end simply with the enthralled contemplation of the shepherdess by the knight. The debate types, however, conclude with a didactic *precepto amoroso*.

The oldest known *pastorela* is Occitanian, but the genre became most widespread in France, with 120 anonymous and 60 by identified authors registered. Nearly all *pastorela* types are found in the *oil* language. In one variant the knight must flee because the lover or other friend of the woman appears. There are a number of French *pastorelas* of a vulgar sort, with a parody of peasant ways as well as of courtly *Platonism. Still, there are lyrical compositions in which a woman truly in love sings her **cantiga*. In some compositions, there is a religious woman who rejects the knight with moralizing arguments. The Occitanian *pastorela* is of an aristocratic orientation: its strength rests on the characters' wit, and there is neither violence nor deception.

There are also Latin compositions related to the *chansons de rencontre* and some with formats similar to the *oil* works of the "interested" type. Sometimes called a subtype of the *cantiga de amigo*, the eight Galician-Portuguese *pastorelas* are also sometimes considered to be formally a separate genre, with the perspective more often that of the woman. Among the authors are Joan Pérez de Aboin, Airas Nunes, Lourenco, and Pero Amigo.

The musical notation of the *pastorelas* has been lost, perhaps due to the insufficient popularity among those who passed them on to subsequent generations. *See also* Gallic Portuguese Poetry.

BIBLIOGRAPHY

Criticism

Flores, C., and María Xosé Ríos. "Pastorela." *Gran Encyclopedia Gallega*. Guijón: Silverio Cañada Editor, 1974 ff. 25: 61–62.

Le Gentil, P. *La Poésie lyrique espagnole et portugaise a la fin du Moyen Âge*. Rennes: Plinon, 1949.

Lesser, A. T. *La pastorela medieval hispánica. Pastorelas y serranas galaico-portuguesas*. Vigo: Galaxia, 1970.

Rivière, J. Cl. *Pastourelles*. Geneva: Droz, 1974–76.

Tavani, Guiseppe. "La poesía lírica galego-portoghese." *Gundriss der Romanischen Literaturen des Mittelalters*. vol. 2. Heidelberg: n.p., 1980.

Kathleen March

PATRAÑA, a fictitious tale or story. Also *patrañuela*. *Timoneda uses the term in the title to his collection of short stories, most of which are of "Italian" style.

PATRAÑUELA. *See Patraña.*

PATRÍCIO, António (1878, Porto–1930, Macau), Portuguese playwright and poet. After two false starts studying mathematics at Porto and one year spent in Lisbon at the Naval Academy, Patrício graduated in medicine in the U of Porto but then decided to enter the diplomatic service. He successively held the post of Portuguese consul in La Coruña, Spain; Canton, China; Manaus, Brazil; Bremen, Germany; Athens, Greece; and Constantinople, Turkey. Thereafter he was special envoy in London and minister in Caracas, Venezuela. He was en route to a similar post in Beijing, China, when he died unexpectedly in Macao.

The first of his books of poetry, *Oceano* (1905; The Ocean), appeared while he was still a student, *Poesias* (1942; Poems), published posthumously, being the second. He also wrote a collection of short stories under the title *Serão Inquieto* (1910; Unquiet Eve). They are written in an allusive poetic style focusing on problems central to the human condition through an astute use of symbols and an allegorical style. This can be seen to advantage in the first story in the collection, "Diálogo com uma Águia" (Conversation with an Eagle), which implicitly centers on the delight, danger and dismay of freedom.

The greater part of his writing was, however, destined for the theater. *O Fim* (1909; The End), which draws its inspiration from Nietzsche, foreshadows the end of the monarchy in tableau form and in symbolic terms, pointing up the ways in which it was existing in a vacuum. *Pedro o Cru* (1918; Peter the Cruel) and *Dinis e Isabel* (1919; Denis and Elizabeth) have subjects drawn from well-known episodes in Portuguese history, while his "tragic fable" *D. João e a Máscara* (1924; D. Juan and the Masked Guest) is a variant on the *Don Juan theme. He was an occasional contributor to *A Águia* and left an unpublished novel "Teodora, Imperatriz de Byzancio" (Theodora, Empress of Byzantium) and fragments of two further plays.

Throughout his writing Patrício seeks self-knowledge through art by placing before his protagonists the prospect of imminent death or ending. His work has fallen into neglect at present, but he was nevertheless one of the best exponents of symbolism in Portugal.

BIBLIOGRAPHY

Primary Texts

Dinis e Isabel. 2nd ed. Lisbon: Aillaud and Bertrand, 1919.
D. João e a Máscara. Lisbon: Aillaud and Bertrand, 1924.
O Fim. Porto: Livraria Chardron, 1909.
Oceano. Porto: Livraria Nacional and Estrangeira, 1905. Poetry.
Pedro o Cru. 2nd ed. Porto: Aillaud and Bertrand, 1919.
Poesias. Lisbon: Ática, 1942. Poetry.
Serão Inquieto. 2nd ed. Porto: Magalhães e Moniz, 1956. Short stories.

Criticism

Correia, Manuel Tanger. "António Patrício, poeta trágico." *Ocidente* 57 (1959): 261–79 and 316–25; 58 (1960): 4–18, 65–80 and 293–308; and 59 (1960): 93–99. (This set of articles was also published under one cover as a "separata" or offprint.)
Lima, Fernando de Araújo. *António Patrício*. Lisbon: Bertrand, 1943.

Peter Fothergill-Payne

PAZ, Enrique. *See* Enríquez Gómez, Antonio

PAZ Y MELIA, Antonio (1842, Talavera de la Reina, Toledo–1927, Madrid), Spanish archivist, literary historian and bibliographer. He contributed to the cataloging and preservation of many historical mss., unpublished documents, and erudite periodicals. Among his publications are *Catálogo de las piezas de teatro manuscritas de la Biblioteca Nacional* (Catalog of the Manuscript Plays in the National Library) and catalogs of the private ducal archives of the houses of Alba and of Medinaceli. He collaborated in producing the bibliographies *Colección de documentos inéditos para la Historia de España* (Collection of Unpublished Documents Concerning Spanish History), *Colección de Escritores Castellanos* (Collection of Castilian Writers), *Bibliófilos españoles* (Spanish Bibliophiles), and edited obscure texts and chronicles from the fourteenth to the sixteenth centuries, including works of *Rodríguez de la Cámara, Gómez *Manrique, and many lesser writers.

PEDRAZA, Juan de (sixteenth c., Segovia?–Segovia?), dramatist. He is remembered for his dramatic farce *Danza de la muerte* (1551; Dance of Death), written for the Corpus Christi celebration in Segovia, in which five representative types (from the pope down to a shepherd) learn that death pardons no one. He probably also wrote a play titled *Santa Susana* (1551); it lists as its author Juan de Rodrigo Alonso, who was also called "de Pedraza." *See also Dança general de la muerte.*

BIBLIOGRAPHY

Primary Texts

Comedia de Sta. Susana. Ed., intro. A Bonilla y San Martín. In "Cinco obras dramáticas anteriores a Lope de Vega." *RH* 27 (1912): 390–97 and 423–36.

Danza de la muerte. In BAE 59.

PEDRO DE ALCÁNTARA, San (1499, Alcántara [Extremadura]–1562, Arenas de San Pedro [Avila]), Franciscan mystic and religious reformer, influential for his writings, preaching, and exemplary life. Educated at Salamanca, he joined the order at the age of 16. Alcántara engaged in the apostolic life of the Franciscan order, in writing and preaching, and also participated in the reform of his order in Castile and Extremadura. After election to the post of provincial in 1538, he settled in a solitary spot in the mountains near Arábida and established a custody (a small group of Franciscan friars ruled by a Custos) composed of austere, contemplative Franciscans. This reform movement spread to other Franciscan communities of Spain.

In 1556 Alcántara withdrew to complete, contemplative retirement near Badajoz where he wrote his important devotional-meditative work, *Tratado de la oración y meditación* (Lisbon, 1557–58; *Treatise of Prayer and Meditation*, 1632), a didactic, devotional manual treating the exercise of prayer and meditation; in effect, it is a guide to inner spiritual life. Inspired by *Osuna's *Abecedario Espiritual*, the monk describes in detail the spiritual path that commences with prayer and meditation through which the individual hopes to achieve ultimate union with God in contemplation. In this *tratado* (treatise) Alcántara distinguishes between active prayer, which thinks, reflects and weighs divine precepts, and meditation, which is capable of lifting the soul toward God assisted by the affections. In Part 1 the author outlines the mysteries on which the individual is to meditate including the hour of the day and the days of the week. Part 2 treats the nature of devotion.

In the final period of his life Alcántara entered into an intimate spiritual relationship with St. *Teresa de Jesús. Often and in generous terms she acknowledged his constant assistance and guidance in her own reform movement. Pedro de Alcántara was beatified in 1622 and canonized in 1669. Apart from some letters, a short work on St. Teresa, and the Constitution of his reform, the *Tratado* is his sole work left to posterity. *See also* Ascetical Literature; Mysticism.

BIBLIOGRAPHY

Primary Text

Tratado de la oración y meditación. Madrid: Rialp, 1958.

English Translation

Treatise on Prayer and Meditation. Tr. Dominic Devas. Westminster, MD: Newman, 1949.

Criticism

Pérez, L. "Información sobre el *Tratado de la oración y meditación*." *Archivo Iberoamericano* 7 (1917): 290–97.

Sala Balust, L. "Textos desconocidos de San Pedro de Alcántara y del Beato Diego José de Cádiz." *Salamanticensis* 2 (1955): 151–63.

Stephane, P., and J. Piat. *Le maître de la mystique. Saint Pierre d'Alcántara*. Paris: Franciscaines, 1959.

Angelo DiSalvo

PEDROLO, Manuel de (1918, L'Aranyó, Segarra–), Catalan novelist, playwright, essayist, short story writer and poet. Most of his early life was spent in Tárrega, ancestral residence of his family (impoverished rural landowners). His father was president of Acció Catalana, a party favoring the autonomy of Catalonia. Pedrolo studied in Tárrega until the end of 1935, when he moved to Barcelona. A voracious reader from childhood, he was especially fond of the works of Pío *Baroja, *Valle-Inclán, and *Pérez de Ayala, as well as an early reader of detective fiction (both the realistic tradition and the interest in mysteries appear as enduring influences in his mature work). He intended to study medicine, but was interrupted by the outbreak of the Spanish Civil War (1936–39). He served in the Artillery Corps, subsequently making his living in a wide variety of jobs (teacher, insurance agent, traveling salesman, editorial assistant, translator, and private investigator). His publishing commenced in 1949 with a book of poetry, *Esser en el mon* (Being in the World). Because of his wartime service with the Republic, he was treated with special harshness by the Franco censors, hostile to writings in Catalan generally. He wrote his first novel in 1940, but it would be many years before any book of his was published. An extremely prolific writer, the most widely read Catalan author in Catalonia, Pedrolo is essentially unknown outside his own linguistic orbit. He could just as well have written in

Spanish, but like Salvador *Espriu, he has stubbornly and idealistically devoted his entire literary career to preserving the Catalan cultural heritage and linguistic tradition and contributing to their growth.

Pedrolo's dramatic period began in 1954 with *Els hereus de la cadira* (The Heirs of the Easy-Chair), and lasted until 1966, ending with *La sentencia* (The Sentence), although some works appeared after that time: *Aquesta matinada i potser per sempre* (1976; This Morning and Maybe Forever); *D'ara a demà* (1977; From Now to Tomorrow); and *Aquesta nit tanguem* (1978; Tonight We Close). Pedrolo's theater has considerable internal coherence, being his investigation of the human condition in essential aspects such as liberty, communication, and death. *La nostra mort de cada dia* (1958; Our Daily Death) attempted an analysis of time, as each character facing death demanded ''his'' time. *Cruma* (1958) depicts existence on a skeletal level with mankind as a symbolic Resident in a bare room with blank walls, with one daily Visitor, obliged each day to invent a game to prevent thought. In *Sóc el defecte* (1959; I'm the Defect), Pedrolo portrays mankind removed from the cocoon/room, in a world which is a maze of staircases. In *Tècnica de cambra* (1959; Chamber Technique), a dormitory room in a hostel represents the world as well as life, in which seven characters symbolize the human microcosm, appearing and leaving at the command of an invisible landlady (birth, death). The room is again used as a symbol in *Darrera versió, per ara* (1958; Last Version, For Now), where another bare white room is furnished only with a black-and-white sphere. The two characters (symbolically Adam and Eve) re-enact the fall but implicitly proclaim their own independence as they reject both angel (white) and devil (black). This act of rebellion, in existential terms, negates the supernatural. The absurd format is used for political criticism in *Homes i no* (1957; Men and No), *Situació bis* (1958; *Full Circle*, 1958) and *L'ús de la matèria* (1963; The Use of Matter). Pedrolo's significance for the theater of the absurd was first recognized by Martin Esslin, who ranked him on a par with other major European dramatists in the 1960s, comparing him favorably with Beckett, Pinter and Sartre (while employing the absurdist style, Pedrolo has always adapted it to his own purposes). At other times, he has portrayed the horrors of contemporary dehumanization in the guise of farce, or satirized bureaucracy in hilarious fashion. Several of his plays have been translated into English and published in *Modern International Drama Magazine*. Additional plays include *Pell vella al fons del pou* (1975; Old Skin at the Bottom of the Well), *Algù a l'altre cap de peça* (1975; Someone at the Other Edge of the Room), *Acompanyo qualsevol cos* (1962; I'll Accompany Whatever Body); and *Bones notícies de Sister* (1979; Good News from Sister), most of which were written considerably earlier.

Pedrolo's brief fiction was collected in three volumes entitled *Contes i narracions* (1974–75; Stories and Novelettes), vol. 1 comprising 1938–54; vol. 2, 1954–55; and vol. 3, 1956–74. Selected articles over a decade were collected in *Els elefants són contagiosos: Articles (1962–1972)* (1974; Elephants Are Contagious). Among critical articles written by Pedrolo was one on Hemingway, who initially attracted him as a technical model. Of probable help to the critic or student is *Si em pregunten, responc* (1974; If They Ask Me I Answer), a collection of interviews of Pedrolo by various authors. An example of his later poetry is found in *Arreu on valguin les paraules, els homes* (1975; Wherever Words Are Valued, Men . . .). Major aspects of his work, which includes more than sixty volumes (without counting his extensive work as a translator of such writers as Faulkner, Dos Passos and Miller), remain unstudied.

It is in the novel that Pedrolo has made his most significant and extensive contribution, cultivating many of the major contemporary variants of the novel, among them science fiction, detective fiction, political allegory, the novel of humor, symbolism, fantasy, the psychological novel, historical and rural fiction, etc. As an experimental novelist, he is Catalonia's most important, for he has consciously and consistently innovated throughout his narrative career, deliberately avoiding established patterns of the novel in Catalan (as set by Narcís *Oller, Víctor *Català, Mercè *Rodoreda and Llorenç *Villalonga). He has distanced himself from novelistic currents in Spain, preferring to find his models in major figures of contemporary European fiction, adapting aspects of writers as different as Joyce, Proust, Céline, Italo Svevo, Broch and Musil, or Henry James. His most important initial influence came from the American novel, but works of the late 1960s and early 1970s were influenced by French criticism and the novelistic practice of Robbe-Grillet, Simón, or Philippe Sollers, in particular. Independently of the variety of styles and techniques, Pedrolo's novels represent his eclectic and highly original attempt to construct a coherent overview of modern and contemporary Catalan history. Within the overall novelistic panorama are several cycles comprising trilogies, tetralogies, or larger numbers of collected novels, for example, *Temps obert* (Open Time), a series of at least ten novels, whose first three appeared in a single volume with the overall series title, followed by others independently titled and including *Situació analítica* (1971; Analytic Situation), *Des d'uns ulls de dona* (1972; From a Woman's Eyes), *Unes mans plenes de sol* (1972; Hands Full of Sun), *Un camí amb Eva* (1968; A Walk with Eva, published out of sequence), *Falgueres informa* (1968; Falgueres Reports), *L'ordenació dels maons* (1974; Placing the Bricks), *S'alcen veus del soterrani* (1976; Voices Rise from the Underground), *Pols nova de runes velles* (1977; New Dust from Old Runes), *Cartes a Jones Street* (1978; Letters to Jones Street), and *"Conjectures" de Daniel Bastida* (1980; "Conjectures" by Daniel Bastida). Although some titles appeared out of intended order due to censorship as well as publishing difficulties, the cycle was planned as the most lengthy ever written in Catalan. Employing a multiplicity of perspectives and viewpoints and playing with the many possible futures and variable genealogies of a single major character, the cycle constitutes a kind of primitive Faulknerian saga of the life of Daniel Bastida, a war orphan raised by a rural family. The cyclic narration acquires epic tones, includes social criticism of economic problems in the agrarian sector in the post-war period, and while paying special attention to psychological detail, often approaches neo-naturalism in its documentary aspects, its emphasis upon sexuality and other instinct-driven behavior, and its political intent. It is a vast project comparable, for example, to Balzac's *Comédie Humaine*, updated to the twentieth c. and transported to Catalonia.

Representative of Pedrolo's science fiction is *Mecanoscrit del segon origen* (1974; Manuscript of the Second Origin), which presents a post-holocaust world in which humanity has been almost completely eliminated by an extraterrestrial attack, with only a nine-year-old black boy and an adolescent Catalan girl (Alba) escaping. Their eventual sexual awakening produces a son, Mar, and soon afterwards the father meets accidental death, leaving Alba—the new Eve—to become the consort of her son in due time. The account (Alba's diary) is published some seven millennia afterward in a new society whose members either revere Alba as the Mother of Mankind or view the whole manuscript as apocryphal. This is one of Pedrolo's most popular works, a post-war best-seller in Catalan. *Sòlids en suspensió* (1981; Solids in Suspension) is an experimental novel which intrudes on the realm of fantasy or science fiction as part of a narrative speculation having to do with the revolt or independence of fictional characters, somewhat in the line developed by Pirandello and *Unamuno, with the difference that it is the *real* characters included in the novel who provoke the revolt of the fictional ones, questioning the "reality" of the former. *Trajecte final* (1975; Final Trajectory) contains a series of six science fiction novelettes. Typical detective and mystery creations are *Mossegar-se la cua* (1968; Biting One's Tail) which has to do with burial of a corpse under the name of someone still alive, *L'inspector fa tard* (1960; The Inspector Is Late) and *Joc brut* (1965; Brutal Game), in which a crime of passion is considered in relation to the probability that it would not have happened had any given detail been altered.

Other novels include *Es vessa una sang fàcil* (1954; An Easy Blood Is Spilled), *Cendra per Martina* (1967; Ashes for Martina), *L'interior es al final* (1974; The Inside [Room] Is at the End), *Domicili provisional* (1956; Temporary Residence), *Elena de segona mà* (1967; Secondhand Elena), *El temps a les venes* (1974; Time in the Veins), *Balanç fins a la matinada* (1963; Balance until Dawn), *Avui es parla de mi* (1966; Today They're Talking about Me), *Procés de contradicció suficient* (1976; Trial of Sufficient Contradiction), *Mister Chase, podeu sortir* (1955; Mr. Chase, You May Leave), *Una selva com la teva* (1960; A Forest Like Yours), *Nou pams de terra* (1971; Nine Palms of Earth), *Les finestres s'obren de nit* (1957; The Windows Open at Night), *Introducció a l'ombra* (1972; Introduction to the Shade), *Cops de bec a Pasadena* (1972; Beak Blows in Pasadena), *La mà contra l'horitzó* (1961; Hand against the Horizon), *Entrada en blanc* (1968; Entry in White), *Pas de ratlla* (1972; Crossing the Line), *Un amor fora ciutat* (1970; A Love outside the City), *Tocats pel foc* (1976; Touched by the Fire), *Si són roses floriran* (1971; If They Are Roses, They'll Bloom), *Acte de violència* (1975; Act of Violence), and *S'han deixat les claus sota l'estora* (1978; The Keys Are Left under the Rug). Among Pedrolo's best and most significant works, in the opinion of Catalan critics, is *Totes les bèsties de càrrega*

(1967; All the Beasts of Burden), a symbolic narration of the oppression of a people by an inhuman, absurd bureaucracy. Likewise of special importance are a cycle of novels, ''La terra prohibida'' (The Forbidden Land) related to the return of political exiles and including *Les portes del passat* (1978; Portals of the Past), *La paraula dels botxins* (1978; The Word of the Boxwoods), *Les fronteres interiors* (1979; Internal Frontiers), and *La nit horizontal* (1979; Horizontal Night). *See also* Catalan Literature.

BIBLIOGRAPHY

Primary Texts

Anonim I. Barcelona: Edicions 62, 1981.
Anonim II. Barcelona: Edicions 62, 1981.
Anonim III. Barcelona: Edicions 62, 1981.
Apocrif U: Oriol. Barcelona: Edicions 62, 1982.

Criticism

Coca, Jordi. *Pedrolo, perillòs? Converses amb Manuel de Pedrolo*. Barcelona: Dopesa, 1973.
Esslin, Martin. *El teatro del absurdo*. Barcelona: Seix Barral, 1966. 199–202.
Hart, Patricia. ''Manuel de Pedrolo and the Catalan Connection.'' In *The Spanish Sleuth (The Detective in Spanish Fiction)*. Cranbury, NJ: Associated University Presses, 1987. 51–66.
Pérez, Janet. ''Three Contemporary Cultivators of Science Fiction in Catalan.'' *Discurso Literario* 2.1 (1984): 203–16.
Wellwarth, George. ''Manuel de Pedrolo and Spanish Absurdism.'' *Books Abroad* 46(1972) 380–87.
———. *Spanish Underground Drama*. University Park: Pennsylvania State UP, 1972.

Janet Pérez

PELLICER, Juan Antonio (1738, Encinacorba, Zaragoza–1806, Madrid), bibliographer, literary scholar and critic. He is most remembered for the *Ensayo de una biblioteca de traductores españoles* (1778; Treatise on a Library of Spanish Translators), which compiles names of Castilian translations available then. His biography on *Cervantes contributed new data; his five-volume edition of the *Quijote*, however, has been surpassed by many others.

BIBLIOGRAPHY

Primary Text

Ensayo de una biblioteca de traductores españoles donde se da noticia de las traducciones que hay en castellano. Madrid: Sancha, 1778.

PELLICER DE OSSAU, José de (1602, Zaragoza–1679, Madrid), historian, genealogist, poet, presumed perpetrator of several hoaxes. He wrote an astute, sympathetic commentary of *Góngora's poetry in *Lecciones solemnes a las obras de don Luis de Góngora* (1630; Solemn Lessons to the Works of Luis de Góngora); his own poetry shows the influence of Góngora. As a genealogist, he has been charged with inventing details to enhance the lineage of clients—such as the apocryphal *Libro de las Querellas*, cited in his genealogy for the Sarmiento family, and the *Libro de los* **llantos*. Pellicer also served as chronicler of Castile and Leon (1624) and of Aragon (1640).

BIBLIOGRAPHY

Primary Texts

Anfiteatro de Felipe el Grande. Cieza: A. Pérez Gómez, 1974. Rpt. of 1631 ed.

Avisos históricos. Sel., E. Tierno Galván. Madrid: Taurus, 1965.

Lecciones solemnes a las obras de don Luis de Góngora. Madrid: n.p., 1630. Rpt. Hildesheim/New York: Olms, 1971.

PEMÁN Y PEMARTÍN, José María (1898, Cádiz–1981, Madrid), Spanish poet, playwright, orator, novelist and short story writer. He studied law in Seville and Madrid, and his dissertation was titled "Las ideas filosófico-jurídicas de la 'República de Platón' " (Philosophical-Juridical Ideas in Plato's *Republic*). He was elected to the *Academia Española in 1936 and was named director in 1946. Pemán's prolific production has been so acclaimed that a literary prize has been named after him. Influenced by Juan Ramón *Jiménez, Pemán wrote several books of poetry, such as *De la vida sencilla* (1923; Of Simple Life), *Nuevas poesías* (1925; New Poetry), *Las musas y las horas* (1945; Muses and Time), and *Antología de poesía lírica* (1954; Anthology of Lyric Poetry). A first collection of poetry appeared in 1937, *Poesías, 1923–1937* (Poetry, 1923–1937) and a second collection, *Poesía: nueva antología, 1917–1959* (Poetry: New Anthology, 1917–1959), appeared in 1959. His prose fiction includes the short stories *Volaterías* (1932; Fancy Free), *Claramor y Rosalinda y otros cuentos* (1947; Claramor and Rosalinda and Other Stories), and *Cuentos sin importancia* (1st ed., 1900s, 2nd ed., 1953; Unimportant Stories). As a novelist, he is noteworthy for *Historia del fantasma y doña Juanita* (1927; The Story of the Ghost and Miss Juanita), *De Madrid a Oviedo, pasando por las Azores* (1933; From Madrid to Oviedo, By Way of the Azores), *El vuelo inmóvil* (1941; The Motionless Flight), *Señor de su ánimo* (1943; Owner of His Soul), and *Doña Sol* (1950; Miss Sol [Sun]). Pemán also wrote *Breve historia de España* (1950; A Brief History of Spain) and two travelogues: one concerning America, *El paraíso y la serpiente* (1943; Paradise and the Serpent), and one concerning southern Spain, *Andalucía* (1958; Andalusia). A gifted orator of nineteenth-c. style, he combined poetic devices with flowery eloquence and spoke out strongly in favor of Hispanidad and traditional values. His lectures given in America were well received and are collected in his *Obras completas* (1948; Complete Works). Important books of essays include *Arengas y crónicas de guerra* (1937; Speeches and Chronicles of War), *El agustinismo del pensamiento contemporáneo* (1955; Augustinianism in Contemporary Thought), and *Ensayos andaluces* (1972; Andalusian Essays). Best known for his drama, Pemán has composed more than sixty plays in the categories of history, thesis, farce and comedy of manners. His many translations and adaptations of plays include *Antígona* (1946; Antigone), *Electra* (1949; Electra) and *Edipo* (1953; Oedipus), a version of Sophocles's play performed in the Roman amphitheater in Mérida. His historical plays, which defend his patriotism and Catholic convictions, include *Cisneros* (1934; Cisneros), *Metternich* (1942; Metternich), and *La destrucción de Sagunto* (1954; The Destruction of Sagunto), intended for performance in the ruins at Sagunto. His most successful thesis plays include *Callados como muertos* (1952; Silent as the Dead), *En las manos del hijo* (1953; In the Hands of the Son), *Los monos gritan al amanecer* (1963; Monkeys Cry Out at Dawn), and *Tres testigos* (1970; Three Witnesses). *El divino impaciente* (1933; *A Saint in a Hurry*, 1935), an interpretation of the missionary Saint Francisco Javier, was perhaps his most popular play, with more than fifteen editions in Spanish. Pemán's pre-war successes—such as *Cuando las Cortes de Cádiz* (1934; At the Courts of Cádiz) and *Julieta y Romeo* (1936; Romeo and Juliet)—built up a faithful following which ensured the success of his post-war plays: *La santa virreina* (1939; The Saintly Viceroy's Wife), *Entre el no y el sí* (1951; Between Yes and No), the comic *Los tres etcéteras de Don Simón* (1958; Don Simón's Three Etceteras), *Paca Almuzara* (1968; Paca Almuzara), *Y en el centro, el amor* (1971; And in the Center, Love), and many, many others. Pemán remained active in Madrid's theatrical life until his death in 1981; because of his great literary accomplishments and dedication to the profession, he is remembered as a patriarch of Hispanic letters. *See also* Contemporary Spanish Theater.

BIBLIOGRAPHY

Primary Texts

Obras completas. 7 vols. Madrid: Escelicer, 1947–65.
Obras selectas. Barcelona: Ahr, 1971.
Teatro. Madrid: G. del Toro, 1974.

English Translation

A Saint in a Hurry; El divino impaciente. Tr. Hugh De Blácam. Intro. Rev. C. C. Martindale, S.J. London: Sands, 1935.

Criticism

Berroa, Rei. "Discurso poético y exilio interior: la poesía española en los inicios del franquismo." *Cuadernos americanos* 258.1 (1985): 170–84.
En torno a Pemán. Cádiz: Excma. Diputación Provincial de Cádiz, 1974.
Gascó Contell, Emilio. *Pemán*. Madrid: EPESA, 1974.
Homenaje a José María Pemán. Madrid: Instituto N. de Bachillerato Masculino y Femenino, 1974.
Nin de Cardon, J. M. "José María Pemán: un patriarca de las letras hispánicas." In *Mensajes desde "El Cerro."* By José María Pemán. 1st ed. Madrid: Organización Sala Editorial, 1974. xiii-lxxxiii.

Zatlin, Phyllis Jean. *Themes of Greek Legend in the Theater of José María Pemán and His Contemporaries*. M.A. thesis, U of Florida, 1962. Micro-opaque of typescript, Lexington: U of Kentucky P, 1964.

Jana Sandarg

PENAS GARCIA, Anxeles (1943, Curtis, La Coruña–), Galician poet. After graduation from the Universidad de Santiago de Compostela, Anxeles Penas became a high school professor. Principally a poet, she has written some dramatic works and has practiced journalism. Her third book, *Galicia, fondo val* (1982; Galicia, Deep Valley), deals with her preferred existential theme whose overall orientation is that of political commitment. Penas has been the recipient of several literary awards since 1970. *See also* Galician Literature.

BIBLIOGRAPHY

Primary Texts

Con los pies en la frontera. La Coruña: Moret, 1976.
Galicia, fondo val. Sada, La Coruña: Ediciós do Castro, 1982.
Ya soy para tu muerte. Madrid: n.p., 1980.

Kathleen March

PENYA D'AMER, Victòria (1827, Mallorca–1898, ?), poet and editor. She won a prize in the first Jocs Florals (*juegos florales) with the poem "Amor de Mare" (1865; A Mother's Love) and was named an honorary member of the Academy of Belles Letters of Barcelona in the year 1872. Her poetry ranges from popular and familiar to moralizing and religious. She contributed to several journals, including *Lo Gay Saber*, *La Renaixença*, and *La Ilustració Catalana*. As editor she worked for *La Ilustración Católica* and *El Pensil del Bello Sexo*. She was honored by the publication of *Manat d'homenatge a Victòria Penya d'Amer* (n.d.; A Cluster of Homages to Victoria Penya d'Amer), a book which also includes one of her own poems. She was the sister of Pere d'Alcàntara and married to Miquel Victorià Amer. *See also* Catalan Literature.

BIBLIOGRAPHY

Primary Texts

Poesies. Barcelona: Ilustració Catalana, 1909.
Poetas Baleares S.XIX: Poesías de autores vivientes. Barcelona: Gelabert, 1873. 247–69.
Els Poetes Romantics de Mallorca: Recull antològic amb una introducció i comentaris. Ed. Manuel Sanchis Guarner. Mayorca: Moll, 1950. 113–23.

Kathleen McNerney

PEREDA, José María de (1833, Polanco, Santander–1906, Polanco), journalist, novelist. The twenty-second (and youngest) child born into a conservative family of *hidalgos* (minor aristocrats), Pereda grew up in the remote northern province of Santander. At the age of seven he left the village of Polanco to pursue his education in the seaport of Santander; then in 1852, on to Madrid to embark on a career in the artillery. By 1854 he was ready to go home, his military aspirations thankfully forgotten. From then on, Pereda stuck to his home ground, with rare forays to the outside world. He tended his estate and devoted most of his life to writing. In 1869 he married Diodora de la Revilla Huidobro. In 1871 he was elected a Carlist deputy to the Spanish Parliament, dissolved in 1872—his sole venture into the very real world of politics. In 1896 he became one of the immortals of the *Academia Española, but by then he was finished, worn out and disheartened by the changed literary atmosphere—realism was out, *modernism and other trends were in—and by the personal tragedy of his eldest son's suicide in 1893. Of a noble and kindly character, Pereda also suffered from a neurotic, passionate temperament. His friendships with liberals *Pérez Galdós and Leopoldo Alas (*Clarín), as well as with conservative critic Marcelino *Menéndez Pelayo, were exemplary. Pereda's life and work were molded by the ideological conflict of his age, the division between the "Two Spains," right and left, symbolized in his mind by the traditionalist, Catholic northern countryside of his youth and family and the liberal, progressive, desacralized metropolis, a social and moral body gangrened from within, as he describes it in his masterpiece, *Peñas arriba*. Thus, the capital, scene of his youthful experiences, was eventually to crystallize in his fiction as the arch-enemy of faith and tradition.

Pereda began as a journalist, contributing articles, sketches, and notes to a local magazine, *La Abeja Montañesa* (The Mountain Bee) in 1857–58 and later to a journal he himself founded, *El Tío Cayetano* (Old Cayetano) in 1858–59. He attempted to revive *El Tío Cayetano* in 1869 so that he could vent his outrage at the tumultuous events of the liberal Revolution of 1868. His first book, *Escenas montañesas* (1864; Mountain Scenes), included previously published sketches and pieces: they are *costumbrista* in intention and nature, stressing, however, some of the negative aspects of life in the provinces. This distaste in Pereda for the rudely ignorant was largely to disappear, to be replaced in his fiction by a fervent love for the things and people of Santander. *Tipos y paisajes* (1871; Types and Landscapes) was a continuation of his first book, followed by a collection of three short novels, *Bocetos al temple* (1876; Sketches in Distemper), *Tipos trashumantes* (1877; Nomadic Types), and *Esbozos y rasguños* (1881; Outlines and Sketches). Out of Pereda's passion for the specificity and the uniqueness of his region grew the desire to write more extended works of fiction. His first novel, *El buey suelto* (1878; The Bachelor), is, unfortunately, a dull, weak thing, which reads more like an ideological tract, with its heavy-handed moralizing on the benefits of marriage, any marriage, compared to the presumably unmitigated misery of bachelorhood. Pereda could not yet make the transition from sketch to novel: witness his inability to create even a moderately interesting character in *El buey suelto* or to link the (rudimentary) elements of plot into a smooth whole. Steadily, though, he made progress, as, for example, in the political satire, *Don Gonzalo González de la Gonzalera* (1879). He retrogressed in *De tal palo, tal astilla* (1880; A Chip off the Old Block), reverting to a Manichean presentation of reality in this melodramatic, unconvincing thesis novel. Only the Catholic traditionalists are good—liberals are wicked unbelievers—in this heated response to Pérez Galdós's novel *Gloria*. Characterization is wooden, situations contrived, and there is no subtlety at all in Pereda's tendentious preaching. In 1882, however, he came out with *El sabor de la tierruca* (The Feel of the Good Earth), a fervent prose poem to his native soil, beginning with a magnificent description of an oak tree, *la cajiga*. In 1883, he published *Pedro Sánchez*, a fine *Bildungsroman*, narrated in first person, on the molding of a provincial youth by the combined forces of politics, money, and sex in the capital. Balzac's Rastignac surely served as a model. The superb *Sotileza* (1885; *Fine Spun*, 1959) demonstrated Pereda's first-rate control of popular language and, finally, a sureness in creating stimulating characters, such as the animalistic Muergo, the understanding and earthy priest Father Apolinar, and the enigmatic Sotileza herself. In *Sotileza* he successfully merges the collective and individual strands of plot, character, and setting, in the epic depiction of Santander's fishermen and their unending struggle with the sea, and the complications of Sotileza's relationship with her three suitors. Structured round a series of contrasts—la Calle Alta versus la Calle Baja; the pure and refined versus the impure and coarse; popular class versus midle class—*Sotileza* is a nostalgic re-creation of a pre-industrialized Santander, an idealized remembrance of things past. Also noteworthy is *La puchera* (1889; The Stew; see ed. by L. Bonet, 1980). Pereda's other high point in fiction, *Peñas arriba* (The Peaks Above) appeared in 1895 and was dedicated "to the holy memory of my son." An extremely popular novel in its day, *Peñas arriba* exalts a simple, rural way of life, ruled by precedence, continuity, hierarchy, and a belief in transcendence. Marcelo, an untested and ordinary young *madrileño*, comes to the mountains of Santander to see his dying uncle Celso. It is apparent that Marcelo is to take the place of this quintessential patriarch of the mountains. To prepare him for this, Pereda patterns the novel into the classic initiation of a young man into manhood. In the process, Marcelo learns that the struggle upward in *Peñas arriba* represents the dual movement toward the difficult purifying of one's life and of one's death, for in Pereda's moral vision, it is only *how* we have lived and *how* we are to die that matter. Other Peredian novels include *La Montálvez* (1888); *Nubes de estío* (1891; Summer Clouds); *Al primer vuelo* (1891; On the First Flight); and *Pachín González* (1896), his last full-length fiction.

Pereda was not a critical realist of the Flaubertian stripe. It is his *costumbrista* roots which allow him to depict realistically popular types and to use popular language creatively. Montesinos has labeled his vision of the world a form of idyllic—hence, partial—realism, in which he sets up models of ideal behavior and wished-for patterns of living, all based on a conservative, hierarchical view of reality. In this sense, Pereda wrote what could be called exemplary fiction. At its worst, it represents an overt display of ideology, to which the fiction is more or less attached (*El buey suelto*, *De tal palo*). At its best, fiction and beliefs (ideology become refined) blend, convincing us of the legitimacy of Pereda's view of life, even if, ultimately, we do not accept it. In this, *Peñas arriba* is the supreme example. *See also* Romanticism.

BIBLIOGRAPHY

Primary Texts

Obras completas. 17 vols. Madrid: Suárez, 1921–30.
Obras completas. 2 vols. Madrid: Aguilar, 1948.

English Translations

The Last of the Breed, and Other Stories. Tr. D. Freeman. London: Nutt, 1916. Five stories.
La puchera. Ed. L. Bonet. N.p.: n.p., 1980.
Sotileza, Fine Spun. Tr. G. Barr. New York: Exposition, 1959.

Criticism

Eoff, S. *The Modern Spanish Novel*. N.p.: n.p., 1961. 21–50.
Klibbe, L. H. *José María de Pereda*. N.p.: n.p., 1975.
Montesinos, J. F. *Pereda o la novela idilio*. 2nd ed. N.p.: n.p., 1969.
Pérez Gutiérrez, F. *El problema religioso en la generación de 1868*. N.p.: n.p., 1975. 131–80.
Valis, N. M. "Pereda's *Peñas arriba*: A Re-examination." *Romantistisches Jahrbuch* 30 (1979): 298–308.

Noël M. Valis

PÉREZ, Alonso (sixteenth c., Salamanca–?), physician, *pastoral author. A personal friend of *Montemayor, Pérez published his continuation to Montemayor's *Diana* in 1564; it enjoyed the good fortune of often being published along with Montemayor's work throughout the sixteenth and seventeenth centuries. Modern publications have not been so generous. His continuation was also customarily translated with the original *Diana*, into French, German and English, making it more popular, although not more worthy, than Gil *Polo's *Segunda Diana*. In the *Quijote*, *Cervantes's priest condemned Pérez's continuation to the fire.

BIBLIOGRAPHY

Primary Text

Los siete libros de la Diana. By J. Montemayor. 2 vols. Antwerp: Bellero, 1580–81. Vol. 2 contains the *Segunda parte* by Alonso Pérez.

English Translation

Diana of George of Montemayor. . . . Tr. B. Yong. London: Bollifant, 1598. Includes second part by Pérez, and also the continuation of Gil Polo.

Criticism

Avalle-Arce, J. B. *La novela española pastoril*. 2nd ed. Madrid: Istmo, 1974.
Smieja, F. "La señora no es para la hoguera: El caso de *La segunda parte de la Diana* de Alonso Pérez." In *Actas del Sexto Congreso Internacional de Hispanistas*. Ed. A. M. Gordon and E. Rugg. Toronto: U of Toronto, 1980.

PÉREZ, Andrés (fl. 1601, León–1622, León), Dominican religious writer. He entered the order at age fourteen, and began preaching in 1592. His first-known work is *Vida de San Raymundo de Peñafort* (1601; Life of St. Raimundo of Peñafort); several years later his *Sermones de Quaresma* (1618; Lenten Sermons) appeared, followed by *Sermones de los Santos* (1622; Sermons on the Saints). He has been proposed as a possible author of the **Pícara Justina*, but most criticism considers *López de Úbeda the most likely possibility.

BIBLIOGRAPHY

Primary Texts

Sermones de Quaresma y de Santos. Valladolid: n.p., 1621–22.
Vida de san Raymundo de Peñafort. Salamanca: n.p., 1601?

PÉREZ, Antonio (c. 1532, Madrid–1611, Paris), writer, statesman, secretary to Philip II. A consummate practitioner of palace intrigue, Antonio Pérez was throughout his life surrounded by controversy and mystery. Presumably the son of Gonzalo Pérez, royal secretary to Charles V and Philip II, he received the protection of the prestigious Eboli family and attended the Universities of Alcalá, Louvain, Padua, and Salamanca. His courtly manners, extensive education, and connections with those in high places made it possible for him to succeed his father as secretary of state in 1567. For the next decade his influence on Philip II was extensive. In 1578, however, Juan de Escobedo, secretary to don Juan de Austria, was assassinated, and Antonio Pérez became the prime suspect. He was eventually arrested and tried, but his friends helped him to escape to Aragon in 1590. When his capture by the king's forces was imminent in 1591, he fled to France, where he spent the remainder of his life.

During his exile he published his famous memoirs, *Relaciones de su vida* (1592; An Autobiography), which vilified Philip II and did much to propagate the *Black Legend against Spain, especially after a second edition was printed in London in 1594. His vindictiveness toward Philip was reaffirmed through the friendship of Pérez with the Earl of Essex of England and Henry IV of Navarre, as well as through his service as a spy for both nations. Before his painful death in 1611, he also published *Cartas a diferentes personas* (1598 and 1603; Letters to Diverse Individuals). *See also* Siglo de Oro.

BIBLIOGRAPHY

Primary Texts

Cartas de Antonio Pérez. Epistolario español. Ed. Eugenio de Ochoa. BAE 13.

Criticism

Marañón, Gregorio. *Antonio Pérez: El hombre, el drama, la época.* 3rd ed. 2 vols. Madrid: Espasa-Calpe, 1951.
Pérez Gómez, A. *Antonio Pérez, escritor y hombre de estado.* Cieza: La Fonte que mana y corre, 1959.
Pfandl, Ludwig. *Historia de la literatura española en la Edad de Oro.* Barcelona: Gustavo Gili, 1952.

Selig, Karl Ludwig, and G. Ungerer. "Letters by Antonio Pérez to don Juan de Zúñiga, 1577." *Bibliothèque d'Humanisme et Renaissance* 27 (1965): 672–81.

Ungerer, Gustav. *A Spaniard in Elizabethan England: The Correspondence of Antonio Pérez's Exile*. 2 vols. London: Tamesis, 1974.

C. Maurice Cherry

PÉREZ CLOTET, Pedro (1902, Villaluenga del Rosario, Cádiz–), Spanish poet. One of the most determined voices of Andalusian poetry, he founded and directed the poetry review, *Isla*. An independent poet who remained apart from the currents of his day (the *Generation of 1927, vanguardism, and later social currents), he occasionally echoes some of the classical Spanish poets of the *Siglo de Oro. Important poetic collections include *Signo del alba* (1929; Sign of the Dawn), *Trasluz* (1933; Against the Light), *Invocaciones* (1942; Invocations), *A orillas del silencio* (1943; On the Shores of Silence), *Presencia fiel* (1944; Faithful Presence), *Soledades en vuelo* (1945; Solitudes in Flight), and *Noche del hombre* (1950; The Night of Man). He published an important study on *Quevedo (1928), and has also written prose, as in *Bajo la voz amiga* (1949; Beneath the Friendly Voice).

PÉREZ DE AYALA, Ramón (1880, Oviedo–1962, Madrid), Asturian novelist, critic, and poet. The author himself confirmed that his date of birth was August 9, 1880, thus solving a polemic concerning the year of his birth. He studied with the Jesuits. He received his law degree in Oviedo, where he was a student of *Clarín. He traveled in France, Italy, England, Germany, and the United States (where he married the American Mabel Rick in 1913), and was a war correspondent for the Buenos Aires newspaper *La Prensa* during World War I. From his visit to the battlefields came his work *Hermann, encadenado* (1917; Herman, in Chains). In 1928 he was elected to the *Academia Española, but never delivered his inaugural address. He served as ambassador to England during the Second Republic (1931–36). After the Spanish Civil War, he and his family spent three years in Biarritz and in Paris. He then moved to Argentina in 1940 where he remained until his return to Spain in 1954. He continued to study the classics and write for *ABC* until his death on August 5, 1962.

Ayala was a novelist, lyric poet and essayist. His poetry is uneven, at times becoming prosaic. His verses are—like those of *Unamuno—ideological and conceptual. Nonetheless, they are not devoid of human emotion. *La paz del sendero* (1904; The Peaceful Path) is the title of his first collection of poems, in which there is something of *modernism, of *Berceo and of Francis Jammes, according to Valbuena. It is his poem of the earth. *El sendero innumerable* (1916; The Path of Infinite Variations) is his poem of the sea and is the best technically. *El sendero andante* (1921; The Flowing Path) is the poem of rivers and is modernist in style.

Ayala's most famous essay, *Las máscaras* (1917–19; The Masks), is about plays, playwrights, and the theory of tragedy. At times the author is excessively harsh or biased in his criticism of theatrical works. In another book of criticism, *Política y toros* (1918; Politics and Bulls), he explores the Spanish penchant for considering oneself an expert on all topics, especially the two mentioned in the title. *El libro de Ruth* (1928; The Book of Ruth) is an anthology of essays extracted from his novels. José García Mercadal has collected many other Ayalan critical essays in *Ante Azorín* (1964; In the Presence of Azorín), *Amistades y recuerdos* (1961; Friendships and Memories), *Divagaciones literarias* (1958; Literary Musings), *Más divagaciones literarias* (1960; More Literary Musings), *Pequeños ensayos* (1963; Little Essays), *El país del futuro: Mis viajes a los Estados Unidos, 1913–1914, 1919–1920* (1959; The Country of the Future: My Voyages to the United States), *Nuestro Séneca* (1966; Our Seneca), *Tributo a Inglaterra* (1963; Tribute to England), *Tabla rasa* (1963; The Table Cleared), *Principios y finales de la novela* (1958; Beginnings and Ends of the Novel), *Fábulas y ciudades* (1961; Fables and Cities), *Viaje entretenido al país del ocio* (1975; Entertaining Voyage to the Land of Leisure), and *Apostillas y divagaciones* (1976; Annotations and Musings). Most of these essays appeared first in Latin-American and Spanish newspapers and literary journals.

Pérez de Ayala is best known as a novelist. His novels are *Tinieblas en las cumbres* (1907; Darkness on the Heights), a crude history of libertine living, published under the pseudonym Plotino Cuevas; *La pata de la raposa* (1912; *The Fox's Paw*, 1924), part two of the above novel; *A.M.D.G.* (1910; To the Greater Glory of God), a novelistic description of life in a Jesuit boarding school, which caused a furor in Spain and which was eventually banned; and *Troteras y danzaderas* (1913; Mummers and Dancers), which is a *roman à clef* about the bohemian literary life in Madrid. Novels which show more maturity include *Luna de miel, luna de hiel* (1923; *Honeymoon, Bitter Moon*, 1972); its sequel *Los trabajos de Urbano y Simona* (1923; *The Labors of Urbano and Simona*, 1972); *Belarmino y Apolonio* (1921; *Belarmino and Apolonio*, 1971); *Tigre Juan*, and its second part, *El curandero de su honra* (1926; *Tiger Juan* and *The Healer of His Honor*, 1933). The latter two books won the National Prize for Literature in 1926, and, along with *Belarmino*, are considered Ayala's best works. He published his last short novel in 1928—*Justicia* (Justice).

Ayala was also the author of monographs on art—*Julio Antonio* and *Miguel Viladrich*; two collections of short novels, *Bajo el signo de Artemisa* (1924; Under the Sign of Artemis) and *El ombligo del mundo* (1924; The Umbilical Center of the World); and three short "poematic novels": *Prometeo, Luz de domingo*, and *La caída de los Limones* (1916; *Prometheus*, *Sunday Sunlight*, and *The Fall of the House of Limon*, 1920). Poems are interpolated into the structure of the latter three novels. Four volumes of his Complete Works were published by José García Mercadal between 1964 and 1969.

He is one of the best novelists of the twentieth c.; some of his novels rank among the best in all of Spanish literature. He was an admirer of *Pérez Galdós, from whose masterful novelistic technique he adapted elements for his own personal style. A member of the *novecentistas*, a transitional group between the better-known *Generation of 1898 and *Generation of 1927, Ayala shared much of the ideology and intellectualism of the former while his attention to style and his more cosmopolitan worldview made him a precursor of the latter. Ideas and narration are equally important in his novels. His ample knowledge of classical culture lessens neither the authenticity of his works nor his deep understanding of human nature and his careful observation of nature. His humor is often mixed with melancholy, and Asturias and Oviedo are the setting of his narratives. His fictional city Pilares is based on Oviedo.

In his early works, realism and *costumbrismo* predominated, and he combined skepticism, satire and pessimism with his humor. From *Belarmino* on, the novels become more intellectual and less realistic, though his symbolic characters remain believable and very human. Descriptions tend to be caricatures or are used to illustrate the author's belief in perspectivism—in which all points of view are correct, though partial, renderings of reality. The narrative conflict is usually between ideologies. *Belarmino y Apolonio*, for example, presents the problem of doubt and faith versus reason, and the two books about Tigre Juan treat the theme of traditional honor. His style is polished and precise; his words are carefully chosen and often evince his extensive knowledge of Latin and Greek. In addition to the honor of being a member-elect of the Spanish Academy, he also received many literary awards including the Premio Nacional, the national prize for literature (1926) and the Juan March Prize for Creative Writing (1960).

BIBLIOGRAPHY

Primary Texts

A.M.D.G. Ed. Andrés Amorós. Madrid: Cátedra, 1983.

Escritos políticos. Ed. P. Garagorri. Madrid: Alianza, 1967.

Obras completas. Ed. José García Mercadal. 4 vols. Madrid: Aguilar, 1963–69.

Obras selectas. Prol. Néstor Luján. Barcelona: AHR, 1957.

Poesías completas. 3rd ed. Buenos Aires: Espasa-Calpe, 1944.

Ramón Pérez de Ayala (1880–1980). Antología. Ed. Manuel Fernández Avello. Oviedo: ALSA, 1980.

English Translations

Belarmino and Apolonio. Tr. Murray Baumgarten and Gabriel Berns. Berkley: U of California P, 1971. (Also French translation in 1923, Russian, 1925, German, 1958, and Italian and Japanese.)

The Fox's Paw. Tr. Thomas Walsh. Intr. A. Livingston. New York: Dutton, 1924.

Honeymoon, Bitter Moon and *The Labors of Urbano and Simona*. Tr. Barry Eisenberg. Berkeley: U of California P, 1972.

Prometheus. The Fall of the House of Limon. Sunday Sunlight. Tr. Alice P. Hubbard and Grace Hazard Conkling. Intro. H. Keniston. New York: Dutton, 1920.

Tiger Juan and *The Healer of His Honor*. Tr. and intro. Walter Starker. New York: Macmillan, 1933.

Criticism

Amorós, Andrés. *La novela intelectual de Ramón Pérez de Ayala*. Madrid: Gredos, 1972.

Best, Marigold. *Ramón Pérez de Ayala: An Annotated Bibliography of Criticism*. London: Grant and Cutler, 1980.

Bobes Naves, María del Carmen, and others. *Homenaje a Ramón Pérez de Ayala*. Universidad de Oviedo: Servicio de Publicaciones, 1980.

Derndarsky, Roswitha. *Ramón Pérez de Ayala: Zur Thematik und Kunstgestalt seiner Romane*. In *Studien zur Philosophie und Literatur des neunzehnten Jahrhunderts*. vol. 8. Frankfurt: Vittorio Klosterman, 1970.

Fernández, Pelayo Hipólito. *Estudios sobre Ramón Pérez de Ayala*. Oviedo: Instituto de Estudios Asturianos, 1980. Includes critical bibliography, pp. 153–204.

Rand, Marguerite C. *Ramón Pérez de Ayala*. TWAS 138. New York: Twayne, 1971. In English.

Simposio Internacional Ramón Pérez de Ayala. Ed. Pelayo H. Fernández. Gijón, Spain: Flores, 1981.

Weber, Frances Wyers. *The Literary Perspectivism of Ramón Pérez de Ayala*. UNCSRLL 60. Chapel Hill: U of North Carolina P, 1966.

Eunice D. Myers

PÉREZ DE GUZMÁN, Fernán (c. 1378–1460?), Lord of Batres, nobleman and author related to both Chancellor Pero *López de Ayala and the Marquis of *Santillana. After the battle of Higueruela, a declared enemy of the powerful don Alvaro de *Luna, Fernán Pérez de Guzmán was imprisoned (1432). After eight months he was released with the others. It is difficult to pinpoint the cause, but shortly after this political mishap, he retired to his estate where he laid down the sword and took up the pen. He carried on in his retirement a long, ascetic, philosophic, and literary correspondence with the bishop of Burgos, don Alonso de *Cartagena.

Although he did write poetry as a younger man, some of it collected in the *Cancionero de *Baena* (Baena's Songbook); critics differ on which they think the best or the most lyrical. All agree, however, that his *Generaciones y semblanzas* (c. 1450; Noble Lineage and Sketches) is a veritable fifteenth-c. prose masterpiece. It compares interestingly with his *Mar de Historias* (A Multitude of Histories) which precedes it. In *Mar de Historias* Pérez de Guzmán treats historical figures, ancient and medieval—Alexander the Great, Julius Caesar, and Charlemagne, for example—and literary figures—King Arthur and Tristan—without distinguishing between the two. This he accomplishes in the first part; in the second he deals with holy men, sages, and their works. An erudite compendium, its only cohesion is the deep belief in the continuity of the Holy Roman Empire under emperor and pope. Its style and manner of exposition foreshadow that of *Generaciones y semblanzas*. This work is based on and is in part a translation of the fourteenth-c. *Mare historiarum* by Giovanni della Colonna.

In the *Generaciones* one sees an astute observer of human nature, a historian, or biographer perhaps, in search of truth. For this reason he refuses to use his subjects, men he knew during his lifetime, as *exempla* of virtues or vices, since he feels that men are a mixture of both. Two basic ideas are presented in his prologue: the efficacy of fame as a moral vector and the historian's responsibility toward the redaction of history. Three rules of thumb for accurate historical prose are that (1) historians should be discrete and should have a pleasing style; (2) they should witness the events about which they write or at least discretely choose a reliable source; (3) they should publish their historical prose only after the death of the subjects in order to ensure objective truthfulness throughout the work. In this prologue, the first treatise on the nature of history and the duty of the historian, Fernán Pérez de Guzmán does for historical prose what his relative the Marquis of Santillana does for poetry.

Even so, absolute objectivity is an ideal which the author fortunately cannot attain, thereby revealing himself as well to his reader.

BIBLIOGRAPHY

Primary Text

Generaciones y Semblanzas. Ed. R. B. Tate. London: Tamesis, 1965.

Criticism

Castillo Mathieu, Nicolás del. "Breve análisis de las *Generaciones y semblanzas* de Fernán Pérez de Guzmán." *Thesaurus* 33 (1978): 422–45.

Deyermond, A. D. *A Literary History of Spain: The Middle Ages*. London: Benn; New York: Barnes and Noble, 1971. 153–54.

Entwistle, W. J. "A Note on Fernán Pérez de Guzmán's *Mar de Historias*, Cap. XCVI (Del stõ grial)." *MLR* 18 (1923): 206–8.

Anthony J. Cárdenas

PÉREZ DE HERRERA, Cristóbal (1558, Salamanca–1625, Madrid), physician, author. Aside from various medical works (he was physician to Philip III), he published a collection of erudite, popular enigmas, all written in verse, called *Proverbios morales* (n.d., Moral Proverbs). They attest to the prevailing taste for the obscure, the difficult and the indirect. Of even greater interest is his work on beggars, the *Discurso del amparo de los legítimos pobres* (1598; Discourse on Aid for the Legitimate Poor). He recounts fascinating examples of how false beggars swindle, cheat, and conduct immoral lives, and argues for clamping down on such abuse and establishing hospices for retraining such people for useful employment. He contributed his own funds to a Madrid poorhouse.

BIBLIOGRAPHY

Primary Text

Amparo de pobres. Ed., intro., M. Cavillac. Clásicos Castellanos 199. Madrid: Espasa-Calpe, 1975.

Criticism

García del Real, E. "Cristóbal Pérez de Herrera y la Decadencia de España Bajo el Gobierno de los Austrias." *Las Ciencias* (Madrid) 14 (1949): 692–715.

PÉREZ DE HITA, Ginés (1544?, Mula–1619?, ?), novelist, poet, and historian. Little is known about him. Although Pérez de Hita was believed to have been a shoemaker in Murcia, his writings firmly establish him as a man of learning. He fought against the *moriscos during their 1568–71 uprising and later developed the prototype of the Moor as brave, spirited, courtly, and honorable, idealizing him as a model of chivalrous behavior. His major work, *Historia de los bandos de los Zegríes y Abencerrajes* (Story of the Zegri and Abencerage factions), better known as *Historia de las guerras civiles de Granada* (1595; *The Civil Wars of Granada*, 1803), gives a powerful description of the rivalry among opposing noble families in Granada and of the continuous feuds which weakened the kingdom before its 1492 conquest by the Catholic kings. Characteristic of both the historical novel and the novel of chivalry, it is the best example of the *novela morisca* (Moorish novel), a genre which originated in Spain and treated a uniquely Spanish theme. The work combines historic reality with fictional episodes of romantic love inspired in the *romances moriscos* and *fronterizos* (Moorish and frontier ballads). Some forty ballads are included, selected from oral tradition and from the more recent literary production. Pérez de Hita presented a brilliant and enchanting tableau of courtly life in Granada, with its colorful festivals, tournaments, and amorous intrigues, identifying his source as the Arab chronicler, Aben Hamin. Today, scholars believe that he used Christian chronicles compiled by Esteban de *Garibay and Hernando del *Pulgar. Part 2 of the book, *Guerras civiles de Granada* (1619; Civil Wars of Granada), neglected the fictional element while strengthening the historical narrative of the revolt of the moriscos. Literarily, it is inferior to Part 1. Here, again, the author inserted ballads, of which some are of his own creation. Other works of lesser impact are *Bello troyano* (Handsome Trojan) and *Libro de la población y hazañas de la ciudad de Lorca* (Book on the People and Feats of the City of Lorca), an epic poem outlining *Guerras civiles*. The latter became very popular during the Spanish *Siglo de Oro (Lope de *Vega, *Calderón) and with the neo-classic, Romantic, and post-Romantic writers, such as Pedro Antonio de *Alarcón (*La Alpujarra*), *Martínez de la Rosa (*Morayma*, *Aben Humeya*), *Fernández y González (*Monfíes de las Alpujarras*, Highwaymen of the Alpujarras), *Moratín father (in his Moorish ballads) and son (''La toma de Granada,'' The Conquest of Granada). The book had an impact on international literary figures in Europe and in the United States as well. In France, it inspired Madeleine de Scudéry (*Almahide*) and Mme. de Lafayette (*Zaide. Histoire espagnole*, seventeenth c.), while, during the Romantic period, it served as the source of the Moorish novel for Chateaubriand's *Les aventures du dérnier Abencérage* and provided the Oriental theme for Victor Hugo's ode, ''La guerre d'Espagne'' and ''Grenade'' in *Les Orientales*. In England, John Dryden produced a heroic drama, *The Conquest of Granada* (seventeenth c.) and, in the United States, the book influenced Washington *Irving's *The Conquest of Granada* and *Legends of the Alhambra* (nineteenth c.). *Guerras Civiles* was translated into French, English, and German during the early nineteenth c. *See also Romancero*.

BIBLIOGRAPHY

Primary Texts

Ginés Pérez de Hita. Guerras civiles de Granada. Ed. P. Blanchard-Demouge. Madrid: Bailly-Ballière, 1913.

Guerras civiles de Granada. BAE 3.
Pérez de Hita, Ginés. Guerras civiles de Granada, Primera Parte. Ed. S. M. Bryant. Newark, DE: Juan de la Cuesta, 1982.

English Translation

The Civil Wars of Granada. Tr. T. Rodd. London: Ostell, 1803.

Criticism

Carrasco Urgoiti, María Soledad. *El moro de Granada en la literatura. (Del siglo XV al XX)*. Madrid: RO, 1956.
———. *The Moorish Novel: El Abencerraje and Pérez de Hita*. TWAS 375. Boston: Twayne, 1976.
Cirot, Georges. "La maurophilie littéraire en Espagne au XVième siècle." *BH* 40 (1938): 150–57, 281–96, 433–47; 41 (1939): 65–68, 345–451; 42 (1940): 213–27; 43 (1941): 265–89; 44 (1942): 96–102; 46 (1944): 5–25.
Espín Rael, J. *De la vecindad de Pérez de Hita en Lorca desde 1568 a 1577*. Lorca: n.p., 1922.
Fustugière, P. "Ginés Pérez de Hita. Sa personne. Son oeuvre." *BH* 46 (1944): 145–83.
Huré, Jacques. "A propos de l'influence de Pérez de Hita sur la littérature française." *Recherches et Etudes Comparatistes Ibéro-Francophones de la Sorbonne Nouvelle*. 4 vols. Paris: Crecifs, U of Paris, 1982. 4: 5–11.
Menéndez Pidal, Ramón. "Romancero nuevo y maurofilia." *España y su historia*. 2 vols. Madrid: Minotauro, 1957. 2: 253–79.
Menéndez y Pelayo, Marcelino. "*Las guerras civiles de Granada* de Ginés Pérez de Hita." *Orígenes de la novela*. vols 13–16 of his *Obras completas*. Santander: CSIC, 1940–74. 2: 134 ff. (Vol. 2 of *Orígenes*, which is vol. 14 of the *Obras completas*.)
Ruta, Emelina. *Ariosto y Pérez de Hita*. Rome: Archivum Romanicum, 1933.
Valli, Giorgio. "Ludovico Ariosto y Ginés Pérez de Hita." *RFE* 30 (1946): 23–53.

Reginetta Haboucha

PÉREZ DE LA OSSA, Huberto (1897, Albacete–), Spanish novelist and poet. He first came to the attention of the literary world with *El ancla de Jasón* (1921; Jason's Anchor), an updating of the myth of the Golden Fleece. *Polifonías* (1922; Polyphonies) is a collection of poetry in the post-modernist vein. His novels include *La lámpara del dolor* (1923; The Lamp of Pain), *El opio del ensueño* (1924; The Opium of Daydreaming), *La santa duquesa* (1924; The Sainted Duchess), *La casa de los masones* (1927; The Masonic House), *Obreros, zánganos y reinas* (1928; Workers, Drones and Queens), and *Los amigos de Claudio* (1931; The Friends of Claudius). He published a collection of short stories with the title *Veletas* (1926; Weathervanes), and tried his hand at the theater in *En el kilómetro 13* (published 1945; On the 13th Kilometer). He was a distinguished stage director, and in collaboration with Luis *Escobar, did an adaptation of *La Celestina* (1957; The Bawd).

PÉREZ DE MIRANDA, Gregorio. *See* López Soler, Ramón

PÉREZ DE MONTALBÁN, Juan (1601 or 1602, Madrid–1638, Madrid), dramatist, writer, notary for the *Inquisition. A close, loyal friend of Lope de *Vega, he was also his first biographer by virtue of his *Fama póstuma* (1636; Posthumous Fame), an homage which included collaborations by most poets of the day. Pérez de Montalbán was of **converso* background; in the early 1620s he was ordained a priest, and by 1633 he became a notary of the Inquisition. *Quevedo disliked him vehemently and attacked him in print. Pérez de Montalbán also participated in literary polemics with *Villayzán and *Jauregui, but he had many loyal friends, too.

Montalbán was popular and prolific in his short life. Leaving various questions of authorship and chronology aside, his works include a long epic poem, *Orfeo en lengua castellana* (1624; Orpheus in Castilian), a worthy collection of exemplary novels titled *Sucesos y prodigios de amor* (1624; Happenings and Prodigies of Love), and a miscellany of plays, novels, and sundry other compositions titled *Para todos. Exemplos morales, humanos y divinos* (1632; For Everybody. Moral, Human and Divine Lessons). The latter merited six editions in the space of two years. But Pérez de Montalbán is most remembered for his drama, about forty-five plays in all, and twelve *autos sacramentales* (**auto*). The plays are of all type, notable are *De un castigo dos venganzas* (For One Punishment a Double Vengeance), a well-written, violent honor play where an unfaithful wife and lover are murdered by the lover's ex-mistress; *No hay vida como la honra* (There Is No Life Like Honor), an action-filled tale with happy resolution; *Como amante y como honrada* (Like a Lover and Like An Honorable Woman), a suspenseful cloak-and-dagger story; and *Los *amantes de Teruel* (Lovers of Teruel), one of the finest *Siglo de Oro versions of this tragic legend of faithful lovers. Pérez de Montalbán's drama is generally entertaining and moralistic in intent, and clearly modeled on Lope's precepts. *See also* Theater in Spain.

BIBLIOGRAPHY

Primary Texts

Los amantes de Teruel. Ed. C. Iranzo. Valencia: Albatrós Hispanófila, 1983.

Dramáticos contemporáneos de Lope de Vega. In BAE 45. Contains seven plays.

Juan Pérez de Montalbán. Novelas ejemplares. Ed. F. Gutiérrez. Barcelona: Selecciones Bibliófilos, 1957.

Orfeo. Ed. P. Cabañas. Madrid: CSIC, 1948.

Para todos. Seville: Gómez, 1736.

Sucesos y prodigios. Ed., intro., A. González de Amezúa. Madrid: Sociedad de Bibliófilos españoles, 1949.

El sufrimiento premiado. Ed. V. Dixon. London: Tamesis, 1967.

Vida y purgatorio de San Patricio. Ed. M. G. Profeti. Pisa: U of Pisa, 1972.

English Translation

The diverting works of . . . Cervantes. Tr. E. Ward. London: Round, 1709. Actually a selection from *Para todos*.

The effect of being undeceived and *The test of friendship*. In Roscoe, T. *The Spanish Novelists*. London: n.p., 1832. 2: 165–267.
The nun ensign. Ed., tr. J. Fitzmaurice Kelly. London: Unwin, 1908.
A weeks entertainment. Tr. E. Ward. London: Woodward, 1710. Wrongly attributed to Cervantes.

Criticism

Dixon, V. "Juan Pérez de Montalbán's *Segundo tomo de las comedias*." *HR* 29 (1961): 91–109.
———. "Juan Pérez de Montalbán's *Para todos*." *HR* 32 (1964): 36–59.
Parker, J. H. *Juan Pérez de Montalbán*. TWAS 352. Boston: Twayne, 1975.
Profeti, M. G. *Montalbán: un commediografo dell 'eta' di Lope*. Pisa: U of Pisa, 1970.

Maureen Ihrie

PÉREZ DE MOYA, Juan (1513?, Santiesteban del Puerto, Jaén–1597?, Granada), mathematician, author, canon of Granada. He studied in Salamanca, and lived in Alcalá from 1572 until at least 1585. His primary literary work is a collection, with commentary, of Greek and Roman myths in which each fable is accompanied by an astute moral or other pertinent observation. Titled *Philosophia Secreta* (1585; Secret Philosophy), its didactic aims are achieved in charming fashion.

Pérez de Moya also wrote several books on mathematics, the most memorable of which is *Aritmética práctica y especulativa* (1562; Practical and Theoretical Arithmetic), as well as a *Varia historia de Sanctas e ilustres mujeres* (1583; Selected History of Holy and Illustrious Women), and *Comparaciones símiles de vicios y virtudes* (1584; Similar Comparisons of Vices and Virtues).

BIBLIOGRAPHY

Primary Texts

Aritmética práctica y especulativa. 15th ed. Madrid: López, 1798.
Philosophia secreta. Ed. E. Gómez de Baquero. 2 vols. Madrid: Compañía ibero-americana, 1928.

PÉREZ DE OLIVA, Fernán (1494, Córdoba–1531, Córdoba), humanist, dramatist and poet. He was a student at the U of Salamanca, and Alcalá; his formal training then continued in schooling abroad, in Rome and Paris. He returned to Salamanca in 1524, was named rector of the U of Salamanca in 1529, and a year later gained the chair of nominalist theology. Because Pérez de Oliva was widely recognized for his erudition, the king appointed him tutor to Prince Philip (though he died before the prince came of age). His dialogues, his superb prose translations of classical Greek plays, and his poetry reflect clearly a *Renaissance view of man. All were published posthumously, mostly by his nephew, Ambrosio de *Morales. His most famous work is the *Diálogo de la dignidad del hombre* (?, pub. 1546; Dialogue on the Dignity of Man), a discussion of man's good and evil qualities which concludes according to Christian truth. It was continued by *Cervantes de Salazar. *See also* Humanism; Renaissance.

BIBLIOGRAPHY

Primary Texts

Diálogo de la dignidad del hombre. Ed. L. Abellán. Barcelona: Clarasó, 1967. Includes preliminary study and bibliography.

Diálogo. . . . BAE 65.

Las obras del Maestro Fernán Pérez de Oliva. 2nd ed. 2 vols. Madrid: Benito Cano, 1787.

Criticism

Atkinson, W. ''Hernán Pérez de Oliva. A Biographical and Critical Study.'' *RH* 71 (1927): 309–484.

''Un Dialogue de Hernán Pérez de Oliva et une lettre d'Ambrosio de Morales: Un Latin à l'espagnole.'' Ed. Jean Claude Margolin. *Acta Conventus. Neo-Latini Turonensis*. Paris: Vrin, 1980. 495–500.

PÉREZ DE URBEL, Justo (1895, Burgos–1979, Madrid), Spanish essayist, poet, medievalist, translator. A Benedictine monk, Pérez de Urbel began his literary life as a collaborator in the bulletin published by the Abbey of Santo Domingo de Silos, and translating books from the English and German. His name became known with the publication of his *Semblanzas literarias* (1927; Literary Portraits) and *San Eulogio de Córdoba* (1927). Thenceforth, he devoted himself to lecturing, contributing to newspapers and magazines, to poetry (e.g, *In terra pax* [1941; Peace on Earth]), and to writing the lives of saints. As a hagiographer, he published five tomes of *El año cristiano* (The Christian Year) beginning in 1934, as well as *San Isidoro de Sevilla*, *Vida de Cristo* (The Life of Christ), *Vida de San Pablo* (Life of St. Paul), and his *Itinerario litúrgico* (Liturgic Itinerary). As a historian, he is noted for a number of books of investigation, including *Los monjes españoles en la Edad Media* (1939; Spanish Monks in the Middle Ages) and *Historia del condado de Castilla* (1945; History of the Counts of Castile). He was made abbot of the Benedictine community in the Valle de los Caídos (Valley of the Fallen; a monument established by the Franco regime in memory of Civil War dead).

PÉREZ DEL PULGAR, Hernán (1451, Ciudad Real, Ocaña?–1531, Granada), heroic soldier, author of a historical account. He fought with the legendary Gran Capitán Gonzalo Fernández de Córdoba in the final years of the Reconquest. Charles V later requested Pérez del Pulgar to record these events, and they were so annotated in the *Breve parte de las hazañas del excelente nombrado Gran Capitán* (1527; Brief Account of the Deeds of the Excellently Named Great Captain). It suffers from an overabundance of learned references and exaggeration at certain moments.

BIBLIOGRAPHY

Primary Text

Crónicas del Gran Capitán. Ed. A. Rodríguez Villa. In NBAE 10.

PÉREZ ESCRICH, Enrique (1829, Valencia–1897, Madrid), novelist and playwright. Pérez Escrich began his theater career in his hometown, but due to financial difficulties occasioned by an early marriage, he decided to try his fortune in Madrid. A string of plays furthered his reputation among other writers, but failed to bring him immediate popular acclaim. Little by little, the prolific Pérez Escrich achieved popular success in the theater, cultivating dramatic works, comedies, and **zarzuelas*. His true fame, however, rests on his production of serialized novels, which were beginning to come in vogue at the time. Like Manuel *Fernández y González, Pérez Escrich reduced the Romantic novel to mere melodrama, sentimentality, and a contrived plot, which, nevertheless, appealed to the mass public and earned a fortune for the author. In 1865, Pérez Escrich adapted his play *El cura de aldea* (The Village Priest) as a novel, but was accused of plagiarism and prosecuted by Luis Mariano de *Larra, son of Mariano José de *Larra; Pérez Escrich was acquitted. Despite his acquired wealth, he ended his life in poverty due to his free-spending.

BIBLIOGRAPHY

Primary Texts

La caridad cristiana. 2 vols. Madrid: Romero, 1906. Sequel to *El cura de aldea*.
El cura de aldea. Madrid: Rodríguez, 1860. Play.
El cura de aldea. 3 vols. Buenos Aires: Sopena, 1939.
El mártir del Gólgota; tradiciones de Oriente. 2 vols. Mexico City: Cicerón, 1947.
La mujer adúltera, novela de costumbres. 2 vols. Madrid: Romero, 1904.

English Translation

The Martyr of Golgotha. Tr. Adèle Josephine Godoy. New York: W. S. Gottsberger, 1887.

Criticism

Alborg, Juan Luis. *Historia de la literatura española*. vol. 4. Madrid: Gredos, 1980.

Linda Maier

PÉREZ FERRERO, Miguel (1905, Madrid–), Spanish poet, biographer, editor and movie critic. Although he holds a doctorate in law, most of his activities have been literary, as part of the group associated with *La Gaceta Literaria* in the vanguard years, and editor of a broad variety of periodicals in successive epochs. He was one of the editors of the literary yearbook *Almanaque literario*, and a contributor to *Cruz y raya*. As a biographer, he published a *Vida de Ramón* (1935; Life of Ramón [*Gómez de la Serna]), the *Vida de Antonio Machado y Manuel* (1947; The Life of Antonio Machado and Manuel), and several biographical studies of Pío *Baroja. He was known as an important cinema critic, writing under the pseudonym Donald.

PÉREZ GALDÓS, Benito (1843, Las Palmas de Gran Canaria–1920, Madrid). Although he spent his youth on Grand Canary Island, Galdós in his life and works was to become closely identified with the capital, scene of many of his finest novels. He was a talented youngster who excelled in writing and the visual arts, yet was an indifferent student in school. His mother, a strong-willed matriarchal power of the household—she probably inspired one of his more unforgettable characters, doña Perfecta—wanted her tenth and youngest child to become a lawyer, the quintessential symbol of middle-class prosperity and stability in nineteenth-c. Spain. Benito demurred; she insisted; and the result was that Galdós found himself studying law—this was soon to be mere pretense—at the U of Madrid (1862). Yet the novelist did apply himself: not to the law of course, but to the observation of life teeming about him in Madrid. There it was: all the corruption and exuberance of life in the making, ready for the sharp yet always eminently human dissection of the future novelist. He became a journalist for *La Nación* (1865; The Nation), which served as an apprenticeship for his creative impulses. He went to Paris (1867), soaked up some of the heady literary atmosphere there, and wrote his first novel, *La Sombra* (1871; *The Shadow*, 1980), a curious piece of psychological fantasy. Another early novel, *La fontana de oro* (1871; The Golden Fountain), is a historical fiction that takes place in 1821 during the interim constitutional government to which the despot Fernando VII reluctantly acceded. This novel and the next one, *El audaz* (1871; The Bold One), established Galdós's fervent and abiding interest in Spain's past as an explanation and anticipation of her present and future. In 1873 he began the first (and most popular) of five series of *Episodios nacionales* (National Episodes). Between 1876 and 1879 he had come out with the remaining four Novels of the First Period, or *Novelas de la primera época*: *Doña Perfecta* (1876; *Doña Perfecta*, 1960), *Gloria* (1877; *Gloria*, 1879), *Marianela* (1878; *Marianela*, 1883), and *La familia de León Roch* (1879; *Leon Roch, a romance*, 1888). The year 1881 signals a high point for Galdós: he published the first of his twenty-four volumes of *Novelas contemporáneas* (Contemporary novels), *La desheredada* (*The Disinherited Lady*, 1957), a splendid analysis of his country's capacity for self-delusion and dream making. This and the next five novels—*El amigo Manso* (1882; *Our Friend Manso*, 1987), *El doctor Centeno* (1883; Doctor Centeno), *Tormento* (1884; *Torment*, 1952), *La de Bringas* (1884; *The Spendthrifts*, 1951), and *Lo prohibido* (1884–85; The Forbidden)—constitute the novelist's most naturalistic phase of his writing and an advance over the earlier thesis novels, such as *Doña Perfecta* and *Gloria*. Writing steadily and indefatigably, Galdós relentlessly churned out novel after novel—and later, more national episodes, plays, and essays—till his final days. Along the way, he produced some of his best fiction, the masterpiece *Fortunata y Jacinta* (1886–87; *Fortunata and Jacinta*, 1986), *Miau* (1888; *Miau*, 1963), *Ángel Guerra* (1890–91), *Nazarín* (1895), and *Misericordia* (1897; *Compassion*, 1966). These last three novels reflect a growing preoccupation with things of the spirit and faith. And he still found time to pursue politics, becoming a deputy in the Spanish Parliament, first in 1886–90, and, later, in 1907 and 1914, his Republican phase. Galdós also traveled extensively, exploring England, Portugal, the Rhineland, Italy, and other parts of Europe. He was elected to the *Academia Española in 1889. It was that same august body which steadfastly refused to support Galdós's candidacy for the Nobel Prize for Literature. The last decade of his life was marked by a weakened creativity, declining health, and economic difficulties. Yet thousands gathered at his funeral to pay homage to the (now) undisputed master of the last century's narrative form (see P. Beltrán de Heredia, "España en la muerte de Galdós," *Anales Galdosianos* 5 [1970]: 89–101). Galdós was a quiet, unassuming man, an attentive listener, not one to talk about himself. But behind that reticent mask was an energetic, complex personality driven, as C. P. Snow highlights in *The Realists* (1978), by the two great passions of his life, literature and, as we know now from recently published correspondence and other sources, women.

Works

Galdós produced an incredible amount of work in his lifetime: forty-six National Episodes, thirty-one novels, twenty-three plays, and fifteen volumes of articles and other miscellaneous writings, much of the latter published posthumously, such as *Memoranda* (1906), *Arte y crítica* (1923; Art and Criticism), and *Toledo: Su historia y su leyenda* (1924?; Toledo: Its History and Its Legends). Also published were a number of collections of his newspaper contributions: *Crónica de la quincena* (1948; Fortnightly Chronicle); *Los artículos de Galdós en "La Nación." 1865–1866, 1868* (1972; Articles of Galdós in *The Nation.* 1865–1866, 1868); *Las cartas desconocidas de Galdós en "La Prensa" de Buenos Aires* (1973; Unknown Letters by Galdós in *The Press* of Buenos Aires), all edited by W. H. Shoemaker. His Complete Works, six volumes—by no means complete—were published by Aguilar.

National Episodes

As a chronicler of his country's historical past, don Benito ranks supreme. His first series of ten *episodios nacionales*, composed rapidly in only three years (1873–75), vibrates with the patriotic intensity that infuses this aesthetic recreation of Spanish history, from the battle of Trafalgar (1805) to the battle of Los Arapiles during the War of Independence (1812). The second series, also ten volumes (1875–79), deals with the period following the French defeat in Spain, that is, the capricious and cruel reign of Fernando VII and the increasingly bitter struggle between the "Two Spains," between conservative and liberal factions already splintering within their own ranks. B. Dendle observes that "in the *episodios* written between 1898 and 1912, Galdós's ordering of the past reflects a vision born of the present" (*Galdós: The Mature Thought*, 1980); and this, in turn, reflects a Galdosian notion of history treated not in itself and as itself, but as an imaginative instrument of moral and spiritual enlightenment. The last three series of *episodios nacionales* (twenty-six volumes) cover the historical period from 1834 to 1879, and are imbued with the fervor of a regenerationist and the subsequent disillusionment of a man who needed to believe in ultimate redemption but who—apparently—could not do so. These episodes are not mere history, or even the aesthetic reconstruction of Spanish history:

they are history transcended through the power of moral imagination. In these, as Dendle says, "the mature Galdós is now less concerned with detailing historical 'facts' than in the earlier series; the imagination—rather than sources—increasingly directs his recreation of the past." Thus, the third series, written between the years 1898 and 1900, reflects both Galdós' regenerationist hopes of a reformed Spain and the disheartening sight of wounded veterans of the Cuban war. The fourth series, though it ostensibly treats the historical period 1848–68, in reality has its true referent in the years 1902–07 when life in Spain seemed to be drifting and the resurgence of anti-clericalism —almost an obsession in Galdós—was uppermost. The fifth and last series, of which only six novels were completed, echoes back to us the quarreling and fragmentation of Spanish Republicans (Galdós's political allegiance then) during the period 1907–12, as well as the Canarian novelist's own marked anti-clericalism.

Theater

As a playwright Galdós was a failure in one sense. He never could quite make the transition from novelist to dramatist when it came to technique. He was used to the slow tempo and narrative interiority of the novel form, and he found it irksome to infuse theatricality and a "show and tell" format into what were most often dramatic adaptations of his novels—for example: *Realidad* (1892; Reality), *Doña Perfecta* (1896), *El abuelo* (1904; *The Grandfather*, 1910), and *Casandra* (1910). On the other hand, despite these limitations, Galdós, following the example of Ibsen, introduced a sense of symbolic planes into the generally abysmal theater of his day. And at his best, he suggests deeper psychological realities, hints of the subconscious, invisible forces which had scarcely been tapped by contemporary Spanish dramatists. At his worst, Galdós displays political demagoguery in his insistence on message-ridden plays such as the *succès de scandale*, *Electra* (1901; tr., 1911).

Novels

Society and its interconnectedness are the substance of Galdós's novelistic art. Even when he focuses on the multiple layers of an individual personality, the novelist never fails to situate his character within the inextricable web of social relationships. His finest example of the dynamic interplay between individual and society is *Fortunata y Jacinta*. As A. Amado observes, "Galdós . . . is always plunged into collective and social life, poured into other peoples' lives, into that special life which comes about from having to live together . . . " ("Lo español y lo universal en la obra de Galdós," *Materia y forma en poesía*, 3rd ed., 1969). All of this means don Benito, as an observer of social realities, is a superb example of the past century's realist novelists (and specifically, a member of the Generation of 1868, along with *Clarín, *Pereda, Jacinto Octavio *Picón, *Palacio Valdés, and so on). Although he seldom formulated his ideas about the novel, he did say, late in his career, that "the novel is an image of life, and the art of writing novels consists of reproducing human character, passion and weakness, greatness and meanness, souls and their physiognomy, all the spiritual and physical forces that are part of us and surround us; language, which is the sign of a people; living space, the symbol of the family; and dress, the mark of the most external traces of personality: all this without forgetting that there must exist a perfect balance between precision and beauty of that reproduction" ("La sociedad presente como materia novelable," *Discurso leído ante la Real Academia Española*, 1897; Present-day Society as Novelistic Material, Speech Read Before the Royal Spanish Academy). Other critical writings of Galdós on the novel include his essay "Observaciones sobre la novela contemporánea en España" (1870; Observations on the Contemporary Novel in Spain), the prologue to José María de Pereda's *El sabor de la tierruca* (1882), and the prologue to the second edition of Leopoldo Alas's *La Regenta* (1901). But Galdós is more than simply an exemplary realist. R. Gullón says of him that "he is the connecting door between two centuries and two trends: realism and symbolism." And he goes on to observe that in Galdós "reality furnishes the starting point, but from there on, the novelist seeks to find the determining impulse beneath that reality, plunging into the shadowy zones of consciousness and exploring the currents of abnormality and dreams. For this reason Galdós may be considered 'modern' and the head of the most noteworthy line of our present-day novel" ("The Modern Spanish Novel," *Texas Quarterly*, Spring 1961). In the early novel *Doña Perfecta* Galdós would write of how his hero, Pepe Rey, "contemplated the immense blackness of the night. You couldn't see anything. . . . That same almost total lack of clarity produced the effect of an illusory movement in the masses of trees, which seemed to stretch outward, lazily went forward and returned encoiled, like the surge of waves in a sea of shadows. A formidable flux and reflux, a battle among forces scarcely understood agitated the silent sphere." This conflict of cosmic and mysterious proportion is emblematic of the novelist's dramatic imagination. Like Balzac, Galdós is a visionary bent on revealing to his readers a series of hidden and unstable relationships and the unresolved dialectical tensions of the *arcanum* which constitutes our world. *See also* Naturalism.

BIBLIOGRAPHY

Primary Texts

Los artículos de Galdós en "La Nación." 1865–1866, 1868. Ed., study W. H. Shoemaker. Madrid: Insula, 1972.

Las cartas desconocidas de Galdós en "La Prensa" de Buenos Aires. Ed., study W. H. Shoemaker. Madrid: Cultura Hispánica, 1973.

Crónica de la quincena. Ed., study W. H. Shoemaker. Princeton: Princeton UP, 1948.

Obras completas. 6 vols. Madrid: Aguilar, 1950–54.

English Translations

Compassion, a novel. Tr. T. Talbot. New York: Ungar, 1962.

The Disinherited Lady. Tr. G. E. Smith. New York: Exposition, 1957.

Doña Perfecta. Tr., intro. H. de Onís. Great Neck, NY: Barron's, 1960.

Fortunata and Jacinta. Tr. A. Moncy Gullón. Athens: U of Georgia P, 1986.

Gloria. Tr. C. Bell. New York: Gottesberger, 1882.

The Grandfather. Tr. E. Wallace. In *Poet Lore* 21.3 (1910): 161–233.
Leon Roch, a romance. Tr. C. Bell. New York: Gottsberger, 1888.
Marianela. Tr. H. W. Lester. New York: Translation P, 1923.
Miau. Tr. J. M. Cohen. London: Methuen, 1963.
Our Friend Manso. Tr. R. Russell. New York: Columbia UP, 1987.
The Shadow. Tr. and ed. K. O. Austin. Athens: Ohio UP, 1980.
The Spendthrifts. Tr. G. Woolsey. London: Weidenfeld and Nicolson, 1951.
Torment. Tr. J. M. Cohen. London: Weidenfeld and Nicolson, 1952.

Criticism

Alas, Leopoldo. *Galdós*. Madrid: Renacimiento, 1912.
Anales Galdosianos. 1966-
Berkowitz, H. Chonan. *Pérez Galdós. Spanish Liberal Crusader*. Madison: U of Wisconsin, 1948.
Casalduero, J. *Vida y obra de Galdós*. 4th ed. Madrid: Gredos, 1978.
Correa, G. *El simbolismo religioso en las novelas de Pérez Galdós*. Madrid: Gredos, 1962.
Eoff, S. H. *The Novels of Pérez Galdós*. St. Louis: Washington U, 1954.
Gilman, S. *Galdós and the Art of the European Novel. 1867–1887*. Princeton: Princeton UP, 1981.
Gullón, R. *Técnicas de Galdós*. Madrid: Taurus, 1970.
Hafter, M. Z. "Ironic Reprise in Galdós' Novels." *PMLA* 86 (1961): 233–39.
Hinterhäuser, H. *Los "Episodios nacionales" de Benito Pérez Galdós*. Tr. to Spanish J. Escobar. Madrid: Gredos, 1963.
Montesinos, J. F. *Galdós*. 3 vols. Madrid: Castalia, 1968–72.
Nimitz, M. *Humor in Galdós*. New Haven: Yale UP, 1968.
Pattison, W. T. *Benito Pérez Galdós and the Creative Process*. Minneapolis: U of Minnesota P, 1954.
Ribbans, G. *Pérez Galdós: "Fortunata y Jacinta."* London: Grant and Cutler, 1977.
Rodgers, E. *Pérez Galdós: "Miau."* London: Tamesis, 1978.
Sackett, T. A. *Pérez Galdós. An Annotated Bibliography*. Albuquerque: U of New Mexico, 1968.
Snow, C. P. *The Realists*. London: Macmillan, 1978. 167–94.
Varey, J. E. *Pérez Galdós: Doña Perfecta*. London: Tamesis, 1971.
Woodbridge, H. C. *Benito Pérez Galdós: A Selective Annotated Bibliography*. Metuchen: Scarecrow, 1975.

Noël M. Valis

PÉREZ GÓMEZ NIEVA, Alfonso (1859, Madrid–1931, Badajoz), prolific novelist, journalist. Aside from many contributions to contemporary magazines and newspapers, he composed fifteen novels, ten short story collections, several travel books and sundry other pieces. His writing is clear, somewhat sentimental, and realistic. Although his plots are not original, descriptions of people and places are well-executed.

BIBLIOGRAPHY

Primary Texts

Agata. Barcelona: Gili, 1897.
Historias callejeras. 2nd ed. Madrid: Fe, 1888.

Para la noche. Novelas cortas. Valencia: Aguilar, 1891.
Un viaje a Asturias, pasando por León. Madrid: Suárez, 1895.

PÉREZ LUGÍN, Alejandro (1870, Madrid–1926, El Burgo, La Coruña), Spanish journalist, novelist and essayist. He studied law in Santiago de Campostela, and was later named an adoptive son of the city. As a journalist, his specialty was reviews of bullfights, which he signed with the pseudonym Don Pío. As a novelist, he is an heir of nineteenth-c. realism, and his works exhibit both *costumbrismo* (paintings of regional customs, language, food and dance, etc.) and an occasional sentimentalism. Among his more famous works is *La casa de la Troya* (1915; The Trojan Woman's House), adapted for both the stage and cinema, and awarded a prize by the *Academia Española. It evokes university student life in Santiago, together with the plot of a romantic idyll, and has become one of the most popular novels of all time in Spain. Another successful work by this author is *Currito de la Cruz* (on the theme of the bullfight). Both works were adapted for the theater by *Linares Rivas.

PÉREZ PASTOR, Cristóbal (1833, Horche, Guadalajara–1906, Horche), archivist, literary historian, chaplain to the convent of Descalzas Reales in Madrid. His literary investigations are among the best of the nineteenth c. They include *La imprenta en Toledo* (1887; Printing in Toledo), *La imprenta en Medina del Campo* (1895; Printing in Medina del Campo), the 3 volume *Bibliografía madrileña del siglo XVI* (1891, 1906, 1907; Madrid Bibliography of the Sixteenth C.) and *Proceso de Lope de Vega* (1901; Trial of Lope de Vega). Pérez Pastor also published biographical documents concerning *Cervantes, *Calderón and others, and a very interesting work on acting, *Nuevos datos acerca del Histrionismo español en los siglos XVI y XVII* (1901; New Facts Concerning Spanish Acting in the Sixteenth and Seventeenth Centuries).

BIBLIOGRAPHY

Primary Texts

Bibliografía madrileña. 3 vols. Madrid: Tip. de huérfanos, 1891–1907.
Documentos cervantinos. . . . 2 vols. Madrid: Fortanet, 1897–1902.
Documentos para la biografía de Calderón. Madrid: Fortanet, 1905.
La imprenta en Medina del Campo. Madrid: Rivadeneyra, 1895.
La imprenta en Toledo. Madrid: Tello, 1887.
Noticias y documentos . . . recogidos por . . . Pérez Pastor. 4 vols. Madrid: Revista de legislación, 1910–26.
Nuevos datos acerca del Histrionismo. Madrid: Revista Española, 1901.

Criticism

Zamora, F. ''Un gran bibliófilo: Pérez Pastor.'' *RABM* 67 (1959): 661–75.

PÉREZ SÁNCHEZ, Manuel Antonio (1900, Rianxo–1930, Rianxo), Galician poet. Born in a coastal village, Manuel Antonio was a merchant marine by profession, although he was well informed of literary currents of the time, including those of other countries. He participated in Galician nationalist activities while maintaining contact with a number of important intellectuals and leaving a valuable volume of correspondence. A collaborator for a number of journals, such as *Suevia* and *Alborada*, he published the aesthetic manifesto *Maís alá* (Beyond) with the artist Alvaro Cebreiro. This became an important call to renovation of Galician literary creation. During his lifetime he published only *De catro a catro* (1928; From Four to Four) and thus was little known until the publication of his *Poesías* (Poems) in 1972. Pérez Sánchez has since become one of the most recognized poets in the Galician language. In great measure due to his influence, and supported by the visits of F. *García Lorca and Gerardo *Diego to Galicia, the regional writing, long of folkloric, modernist or other traditional nature, acquired avant-garde features. Manuel Antonio himself was an accomplished *creacionista* (creationist) whose work contains elements reflecting his work as sailor: nature, marine images, the practice of navigation. In 1979 *O día das letras galegas* (The Day of Galician Letters) was dedicated to him and critical studies have since been increasing. *See also* Galician Literature.

BIBLIOGRAPHY

Primary Texts

Correspondencia. Vigo: Galaxia, 1979.

De catro a catro. La Coruña: n.p., 1928.

Poesías. Vigo: Galaxia, 1972. Contains the books organized by author: *Con anacos do meu interior*, *Foulas*, *Sempre e máis despóis*, *Viladomar*.

Criticism

Cristobo Vicente, José Luis. "Manuel Antonio, poeta del mar." *Cuadernos de Estudios Gallegos* 25.76 (1970): 200–209.

March, Kathleen N. "As invariantes creacionistas na obra de Manoel-Antonio." *Grial* 63 (Jan.-Feb.-Mar. 1979): 1–17.

———. "Espacialidade e temporalidade na poesía de Manoel Antonio." *Grial* 68 (Apr.-May-June 1980): 129–43.

Pena, X. Ramón, *A poesia de Manuel António. Nas literaturas galegas de vanguarda*. La Coruña: La Voz de Galicia, 1979.

Pérez-Barreiro Nolla, F. "Acenos náufragos. Lendo a Manoel-Antonio." *Grial* 39 (1973): 93 ff.

Kathleen March

PÉREZ VALIENTE, Salvador (1919, Murcia–), Spanish poet and essayist. He studied philosophy and literature at the university level, and belonged to the post-war poetic group Garcilaso, a conservative tendency patronized by the Franco regime which produced somewhat anachronistic *pastoral eclogues in imitation of the *Renaissance poet whose name they adopted. His first book of poems was *Cuando ya no hay remedio* (1947; When There's No Longer Any Help), followed by *Por tercera vez* (1953; For the Third Time), a runner-up for the Adonais Poetry Prize. He also wrote *El libro de Elche* (1949; The Book of Elche) in prose.

PÉREZ Y GONZÁLEZ, Felipe (1846, Seville–1910, Madrid), Spanish journalist, lawyer, poet and dramatist. He appears as a somewhat facile versifier in the posthumous collection, *Un año en sonetos* (A Year in Sonnets), occasionally reminiscent of the style of Lope de *Vega. As a playwright, he produced one exceptionally popular piece, *La Gran Vía* (1886; The Great Boulevard), a sort of musical review. Other works for the stage are *Simón por horas* (Simon by the Hour), *La villa del oso* (The Villa of the Bear), *Pasar la raya* (Going Too Far), *Los vecinos del segundo* (The Neighbors on the Second Floor), *Los cortos de genio* (Short-Tempered), *Oro, plata, cobre y nada* (Gold, Silver, Copper and Nothing), *Dona Inés del alma mía* (My Dearest Inés), etc. He outlined but did not complete a biography of Luis *Vélez de Guevara.

PÉREZ Y PÉREZ, Rafael (1891, Cuatretondeta, Alicante–1984, Alicante), novelist and journalist. A prolific and facile writer of popular romances, he became one of the best-known novelists of the Spanish-speaking world during many years of this century. Officially, his profession was that of schoolteacher; he was also a newspaperman for some time in Alicante. His novels are numerous, and nearly all can be classified as sentimental or erotic, or mild apologies for middle-class morality. Among his many novels, still uncataloged, are *El hada alegría* (1931; The Good Fairy, Joy); *La clavariesa* (1931); *Almas recias* (1932; Stout Souls); *Los cien caballeros de Isabel la católica* (1935; The Hundred Knights of Queen Isabella); *Doña Sol* (1935; 2nd ed., 1959); *Duquesa Inés* (1935; 2nd ed., 1942); *Los dos caminos* (1935; The Two Paths); *La ciénaga* (1940; The Swamp); *Al borde de la leyenda* (1939; Bordering upon Legend); *Cabeza de estopa* (1941; 11th ed., 1957; Straw-Head); *Esperanza* (2nd ed., 1942; Hope); *Dos Españas* (1941; The Two Spains); *Cuando pasa el amor* (1942; When Love Goes By); *Alfonso Queral* (1946); *Aquella noche* (1952; That Night); *La beata Zaragata* (1957; That Devout Zaragata); *Aquella mujer* (1961; That Woman); *Almas a la deriva* (1961; Souls Drifting with the Current); *Los dos almirantes* (1962; The Two Admirals); *El "hereu" de En Sarrià* (1963; The Heir of the Sarrià Manor); *A espaldas del amor* (1965; Behind the Back of Love); *Una boda extraña* (1966; A Strange Wedding); *Un caballero leonés* (1966; A Leonese Gentleman); *La casa maldita* (1967; The Accursed House); *La bruja de la ermita* (1967; The Witch of the Hermitage); and *El doncel de doña Urraca* (1968; The Squire of Lady Urraca).

Janet Pérez

PÉREZ ZÚÑIGA, Juan (1860, Madrid–1938, Madrid), Spanish poet, narrator and humorist. Pérez Zúñiga obtained his law degree in 1882, and was an amateur violinist, but his true forte was comedy. He published approximately fifty festive works, whose cleverness brought him enormous popularity in his day. A facile versifier, he produced the parody *El arte de hacer curas* (no year; The Art of Making Priests [or of Curing]); published the series *El relato humorístico* (Humorous Tales), and above all, his most celebrated burlesque, the four-volume

Viajes morrocotudos (1901–2; Travels of Great Importance; a probable parody of Montesquieu's *Cartes persanes* [1721], and of José *Cadalso whose *Cartas marruecas* [1789], are alluded to by the title's play on words). In 1935, he published his memoirs under the title *El placer de recordar* (The Pleasure of Remembering).

PEROJO Y FIGUERAS, José del (1852, Santiago de Cuba–1908, Madrid), intellectual, politician, writer. Educated in France, Germany and England, greatly influenced by the thought of Kant (having even translated part of the *Critique of Pure Reason*), he urged Spain to join the culture of Europe in *Ensayos sobre el movimiento intelectual en Alemania* (1875; Essays on the Intellectual Movement in Germany). Most of his articles found their outlet in the *Revista Contemporánea* (Contemporary Magazine) which he founded in 1880, and which lived until 1907. He also wrote *La ciencia española bajo la Inquisición* (1877; Spanish Science under the Inquisition), and maintained a polemic with *Menéndez y Pelayo regarding the worth of science in Spain.

BIBLIOGRAPHY

Primary Text

Ensayos sobre el movimiento intelectual en Alemania. Madrid: Medina y Navarro, 1875.

PERSIA, Juan de (c. 1567?, Persia–1640?, ?), Christian name of Uruck Bec, son of the sultan of Persia, Ali Bec. He converted to Catholicism after arriving in Spain in 1601 as part of a Persian embassy visit to the court of Philip III. Fray Alonso *Remón helped him compose a narrative about Persia, its history, geography and people, and his own travels and conversion, titled *Relaciones de Don Juan de Persia* (1604; Accounts of Don Juan of Persia).

BIBLIOGRAPHY

Primary Text

Relaciones. Ed. N. Alonso Cortés. Madrid: Gráficas Ultra, 1947.

English Translation

Don Juan of Persia. Ed. and tr. G. Le Strange. London: Routledge, 1926.

PERUCHO, Juan (1920, Barcelona–), Catalan and Castilian novelist, poet, short story writer and essayist. A very original and profound, imaginative writer, Perucho became one of the most distinctive personalities of the Catalan intellectual and cultural scene during the Franco era, but was almost unknown outside this linguistic orbit. With the liberalization of the dictator's final years and especially after Franco's death, Perucho gained recognition in the rest of the peninsula, and many of his works were published in Castilian. Since this is a phenomenon of the last decade, for the most part, Perucho has received relatively little critical notice.

Among this writer's novels are *Libro de caballerías* (1957; Book of Chivalry),

Les històries naturals (1960; *Natural History*, 1988), and *Las aventuras del caballero Kosmas* (1981; The Adventures of the Knight Kosmas), whose titles suggest peculiar and characteristic aspects of Perucho's work, his erudition, humor and boundless fantasy. More recent novels include *Pamela* (1983), *Los laberintos bizantinos* (1984; Byzantine Labyrinths), and *Dietario apócrifo de Octavio de Romeu* (1985; Apocryphal Diary of Octavio de Romeu). The latter pretends to be the journal of an alter ego of the early twentieth-c. Spanish essayist, art critic and intellectual modernist Eugenio d'*Ors, and presents a curious combination of genuine cultural preoccupations of this writer together with jokes, apocryphal references and citations.

Perucho's short fiction includes numerous collections, among them *Galería de espejos sin fondo* (1965; Gallery of Bottomless Mirrors), *Rosas, diablos y sonrisas* (1965; Roses, Devils and Smiles), *Botánica oculta* (1969; Occult Botany), *Historias secretas de balnearios* (1972; Secret Histories of Spas), *Bestiario fantástico* (1977; Fantastic Bestiary), and most recently, *Nicéforas y el Grifo* (1987; Nicéforas and the Griffin). Again, the titles are eminently indicative, with their references to the secret, occult, mysterious, fantastic and mythological, suggesting the immense erudition and vast culture of Perucho's personal and poetic universe, which combines reality with fantasy, past with present to create curious and extraordinary texts. In addition, Perucho has published many collections of poetry, gathered together and reissued in his *Obra poética completa* (1978; Complete Poetic Works), of which there have been various editions. An exemplary recent essay is his *Teoría de Cataluña* (1987; Theory of Catalonia) in which Perucho—an inveterate bibliophile—brings together both rare and curious historical writings, real or alleged oral traditions and customs with apocryphal, fantastic or magic chronicles, creating a work which is both erudite and ironic, a sensitive tribute to Catalonia and an ambiguous jest for cultured readers.

BIBLIOGRAPHY

Primary Texts

Botánica oculta. Barcelona: Plaza y Janés, 1986.
Historias secretas de balnearios. Barcelona: Plaza y Janés, 1987.
Les històries naturals. Barcelona: Destino, 1960.
Libro de caballerías. Madrid: Cupsa, 1977.
Poesía, 1947–1973. Barcelona: Edicions 62, 1978.

English Translation

Natural History: A Novel. Tr. D. H. Rosenthal. New York: Knopf, 1988.

Janet Pérez

PESSANHA, Camilo (1867, Coimbra, Portugal–1926, Macau), Portuguese Symbolist poet. The first child of an illegitimate union between a young law student, Francisco Antonio de Almeida Pessanha, and a domestic servant, Maria de Espírito Santo Duarte Nunes Pereira, Camilo Pessanha was legally recognized by his father at the age of sixteen. He spent his childhood in the company of his mother and four other children of the same union, moving often from their modest Coimbran home to small provincial towns to be near Pessanha's father, whose post of municipal judge resulted in frequent transfers. The family settled permanently in Coimbra when Pessanha entered law school in 1884.

At the university he was active in the bohemian life of Coimbra students although he contributed little to the two fashionably controversial magazines of youthful rebellion, *Bohemia Nova* and *Os Insubmissios*. Following his graduation from law school in 1891, he accepted two minor job assignments in Portugal before proceeding to Macao in 1894 to accept a permanent position as a lecturer of philosophy and law at the Portuguese Liceum. He continued his private law practice, which eventually led to the post of government recorder and judge.

While leading the life of a Chinese mandarin, he took a Chinese concubine, whose daughter by a previous union took care of Pessanha's needs until his death in 1926. He collected Chinese memorabilia, studied Chinese culture and language, translated Chinese poetry and wrote essays about the Chinese way of life.

His stay in Macao was interrupted by frequent visits to Portugal for treatment of a nervous condition aggravated by heavy use of opium and alcohol. After his last visit in 1915 he did not return to Portugal; depressed and weak with illness, he remained confined to his bed the final years of his life. He died of tuberculosis in 1926.

Pessanha's small but significant literary output has been preserved through the devotion and perseverance of his lifelong friends, especially João de Castro Osório. Osório persuaded Pessanha to put in writing the poems he recited at social gatherings, during his visits in Portugal. Adding the poems he copied himself to those sent to him by Pessanha, Osório published the first edition of *Clepsidra* in 1920. Following the poet's specifications, he published expanded volumes in 1945 and 1956, and finally in 1969 he was able to bring out *Clepsidra e Outros Poemas*. Included in this edition are additional items found in obscure magazines or donated by individuals from their personal collections. Reprinted many times since 1969, this has become the definitive collection of the poet's works.

Through this small opus, Pessanha became one of the foremost exponents of Portuguese Symbolism and turn of the century European Decadentism. His poetry marks the beginning of the Modernist revolution. The language, which he designed to express the instability of life without absolutes, characterized by its disintegrative fluidity, elusive metaphor and cosmic ellipses, later became an essential tool of the modernist writers.

Through an irrationalist probe of the objective world, he attempted to establish correspondences between that world and the self. Ultimately, however, he showed that all correspondences are overcome by the disintegrative power of time and death, underscored in his poetry through the unsettling images of flowing water and moving sand, which deny man any hope of a stable foundation. The sonnet "Oh Images That Float" translated below illustrates more clearly this unsettling notion of a universe in flux, moved by the principles of time and death.

Oh images that float through the iris
Of my eyes, why do you not remain fixed?
Flowing constantly like crystalline waters
That spring toward the nevermore! . . .

Or to the darkened lake where
Your course leads, silent with jonquils,
And the vague anguished fear takes over,
—Why do you move on without me, carrying
me not with you?

Without you my open eyes are
But a useless mirror, my pagan eyes!
A succession of draught-stricken deserts . . .

All that remains is the shadow of my hands,
The casual flexing of my trembling fingers.
—A strange shadow in a vain motion.

BIBLIOGRAPHY

Primary Texts

Camilo Pessanha, Poesia e Prosa. Ed. Bernardo Vidigal. Rio: Agir, 1965.
China, Estudos e Traduções. Lisbon: Agencia Geral das Colonias, 1944.
Clepsidra. Lisbon: Lusitânia, 1920.
Clepsidra. Lisbon: Atica, 1945, 1956.
Clepsidra e Outras Poemas. Ed. João de Castro Osório. Lisbon: Atica, 1969.

Criticism

Barreiros, Danilo. *O Testamento de Camilo Pessanha*. Lisbon: Bertrand, 1961.
Gomes, Alvaro Cardoso. *A Metáfora Cósmica em Camilo Pessanha*. São Paulo: U of São Paulo P, 1977.
Miguel, Antonio Dias. *Camilo Pessanha. Elementos para o Estudo da sua Biografia e da sua Obra*. Lisbon: Alvaro Pinto (Ocidente), 1955.
Simões, João Gaspar. *Camilo Pessanha, A Obra e o Homem*. Lisbon: Arcadia, n.d.
Spaggiari, Barbara. *O simbolismo na Obra de Camilo Pessanha*. Lisbon: Instituto de Cultura e Lingua Portuguesa, 1982.

Raymond Sayers

PESSARRODONA I ARTIGUÉS, Marta (1941, Terrassa, Barcelona–), Spanish and Castilian poet and journalist. The only child of a middle-class family, Pessarrodona attended the U of Barcelona, studying history and Romance languages. Until her early twenties, she wrote only in Castilian, but she made the decision in 1964 to switch to Catalan. From 1972 to 1974, she served as a lecturer in Spanish at the U of Nottingham, and has written some poems in English. Among her collections of poetry are *Setembre 30* (1969), *Vida privada* (1972; Private Life), *Memòria* (1979; a nostalgic recollection of her homeland, written during a London winter), and *A favor meu, nostre* (1982; In My Favor, or Ours). Most if not all of these are reprinted in *Poemes 1969–81* (1984), which in addition to selections from all the foregoing collections, has a prologue by R. Pinyol-Balasch, an epilogue concerning new works, and illustrations, making it the best introduction to the poet's work and development; a Castilian translation has been announced. Subsequently, Pessarrodona published *Berlin Suite* (1985); she had gone to Berlin in January of 1984, and her stay there inspired the book's eight compositions. She conceives of poetry as a means of unveiling the moral meaning of existence, of attempting to understand experience in rational terms and evaluating it, a concept resembling that of such English poets as T. S. Eliot and W. H. Auden, and in recent Spanish poetry, of Luis *Cernuda and Jaime Gil de Biedma. Some of her poems are erotic, some feminist, and others inspired by memories, especially evocations of childhood. At times, her writing can be ideological and tendentious, motivated by socio-political *engagement*.

Janet Pérez

PESSOA, Fernando António Nogueira (1888, Lisbon–1935, Lisbon), Portuguese poet. The first son of Joaquim de Seabra Pessoa and Maria Madalena Pinheiro Nogueira, Fernando Pessoa spent the first five years of his life in a comfortable and cultured home in a fashionable district of old Lisbon. His mother had to move the family to more modest quarters following his father's death in 1893, and in 1896 she moved the family to Durban, South Africa, to join her new husband, Comandant João Miguel Rosa, who had the post of Portuguese consul in South Africa. There Pessoa attended English boarding schools in Durban, where he was an excellent student, especially in French and Latin.

In 1905, he returned to Lisbon to begin his university studies in Portuguese literature. In Lisbon, he shared with his father's two sisters the home of his somewhat deranged and often hospitalized paternal grandmother. He earned his living by handling commercial correspondence in many languages for several firms in Lisbon, devoting the rest of his time to literary activity and activism until his death in 1935 at age forty-seven. He never married, and the story of his limited and sad love life appears in the fifty letters he wrote to Ofelia Queiroz, the woman with whom he imagined he was in love.

Although many of Pessoa's works were published during his lifetime, it was only after an initial compilation of his unpublished work in 1946 that the enormity of his writing enterprise became apparent. Complete poetic works by Fernando Pessoa, under the title *Obras Completas*, have been published posthumously in eleven volumes by Atica, which is now in process of publishing a compilation of Pessoa's prose: the first two volumes, published in 1982, contain *O Livro do Desassossego*.

Considered by many as the best Portuguese writer since *Camões, Pessoa tuned his poetic craft against the background of unprecedented turbulence in Portuguese history, including the socio-political fermentation spun by the revolution and the advent of the republic in 1910, which culminated with the *Estado Novo* and the rise to power of fascist dictator Antonio Salazar.

The turbulence observed in Portugal reflected that of all Europe. European cultural and intellectual life was dominated by the explosive emergence of *Modernism. Characterized by a total rejection of nineteenth-c. *Romanticism and positivism and an active desire and search for something modern, something completely new and different from the old models, Modernism found its expression in the many "ism" movements of the pre-war years (e.g., Futurism, Fauvism, Dadaism).

Fernando Pessoa became integrated into the mainstream of Modernist thought and creativity, furthermore, having engineered new movements and created new literary artifacts, such as the "heteronyms," he became one of the main exponents of Modernism.

While Pessoa's literary activity began in 1912 with articles published in the *Aguia*, a journal of the Portuguese Renaissance, he quickly established his independence from the group with a violent satire written against one of its leaders, Afonso Lopes *Vieira, followed by his official repudiation of the *Aguia* in 1913 for its refusal to publish his drama *O Marinheiro*. His ensuing collaboration in the controversial art journal *O Orpheu* (The Orpheus) clearly established him as a force for Modernist change in Portuguese and European intellectual circles. Yet his creation of new literary movements (*Paúlismo*, *Interseccionismo*, *Sensacionismo*) and his collaboration in The Orpheus, which had an enormous contemporary effect, are overshadowed by his creation of "heteronyms," the fictional products of Pessoa's imagination. He brought to life the first heteronym, Alberto Caeiro, in 1914 as a joke on Mario *Sá-Carneiro. The latter, who was a member of a group of innovative young poets, had become a close friend of Pessoa following his break with the *Aguia*.

Heteronyms

The history-making birth of Alberto Caeiro, created as a "bucolic poet of the complex type," was followed by others. The most fully developed heteronyms had recorded life histories and individual personalities while their published and unpublished writings showed consistent, distinctive styles and philosophies. Although many of the fictitious heteronymic artifacts, such as Abílio Quaresma, António Mora, Alexander Search, Vicente Guedes, O Barão de Teive, and others, never reached full development, they are nonetheless responsible for an interesting portion of Pessoa's literary output, and their writings contain meaningful data about the other heteronyms. Among these less developed heteronyms the most interesting is Bernardo Soares. Called a "semiheteronym" by the critics, Soares is the author of Pessoa's best prose in the form of the recently reconstituted *Livro do Desassossego* (Book of Restlessness), whose most famous quote "My country is the Portuguese language" provides an important clue to Pessoa's relationship and preoccupation with language.

The other, fully developed heteronyms express a variety of options and attitudes toward modern life. Alberto Caeiro, the master, and his disciple and biographer Ricardo Réis, predicate a simple life and a return to classical paganism. Alvaro de Campos, perhaps the most famous of heteronyms, exudes modernist iconoclasm and a state of fragmentation in his attitude of dissatisfaction with the contemporary condition of life and thought in Europe. The poetry of Fernando Pessoa himself, called "orthonymous" by the poet, may be seen as constituting the fourth major heteronym. The feature that distinguishes this heteronym is a claim to a non-fictitious life history. Fernando Pessoa, either as a heteronym or as an orthonym, and the other heteronyms are the multiple authors of a uniquely complex opus, that in its entirety combines and expresses those concerns which have become central in twentieth-c. European cultural thought: self, language and reality. Pessoa's consistently modern treatment of these pivotal themes ensures that the form, method and content of his writings will interest scholars for generations to come.

In his ontological treatment of these themes, Pessoa pursued many paths of analysis that have since become validated by scientific and philosophical inquiry. Among these is the suggestion of the elusive nature of self, the dependence of reality on the subject, and the primacy of language in the construction of a poetic and a non-poetic reality.

Pessoa's concern with defining the purpose and nature of self creates a most complicated topology of a self whose very existence is placed in doubt. What places its existence in doubt is man's inability to apprehend it in order to define it. Constantly fragmented by time and space, the self evades all efforts to circumscribe it.

While it can be neither fixed nor defined, the self can be reduced to an ineffable, inexplicable element: the awareness from the margins of being of awareness of the self. "There exists only that of mine which now sees me." Having thus reduced the nature of self, Pessoa's ontological argument proceeds no further.

Yet, in much of Pessoa's writing on reality, the latter is established as being dependent upon that tenuous, marginal inexplicable self.

Pessoa's anticipation and understanding of the concept of the primacy of language in the act of creating a poetic or a non-poetic reality, are evident in his two most famous creations: the heteronyms, which in themselves are but language constructs, and the poem "Autopsicografia," in which he states that the poet, by constructing a reality with words, is constructing a feigned emotion, for any emotion, whether real or imaginary, once expressed in words, is always only a language construct.

In his diachronic treatment of these themes, Pessoa suggested a view of contemporary Western civilization as having reached the state of ultimate desacralization. Recognizing the existential anguish produced in the self by such a state of desacralization, Pessoa devoted much of his opus to suggesting various remedies. One remedy would simply reverse the process of desacralization by returning man to the simple life of paganism. Another remedy would allow man to understand the purpose of it all through an expansion of his knowledge of the ultimate reality by probing the occult mysteries or by engaging in a Faustian enterprise. Part of Pessoa's opus is devoted to a discussion of yet another alternative in which the self, identified and fused with the motherland, shares in its glory, both past and future, thus acquiring immortality through the glorious national mission.

Of the remedies Pessoa suggested to the nihilist despair and existential *saudade* (nostalgia) the one that seems to be most acceptable to modern man is that of a choice of aesthetic creation as the one act which holds the last vestiges of that which was once sacred in the universe. This suggestion clearly places him in the line of aesthetic thought that stretches from Nietzsche to Sartre and Mallarmé to Derrida.

In these profound considerations of seminal themes of the twentieth c., Pessoa's work suggests a myriad of options and possible positions. His invitation to the reader is to consider them all with him.

BIBLIOGRAPHY

Primary Texts

Obras Completas. 11 vols. Lisbon: Atica, 1942–1974. Complete poetic works.

O Libro do Desassossego. 2 vols. Lisbon: Atica, 1982. Prose.

English Translation

Fernando Pessoa. Tr. Jonathan Griffin. Oxford: Carcanet, 1971.

Fernando Pessoa. Tr. Jonathan Griffin. Suffolk: Chaucer, 1982.

Fernando Pessoa, Selected Poems. Tr. Peter Rickard. Edinburgh: Cambridge UP, 1971.

"Pessoa. The Messenger." Tr. R. W. Sousa. In *The Rediscoverers*. State College: Pennsylvania State UP, 1981.

"Poems by Fernando Pessoa." Tr. J. Longland. *Poet Lore* (Fall 1970): n.p.

"Portuguese Sea" and "Epitaph for Bartolomeu Dias." In *Portuguese Poems and Translations*. Tr. Leonard S. Downs. Lisbon: n.p., 1947.

Selected Poems by Fernando Pessoa. Tr. E. Honig. Intro. O. Paz. Chicago: Swallow, 1971.

"Seven Poems of Fernando Pessoa and Two Poems of A. Caeiro." Tr. J. L. Agneta. In *Portuguese Essays*. Lisbon: n.p., 1963.

Three Twentieth Century Portuguese Poets. Tr. J. M. Parker. Johannesburg: Witwatersrand UP, 1960.

Criticism

Actas do 1º Congresso de Estudos Pessoanos. Porto: Centro de Estudos Pessoanos, 1979.

Actas do 2º Congresso Internacional de Estudos Pessoanos. Porto: Centro de Estudos Pessoanos, 1985.

Antunes, Alfredo. *Saudade e Profetismo em Fernando Pessoa*. Braga: Faculdade de Filosofia, 1983.

Centeno, Yvette K. *Fernando Pessoa—Tempo, Solidão, Hermetismo*. Lisbon: Livraria Morais, 1978.

Galhoz, Maria Iliette. "Introdução." *Fernando Pessoa: Obra Poética*. Rio de Janeiro: Aguilar, 1960.

Guntert, Georges. *Fernando Pessoa, O Eu Estranho*. Lisbon: Dom Quixote Publishers, 1982.

Guyer, Leland Robert. *Imagery of Closed Space in the Poetry of Fernando Pessoa*. Diss., U of California, Santa Barbara, 1979.

Lind, Georg Rudolf. *Teoria Poética de Fernando Pessoa*. Porto: Inova, 1970.

Lopes, Maria Teresa Rita. *Fernando Pessoa et le drame symboliste*. Paris: Centro Cultural Português, Fundação C. Gulbenkian, 1977.
Lourenço, Eduardo. *Fernando Pessoa Revisitado*. Porto: Inova, 1973.
Moisés, Carlos Felipe. *O poema e as Máscaras*. Coimbra: Almedina, 1981.
Monteiro, Adolfo Casais. *Estudos sobre a Poesia de Fernando Pessoa*. Rio de Janeiro: Agir, 1958.
Monteiro, George, ed. *The Man Who Never Was*. Providence: Gavea Brown, 1982.
Padrão, Maria da Gloria. *A Metáfora em Fernando Pessoa*. Porto: Inova, 1973.
Pereira da Costa, Dalila L. *O Esoterismo de Fernando Pessoa*. Porto: Lello e Irmão, 1971.
Persona. Ed. Arnaldo Saraiva. A journal devoted to Fernando Pessoa. Centro de Estudos Pessoanos. Porto, continuous publication since 1977.
Pina Coelho, Antonio. *Os Fundamentos Filosóficos da Obra de Fernando Pessoa*. 2 vols. Lisbon: Verbo, 1968.
Prado Coelho, Jacinto de. *Diversidade e Unidade em Fernando Pessoa*. 2nd ed. Lisbon: Verbo, 1963.
Quadros, António. *Fernando Pessoa*. 2nd ed. Lisbon: Arcadia, 1968.
———. *Fernando Pessoa, A obra e o homem*. 2 vols. Lisbon: Arcadia, 1981.
Rosa, Pradelino. *Uma Interpretação de Fernando Pessoa*. Lisbon: Guimarães, 1971.
Seabra, José Augusto. *Fernando Pessoa ou o Poetrodrama*. São Paulo: Perspectiva, 1974.
Sena, Jorge de. *Fernando Pessoa e Ca Heterónima*. Lisbon: Edições 70, 1984.
Severino, Alexandrino. *Fernando Pessoa na Africa do Sul*. Lisbon: Publicações Dom Quixote, 1983.
Silva, Agostinho da. *Um Fernando Pessoa*. Lisbon: Guimarães, 1959.
Simões, João Gaspar. *Fernando Pessoa perante Bernardo Soares*. Lisbon: Difedi Difusão, 1983.
———. *Heteropsicografia de Fernando Pessoa*. Porto: Inova, 1973.
———. *Vida e Obra de Fernando Pessoa*. Rio de Janeiro: Livraria Bertrand, 1981.

Joanna Courteau

PETRARCHISM. *See* Italian Literary Influences

PETRUS ALFONSI. *See* Alfonso, Pero

PI Y MARGALL, Francisco (1824, Barcelona–1901, Madrid), literary scholar, orator, historian, politician, father of Spanish federalism. A precocious youth, at age thirteen he enrolled at the U of Barcelona—supporting himself by tutoring as he studied. He later completed his doctorate in law at the U of Madrid. Before 1854, most of his publications were of a literary bent: he continued the *Recuerdos y bellezas de España* (Memories and Beauties of Spain) begun by *Piferrer; he collaborated on various encyclopedias; he completed an edition of Father *Mariana's works for the *Biblioteca de Autores Españoles; he wrote *Historia de la pintura en España* (1851; History of Painting in Spain), which was censored by the church for its anti-religious radicalism. Although his literary activities continued throughout his life, after 1854 politics became the primary focus of Pi y Margall's life. His tumultuous political fortunes ran from exile to serving, briefly, as president of the first Spanish Republic, in 1873. Pi y Margall's legacy of political essays, historical studies, and literary research continues to be of interest to this day.

BIBLIOGRAPHY

Primary Texts

Granada, Jaén, Málaga y Almeria. Barcelona: Cortezo, 1885.

Las nacionalidades. Barcelona: Producciones Editoriales, 1979.

La qüestió de Catalunya. Barcelona: Alta Fulla, 1978.

La reacción y la revolución: estudios políticos y sociales. Ed., study A. Jutglar. Barcelona: Anthropos, 1982.

Criticism

Dihigio y Mestre, Juan Miguel. *Pi y Margall y la revolución cubana*. Havana, Cuba: Siglo XX, 1928.

Jutglar, Antoni. *Pi i Margall y el federalismo español*. Madrid: Taurus, 1975.

Joan Gilabert

PÍCARA JUSTINA, La, *picaresque novel. *El libro de entretenimiento de la Pícara Justina* (1605; *The Life of Justina, The Country Jilt*, 1707) was first published in Medina del Campo. The author is now acknowledged to be a physician, Francisco *López de Ubeda, and the book is dedicated to a powerful courtier, Rodrigo Calderón. It is the first picaresque novel with a female protagonist although *La *Celestina* (1499; *The Spanish Bawd*, 1964) and *La Lozana Andaluza* (1528; The Lusty Andalusian Wench) may to some degree be considered precursors. The author was employed in the court of Philip III, not only for his medical expertise but also for his sense of humor. The text was probably composed between 1602 and 1603 as a parodic response to Mateo *Alemán's exemplary picaresque novel *Guzmán de Alfarache* (1599) and also to commemorate satirically the court's sojourn in León in 1602. In large part the work is a *roman à clef* addressed to the courtiers able to comprehend its intricate web of witty allusions and double entendres. Even some of the most obvious of these were lost on many modern critics and readers until Bataillon and others reinterpreted and reevaluated the work. For example, Justina was generally understood to have been a chaste protagonist because she says she is, an improbable assertion given her parentage, social class, activities, and friends. A picaresque tale is usually the confession of a liar narrating his own life so as to seem better than he actually is. It follows that when Justina labels herself the "pícara romera" (pilgrim rogue) the reader is expected to react with skepticism and catch the implied pun "romera/ramera" (pilgrim/whore). This is but one of the numerous examples of the text's ribald humor and linguistic playfulness.

La Pícara Justina is divided into three ironic prologues and four books with a complex scheme of subdivisions into chapters, parts, and numbers. The complicated structure is probably a parodic reference to *Guzmán* and other contemporary texts, as are many other aspects of the work. Justina is a good-natured, though maliciously glib, protagonist who loves to dance and offers a contrast to the embittered, defensive Guzmán. The moralizing passages seem absurdly inapplicable, an implied criticism of Guzmán's claim that he is narrating his sordid life with a didactic intent. In the first book, "La Pícara Montañesa" (The Highlander Rogue), Justina recounts her genealogy (full of ironic references to her Jewish ancestry), early life, and education. The remaining three books, "La Pícara Romera" (The Pilgrim Rogue), "La Pícara Pleitista" (The Litigating Rogue), and "La Pícara Novia" (The Betrothed Rogue), treat her picaresque adventures until the time of her marriage to a gambling man of arms named Lozano. Finally, the protagonist promises a second volume of adventures in which she will marry twice more, once to a decrepit old man, Santoloja, and later to Guzmán de Alfarache.

Because of the rhetorical virtuosity of the author, *La Pícara Justina* is still one of the most enigmatic and difficult of all picaresque novels. Replete with obscure allusions, puns, jargon, colloquialisms, witty poems in fifty-one different meters, and facetious apologues and hieroglyphics, the text is a burlesque with misogynist overtones—not a novel of social protest, but an entertainment to amuse an aristocratic public.

BIBLIOGRAPHY

Primary Texts

La Pícara Justina. Ed. Bruno Mario Damiani. Madrid: Porrúa, 1982.

La Pícara Justina. Ed. Antonio Rey Hazas. Madrid: Nacional, 1977.

English Translation

The Life of Justina, the Country Jilt. The Spanish Libertines. Tr. Captain John Stevens. London: Samuel Bunchley, 1707.

Criticism

Bataillon, Marcel. *Pícaros y Picaresca: La Pícara Justina*. Madrid: Taurus, 1969.

Damiani, Bruno. *Francisco López de Úbeda*. TWAS 431. New York: Twayne, 1974.

Friedman, Edward. *The Antiheroine's Voice: Narrative Discourse and Transformations of the Picaresque*. Columbia: U of Missouri P, 1987.

Jones, Joseph R. "Hieroglyphics in *La Pícara Justina*." *Estudios Literarios de los hispanistas norteamericanos dedicados a Helmut Hatzfeld*. Ed. Josep Solá-Solé, Alessandro Crisafulli, and Bruno Damiani. Barcelona: Hispam, 1974. 415–29.

Rey Hazas, Antonio. "La compleja faz de una pícara: Hacia una interpretación de *La Pícara Justina*." *Revista de Literatura* 45 (1983): 87–109.

Ronquillo, Pablo J. *Retrato de la Pícara. La protagonista de la picaresca española del siglo XVII*. Madrid: Playor, 1980.

Helen H. Reed

PICARESQUE, a type of fiction. The term *picaresque novel* has been applied to numerous long narrations written in the sixteenth and seventeenth centuries in Spain, that is, as an historical designation, and also, by extension, to texts similar to them in European letters up to the present. These narratives, usually the fictional autobiographies of humbly born individuals, are among the most innovative and influential texts in Spanish literary history. The protagonists are often anti-heroes that begin their lives as victims of circumstance, but through experience become rogues and rascals. The fictional rogue or ''pícaro'' narrates his (or occasionally her) tale from its ignominious beginnings to his present vantage point. He has been born to unsavory parents and orphaned, or for some other reason compelled to leave home, at an early age. Almost immediately, the *pícaro* suffers a bad experience, a rude awakening to the harshness of existence, that makes him realize that he, alone, must fend for himself in the world. He moves from one master to another, often mistreated and hungry, and learns to survive through stealth and guile. During this educational process, the *pícaro* becomes an adept trickster, even exchanging roles with his deceivers. Yet his social and economic ambitions are generally frustrated, and real advancement eludes him. In the meantime, he observes society with a satirical eye and amuses the reader with his episodic adventures, linguistic virtuosity, and sardonic views. At the point where he is writing his tale, he has usually reached a milestone in his life that gives him pause for reflection—marriage, economic change, imprisonment, some other disaster, or emigration to America. Moreover, he has gained sufficient self-knowledge to offer an explanation for his present state, frequently dishonorable.

The first text in which the form and essential features of the genre appear is the anonymous *La Vida de Lazarillo de Tormes y de sus fortunas y adversidades* (1554; *The Life of Lazarillo de Tormes. His Fortunes and Misfortunes*, 1973). Antecedents of **Lazarillo* may be recognized in the characters, style, and episodes of *El libro de buen amor* (1343; *The Book of Good Love*, 1972), el *Arcipreste de Talavera's *Corbacho* (1498; *Little Sermons on Sin*, 1959), and the **Celestina* (1499; *The Spanish Bawd*, 1964), or in the tone and structure of Apuleius's *The Golden Ass*. Nevertheless, the originality of *Lazarillo* is remarkable, especially if one takes into account the chivalric, *pastoral and sentimental novels in vogue during the *Renaissance. *Lazarillo* displays many features in parodic response to heroic and idealistic fiction, for example, the *pícaro*'s ignoble birth and materialistic values. *Lazarillo* is a short, ironic work with a circular structure, consisting of seven *tratados* or chapters in which Lazarillo serves various masters, first a crafty blind man, an avaricious priest, and a squire as poor as himself. His childhood is recounted in sympathetic and humorous detail, and his adult life, subtly implied to be more reprehensible, glossed over rapidly. The entire narrative is directed to a fictitious reader, *Vuestra Merced* (Your Worship), who has requested an explanation of the *caso* (case or affair), in the final *tratado* implied to be Lazarillo's sharing of his wife with his patron the archpriest. The tale is narrated so that the reader comprehends how Lazarillo arrived at his final state of dishonor, ironically referred to as the height of his good fortune, and that his version of his life is selective and does not disclose all.

The publication history of the picaresque is curious. Although *Lazarillo* enjoyed some immediate success, it was not seriously imitated until Mateo *Alemán incorporated most of its essential features into his own quite different literary project, *Guzmán de Alfarache* (1599; *The Rogue; or the Life of Guzmán de*

Alfarache, 1622–23), nearly fifty years later. *Lazarillo* was banned by the *Inquisition during the latter part of the sixteenth c., but was reissued with *Guzmán* in 1599. *Guzmán* was a resounding success, and there quickly followed a proliferation of picaresque texts in Spain that imitated or varied characteristics of the two earliest works. One might say the genre was born when readers, some of whom were writers, recognized in the similarities between *Lazarillo* and *Guzmán* identifiable attributes of a type of fiction; that is, they intuited the unwritten poetics of an incipient genre. Very soon, literary influence followed political expansion. Spanish texts were translated, and new picaresque works were written in response to them in England, France, Germany, and Latin America. Finally, reminiscences of picaresque characters, structures, themes, or myths still surface in some works of modern fiction, to whose development the tradition undoubtedly contributed in the first place.

Guzmán de Alfarache is a lengthy baroque work in which the garrulous and defensive protagonist narrates his life to a fictitious reader, ''tú.'' The emotionally fraught, rhetorically complex autobiography is punctuated with moralizing digressions, good advice that is contradicted by the bad example of the narrator's own behavior. Guzmán cannot practice what he preaches, and his consistently vengeful and embittered attitudes have caused many readers to doubt the sincerity of his final conversion. In some ways, *Guzmán* is a typical baroque compendium of moral and philosophical wisdom whose great innovation is to include as exemplary material the unified narrative of a *pícaro's* life. Mateo Alemán published a second part to *Guzmán* in 1604, following a spurious sequel by Juan *Martí in 1602, to which he makes justifiably angry reference in his text. Also written in 1604 was *El Guitón Honofre* (The Rogue Honofre), a lighthearted entertainment with brief moralizations in verse by Gregorio González. Two other comic or burlesque picaresque works followed, in part parodic responses to *Guzmán* and stylistic tours de force by brilliant satirists. *Quevedo's *La Vida del Buscón llamado Don Pablos* (1626; *The Life and Adventures of Don Pablos the Sharper*, 1957) was probably written in 1603 or 1604, and *El libro de entretenimiento de La *Pícara Justina* (1605; *The Life of Justina, the Country Jilt*, 1707) is the first picaresque novel with a female protagonist. In these works the convention of autobiography functions differently than in *Lazarillo* and *Guzmán* in that a greater and less ambivalent ironic distance is maintained between author and protagonist. The *pícaros* are less evolving individuals attempting to cope with their predicament than vehicles of satire that voice their authors' jokes, conceits, and social criticism. Both Quevedo's Pablos and *el guitón* Honofre aspire to be gentlemen, but are not allowed to escape the destiny decreed to them by birth. Rather, their social pretensions are presented as absurd and outrageous. During the next decade the picaresque was somewhat eclipsed by the popularity of *Cervantes's *Quijote* and his *Novelas ejemplares* (1613; *The Deceitful Marriage and Other Exemplary Novels*, 1963), though some of the latter (*Rinconete y Cortadillo*, *La ilustre fregona* [The Illustrious Kitchen Maid], *El casamiento engañoso* [The Deceitful Marriage]; and *El coloquio de los perros*

[The Dogs' Colloquy]), might be considered variations of the picaresque. Other authors such as *Castillo Solórzano and María de *Zayas y Sotomayor also wrote short Italianate novels on picaresque themes or including picaresque elements.

Cervantes also makes ironic allusion to *Guzmán de Alfarache* and the picaresque in the episode of Ginés de Pasamonte in the *Quijote*, which is in its entirety partly written in response to its influential predecessor.

In the picaresque novels that follow there is great variety. The protagonists of *La Vida del Escudero Marcos de Obregón* (1618; *The History of the Life of the Squire Marcos de Obregón*, 1816) by Vicente *Espinel and *El Donado Hablador o Alonso, mozo de muchos amos* (1624–26; *The Chattering Lay Brother or Alonso, Servant of Many Masters*, 1844–45) by the doctor Jerónimo de *Alcalá Yáñez are less *pícaros* than honest bourgeois conformists. The first abandons the usual urban setting of the picaresque to embark on a series of byzantine adventures, a mixture of fiction and the idealized autobiography of the author himself. The latter, as the title implies, is a loquacious lay cleric that exhaustively comments on his narration of picaresque adventures. In other works, satiric elements predominate over the picaresque to such a degree that they might be better designated anatomies or Menippean satires. Examples are *La desordenada codicia de bienes ajenos* (1619; *The Sonne of the Rogue; or the Politick Theefe*, 1638) by Carlos García and *El diablo cojuelo* (1641; *The Limping Devil*, 1898) by Luis *Vélez de Guevara. The terminal Spanish picaresque novel, *La Vida y hechos de *Estebanillo González, Hombre de buen humor* (1646; *The Life of Estebanillo González, the Pleasantest and Most Diverting of all Comical Scoundrels*, 1707), is a cynical, subversive, and linguistically exuberant work replete with historical events and persons from the time of the Flemish Wars. The protagonist is a *pícaro*, soldier, and buffoon perhaps recounting the genuine memoirs of the author himself adjusted to a picaresque framework.

The *pícaro* is an inconsistent, tragicomic character in conflict with the corrupt society he satirizes, yet in part emulates in order to survive. He inspired a wide spectrum of attitudes on the part of authors and readers, who alternately regarded him as scoundrel, parvenu, rebel, outsider, carnival clown, existential hero, or victim of injustice. Perhaps for these reasons as well as others, authors of picaresque narratives often elaborated complicated rhetorical structures in regard to the reader that encourage ambiguity or indicate multiple levels of meaning. Historical and individual differences in reader expectation and taste, as well as the ironic tone and linguistic complexity of picaresque discourse, have occasioned diversity in interpretation.

The generalized overview of the picaresque presented at the beginning of this essay is based on characteristics encountered in *Lazarillo* and *Guzmán*, frequently imitated in texts that follow, and adapted by modern writers and critics to form their idea of the picaresque; that is, it is a composite arrived at with the benefit (or limitations) of a modern perspective. However, some seventeenth-c. texts don't partake of even most of these generic attributes. Strictly speaking, they are neither novels nor picaresque. Many authors overburden their particular versions of the picaresque with moral commentary, social satire, a burlesque treatment, and other forms of autobiography. Only *Lazarillo* and *Guzmán* conform well to the stipulation that the protagonist develop through his experience like the hero of a modern novel.

These are some of the conundrums that have caused a certain theoretical disarray in picaresque criticism. At the risk of being reductive, one might say that views of the genre have polarized, though there exist various strict and broad definitions and some gradations in between. One extreme is a taxonomy of characteristics that links a picaresque *Weltanschauung* to its narrative structure and relates both to similar modern novels dealing with the tribulations of the social outcast. Hence, the unitary point of view, episodic form, and Sisyphean action are associated with the pessimism, frustration, and cynicism of the *pícaro*, who is attempting to learn how to survive in a hostile environment. At the opposite pole is a far less restrictive idea of the picaresque that allows for ideological and formal variation. It regards the picaresque as a protean genre, treating as essential only the bare bones of the narrative: a picaresque subject matter and action. Also germane to this view of the picaresque is a self-conscious quality. The author's frame of reference as he composes his text is derived from other picaresque narrations, though he may reject some conventions and embrace others. The second view allows for comic or serious treatment of the *pícaro*—hence *El Buscón* and *La Pícara Justina* fall within the taxonomy, as do the picaresque exemplary novels of Cervantes, usually banished for being inconsistently autobiographical or fundamentally dialogical, open, tolerant, and representative of a multitude of points of view. Yet they are obviously written in response to previous picaresque texts.

Another area of debate is the nature of picaresque "realism," often touted as an essential characteristic. It has been suggested that its importance does not stem from providing an accurate depiction of seventeenth-c. Spanish lowlife or urban poverty, the world of thieves, delinquents, and vagabonds, but rather from its reflecting a mental universe of social marginality. The *pícaro* pretends to be what he is not and exposes the greater society's false code of honor, according to which achieving social aspirations depends on deceiving others with appearances.

BIBLIOGRAPHY

Primary Texts

Alemán, Mateo. *Guzmán de Alfarache*. Ed. Benito Brancaforte. Madrid: Cátedra, 1981.

———. *Guzmán de Alfarache*. Ed. Francisco Rico. Madrid: Planeta, 1983.

Anon. *Lazarillo de Tormes*. Ed. Alberto Blecua. Madrid: Castalia, 1972.

González, Gregorio. *El Guitón Honofre* (ms.). Ed. Hazel G. Carrasco. Chapel Hill, NC: Estudios de Hispanófila, 1973.

Quevedo, Francisco de. *La Vida del Buscón llamado Don Pablos*. Ed. Fernando Lázaro Carreter. Salamanca: CSIC, 1965.

Valbuena y Prat, Angel, ed. *La Novela Picaresca Española*. Madrid: Aguilar, 1968.

Most extensive collection available. Does not contain *El guitón Honofre*. Spare notes.

English Translations

Blind Man's Boy. Tr. J. M. Cohen. London: New English Library, 1962. (*Lazarillo*)

The Deceitful Marriage and Other Exemplary Novels. Tr. Walter Starkie. New York: New American Library, 1963.

The Life and Adventures of Don Pablos the Sharper. In *Masterpieces of the Spanish Golden Age*. Tr. Mack Hendricks Singleton et al. Ed. Angel Flores. New York: Holt, Rinehart, and Winston, 1957.

The Life of Lazarillo de Tormes. His Fortunes and Misfortunes. As Told by Himself. Tr. Robert S. Rudder. New York: Frederick Ungar, 1973.

The Rogue; or The Life of Guzmán de Alfarache. Tr. James Mabbe. London: G. E. Blount, 1622, 1623. London: Constable; New York: Knopf, 1924. New York: AMS, 1967.

Two Spanish Picaresque Novels. Tr. Michael Alpert. Harmondsworth: Penguin, 1969. (*Lazarillo* and *El Buscón*)

Criticism

Bjornson, Richard. *The Picaresque Hero in European Fiction*. Madison: U of Wisconsin P, 1977. Contains a useful typology of picaresque novels.

Dunn, Peter N. "Problems of a Model for the Picaresque and the Case of Quevedo's *Buscón*." *BHS* 59 (1982): 95–105. Stresses differences between *Lazarillo* and *Guzmán* and difficulties of genre theory.

———. *The Spanish Picaresque Novel*. Boston: Twayne, 1979. An excellent survey.

Guillén, Claudio. "Toward a Definition of the Picaresque" and "Genre and Countergenre: The Discovery of the Picaresque." *Literature as System*. Princeton: Princeton UP, 1971. Two fundamental and influential theoretical articles.

Laurenti, Joseph L. *Bibliografía de la literatura picaresca*. Metuchen, NJ: Scarecrow, 1973.

Lázaro Carreter, Fernando. *Lazarillo de Tormes en la Picaresca*. Barcelona: Ariel, 1972. Formalist criticism at its best. Discusses diachronic idea of genre.

Mancing, Howard. "The Picaresque Novel: A Protean Form." *College English* 6 (1979–80): 182–204.

Parker, Alexander. *Literature and the Delinquent. The Picaresque Novel in Spain and Europe 1599–1753*. Edinburgh: Edinburgh UP, 1967. A thematic study giving primacy to *Guzmán* in the formation of the genre and stressing the ideology of the Counter-Reformation.

Reed, Walter L. *An Exemplary History of the Novel: The Quixotic versus the Picaresque*. Chicago: U of Chicago P, 1981.

Ricapito, Joseph V. *Bibliografía Razonada y anotada de las obras maestras de la Picaresca Española*. Madrid: Castalia, 1980.

Rico, Francisco. *The Picaresque Novel and Point of View*. Tr. Charles Davis with Harry Sieber. Cambridge: Cambridge UP, 1983. Fundamental study of narrative structure of major picaresque texts and relation to modern novel.

Sieber, Harry. *The Picaresque*. London: Methuen, 1977. A good brief survey of Spanish and European picaresque fiction.

Wicks, Ulrich. "The Nature of Picaresque Narrative: A Modal Approach." *PMLA* 89 (1978): 240–49.

Helen H. Reed

PÍCARO. *See* Picaresque

PICÓN, Jacinto Octavio (1852, Madrid–1923, Madrid), novelist, prose author. Both his life and works reflect a dual French-Spanish heritage. His French mother and sojourns in France imbued him with a sense of elegant Gallic irony and refined wit, as well as a very nearly Jacobin ideology. (Both sides of the family were liberal in politics and attitudes.) But Picón was equally a son of Madrid, following in the footsteps of his beloved uncle, José *Picón, well known in his day for such **zarzuelas* as *Pan y toros* (1864; Bread and Bulls). Like the uncle in his plays and *zarzuelas*, the nephew, too, re-created in his fiction the settings and flavor of the Spanish capital. Picón began his literary career as a journalist, contributing pieces to such newspapers as *El Correo*, *El Imparcial*, and *La Ilustración Española y Americana*, but he is best known as a novelist and short story writer—along with Leopoldo Alas (*Clarín), *Pérez Galdós, *Pereda, Juan *Valera, etc., he is considered a member of the illustrious Generation of 1868. He was also an art critic, producing, for example, studies on the history of caricature, Velázquez, and the nude in Spanish art. He was a member of the *Academia Española (1900), to which he delivered an acceptance speech on his much admired predecessor, politician-statesman Emilio *Castelar; and of the San Fernando Royal Academy of Fine Arts (1902).

Picón's first novel, subtitled "Almost a Novel," was the modest-sized *Lázaro* (1882; Lazarus), in which his anti-clerical tendencies and a critical-moral vision predominate. *Juan Vulgar* (1885), another "little" novel, reflects this same moral stance, this time heavily laced with irony and satire, and in its main character, anticipates the abulic and narcissistic daydreamers of *Azorín, *Unamuno, and Pío *Baroja. *El enemigo* (1887; The Enemy) is Picón's most harshly anti-clerical piece of fiction. In other novels—*La hijastra del amor* (1884; The Step-Child of Love), *La honrada* (1890; The Honorable Lady), *Dulce y sabrosa* (1891; Sweet and Delectable, probably his best work), *Juanita Tenorio* (1910) and *Sacramento* (1914; Sacrament)—he criticizes the stuffy and hypocritical, sexually repressed society of Restoration Spain, in which men and women enter into the marriage contract out of ignorance or questionable motives, in which love, juxtaposed to the usually unsatisfactory state of matrimony in Picón's novels, is radically misunderstood or not experienced at all until circumstances, ill-timed and usually untenable in the long run, allow his characters to become illuminated by love as both a passion and an ideal. Within the self-imposed limits of his particular vision of Restoration society—the Spanish bourgeoisie, the entrapment of marriage, and sex—Picón does a quite decent job in analyzing the duplicitous code of behavior of his times. He lacks depth, that capacity and daring to surpass the circle of rational knowing, but he writes well of those things he is familiar with, delineating with an elegant, often incisive pen his middle-class characters and world. His style, clear and frequently ironic, shows the influence of his readings in the classic writers of Spain's Golden Age. Some of his best short stories appeared in such volumes as *Cuentos de mi tiempo* (1895; Stories of My Time), *Desencanto* (1925; Disenchantment), and *Mujeres* (1911; Women).

BIBLIOGRAPHY

Primary Texts

Dulce y sabrosa. Ed. G. Sobejano. 2nd ed. Madrid: Cátedra, 1982.
Obras completas. Madrid: Renacimiento, 1909–28.

Criticism

Amezúa y Mayo, A. G. de. *Apuntes biográficos de don Jacinto Octavio Picón*. N.p.: n.p., 1925.
Clemessy, N. ''*Lázaro*. La primera novela de Jacinto Octavio Picón.'' *CH* 319 (1977): 37–48.
Peseux-Richard, H. ''Un romancier espagnol: Jacinto Octavio Picón.'' *RH* 30 (1914): 515–85.
Valis, N. M. ''Una primera bibliografía de y sobre Jacinto Octavio Picón.'' *Cuadernos Bibliográficos* 40 (1980): 171–209.
———. *The Novels of Jacinto Octavio Picón*. Lewisburg, PA: Bucknell UP, 1986.

Noël M. Valis

PICÓN, José (1829, Madrid–1873, Valladolid), dramatist. An architect by profession, José Picón y García was ardently devoted to literature and the arts; in 1859; he finally committed himself once and for all to the theater with a one-act play called *El Solterón* (The Old Bachelor). He quickly gained renown for his graceful and witty **zarzuelas*, a form of Spanish light opera which centers round sketches of local customs and scenes. His best and most popular creation is *Pan y toros* (1864; Bread and Bulls), which was banned in 1867 by Isabel II. José Picón's strong liberalism and his criticism of a stagnated, atrophied Spain, as embodied in *Pan y toros* and other dramatic works, undoubtedly provided a political and moral ideal for his nephew, novelist Jacinto Octavio *Picón. Some of his other works include *La guerra de los sombreros* (1859; The War of the Hats), *Anarquía conyugal* (1861; Conjugal Anarchy), *La Corte de los Milagros* (1862; Court of Miracles), and *Gibraltar en 1890* (1866; Gibraltar in 1890). A good man, independent and passionate, he was, however, to die on July 4, 1873, in the insane asylum of Valladolid.

BIBLIOGRAPHY

Primary Texts

Anarquía conyugal. Madrid: González, 1861.
La Corte de los Milagros. Madrid: Rodríguez, 1862.
Gibraltar en 1890. Madrid: Centro General de Administración, 1866.
La guerra de los sombreros. Madrid: Rodríguez, 1859.
Pan y toros. Madrid: Centro General de Administración, 1864.

Criticism

Lustonó, Eduardo de. "José Picón." *La Ilustración Española y Americana* 47.28 (July 30, 1903): 70, 74.

Picón, Jacinto Octavio. "Prohibición de *Pan y toros* en tiempo de Isabel II." *RH* 40 (1917): 1–46.

Valis, Noël M. *The Novels of Jacinto Octavio Picón*. Lewisburg, PA/London: Bucknell UP, 1985. 22–25.

Noël M. Valis

PIDAL Y CARNIADO, Pedro José, Marqués de Pidal (1799, Villaviciosa, Asturias–1865, Madrid), politician, journalist, literary critic and historian. A political moderate influenced by constitutionalism, Pidal received appointments in the governments of Narváez and Istúriz and served as Spain's ambassador to Rome (1857–58). Pidal devoted equal energies to his literary and journalistic endeavors and regularly contributed to *El Espectador* (The Spectator), *El Faro* (The Lighthouse), and the *Revista de Madrid* (Journal of Madrid), in which he participated in a polemic concerning the three dramatic unities, defending their applicability as late as 1839, after *Romanticism had supposedly triumphed. His great interest in medieval Spanish literature led him to the discovery of rare mss. located in the library of El Escorial, including those of the *Vida de Santa *María Egipcíaca* (Life of Saint Mary of Egypt) and the *Libro de *Apolonio* (Book of Apollonius), which he edited under the title *Colección de poesías castellanas anteriores al siglo XV* (1864; Anthology of Pre-Fifteenth Century Castilian Poetry). His famous prologue "De la poesía castellana en los siglos XIV y XV" (Concerning Fourteenth and Fifteenth-Century Castilian Poetry) precedes his edition of the *Cancionero de *Baena* (1851; The Ballad Collection of Baena).

BIBLIOGRAPHY

Primary Texts

El cancionero de Juan Alfonso de Baena (siglo XV) ahora por primera vez dado a luz, con notas y comentarios. Madrid: Rivadeneyra, 1851.

Estudios literarios de d. Pedro José Pidal, primer marqués de Pidal. 2 vols. Madrid: Tello, 1890.

Poetas castellanos anteriores al siglo XV. BAE 57.

Criticism

Amezúa y Mayo, Agustín González de. *Don Pedro José Pidal, marqués de Pidal (1799–1865). Bosquejo biográfico*. Madrid: Hernández, 1913.

Navas Ruiz, Ricardo. *El Romanticismo español*. 3rd ed. Madrid: Cátedra, 1982.

Peers, E. Allison. *A History of the Romantic Movement in Spain*. 2 vols. Cambridge: Cambridge UP, 1940.

Romero Mendoza, Pedro. *Siete ensayos sobre el Romanticismo español*. vol. 2. Cáceres: Servicios Culturales de la Excma. Diputación Provincial de Cáceres, 1960.

Phoebe Porter Medina

PIE QUEBRADO, Versos de (limping verse), a form of poetry. *Pie quebrado* stanzas usually are composed of six lines in which lines 1, 2, 4, and 5 are eight syllables long, and lines 3 and 6 contain four syllables each. The pattern of rhyme may vary. Early examples of *pie quebrado* verse are found in writings of *Alphonse the Wise, *Berceo, the *Arcipreste de Hita, etc., but the form was popularized and regularized by the Marqués de *Santillana. Although the form has been employed through the centuries, it was most popular in the *Renaissance. Later poets varied the line lengths; twelve and six syllables, fourteen and seven syllables, sixteen and eight syllables, etc.

PIERRES Y MAGALONA (Pierres de Provenza and the Pretty Magalona), sixteenth-c. Spanish translation of a novel of chivalry. The Spanish version, translated from a fifteenth-c. French text, first appeared in 1519 in Burgos and Seville. The tender love story spiked with adventure was popular throughout Europe as well as in Spain.

PIFERRER, Pablo (1818, Barcelona–1848, Barcelona), poet and prose author. Although he wrote only in Castilian, he formed part of the group of Catalan writers (*Milà i Fontanals, *Rubió i Lluch, *Ors, etc.) who championed regional values of Catalonia as well as those of the nation. Piferrer was a victim of tuberculosis; his sixteen extant poems were published posthumously by Milà. The most famous are ''Canción de la primavera'' (1843; Song of Spring), ''El ermitaño de Montserrat'' (1842–45?; The Hermit of Montserrat), and the legend ''Alina y el genio'' (c. 1845; Alina and the Genie). He also left a collection of articles, many of which were later published with the title *Estudios de crítica* (1859; Critical Studies), and served as editor or collaborator in various journalistic activities. With *Quadrado, Parcerisa and *Pi y Margall, he undertook publication of a narrative *Recuerdos y Bellezas de España* (1839–43; Souvenirs and Beauties of Spain), of uneven merit. *See also* Catalan Literature.

BIBLIOGRAPHY

Primary Texts

Estudios de crítica. Barcelona: Diario de Barcelona, 1859.
Poetry. See Carnicer, in Criticism.
Recuerdos y Bellezas de España. vol 1. Barcelona: Barcino, 1939. Facs.
Recuerdos y Bellezas de España. vol. 2. Barcelona: Barcino, 1948. Facs.

Criticism

Carnicer, R. *Vida y obra de Pablo Piferrer*. Madrid: CSIC, 1963.

PILARES, Manuel (1921, Oviedo–), Spanish poet and short story writer. Of the working class, Pilares worked in the mines in Asturias and also sketched commercially before going to work for the railroads. As a poet, he is inspired by his own experience and the environments in which he has lived, as seen in the collections *Poemas mineros* (n.d.; Mining Poems) and *Sociedad Limitada* (1950; The Corporation). His story collections include *Historias de la Cuenca Minera* (n.d.; Tales of the Mining Region) and *El Andén* (1951; Railway Platform), which was awarded the Café Gijón Prize.

PIMENTÁ, (José) Alberto (Resende de Figueiredo) (1937, Porto–), poet, essayist, editor, creator of and participant in theatrical productions, translator. Pimentá is an independent vanguardist who even remained marginal to the experimental poetry of the 1960s and 1970s, and who rehabilitated the Baroque in contemporary Portuguese poetry, as in *Ascenção de dez gostos à boca* (1977; The Ascencion of Ten Pleasures to the Mouth). He is famous for his morphological mannerism and allegory that satirize established culture, as in *Discurso sobre o filho-da-puta* (1977; Discourse about the Son-of-a-Bitch), *Homo Sapiens* (1977), and *Bestiário Lusitano* (1980; Lusitanian Bestiary). Recently, his poetry has been playfully complex in form and bitingly critical of the post–1978 political crisis, as in *Canto nono* (1981; Ninth Canto). With his 1984 *Read & Mad*, Pimentá presents an intertextual montage of images and problems from *Camões and Fernando *Pessoa. His 1986 *Metamórfoses do vídeo* (Metamorphoses on Video) gathers together his best poetic critiques of absurd and pretentious culture from 1970 to 1984, with his best collages, concretist works and graphics. He studied German at the U of Coimbra and taught Portuguese and Romance philology at the U of Heidelberg. He has written critical essays in German, Italian and Portuguese, and publishes in many European journals. He conducts ongoing research on cultural topos in Coleridge, Gil *Vicente and António Vieira.

BIBLIOGRAPHY

Primary Texts

A Ascenção de dez gostos à boca. Lisbon: Autor, 1977.

Discurso sobre o filho-da-puta. Lisbon: Teorema, 1977. Criticism.

O Jogo de pedras [: antologia 1970–1980]. Lisbon: Sociedade Industrial Gráfica Telles da Silva, 1980.

Metamórfoses do vídeo. Rio de Janeiro: José Ribeiro, 1986.

Read & Mad. Lisbon: Ed. & etc, 1984.

English Translations

Five poems in *Micromegas: A Poetry Magazine: Portuguese issue* 12.1 (1985): 29–31.

Criticism

Hatherly, Ana. ''Situação da vanguarda literária em Portugal (a propósito dum livro de Alberto Pimentá).'' *Colóquio: Letras* 45 (Sept. 1978): 57–61.

Robert R. Krueger

PINEDA, Juan de (1515? Medina del Campo–1597, Medina del Campo?), Franciscan scholar. His major work is *Los treynta y cinco diálogos familiares de la agricultura christiana* (1589; Thirty-Five Personal Dialogues of Christian Agriculture), which gives his detailed view of contemporary Spanish life. He also penned the *Historia maravillosa . . . de San Juan Bautista* (1574; Wondrous History of St. John the Baptist) and *Los treynta libros de la monarquía eclesiástica o historia universal del mundo* (1576; Thirty Books of the Ecclesiastic Monarchy or Universal History of the World). Pineda's impressive erudition and rich vocabulary are marred by a rather leaden style.

BIBLIOGRAPHY

Primary Texts

Los treynta libros de la Monarchia. . . . 5 vols. Barcelona: Margarit, 1620.
Los treynta y cinco diálogos familiares. . . . In BAE 161–63 and 169–70.

PINTO GROTE, Carlos (1923, Tenerife, Canary Islands–), Spanish poet and short story writer. Trained as a psychiatrist, he has written several poetry collections: *Elegía por un hombre muerto en un campo de concentración* (1956; Elegy for a Man Who Died in a Concentration Camp), *El llanto alegre* (1957; Happy Sobbing); *Como un grano de trigo* (1965; Like a Grain of Wheat); and *Sin alba ni crepúsculo* (1967; With Neither Dawn Nor Dusk). His prose fiction includes *Las horas del hospital y otros cuentos* (1956; Hours at the Hospital, and Other Stories).

PIQUER, Andrés (1711, Fórnoles, Teruel–1772, Madrid), philosopher, physician, erudite. He studied at the U of Valencia, later teaching anatomy there. In 1751, Piquer became a court physician to Ferdinand IV, and moved to Madrid. He published several medical works, including *Medicina vetus et nova* (1735; Ancient and New Medicine) in Latin, and *Tratado de las calenturas* (1751; Treatise on Fevers), but his most significant effort was the *Física moderna, racional y experimental* (1745; Modern Physics, Rational and Experimental)—the first Spanish book on physics. It earned him international attention. Piquer also published a trilingual edition of Hippocrates, in Spanish, Greek and Latin.

BIBLIOGRAPHY

Primary Texts

Andreae Piqueri; archiatri Medicine vetus, et nova. 5th ed. Madrid: Ibarra, 1776.
Discurso sobre la enfermedad del rey nuestro señor d. Fernando. In *Colección de documentos inéditos para la historia de España.* 112 vols. Madrid: n.p., 1842–96. vol 18: 156–226.
Física moderna. . . . 2nd ed. Madrid: Ibarra, 1780.
Tratado de calenturas. 4th ed. Madrid: Ibarra, 1777.

PIRES, José Cardoso (1925, ?–), Portuguese prose writer. One of Portugal's best contemporary writers, Cardoso Pires assimilated the art of the American short story, rejecting the sentimentality of his national tradition that characterized many neo-realistic authors. Among his influential sources are Hemingway and Roger Vaillard.

A sophisticated observer of human sentiment and awareness of social status, Cardoso Pires has created novels such as *O Anjo Ancorado* (1958; The Anchored Angel), whose almost exaggerated Realism nonetheless results in a controlled portrayal of coastal life at different social levels of experience. Yet the author rejected the "populistic" neo-realism of Portuguese literature, even though he shared its goals of denouncing the absurdity of the political system with its oppressive fascism and subsequent class inequalities. Cardoso Pires's reality is expressed more allegorically and is incisive. Rather than the rural culture, his is the cruel city world of the alienated well-to-do and the marginals who co-exist within the same spheres. The intention of this literature is moralistic, the tone at times deliberately accusing. This takes the author beyond historical realism toward the creation of symbolic situations and characters which the reader must make a greater effort to interpret, often being left abruptly with an unexpected ending.

BIBLIOGRAPHY

Primary Texts

E agora, José? N.p.: n.p., 1977.
O Anjo Ancorado. Lisbon: Ulisseia, 1958.
Balada da Praia dos Cães. Lisbon: Edições O Jornal, 1982.
Os Caminheiros e Outros Contos. Lisbon: Centro Bibliográfico, 1949.
Cartilha do Marialva. Lisbon: Ulisseia, 1960.
O Delfim. Lisbon: Moraes, 1968.
Dinossauro Excelentíssimo. Maio: Arcádia, 1972.
Histórias de Amor. Lisbon: Gleba, 1952.
O Hóspede de Job. Lisbon: Arcádia, 1963.
Jogos de Azar. Lisbon: Arcádia, 1963.
O Render dos Heróis. Lisbon: Gleba, 1960.

Criticism

Campelo, Juril do Nascimento. ''Aspectos da Temporalidade em *O Delfim.*'' *Revista de Letras* (Paraná) 28 (1979): 61–66.
Keats, L. W. *Thesis and the Craft of Prose Fiction in the Work of José Cardoso Pires.* Leeds: U of Leeds, 1966.
Melo, João. ''As Funções do Narrador em *O Delfim* de José Cardoso Pires.'' *Colóquio* 59 (Jan. 1981): 30–41.
Ornelas, José N. ''Técnica e Estrutura d'*O Anjo Ancorado.*'' *REH* 15.3 (Oct. 1981): 323–38.

Kathleen March

PLÀ I CASADEVALL, Josep (1897, Palafrugell–1981, Llofriu), narrator and journalist. Born into a well-to-do rural family of the Costa Brava, young Plà studied medicine and law, but at a very early age he discovered his true vocation in literature. Like many Catalan writers of the twentieth c. he began his literary apprenticeship writing for several local magazines: *Revista de Girona*, *Baix Empordà*, *Manresa*, etc. After World War I, he devoted himself exclusively to writing and until his death wrote no less than thirty thousand pages of narrative, considered by most critics as the best of twentieth-c. *Catalan literature. In his younger years his production was mostly journalistic, though of the highest quality, and later, especially during the last forty years of his life, it consisted of essays and narrations on the most varied topics: biographies, politics, cultural events, descriptions of towns and Catalan landscapes, etc. Although he traveled widely as a correspondent to different European capitals, Plà basically remained, in the words of the critic *Castellet, a ''sophisticated peasant.'' Profoundly conservative, his writings reflect a deep distrust of the most basic truisms of Western civilization and a skepticism concerning the goodness of the human condition. During the Spanish Civil War of 1936–39 he was one of the very few Catalan intellectuals who sided with Franco, returning with the fascist troops in 1939. The irony of ironies was the fact that because he was a Catalan he was treated as one of the defeated. He could not write in his own language nor be a "Catalan fascist." Plà's bitterness and disillusion with the human condition became almost morbid. It is in those years, self-exiled to his small hometown, that he wrote true masterpieces of narrative literature like *El quadern gris* (The Gray Notebook), included as the first volume of *Obra completa* (1966; Complete Works), and *Homenots* (1956; Men), biographies of prominent Catalans in all walks of life. His solitude and isolation from the mainstream of Catalan culture left Plà undisturbed, patiently and stubbornly compiling his literary works and going deeply into the almost mystical Catalan earth of which he, like a grain of sand, felt himself a part: "Quin pais més agradable! Quina permanent sensacio de no viure a Espanya, de trobar-se totalment separat!" (What a beautiful country! What a permanent feeling of not living in Spain, of finding oneself completely cut off!) In simple, clear and yet beautiful prose, Plà strove to write in flashed impressions and at the same time with careful precision. His prose—with the vivid and clear colors of the classic Mediterranean—is not only to be read but also to be felt, seen and touched. Plà, stoic and humanist, saw beauty and time passing by, the memory of civilization only capturable in art (i.e., literature). Thus, very persistently and always unassumingly, he wrote to defeat the miseries of daily life. Enormously popular with the public, he is considered today one of the true masters of modern Catalan prose. His opus is enormous and faithfully depicts the social and cultural life of contemporary Catalonia: its historical events and customs, its cities and villages, its men and women. As with *Azorín in Castilian literature, Plà's gentle irony and refined skepticism never crystalize into a full-fledged novel, although he attempted the genre several times, most notably in *El carrer estret* (1951; Narrow Street). Other important works are *Llanterna màgica* (1926; The Magic Lantern), *Cartes de lluny* (1928; Letters from Afar), *Francesc Cambó* (1928–30), *Viatge a Catalunya* (1934; Journey to Catalonia), *Guía de la Costa Brava* (1941; Guide to the Costa Brava), *La huida del tiempo* (1945; The Flight of Time), *Cadaqués* (1947), *Pa i raïm* (1951; Bread and Grapes), *Els pagesos* (1952; The Peasants), *Les hores* (1953; The Hours), *Week-end d'estiu a Nova York* (1955; Summer Weekend in New York), *Notes disperses* (1969; Scattered Notes), *Notes de capvespral* (1979; Evening Notes).

BIBLIOGRAPHY

Primary Texts

Obra completa. Intro. Joan Fuster. 2nd ed. 14 vols. Barcelona: Destino, 1966–72.

Criticism

Castellet, Josep. M. *Josep Plà o la raó narrativa*. Barcelona: n.p., 1978.

———. "Perfil de Josep Plà amb motiu de la seva mort." *Serra d'Or* (July-Aug. 1983): 439–41.

Destino. Several authors. No. 1,545 (1967) and No. 1,796 (1972).
Manent, A. *Carner, Riba, Plà*. Madrid: n.p., 1973.
Molas, Joaquim. ''Les obres completes de Josep Plà.'' *Serra d'Or* (Oct. 1966): 59–62.

Joan Gilabert

PLATONISM. In the Iberian literatures as in others Plato has been an important presence, though the direct exposition of his thought has contributed less to this than the enduring substratum of commonly held, semi-Platonic beliefs: the primacy of spirit over matter; the analogical ordering of nature; the human microcosm; unity as the goal of thought. Such assumptions—in some cases derived from St. Paul, in others serving as common ground among medieval Christians, Moslems and Jews—went largely unchallenged until modern times. A second indirect source of influence was Renaissance Neoplatonism. Ancient Neoplatonic thought, like Platonism itself, made its impact in the peninsula mainly through these intermediaries.

European responses to Plato from the twelfth-c. renaissance onwards, found echoes in Spain, though these were often transformed by local factors. Spain's more intensive Oriental contacts embraced philosophical work of real substance, such as the *Fons Vitae* of the Andalusian Jew Ibn Gabirol. But Eastern wisdom literature like the *Buenos proverbios* or *Bocados de oro* was more apt to promote esoteric images of Plato as aphorist, ascetic or even magician. Twelfth-c. and later translators could tell Spain something of the *Timaeus* and of Neoplatonic thought; the Platonist philosophy expounded at Chartres and Paris was not unknown there. But university philosophical teaching was slow to emerge in Castile; without native institutions to sustain it such interest soon faded. In Catalonia, by contrast, a more creative response to Platonic thinking began with Ramón *Llull and continued, from Martí to Sibiuda, among teaching friars in closer touch with the Parisian schools.

Fifteenth-c. Aragonese political involvement in Italy favored contact with early humanist interpreters of Plato. Yet Castilian sentence-literature old and new preserved his misleading popular image. Professional scholars like El Tostado (*Madrigal, Alfonso de), though better-informed, were limited by their own rigorously Aristotelian method, and by the range of texts traditionally available in the Latin West: *Timaeus*; *Phaedo*; *Meno*; parts of the *Republic*. The mid-century cultural movement did become aware of recent Italian humanist translations into Latin, two of which (*Phaedo* and the spurious *Axiochus*) were rendered into Castilian for Santillana in the 1440s by Pero Díaz de Toledo. But these pioneer efforts bore little fruit (except perhaps in the re-emergence of the dialogue as a literary form). To the end of the century such figures as Alonso Ortiz, who knew the *Gorgias*, and the unnamed copyist of a Latin *Phaedrus* and *Apology* remained untypical. Only a few Spaniards—mostly visitors to Italy—knew anything of Ficino.

The influence of Ficino's Neoplatonism began to be seriously felt in certain Hispano-Jewish writers of the early sixteenth c. The Portuguese **converso*

Bernardim *Ribeiro drew upon its hermetic elements; the *Dialoghi d'Amore* of León *Hebreo (the exiled Judah Abravanel) developed its harmonious cosmology and teaching about love. This last was historically opportune. Both the courtly and Petrarchan poetic traditions regarded love as an ennobling discipline, a source of spiritual worth. The ascent of chaste, "Platonic" love from desire of physical beauty, through adoration of a virtuous soul, to contemplation of the godhead served to define and dignify such notions. Abravanel's dialogues were published in the mid 1530s; so was *Boscán's translation of *Castiglione's *Courtier*, a blander, more socially assimilable version of similar doctrines on love. These doctrines supplied the *pastoral genre with most of its themes. Their fusion of amorous and religious discourse lent itself well to the expressive needs of sixteenth-c. *mysticism. Above all, their influence, patent already in *Garcilaso de la Vega, was to affect most sixteenth and seventeenth-c. poets. In such poet-philosophers as *Aldana or Luis de *León a recognizably Neoplatonic world harmony was presented as the vehicle of a Christian message.

These writers were able to profit from the improved state of knowledge about Plato, made possible by *Renaissance scholarship. So did radical thinkers (*Vives; *Servet) in search of some alternative to the prevailing Aristotelian orthodoxy. The more cautious *Fox Morcillo tried to prove that Plato and Aristotle could, after all, be reconciled. At a more modest level Pedro Simón *Abril translated the *Gorgias* and *Cratylus* for teaching purposes; the Bachiller Rúa remodeled Pero Díaz's early versions. The scholarly tradition, then, is not negligible. Platonic topics even helped to shape the debate among Spaniards about the legitimacy of fiction. But it was, perhaps significantly, the Aristotelian notion of exemplarity which prevailed in that argument. Platonist scholarship in Spain was never as important as the wider diffusion of broadly Platonic (or Neoplatonic) attitudes. Nor did it seriously contest the philosophical primacy of Aristotle in the age of the Counter-Reformation.

After the Renaissance period there are no Platonist movements to be registered. Yet individual writers were always liable to revert to a Platonist outlook or to Platonist themes. There is the consciously archaizing philosophical idealism of Juan *Valera in the nineteenth c.; in the twentieth the humanism of *Pérez de Ayala and the hermeticism of *Pessoa bear obvious Platonist traces. Indeed the polarities of symbolism and realism, between which so much post-romantic literature is ranged, can be seen as reflecting the more ancient opposition between Plato and Aristotle. The division runs through Spanish and Portuguese culture as through all the cultures of the West. *See also* Aristotelianism.

BIBLIOGRAPHY

Criticism

Abellán, José Luis. *Historia crítica del pensamiento español.* Madrid: Espasa-Calpe, 1979.

Green, Otis H. *Spain and the Western Tradition.* 4 vols. Madison: Wisconsin UP, 1963–66.

Ife, Barry W. *Reading and Fiction in Golden-Age Spain: A Platonist Critique and Some Picaresque Replies*. Cambridge: UP, 1985.

Maravall, José Antonio. "La estimación de Sócrates y de los sabios clásicos en la Edad Media española." In *Estudios de historia del pensamiento español*. vol. 1. Madrid: Cultura Hispánica, 1973.

Parker, Alexander A. *The Philosophy of Love in Spanish Literature, 1480–1680*. Edinburgh: UP, 1985.

Rico, Francisco. *El pequeño mundo del hombre: varia fortuna de una idea en las letras españolas*. Madrid: Castalia, 1970.

Round, Nicholas G. "The Shadow of a Philosopher: Medieval Castilian Images of Plato." *JHP* 3 (1978–79): 1–36.

Nicholas Round

POLO, Gaspar Gil (?, ?–1585, Barcelona), poet and *pastoral prose author. Very little biographical data is known about the continuator of *Montemayor's *Diana*. He was appointed to a distinguished post in the royal treasury by Philip II in 1572. He was also a notary in Valencia. He renounced the position in 1579 in favor of his son Julián; in 1580 he went to Barcelona to oversee the affairs of the royal patrimony, and died there. He had another son, also named Gil Polo, who was a jurist and wrote law texts. The son has been confused with the author of the *Diana*, as likewise occurred with another Gil Polo, who taught Greek in Valencia (1566–73).

With the exception of a few pieces of verses at the beginning of certain texts (a sonnet praising the *Carolea* of Jerónimo Semperse, 1560, and other poetry of the same style), Gil Polo's only work is *Los cinco libros de la Diana enamorada* (Valencia, 1564; *The Five Books of the Enamored Diana*, 1968). In this exquisite work of art, Gil Polo continues the amatory matters of Montemayor's *Diana*, but resolves the impossible and objectionable elements contained therein. Although married to Delio, Diana is still enamored of Sireno. The two embark on separate journeys to the palace of Felicia and are reunited in their love after the death of Delio. The novelistic structure has often been criticized because of its elementary nature. It serves as a simple backdrop upon which Gil Polo raises scenes of ardent lyricism with his elegant descriptions of the Levantine landscape.

Gil Polo intersperses a variety of lyrics throughout the narrative. Among the most notable poems are "La canción de Nerea" (The Song of Nerea) and "Epitalamio de Diana y Sireno" (Epithalamium of Diana and Sireno), written in alexandrine verse, a rare form in the sixteenth c. He also composed new poetical forms, such as the *versos provenzales*, Provençal verses, combinations of hendecasyllables and pentasyllables in twelve-line stanzas. In addition, there are numerous examples of short meters.

The "Canto de Turia" (Song of Turia) figures prominently in the *Diana enamorada* (Enamored Diana). Composed of *octavas reales*, it is one of many catalogs of illustrious men of the time. The river Turia, personified in the mythological manner, leaves its cave to speak of Borjas y Moncada, Lluís *Vives, Ausiàs *March, and other eminent Valencians. It is reminiscent of the analogous

"Canto de Orfeo" (Song of Orpheus) of Montemayor's *Diana* and served as a model for *Cervantes's "Canto de Caliope" (Song of Caliope) in *La Galatea*.

The *Diana enamorada* was well received in the sixteenth and seventeenth centuries, although its success was eclipsed slightly by Alonso *Pérez's pastoral romance published one year earlier. Bartholomew Yong published an English translation in 1598, and the German humanist Gaspar Barth produced a translation in Latin (1625). Despite the subsequent decline of the genre, the *Diana enamorada* continued to be highly acclaimed and was re-edited in the eighteenth c. More recently the work has been praised for the beauty of its prose and verse.

BIBLIOGRAPHY

Primary Text

Diana enamorada. Ed. R. Ferreres. Madrid: Espasa-Calpe, 1973.

English Translations

A Critical Edition of Yong's Translation of George of Montemayor's "Diana" and Gil Polo's "Enamored Diana." Ed. J. M. Kennedy. Oxford: Clarendon, 1968.

Diana enamorada (1564) together with the English Translation (1598). Ed. R. Grismer and M. Grismer. Minneapolis: Burgess, 1959.

Criticism

Avalle-Arce, Juan Bautista. *La novela pastoril española*. 2nd ed. Madrid: Istmo, 1974.

Deborah Compte

POLO Y PEYROLÓN, Manuel (1846, Cañete, Cuenca–1918, Valencia), novelist, professor. He taught psychology, logics and ethics at the Institute in Teruel and later in Valencia, and published various scholarly works in these areas. As a strong, traditional Catholic, he opposed *Naturalism, following instead the lead of *costumbristas* in his fiction. *Los mayos* (1879; May Games) is a charming love story filled with Aragonese customs and color. Another *costumbrista* work is *Costumbres populares de la sierra de Albarracín* (Popular Customs of the Sierra of Albarracin), the first part of which appeared in 1873, and the second in 1910. *See also* Romanticism.

BIBLIOGRAPHY

Primary Texts

Costumbres populares. 3rd ed. Barcelona: Católica, 1876.

Los mayos; los mellizos; el sí de una serrana; la tía Levítico. N.p.: Católica Casals, 1917.

POMBO, Álvaro (1939, Santander–), Spanish novelist and poet. He obtained a degree in philosophy from the U of Madrid, as well as another bachelor's degree in philosophy from Birbeck College in London, living in England from 1966 until the end of 1977. He was unknown in Spanish literary circles before that date, but published two books that year, one of poetry, *Variaciones* (Variations), winner of the El Bardo Prize for Poetry, and one of short fiction, *Relatos* *sobre la falta de sustancia* (Tales of Lack of Substance; repub. 1985). Many of these stories contemplate aspects of homosexuality, and are expressed in a style hailed as absolutely original, rhetorically exemplary, evocative and yet absolutely emotionless. *El parecido* (1979; 2nd ed., rev., 1985; The Resemblance) is a novel which, like its predecessors, was overlooked upon first publication. Jaime, son of an upper-class family in northern Spain, is killed in a freak motorcycle accident; the three days following his funeral are given over to debates as to the ''real'' identity of the deceased, that is, his real personality among the several facades or schizophrenic selves he projected for those who knew him, including his uncle Gonzalo, a fashionable writer secretly enamored of his nephew; his proud mother with her repressed sexuality; and Pepelín, the family chauffeur who is a look-alike of Jaime, encouraged by the mother to ''become'' her son. In 1984, Pombo won the first Herralde Novel Prize awarded by Editorial Anagrama, which initiated with this title a series of ''new'' novels by new or little-known writers, and Pombo became an overnight literary sensation, considered the revelation of the decade. The prize-winning novel is entitled *El héroe de las mansardas de Mansard* (The Hero of Mansard's Garret Roofs), a work combining irony and humor, cultured or esoteric and colloquial language, circular or peripheral and distant narrative with hyper-realist monologues. Themes include robbery, blackmail, betrayal, unorthodox sexuality, and rites of passage. The protagonist is a gnome-like boy, Kus-Kus, of the upper bourgeoisie of northern Spain, with a circle of relatives and servants each more extravagant, eccentric and deviant than the last. *El hijo adoptivo* (1984; The Adopted Son) tells the story of two proud unpublished writers, a mother (already deceased) and her son Pancho, isolated in a decrepit country house near the seacoast of northern Spain. A man from the past, a former secretary of Pancho's mysteriously fired by the mother, appears with a child, his son, who is installed in the crumbling mansion. It is a tale of mystery and of ghosts but also a love story, told with a certain humor up to its sudden, unexpected, tragic and ironic ending. This novel was also submitted to the Herralde Prize competition and was a finalist. The focus of *Los delitos insignificantes* (1986; Insignificant Crimes) is once again homosexuality, re-creating the relationship between Ortega, a middle-aged homosexual and frustrated writer, and Quirós, a good-looking, light-headed young man who is temporarily unemployed. Histrionic notes are introduced with the mother of Quirós, a pretentious widow about to remarry, whose behavior is that of an aging prima donna. The humor usually associated with her appearances fades as the eruption of eroticism precipitates a tragic end. Much admired by fellow writers and contemporary critics, Pombo is considered the most original literary personality to have appeared thus far in post-Franco Spain.

Janet Pérez

POMPEIA, Núria (1938, Barcelona–), journalist, cartoonist and short story writer. She contributed regularly to *Triunfo* and was managing editor of *Por Favor*. Most of her work is both graphic and literary, a blend of cartoons and text. Her themes are predominantly feminist; *La educación de Palmira* (1972; The Education of Palmira) introduces us to one of the best-known cartoon characters in the Spanish-speaking world. Through Palmira, the author shows how traditional education deforms the female's natural impulses and intellect. In *Mujercitas* (1975; Little Women) she juxtaposes traditional stereotypes with feminist reality, making her points with humor and insight. *Y fueron felices comiendo perdices* (1970; And They Lived Happily Ever After) confronts the myth of the blissful wife and mother with the everyday realities which constitute life once the honeymoon is over. *Cinc cèntims* (1981; Five Cents) is a collection of twelve short stories, her first entirely verbal work, written in Catalan. The stories underscore the lack of real change beneath the appearance of modernization and progress, keeping intact her feminist viewpoint and satiric sense of humor.

BIBLIOGRAPHY

Primary Texts

Cinc cèntims. Barcelona: Edicions 62, 1981.
La educación de Palmira. Barcelona: n.p. 1972.
Maternasia. Barcelona: Kairós, 1967.
Mujercitas. Barcelona: Kairós, 1975.
Pels segles dels segles. Barcelona: Edicions 62, 1971.
Y fueron felices comiendo perdices. Barcelona: Kairós, 1970.

Kathleen McNerney

PONCE, Bartolomé (fl. 1600, Aragón–?), Cistercian monk, author of religious works. His most famous writing is the *Primera parte de la clara Diana a lo divino* (1599; First part of the Celebrated Diana in Religious Style), a religious allegory inspired by Jorge de *Montemayor's *Diana*. The pastoral anecdote is all but lost in Ponce's complex allegorization: entertaining tales of human love are labeled in passing as lessons in the temptations of the World and the Flesh and are weakly contrasted with homilies of post-Tridentine nature. The spiritual adventures of Barpolio (rational man) are related in pedantic, ornate style through emblematic symbolism which, although foreign to modern taste, was quite attractive to sixteenth- and seventeenth-c. readers. The sequel promised at the end of the volume (''if this first part is acceptable'') was evidently never published and perhaps never written. *Clara Diana* has not been published since 1599. *See also* A lo divino; Pastoral.

BIBLIOGRAPHY

Criticism

Avalle-Arce, J. B. *La novela pastoril española*. 2nd ed. Madrid: Istmo, 1974. 269–70.
Solé-Leris, A. *The Spanish Pastoral Novel*. TWAS 575. Boston: Twayne, 1980. 138–39.

Elizabeth Rhodes

PONCE DE LA FUENTE, Constantino (c. 1502, San Clemente de la Mancha, Cuenca–c. 1560, Seville), preacher, evangelist, religious writer. Of Jewish lineage, he rose to the position of royal preacher for Charles V and accompanied

Prince Philip on European travels. His published writings, appearing from 1543 to 1556, were very popular and underwent multiple editions. Yet, by 1558, he was imprisoned by the *Inquisition in Seville on charges of heresy and Lutheranism. He died in prison, and was burned in effigy in 1560. His writings are suffused with a very spiritual Christianity, with individual faith in Christ as the cornerstone; María Paz Aspe correctly observes that his life synthesizes many of the complex interactions of sixteenth-c. religious movements in Spain. *See also Converso.*

BIBLIOGRAPHY

Primary Texts

Suma de la Doctrina cristiana. Barcelona: D. Gómez Flores, 1983.
Beatus vir, carne de hoguera: Exposición del primer salmo. . . . Madrid: Nacional, 1977.

English Translation

The Confession of a Sinner. Tr. John T. Betts. London: Bell and Daldy, 1869.

Criticism

Aspe, María Paz. ''Constantino Ponce de la Fuente, Escritor 'Evangelista' del Siglo XVI.'' In *Actas del Sexto Congreso Internacional de Hispanistas.* Ed. A. M. Gordon and E. Rugg. Toronto: U of Toronto, 1980. 73–77.

PONCE DE LEÓN, Basilio (1560, Granada–1629, Salamanca), poet and orator. An Augustinian, he taught theology in Alcalá and Salamanca and wrote numerous theological treatises in Latin that were celebrated by his contemporaries in *Fama póstuma* (1630; Posthumous Fame). Some of his poems were attributed to his uncle, Fray Luis de *León. His main literary contribution, the *Sermones de Cuaresma* (1605–10; Lenton Sermons), is written in an elegant prose replete with familiar and colloquial expressions. *De Agno Typico* (1604) is a text in defense of his uncle when he was persecuted by the *Inquisition.

BIBLIOGRAPHY

Primary Texts

Fama póstuma. Ed. F. Montesdoca. Salamanca: n.p., 1630.
For other primary sources, consult Palau y Dulcet, A. *Manual del librero hispanoamericano* 13 (1961): 411–13.

José Ortega

PONDAL, Eduardo (1835, Ponteceso–1916, La Coruña), poet. Together with Rosalía de *Castro and *Curros Enríquez, Pondal is regarded as one of the most important Galician poets of the nineteenth c. He was born, raised and lived most of his life in one of the archetypical parts of Galicia, the region of Bergantiños where the mountains meet the sea and the green landscape is forever shrouded in mist. He was a friend of the historian Manuel *Murguía, Rosalía's husband. Pondal's verse is steeped in the most ancient Celtic tradition of his Galician ancestry. The poems of his only book, *Queixumes dos pinos* (1886; Laments of the Pines), are typically Ossian-like in their fixation upon a heroic past, their intensity, the mythology of the native land and the rough-hewn nature of their strophes. *See also* Galician Literature.

BIBLIOGRAPHY

Primary Texts

Queixumes dos pinos. Buenos Aires: EMECE, 1940.

Criticism

Carballo Calero, R. *Historia da literatura galega contemporánea*. Vigo: Galaxia, 1973. 802.

———. *Versos inorados ou esquecidos de Eduardo Pondal*. Vigo: Galaxia, 1960.

Ricardo Landeira

PONZ, Antonio (1725, Bechi, Valencia–1792, Madrid), writer. He studied theology and then art, attending the Real Academia de Bellas Artes de San Fernando in Madrid, and continuing study in Rome. He wrote the monumental, eighteen-volume *Viaje de España* (1772–74; Journey through Spain) and the two-volume *Viaje fuera de España* (Journey Outside of Spain) in which he compiles a record of the art and architecture he sees in his travels through much of Spain. Many of these pieces have subsequently disappeared. Despite his lack of literary talent, and his strong neo-classical prejudices, the *Viaje* is the first attempt to amass an inventory of Spain's enormous, varied artistic wealth.

BIBLIOGRAPHY

Primary Text

Viaje de España; seguido de los dos tomos de Viaje fuera de España. Ed. C. María del Rivero. Madrid: Aguilar, 1947.

Criticism

Puente, Joaquín de la. *La visión de la realidad española en los ''Viajes'' de Don Antonio Ponz*. Madrid: Moneda y Crédito, 1968.

PORCEL, Baltasar (1937, Andratx, Mallorca–), novelist, playwright and journalist. Some of his novels are *Solnegre* (1961; Blacksun), *La lluna i el ''Cala Llamp''* (1963; The Moon and the Sail Boat), *Els escorpins* (1965; The Scorpions), *Els argonautes* (1967; The Argonauts), *Difunts soto els ametllers en flor* (1970; Dead Men under the Budding Almond Trees), *Cavalls cap a la fosca* (1975; Horses toward the Night), *Las manzanas de oro* (1980; The Golden Apples) and *Todos los espejos* (1981; All the Mirrors). He is also the author of a collection of short stories, *Crònica d'atabalades navegacions* (1971; Chronicle of Stupefied Navigators), travel books on the Balearic Islands, and numerous articles and books on political and cultural topics. His plays, including *Els condemnats* (1959; The Condemned), *Historia d'una guerra* (1963; History of a War) and five other titles, were published in 1965. His prose works in Mallorquin or Catalan have been translated to Castilian.

BIBLIOGRAPHY

Primary Texts

Els argonautes. Barcelona: Edicions 62, 1979.
Cavalls cap a la fosca. Barcelona: Edicions 62, 1978.
Crònica d'atabalades navegacions. Barcelona: Edicions 62, 1971.
Solnegre. Barcelona: Edicions 62, 1973.
Teatre. Palma de Mallorca: Daedalus, 1965.

Criticism

Gimferrer, Pere. Prologue to *Solnegre*. By B. Porcel. Barcelona: Edicions 62, 1973.
Laín Entralgo, Pedro. Prologue to *Las sombras chinescas*. By B. Porcel. Barcelona: Táber, 1968. 11–14.
Molas, J. Prologue to *Teatre*. By B. Porcel. Palma de Mallorca: Daedalus, 1965. 9–25.
Soldevila, L. *El misteri de l'alzinar i altres contes*. Barcelona: Edicions 62, 1982.

Kay Pritchett

PORCEL Y SALABLANCA, José Antonio (1720, Granada–1794, ?), poet, playwright, erudite, orator. He studied at the Colegio de San Dionisio del Sacromonte in Granada and occupied important positions in different religious institutions. Porcel also founded and participated in the literary group Academia del Trípode (Tripod Academy) in Granada, and was a member of the Academia de Buen Gusto.

Porcel was a late follower of *Góngora; his best work is *Fábulas de Adonis,* a fable of Adonis and Venus narrated by Anaxarte in four loving *pastoral eclogues. The delicacy of this composition is impaired by the exuberance and lack of musicality.

BIBLIOGRAPHY

Primary Texts

El árbol de las lises. Málaga: F. de Casas y Martínez, 1784.
Gozo y corona de Granada. Granada: Real, 1762.
Fábulas del Adonis. In BAE 65.

Criticism

Arco y Molinero, A. "El mejor ingenio granadino del siglo XVIII, D. José Antonio Porcel y Salablanca." *Alhambra* 478–82 (1918): 73–75, 95–97, 121–23, 145–57, 169–71.
Orozco Díaz, E. "Porcel y el barroquismo literario del siglo XVIII." *Cuadernos de la Cátedra Feijoo* 21 (1968): 20–36.

José Ortega

PORIDAT DE PORIDADES (Secret of Secrets), a moral treatise in the form of letters ostensibly written by Aristotle to Alexander the Great advising him on the qualities and duties of the ideal king. Anonymously translated from the Arabic *Sirr al-asrar*, it appeared in Spain in the thirteenth c., the Spanish counterpart of the *Secretum secretorum*, a widely known Latin version by Philip of Tripoli. Both texts greatly influenced medieval Spanish political-moral writings. The best-preserved ms. consists of twenty-six folios comprising an introduction and eight treatises on such matters as justice, military defense and proper selection of royal aides. It contains proverbs, Oriental fables and even a lapidary. In two mss. it is followed by the *Libro de los buenos proverbios* (Book of Good Proverbs), reordered so that the section known as *Ensennamientos de Alexandre* (Teachings of Alexander) is contiguous to the similar material of the *Poridat.*

BIBLIOGRAPHY

Primary Text

Secretum Secretorum. Poridat de las poridades de Seudo Aristoteles. Ed. Lloyd A. Kasten. Madrid: HSMS, 1957.

Criticism

Kasten, Lloyd A. " 'Poridat de las poridades': a Spanish Form of the Western Text of the *Secretum secretorum.*" *RPH* 5 (1951): 180–90.

Kathleen L. Kirk

PORLÁN, Rafael (1889, Córdoba–1945, Jaén), Spanish poet belonging to the Andalusian school. His first book was *Pirrón en Tarifa* (1926; Pyron in Tarifa), followed by *Romances y canciones* (1936; Ballads and Songs), and the posthumous *Poesías* (1948; Poetry).

PORTAL NICOLÁS, Marta (1930, Nava, Asturias–), Spanish journalist, essayist and novelist. Portal, who has been a professor of literature, studied in Colombia with a grant from the March Foundation, and has written literary criticism in addition to her fiction. Her first novel was *A tientas y a ciegas* (1966; Blindly and Gropingly), which won the Planeta Prize. The theme is a feminist one: a thirty-year-old married "sex object" decides to finish her university degree; formerly frigid with her faithless Don Juan husband, she has a sensual affair with a professor, but is unable to go against patriarchal norms and tradition to leave her husband. She returns to him, planning to have children and be a more generous wife. Other early literary efforts are novelettes collected in *El malmuerto* (1967; Murdered), followed by *A ras de las sombras* (1968; At the Level of the Shadows). Portal was much impressed by her time in Latin America, and produced at least two works as a result, *El maíz, grano sagrado de América* (1970; Corn, America's Sacred Grain) and *Proceso narrativo de la Revolución mexicana* (1977; Narrative Process of the Mexican Revolution), a study of the contemporary Mexican novel. She returned to the theme of adultery in *Ladridos a la luna* (1970; Howling at the Moon), which again ends with the woman unable to break the bonds of matrimony, deciding to break off the affair instead and return to a less than satisfactory marriage. *La veintena* (1973; Two Score) is a collection of twenty stories, and *El buen camino* (1975; The Good Road), another novel.

Janet Pérez

PORTUGAL, Condestable don Pedro de (1429–1466), poet and author. He wrote two works combining prose and verse: *Sátira de felice e infelice vida* (Satire on the Happy and Sad Life) and *Tragedia de la insigne reyna Doña Isabel* (Tragedy of the Celebrated Queen Isabelle), not published until 1899. Another important work is the poem *Coplas de contempto de las cosas fermosas del mundo* (c. 1490; In Contempt of the World's Beautiful Things). Although don Pedro was Portuguese, he wrote in Castilian, and is best known for *Sátira de felice e infelice vida*, which is generally included in the category of sentimental romances, tales of unhappy or tragic love that flourished in the fifteenth and sixteenth centuries.

BIBLIOGRAPHY

Primary Texts

Obras completas. Ed. Luis Adão de Fonseca. Lisbon: Fundação Calouste Gulbenkian, 1975. 1–75.

Sátira de felice e infelice vida. In *Opúsculos literarios de los siglos XIV a XVI*. Ed. A. Paz y Melia. SBE 29. Madrid: SBE, 1892. 47–101.

Criticism

Gascón Vera, Elena. *Don Pedro, Condestable de Portugal*. Madrid: Fundacion Universitaria Española, 1979.

Patricia Grieve

PORTUGAL, José Bernardino Blanc de (1914, Lisbon–), poet, editor, critic, musicologist. Born in Lisbon of noble ancestry (as his name denotes) on March 8, 1914, José Blanc de Portugal graduated from the U of Lisbon with a master's degree in geological sciences. His long career as a geo-physicist working for the National Meteorological Service afforded him an opportunity to live and travel extensively throughout mainland Portugal, the Azores, Angola and Mozambique. He eventually became the director of the service.

Beginning with his studies at the university, and parallel with his commitment to science, has been a lifelong interest in the arts and literature in particular. For many years he has been a recognized music critic, with reviews appearing regularly in Portugal's leading newspapers and journals, and, at various times, he has also been a critic of literature, especially of poetry and theater, as well as film and ballet. In addition, he has been active as a translator of English, German and Italian authors, with special acclaim for his rendering of Shakespeare's *Hamlet*.

He was appointed Portugal's cultural attaché to Brazil, and came out of retirement to serve first as vice-president and then as acting president of the Instituto de Cultura e Língua Portuguesa, the major cultural arm of the Portuguese government.

José Blanc de Portugal began his poetic career in college where he was an editor of the student literary paper, *Movimento*. He became one of the founding editors and contributors, with Tomás Kim and Ruy Cinatti (and later with Jorge de *Sena) of the *Cadernos de Poesia*, an important journal which published works by the leading writers of the day, making no distinction as to aesthetics or political persuasion, but only of quality. His poems also appeared in *Aventura*, *Litoral* and *Tricórnio*. He was not published in volume until his forty-sixth year, when he allowed close friends to select some of his poems for publication so that he could compete for the prestigious, one-time only, Fernando Pessoa Prize. He won the award in 1959, with *Parva Naturalia*, which was subsequently published in 1960. A second volume of poetry and a volume of essays appeared later that year.

José Blanc de Portugal's poetry reflects his vast scientific, cultural and religious knowledge, all the way from lyrically incorporating the four laws of cristalography into a poem, through references to such disparate philosophies as Persian, Greek, Chinese, Arabic and Mexican, to Roman Catholic indoctrination and the gifts of the Holy Ghost. His poetry presents a holistic, even ecumenical vision of the world, with all of man and nature's material as well as spiritual aspects accounted for. Although pained by the tragic contradictions between man's potential and his behavior, he does not belittle or satirize him, nor is he didactic or condescending, preferring instead to observe and offer occasional and discreet comments in a reasoned, often understated, but always dignified manner. The poet's acute awareness of the ongoing tensions between dissimilar phenomena (spiritual/material; good/evil; potential/performance) constitutes the very essence of human existence. For the poet, life demands some sort of resolution or balance which at best will be precarious, often ironic and not infrequently tragic. To record in measured and succinct language the endless varieties of nature and the way man has or has not come to grips with his total environment forms part of José Blanc de Portugal's poetic legacy.

BIBLIOGRAPHY

Primary Texts

Anticrítico. Lisbon: Ática, 1960.

O Espaço Prometido. Lisbon: Morais, 1960.

Odes pedestres precedidas de auto poética, e seguidas de música ficta e outros poemas. Lisbon: Ulisseia, 1965.

Parva Naturalia. Lisbon: Ática, 1960.

Criticism

Menéres, M. Alberta, and E. M. de Melo e Castro. *Antologia da Poesia Portuguesa 1940–1977*. vol. 2. Lisbon: Moraes, 1979.

Rocha, Clara. *Revistas Literárias do Século XX em Portugal*. Lisbon: Imprensa Nacional-Casa da Moeda, 1985.

Saraiva, António José and Óscar Lopes. *História da Literatura Portuguesa*. 10th ed. Porto: Porto, 1978.

Sena, Jorge de, ed. *Líricas Portuguesas*. 3rd series, vol. 1. Lisbon: Portugália, 1972, 171–89.
Williams, Frederick G. "A Conversation with José Blanc de Portugal." Video-tape interview in color conducted in December 1980 at the U of California, Santa Barbara.

Frederick G. Williams

POZO GARZA, Luz (1922, Ribadeo, Lugo–), Galician poet. Pozo Garza's studies in music are readily apparent in her verses. She is editor of the journal *Nordés* (Northeast), since 1975 an important journal of Galician poetic creation and criticism. The predominant theme of her poetry is love, which has a sensual dimension that seeks to fuse itself with the natural surroundings. Over the years the passage of time becomes more evident in Pozo Garza's poems, leading to greater uneasiness, breaks with logical structures, and increasing concentration on existential themes. In *Concerto de outono* (1981; Autumn Concert), music is a symbol of vitality which contrasts with references to an approaching finale, and the precursor Rosalía de *Castro is linked with Galician cultural identity, while the overall cadence becomes one of love, death, country, freedom, anger and rebellion in search of absolute beauty. *See also* Galician Literature.

BIBLIOGRAPHY

Primary Texts

Ánfora. N.p.: n.p., 1949.
Cita en el viento. N.p.: n.p., 1962.
Concerto de outono. Sada, La Coruña: Castro, 1981.
O paxaro na boca. Lugo: Xistral, 1952.
El vagabundo. N.p.: n.p., 1952.
Verbas derradeiras. La Coruña: Nordés, 1976.

Criticism

Conde, Carmen. *Poesía femenina española viviente*. Madrid: n.p., 1954.
"Mapa literaria de Galicia." *La estafeta literaria* 320–25 (1965).
Martul Tobío, Luis. "Luz Pozo Garza." In *Gran Enciclopedia Gallega*. Santiago-Gijón: Silverio Canada Editor, 1974 ff.
Moreiras, Eduardo. "Limiar." In *Concerto de outono*. Sada, La Coruña: Castro, 1981.
Saínz de Robles, F. *Historia y antología de la poesía castellana*. 2nd ed. Madrid: Aguilar, 1956.

Kathleen March

PRADILLA, Bachiller de la (fl. 1517, ?–?), author. Thus signed the composer of an *Egloga real* (1517; Royal Eclogue) written to commemorate the arrival of Charles V to Valladolid that year. The ms. in the *Biblioteca Nacional includes prose commentary of the poem and its translation in Latin. Hernán *López de Yangüas has been suggested as the true writer behind the pseudonym.

BIBLIOGRAPHY

Criticism

Bonilla, A. "Fernán López de Yangüas y el Bachiller de la Pradilla." *Revista Crítica Hispanoamericana* 1 (1915): n.p.

PRADOS, Emilio (1899, Málaga–1962, Mexico), Spanish poet connected with the *Litoral* group. Within a delicate aestheticism Prados maintains a voice with intimate human resonances, expressing immediate emotions; his form is almost always perfect. Poetry collections include *Tiempo* (1925; Time), *Canciones del farero* (1926; Songs of the Lighthouse Keeper), *Vuelta* (1927; Return), *Llanto subterráneo* (1936; Subterranean Weeping). In the Americas, where he resided following the Spanish Civil War, appeared *Mínima muerte* (1939; Minimum Death), *Memoria del olvido* (1940; Remembrance of Forgotten Things), *Jardín cerrado* (1946; Closed Garden), *El dormido en la yerba* (1953; Sleeper on the Grass), *Circuncisión del sueño* (1957; Circumcised Dreams), and *Antología 1923–1953* (1954; Anthology, 1923–53). Published posthumously were *Diario íntimo* (1966; Intimate Diary), and *Cuerpo perseguido* (1971, ed. Carlos Blanco Aguinaga; Persecuted Body). There is also an edition of Prado's complete works by Blanco Aguinaga.

BIBLIOGRAPHY

Primary Texts

Antología, 1923–1953. Buenos Aires: Losada, 1954.
Circuncisión del sueño. Mexico: Tezontle, 1957.
Cuerpo perseguido. Ed. Carlos Blanco Aguinaga. Barcelona: Labor, 1971.
Diario íntimo. Málaga: Librería Anticuaria el Guadalhorce, 1966.

Criticism

Blanco Aguinaga, Carlos. *Emilio Prados: vida y obra*. New York: Hispanic Institute in the United States, 1960.

Genaro J. Pérez

PRAT DE LA RIBA, Enric (1870, Castelltercol–1917, Castelltercol), Catalan journalist and essayist. The son of a wealthy family, trained as a lawyer and involved from an early age in politics, Prat de la Riba was an avid proponent of Catalan nationalism, an exceptionally effective orator, cultural leader, and ethnic historian. Essentially his entire life was devoted to the cause of Catalan culture and autonomy (statehood). Early writings include *La nació com asubjecte de Dret Natural* (1890; The Nation as Subject to Natural Law), *Compendi de doctrina catalanista* (1894; Compendium of Doctrines Favoring Catalonian Independence), in collaboration with Pere Muntanyola, and *La nacionalitat catalana* (1906; Catalonian Statehood). His promulgation of the "Noucentisme" movement brought Catalan culture closer to modern Europe, and he was able to provide important support for cultural growth as president of both the Diputacio Provincial de Barcelona (similar to the Catalan State Senate) and of the larger

Mancomunitat de Catalunya. As founder of the important political party La Lliga, he set down his political thought in *Manifestos Als Catalans* (Manifests for the Catalan People), *Al Poble Catalá* (To the People of Catalonia) and *Per Catalunya i l'Espanya gran* (1916; For Catalonia and a Great Spain). His major works of history are *Compendi de la Historia de Catalunya* (1898; Compendium of Catalonian History) and *Historia de la nació catalana* (1917; History of the Catalan Nation). *See also* Catalan Literature.

Janet Pérez

PREOCUPACIÓN DE ESPAÑA (Spain's Worry). The theme of Spain as a problematic nation in need of redefinition or reform has been a perennial concern in Spanish letters. It is a leitmotif of texts too numerous to mention and has been the subject of intense scrutiny by some of Spain's major writers and thinkers. The topic has often become a focus of passionate attention during periods of economic decline or loss of political power, and the standard of comparison has sometimes been the rest of Europe.

In the seventeenth c. the theme surfaces in the works of *Cervantes, *Quevedo, *Saavedra Fajardo, and *Gracián y Morales and may be linked with Baroque disillusion as Spain's empire deteriorated. The thinkers of the eighteenth-c. Enlightenment—such as *Feijoo, *Cadalso, *Forner and *Jovellanos—were less anguished and more analytical in their approach. Later, the Romantic, Mariano José de *Larra wrote *Artículos de Costumbres* (1832–35; *Customs of Spain*, 1963), evocative descriptions of customs peculiar to Spain, alternately expressing delight and pessimism.

The national problem received the most subtle and exhaustive investigation by the *Generation of 1898, following the loss of the remainder of Spain's colonies. They shared the common assumption that Spain's historically and geographically determined national character needed to be redefined and remedied. The earliest attempts to address the issue were five essays by *Unamuno, ultimately collected in *En Torno al Casticismo* (1902; Concerning Purism), and *Ganivet's *Idearium Español* (1897; *Spain: An Interpretation*, 1946). Unamuno's search for the essentials of Spain as a spiritual and historical entity continued in *La Vida de don Quijote y Sancho* (1905; *The Life of Don Quijote and Sancho*, 1967), where literary characters symbolize national values, and in his philosophical masterpiece *Del sentimiento trágico de la vida en los hombres y los pueblos* (1912; *The Tragic Sense of Life in Men and Nations*, 1972). Another writer of the Generation of 1898, *Azorín, wrote several nostalgic yet critical books lyrically describing backward, provincial Spain.

Subsequently, *Ortega y Gasset undertook a profound phenomenological meditation on Don Quijote as representative of Spain's contradictory nature in *Meditaciones del Quijote* (1914; *Meditations on Quixote*, 1961). Later, he applied a biological metaphor to historical evolution in *España Invertebrada* (1921; *Invertebrate Spain,* 1937), concluding that Spain lacked a feudal phase of development and recommending Europeanization.

Since the Spanish Civil War, contemporary thinkers, writers, and essayists have continued to debate and reinterpret Spain's character and place in the modern world. *See also* Essay.

BIBLIOGRAPHY

Primary Texts

Azorín. *Obras completas*. Madrid: Aguilar, 1975.
Ganivet, Angel. *Obras completas*. 2 vols. Madrid: Aguilar, 1951.
Larra, Mariano José de. *Artículos de costumbres*. Madrid: Espasa-Calpe, 1942.
Ortega y Gasset, José. *Obras completas*. 2nd ed. 6 vols. Madrid: RO, 1950–52.
Unamuno y Jugo, Miguel de. *Obras completas*. 6 vols. Madrid: Escelier, 1966.

English Translations

Crow, John A. *Spain: The Root and the Flower*. New York: Evanston; London: Harper and Row, 1963. Excerpts from *Artículos de Costumbres*.
Ganivet, Ángel. *Spain: An Interpretation*. Tr. J. R. Carey. London: Eyre and Spottiswoode, 1946.
Ortega y Gasset, José. *Invertebrate Spain*. Tr. Mildred Adams. New York: Norton, 1937.
———. *Meditations on Quijote*. Tr. Evelyn Rugg and Diego Marín. New York: Norton, 1961.
Unamuno, Miguel de. *Our Lord Don Quijote. The Life of Don Quijote and Sancho with Related Essays*. Tr. Anthony Kerrigan. London: Routledge, 1967.
———. *The Tragic Sense of Life in Men and Nations*. Tr. Anthony Kerrigan. Princeton: Princeton UP, 1972.

Criticism

Franco, Dolores. *España como preocupación*. Madrid: Guadarrama, 1961.
Laín Entralgo, Pedro. *España como problema*. Madrid: Aguilar, 1960.
———. *La generación del 98*. Madrid: Diana. Artes Gráficas, 1945.
Martínez-López, Ramón, ed. *Image of Spain*. Austin: U of Texas P, 1961.
Shaw, Donald L. *The Generation of 1898 in Spain*. London: Benn; New York: Barnes and Noble, 1975.

Helen H. Reed

PRIETO, Antonio (1930, Almería–), Spanish novelist. Unlike many future writers who were children during the war and had their lives scarred and writings marked as a result, Prieto seems to remember little of the war, which began when he was six (and is not reflected in his fiction). He attended the U of Madrid, beginning the study of medicine, which he dropped to switch to humanities, and began to write. His first novel, *Tres pisadas de hombre* (1955; Three Steps by a Man), won the economically significant Planeta Prize and was praised for its style and imagination. *Buenos días, Argüelles* (1956; Good Morning, Argüelles [a Madrid neighborhood near the university]) is a blend of neo-realism and *costumbrismo*, painting many Madrid types and characteristic settings. *Vuelve atrás, Lázaro* (1958; Turn Back, Lazarus), another novel, was followed by *Encuentro con Ilitia* (1961; Encounter with Ilitia), *Prólogo a una muerte* (1965; Prologue to a Death), and *Elegía por una Esperanza* (1969; Elegy for [a] Hope).

He married Pilar Palomo, a professor and critic, and both spend much of their time in literary research. He has also served as director of the magazine *Prohemio*, and contributes to various magazines, journals and reviews.

Janet Pérez

PRIETO ROUCO, Carmen (1901, Vilalba–1977, Vilalba), Galician poet. Although Prieto Rouco's work is not abundant, her importance rests strongly on the way in which she represents the condition of being a woman writer in Galicia and a successor to Rosalía de *Castro. Her subjective, descriptive lyrics concern Galician rural society and include protests against the economic situation of the peasants. Surprisingly, there is little love poetry, except as a literary exercise or in monologue form. Prieto Rouco's Galician is somewhat forced, as if she were making an effort to avoid incorrect usages due to Spanish influence.

Prieto Rouco also is the author of theatrical works such as *A virxe viuda (Hestoria dun amor)* (1963; The Widowed Virgin. A Love Story); *A loita* (1923; The Struggle); *O embargo* (The Embargo), a tragedy in verse form; *Treidores celos* (Betraying Envies), a Galician **zarzuela* (light opera); *Nubes de verano* (Summer Clouds), a *zarzuela*; *Madrastra* (Mother-in-law); *Amor y ambición* (Love and Ambition); *Na boda do afillado* (At the Godson's Wedding); and *O secreto da bruxa* (The Witch's Secret), all works of a dramatic type. *See also* Galician Literature.

BIBLIOGRAPHY

Primary Texts

Horas de frebe. Lugo: El Progreso Vilalbés, 1926.
Lluvia menuda. Ortigueira: n.p., 1956.
Violetas. Lugo: n.p., 1954.

Criticism

Carballo Calero, Ricardo. *Historia da literatura galega contemporánea*. 3rd ed. Vigo: Galaxia, 1981.

Kathleen March

PRIMO DE RIVERA Y SÁENZ DE HEREDIA, José Antonio (1902, Madrid–1936, Alicante), Spanish essayist and politician. Founder of the Spanish Falange, a national syndicalist party, on October 29, 1933, he was the son of the dictator General Miguel Primo de Rivera and disciple of José *Ortega y Gasset, and came to find himself caught between the imperatives of action and thought symbolized by his father and intellectual mentor respectively.

As a follower of the Ortega of *La rebelión de las masas* (1930), José Antonio was familiar with the theoretical division of labor established in that book between the tasks of the intellectual and the tasks of the practical politician. While the first would plan the best goals of political activity as a sub-discipline of philosophy, the latter would be guided by those goals to develop the best practical means to implement them. By late 1935, however, José Antonio was thoroughly embroiled in doing what Ortega had said was not possible: being both theoretician and political leader of the Falange in its ever more violent confrontations with the supporters of the Republic and groups of the extreme left. At this time José Antonio wrote a short, famous address titled "Homenaje y reproche a don José Ortega y Gasset" (Homage and Reproach of don José Ortega y Gasset). In it he acknowledged and praised Ortega as the person most responsible for bringing Spaniards born after 1898 to the awareness of the great problems of the "Fatherland." But he also criticized Ortega for not fulfilling the implicit—from his viewpoint—obligation to lead those younger Spaniards in "re-vertebrating" what Ortega, in a book of the same title, called "invertebrate Spain" in 1921.

On November 20, 1936, José Antonio paid the price for his adhesion to his ideals when he was executed in Alicante by Republican forces in the early days of the Spanish Civil War. It is generally assumed that General Francisco Franco, leader of the Nationalist rebellion, and future dictator of Spain, could have bargained for the life of José Antonio, but that he preferred a dead martyr to a live rival for moral authority and political power. Nonetheless Franco did take over the Falange for the purpose of legitimizing his oligarchy both during and after the Civil War.

José Antonio's writings are easily found in complete and selected Spanish editions of his work. Because his theories were canonized and perverted at the same time, and then became merely pretexts, they constitute the only authoritative source for his idealistic, if somewhat nebulous ideas describing a patriarchal national collectivism in which all groups had mutual responsibilities and obligations. *See also* Essay.

BIBLIOGRAPHY

Primary Texts

Obras completas de José Antonio Primo de Rivera. Madrid: Publicaciones Españolas, 1952.

Textos inéditos y epistolario de José Antonio. . . . Madrid: Ediciones del Movimiento, 1956.

Criticism

Payne, Stanley G. *Falange: A History of Spanish Fascism.* Stanford: Stanford UP, 1961.

Stephen Miller

PRÍNCIPE, Miguel Agustín (1811, Caspe–1863, Madrid), professor of literature, lawyer, librarian, prolific playwright and writer. A multifaceted individual, he experimented with many literary genres. As a journalist he employed the pseudonyms Don Yo (don I) and Miraveque (Lookseethat). Dramatic works include *El conde don Julián* (1839; Count don Julian) and *Periquillo entre ellos* (1844; Periquillo among Them).

BIBLIOGRAPHY

Primary Texts

Cerdán, justicia de Aragón. Madrid: Repullés, 1841. Rpt. Louisville, KY: Falls City Microcards, 1960.

El desván. Madrid: Repullés, 1851. Rpt. Louisville, KY: Falls City Microcards, 1960.

Fábulas de Miguel Agustín Príncipe. Barcelona/Buenos Aires: Molino, 1941.

Obras dramáticas. 4 vols. Madrid: Repullés, 1840–51.

Tirios y troyanos. 2 vols. Madrid: Soler, 1845–48.

PRÍNCIPES, Consejo y consejeros de (Advice for Princes), fourteenth-c. didactic work. It treated moral issues and political philosophy, and is but one example of this popular fourteenth-c. genre. The ms., now in the Escorial Library, is attributed by Father Zarco to Pedro Gómez de Albornoz, who was born in Cuenca and eventually became archbishop of Seville. Rodríguez de Castro proposes Pedro Gómez Barroso, another archbishop of Seville who died in 1390, as a possible author.

BIBLIOGRAPHY

Criticism

Zarco Cuevas, J. *Catálago de los manuscritos castellanos de la Real biblioteca de el Escorial*. 3 vols. Madrid: Real Monasterio, 1924–29.

Lucy Sponsler

PRINTING IN SPAIN. The study of literature as we have known it in modern times was made possible by the development of printing in a print-oriented society and by the concomitant decline in scribal culture. The very establishment of a literary canon has been determined, in part, by the decisions of printers and publishers to make editions of literary works available. In Spain the history of printing is conditioned by complex socio-cultural and politico-economic factors as well as by developments in literary style and taste. The advent of printing in Spain was somewhat late, but it spread quickly to several major cities. Spain's recorded output of incunabula is exceeded only by Italy, Germany, France and Holland, and it is greater than the pre–1500 production in England, Belgium and all other European nations. As elsewhere in Europe, the first printers in Spain were Germans, but the printing art the immigrants developed quickly took on a national style which bibliophiles have characterized as "rugged yet effective and reminiscent of [Spain's] rough, careless splendor, its grave, sad magnificence" (Updike, 2: 102). The severe quality of Spanish typography and the similarly rugged splendor of Spanish illustrations may have been due to the superiority of Spanish ink, which was considerably blacker than Italian or Flemish contemporary examples. Another practice followed by some Spanish presses, the application of Islamic-style ornamentation, was admired and quickly adapted for title page decoration by European printers.

Controversy still surrounds the matter of dating the first works to be printed in Spain. Incomplete and erroneously dated colophons have suggested dates as early as 1468 for a Barcelona edition of Mates's Latin *Grammatica*. Historical records indicate that Juan Parix published in Segovia the proceedings of a Constitutional Synod in 1472. Other sources suggest that in 1473 a printer in Zaragoza, Valencia, or Barcelona produced a Latin edition of Aristotle's political works. It is likely, however, that the first contemporary literary work to be printed was the collection of forty-five Marian poems written for a competition celebrated in Valencia in 1474, and printed by Lamberto Palmart the same year, *Les Obres e* **trobes en lahors de la sacratissima Verge Maria*. Other early works produced in Valencia include a Bible in Valencian (1478, Palmart) and Nicolás Spindeler's 1490 printing of *Tirant lo Blanch* (*Martorell, Joanot), an edition with rich border decoration in a somewhat Oriental style. Rivaling Valencian claims to primacy was Zaragoza with the *Manipulus curatorum* printed in 1475 by Mateo Flandro. Other firsts in Zaragoza include the appearance of Jorge *Manrique's *Coplas* (verse compositions) printed by Pablo de Hurus in 1492, whose printing house was the first Spanish one to use a printer's mark. The first Spanish book with illustrations by a Spanish artist was Enrique de *Villena's *Los trabajos de Hércules* (The Labors of Hercules), printed in Zamora by Antonio de Centenera in 1483. The eleven woodcuts accompanying the text have been praised for their "extraordinary vigor" (Harthan, 70). Zamora was also the site of one of the earliest and most productive Hebrew presses in Spain. Working quietly in small towns such as Zamora, Montalbán, Guadalajara and Híjar, the Jewish printers produced Hebrew texts of generally high quality from the mid–1470s until the Expulsion in 1492. Seville was distinguished as the site of the first printing by an entirely Spanish printing house. In 1477 Clemente *Sánchez de Vercial's *Sacramental* was issued there by three Spanish printing partners: Antonio Martínez, Bartolomé Segura and Alfonso del Puerto. The last of the three associates also printed Diego de *Valera's *Crónica de España* in 1482. Printing houses founded by German immigrants issued several major incunabula in Seville: Alfonso de *Palencia's *Vocabulario universal* (1490), Diego de *San Pedro's *Cárcel de amor* (Prison of Love) and Fernán *Pérez de Guzmán's *Coplas* in 1492. Barcelona also has a long history of printing, but the oldest extant texts published there are a 1479 edition of *Manipulus curatorum* and the 1480 Catalan translation *Regiment dels princeps* (a guide for princes). Another notable Catalan translation was the 1484 edition of Alfonso de la *Torre's *Visión deleitable de la filosofía y artes liberales* (an encyclopedic work). One of the most politically and culturally significant incunabula was Christopher Columbus's Barcelona-printed *Epistola de insulis nuper inventis*, the so-called Columbus Letter of 1493. The letter, the first document to notify Europe of the discovery of the New World, was printed by Pedro Posa. Nine separate editions of the document would be printed before 1500. Presses were probably functioning in Burgos in the early 1480s but the major incunabula printed there were Hernando del *Pulgar's glossed *Coplas de Mingo Revulgo* in 1485, the 1487 *Doctrinal de caballeros* (a handbook for noblemen and princes) of García de Santa María and the disputed first edition of Fernando de *Rojas's *Comedia de Calixto y Melibea* in 1499. Early Toledo-imprinted works of importance were the 1486 edition of Pulgar's *Claros varones de Castilla* (biographical sketches of his Castilian contemporaries) and the first volumes of Alfonso Martínez de Toledo's (*Arcipreste de Talavera) *El corbacho* (a misogynist work condemning worldly love) in 1499.

Along with Barcelona and Sevilla, Salamanca was one of the three major incunabula centers to become a printing hub in the sixteenth c. Much of the printing activity in Salamanca, a university town, produced patristic, theological, legal, and humanistic texts for student consumption. Due to intense competition from foreign presses producing inexpensive classical texts, university presses in Salamanca and Alcalá de Henares came to specialize in printing works of Spanish authors. Examples of the craftsmanship in Salamanca presses in the period are Antonio de *Nebrija's *Introductiones latinae* of 1481, a five-volume commentary on Eusebius by El Tostado (Alfonso de *Madrigal) in 1506, and the first edition of **Palmerín de Oliva* in 1511. Much of the ferment in sixteenth-c. printing emanated from the Sevillan presses of Jacob Cromberger, the Aldus Manutius of Spain. Perhaps because "he addressed himself in the first place to the common reader" (Norton, 12), he produced many well crafted prose romances and chronicles illustrated by woodcuts. Cromberger and his Spanish descendants are also to be remembered for introducing the printing press into the New World by their establishment of a branch office in Mexico in 1539. Other milestones of the era were Jorge Coci's production in Zaragoza of the four-volume **Amadís de Gaula* in 1509 and the 1521 *Flos sanctorum* of Pedro de *Vega, "one of the most remarkable examples of multicolor printing in Europe" (Lyell, 163). Spain's greatest claim to printing fame in the first century of the industry's history was the Complutensian Polyglot Bible (*Bible of Alcalá), the first and the most beautiful of the four great multilingual Bibles. The Alcalá Polyglot was printed 1514–17 with the high-quality types of Arnao Guillén de Brocar and under the careful supervision of Cardinal Francisco Jiménez de *Cisneros and the team of erudite scholars he maintained.

While perhaps one-fourth of the works produced during the first century of printing in Spain were vernacular literary works, over one-third of the materials printed were theological, liturgical or ecclesiastical. The founding of new religious orders or new convents such as those of the Jesuits and the institution of reforms by the Council of Trent created a demand for new breviaries and related liturgical publications. Printers, who were often booksellers, might prefer to accept lucrative ecclesiastical contracts rather than engage in printing a literary work whose profitableness would be speculative. Since the 1480s, printers in Toledo and Valladolid had enjoyed a virtual monopoly in the printing of Crusade indulgences. The rapidity of press production accelerated the clandestine traffic in indulgences—a development which in turn was recognized in literary works such as the **Lazarillo de Tormes* (1544). The patronage of ecclesiastical authorities and other powerful individuals was indispensable to the founding and early support of Spanish presses, but only the presses that benefited from monopolistic contracts—such as ecclesiastical or government commissions—were the most likely to survive. Several economic factors conditioned the printer-booksellers to avoid publishing literary texts of speculative profitability: (1) the high cost of paper, most of which was imported; (2) the monetary charges imposed by governmental regulatory agencies; and (3) the increasing risk that a work would be prohibited by the *Inquisition after its printing.

Although the earliest printed works resembled mss., later incunabula began to include pagination and information about the author and printer, as well as the place and date of publication. The early printers were also most frequently the editors, bookdealers and instigators of publication for the works they printed. At times a merchant would commission a printed work, and the book's colophon would indicate that the publication was made ''at the expense of'' a second party. By the middle of the sixteenth c., Spanish books included printed information reflecting the increased governmental and Inquisitorial regulation of the printing and book trade. An author or, more frequently, the printer to whom he sold his work had to receive authorization from the Royal Council to have the work published. The royal certification was granted only after ecclesiastical and Inquisitorial censors had carefully examined the first printed copy by comparing it with the ms. and searching for objectionable material. Only after the conditions demanded by the censors had been met would a printer receive authorization to add the title page and other publication data and to print additional copies of the work. Authorities also designated the work's price and granted exclusive printing privileges for periods of ten to twelve years. There was no true copyright, however, since foreign printing firms would reproduce popular or profitable books without regulation. The situation was particularly problematic for playwrights whose staged works might be transcribed and sold by a copyist attending the performances of his plays.

The increased regulation of printing and related aspects of book production coincided with the decline in the craftsmanship of printed works. By the mid-sixteenth c. when Madrid became the seat of government and the nascent printing center of Spain, the number of carefully printed books had diminished.

The diffusion of crudely printed and inexpensive chapbooks, however, was making the acquisition of popular ballads, proverbs and rhymed prayers more accessible to individuals who might hesitate to purchase books bound in the customary pigskin or vellum. The folio-sized books of the incunabula period gave way to works produced in quarto or octavo and, less frequently, in the sextodecimo format. By the end of the sixteenth c., the angular gothic types were largely replaced by round roman fonts. It is perhaps ironic that some of the classical literary works of Spain's *Siglo de Oro first appeared in very modest or poor-quality editions in the seventeenth c. The 1615 printing of *Cervantes's *Don Quixote* Part 2 by Juan de la Cuesta in Madrid has been judged to be a ''respectable production'' (Updike, 67), but the collection of the author's stage-works printed in the same year is an example of cheap workmanship using ''broken or used types and detestable paper'' (Millares Carlo, 149). Spain did produce one magnificently illustrated seventeenth-c. work in Seville: a festival book with striking engravings to commemorate the canonization of King Ferdinand in 1671. In the following c., printing experienced a revival in Spain as it did elsewhere in Europe. The increased vigor of the Spanish printing industry in the period 1760–90 was due largely to the favorable policies established during the reign of Charles III and to the successful cooperation among the printers affiliated with the Royal Company of Printers. One associate of the company, Joaquín Ibarra, has been recognized as one of the foremost printers in eighteenth-c. Europe. His 1780 edition of *Don Quixote* and his 1772 splendid publication of the works of Sallust are among the finest volumes produced by any nation during the century. By the nineteenth c. the modern notion of a printer's role had become established and the formerly intimate association between printer and literary production had faded. Although printing had become a more strictly commercial venture, some members of the printing industry continued to contribute to the study of Spanish literature by editing less frequently read works along with those of the established canon. An example is the work of Rivadeneyra for the *Biblioteca de Autores Españoles or the Biblioteca Rivadeneyra. *See also* Censorship.

BIBLIOGRAPHY

Criticism

Bloch, Joshua. "Early Hebrew Printing in Spain and Portugal." *Bulletin of the New York Public Library* 42 (1938): 371–418.

Haebler, Konrad. *The Early Printers of Spain and Portugal*. London: Bibliographical Society, 1897.

Harthan, John. *The History of the Illustrated Book*. London: Thames and Hudson, 1981.

Historia de la imprenta hispana. Madrid: Nacional, 1982.

Lyell, James P. R. "Spain and Portugal." In *Printing, A Short Story of the Art*. Ed. R. A. Peddie. London: Grafton, 1927.

Millares Carlo, Agustín. *Introducción a la historia del libro y de las bibliotecas*. Mexico: Fondo de Cultura Económica, 1971.

Norton, Frederick. *Printing in Spain, 1501–1520*. Cambridge: Cambridge UP, 1966.

Thomas, Diana. *The Royal Company of Booksellers of Spain, 1763–1794*. Troy, NY: Whitson, 1984.

Updike, Daniel Berkeley. *Printing Types*. 3rd ed. 2 vols. Cambridge, MA: Harvard UP, 1962.

Catherine Swietlicki

PROAZA, Alonso de (c. 1445?, Asturias–c. 1519, Valencia), humanist, poet, translator. Probably educated in Salamanca, he served as secretary to the bishop of Tarazona later in life. In 1504 he was elected professor of rhetoric at the U of Valencia. Proaza today is most remembered for his editorial work; with the encouragement of Cardinal Jiménez de *Cisneros, he translated and commented on the scholastic works of Ramón *Llull. As *corrector* (proofreader) for many years, he edited two of the masterworks of the *Renaissance, the *Sergas de Esplandián* (1505; Deeds of Esplandian), and the **Celestina* (1500). Some critics once felt Proaza intervened heavily in his editing, and actually wrote the additional five acts of the *Tragicomedia de Calixto y Melibea*; D. W. McPheeters rejects this hypothesis. Three anonymous plays have also been attributed to Proaza, with little substantiation. His poetry is found principally in the 1511 and 1514 editions of the *Cancionero general*. *See also* Humanism.

BIBLIOGRAPHY

Criticism

McPheeters, D. W. *El humanista español Alonso de Proaza*. Madrid: Castalia, 1961.

PROENÇA, Raul Sangreman (1881, Caldas da Rainha–1941, Porto), Portuguese political journalist and man of letters. He studied economics and finance at the Instituto Industrial of Lisbon, graduating in 1905 and taking up teaching thereafter. He practiced journalism from his student years. Throughout he wrote to publicize his republican convictions. In 1910 (the year in which the Republic was proclaimed) he contributed to *A República*, *Vanguarda* and *Alma Nacional*. In 1912 he was active in setting up *A Águia*, the organ of the Renascença Portuguesa, and became involved in *Norte*, which was published by Jaime *Cortesão. Leonardo *Coimbra was instrumental in appointing him to the Biblioteca Nacional (National Library) in Lisbon where he had a productive and successful career, rising to become chief of technical services. While he was there and during the time that Jaime Cortesão was director, he was an active member of the Grupo da Biblioteca, a group that included in its number many influential Portuguese writers and thinkers, among them António *Sérgio, Aquilino *Ribeiro, Afonso Lopes *Viera, Reinaldo dos Santos and José de Figueiredo. In 1921, with Jaime Cortesão, Aquilino Ribeiro and Câmara Reys, he helped to found *Seara Nova*, an influential and remarkably long-lived critical review. The foundation of the library's press (Imprensa da Biblioteca Nacional) and its publications were among the direct results of the group's activities. Particularly worthy of note and stemming directly from Proença's efforts are the review *Lusitânia* and the *Guia de Portugal*, an authoritative guide to Portugal and particularly to its art treasures. When the military seized power in 1926 Proença was forced into exile and only allowed to return on compassionate medical grounds shortly before his death.

BIBLIOGRAPHY

Primary Texts

Antologia. Pref. and ed. António Reis. Lisbon: Ministerio da Cultura, 1985—.

Páginas de Política. Pref. and ed. Câmara Reys. 2 vols. Lisbon: Seara Nova, 1939.

Criticism

Dionísio, Sant'Ana. *O Pensamento Especulativo e Agente de Raul Proença*. Lisbon: Seara Nova, 1949.

Jaime Cortesão, Raul Proença. Catálogo da Exposição Comemorativa do Primeiro Centenário (1884–1984). Lisbon: Biblioteca Nacional, 1985. Extensive bibliography.

Moser, Gerald. ''The Campaign of *Seara Nova* and Its Impact on Portuguese Literature, 1921–1961.'' *Luso-Brazilian Review* 2 (1964): 15–42.

Peter Fothergill-Payne

PUÉRTOLAS VILLANUEVA, Soledad (1947, Zaragoza–), Spanish novelist. She studied journalism at the U of Zaragoza, and later did graduate work in Spanish literature at the U of California–Santa Barbara, where she obtained a master's degree. She is a literary critic who collaborates with a number of newspapers, and also published a critical study entitled *El Madrid de La lucha por la vida* (1971; Madrid as Seen in [Baroja's] ''Struggle for Life''). Among her novels are *El bandido doblemente armado* (1980; The Doubly Armed Bandit), winner of the 1979 Sésamo Prize, a work structured in the form of ten stories all about the same family and told by the same narrator. *Una enfermedad moral* (1982; A Moral Illness) is a short story collection, with a thematic nucleus of moral problems (although the title also constitutes a pun on the fixed phrase ''mortal'' illness). Covering a wide variety of times and places, the stories range from melancholy psychological analysis to intimacy to autobiography and a certain humor. *Burdeos* (1986; Bourdeaux) moves away from the adolescents found in the writer's first novel to mature characters, unable to solve the mysteries of their own disillusionment, loneliness, lack of confidence, weakness and aging. *Todos mienten* (1988; They're All Liars) is a sometimes humorous view of the frivolity of present-day Madrid, sketching the adolescence and rites of passage to maturation of a young man raised in two contrasting environments, the home of his widowed, but smiling and optimistic mother, and that of his somber and even tragic paternal grandparents, beset by sickness, death and madness. The narrator comes to the conclusion that the only way to survive in such contrasting environments is by lying.

Janet Pérez

PULGAR, Hernando del (1430?, ?–1493?, Toledo?), biographer, chronicler, and author of letters and essays. The son of **conversos*, he served Henry IV (1450–68) and was later secretary to the Catholic monarchs (1471) and their ambassador to France (1474–75). Chronicler of the reign of Ferdinand and Isabel up to 1490, he enjoyed great prestige at court. This history, the *Chrónica de los muy altos y esclarecidos Reyes Cathólicos don Fernando y doña Isabel, de gloriosa memoria* (Chronicle of the Very Powerful and Excellent Catholic Kings, Ferdinand and Isabel, of Glorious Memory), was first published in a Latin translation attributed to Antonio *Nebrija in Granada, 1545; the Castilian text, in Pulgar's name, appeared in Zaragoza, 1567. The *Chrónica*, a panegyric, is divided into three books, or parts. In the manner of Titus Livy, Pulgar places heroic speeches in the mouths of his characters, achieving thereby a successful literary and dramatic effect. This was an extremely influential history, being an important source for later writers like Ginés *Pérez de Hita and his *Guerras civiles de Granada* (1595; The Civil Wars of Granada).

Pulgar's most valuable contribution for both literature and history, however, is the series of twenty-four portraits offered in the collection *Claros varones de Castilla* (1486; The Illustrious Nobility of Castile). In the prologue, he notes that his models are the classical authors Valerius and Plutarch, the French Vernade, and Spain's *Pérez de Guzmán, whom Pulgar affectionately remembers. These brief biographies of the illustrious figures of his time, for example, the Marquis of *Santillana, the Count of Haro, and Rodrigo de Villandrando, are less severe and more complete and literary than those of Pérez de Guzmán, whom Pulgar surpasses in vividness and agility of narration. Santillana is described, for example, as being a handsome man, sharp, discreet, and valiant to the point that "ni las grandes cosas le alteraban ni en las pequeñas le placía entender" (neither did great things disturb him, nor did it please him to worry about small ones). The biographical sketches of Pulgar have more character than those of Pérez de Guzmán, although they may weaken at times through excessive moralization; on the other hand, they reflect a preoccupation with distilling the essence of the individual, effectively using psychological penetration and irony in many descriptions where candor is subordinated to diplomacy.

Interesting, too, are the thirty-two *Letras* or *Cartas* (c. 1485; Letters), published in Burgos. Herein can be seen the humorist and satirist, who frequently attacks his victims with mordacity, for example, the harsh censure he directs at the rebellious Archbishop Carrillo. Notable, moreover, is his "Carta XI" to Queen Isabel, which informs her that he will accept the commission for writing the *Chrónica* of the reign of the Catholic monarchs. Pulgar's flattering commentary on the *Coplas* (couplets) of **Mingo Revulgo*, a satirical work perhaps written by the Franciscan friar Iñigo de *Mendoza, led Padre *Mariana in his *Historia general de España* to believe that he was their author.

BIBLIOGRAPHY

Primary Texts

Claros varones de Castilla. Ed. J. Domínguez Bordona. Madrid: Espasa-Calpe, 1954.

Claros varones de Castilla. Ed. R. B. Tate. Temas de España 160. Madrid: Taurus, 1985.

Crónica de los Reyes Católicos, por su secretario Fernando del Pulgar. Ed. Juan de Mata Carriazo. 2 vols. Madrid: Espasa-Calpe, 1943.

Letras.—Glosa a las coplas de Mingo Revulgo. Ed. J. Domínguez Bordona. Madrid: Espasa-Calpe, 1958.

Letras. Ed. Paola Elia. Collanadi Testi e Studi Ispanici, 1; Testi Critici, 3. Pisa: Giardini, 1982.

Criticism

Cantera, F. "Fernando de Pulgar y los conversos." *Sefarad* 4 (1944): 295–348.

Faulhaber, Charles B., et al. "Pulgar, Hernando del." In *Bibliography of Old Spanish Texts*. 3rd ed. Madison: HSMS, 1984. 291. [Documentation of extant mss. of his works.]

Romero, J. L. "Sobre la biografía española del s. XV y los ideales de la vida." *Cuadernos de historia de España* 1–2 (1944): 115–38.

Simón Díaz, José. ''Pulgar (Hernando de).'' In *Manual de bibliografía de la literatura española*. 3rd ed. Madrid: Gredos, 1980. 158, nos. 3698–3705.

Dennis P. Seniff

Q

QUADRADO, José María (1819, Ciudadela, Menorca–1896, Palma de Mallorca), historian and archaeologist. A traditionalist thinker and follower of *Balmes, he founded the magazine *La Palma* (1840–41; The Palmtree) and the newspapers *El Católico* (1842; The Catholic) and *La Fe* (1844; The Faith). Quadrado was an erudite endowed with artistic taste. He contributed to the collection *Recuerdos y bellezas de España* (1844–48; Memories and Beauties of Spain), directed by Parcerisa, with the volumes on Aragón, New Castile, Asturias, and León, Valladolid, Palencia, Zamora, and Salamanca, Avila and Segovia. He also wrote a documented *Historia de la conquista de Mallorca* (1893–96; History of the Conquest of Mallorca). Some of his works were collected as *Ensayos religiosos, políticos y literarios* (1893–96; Religious, Political and Literary Essays) with a foreword by Marcelino *Menéndez y Pelayo.

BIBLIOGRAPHY

Primary Texts

Ensayos religiosos. Intro. Menéndez Pelayo. 2nd ed. 4 vols. Palma: Armengol y Muntaner, 1893–96.

Historia de la conquista de Mallorca. Palma: Esteban Trías, 1850.

Recuerdos y bellezas de España. Aragón. Madrid-Barcelona: R. Indar, 1844–48. *Asturias y León*. Madrid: Repullés, 1855–59. *Castilla la Nueva*. Madrid: Repullés, 1848–53. *Salamanca, Avila y Segovia*. Madrid-Barcelona: D. Tasso, 1865–72. *Valladolid, Palencia y Zamora*. Madrid: Cebría López, 1861–65.

Criticism

Alcover, A. M. *Don Jusep María Quadrado: sa vida, ses obres*. Mallorca: Amenagual i Muntaner, 1919.

Oliver, Miguel de los Santos. *Quadrado, un colaborador de Balmes*. Barcelona: n.p., 1910.

Salvador García Castañeda

QUADROS, António, pseudonym of João Pedro Grabato Dias (1933, Viseau–), Portuguese poet and painter. He has resided in Mozambique since 1968. Since his first poetry book, *40 e tal sonetos de amor e circunstância e uma cancio desesperada* (1970; Some Forty Love and Occasional Sonnets and one Song of Despair), he has been considered among Portugal's most brilliant poets. *Uma meditação* (1970; A Meditation) was followed by two so-called didactic odes in free verse, *O morto* (The Dead Man) and *A arca* (The Ark), the same year. An extremely personal poet with a lyric sweep, he ranges from violence to humor. *Quybyrycas* (1972) parodies Renaissance epics and spoofs the Portuguese adventure in Africa, while *A presaga* (1974; The Foreboding) employs a collage of intertextuality in celebration of Mozambican independence.

BIBLIOGRAPHY

Primary Texts

A arte de continuar Português. Lisbon: Templo, 1978.
Crítica e verdade. Lisbon: Livraria Classica, Teixeira, 1964.
Portugal, razão e mistério. Lisbon: Guimarães, 1986—.

Janet Pérez

QUART, Pere, pseudonym of Joan Oliver Sallarés (1899, Sabadell, Barcelona–1986, Barcelona), Catalan poet, novelist, and dramatist. The son of a well-to-do bourgeois family, he was trained as a lawyer, and practiced for a time, as well as writing for the periodical press and founding a publishing house, La Mirada, with Francesc Trabal. The Spanish Civil War resulted in his exile to France and subsequently Chile, where he founded a journal, *Germanor*, and continued his publishing activity. He began his literary activity with a play, *Gairebé un acte o Joan, Joana i Joanet* (1929; Almost an Act, or John, Joan and Janet). Use of the pseudonym dates from 1934, when he published *Les decapitacions* (Decapitations). Several other works followed in quick succession: *Cataclisme* (1935; Cataclysm); *Allò que tal vegada s'esdevinqué* (1936; What Might Happen); *Bestiari* (1937; Bestiary); *Contraban* (1937; Contraband); and *Cambrera nova* (1937; The New Waitress). Some works of the war years are direct reflections of the conflict: *Oda a Barcelona* (1936; Ode to Barcelona) and *La fam* (1938; Hunger). He spent well over a decade in exile, and while in Chile published *Saló de tardor* (1947; Autumn Salon). The exile experience finds echoes in *Terra de naufragis* (1956; Land of the Shipwrecked), published after he had returned to Catalonia. During the 1960s, several additional works appeared: *Vacances pagades* (1960; Vacations with Pay); *Les dotze aiguaforts de Granyer* (1962; Granyer's Dozen Etchings); *Circumstàncies* (1968); and *Tros de paper* (1970; A Bit of Paper).

BIBLIOGRAPHY

Primary Text

Obres completes. 4 vols. Barcelona: Aymà, 1975–82.

QUERELLAS, Libro de las (Book of Complaints), an apocryphal work, attributed to *Alphonse the Wise. *Pellicer de Ossau listed it in his report on the Sarmiento home. It is but one of several falsifications engineered by Pellicer to flatter his clients and to increase his own stature.

QUEIRÓS, Carlos or more fully Jose Carlos Queirós Nunes Ribeiro (1907, Lisbon–1949, Paris), Portuguese poet, literary and art critic. He studied law at the U of Coimbra but did not qualify. He forms the link between the group that set up *Orpheo* and that which set up and propagated the ideas embodied in the review *Presença*, to which he was a frequent contributor. He was active in several more of the literary reviews in which Portugal abounded at that time, including *Aventura*, *Variante Revista de Portugal*, *Contemporânea*, *Atlântico*, *Litoral* and *Panorama*, the last of which he edited. He was much admired in his own time for his lucid and sensuous poetry. Adolfo Casais *Monteiro considered his work "the most musical poetry of contemporary Portugal." He wrote in several forms but favored the sonnet, ode, "canção" (song) and pastoral. His shorter poems have an epigrammatic ring to them.

David Mourão-Ferreira sees in Queirós a close follower of Rimbaud and Mallarmé, pointing to *Desaparecido* (1935; Gone Away) and *Breve Tratado de Não-Versificação* (1948; Short Treatise on Non-Verse) as being of a piece and demonstrating Queirós's symbolist inheritance. The rest of his oeuvre is scattered among the various periodicals to which he contributed. To that should be added some hundred or so poems unpublished at his death, most of which have been gathered together in an as yet unpublished thesis by Maria Evelina Carreiro Duarte, *Carlos Queirós, Subsídios para o Estudo de Sua Obra*, U of Lisbon, 1960.

BIBLIOGRAPHY

Primary Texts

Breve Tratado de Não-Versificação. Lisbon: Oficina Gráfica, 1946.
Desaparecido e outros poemas. Lisbon: Bertrand, 1950.
Homenagem a Fernando Pessoa. Coimbra: Atlântida, 1936.
Ode a Arthur Rimbaud. Lisbon: author, 1942.

Criticism

Nemésio, Vitorino. "À memoria de Carlos Queirós." In *Conhecimento de Poesia*. Bahia: Livraria Progresso, 1958. 217–21.
Simões, João Gaspar. "Carlos Queirós." In *Crítica II*. Lisbon: Delfos, 1961. 1: 239–48.

Peter Fothergill-Payne

QUEIZÁN, María Xosé (1939, Vigo–), prose and poetry writer. Queizán participated in the renovation movement in Galician culture which began in the 1960s. A professor of Galician language and literature, she has produced in almost all genres and has maintained a long participation in theatrical projects. In addition to two novels, several short stories, two books of feminist essays, and a literary study, Queizán has published poetry in the journal *Nordés* (Northeast) and in collective books such as *Festa da palabra silenciada* (Festival of the Silenced Word) and the *Libro de amor* (Book of Love). She has also written a filmscript for ''Con hoxe e con mañá'' (1976; With Yesterday and Today) and the as yet unpublished *Non convén chorar máis* (It's Not Good to Cry Any More), a play. *See also* Galician Literature.

BIBLIOGRAPHY

Primary Texts

Amantia. Vigo: Xerais, 1984. Novel.
A muller en Galiza. Sada, La Coruña: n.p., 1977. Essay.
A nova narrativa galega. Vigo: n.p., 1979.
A orella no buraco. Vigo: Galaxia, 1965; 2nd ed. 1984. Novel.
Recuperemos as mans. Santiago de Compostela: n.p., 1980. Essay.

Kathleen March

QUEROL, Vicente Wenceslao (1836, Valencia–1899, Bétera, Valencia), poet in Castilian and Valencian. After obtaining a law degree (1860) he joined the railway company, rising to the rank of vice-director of the Madrid-Zaragoza and Alicante railways (1888). He was a bilingual poet, appreciated by a select minority. His poetry can be divided into two periods: the first, mostly romantic, incorporates legendary themes; the second is more lyrical and reveals the poet's sentiments. He was a friend of Teodor *Llorente, who wrote a prologue to Querol's *Rimas* (1877; Rhymes).

BIBLIOGRAPHY

Primary Texts

Obres valencianes completes. Ed. Luis Guarner. Valencia Sicania. Castellón de la Plana: T. G. Fills de F. Armengot, 1958.
Poesías. Ed. Luis Guarner. Madrid: Espasa-Calpe, Clásicos Castellanos, 1964.
Poesías desconocidas. Ed. Luis Guarner. Madrid: CSIC, 1967.

Criticism

Guarner, Luis. *Poesía y verdad de Vicente Wenceslao Querol*. Madrid: CSIC, 1967.

Salvador García Castañeda

QUESADA, Alonso (1886/1888, Las Palmas de Gran Canaria–1925, Santa Brígida, Canary Islands), Spanish poet. A member of the post-modernist group in the Canaries, his real name was Rafael Romero. He worked as an employee in the office of an English company, and his difficult life produced a resigned, ironic, quotidian echo in his poetry. His 1915 poetry collection *El lino de los sueños* (Linen of Dreams) was distinguished by a prologue written by no less an intellectual leader than *Unamuno. He published *Crónicas de la ciudad y de la noche* (1919; Chronicles of the City and the Night) and a dramatic poem, *La umbría* (1923; Shadows). He is associated with two fellow poets and friends, also Canary Island post-modernists, Tomás *Morales and Saulo *Torón.

QUEVEDO, Francisco de (1580, Madrid–1645, Villanueva de los Infantes), poet, novelist, dramatist, satirist, philosopher, and translator. Francisco Gómez de Quevedo y Villegas was born in Madrid on September 17, 1580. His father, Pedro Gómez de Quevedo (d. 1586), belonged to the lower nobility and served as secretary to Princess Maria, daughter of Charles V, and to Queen Ana of Austria, wife of Philip II; his mother, María de Santibáñez (d. 1601), was a lady-in-waiting for Queen Ana and Princess Isabel Clara Eugenia. Quevedo probably received his early education at the Jesuit-run Imperial College of Madrid. By 1596 he had entered the U of Alcalá, from which he received both the bachelor's degree (1600) and the licentiate. He began to study theology at Alcalá, but in 1601 followed the royal court to Valladolid before finishing. There he renewed his theological studies, but became considerably more engrossed in making his mark in the courtly literary milieu. Eighteen of his early poems appeared in Pedro *Espinosa's important anthology, *Flores de poetas ilustres* (1605; Flowers of Illustrious Poets).

Having gone back to Madrid after the return of the court in 1605, Quevedo initiated an intense creative period which gave flower to several of the *Sueños* (*Visions*, 1963), translations of Anacreon, Phocilides and the lamentations of Jeremiah, various satirical tracts and possibly *El buscón* (*The Scavenger*, 1962). From 1610 to 1613 Quevedo retired on a number of occasions to La Torre de Juan Abad (a town in La Mancha where his mother had left him an estate), apparently suffering from an inner crisis of sorts, and there wrote several works reflecting his religious anguish and despair about humanity in general. The most important is *Heráclito cristiano* (Christian Heraclitus), probably the greatest set of metaphysical and religious poems of the age.

Toward the end of 1613 Quevedo joined Pedro Téllez de Girón, Duke of Osuna, in Sicily, where the latter had been named viceroy. For the next five years he served his friend and benefactor in various capacities; as a reward for his endeavors, Quevedo was appointed to the Order of St. James by Philip III in 1618. Eventually, however, he fell victim to the increasing political difficulties in which the duke was embroiled, and was forced to return to Madrid. His troubles came to a head following his friend's disastrous fall from power. In 1620 he was banished from the court, suffering imprisonment both in his own house at La Torre and at Uclés. After the death of Philip III, Quevedo enjoyed a short respite under the new king, Philip IV, and the all-powerful Count-Duke of Olivares, but was again banished to La Torre in 1622 because of revelations regarding his role in the Osuna affair.

After receiving permission to return to Madrid, Quevedo entered a period of relative calm, the result in large part of his unabashed adulation of the king and the count-duke. In 1628, however, he was again enmired in controversy, this time over whether St. *Teresa of Avila should be allowed to join St. James as Spain's patron saint. His resistance to the proposal (which was favored by the king) earned him a brief period of exile at La Torre, palliated by the eventual victory of his position on the subject.

A campaign mounted by several friends led to Quevedo's marriage to Esperanza de Mendoza on February 29, 1634. The two lived together for very little time, and separated permanently after 1636. (It should be noted that Quevedo apparently maintained a long extramarital relationship with a lower-class woman referred to as "la Ledesma" by his enemies, and may even have had children by her.) In 1635 Quevedo moved again to his estate at La Torre, possibly because he did not have sufficient money to support himself at the court, and stayed there almost continuously until the beginning of 1639.

On December 7 of that year Quevedo was arrested in Madrid and sent off to prison in the city of León. The exact reason for his imprisonment still remains unknown. The traditionally accepted theory—that he left a poem critical of the king under the latter's napkin one evening—is now no longer accepted. Whatever the true motive, it was sufficient to earn him imprisonment for the next three and a half years. The adverse surroundings took a severe toll on his health, and on his release in June of 1643 after the fall of the count-duke, it was clear that he did not have long to live. After stays in both Madrid and La Torre, Quevedo finally succumbed on September 8, 1645, in Villanueva de los Infantes.

Recognized today as one of the true geniuses in the history of Hispanic letters, Quevedo exploited the possibilities of the Spanish language in a way very few writers can approximate. In the words of Jorge Luis Borges, "Francisco de Quevedo is less a man than a vast and complex literature."

Poetry

While the great majority of Quevedo's poetry never appeared in print during his lifetime, its impact was still enormous because of its circulation in ms. form. After Quevedo's death, José *González de Salas, a close friend, edited the mss. willed to the poet's nephew, Pedro Alderete Villegas. The first volume of what was to be a two-volume edition appeared under the title *El Parnaso español, monte en dos cumbres dividido, con las nueve musas castellanas* (1648; Spanish Parnassus, Mount Divided in Two Summits, with the Nine Castilian Muses), and contained some 550 poems. González de Salas died before completing the second volume, eventually published by Pedro Alderete as *Las tres musas últimas castellanas, Segunda cumbre del Parnaso español* (1670; The Last Three Castilian Muses, Second Summit of the Spanish Parnassus). Its 234 compositions were poorly edited, there being numerous errata, false attributions, etc.

Quevedo's reputation as one of Spain's greatest poets rests on a creative outpouring of great thematic and stylistic variety. While the distinctions traditionally drawn between the "cultista" and "conceptista" styles of poetic expression have come under increasing criticism, we should, nevertheless, note Quevedo's role as the principal champion of the second. He consistently rejected the use of the Latinate vocabulary and violent hyperbaton so favored by *Góngora, preferring instead to cultivate the conceit and wordplay.

His more serious poetry can be divided (following J. M. Blecua's criteria) into the metaphysical, the moral, and the religious. The first category embraces a series of poems in which Quevedo addresses themes revolving around the problematic nature of human existence, particularly our mortality and our manner of confronting it. In these anguish-ridden poems, which often stress that life is simply a form of death, Quevedo transcends the manifest neo-Stoic influence, sometimes striking chords of stunning modernity (see Alonso): ''soy un fue, y un será, y un es cansado'' (I am a was, a will be, and an is tired), he laments in one. Quevedo's moral poems belong to a tradition stretching back to classical antiquity. Attacking the usual vices (avarice, pride and ambition, adulation, etc.) as well as the shortcomings of his fellow Spaniards, he displays once again his affinities with the Stoics as well as a thorough knowledge of the Roman satirists, such as Juvenal, Persius and Martial. Much of Quevedo's best religious poetry belongs to the aforementioned collection, *Heráclito cristiano*. Together with several poems which deal with the ineluctable flow of time and human mortality in a way not specifically Christian in focus, there are many which express Quevedo's repentance for past sins, his affliction over the distance created between him and God by his misspent life, etc. His other religious poetry includes works on the life and sayings of Christ (including an epic poem about the harrowing nature of Hell), the lives of the apostles and various other saints, and a beautiful version of the Song of Songs.

His works of a more serious nature also encompass a large number of eulogies and epitaphs. The subjects range from both real and mythical figures of antiquity to his own contemporaries, including friends, political personages, and fellow writers.

Quevedo's love poetry is considered among the best in Spanish literature. While critics have noted strains of Petrarchism, Neoplatonism, and courtly love in its language and sensibility (see Green and Olivares), Quevedo transcends not only the conventions of these traditions, but also virtually all others prevalent in the rhetoric of his day. His astonishingly original use of language highly charged with searing emotion reaches its most remarkable achievements in the poems where he fuses the theme of love with that of death (''Cerrar podrá mis ojos''—''My eyes may be closed'' being the best example). In them he speaks of how his love will survive his death, yet in a curiously materialistic way. Most of these are dedicated to ''Lisi,'' the great passion of his life whose identity has never been definitively established. It should also be noted that Quevedo wrote many love lyrics in a lighter vein, both to Lisi and the many other women celebrated under the guise of pseudonyms.

It is within the enormous body of Quevedo's satirical and burlesque poetry where his pure inventiveness with language and ability in the creation of conceits and metaphors reach their highest manifestations. Showing an unmitigatedly cruel tendency toward grotesque deformation and an overpowering desire to exercise wit in all its forms (see Iffland), he launches savage attacks on a vast range of targets: old women, doctors, tradesmen, innkeepers, cuckolds, social arrivistes, duennas, prostitutes, dandies, foreigners, women who use cosmetics, personal enemies (Góngora, *Ruiz de Alarcón), *ad infinitum*. Another important set of poems is that in which he burlesques Greco-Roman myths with ferocious relish. Quevedo's major effort at parody is his "Poema heroico de las necedades y locuras de Orlando el enamorado" (Heroic Poem of the Foolishness and Idiocies of Orlando in Love), based on Boiardo's *Orlando Innamorato*; though the poem contains moments of marked lyricism, its overall vision is hyperbolically grotesque. In a separate category belong Quevedo's **jácaras*: compositions normally presented as the correspondence between members of the "underworld" and their paramours using the special slang ("germanía") characteristic of the criminal element.

Quevedo's activity as a translator extended to his poetry: Anacreon, Martial, Jeremiah, Epictetus and Phocilides were the subjects of translations or imitations of varying sorts. He also brought back into circulation the poetry of Fray Luis de *León and Francisco de la *Torre, publishing editions of their works as an "antidote" to Gongorism.

Prose

The Picaresque Novel. La vida del buscón llamado don Pablos (The Life of the Con Man Named Don Pablos, tr. as *The Scavenger*, 1962, or *The Swindler*, 1969, etc.), Quevedo's extraordinary contribution to the *picaresque, was probably written before 1610 (conceivably as early as 1602–3), and may have undergone a substantial revision some years later (according to the widely accepted theory F. Lázaro Carreter expounds in his critical edition of the text). It circulated in ms. form until 1626, when it was published in Zaragoza without Quevedo's authorization.

Like its predecessors, **Lazarillo de Tormes* and *Alemán's *Guzmán de Alfarache*, *El buscón* is presented as the autobiography of a member of Spain's multifarious class of social outcasts and low-life types generally designated as *pícaros*. Pablos de Segovia is the son of a barber, who also practices thievery, and a procuress, whore and witch of **converso* extraction. As a child he determines to leave behind his ignominious origins and achieve a higher social rank, preferably that of a *caballero* ("gentleman"). Once he has severed from his parents, he sets out on a career whose roller-coaster trajectory begins with his becoming the servant of a young noble and ends with his escape to the Americas as a hardened criminal of the Sevillian underworld.

In between he finds himself playing such roles as virtuosic trickster and petty thief in the student circles of Alcalá and scarecrow-like pseudo-gentleman in Madrid. Checkering the episodic flow of the narrative are such experiences as being spit upon by over a hundred students and being served a piece of his father's flesh in a meatpie. While many social types are satirized in the course of the novel, Quevedo's principal butt is seemingly Pablos himself. In having him end as he does, Quevedo would seem to imply that people of befouled origins will inevitably be drawn back to them.

Rather than the narrative content per se, it is the novel's mode of expression which is at the root of its undeniable originality. Quevedo has endowed Pablos with his own verbal inventiveness and wit, thus making him by far the most entertaining of all *pícaro*-narrators. The entertainment, however, is not the innocent or lighthearted variety: the wit is most often used to wound and belittle. The relentlessly grotesque vision of the world which emerges from these pages, fraught with scatology and characters who verge on being puppets, make it a forerunner of the darker vein in twentieth-c. fiction.

Other Satire. The *Sueños* (*Visions*) are without doubt Quevedo's most widely known satirical works. Five in number, they were composed from roughly 1605 to 1622. They first circulated as mss., only to be published in a pirated edition in Barcelona in 1627; this volume carried the title *Sueños y discursos de verdades descubridoras de abusos, vicios, y engaños, en todos los oficios y estados del mundo* (Visions and Discourses of Truths Which Reveal Abuses, Vices, and Deceit in all the Occupations and Estates of the World). Conceivably spurred by a clique of Quevedo's enemies, the *Inquisition forced him to revise several of the texts; the modifications consist mainly of a transformation of the Judeo-Christian context of the narrative (which the censors deemed irreverent) to a classical, pagan one. This ''approved'' version (full of patent inconsistencies) appeared in Madrid in 1631 under the unlikely title of *Juguetes de la niñez y travesuras del ingenio* (Childhood Jests and Witty Mischief).

El sueño del Juicio Final (Vision of the Final Judgment) was probably composed in 1605. In it Quevedo narrates a dream about Judgment Day, catalyzed by the reading of a text on just this subject. The first part describes the dead bodies rising from the graves and their subsequent march toward the place where they will be judged; the second narrates the Judgment itself.

El alguacil endemoniado (The Bedeviled Constable) was written at some time between 1605 and May of 1608. Unlike its predecessor, it is not presented as a dream, but as an actual occurrence. Quevedo enters a church where the exorcism of a constable is being carried out. He proceeds to engage in a dialogue with the demon who inhabits the latter's body, and thereby learns about many of the inhabitants and customs of Hell.

El sueño del infierno (Vision of Hell) was completed on April 30, 1608. This time Quevedo also eschews the oneiric framework, saying that all he narrates was seen thanks to his Guardian Angel and divine Providence. It begins in allegorical fashion: Quevedo finds himself in the middle of a garden out of which lead two paths, one narrow and full of obstacles, the other wide and flooded with people. After a short-lived attempt to follow the narrow path, he switches over to the other and soon finds himself at the gates of Hell. What follows is a tour of the latter in which Quevedo speaks with the damned and the devils who torment them. It ends with a description of Lucifer's personal chambers.

Quevedo dedicated *El mundo por de dentro* (The World from Within) to his friend and benefactor, the Duke of Osuna, on April 26, 1612 (1610 in *Juguetes*). Using the rhetoric of allegory, he begins with a description of the terrible confusion in which he is living. One day he runs into an old man who turns out to be ''Desengaño'' (Disillusion); he invites Quevedo to go on a tour of the ''main-street of the world,'' whose name is ''Hypocrisy.'' In the ensuing episodes the old man peels away fraudulent appearances, and shows the ingenuous Quevedo the disagreeable realities lying behind them.

El sueño de la Muerte (The Vision of Death), dedicated on April 6, 1622, returns to the dream-format of the first work in the series. This time induced by a reading of Job and Lucretius, it narrates Quevedo's encounter with the strangely allegorical figure of Death, who introduces him to her kingdom. The initial targets are several of the professional groups which are perpetual targets in these works, but it ends up dealing mainly with various figures from popular culture (Pero Grullo, Mateo Pico, etc.).

A work related to the *Sueños* in spirit, as well as by its inclusion in *Juguetes*, is the *Discurso de todos los diablos o infierno enmendado* (The Discourse of All Devils or Hell Reformed). It was written in 1627 and published the following year. Unlike its predecessors, it is not narrated in the first person. It begins with a description of the confusion created in Hell by a duenna, a busybody and a "stool pigeon," and proceeds to present a series of scenes in which politically related themes tend to dominate (Julius Caesar, Brutus, Nero and *Seneca are among those who appear).

As found throughout his satirical works, there is a tendency in the *Sueños* to return to certain targets with obsessive frequency. The disdainful resentment toward the trades and the professions Quevedo harbored appears in the repeated assaults on tailors, pharmacists, doctors, lawyers, taverners, merchants, etc. His blatant misogynism surfaces in the prolific attacks on different varieties of women. Attacks on foreigners and heretics display Quevedo in his oft-adopted role of defender of Counter-Reformation, imperial Spain.

Overflowing with puns, clever turns of phrase, comic allusions, paradoxes, etc., the *Sueños* share stylistic similarities with all his satirical and burlesque creations. The strong strain of the grotesque has led critics to compare these works with the paintings of Bosch (popular in Spain from the time Philip II began to collect them), but true resemblances are few. Much more to the point are the parallels critics have drawn between these works and the genre of the **entremés*. The satirical parades of standard social types, the slapstick humor, the often dizzying pace and the puppet-like insignificance of so many of the characters all recall this popular theatrical form of which Quevedo himself was a master.

Quevedo's most extensive satirical work in prose is *La Hora de todos y la Fortuna con seso* (The Hour of All Men and Fortune in Her Wits), which he calls a "fantasía moral" (a moral fantasy). Written in 1635, it was published posthumously in 1650. The work begins with a meeting of a grotesquely presented set of Greco-Roman gods during which it is decided that for once Fortune should give each person what he or she deserves. A long series of scenes follows, all depicting a world turned upside down. The offenders appear in the midst of their reprehensible activities, and are then suddenly exposed or punished by the apocalyptic effect of the Hour, often fantastic in nature. Many of the early scenes involve Quevedo's pet targets: doctors, lawyers, pharmacists, poets, prostitutes, women who use cosmetics, etc. Eventually a concern for political and international matters takes precedence, and Quevedo once again assumes the role of the polemicist at battle with Spain's putative enemies. Perhaps the most interesting of these tracts is that of the "Monopantos," in which he suggests, in veiled terms, that the Count-Duke of Olivares is collaborating with Jewish financial interests abroad. Also of note are those in which the plight of Indians, blacks, and, strangely enough, women, is protested.

Several of the innumerable short satirical and burlesque works in prose are worthy of mention for the pronounced level of their artistry or their place in the development of his thematic repertoire. They include *Vida de la Corte y oficios entretenidos en ella* (written 1599?; Life at the Court and Entertaining Occupations There), an early display of his inclination toward satirizing standard types (or *figuras*) of the urban, courtly milieu; *El caballero de la Tenaza* (written 1606?; The Knight of the Pincers), the archetype for the many works representing battles between money-grubbing women and men intent on protecting their purses; his scatological masterpiece, *Gracias y desgracias del ojo del culo* (Favors and Misfortunes of the Nether-eye); *Aguja de navegar cultos* (Compass for Navigating as Cultured People) and *La culta latiniparla* (The Latin-jabbering Cultured Woman), savage satires of the *gongoristas* written in the late 1620s; and finally, his numerous pieces of mock legislation (*premáticas*) in which he attacks irritating social habits, linguistic clichés, etc.

Philosophical and Religious Works. Quevedo is considered one of the first representatives of the neo-Stoic movement in Spain (see Ettinghausen). The basic intent of his efforts was to reconcile the precepts of the classical Stoic thinkers, particularly Seneca, with the teachings of Christianity. The ultimate "Stoic hero" for him was Job, who combined the much-valued indifference to adversity with a faith in God. Among his writings are *De los remedios de cualquier fortuna* (written 1633; On the Remedies of Any Fortune), a translation and commentary of this work wrongly attributed to Seneca; *Nombre, origen, intento, recomendación y descendencia de la doctrina estoica* (written 1633–34; Name, Origin, Purpose, Recommendation and Lineage of the Stoic Doctrine), a history and explanation of the Stoic movement (which he says derives originally from Job), along with a defense of Epicurus; *La cuna y la sepultura* (1634; The Cradle and the Grave), a work of ascetic teachings, focusing predominantly on the way human beings should confront their own mortality; and *La constancia y pacienca del santo Job* (written 1641; The Constancy and Patience of St. Job), a philosophizing commentary on passages from the Book of Job.

Quevedo's religious treatises include two biographies, *Vida de Fray Tomás de Villanueva* (1620; The Life of Brother Tomás de *Villanueva) and the much more significant *Vida de San Pablo apóstol* (dedicated in 1644; The Life of St. Paul the Apostle); *Providencia de Dios* (written 1641; God's Providence), which strives to establish that God and Providence exist and that the human soul is immortal; and *Virtud militante* (written in the mid–1630s;

Militant Virtue), which attacks the ''four plagues of the world'': envy, ingratitude, pride and avarice. Provoked by the decision to name St. Teresa of Avila as co-patron saint of Spain, Quevedo wrote his *Memorial por el patronato de Santiago* (Brief in Favor of the Patronage of St. James) and *Su espada por Santiago* (His Sword for St. James), arguing the latter should remain the sole patron.

Political Works. Quevedo's most important work treating political theory is by far his *Política de Dios, Gobierno de Cristo Nuestro Señor* (Politics of God, Government of Christ Our Lord), the first part of which was completed and dedicated to the Count-Duke of Olivares in 1621. After a pirated edition appeared in 1626, Quevedo himself published a corrected and enlarged version, which came out that same year; the second part of the work was published in 1655. The treatise attempts to establish the theoretical groundwork for a governmental system based on Christian ideals. The best form of government, according to Quevedo, is a monarchy, one whose authority is absolute because it issues from divine will. The king should govern using Christ as his supreme model. Much attention is paid to the qualities required of the king's counselors, they being probably as important as the king himself. Quevedo rejects tyrannicide as the solution for an evil monarch, choosing instead to present the latter as a form of divine punishment which must be suffered in silence. The work contains few truly original ideas, its significance stemming principally from the mastery of its style as well as the great popularity it achieved.

Among his other noteworthy treatises are *España defendida y los tiempo de ahora* (written 1609; Spain Defended and Modern Times) and *Marco Bruto* (started 1631, completed 1644). The first is a nationalistic defense of Spain and Spanish culture in general, elicited by what Quevedo calls the ''calumnies of foreigners''; the second is a running commentary on a translation of Plutarch's text on Marcus Brutus, distilling from it the ethical and political implications.

Theatre

The only extant *comedia* available—*Cómo ha de ser el privado* (written 1627–28; How the King's Favorite Should Be)—is a rather ungainly attempt at embodying in dramatic form some of the ideas expressed in *Política de Dios* (in a way that would prove flattering to the count-duke and Philip IV). His *entremeses*, to the contrary, are masterful examples of their genre, on a par with those of *Quiñones de Benavente and *Cervantes in many respects. Most seem to belong to the period from 1610 to 1630. Primarily satirical in nature, their butts range from people who try to cover their old age and physical defects (*La ropavejera*, The Old Clothes Dealer) to the complaisant cuckold (*Diego Moreno*), from parasitical women (*El niño y Peralvillo de Madrid*, The Little Boy and the Peralvillo of Madrid) to dishonest innkeepers (*La venta*, The Inn). Quevedo also excelled in the composition of *bailes*, short dramatic pieces in the form of monologues or dialogues, often sung and accompanied by dance. They are predominantly populated by the low-life types characteristic of the picaresque, and show the same ludic impulse and wittiness found in the *entremeses*. *See also* Conceptismo.

BIBLIOGRAPHY

Primary Texts

La Hora de todos y la Fortuna con seso. Ed. Luisa López-Grigera. Madrid: Castalia, 1975.

Obras completas. Ed. Felicidad Buendía. 2 vols. Madrid: Aguilar, 1969.

Obra Poética. Ed. José Manuel Blecua. 3 vols. Madrid: Castalia, 1969–71.

Poesía original. Ed. José Manuel Blecua. Barcelona: Planeta, 1963.

Política de Dios. Ed. James O. Crosby. Madrid: Castalia, 1966.

Sueños y discursos. Ed. Felipe C. R. Maldonado. Madrid: Castalia, 1973.

La vida del buscón llamado don Pablos. Ed. Fernando Lázaro Carreter. Salamanca: CSIC, 1965.

English Translations

Quevedo: The Choice Humorous and Satirical Works. Tr. Charles Duff. New York: E. P. Dutton, 1926; rpt. Westport, CT: Hyperion, 1977. (Tr. of *El buscón*, *Sueños* and other works, based on earlier tr. by Sir Roger L'Estrange and John Stevens.)

The Scavenger. Tr. Hugh A. Harter. New York: Las Américas, 1962.

Two Spanish Picaresque Novels: "Lazarillo de Tormes" and "The Swindler." Tr. Michael Alpert. Harmondsworth, England: Penguin, 1969. (Tr. of *El buscón*.)

Visions. Tr. J. M. Cohen. Carbondale: Southern Illinois UP, 1963.

Criticism

Works covering several areas

Ayala, Francisco. *Cervantes y Quevedo*. Barcelona: Seix-Barral, 1974.

Bleznick, Donald. *Quevedo*. TWAS 153. New York: Twayne, 1972.

Carilla, Emilio. *Quevedo (entre dos centenarios)*. Tucumán, Argentina: Universidad Nacional de Tucumán, 1949.

Crosby, James O. *Guía bibliográfica para el estudio de Quevedo*. London: Grant and Cutler, 1976.

Iffland, James. *Quevedo and the Grotesque*. 2 vols. London: Tamesis, 1978 and 1982.

———, ed. *Quevedo in Perspective: Eleven Essays for the Quadricentennial*. Newark, DE: Juan de la Cuesta, 1982.

Lida, Raimundo. *Prosas de Quevedo*. Barcelona: Crítica, 1981.

Sobejano, Gonzalo, ed. *Francisco de Quevedo*. Madrid: Taurus, 1978.

Poetry Criticism

Alonso, Dámaso. "El desgarrón afectivo en la poesía de Quevedo." In *Poesía española*. Madrid: Gredos, 1952. 497–580.

Crosby, James O. *En torno de la poesía de Quevedo*. Madrid: Castalia, 1967.

Green, Otis H. *Courtly Love in Quevedo*. Boulder: University of Colorado Press, 1952.

Navarro de Kelley, Emilia. *La poesía metafísica de Quevedo*. Madrid: Guadarrama, 1973.

Olivares, Julián. *The Love Poetry of Francisco de Quevedo: An Aesthetic and Existential Study*. Cambridge: Cambridge UP, 1983.

Parker, Alexander A. "La 'agudeza' en algunos sonetos de Quevedo." In *Estudios dedicados a Menéndez Pidal*. 8 vols. Madrid: n.p., 1950–1952. 3: 345–60.

Pozuelo Yvancos, José M. *El lenguaje poético de la lírica amorosa de Quevedo*. Murcia: Universidad de Murcia, 1979.

El buscón Criticism

Cros, Edmon. *Ideología y genética textual: El caso del ''Buscón.''* Madrid: Cupsa, 1980.
Díaz Migoyo, Gonzalo. *Estructura de la novela: Anatomía del ''Buscón.''* Madrid: Fundamentos, 1978.
Lázaro Carreter, Fernando. ''Originalidad del *Buscón.*'' In *Estilo barroco y personalidad creadora: Góngora, Quevedo, Lope de Vega*. Salamanca: Anaya, 1966. 11–59.
Molho, Maurice. *Introducción al pensamiento picaresco*. Salamanca: Anaya, 1972.
Parker, Alexander A. *Literature and the Delinquent: The Picaresque Novel in Spain and Europe, 1599–1753*. Edinburgh: Edinburgh UP, 1967.
Spitzer, Leo. ''Sobre el arte de Quevedo en el *Buscón.*'' In *Francisco de Quevedo*. Ed. Gonzalo Sobejano. Madrid: Taurus, 1978. 123–84.

Sueños Criticism

Levisi, Margarita. ''Hieronymus Bosch y los *Sueños* de Francisco de Quevedo.'' *Filología* 9 (1963): 163–200.
Nolting-Hauff, Ilse. *Visión, sátira y agudeza en los ''Sueños'' de Quevedo*. Madrid: Gredos, 1974.

La hora de todos Criticism

Bourg, Jean; Pierre Dupont, and Pierre Geneste. Introduction to their French translation entitled *L'heure de tous et la fortune raisonable*. Paris: Aubier, 1980.
Iffland, James. ''Apocalypse Later: Ideology and Quevedo's *La hora de todos.*'' *REH* (U of Puerto Rico) 7 (1980): 87–132.
López-Grigera, Luisa. *Relección de ''La hora de todos.''* Bilbao: Universidad de Deusto, 1971.

Criticism of Philosophical works

Ettinghausen, Henry. *Francisco de Quevedo and the Neostoic Movement*. Oxford: Oxford UP, 1972.

Theater Criticism

Asensio, Eugenio. *Itinerario del entremés*. Madrid: Gredos, 1965.

James Iffland

QUILES, Eduardo (1940, Valencia–), Spanish dramatist and short story writer. Most writers of what theatrical historian George Wellwarth termed *Spanish Underground Drama* (1972) were maintained in a state of virtual anonymity by the Franco *censorship and the theatrical commercial establishment. More than a dozen experimental playwrights of the 1960s and 1970s, including José *Ruibal, Martín Elizondo, Manuel *Martínez Mediero, Miguel *Romero Esteo, Antonio *Martínez Ballesteros, and others were excluded from Spanish stages even after the death of Franco. Hence, Quiles (like many other writers of this radically subversive theatrical variant) spent a good deal of time as a voluntary expatriate. He lived in North Africa, France and Mexico, working for cultural periodicals, in radio and television, and for an agency of Unesco. Many of his stories were published in Mexican magazines, and he also wrote stories and theater for children, and scripts for Mexican and U.N. television productions. His is vanguardist theater, but based upon principles of the classical theater, incorporating major contemporary themes. Thus, for example, he provides a visual image of tyranny in *La concubina y el dictador* (1978; The Concubine and the Dictator), of the notion of peaceful revolution in *Pigmeos, vagabundos y omnipotentes* (1971; 2nd ed., 1975; Pygmies, Vagabonds and Omnipotents), and of man's economic exploitation of his fellows in *El asalariado* (1969; *The Employee*, 1972).

Quiles first began to write for the theater in 1964, and by 1979 (when his first volume of theater in Spanish appeared), he had written more than forty plays, none of which had been produced in Spain, although he had had productions in Mexico, Canada and the United States, the latter two in English translations. The years spent in Mexico (1972–75) affected Quiles deeply, as he came face-to-face with misery, poverty and Third World problems, turning away from earlier more abstract, philosophical or metaphysical themes to more specifically socio-political concerns. His plays are often brief, one- and two-act pieces, conceived as dramatic monologues or (given his exclusion from Spain's theaters) intended for the dinner-theater, café-theater and experimental salons or dramatic studios. His repertoire is broad both technically and thematically, ranging from farcical comedy, for example, *Los faranduleros* (1971; The Strolling Players), to an absurdist burlesque of conformist education resulting in perpetual immaturity as in *El hombre-bebé* (1969; Baby-Man), or a futuristic vision of dehumanized man as an automatically controlled type of robot *(Rebelde-robot* [1972; Robot Rebel]). Other works are bitter satire or grotesque farce, usually redeemed by pity for the human condition or by humor. Quiles views the human race as having failed in its attempts at humanity, existentially bankrupt and largely isolated by the deterioration of interpersonal relationships in the professional environment (as portrayed in *La navaja* [1972; The Knife]). His skepticism as to mankind's authenticity produces *El hombre y la máscara* (1967; The Man and the Mask) in which personality and identity are variable according to the role assigned by society. He is especially critical of consumerism and materialism, portraying modern life—eased by technological progress—as empty leisure where man has become a useless drone surrounded by unnecessary, unsatisfying abundance (*Su majestad la moda* [1973; Her Majesty, Fashion]), perceptibly derived from the guignol. At least two plays are devoted to the passion for football (or soccer), seen as Spain's "opiate of the masses," El *balón* (The Ball) and *Regreso de Dimitri Goss* (The Return of Dimitri Goss), both 1971.

Quiles has also written a number of works which might accurately be termed feminist, including *El tálamo* (1973; *The Bridal Chamber*, 1973), *Diario de una mujer galante* (1976; Diary of a Gallant Woman)—whose production was canceled by the Franco censors—and *La ira y el éxtasis* (1974; Anger and Ecstasy). In each case, woman is portrayed as the victim of *machismo*, as well as of her social conditioning which has made her concept of self-worth depend upon masculine desire or admiration. In *La ira y el éxtasis*, an aging diva, terminally ill, fights a lonely battle against total isolation, while in the dramatic monologue *El tálamo*, a once-attractive secretary whose jobs often depended more on her sexual receptivity than her stenographic skills performs her nightly ritual of "rejecting" importunate employers or ex-lovers in a one-way phone conversation. *El jardín del varón* (1974; The Male's Garden) is a protest against masculine dominance and a cry for feminine liberation, a note which is unmistakable even in works with other major themes such as *La concubina y el dictador*, or *Pigmeos, vagabundos y omnipotentes*. No matter how abrasive his humor, despite occasionally scathing sarcasm, Quiles is something of a Utopian idealist who aspires to a future community where man will no longer be a wolf to his own kind, a society with neither privilege nor manipulations, without misery or pain, with liberty, justice and equality for all. His bitterness is for those who have lost sight of those goals, or never held them, but this is tempered by pity and mercy for the suffering, the exploited, the lonely. He is among the most profound, most lyric and complex of the writers of his generation. *See also* Contemporary Spanish Theater.

BIBLIOGRAPHY

Primary Texts

La concubina y el dictador, Pigmeos, vagabundos y omnipotentes y El asalariado. Preliminary Study, Klaus Pörtl. Valencia: Prometeo, 1979.

Motín de cuentos. Valencia: Prometeo, 1979.

El tálamo. In *Contemporary Spanish Theater.* Ed. Patricia W. O'Connor and Anthony M. Pasquariello. New York: Scribner's, 1980.

Teatro tragicómico. Valencia: Prometeo, 1980.

English Translations

The Refrigerator and *The Bridal Chamber.* In *Modern International Drama* 7.1 United States. (1973). *The Employee*, in *Modern International Drama* 9.1 (1975). *The Cripples* in *Modern International Drama* 12.2 (1979).

New Generation Spanish Drama. An Anthology. Ed. George Wellwarth. Montreal: n.p., 1976. Contains *The Employer*, *The Refrigerator*, and *The Bridal Chamber.*

———. *Spanish Underground Drama.* University Park: Pennsylvania State UP, 1972.

Criticism

Pérez, Janet. "The Dramatic Rhetoric of Eduardo Quiles." *Gestos* 3 (1988): 67–79.

Wellwarth, George. "Teatro 1, Eduardo Quiles." *World Literature Today* 53.4 (Autumn 1979): 653.

Janet Pérez

QUIÑONES, Suero de. *See* Paso Honroso, Libro del

QUIÑONES DE BENAVENTE, Luis (1589?, Toledo–1651, Madrid), most prolific and influential writer of *entremeses* of his day. He never attempted to write a full-length play, and sixteen poems written for competition constitute his only other literary efforts. Although he enjoyed great popularity in his time, very little is known of his life: his date of birth is not known, nor is his principal occupation, but a death certificate of August 25, 1651, makes reference to his priesthood.

Benavente's role in the development of the **entremés* was comparable to that of Lope de *Vega in drama. Besides writing more *entremeses* than any of his contemporaries (150 are attributed to him), Quiñones de Benavente was the major innovator in that genre. Those who followed merely continued the precepts he originated. He began writing just as the *entremés* form was changing from prose to verse, but all of his works, even the earliest, were entirely in verse. The first published was *Los coches* (The Coaches), included by *Tirso de Molina in the *Segunda Parte* of his plays (1634). From 1640 on, other *entremeses* by Benavente were published in various collections of different authors. In 1645 a collection of Benavente's works was published with the title *Jocosería, Burlas veras o reprensión moral y festiva de los desórdenes públicos* (Jocoseria, Truth in Jest, or Moral and Humorous Reproof of Public Abuses). It is assumed that the plays in this volume are Benavente's.

Benavente's plays can be divided into two basic categories; the first is the spoken interlude written in the realistic manner, where the characters usually belong to the lower classes and the setting is urban. Deception is an important element in these works. Two examples of this type are *El borracho* (The Drunk) and *Los vocablos* (Words). The latter anticipates Molière's *Les précieuses ridicules* in its mockery of overly elegant language. The second category, the *entremés* cantado (sung interlude), is considered Benavente's most original contribution to the theater. The content of these plays is usually completely imaginative, and the characters are designated either as "voices" or by the proper names of the actors. Dance is an important feature in them.

Quiñones y Benavente probably wrote more than the 150 plays now attributed to him. Some of these might be found among anonymous works or might have been published under another playwright's name. The most important source of newly discovered interludes by Benavente is a book called *Ramillete gracioso* (1643; Witty Bouquet), the only copy of which is in the Museo del Arte Escénico del Instituto del Teatro in Barcelona. The same museum has other mss. with Benavente's name. The full extent of Benavente's output and influence clearly has yet to be ascertained. *See also* Theater in Spain.

BIBLIOGRAPHY

Primary Texts

Colección de entremeses, loas, bailes, jácaras y mojigangas desde fines del siglo XVI a mediados del XVIII ordenada. Ed. E. Cotarelo Mori. NBAE 17&18.

Navidad y Corpus Christi festejados por los mejores ingenios de España en diez y seis autos a lo divino, diez y seis loas, y diez y seis entremeses. Madrid: n.p., 1664. Microfilm of orig. in Boston Public Library, Ticknor Collection, 1969.

Criticism

Bergman, Hannah E. "Algunos entremeses desconocidos de Luis Quiñones de Benavente." In *Homenaje a Casalduero: Crítica y Poesía*. Ed. Rizel Pincus Sigele and Gonzalo Sobejano. Madrid: Gredos, 1972.

———. *Luis Quiñones de Benavente*. TWAS 216. New York: Twayne, 1972.

Nina Shecktor

QUINTANA, Manuel José (1772, Madrid–1857, Madrid), poet, dramatist, and biographer. Quintana's long life spanned years of enormous upheavel in Spain and profound changes in his country's political and social structures. The form of his literary endeavors tended to adhere to the precepts of neo-classicism, but the content of those writings was frequently revolutionary. He is remembered as one of the first great liberal poets of nineteenth-c. Spain.

Quintana studied rhetoric, Latin, and philosophy in Madrid and Córdoba before entering higher studies at the U of Salamanca, where his father had been a professor of canon law. The elder Quintana's position enabled him to secure and read books which were strictly prohibited by the *Inquisition—books by the "heretics" Voltaire, Montesquieu, Condillac, Smith, Bacon, Rousseau, Erasmus—and the young Quintana had access to them. He read these authors avidly, became passionately interested in the ideas expressed by the most liberal among them, and left markings of those readings both implicitly and explicitly throughout his works. In Salamanca he became a disciple and friend of the poet *Meléndez Valdés, and established contacts which would become useful later on. Already attracted to poetry, in Salamanca he received guidance and encouragement. In 1788, at the age of sixteen, he published his first volume of verses, and Batilo's philosophical ideas were apparent in them.

After graduating from Salamanca, Quintana returned to Madrid, worked as a lawyer, and continued to write. The newly recovered relations between his two favorite countries in 1795 prompted his Ode "A la paz entre España y Francia" (To the Peace Between Spain and France). Between that year and 1802, when he published another collection of poems, he wrote a number of the works he is best remembered for today: odes to Meléndez, to *Jovellanos, to Nicasio *Alvarez de Cienfuegos; passionate defenses of freedom ("A Juan de Padilla," 1797; To Juan de Padilla); elegies ("A la muerte de un amigo," 1798; On the Death of a Friend); stirring philosophical musings ("A la invención de la imprenta," 1800; To the Invention of the Printing Press); and a drama, *El duque de Viseo* (1801; The Duke of Viseo). His popularity rose rapidly and was confirmed by the time the 1802 collection appeared. From then on Quintana's fame was assured: his work as a critic in the newspaper he founded in 1803; as a dramatist in *Pelayo* (1805); as a biographer of past heroes in the *Vidas de españoles célebres* (1807; *Lives of Celebrated Spaniards*, 1833); and as a poetry editor in the first edition of the *Poesías selectas castellanas* (1807; Selected Spanish Poetry) all displayed the intelligence of a man deeply committed to Spanish nationalism and humanitarian ideals. His ode "El panteón del Escorial"

(1805; The Pantheon in the Escorial) revealed his rejection of the facile codes of imperialism and his willingness to criticize what he considered inglorious events in Spain's past. After being named theatrical censor in Madrid in 1806, he opened his home to the capital's most important literary and political figures, and his *tertulia* became an important center of liberal thought.

The patriotism which Quintana had been expressing in his literature was put into practice in 1808. The French attempted to enlist him in their cause (as they had Meléndez), but instead Quintana adopted a stance of fierce opposition. He published his radical *Poesías patrióticas* (1808; Patriotic Poems) and a newspaper called *Semanario Patriótico* (Patriotic Weekly). The Patriotic Poems contain some of his most revolutionary and dramatic odes. In ''A España después de la revolución de marzo'' (To Spain, Following the March Revolt) he raised the cry of ''¡guerra, guerra, españoles!'' (war, war, Spaniards!), even though war was a ''barbarous'' and frightening thing. Still, he pleaded with his countrymen to pledge ''¡antes la muerte que consentir jamás ningún tirano!'' (Death before we accept a tyrant!). ''Despierta, España'' (Wake up, Spain), he demanded in ''Al armamento de las provincias españolas contra los franceses'' (To the Arming of Spanish Provinces against the French), since ''no hay majestad para quien vive esclava'' (there is no majesty for he who lives enslaved). Revolution was at hand, and Quintana dreamed of freedom from the approaching despotism.

As the French advances forced liberals toward Seville and then into Cádiz, Quintana, in the service of the Junta Central, published a huge stream of manifestos, declarations, challenges, and calls-to-arms to his compatriots, exhorting them to resist the French invaders. During the War of Independence he accepted numerous posts in the government-in-exile. Nonetheless, his participation in that liberal government earned him Ferdinand VII's disfavor. Upon the king's return, Quintana was stripped of the honors he had accumulated (he had been elected to the *Academia Española, for example), persecuted by the *Inquisition, and finally jailed in Pamplona for six years (1814–20). He enjoyed a three-year freedom when constitutional government was re-established by Riego, but upon Ferdinand's second return in 1823, Quintana was banished to a small town in Extremedura. He was not inactive, though, and he kept in contact with friends in Madrid, where he was allowed to relocate in 1828. He spent time writing more *Lives* in 1830 and 1832, and as soon as Ferdinand died in 1833 Quintana once again enjoyed official favor, taking on many of the positions he had held previously. For the next two decades he worked on government commissions, received countless honors, and was revered for the deep patriotism and heroic liberalism he had expressed so forcefully in the first years of the century. The *Biblioteca de Autores Españoles honored him by publishing a volume of his *Obras completas* (Complete Works) in 1852, and Quintana became a quasi-institution in himself. He was even crowned Spain's first poet laureate by Queen Isabel II in a large celebration in Madrid in 1855. His best work, however, had been done many years before. He died, at eighty-five, in 1857. A nephew published some *Obras inéditas* (Unpublished Works) in 1872, and a more complete three-volume *Obras completas* (Complete Works) appeared in Madrid in 1897–98, but Quintana's work in poetry and prose was voluminous and much has been lost or has remained uncollected.

BIBLIOGRAPHY

Primary Texts

Obras completas. Madrid: Rivadeneyra, 1852.
Obras completas. 3 vols. Madrid: González Rojas, 1897–8.
Poesías. Ed. Narciso Alonso Cortés. Madrid: Espasa-Calpe, 1958.
Poesías completas. Ed. Albert Dérozier. Madrid: Castalia, 1969.

English Translation

Lives of Celebrated Spaniards. Tr. T. R. Preston. London: Fellowes, 1833.

Criticism

Dérozier, Albert. *Manuel José Quintana y el nacimiento del liberalismo en España*. Madrid: Turner, 1978.
Luis, Leopoldo de. ''La oda 'El panteón del Escorial,' de Quintana.'' *RO* 39 (1972): 363–77.
Monguió, Luis. ''Don Manuel José Quintana y su oda 'A la expedición española para propagar la vacuna en América'.'' *Boletín del Instituto Riva-Aguero* (Lima) 3 (1956–57): 175–84.
Pageaux, Daniel-Henri. ''La genèse de l'oeuvre poétique de Manuel José Quintana.'' *Revue de Littérature comparée* 37 (1963): 227–67.
Sebold, Russell P. '' 'Siempre formas en grande modeladas': Sobre la visión poética de Quintana.'' *Homenaje a Rodríguez-Moñino* 2 (1969): 177–84.
Vila Selma, J. *Ideario de Manuel José Quintana*. Madrid: CSIC, 1961.

David Thatcher Gies

QUINTO, José María de (1925, Madrid–), Spanish playwright and drama critic. A theorist and experimental dramatist, Quinto was associated with Alfonso *Sastre in founding the ''revolutionary'' social theater movement in Madrid in the late 1950s and early 1960s. He participated in drafting manifestos, as well as writing theoretical studies and justifications. He was a founder of La Carátula, a little theater group, and also wrote a number of original plays, including the one-act drama *Sed* (n.d.; Thirst). He translated contemporary French and American playwrights, including Jacques Bernard and Tennessee Williams, and also wrote short stories and a novel, *Toque de silencio* (1965; Call to Silence). *See also* Contemporary Spanish Theater.

QUIROGA, Elena (1921, Santander–), Spanish novelist and short story writer. The sixteenth of seventeen children of a minor Galician nobleman, Elena Quiroga spent her childhood with her father and siblings in Villoria (Galicia); her mother died before she was two years old. She was educated in a Catholic girls' school in Bilbao, completing her high school in Rome in 1936, just before the outbreak of the Civil War. After some time in southern France, she returned to Spain in 1938, where she spent the remainder of the war in Galicia. The winters of 1941 and 1942 (especially difficult in famine-plagued Galicia) were spent in Barcelona. In 1942, she and her father moved to La Coruña, where she began to interest herself in literature. Her first novel, *La soledad sonora* (1949; Sonorous Solitude), was of a conventional, traditional cut and subsequently excised by the novelist from her collected works. In 1950, she married a historian and specialist in heraldry, Dálmiro de la Válgoma, and moved to Madrid, where she has since resided.

Viento del norte (1951; North Wind) won the Nadal Prize and brought considerable publicity. It is a novel in the vein of *Pardo Bazán, a kind of family chronicle of rural decadence, also traditional in style and technique. *La sangre* (1952; Blood) is more experimental in narrative perspective, as the viewpoint is that of a chestnut tree. The conservative outlook of the early novels also appears in the novelettes *La otra ciudad* (The Other City) and *Trayecto uno* (Bus #1), both published in 1953. *Algo pasa en la calle* (1954; Something's Happening in the Street) initiates a more experimental period, characterized by a more progressive and critical attitude. This novel is Quiroga's most sophisticated accomplishment of the 1950s, with multiple perspectives employed to reconstruct the enigmatic personality of the dead protagonist, and featuring interior monologue-techniques which reappear in *La enferma* (1955; The Sick Woman), whose protagonist is not dead, but mute and immobilized. *Plácida la joven* (1956; Young Plácida), a moderately feminist portrait of a young Galician fishwife who dies in childbirth, and *La última corrida* (1958; The Last Bullfight) are less noteworthy.

Quiroga's best novels are *Tristura* (1960; Sadness), winner of the Critics' Prize, and *Escribo tu nombre* (1956; [Liberty], I Write Your Name), Spain's entry in the 1967 international competition for the Rómulo Gallegos Novel Prize. These two novels are the first parts of a longer cycle also comprising *Se acabó todo, muchacha triste* (It's All Over Now, Baby Blue), and perhaps another title or two yet unfinished. The novels of the cycle are unified by a common protagonist, Tadea, seen at a different stage of life in each: childhood (*Tristura*), life in the convent boarding school (*Escribo tu nombre*), and the Civil War (*Se acabó todo*).

Presente profundo (1973; Profound Present) is one of Quiroga's most significant and successful novels, and although relatively short, one of the most complex in structure. It re-creates the lives and deaths of two female suicides, very different women who are joined only by association in the mind of a young Galician doctor who investigates and contrasts their lives. It includes many of Quiroga's enduring concerns: time, moral issues, the positive and negative manifestations of religion, female psychology and feminist problems, existential awakening, the themes of freedom and solitude and the meaning of life and death. This independent and multifaceted novelist continues to interest because of her abiding concern with technique and self-improvement, and for insights into Galicia, the social structure in Spain, and her portraits of women. She has had a number of French and German translations, but none to English.

BIBLIOGRAPHY

Primary Text

La careta. Barcelona: Noguer, 1955.

Criticism

Boring, Phyllis [Zatlin]. *Elena Quiroga*. TWAS 459. Boston: Twayne, 1977. In English.
Brent, Albert. "The Novels of Elena Quiroga." *Hispania* 42 (1959): 210–13.
Delano, Lucile K. "The Novelistic Style of Elena Quiroga." *Kentucky Foreign Language Quarterly* 9 (1962): 61–67.
———. "Sensory Images in the Galician Novels of Elena Quiroga." *Kentucky Foreign Language Quarterly* 10 (1963): 59–68.
Villegas, Juan. "Los motivos estructurantes de *La careta*, de Elena Quiroga." *CH* 75 (1968): 638–48.

Janet Pérez

QUIROGA, Pedro de (sixteenth c., Peru–?, Peru), priest and writer. He is the author of four dialogues, *Los coloquios de la verdad* (c. 1583; Colloquies on Truth), that deal with the issues and consequences of the Conquest of Peru. In the dialogues a hermit, a Spaniard, and an Indian discuss both the reasons for and difficulties in converting the Indians to Christianity. The *Coloquios* contain numerous facts about the culture and customs of the Indians; the harm, grievances and injustices they have suffered are also enumerated. An apologist for the Indians, Quiroga was influenced by the passionate anti-imperialism of Bartolomé de las *Casas's chronicle, *Relación de la destrucción de las Indias* (1552). *See also* Black Legend.

BIBLIOGRAPHY

Primary Texts

Coloquios de la Verdad. Ed. Julián Zarco Cuevas. Biblioteca Colonial Americana, 7. Seville: Centro Oficial de Estudios Americanistas de Sevilla, 1922.

Criticism

Apuntes biográficos de Pedro Quiroga. No editor. Buenos Aires: Buffel and Bosch, 1887.

Helen H. Reed

QUIROGA PLA, José María (1902, Madrid–1955, Geneva), Spanish essayist and poet. Most of his essays remain uncollected, spread among reviews and newspapers. He also wrote poems, many appearing first in the poetry magazine *Litoral*, of Málaga, and collected in the volume *Baladas para acordeón* (n.d.; Ballads for an Accordion). He was a son-in-law of *Unamuno.

QUIRÓS, Pedro de (159?, Seville–1657, Madrid), poet in the **conceptismo* tradition. He was one of the first to join the Comunidad de Clérigos Menores (Community of Minor Clerics) when the order first appeared in Seville in 1624. He became provost of the College of San Carlos of the U of Salamanca and later was elected inspector general of the order in Spain.

Quirós is known primarily as a poet, although his poetry remained unpublished until 1887, when it appeared in *Bibliófilos Andaluces* with a prologue by Marcelino *Menéndez y Pelayo. The collection is entitled *Poesías divinas y humanas del Padre Pedro de Quirós* (Divine and Worldly Poetry by Father Pedro de Quirós), and contains sonnets, songs and madrigals in the style of the poets from Madrid rather than those from Seville. His religious poems are similar to those of Lope de *Vega, and he also translated hymns from the Latin. The sonnet "A Itálica" (To Italica) and the madrigal "Tórtola amante que en el roble moras" (Turtledove Who Lives in the Oak Tree) have acquired fame by being included in several anthologies of Golden Age poetry. The poetry of Quirós often contrasts worldly beauty and death, illustrating the illusory nature of everything in this world. He also attempts to show that *desengaño* (knowledge of truth) is most important.

Quirós occasionally wrote prose as well. While in Salamanca, he wrote *Presentación real* (Royal Presentation), an account of the tribute paid to King Philip IV by the U of Salamanca upon his death. He also edited a work called *Comentarios al profeta Jonás* (Commentaries on the Prophet, Jonas).

BIBLIOGRAPHY

Primary Texts

Obras. In BAE 32.

Criticism

Wardropper, Bruce. *Spanish Poetry of the Golden Age*. New York: Appleton-Century-Crofts, 1971.

Nina Shecktor

R

RADA Y DELGADO, Juan de Dios de la (1827, Almería–1901, Madrid), archaeologist, professor at the U of Madrid, writer. He was director of the Archaeological Museum and a member of the Academies of History and of Fine Arts. He directed *La Revista Universitaria* (1856–61; The University Review), and contributed to newspapers such as *El Teatro* (The Theater) and *La Ilustración Española y Americana* (The Illustrated Spanish and American News). In co-operation with *Amador de los Ríos, he wrote *Historia de la villa y Corte de Madrid* (1861–64; A History of Madrid, Township and Court); and with Aureliano *Fernández Guerra, *Historia de España* (History of Spain) up to the Visigothic period. He is also author of *Historia de la orden de María Luisa* (1865; History of the Order of Maria Luisa), *Mujeres célebres de España y Portugal* (1868; Illustrious Women of Spain and Portugal). *Crónica de la provincia de Granada* (1869; Chronicle of the Province of Granada), and *Frescos de Goya en San Antonio de la Florida* (1888; Goya Frescos at the San Antonio de la Florida Church). Rada also wrote some poetry, the historical novels *Don Ramón Berenguer el viejo* (1858; Don Ramón Berenguer, the Old One) and *Wifredo II, conde de Barcelona* (1865; Wifredo II, Count of Barcelona), and a drama entitled *Cristóbal Colón* (1863; Christopher Columbus).

BIBLIOGRAPHY

Primary Texts

Cristóbal Colón. Drama. Madrid: José Rodríguez, 1863.
Don Ramón Berenguer el Viejo. Novela histórica original. Barcelona: Manero, 1858.
Frescos de Goya en San Antonio de la Florida. Madrid: Tello, 1888.
Mujeres célebres de España y Portugal. 2 vols. Barcelona: Víctor Pérez, 1867–68.
Wifredo II, Conde de Barcelona. Novela histórica. Madrid: Jerez, 1865.

Salvador García Castañeda

RAIMUNDO, Archbishop (?, Gascony–1152, Toledo), Archbishop of Toledo and lord chancellor to Alphonse VII of Spain. A cleric of the French Cluniac order, he founded the famous *Escuela de Traductores de Toledo (School of

Translators of Toledo), gathering a great library of Oriental mss. and organizing a team of scholars, translators and scribes, making available for the first time in medieval Europe Latin versions of Arabic and Hebrew mss. on philosophy, astronomy, mathematics, medicine, alchemy, etc. These included Arabic translations of Persian and Indian works and of Greek writings previously lost to Western tradition.

The most famous of Raimundo's translators, Domingo González (Dominicus Gundisalvi), Archdeacon of Segovia, and Juan Hispalense (Johannes Hispalensis), collaborated in what seems to have been a standard translating procedure: from the Arabic, Hispalense produced an intermediate translation, probably oral, in the Spanish vernacular; González converted the vernacular to Latin. The philosophical writings of Avicena (Avicenna), Avicebrón (Ibn Gabirol) and Algacel (al-Gazzali) were among the works translated by this team. The Averroist movement in Europe is attributed to the dissemination of the writings of Averroës through the School of Translators. *See also* Hispano-Judaic Literature.

BIBLIOGRAPHY

Criticism

Brasa Díez, Mariano. "Traducciones y Traductores Toledanos." *Estudios filosóficos* 62 (1974): 129–37.

González Palencia, Angel. *El Arzobispo don Raimundo de Toledo*. Barcelona: Labor, 1942.

Kathleen L. Kirk

RAMÓN Y CAJAL, Santiago (1852, Petilla de Aragón, Navarra–1934, Madrid), physician, histologist, scientist who received the Nobel Prize (1906) in recognition of his discoveries in neurology. Although his fame rests mainly on scientific achievements, his contribution to the world of letters is not negligible. An enlightened man of ideas, he was akin to his contemporaries Francisco *Giner de los Ríos, Joaquín *Costa and *Pérez Galdós of liberal ideology and for that reason has been considered a precursor of the *Generation of 1898. His non-scientific work encompasses short stories, anecdotes, thoughts and biographical memoirs. Literary and enlightening are his short stories *Cuentos de vacaciones* (1905; Vacation Stories) and his essays *Charlas de café, pensamientos, anécdotas y confidencias* (1920; Café Babble, Thoughts, Anecdotes and Confidences). His memoirs transcend simple reminiscences, providing reflections on Spanish matters as well as a scientist's intellectual testimony: *Recuerdos de mi vida* (1901–23; *Recollections of My Life*, 1966), *Cuando yo era niño* (1921; My Childhood), *El mundo visto a los ochenta años* (1934; A View of the World at Eighty). Reflections on Spain include *Reglas y consejos sobre la investigación científica* (1897; *Precepts and Counsels on Scientific Investigation*, 1951), *Psicología de D. Quijote y el quijotismo* (1905; Psychology of d. Quixote and Quixotism).

BIBLIOGRAPHY

Primary Texts

Obras literarias completas. Madrid: Aguilar, 1950.
Charlas de café. Madrid: Aguilar, 1948.
Mi infancia y juventud. Madrid: Calpe, 1976.
El mundo visto a los ochenta años. New York: Arno, 1979.
Recuerdos de mi vida. Madrid: Alianza, 1981.

English Translations

Precepts and Counsels on Scientific Investigation. Tr. Cyril B. Cournville. Mountain View, CA: Pacific Press, 1951.
Recollections of my Life. Tr. Horne Craigie. Cambridge, MA: MIT, 1966.

Criticism

Albarracín Teulón, Agustín. *Santiago Ramón y Cajal o la pasión de España*. Barcelona: Labor, 1978.
Cannon, Dorothy. *Explorer of the Human Brain*. New York: Schuman, 1949.
Laín Entralgo, Pedro. *Nuestro Cajal*. Madrid: Rivadeneyra, 1967.
Tzitsikas, Helene. *Ramón y Cajal: su obra literaria*. México: De Andrea, 1965.

Pilar Sáenz

RAMOS CARRIÓN, Miguel (1845, Zamora–1915, Madrid), Spanish journalist and dramatist. He began his literary career as a collaborator with *El Museo Universal* under the direction of *Hartzenbusch, and later founded the weekly *Las Disciplinas*, to which he contributed under the pseudonym Boabdil el Chico. His first dramatic work, *Un sarao y una soiree* (1866; A Spanish Evening Party and a [French] Soiree), was written for a troupe of *Arderius. He wrote a number of books for **zarzuelas* (musical comedy or light opera), including *La tempestad* (1882; The Storm) and *La bruja* (1887; The Witch) among the more memorable. He also wrote for the **género chico* stage (featuring short comic or satiric plays usually of one act) with *El chaleco blanco* (1890; The White Vest) and *Agua, azucarillos y aguardiente* (1897; Water, Sugar Cubes and Liqueur). Among his full-length comedies are *Los señoritos* (1874; The Playboys), *Cada loco con su tema* (1874; Each Madman Has His Theme), *León y leona* (1874; Lion and Lioness), and *El noveno mandamiento* (1879; The Ninth Commandment). He also wrote the book for the theatrical review *Los sobrinos del capitán Grant* (1877; Capt. Grant's Nephews), and collaborated on various other musicals and stage productions with authors such as *Camprodón, Vital Aza, *Estremera, Campo Arana and Lustonó.

RAMOS OREA, Tomás (1936, Madrid–), Spanish poet and professor. His collections of poetry include *La fuente o Ella* (1962; She or the Fountain), *Amor venidero* (1964; Future Love), and *Vocación y destino* (1968; Vocation and Destiny). Other works are textbooks, a poetry anthology, and a collection of prose essays in the nature of brief memoirs, *En marcha (viajes y reflexiones* (1968; Underway [Travels and Reflections]).

RAMOS PÉREZ, Vicente (1919, Guadamar del Segura, Alicante–), poet, essayist, historian and professor. A prolific writer in several fields, Ramos has published books of poetry, has written biographies of Alicantine authors, and has contributed to historical studies of his native region. His most important literary criticism focuses on Gabriel *Miró.

BIBLIOGRAPHY

Primary Texts

Destino de tu ausencia. Valencia: Institución Alfonso el Magnánimo, Diputación Provincial de Valencia, 1957. Poetry.

Gabriel Miró. Alicante: Instituto de Estudios Alicantinos, 1979. Biography.

La Guerra Civil 1936–1939 en la provincia de Alicante. 3 vols. Alicante: Biblioteca Alicantina, 1973–74. History.

El mundo de Gabriel Miró. 2nd ed. Madrid: Gredos, 1970. Criticism.

Rafael Altamira. Madrid: Alfaguara, 1968. Biography.

Roberta Johnson

RAZÓN DE AMOR (Lyric Poem on the Subject of Love) (early thirteenth c.). Also known as the *Razón feita de amor*, this anonymous work is considered the earliest extant lyric poem in Castilian. It is found in the Bibliothèque Nationale, Paris, in a *ms.* together with the **Denuestos del agua y el vino* (Debate between Water and Wine) which follows the poem. Although signed by Lupus de Morus, it is likely that he was the scribe rather than the author. The language of the poem contains numerous forms from the Aragonese dialect and the lines are principally eight or nine syllables long. Of a popular rather than learned style, it tells of two lovers who meet, declare themselves and eventually part in one brief encounter. Although probably derived from a French poem, the *Razón* has its own unique, delicate sensuality, grace and colorful imagery.

BIBLIOGRAPHY

Primary Texts

Jacob, Alfred B. "Edition and Evaluation of the *Razón de amor*." Diss., U of Pennsylvania, 1956.

See also English Translations.

English Translations

"The *Razón de amor*: An Old Spanish Lyrical Poem of the 13th Century." Ed. and tr. Charles C. Stebbins. *Allegorica* 2.1 (1977): 144–71. Spanish and English texts.

Criticism

de Ferraresi, A. C. "Locus Amoenus y vergel visionario en *Razón de amor*." *HR* 42 (1974): 173–83.

DeLey, Margo. "Provençal Biographical Tradition and the *Razón de amor*." *JHP* 4 (1979–80): 1–17.

Impey, O. T. "La estructura unitaria de *Razón de amor*." *JHP* 1 (1976): 1–24.
Van Antwerp, M. "*Razón de amor* and the popular tradition." *RPH* 32 (1978): 1–17.

Lucy Sponsler

REBOLLEDO, Bernardino de (1597, León–1676, Madrid), didactic poet. Before beginning his writing career, Rebolledo spent the major portion of his life as a soldier and diplomat. He took part in the fight against the Turks and in the Thirty Years' War. Later he spent twenty years in Denmark as ambassador from Spain. In 1638, the king of Spain conferred upon him the title of count as reward for his many years of loyal service. Since most of his poetry was written abroad, its style has little in common with the movements prevalent in Spain at the time. He especially admired and attempted to imitate the *Argensola brothers. Because of its didactic nature, Rebolledo's work was later praised by the dramatist Leandro Fernández de *Moratín.

In 1650, his poetry was published in a collection entitled *Ocios* (Idle Pastimes). In one long poem called *Selva militar y política* (1652; The Military and Political Jungle), Rebolledo explains his military and diplomatic theories. Another long narrative poem, *Selvas dánicas* (1655; Danish Jungles), uses the genealogy of the Danish royal family as a pretext for a diatribe against Lutheranism and glorification of the Catholic church. The poem proclaims the glory of the family while they were Catholic, and it is believed that his unequivocal criticism of their conversion to Protestantism led to his dismissal as ambassador. Rebolledo also wrote religious poetry, including the third volume of his Obras poéticas (1660–61, Poetry) which is called *Rimas Sacras* (1661; Sacred Rhymes), and translations into Spanish of the Psalms.

His only attempts at other genres are the *Discurso sobre la hermosura y el amor* (1652; Discourse on Beauty and Love), one of the last manifestations of *Renaissance Neoplatonism, and the *Entremés de los maridos conformes* (Interlude of Agreeable Husbands), which was included in the *Obras poéticas*, published in Antwerp in 1660. *See also* Platonism; Siglo de Oro.

BIBLIOGRAPHY

Primary Texts

Ocios, and other works. In *BAE*, 42 (1857) and 35 (1855).

Criticism

Río Alonso, F. *El Conde de Rebolledo y sus obras*. Leon: Religiosa de Jesús López, 1927.

Nina Shecktor

REFRÁN. *See Refranero*

REFRANERO (Book of Proverbs). These book-length collections of *refranes* (proverbs) comprise an exceedingly rich aspect of the Spanish language. The age-old, pithy utterances of popular wisdom, often rhythmic and with rhyme, became very popular in *Siglo de Oro Spanish literature. While it is difficult and dangerous to typecast a Spanish profile on the basis of the nation's proverbs, A. A. Parker has pointed to a unique "astringent humor" as the essential way in which many subjects are approached by the *refrán*.

The first published collection of proverbs in Spain was compiled by the Marqués de *Santillana and titled *Refranes que dizen las viejas tras el fuego* (1508; *The Proverbs of Sir James López de Mendoza*, 1579). It was followed by Pedro Vallés's *Libro de refranes* (1594; Book of Proverbs), which contained 4,300 *refranes*. The most important source for sixteenth- and seventeenth-c. writers was Hernán *Núñez de Guzmán's *Refranes o proverbios en romance* (1555; Proverbs in the Romance Language), which was reprinted eight times. Subsequent collections include Gonzalo *Correas's *Vocabulario de refranes* (c. 1626; Proverb Vocabulary), J. M. *Sbarbi's ten-volume *El refranero general español* (1874–78; General Spanish Proverb Book), *Coll y Vehí's *Refranes del "Quijote"* (1874; *Quijote* Proverbs), and *Rodríguez Marín's multivolume efforts which span almost two decades of research, and are listed in the bibliography.

BIBLIOGRAPHY

Primary Texts

Coll y Vehí, J. *Los refranes del "Quijote."* Barcelona: Diario de Barcelona, 1874.

Correas, G. *Vocabulario de refranes y frases proverbiales.* Ed. L. Combet. Bordeaux: U of Bordeaux, 1967.

Núñez, H. *Refranes, o proverbios en romance. . . .* Ed., study, sel., notes F. Sáinz de Robles. Madrid: Aguilar, 1950.

Rodríguez Marín, F. *Más de 21,000 refranes castellanos.* Madrid: RABM, 1926.

———. *Dos mil seiscientos refranes más.* Madrid: RABM, 1930.

———. *Los 6,666 refranes de una última rebusca.* Madrid: Bermejo, 1934.

———. *Todavía diez mil setecientos refranes más.* Madrid: Prensa Española, 1941.

Santillana, M. de. *Refranes que dizen las viejas tras el fuego.* Ed. U. Cronan. In *RH* 25 (1911): 134–76.

Sbarbi, J. M. *Refranero general español.* Madrid: Gómez Fuentenebro, 1874–78.

Vallés, P. *Libro de refranes copilado por el orden del a.b.c.* Madrid: García, 1917. Facs.

English Translations

The Book of Spanish Proverbs. Sel., tr. C. H. Calloway. New York: Spanish American Printing, 1944.

The Proverbs of Sir James López de Mendoza. Tr. Barnabe Googe. London: Watkins, 1579.

Criticism

Parker, A. A. *The Humor of Spanish Proverbs.* Cambridge: Heffer and Sons, 1963.

Rosal, F. del. *La razón de algunos refranes.* Intro., ed., notes B. Bussell Thompson. London: Tamesis, 1975.

RÉGIO, José (1901, Vilo do Condo, Portugal–1969, Vilo do Condo), pseudonym of José Maria dos Reis Pereira. Portuguese poet, novelist, dramatist, essayist. Although he studied Romance philology, he became interested in poetry while still a student, publishing his first book of poetry, *Poemas de Deus e do diabo* (Poems of God and the Devil) in 1925. He was a co-founder of the modernist literary magazine *Presença* with João Gaspar Simões and Antonio Branquinho da *Fonseca. The duality indicated by the title of his first collection of poems is part of a constant dualism or conflict between good and evil, life and death, sanity and madness, and a variety of moral dichotomies found in Régio's works. *Biografia* (1929), *Críticos e criticados* (1936; Critics and the Criticized), *Em torno da expressão artística* (1940; Concerning Artistic Expression), *Pequena historia da moderna poesia portuguesa* (1941; Brief History of Modern Portuguese Poetry), *Ensaios de interpretação crítica* (1964; Essays in Critical Interpretation), and *Três ensaios sobre arte* (1967; Three Essays on Art) are among his professional treatises.

In his novels, Régio pays special attention to the rural gentry, people who live in the only big house in small, sleepy villages, emphasizing psychological aspects, moral issues, timeless virtues, and interpersonal relationships, and including large doses of local color. His style is somewhat dated, his rhetoric a thing of the past, but they harmonize with his traditional and conservative values. He created a major novelistic cycle, a pentalogy with the overall title *A velha casa* (1945–66; The Old House), comprised of *Uma gota de sangue* (1945; A Drop of Blood); *As raízes do futuro* (1947; Roots of the Future); *Os avisos do destino* (1953; Destiny's Warnings); *As monstruosidades vulgares* (1960; Everyday Monstrosities); and *Vidas são vidas* (1966; Lives are Lives). His preoccupation with good and evil is especially evident in the novel, *O príncipe com orelhas de burro* (1942; The Prince with Donkey's Ears) and a theatrical work, *Benilde; ou, A Virgem Mãe* (1947; Benilde, or the Virgin Mother). He was especially interested in feminine characters, and devoted one book of short fiction to them, *Histórias de mulheres* (1946; Stories about Women). Other titles are *Jogo da cabra cega* (1934; Blind-man's Bluff); *As encruzilhadas de Deus* (1936; The Crossroads of God); *António Botto e o amor* (1938; Botto and Love); *Mas Deus é grande* (1945; But God is Great); *El Rei Sebastião* (1949; King Sebastian); *A salvação do mundo* (1954; Salvation of the World); *Tres peças em um acto* (1957; Three One-Act Plays); *Filho do homem* (1961; The Son of Man); *Há mais mundos* (1962; There are Other Worlds); *Cântico suspenso* (1968; Suspended Canticle); *Música ligeira* (1970; Light Music); *Confissão dum homem religioso* (1971; Confessions of a Religious Man).

BIBLIOGRAPHY

Parker, J. M. *Three 20th-Century Portuguese Poets.* Johannesburg: Witwatersrand UP, 1960. 48–64.

REINA, Casiodoro de (c. 1520, Seville?/Reina, Extremadura–1594, Frankfurt, Germany), theologian, priest, Protestant reformer. After attending the U of Seville he joined the Hieronymite order, living at the monastery of San Isidro del Campo. There, he became a strong proponent of Protestant beliefs. The *Inquisition viewed the activities of this and other "new" groups with increasing suspicion; in 1557, Reina and the ten or eleven others in his conventicle made the decision to flee Seville. Many were caught and burned at the stake, imprisoned, etc.; Reina, however, succeeded in reaching Geneva. By 1559 he was in England, conducting informal services for a group of fellow Spanish religious refugees. He also began translation of the Bible into vernacular Spanish. Published in 1569, it is the first complete Bible in Spanish to be translated from original tongues—an amazing feat for one individual. The translation attests to Reina's fine command of Hebrew, Syriac, Latin and Greek, and continues to be the translation used by most Spanish Protestants to this day.

Reina was persecuted and harassed for his religious convictions the rest of his life—charges of Servetism (Miguel *Servet), etc., resurfaced time and again. Apart from some correspondence in French, the balance of Reina's letters and a few extant publications are in Latin. They bear witness to the breadth of his knowledge and to his keen interest in questions of theology. *See also* Bible in Spain; Corro, Antonio del.

BIBLIOGRAPHY

Primary Text

La Santa Biblia: Antiguo y Nuevo Testamento: Antigua Versión de Casiodoro de Reina. . . . . Charlotte, NC: C. D. Stempley, 1977.

Criticism

Kinder, A. G. *Casiodoro de Reina.* London: Tamesis, 1975.

Maureen Ihrie

REINA, Manuel (1856, Córdoba–1905, Madrid), Spanish poet. Born in Puente Genil, Córdoba, Reina studied law in Seville, Granada, and Madrid. An active member of the Liberal party, he served several terms as a representative to the Spanish Parliament. His poetry appears in press as early as 1874, with the most important following a few years later: *Andantes y allegros* (1877), *Cromos y acuarelas* (1878; Lithographs and Watercolors), *La vida inquieta* (1894; Unsettled Life), *Poemas paganos* (1896; Pagan Poems), and *El jardín de los poetas* (1899; The Garden of the Poets). The initial works show the influence of *Bécquer, Heine, and the Romantic and post-Romantic writers. The later poetry of Reina, an avid reader with a solid knowledge of French, English, and German writers of the period, incorporates themes, meters, lexical items, and attitudes that are decidedly Parnassian and pre-Modernist. With Salvador *Rueda, Reina represents the transition from *Romanticism to *Modernism.

BIBLIOGRAPHY

Primary Text

Sus mejores versos. Madrid: n.p., 1928.

Criticism

Aguilar Piñal, Francisco. *La obra poética de Manuel Reina.* Madrid: Nacional, 1968.
Cardwell, Richard. *La vida inquieta.* Exeter: U of Exeter P, 1978.

Cossío, María José de. *Cincuenta años de poesía española*. Madrid: Espasa-Calpe, 1960.
Díaz-Plaja, Guillermo. *Modernismo frente a noventa y ocho*. Madrid: Espasa-Calpe, 1966.

Mary Lee Bretz

REINA DE MALLORCA, La (1313, ?–1346, ?), poet. *Milà i Fontanals identifies her as Costança d'Aragó, daughter of Alfons el Benigne of Catalunya-Aragó and sister of Pere III el Ceremoniós. While most critics agree with this identification, Martín de Riquer believes she could be Violant de Vilaragut, the second wife of Jaume III de Mallorca. Only a few examples of her work are extant.

BIBLIOGRAPHY

Primary Texts

Antología General de la Poesía Catalana. Ed. J. M. Castellet and J. Molas. Barcelona: Edicions 62, 1979. 25–26.
Manat d'homenatge a La Reina Costança de Mallorca. Barcelona: Esteve Albert, 1975. 5–8.

Kathleen McNerney

REINOSO, Félix José (1772, Seville–1841, Madrid), priest, poet. His neo-classical verse was published with the title *Poesías de una Academia de las Letras Humanas* (1797; Poems of a [Classical] Literature Academy). His poem "La inocencia perdida" (1804; Lost Innocence) received a prize in a poetry competition.

Reinoso must also be remembered for his defense of the *afrancesados*—Spaniards who cooperated with the French invaders—titled *Examen de los delitos de infidelidad a la patria imputados a los españoles sometidos bajo la dominación francesa* (1816; Examination of the Crimes of Treason to the Nation Imputed to Spaniards Placed under French Rule).

BIBLIOGRAPHY

Primary Texts

Examen de los delitos de infidelidad. . . . Auch: Duprat, 1816.
"La inocencia perdida." In BAE 67.
Obras. Ed. A. Martín Villa and F. de B. Palomo. 2 vols. Seville: n.p., 1872–79.

REIS D'ORIENT, Libre dels tres. *See Reys D'Orient, Libre dels tres*

REJÓN DE SILVA, Diego Antonio (1740, Murcia–1796, Murcia), politician, writer. Secretary of state for Charles III, he wrote a *picaresque narrative, *A-venturas de Juan Luis* (1781; Adventures of Juan Luis), using the pseudonym Don Diego Ventura Rexón y Lucas. Also his are a *Fábula de Céfalo y Procris* (1763; Fable of Cephalus and Procris) and a didactic poem, *La pintura* (1786; Painting).

BIBLIOGRAPHY

Primary Texts

Aventuras de Juan Luis. Madrid: n.p., 1781.

La pintura. Poema didáctico en tres cantos. Segovia: Espinosa de los Monteros, 1786.

Poesías. In BAE 67.

RELACIÓN, literary term. It is used to denote historical narratives, or chronicles. *Relación* may also apply to a long narrative speech in a play.

REMÓN, Alonso (1565?, Cuenca–1632, ?), chronicler for the Mercedarian order and dramatist. Not much is known about his life before he entered the U of Alcalá in 1577. In 1601, he signed himself "licentiate," and in 1606, "Doctor Remón." It is unknown exactly when he took vows, but his name appears as a friar of the order in 1605, and by 1612, he is referred to as general chronicler of the order. His first book was *De la concepción puríssima de Nuestra Señora, ocho discursos predicables* (1616; Eight Preachable Discourses on the Immaculate Conception of Our Lady). For writing two parts of the history of the order (the first part was published in 1619, and the second part was published posthumously in 1633) and for other services, Remón received the title of "maestro" (master) of the order, probably in 1629. Also published posthumously was Remón's edition of Bernal *Díaz del Castillo's *Historia verdadera de la conquista de Nueva España* (1632; True History of the Conquest of New Spain).

Of his dramatic production, there are nine extant works, among them the *Auto de el hijo pródigo* (1599; Play of the Prodigal Son) and the *Comedia de las tres mujeres en una* (1640; Comedy of the Three Women in One). Some critics believe that Remón also wrote under the pseudonym Antonio de *Liñán y Verdugo. He received praise from both Lope de *Vega and *Cervantes, but his name is never mentioned by his fellow Mercedarian, *Tirso de Molina. In addition, when Tirso succeeded Remón as chronicler of the order, he started from the beginning rather than continue his predecessor's work.

BIBLIOGRAPHY

Primary Text

Comedia de las tres mujeres en una. In *Parte 32 con doce comedias de diferentes autores*. Zaragoza: n.p. 1640.

Criticism

Fernández Nieto, Manuel. *Investigaciones sobre Alonso Remón, dramaturgo desconocido del siglo XVII*. Madrid: Retorno, 1974.

Nina Shecktor

RENAISSANCE IN SPAIN. In Spain, the advent of the Renaissance coincides approximately with the political unification of Aragón and Castille. Even before that, during the reign of John II, there had been signs of deep cultural change, particularly in the generalized adoption of Castilian as a national language. Poets begin to experiment with Italianate meters and forms—heptasyllables and hendecasyllables, sonnets, *silvas*, *octavas reales* (*Octavas)—and at the same time show a willingness to incorporate previously uncongenial themes, such as the courtly love tradition of Petrarch and his followers. These tendencies are generally restricted to the literature of the aristocracy, which felt the effects of the Renaissance from the fifteenth c. onward; in popular literature, by contrast, the medieval modes persist well into the seventeenth c. It is not uncommon during this period to find educated poets using Italianate and traditional forms side by side, fitting each to a subject appropriate to its station—traditional poetic forms for humble or comic themes, and the resonant Italian meters for nobler matters such as courtly love or the affairs of state.

Renaissance Spanish literature differs from what preceded it in several important respects. As in the rest of Europe, there was an enormous increase in both the production and the dissemination of literature, together with a more cosmopolitan willingness to accept foreign literatures as models for imitation—a phenomenon that explains the accelerated pace of literary evolution in these years. A new ideological complexity is also evident, and is reflected in the growing variety of themes used and the appearance (or further development) of literary genres, especially the enormous enrichment of the still-embryonic medieval *theater. The predominance of the educated (*culto*) style and its aristocratic trappings, mythological allusions, Latinisms, and rhetorical devices such as hyperbaton were the fruits of a strong humanistic influence; the cultural presence of classical antiquity was more frequent and immediate than in the preceding centuries; the Italianate style, from the time of *Boscán and *Garcilaso de la Vega, predominated in poetry; Latin continued to be used as a literary language, but side by side with a conscious cultivation of the popular tongue, an interest in its lexical forms and expressive capabilities (see Juan de *Valdés, *Diálogo de la lengua*, for a brilliant contemporary discussion of this topic). On the negative side, Renaissance literature lost immediacy and freshness. From very early on, it showed a fatal tendency toward mannerism; tortuous artificiality was always ready to replace spontaneous invention. Writers adopted a dogmatic tone and tended toward a pedantic gravity. Only the very greatest literature of this period was able to achieve the heights of dignity and tranquility without loss of warmth, passion, joy. It is not surprising, in retrospect, that the seeds of seventeenth-c. **culteranismo* and **conceptismo* were already present, if one looks with care, in the very first works of the Spanish Renaissance.

In terms of humanistic learning—perhaps its most characteristic aspect—the Renaissance in Spain may be seen as a brief and glorious parenthesis between two unyieldingly theocentric periods. The generations of the early sixteenth c., influenced by the exuberant Christian *humanism of Erasmus of Rotterdam, were shortly to witness the marshaling of Spain to the cause of the Counter-Reformation; the authors of this latter era lived and worked against the background of a conservative religious movement in which they were, to varying degrees and in varying senses, active participants. The effect on literature was profound.

Apart from the great proliferation of specifically religious works, from the second half of the sixteenth c. onward, we should mention two related phenomena: the frequent appearance of profane literature on religious themes (plays based on the lives of saints, *autos sacramentales* (**auto*), poems like Lope de *Vega's *Isidro* or his *Pastores de Belén*, which take religious material as their source of inspiration but which are meant to be recreational or diverting in the profane sense, rather than oriented toward spiritual life as an ecclesiastic would understand it), and the use of contemporary religious ideas as points of reference in works that otherwise were far removed from any concrete religious purpose. Transpositions **a lo divino* are a striking manifestation of these tendencies. *See also* Erasmism; Italian Literary Influences; Printing in Spain; Siglo de Oro.

BIBLIOGRAPHY

Criticism

Bataillon, Marcel. *Erasmo y España. Estudios sobre la historia espiritual del siglo XVI*. Tr. Antonio Alatorre. Mexico: Fondo de Cultura Económica, 1966.

Blanco Aguinaga, Carlos, Julio Rodríguez Puértolas, and Iris M. Zavala. *Historia social de la literatura española*, vol. 1: *Edad conflictiva*. Madrid: Castalia, 1978. 195–361.

Blecua, J. M. *Sobre poesía de la Edad de Oro*. Madrid: Gredos, 1970.

Clavería, Carlos. "Humanistas creadores." *Historia general de las literaturas hispánicas*. Ed. Guillermo Díaz-Plaja. Barcelona: Barna, 1951. 2:437–88.

Fernández Alvarez, Manuel. *La sociedad española del Renacimiento*. Madrid: Cátedra, 1974.

Gilman, Stephen. "The Problem of the Spanish Renaissance." In *Studies in the Literature of Spain: Sixteenth and Seventeenth Centuries*. Ed. Michael J. Ruggerio. Brockport, NY: Department of Romance Languages, SUNY, 1977.

Jones, R. O. *A Literary History of Spain. The Golden Age. Prose and Poetry. The Sixteenth and Seventeenth Centuries*. London: Benn; New York: Barnes and Noble, 1971.

Pfandl, Ludwig. *Historia de la literatura española en la Edad de Oro*. Barcelona: Gili, 1952.

Río, Angel del. *Historia de la literatura española*. New York: Holt, Rinehart and Winston, 1948. 1: 103–205.

Vossler, Karl. *Introducción a la literatura española del Siglo de Oro*. Madrid: Cruz y Raya, 1934.

William Ferguson

RENGIFO, Juan Díaz (fl. 1592, ?–?), poet. A member of the Jesuits, he composed a very popular poetics, the *Arte poética española con una fertilísima silva de consonantes comunes*... (1592; Spanish Art of Poetry with a Rich Collection of Common Rhymes). He emphasizes the didactic function of poetry, and included a rhyming dictionary. Despite its general lack of originality, it underwent many editions in seventeenth- and eighteenth-c. Spain.

BIBLIOGRAPHY

Primary Text

Arte poética española. Salamanca: Serrano de Vargas, 1592.

RÉPIDE, Pedro de (1882, Madrid–1948, Madrid), novelist, newspaperman, and chronicler of life in Madrid. Although he studied law and philosophy and letters, his literary vocation made him dedicate his total attention to writing. He published his first book, *Las canciones* (1901; Songs), before age nineteen. Shortly afterwards he moved to Paris, where he audited classes at the Sorbonne. The exiled Spanish queen, Isabel II, put him in charge of her library, and he remained in Paris until her death. After he returned to Spain his fame became established when his novel *La enamorada indiscreta* (1921; The Indiscreet Lover) won the literary prize offered by the newspaper *El Liberal*. From then on he became a regular contributor to this and several other papers. Through their pages he became known as an interpreter of the history, life, and customs of Madrid. Because of his colorful and *castizo* style he was regarded as a master of *costumbrismo*. His worth was recognized when the *Ayuntamiento* proclaimed him "Cronista Oficial de la Villa." With the Civil War (1936) Répide went into exile in Latin America; he returned in 1947, the year before his death.

Répide's literary value rests on his work as a chronicler and interpreter of life in Madrid. Sáinz de Robles considers his works as equal to those of *Mesonero Romanos and Fígaro (Mariano José de *Larra). Some of his best sketches are collected in the posthumous *Las calles de Madrid* (1972; Madrid Streets), but many of his earlier full-length works are also dedicated to Madrid, for example, the novels *Del Rastro a Maravillas* (1907; From the Flea-Market to Maravillas Street), a blend of picaresque and romantic themes, and *Los cohetes de la verbena* (1911; The Fireworks at the *verbena*); the one-act plays *La casa de la Araceli* (1911; Araceli's House) and *Cadena de rosas* (1913; Chain of Roses); the essay *La corte de las Españas* (1913; The Court of Spain); and the series of lectures *Imágenes de Madrid* (1926; Images of Madrid). In addition, Répide wrote on the "Restauración" period of Alfonso XII's reign, and published a biography of Isabel II, where, once again, the protagonists are the city and its atmosphere rather than the monarchs. He wrote about his travels in *Del Mar Negro al Caribe* (From the Black Sea to the Caribbean) and about the Civil War in *Memorias de un aparecido (1936–1937)* (1937; Memoirs of a Ghost).

BIBLIOGRAPHY

Primary Texts

Las calles de Madrid. Ed., prol. F. Romero. 2nd ed. Madrid: Aguado, 1972.
Los cohetes de la verbena. Madrid: Pueyo, 1911.
La enamorada indiscreta. Madrid: Pueyo, 1921.
Imágenes de Madrid. Madrid: Blas, 1926.
Del rastro a Maravillas. Madrid: Nuestra raza, 1935.
Memorias de un aparecido. Caracas: Tipografía Americana, 1937.

Criticism

Cansinos Assens, Rafael. "Los madrileñistas." In *La nueva literatura,* vol. 2: *Las escuelas.* Madrid: Páez, 1925. 159–79.
Romero, Federico. Prólogo to *Las calles de Madrid.* By Pedro de Répide. 2nd ed. Madrid: Afrodisio Aguado, 1972.
Sáinz de Robles, Federico. *Ensayo de un Diccionario de la Literatura.* Madrid: Aguilar, 1964. 2: 964–65.

María A. Salgado

RESENDE, García de (c. 1470, Evora–1536, ?), verse anthologist, poet, historian. Following the example of the 1511 **Cancionero general* (General Songbook), García de Resende published a collection of poems by 286 Portuguese lyricists titled *Cancioneiro geral* (1516; General Songbook). Twenty-nine of the poets included poems both in Portuguese and Castilian. The majority of these poems follow the allegorical and Italianate style of *Mena and the Marquis of *Santillana. Resende also wrote a *Chronica de D. João II* (n.d.; Chronicle of John II), a *Miscelánea* (Miscellany), and a *Breve memorial de peccados* (Brief Book on Sins). *See also* Cancionero.

BIBLIOGRAPHY

Primary Texts

Cancioneiro geral. 3 vols. Stuttgart: Literarischer, 1846–52.
Cancioneiro geral. New York: De Vinne, 1904. Facs. by A. M. Huntington.
Chronica de el-rei D. João II. Lisbon: Escriptorio, 1902. Also contains *Miscelánea.*

Criticism

Scudieri Ruggieri, J. *Il Canzoniere di Resende.* Geneva: Olschki, 1931.

REVELACIÓN O VISIÓN DE UN ERMITAÑO (Revelation, or Vision of a Hermit), anonymous moral-didactic debate poem from the late fourteenth c. (1382, according to the poem's first stanza), written in **arte mayor*. Deriving from the Latin *Visio Philiberti*, its theme is that of the **Disputa del alma y el cuerpo* (Debate of the Soul and the Body). The influence of Dante is apparent in the writer's use of allegory and asceticism to recount the dream of the hermit. *See also* Italian Literary Influences.

BIBLIOGRAPHY

Primary Text

"Revelación o visión de un ermitaño." *Poesía española medieval.* Ed. Manuel Alvar. Hispánicos Universales 14. Madrid: Cuspa, 1978. 393–97.

Criticism

Sugarman, Miriam DeCosta. ''The Debate between the Body and the Soul in Spanish Medieval Literature.'' *DA* 28 (1967): 1829A, Johns Hopkins U.

Kathleen L. Kirk

REVILLA Y MORENO, Manuel de la (1846, Madrid–1881, El Escorial), literary critic and essayist. Revilla graduated from the U of Madrid with a degree in law, philosophy, and literature. He was co-founder of the magazines *El Amigo del Pueblo* and *La Ética* and a contributor to *El Pueblo* and *El Globo*. An outstanding orator, he gave lectures at the *Ateneo in Madrid. From 1876 until his premature death in 1881, he held the chair of literature at the U of Madrid. In 1876 he entered the debate on science in Spain against Marcelino *Menéndez y Pelayo. Most of his articles on philosophy and literature appeared in two of the most important magazines of the time: *Revista de España* and *Revista Contemporánea*. The latter articles, along with other works, were collected posthumously in *Obras* (1883; Complete Works) and published by the Ateneo of Madrid. A sharp, penetrating, and argumentative critic who was feared and revered among his contemporaries, Revilla manifested an ideological restlessness which originated principally from the philosophies of *Krausism, neo-Kantism, and positivism and which caused much controversy and debate among Spanish intellectuals. His early death prevented the full development of his potential in his philosophical and literary writings.

BIBLIOGRAPHY

Primary Texts

Críticas. 2 vols. Burgos: D. Timoteo Arnaiz, 1884.
Obras. Madrid: El Ateneo Científico, Literario y Artístico, 1883.

Criticism

Blanco García, P. Francisco. *La literatura española en el siglo XIX*. 2nd ed. Madrid: Saenz de Jubera Hermanos, 1910.
Cejador Y Frauca, Julio. *Historia de la lengua y literatura españolas*. vol. 11. Madrid: RABM, 1915–22.

Gilbert Paolini

REY DE ARTIEDA, Andrés (1549, Valencia–1613, Valencia), soldier, poet, dramatist. In addition to a successful military career for over 30 years, Rey de Artieda (as *Centinela* [Sentinel]) was one of the most distinguished members of the *Academia de los Nocturnos* (Academy of Night Revelers). His precocious poetic talent was praised by Gaspar Gil *Polo in *Canto de Turia* (Song of Turia) when Artieda was only fourteen. In 1605, he published various pieces in *Discursos, epístolas y epigramas de Artemidoro* (Discourses, Epistles and Epigrams of Artemidoro). His sonnets are particularly powerful.

Although various titles are attributed to him (*Los encantos de Merlín,* The Spells of Merlin; *El príncipe vicioso*, The Decadent Prince; **Amadís de Gaula*,

Amadis of Gaul), Artieda's dramatic reputation rests on *Los Amantes* (The Lovers), his only extant drama. It is based on the popular legend of the lovers of Teruel, which later inspired works by *Tirso, *Pérez de Montalbán, *Hartzenbusch, etc. Divided into four acts, Artieda's work is the first serious consideration in Spanish drama of the fatal consequences of obstructed love. *See also* Academia; Amantes de Teruel, Leyenda de los.

BIBLIOGRAPHY

Primary Texts

Los amantes. Ed. Agustín González de Amezúa. Madrid: La Arcadia, 1947.

Poesías. In *BAE* 17, and 25.

Criticism

Weiger, John C. *The Valencian Dramatists of Spain's Golden Age*. TWAS 371. Boston: Twayne, 1976.

REYES, Matías de los (1581, Borox, Toledo–after 1640, Madrid), writer. Born to an undistinguished **converso* family, Matías evidently moved to Madrid at an early age and subsequently claimed that city as his birthplace. His extant works include six plays, an **auto*, and an ambitious piece of prose titled *El Menandro* (1630), which combines characteristics of the Byzantine novel, the *comedia*, and the Italian *novella*. Carroll Johnson argues that despite the mediocrity of his literary production as a whole, Reyes does merit study for his "artistic presentation of spiritual values" and the overriding importance he allots to the role of form in his writing.

BIBLIOGRAPHY

Primary Text

El Menandro. Ed. Emilio Cotarelo y Mori. In *Colección Selecta de Antiguas Novelas Españolas*. vol. 12. Madrid: Bibliófilos españoles, 1909.

Criticism

Johnson, Carroll B. *Matías de los Reyes and the Craft of Fiction*. Berkeley and Los Angeles: U of California P, 1973. Contains biography, bibliography, and discussion of extant works.

REYES AGUILAR, Arturo (1864, Málaga–1913, Málaga), Spanish short story writer and novelist of the regional Andalusian school. His works emphasized local color, and "typical" scenes such as the courtship through wrought-iron grill-work, flamenco music and dancing, and quarrels motivated by jealousy, with large doses of folklore and the picturesque. He was also a poet, with such titles as *Intimas* (1891; Intimate Poems), *Otoñales* (1904; Autumn Verse), *Béticas* (1910; Poems of Betis), *Romances andaluces* (1912; Andalusian Ballads), and *Del crepúsculo* (1914; Concerning Twilight), which appeared after his death. *Cosas de mi tierra* (1893; Things about My Land) is a collection of stories of regional inspiration, as are the novels *Cartucherita* (1898; Pistol-Toting Mama),

Sangre torera (1912; Bullfighting Blood), *El niño de los caireles* (1908; The Boy with the Fringes [Wig]), *Sangre gitana* (1911; Gypsy Blood) and *Oro de ley* (1913; "Legally" Gold).

REYS D'ORIENT, Libre dels tres (Book of the Three Kings of the East), anonymous poem of 242 lines of short, irregular verse, in rhyming couplets, probably written between 1225 and 1260. Only the opening verses touch upon the journey of the Magi; the body of the poem recounts the holy family's flight into Egypt, their encounter with two robbers, one evil, one merciful, and ultimately the scene of the Crucifixion, when the son of the good robber accepts Christ and is saved while the son of the bad robber mocks him and is damned. The crux of the poem is the action of divine grace, conferred by Mary in what amounts to a symbolic baptism when she bathes the child of the good robber.

Its meter and some linguistic similarity to the *Vida de Santa *María Egipciaca* (Life of St. Mary of Egypt) suggest French derivation, although there are also definite Aragonese features. The apocryphal Gospels are an important source. Focusing on the poem's actual content, Manuel Alvar has renamed it the *Libro de la infancia y muerte de Jesús* (Book of the Infancy and Death of Jesus). *See also* Hagiography.

BIBLIOGRAPHY

Primary Text

Libro de la infancia y muerte de Jesús (Libre dels tres Reys d'Orient). Ed. Manuel Alvar. Madrid: CSIC, 1965.

Kathleen L. Kirk

RIAL, José Antonio (1911, Cádiz, Spain–), prose writer. He has lived in Venezuela since 1950, where he attained citizenship in 1955. Although not an exile, he considers himself a *transterrado* who left Spain after seven years in prison for political reasons (1936–43) and set down new roots in the American continent. His training in Spain was in business administration, and he also worked as an expert for the Spanish navy. Although he was already interested in intellectual pursuits, it was while he was in jail that he began to study modern and classical languages and to read extensively European and Hispano-Arabic literatures. Once free and in his new American abode he studied journalism in the Universidad Central in Caracas; later on he worked for *El Universal*, whose editor he became in 1966. He is now considered a Venezuelan writer, although he has not lost his Spanish identity; indeed, defense of the Iberian legacy in the Americas is present in all of his writings. He has traveled in the United States, Europe and the Middle East as a journalist and his cosmopolitan outlook adds another dimension to his work. He received an award in the Canary Islands in 1947 for his novel *Gentes de mar* (People of the Sea) and in Caracas in 1951 for his play *Los armadores de la goleta "Ilusión"* (The Building of the Ship *Illusion*). Rial's published books include *Venezuela-Imán* (1955), *Jezabel* (1965) and *La prisión de Fyffes. Memorias carcelarias* (1969; Fyffes Prison. Jailhouse

Memoirs). Another novel, *Segundo Naufragio* (Second Shipwreck), will appear soon. His play *La muerte de García Lorca* (1975; The Death of García Lorca) was to be staged in New York in 1986 in Spanish and in its English translation. His best known novels are *Venezuela-Imán* and *Jezabel*. The former explores the plight of refugees and their effort to rebuild their lives, and finds them all in the same existential vise, whether they are Spaniards, Jews or even defeated German Nazis. Yet, for the group he depicts, Venezuela is a country full of promise and contradictions, a magnet that will allow newcomers neither indifference nor detachment. In *Jezabel* the young Venezuelan protagonist must scrutinize his father's traditional upper-class liberalism and decide whether it is viable in the present circumstances of his country. Simultaneously he comes in contact with two European women who introduce him to Marxism, Oriental philosophies and a lifestyle completely different from that of his Hispanic heritage. At home, his stepfather, an ambitious, enterprising businessman, not lacking in kindness and generosity, embodies the Venezuelan version of American pragmatism; his surname, significantly, is Travieso (mischievous). Rial's message is that Spanish American countries should not renounce their values and identity, but revise them, and be fulfilled in the knowledge that they belong to a historical community of nations that has everything to gain by its fraternal ties. Rial's style is sometimes abstract, and his stories take the reader through a labyrinth of cerebral and emotional paths; his characters are interesting and intense. It is to his credit that although he has a didactic purpose, his narrative is never dogmatic or narrow. A book of journalistic essays, *La destrucción de hispanoamérica* (1976; The Destruction of Spanish America), deals directly with his political ideas in relation to American cultural imperialism and what he perceives as self-destructive anti-Spanish attitudes in Hispanic countries.

BIBLIOGRAPHY

Primary Texts

La destrucción de hispanoamérica. Caracas: Monte Avila, 1976.
La muerte de García Lorca. Caracas: Monte Avila, 1975.
La prisión de Fyffes. Caracas: Monte Avila, 1969.
Venezuela-imán. Esplugas de Llobregat: Plaza y Janés, 1973.

Criticism

Zaleya Kolker, Marielena. *Visiones americanas de los transterrados españoles de 1939*. Madrid: Instituto de Cooperación Iberoamericana, 1985.

Marielena Zelaya Kolker

RIAZA, Luis (1925, Madrid–), playwright and postal worker. Economic demands have always placed limitations on the time and energy he could devote to the theater. Forced idleness resulting from an illness in 1966 effected his return to writing, and a number of prize-winning plays ensued. Riaza's theater is anti-commercial, however, and his works have been produced largely by independent groups and at festivals, especially Sitges. The only major commercial production accorded one of his plays was the 1979 staging of *Retrato de dama con perrito* (1976; Portrait of a Lady with a Little Dog) directed by Miguel Narros at the National Dramatic Center in Madrid. Riaza divides his own dramatic production into two groups—larger scale spectacles and more intimate, personal works. The best known example of the former is *El palacio de los monos* (1978; The Palace of the Monkeys), while the latter would include the aforementioned *Retrato de dama con perrito* and *El desván de los machos y el sótano de las hembras* (1974; The Attic of the Males and the Basement of the Females). Riaza's work is deliberately anti-realistic, anti-literary and anti-poetic (in a manner which produces a kind of inverse poetry). Ritual and ceremony are essential elements of his unique brand of avant-garde drama. His utilization of the grotesque and his visual deformations and emphasis on the plastic arts suggest a strong debt to Ramón del *Valle-Inclán. In his best works, Riaza utilizes women from the popular classes as symbols of the oppressed. Dualities abound, and are reflected in his use of divided sets, the metamorphosis of characters and the instability of sex roles. These devices are directed toward a search for freedom and concomitant examination of the nature of power. Although his audience may be limited, Riaza's evocative language and utilization of stage space to project haunting visual images have established his importance as an innovative voice in *contemporary Spanish theater of the avant-garde.

BIBLIOGRAPHY

Primary Texts

Antígona . . . cerda! Mazurka. Epílogo. Madrid: Colección la Avispa, 1983.

El desván de los machos y el sótano de las hembras y *El palacio de los monos*. Madrid: Cátedra, 1978.

Retrato de dama con perrito. Madrid: Fundamentos, 1976. 2nd version. Madrid: Voz, 1980.

Criticism

Boym, Svetlana. "Los modelos y los copiadores en *Retrato de dama con perrito* de Luis Riaza." *Estreno* 10.1 (Spring 1984): 29–31.

Cazorla, Hazel. "The Theater of Luis Riaza." *Modern Drama* 24.1 (March 1981): 36–43.

Pérez-Stansfield, María Pilar. *Teatro español de posguerra*. Madrid: José Porrúa Turanzas, 1983.

Podol, Peter. "Ritual and Ceremony in Luis Riaza's Theater of the Grotesque." *Estreno* 8.1 (Spring 1982): 7–8, 17.

Ramos, Alicia. "Luis Riaza: el dramaturgo y su obra." *Estreno* 8.1 (Spring 1982): 18–21.

Peter L. Podol

RIBA, Carles (1893, Barcelona–1959, Barcelona), poet, prose writer, translator, and husband of Clementina *Arderiu. Riba was the son of a Carlist officer. He learned Latin and German in high school, and as early as 1911 he published a Catalan version of Virgil's *Bucolics*. In 1914 he received the doctorate in humanities. About the same time he also learned classical Greek and wrote his first critical essays. His early poems reflect influences that would dominate his lyrical production—the Greek and Roman classics, Joan *Maragall, Ausiàs *March, and the ideas of the "noucentisme" with its particular emphasis on the complete "homme de lettres," simple but highly polished style, and total devotion to intellectual pursuits. Riba's relation to Catalan poetry is similar to that of Valéry in French poetry and Jorge *Guillén or Pedro *Salinas in Castilian poetry. According to the Castilian humanist Tovar, Riba was the most sophisticated and humanistically knowledgeable of the twentieth-c. Iberian poets. But Riba is not only a coldly intellectualized poet. Quite often he reveals a delicate yet powerful sensibility dominated, however, by classical reason and a preference for the most learned and exquisite forms. Somewhat later in his life (in 1922) he resided in Munich and studied the rigorous methodological school of criticism with Karl Vossler, its founder. There he became familiar with the German classics, following an old tradition of Catalan intellectuals since the early Renaixença (nineteenth-c. Catalan renaissance), but in 1932 he described the excesses of intellectualism in an excellent essay, *Els poetes i la llengua comuna* (Poets and Everyday Language). During the Civil War he remained faithful to the Republic and in 1938 read his doctoral thesis on Joan Maragall's *Nausica* at the U of Barcelona. It was published in the volume . . . *Més els poemes* (1938; . . . And the Poems), probably his best prose essay. He left Catalonia, like many others, in 1939, residing in occupied France (Bierville, Bordeaux, Montpellier, etc.) until 1943 when he returned to Barcelona. In France he began to write the poems that constitute the best of his poetry; masterfully transforming concepts of Catalan language, culture and form into the rough feelings of spiritual pain, desolation and longing, compressing everything into the most essential terms. As a poet he descends, as far as he is able, to the collective tragedy of the defeated Catalonia of the forties. The first edition of *Elegies de Bierville* (1943; Elegies of Bierville) had to be published abroad in Buenos Aires, the second edition with a prologue by himself, in Santiago, Chile, and finally, the third edition could be published in Barcelona (1951). One can still trace the influences of Valéry and Mallarmé but increasingly the deep melancholy of Hölderlin (whom he translated in 1944) makes itself manifest. Riba's "Selensuch" (the search for the ultimate meaning) impels the poet to the spiritual odyssey of the poet returning, like Ulysses, to his Ithaca (Catalonia) and his god (the final poem of the book deals specifically with Ulysses' return to Ithaca). The *Elegies* gave Riba immense prestige throughout Spain, and his numerous translations of the classics—Plutarch, Sophocles and, above all, his masterful second version of the *Odyssey*—established him as the leading humanist of the Iberian Peninsula in one of the darkest periods of its culture. His death in 1959 closes the epoch of Catalan symbolist poetry. As a poet he never reaches the heights of *Verdaguer, Maragall or *Carner, but as an intellectual he was faithful and devoted to the Catalan language and throughout his life defended, successfully and masterfully, the best tradition of Western humanistic civilization. *See also* Catalan Literature.

BIBLIOGRAPHY

Primary Texts

Obres completes. Intro. Arthur Terry. Barcelona: Edicions 62, 1965.

English Translations

Poems by Carles Riba. Tr. J. L. Gili. Oxford: Dolphin, 1964.

Criticism

Boixareu, Mercè. *El jo poètic de Carles Riba i Paul Valéry*. Barcelona: n.p., 1978.
Ferraté, Joan. *Carles Riba, avui*. Barcelona: n.p., 1955.
Plà, Josep. "Carles Riba." In *Homenots. Primera sèrie*. Barcelona: n.p., 1966.
Serra d'Or. September 1979. Special issue dedicated to Riba.
Triadú, Joan. *La poesía segons Carles Riba*. Barcelona: n.p., 1954.

Joan Gilabert

RIBADENEYRA, Pedro de (1526, Toledo–1611, Madrid), Jesuit priest, biographer, historian, ascetic writer. Having spent the first thirteen years of his life in Toledo, he then traveled to Rome (1539) to become a page for Cardinal Alexander Farnese. There, he soon met, and later became a close friend and disciple of, St. *Ignacio de Loyola. From 1545 to 1549, Ribadeneyra studied at the U of Padua; in 1553 he was ordained. Following three more years of study, in 1556 he began to function as an orator and official representative of the growing Jesuit organization, traveling to Netherlands (1556–60), England (winter of 1558–59), and throughout Italy (1560–72). The year 1573 marks his return to Spain, in part for reasons of health; from this moment on his literary career blossomed. The Ribadeneyra canon includes saints' lives, church history, histories of the Jesuit order, ascetic works, and writings offering political counsel to government leaders. The finest biography is the *Vida del Padre Ignacio de Loyola* (1583; *The Life of B. Father Ignatius of Loyola*, 1616). First published in Latin (1572), this compelling narration benefits from Ribadeneyra's personal understanding of the saint, his objectives and philosophy. Also worthy of mention are the *Vida del Padre Francisco de Borja* (1592; Life of Father Frances of Borgia), and the *Vida del Padre Maestro Diego Laínez* (1594; Life of Father Diego Laínez). The *Flos sanctorum* (1599; Saints' Lives) was quite popular, as was the *Historia eclesiástica del Cisma del reino de Inglaterra* (1588 and 1593; Ecclesiastic History of the Schism of England). Here again Ribadeneyra supplements historical narration with his personal knowledge of events in England. Ribadeneyra's ascetical works are the most "original" part of his writing. The *Tratado de la tribulación* (1589; Treatise on Tribulation) is his most spontaneous and vigorous work. Falling within the *Senequism tradition, it offers counsel for the adversities of life. There are some lovely poetic passages in it, and the entire work is infused with a gentle sadness. *See also* Ascetical Literature; Hagiography.

BIBLIOGRAPHY

Primary Texts

Historias de la contrarreforma. Intro., notes E. Rey. Madrid: Sáenz, 1945. Contains the *Vida de San Ignacio, Vida de Diego Laínez, Vida de Alfonso Salmerón*, *Vida de Francisco de Borja*, *Historia del Cisma*, and the *Exhortación*.

Flos sanctorum. 3 vols. Barcelona: Sierra, Oliver y Martí, 1790.
Obras escogidas. In BAE 60.
Tratado de la religión. Intro. J. Puig. Buenos Aires: Sopena, 1942.
Tratado de la tribulación. Madrid: La España, 1900.
Vida de Ignacio Loyola. Buenos Aires: Espasa-Calpe, 1946.

English Translations

The Lives of the Saints. . . . Tr. William Petre. 2nd ed. 2 vols. London: BS, 1730.
The life and death of . . . Virgin Mary. . . . Montreal: Maguire, 1835.
Religion and the Virtues of the Christian prince; against Machiavelli. Abridged. See. Botero, G. *Practical Politics*. Tr. and ed. G. A. Moore. Chevy Chase, MD: Country Dollar P, 1949.

RIBEIRO, Aquilino (1885, Carregal de Tabosa–1963, Lisbon), Portuguese novelist. The mountainous Beira Alta was to find its supreme interpreter in Aquilino Ribeiro. This is more important and less regionalist than it would seem at first glance, since ''beirão'' has been in Portuguese letters an archetypal opposite to city-dweller. This mythical sense of ''rustic, almost barbarian'' is outlined in *Cancioneiro Geral* and in Gil *Vicente, re-enforced in the nineteenth c. by Camilo Castelo Branco and Abel Botelho, but it would find its complex, often ambivalent character most fully in Ribeiro's prose, with all its sensory wealth, vigor and violence, especially in *Terras do Demo* (1919; The Devil's Lands), *Andam Faunos pelos Bosques* (1926; Pan Walks in the Forest) or *Quando os Lobos Uivam* (1958; *When the Wolves Howl*, 1963), the latter of which had its circulation harassed by the secret police. In 1960, however, Aquilino Ribeiro was the Portuguese candidate for the Nobel Prize for Literature. He had earlier been the subject of a warm public homage in Brazil, and it is perhaps no coincidence that a volume on Ribeiro (compared to Guimarães Rosa by Fernando Mendonça) was the one chosen to start Portuguese and Brazilian collections on contemporary writers. In several aspects Aquilino's was the temper, life, verbal (though literate and educated) talent of his most famous character, a lively, experienced muleteer whose autobiographical monologue, first published as part of *Estrada de Santiago* (1922; Milky Way) was later reprinted under its own separate title—*O Malhadinhas*, the character's nickname—on the anthological strength of its 150 pages born out of the best Iberian tradition of *picaresque literature.

Works

Aquilino Ribeiro's first in a series of about sixty books was *Jardim das Tormentas* (1913; Garden of Torments). This collection of short stories hints at the main lines along which his oeuvre would develop: natural instinct, life of the senses versus social, religious or political obstacles, often satirized; cosmopolitan experience and foreign influences (Anatole France, Nietzsche) integrated in his own *Weltanschauung*; historical or hagiographical legends as background to the baroque contrast between sensual joy and physical degradation (old age, illness, death). Some of Ribeiro's books are not far from autobiographical. *Cinco Réis de Gente* (1948; Little Ones) evokes childhood spent in the mountains of Beira; *Uma Luz ao Longe* (1949; A Light in the Distance) resumes the narrative with the boy, like the author himself, being taken for secondary education into a college run by priests. Indeed, much of Ribeiro's fiction relies on landscapes, characters, places (Beira, Lisbon, also Paris and Spain) the author had grown well acquainted with. Faithful, however, to his own image of the novelist as a bee, he tends to mix the elements of real life in producing the honey of art. Still, *A Via Sinuosa* (1918; The Sinuous Way), *O Homem que Matou o Diabo* (1930; The Man Who Killed the Devil) and *Lápides Partidas* (1945; Broken Tombstones) draw recognizably from Ribeiro's own life. As a young man he left the seminary, settled in Lisbon, wrote for the Republican press and engaged in revolutionary activity, in consequence of which he was imprisoned, but escaped into exile (this period of 1901–8 is covered in his posthumous memoirs *Um Escritor Confessa-se* [1974; A Writer's Confessions]). In 1914, after half a dozen years of Paris and the Sorbonne, Ribeiro returned to Lisbon, became a teacher at Liceu Camões and then a librarian at the Biblioteca Nacional; there he joined Jaime *Cortesão, Raul *Proença, António *Sérgio and others in what came to be known as the group of *Seara Nova*. Ribeiro was involved in the 1927 and 1928 armed rebellions against dictatorship. Once more he found himself in jail, but again he managed to flee into exile, returning in 1932. There followed three decades of continuous literary output: Ribeiro translated *Cervantes and Xenophon; studied Camilo, Cavaleiro de Oliveira, *Camões, Fernão Mendes Pinto, António José da Silva (''O Judeu''), Leal da Câmara, Eça, Raul *Brandão; researched history and hagiography, though it was more in his vein to fictionalize them as in *Aventura Maravilhosa de D. Sebastião* (1936; Wondrous Adventure of King Sebastian) or in *S. Banaboião, Anacoreta e Mártir* (1937; Saint Banaboião, Hermit and Martyr). Fiction kept being Ribeiro's most distinctive literary contribution, whether he was writing for children as he had done in *Romance da Raposa* (1924; The Fox's Tale) or pursuing his main work of novel writing. Besides the ones noted above, reference should be made to *Mónica* (1938), *O Arcanjo Negro* (1947; The Black Archangel) and *A Casa Grande de Romarigães* (1957; The Mansion at Romarigães); the latter could be the subject of an interesting comparison with Eça's *A Ilustre Casa de Ramires* (1987).

Aquilino's Prose

''Every literature has the writers it deserves,'' wrote João Gaspar Simões. Thanks to Ribeiro, it was claimed, Portuguese fiction has been kept at the level it reached in the previous c. with Camilo and Eça. Indeed, Ribeiro commands a great lexical wealth (from archaisms to modern colloquialisms) in an ever appropriate variety of rhythms, and is generally acknowledged as the best stylist in Portuguese letters since Camilo. Ribeiro's strong individuality, mirrored in his style, caused him at times some ill-will from literary movements. He was labeled ''regionalist'' and replied ''if being regionalist means that you described something else besides Lisbon, then I would not claim any better''

(1926). Later, he would say, "I was recently stuck another label, the one of prose-writer, thus being excluded from the novelists' class. . . . I would like to be told what my prose, if emptied of its human document, is" (1944). Being especially sensitive to nature, Ribeiro excels in bringing to life the microcosmos of Beira Alta—namely, his native Serra da Nave in its triple identity of land, men, and animals—imbued in the author's best pages with universal value. But also in his urban (mainly related to Lisbon) fiction Ribeiro tends to keep an observant eye out for physical, sociological and psychological detail and its subtle verbal expression. Among Ribeiro's limitations are the too passive role accorded to some of his women characters, as A. J. Saraiva and Oscar *Lopes noted, and that, as was said of Dickens, "his parts are better than his wholes"—meaning that he tends to concentrate on the episode as the writing unit, the architecture of his longer fiction often being (as in *Quando os Lobos Uivam*) unequal to his powerful prose. To conclude with Gaspar Simões: "Our typical writers, those who represent us most fully, do not unfold themselves into their characters—they project themselves into their prose"; and he illustrates with Camilo's and Aquilino's prose.

BIBLIOGRAPHY

Primary Texts

Andam Faunos pelos Bosques. Lisbon: Bertrand, 1926.
A Casa Grande de Romarigães. Lisbon: Bertrand, 1957.
Estrada de Santiago. Lisbon: Bertrand, 1922.
O Malhadinhas. Lisbon: Bertrand, 1946.
Obras Completas de Aquilino Ribeiro. Lisbon: Bertrand, [in press].
Quando os Libos Uivam. Lisbon: Bertrand, 1958.
Terras do Demo. Lisbon: Bertrand, 1919.

English Translation

When the Wolves Howl. Tr. P. McGowan Pinheiro. London: Cape, 1963. New York: Macmillan, 1963.

Criticism

Lopes, Óscar. *Cinco Personalidades Literárias. . . .* Porto: Divulgação, 1961.
———. "O mundo pícaro de Aquilino Ribeiro." *Vértice* 25 (Dec. 1965): 885–96.
Mendes, M. ed. *Aquilino Ribeiro*. Lisbon: Arcadia, 1960.
Novaes Coelho, Nelly. *Aquilino Ribeiro: Jardim das Tormentas; gênese da ficção aquiliniana*. São Paulo: Quíron, 1973.
Vasconcelos, Taborda de. *Aquilino Ribeiro*. Lisbon: Presença, 1965.

RIBEIRO, Bernardim (1482, Torrao, Alemtejo, Portugal–1552, Lisbon), poet, prose author. His father was assassinated by royal order for involvement in a conspiracy against John II. Friend of *Sá de Miranda, Bernardim may have been in Italy with *Garcilaso de la Vega and Sá from 1520 to 1524. Ribeiro wrote exclusively in Portuguese. Several of his poems appeared in the *Cancionero de Resende* (1516; Resende's Songbook), and in 1536 he published the *Trovas de dous pastores Silvestre y Amador* (Songs of Two Shepherds, Silvestre and Amador), which clearly follows Petrarchist tradition. Ribeiro's fine eclogues make him creator of Portuguese bucolic verse. In 1554, posthumously, the *História de Menina e Moça* (Story of the Maiden and Lass) appeared. Leaving aside various bibliographic and textual puzzles, this singular work is comprised of a unique combination of chivalric, sentimental and *pastoral elements, all unified through a delicately feminist attitude. Its sentimental psychological landscape clearly belongs to the *saudade* tradition. *See also* Italian Literary Influences.

BIBLIOGRAPHY

Primary Texts

"B. Ribeiro. Eglogas." Ed. M. Braga. *RFE* 25 (1941): 276–79.

Eclogas. Sel., pref. Rodrigues Lapa. Lisbon: Rua da Rosa, 1947.

Historia de menina e moça. Ed., intro. D. E. Grokenberger. Lisbon: Studium, 1947.

Obras. Ed. A. Braamcamp. Pref. C. Michaëlis de Vasconcelos. 2 vols. Coimbra: Universidade, 1923.

Trovas de dous pastores. Lisbon: Livraria Civilização, 1963. Facs. of 1536 ed.

Criticism

Gallego Morell, A. *Bernardim Ribeiro y su novela Menina e moça*. Madrid: CSIC, 1960.

RIBERA, Anastasio Pantaleón de (1600, Madrid?–1629, Madrid), poet. A follower of *Góngora and **culteranismo*, he was an active participant in literary academies, especially the Academy of Mendoza. A renowned skirt-chaser, he seems to have died of syphilis. His *Obras* (1634; Works) were collected by friends and published posthumously—in the prologue to this work, his death is attributed to a wound he received as victim in a case of mistaken identity. Many of the poems are humorous or satirical. *See also* Academia.

BIBLIOGRAPHY

Primary Texts

Obras. Ed. R. Balbín Lucas. 2 vols. Madrid: CSIC, 1944.

Criticism

Brown, K. *Anastasio Pantaleón de Ribera (1600–1629)*. Madrid: Porrúa Turanzas, 1980. Includes reproduction of various mss.

RICO Y AMAT, Juan (1821, Elda, Alicante–1870, Madrid), attorney, journalist, playwright. His dramatic efforts include *Costumbres políticas* (Political Customs) and *Misterios de palacio* (Palace Mysteries). His first work was lyric: *Poesías serias y satíricas* (1842; Serious and Satiric Poems), which contains a prologue by *Hartzenbusch. Rico y Amat also wrote a historical study: *Historia política y parlamentaria de España* (1860; Political and Parliamentary History of Spain) and a *Diccionario de los políticos* (1855; Dictionary of Politicians).

BIBLIOGRAPHY

Primary Texts

Costumbres políticas. Madrid: Rodríguez, 1885.

Diccionario de los políticos. Ed., notes D. Sevilla Andrés. Madrid: Narcea, 1976.

Historia política y parlamentaria de España. 3 vols. Madrid: Escuelas pías, 1860–61.
Poesías serias y satíricas. Madrid: Repullés, 1842.

RIDRUEJO, Dionisio (1912, Burgo de Osma, Soria–1975, Madrid), law student, poet of the *Generation of 1936, essayist, journalist, translator, artist, and teacher. He also wrote prologues and introductions to works by such writers as Camilo José *Cela, Leopoldo *Panero, and Francisco *Fernández-Santos. He studied Dante, Petrarch, and classical Spanish literature. His poetry is at once traditional and a product of its time, ranging from sonnets in the manner of *Garcilaso de la Vega to blank verse and encompassing a broad spectrum of subjects. His major political statement, *Escrito en España* (1962; Written in Spain), did not appear in Spanish bookstores until the 1970s, and his poetry, which was not well known for several decades, is now gaining well-deserved appreciation.

Because of his political views, he suffered persecution in his native country. He was an early supporter of José Antonio Primo de Rivera and of the ideals of the Falange, but later incurred the enmity of the Franco government and was imprisoned initially for reading over the air a prohibited speech written by Primo de Rivera. Later he joined Franco and was named director of propaganda. At the age of twenty-six he entered a sanatorium because of ill health and depression, and it was there that he wrote patriotic sonnets and steeped himself in the writings of Plato, Machiavelli, Hegel, and Mann. His only heroic political poems are those which appeared in 1940 with the title *Poesía en armas* (Poetry at Arms). He left the post of director general that year and co-founded with Pedro *Laín Entralgo the journal *Escorial*, which published contributions by the major literary and intellectual figures of the time. In 1946 he married Gloria de Ros Ribas and dedicated himself to writing, completing *Elegías* (Elegies), four dramatic works (*La fundación del reino* [The Founding of the Kingdom], *El hijastro del tiempo* [Time's Stepson], *El pacto con la vida* [Contract with Time], and *Don Juan*), and a novel, *La juventud de Diego Manrique* (The Youth of Diego Manrique), which was never published. His poetic works were gathered and published under the title *En once años: Poesías completas de juventud, 1935–1945* (1950; In Eleven Years: Complete Poetry of Youth, 1935–1945), for which he was awarded the Premio Nacional de Literatura.

After a hiatus that included an assignment in Rome as a correspondent for the newspaper *Prensa del movimiento*, he returned to Madrid in 1951 and published a handful of poems inspired by the birth of his daughter, *Los primeros días: Idilios de la hija reciente* (1952; The First Days: Idylls of the New Daughter), which he considered his best collection. He continued his political activism, refusing to accept any political posts in the Franco government, acting instead as director of Radio Intercontinental and defending the exhibition of works by Picasso, Dali, and other artists considered subversive by the art, political, and religious establishment in Spain. After a student rally in which a government official was injured, he was imprisoned for a month and a half in the Carabanchel jail, where he continued to write and to paint. Upon his release, he and a group of young people formed the Partido Social de Acción Democrática, a progressive, culturally liberal, politically democratic, and economically neo-socialist organization. Jailed again for statements made to a Havana weekly and for conspiring against the regime, he wrote satirical political poetry and painted until his release, continuing afterwards his relentless opposition to the Franco regime. He lost his position as director of Radio Intercontinental and incurred a steep penalty because of the statements he had made to the press in Havana. Since he was unable to pay, his personal belongings were inventoried and seized. For two years he was exiled in Paris, where he completed the writing of *Escrito en España*, attacking the Franco government for executing the communist leader Julián Grimau. His arrest in 1964, upon his return to Spain, led to a protest in Paris, but two weeks later he was released after the apparent intervention of General De Gaulle. There remained, however, an action against him for his article supporting Grimau, and he was fined and sentenced, then released provisionally. What little writing he did between 1950 and 1964 was published abroad and unavailable in Spain.

While continuing to work with the Acción Democrática party, Ridruejo wrote *Cuaderno catalán* (1965; Catalan Notebook), a series of translations and prologues, and *Guía de Castilla la Vieja* (1973, 1974: Guide to Old Castille), a magnificent collection in two volumes of information, lyrical prose, and photographs. He began to write poetry again in 1968, while in residence as a visiting professor at the U of Wisconsin, where he wrote *Cuadernos de Madison*. Because of failing health, he returned to Spain less than a year later in order to rest and recuperate in Alicante. He grew increasingly pessimistic about the political situation. Through the efforts of Ricardo Gullón, he was invited to teach at the U of Texas, where he wrote *Los cuadernos de Austin* and the second part of *Casi en prosa*. He returned to Madrid in 1970, only to face more fines and imprisonment. While there, he wrote his memoirs, published articles and began to write in installments in *Destino*, and founded the Unión Social Demócrata Española. In Portugal, he wrote the *Cuadernillo de Lisboa*, then translated Josep *Plà's *Cuaderno gris*. He had plans to write another book, but died before he was able to fulfill his goal.

Ridruejo's poetry may be divided into three stages, the first a return to traditional forms, counted syllables, and beautiful expression, the second more intimate, more global, broader in scope, and the third anguished and disillusioned—a reflection of hardships he endured. There is a growing existential anguish throughout the development of his work. His memoirs, together with a chronology of his life, interviews, personal opinions on a myriad of matters, letters, and photographs were published under the title *Casi unas memorias* (1976; Almost Memories). Also published posthumously is *Sombras y bultos* (1977; Shadows and Shapes), a collection of his essays, biographical and literary rather than political.

BIBLIOGRAPHY

Primary Texts

Casi unas memorias. Ed. César Armando Gómez. Prol. Salvador de Madariaga. Barcelona: Planeta, 1976.

Cuadernos de Rusia, *En la soledad del tiempo*, *Cancionero en ronda*, and *Elegías*. Intro. and bibliog., Manuel A. Penella. Madrid: Castalia, 1981.

En once años: Poesías completas de juventud, 1935–1945. Madrid: Nacional, 1950.

Escrito en España. Buenos Aires: Losada, 1962.

Guía de Castilla la Vieja. Barcelona: Destino, 1973, 1974.

Hasta la fecha, 1934–1959. Prol. Luis Felipe Vivanco. Madrid: Aguilar, 1961.

Sombras y bultos. Barcelona: Destino, 1977.

English Translations

"A ti, yunque del aire pensativa." In *Spanish Poetry since 1939*. Tr. C. D. Ley. Washington, DC: Catholic U of America, 1962.

"A una piedra de molino en tierra." In *The Collected Poems of Roy Campbell*. Tr. R. Campbell. vol. 3. London: Bodley Head, 1960.

Criticism

Aguirre, Jesús. Introduction. *Dionisio Ridruejo, de la Falange de la oposición*. Madrid: Taurus, 1976.

Domenich Mira, Francisco J. *Bibliografía de Dionisio Ridruejo*. Madrid: Universidad Complutense, 1982.

Schmidt, Hans-Peter. *Dionisio Ridruejo, ein Mitglied der Spanischen "Generation von 36"* (Dionisio Ridruejo, a Member of the Spanish "Generation of 1936"). Bonn: Romanische Seminar der Universitat Bonn, 1972.

Vidal, Alejandra. *Homenaje a Dionisio Ridruejo* (Homage to Dionisio Ridruejo). Madrid: Labor y Moneda y Crédito, 1977.

Vivanco, Luis Felipe. "El desengaño del tiempo en la poesía de Dionisio Ridruejo." In *Introducción a la poesía española contemporánea*. Madrid: Guadarrama, 1951. Also in the prologue to *Hasta la fecha*.

Esther Nelson

RIERA, Carme (1949, Mallorca–), short story writer and novelist in Catalan (and in the Majorcan dialect), essayist and critic in Castilian, professor of Castilian literature at the Autónoma U of Barcelona. She earned a degree in Filología Hispánica (Castilian language and literature) from the U of Barcelona and continued her Ph.D. studies (in Castilian Golden Age literature) at the Autónoma. Riera may be considered one of the most important young writers and stylists to emerge in Catalonia since the death of Franco in 1975. The exceptional intellectual rigor of her work is complemented by a graceful, innovative prose style; its clear engagement of the issues raised by the Catalanist and feminist movements of the 1960s and 1970s have won it great popular appeal in Catalonia and among Spanish women.

Riera won her first literary prize (the Recull) in 1974, for the lyrical and startling short story "Te deix, amor, la mar com a penyora" (I Leave You, Love, the Sea as Token), subsequently published as the eponymous work in a collection of her stories and narrations in Catalan and Majorcan. While the critics took no notice of this book when it was published, *Te deix, amor, la mar com a penyora*—with its supple, sensuous prose and feminist inspiration—became a best-seller in Catalonia, running through nineteen printings by 1983. In 1977 she published an equally successful second collection of short narrative pieces, *Jo pos per testimoni les gavines* (Let the Seagulls Be My Witness); the eponymous story is a sequel to "Te deix. . . ." Riera translated most of these pieces into Castilian for publication under the title *Palabra de mujer* (1980; The Woman Speaks; also tr. into Greek, 1981). Four of these short fictional works have also been translated into Russian for inclusion in an anthology of Castilian and Catalan short stories of the 1970s.

Riera received the literary prize Prudenci Bertrana in 1980 for her novel *Una Primavera per a Domenico Guarini* (A "Primavera" for Domenico Guarini). Stylistically, structurally, and thematically complex, this novel narrates a double search for truth on the part of a Majorcan journalist. It leads her in circles around Boticelli's "La Primavera" until she can decipher the hidden or ill-interpreted truths of that cultural artifact. Most of the novel is written in (several registers of) standard Catalan, but the Valencian and Majorcan dialects figure importantly in some sections as well.

Epitelis tendríssims (1981; Exquisite Epithelia) is another collection of short fiction, at once playful and erotic; all share the same initial setting, a small Majorcan hotel; each purports to tease out the secret life of one guest. This work evidences once again Riera's strong interest in the problems and the promise of language, both as literary instrument and as vehicle for self-fulfillment.

El cementiris de Barcelona (1980; The Cemeteries of Barcelona), is a narrative tour of Barcelona's historic cemeteries, illustrated with photographs by Colita. *Quasi bé un conte, la vida de Ramon Llull* (1980; Just Like a Story: The Life of Ramon Llull) is a children's biography of this multifaceted thirteenth-c. writer, the first great European thinker to write extensively in the vernacular (Majorcan, in his case).

Riera has been a regular contributor to the newspaper *El País*, and to the literary magazines *Serra d'Or* and *Quimera*. She has published in *Revista de Occidente*, and worked in the Catalan section of TVE (Spanish television).

BIBLIOGRAPHY

Primary Texts

El cementiris de Barcelona. Barcelona: EDHASA, 1980.
Epitelis tendríssims. Barcelona: Edicions 62, 1981.
Jo pos per testimoni les gavines. Barcelona: Laia, 1977.
Palabra de mujer. Barcelona: Laia, 1980.
Te deix, amor, la mar com a penyora. Barcelona: Laia, 1975.
Una primavera para Domenico Guarini. Spanish tr. L. Cotoner. N.p.: n.p., 1981.
Una Primavera per a Domenico Guarini. Barcelona: Edicions 62, 1980.

Criticism

Campillo, Maria. "L'art com a revelació." *Serra d'Or* 23.265 (1981): 652–53.

Cotoner, Luisa. "*Una primavera per a Domenico Guarini* de Carme Riera." *Mirall de glaç. Quaderns de literatura* (Terrassa, Spain) 1982: 52–57.

Gabancho, Patrícia. *La rateta encara escombra l'escaleta*. Barcelona: Edicions 62, 1982.

Nichols, Geraldine C. "Mitja poma, mitja taron ja: Génesis y destino literarios de la catalana contemporánea." *Anthropos* 60–61 (1986): 113–23.

Ordóñez, Elizabeth. "Beginning to Speak: Carme Riera's *Una primavera para Domenico Guarini*." *La Chispa '85. Selected Proceedings*. Ed. Gilbert Paolini. New Orleans: Tulane UP, 1985. 285–93.

Geraldine Nichols

RÍO SAINZ, José del (1886, ?–1964, ?), Spanish journalist, poet and essayist. Some of his newspaper articles are collected in book form with the title *Aire de la calle* (1933; Airs of the Street), the title of his daily column in *La Voz de Cantabria*, a northern regional newspaper which he founded. He studied naval science and spent a number of years as a sailor; the sea, its people and its ports are constant themes in his poetry, as exemplified in such sonnets as "Las peñas del naufragio" (Shipwreck Rocks) and "Las tres hijas del capitán" (The Captain's Three Daughters). His poetry appears to have been influenced by another poet of the sea, the Canary Islander Tomás *Morales and by the Modernist poet Rubén Darío.

RIOJA, Francisco de (1583, Seville–1659, Madrid), baroque lyric poet in the tradition of Fernando de *Herrera, theologian, scholar, jurist, and protégé of Count-Duke Olivares whom he accompanied into exile at Loeches and Toro. Upon his patron's death, Rioja returned, disillusioned, to Seville. In 1654 he was named envoy of the Seville City Council to Madrid where he resided until his death. As librarian of Philip IV and historian of Castile, he associated with many noblemen and with authors including *Cervantes, Lope de *Vega and *Pérez de Montalbán.

Once erroneously thought to be the author of two masterpieces of Spanish lyric poetry—the *Canción a las ruinas de Itálica* (Ode to the Ruins of Italica) and the **Epístola moral a Fabio* (Epistle to Fabius)—his reputation has rested upon the subtle verbal elegance accentuated by deep undertones of melancholy, despair and disillusion which are expressed almost as understatement. Nature predominates in his lyric vision which exalts the intrinsic worth of the most insignificant forms of creation and stands in awe of the brevity of its existence. A master of floral imagery and the symbols of time forever lost, his images of the rose, the carnation, and the jasmine in his exceptional *silvas* have distinguished him as an original and sensitive poet. His sonnets in the manner of *Góngora reveal both a stoic temperament and the chiding impatience of the moralist. As principal poet of the group centered in Seville in the first third of the seventeenth c. (**Escuela Sevillana*), Rioja shared a heritage common to them all, the inability to completely cast off the formal classical trappings of Gongorism. As did his contemporaries, Rioja retained much of the *culto* spirit while being assimilated into the mainstream of a growing contemporary malaise. The result of the opposing tendencies was a generation of transitional poets whose works contain both classical and revolutionary voices.

Also noteworthy are Rioja's longer poems *A la constancia* (In Praise of Loyalty), *A la riqueza* (On Wealth), and *A la Pobreza* (On Poverty). Several of his sonnets express nostalgia for lost civilizations and cultures: ''Este ambicioso mar que un leño atado'' (This Proud Sea Which [Devours] a Winged Timber) and ''A las ruinas de la Atlántida'' (To the Ruins of Atlantis).

Rioja was also the author of several prose works of little significance which include treatises on rhetoric and literary criticism, for example *Avisos de las partes que ha de tener un predicador* (Advice on How to be a Good Preacher).

BIBLIOGRAPHY

Primary Texts

Poesías inéditas de Francisco de Rioja y otros poetas andaluces. Ed. Pedro Estala. Colección de Poetas Españoles, 18. Madrid: n.p. 1797.

Poesías de D. Francisco de Rioja. Ed. Cayetano Alberto de la Barrera y Leirado. Madrid: Sociedad de Bibliófilos Españoles, 1867 (supp. Seville, 1872).

Poesía sevillana en la Edad de Oro. Edición y estudio de Alberto Sánchez. Madrid: Clásicos Castilla, 1948.

Poetas líricos de los siglos XVI y XVII. vol. 1. Ed. Adolfo de Castro. BAE 32.

Richard Glenn

RÍOS, Fernando de los (1879, Ronda–1949, New York), Spanish essayist. An important socialist thinker, minister of education for the Second Republic, as well as an ambassador and university professor, he had a significant effect on culture, creating a number of centers of study which managed to survive the Civil War and weather subsequent political storms: the Centers of Arabic Studies in Granada and Madrid, the Center of Spanish American Studies in Seville, the International Summer University in Santander, etc. He was a mentor of *García Lorca, sponsoring the latter's traveling theater, La Barraca. Important works of Fernando de los Ríos include *Mi viaje a la Rusia soviética* (1922; My Trip to Soviet Russia), which went through many editions, and *Estado e Iglesia en la España del siglo XVI* (1928; Church and State in sixteenth-c. Spain), republished in 1957 with the title *Religión y estado* (Religion and State). *See also* Essay.

RÍOS Y NOSTENCH, Blanca de los (1859, Seville–1956, Madrid), Spanish poet, journalist and critic. She became known as a lyric poet while still quite young with such works as *Romancero de don Jaime* (Ballad-book of Lord James) and *Esperanzas y recuerdos* (Hopes and Recollections), both published in 1881, and *La novia del marinero* (1886; The Seaman's Sweetheart). She also wrote novels, including *La niña de Sanabria* (1907; The Girl from Sanabria) and *Melita Palma*, and a collection of Andalusian tales entitled *La rondeña* (1902; The Woman from Ronda). She was well known as a lecturer and newspaper writer, and contributed to numerous reviews as well as working as director of the magazine *Raza española*, in which many of her articles and essays appeared. In 1889, the *Academia Española recognized her *Estudio biográfico y crítico de Tirso de Molina* (Biographical and Critical Study of Tirso) with an award. This was a landmark for *Tirso scholarship, revealing new biographical data and clarifying the chronology of his works. Tirso has been the favorite subject of her critical investigations, which also include *El Don Juan de Tirso* (Tirso's Don Juan) and *Las mujeres de Tirso* (1910; Tirso's Women), as well as critical studies of other aspects of his work and an authoritative critical edition of this dramatist's complete works. Other essays include *Del Siglo de Oro* (1910; About the Golden Age) and *De la mística y de la novela contemporánea* (1909; Concerning Mysticism and the Contemporary Novel), an outgrowth of articles and lectures devoted to the literary personality of St. *Teresa.

RISCO, Vicente (1884, Orense–1963, Orense), Galician novelist and poet; author of essays in Spanish. Risco was a professor in the Normal School of Orense, and devoted much of his literary energy to the attempt to preserve Galician culture and language. He was also a well-known ethnologist, and in this specialty wrote several significant studies including his *Historia de los judiós desde la destrucción del Templo* (1944; History of the Jews Following the Destruction of the Temple), and *Biografía de Satanás* (1948; The Biography of Satan). *See also* Galician Literature.

RIVADENEYRA, Pedro de. *See* Ribadeneyra, Pedro de

RIVAS, Ángel de Saavedra, Duque de (1791, Córdoba–1865, Madrid), Romantic dramatist and poet. Rivas is best known for his stunning Romantic play *Don Alvaro o la fuerza del sino* (1835; Don Alvaro or the Force of Destiny), although the entire body of his work is substantial and varied. Verdi added to *Don Alvaro*'s fame by using it as the source for his opera *La forza del destino*.

Born into a titled and wealthy Andalusian family, Angel de Saavedra received the standard upper-class education of his day—broad studies in the humanities taught by French professors who had fled France following the Revolution of 1789. Poetry and painting were his favorite subjects as well as his greatest strengths. When his father died in 1802, the noble title fell to Ángel's older brother and the family moved to Madrid, where Angel continued his studies at the important Real Seminario de Nobles until 1806. At the age of fifteen he joined the Royal Guards, a suitable profession for second sons, and was swept into action when the French invasion of 1808 precipitated the six-year War of Independence. In 1809 he was gravely wounded on the battlefield when his horse was shot out from beneath him (an incident reflected later in *Don Alvaro*); during his recovery he composed his lovely ballad ‘‘Con once heridas mortales’’ (With eleven mortal wounds). Once his health had been regained he returned to his native Córdoba, but the French advances forced him to flee, accompanied by his mother, to Cádiz, the home of numerous dispossessed liberals (*Quintana and *Martínez de la Rosa were there). Saavedra's military service and his literary avocation mixed well in Cádiz, and he composed poems which drew on his neo-classical education, his deep patriotism, his attraction to Spanish medieval heroes, and his strict adherence to the code of honor. The last three characteristics were to become hallmarks of the *Romanticism Rivas would discover in himself in later years. His long narrative poem ''El paso honroso'' (1812; The Honorable Crossing) contains seeds of these characteristics, as do the thirty short pieces published in his *Poesías* (1814; Poems).

Saavedra's family prestige seems to have protected him against Ferdinand VII's reprisals. Between 1814 and 1820, Saavedra's fortunes rose, and he wrote a series of tragedies following the neo-classical rules of drama—*Ataúlfo* (1814), *Aliatar* (1816), *El duque de Aquitania* (1817; The Duke of Aquitaine), and *Malek-Adhel* (1818). Riego's uprising in 1820 enabled him to test his liberal ideas, and he actively supported Riego's constitutional government. He was elected to the new parliament in 1821, published a second, augmented edition of his poetry, and successfully staged a political tragedy, *Lanuza* (1822) in Madrid. He did not escape Ferdinand's enmity twice, and in late 1823 he fled Spain to avoid harsh punishment for his progressive political views. He went to Gibraltar, then to London, then back to Gibraltar and finally, in 1825, to the island of Malta, where he settled with Encarnación Cueto y Ortega (whom he had married during his second stay in Gibraltar). He continued to write. His long narrative poem *Florinda* (1826) reflects increasing Romantic tensions, heightened perhaps by his contact with the Spanish liberals and English Romantics in London. On Malta he developed an important friendship with John Hookham Frere, whose vast library provided Saavedra with access to Spanish and European classics. In the five years he spent in Malta, Saavedra read and wrote extensively, all the while moving away from the neo-classicism of his youth toward the emotional and personal *Romanticism of his middle years. On Malta he wrote another patriotic tragedy, *Arias Gonzalo* (1827), the poem ''El faro de Malta'' (1828; The Lighthouse of Malta), the comedy *Tanto vales cuanto tienes* (1828; You Are What You Own)—which takes as a model the style of Leandro Fernández de *Moratín—, and there he began his very famous narrative poem, ''El moro expósito'' (begun in 1829, published in 1834; The Foundling Moor).

In 1830, Saavedra moved with his family to France (Orleans, Paris, Tours), where he was reunited with old friends and Spanish exiles, in particular Antonio *Alcalá Galiano. In 1832, in Tours, he wrote the first draft of *Don Alvaro*, in prose, which Alcalá Galiano, after having translated into French, tried (unsuccessfully) to have staged in Paris. But ''El moro expósito,'' with its stirring prologue by Alcalá Galiano on the new Romanticism, did achieve popularity, and Saavedra, taking advantage of the amnesty declared by Ferdinand VII's widow, María Cristina, returned to Spain in January 1834. Several months later his older brother died and Angel inherited the title, Duke of Rivas, which brought with it a seat in Parliament. That same year he was elected to the *Academia Española.

Rivas reworked parts of his *Don Alvaro* into verse, and had it staged in Madrid on March 22, 1835. The play was well received, although it was not a major hit. People did talk about it and it gradually became a symbol of the Romantic movement—wild, rebellious, emotional, radical, exaggerated. The neo-classicists, who witnessed the rejection of their orderly world and an open challenge to their literary precepts, hated it. To their disappointment, though, it set the tone for much Spanish playwriting and versification for the next decade. Interestingly, Rivas's own youthful liberalism began to weaken soon after the appearance of *Don Alvaro*, and while his play initiated a series of similarly rebellious plays, his position in Spanish society moved him away from the radicalism of his past toward a more moderate political and literary stance. He served the queen regent as a moderate liberal, and even suffered exile again in 1836 when the progressive liberals came to power. On his return to Spain in 1837, he settled into a type of early retirement in Seville, pursuing his literary interests and tending to his family. In the exquisite *Romances históricos* (1841; Historical Ballads) his attraction to the solid, popular values of Spain's heroic past (the past glorified by*Durán) is clearly evident, and in the ballads he eschews the bizarre emotionalism of the melodramatic *Don Álvaro*. These ballads are considered by some to be his most serious contribution to Spanish letters. In them he reviews popular legends and historical incidents, rewriting them with confident description and colorful narrative style, and infusing the whole with an exuberant nationalism that was a fundamental part of the Spanish Romantic movement.

More plays and poems followed, although none ever reached the level of popularity of "El moro expósito," *Don Alvaro*, or the *Romances históricos*. *Solaces de un prisionero* (1841; Relaxations of a Prisoner), *La morisca de Alajuar* (1841; The Moorish Girl from Alajuar), *El crisol de la lealtad* (1842; The Test of Loyalty), and *El parador de Bailén* (1844; The Inn at Bailén) are all but forgotten today. Only one, *El desengaño en un sueño* (1844; Disillusionment in a Dream)—which Rivas claimed as his own favorite—has been praised for its originality. By 1844 Rivas was back in the government, serving the conservative regime of General Narváez as ambassador to Naples and Sicily. He returned to Madrid in 1850, continued to write poems—the most successful of them were the long narrative legends, "La azucena milagrosa" (written in Naples in 1847; The Miraculous Lily), "Maldonado," and "El aniversario" (The Anniversary), all published in the book *Leyendas* (1854; Legends), and oversaw the publication of his incomplete five-volume collected works (Madrid: Biblioteca Nueva, 1854–55). He spent a short time as ambassador to France in 1859–60, then returned to Madrid for good, where he was named director of the Spanish Royal Academy (1862), president of the Council of State (1863), and member of the Order of the Golden Fleece (1864). He died on June 22, 1865. His son published his *Obras completas*.

BIBLIOGRAPHY

Primary Texts

Don Alvaro o la fuerza del sino. Ed. Ermanno Caldera. Madrid: Taurus, 1986.

Don Alvaro o la fuerza del sino. Ed. Donald L. Shaw. Madrid: Castalia, 1986.

Don Alvaro o la fuerza del sino. Ed. María Socorro Perales. Madrid: Burdeos, 1988.

Don Alvaro o la fuerza del sino. Lanuza. Ed. R. Navas-Ruiz. Madrid: Espasa-Calpe, 1975.

Obras completas. 7 vols. Madrid: Rivadeneyra, 1894–1904.

Obras completas. Ed. Jorge Campos. Madrid: Rivadeneyra, 1957.

English Translations

Don Alvaro. Tr. Robert Lima. In *Spanish Plays of the Nineteenth-Century*. New York: Las Américas, 1964.

Don Alvaro or the Power of Fate [Don Álvaro o la fuerza del Sino]. Tr. Luis Soto-Ruiz and Georgia Pappanastos. In *Three Spanish Romantic Plays*. Intro. A. Pasero. Milwaukee: Marquette UP: 1990.

Criticism

Andioc, René. ''Sobre el estreno de *Don Alvaro*.'' *Homenaje a Juan López-Morillas*. Madrid: Castalia, 1982. 63–86.

Cardwell, Richard. ''Don Alvaro or the Force of Cosmic Injustice.'' *Studies in Romanticism* 12 (1973): 559–79.

Lovett, Gabriel. *The Duke of Rivas*. TWAS 452. Boston: Twayne, 1977.

Pattison, Walter. ''The Secret of Don Alvaro.'' *Symposium* 21 (1967): 67–81.

Shergold, N. D. ''The *Romances* of the Duque de Rivas.'' *Studies of the Spanish and Portuguese Ballad*. London: Tamesis, 1972. 127–39.

David Thatcher Gies

RIVAS CHERIF, Cipriano de (1891, Madrid–1969, Mexico), lawyer, theater director and writer. Rivas Cherif collaborated in journals such as *La Pluma* and the weekly *España*. He began to publish at a very early age and translated a numerous number of works.

BIBLIOGRAPHY

Primary Texts

Breviario de teatro. Guatemala: Ed. del Ministerio de Educación Pública, 1953.

Un camarada más. N.p.: n.p., 1922.

Pepita Jiménez (novela famosa de D. Juan Valera, refundida en tres actos de teatro). Madrid: Prensa Moderna, 1929.

Versos de abril. N.p.: n.p., 1907.

Kathleen March

ROBLES, Antonio (1897, Robledo de Chavela, Madrid–), novelist and author of children's literature who wrote under the pseudonym Antoniorrobles. His first novel, entitled *Tres* (1926; Three), reflects the ''dehumanized'' vogue of the day. Other works of interest are *Novia, partida por dos* (1931; Bride Divided between Two), *Torerito soberbio* (1932; Haughty Bullfighter), and *Aleluyas de*

Rompetacones (1939; Heelbreaker's Allelujah). Short fiction comprises the following collections: *Cuentos de las cosas de navidad* (1932; Tales of Christmas Happenings), and *Cuentos de los juguetes vivos* (1931; *Tales of Living Playthings*, 1938).

BIBLIOGRAPHY

Primary Texts

Aleluyas de Rompetacones. Mexico: Estrella, juventud, 1939.
Albéniz, genio de "Iberia." N.p.: Constancia, 1953.
La bruja de doña Paz. N.p.: Instituto Mexicano Norteamericano de Relaciones Culturales, 1960.
Cuentos de las cosas que hablan. Madrid: Espasa-Calpe, 1983.
Cuentos de los juguetes vivos. Madrid: Compañía Iberoamericana de Publicaciones, 1931.
Diario de Sucesos Notables (1665–1703). Madrid: Porrúa, 1972.
Historias de Azulita y Rompetacones: Cuentos infantiles. N.p.: Secretaría de Educación Pub., 1968.

English Translations

Merry Tales from Spain. Tr. Edward Huberman. Philadelphia: John C. Winston, 1939.
The Refugee Centaur. Tr. and adapted by Edward and Elizabeth Huberman. Illus. John Resko. New York: Twayne, 1952.
Tales of Living Playthings. Tr. Edward Huberman. New York: Modern Age Books, 1938.

Genaro J. Pérez

ROCA DE TOGORES, Mariano. *See* Molíns, Marqués de

ROCABERTI, Isabel de (1551, ?–1624, ?), mystic, nun. Largely self-taught, she professed with the Dominicans at a young age. At the request of her confessor, she set down an account of her mystical visions, which was later edited and published by her nephew, the Archbishop Juan Tomás de Rocaberti. *See also* Mysticism.

BIBLIOGRAPHY

Primary Text

Libro de su admirable vida y doctrina, que escribió de su mano. Ed. J. T. de Rocaberti. 4 vols. Valencia: Mestre, 1679–85.

RODOMONTADAS. Collections of sayings and anecdotes of oaths, bluster, and bravado attributed to Spanish soldiers by French writers of the sixteenth c. A series of Spanish victories led to this French perception of Spain and Spanish types, a view guided by a spirit of joking, satire, and caricature. The term originates with the braggart of Boiardo's *Orlando Innamorato*, Rodomonte. Nicolas Baudouin published *Rodomontadas castellanas, recopiladas de diversos autores y mayormente del capitán Escardón Bombardón* (Castilian Rodomontades, Copied from Diverse Authors, Especially Captain Escardón Bombardón), which appeared in at least eighteen editions and which is, in general, the same text as *Rodomontadas castellanas, recopiladas de los comentarios muy espantosos, terribles e invencibles capitanes Matamoros, Crocodillo y Rajabroqueles* (1607; Castilian Rodomontades, Copied from the Commentaries of the Frightening, Terrible, and Invincible Captains Matamoros, Crocodillo, and Rajabroqueles). In addition, several Spanish political refugees cultivated the genre, an example being Francisco de Cáceres's *Nuevos fieros españoles.* These books mixed characterizations of the ruffian and the soldier.

The *Rodomontada* is comical due to linguistic misfirings and exaggerated situations. The most noteworthy examples are found in the *Discours d'aucunes rodomontades . . . espagnolles* (Discourse on Spanish . . . Rodomontades) of Pierre de Brantôme (1540–1614), which blends satire and affection in praise of the Spanish soldier. Brantôme was the first to collect the *Rodomontadas* without translating them, since he felt that any educated Frenchman should be able to read them in Spanish. The collection was dedicated to Queen Margarita, the sister of Isabel de la Paz. Brantôme's *Rodomontadas* show admiration for all things Spanish; other versions exhibit more ill will.

BIBLIOGRAPHY

Primary Texts

Baudouin, Nicolas. *Rodomontadas castellanas.* Paris: Chevalier, 1607.

Brantôme, Pierre de Bourdeille de. *Discours d'aucunes rodomontades et gentilles rencontres et parolles espagnolles.* In *Oeuvres Complètes.* Paris: Renouard, 1873.

English Translation

Baudouin, Nicolas. *Rodomontados.* London: Iaggard, 1610.

Criticism

Cioranesco, A. *Las ''Rodomontadas Espagnoles'' de N. Baudouin. BH* 39 (1937): 339–55.

Cottrell, Robert D. *Brantôme: The Writer as Portraitist of His Age.* Geneva: Droz, 1970.

López Barrera, Joaquín. *Brantôme y el género bufo y grotesco de las ''Rodomontadas Españoles'' en la literatura francesa. RABM* 27 (1923): 56–81.

Catherine Larson

RODOREDA, Mercè (1909, Barcelona–1983, Girona), novelist. Daughter of a somewhat typical Catalan middle-class family, she had a very lonely childhood and from a young age was an avid reader. As with many other Catalan writers of her generation, her apprenticeship was done writing in magazines and newspapers: *Revista de Catalunya*, *Mirador*, *Meridià*, etc. She wrote several short stories and novels, among them *¿Soc una dona honrada*? (1932; Am I an Honest Woman?) and *Un día en la vida d'un home* (1934; A Day in the Life of a Man). They were all rejected later on by Rodoreda herself. Her first important novel is *Aloma* (1938), a symbolic and poetic novel centered on the character of a woman, a theme that she never again abandoned. Nonetheless, this novel is a milestone in Rodoreda's novelistic career. The Catalan defeat in the Spanish Civil War of 1939 exiled and demoralized her. Living in Bordeaux, Paris and

Geneva, she struggled to make a living and wrote only scattered short stories in Catalan magazines of the diaspora. Once her economic and existential situation was finally stabilized in Geneva, she resumed her literary production, in about 1954. From then on her novelistic production was brilliant. Her first important book of this post-war era is *Vint-i-dos contes* (1957; Twenty-two Stories). It was followed by an absolute masterpiece of European literature, *La plaça del Diamant* (1962; *The Time of Doves*, 1984). A novel of only apparent simplicity, it is the story of a woman of humble state who with her strong vision of the world dominates it. As the years pass by this woman, one can notice the vitality and idealism of adolescence, the vitality of youth, the epic of the Civil War and the hopelessness and sterility of the defeat in the post-war years. It has had enormous success in Catalonia and in many countries around the world. Another masterpiece of the contemporary Catalan novel is *El carrer de les camèlies* (1966; The Street of Camellias), a continuation of Rodoreda's constant themes: the margination of women, frustrated love relations, etc. *Jardí vora el mar* (1967; Garden Near the Sea) breaks with the realism of her former novels; and *Mirall trencat* (1974; Broken Mirror) is the culmination of this evolution, a beautiful novel centered on the myth of childhood with symbolistic overtones. However, this novel represents a closed narrative world, a truly brilliant end to Rodoreda's novelistic world. She is acclaimed as the greatest narrator of twentieth-c. *Catalan literature.

BIBLIOGRAPHY

Primary Texts

Obres completes. 2 vols. Barcelona: Edicions 62, 1976 and 1978.

English Translation

The Time of Doves. Tr. David Rosenthal. New York: Taplinger, 1984.

Criticism

Arnau, Carme. *Introducció a la narrativa de Mercè Rodoreda*. Barcelona: n.p., 1979.
Coll, Carme. "Mort de Mercè Rodoreda a setanta-tres anys." *Avui*, 14 July 1983.
Molas, Joaquim. "Mercè Rodoreda i la novel·la psicològica." *El Pont* 31 (1969): n.p.
Porcel, Baltasar. "Mercè Rodoreda o la força lírica." *Serra d'Or* (May 1966): 231–35.
Triadú, Joan. "Una novel·la excepcional: *La plaça del Diamant* de Mercè Rodoreda." In *Llegir com viure*. Barcelona: n.p., 1963. 132–39.

Joan Gilabert

RODRIGO, Cantar de (Song of Rodrigo), medieval epic poem. Also known as the *Mocedades de Rodrigo* (The Youthful Deeds of Rodrigo), this anonymous poem, set down during the second half of the fourteenth c., is the principal survivor of the tradition dealing with the wholly fictitious deeds of the young Cid. It is a reworking of a lost epic which survives in chronicles and ballads and inspired Guillén de *Castro's *Mocedades del Cid*. Among its fantastic episodes are the death of Ximena's father at the hands of Rodrigo, the intervention of St. Lazarus in the form of a leper, and the defeat by Rodrigo of the coalition of the king of France, the Holy Roman Emperor, the Patriarch, and the Pope. The character of Castro's Rodrigo, when compared to Rodrigo in the **Cantar del Cid*, has been completely transformed; the virtues of loyalty and moderation have been replaced by erratic behavior, belligerance and arrogance. The *Cantar de Rodrigo* is not devoid of interest in its narrative action, which, as Armistead has shown, hinges on Rodrigo's vow not to marry Ximena, as the king has ordered, until he has won five battles. Nevertheless, it reflects the epic in decline. This state of decline, which has been systematically studied by Deyermond, is patent both in the poet's treatment of the material and in formal aspects. Notable are the deterioration of character portrayal, increased erotic interest, and faulty versification. Concomitant with these is a clear clerical or learned reworking of the material similar to the *Poema de *Fernán González*. This is attested by a rather extensive historical introduction, in contrast with the beginning *in medias res* of the earlier epics, the frequent references to documents of grants and privileges, and an interest in the fortunes of the diocese of Palencia.

BIBLIOGRAPHY

Primary Text

Deyermond, A. D. *Epic Poetry and the Clergy: Studies on the "Mocedades de Rodrigo."* London: Tamesis, 1969.

Criticism

Armistead, Samuel G. "The Structure of the *Refundición de las Mocedades de Rodrigo.*" *RPH* 17 (1963–64): 338–45.

———. "The *Mocedades de Rodrigo* and Neo-Individualist Theory." *HR* 46 (1978): 313–27.

Chalon, Louis. *L'Histoire et l'épopée castillane du Moyen Age: Le cycle du Cid, le cycle des comtes de Castille*. Paris: Champion, 1976.

Deyermond, A. D. See Primary Text, above.

———. *A Literary History of Spain. The Middle Ages*. London: Benn; New York: Barnes and Noble, 1971.

———. "The *Mocedades de Rodrigo* as a Test Case: Problems of Methodology." *La corónica* 6 (1978): 108–12.

Webber, Ruth House. "Formulaic Language in the *Mocedades de Rodrigo.*" *HR* 48 (1980): 195–211.

Porter Conerly

RODRÍGUEZ, Alonso (1538, Valladolid—1616, Seville), Jesuit ascetic writer. He studied arts and philosophy at the U of Valencia, theology at the U of Salamanca, and entered the order in 1557, holding various posts therein. His treatise *Ejercicio de perfección y virtudes cristianas* (1609; *The Christian Man's Guide*, 1630) has enjoyed about fifty complete Spanish editions (and more partial publications), and has been fully or partially translated to twenty-three languages. Composed of three parts, each of which contains eight treatises with titles such as "A Treatise of Humility," "A Treatise of Indulgences," and "A Treatise of Mental Prayer," it is intended for novices, and emphasizes how to acquire and practice the virtues. He also wrote *Tratado de la conformidad con la voluntad de Dios* (1608; Treatise on Conforming to God's Will). *See also* Ascetical Literature.

BIBLIOGRAPHY

Primary Texts

Ejercicio de perfección y virtudes cristianas. 8th ed. Madrid: Apostolado de la Prensa, 1954.
Autobiografía; o sea, memorial o cuentas de la conciencia. . . . Ed. V. Segarra. Barcelona: Borgiana, 1956.
Magisterio espiritual, ascético y místico de s. Alonso Rodríguez. Ed. J. Tárrago. Barcelona: Librería religiosa, 1935.

English Translations

Autobiography. Tr. W. Yeomans. London: Chapman, 1964.
The Christian Man's Guide, 1630. The Two First Treatises. Ilkley: Scolar, 1977.
A Short and Sure Way to Heaven. Ilkley: Scolar, 1975.
A Treatise of Humility, 1632. Ilkley: Scolar, 1977.
A Treatise of Indulgences, 1623. Ilkley: Scolar, 1973.
A Treatise of Mental Prayer. Ilkley: Scolar, 1976.

RODRÍGUEZ CORREA, Ramón (1835, Havana, Cuba–1894, Madrid), journalist, politician, and friend of poet Gustavo Adolfo *Bécquer. Rodríguez Correa gained fame as a political satirist and served on the editorial boards of various newspapers, including *El Contemporáneo* (The Contemporary), *El Gobierno* (The Government), *El Mediodía* (The Mid-day), and *Las Noticias* (The News), the latter two which he helped to found. He also held several political offices and was an unsuccessful mediator at the outbreak of the Ten Years' War in Cuba in 1868. A prologue by Rodríguez Correa, denying his friend's presumed imitation of Heine while recognizing the similarities between their work, precedes a posthumous collection of Bécquer's poetry. Under the pseudonym Adolfo Rodríguez, Rodríguez Correa and Bécquer collaborated on several theatrical productions, including the *zarzuelas *El nuevo Fígaro* (1862; The New Figaro) and *Clara de Rosemberg* (1863). He alone published a collection of novelettes, *Agua pasada* (1894; Water under the Bridge), and a novel, *Rosas y perros* (1872; Roses and Dogs), which contains a prologue by Bécquer.

BIBLIOGRAPHY

Primary Texts

Agua pasada. Madrid: Fe; Havana: La Propaganda Literaria, 1894.
Rosas y perros. Orizaba, Mexico: "La Luz," 1883.
His prologue to Bécquer's works appears in *Obras de Gustavo A. Bécquer*. 2 vols. Madrid: Fortanet, 1871.
His theatrical collaborations with Bécquer have been collected in *Teatro de Gustavo Adolfo Bécquer*. Ed. J. A. Tamayo. RFE Anejo 42. Madrid: CSIC, 1949.

Criticism

Alborg, Juan Luis. *Historia de la literatura española*. vol. 4. Madrid: Gredos, 1980.

González-Blanco, Andrés. *Historia de la novela en España desde el romanticismo a nuestros días*. Madrid: Saenz de Jubero, 1909.

Romero Mendoza, Pedro. *Siete ensayos sobre el Romanticismo español*. vol. 1. Cáceres: Servicios Culturales de la Excma. Diputación Provincial de Cáceres, 1960.

Phoebe Porter Medina

RODRÍGUEZ DE ALMELA, Diego (1426?, Murcia–1492, ?), priest, didactic and historical writer. Chaplain to Queen Isabella, student of Alonso de *Cartagena, he wrote a *Compilación de las batallas* (1487; Compilation of Battles), and a *Valerio de las estorias escolásticas y de España* (1487; Valerian of Scholastic Histories and of Spain), which was for a time erroneously attributed to *Pérez de Guzmán. His *Compilación de las crónicas et estorias de España* (written before 1479; Compilation of Spain's Chronicles and Histories) was presented to the monarchs in 1491. The *Compilación de los milagros de Santiago* (1491; Compilation of Miracles of St. James) remained in ms. form until very recently.

BIBLIOGRAPHY

Primary Texts

Compilación de las batallas. Murcia: Lope, 1487.

Compilación de los milagros de Santiago. . . . Ed., study, J. Torres Fontes. Murcia: Nogués, 1946.

Colección de los hechos más notables de la Sagrada escritura . . . a imitación del Valerio. Ed. J. Antonio Moreno. Madrid: Román, 1793.

RODRÍGUEZ DE CUENCA, Juan (fourteenth c.?,–?), historian. He is credited with a *Sumario de los reyes de España* (pub. 1781; Summary of the Monarchs of Spain), which begins with Pelayo and concludes with his own monarch, Henry III.

BIBLIOGRAPHY

Primary Text

Sumario de los reyes de España. Ed. E. de Llaguno. Madrid: Sancha, 1781.

RODRÍGUEZ DE LA CÁMARA (or DEL PADRÓN), Juan (?, El Padrón, Galicia–c. 1450, El Herbón, Galicia), poet, novelist and priest. A member of the minor Galician nobility who traveled widely and may have accompanied Cardinal Cervantes to the Council of Basel (1431–49), Juan Rodríguez figures in literary history as a troubadour in the tradition of his countryman *Macías, el enamorado. It is believed that Juan Rodríguez indiscreetly revealed his love to an important lady at court, and after being angrily rejected, he abandoned courtly life and entered the Franciscan monastery of El Herbón.

His prose works include a treatise on nobility, the *Cadira del honor* (1438;

The Seat of Honor), in which he defends the traditional view that lineage determines true nobility; a defense of women, the *Triunfo de las donas* (1438; The Triumph of Women), which offers fifty reasons for the superiority of women; a partial translation of Ovid's *Heroides,* the *Bursario* (Pocket Novel); and, most significantly, *El siervo libre de amor* (1439–40; The Emancipated Slave of Love). The latter, prototype of the sentimental romance, combines an autobiographical narration, a sentimental tale with tragic ending (the "Estoria de los dos amadores Ardanlier e Liesa" [Story of the Two Lovers Ardanlier and Liesa]), and courtly poems. Other courtly poems by Juan Rodríguez appear in songbooks such as the *Cancionero de *Baena* and the *Cancionero General.*

BIBLIOGRAPHY

Primary Texts

Obras completas. Ed. César Hernández Alonso. Madrid: Nacional, 1982.

Criticism

Andrachuk, Gregory P. "A Re-examination of the Poetry of Juan Rodríguez del Padrón." *BHS* 57 (1980): 299–308.

Cocozzella, P. "The Thematic Unity of Juan Rodríguez del Padrón's *Siervo libre de amor.*" *Hispania* 64 (1981): 188–98.

Gilderman, M. S. *Juan Rodríguez de la Cámara.* TWAS 423. Boston: Twayne, 1977.

Herrero, J. "The Allegorical Structure of the *Siervo libre de amor.*" *Speculum* 55 (1980): 751–64.

Impey, O. "The Literary Emancipation of Juan Rodríguez del Padrón: From the Fictional 'Cartas' to the *Siervo libre de amor.*" *Speculum* 55 (1980): 305–16.

James Ray Green

RODRÍGUEZ DE LENA, Pero (fl. 1434, ?–?), notary. He is remembered for having witnessed the competition of the *Paso honroso de Suero de Quiñones,* and subsequently editing the above-mentioned account. *See also Paso honroso, Libro del.*

BIBLIOGRAPHY

Primary Text

Libro del passo honroso defendido por el Excelente Cavallero Suero de Quiñones. Ed., intro., A. Labandeira Fernández. Madrid: Fundación Universitaria Española, 1977.

RODRÍGUEZ DE MONTALVO, Garci. *See* Montalvo, Garci Ordóñez [or Rodríguez] de

RODRÍGUEZ DE VILLAVICIOSA, Sebastián (1618?, Tordesillas–after 1660, ?), dramatist. He collaborated with *Cáncer, *Moreto, Francisco de *Avellaneda, and others. With Avellaneda he composed his most famous play, *Cuantas veo, tantas quiero* (n.d.; However Many I See, That's How Many I Love). His play *La dama corregidora* (n.d.; The Lady Magistrate) influenced

Montfleury's *La femme juge et partie*. Rodríguez de Villaviciosa's *entremeses* are also of the first order.

BIBLIOGRAPHY

Primary Texts

Cuantas veo, tantas quiero. In BAE 47.

Various *entremeses* in *Colección de entremeses, loas, bailes, jácaras y mojigangas desde fines del siglo XVI*. Ed. E. Cotarelo y Mori. 2 vols. In NBAE 17 and 18.

RODRÍGUEZ FER, Claudio (1956, Lugo–), Galician poet and critic. After studying at the U of Santiago, he began teaching literature. He has published four books of poetry and several short stories, as well as studies of Galician writers. The prologue to *Poemas de amor sen morte* (1979; Love Poems without Death) is important to understanding his creative orientation. In it Rodríguez Fer refers to the basic musical nature of poetry, to the need to return to Galician-Portuguese verse for inspiration, and to love as a means of achieving harmony with the world. The key to this harmony is woman. At the same time, the poet purposely establishes an intertextual mode which helps extend Galician poetry beyond its own linguistic and geographic confines toward that of other countries, in a sort of validation process. In particular, one finds constant evidence of his familiarity with Latin American writers. There is also evidence of modern-day formalism, and an avant-garde interest in combining the visual with the written mode. Except for the somewhat experimental *Cinepoemas* (1983; Filmpoems), there is always an underlying reference to Galicia as place of origin, with its geography, landscapes, climate, human and animal inhabitants, and historical identity. *See also* Galician Literature.

BIBLIOGRAPHY

Primary Texts

Cinepoemas. La Coruña: Xerais, 1983.

Historia da lúa. Vigo: Galaxia, Colección Ronsel, 1984.

Poemas de amor sen morte. Granada: Antonio Ubago, 1979.

Tigres de ternura. Santiago de Compostela: Sociedade Cooperativa ''Reprografía 1846,'' 1980?

Criticism

March, Kathleen N. ''Claudio Rodríguez Fer.'' *Gran Enciclopedia Gallega*. Santiago-Gijón: Silverio Canada Editor, 1974 ff.

Kathleen March

RODRÍGUEZ MARÍN, Francisco (1865, Osuna, Seville–1943, Madrid), Spanish essayist, poet, critic and folklorist. After obtaining a law degree, he was obliged to abandon the practice of law after almost completely losing his voice after an operation. He became director of the National Library (*Biblioteca Nacional), and was elected a member of the *Academia Española in 1905. His poetry collections, *Madrigales* (Madrigals) and *Sonetos* (Sonnets), are classic in style and theme, recalling works of the sixteenth and seventeenth centuries. He also imitated certain literary classics in some of his stories, as seen in *Nueva premática del tiempo* (1891; New Prematics of Time). He collected and published popular sayings, folk songs, and Andalusian proverbs, and compiled extensive repertoires of words not included in the Dictionary of the Academy, for example, *Dos mil quinientas voces castizas y bien autorizadas que piden lugar en nuestro léxico* (1922; 2,500 Authentic and Authoritative Words Which Demand a Place in Our Lexicon). Even more important are his contributions to bibliographies of classical Spanish writers and the annotation of their works. He edited many Renaissance texts, including Pedro de *Espinosa's *Flores de poetas ilustres* (Flowers of Illustrious Poets), the poetry of Baltasar del *Alcázar and Luis *Vélez de Guevara's *El diablo Cojuelo* (The Limping Devil). He wrote a biography of Luis *Barahona de Soto, and published many findings on the life of Mateo *Alemán and notes on many other *Siglo de Oro writers. He is especially known for work in Cervantine studies, his editions of *Cervantes's *Novelas ejemplares* (Exemplary Novels), and extensive commentaries of *Don Quixote*, as well as numerous articles and studies of lesser works by Cervantes.

BIBLIOGRAPHY

Criticism

Río y Rico, G. M. del. *Biografía y Bibliografía de don Francisco Rodríguez Marín.* Madrid: n.p., 1947.

RODRÍGUEZ MÉNDEZ, José María (1925, Madrid–), Spanish playwright, novelist, short story writer, essayist, and theater critic. After earning a law degree, traveling through Argentina as a journalist, serving in the Spanish Legion in North Africa, and then emigrating from Madrid to Barcelona—all experiences to be reflected in his drama and fiction—Rodríguez Méndez became active for six years with La Pipironda, a group that carried popular theater, including his own short pieces, to Barcelona's working-class districts.

Rodríguez Méndez's dramas of critical realism written in the 1950s and 1960s show the tragedy of the common people of Spain, especially its youth—whom he always presents as victims. These plays include *Vagones de madera* (1963; The Wooden Train Cars), where he portrays soldiers recruited to serve as cannon fodder in the 1921 colonial war of Melilla, and *Los inocentes de la Moncloa* (1961; The Innocents of Moncloa), winner of the Larra Award after its Madrid premiere in 1964. Considered one of the key works of Rodríguez Méndez's generation, *Los inocentes* depicts the sordid existence of Spanish students of the 1950s, forced to compete for professional posts in a degrading, dehumanizing system. *La batalla del Verdún* (1966; The Battle of Verdun) portrays Andalusian emigrants to Barcelona obliged to struggle daily for survival, and *Los quinquis de Madriz* (1982; The Low-life of Madrid) dramatizes the adventures of a youth who is finally executed after a shoot-out with the police that he does not initiate.

The latter two dramas, like Rodríguez Méndez's history plays, have their roots in the popular tradition of Lope de *Vega and *Cervantes, the *picaresque, the *sainete or brief farce, and the *esperpento* or distorted image of *Valle-Inclán. *Historia de unos cuantos* (1982; Tale of Some Few People) and *Bodas que fueron famosas del Pingajo y la Fandanga* (1979; The Famous Nuptials of Pingajo and Fandanga) are popular chronicles that show history "from below," from the viewpoint of the ordinary people who are its victims. The former drama depicts ten moments of Spain's history, from 1898 to the 1940s, seen through the eyes of popular Madrid characters taken from *zarzuelas* or light operas and from a musical review of the 1930s. These same characters are the subjects of his *Ensayo sobre el machismo* (1971; An Essay on Machismo). *Bodas que fueron famosas*, a tragi-comedy set in Madrid's *arrabales* or shantytown of 1898, with its illiterate and degraded masses, was selected to inaugurate the new Centro Dramático Nacional in 1978. *Flor de Otoño* (1974; Autumn Flower), which incorporates cabaret music of the 1930s, opened at Madrid's Español Theater in 1982. These chronicles, with their succession of popular sketches and narrative structure, represent a new dramatic model in post–Civil War Spain.

Rodríguez Méndez turned to the dramatic monologue in *Teresa de Avila* (1982), performed by actress María Paz Ballesteros in Madrid's Capilla del Arzobispo, in 1982. Most recently, he has directed productions of his dramatic anthology of poetry and music, *Castilla, pequeño rincón* (Castille: A Small Corner) performed throughout central Spain by a group from Barco de Avila. Rodríguez Méndez, now a resident of Madrid, where he moved from Ávila, has published award-winning fiction and several essays, including two polemical books of theater criticism: *Comentarios impertinentes sobre el teatro español* (1972; Impertinent Commentaries on the Spanish Theater) and *La incultura teatral de España* (1974; The Lack of Theatrical Culture in Spain). *See also* Contemporary Spanish Theater.

BIBLIOGRAPHY

Primary Texts

Bodas que fueron famosas del Pingajo y la Fandanga. Flor de Otoño. Madrid: Cátedra, 1979.

Ensayo sobre la "inteligencia" española. Barcelona: Península, 1972.

Ensayo sobre el machismo español: Del Escarramán al "Pichi." Barcelona: Península, 1971.

Literatura española. Ed. Antonio Morales. Murcia: Universidad de Murcia, 1989.

Los inocentes de la Moncloa. Ed. Martha T. Halsey. Salamanca: n.p., 1980.

Los quinquis de Madriz. Historia de unos cuantos. Teresa de Avila. Murcia: Godoy, 1982.

Criticism

Fernández Insuela, Antonio. "*Bodas que fueron famosas . . .*: Degradación e ironía." *Archivum* (Oviedo) 31–32 (1981–82): 289–304.

Martín Recuerda, José. *La tragedia de España en la obra dramática de José María Rodríguez Méndez (desde la restauración hasta la dictadura de Franco.)* Salamanca: Universidad de Salamanca, 1979.

Monleón, José. ''Teatro popular: la respuesta de Rodríguez Méndez.'' In *Teatro*. By J. M. Rodríguez Méndez. Madrid: Taurus, 1968. 21–55.

Oliva, César. ''Rodríguez Méndez.'' In *Cuatro dramaturgos ''realistas'' en la escena de hoy*. Murcia: U of Murcia, 1978. 77–113.

Ruiz Ramón, Francisco. ''Rodríguez Méndez.'' In *Historia del teatro español. Siglo XX*. Madrid: Cátedra, 1975. 509–16.

Martha T. Halsey

RODRÍGUEZ MOHEDANO, Rafael and Pedro (between 1725 and 1730, ?–between 1795 and 1800, Granada?), Franciscan friars, literary historians. They dedicated their lives to compiling the *Historia literaria de España* (1766–91; Literary History of Spain), a ten-volume opus which, with admirable erudition, only reaches Lucan (AD 39–65). The work provoked criticism by Ignacio *López de Ayala, but was defended by J. Suárez de Toledo, and the two brothers.

BIBLIOGRAPHY

Primary Texts

Historia literaria de España. 2nd ed. 10 vols in 12. Madrid: García, 1769–91.

RODRÍGUEZ MOÑINO, Antonio (1910, Calzadillo de los Canos, Badajoz–1970, Madrid), Spanish philologist and bibliographer, critic and literary historian. Librarian of the Lázaro Galdiano Museum in Madrid, he concentrated his attention upon literati of Extremadura. He served for a time as a professor of Spanish at the U of California (Berkeley), and was elected to the *Academia Española. Rodríguez Moñino authored more than fifty works in addition to his numerous editions of the works of other unknown or forgotten writers, for example, *Poesías* (Poetry) of Gregorio *Silvestre, *Poetas extremeños del siglo XVI* (Extremaduran Poets of the Sixteenth C.), *Joaquín Romero de Cepeda, poeta extremeño del siglo XVI* (Joaquín Romero de Cepeda, Extremaduran Poet of the Sixteenth C.), etc. He also worked on a history of literature in Extremadura, *Historia de la literatura extremeña*, of which he completed only the part up to the Renaissance. He served as editor of the Gallardo collection for bibliophiles, and later of the Castalia publishing house. His studies of Cristóbal de *Mesa, published from 1949 to 1952, are considered of special importance. In 1953, he founded the *Revista española,* perhaps the most important literary organ in Spain during the 1950s and early 1960s for new writers in the fields of essay, criticism and short fiction. He edited the twelve-volume series *Las fuentes del Romancero General* (1957; Sources of the General [Medieval] Ballad Book) with notes, indexes and supplements, a work which alone would have confirmed his position as a major philologist. He was vice-president of the Hispanic Society, and founder of the Clásicos Castalia collection, still in existence, in which the world's most distinguished Hispanists have collaborated in the annotation and publication of definitive or critical editions of important classical and modern texts. His disciples and colleagues prepared a festschrift in his honor entitled *Antonio Rodríguez Moñino: Estudios sobre su labor científica* (1968; Studies

On the Scientific Labors of Antonio Rodríguez Moñino). Other important titles include *Don Bartolomé José Gallardo (1776–1852)* (1955); *Construcción crítica y realidad histórica de la poesía española de los siglos XVI y XVII* (1965; Critical Construction and Historical Reality of Spanish Poetry of the Sixteenth and Seventeenth Centuries), translated to English by L. B. Simpson (1968); *Historia de una infamia bibliográfica. La de San Antonio de 1823* (1965; A History of the Bibliographical Infamy of San Antonio, 1823); *Catálogo de los manuscritos poéticos castellanos existentes en la biblioteca de The Hispanic Society of America* (3 vols., 1965; Catalog of the Poetic Manuscripts in Castilian in the Library of the Hispanic Society), in collaboration with his wife, Maria Brey Mariño; *La Silva de romances de Barcelona, 1561* (1969; The Barcelona Ballad Collection of 1561), and *Diccionario bibliográfico de pliegos sueltos poéticos (siglo XVI)* (1970; A Bibliographic Dictionary of Unbound Poetry Manuscripts of the Sixteenth C.).

RODRÍGUEZ RUBÍ, Tomás (1817, Málaga–1890, Madrid), politician, playwright and poet. A political figure of moderate tendencies, he was the overseas minister until the September Revolution of 1868, when he was forced to emigrate. After the Restoration he became the royal commissar of finance in Cuba. He became a member of the *Academia Española in 1860. In 1841 he published *Poesías andaluzas* (Andalusian Poems), his only book of verse. He is best known for his dramatic works. Highly esteemed as a dramatist during his lifetime, he has since fallen into oblivion. He wrote historical plays such as *Isabel la católica* (1843; Isabella the Catholic), *Bandera negra* (1844; Black Flag) about Philip IV's epoch, *La rueda de la fortuna* (1845; The Wheel of Fortune) about Ensenada, and *La corte de Carlos II* (1846; The Court of Charles II). He also composed comedies of customs with a didactic intention. In this category fall *Casada, virgen y mártir* (1843; Married, Virgin and Martyr) and *La feria de Mairena* (1843; The Fair of Mairena). Over two dozen other plays are comedies of manners, many of which take place in an aristocratic atmosphere and contain ironical drawing room dialogue. On occasions, the ideas in his works are superficial, but he has his moments of humorous and penetrating observation such as in *El agua mansa* (1854; The Calm Water) and *Fiarse del porvenir* (1874; Confide in the Future). He also wrote romantic dramas such as *Borrascas del corazón* (1847; Storms of the Heart) and *La escala de la vida* (1858; The Ladder of Life). Most of his dramatic works are written in verse.

BIBLIOGRAPHY

Primary Texts

Obras dramáticas de T. Rodríguez Rubí. 35 vols. Madrid: n.p., 1840–79.
Poesías andaluzas. 3rd ed. Paris: Lefevre, 1853.

Criticism

Burgos, Ana María. ''Vida y obra de Tomás Rodríguez Rubí.'' *Revista de Literatura* 23 (1963): 65–102.

Smith, W. F. "Contributions of Rodríguez Rubí to the Development of the Alta Comedia." *HR* 10 (1942): 53–63.

Phoebe Porter Medina

RODRÍGUEZ SPITERI, Carlos (1911, Málaga–), poet. An attorney who began his poetic endeavors with *Choque Feliz* (1935; Happy Shock), he thereafter published many volumes of poetry, including the following: *Hasta que la voz descanse* (1943; Until the Voice Rests), *Amarga sombra* (1947; Bitter Shadow), *Las voces del ángel* (1950; Angel's Cries) and a tribute to his native city entitled *Málaga* (1953). He was founder and sponsor of the review *Caracola*, published in Málaga. Other titles include *Ese día* (1959; That Day), *Una puerta ancha* (1962; A Wide Door), *Los espejos* (1964; The Mirrors), *Las cumbres* (1966; Summits), *Cinco poemas* (1966; Five Poems), and *Callar juntos* (1967; Silent Together).

BIBLIOGRAPHY

Primary Texts

Ese día. Madrid: Rialp, 1959.
Una puerta ancha. Málaga: El Guadalhorce, 1962.
Los espejos. Málaga: El Guadalhorce, 1964.
Las cumbres. Málaga: Librería Anticuaria El Guadalhorce, 1965.
Callar juntos. Málaga: Librería Anticuaria El Guadalhorce, 1967.

Genaro J. Pérez

ROF CARBALLO, Juan (1905, Lugo–), Spanish physician and essayist. Founder of the Institute of Psychosomatic Studies, he possesses an ample preparation in psychology, history, humanistic studies and literature, and many of his professional essays are of solid literary quality, including *El hombre a prueba* (1951; Man under Examination), *Patología psicosomática* (1954; Psychosomatic Pathology), *Cerebro interno y mundo emocional* (1952; Inner Brain and the Emotional World), *La medicina actual* (1943; Present-Day Medicine), *Urdimbre afectiva y enfermedad. Introducción a una medicina psicosomática* (1960; Scheme of Affective Relationships and Illness. Introduction to Psychosomatic Medicine), *Entre el silencio y la palabra* (1960; Between Silence and the Word), *Niño, familia y sociedad* (1960; Child, Family and Society), and *El hombre como encuentro* (1968; Man as Encounter).

ROGERIO SÁNCHEZ, Jośe (1876, Valladolid–1950, Madrid), Spanish novelist and philologist. He taught literature for many years at the San Isidro Institute in Madrid, wrote textbooks, published editions of classical works (e.g., the *Gramática* of *Nebrija), and authored several novels, including *Almas de acero* (1904; Souls of Steel), *En busca de la vida* (1906; In Search of Life), and *Tristes destinos* (1908; Sad Destinies).

ROIG, Jaume (?, Valencia–1478, Benimàmet), poet. He probably studied in Barcelona and France. A physician by profession, in this capacity he occupied prestigious jobs, public and private. Aside from *Spill* he produced only minor works such as *Trobes en lahors de la Verge Maria* (Poems Eulogizing the Virgin Mary). Having fled the black plague which afflicted Valencia in April of 1460, he began writing *L'Spill* (The Mirror), also known as *Llibre dels consells i Llibre de les dones* (Book of Good Counsel and Book of Women), which is a furious diatribe against the feminine sex. It is a book strange in form, for although it could be construed as a full-fledged novel, it uses poetic form with a very short meter. It has sixteen thousand lines of four syllables and is divided into a preface and four volumes. Riquer believes Roig was a frustrated narrator because he used a medium unsuited, even in his time, to his objective.

L'Spill is one of the main works of misogynous European literature along the lines of the *Corbaccio* by Boccaccio, *El Corbacho* by the *Arcipreste de Talavera and the *Mathéolus* translated by Jean Le Fevre. The book can be read at two levels, the fantastic relating to the adventures of the hero, and the "true-real" of the locations and ambience of these adventures. With a tremendously realistic attitude and in mostly popular language, the author expresses a very pessimistic view of the world and offers a somber vision of the social milieu he experiences. It is the typical *picaresque story of a child forced into the cruel world by his mother; he ends his literary life in an ambiguous marriage to a virtuous woman, Isabel de Pellisser, who happens to have the same name as the true wife of Roig. *L'Spill* is considered by many as one of the most important precursors of the Spanish picaresque novel; its autobiographical and episodic format is typical of picaresque art, and it depicts the harshest aspects of life. On the other hand, it lacks the moralizing sense of the classic picaresque narrator. Roig's work is literarily valuable for its easygoing humor and the manner in which he takes advantage of the incisive and mordant popular expressions of the Catalan of his time. *See also* Catalan Literature.

BIBLIOGRAPHY

Primary Text

Spill. Ed. Miguel i Planas. 2 vols. Barcelona: Biblioteca Catalana, 1929–50.

Criticism

Agüera, V. G. *Un pícaro catalán del siglo XV (El "Spill" de Jaume Roig y la tradición picaresca)*. Barcelona: Hispam, 1975.

Chabás, R. *Spill o "Llibre de les dones" per Mestre Jaume Roig*. Barcelona-Madrid: L'Avenc, 1905.

Fuster, J. "Jaume Roig i sor Isabel de Villena." *Obres Completes*, I. Barcelona: Ediciones 62, 1968.

Joan Gilabert

ROIG, Montserrat (1946, Barcelona–1991, Barcelona), novelist and short story writer in Catalan, journalist in Catalan and Castilian.

Daughter of Catalan writer Tomàs Roig i Llop, she graduated from the U of

Barcelona (1968) with a degree in Spanish (Castilian). She also participated in the 1966 anti-Franco student occupation of the Capuchin monastery in Barcelona (the Caputxinada), a collective action signaling the open resurgence of Catalan nationalism which would mark her generation. While for pragmatic reasons she has done most of her journalistic work in Castilian, Roig writes her fiction in Catalan, and cites Catalan authors such as *Oller, *Rodoreda, *Villalonga, and *Plà as her principal models. Considered a member of the Catalan literary generation of the 1970s, Roig is a popular writer and a very well-known figure in Spain.

Her literary career was launched when one of her short stories won first prize for narrative fiction at the Jocs Florals (**juegos*) in Caracas, 1966. In 1969 she won three more prizes: the Recull and the Sant Adrià for short stories, and the Serra d'Or for reporting. In 1970 her collection of short stories, *Molta roba i poc sabó i . . . tan neta que la volen* (1971; Lots of Clothes and Little Soap and . . . So Clean They Love It [Spanish tr. *Aprendizaje sentimental*, 1981]), won the important Víctor Català Prize for Fiction. These stories introduce many of the fictional denizens of l'Eixample or El Ensanche (the conservative bourgeois section of Barcelona where Roig grew up) who would reappear in a trilogy exploring the difficult question of Catalan identity in the modern world. Beginning with *Ramona, adéu* (1972; Ramona, Good-Bye [Spanish tr. *Ramona, adiós*, 1981]), this trilogy follows the fortunes of the Miralpeix and Claret families from 1894 to 1979, concentrating particularly on the women of the family; their lives, thoughts, and perceptions of local and world history are privileged over those of their male relatives. The second novel in the trilogy, *El temps de les cireres* (1977; Cherry Time [Spanish tr. *Tiempo de cerezas*, 1981]), won the prestigious Sant Jordi Prize in 1976. The third novel, *L'hora violeta* (1980; *The Violet Hour*, n.d. [Spanish tr. *La hora violeta* 1980]) is undoubtedly the most feminist of the trilogy in inspiration. *L'òpera quotidiana* (1982; The Daily Opera [Spanish tr. *La ópera cotidiana*, 1982]), is Roig's fourth and best novel to date. It returns to l'Eixample, and uses a by now familiar member of the Miralpeix clan as structural axis for its exploration of the changes in Catalan society.

Roig has been a prolific journalist, both print and electronic. She has had three different television interview programs, and has written the following books of reportage: *Rafael Vidiella, l'aventura de la revolució* (1974; Rafael Vidiella, The Adventure of Revolution); *Els catalans als camps nazis* (1977; Catalans in Nazi Concentration Camps [Spanish tr. *Noche y niebla: los catalanes en los campos nazis*, 1978]); *El feminismo* (1981; Feminism); *Mujeres en busca de un nuevo humanismo* (1981; Women in Search of a New Humanism); and *Mi viaje al bloqueo* (1982; My Trip to the Siege), a book about the siege of Leningrad commissioned by its Russian publisher. *¿Tiempo de mujer?* (1980; A Woman's World?) is a collection of Roig's previously published articles on women. She has published six books of interviews: *Retrats paral.lels*, in three volumes (1975, 1976, 1978; Parallel Portraits); *Los hechiceros de la palabra* (1975; Word Wizards); *Personatges* and *Personatges, segona sèrie* (1979 and 1980; Personalities, and Personalities, Part 2).

L'agulla daurada (1985; The Golden Needle [Spanish tr. *La aguja dorada*, 1985]), is a sort of intellectual journal of her experiences in and reflections on Leningrad.

Roig and Isabel-Clara *Simó, a Valencian writer, are the joint subjects for Book 5 in the series Diàlegs a Barcelona (Dialogues in Barcelona); the book is an (edited) transcription of a day-long conversation between the two.

BIBLIOGRAPHY

Primary Texts

L'agulla daurada. Barcelona: Edicions 62, 1985.
Els catalans als camps nazis. Barcelona: Edicions 62, 1977.
El feminismo. Barcelona: Salvat, 1981.
Los hechiceros de la palabra. Barcelona: Martínez Roca, 1975.
L'hora violeta. Barcelona: Edicions 62, 1980.
Mi viaje al bloqueo. Moscow: Progreso, 1982.
Molta roba i poc sabó i . . . tan neta que la volen. Barcelona: Edicions 62, 1978.
Mujeres en busca de un nuevo humanismo. Barcelona: Salvat, 1981.
L'opera quotidiana. Barcelona: Planeta, 1982.
Personatges and *Personatges, segona sèrie*. Barcelona: Pòrtic, 1979, 1980.
Rafael Vidiella, l'aventura de la revolució. Barcelona: Laia, 1974.
Ramona, adéu. Barcelona: Edicions 62, 1972.
Retrats paral.lels. 3 vols. Montserrat: Abadia de Montserrat, 1975, 1976, 1978.
El temps de les cireres. Barcelona: Edicions 62, 1977.
¿Tiempo de mujer? Barcelona: Plaza and Janés, 1980.

English Translations

''Mar'' (''Sea''). In an international anthology of women's fiction published in nine countries and eight languages. British tr. *Sex and Sensibility*. London: Sidwick Jackson, 1981.
The Violet Hour. London: Virago Press, n.d.

Criticism

Busquets i Grabulosa, Ll. *Plomes catalanes contemporànies*. Barcelona: Mall, 1980. 177–84. Interview.
Graells, Guillem-Jordi, and Oriol Pi de Cabanyes. ''De la requesta que fou feta a Montserrat Roig.'' *Serra d'Or* 13.138 (1971): 27–29. Interview.
Nichols, Geraldine C. ''Mitja poma, mitja taronja: Genésis y destino literarios de la catalana contemporánea.'' *Anthropos* 60–61 (1986): 118–23.

Geraldine Nichols

ROJAS, Carlos (1928, Barcelona–), Spanish novelist. Rojas belongs to a group christened by Manuel García Viño as ''intellectual'' novelists, although most of his works belong to the subgenre of the historical novel, or a variant in which history is treated largely as a point of departure, with little regard for ''fact'' as generally conceived: history in the novels of Rojas is a malleable substance in flux, in which critical events are subject to different outcomes with obvious consequences for subsequent happenings. He is a prolific writer, who for many years has been an expatriate, living in the United States and teaching Spanish at Emory U. His early works attracted little attention: *Adolfo Hitler está en mi casa* (1965; Hitler Is in My House); *Rei de Roma* (1966; King of Rome; in Catalan); *Auto de fe* (1968; Act of Faith [the title refers to the ceremonies in which the *Inquisition burned those accused of heresy]); *Aquelarre* (1970; Witches' Sabbath); and *Luis III el Minotauro* (1970; Louis III, the Minotaur). His first significant critical success came when *Azaña* (1973) won the Planeta Prize. This portrait of the controversial president of the Spanish Republic depicts the aging politician in the last months of his life, in exile in France, as he remembers crucial moments of his regime from the disastrous revolt of the Andalusian peasants in Casas Viejas (1934) until the retreat across the Pyrenees (1939), and includes many of the better-known historical figures of the period. More than history or biography, this novel stresses the interpersonal relationships (undocumented but personal) between Azaña and many of these personages, and manages to capture faithfully the idiosyncrasies of Azaña's personal style of speaking and writing. In 1975, Rojas published *Mein Führer, mein Führer*, the second of his novels to focus upon Hitler, but conceived as part of a ''trilogy of power'' together with *Auto de fe* and *Azaña* (somewhat in the manner of Francisco *Ayala in *Los usurpadores*). It is not only the abuse of power, but a symbolic modernization of the medieval theme of the Dance of Death in which the observer questions human passions and destiny, the meaning of human life, and the contradictions of personal and historical existence.

In 1977, Rojas published *Memorias inéditas de J. A. Primo de Rivera* (Unpublished Memoirs of José Antonio *Primo de Rivera —founder of the Falange). José Antonio—political ideologue and ''hero'' or ''martyr'' of Spanish Fascism, executed in 1936—is a logical figure to consider alongside Hitler and Azaña, and necessary to complete the political panorama. Here, however, Rojas takes further poetic license, postulating a version in which José Antonio did not die in Alicante in 1936, but lived to hold a series of conversations with Stalin (and later took the place of Trotsky in Mexico where he would eventually be assassinated by Mercader).

In *El Valle de los Caídos* (1978; Valley of the Fallen), Rojas turns to a topic belonging to the Franco era: the title refers to the monumental mausoleum carved out of living rock for Franco, to serve as a memorial to himself and those who served with him and died in the Civil War. Rojas presents two temporal planes, the present and the Spain of Goya and Ferdinand VII (late eighteenth and early nineteenth centuries) which form a counterpoint indicating that the struggle between liberals and conservatives which began at that time and the slaughter of the Spanish people in their strivings for democracy have not changed. *El ingenioso hidalgo y poeta Federico García Lorca asciende a los infiernos* (1979; The Ingenious Gentleman and Poet, Federico García Lorca, Ascends to Hell) won the Nadal Novel Prize for the year of its publication, Rojas's most prestigious prize to that point. Here Rojas does not change the historical facts of Lorca's assassination but focuses on the poet after death, where his life's most obsessive fear—the terror of dying and the total annihilation of consciousness—is replaced by a ''No Exit'' situation in hell where each soul receives a theater and stage on which memories, dreams and strivings of his/her life are endlessly replayed. *El sueño de Sarajevo* (1982; The Dream of Sarajevo), together with the two immediately preceding novels, constitutes another trilogy, the so-called trilogy of Sandro Vasari (an alter ego of Rojas). The crucial historical event which forms the focal point of this novel is the assassination of Archduke Ferdinand in the Balkans, leading to the outbreak of World War I.

Janet Pérez

ROJAS, Fernando de (c. 1474?, Puebla de Montalbán, Toledo–1541, Talavera), attorney, author of the *Celestina. Much of the life of Rojas, creator of one of Spain's literary jewels, can only be conjectured. Of a **converso* family, he attended the U of Salamanca, probably graduating around 1498 or 1499. He then practiced law in Talavera until his death. The inventory of his will indicates modest yet comfortable circumstances, and a standard library. The *Celestina* is his only work; written when he was about twenty years old, the masterful dialogue in prose closes the door to the Middle Ages (see Edad Media, Literatura de la) as it opens that to the *Renaissance, and creates one of Spain's most enduring archetypes.

BIBLIOGRAPHY

Primary Text

La Celestina. Ed. D. S. Severin. Intro. S. Gilman. Madrid: Alianza, 1969.

English Translation

The Spanish Bawd. Tr. J. M. Cohen. Harmondsworth and Baltimore: Penguin, 1964.

Criticism

Dunn, Peter N. *Fernando de Rojas.* TWAS 368. Boston: Twayne, 1975.
Gilman, S. *The Spain of Fernando de Rojas.* Princeton: Princeton UP, 1973.

ROJAS VILLANDRANDO, Agustín de (1572, Madrid–before 1635?, Paredes de Nava), writer, actor and dramatist. He journeyed from city to city, and was known as ''el caballero del milagro'' (the miracle-knight), as it was not known how he supported himself. In addition to travels throughout Spain, he spent time as a soldier in France, as a pirate against the English, and in Italy. In 1603, he married Ana de Arceo and left the world of acting he had inhabited the previous six or seven years. One of his most ardent desires was to prove his noble lineage; he pursued this goal in vain. The last document in which he is described as living is dated 1618, and is a request for proof of nobility. In 1635 Ana de Arceo, as the author's widow, petitioned for the documents—thus Rojas Villandrando is presumed to have died before then.

His many travels and strong curiosity about the world gave Rojas much knowledge to share with his reading public. His drama *El natural desdichado* (n.d.; The Unfortunate Native) is important as a precursor of *Calderón's *La vida es sueño*. The prose work *El buen repúblico* (1611; The Good Republic) is primarily a didactic proposal of principles of good government. Within several months of its publication, the book was banned by the *Inquisition because of several pages dealing with astrology.

The work for which Rojas is best known is *El viaje entretenido* (1603; The Entertaining Journey); it presents a panorama of life in the theatrical companies of that time. The work also served as a vehicle for publication of Rojas's own **loas*. The *Viaje* uses dialogue, drama and narrative, and combines experiences from Rojas's life and his wide readings. A sentimental novel, the story of Leonardo and Camila, is also included in the work. It met with great success, being published in 1603 and then again in 1604, 1611 (two editions), 1614, 1615, 1624, and 1625. The *Viaje* today holds clear historical value for the information it provides about the details of theatrical life of the day and the topics of interest to the learned reader of the era.

BIBLIOGRAPHY

Primary Texts

El buen repúblico. Salamanca: A. Ramírez, 1611.
El viaje entretenido. Ed. Jean Pierre Ressot. Madrid: Clásicos Castalia, 1972.

Criticism

Joset, J. "De Fernando de Rojas a Agustín de Rojas: Presencia de *La Celestina* en *El viaje entretenido*." In *La Celestina y su contorno social: Actas del I Congreso Internacional sobre La Celestina*. Ed. M. Criado de Val. Hispam: Colección Summa, Barcelona; Borrás, 1977. 347–57.

———. "Un falso libro picaresco: Sobre el género literario de *El viaje entretenido* de Agustín de Rojas Villandrando." In *La picaresca: Orígenes, textos y estructuras*. Ed. M. Criado de Val. Madrid: Fundación Universitaria Española, 1979. 825–31.

Osuna, R. "El estilo enumerativo en el *Viaje entretenido* de Rojas Villandrando." *Neophilologus* 62 (1978): 386–91.

Nina Shecktor

ROJAS ZORRILLA, Francisco de (1607, Toledo–1648, Madrid), dramatist and poet. The most acclaimed playwright of the *Calderón school, he was thoroughly imbued with the spirit of court life in Madrid, and enjoyed the patronage of Philip IV. At the age of twenty-four he contributed a sonnet to an homage volume dedicated to the king (*Anfiteatro de Felipe el Grande*; Amphitheater of Philip the Great) on the occasion of his having shot a bull from a palace window. A poet of the Buen Retiro, he frequented the literary circles of the court and was often in the company of the leading authors, among them Antonio *Coello, *Pérez de Montalbán and Calderón de la Barca. Early in his career he collaborated with various contemporaries in the composition of plays, some of which were well received by the public. His *Los bandos de Verona, Montescos y Capeletes* (pub. 1645; The Factions of Verona, Montesques and the Capulets) was selected to inaugurate the Buen Retiro Coliseum in 1640. The same year, he married Catalina Yáñez Trillo de Mendoza. Their son, Antonio de Rojas, became a judge in the Mexican High Court. He had an extramarital affair with María Escobedo, the wife of an actor also named Francisco de Rojas. His illegitimate daughter, Francisca Bezón (nicknamed La Bezona), became a noted actress. In 1643 his eligibility for knighthood was established and the king was able to have him inducted into the Order of Saint James. Francisco de *Quevedo presided as scribe at the second inquiry, at which time the doubts which had at first delayed his admission to the order were dispelled.

Most of Rojas's plays were published in two *partes* (anthologies) during his lifetime. Some not included in these collections were published later in various anthologies and separately (*sueltas*). The first collection (Madrid: María de Quiñones, 1640) contains a dozen plays: *No hay amigo para amigo* (Point of Honor), *No hay ser padre siendo rey* (Venceslas), *Donde hay agravios no hay celos* (The Servant Master), *Casarse para vengarse* (Vendetta Marriage), *Obligados y ofendidos* (The Generous Enemies), *Persiles y Sigismunda o hallarse para perderse* (Persiles and Sigismunda or The Found Lost), *Peligrar en los remedios* (The Risk of Rescue), *Los celos de Rodamonte* (Rodamonte's Jealousy), *Santa Isabel, reina de Portugal* (St. Isabel, Queen of Portugal), *La traición busca castigo* (*The False Friend*, 1702), *El profeta falso Mahoma* (Mohammed the False Prophet), *Progne y Filomena* (Procne and Philomela).

The second collection of Rojas's plays (Madrid: Francisco Martínez, 1645), also contains a dozen works: *Lo que son las mujeres* (Women Defined), *Los bandos de Verona* (The Factions of Verona), *Entre bobos anda el juego* (Don Lucas del Cigarral), *Sin honra no hay amistad* (No Friendship without Honor), *Nuestra Señora de Atocha* (Our Lady of Atocha), *Abrir el ojo* (Keep a Close Watch), *Los trabajos de Tobías* (The Hardships of Toby), *Los encantos de Medea* (Medea's Spells), *Los tres blasones de España* (The Three Glories of Spain), *Los áspides de Cleopatra* (Cleopatra's Asps), *El más impropio verdugo* (The Most Inappropriate Executioner), *Lo que quería ver el Marqués de Villena* (What the Marquis of Villena Wanted to See).

Other plays by Rojas include *El Caín de Cataluña* (The Catalan Cain), *Cada cual lo que le toca* (To Everyone His Due), *El desafío de Carlos V* (The Challenge of Charles V), *Primero es la honra que el gusto* (Honor over Pleasure), *La vida en el ataúd* (Life in the Coffin), *Morir pensando matar* (Deathbed Vengeance), *Numancia cercada* and *Numancia destruida* (Numantia Beseiged and Numantia Destroyed), and his most famous drama, *Del rey abajo, ninguno o el labrador más honrado, García del Castañar* (*None beneath the King*, 1924).

Rojas's contribution to the evolution of Spanish drama is considerable. He sharpens and concentrates tragic confrontations, dramatizing attitudes which challenge the traditional view of the personal honor code. His revolutionary bent was not at first appreciated by the public. His *Cada cual, lo que le toca* was booed because it questions the time-honored view of male superiority by elevating woman to a status of equal authority and respect. In this play the wife takes personal vengeance herself after being raped. The husband is seen as a weak, spineless wretch, incapable of taking decisive action to right a wrong which occurred before the marriage vows were spoken. Américo *Castro saw in this drama, as well as in *El Caín de Cataluña*, echoes of Erasmus's philosophy. In each work the protagonist—torn between duty to country and love for family—opts for a compromise solution to the crisis which leaves both intact. In this and other of Rojas's plays, woman is emanicipated and the inflexible grip of the honor code is relaxed to a degree rarely seen on the stage previously. Woman is man's equal if not his superior in many of Rojas's most entertaining plays in which duty to the public order can be fulfilled without the sacrifice of family ties. Women assume the decisive role in *Progne y Filomena* and in *La traición busca la venganza* in which the deceitful lover is executed and the wife allowed to live. In *No hay ser padre siendo rey*, a father refuses to execute his homicidal son. He abdicates in favor of the latter, in this way avoiding having to choose between adherence to the law and love of family. A similar choice must be made in *El Caín de Cataluña*, which dramatizes the case of a fratricidal son. In this interesting play, the father releases his son from prison but justice is still served when the guards—unaware that the escape had been authorized—fire upon the fleeing criminal, who is killed.

Rojas's best known work, *Del rey abajo, ninguno*, is more traditional in the treatment of the honor code. As in several earlier dramatizations of the motif, Rojas reaffirms the absolute authority of the monarchy and the power of an aggrieved husband over his wife. Once García realizes that the intruder is not the king, he is free to take vengeance against both his wife and the nobleman who threatens his personal honor. The scene in which García contemplates murdering his innocent wife is inconsistent with Rojas's usual portrayal of victimized women. Another exception is found in his *Casarse por vengarse*, which has similarities of plot with Calderón's *El médico de su honra* (The Physician of His Own Dishonor). In *Del rey abajo, ninguno* Rojas combines highly original descriptions of bucolic life, the hunt, and matrimony in lyrical songs which provide a marked contrast to the aura of horror and bitterness implicit in the unfolding tragedy. The reapers' songs and the sonnets exchanged by the married couple are especially fine. These compositions contribute a contemporary immediacy to the historical framework of the material dramatized.

Several of the plays based on mythology or ancient history are worthy of mention. In *Los áspides de Cleopatra*, the intervention of fate in love affairs is well dramatized. The metaphoric language resembles that of the post-Gongorine generations of poets as well as the stylistic imprint of Calderón.

A peculiar structural characteristic of some plays is the inclusion of exaggerated character types in isolated vignettes, which appear as if independent of the primary action. They are not unlike extended **entremeses* (interludes) which tend to momentarily suspend the progression of the play. The character Don Lucas in *Entre bobos anda el juego* is among the most amusing of these caricatures. The motif of the old man married to a much younger woman provides clever yet grotesque episodes in the manner of interludes.

Rojas also composed some eight *autos sacramentales* (**auto*) in which the

Calderón model is easily detected though in lesser dimension. Among this group of dramas are included *Galán, valiente y discreto* (Handsome, Brave and Wise), *El rico avariento* (The Wealthy Beggar), *La viña de Nabot* (Naboth's Vineyard), and *El gran patio de palacio* (The Great Palace Courtyard), which hinges upon the metaphor of the world as a palace where all must go to present petitions to God.

Imitations of Rojas's works were frequent in other languages, especially in French. Lesage based his *Le point d'honneur* on *No hay amigo para amigo*. Scarron imitated his *Obligados y ofendidos* in *L'écolier de Salamanque* as did Corneille in his *Les illustres ennemis* and Lesage in his *Le Diable boiteux*. Beaumarchais used it for his *Eugenia*. *Entre bobos va el juego* is the model for Scarron's *Don Japhet d'Armenie* and for Corneille's *Don Bertrand du Cigarral*. *See also* Theater in Spain.

BIBLIOGRAPHY

Primary Texts

Cada cual lo que le toca. Ed. Américo Castro. Teatro Antiguo Español II. Madrid: Sucesores de Hernando, 1917.

Comedias escogidas de Don Francisco de Rojas Zorrilla, ordenadas en colección por don Ramón de Mesonero Romanos. BAE 54.

Del rey abajo, ninguno. Entre bobos anda el juego. Ed. F. Ruiz Morcuende. Clásicos Castellanos 35. Madrid: Espasa-Calpe, 1917.

Morir pensando matar. La vida en el ataúd. Ed. Raymond R. MacCurdy. Clásicos Castellanos 153. Madrid: Espasa-Calpe, 1961.

Numancia cercada y Numancia destruida. Ed. Raymond R. MacCurdy. Madrid: Porrúa Turanzas, 1977.

English Translations

The False Friend. Tr. Sir John Vanbrugh. London: n.p., 1702.

The Man's the Master. Tr. William D'Avenant. London: Herringmen, 1669.

None beneath the King. Tr. Isaac Goldberg. Girard, KS: Haldeman-Julias, 1924.

Criticism

Cotarelo y Mori, Emilio. *Francisco de Rojas Zorrilla, noticias biográficas y bibliográficas*. Madrid: Revista Archivos, 1911.

MacCurdy, Raymond R. *Francisco de Rojas Zorrilla and the Tragedy*. Albuquerque: U of New Mexico P, 1958.

———. *Francisco de Rojas Zorrilla. Bibligrafía crítica*. Madrid: CSIC, 1965.

———. *Francisco de Rojas Zorrilla*. TWAS 64. New York: Twayne, 1968.

Reichenberger, Arnold G. "Recent Publications Concerning Francisco de Rojas Zorrilla." *HR* 32 (1964): 351–59.

Richard Glenn

ROLDÁN, José María (1771, Seville–1828, Seville), priest, poet. Religious and neo-classical themes dominate his poems, which were published in the Seville magazine *El correo literario*.

BIBLIOGRAPHY

Primary Texts

Poesías. In BAE 67.

ROMANCE. *See Romancero*

ROMANCERO. The *Romancero* is the complete corpus of Hispanic ballads (Spanish, Hispano-American, Portuguese, Catalan, and Judeo-Spanish). The *romance* can be defined as a relatively short, epico-lyric narrative poem, in sixteen-syllable usually monorhymed verses divided into two octosyllabic hemistichs, with assonant rhyme in each second hemistich. In practice, however, a number of poems that are neither octosyllabic nor monorhymed (assonant parallelistic couplets, for example) have also been accepted into the *Romancero* canon. The eight-syllable *romance* verse ultimately derives from the anisosyllabic assonant verse of the medieval Spanish epic. The generally accepted theory, as demonstrated by Ramón *Menéndez Pidal, is that the earliest *romances* began as fragments, isolated scenes, of **cantares de gesta* (traditional epics)—always the most dramatic, peak points of the narrative—which, because of their special interest, came to be sung separately and eventually evolved into independent poems in their own right. But, in addition to such epic beginnings, it is clear that traditional lyric poetry also played a significant role in the origins of the *Romancero* and that, in addition, strophic ballads current in other European speech communities, notably France, soon began to be taken over and adapted in *romance* form. Continuing one of the essential functions of the medieval epic, *noticierismo* (retelling current history in verse form), the *romances* were also used early on as a vehicle for narrating and commenting on contemporary events. Spanish ballads can be documented from as early as 1421, but there is convincing secondary evidence that they were already being sung a century before, in the early 1300s.

Throughout the fifteenth c. there is only sporadic documentation, but in the early 1500s, *romances* began to become enormously popular and were published in cheap, and ephemeral, popular broadsides (*pliegos sueltos*). Though we know of at least one early attempt to bring ballads together in book form, the *Libro en el qual se contienen cincuenta romances* (Barcelona, c. 1525; A Book Containing Fifty Ballads) and *romances* are also included in Hernando del Castillo's *Cancionero general* (General Anthology of Poems and Songs), published in 1511, the period from around 1510 to 1550 can be considered the epoch of the *pliegos sueltos*. Around 1548, Martín Nucio, a printer in Antwerp, published his undated *Cancionero de romances* (Ballad Anthology), thus initiating a new stage in early ballad documentation: the **cancioneros*. Following Nucio's collection, the printing of ballads in book form came into vogue, though *pliegos* continued to be published as well. The ballads perpetuated in both *pliegos* and *cancioneros* appear to be surprisingly uniform. In most cases, we have but a single version of any given ballad. If a ballad had previously been printed, the printed text was usually given preference over any variant version that might have been known from oral tradition. Thus the early *Romancero* seems to consist of a series of identical versions which are monotonously reprinted, with only minimal textual variations from one *cancionero* to another. But such apparent uniformity is misleading. Besides the *pliegos sueltos* and *cancioneros*, there is abundant additional evidence concerning the *romances*' traditional existence during this period: literary quotations of isolated verses; *ensaladas* (miscellany poems combining single verses from different ballads and songs); citations of verses and even entire ballads in *Siglo de Oro dramas; Portuguese song books, independent of the Castilian printed canon; proverbialization of ballad lines; ballads cited and adapted in guitar manuals (*vihuelistas*); verses used as tune indicators in Hebrew hymnals (*piyûtîm*); and the crucial testimony of the modern oral tradition all provide indispensable evidence concerning the *romancero viejo* (early balladry) and its traditional variability. Despite the seeming uniformity of the early printed texts, ballads in the fifteenth and sixteenth centuries were, then, just as multiplex and as protean as are those which can be documented in oral tradition today.

In the 1580s, with the publication of the *Flores de romances* (Bouquets of Ballads), Spanish balladry entered yet another phase. From its very first use in printed form (in Hernando del Castillo's *Cancionero*), *romance* verse had been used by learned poets, but in the *Flores*, this adaptation of the traditional verse to the purposes of learned poetry took on a new importance. The result was a plethora of ballads of learned origin: *el romancero nuevo* (new balladry). Though the old traditional ballads, in both *pliegos sueltos* and *cancioneros*, continued to be printed well into the seventeenth c. (and, in a few exceptional cases, even later), the 1580s and 1590s are the *grande époque* of the *romancero nuevo*, culminating in the *Romancero general* (1600). In the early seventeenth c., the *romance*'s use among cultured poets began to decline and, for the next two centuries, it was largely relegated to an almost "underground" existence: *Romances* continued to be sung, as oral poetry, wherever Hispanic languages were spoken, and they also continued to circulate in printed form in popular broadsides distributed and sung by itinerant blind men. In the eighteenth c., ballad meter was still cultivated by learned poets and to a greater extent than has usually been recognized, but, in general, the late seventeenth, eighteenth, and early nineteenth centuries are an apparently regressive time for the *Romancero*. During these years, just as during the fourteenth and fifteenth centuries, oral *romances* existed essentially in what Menéndez Pidal defined as an *estado latente* (latent state): that is, a cultural feature may exist and may even be very popular among the common people, but will go unrecognized by literate cultural media. Scholarly interest in the ballad was awakened in the nineteenth c., with *Romanticism's concern for popular culture. Extensive collections of traditional *romances* began to be brought together, first in Portugal, then in Catalonia, Brazil, Spain, and the Sephardic communities, later in Spanish America, and later still in the Canary Islands.

In the early 1900s, Menéndez Pidal began a sustained campaign, which continues even today, to rediscover the Hispanic ballad tradition in all its diverse geographic and linguistic ramifications. This research initiative led to the formation, in Madrid, of a monumental ballad archive, embodying many thousands of variant texts, which today make possible minutely detailed studies of the *Romancero* in its many geographic and chronological varieties. One of the most striking features of the *romance* is its Pan-Hispanic character, its essentially universal distribution throughout the Hispanic world. It is safe to say, as Menéndez Pidal theorized years ago—and subsequent research has repeatedly confirmed his theory—that *romances* will be found wherever Spanish, Portuguese, Catalan, and Judeo-Spanish are spoken. As a consequence, it is impossible to study the *Romancero* in a complete and satisfactory way without taking into account all its geographic and chronological modalities. Another notable feature is the *Romancero*'s continued existence on both the traditional and learned levels: while the *romance* has lived for centuries as an essentially oral genre, it has, at the same time, also been cultivated as an artistic medium by some of the most brilliant Spanish poets, from Lope de *Vega and *Góngora to Antonio *Machado and Federico *García Lorca. The most practical classification system currently in use for Hispanic ballads—though certainly not without its flaws—combines origins for some categories with thematic content for others. By the time the ballad tradition emerged from its centuries of *estado latente* (c. 1328–1510) to achieve universal popularity among all social classes—from kings to stable boys—in the sixteenth c., the *romance*, in terms of its thematic diversity, was already an enormously complex poetic genre, embodying compositions devoted to the most variegated topics: stories dating back to medieval Spanish and French epics; events derived from Spanish history; narratives from the Bible and the Apocrypha; legends from classical antiquity; stories based on medieval *romans d'aventure*; and novelesque adventures, either created in Spain or adapted from the balladry of other European peoples. the thematic range of such novelesque *romances*—the most popular in the modern oral tradition—is impressively diverse and covers a wide range of human experiences and emotions, both good and bad: marital fidelity and infidelity; amorous adventures and the misfortunes of love; the husband's return; the unfortunate wife; the evil mother-in-law; tricks and deceptions; rape and abduction; incest and infanticide; murder, mayhem, and bloody vengeance.

Scholarship concerning Pan-Hispanic balladry has burgeoned during the last fifteen years. From a generally neglected and little known field, cultivated by a few specialists, ballad studies have emerged as a fully recognized and notably productive branch of Hispanism. The pathfinding research of Menéndez Pidal laid the groundwork for the rigorous study of early ms. and printed evidence and also led to the rediscovery of the modern oral tradition. *Rodríguez Moñino's monumental contributions have made it possible to study the early printed evidence with renewed attention to the smallest textual details. Paul Bénichou's crucially important work has led to a re-evaluation of the oral tradition as a dynamic, creative process. The massive field expeditions carried out by Diego Catalán and other researchers at the Seminario Menéndez Pidal, as well as their innovative approaches to the analysis of ballads and ballad poetics, have produced dramatic discoveries and important critical insights. Currently the *Romancero* is being studied from a variety of perspectives: the early *Romancero* and the search for previously unknown *pliegos* and *cancioneros*; early fragmentary evidence: literary allusions, *ensaladas*, etc.; the *Romancero* and Golden Age drama; historical studies: connections with the epic, *noticierismo*, the origins and development of individual themes; Pan-European analogues; fieldwork on the modern tradition; ballad music; bibliography and cataloging; literary criticism; creativity in oral tradition; ideological and sociological perspectives; semiotics; formulaic diction; and computer-based research. Such a multi-faceted scholarly effort bodes well for the future of *Romancero* studies as a healthy new sub-discipline of Hispanism.

BIBLIOGRAPHY

Primary Texts

Amades, Joan. *Folklore de Catalunya: Cançoner*. Barcelona: Selecta, 1951.

Beutler, Gisela. *Estudios sobre el romancero español en Colombia*. Bogotá: Caro y Cuervo, 1977.

Costa Fontes, Manuel da. *Romanceiro da Ilha de S. Jorge*. Coimbra: Universidade, 1983.

Menéndez Pidal, Ramón, et al. *Romancero tradicional de las lenguas hispánicas*. Ed. Diego Catalán et al. 12 vols. Madrid: Gredos, 1957–85.

Rodríguez Moñino, Antonio. *Diccionario de pliegos sueltos poéticos (Siglo XVI)*. Madrid: Castalia, 1970.

———. *Manual bibliográfico de cancioneros y romanceros*. 4 vols. Madrid: Castalia, 1973–78.

Sánchez Romeralo, Antonio, et al. *Bibliography of the Hispanic Ballad in Oral Tradition*. Madrid: Seminario Menéndez Pidal, 1980.

Wolf, Fernando J., and Conrado Hofmann. *Primavera y flor de romances*. Ed. Marcelino Menéndez Pelayo. Santander: CSIC, 1945.

English Translations

Armistead, Samuel G., and Joseph H. Silverman (musical transcriptions: Israel J. Katz). *Folk Literature of the Sephardic Jews*. 2 vols. Berkeley and Los Angeles: U of California P, 1971–86. English translations or detailed abstracts.

———, et al. *Judeo-Spanish Ballads in the Menéndez Pidal Archive*. 3 vols. Madrid: Seminario Menéndez Pidal, 1978. Detailed plot summaries in Spanish and English.

Bryant, Shasta M. *The Spanish Ballad in English*. Lexington: UP of Kentucky, 1973.

Catalán, Diego, et al. *The Pan-Hispanic Ballad: General Descriptive Catalogue*. 3 vols. Madrid: Seminario Menéndez Pidal, 1982–84. Exhaustive plot summaries in Spanish and English.

Merwin, W. S. *Some Spanish Ballads*. New York: Abelard-Schumann, 1961.

Wright, Roger. *Spanish Ballads*. Warminster, England: Aris and Phillips, 1987.

Criticism

Bénichou, Paul. *Creación poética en el romancero tradicional*. Madrid: Gredos, 1968.

Catalán, Diego. ''El romancero medieval.'' *El comentario de textos, 4*. Madrid: Castalia, 1983. 451–89.

Catalán, Diego, et al. *Catálogo General del Romancero.* 4 vols. Madrid: Seminario Menéndez Pidal, 1982–88.
Débax, Michelle. *Romancero.* Madrid: Alhambra, 1982.
Menéndez Pidal, Ramón. *Romancero hispánico.* 2 vols. Madrid: Espasa-Calpe, 1953.
Petersen, Suzanne H., et al. *Voces nuevas del romancero castellano-leonés.* 2 vols. Madrid: Seminario Menéndez Pidal, 1982.
Sánchez Romeralo, Antonio, et al. *The Hispanic Ballad Today.* 3 vols. Madrid: Seminario Menéndez Pidal, 1979.
Webber, Ruth H. *Hispanic Balladry Today.* New York: Garland, 1989.

Samuel G. Armistead

ROMANCILLA. *See Endecha*

ROMANTICISM, a cultural movement. The term designates the modes of thinking, feeling, and creating that replaced the modes of the Enlightenment, the Age of Reason, and came to prevail in all areas of cultural activity in the Western World around the end of the eighteenth c. While some representatives of the movement lived almost till the end of the nineteenth c., new writers still moved by the fundamental Romantic impulses and appearing after about 1850 are usually thought of as epigonic, post- or late-Romantic. Still, if the time of its origin is relatively easy to fix, many critics would claim that the end of the movement is nowhere in sight, that even the self-styled reactions against it are expressions of the Romantic spirit. If no legislation can prevent the use of the adjective *romantic* to characterize cultural phenomena originating in earlier periods or in lands untouched by eighteenth-c. rationalism and the rebellion against it, the adjective with a capital R (in English: some other languages, e.g., Spanish, lack the advantage of this distinction) had, in the interests of sanity, best be restricted to the movement historically defined. But agreed as we all may be on such a historical delimitation, we shall find it virtually impossible to achieve a satisfactory qualitative definition, for it was a movement rife with contradictions and paradoxes as it endeavored in numberless ways to build a new culture out of the shards of the Enlightenment, that age which by applying to itself its own principles of rational analysis (Berkeley, Kant), committed, so to speak, cultural suicide. The supremacy of reason both as the logical faculty capable of understanding reality and as everyday common sense; the assumption that rules not only for ethical conduct but for artistic creation (the much misunderstood unities, among others) were not only discoverable but, in the arts, had been discovered once and for all "out there"; the consequent advocacy of the imitation not of nature but of classical models (wherefore "neo" classicism) in the arts, with their objectively pleasing qualities of proportion and balance, what sensible men would naturally prefer as a matter of good taste as they pursued the common goal of human (social) perfectibility—in place of this unitary, cosmopolitan project, which we call the Enlightenment (*Ilustración* in Spanish) and of which the enduring verbal monuments are in the realm of thought (Locke, Hume, Leibniz, Kant, Descartes, Diderot, to name but a few) and in didactic, critical, and satirical prose (Lessing, Voltaire, Swift, Johnson) and not in the pallid neoclassic imitations of Roman imitations of Greek tragedy or the equally pallid, uninspired lyric poetry—in place of this project Romanticism offered what may properly be called a counterproject that starts with the individual, whose reason, if not denigrated, is subservient to his imagination and emotions, who belongs not to an abstraction called society but to a people, a nation (wherefore nationalism and, in the sense in which we use the word today, patriotism) and who is by nature *free* (of despots in politics, of rules in the arts, of constraints in economics) and whose inner soul and its motions are the proper subject of expression and object of imitation in the arts. It can be seen at once why the artifacts of Romanticism are so multifarious that a definition will be either so ample as to be useless or so precise as to exclude what must be included.

In recent years, Professor Russell P. Sebold has tried to make of Spain the first, rather than the last, European nation to espouse and exemplify Romantic doctrine, by relentlessly asserting that *Cadalso's *Noches lúgubres* (1789; Funereal Nights) is a thoroughly Romantic work and therefore the earliest specimen in existence of Romantic literature, and by claiming, with similar relentlessness, that long before *Weltschmerz* was coined in German and *mal du siècle* in French, *Meléndez Valdés had named the Romantic malady *fastidio universal* in his second elegy (1794). The argument is neither original (*Azorín said the same thing citing the same texts, more than half a century ago) nor sustainable. Meléndez is not describing his alienation from the world—no amount of torturing the text of the elegy can extract this sense from it—but complaining about the way things have worked out for him. To his friend *Jovellanos—to whom the poem is addressed—he says, "You can save me." Real *Weltschmerz* has no remedy. "Along with Cadalso, Meléndez," as Professor Emilio Palacios says, "becomes the authentic creator of Romantic language, . . . which does not mean that he was a Romantic. His ideas continue to be those of the Enlightenment." Such literary deportment constituted what for generations critics have sensibly called pre-Romantic. Romanticism in Spain began elsewhere.

The Spanish nineteenth c. from its beginning to its end was marked by political turbulence. In 1808, Napoleon invaded and placed his brother Joseph on the throne, where he remained till 1814, when Ferdinand VII brought the Bourbon dynasty back to power. The intellectual heirs to the Enlightenment divided into two groups, the *liberales*—those who wanted a Spanish king to head a Spanish democracy—and the *afrancesados* (the beFrenched)—those who saw good in the Europeanizing influence of the foreign king. A less ideological label also came into use, *patriotas*, who took the side of the *patria* against the Napoleonic invaders and were the main actors in the *guerrillas* that finally brought an end to Joseph's reign. Three words, thus, that were not in the first instance inspired by the Romantic movement were very soon associated with it and entered into general European usage from the Spanish situation—*liberal* (in the political sense), *patriot* (the person who is for his country right or wrong because it is his), and *guerrilla* (little war, i.e., warfare waged without central direction).

Vis-à-vis the stolid resistance of the church and the generally conservative establishment, *liberales* and *afrancesados*, as circumstances permitted, continued the effort to achieve enlightenment in Spanish intellectual life, and so, in literary matters the doctrines of neo-classicism were still being advocated by the best Spanish minds at a time when Romanticism had gained the day in Germany, France, and England. This obduracy led to a tiresome quarrel which cannot be kept out of any account of Spanish Romanticism. Taking up in an extremely selective way the doctrines of A. W. Schlegel, Johan Nikolas Böhl von Faber (in Spain, Juan Nicolás *Böhl de Faber), a German who had become a Spanish citizen, published a series of newspaper articles in which he sought to persuade Spanish writers to abandon neo-classicism with all its rules, go back to the great "Romantic" theater of *Calderón, and thus fall into line with the most advanced literary practice of Europe. The ill-concealed intention of Böhl's campaign was to support the absolutist reactionary Catholic government of Ferdinand VII, an intention that had nothing to do with Schlegel, who admired Calderón not for conservative political reasons but because, like Shakespeare, the Spanish dramatist represented freedom from rules, inner spiritual realities, national spirit, etc. Entering the debate on the neo-classic side, the *liberal* José Joaquín de *Mora, seconded occasionally by Antonio *Alcalá Galiano, argued in a hit-or-miss way against the abandonment of Enlightenment ideals, which had yet to be fulfilled in Spain. It was an argument between mediocrities, won by neither side, since, as Professor Donald Shaw has pointed out in an extremely perspicacious article, it went on in a void: during the years of the so-called *querella calderoniana* (Calderón question), 1813–20, no significant literary life was going on in Spain; there was no one to convince.

Although Böhl retired from the polemic to become an honorary member of the Spanish Academy (*Academia Española) and Mora in time changed sides, the quarrel was taken over by other spokesmen expressing their views in pamphlets and in the periodical press. Two names will suffice as representatives, one an intelligent defender of classicism, Alberto *Lista, the other, Agustín *Durán, a scarcely coherent advocate of the great Spanish theater of the past. As the late Vicente Llorens explains, between the classicistic pedants and the official censorship under Ferdinand VII, there was little breathing space for those inclined to original literary activity. "For the Spanish government there was no critical authority more competent than that of the churchmen. And it is they, from the Archbishop of Toledo . . . to the Queen's confessor, who determined not the literary value but the morality of a work, simply on the basis of such details as the presence of a *lip* in a verse of Moratín's or a passage in which *breasts* are mentioned."

Not only for *afrancesados* but also for *liberales*, Ferdinand VII's unenlightened despotism meant either prison or exile, and, especially from the fall of the Liberal government in 1823 till the death of Ferdinand in 1833, virtually the entire intellectual class of Spain was to be found in exile, mostly in France, with some 8,000 *afrancesados* and uncounted *liberales*, but also in England, where some

1,000 Liberal families are estimated to have found refuge (see Llorens, *Liberales y románticos*). If there was to be a significant Romantic movement in Spain, it would have to be produced largely by these people. And so it was. Cultural life inside Spain was saved from extinction by a handful of *afrancesados*, Llorens observes, who were able to adapt to the situation—Lista, *Gómez Hermosilla, *Miñano, Narganes. *Espronceda, Ventura de la *Vega, and other figures of the Romanticism-to-be got their classical education from Alberto Lista in the Colegio de San Mateo in Madrid. "Between those that stayed behind and those abroad [Llorens again] there was at first no contact and at best very little. . . . While the expatriates could work in freedom, those at home were subject to *censorship, so that two Spanish literatures came into existence, each going its own way." The analogy with the Franco decades is too striking to pass unmentioned.

Awaiting the expatriates in London was the remarkable ex-priest José María *Blanco White, a true voluntary emigré, who had been living there since 1810. Without ceasing to be a Spaniard he had become not only an Englishman but an English man of letters at the time of Romanticism's great flowering in his adopted country, in both poetry and literary criticism—Wordsworth's decisive preface to the *Lyrical Ballads* (1798), Hazlitt's *Lectures on the English Poets* (1818), Mme de Staël's *De l'Allemagne* (1810; *On Germany*, 1813). A. W. Schlegel's *Vorlesungen über Dramatische Kunst und Literatur* (*Lectures on Dramatic Art and Literature*) came out in English in 1815 as did Friedrich Schlegel's *Geschichte der Alten und Neuen Literatur* (*History of Ancient and Modern Literature*) in 1818, and most important of all, Coleridge's *Biographia Literaria* (1817) offered its brilliant exposition (often mere plagiarism, as is now well known) of German Romantic philosophy as it related to literature (Kant, Schiller, Schelling, etc.). All this Blanco took in, thoroughly digested, and transmitted to the Spanish emigrés both through direct contact and through his numerous essays on Spanish literature contributed to British periodicals usually in English but sometimes in magazines that catered to Spanish readers in their native language. It soon became evident that where Böhl von Faber had failed with the Liberals in Spain, Blanco succeeded in England, by showing them that they could be Romantics as writers without abandoning the political legacy of the Enlightenment. No Spanish writer of consequence failed to be influenced, either through direct contact in exile or through contact with the returning exiles, by the authentic Romantic movement in France and especially England.

It is customary to take the publication of *El moro expósito* (1834; The Foundling Moor) by the Duke of *Rivas (Angel de Saavedra) as the beginning of Romanticism in Spain. (It is also customary to protest over the absurd precision of such dating, but if one remembers the situation in Spain—censorship and the massive exile of the adult educated class till the death of Ferdinand in 1833—the precision becomes understandable. The example of the naturally precise opening date is no doubt partly responsible for the widely accepted but truly absurd closing date, 1844, the year of *Zorrilla's *Don Juan Tenorio*.) Rivas's work had an anonymous preface known to have been written by Blanco's most adept associate, Antonio Alcalá Galiano, a preface that amounts to a Romantic apologia: It is a mistake to call the works of Shakespeare, Calderón, and others of earlier centuries Romantic. Romanticism is the literature of today (i.e., the early nineteenth c.) and has its origins in Germany. The writer must be of his time and society: like the writer of any other epoch, the Romantic is historically and nationally contingent. The servile imitation of foreign models and literary doctrine (the unities) has been a blind alley for the Spaniard, who must reject neo-classical authoritarianism and the myths and models of antiquity and devote himself to the inner movements, the passions, of the soul and seek out subjects from the life of his own times. Except for the advocacy of literary nationalism, the preface was curiously unrelated to the poem, and pointed rather to some kind of "realism." No matter. There is no evidence that this preface had any influence at all.

For the Romantic movement as commonly defined there is no better guide than Vicente Llorens and his posthumous work *El romanticismo español* (Spanish Romanticism). The clearest sign of new life in Spanish culture after the death of Ferdinand VII was the proliferation of periodicals, some ephemeral, some fairly long-lived, all of them outlets for the burgeoning new school of writers. Only the most important can be mentioned: *El Artista*, *El Semanario Pintoresco*, *No Me Olvides*, *El Iris*, and *El Pensamiento*. Poetry, short fiction, educational (i.e., informative) articles, and literary, music, art, and theater criticism filled their columns as their contributing authors, elaborating for the general public the various aspects of Romantic doctrine, established themselves as the acknowledged representatives of the movement: *Escosura, Ventura de la Vega, Roca de Togores (*Molíns), *Pastor Díaz, Pedro de Madrazo, *Cueto, Zorrilla, *García Tassara, *Fernán Caballero (the first Romantic "woman of letters," signing herself here with the initials of her real name, Cecilia Boehl), *Mesonero Romanos, *Gil y Carrasco, *Quadrado, Salas y Quiroga, Espronceda, Miguel de los Santos *Alvarez, *Ros de Olano.

Novel

In the other European countries, novelists, some of them in but not precisely of the Romantic movement, others declared advocates of the new doctrine, produced a body of works that we still read as the first great modern novels—Goethe, Jane Austen, Balzac, Stendhal, etc. In Spain, where, it is generally agreed, *Cervantes invented the novel, those who sought to bring the genre back to life could produce nothing but embarrassing imitations of Sir Walter Scott's romances. It is customary to accord these writers the merit, at least, of introducing the Scottish-English writer's influence into Spain, but the consequences, for example, the hundreds of historical romances ground out by *Fernández y González, are no justification even for the attribute of historical importance. Forerunner of the novels in question was Rafael Húmara's *Ramiro, Conde de Lucena* (1823). Then came Ramón *López Soler's *Los bandos de Castilla* (1830; Castilian Factions), Estanislao de Cosca Vayo's *La conquista de Valencia por el Cid* (1831; The Cid Conquers Valencia), Patricio de la Escosura's *Ni rey ni roque* (1835; Neither King nor Castle), Juan Cortada's *La heredera de Sangumí* (1835;

Sangumi's Heiress), and José *García de Villalta's *El golpe en vago* (1835; Aimless Flight). Even writers as gifted in other genres as Larra and Espronceda could not, when they tried to, produce historical novels readable today (respectively, *El doncel de don Enrique el doliente* [1834; Henry the Sorrowful's Page]; *Sancho Saldaña* [1834]). Only Enrique Gil y Carrasco's *El Señor de Bembibre* (1844; The Lord of Bembibre), saturated with Romantic sentiment that joins characters and nature in an almost mystical unity and borne along by the author's evident love of the medieval scene he depicts, is an exception to the rule of clumsy mediocrity. (*Pérez Galdós was to come along later to confer artistic dignity upon the historical novel, but he did not take his Spanish antecedents as models.)

Costumbrismo

Not quite absolutely peculiar to Spanish Romanticism but certainly so in the high degree of importance it enjoys there is the literary phenomenon known as *costumbrismo*, the art of depicting in verbal sketches the manners, customs (*costumbres*, wherefore *costumbrismo*), types, games, and such, of particular localities. *Castizo*—''pure'' (Spanish, Andalusian, Sevillian, of a particular quarter of town)—was the catchword, and the literary style, to be *castizo*, had (in the most extreme case, *Escenas andaluzas*, 1846 [published earlier in various magazines], by Serafín *Estébanez Calderón) to be so loaded with localisms and dialectal expressions that what was written by a native about Andalusia would be to a considerable extent unintelligible to a reader in Old Castile. As Larra was the first to point out, the *cuadro* or *artículo de costumbres*, to use the terms early assigned to the genre, looked outside of Spain for its models, notably to Addison in England and Jouy in France, but did so in part not to imitate so much as to correct the errors that foreign visitors had introduced into their pictures of ''Romantique Espagne,'' so that a critical anti-Romantic spirit entered into conflict with the sentimental Romantic localism of *Escenas matritenses* (Madrid Scenes) that Mesonero Romanos published in his *Semanario Pintoresco*, and the genre that had started as a superficial celebration of Spanish picturesqueness became for Mariano José de *Larra—himself often at odds with the movement of which he was the most striking and authentic embodiment—a vehicle for mordant satire of the peculiarly Spanish manners and customs: to be Spanish was to be ridiculous, incompetent, uncivilized. A less bitter but still critical attitude is reflected by an assembly of writers ranging from those too young to have a reputation (Antonio *Flores) to well-established figures like Rivas and *Hartzenbusch and including almost all the (male) Romantics one can think of, who devoted their talents to compiling a gallery of portraits—types, not scenes—entitled *Los españoles pintados por sí mismos* (1843–44; Spaniards Depicted by Themselves), a title obviously imported from France (*Les Français peints par eux mêmes*), in which the introduction of woodcut illustrations showing the types described in the text, as Llorens astutely observes, made the words and the genre superfluous.

Theater

More than a hundred tried their hand at writing for the theater during the Romantic decade, and since demand for new works (in Madrid) was greater than the dramatists' originality could supply—the run of a play was about three evenings—it was often satisfied by translations from the French, mostly melodramas and comedies by Scribe, Ducange, Bouilly, and others. (The true French Romantics—Hugo, A. Dumas, Delavigne—were less favorably received by Madrid, as were the other foreign playwrights, classic and contemporary.) Serious dramas by Spanish dramatists that enjoyed some success were, in first place, *Martínez de la Rosa's *La conjuración de Venecia* (The Venice Conspiracy), followed by *El trovador* (The Troubadour) by *García Gutiérrez and *Los amantes de Teruel* (The Teruel Lovers) by Hartzenbusch, but the public taste really favored lighter fare: a comedy of magic, *La redoma encantada* (The Enchanted Phial), by Hartzenbusch, had the extraordinary number of thirty performances in a row. Nor did the great classics—Lope de *Vega, Calderón, etc.—drastically rewritten (*refundidos*) to please the palate of the times, live up to the expectations held out for them by such advocates as Boehl de Faber and Durán. Larra and Gil y Carrasco, the best critics of the day, found much to admire in the theater of their contemporaries, but later writers, looking for values that transcend the mere fashions of Romanticism, have ridiculed their preposterous plots, their excess of incident, and their ranting dialogue. Still, others would say, if dramas by García Gutiérrez (*El trovador*, *Simón Bocanegra*) and the Duke of Rivas (*Don Alvaro, o la fuerza del sino* [Don Alvaro, or the Power of Fate]) were able, like certain plays of Hugo (*Hernani*, *Le Roi s'amuse*) and Schiller (*Don Carlos*), to inspire some of Verdi's most thrilling operas, there must be more to them than their belittling critics have been willing to allow. The truth is, however, that the inner meaning, the emotion, of the plots and dialogues not only of the Spanish Romantics but of the French and German as well, could only be convincingly expressed in the non-verbal language of the great Italian composer. It is obligatory to close even the briefest account of the Romantic theater with the name of José Zorrilla, whose *Don Juan Tenorio* (1844) is the only Romantic play still performed (on All Souls' Day and in the ensuing week or so), a vulgar sentimentalization of the famous legend, in verse that rarely rises above the level of doggerel and is generously imprinted on the memory of Spanish speakers the world over. *See also* Don Juan, Legend of.

Poetry

Although Rivas's book of poems *El moro expósito* signaled the beginning of official Spanish Romanticism, other poets writing during the first Carlist war (1833–39) were content to publish fragments and short works in the periodicals. Then, suddenly (Llorens once more) there was a flood of poetry books in two or three years. Their authors' names are mostly familiar to us: Espronceda (*El diablo mundo* [The Infernal World]), Rivas (*Romances históricos* [Historical Ballads]), Mora (*Leyendas españolas* [Spanish Legends]), Zorrilla (*Cantos del trovador* [Songs of the Troubadour]), and numerous other volumes, often titled simply *Poesías* (Poems) by *Arolas, Pastor Díaz, *Campoamor, Eugenio de *Ochoa, Salvador *Bermúdez de Castro, Miguel de los Santos Alvarez. Also, for the first time since Sor Juana Inés de la Cruz we encounter a woman among the significant poets, Gertrudis *Gómez de Avellaneda, who would in later decades take up feminist positions clearly anticipating those of our own day. The rhetorical freedoms of Romanticism (verse forms, lexicon, extended structures) that had amounted to a scandalous revolution in France had never been unavailable to Spanish poets; what was new for them was the expressive intent, the fundamental Romanticism outlined at the beginning of this article. One cannot, alas, read most of this poetry without being reminded of various European writers (chiefly Byron but also Goethe, Hugo, and others) evidently the objects of its imitation, and even where no such poetic sycophancy is noticeable—in the widely cultivated narratives of traditional Spanish legends—the sense of padding to fill out the lines, complete the rhymes, and finish the story is inescapable. This is why they do not enjoy copious representation in the one-volume anthologies of Spanish verse where, with the equally derivative eighteenth-c. fabulists, they are dutifully included as stepping stones from the splendid poetry of the Golden Age to the no less splendid poetry of the *Generation of 1898 and its epigones. Espronceda is the notable exception: he is no better than the rest if we judge him by his faults, but these seem trivial beside his powerful originality in invention, imagery, and existential daring, not to mention his fluency and dazzling skill at versification.

Anti-Romanticism

Corresponding to Romanticism in literature was what might be called the political Romanticism of the Progressives (*progresistas*), the party generally speaking of our writers. The installation of the government of the Moderates (*moderados*) in May of 1844 provides a terminal date perhaps less arbitrary and artificially decimal than at first one is inclined to think, inasmuch as the newly empowered bourgeoisie quickly showed its aversion to what it regarded as the excesses of Romanticism particularly in the theater, and its preference for the tidier, less disturbing plays of what might be dubbed neo-neo-classical playwrights (e.g., *El hombre del mundo* [1845; A Man of the World] by Ventura de la Vega, in which the social institution of marriage is held inviolable and the would-be Don Juan is sent packing, to the great satisfaction of public and critics alike: bourgeois Romanticism, a contradiction in terms). The major periodicals serving as instruments of the anti-Romantic reaction, whether they favored or deplored the material progress of the new society, were *El Siglo Pintoresco*, *Revista de los Intereses Materiales y Morales*, *Revista Literaria de El Español*, *Semanario Pintoresco Español*, and *La Censura*. To be sure, the Romantic writers did not suddenly cease to exist merely because the new political climate was less friendly toward them. Indeed, novelists and social critics began to find their *raison d'être* precisely in writing *against* the new smug plutocracy, some advocating the extension of freedom's benefits to the lower classes (*Ayguals de Izco, the author of numerous works modeled after Eugène Sue's social novels, e.g., *Pobres y ricos o La bruja de Madrid*, [1849; Rich and Poor or the Witch of Madrid]), others denouncing both the plutocracy and any kind of socialist (ameliorative) reform, and advocating in its stead regression to the perfectly balanced "beautiful"—the aesthetic criterion is appealed to constantly—Catholic medieval society (Juan *Donoso Cortés, *Ensayo sobre el catolicismo, el liberalismo y el socialismo* [1848; Essay on Catholicism, Liberalism and Socialism]), or still others, principally Fernán Caballero in *La gaviota* (1849; The Seagull), in precise antithesis to Ayguals de Izco, celebrating the society in which the rural rich and poor in Andalusia, under the shelter of a common religious faith, lived in idyllic harmony. (In addition to the women writers already mentioned—Fernán Caballero and Gertrudis Gómez de Avellaneda—two others also achieved distinction under the aegis of Romanticism in Spain: the poets Carolina *Coronado and Rosalía de *Castro.)

Post-Romanticism

Although those writers continuing in the Romantic veins in spite of bourgeois hostility and ecclesiastical censure might, for chronological reasons, properly be labeled post-Romantic—epigones of the movement—that label is customarily reserved for a slightly later group, among whom are to be counted two of the most authentically Romantic writers of the century, the previously mentioned Galician Rosalía de Castro and the Andalusian Gustavo Adolfo *Bécquer, whose *rimas* have so totally occupied the sensibilities of the Spanish-speaking world as to enjoy, much as Heine's *Buch der Lieder* (Songbook) has done among German speakers, the status of folk poetry—short songs of erotic anguish that literally millions know by heart.

The Romanticisms of all European cultures are deeply interconnected and have provided scholars endless opportunities for often very shallow "influence" studies, happily now out of fashion. France, Germany, England, and even Russia suffered the crisis of consciousness in the eighteenth c. that precipitated the Romantic movement in Europe. Spain did not go through this crisis till the end of the nineteenth c. (*Krausism). Some critics, including the present writer, have therefore argued that the writers of the Generation of 1898 are Spain's authentic Romantics. But for all the apologies that are made for it, the conventionally established Romantic movement in Spain cannot be relegated to contempt and oblivion. Indeed, it is very much worth visiting and studying. Why? First, because it is there: it is what occupies the cultural arena for several decades of the nineteenth c. as Spain's best minds continue to struggle to participate in the life of Europe without losing their own souls. Second, because in the welter and cascade of mediocre literary production—from the beginnings of the empire, Spain has always had more literature than she knew what to do with, from illiterate street-corner minstrels to physicians who think the pen is mightier than the scalpel—a few writers emerge as no less important, interesting, and moving in their several ways than the major Romantic figures in the rest of Europe: Blanco White, perhaps the most Romantic of them all, as from his permanent exile in England he lectures both the English and his compatriots in pages of literary and historical criticism that can be read with profit still today (he may have been the first writer to use ''realistic'' as a term of literary criticism [in ''Recent Spanish Literature,'' *London Review*, I, 1835]); Larra, who, as Fernando Savater would have it, invented the newspaper article (a Russel Baker of his time), if not for the whole world, at least for Spain, Voltairean like Goya in his satirical attitude but Romantic in his etched Goyesque descriptions and the movement of his prose—one has but to compare his *artículos* with Cadalso's *Cartas marruecas* (Moroccan Letters) to see what the phrase ''Romantic prose style'' can mean; Espronceda, who, if he does not surpass his two evident models, Byron and Goethe, easily outdoes Hugo when he appropriates the famous trick of mimicking the approach and departure of the *djinns* (*Les Orientales*) with lines first of increasing and then of decreasing length and uses it much more expressively as a metrical correlative, so to speak, of Montemayor's orgasmic encounter with death in *El estudiante de Salamanca* (The Salamanca Student); Enrique Gil y Carrasco, of the innumerable imitators of Sir Walter Scott the only one who truly surpasses his model and in *El Señor de Bembibre* (The Lord of Bembibre) writes a ''medieval'' novel that can absorb the adult reader today as none of Scott's novels can do; Bécquer, the most influenced poet in all Spanish literature if scholars are to be believed, and yet, in whose brief poems one hears not the influences but an original lyric voice, using everyday language to image the poignant expectations and frustrations of love and poetizing.

BIBLIOGRAPHY

Criticism

Del Río, Angel. ''Present Trends in the Conception and Criticism of Spanish Romanticism.'' *RR* 39 (1948): 229–48.

Eichner, Hans, ed. *Romantic and Its Cognates: The European History of a Word*. Toronto: U of Toronto P, 1972. See Shaw below.

Jacobsen, Margaret. *The Origins of Spanish Romanticism: A Selective Annotated Bibliography*. Lincoln, NE: Society of Spanish and Spanish American Studies, 1986.

Llorens, Vicente. *Liberales y románticos: una emigración española en Inglaterra, 1823–1834*. 2nd ed. Madrid: Castalia, 1968.

———. *El romanticismo español*. Madrid: Fundación March/Castalia, 1979.

Peers, Edgar Allison. *A History of the Romantic Movement in Spain*. 2 vols. Cambridge: Cambridge UP, 1940.

The Romantic Movement Bibliography, 1936–1970. Compiled by various hands. 7 vols. Ann Arbor: Pierian P with R. R. Bowker, 1973.

Sebold, Russell P. *La trayectoria del romanticismo español*. Barcelona: Crítica, 1983.

Shaw, Donald L. ''Spain: Romántico—Romanticismo—Romancesco—Romanesco—Romancista—Románico.'' In *Romantic and Its Cognates*. Ed. H. Eichner. Toronto: U of Toronto P, 1972. 341–71.

Edmund L. King

ROMEA, Julián (1813, San Juan, Murcia–1868, Loeches), actor, poet. He also taught acting at the Royal Conservatory in Madrid. His verse—both lyric and religious—was collected in the volume *Poesías* (1846; Poems); Romantic tendencies are avoided, and the influence of *Meléndez Valdés is clear. Romea's *Ideas generales sobre el arte del teatro* (1858; General Ideas on the Art of the Theater) and *Los héroes en el teatro, reflexiones sobre la manera de representar la tragedia* (1866; Heroes in the Theater, Reflections on How to Represent Tragedy) demonstrate his ability as a critic.

BIBLIOGRAPHY

Primary Texts

Los héroes en el teatro, reflexiones. . . . Madrid: Abienzo, 1866.
Ideas generales sobre el arte del teatro. Madrid: Abienzo, 1858.
Poesías. Madrid: Rivadeneyra, 1846.

Criticism

Ferrer del Río, A. "Julián Romea." *Revista española* 3 (1868): n.p.

ROMEA, Julián (1848, Zaragoza–1903, Madrid), actor, **autor*, librettist. Nephew to Julián Romea (1818–1868), he also devoted his life to the theater. Many of his librettos are worthy of remembering, including *El señor Joaquín* (1898; Mr. Joaquín) and *El padrino de "El nene" o todo por el arte* (1896; Baby's Godfather, or Everything for Art).

BIBLIOGRAPHY

Primary Texts

El padrino de "el nene". . . . In *Spanish Plays* 333.
El señor Joaquín. In *Spanish Plays* 387.

ROMERO, Luis (1916, Barcelona–), novelist and short story writer of realist tendencies. He won the Nadal Prize in 1951 with his novel *La noria* (1952; The Treadmill). Other publications include *Cuerda tensa* (1950; Tense Cord), *Carta de ayer* (1953; Letter from the Past), *Las viejas voces* (1955; The Old Voices), *Los otros* (1956; The Others), *La nochebuena* (1960; Christmas Eve), *La corriente* (1962; The Current), *El cacique* (1963; The Boss; winner of the Planeta Prize), *Tudá* (1957), *Esas sombras del trasmundo* (1957; Shadows from Beyond) and two short novels in Catalan. In recent years, Romero has written pseudo-historical and historical accounts of the Spanish Civil War.

BIBLIOGRAPHY

Primary Texts

El cacique. Barcelona: Planeta, 1976.
Cuerda tensa. Lincoln, NE: Society of Spanish and Spanish American Studies, 1979.
La noria. Barcelona: Destino, 1981.

Criticism

González-del-Valle, Luis, and Bradley Shaw. *Luis Romero*. TWAS 520. New York: Twayne, 1979.

Luis T. González-del-Valle

ROMERO ESTEO, Miguel (1930, Montoro, Córdoba–), Spanish playwright and essayist. A member of the "underground" dramatists together with such others as José *Ruibal and Eduardo *Quiles, Romero Esteo spent six years in a seminary before deciding to renounce studies for the priesthood; he subsequently studied organ, piano, musical composition, philosophy, and—during a year in England—theology. Then, at the U of Madrid, he moved from journalism to economics to political science, in which he received his degree, meanwhile working in a wide variety of jobs, including one which is directly reflected in his plays, that of assistant to the chef of the officers club at the American air base at Torrejón, a background much in evidence in *Fiestas gordas del vino y el tocino* (1975; Fat Fiesta of Wine and Bacon), and *Paraphernalia de la olla podrida, la misericordia y la mucha consolación* (1975 [shortened version]; Paraphernalia of the Stew-pot, Mercy and Great Consolation), which was performed by non-professional companies in Spain in 1972 (Sitges Festival) and in 1973, receiving somewhat ambiguous reviews because of the play's unmistakable denunciation of the Franco regime. The action is set in a restaurant kitchen (which is actually an insane asylum) whose employees are psychopaths, run by the absolute authority of the Chef (Franco) who is blindly worshipful of the mythical culinary perfection of "el garbanzo" (Spanish chick-pea), a devotion echoed by all but Marmitón (the scullion), who dares to suggest other fare (provoking a charge of subversion), a crime punishable by death, carried out by forcing water into him through a funnel, torturing him and coating the body with tomato sauce, while a choir sings hymns and operatic arias. Other works include *Pasodoble* (1973; Spanish Two-Step), *Pizzicato irrisorio y gran pavana de lechuzos* (1978; Derisive Pizzicato and Pavane [Court Dance] of Demons and Dimwits), both of which reflect his studies of music, and *El vodevil de la pálida, pálida, pálida, pálida Rosa* (1979; Vaudeville of the Pale, Pale, Pale, Pale Rose); and a "grotesque opera," *Pontifical* (published in German translation [1971]).

BIBLIOGRAPHY

Criticism

O'Connor, Patricia, and Anthony Pasquariello, eds. *Contemporary Spanish Theater: Seven One-Act Plays*. New York: Scribner's, 1980.
Valdivieso, L. Teresa. *España: bibliografía de un teatro silenciado*. Lincoln, NE: Society of Spanish and Spanish American Studies, 1979.

Wellwarth, George. *Spanish Underground Drama*. University Park: Pennsylvania State UP, 1972. 83–90.

Janet Pérez

ROMERO LARRAÑAGA, Gregorio (1814, Madrid–1872, Madrid), second-rate Romantic novelist, playwright, and poet. Romero Larrañaga studied law at the U of Alcalá de Henares and worked as a librarian at the National Library (See Biblioteca Nacional) in Madrid. With the publication of his short story in verse, "El sayón" (The Bailiff), an imitation of Patricio de la *Escosura's *El bulto vestido del negro capuz* (The Ghost in the Black Cloak) and originally published in the *Semanario Pintoresco Español*, he made a name for himself, and he continued to publish imitative poetry—*El de la cruz colorada* (He of the Red Cross) and *Alcalá de Henares*, modeled after *Zorrilla's *Oriental* and *Toledo*, respectively. In 1841, he published two distinctly Romantic collections, *Poesías* (Poetry) and *Cuentos históricos, leyendas antiguas y tradiciones populares de España* (Historical Stories, Ancient Legends, and Popular Traditions of Spain), and in 1843, he published a volume of three narrative poems on the Middle Ages, *Historias caballerescas españolas* (Spanish Stories of Chivalry). Romero Larrañaga's attempts to achieve more popular success in the theater met with dismal failure until his collaborations with Eduardo and Eusebio *Asquerino on such historical dramas as *Felipe el Hermoso* (1845; Philip the Handsome), *El gabán del rey* (1847; The King's Cape), and *Juan Bravo* (1849). *See also* Romanticism.

BIBLIOGRAPHY

Primary Texts

Cuentos históricos, leyendas antiguas y tradiciones populares de España. Madrid: Boix, 1841.
Felipe el Hermoso. With Eusebio Asquerino. Madrid: Repullés, 1845.
El gabán del rey. With Eduardo Asquerino. Madrid: Repullés, 1847.
Poesías. Madrid: Lalama, 1841.
El sayón: Cuento romántico en verso. Madrid: Sancha, 1836.

Criticism

Navas Ruiz, Ricardo. *El Romanticismo español*. 3rd ed. Madrid: Cátedra, 1982.
Peers, E. Allison. *A History of the Romantic Movement in Spain*. 2 vols. Cambridge: Cambridge UP, 1940.
Varela, José Luis. *Vida y obra literaria de Gregorio Romero Larrañaga*. Madrid: CSIC, 1948.

Phoebe Porter Medina

ROMO ARREGUI, Josefina (1913, Madrid–), Spanish poet and critic. Romo's doctoral dissertation for the U of Madrid (1944) received a prize for her study of the nineteenth-c. dramatist Gaspar *Núñez de Arce, and much of her effort has been devoted to academic research and critical essays. For many years she has been a professor of Spanish literature at the U of Connecticut, while continuing to write and publish poetry. Among her verse collections are *La peregri-*

nación inmóvil (1932; Motionless Pilgrimage), *Acuarelas, no venal* (1935; Watercolors, Not Venal), *Romancero triste, no venal* (1936; Collection of Sad Ballads, Not Venal), *Aguafuertes y otros poemas, no venal* (1940; Engravings and Other Poems, Not Venal), *Cántico de Mariá Sola. 1946–1948* (1950; Canticle of Maria Alone. 1946–48), *Isla sin tierra* (1955; Island without Land), *Elegías desde la orilla del triunfo* (1964; Elegies from the Triumphal Shore), *Poemas de América* (1967; American Poems), and *Autoantología* (1968; Self-Anthology). Romo's poems are often extremely personal, imaginative and mystical when not melancholy, estranged and terribly alone. Religious preoccupations, autobiographical incidents and reactions to expatriation are other frequent themes.

BIBLIOGRAPHY

Criticism

Autoantología. New York: Academia de la Lengua Española de Nueva York, 1968.
Elegías desde la orilla del triunfo. New York: n.p., 1964.
Isla sin tierra. New York: n.p., 1955.
Poemas de América. Madrid: n.p., 1967.

Janet Pérez

RONCESVALLES, Cantar de (Song of Roncesvalles), epic poem. Fragment of a thirteenth-c. **cantar de gesta* comprised of 100 lines of verse and recounting the lament of the Emperor Charlemagne over the corpses of Oliver, the Bishop Turpin, and the emperor's nephew Roland at the battle of Roncesvalles. Composed in irregular meter, like the **Cantar de Mio Cid* (Song of the Cid), and containing traces of Navarro-Aragonese dialect, the fragment corresponds in theme to the latter part of the French *Chanson de Roland* (Song of Roland), yet differs substantially in its style, which is more characteristic of the Spanish *gestas*. Discovered in 1916 and published the following year by Menéndez Pidal (*Revista de filología española* 4, 1917), the *Roncesvalles* fragment is the earliest known forerunner of the Carolingian cycle which flourished in fifteenth-c. Spain.

BIBLIOGRAPHY

Primary Text

"Cantar de Roncesvalles." *Poesía española medieval*. Ed. Manuel Alvar. Hispánicos Universales 14. Madrid: Cuspa, 1978. 71–75.

Criticism

Horrent, Jules. "*Roncesvalles*": *Etude sur le fragment de cantar de gesta conservé à l'Archivo de Navarra (Pampelune)*. Paris: Bibliothèque de la Faculté de Philosophie et Lettres de l'Université de Liège 120, 1951.

Kathleen L. Kirk

ROS, Félix (1912, Barcelona–), poet and critic. Professor of literature, he initiated his writing career as a journalist in *Cruz y raya*. His writings include poetry, critical works, anthologies and translations. Among the books of poetry are *Verde voz* (1934; Green Voice), *Nueve poemas de Valéry y doce sonetos de la muerte* (1939; Nine Poems of Valéry and Twelve Sonnets of Death), *Elegías* (1952; Elegies), *Condenado a muerte, poema* (1967; Condemned to Death, a Poem).

BIBLIOGRAPHY

Primary Texts

Condenado a muerte, poema. Madrid: Nacional, 1967.
El Conde-Duque de Olivares. Madrid: G. del Toro, 1971.
De Acapulco a Nueva York, pasando por los Balcanes. Madrid: Prensa Española, 1971.

Genaro J. Pérez

ROS, Samuel (1905, Valencia–1945, Madrid), novelist and dramatist. An attorney by profession, Ros wrote long and short fiction as well as theater. His writing often combines humor with lyricism. Among his works are the novels *Las sendas* (1930; The Paths), *El ventrílocuo y la muda* (1930; The Ventriloquist and the Mute), the stories *Marcha atrás* (1931; Backwards March), the farces *En Europa sobra un hombre* (In Europe a Man is Left Over) and *Víspera* (The Day Before). A collection of his narrations was published as *Cuentas y cuentos, antología 1928–1941* (1942; Accounts and Stories, Anthology 1928–1941).

BIBLIOGRAPHY

Primary Texts

Cuentas y cuentos, antología 1928–1941. Madrid: Nacional, 1942.

Genaro J. Pérez

ROS DE OLANO, Antonio (1808, Caracas, Venezuela–1886, Madrid), prose writer and poet. As a professional soldier he served during the first Carlist War (1833–40), commanded an army corps during the African War (1859–60), and became one of the most prestigious generals and public men of his time. One of José de *Espronceda's closest friends, Ros wrote the prologue to the *Diablo Mundo* (1840; Devil World) and contributed to the most important literary magazines of his time. His collected poems appeared under the title *Poesías* (1886; Poetry). His prose is more successful. On one hand, he wrote works of a realistic nature: *Episodios de la Guerra Civil* (1868–70; Episodes of the Civil War), which appeared in *Revista de España*; memoirs from childhood or from the African War; and the novel *El diablo las carga* (1840; The Devil's to Blame). On the other hand, Ros acquired a well-deserved reputation as an unconventional writer (''escritor raro'') with his outlandish and fantastic stories, and a strange fiction work entitled *El doctor Lañuela* (1863; Doctor Lañuela).

BIBLIOGRAPHY

Primary Texts

Cuentos estrambóticos y otros relatos. Ed. Enric Cassany. Barcelona: Laia, 1980.
El diablo las carga. Madrid: Compañía Tipográfica, 1840.
El doctor Lañuela. Madrid: Galiano, 1863.
Leyendas de Africa. Madrid: Gaspar y Roig, 1860.

Criticism

Baquero Goyanes, Mariano. *El cuento español en el siglo XIX*. Madrid: RFE, 1949.

Blanco García, Francisco. *La literatura española en el siglo XIX*. vol. 1. Madrid: Saenz de Jubera, 1891.

Cortón, Antonio. "Ros de Olano y su tiempo." In *Pandemonium (Crítica y sátira)*. Madrid: Suárez, 1889. 163–74.

Valera, Juan. "Notas biográficas y críticas." In *Obras completas*. Madrid: Aguilar, 1942.

Salvador García Castañeda

ROSA, António Ramos (1924, Faro, Algarve–), Portuguese poet, translator and critic. Co-director of the literary magazines *Arvore* (1952–54), *Cassiopeia* (1956), and *Cadernos do Meio-Dia* (1958–60). He has published critical essays in *Seara Nova*, *Ler*, *Vértice*, *O Tempo e o Modo*, *Artes e Letras*, *Colóquio*, *Loreto 13*, *Silex*, *Sema*, *Nova Renascença*, *Raiz e Utopia*, *Cadernos de Literatura*. He has also collaborated in other foreign magazines: *Sud*, *Revista Brasileira de Lingüística*, *Anima*, *Obsidiane*, *Argile* (France), *Poesía* (Spain), *Europa Letteraria* (Italy), *Poesía 29* (Argentina), and *O Estado de São Paulo* (Brazil). Rosa was awarded the Hautvilliers Foundation Prize for translation in 1976.

Rosa's extensive reading of Portuguese and foreign poets, as well as the correspondence he has maintained with many of them, contributes to the rigor and the lucidity of his prose essays and makes his poetry an original voice to be read in the light of poetry written in Portuguese, French, Spanish and Italian. A reader of English and American poetry, however, will undoubtedly recognize that his poems breathe the familiar atmosphere of the great originals of the American and English Romantic tradition, from Shelley, Emerson, and Whitman to Stevens's fertile barrenness, absences and repetitions.

His early poems, namely those in *Grito Claro* (1958; The Clear Cry) and *Viagem Através duma Nebulosa* (1960; Voyage through a Nebula), construct an empty space of desire where the poet inscribes his outraged cry of rebellion against the solitude imposed by the system, his poetry is a mark of discordance in a society where there is truly no communication. This is best exemplified in one of his most famous poems, "O Boi da Paciência" (The Ox of Patience).

Ramos Rosa dedicated his book *As Marcas no Deserto* (1978; The Marks on the Desert) "To the eighty thousand young people who rallied in Bologna in 1977," and he explained in an interview, "I sympathize with all movements that attempt to break the system." As a young man, he himself was imprisoned for some months when he joined the Movimento de Unidade Democrática Juvenil, a cultural and political group which acted as a catalyst of intellectual resistance against the dictatorial regime (1926–74). But Ramos Rosa's mark of rebellion can by no means be limited to specific political events or circumstances; he aims at total communication, that is, total love, which is the goal of his poetic discourse as seen in the title poem from *Não Posso Adiar o Coração* (1974; I Cannot Postpone Love).

All Rosa's poetry is a quest for transparency in language, a desire for a language as "the origin of all / the complete creation." From *Ocupação do Espaço* (1963; The Space Habitation) onwards, the cry of revolt in his poetry is replaced by the meticulous construction of a poetic space through constant probings of or approximations to the real, that is, the knowable. Rosa's poetry is then constructed in the oppressive awareness that, even if it is not possible to change actuality, the constant redefinition of our fictions remains a necessity. This construction, or these probings into the limits of language, is a tortured journey where the poet struggles for breath, while always on the verge of silence. It is a language on the point of revealing its secret without ever actually doing so. Thus Ramos Rosa's poetry has an unfinished quality ("The Most Simple Words Remain to Be Said"), a conscious and sought for poverty wrought of words that gravitate around a center impossible to define in words. That is possibly the reason why the interrogative and the vocative are his two main characteristic modes.

His essays *Poesia Moderna: Interrogação do Real*, like most of his poems, are a call to the reader to share the writer's questionings. In *Poesia, Liberdade Livre* (1962; Poetry, Freedom Free) the poet reiterates Maurice Blanchot's conception of poetry as a changing reality where the poem is the creator of the poet; that is, the poetic identity of the poet emerges from the very process of writing.

Ramos Rosa's poetic evolution shows an increasing awareness that the poetic word is a liberator of meaning and that the process of writing is an ontological adventure. In his most recent books, such as *O Incêndio dos Aspectos* (1980; The Fire of Aspects), *Incerto Exacto* (1982; The Exact Uncertainty), *Quando o Inexorável* (1983; Facing the Inexorable), *Ficção* (1984; Fiction), *Mediadoras* (1985; Mediators), and *Volante Verde* (1986; Green Flyer), Ramos Rosa takes poetry a step further. When we read poems like "Ficção" we are confronted with a series of arresting, palpable images that seem to coalesce for a moment in a sketch of a plot on the brink of disclosure. However, ambiguity is irreducible—each reader will find in it something to fit his deepest preoccupations.

The reasons behind this poetic strategy were given by the poet in a recent talk: "The poetic word is not a mere sign or message, it is a body which grows in accordance to desire—in the past the poet would depart from inspiration to the work, today he departs from the writing to inspiration. The poet does not express, nor does he reproduce, nor represent because the writing of poetry is a living experience of the unknown that manifests itself through the very process of writing."

Doubtless one of the most prolific of Portuguese poets, Ramos Rosa is usually considered to be one of the leading innovators of poetry nowadays. He lives in Lisbon where he dedicates himself solely to writing.

BIBLIOGRAPHY

Primary Texts

Ciclo do Cavalo. Porto: Limiar, 1975.
Dinâmica Subtil. Lisbon: Ulmeiro, 1984.
Horizonte Imediato. Lisbon: Dom Quixote, 1974.

Não Posso Adiar o Coração. Pref. E. Lourenco. Lisbon: Plátano, 1974.
Nos Seus Olhos de Silêncio. Lisbon: Dom Quixote, 1970.
O Incêndio dos Aspectos. Pref. V. Ferreira. Porto: A Regra do Jogo, 1980.
Ocupação do Espaço. Pref. E. M. de Melo Castro. Lisbon: Portugàlia, 1963.
Quando o Inexorável. Porto: Limiar, 1983.

Criticism

Besse, Maria Graciette. ''A Palavra e o Silêncio na Poesia de A. Ramos Rosa.'' In *Colóquio/Letras* (Lisbon) 61 (May 1981): 30–38.
Centeno, Yvette K. ''Ciclo do Cavalo de Antonio Ramos Rosa: uma leitura.'' In *Colóquio/Letras* (Lisbon) 35 (Jan. 1977): 41–46.
Cruz, Gastão. ''Nudez, Evidência, Paobreza, nas Palavras de A. Ramos Rosa.'' In *A Poesia Portuguesa Hoje*. Lisbon: Plátano, 1973. 121–26.
Guimarães, Fernando. ''Antonio Ramos Rosa—A Poesia em forma de Ciclo.'' *Colóquio/Letras* (Lisbon) 45 (Sept. 1978): 28–35.
Simões, João Gaspar. ''A. Ramos Rosa—Voz Inicial.'' In *Critica II-Poetas Contemporáneos*. Lisbon: Delfos, n.d. 273–77.
Torres, Alexandre Pinheiro. ''A Poesia de A. Ramos Rosa ou: onde se mostra que tambem se passa do concreto para o abstrato.'' In *Programa para o Concreto*. Lisbon: Ulisseia, 1966. 187–212.

Manuela Renata Valente de Carvalho

ROSALES, Luis (1910, Granada–), poet and literary critic, doctor in letters, U of Madrid. He has been a member of the *Academia Española since 1964 and has received numerous prizes, including the Premio Nacional de Poesía, Premio Mariano de Cavia, Premio de Crítica, and Premio Cervantes. His first poems appeared in 1933 in *Los cuatro vientos*, and he later collaborated on *Cruz y Raya*, *El Gallo Gris*, etc. He has directed the literary magazines *Cuadernos Hispanoamericanos* and *Nueva Estafeta*. In 1940 Rosales was named secretary of the literary magazine *Escorial*, a publication that played an important role in the post-war recuperation of liberal writers. During the same period he produced a number of works of literary criticism: The two-volume *Poesía heroica del imperio* (1940–43; Heroic Poetry of the Empire); *Juan de Tassis, conde de Villamediana* (1944; Juan of Tassis, Count of Villamediana); *Cervantes y la libertad* (1960; Cervantes and Freedom); *El sentimiento de desengaño en la poesía barroca* (1960; The Feeling of Disillusion in Baroque Poetry), and *La poesía de Neruda* (1978; The Poetry of Neruda).

Rosales, a member of the *Generation of 1936, attempted to restore the lyric tradition of the Renaissance. *Abril* (1935) is a love chant in Catholic spirituality. Basically this collection of poems is a manifesto for humanism in reaction to neo-Gongorism and the ''pure'' poetry of the *Generation of 1927. Rosales's preoccupation with religious themes appears in *Retablo sacro del nacimiento del Señor* (1940; Retable of the Birth of Christ), while in *Rimas* (1937–51) a neo-romantic tone prevails. In *La casa encendida* (1949; The Lighted House), daily experiences are raised to a universal dimension, and *El contenido del corazón* (1969; The Content of the Heart) constitutes a poetic search into love and friendship. *Diario de una resurrección* (1979; Diary of a Resurrection), perhaps his best collection of poems, is a brilliant synthesis of conceptual and linguistic clarity concerning man's search for freedom. *Un rostro en cada ola* (1982; A Face in Each Wave) is a testimony of Rosales's experience during the Civil War. *Oigo el silencio universal del miedo* (1984; I Hear the Universal Silence of Fear) is a series of reflections, in poetic prose, dealing with love, aesthetics, friendship and politics.

Rosales's lyrics capture the pulse of life with simplicity. Linguistically his work reflects a direct and spontaneous communication with the reader.

BIBLIOGRAPHY

Primary Texts

La casa encendida. Madrid: Seminario de Problemas Hispanoamericanos, 1949.
El contenido del corazón. Madrid: Cultura Hispánica, 1969.
Diario de una resurrección. Madrid: Fondo de Cultura Económica, 1979.
Rimas (1937–51). Madrid: Cultura Hispánica, 1951.
Un rostro en cada ola. Melilla: "Rusadir," 1982.

Criticism

"Homenaje a Luis Rosales." *CH* 257–58 (May-June 1971): n.p.
Vivanco, Luis Felipe. *Introducción a la poesía española*. Madrid: Guadarrama, 1971. 2: 113–49.

José Ortega

ROSELL Y LÓPEZ, Cayetano (1817, Aravaca, Madrid–1883, Madrid), bibliographer, dramatist, editor, professor. He began working at the *Biblioteca Nacional in 1845, and in 1880 succeeded *Hartzenbusch as head of the archives section. Rosell y López edited and wrote the prologues to various volumes of the *Biblioteca de Autores Españoles, and contributed historical and biographical articles to many magazines of the day.

ROSETE NIÑO, Pedro (1608, Madrid–after 1659, ?), poet, playwright. Very little is known of his life. A student at the U of Alcalá, apparently afflicted with health problems throughout his life, he collaborated with many dramatists, including *Moreto, *Rojas Zorilla, and Jerónimo de *Cáncer. Some twenty-five plays comprise his extant production. They are of all types, historical, religious, mythological, and "sword and cape."

BIBLIOGRAPHY

Primary Texts

El arca de Noé. Madrid: Sanz, 1757.
Comedia famosa de Píramo y Tisbe. Ed., study, P. Correa Rodríguez. Pamplona: U of Navarre, 1977.
El triunfo del Ave María. In BAE 49.

Criticism

See Correa Rodríguez, in *Comedia famosa*, above.

Frances Bell Exum

ROSETTI, Ana (1950, San Fernando, Cádiz–), Spanish poet and novelist. Of a well-to-do traditional family, Rosetti was convent-educated, but adolescent discovery of art and beauty in multiple forms (from religious statuary to silks, from the music of Mozart or Handel to poetry) exercised a powerful influence on her sensuality and aesthetic sensibilities. Via travels in Europe and Africa, she evolved like other rebels of the late sixties, attracted by peace movements and free love (not only "make love, not war," but a philosophic exaltation of eroticism as the only truth, one of life's few realities). Rosetti's formation is to a considerable extent autodidactic, including extensive reading and a bohemian period with several temporary jobs, notably (because of literary echoes) one in a cabaret or music-hall. She is an exceptionally erotic poet, noteworthy not merely because she is a woman, but because Spain lacks a tradition of erotic poetry.

Her first book of poems, *Los devaneos de Erato* (1980; The Frenzies of Erato [muse of lyric poetry]), has an acknowledged autobiographical basis, with insistent evocations of the past. *Dióscuros* (1982; Dioscuri [allusion to Castor and Pollux]), conceived as an integrated volume, contains nine poems evincing increased concern with form and language. *Indicios vehementes* (1985; Vehement Signs), an anthology of Rosetti's poetry from 1979 to 1984, includes *Los devaneos* and *Dióscuros* plus previously unpublished pieces. *Devocionario* (1985; Devotionary) was awarded the King Juan Carlos International Prize for Poetry in 1985, the most significant recognition accorded Rosetti to date. *Devocionario* evokes the language of the most impassioned *mysticism, but Rosetti's mysticism is not metaphysical: a palpably physical, corporeal mysticism of the senses, it is expressed in violent, sometimes extreme language, with occasionally brilliant metaphors, incorporating elements from Catholic liturgy.

Plumas de España (1988; Plumes of Spain), Rosetti's first novel, is a modern variant of the *picaresque tradition in which the characters are homosexuals, music-hall dancers, variety show artists and eccentrics. The writer—or her persona—functions as the first-person narrator, a well-known woman poet thinking of writing a novel. With humor, irony, and vivacious, colorful language, Rosetti playfully toys with the contemporary vogue for metafiction. *Yesterday* (1988), her latest collection of poetry, and a cumulative anthology, contains intertextuality, allusions to other cultures (ranging from classical mythology to contemporary advertisements for blue jeans and undergarments), titles or phrases drawn from other languages—English, Latin, French, Italian—Spanish and Latin American poets and novelists, popular songs, movies, and the mass media.

BIBLIOGRAPHY

Primary Texts

Aquellos duros antiguos. Málaga: Librería Anticuaria "El Guadalhorce," 1987.
Los devaneos de Erato. Valencia: Prometeo, 1980.

Devocionario. Madrid: Visor, 1985.
Dióscuros. Málaga: Jarazmín, 1982.
Indicios vehementes. Madrid: Hiperion, 1985.
Plumas de España. Barcelona: Seix Barral, 1988.
Yesterday. Madrid: Torremozas, 1988.

Janet Pérez

RUBIÓ I LLUCH, Antoni (1856, Valladolid–1937, Barcelona), historian, critic, poet and diplomat; son of Joaquim *Rubió i Ors. He studied law and humanities in Barcelona, receiving his doctorate in 1878 with a memorable thesis, *Estudio crítico-bibliográfico sobre Anacreonte y la colección anacreóntica* (1879; Critical-Bibliographical Study of Anacreon and the Anacreontic Collection). A disciple of *Milà i Fontanals, Rubió i Lluch succeeded him at the U of Barcelona in 1885. He also occupied the chair of Catalan literature (1904) of the Estudis Universitaris Catalans (Catalan University Studies). For long periods of time he served as consul of Spain in Greece and Italy where he was sent to facilitate his scholarly research. Like his mentor Milà, he wrote prodigiously in the best known magazines of his time: *La Renaixenca*, *La Ilustració catalana*, *Catalunya*, and in Madrid, Central America, and Greece; his most important essays were published in *Estudis Universitaris Catalans* and the *Anuari de l'Institut d'Estudis Catalans* (Annual of the Institute of Catalan Studies). Though primarily a classical scholar, he also translated, into Castilian, modern Greek writers: *Novelas griegas* (1893; Greek Novels). As a result of his Hellenic interests he became the greatest scholar of the Catalan presence in Greece after the conquest by the Almogàvers: *La expedición y dominación de los Catalanes en Oriente juzgados por los griegos* (1883; The Expedition of the Catalans in the Levant Judged by the Greeks); *Catalunya a Grècia, estudis literaris i històrics* (1906; Catalonia and Greece, Literary and Historical Studies); and *La llengua catalana a Grècia* (1907; The Catalan Language in Greece). Even after his death Rubió i Lluch continued the Greco-Catalan connection: *Diplomatari de l'Orient català* (Diplomatic Events of the Catalan Levant) was published posthumously in 1947.

On Catalan classical literature Rubió i Lluch wrote perhaps his most seminal books: *El Renacimiento clásico en la literatura catalana* (1889; Classical Renaissance in Catalan Literature); *Sobre el valor literario de "Tirant lo Blanch"* (1907; On the Literary Value of *Tirant lo Blanch*); *Estudi sobre l'elaboració de la crònica de Pere el Cerimoniós* (1910; Study of the Elaboration of the Chronicle of Pere el Cerimoniós); *Ramon Llull* (1911); the critical edition of **Curial i Güelfa* (1901); and others. Also, his studies on Milà i Fontanals: *Manuel Milà i Fontanals, notes biogràfiques* (1918; Manuel Milà i Fontanals, Biographical Notes); *Milà i Fontanals i Rubió i Ors* (1919); and, above all, his magnificent prologue-study to the poetry of his father, Rubió i Ors, *Lo Gayter del Llobregat* (1902). Last but not least, Rubió i Lluch also wrote definitive monographs on Castilian literature: *El sentimiento del honor en el teatro de Calderón* (1882; The Sense of Honor in the Theater of Calderón); and others on Fray Luis de

*León, *Cervantes and Marcelino *Menéndez y Pelayo. Without reading Rubió i Lluch, one cannot fully understand Spanish Peninsular culture, and Catalan culture, not at all. He was one of the greatest humanists of the modern Catalan Renaixença. *See also* Catalan Literature.

BIBLIOGRAPHY

Primary Texts

Los catalanes en Grècia; últimos años de su dominación, cuadros históricos. Madrid: Voluntad, 1927.

Curial y Güelfa; novela catalana del quinzen segle. Ed., annotated by Rubió y Lluch. Barcelona: Redondo, 1901.

Documents per l'historia de la cultura catalana migeval. 2 vols. Barcelona: Institut d'Estudis Catalans, 1908–21.

El sentimiento del honor en el teatro de Calderón. Barcelona: J. Subirana, 1882.

Criticism

Cabré, M. D. "Don Antonio Rubió i Lluch." *Argensola* 7 (1956): 363–66.

Guilleumas, R. *La llengua catalana segons Antoni Rubió i Lluch*. Barcelona: n.p., 1957.

d'Olwer, Nicolau. *Caliu*. Mexico: n.p., 1958.

Joan Gilabert

RUBIÓ I ORS, Joaquim, pseudonym Lo Gayter del Llobregat (1818, Barcelona–1899, Barcelona), poet, playwright, historian and critic; father of *Rubió i Lluch. After ecclesiastical studies in a seminary, Rubió i Ors entered the U of Barcelona to study law and humanities. In 1847 he taught at Valladolid, and in 1858 he obtained a professorship at the U of Barcelona, eventually becoming its president. In 1839 he began to publish poetry in Catalan in the *Diario de Barcelona* (Barcelona News Daily) under the pseudonym of Lo Gaiter del Llobregat (The Bagpiper of Llobregat), which happened to be the title of his first poem. All these poems were collected in the volume *Lo Gayter del Llobregat* (1841) with a very famous prologue in which he urged all Catalan writers to use their native language. This prologue became the bible of the Catalan Renaixença (nineteenth-c. renaissance); it has clear romantic, Catholic and conservative overtones. In many ways it paved the way for the ideology of the modern Catalan literary movement until quite recent times. A few years later he issued a much enlarged second edition of the book (1858). Rubió i Ors also attempted epic poetry—*Roudor del Llobregat* (1842; Roudor from Llobregat)—perhaps trying to imitate the famous Chronicle of *Muntaner dealing with the exploits of the Almogàvers (Catalan Mercenary Troops) in the Levant. Very active in the restoration of the Jocs Florals (*juegos), he wrote a great deal of poetry with influences from the French and Castilian romantics. In general, his literary production is studied today only for its historical value; his works as a scholar and historian of Catalan language and literature are more valuable. Of historical importance are *Breve reseña del actual renacimiento de la lengua y literature catalana* (1877; Brief Review of the Present Renaissance of the Catalan Language and Literature) and his books *Ausiàs March y su época* (1882; Ausiàs March and His Time) and *Noticia de la vida y escritos de D. Manuel Milà i Fontanals* (1887; Biography and Works of Mr. Milà i Fontanals). Throughout his life he contributed frequently to *El Vapor* and to lesser known conservative and Catholic Catalan magazines. *See also* Catalan Literature.

BIBLIOGRAPHY

Primary Texts

Obres escollides. Ed. Joan Sardà. Barcelona: n.p., 1914.

Criticism

Capdevila, J. M. "Joaquim Rubió i Ors." In *Estudis i lecturas*. Barcelona: Selecta, 1965.

Jordán de Urries y Azara, J. *Rubió y Ors, poeta castellano*. Barcelona: n.p., 1912.

Menéndez Pelayo, M. *Estudios y discursos de crítica histórica y literaria*. vol. 5. Madrid: CSIC, 1942.

Rubió i Lluch, A. "Pròleg." To J. Rubió i Ors, *Lo Gayter del Llobregat, Poesies*. vol. 4. Barcelona: n.p., 1902.

Joan Gilabert

RUEDA, Lope de (1505?, Seville–1565, Córdoba), actor, playwright, talented speaker, also from a family of craftsmen, and a goldsmith by trade. Rueda was praised by *Cervantes as an outstanding poet and actor who played with equal skill the roles of blacks, clowns, braggarts and especially that of the Basque. It is assumed that during his career as an actor he visited many Spanish cities and probably traveled to Italy whose language he knew well. By 1551 he resided in Valladolid, and the following year the city government granted him a fixed salary to perform his works on permanent stages. In 1552 he married an actress named Mariana who had been in the service of the Duke of Medinaceli at his palace in Cogolludo. Upon the duke's death, Lope de Rueda sued the estate for his wife's salary. In 1554 the Count of Benavente selected him to perform for the king on the occasion of his departure for England. He also performed in Segovia upon the completion of construction of the cathedral in 1558, and during the 1559 Corpus celebrations several of his works were mounted in the streets: *El hijo pródigo* (The Prodigal Son) and the *Auto de Naval y Abigail* (Play about Naval and Abigail). Two other works were performed in Toledo during Corpus of 1560. By a second wife, a Valencian named Rafaela, he had a daughter, born in Seville in 1564. Upon his death in Córdoba in 1565, he was buried between the choirs of the cathedral. His works were published posthumously in Valencia (1567) by the writer Juan de *Timoneda.

Although his dramatic compositions were thoroughly imbued with the spirit of Italianate drama and its technical and theatrical innovations, it is in the short **pasos* (sketches) that Lope de Rueda achieves his greatest success. In these works he brings to the stage a convincing combination of the language, ways, and superstitions of many previously undramatized stereotypes of a wide variety of social elements. The light, fast-paced dialogue of the prose sketches sometimes echoes the language of the **Celestina*. Rueda's characters include amusingly depicted physicians, students, laborers, and often grotesquely exaggerated caricatures of provincials. The most memorable character to populate the *paso* is the **bobo* (buffoon), whom many consider to be the most immediate forerunner of the stock **gracioso* character of the full-blown *comedia*. Several editions of Rueda's *pasos* were published during the sixteenth c. *El deleytoso* (Valencia, (1567; The Delight) contains seven sketches. A *pastoral colloquy is included in the second edition (Logroño, 1588). This pastoral colloquy was also deemed worthy of inclusion in the second collection of *pasos*, the *Registro de representantes* (1570; Registry of Performers). The best and most often cited *pasos* include *El convidado* (The Guest), *La carátula* (The Mask), *Las aceitunas* (*The Olives*, 1928), *El rufián cobarde* (The Cowardly Braggart), *Los lacayos ladrones* (The Thieving Footmen), *La generosa paliza* (The Sound Thrashing), and *Cornudo y contento* (The Complaisant Cuckold).

Essential to Lope de Rueda's art is an authenticity of colloquial language and an accurate portrayal of believable comic types. His objective is pure entertainment calculated upon a keen intuition of precisely which comic elements would move the public to unbridled laughter. This brand of comedy, unencumbered by psychological nuance or rhetorico-ideological trappings, soon set the precedent for a genre of drama which would culminate in the **entremés* (interlude) of the seventeenth c. Lope de Rueda excels in the composition of drama charged with traditional language, superstitions, folk sayings, curious prayers and regional anecdotes.

Only in the shepherds' dialogues—a genre for which Lope de Rueda felt a great affinity—did he indulge in intellectual speculations. These more formal works were commissioned for private performances before noblemen and royalty. Consequently, they appear more pretentious and are marked by a style that is both stilted and solemn. Two of the colloquies are in prose (*Camila* and *Tymbria*), and one is in verse (*Prendas de amor*; Cupid's Tokens). In the tongue-in-cheek *Diálogo sobre la invención de las calzas* (Conversation about the Invention of Tights), footmen make light of the latest vogue in fashion.

For his four longer plays and for some of the *pasos*, Lope de Rueda drew upon various Italian sources—both dramatic and novelistic—for inspiration. A tale by Boccaccio is the source for the third *paso* of the *Deleytoso* which Leandro Fernández *Moratín named *Cornudo y contento* (The Complaisant Cuckold). Another (the ninth tale of the second day) provides the plot for the play *Eufemia* (*Eufemia*, 1958–59), which contains the exceptionally accomplished dramatization of the negress Eulalia. The Plautine motif of the Menechmos (The Identical Brothers) inspired several versions before that of Rueda: one by Giovani M. Cecchi and an anonymous play *Gli ingannati* (Siena, 1531), which is attributed to A. Piccolomini. Lope de Rueda's adaptation bears the same title as that 1531 work, *Los engañados* (The Deceived). His version of the material also includes the memorable black Guiomar. Rueda's *Armelina* is based on Cecchi's *Il Servigiale* and A. Francesco Raineri's *Attila*. Rueda's *Medora* derives from a work by Luis A. Giancarli (*La Cigganna*). Lope de Rueda's dependence upon the model for a framework upon which to hang the more contemporary dialogue results at times in an unsettling, seemingly arbitrary scenic partitioning. To the rigid archetypal framework, Lope often adds realistic vignettes which appear as miniature, isolated *pasos* within the larger dramatic piece. More than half a dozen of these separable sketches are contained within the four long plays.

Lope de Rueda's lyric poetry is limited to several compositions. A poem in *quintillas*, the *Disputa y cuestión de amor* (Love Argued), is of doubtful attribution. Lope de Rueda's main contribution to the evolution of a Spanish national drama was to tip the balance away from the frozen classical paradigms which were all too apparent in many other sixteenth-c. playwrights. He was instrumental in the canonization of a unique dramatic form, the *paso*, which contained all the best elements of popular comedy. *See also* Italian Literary Influences; Theater.

BIBLIOGRAPHY

Primary Texts

Eufemia y Armelina. Ed. F. González Ollé. Salamanca: Anaya, 1967.
Obras. Ed. Emilio Cotarelo y Mori. 2 vols. Biblioteca Selecta de Autores Clásicos Españoles, vols. 10 and 11. Madrid: Sucesores de Hernando, 1908.
Pasos completos. Prol. F. García Pavón. Madrid: Taurus, 1970.
Pasos de Lope de Rueda. Ed. Manuel de la Rosa. Madrid: Escelicer, 1973.
Teatro completo. Ed. Angeles Cardona de Gibert and Garrido Pallardó. Barcelona: Bruguera, 1967.

English Translations

Eufemia. Tr. W. S. Merwin. *Tulane Drama Review* 3 (1958–59): 57–79.
The Olives. Tr. W. Knapp Jones. *Poet Lore* 39 (1928): 310–13.

Criticism

Sáez Godoy, Leopoldo. *El léxico de Lope de Rueda: clasificaciones conceptuales y estadísticas*. Bonn: Rheinsiche Friedrich Wilhelms Universität, 1968.
Tusón, Vicente. *Lope de Rueda. Bibliografía crítica*. Cuadernos Bibliográficos 16. Madrid: CSIC, 1965.
Veres D'Ocon, Ernesto. "Juegos idiomáticos en las obras de Lope de Rueda." *RFE* 34 (1950): 195–237.

Richard Glenn

RUEDA Y SANTOS, Salvador (1857, Málaga–1933, Madrid), Spanish poet. Rueda was born in the small rural village of Benaque, Málaga. Of humble origin, he had little formal schooling. He began to write poetry at an early age, inspired initially by the oral poetry he had learned as a child. As a young man he moved to Málaga, where he continued to write while he sought to improve his economic situation. In Málaga and later Madrid his work appeared in leading journals of the day (*Málaga*, *Andalucía*, *La Gaceta de Madrid*, *El Imperial)*. Rueda moved to Madrid at the suggestion of the poet Gaspar *Núñez de Arce, who offered him a post at *La Gaceta de Madrid*. Subsequently, Rueda worked as librarian at the U of Madrid, the National Library (*Biblioteca Nacional), and the Provincial Library of Málaga.

Rueda's importance as a poet is primarily historical. During the years between 1880 and 1892 he was the most important of a number of poets who sought new modes of poetic expression. His major books of poetry are *Noventa estrofas* (1883; Ninety Stanzas), *Aires españoles* (1890; Spanish Airs), *En tropel* (1892; In a Rush), and *Piedras preciosas* (1900; Precious Stones). In the experimentation with new metric combinations and the use of color and musicality, Rueda is clearly a precursor of Rubén Darío and the Modernist revolution in Spanish poetry. He does not, however, sustain the innovative impulse of his early poetry and is rapidly surpassed by Darío and subsequent poets. In his use of neologisms to express popular themes and in the alteration of popular verse forms, Rueda has more recently been considered a forerunner of such poets as Federico *García Lorca, Luis *Cernuda, and Miguel *Hernández.

BIBLIOGRAPHY

Primary Texts

Antología poética. Madrid: Aguilar, 1962.
Poesías completas. Barcelona: Maucci, 1911.

Criticism

Cernuda, Luis. *Estudios sobre poesía contemporánea*. Madrid: Guadarrama, 1959.
Cossío, José María de. *Cincuenta años de poesía española*. Madrid: Espasa-Calpe, 1960.
Díaz-Plaja, Guillermo. *Modernismo frente a noventa y ocho*. Madrid: Espasa-Calpe, 1966.
Prados y López, M. *Salvador Rueda, el poeta de la Raza*. Málaga: Zambrana, 1941.

Mary Lee Bretz

RUFO, Juan (1547, Córdoba–after 1620, Córdoba), known for two works, entirely different: the *Austríada* (Austriade), an epic poem, and *Los seiscientos apotegmas* (The Six Hundred Apothegms), a book of proverbial sayings.

Second child of Luis Rofos, a dyer of cloth, he at times used the surname Gutiérrez, taken from a paternal uncle; calling himself either Juan Gutiérrez or Juan Rufo Gutiérrez. Gambling was one of his favorite pastimes. His father usually paid off the son's gambling debts; at one point the youth stole 500 ducats worth of goods from his father.

He went to Salamanca, probably in 1561, to study at the university, but his name is never mentioned in the registration lists. By 1568, he had returned to Córdoba, where he obtained a government post. The following year he stole 600 *fanegas* (about 900 bushels) of wheat designated for the poor. He married María Carrillo in 1581, and the following year a son, Luis, was born.

In 1571 Rufo enlisted in the Armada and accompanied don Juan of Austria in the royal galley. Historical facts given to him by Juan de Soto, secretary of don Juan, inspired the epic poem, *Austríada.* Another source was *Hurtado de Mendoza's *Guerra de Granada.* After its initial publication in 1584, it was reissued twice. The poem treats the intervention of don Juan of Austria in the war of Granada and in the battle of Lepanto.

The second work, *Los seiscientos apotegmas,* was published in Toledo in 1596. For the title, Rufo purposely selected a rarely used word in Spanish which denotes sayings or proverbs. The history of the apothegm in Spanish begins in 1533, when Diego *Gracián de Alderete published a translation of the *Apophthegmata* of Plutarch. The term was also used by Erasmus, and by Melchor de *Santa Cruz, the first to compile a collection of Spanish national apothegms. Juan Rufo was one of the first in Spanish to drop the ''h'' from the word, and also one of the first to use the word without an explanation of its meaning. The most immediate precedent for Rufo's work was the *Floresta española de apothegmas* by Santa Cruz. Rufo places greater emphasis on the moral element than his predecessor, and his sayings are not grouped according to topic. In spite of its title, the work actually contains 707 apothegms.

BIBLIOGRAPHY

Primary Text

Los seiscientos apotegmas y otras obras en verso. Ed. Alberto Blecua. Madrid: Espasa-Calpe, 1972.

Nina Shecktor

RUFO, Luis (1582?, Córdoba–1653, Córdoba), poet and painter. In Italy he won over Caravaggio in a painting competition. Like his father, Juan *Rufo, he produced a collection of apothegms called *Los quinientos apotegmas* (The Five Hundred Apothegms. This collection remained unpublished until 1875, when it was published by *Sbarbi. The work was reissued in 1882 in Madrid with the title *Los quinientos apotegmas de Don Luis Rufo*. Luis Rufo was the bearer of a letter written in verse by his father concerning the art of governing well, to be presented to King Philip III. In Madrid he entered the service of Prince Filiberto of Savoy.

BIBLIOGRAPHY

Primary Text

Los quinientos apotegmas de Don Luis Rufo. Madrid: Gómez Fuentenebro, 1882.

Nina Shecktor

RUIBAL, José (1925, Pointevedra–), playwright. While working as a journalist in South America in the 1950s, Ruibal became acquainted with the theater of the absurd and began to write plays. His writings also show a familiarity with the French avant-garde dramatist Antonin Artaud as well as Greco-Roman animal fables and Spanish medieval and Calderonian allegory. The unconventionality and dissident stance of his writing made both production and publication of his work in Spain extremely difficult; his work and that of a number of his colleagues is part of what has been termed Spain's underground theater. His early plays, *Los mendigos* (1957; The Beggars), *El bacalao* (1960; *The Codfish*, 1972) and *El asno* (1962; *The Jackass*, 1970) are satires of bureaucracy and economic exploitation. In *El hombre y la mosca* (written in 1968; first Spanish ed. 1977;

The Man and the Fly, 1970), considered by critics his most important work, Ruibal has created a complexly structured allegory devoid of a traditional dramatic structure and open to numerous interpretations. Critics have seen in this work a paradigm of the Franco dictatorship, a rite of initiation, and a case study of a split personality. *La máquina de pedir* (1969; *The Begging Machine*, 1975), a satire of attempts by the intrinsically selfish to end poverty, is, like *El hombre y la mosca*, a work of social protest characterized by satiric language and an extremely complicated structure in which animals, humans and mechanized creations all play important roles. In 1971 Ruibal moved to the United States. *See also* Contemporary Spanish Theater.

BIBLIOGRAPHY

Primary Texts

El Bacalao. A Reader in Spanish Literature. Ed. Anthony Zahareas and Barbara Kaminar de Mujica. New York: Oxford UP, 1976.

El hombre y la mosca, España en el siglo XX. Madrid: Fundamentos, 1977.

La máquina de pedir, El asno y La ciencia del birlibirloque. Madrid: Siglo XXI, 1970.

Teatro sobre teatro (La máquina de pedir, Los mendigos, La secretaria, Los mutantes, El rabo, Los ojos, El padre, El superagente). Madrid: Cátedra, 1975.

English Translations

"The Codfish." Tr. J. Pearson. In *Modern International Drama* 5.2 (1972): 5–18.

"The Jackass" and *The Man and The Fly*. Tr. J. Zelonis. In *The New Wave Spanish Drama*. Ed. G. Wellwarth. New York: New York UP, 1970.

Criticism

Castellví de Moor, Magda. "Esquematización y objetivación simbólica en el teatro de Ruibal." *Journal of Spanish Studies, Twentieth Century* 3.1 (Spring 1975): 45–49.

Cramsie, Hilde. *Teatro y censura en la España franquista: Sastre, Muñiz y Ruibal*. New York: Peter Lang, 1984.

Wellwarth, George. *Spanish Underground Drama*. University Park: Pennsylvania State UP, 1972.

Judith Ginsberg

RUIZ, Juan. *See* Arcipreste de Hita

RUIZ AGUILERA, Ventura (1820, Salamanca–1881, Madrid), Salamancan man of letters. After studying and giving up medicine, he went to Madrid in 1843 to begin a literary career which produced a wide variety of work—collections of poems: the *Ecos nacionales* (1849, 1854, 1873; National Echoes) and *Elegías* (1862, 1873; Elegies); novels: *El conspirador de a folio* (1848; The Folio-size Conspirator) and *El mundo al revés* (1865; Upside-down World); collections of shorter fiction: *Proverbios ejemplares* (1864; Exemplary Proverbs), *Limones agrios* (1866; Bitter Lemons) and *Proverbios cómicos* (1870; Comic Proverbs); and, in the styles of *Calderón, Leandro Fernández de *Moratín and the sentimental drama of the time, staged plays: *Del agua mansa nos libre Dios*

(1847; May God Protect Us from Still Waters), *Bernardo de Saldaña* (1848), *Camino de Portugal* (1849; The Road to Portugal), and *Flor marchita* (1853; Faded Flower); and, in collaboration, a liberal historical study, *Europa marcha* (1849; Europe on the Move). He also founded and/or edited various weekly publications; of these the most important was *El Museo Universal*. Despite all this steady output, Aguilera, like many another literary man of his time, had to accept for economic reasons the directorship of the National Museum of Archaeology.

Aguilera presents the case of both a typical literary figure of his time and of one truly important for a comprehension of literary history. He was a transitional figure between neo-classicism and Realism/*Naturalism; his two collections of *Proverbios*, the *Ecos* and satiric poems, especially *La Arcadia moderna* (1867, 1873; The Modern Arcadia) were studied and written about by *Pérez Galdós. By 1870, on the eve of his flowering as a novelist, he saw in those works by Aguilera the most important and immediate models for the kind of national novel France and England had produced through Balzac and Dickens. For Galdós, Aguilera was the contemporary Spanish writer closest to the great socio-mimetic national tradition of *Cervantes, *Quevedo, Velázquez, Goya, Ramón de la Cruz and *Mesonero Romanos. And, hence, Aguilera was the writer whose work could best serve as a model for those who, like Galdós, wanted to put a novel of national manners in the service of the liberal social movement signified by the Spanish Revolution of 1868.

BIBLIOGRAPHY

Primary Texts

Obras completas. 3 vols. Madrid: Biblioteca de Instrucción y Recreo, 1873–74.

Criticism

Brown, Reginald F. ''Una relación literaria y cordial: Benito Pérez Galdós y Ventura Ruiz Aguilera.'' In *Actas del Quinto Congreso Internacional de Hispanistas*. vol. 1. Ed. M. Chevalier et al. Bordeaux: Instituto de Estudios Ibéricos e Iberoamericanos, 1977. 223–33.

Miller, Stephen. *El mundo de Galdós*. Santander: Sociedad Menéndez Pelayo, 1983. 14–22, 73–78.

Pérez Galdós, B. ''Observaciones sobre la novela contemporánea en España.'' In *Ensayos de crítica literaria*. Barcelona: Península, 1972. 115–32.

Sena, Enrique de. ''Prologo.'' *Ecos nacionales (Selección)*. Salamanca: Librería Cervantes, 1981. 7–17.

Stephen Miller

RUIZ DE ALARCÓN Y MENDOZA, Juan (1580/81, Mexico City–1639, Madrid), dramatist, lawyer, government servant. Among the numerous playwrights in the first third of the seventeenth c. in Spain, Alarcón, Lope de *Vega, and *Tirso de Molina are the major stars. Born in Mexico City in late 1580 or 1581, Alarcón was the third son of Pedro Ruiz de Alarcón, a recent immigrant to the viceroyalty of New Spain and member of a Manchegan family belonging to the landed gentry in the province of Cuenca (Spain), and Leonor (Hernández de Cazalla) de Mendoza, daughter of a Spaniard who had come to the Taxco (Mexico) mining area in the 1540s. Proud of his father's lineage (distantly related to the powerful clans of Pacheco and Girón, headed respectively by the Marquis of Villena and the Duke of Osuna), Alarcón seldom spoke of his mother's less distinguished mercantile and mining family, partly because of Spanish prejudice against trade and commerce, partly because it was politic to silence his Creole background in view of the frequently contemptuous attitude in Spain toward colonials. In only one of his plays, *El semejante a sí mismo* (The Man Who Was Like Himself), is there any mention of events or scenes in New Spain. Still, various scholars in this century have claimed to detect in his work attitudes and values indicative of Mexican, as opposed to Spanish, national character and psychology; others have as stoutly denied these claims. One further distinctive mark, his hunchback, set Alarcón off from his fellows and made him always the object of sneers and laughter.

After grammar school studies, probably with the Jesuits, in Mexico City Alarcón completed between 1596 and 1600 the required curriculum for the degree of bachelor in canon law. In that year he sailed for the first time to Spain and enrolled in the famed law faculty of the U of Salamanca, where the degree was actually conferred in October 1600. Two years later he earned the degree of bachelor of civil law; he probably remained at the university until 1606 to continue graduate study in law. From 1606 to 1608 he lived in Seville—where he had relatives—practiced law, and joined in the activities and amusements of young literati.

Returning to Mexico City in 1608 with the same fleet that carried Mateo *Alemán, author of *Guzmán de Alfarache*, he successfully passed the oral examinations at the U of Mexico for the degree of licentiate in canon and civil law in 1609. Between 1609 and 1613 he practiced his profession in his natal city and for a time served as legal adviser to the *corregidor*, the highest royal appointee in the Mexico City government. Meanwhile he competed unsuccessfully four times for a chair on the faculty of law at the U.

Once again in Spain in 1613, he settled in Madrid and joined the swarm of courtiers seeking royal favors and posts in the government bureaucracy. Not until 1626 were his efforts crowned with success when he was named *relator interino* (supernumerary court reporter) on the Council of the Indies (the official recommendation excluded him from the more distinguished post of magistrate of a colonial court because of his physical deformity); he officially held this position, converted into a regular appointment in 1633, until his death on August 4, 1639. In 1617 his one child, Laurencia, was born of his common-law union with Angela de Cervantes. To this daughter, married to a distant relative living in La Mancha, Alarcón left the bulk of his estate.

Between 1613 and 1625 (according to the best estimate of dates of composition, made by Courtney Bruerton), during the long years of waiting for a royal appointment, Alarcón wrote the twenty plays published by him during his lifetime, eight in 1628, the remaining twelve in 1634. Three other plays are attributed to him with considerable certainty, the most notable being the excellent drama *No hay mal que por bien no venga* (1653; It's an Ill Wind That Blows No Good).

Among the major playwrights of his day Alarcón stands out for the relatively small number of his dramas, yet he essayed—always within the limits of the conventions established by Lope de Vega for his "new comedy"—surprisingly diverse subjects and types of drama, which may be loosely classified as follows: (1) two dramas dealing with religious conflict and the psychology of religious conversion—one, *El Anticristo* (The Antichrist), a sweeping, ambitious dramatization of the conflict between the forces of good and evil (led by the false Messiah and the false prophet Elijah) in the last days of the world, the other, *La manganilla de Melilla* (The Stratagem of Melilla), dealing with a sixteenth-c. battle between Christians and Muslims in North Africa; (2) eight heroic dramas set in the past, most of them treating the relations in an absolutist state between the sovereign, his chief minister and vassals, and the law (reflecting in greater or lesser degree Spanish preoccupation between 1617 and 1623 with governmental and economic reforms)—*Los favores del mundo* (The Favors of the World), *Ganar amigos* (Winning Friends), *El dueño de las estrellas* (The Master of the Stars), *La amistad castigada* (Friendship Punished), *Los pechos privilegiados* (Privileged Breasts), *La crueldad por el honor* (Cruelty for the Sake of Honor), *El tejedor de Segovia*, Part 2 (The Weaver of Segovia), and *No hay mal que por bien no venga*; (3) eleven comedies of intrigue and of contemporary customs and manners—*El desdichado en fingir* (The Unlucky Feigner; though set in Bohemia, the customs and manners are wholly those of Alarcón's Spain), *El semejante a sí mismo* (The Man Who Was Like Himself), *La cueva de Salamanca* (The Cave of Salamanca), *Mudarse por mejorarse* (Changing Love to Improve One's Fortune), *Todo es ventura* (Everything Is Chance), *La industria y la suerte* (Scheming Versus Luck), *Las paredes oyen* (The Walls Have Ears), *Los empeños de un engaño* (The Entanglements of a Falsehood), *La prueba de las promesas* (The Test of Promises), *La verdad sospechosa* (Suspect Truth), *El examen de maridos* (The Examination of Husbands).

Among the historical dramas, *Ganar amigos* stands out for the masterful manipulation of plot and characters to illustrate the great theme of the sacredness and obligations of friendship; but the one which has been most frequently revived is *El tejedor de Segovia*, a play filled with heroic and violent actions as well as a hint of social protest against the oppression of the people by arrogant nobles. For this reason it appealed to nineteenth-c. Romantics and is his only play to appear in Russian translation (1946). Still, Alarcón's major achievement does not lie in the historical dramas; he had little sense of the poetry of the past and no apparent interest in imagining medieval Spanish or ancient Greek society. Thus blatant anachronisms appear in all these plays, for example, in *Ganar amigos* the announcement of the final fall of Granada to the Christians (1492) during the reign of Peter I of Castile in the fourteenth c.

Alarcón's most original and best plays are to be found among the comedies of customs and manners, in which his gift for acute and critical observation of society—honed perhaps by his Creole sensibilities and the pain of his deformity—produced true and memorable characters and scenes: the youthful gaiety of university students, rich and poor alike, united in their love of fun and respect for learning (*La cueva de Salamanca*); the mercantile bustle of the cosmopolitan port city of Seville (*La industria y la suerte*); the fawning, lying, and pretentiousness of courtiers, government ministers, and jobseekers in the royal capital at Madrid (*La verdad sospechosa*, *El examen de maridos*, *La prueba de las promesas*).

Some of these plays deepen into genuine comedies of character of the type later made famous by Molière, in which the complications and denouement of the plot are due much less to chance and coincidence than to the failings of human character. Of these the most celebrated is *La verdad sospechosa* (a play twice translated into English), in which the appealing young protagonist García is blocked from achieving the marriage he intensely desires not by the machinations of a rival but by the flaw in his own character, his compulsive, gratuitous lying. Another lawyer-playwright, Pierre Corneille, charmed by this work (nothing in the Spanish language, he said, had ever pleased him more), partly translated and partly adapted it in his comedy *Le Menteur* (1644; The Liar), which, according to Voltaire, was the principal force behind Molière's new conception of comedy.

Among the playwrights of the period, many of them priests, some ex-soldiers, Alarcón was the only practicing lawyer, the only representative of Spain's small professional bourgeoisie. His plays show the stamp of that lengthy professional training: the use of legal vocabulary, the subtle distinctions and paradoxes developed in argument and dialogue, the concern for logicality and proofs, the syllogistically ordered debates which close two plays (*La cueva de Salamanca* and *El examen de maridos*), the prominence given to lawmakers (Lycurgus in *El dueño de las estrellas*), and the examination of the conflicts in an absolutist state between the king as source of all law and the king as upholder of the law (*Ganar amigos*). Lacking in lyricism, *mysticism, or deep religious fervor, little interested in the epic events of the Reconquest or the idealization of the Spanish peasantry (all dominant aspects of the theater of Lope de Vega and Tirso de Molina), Alarcón speaks for and to the urban bourgeoisie and its values: loyalty to the king above all, the exaltation of friendship over romantic love, the importance of marriage and family and father-son relationships, no idealization of women but the refusal to castigate their failings by raising a violent hand against them, the insistence on truth-telling, prudence, caution, keeping one's word, and an honor code which asks even of the highest-born noble that his actions be virtuous. Alarcón is the creator in the theater of his time of urban comedy at its best. *See also* Theater in Spain.

BIBLIOGRAPHY

Primary Texts

Obras completas de Juan Ruiz de Alarcón. Ed. Agustín Millares Carlo. 3 vols. Mexico: Fondo de Cultura Económica, 1957, 1959, 1968.

English Translations

The Truth Suspected. Tr. Julio del Toro and Robert V. Finney. In *Poet Lore* 38 (1927): 475–530.

The Truth Suspected. Tr. Robert C. Ryan. In *Spanish Drama*. Ed. Angel Flores. New York: Bantam Books, 1962. 135–89.

Criticism

Alatorre, Antonio. ''Para la historia de un problema: la mexicanidad de Ruiz de Alarcón.'' *Anuario de Letras* [de la Universidad Nacional de México] 4 (1964): 161–202.

Casalduero, Joaquín. ''El gracioso de *El Anticristo*.'' In *Estudios sobre el teatro español*. Madrid: Gredos, 1962. 131–44.

Castro Leal, Antonio. *Juan Ruiz de Alarcón, su vida y su obra*. México: Cuadernos Americanos, 1943.

King, Willard F. ''La ascendencia paterna de Juan Ruiz de Alarcón y Mendoza.'' *NRFH* 19.1 (1970): 49–86.

———. *Juan Ruiz de Alarcón: su mundo mexicano y español*. Mexico City, Mexico: El Colegio de México, 1989.

Poesse, Walter. *Ensayo de una bibliografía de Juan Ruiz de Alarcón y Mendoza*. Valencia: Castalia, 1964 (supplement in *Hispanófila* 27 [1966]: 23–42.

———. *Juan Ruiz de Alarcón*. TWAS 231. New York: Twayne, 1972.

Staves, Susan. ''Liars and Lying in Alarcón, Corneille, and Steele.'' *Revue de Littérature Comparée* 46.4 (1972): 514–27.

Willard F. King

RUIZ IRIARTE, Víctor (1912, Madrid–1982, Madrid), Spanish playwright and journalist. Best known for his comedies, he was the first new playwright to emerge on the Madrid stage following the Civil War (1936–39). His early works—*El puente de los suicidas* (1945; Suicide Bridge), *Academia de amor* (1946; Academy of Love), and *El aprendiz de amante* (1949; The Apprentice Lover)—established his reputation and identified him as a writer of poetic fantasy, reminiscent in some respects of the theater of Pirandello, Evreinov, Anouilh, and *Casona. His 1950 hit, *El landó de seis caballos* (The Six-Horse Landau), a whimsical interweaving of illusion and reality, is considered the prototype of the escapist comedy favored by the Spanish bourgeois audience in the difficult post-war years.

Ruiz Iriarte's approach to comedy, however, was not monolithic. His *El gran minué* (1950; The Grand Minuet), set in the eighteenth c. in an unidentified European court, is a fine example of political and social satire. His *Juego de niños* (1952; Child's Play), recipient of the National Theater Prize, marks the beginning of a series of comedies of manners that likewise contain a satirical current. Although his satire is usually gentle in tone, Ruiz Iriarte stood as an observer and critic of a changing Spanish society. In particular he noted the disintegration of the traditional family structure, the hypocrisy of middle-class morality and the double standard in moral values, the generation gap; the overemphasis on material possessions and social status, and society's tendency to judge people by external appearance rather than by inner worth. His criticism became more outspoken in his later works, starting with *Esta noche es la víspera* (1958; Tonight Is the Prelude) and culminating in his two major serious dramas: *El carrusell* (1964; The Carousel) and *Historia de un adulterio* (1969; Story of Adultery).

Ruiz Iriarte vigorously defended comedy for comedy's sake. His farce *La guerra empieza en Cuba* (1955; The War Begins in Cuba), built on a classic use of identical twins, is the epitome of theater for fun. On the other hand, he also saw the possibility of using comedy to convey a message. His *La muchacha del sombrerito rosa* (1967; The Girl in the Little Pink Hat), winner of the National Literature Prize, and its sequel *Primavera en la Plaza de Paris* (1968; Springtime in the Plaza de Paris) dealt with the return to Spain of political exiles and was an open plea for reconciliation between the conservative and liberal factions.

A polished craftsman, Ruiz Iriarte excelled in careful play construction and in the creation of sparkling dialogue. In addition to achieving critical and commercial success in Spain and Latin America, several of his plays have been translated to other languages, including English, German, Japanese, and Portuguese. Active in the theatrical and literary world of Madrid, Ruiz Iriarte directed his own plays, collaborated on movie scripts, wrote television plays, and, over a forty-year period, contributed numerous articles to major newspapers and literary journals. He served as president of the Sociedad General de Autores de España (Association of Spanish Authors) and of the Spanish authors' pension fund.

BIBLIOGRAPHY

Primary Texts

Buenas noches, Sabina. Madrid: Preyson, 1983.

La pequeña comedia. Madrid: Escelicer, 1967. Television comedies.

Un pequeño mundo. Madrid: Sociedad General Anónima Española, 1962. Newspaper articles.

Teatro selecto de Victor Ruiz Iriarte. Madrid: Escelicer, 1967.

See also *Teatro español*. Ed. F. Sáinz de Robles. Madrid: Aguilar, for seasons 1949–50, 1950–51, 1951–52, 1952–53, 1955–56, 1958–59, 1964–65, 1965–66, 1966–67, 1967–68, 1968–69.

Criticism

Holt, Marion P. "Victor Ruiz Iriarte." In *The Contemporary Spanish Theater (1949–1972)*. TWAS 336. Boston: Twayne, 1975.

Schevill, Isabel Magana. Intro. to *Juego de niños*. Englewood Cliffs, NJ: Prentice-Hall, 1965. viii-xxiii.

Spencer, Janie. "Fantasy Used and Abused in Ruiz Iriarte's Theater." *Estreno* 10.1 (1984): 7–9.

Zatlin-Boring, Phyllis. *Victor Ruiz Iriarte*. Boston: Hall, 1980.
———. "The Pirandellism of Victor Ruiz Iriarte." *Estreno* 4.2 (1978): 18–21.

Phyllis Zatlin

RUIZ-RICO, Juan José (1948, Granada–), narrator, essayist, and poet, doctor in law and master of arts in political science. Ruiz Rico studied social science in Paris, London, and Manchester. He teaches political science at the U of Granada.

As a poet, he is the author of *Mass Society* (1971), and *Puñal de luz* (1972; Light of Knife). His essays include *El papel político de la Iglesia Católica en España* (1977; The Political Role of the Catholic Church in Spain).

Ruiz Rico's first novels—*La culpa de Cairós* (1978; Cairós's Guilt) and *Inmutator Mirabilis* (1980)—have as a main theme the cynicism and immorality in contemporary Spanish society. *Ejercicio para romper una muñeca* (1981; Exercise to Break a Doll) deals with the problem of abortion, and is written in an erotic language, combining dialogues from different texts. *Al sur son las hogueras* (1982; In the South Are the Bonfires) is perhaps Ruiz Rico's best narrative; he utilizes material taken from social anthropology to reveal the superstitious social and psychological practices of an Andalusian community. *Nocturno de febrero junto al Bósforo* (1985; February Nocturne near the Bosforo) is a political history about the supposed triumph of the coup d'état that took place in Spain on February 23, 1982.

BIBLIOGRAPHY

Primary Texts

Al sur son las hogueras. Granada: Don Quijote, 1982.
La culpa de Cairós. Madrid: Las Ediciones del Espejo, 1978.
Ejercicio para romper una muñeca. Madrid: Grijalbo, 1981.
Inmutator mirabilis. Barcelona: V. Pozanco, 1980.
Mass Society. Jaén: Diego Sánchez del Real, 1971.
Nocturno de febrero junto al Bósforo. Extremadura: Regional, 1985.
Puñal de luz. Burgos: Artesa, 1972.

José Ortega

RUSIÑOL Y PRATS, Santiago (1861, Barcelona–1931, Aranjuez), novelist, essayist, poet, playwright, and painter. The son of a Catalan businessman, Rusiñol decided at the age of twenty-five to follow his artistic inclinations instead of continuing in his family's business. His largely autobiographical novel, dramatized in 1917, *L'auca del senyor Esteve* (1907; Spanish tr. *Aleluyas del Señor Esteban*, 1909; Mr. Esteve's Praise), describes this early period of his life and the world of commerce and factories of the Barcelona bourgeoisie. Rusiñol wrote almost exclusively in Catalan and his works, which enjoyed considerable popularity, were translated into Spanish. The distinguished authors Gregorio *Martínez Sierra, Eduardo *Marquina, Jacinto *Benavente, and Joaquín *Dicenta were among his translators. Rusiñol's world view, imbued with both a joy for life and a wry skepticism, with notes of harsh realism as well as romantic idealism, humor, and sentimentality, found great favor in Spain. His collected essays on life, travel and landscape include *Anant pel mon* (1896; A Traveler in the World), and *Fulls de la vida* (1898; Pages from My Life). His early *Oracions* (1898; Prayers) are prose poems dedicated to ruins, abandoned gardens, and elements of nature. In the late 1890s Rusiñol participated in the collective cultural activities, exhibitions, concerts, theater, of the Catalan group of artists and writers known as Cau Ferrat (The Den of Ferrat) and he later turned his home in Sitges, where many of the group's activities were held, into a museum also called Cau Ferrat. Rusiñol spent a considerable amount of time in Paris, and he traveled through much of Spain.

Rusiñol's best known and most accomplished novel is the satirical *El poble gris* (1902; Spanish tr. *El pueblo gris*, 1904; The Gray Town), a biting description of provincial life. But his theater won for him his greatest acclaim. Such works as the operetta *L'alegria que passa* (1898; Spanish tr. *La alegría que pasa*, 1906; Transient Happiness), with music by N'Enric Morera, and the dramas *El pati blau* (1903; Spanish tr. *El patio azul*, 1909; The Blue Patio) and *El mistic* (1904; Spanish tr. *El místico*, 1904; The Mystic) were the best known. The latter work, of considerable historical significance, treated the life of the great Catalan poet, the priest Jacint *Verdaguer, and achieved enormous popularity throughout Spain.

Also a distinguished painter, noted particularly for his landscapes, Rusiñol was, together with Ramón Casas, the principal animator of the Catalan Modernist movement in the 1890s, a school of painting inspired by the French Naturalists. He was also associated with Els Quatre Gats (The Four Cats), a Barcelona tavern frequented by prominent artists, including Pablo Picasso, after its opening in 1897. Rusiñol's book *Jardins d'Espanya* (1903; Spanish tr. *Jardines de España*, 1914; Gardens of Spain) contains forty reproductions of these paintings with comments by the author. His *L'illa de la calma* (1922; Spanish tr. *La isla de la calma*, 1925; *Majorca, the Island of Calm*, 1958), a prose study of the island of Mallorca, very much resembles his landscape paintings in theme and techniques. He died at Aranjuez, the Spanish royal country palace whose gardens he was particularly fond of painting. *See also* Modernism; Naturalism.

BIBLIOGRAPHY

Primary Texts

Obres completes. 3rd ed. 3 vols. Prol. Carles Soldevila, notes Donald Samuel Abrams. Barcelona: Selecta, 1973.

English Translation

Majorca, the Island of Calm. English version by Mary Lake. New ed., rev. by Dooreann MacDermott and J. F. Llatjos. Barcelona: Pulido, 1958.

Criticism

Ferrer Gilbert, Pedro. *El archiduque Luis Salvador, Rubén Darío y Santiago Rusiñol en Mallorca*. Inca-Palma: Vich, 1943.

Francés, José. *Santiago Rusiñol: y su obra.* Gerona Dalmau: Carles Pla, 1945.
Irizarry, Estelle. *Writer-Painters of Contemporary Spain.* TWAS 721. Boston: Twayne, 1984.
Pla, José. *Santiago Rusiñol: el seu temps.* Barcelona: Selecta, 1955.
Rusiñol, Maria. *Santiago Rusiñol visto por su hija.* Barcelona: Juventud, 1963.

Judith Ginsberg

S

SÁ-CARNEIRO, Mário (1890, Lisbon–1916, Paris), poet and short story writer of the Portuguese Modernist group, also known for one early play, *Amizade* (1912; Friendship), written in collaboration with Tomás Cabreira Júnior, and one novella, *A Confissão de Lúcio* (1914; Lucio's Confession). Always prey to emotional instability, he committed suicide in 1916 at the second attempt, after warning his friend and confidant, Fernando *Pessoa, by letter that he was about to do so. His letters to Pessoa from Paris, where he lived for much of the time between October 1912 and his death, are relevant to his artistic production as well as being personally revealing. Most, but not all, have been published in the two-volume *Cartas a Fernando Pessoa* (1958 and 1959; Letters to Fernando Pessoa). His other published correspondence is equally helpful: he was an essentially confessional author and a self-conscious artist, and everything he wrote is pervaded by his tastes and ideology as well as by his tormented sensibility.

His truly productive period lasted for only three years (1913–16), though his second book, *Princípio* (1912; Beginning), a collection of short stories, was started in 1908, and there was also some early poetry, notably a short elegy to the young co-author of *Amizade*, who committed suicide in 1911. In effect, his fame depends on the one novella, a group of short stories published under the title *Céu em Fogo* (1915; Heaven Ablaze) and, above all, on his uneven, but sometimes very impressive poetry, which was written sporadically throughout his Paris years and eventually published in 1946 (*Poesias*; Poems). In a list of his works compiled by Fernando Pessoa and published in the journal *Presença* in November 1928, the juvenilia is ignored.

In common with their counterparts in other countries, the Portuguese Modernists were determined to bring about change in their cultural ambience, and Sá-Carneiro, temporarily back in Lisbon because of the Great War, was one of the founders and, in the second and last issue, editors of their iconclastic journal *Orpheu* (March and June 1915; Orpheus). A third number was prepared, but this was abandoned because of financial problems: the project ran at a loss and Sá-Carneiro, who had injudiciously given his father's name as its financial guarantor, fled back to a secret address in Paris. There he killed himself nine months later, claiming in a letter to Pessoa that lack of money was his only motive.

Though undeniable that he was financially embarrassed (he never worked, and the allowance that he received from his father was insufficient to maintain the lifestyle that suited him), this cannot in fact be judged the principal cause of his early death. He had always been obsessed by suicide, his sexual orientation was ambivalent, he was chronically insecure and he was the victim of continuously increasing mental anguish. The later poems—the "Sete Canções de Declínio" (Seven Songs of Decline), followed by "Crise Lamentável" (Pitiful Crisis), "O Fantasma" (The Ghost), "El-rei" (The King), "Aqueloutro" (That Other One) and "Fim" (End)—all bear witness to his emotional state, and are redolent of sardonic and self-deprecatory bitterness.

In spite of all the new isms created by the Modernists, and their avowed enthusiasm for cultural novelty, much of Sá-Carneiro's work has its roots in earlier artistic movements, albeit those that came from abroad, rather than Portugal. *Amizade* is sentimentally romantic, while the short stories and *A Confissão de Lúcio* testify to the influence of E. T. A. Hoffmann, the French *conte fantastique* and Edgar Allan Poe's *Tales of Mystery and Imagination*, as well as that of French decadentism and English aestheticism. This is not to say that there is no originality in his writings however, especially where the poetry is concerned, even if much of it is incontrovertibly post-symbolist. Furthermore, it should be borne in mind that what was essentially passé in Paris when Sá-Carneiro lived there—the Art Nouveau movement, together with several other aspects of fin-de-siècle sensibility and activities—was, by and large, new and shocking in Portuguese circles. He was almost abnormally devoted to the French capital and all it contained, represented or had given birth to, even though at heart he was lonely and homesick there, and he brought to Portuguese letters a flavor of what was, to him if not to the real Parisian avant-garde, urban sophistication and European modernity. And in fact the results were often authentically new, not only because some of the areas of inspiration, such as the theater, the dance, painting and kinetic art, really were breaking new ground all around him, but also because he possessed the ability to effect a telling symbiosis between cultural elements and his own tormented personality. In true aesthetic fashion, he determined to make life art, but he discovered at a tragically early age that this was an impossible aim. His writings act as a kind of metaphor for his attempt to do so and his gradual realization of defeat.

BIBLIOGRAPHY

Primary Texts

Cartas a Fernando Pessoa. Ed. U. Tavares Rodrigues. Lisbon: Atica, 1958 and 1959.

Cartas de Mário de Sá-Carneiro a Luís de Montalvor/Cândida Ramos/Alfredo Guisado/José Pacheco. Ed. A. Saraiva. Oporto: Limiar, 1977.

Correspondência Inédita de Mário de Sá-Carneiro a Fernando Pessoa. Ed. A. Saraiva. Oporto: Centro de Estudos Pessoanos, 1980.

Mário de Sá-Carneiro e a Génese de ''Amizade.'' Ed., study François Castex. Coimbra: Livraria Almedina, 1971.

Obras Completas de Mário de Sá-Carneiro. Lisbon: Atica, 1940—.

Poesias. Ed. João Gaspar Simões. Lisbon: Atica, 1946.

Todos os Poemas. Rio de Janeiro: Aguilar, 1974.

Criticism

Bacarisse, Pamela. *A Alma Amortalhada. Mário de Sá-Carneiro's Use of Metaphor and Image.* London: Tamesis, 1984.

Carpinteiro, Maria da Graça. *A Novela Poética de Mário de Sá-Carneiro.* Lisbon: Publicações do Centro de Estudos Filológicos, 1960.

Figueiredo, João Pinto de. *A Morte de Mário de Sá-Carneiro.* Lisbon: Publicações Dom Quixote, 1983.

Galhoz, Maria Aliete. *Mário de Sá-Carneiro.* Lisbon: Presença, 1963.

Woll, Dieter. *Realidade e Idealidade na Lírica de Sá-Carneiro.* Lisbon: Delfos, 1968.

Pamela Bacarisse

SÁ DE MIRANDA, Francisco (1481, Coimbra–1558, Quinta da Tapada, between the Douro and Minho valleys, Portugal), renowned lyric poet who introduced Italian verse forms into Portugal. Born the illegitimate son of a canon of Coimbra, Sá does not seem to have been caused professional or personal difficulties by his irregular origins. He graduated from the university in Coimbra as a doctor of law, a career he never pursued. His first poems date from 1510–15 and were published in the *Cancioneiro Geral* (General Songbook) of 1516. From 1521 to 1526 he traveled in Italy, perhaps meeting with his distant relative Vittoria Colonna. In 1527 he returned to Portugal and by 1530 had retired from court life to voluntary exile in Minho (northern Portugal), where he wrote most of his works. In 1552, at the insistence of Prince John, he sent a copy of his works to the court, thus increasing their already substantial popularity. In the final years of his life, Sá was plagued by the deaths of his son (1553), Prince John (1554), and his wife (1555). His poetry was first published in 1595.

Sá is considered to represent to Portuguese poetry what *Garcilaso de la Vega does to Spanish verse; however, his works show evidence of a strong alliance to traditional verse forms, and his love poetry never develops beyond the medieval complaint. Although his lovers do not find any joy in their suffering, neither do they value their pain as uplifting or purifying. His poetry consistently expresses a suspicion of beauty and love as sources of man's downfall that throw him into confusion, an attitude in direct contrast with the spirit of the age, which tended to interpret love's suffering as a source of moral perfection.

Sá's pessimistic attitude about love is vented through misogyny. The only women praised in his works are Celia, celebrated in an eclogue by that name, and his wife, to whom he dedicated the sonnet ''Aquelle espirito ja tam bem pagado.'' Celia may represent Isabel Freyre, muse of Garcilaso. Both works celebrate dead women who have escaped from the evils of this world.

Over half of Sá's poetry is in Spanish, and he clearly preferred Spanish to Portuguese when writing hendecasyllabic verse. His works, which include two *comedias,* reflect a humanistic education, respect for and integration of classical and Italian sources, and a decidedly Stoic tone. Sá's nine well-known eclogues and his *epístolas* reflect the poet's distrust of man as a social animal and express his quiet exaltations of the ascetic life he made his own.

BIBLIOGRAPHY

Primary Texts

Obras completas. Ed. M. Rodrigues Lapa. 2 vols. Lisbon: Livraria Sá da Costa, 1942.

Poesías de Francisco de Sá de Miranda. Ed. C. Michaëlis Vasconcellos. Halle: Niemeyer, 1885.

Criticism

Earle, T. F. *Theme and Image in the Poetry of Sá de Miranda*. Oxford: Oxford UP, 1970.

Pina Martins, J. V. *Sá de Miranda e a cultura do renascimento*. 2 vols. Lisbon: Bibliografía, 1972.

Elizabeth Rhodes

SAAVEDRA FAJARDO, Diego de (1584, Algezares, Murcia–1648, Madrid), diplomat, political analyst, historian, and writer. Saavedra was from a rich and noble family. He studied law in Salamanca and began his diplomatic career as the secretary of Cardinal Gaspar de Borja, Spanish ambassador to the Vatican (1600), whom he accompanied to Rome and Naples and whom he later succeeded. Saavedra became a member of the Order of Santiago, and although he did not take major orders, he was named canon of Santiago (1617). He attended the conclaves electing Gregory XV (1621) and Urbane VIII (1623). From this last date on, his diplomatic career never faltered. He became ambassador to Rome (1631) and to Germany (1633), Indies consultant, and plenipotentiary representative to the Peace Conference of Münster (1643); he was said to be the man behind a number of the major treaties forged at that conference. Saavedra carried out various diplomatic missions in Munich (1637). His influence was felt in Franche-Comté, the Swiss cantons, Regensburg (Ratisbon), Brussels, Vienna, etc. He died in 1648, while filling the post of consultant on the Indies. In foreign service for forty years, Saavedra was regarded as one of the wisest and most capable diplomats in Europe.

Saavedra Fajardo was a noted and prolific writer, analyst, and theorist in the areas of politics and history. His long diplomatic career put great resources at Saavedra's disposal. Writing as a historian, he conceived *Corona gótica, castellana y austríaca* (1646; The Gothic, Spanish, and Austrian Crown); only the first part, in which Saavedra narrates the history of the Visigoths, was completed. Toward the end of the seventeenth c. the project was finished by Alonso Núñez de Castro (1671 and 1677; *Corona castellana y austríaca)*.

Saavedra's political ideas appear in detail in his *Empresas políticas o Idea de un príncipe cristiano representada en cien empresas* (1640; Political Enterprises or The Idea of a Christian Prince Represented in a Hundred Emblems). Each chapter was preceded by an emblem or drawing that graphically described its theme. Saavedra's book closely follows Jacobo Bruck Angermunt's *Emblemata politica* (1618); the genre was in favor in Europe at that time, but Saavedra gave it more serious treatment. The book's rich shading, displays of erudition, and eloquent expression make the *Empresas* the best European example of the genre. It is a guidebook for the education of the Christian prince, in open opposition to the secular cynicism of Machiavellianism. In its pages, one can see Saavedra's animosity toward those writers of treatises who were not guided by what he termed the positive examples of religion and who favored a utilitarian approach to politics. An exalted patriotism flows throughout the book, stressing nationalistic strengths and virtues and attacking such negative influences as the power of favorites in the court, the economic decline within Spain, and European conspiracies against the Spanish Empire abroad. Further, the book puts forward the supremacy of the law over any individual person. Stoicism and an analysis of biblical, classical, and contemporary culture are also explored in the *Empresas*, which has undergone numerous editions and printings.

Saavedra's second important work is *República literaria* (1655; Literary Republic), probably written in 1612 and published after his death under the title *Juicio de Artes y Sciencias*. Claudio Antonio de Cabrera appeared as the author of the first edition (Madrid, 1655); Saavedra's authorship was not discovered until years later. This burlesque satire presents a dream, in Lucianesque style, describing a fantastic city inhabited by the arts and sciences; the sciences are completely discredited in the work. The book presents a sharp and refined critique, which is more interesting due to what it illustrates about the epoch's aesthetic attitudes than because of Saavedra's own personal judgments. Juan de *Mena, Fernando de *Herrera, *Camões, *Góngora, Michelangelo, and *Velázquez are among the figures explored in the *República*. A number of major omissions may be found, however: *Cervantes, *La *Celestina*, and *theater in general. Still, the *República* does note men of science (Vesalius, Galen), lawyers, artists, etc.

The Lucianesque style reappears in *Locuras de Europa* (1748; Europe's Madness), a satiric dialogue between Mercury and Lucian in which Saavedra puts forward his political theories on the relationship between Spain and the rest of Europe; it specifically explores the intrigues of other European nations against Spain and discusses the idea of peace among nations. Like *Gracián y Morales, Saavedra also wrote on King Ferdinand in *Política y razón de estado del Rey Católico don Fernando* (1631; The Politics and Reason of State of the Catholic King, don Ferdinand). The central idea is that Ferdinand was the model Christian prince, particularly since he was noted for being fair and just. The book is also a brief treatise on the art of ruling, synthesizing the ideas of Aristotle and the Thomists. Saavedra's style is terse and tight. Critics have generally noted pleasantness and deliberation in Saavedra's works, mixed with a tendency toward sententiousness. A number of works are lost, including *Guerras y movimientos de Italia de cuarenta años a esta parte*, *Suspiros de Francia*, and *Ligas de Francia con holandeses y sueceses*. Saavedra Fajardo represents a key moment in the European Baroque era; his works reflect his extraordinary diplomatic activity, giving his political treatises universal and human value.

BIBLIOGRAPHY

Primary Texts

Empresas políticas. Salamanca: Anaya, 1972.
Locuras de Europa. Ed. J. M. Alejandro. Salamanca: Anaya, 1965.
Obras completas. Ed. Angel González Palencia. Madrid: Aguilar, 1946.
República literaria. Ed. John Dowling. Salamanca: Anaya, 1967.

Criticism

Dowling, John. *Diego de Saavedra Fajardo*. TWAS 437. Boston: Twayne, 1977.
———. *El pensamiento político-filosófico de Saavedra Fajardo*. Murcia: n.p., 1957.
Fernández Santamaria, J. A. "Diego de Saavedra Fajardo: Reason of State in the Spanish Baroque." *Il Pensiero Politico* 12 (1979): 19–37.
Fraga Iribarne, Manuel. *Diego de Saavedra Fajardo y la diplomacia de su época*. Madrid: Dirección General de Relaciones Culturales del Ministerio de Asuntos Exteriores, 1955.
Hafter, Monroe Z. "Saavedra Fajardo: The Serpent and the Dove, the Lion and the Fox." In *Gracián and Perfection: Spanish Moralists of the 17th Century*. Cambridge: Harvard UP, 1966. 43–73.
Lundelius, Ruth. "Concerning Diego de Saavedra Fajardo: Baroque Essayist." *Revista Canadiense de Estudios Hispánicos* 4 (1980): 206–17.

Catherine Larson

SABUCO DE NANTES, Oliva (1562, Alcaraz–1622, Albarete?), author. Daughter of one Bachelor Miguel de Sabuco, two works are signed by her. In 1587, there appeared the *Nueva filosofía de la naturaleza del hombre* (New Philosophy Concerning the Nature of Man), in which human anatomy, human knowledge, the social structure, and medical questions are discussed. Appended to the *Nueva filosofía* was the *Vera medicina y vera filosofía . . .* (True Medicine and True Philosophy . . .) which criticizes current medical theory and practice. Human emotions and behavior are attributed to the condition and action of the brain, somewhat along the same current of inquiry found in Juan *Huarte de San Juan's *Examen de ingenios* and Francisco *Sánchez's *Que nada se sabe*. In the last century, some critics have rejected Doña Oliva as author, attributing the work instead to her father, Miguel de Sabuco.

BIBLIOGRAPHY

Primary Texts

Nueva filosofía de la naturaleza del hombre. Madrid: Nacional, 1981.
Nueva filosofía y vera medicina. Ed. Octavio Cuartero. Madrid: Fé, 1888.
Obras. In BAE 45.

Criticism

Galerstein, C. and K. McNerney. *Women Writers of Spain*. Westport, CT: Greenwood, 1986.

Guy, A. "Modernité du philosophe Sabuco." In *Les cultures ibériques en devenir. Essais publiés en homage à la memoire de Marcel Bataillon (1895–1977)*. Paris: Singer Polignac, 1979.
Marcos, B. *Miguel Sabuco; antes doña Oliva*. Madrid: Caro Raggio, 1923.

Maureen Ihrie

SÁENZ-ALONSO, Mercedes (1917, San Sebastián–), Spanish novelist, critic, essayist and journalist. A professor at the U of Navarra and international lecturer on subjects ranging from art to history and literature, Sáenz-Alonso has written travel books (*Del Bosforo a Gibraltar* [1963; From the Bosphoros to Gibraltar] and *Del Molino al Minarete* [From the Mill to the Minaret]) as well as several critical studies: *Don Juan y el donjuanismo* (1969; Don Juan and "donjuanism"), her best-known essay; *La poesía Pre-renacentista española* (Pre-Renaissance Spanish Poetry) and *Breve estudio de la novela española* (1972; Brief Study of the Spanish Novel). *Hekate. Noche. Muerte. Mujer* (Hecate. Night. Death. Woman) is a study of witchcraft. Most of Sáenz-Alonso's novels deal with war and its destruction and resulting individual failures and frustrations. *Bajos fondos* (1949; The Depths), set in lower-class London just prior to World War I, portrays several families living in the same building, including some grotesquely abnormal characters. A sequel, *Altas esferas* (1949; High Spheres), a novel of espionage, intrigue and treason set during the war, traces one of the children from the previous novel, so embittered by her miserable childhood that she eventually betrays England and kills her father. *El tiempo que se fue* (1951; The Time That Is Gone), with a greater autobiographical basis, returns to San Sebastián to study the war's role in the decadence and downfall of a noble Basque family. The loss of family and spiritual values identified as a central problem in this novel is further examined in *La pequeña ciudad* (1952; The Small Town), which investigates ambition and the effects of failure and frustration on varying personalities in situations where family relationships are the significant variable.

BIBLIOGRAPHY

Primary Texts

Altas esferas. Barcelona: Caralt, 1949.
Bajos fondos. Barcelona: Caralt, 1949.
La pequeña ciudad. Barcelona: Caralt, 1952.
El tiempo que se fue. Barcelona: Caralt, 1951.

Janet Pérez

SAETAS, a type of popular Andalusian verse. Each stanza may be comprised of two to six octosyllabic lines. Sung during religious festivals, especially during Holy Week, they narrate the Passion of Christ, and recall the need for repentance.

SÁEZ DE MELGAR, Faustina (1834, Villamanrique de Tajo, Madrid–1895, Madrid), novelist, feminist, poet and lecturer. She came from a Castilian landowner family which, as Pilar *Sinués indicated, strongly opposed her literary vocation. That could explain her tireless, lifelong struggle in favor of women's education. In 1855 she married and moved to Madrid, and in 1859 her first book, *La Lira del Tajo. Poesías de* (The River Tajo's Lyre. Poems of), appeared. By 1890 she had published as many as thirty books, including *Africa y España. Cantos poéticos* (1859; Africa and Spain. Poetic Songs), poetry; *La Higuera de Villaverde* (1860; The Fig Tree of Villaverde), traditional legend; *Ecos de gloria* (1863; Echoes of Glory), historical legends; and many novels, such as *La Pastora de Guadiela* (1860; The Shepherdess of Guadiela), and *Rosa la cigarrera de Madrid* (1872; Rosa the Cigar Seller of Madrid). Many of her novels were reprinted several times, and *La Marquesa de Pinares* (1861; The Marchioness of Pinares) reached ten editions.

She wrote two short stories for children, readings for school boys and studies about the feminine question. She managed many magazines, such as *La Violeta*, which gave women the opportunity to publish. In 1860 she founded in Madrid the Ateneo Artístico y Literario, the first feminine lyceum in Spain and the origin of the Asociación para la Enseñanza de la Mujer (Association for the Education of Women), a leader institution in the organization and promotion of women's education in Spain.

For Cossío, her most important lyrical work is *La Lira del Tajo*, which, although essentially Romantic, shows some new features that overpass *Romanticism, such as the preference for regular strophes and the limitation of pathos.

BIBLIOGRAPHY

Primary Texts

Africa y España. Cantos poéticos. Madrid: B. Fernández, 1859.

La Lira del Tajo. Poesías de. Madrid: B. Fernández, 1859.

La Marquesa de Pinares. Madrid: B. Fernández, 1861.

Memorias del Ateneo de Señoras. Por la Presidenta y Fundadora Doña. . . . Madrid: Señores Rojas, 1869.

Las mujeres españolas, americanas y lusitanas vistas por sí mismas. Dir. by F.S.M. Barcelona: Juan Pons, n.d.

Criticism

Cejador y Frauca, Julio. *Historia de la lengua y literatura castellana*. 14 vols. Madrid: Tipología de Archivos, 1915–22.

Cossío, José María. *Cincuenta años de poesía española (1850–1900)*. 2 vols. Madrid: Espasa-Calpe, 1960.

Ferreras, J. I. *Catálogo de novelas y novelistas españolas del s. XIX*. Madrid: Cátedra, 1979.

Sinués de Marco, Pilar. *Biografía de Faustina Sáez de Melgar*. In *La Higuera de Villaverde*. By Faustina Sáez de Melgar. Madrid: Bernabé Fernández, 1860.

Cristina Enríquez

SAFINIO. *See* Estébanez Calderón, Serafín

SAGARRA I CASTELLARNAU, Josep María de (1894, Barcelona–1961, Barcelona), Catalan poet, playwright and novelist. Sagarra belonged to an ancient aristocratic family, and like others of his class, was educated in a private Jesuit school. He studied law at the U of Barcelona, but never practiced, preferring to devote himself to literature from a very early age (his first poems were published when he was twelve). *Primer llibre de poemes* (1914; First Book of Poems), published when he was twenty, was followed in quick succession by *El mal caçador* (1916; The Bad Hunter), *Cançons d'abril i de novembre* (1918; Songs from April to November), *Cançons de taverna i d'oblit* (1922; Songs of Tavern and Oblivion), *Cançons de rem i de vela* (1924; Songs of Oar and Sail), and *Cançons de totes les hores* (1925; Songs for All Hours). Unlike the writers of the Catalan Renaixenca period with their artificially archaic lexicon and syntax, Sagarra followed the example of *Verdaguer and *Maragall in using popular language, the contemporary idiom, unaffected, simple and direct. Sagarra's popularity was enormous, matching his facility as a versifier, bringing him many prizes as well as imitators.

Sagarra's theatrical works are varied, ranging from dramatic poems to lyric theater, from farce to the tragic poem, characterized by the same facility as his lyric poetry, but with a greater tendency to repetition and the use of stock types. He is a key figure of Catalan theater of the 1920s and 1930s, despite a tendency to neo-Romanticism and even occasional near-melodrama or sentimentality. Among his theatrical works are *Rondalla d'esparvres* (1918; Serenade by Blackbirds), *Dijous Sant* (1919; Maundy Thursday), and *L'estudiant i la pubilla* (1921; The Student and the Maiden). More significant plays are *Les veus de la terra* (1923; Voices of the Soil); *Marçal Prior* (1926); *L'assassinat de la senyora Abril* (1927; The Murder of Lady April), in prose; and *L'hostal de la glòria* (1931; The Glory Inn), awarded the important Ignasi Iglesies Prize. Examples of his farces are *La Llúcia i la Ramoneta* (1928; Lucia and Little Ramona), and *Amàlia, Emèlia i Emilia* (1929), while *Judit* (1929) and *La filla del carmesí* (1930; The Crimson Daughter) are tragic poems.

Sagarra also wrote a number of very popular novels, including *Paulina Buixareu* (1919), *All i Salobre* (1929; Garlic and Salt), *Cafè, copa i puro* (1929; Coffee, Brandy and Cigar), and his greatest critical success, *Vida privada* (1932; Private Life), winner of the Crexells Prize. His most famous work is the long poem, *El Comte Arnau* (1928; Count Arnold), which re-creates the legend of a medieval hero of ballads and tales (not coincidentally, a maternal ancestor of

Sagarra's). Most of this writer's important writing was done before the Civil War, as his last collection of poetry, *La rosa de cristall* (The Crystal Rose), appeared in 1936; he had no significant work in the theater after *Roser florit* (1935; The Flowering Rose). Throughout his work, he portrays much the same popular types, the same identical passions, with an unwavering continuity of poetic vision. An essentially traditional and egocentric writer, he remained apart from vanguard experimentalism and the stylized culturalism and civil aesthetics of *noucentisme* alike. *See also* Catalan Literature.

BIBLIOGRAPHY

Primary Texts

Obres completes. 4 vols. Barcelona: Selecta, 1967–81. Vol. I. *Poesía*. 2nd ed. Prol. O. Saltor. Vol. 2. *Prosa*. 2nd ed. Prol. Domènc Guansé. Vol. 3. *Teatre I*. 2nd ed. Vol. 4. *Teatre II*.

Criticism

Aleixandre, Vicente. "José María de Sagarra, entre mis amigos." *Los encuentros*. Madrid: Guadarrama, 1958. 129–35.

Carbonell, Jordi. "L'obra dramàtica de Josep María de Sagarra." *Teatre complet, IV*. Barcelona: Selecta, 1964. 1345–1406.

Molas, Joaquim. "El cas Sagarra." *La literatura catalana de postguerra*. Barcelona: Dalmau, 1966. 39–53.

Serrahima, Maurici. "Josep M. de Sagarra." *Dotze mestres*. Barcelona: Destino, 1972. 333–65.

Vilanova, Antonio, "La obra poética de Josep M. de Sagarra." In *Panorama de la literatura del siglo XX*. Ed. A. Rousseaux. Madrid: Guadarrama, 1960. 799–801.

SAHAGÚN, Carlos (1938, Onil, Alicante–), poet and critic. Included in Francisco Ribes's *Poesía última* (1963; Latest Poetry), he is a member of Spain's second post-war generation of poets. The depiction of experiences from childhood and adolescence, expressed in a simple, concise language, is a common thread in his poetry. Although concerned with social themes, he believes that form should take precedence over message in poetry. He has received several important literary awards: José Luis Hidalgo (1956), Adonais (1957), Boscán (1960), and the coveted National Prize for Literature (1980). His collections of poetry include *Hombre naciente* (1955; Naissant Man); *Profecías del agua* (1958; Prophecies of Water); *Como si hubiera muerto un niño* (1961; As If a Child Had Died); *Estar contigo* (1973; To Be With You), his collected works; *Memorial de la noche (1957–1975)* (1976; Recollections of Night); and *Primer y último oficio (1973–1977)* (1979; First and Last Craft). He is also the editor of an anthology of early twentieth-c. Spanish poetry, *Siete poetas contemporáneos* (1959; Seven Contemporary Poets).

BIBLIOGRAPHY

Primary Texts

Como si hubiera muerto un niño. Barcelona: Instituto de Estudios Hispánicos, 1961.

Hombre naciente. Onil, Alicante: Silbo, 1955.

Memorial de la noche (1957–1975). Barcelona: El Bardo, Lumen, 1976.
Primer y último oficio (1973–1977). León: Provincia, 1979.
Profecías del agua. Madrid: Rialp, 1958.

English Translations

''Manantial'' (Fountain-Head). In *Spanish Poetry since 1939*. Tr. Charles David Ley. Washington, DC: Catholic U of America P, 1962.
Poems. In *Recent Poetry of Spain*. Tr. Louis Hammer and Sara Schyfter. Old Chatham, NY: Sachem Press, 1983. 214–23.
''Unforgettable Things.'' Anon. tr. *Arena* 23 (1965): 69–70.

Criticism

Beltrán Pepió, V. ''Poética y estadística: nuevos y novísimos poetas españoles.'' *Revista de Literatura* 88 (1983): 123–44.
Debicki, Andrew P. ''Carlos Sahagún: Metaphoric Transformations.'' In *Poetry of Discovery: The Spanish Generation of 1956–1971*. Lexington: U of Kentucky P, 1982. 142–64.
Manrique de Lara, José Gerardo. ''La poesía de Carlos Sahagún.'' In *Poetas sociales españoles*. Madrid: EPESA, 1974. 161–67.
Miró, Emilio. '' 'Primer y último oficio,' de Carlos Sahagún.'' *Insula* 402 (1980): 6.
Rodríguez Puértolas, Julio. ''La poesía de Carlos Sahagún: niños y ríos.'' *Norte* 3 (1969): 45–52.

Kay Pritchett

SAID ARMESTO, Víctor (1871, Pontevedra–1914, Madrid), Spanish critic and essayist. Professor of Spanish literature in several schools and of Galician-Portuguese literature at the U of Madrid, he published numerous critical articles in journals and newspapers dealing with literature and philosophy. His critical approach was mainly historical with preference for folkloric themes such as *La leyenda de don Juan* (1908; Don Juan's Legend) and *Tristán y la literatura rústica* (1911; Tristan and Rustic Literature). Said Armesto examines especially the popular backgrounds of literary works. His philological studies produced critical editions of *Las Mocedades del Cid* by Guillén de *Castro (1913) and *Cigarrales de Toledo* by *Tirso de Molina. Said Armesto left many unpublished mss. dealing with Galician literature.

BIBLIOGRAPHY

Primary Texts

La leyenda de Don Juan. Buenos Aires: Espasa-Calpe, 1946.
Téllez, Gabriel [Tirso de Molina]. *Cigarrales de Toledo*. Ed. V. Said Armesto. Madrid: Renacimiento, 1913.

Genaro J. Pérez

SAINETE, a type of drama. Derived from the **entremés* and the **paso*, these one-act sketches, often comic, served as a counterpoint to the full-length plays with which they were performed. They reached the height of their popularity in the eighteenth c. The inclusion of music and the depiction of urban life scenes and types became defining characteristics, especially in the *sainetes* of Ramón de la *Cruz.

SALADRIGAS, Robert (1940, Barcelona–), Catalan journalist, essayist, novelist, story writer, and children's author. After inconclusive work in economics, Saladrigas began writing for newspapers in Barcelona. He has written for the country's most important reviews and dailies, and is presently the critic in charge of the book section of *La Vanguardia*. Although he writes in Catalan, all of his works have appeared in Castilian translations. His story collections include *Boires* (1970; Beverages), *Néixer de nou, cada dia* (1979; To Be Born Anew, Each Day), *Sota la volta del temps* (1980; Beneath the Curve of Time), and *Imatges del meu mirall* (1983; Images from My Mirror). Among his novels are *El cau* (1967; The Den), *52 hores a través de la pell* (1970; 52 Hours across the Skin), *Aquell gust agre de l'estel* (1977; That Bitter Star Taste; tr. to Spanish as *El vuelo de la cometa* [The Flight of the Kite]), *Pel camí ral del nord* (1980; Along the Northern High-Road), and *Sóc Emma* (1983; I'm Emma). *Memorial de Claudi M. Broch* (1986; Memoir of Claude Broch) won the prestigious Critics' Prize for the year of publication. Saladrigas is one of the most original and innovative of contemporary Catalan narrators, and an important chronicler of his generation. His characters at times symbolize a divided Spain, a disunited Catalonia, both torn by hatred, political dissension and the rancors left by the Civil War. They incarnate the search for individual and collective identity, the attempt to recover lost values, and his generation's struggle with intellectual and personal maturation in the post-war years.

Janet Pérez

SALAMANCAN SCHOOL. *See* Escuela Salmantina

SALAS, Francisco Gregorio de (1727, Jaraicejo, Extremadura–1807, Madrid), bucolic poet and fabulist. A clergymen, he spent most of his life in Madrid as chaplain to a convent. Although very well connected, he always refused advantageous appointments. Salas owned a small cabin outside Madrid, and spent all his free time enjoying the peace and solitude of the countryside. He left several religious works that were quite popular for an extended period, but he was even better known for his *Observatorio rústico* (1772; Rural Observatory) and his *Poesías* (1773; Poems); both underwent ten editions. Although contemporaries attacked him for his prosaism, modern critics like *Azorín, Gerardo *Diego, and Joaquín Arce revindicated his lyricism, authenticity and sense of nature.

BIBLIOGRAPHY

Primary Texts

Dalmiro y Silvano. Egloga amorosa y elogio de la vida del campo. . . . Madrid: Andrés Ramírez, 1780.

Observatorio rústico, en donde se hace una descripción de la vida del campo y sus ventajas. Madrid: Sancha, 1772. [10th ed. from Madrid: Borbon, 1830.]

Poesías. In BAE 67 (1875).
Poesías. 2 vols. Madrid: Ramón Ruiz, 1797.

Criticism

Arce, Joaquín. *La poesía del siglo ilustrado*. Madrid: Alhambra, 1980. 260–62.
Azorín. "Los españoles." In *Los valores literarios*, vol. 2 of *Obras completas*. Madrid: Aguilar, 1947. 1100–1105.
García Castañeda, S. "La obra fabulística de Francisco Gregorio de Salas." *Spicilegio Moderno* (Universitá di Bologna) 15–16 (1981): 3–13.

Salvador García Castañeda

SALAS BARBADILLO, Alonso Jerónimo de (1581, Madrid–1635, Madrid), satirist, novelist. He is best-known for his *picaresque novel, *La hija de Celestina* (1612; *The Daughter of Celestina,* 1912). The first born of seven children of Diego de Salas Barbadillo and María Parras, he attended the U of Alcalá and later the U of Valladolid, where he studied canon law. When his father died in 1603, Alonso's life changed dramatically. The youth left the university to dedicate himself to poetry and adventure. Unfortunately, he made several unpropitious acquaintances: a friendship with a Persian, Don Diego de Persia, evolved into an argument which provoked lengthy court testimony; he was charged with libel against three constables and their wives; he was accused of slander by about a dozen women. Alonso's punishment included a fine and exile from Madrid. He later joined a *cofradía*, the Brotherhood of Slaves of the Holy Sacrament. He never married, tried unsuccessfully to claim family lands in Italy, and was deaf for ten years before dying at age fifty-four.

Salas was commissioned as censor for the *Novelas ejemplares* of *Cervantes, the writer who perhaps influenced Salas most decisively. Although Salas's writing varies widely in terms of style and quality, M. Peyton divides his work into four categories: picaresque novels; framework novels; dialogued novels; and interludes. His most famous work, *La hija de Celestina*, was published in two separate editions, both in 1612, one at Zaragoza and the other at Lérida. The Zaragoza edition is considered the *princeps*. The work was reissued in 1614, with several additions and a new title, *La ingeniosa Elena, hija de Celestina*. (*The Daughter of Celestina*, 1912). María, or Zara, is the mother who comes to be known as the "second Celestina" when she decides to become a witch like her own mother. A laundress, she is sought after by Christian gentlemen, but only has affairs with Moors. At age forty, she finally marries an alcoholic Galician and begins practicing witchcraft. She sells her daughter Elena three times as a virgin; after this point, the novel deals with Elena's life after leaving her mother, as she travels around trying to swindle people.

Other works by Salas Barbadillo include: *Don Diego de noche* (1623; Don Diego, Nocturnal Adventurer); *La casa del placer honesto* (1620; The House of Virtuous Pleasure); *El necio bien afortunado* (1621; *The Fortunate Fool*, 1670); and *La estafeta del dios Momo* (1627; The Post Office of the God Momus). In *Don Diego de noche*, the protagonist decides to leave ordinary daytime life to become a night adventurer. In order to produce the effect of constant nighttime, he seals off his house in Toledo from daylight. He then sets out for adventure, "mischievous but moral."

Salas's writing is satirical and critical, but not gloomy; a moralizing intent is usually present, and also a strong aversion to hypocrisy. According to Peyton, Salas "reveals his own time of life: the crafty, preying, decadent side of a Madrid turned frivolous and vicious in many of her aspects. . . ." *See also Celestina, La.*

BIBLIOGRAPHY

Primary Texts

Don Diego de Noche. Madrid: Atlas, 1944.
Obras. 2 vols. Madrid: Pérez Dubrull, 1907–9.
La peregrinación sabia y El sagaz Estacio. Prol. F. A. Icaza. Madrid: La Lectura, 1924.

English Translations

Don Diego de Noche. Critical ed. Myron Peyton. Diss. Northwestern University, 1942.
The Daughter of Celestina. Tr. F. Holle. Strasbourg: Heitz; New York: Steckert, 1912.
The Fortunate Fool. Tr. P. Ayres. London: Pit, 1670. Rpt. 1983. (Microfilm).

Criticism

Listerman, R. W. "*La hija de Celestina:* Tradition and Morality." *Language Quarterly* 22.1–2 (Fall-Winter 1983): 52–53, 56.
Peyton, M. A. *Alonso Jerónimo de Salas Barbadillo*. TWAS 212. New York: Twayne, 1973.

Nina Shecktor

SALAVERRÍA, José María (1873, Vinaroz, Castellón–1940, Madrid), prose writer. A native of the Basque area, he spent his childhood in San Sebastián. Although he wrote fiction, for instance *La virgen de Aránzazu* (1909; The Virgin of Aranzazu), Salaverría is known mainly for his essays and journalism. He traveled extensively through Europe and America. Spanish-American themes and the defense of Hispanic America appear throughout his work, which includes *La afirmación española* (1917; The Spanish Affirmation), *Vieja España* (1907, with a prologue by *Pérez Galdós; Old Spain), *Las sombras de Loyola* (1911; Loyola's Shadows), *España vista desde América* (1914; Spain Observed from America), *Los fantasmas del museo* (1920; Museum Ghosts), *El muchacho español* (1917; The Spanish Kid), *Martín Fierro y el criollismo español* (1918; Martín Fierro and Spanish criollismo), *Alma Vasca* (1920; Basque Soul), *Santa Teresa* (1921; Saint Therese), *Bolívar el Libertador* (1930; Bolivar the Liberator). In his last years occurs an exaltation (like that of *Maeztu) of Spanish national values. Like Ramiro de Maeztu, also, Salaverría in his work emulates the essence of the spirit of the *Generation of 1898.

BIBLIOGRAPHY

Primary Texts

Los conquistadores: el origen heróico de América. Madrid: Caro Raggio, 1918.
Bolívar el Libertador. Madrid: Espasa-Calpe, 1930.
Alma Vasca (Itinerarios españoles). Madrid: Rivadeneyra, 1923.

Criticism

Del Río, Angel. *El concepto contemporáneo de España; Antología de ensayos, 1895–1931*. Buenos Aires, Losada, 1936.
Petriz Ramos, Beatriz. *Introducción crítico-biográfica a José María Salaverría*. Madrid: Gredos, 1960.

Genaro J. Pérez

SALAZAR, Ambrosio de (1575?, Murcia–after 1640, France), grammarian, anthologist, scholar. He lived most of his life in France, teaching Spanish at various schools there. He also served as interpreter for the French king, and as secretary to Queen Anne of Austria in Paris. Salazar's anthologies, all published in France and bilingual in Spanish and French, were compiled with a pedagogical end. They include *Las clavellinas de recreación* (1614: Entertainment Pinks), *Espejo general de la gramática en diálogos* (1614: General Model of Grammar in Dialogues), *Thesoro de diversa lición* (1636; Treasure of Various Lessons) and *Secretos de la gramática española* (1640; Secrets of Spanish Grammar). His sources for these stories include Melchor de *Santa Cruz's *Floresta* and Pero *Mexía's *Silva*.

BIBLIOGRAPHY

Primary Texts

Espejo general de la gramática. Rouen: Cailloüe, 1636.
Las clavellinas de recreación. Rouen: Morront, 1614.
Secretos de la gramática española. Rouen: Cailloüe, 1640.
Thesoro de diversa lición. Paris: Boullanger, 1637.

Criticism

Morel Fatio, A. *Ambrosio de Salazar et l'étude de l'espagnol en France sous Louis XIII*. Paris: Picard, 1901.

SALAZAR, Diego de (fl. 1546, Toledo–?), soldier, translator, poet. He fought with the Gran Capitán Gonzalo Fernández de Córdoba in Italy. With Diego López de Ayala and Blasco de Garay, Salazar published in 1546 a version of Boccaccio's *Filocolo*, and three years later, they produced a translation of *Sannazaro's *Arcadia*. Salazar also translated various classical historical works, and composed a dialogue, *Tratado de re militari* (1536; Treatise on War), which clearly imitates Machiavelli's *The Art of War*.

BIBLIOGRAPHY

Primary Texts

La Arcadia. Valencia: n.p., 1966.
Tratado de re militari. Brussels: Velpius, 1590.

SALAZAR CHAPELA, Esteban (1902, Málaga–1965, London), Spanish journalist, essayist, and novelist. Salazar Chapela belonged to the group associated with *Ortega y Gasset and collaborated on some of the same publications, both as an editor of *El Sol* (a liberal newspaper under the aegis of Ortega's family) and as a frequent contributor to Ortega's *Revista de Occidente*, the major intellectual organ of Spain during the late 1920s and early 1930s. Because of this group's close ties to the Spanish Republic, Salazar Chapela was exiled after the Spanish Civil War, and died in England. His work is little known in Spain because of political silencing and the circumstances of exile, and similarly unknown in his land of exile for linguistic reasons. Among his early fiction, *Pero sin hijos* (1931; But without Children) was very well received; notable among his novels written as an expatriate is *Perico en Londres* (n.d.; Expert on London), a novel reflecting the exile experience.

SALCEDO ARTEAGA, Emilio (1929, Salamanca–), journalist, essayist, and novelist. He began publishing in the Salamanca newspaper *El Adelanto* (Progress) at the age of sixteen, moving to another Salamanca paper, *La Gaceta Regional* (The Regional Gazette), the next year. He studied medicine for a while, then law and later Romance philology at the U of Salamanca. Later he worked as an insurance agent. He served as director of the Teatro Universitario de Salamanca (University Theater of Salamanca) during that university's seventh centennial. In 1967 he moved to Valladolid to become an editor of *El norte de Castilla* (The North of Castille), a newspaper of which he became the editor-in-chief in 1968. He has written a well-received book on the nineteenth-c. poet José *Gabriel y Galán, and a 1965 grant from the Fundación March (March Foundation) supported his book *Vida de Espronceda* (1967; Life of Espronceda). His other works of literary history, criticism and biography include *Literatura salmantina del siglo XX* (1960; Salamancan Literature of the Twentieth C.), *Teatro y sociedad en el Valladolid del siglo XIX* (1978; Theater and Society in Nineteenth-C. Valladolid), and his very valuable *Vida de Don Miguel de Unamuno* (1964; Life of Don Miguel de Unamuno), which won a special prize from the Spanish Ministry of Education on the occasion of the centennial of Unamuno's birth. He is also the author of *Márgenes de Unamuno* (1967; Unamuno's Margins) and *Relatos y paisajes* (1964; Narratives and Landscapes). His novels include *Puesto en la vida* (1961; Placed in Life) and *El cochecito rojo* (1961; The Little Red Car).

BIBLIOGRAPHY

Primary Texts

El cochecito rojo. Madrid: Aguilar, 1961.

Literatura salmantina del siglo XX. Prol. Manuel García Blanco. Salamanca: Centro de Estudios Salmantinos, 1960.

Relatos y paisajes. Madrid and Salamanca: Ciadi, 1964.

Teatro y sociedad en el Valladolid del siglo XIX. Valladolid: Ayuntamiento de Valladolid, 1978.

Vida de Don Miguel de Unamuno. Salamanca: Anaya, 1964.

Judith Ginsberg

SALCEDO CORONEL, José García de (?, Seville–1651, Madrid), poet, editor of the works of *Góngora. Active in military and political positions in Italy, he later entered the service of the *cardenal infante* Ferdinand of Austria. His four-volume critical edition of the works of Góngora, *Obras de don Luis de Góngora comentadas* (1636–48; Works of don Luis de Góngora with Commentary), holds literary and historical value for its information about the extent and influence of Gongorism, including debates among poets and readers of poetry in the first half of the seventeenth c. Salcedo Coronel admired Góngora's elaborate style and attempted to imitate it in his own verse, which received the praise of Lope de *Vega and Luís *Vélez de Guevara. His collections of poetry include *Rimas* (1624; Rhymes), *Ariadna* (1624; Ariadne), *Cristales de Helicona o Segunda Parte de las rimas* (1642; Crystals of Helicon or the Second Part of the Verses) and *Panegírico al serenísimo Infante Cardenal* (1636; Panegyric to His Serene Highness the Infante Cardenal). *See also Culteranismo*.

BIBLIOGRAPHY

Primary Texts

Cristales de Helicona, rimas. Madrid: Díaz de la Carrea, 1650. (Microfilm at the Hispanic Society in New York City.)

Obras de Don Luis de Góngora, comentadas por Don García de Salzedo. Madrid: Real, 1636–48.

Nina Shecktor

SALINAS, Pedro (1891, Madrid–1951, Boston), scholar, poet, playwright. Madrid born and educated—he earned a doctorate in literature from the U of Madrid in 1917—Salinas was the eldest of the group of poets known as the *Generation of 1927 whose other members include Dámaso *Alonso, Federico *García Lorca, Jorge *Guillén, Luis *Cernuda, Rafael *Alberti, and Vicente *Aleixandre. Salinas, like several others of this generation, most notably Dámaso Alonso and Jorge Guillén, was also a productive scholar and teacher of literature, lecturing at many universities in North and South America and holding posts at several Spanish universities as well as at the Sorbonne (1914–17); Cambridge U (1922–23); Wellesley College (1936–40); U of Río Piedras, Puerto Rico (1942–45) and Johns Hopkins U (1940–45; 46–50); and the Middlebury Language

School where he taught for many summers. His scholarly and critical work includes *Jorge Manrique, o tradición y originalidad* (1947; Jorge Manrique, or Tradition and Originality), an insightful analysis of the medieval concept of literary tradition and creation; *Reality and the Poet in Spanish Poetry* (1940; tr. into Spanish, *La realidad y el Poeta*, 1976); in which he viewed the poet as placing ''himself before reality . . . in order to create something else''; *Literatura española: siglo XX* (1949; Spanish Literature: Twentieth Century), a collection of short articles, in one of which he puts forth one of the clearest and most precise definitions of the Spanish *Generation of 1898; and *La poesía de Rubén Darío* (1948; The Poetry of Rubén Darío), an innovative study of the modernist poet. In 1948 Salinas published *El defensor* (1948; The Defender), a collection of five essays on modern culture, in which he strongly criticizes the modern fixations with money, efficiency and material success that have led to the individual's growing isolation from his surroundings and his fellow human beings. Salinas is troubled by the diminished importance of the spoken and written word which he finds to be an indication of the spiritual impoverishment of modern life.

Salinas also directed Spanish language and literature courses for foreigners, first in Madrid and then in Santander at the Universidad Internacional Menéndez y Pelayo, which he organized in 1933. He also founded the Contemporary Literature Section of the Centro de Estudios Históricos (Center for Historical Studies) and edited its journal, *Indice Literario*, from 1932 until 1936. He left Spain in 1936 to teach at Wellesley and, after the victory of Francisco Franco in the Civil War, he remained in exile in the United States until his death.

In Gerardo *Diego's anthology, *Poesía española contemporánea* (1934; Contemporary Spanish Poetry) Salinas defined poetry as ''una aventura hacia lo absoluto'' (an adventure toward the absolute). In formal terms his poetry is characterized by his use of short verse forms of six, seven or eight syllables, usually combined in the same poem. He rarely uses consonant rhyme although he is agile with assonance, and he generally avoids classical poetic forms, with the exception of a few sonnets.

Critics have seen three distinct periods of Salinas's poetic production. The first, including *Presagios* (1923; Presages), *Seguro Azar* (1929; Steadfast Chance), and *Fábula y signo* (1931; Fable and Sign), explores the relation between inner and outer reality with a certain metaphysical anguish in light of the unreliability of appearances. At the same time, in the latter two works especially, there is a reflection of some of the frivolity and exuberance of the twenties—typewriters, cinemas, electric lights, radiators, telephones, and fast cars. Two collections of love poems, *La voz a ti debida* (1933; *My Voice Because of You*, 1976) and *Razón de amor* (1936; Love's Reason), both written before his exile, are widely acknowledged to be his greatest works. In *La voz a ti debida* Salinas describes the common human feelings in a real love affair with a real woman, defining the details of this experience with great subtlety and sensitivity. He delves deeply into the lived experience of the love he has profoundly felt, and he attempts to understand what it is that he loves in this one particular woman. *Razón de amor* continues the exploration of love of the previous work, although critics have pointed to a thread of anguish about fleeting time and happiness in the later work. While the theme of love is still present in *El contemplado* (1946; The Contemplated Sea), written in Puerto Rico, this long poem (which Salinas recorded for the Library of Congress in 1946) marks a change in Salinas's subject matter. *El contemplado* is a dialogue with the sea, which is portrayed as a symbol of essential reality, constantly changing, yet eternal.

Salinas's third period is most clearly seen in *Todo más claro* (1949; All Things Made Clearer), considered the most important work he wrote in exile. Here Salinas is sharply critical of modern society and its materialistic values. The optimism of the love poems has vanished in his long exile. He protests war in "Cero" (Zero) and turns to satire in "Nocturno de los Avisos" (Nocturne of the Signs) depicting Times Square in New York City as a symbol of a distorted, dehumanized and valueless world. The atom bomb, foreseen in "Cero," is the sober topic of Salinas's novel *La bomba increíble* (1950; The Incredible Bomb) as well as a haunting presence in his play *Caín, o una gloria científica* (1957; Caine, or a Glory of Science).

BIBLIOGRAPHY

Primary Texts

Cartas de amor a Margarita (1912–1915). Ed. Soledad Salinas de Marichal. Madrid: Alianza, 1984.

Jorge Manrique, o tradición y originalidad. Barcelona: Seix Barral, 1974.

Poesías completas. Ed. Soledad Salinas de Marichal. Prol. Jorge Guillén. 2nd ed. Barcelona: Barral, 1975.

La responsabilidad del escritor. 3rd ed. Barcelona: Seix Barral, 1970.

Teatro completo. Madrid: Aguilar, 1957.

English Translations

My Voice Because of You. Tr. Willis Barnstone. Pref. Jorge Guillén. Albany: State U of New York P, 1976.

To Live in Pronouns: Selected Love Poems. Tr. Edith Helman and Norma Farber. New York: Norton, 1974.

Criticism

Crispin, John. *Pedro Salinas.* New York: Twayne, 1974.

Debicki, Andrew P., ed. *Pedro Salinas.* Colección El Escritor y La Crítica. Madrid: Taurus, 1976.

Feal Deibe, Carlos. *La poesía de Pedro Salinas.* Madrid: Gredos, 1965.

Insula (Madrid) November-December 1971. Issue dedicated to Salinas.

Zubizarreta, Alma de. *Pedro Salinas: el diálogo creador.* Madrid: Gredos, 1970.

Judith Ginsberg

SALINAS DE CASTRO, Juan (1562?, Seville–1643, Seville), presbyter of the Seville Cathedral, poet. Of a wealthy family, he studied at Salamanca and Logroño, and traveled to Italy before settling in Seville. His early poetry falls within the *Renaissance tradition—**conceptismo* is apparent in his later verse.

BIBLIOGRAPHY

Primary Texts

Poesías. 2 vols. Seville: Geofrin, 1869.

Poesías. Sel., prol., R. Laffón. Valencia: n.p., 1942.

Criticism

Bonneville, H. *Le Poète sévillan Juan de Salinas, 1562?–1643: vie et oeuvre*. Paris: PUF, 1969.

SALISACHS, Mercedes (1916, Barcelona–), novelist. From a well-to-do Barcelona family, Salisachs was educated in a convent school and later earned a degree in business. Some of her early writings, including her first novel, *Primera mañana, última mañana* (1955; First Morning, Last Morning), appeared under the pseudonym María Ecín. In the mid–1950s she worked on a weekly art program on the radio and later briefly with Spanish television. She also contributed to a variety of newspapers and magazines and wrote television screenplays as well. Her writing is characterized by its intelligence, its lack of sentimentality, and a strong sense of irony. Her subsequent novels include *Carrera intermedia* (1956; Intermediate Career), a finalist for the prestigious Planeta Prize; *Una mujer llega al pueblo* (1957; *The Eyes of the Proud*, 1960), a sharp portrayal of Catalan sexual hypocrisy, which won the City of Barcelona Prize; *Más allá de los railes* (1957; Beyond the Rails); *Adán Helicóptero* (1957; Adam Helicopter); *Pasos conocidos* (1957; Known Steps); *Vendimia interrumpida* (1960; Interrupted Grape Harvest); *La estación de las hojas amarillas* (1963; The Season of Yellow Leaves); *El declive y la cuesta* (1966; The Road Down and the Hill); *La última aventura* (1967; The Last Adventure); *Adagio confidencial* (1973; Confidential Adagio); *La gangrena* (1975; Gangrene); *Viaje a Sodoma* (1977; Voyage to Sodom); *El proyecto* (1978; The Project); *La Presencia* (1979; The Presence); *Derribos* (1981; Debris). Salisachs is quite well traveled, and she has lectured throughout Spain and in a number of foreign countries. Her novels have been translated into French, English, Swedish, German, Finnish, and Italian.

BIBLIOGRAPHY

Primary Texts

Adagio confidencial. Barcelona: Planeta, 1973.

La estación de las hojas amarillas. 2nd ed. Barcelona: n.p., 1963.

La gangrena. Barcelona: Planeta, 1975.

Pasos conocidos. Barcelona: Pareja y Borras, 1957.

Una mujer llega al pueblo. Barcelona: Planeta, 1975.

English Translation

The Eyes of the Proud. Tr. Delano Ames. New York: Harcourt Brace, 1960.

Judith Ginsberg

SALOM, Jaime (1925, Barcelona–), Spanish playwright. Although he began writing theater in the 1940s while still a medical student at the U of Barcelona, Salom did not achieve his first stage production until 1955 and did not fully enter into the theater world until the 1960s. His first real theatrical success was *Culpables* (1961; Guilty), a murder drama reflecting the influence of J. B. Priestley and Agatha Christie, which was translated and staged in Germany, Belgium, Switzerland, Austria, and Czechoslovakia, as well as Latin America. In 1984 it was successfully revived in Madrid. Salom's first play to bear the stamp of his own originality was *El baúl de disfraces* (1974; The Trunk of Disguises). A poetic fantasy dealing with man's life stages and the eternal feminine, the play calls for the doubling of three actors in all of the roles in several episodes. Salom has made no effort to write a second play in this current, but the theatricalist tendencies introduced here are repeated in several of his later, mature works. The culmination of this first period was *La casa de las Chivas* (1968; The House of the Chivas), a psychological drama of the Spanish Civil War that holds the Madrid box office record with its 1,343 continuous performances in a single theater. Winner of several major prizes, the play has been turned into a novel, was successfully televised in Spain in 1978, and has been well received in German and Portuguese translations.

In the plays of his second period, beginning in the late 1960s, Salom began to raise political, social, and religious questions, albeit veiled by an allegorical or historical framework. Continuing his experimentation with innovative, theatricalist kinds of theater, he also began to introduce psychological expressionism, a technique that links him to Arthur Miller and, in Spain, to Antonio *Buero Vallejo. His major plays in this group include *Los delfines* (1969; The Heirs Apparent), an allegorical commentary on the impending end of the Franco regime; *La noche de los cien pájaros* (1972; The Night of the Hundred Birds), an expressionistic evocation of the past by a man who feels himself guilty of his wife's death; and *Tiempo de espadas* (1972; Time of Swords), a religio-political drama, presenting an anachronistic interpretation of the events leading up to the Last Supper.

Starting with the 1975–76 theatrical season and following the death of the dictator Francisco Franco, Salom's theater has become openly ideological and increasingly liberal. His two most important works thus far in Democratic Spain are *La piel del limón* (1976; Bitter Lemon), an impassioned plea for divorce reform, and *El corto vuelo del gallo* (1980; *The Cock's Short Flight*, 1985), a presentation of the life of Franco's liberal, libertine father. Both of these two recent plays continue in the expressionistic mode.

Many of Salom's works have been awarded major prizes and have been among the longest-running plays of their respective seasons. *See also* Contemporary Spanish Theater.

BIBLIOGRAPHY

Primary Texts

El corto vuelo del gallo. Barcelona: Grijalbo, 1981.
La piel del limón. Salamanca: Almar, 1980.
Teatro/Jaime Salom. Madrid: G. del Toro, 1974.
Teatro selecto de Jaime Salom. Madrid: Escelicer, 1971.

English Translation

The Cock's Short Flight. Tr. Marion P. Holt. In *DramaContemporary: Spain*. Ed. Marion P. Holt. New York: Performing Arts Journal Publications, 1985.

Criticism

Estreno 8.2 (1982), issue devoted to theater of Salom.

Holt, Marion P. ''Jaime Salom.'' In his *The Contemporary Spanish Theater* (1949–1972). Boston: Twayne, 1975. 156–69.

Marquerie, Alfredo. *Realidad y fantasía en el teatro de Jaime Salom*. Madrid: Escelicer, 1973.

Zatlin-Boring, Phyllis. ''Expressionism in the Contemporary Spanish Theatre.'' *Modern Drama* 26.4 (1983): 555–69.

———. *Jaime Salom*. Boston: G. K. Hall, 1982.

Phyllis Zatlin

SALUCIO DEL POYO, Damián (?, Murcia–1614, Murcia), playwright. A follower of Lope de *Vega, praised by *Cervantes in the *Viaje del Parnaso*, most of his works were historical, such as *La privanza y caída de don Álvaro de Luna* (n.d.; The Preference and Fall of don Alvaro de Luna) and *La próspera fortuna del famoso Ruy López de Avalos el Bueno* (n.d.; The Good Fortune of the Famous Ruy López . . .) and *La adversa fortuna del muy noble caballero Ruy López de Avalos el Bueno* (The Adverse Fortune of the Very Noble Knight Ruy López . . .). The religious play *La vida y muerte de Judas* (Life and Death of Judas) is also his; later dramatists such as A. *Zamora and *Hartzenbusch repeat this theme.

BIBLIOGRAPHY

Primary Texts

La próspera fortuna . . . and *La adversa fortuna*. . . . In BAE 48.

El rey perseguido y corona pretendida. Ed., intro. K. Toll. Leipzig: Noske, 1937.

La vida y muerte de Judas. In *Ocho comedias desconocidas*. . . . Ed. A. Schaffer. Leipzig: Brockhaus, 1887.

Criticism

García Soriano, J. *Damián Salucio del Poyo*. *BRAE* 13 (1926): 269–82 and 474–506.

SALVÀ, Maria Antònia (1869, Llucmajor, Mallorca–1957, Llucmajor), poet and translator into Catalan. She spent all her life in her ancestral home, L'Allapassa, on the Island of Majorca; she only traveled once to the Holy Land and a few times to the Spanish mainland. She was self-taught. Her formation as a poet is rooted in the Majorcan oral tradition of the ''glosadors,'' country folk who recite improvised rhymed poems on any conceivable subject: love, satire, farm work, the seasons, the weather, etc. This tradition is evident throughout her poetry, especially in her choice of poetic matter, which is drawn mostly from her immediate surroundings and the Majorcan landscape. She is considered a member of the Escola mallorquina (Majorcan school), a literature that is parallel to that of Catalonia. Together with Miguel *Costa i Llobera and Joan *Alcover, she is one of its most distinguished modern poets. Salvà translated works by Manzoni, Jammes, Pascoli, Saint *Teresa and Gabriela Mistral. They all had an effect on her development as a poet, particularly Mistral. First known as a translator, she published her first original work, *Poesies* (Poems), in 1903. From then on she devoted herself primarily to poetry. Her style remains constant throughout her production. Her poetic language is spontaneous and of an apparent simplicity which reveals an accomplished poetic technique built over a lifelong dedication to poetry. The main themes of her poetry are lyrical descriptions of country life and the Mediterranean landscape, presented in a great variety of rhymes and meters. Her three main publications are *Poesies* (1903; Poems), *Espigues en flor* (1926; Blossoming Wheat) and *El retorn* (1934; Returning). In them, she achieves a great lyrical effect by balancing sonority and lexical accuracy. Writing in standard Catalan, she also draws words from the Majorcan vernacular, which adds to the natural flow of images in her poems. *Entre el record i l'enyorança* (1955; Between Memories and Nostalgia) is her only work in prose. It is a retrospective look at her life and poetry. Even in prose, her writing maintains a sustained lyrical tone. *Antologia poètica* (1957; Poetic Anthology) and *Al cel será poeta!* (1981; In Heaven She Will Be a Poet) are both selections of poems from her previous publications.

BIBLIOGRAPHY

Primary Texts

Al cel será poeta! Barcelona: EDHASA, 1981.
Antologia poètica. Barcelona: Selecta, 1957.
Cel d'horabaixa. Mallorca: Moll, 1948.
Entre el record i l'enyorança. Mallorca: Moll, 1955.
Espigues en flor. Barcelona: Impremta Altés, 1926.
Llepolies i joguines. Mallorca: Biblioteca "Les Illes d'Or," 1946.
Lluneta del pagès. Mallorca: Moll, 1952.
Poesies. Palma de Mallorca: Joan Alcover, 1910.
El retorn. Barcelona: Lluís Gili, 1934.

Criticism

Alemany Vich, Luis. "Escritores Baleares (Fichas bibliográficas)." *Estafeta Literaria* 426–28 (1969): 104–19.
Carner, Josep. "La poesia de Maria Antònia Salvà." *Antologia poètica*. By Maria Antònia Salvà. Barcelona: Selecta, 1957. 7–18.
Galerstein, Carolyn, ed. *Women Writers of Spain*. Westport, CT: Greenwood, 1986.

Anna Sánchez Rue

SALVADOR, Álvaro (1950, Granada–), poet, playwright, essayist, doctor in philosophy and letters. He teaches literature at Granada U. One of the founding members of the cultural group Colectivo 77, which produced the collective book of poems *La poesía más transparente* (1976; The Most Transparent Poetry), and the short story book *Se nos murió la Traviata* (1969; We Lost the Traviata), Professor Salvador has directed the literary magazine *Tragaluz* (1968–69), and has collaborated in *Nefelibata, Letras del Sur, Insula, Papeles de Son Armadans, Litoral, Hora de Poesía, Cuadernos Hispanoamericanos,* etc.

Alvaro Salvador has published the following books of poetry: *Y* . . . (1971); *La mala crianza* (1978; Bad Breeding); *De la palabra y otras alucinaciones* (1974; On Words and Other Hallucinations); *Los cantos de Ilíberis* (1976; Ilíberis's Songs), and *Las cortezas del fruto* (1980: Fruit Peels), his best collection of poetry.

In collaboration with García Montero, he wrote *Tristia* (1982), and with the same author and Javier Egea, the poetic manifesto *La otra sentimentalidad* (1983; The Other Sentimentality). Alvaro Salvador has written several theatrical pieces: "Don Fernando de Córdoba y Válor. Aben Humeya"; "La mirada hacia Oriente" (The Lost Look Toward Orient), and "Paraíso perdido" (Lost Paradise). The latter play, based on Luis *Cernuda's life, was performed in 1983.

Alvaro Salvador's poetry constitutes an ironic and devastating reflection on the cultural principles of Spain as it moved from dictatorship to democracy after Franco's death. His rebellious attitude is projected into a radical transformation of the language as he seeks innovative linguistic resources to express the new generational feeling ("sentimentalidad") with its different values of time, history, and literature.

BIBLIOGRAPHY

Primary Texts

Los cantos de Ilíberis. Jaén: Pliegos Poesía Andaluza "El Olivo," 1976.

Las cortezas del fruto. 1973–1979. Madrid: "Endymión," Ayuso, 1980.

De la palabra y otras alucinaciones. Vélez-Málaga: Publicaciones de Arte y Cultura, 1974.

La mala crianza. Ed. A. Caffarena. Málaga: Librería Anticuaria El Guadalhorce, 1978.

La otra sentimentalidad. Granada: Don Quijote, 1983.

Tristia. 1978–1981. Melilla: Ediciones del Ayuntamiento, 1982.

Y. . . . Granada: Editorial Universitaria, 1971.

Criticism

Jiménez Millán, A. "Una reflexión lúcida sobre la poesía: *Las cortezas del fruto*." *CH* 388 (Oct. 1982): 215–22.

Rodríguez, Juan Carlos. "La guarida inútil," prologue to *Las cortezas del fruto*: 15–25.

José Ortega

SALVADOR, Tomás (1921, ?–), Spanish novelist and editor. His first literary success came with *Historias de Valcanillo* (1951; Tales from Valcanillo), a finalist for the Nadal Prize. His next two books were written in collaboration with José Vergés, *Garimpo* (1952) and *La virada* (1954; The Turn-Around). *Cuerda de presos* (1953; Chain Gang) was his greatest critical success, winning him the City of Barcelona Prize and a National Literary Prize. Two additional books of fiction are *El charco* (1953; The Puddle) and *Esta noche estará solo* (1954; Tonight, He'll Be Alone), a collection of stories. Among his other works are *División 250* (1954), a novel based on the Spanish Blue Division which fought in Russia, *Los atracadores* (1955; The Ambushers), *Hotel Tánger* (1955), and *Cabo de vara* (1958; Lance Corporal [the title involves an untranslatable play on words]), one of Salvador's most characteristic and personal narratives. More recent works include *Dentro de mucho tiempo . . .* (1961; In a Long Time . . .).

Diálogos en la oscuridad (1956; Dialogues in the Darkness) is essentially a love story, the dense, suggestive conversations between a man and a woman in the shadows, while the dialogues between other characters are structured in counterpoint. In *El haragán* (1957[?]; The Idler), Salvador attempts a somewhat experimental presentation as the protagonist interrogates his past via five key episodes in his life, five narrative levels, each keyed to a character: José, the Idler, his wife Andrea, his grandfather Remigio, his father Carlos, and the Bestia Desconocida (unknown beast), a killer. *La nave* (The Ship) is a futuristic novel, based on the theme of extraterrestrial visitors. *El agitador* (1960; The Agitator) deals with political agitation on the contemporary scene from the anti-communist stance. Salvador is self-taught, and his novels usually lack polishing, in spite of attempts at innovation.

Janet Pérez

SALVAT-PAPASSEIT, Joan (1894, Barcelona–1924, Barcelona), poet and prose writer. He was born into a working-class family (unusual circumstance for any European writer but especially so for a Catalan writer). His father died in 1901, and Salvat-Papasseit grew up in an orphanage. Autodidactic, he did his extensive readings thanks to friends and especially Mr. Emili Eroles, owner of a bookstore. He never had a stable job, and in the winter of 1915–16 he even worked as a night watchman. In 1917 he obtained his first steady job as a bookseller at the Galerias Laietanes (a Barcelona department store), but a year later, and after having been married, he contracted tuberculosis. He died in utter poverty, helped only by the few friends who understood his greatness. As a youth he was a radical and a revolutionary much involved with social issues; for example, in 1917 he founded and edited the magazine *Un enemic del poble* (An Enemy of the People), which lasted only until 1919. Its issues, largely written by him, contain the articles that explain his basic ideology: "Manca de joventut" (Lack of Youthfulness) in no. 3, "Despertarem d'entre els morts?" (Shall We Awaken among the Dead?) in no. 4, "Massa Seny" (Too Much Common Sense) in no. 11, "Sóc jo, que parlo als joves" (I Am the One Who Talks to the Youth) in no. 16, and many others. Like Miguel *Hernández in Castilian poetry, Salvat-Papasseit is a twentieth-c. romantic who impresses the reader with his sincerity and, most importantly, with his powerful art. Like Mayakowski, he combines revolutionary ideology with revolutionary art form and content. In 1920 he published his aesthetic manifesto *Contra els poetes en minúscula* (Against the Poets in Lower Case Letters), of enormous importance for all Catalan avant-garde poetry. With enormous enthusiasm he edits futuristic reviews: *Arc voltaic* (Voltaic Arch), *Proa* (Bow); and he wrote one of the seminal books of avant-garde poetry in Catalonia, *Poemes en ondes herzianes* (1919; Poems in Herzian Waves). A social pariah, in a wretched state of health, he sings the joy of life and the sensuality of love as no one else, except perhaps Ausiàs *March and his greatest lyrical mentor, Joan *Maragall, in *El poema de la rosa als llavis* (1923; The Poem of the Rose to the Lips). Life and art are a mystical unity in Salvat; under the pillow of his deathbed was found his last ms.: *Óssa Menor* (1924; Ursa Minor) with the commentary ''Fi dels poemes d'avantguarda'' (End of the Avant-garde Poems). He goes through life like a brilliant meteor, contradictory and at times erratic, but full of rough vitality. In the midst of the general pretensions and frivolity of his time he longs for opposing and absolute desires; life for him is a path of uncertain glory. Some of his poems are the best of modern Catalan literature: ''La meva amiga com un vaixell blanc'' (My Girlfriend Like a White Ship), ''Canto a la lluita'' (I Sing to the Struggle), ''L'enamorat li deia'' (The Lover Would Tell Her), and the song of unity among all Catalans, ''Les conspiracions'' (The Conspiracies). Even his erotic poetry, like that of Ausiàs March, possesses a powerful and transcendent meaning. Like Maragall, to whom he owes so much, but to a greater degree, Salvat is a true popular poet. Today, more than sixty years after his death, no young troubador of the contemporary Nova Cançó (The New Catalan Song) omits from his or her repertoire the poetry of Salvat-Papasseit. Like Antonio *Machado Ruiz, *García Lorca, Hernández, Ausiàs March, Maragall, Jordi de *Sant Jordi and others, Salvat lives on through his poetry. *See also* Catalan Literature.

BIBLIOGRAPHY

Primary Texts

Cincuenta poemas. Sel., tr. José Batlló. Bilingual ed. Barcelona: Lumen, 1977.

Epistolari de Joan Salvat-Papasseit. Ed. A. J. Soberanasi Lleó. Barcelona: Edicions 62, 1984.

Poesies. Intro. Joan Fuster. Barcelona: Ariel, 1962.

Poesies completes. Ed. Joaquim Molas. Barcelona: Ariel, 1978.

English Translations

Selected Poems. Sel., tr., intro. D. Keown and T. Owen. Wales: Llandysul, 1982.

Criticism

Castellet, J. M. ''Salvat-Papasseit i l'introduccio del realisme a la poesia catalana.'' In *Poesia, realisme, historia*. Barcelona: n.p., 1965. 58–64.

Garcés, Tomás. *Sobre Salvat-Papasseit i altres escrits*. Barcelona: n.p., 1972.

Revista de poesia 1.5–6, (1925). Special issue devoted to Salvat.

Serra d'Or 16.179 (August 1974).

Teixidor, Joan. ''Joan Salvat-Papasseit.'' In *Cinc poetes*. Barcelona: n.p., 1969. 49–89.

Joan Gilabert

SAMANIEGO, Félix María (1745, La Guardia, Alava–1801, La Guardia), fabulist, literary critic, poet. He and contemporary Tomás de *Iriarte are the two most famous Spanish fabulists. Of a distinguished Basque family, he became an active member of both formal and informal literary gatherings of the day. In

1781 he published the work which garnered him unexpected, resounding success, the *Fábulas en verso* (Fables in Verse), a collection of 137 fables. They have been reissued countless times over the years and are still popular.

The next few years find him in Madrid, where he pens various articles, poems, parodies, or criticism, such as "Continuación de las memorias críticas," which initiated a lengthy polemic with *García de la Huerta; a parody of Nicolás Fernández de *Moratín's *Guzmán el Bueno*; a parody of Father Diego *González's *El murciélago alevoso,* and one of Iriarte's *Poema de la música*. These writings were later collected in *Obras críticas* (1898; Critical Works) and *Obras inéditas o poco conocidas* (1866; Little Known Unedited Works). Samaniego eventually withdrew from Madrid, and from such activities. Some time before 1793 he began to write, and circulate in ms. form only, some immoral fables in verse—very risqué erotic anecdotes which also poked fun at the clergy. Someone denounced him to the *Inquisition, and he underwent a difficult period before emerging unscathed. He lived out his remaining years quietly.

BIBLIOGRAPHY

Primary Texts

Fábulas. Ed., intro., notes E. Jareño. Clásicos Castalia 7. Madrid: Castalia, 1969.
El Jardín de Venus. Ed. E. Palacios Fernández. Madrid: Siro, 1976.
Obras críticas. Ed., study J. Apraíz. Bilbao: n.p., 1898.
Obras inéditas o poco conocidas. Ed., intro. E. Fernández de Navarrete. Vitoria: Monteli, 1866.
Poesías. In BAE 61.

Criticism

Palacios Fernández, E. *Vida y obra de Samaniego*. Vitoria: n.p., 1975.

SAMPEDRO, José Luis (1917, Barcelona–), novelist, economist, professor of economics. An eminent economist whose works include *Realidad económica y análisis estructural* (1959; Economic Reality and Structural Analysis) and *Las fuerzas económicas de nuestro tiempo* (1967; *Decisive Forces in World Economics*, 1967), a professor of these subjects in both Spain and England, Sampedro for many years presented himself as a Sunday writer. With the 1981 publication of *Octubre, octubre* (October, October), he has emerged as one of his country's important novelists. The fact is that the literary vocation which antedates Sampedro's interest in economics, and which may now overshadow his success in the social sciences, was never dormant. After obtaining a second prize in a first novel competition in 1947 with *La sombra de los días* (unpublished; The Shadow of the Days), Sampedro has published *Congreso en Estocolmo* (1952; Convention in Stockholm), *El río que nos lleva* (1961; The River That Carries Us), *El caballo desnudo* (1970; The Naked Horse), *Octubre, octubre*, and most recently, *La sonrisa etrusca* (1985; The Etruscan Smile). He has also written plays, *La paloma de cartón* (1950; Cardboard Dove; Calderón de la Barca Prize) and an ecology drama *avant la lettre* titled *Un sitio para vivir* (1955; A Place to Live).

Sampedro's way of characterizing his life—born in 1968, died in 1977—is symptomatic of a pervasive theme in his novels, that of existential self-creation. This vitalistic concern receives a more spiritual accent in the so-called posthumous novels he has written after having outlived his projected sixty-year lifespan. Throughout his narrative, Sampedro's vitalism commonly takes on erotic, romantic, as well as anthropological forms whose expression, in turn, is rich with literary echoes of Spanish (Jorge *Manrique, Pío *Baroja, *García Lorca, *Cela) and non-Hispanic origin (Lawrence, Hemingway, Joyce, Durrell).

In *Congreso en Estocolmo*, a middle-aged professor undergoes a vitalistic awakening through contact with elemental Lapland culture and through a sensual if also sentimentalized romance with a young Scandinavian. In *El río nos lleva*, another world-weary protagonist discovers through the anthropologically conceived folk culture of loggers on the Tagus River the meaning of human dignity, although he is ultimately deprived of the earth-moving sex enjoyed by some of his Hemingwayesque fellow characters. *Octubre, octubre*, the next major Sampedro novel, and one described by its author as a ''novela mundo'' (world novel) rather than as the more simple ''novela situación'' (situation novel) of *Congreso* or as the linear ''novela río'' (river novel) of the later work, interprets vitalistic rebirth on many levels—as sentimental romance, as sexual union, and as mystical oneness. Sampedro's world novel is a most learned novel world, one filled with the exotic lore of Sufi, Cabala, and courtly love traditions. The work that breaks ground formally and thematically is *Octubre, octubre*. Although readers tend to be partial to the more traditional pleasures afforded by the neighborhood chronicles in this text, the work as a whole makes an impressively elaborate metafictional statement. This novel of novels within a novel tells of the search to overcome difference and absence in the relations between the sexes. However, the androgynous solution—male Scheherezades—is made structurally problematic since these characters must continually retell and reinvent themselves to claim necessarily elusive identities for themselves and their texts, one of which is a novel titled *Octubre, octubre*.

Sampedro has declared that he will not undertake another nineteen-year project, another *Octubre, octubre*, but he may carry on its spirit of experimentation in his narratives in progress: *Mah* and *La archiduquesa* (The Archduchess).

BIBLIOGRAPHY

Primary Texts

El caballo desnudo. Barcelona: Planeta, 1970.
Congreso en Estocolmo. Madrid: Alfaguara, 1983.
Octubre, octubre. Madrid: Alfaguara, 1981.
El río que nos lleva. Madrid: Alfaguara, 1982.
La sonrisa estrusca. Madrid: Alfaguara, 1985.

Criticism

de Armas, Isabel. ''La vida en el 'Cuartel de Palacio.' '' *CH* 381 (1982): 677–81.
Batlló, José. ''José Luis Sampedro: la escritura como necesidad.'' *Camp de l'arpa* 95 (1982): 32–42.
Quiroga Clérigo, Manuel. ''Erase el lenguaje.'' *Nueva Estafeta* 38 (1982): 91–95.

Sánchez Arnosi, Milagros. ''José Luis Sampedro y su novela 'Octubre, octubre': una teoría del conocimiento.'' *Insula* 424 (1982): 5.

Sunen, Luis. '' 'Octubre, octubre' de José Luis Sampedro.'' *Insula* 425 (1982): 5.

Laura Rivkin-Golden

SAN JOSÉ, Jerónimo de (1587?, Mallén, Zaragoza–1654, Zaragoza), historian, author, poet. A member of the Carmelite order, he wrote the *Historia del Carmen Descalzo* (1637; History of the Discalced Carmen), which encountered *censorship difficulties, and a *Vida de San Juan de la Cruz* (1641; Life of St. John (*Juan) of the Cross). Also his is the *Genio de la Historia* (1651; The Spirit of History). Disciple of Bartolomé Leonardo de *Argensola, he was an avowed foe of **culteranismo*. His poetry is religious and moralistic, and becomes meditative and mystical in his later work.

BIBLIOGRAPHY

Primary Texts

Cartas al cronista Juan F. Andrés de Ustarroz. Ed. J. M. Blecua. Zaragoza: CSIC, 1945.

Compendio de la vida del místico doctor San Juan de la Cruz. In *Obras*. By Saint Juan de la Cruz. N.p.: n.p., 1912. 1: 1–154.

Genio de la historia. 2nd ed. Madrid: Muñoz del Valle, 1768.

Poesías selectas. Zaragoza: Diputación Provincial, 1876.

SAN PEDRO, Diego de (fifteenth c., ?–?), writer. Active in the last quarter of the fifteenth c., he served Juan Téllez-Girón, Count of Ureña. At the court of the Catholic monarchs, San Pedro was a popular writer of sentimental romances and poems for the young nobles. Very little else is known about his life.

San Pedro's first known work is the *Pasión trovada* (1516 [written 1480s]; Christ's Passion Versified), which went through many popular editions well into the nineteenth c., usually without the true author's name. He is best known for his two prose romances, the *Tractado de amores de Arnalte y Lucenda* (1491 [written 1481?]; *A Small Treatice betwixt Arnalte and Lucenda*, 1639) and *Cárcel de Amor* (1492; *Prison of Love*, 1979), both very influential in the development of European fiction because of their psychological analyses of the torments of love. *Arnalte* describes the breaking of the protagonist's mental health after an unrequited infatuation with Lucenda. *Cárcel de Amor* begins with the Author's witnessing an allegorical representation of Leriano being held captive and tortured in Love's castle. With the Author's help Leriano comes into the favor of his beloved Laureola, a princess. A jealous slanderer charges them with lascivious conduct, and Laureola is imprisoned by her father, the king. Leriano rescues the princess by force of arms, and after a long war with the king, clears the lovers' names. However, Laureola then writes Leriano that she can never again see him since such would substantiate the slanders. He lets himself die, a martyr to the religion of Love. A large portion of the novel is in epistolary form or is long rhetorical speeches, with little dialogue. The Author plays a major character role in the work.

In the 1480s, San Pedro wrote for the ladies of the court a *Sermón* (1540?; Sermon), an art of love which employs the form of a learned sermon. He also wrote poetry, such as a panegyric to Isabella and a *Siete angustias de Nuestra Señora* (The Seven Sorrows of Our Lady), both of which appeared in the *Arnalte y Lucenda*. San Pedro's love poems are included in the *Cancionero general* (1511 and 1514, General Songbook). His last known piece, which renounces his earlier erotic works, is the poem *Desprecio de la Fortuna* (1506; Contempt of Fortune), a sensitive interpretation of Boethius's *On the Consolation of Philosophy*. *See also* Renaissance; Siglo de Oro.

BIBLIOGRAPHY

Primary Texts

Obras completas. Ed. K. Whinnom and D. Severin. 3 vols. Clásicos Castalia 39, 54, 98. Madrid: Castalia, 1971 ff.

English Translation

Prison of Love. With the Continuation of Nicolás Núñez. Ed. K. Whinnom. Edinburgh: Edinburgh UP, 1979.

Criticism

Whinnom, K. *Diego de San Pedro*. TWAS 310. New York: Twayne, 1975.

Eric Naylor

SÁNCHEZ, Francisco (1552?, Tuy, Galicia–1623, Toulouse, France), philosopher and physician. Of Jewish heritage, Sánchez and his family moved to France when he was still a youth. He enrolled in the School of Medicine at the U of Montpellier in 1573, and later graduated and became a professor there for eleven years. Subsequently he moved to Toulouse, teaching and practicing medicine, and teaching philosophy, until his death.

Sánchez composed many medical and philosophical works, but his most enduring piece is the skeptical tract *Quod Nihil Scitur* (1581, perhaps written 1576; That Nothing Is Known). Drawing on the ten modes of Sextus Empiricus, Sánchez developed a systematic refutation of all attempts which had been made and could be made by man to attain any sort of knowledge. Richard Popkin considers him ''the only Sixteenth-century skeptic other than Montaigne who has achieved any recognition as a thinker.''(36–7)

BIBLIOGRAPHY

Primary Texts

Que nada se sabe. Ed. M. Menéndez y Pelayo. Buenos Aires: Nova, 1944. (Spanish)
Tratados Filosóficos. Pref. A. Moreira de Sá. 2 vols. Lisbon: Instituto de Alta Cultura, Gaspar Pinto de Sousa, 1955. (Latin and Portuguese)

English Translation

That Nothing Is Known. Ed. Elaine Limbrick and Douglas F. Thomson. Cambridge: Cambridge UP, 1989. Latin and English.

Criticism

Menéndez y Pelayo, M. "De los orígenes del criticismo y del escepticismo y especialmente los precursores españoles de Kant." In *Ensayos de crítica filosófica*. vol. 2. Santander: Artes Gráficas, 1948.

Popkin, R. *The History of Scepticism from Erasmus to Spinoza*. Berkeley: U of California P, 1979.

Solana, M. *Historia de la filosofía española*. vol. 1. Madrid: Asociación española para el progreso de las ciencias, 1941.

Maureen Ihrie

SÁNCHEZ, Miguel (?, ?–before 1609?, Plasencia?), poet and dramatist. Referred to as "el divino" (the divine one), praised by contemporaries such as Lope de *Vega and *Cervantes. Very little is known of Sánchez, and his work subsequently has been largely forgotten. The two poems which have been preserved are "Oíd señor don Gaiferos" (Listen, Sir Gaiferos) and "Canción a Cristo crucificado" (Song to the Crucified Christ). The extant plays are *La isla bárbara* (The Savage Island), *La guarda cuidadosa* (The Zealous Guard), and *El cerco y toma de Túnez y la Goleta por el Emperador Carlos Quinto* (The Surrounding and Capture of Tunisia and Its Capital by Emperor Charles V). They prove that Sánchez was a talented precursor of Lope.

BIBLIOGRAPHY

Primary Texts

"El cerco y toma de Túnez. . . ." National Library, Madrid. Ms. no. 16.832.

"La isla bárbara" and "La guarda cuidadosa." Two comedies by Miguel Sánchez (el Divino). Ed. H. Rennert. Boston: Ginn; Halle: Niemeyer, 1896.

"Oíd señor don Gaiferos." In *Romancero general*. Ed. A. Gonzalez Palencia. 2 vols. Madrid: CSIC, 1947.

Criticism

Williamsen, Vern G. "El teatro de Miguel Sánchez, el Divino." In *Actas del Sexto Congreso Internacional de Hispanistas*. Ed. Alan M. Gordon and E. Rugg. Toronto: U of Toronto, 1980. 803–7.

SÁNCHEZ, Tomás Antonio (1732, Ruiseñada, Santander–1802, Madrid), editor, medieval scholar, poet. The first to recognize the importance of forgotten medieval texts, he brought to light the **Cantar de mio Cid*, the *Libro de *Alejandre*, works by *Berceo, the *Arcipreste de Hita, etc., in his *Colección de poesías castellanas anteriores al siglo XV* (1779–90; Collection of Pre-Fifteenth C. Castilian Poetry). He also collaborated on an edition of Nicolás *Antonio's *Bibliotheca Hispana Nova* (1783–88). Sánchez's own poetry is satirical. He sustained literary polemics with *Forner and *Floranes.

BIBLIOGRAPHY

Primary Text

Poetas castellanos anteriores al siglo XV. Cont. by P. J. Pidal. Expanded, illus., F. Janer. In BAE 57 (1952).

SÁNCHEZ ALBORNOZ, Claudio (1893, Avila–), Spanish philologist, medievalist and essayist. A discipline of Ramón *Menéndez Pidal, he was instrumental in training a whole generation of younger medievalists in Spain. For a period of years, he was a professor at Madrid's Central U and director of the Institute of Medieval Studies. Among his noteworthy historical essays are *Estampas de la vida en León durante el siglo X* (1926; Scenes of Leonese Life in the Tenth C.). He has also done significant studies of feudalism, monetary exchange in the Middle Ages, and an ancient custom of self-rule known as *behetría*. *Lecturas de historia de España* (1929; Readings in the History of Spain) is essentially literary, while one of his most significant contributions is his study of the history of the Arabs in the Iberian Peninsula, *La España Musulmana* (1946; Muslim Spain). Among his latest works is *España, un enigma histórico* (2nd ed., 1962; Spain, A Historical Enigma).

SÁNCHEZ-BARBUDO, Antonio (1910, Madrid–), Spanish essayist, fiction writer, and critic. He began very young as a contributor of articles to *El Sol*, and was associated with a pro-Republican group of intellectuals in Madrid under the general aegis of *Ortega y Gasset, belonging to a circle including *Serrano Plaja and *Azcoaga. His first stories were gathered together in book form with the title *Entre dos fuegos* (1938; Cross-Fire). Following the Civil War, he went into exile in Mexico, where he published his second book, polemic in nature, *Una pregunta sobre España* (1945; A Question about Spain). *Sueños de grandeza* (1946; Dreams of Grandeur) is a novel. After some time in Latin America, he emigrated to the United States, where for many years he served as a professor of Spanish literature at the U of Wisconsin, specializing largely in the *Generation of 1898 and publishing such critical studies as *Estudios sobre Unamuno y Machado* (1959; Studies on Unamuno and Machado); and *La segunda época de Juan Ramón Jiménez (1916–1953)* (n.d.; The Second Period of Juan Ramón Jiménez, 1916–53). He also edited *Cincuenta poemas* (1963; Fifty Poems) of Juan Ramón *Jiménez, and *Dios deseado y deseante* (1965; God Desired and Desiring) by the same poet, and *Los poemas de Antonio Machado* (1967; The Poems of Antonio *Machado), all with commentaries.

SÁNCHEZ-CUTILLAS I MARTÍNEZ, Carmelina (1927, Madrid–), poet, novelist and historian. She studied philosophy and literature, and as a writer, has divided her attention between the history of Valencia, a city with which she has close ties, and works of literary creation. *Matèria de Bretanya* (1976: Themes of Brittany) won the Andròmina Prize; it is fictionalized and lyrical memoirs with a prologue by Pere Maria Orts i Bosch. The author draws a series of vignettes based on childhood memories to paint the society of the late 1920s and early 1930s in a small town.

BIBLIOGRAPHY

Primary Texts

Conjugació en primera persona. N.p.: n.p., 1969.
Els jeroglífics i la pedra de Rosetta. Valencia: Eliseu Climent, 1976.

Llibre d'amic e d'amada. Valencia: Torres, 1980.
Matèria de Bretanya. Valencia: Eliseu Climent, 1976.
Un món rebel. Valencia: Vives Mora, 1964.

Kathleen McNerney

SÁNCHEZ DE BADAJOZ, Diego (c. 1479, Badajoz or Talavera de la Reina–c. 1552, ?), cleric, poet, and dramatist. Brother of the poet Garci *Sánchez de Badajoz, Diego served under Pedro Ruiz de Mota, bishop of Badajoz. Although he composed moralities and allegories, he is best known as a writer of twenty-eight farces and may have been a rival of *Torres Naharro. Despite the ever-present moralizing element in the farces, they are noted for their realistic, satirical, and often *picaresque quality. Because the farces deal with the lives of shepherds and other common folk, indelicate language occurs in several of them; nevertheless, Sánchez de Badajoz has been duly recognized for his contributions to the development of what was eventually to become Spain's *auto sacramental* (**auto*). The principal works of Sánchez de Badajoz were published in Seville by his nephew in the posthumous *Recopilación en metro* (1554; A Compilation of Verse). Among the pieces which best serve to demonstrate his style are the *Farsa del molinero* (The Farce of the Miller), the *Farsa del colmenero* (The Farce of the Beekeeper), the *Farsa del Santísimo Sacramento* (The Farce of the Most Blessed Sacrament), and the *Farsa Teologal* (*Theological Farce*, 1934).

BIBLIOGRAPHY

Primary Texts

Farsas. Ed. J. M. Díez Borque. Letras Hispánicas Series 71. Madrid: Cátedra, 1978.
"Four *Farsas* of Diego Sánchez de Badajoz and the Old Testament: A Critical Edition with Notes." Ed. Rochelle K. Kelz. Diss., Northwestern U, 1971.
Recopilación en metro. Ed. Frida Weber de Kurlat. Buenos Aires: Universidad de Buenos Aires, 1968.

English Translation

"Theological Farce in Which Are Chiefly Discussed the Incarnation and Birth, Etc." Tr. Willis Knapp Jones. *Spanish One Act Plays in English*. Dallas: Tardy, 1934. 31–48.

Criticism

Arias, Ricardo. *The Spanish Sacramental Plays*. TWAS 572. Boston: Twayne, 1980. 66–76.
Crawford, J. P. Wickersham. *Spanish Drama before Lope de Vega*. Rev. ed. Philadelphia: U of Pennsylvania P, 1967.
Gustafson, Donna. "The Role of the Shepherd in the Pre-Lopean Drama of Diego Sánchez de Badajoz." *Bulletin of the Comediantes* 25 (1973): 5–13.
Wardropper, Bruce. *Introducción al teatro religioso del Siglo de Oro: Evolución del auto sacramental antes de Calderón*. Salamanca: Anaya, 1967. 185–209.
———. "The Search for a Dramatic Formula for the *Auto Sacramental*." *PMLA* 65 (1950): 1196–1211.

Wiltrout, Ann E. "Audience Relationship and Pastoral Empathy in Seven *Farsas* by Diego de Sánchez de Badajoz." *RHM* 40.1–2 (1978–79): 1–16.

C. Maurice Cherry

SÁNCHEZ DE BADAJOZ, Garci (1460–80?, Ecija–1526–45?, ?), Andalusian courtly love poet and musician. Scant and conflicting biographical data exist for this poet, whose work is included in various editions of the *Cancionero general* (1511 and ss.). Some of his poems, such as "Lamentaciones" (1511; Lamentations) were sufficiently popular to merit publication in *pliegos sueltos* (popular broadsides). Garci Sánchez was at least equally famous for his love life; multiple anecdotes preserve extravagant behavior stemming from his passionate, unrequited love for a lady. He is said to have literally gone mad for a period of time. As well as being a prisoner of love, he apparently was imprisoned physically for several years, for unknown reasons. Such anecdotes are recounted by authors such as *Timoneda, Lope de *Vega, etc. *See also* Cancionero.

BIBLIOGRAPHY

Primary Texts

The Life and Works of Garci Sánchez de Badajoz. By Patrick Gallagher. London: Tamesis Books, 1968. Contains biography, critical edition of poetry, and analysis.

Criticism

See above.

SÁNCHEZ DE LAS BROZAS, Francisco (1523, Brozas, Cáceres–1600, Salamanca). Sánchez de las Brozas, commonly known as El Brocense, was an influential humanist who occupied a chair in rhetoric at the U of Salamanca. Like Antonio de *Nebrija, a century earlier, El Brocense played a key role in reforming the study of the classics, especially through his *Arte para saber latín* (1595; a Latin grammar), *Grammaticae Graecae Compendium* (1581; a Greek grammar), and *Verae brevesque latinae institutiones* (1587; Principles of Latin Grammar), in which he refines and corrects Nebrija's method. Among many other accomplishments in this field, he published editions of Virgil's *Bucolics* (1591), selected works of Ovid (1546), and translations of Horace.

In the field of Spanish literature, El Brocense's commentaries on Juan de *Mena (1582) and his annotated edition of *Garcilaso de la Vega (1574) are worthy of mention. In the latter work, according to some critics, he had been guilty of denying Garcilaso's "originality" by listing the Greek, Latin and Italian poets in whom the great Spanish poet had found inspiration; but El Brocense, in a much-quoted remark, retorted that anyone worthy of the name of poet would naturally imitate the greatest writers of antiquity ("no tengo por buen poeta al que no imita a los excelentes antiguos"; he who does not imitate the excellent ancients, I do not consider a good poet). The annotated Garcilaso was a landmark of sorts for peninsular literature: it was the first time a Spanish poet had been elevated to the status of a classic (by becoming the object of scholarly commentary and textual criticism, processes ordinarily reserved for ancient authors).

El Brocense wrote numerous poems and commentaries in Latin. His concept of literary beauty depends principally on form, somewhat after the manner of the Italian humanists, as one may see in his treatises *De arte dicendi* (1556; On Public Speaking) and *Organum dialecticum et rhetoricum cunctis discipulis utilissimum et necessarium* (Lyon, 1579; A Manual of Logic and Rhetoric); it should be remembered, moreover, that this great humanist was brought to trial by the *Inquisition (1584) for having dared to criticize the form of the Gospels.

A follower of Erasmus, El Brocense in his scientific works displays the encyclopedic tendency typical of *humanism: *Declaración y uso del reloj español* (1549; Description and Uses of the Spanish Clock), *Pomponii Melae de situ orbis* (1574; Pomponius Mela's Cosmography), *Sphera mundi ex variis auctoribus concinnata* (1579; The World According to Various Authors). Among his philosophical works are the *Doctrina de Epicteto* (1600; The Teachings of Epictetus), *Paradoxa* (1581; Paradoxes), and *De nonnullis Porphyrii aliorumque in Dialectica erroribus* (1588; On Some Logical Errors in Porphyry and Others; translated into Spanish by Alcayde Vilar, 1588). *See also* Italian Literary Influences; Renaissance.

BIBLIOGRAPHY

Primary Texts

Gallego Morell, Antonio, ed. *Garcilaso de la Vega y sus comentaristas. Obras completas del poeta. Acompañadas de los textos íntegros de los comentarios de el Brocense, Fernando de Herrera, Tamayo de Vargas y Azara*. 2nd ed. Madrid: Gredos, 1972.

Pinta Llorente, M. de la, and Antonio Tovar, eds. *Procesos inquisitoriales contra Francisco Sánchez de las Brozas*. Madrid: Instituto Antonio de Nebrija, 1941. With a critical study.

Criticism

Bataillon, Marcel. *Erasmo y España*. Tr. Antonio Alatorre. Mexico: Fondo de cultura económica, 1966. See especially pp. 734–37.

Bell, A. F. G. *Francisco Sánchez el Brocense*. London: Oxford UP, H. Milford, 1925.

García, Constantino. *Contribución a la historia de los conceptos gramaticales; la aportación del Brocense*. RFE Anejo 71. Madrid: CSIC, 1960.

González de la Calle, Pedro Urbano. *Francisco Sánchez de las Brozas. Su vida profesional y académica. Ensayo biográfico*. Madrid: Suárez, 1923.

Merrill, Judith S. ''Las primeras clasificaciones tripartitas de las partes de la oración: Villalón y El Brocense.'' *NRFH* 19 (1970): 105–10.

William Ferguson

SÁNCHEZ DE VERCIAL, Clemente (1370?–1434?), archdeacon of Valderas in León. Author known principally for his *Suma* or *Libro de los exenplos por A.B.C.* (Digest, or Book of Exempla [Ordered] by A.B.C.), the largest compilation of *exempla* in Spanish, containing more than 500 tales under some 450 chapter divisions. The form derives from the Latin *alphabetum* in which alphabetical ordering of tales according to key words (Avarice, Blasphemy, Chastity, etc.) replaces the frame story of earlier collections. A Latin maxim, followed by a rhymed couplet in Spanish summarizing the moral of the tale, heads each chapter. The work has a distinctly ecclesiastical bent and probably served as a source book for vernacular sermons. Sánchez mentions some forty authors and texts in this work, including the *Vitae Patrium* (Lives of the Fathers), Petrus Alphonsi (Pero *Alfonso; *Disciplina clericalis* or Instruction for Clerics), St. Augustine, Gregory the Great (*Dialogues*), Valerius Maximus, *Seneca, Cicero, and Pliny. Other works by Clemente Sánchez are the *Sacramental* and *Breve copilacion de las cosas necesarias a los sacerdotes* (Brief Compilation of Items Necessary for Priests), both writings of instruction and reform for clergy.

BIBLIOGRAPHY

Primary Texts

Libro de los exemplos por A.B.C. Ed. John E. Keller. Madrid: CSIC, 1961.

Kathleen L. Kirk

SÁNCHEZ ESPESO, Germán (1940, Pamplona–), Spanish novelist. Sánchez Espeso studied the equivalent of junior and senior high school in a private Jesuit institution in Pamplona, and joined the Company of Jesus. As a Jesuit, he studied humanities and rhetoric in the monastery of Veruela (Zaragoza) and philosophy in Loyola College (Guipúzcoa). He subsequently served as a professor of literature and oratory in the private Jesuit school in Tudela (Navarre), and studied applied psychology. He obtained a degree in cinematography at the U of Valladolid, and a certificate as a television producer. After studying theology in the monastery of Oña (Burgos) and in Deusto U (Bilbao), he abandoned the order to become a producer of publicity films in Madrid. He then became an initiate in studies of yoga.

Sánchez Espeso's novels include *Experimento en Génesis* (1967; Experiment in Genesis), *Síntomas de éxodo* (1969; Symptoms of Exodus), *Laberinto lerítico* (1972), and *De entre los números* (1978; From among the Numbers), announced as parts of a pentalogy entitled "Pentateuco." His fifth novel, *Narciso* (1979; Narcissus), does not belong to this cycle, but is intended as a pitiless "reflection" of the narcissism within us all. His character is something of a drunkard, a madman, a degenerate, but more than all of these, just as the novel is a tale of love, sexuality and crime, but also transcends these elements.

SÁNCHEZ FERLOSIO, Rafael (1927, Rome–), Spanish novelist, philologist, short story writer. Rafael *Sánchez Mazas (Sánchez Ferlosio's father) was cultural attaché of the Spanish embassy in Rome when the future writer was born; his mother, Liliana Ferlosio, was Roman. He began to study architecture in Madrid, changing to Semitic languages (Hebrew and Arabic) without completing a degree; later he also studied management. *Industrias y andanzas de Alfanhuí* (1951; The Deeds and Wanderings of Alfanhuí) is a singularly artistic neo-picaresque fantasy, independent of all contemporary movements and influences. The title evokes classic *picaresque models, and chapter headings are done in Renaissance style. The picaresque structure (autobiography of a boy who leaves home, serving many masters in the course of losing his innocence) contrasts with the lyric prose and poetic fantasy of many episodes.

Literary fame came with Sánchez Ferlosio's second novel, *El Jarama* (1955; The Jarama River), one of several novels widely publicized because of its winning the Nadal Prize. It is considered (together with *Gran Sol* of Ignacio *Aldecoa) the crowning achievement of Spanish objectivism. Instead of continuing his exceptionally promising novelistic career, Sánchez Ferlosio has devoted himself since 1957 to philology and investigations of linguistic theory. A private person who shuns interviews, he has published only a handful of short stories (in periodicals, during the interim between the two novels), a few articles, and—after two decades of silence following *El Jarama*—two volumes of curious essays or first-person meditations, both entitled *Las semanas del jardín* (1974; Weeks in the Garden). Topics range over many centuries and cultures, from the Bible to the circus and from haiku poetry to computers, but the essays are unified by a common concern for problems of language, expression and communication.

El Jarama (whose title is the name of a river near Madrid, scene of one of the bloodiest battles of the Civil War) is a slice-of-life covering some sixteen hours from early morning to midnight of a summer Sunday during which varied groups of working people try not too successfully to enjoy their day off. Traveling by train or bicycle to the site a few kilometers outside the capital, they swim, picnic and frequent the riverside tavern, returning in the evening or night to the city. *El Jarama* lacks plot and protagonist, has little or no sustained action, and its anodyne characters converse monotonously in popular slang and vulgar clichés exuding banality and triviality. The novel, largely dialogue, is an overpowering tour de force of technical fidelity in transcribing popular speech. The few events are insignificant, lacking transcendence (the one exception, Lucita's death by drowning, is similarly treated, as a bit of an inconvenience, without metaphysical repercussions). The writer's emphasis on ordinariness is deliberate: Spanish neo-realism and objectivism in the 1950s stressed portraiture of daily life (as opposed to exceptional events). Under cinematic influence, objectivism presented characters via words and deeds, with minimal authorial interventions. Descriptions of "scientific" exactness shun subjective adjectivation, psychological analysis and value judgments.

BIBLIOGRAPHY

Criticism

Castellet, J. M. "Notas para una iniciación a la lectura de *El Jarama*." *Papeles de Son Armadans* 2 (*May* 1956): 205–17.

Ortega, José. "Tiempo y estructura en *El Jarama*." *CH* 201 (Sept. 1966): 801–8.

Quiñones, Fernando. "*El Jarama* de Rafael Sánchez Ferlosio." *CH* 80 (Aug. 1956): 128–42.

Villanueva, Darío. *"El Jarama" de Sánchez Ferlosio: su estructura y significado*. Santiago de Compostela: n.p., 1973.

SÁNCHEZ MAZAS, Rafael (1894, Madrid–1966, Madrid), Spanish journalist, poet and novelist. From a family of Basque origin, remotely related to *Unamuno, he studied law, but was better known as a journalist who contributed to several important dailies including *El Sol*, *ABC*, and others. Although his reporting usually had a political slant, he was an original prose stylist. His earliest work, influenced by contemporary French writers as well as by Goethe, was entitled *Pequeñas memorias de Tarín* (1915; Little Memoir of Tarin). Most of his poetry was classical in style. He lived several years in Italy, and this residence was reflected especially in his lyrics (a minor diplomat, he married an Italian woman, and was the father of the contemporary novelist Rafael *Sánchez Ferlosio). His poetry includes *Quince sonetos para quince esculturas de Moisés de Huerta* (n.d.; Fifteen Sonnets for Fifteen Sculptures by Moses Huerta). *Vida nueva de Pedrito de Andía* (1951; The New Life of Pete Andía) is a neo-picaresque narrative; *Lances de boda* (1952; Wedding Adventures) is also a novel.

SÁNCHEZ-SILVA, José María (1911, ?–), Spanish journalist, short story writer and novelist. He began his newspaper work while still quite young, and published his first short story collection in 1934, *El hombre de la bufanda* (The Man with the Scarf). After the Civil War, he returned to the narrative with several titles in rapid succession: *La otra música* (1941; That Other Music); *No es tan fácil* (1943; It Isn't That Easy); *La ciudad se aleja* (1946; The City Moves into the Distance). Although he produced a number of other titles, the one which brought him the most recognition was a short novel which enjoyed international success, *Marcelino, pan y vino* (1952; Marcelino, Bread and Wine). Later he published another short story collection entitled *Historias de mi calle* (1954; Stories from My Street).

BIBLIOGRAPHY

Primary Texts

Obras Selectas. Madrid: Plenitud, 1959.

SANCHO II DE CASTILLA, Cantar de (Song of Sancho II of Castile), medieval epic poem. By reconstructing fragments of this poem which appear in chronicles, scholars have determined that its subject is the struggle in which Sancho II became involved with his brothers García and Alfonso and his sisters Elvira and Urraca. The latter was beseiged in Zamora, and as a consequence Sancho was assassinated by Vellido Dolfos. The *Cid is portrayed as a faithful vassal of Sancho, and the final episode in the *Cantar* may have been a confrontation between the Cid and Alfonso. *See also* Cantar de gesta.

BIBLIOGRAPHY

Primary Text

Puyol, J. *Cantar de gesta de don Sancho de Castilla*. Madrid: Suárez, 1911.

Criticism

Fraker, Charles. ''Sancho II: Epic and Chronicle.'' *Romania* 95 (1974): 467–507.
Reig, Carola. *El cantar de Sancho II y el cerco de Zamora*. *RFE* Anejo 37. Madrid: CSIC, 1947.

James Ray Green

SANDOVAL, Adolfo de (1870, Oviedo–1947, Madrid), Spanish novelist, historian, and biographer. Honored for his work in the history of art and ancient Spanish cities with membership in the Academy of Fine Arts and Toledo's Academy of Historical Sciences, Sandoval was an author of sentimental novels whose primary virtue was their power of evocation of the antiquated, provincial capitals of Spain. Thus he portrays the walled medieval city of Ávila in *La Gran Fascinadora* (1928; The Great Fascinator), *Beatriz Pacheco (una historia de amor)* (1929; Beatrice Pacheco, a Love Story), and *Almas gemelas* (1930; Twin Souls), all having certain touches of *Romanticism in addition to their sentimentality. Segovia is the ancient city re-created as the dreamy background for *Fuencisla Moyano* (1932). *Las supremas revelaciones de la vida* (1932; Life's Supreme Revelations), an autobiographical novel, is set in another old city of Castile, while a third book published in this same year, *Los bellos países, España* (Beautiful Countries: Spain), is descriptive in nature. Among Sandoval's biographical works is a study of the life of Marcelino *Menéndez y Pelayo.

BIBLIOGRAPHY

Primary Texts

!Ahí va un corazón! Madrid: Castro, 1935.
Los amores de un cadete. Madrid: C. Vallinas, 1927.
Carolina Coronado y su época. Zaragoza: Librería General, 1944.

SANDOVAL, Prudencio de (1553, Valladolid–1620, Estella, Navarre), historian. He entered the Benedictine order in 1569, and rose to become bishop of Tuy in 1608, and of Pamplona three years later. His historical works include *Historia de la vida y hechos del emperador Carlos V* (1604 and 1606; History of the Life and Deeds of Emperor Charles V); the *Crónica de Alfonso VII* (1600; Chronicle of Alphonse VII); and the *Historia de los Reyes de Castilla y de Aragón* (1615 and 1634; History of the Monarchs of Castile and Aragon). His work combines legends with fact, and does not verify information garnered from other sources; but he does include original documents.

BIBLIOGRAPHY

Primary Texts

Crónica de Alonso VII. Madrid: Sánchez, 1600.
Historia de la vida y hechos del emperador Carlos V. Ed. C. Seco Serrano. In BAE 80–82.
Historia de los reyes de Castilla y de León. Madrid: Cano, 1792.

English Translation

The history of Charles the Vth. . . . Tr. J. Stevens. London: Smith, 1703. Abridged.

Criticism

Castañeda, V. *El cronista fray Prudencio de Sandoval*. Madrid: Tip. de Archivos, 1929.

SANDOVAL Y CUTOLI, Manuel (1873, Madrid–1932, Madrid), Spanish literary critic and poet. He contributed to *La Epoca*, and came to be a member of the *Academia Española. His poetry was in the style of the nineteenth c., without influences of the modern or contemporary movements and theories. Works include *Aves de Paso* (1909; Migratory Birds), *Cancionero* (1904; Song-Book) and *De mi cercado* (1912; From Inside My Fence), which received the Spanish Academy's Fastenrath Prize.

SANNAZARO, Jacopo (1458, Naples–1530, Naples), *pastoral author, humanist. Descended from a Spanish family, this Italian humanist wrote in 1504 the bucolic composition which became the prototype for all subsequent pastoral literature in Spain and Europe for the next two hundred years. Titled *La Arcadia* (Arcadia), it is an idyllic mixture of prose and verse, with elegant shepherds and shepherdesses evoking a world of sentiment. The first Spanish translation appeared in 1549; its influence is palpable in *Montemayor, Gil *Polo, *Cervantes, and all subsequent pastoral literature.

BIBLIOGRAPHY

English Translation

Arcadia and Piscatorial Eclogues. Tr. R. Nash. Detroit: Wayne State UP, 1966.

Criticism

Avalle Arce, J. B. *La novela pastoril española*. 2nd ed. Madrid: Istmo, 1974.
Bochetta, V. E. *Sannazaro en Garcilaso*. Madrid: Gredos, 1976.
Kennedy, W. J. *Jacopo Sannazaro and the Uses of Pastoral*. Hanover: UP of New England, 1983.
Poggioli, R. *The Oaten Flute*. Cambridge, MA: Harvard UP, 1976.

SANT JORDI, Jordi de (c. 1400, Valencia–c. 1424, ?), poet. Chamberlain of the court of Alphonse the Magnanimous, Sant Jordi's life appears to have been very closely linked to the reign of this monarch, whom he accompanied on many journeys. In 1420 he took part in the military expedition to Sardinia and Corsica together with other famous Catalan poets such as Andreu Febrer and Ausiàs *March. It is known that between 1421 and 1423 he was living in Italy, and around this time he was imprisoned by the famous Condottiere Sforza. By 1425 he was dead. The eighteen poems that have survived show a clear Provençal influence in the language although his *Weltanschauung* is markedly Petrarchan and therefore thoroughly *Renaissance. He is an extremely sensitive and elegant poet who endows his lady, his Provençal muse, with the attributes of highest perfection. In this regard his "estramps" (unrhymed verses) are true masterpieces of Catalan poetry. His love poetry is generally addressed to unknown ladies although "Reina d'honor" (Queen of Honor) was probably inspired by Margarita de Prades, widow of Martí l'Humà. Generally, all the poems are laudatory songs of the troubadour tradition in which sensitivity of feelings relates to concrete events or, less often, examines the love relationship with the lover in a more transcendent mood, as in the famous line "Jus lo front port vostra bella semblança" (Your very forehead mirrors your beautiful countenance). In the allegoric debate, "Un cors gentil que m'ha tant enamorat" (A Gentle Heart with Which I Have Fallen in Love), Eyes, Heart and Thought discuss among themselves which has the most influence on Love. Also allegoric is another debate, "Passio Amoris Secundum Ovidium" (Love's Passion According to Ovid), where Pain flogs the lover and expels him from the castle of the God of Love. This composition shows the poet's predilection for the classical troubadours and also influences from the *Roman de la Rose* by Guillaume of Lorris. Two misogynous poems complete the repertoire.

Jordi de Sant Jordi was much admired by the Marquis of *Santillana, whom he met in the court of Alphonse the Magnanimous; the Castilian poet praised him as a poet and as a musician *(Proemio*, c. 1449) and after Sant Jordi's death composed in his memory a long poem, "Coronación de Mossén Jordi" (Coronation of Mossen Jordi). *See also* Catalan Literature; Italian Literary Influences.

BIBLIOGRAPHY

Primary Texts

Jordi de Sant Jordi. Ed. M. de Riquer. Granada: Universidad de Granada, 1955. Edition and study.

Jordi de Sant Jordi (poesies, dates i comentaris). By N. d'Owler. Barcelona: Biblioteca Filològica de l'Institut de la Llengua Catalana, 1917.

Obres. Ed. M. de Riquer. Barcelona: L'Avenç, 1935.

Obres poétiques. Ed. J. Massó i Torrents. Barcelona-Madrid: L'Avenç, 1902.

Criticism

Riquer, M. de. "Reconstrucción de una poesía de Jordi de Sant Jordi." *Boletín de la Sociedad Castellonense de Cultura* 27 (1952): n.p.

———. " 'Stramps' i 'Midons' de Jordi de Sant Jordi." *Revista Valenciana de Filología* 1 (1951): n.p.

Joan Gilabert

SANTA CRUZ, Alonso de (?, Seville?–1572?, Seville?), sailor, cosmographer, historian. He sailed as treasurer with Cabot to the Strait of Magellan (1525); upon return, he was named cosmographer for the Casa de Contratación (Commerce Building) in Seville. His most important work is the *Crónica de Carlos V* (Chronicle of Charles V), which covers the years 1500 to 1550, and contains excellent material on the War of the Comunidades. He also completed the chronicle of the Catholic monarchs, starting where Hernando del *Pulgar had ceased.

BIBLIOGRAPHY

Primary Texts

Crónica de los reyes católicos (hasta ahora inédita). Ed., study J. de Mata Carriazo. 2 vols. Seville: Escuela de Estudios Hispanoamericanos, 1951.

Crónica del emperador Carlos V. Ed. A. Blázquez and R. Beltrán y Rózpide. 5 vols. Madrid: Real Academia de Historia, 1920–25.

Islario general de todas las islas del mundo. Prol. A. Blázquez. Madrid: Real sociedad geográfica, 1918.

Libro de las longitudenses y. . . . Ed. Blázquez. Seville: Zarzuela, 1921.

English Translation

Map of the world by the Spanish cosmographer Alonso de Santa Cruz 1542. Ed. E. W. Dahlgren. Stockholm: Swedish Staff General, 1892.

SANTA CRUZ, Melchor de (1520, Dueñas–1580, Toledo), anthologist of two important works. The *Floresta española de apotegmas, o sentencias sabia y graciosamente dichas de algunos españoles* (1574; Spanish Collection of Apothegms, or Wise and Witty Maxims Said by Various Spaniards). Indexed according to speakers (royalty, priests, soldiers, students, etc.) and theme, it preserves vivid, piercing impressions of certain personalities and types, and, in a general sense, a panoramic vision of rich folkloric worth. The *Floresta* enjoyed many editions in Spanish, and was translated into French, Italian and German in the early part of the seventeenth c. Two years later, *Cien tratados de notables sentencias assí morales como naturales* (1576; One Hundred Treatises of Notable Maxims, Both Moral and Natural) appeared. It is another collection of maxims, divided into the categories of religion, virtues and vices.

BIBLIOGRAPHY

Primary Texts

Cien tratados. Toledo: Anaya, 1576.

Floresta general. Cont'd by F. Asensio. Madrid: Sociedad de bibliófilos madrileños, 1910–11.

English Translation

Wits fittes and fancies. . . . By A. Copley. London: R. Johnes, 1595. Derived in part from the *Floresta.*

SANTA MARÍA, Pablo de (1350, Burgos–1435, Burgos), eminent theologian, scholar and royal chancellor. Born Selemoh Halevi, of a distinguished Jewish family, he was a Talmudic scholar and a rabbi, but in 1390, influenced largely by the writings of St. Thomas Aquinas, he converted to Christianity, taking the name Pablo de Santa María. He studied theology in Paris and subsequently rose through the church hierarchy until in 1415 he was appointed archbishop of Burgos. His forceful character, erudition and oratory skill earned the favor of Henry III, who made him not only a privy councilor and lord chancellor of Castile, but also his testamentary executor and personal tutor to the prince John II.

Santa María's most valued and scholarly works are Latin treatises arguing points of Christian theology. His best-known work in Castilian is the *Edades trovadas* (Ages in Verse) or *Las siete edades del mundo* (The Seven Epochs of the World), an allegorical poem of some 340 stanzas in **arte mayor*, recounting "everything that has been and happened from the creation of Adam" to the birth of John II (1404). Created perhaps for his royal pupil, the poem is competently written and of archaeological value but of dubious literary worth. The *Suma de crónicas* (Summary of Chronicles) is a rather cursory prose compendium of the more salient events of the *Edades*. It enumerates important figures of Spain beginning with Hercules, "son of King Jupiter," and ending with Fernando de Antequera's succession to the throne of Aragon in 1412. Santa María was formerly credited with partial authorship of the *Crónica de Juan II* (Chronicle of John II), now attributed to his brother Alvar García. *See also Converso*; Hispano Judaic Literature.

BIBLIOGRAPHY

Primary Text

"Edades trovadas." In *Cancionero castellano del siglo XV*. Ed. Raymond Foulché-Delbosc. NBAE 22, 155–88.

Criticism

Cantera Burgos, Francisco. *Alvar García de Santa María y su familia de conversos*. Madrid: CSIC, 1952.

Luciano Serrano, R. P. *Los conversos d. Pablo de Santa María y d. Alfonso de Cartagena*. Madrid: CSIC, 1942.

Kathleen L. Kirk

SANTANA, Lázaro (1940, Las Palmas de Gran Canaria–), Spanish poet and founder of the Tagoro collection of books of poetry and prose. Significant titles of his poetry volumes include *Con la muerte al hombro* (1963; With Death on My Shoulder); *Noticia de un amor* (1964; News Item on a Love Affair); *Siete Elegias personales* (1965; Seven Personal Elegies), winner of the Tomás Morales Prize; and a book of short stories, *Samba para no morir* (1968; Samba to Avoid Dying).

SANTARENO, Bernardo, pseudonym of António Martinho do Rosário (1924, Santarém–1980, Lisbon), Portuguese dramatist. If one is asked to mention a Portuguese dramatist of the 1960s, Santareno is, even more than Romeu Correia or Sttau Monteiro, the likely name to spring to mind. He started by publishing *Teatro* (1957; Drama), a volume containing three plays, the best of which, *A*

Promessa (*The Promise*, 1981), after ten days of being performed at Oporto with great impact, was stopped by the Censorship Services and only allowed to go back onstage ten years later. Santareno's gift for dramatic tension by blending backward religious and social attitudes with repressed eroticism in powerful scenes and often poetic dialogue is also present in *O Crime de Aldeia Velha* (1959; The Crime at Old Village), *António Marinheiro* (1960; António the Sailor), *O Pecado de João Agonia* (1961; The Sin of João Agonia). These plays, not without delay or difficulties, were performed and were influential throughout the decade, their author being significantly and almost unanimously applauded by critics. Meanwhile Santareno, though keeping to the tenor of his previous work, moved toward epic theater in *O Judeu* (1966; The Jew) and *O Inferno* (1967; Hell), taking a more overtly political stance in *A Traição do Padre Martinho* (1969; The Treason of Father Martinho) and *Português, Escritor, Quarenta e Cinco Anos de Idade* (1974; Portuguese, Writer, Forty-Five Years of Age).

Santareno's early books were three volumes of poetry: *A Morte na Raiz* (1954; Death at the Root), *Romances do Mar* (1955; Sea Ballads), *Os Olhos de Víbora* (1957; The Eyes of the Viper). *Nos Mares do Fim do Mundo* (1959; On the End of the World Seas) is the prose account of a year spent as a doctor on board one of those Portuguese vessels that used to go fishing cod by Newfoundland. The play *O Lugre* (1959; The Schooner) also relates to this experience; thereafter Santareno always wrote drama while living and working in Lisbon as a psychiatrist. The link between a popular Lisbon quarter and psychiatric jargon in "O Édipo de Alfama" (The Oedipus of Alfama), the explanatory subtitle to *António Marinheiro*, might be said to hint at Santareno's type of drama, that is, a kind of psychoanalysis of Portuguese society of his day. That is more literally the case in the first period of his oeuvre (1957–62), made of subdued psychodramas, as if Santareno were letting loose in acceptable theatrical molds his and society's latent conflicts. In the best scenes this results in remarkable literary quality, Santareno's work having reminded critics of Tennessee Williams or, on the other hand, of contemporary Spanish poets. This latter affinity may help to explain the unusual fact that his early work was readily translated into Spanish.

Santareno's plays not yet mentioned are *Irmã Natividade* (1961; Sister Natividade), the first act of *A Excomungada* (The Excommunicate), previously published with *O Bailarino* (The Dancer) and *A Promessa* in the volume *Teatro* referred to above; *Os Anjos e o Sangue* (1961; Angels and Blood), written for television; *O Duelo* (1961; The Duel); *Anunciação* (1962; Annunciation); short plays collected under the title *Os Marginais e a Revolução* (1979; Outcasts and Revolution). In *Anunciação* more explicit socio-political references are integrated into Santareno's ingrained themes and thus the play can be viewed as "announcing" his second phase. *O Judeu* and *O Inferno* are both long, carefully crafted, technically ambitious examples of documentary theater. Not that Santareno had done nothing of the kind before: *O Crime de Aldeia Velha*, which shows how villagers in twentieth-c. Portugal came to burn a woman suspected of witchcraft, had its impact reinforced by attaching a piece of news from a Portuguese paper telling of one such case that had in point of fact happened not so long ago. Indeed, Santareno's dramas are always plausible, if not based on fact or experience; but none rely so heavily on documents as *O Judeu* and *O Inferno*, since they both take court cases onto the stage, somewhat as Peter Weiss did with the Nuremberg trials of Nazi war criminals. *O Judeu* (1966) draws much from the processes brought by the *Inquisition against Cavaleiro de Oliveira and the seventeenth-c. playwright António José da Silva, nicknamed "O Judeu"; the audience was to feel the parallel with the ruling inquisitorial Estado Novo regime. *O Inferno* (1967), soberly and more effectively, dramatizes the case of a young couple from Chester who hit the world headlines as "the devilish lovers"; as the trial progresses, the public is given with Brechtian skill the different reactions aroused in the jury by the couple's sadistic, racist murders. Santareno's last major plays, *A Traição do Padre Martinho* (1969) and *Português, Escritor, Quarenta e Cinco Anos de Idade* (1974), stress the dramatist's commitment to political activism and the techniques of epic theater, since the audience is (perhaps too) didactically shown the wrongs of a situation and left to take it into their hands to correct it.

BIBLIOGRAPHY

Primary Texts

Anunciação. Lisbon: Atica, 1962.
O Crime de Aldeia Velha. Lisbon: Atica, 1959.
O Inferno. Lisbon: Atica, 1967.
Obras Completas de Bernardo Santareno. 3 vols. to date. Lisbon: Caminhol, 1984-.
A Promessa. Lisbon: Atica, 1957.
A Traição do Padre Martinho. Lisbon: Atica, 1969.

English Translation

The Promise. Tr., intro., Nelson H. Vieira. Providence: Gávea-Brown, 1981.

Criticism

McNab, George. "Activist Theater in Portugal." In *Roads to Today's Portugal*. Ed. N. H. Vieira. Providence: Gávea-Brown, 1983. 43–54.
Mendonça, Fernando. *Para o Estudo do Teatro em Portugal*. Assis: Faculdade de Filosofia, Ciências e Letras, 1971.
Porto, Carlos. *Em Busca do Teatro Perdido (1958–1971)*. 2 vols. Lisbon: n.p., 1973.
Rebelo, Francisco. "Do Teatro em Portugal." *Colóquio* 54 (June 1969): n.p.
Woodyard, G. W. "A Metaphor for Repression: Two Portuguese Inquisition Plays." *Luso-Brazilian Review* 10 (June 1973): 68–75.

Carlos J. Pereira

SANTIAGO Y PALOMARES, Francisco Javier de (1728, Toledo–1796, Madrid), philologist, calligrapher, artist, historian. Palomares's contribution to the Spanish Enlightenment is an important one frequently overlooked by literary historians of that period. His transcription of works like the *Libro de buen amor* (c. 1753; now in the Bibliothèque Nationale of Paris) by the *Arcipreste de Hita,

Enrique de *Villena's *Arte cisoria* (1763), *Alphonse X's *Cantigas de Santa María* (c. 1750) and *Alphonse XI's *Libro de la montería* (1795) reflects an extraordinary scholarly effort realized over a period of almost fifty years. These editions are superb examples from the nascent period of contemporary critical investigation. Palomares's most significant calligraphic treatise, the *Arte nueva de escribir* (1776; The New Way of Writing), emphasizes the need for the development of a national style of handwriting acquired through precept and example. Significantly for Spanish belles lettres, the *letra de Palomares* (Palomares handwriting) would set the standard for "proper" writing in Spain for most of the nineteenth c.; it is satirized by Ramón de *Mesonero Romanos in his *Escenas matritenses* of 1832.

BIBLIOGRAPHY

Primary Texts

Arte nueva de escribir. Madrid: Sancha, 1776.

Francisco Javier de Santiago y Palomares: Selected Writings, 1776–95. Ed., study, Dennis P. Seniff. Exeter Hispanic Texts, 38. Exeter, England: U of Exeter, 1984.

El maestro de leer; Conversaciones ortológicas. 2 vols. Madrid: Sancha, 1786.

Criticism

Anon. "Noticias biográficas de don Francisco Xavier de Santiago Palomares: *Solicitud*." *BRAH* 76 (1920): 264–67.

Cotarelo y Mori, Emilio. "Palomares (D. Francisco Javier de Santiago y)." In *Diccionario biográfico y bibliográfico de calígrafos españoles* 2, no. 818. Madrid: RABM, 1916. 133–48.

Dennis P. Seniff

SANTILLANA, Íñigo López de Mendoza, Marqués de (1398, Carrión de los Condes, Palencia–1458, Guadalajara), politician, soldier, humanist, poet and prose writer. Santillana was a key figure of vigorous pre-Renaissance culture in Spain both in his personal literary and cultural activities and in his support of humanistic studies by others. He was also deeply involved in the volatile politics of John II's reign; the powerful royal favorite, Alvaro de *Luna, was a lifelong enemy.

Santillana's lineage was illustrious: nephew to Pero *López de Ayala and to *Pérez de Guzmán, his father was Admiral of Castile when he died in 1404. Iñigo's mother, doña Leonor de Vega, and maternal grandmother, doña Mencía de Cisneros, then assumed responsibility of his education. His grandmother was an influential patron of learning and exerted a major role in his intellectual training and development. From 1412 to 1418, the young Iñigo served at the Court of Aragon and formed relationships with leading intellectuals and poets such as Jordi de *Sant Jordi, Enrique de *Villena and Ausiàs *March. Another luminary, Juan de *Mena, was to become, like Luna, his foe. Santillana was not a classicist—although he did read Latin—but he was a linguist, mastering French, Italian, Galician and Catalan. Following his grandmother's example, he became a strong patron of poetry and of humanistic endeavors; he commissioned translations of various classical works into Spanish, and the fine library of mss. he amassed over the years later became part of the *Biblioteca Nacional collection. His interest in languages also led to his collection of proverbs, *Refranes que dicen las viejas tras el fuego* (Proverbs Old Women Say Behind the Fire).

Santillana's multifaceted life well illustrates the strengths, weaknesses, innovations and contradictions of his day. As a soldier he participated in several campaigns: battles against the Moors in the 1430s, and the 1445 Battle of Olmedo, after which the king granted him his title of Marquis of Santillana. Political struggles during John II's rule and Santillana's staunch hatred for Alvaro de Luna led him to participate also in various armed struggles both in defense of and against John II.

Santillana left little prose writing. Most interesting is the *Prohemio é carta* (Prologue and Letter) which was written as a preface to a poetry collection Santillana sent to Don Pedro of Portugal. Divided into twenty-one parts, it gives a rather traditional definition and evaluation of poetry and its style levels, with references to various European literatures he is familiar with. The *Prohemio* is the first literary treatise written in Spanish.

Santillana's poetry, for which he is celebrated, encompasses a wide variety of styles and genres. D. W. Foster classifies his verse into two general categories: 1) courtly Galician-Portuguese poems-songs, *decires, *serranillas, and generally more light-hearted writing, and 2) Italianate poetry—more serious and ambitious, dealing with moral and philosophical concerns, often against a contemporary historical backdrop. Today his serranillas are by far most popular of all, although they are not the most significant part of his verse, and were not the most popular or esteemed part in his day. The serranillas elegantly narrate encounters between a male traveler of noble station and a rustic but physically attractive shepherdess who is a commoner. This basic situation, sketched in rapid, graceful fashion, leaves room for numerous variations to entertain a courtly audience, as Nancy Marino has observed. Santillana is the first writer to use the term "serranillas" to refer to this type of poem, and he is its most accomplished composer.

Santillana's more serious, didactic verse was highly praised in his day. The *Comedieta de Ponça* (Play of Ponza) was probably written around 1436, although it was not made public until 1444. Composed of lines of *arte mayor, the 120 stanzas narrate the unsuccessful battle King Alphonse V of Aragon and his two brothers waged against the Genoese in 1435. The battle functions as a backdrop for consideration of the role of fortune in determining man's fate. Similarly didactic is *Bías contra fortuna* (written 1448, pub. 1502; Bias Against Fortune). Composed of 180 stanzas, it was penned after a cousin of Santillana's was imprisoned by Alvaro de Luna. It is a debate between Bias, a Stoic and one of the seven wise men of Ancient Greece, and Fortune. Bias resists the whims and enticements of Fortune through reason, learning, knowledge of human nature, and a will to resist and to confront death. Influence of this poem is seen in the poetry of Jorge *Manrique.

The *Doctrinal de privados* (1456; The Confidants' Manual) is a scathing portrayal of Alvaro de Luna, after his demise, in which Luna is seen confessing, and literally consuming, his own past sins. The poem's goals are more ambitious than a simple denunciation of the despised adversary, however. As David Foster observes, "certainly from stanza forty on, Luna emerges not only as the ironically repentant image of his historical self, but as an image of Everyman, subject to and dominated by the intense vices of the human condition, aware of the virtues to which he would subscribe, and able at the end to recant his life, confident in the boundless mercy of his God for salvation." (*Marqués de Santillana*, 45)

Santillana's openness to new metrical forms and innovations is also seen in his forty-two sonnets. About half treat themes of love, while the rest consider religious, moral, political or historical questions. They do not attain the mastery of *Garcilaso de la Vega's creations, but they are among the very first written in Spanish, and clearly contribute to the development of the genre in Spain. *See also* Gallic Portuguese Poetry; Humanism; Italian Literary Influences; Renaissance.

BIBLIOGRAPHY

Primary Works

Antología poética: Marqués de Santillana. Ed. D. W. Foster. Madrid: Taurus, 1982.

Marqués de Santillana: Poesías completas. Ed., intro. M. Durán. 2 vols. Madrid: Castalia: 1975, 1980.

Obras completas. Ed., intro., notes A. Gómez Moreno and Maximilian P. A. M. Kerkhof. Barcelona: Planeta, 1988.

Los Sonetos 'Al Itálico Modo' de Iñigo López de Mendoza Marqués de Santillana. Ed., intro., Maximilian P. A. M. Kerkhof and Dirk Tuin. Madison, WI: HSMS, 1985.

Criticism

Durán, Manuel. "Santillana y el prerrenacimiento." *NRFH* 15 (1961): 343–63.

Foster, David. *The Marqués de Santillana.* TWAS 154. NY: Twayne, 1971.

Lapesa, Rafael. *La obra literaria del Marqués de Santillana.* Madrid: Insula, 1957.

Marino, Nancy. *La serranilla española: Notas para su historia e interpretación.* Potomac, MD: Scripta Humanística, 1987.

Pérez Bustamante, R. *El Marqués de Santillana. Biografía y documentación.* Madrid: Taurus, 1983.

Reichenberger, A. "The Marqués de Santillana and the Classical Tradition." *Iberoromana* 1 (1969): 5–34.

SANTO DOMINGO, Sor María de (c. 1470 to 1475?, Aldeanueva, Avila–?, ?), Dominican nun. She joined the order at age seventeen, already having had divine visions. She wrote *Oración y contemplación* (between 1517 and 1522; Prayer and Contemplation). The work urges reformation of the order. Sor María continued to have visions throughout her life; that fact, added to her desires to reform certain aspects of the Dominican convent life, prompted the *Inquisition to investigate her for evidence of Illuminism (*Alumbrados). She gained the protection of such powerful men as Jiménez de *Cisneros, and eventually was absolved of any deviations. Records of her trial reveal an uncommon, vigorous personality.

BIBLIOGRAPHY

Primary Text

Oración y contemplación. Ed. and study, J. M. Blecua. Madrid: Hauser y Menet, 1948. Facs.

SANTOB. *See* Tob, Sem

SANTOS, Francisco (1617, Madrid–1700, Madrid), popular Baroque prose author. He wrote some fifteen prose works, all of which present bleak, bitter depictions of the corruption, decay, violence and sins of seventeenth-c. Spanish society. The specter of Death is everywhere, women are a prime cause of corruption and evil, man is but a collection of uncontrolled appetites. Although not a *picaresque author, Santos uses selected picaresque elements and techniques. His world resembles that of *Alemán, *Gracián y Morales and *Quevedo, all of whom he plagiarized. Santos's didactic, moralizing intent cannot be overemphasized. His best works include *Periquillo, el de las gallineras* (1663; Periquillo, the Henhouse Guy), *Día y noche de Madrid* (1663; Day and Night in Madrid), *La verdad en el potro y el Cid resucitado* (1671; Truth on the Rack and the Cid Brought Back to Life), *El no importa de España . . .* (1667; Spain's I Don't Care . . .) and *El diablo anda suelto, verdades de la otra vida soñadas en ésta* (1677; The Devil's Loose, Truths from the Other Life Dreamt in This One).

BIBLIOGRAPHY

Primary Texts

"A critical edition with notes and variants of Francisco Santos' *Periquillo* . . . together with a study. . . . " By A. Samper. *DAI* 35 (1975): 4552A–4553A. Indiana U.

"Francisco Santos: Edición crítica de *El rey gallo y* . . . y estudio. . . . " By V. Arizpe de León. *DAI* 43.2 (1982): 460A. U of Michigan.

El no importa de España y La verdad en el potro. Ed., study J. Rodríguez Puértolas. London: Tamesis, 1973.

Obras selectas. Ed., intro., notes M. Navarro Pérez. Madrid: Instituto de Estudios Madrileños, 1976. Contains *Día y noche de Madrid* and *Las tarascas de Madrid.*

Criticism

Czyzewski, P. E. "Picaresque and Costumbrista Elements in the Prose Works of Francisco Santos." *DAI* 36 (1976): 6081A–6082A. U of Illinois–Urbana/Champaign.

See also Primary Texts.

Maureen Ihrie

SANTOS TORROELLA, Rafael (1914, Port Bou–), Spanish poet and translator. He was director of *Cobalto*, a poetry review, and took part in numerous poetry congresses. His more significant collections include *Ciudad perdida*

(1949; Lost City); *Altamira* (1949); *Sombra infiel* (1952; Faithless Shadow); *Nadie. Poemas del Avión* (1954; Nobody. Poems from an Airplane); *Hombre antiguo* (1956; Ancient Man), winner of the City of Barcelona Prize; and *Cerrada Noche* (1959; Blackest Night).

SANZ DEL RÍO, Julián (1814, Torre Arévalo–1869, Madrid), philosopher and educator. In 1836, he earned a doctorate in canonical law from the U of Granada, and later he studied civil jurisprudence in Madrid, where he began the practice of law. In 1843, Sanz del Río was appointed provisional professor of the history of philosophy at the U of Madrid under condition that he spend two years abroad with a government-sponsored scholarship to further his studies. Unimpressed by the instruction in Paris, he traveled to Brussels and met with Heinrich Ahrens and later to Heidelberg, where he studied with Carl David August Roeder and devoted himself to the study of the philosophy of "racionalismo armónico" (harmonious rationalism) propounded by Karl Christian Friedrich Krause. When Sanz del Río returned to Spain, he declined to fill his post immediately because he still felt ill-prepared to teach, and until 1854, he remained in seclusion in Illescas. During those years he produced *Lecciones para el sistema de filosofía analítica de K. Ch. F. Krause* (1850; Lessons on K. Ch. F. Krause's System of Analytical Philosophy). In 1854, he assumed his teaching duties, spreading the Krausist doctrine to his students. *Krausism revolutionized Spanish intellectual life in the second half of the nineteenth c. and exerted a strong influence on literature. In 1860, Sanz del Río published *Ideal de la humanidad para la vida* (Humanity's Ideal for Life), a liberal adaptation of Krause's *Das Urbild der Menschheit* (1811), and *Sistema de la filosofía: Metafísica* (System of Philosophy: Metaphysics). Although Sanz del Río was not an original thinker, his propagation of Krausism and his influence on such eminent students as Francisco *Giner de los Ríos, Gumersindo de *Azcárate, and Nicolás Salmerón, led to the practical application of Krausist theories in politics and education and resulted in the founding of the Institución Libre de Enseñanza in 1876. Sanz del Río created a furor when he refused to sign an oath of religious and political faith in 1867, and was dismissed from his university position; he died two years later, leaving a number of unfinished works.

BIBLIOGRAPHY

Primary Texts

Análisis del pensamiento racional. Madrid: Alaria, 1877.
Filosofía de la muerte. Sevilla: Fernández, 1877.
Ideal de la humanidad para la vida. Madrid: Galiano, 1860.
Sistema de la filosofía: Metafísica. Madrid: Galiano, 1860.
Textos escogidos. Barcelona: Cultura Popular, 1968.

Criticism

Jobit, Pierre. *Les éducateurs de l'Espagne contemporaine*. 2 vols. Paris: E. de Boccard, 1936.

López Morillas, Juan. *El krausismo español: Perfil de una aventura intelectual*. Mexico City: Fondo de Cultura Económica, 1956.
Manrique de Lara, Gervasio. *Sanz del Río, siglo XIX*. Madrid: Aguilar, 1935.
Shaw, Donald L. *A Literary History of Spain: The Nineteenth Century*. London: Benn, 1972.

Phoebe Porter Medina

SANZ Y SÁNCHEZ, Eulogio Florentino (1822, Arévalo, Avila–1881, Madrid), journalist, poet, and dramatist. Orphaned at an early age, Sanz was placed in the custody of an unscrupulous, ill-tempered uncle who sent him to study at the U of Valladolid. He later went to Madrid and led a bohemian existence until he was introduced to the Spanish literary world, contributing poetry and criticism to such periodicals as *El Español*, the *Semanario Pintoresco Español*, and *La Patria*, among others, and earning a reputation as a hard-nosed critic. In 1848, his historical drama *Don Francisco de Quevedo*, portraying the poet as a Romantic creator, achieved instant success, but his next dramatic endeavor, the verse comedy *Achaques de la vejez* (1854; Ailments of Old Age), was a disappointment in comparison. From 1854 to 1856, Sanz served as secretary to the Spanish delegation in Berlin, and the following year, his translation of fifteen poems of Heine appeared in the journal *El Museo Universal*, producing a profound impact on the poet Gustavo Adolfo *Bécquer. Sanz also held the post of Spanish minister in Tangiers, but later rejected similar appointments in Brazil and Mexico. His poetry combines elements of the popular and the Germanic, and his best-known poem, "Espístola a Pedro" (Epistle to Peter) has been included among *Las cien mejores poesías (líricas) de la lengua castellana* (1908; The Hundred Best Poems in the Spanish Language) collected by Marcelino *Menéndez y Pelayo. Bitterly affected by the lack of recognition of his talents, Sanz spent his last years in poverty away from the political and literary world, consequently not fulfilling his early literary promise.

BIBLIOGRAPHY

Primary Texts

Achaques de la vejez. Madrid: F. Abienzo, 1854.
Don Francisco de Quevedo. Ed. R. S. Rose. Boston: Ginn, 1917.
"Epístola a Pedro." In *Las cien mejores poesías (líricas) de la lengua castellana*. By M. Menéndez y Pelayo. Madrid: Pueyo, 1908.

Criticism

Alborg, J. L. *Historia de la literatura española*. vol. 9. Madrid: Gredos, 1980.
Díez Taboada, J. M. "Eulogio Florentino Sanz, poeta de transición (1822–1881)." *Revista de Literatura* 13 (1958): 48–78.
Peers, E. A. *A History of the Romantic Movement in Spain*. vol. 2. Cambridge: Cambridge UP, 1940.
Shaw, D. L. *A Literary History of Spain: The Nineteenth Century*. London: Benn, 1972.

Phoebe Porter Medina

SARMIENTO, Martín (1695, Villafranca del Bierzo, León–1772, Madrid), writer. Martín Sarmiento is the Benedictine name for Pedro José García Balboa, an introverted man of science and letters who spent most of his life in his monk's cell in San Martin, Madrid. Sarmiento wrote on hundreds of different subjects from natural sciences to child rearing, from religious meditations to philological essays. Nevertheless, only one of his writings was published during his lifetime—the *Demonstración criticoapologética del Theatro crítico universal* (1732; Critical Apology on the Universal Critical Theater) in which he argues a strong defense of his colleague and friend *Feijoo. Posthumous publication of his works began in 1775 with *Memorias para la historia de la poesía y poetas españoles* (Memoirs for the History of Poetry and Spanish Poets). This volume was the only work published until the BRAE published some of his philological writings in the 1930s. The majority of his mss., as yet unpublished, remain scattered throughout Spain in archives and private collections.

BIBLIOGRAPHY

Primary Texts

Catálogo de voces y frases de la lengua gallega. Ed. J. L. Pensado. Salamanca: U of Salamanca, 1973.

Memorias para la historia de la poesía y poetas españoles. Buenos Aires: Emecé, 1942.

Sobre el origen de la lengua gallega. Vigo: n.p., 1974.

Viaje a Galicia. Ed. J. L. Pensado. Salamanca: U of Salamanca, 1975.

Criticism

Anon. *Guía bibliográfico para el estudio de Fray Martín Sarmiento*. In *Cuadernos de Estudios Gallegos* 27 (1972): 369–79.

Helman, Edith F. ''Viajes de españoles por la España del siglo XVIII.'' *NRFH* 7 (1953): 618–19.

Pensado, J. L. *Fr. Martín Sarmiento, Testigo de Su Siglo*. Salamanca: Universidad, 1972.

Volume 31 (1971–72) of the *Boletín de la Real Academia Española* is dedicated to Sarmiento studies.

Carmen Chaves McClendon

SARMIENTO DE GAMBOA, Pedro (1532, Alcalá de Henares–1592?, ?), navigator, soldier in the New World, author. At age eighteen he enlisted; in 1555 he left for Mexico, and for the next twenty-five years was a soldier in the New World. Sarmiento was involved in many campaigns and expeditions, and struggled valiantly to establish a colony in the Straits of Magellan. He was chastised twice by the *Inquisition for irreverancy and other violations. His autobiographical *Viajes* (n.d.; Journeys) is entertaining and informative, and his *Historia del reino de los incas* (1572; History of the Reign of the Inca) provides valuable, correct chronology not found elsewhere about the Inca defeat, and firsthand information on early traditions. Written under instructions from the viceroy of Peru to justify the Spanish conquest, the account is marred by the blatantly biased condemnation of the Inca Indians as usurpers, tyrants, etc. The *Historia* remained unpublished until 1906.

BIBLIOGRAPHY

Primary Texts

Historia de los incas. Buenos Aires: Emecé, 1942.

Viaje al estrecho de Magallanes por. . . . Prol. A. Braun Menéndez. 2 vols. Buenos Aires: Emecé, 1950.

English Translation

History of the Incas. Tr., ed. C. Markham. Nedeln, Lichtenstein: Kraus, 1967.

Criticism

Morales, E. *Aventuras y desventuras de un navegante, Sarmiento de Gamboa*. Buenos Aires: Futuro, 1946.

SARRÍA, Luis de. *See* Granada, Luis de

SASTRE, Alfonso (1926, Madrid–), playwright and dramatic theorist. Largely influenced by existentialism, Sastre has added to the philosophical outlook a measure of social criticism directed at tyrannical regimes, and in particular, at the government of Franco. In the theater of Sastre, the individual enmeshed in the bureaucratic structure of society emerges as the doomed hero, the relentless protagonist destined to be forever caught in a meaningless web of rules and regulations. To be sure, there is a Kafkaesque element in the expression of seemingly hopeless resolution. Yet, within the context of powerful, overwhelming chains which bind one to society, the audience (or the reader, as the case may be) experiences the inexorable presence of the rebellious individual as he or she strives to rise above the mass of anonymous humanity. The individual is likely to fail ultimately, but the struggle itself endures. It is precisely by means of the act of defiance that one succeeds in feeling alive in complete mastery of one's own soul. The individual who seeks to free himself or herself of the shackles of fear is nobly rewarded as he or she attains a consciousness of human destiny. Such a vision, a true revelation, is denied to the unsuspecting masses who exist in a vacuum, devoid of feeling or purpose.

The importance of Sastre in the Spanish theater of the post Civil War period cannot be overstated. His impact has been felt not only in his creative dramas, such as *Escuadra hacia la muerte* (written 1953; *The Condemned Squad*, 1961), *La mordaza* (written 1954; *The Gag*, n.d.), *Anna Kleiber* (written 1955; English tr. 1962), *En la red* (written 1959; *In the Web*, 1964) to mention but a few, but also, additionally, in his professional commitment to revolutionizing the Spanish stage. For example, he was a co-founder of Arte Nuevo (New Art), a refreshing alternative to the uninspiring theater of the first eight years of the 1940s (in 1949 *Buero Vallejo broke the ice, so to speak, with his explosive *Historia de una escalera* [Story of a Staircase]). In 1950, still dissatisfied, Sastre along with José María de *Quinto, founded a new group, Teatro de Agitación Social (The Theater of Social Agitation). If Hamlet wanted "to catch the conscience of the king," Sastre has dedicated himself to the proposition that the function of the theater is to disturb, not merely "to catch the conscience" of his audiences. In this venture he has been as active outside the stage as he has been in it. Not only did he provoke the government of Franco, but apparently also the government of the United States: although he has been invited by numerous American universities to be a visiting professor or artist in residence, he has been denied entry.

The first major theatrical production of Sastre, *Escuadra hacia la muerte*, took place in Madrid in 1953. The play is disturbing, indeed. It deals with a squad of soldiers destined to die in their impossible task to fend off the enemy. The squad is composed of soldiers who have committed, in the eyes of the army, unpardonable crimes. The corporal in charge of the squad is a sadistic leader who makes life unbearable. The soldiers decide to murder their corporal, but once the deed is done, the perpetrators experience an emptiness which is more destructive than the agony of living under a tyrant. ''There is no exit.'' All that is left is the memory of their collective crime. Senseless destruction is self-defeating. Before their crime, the soldiers were headed for death; now what awaits them is far worse, inextricable emptiness in a life devoid of purpose or direction. An act of defiance must be constructive in order to have meaning, and to accrue benefits to society. ''Agitation'' must be for the good of all. In this play the individuals surrendered their identity and became a mob, a headless monster of a sort. Is Goban, the corporal, a symbol of a despotic almighty? Possibly.

From 1953 on, Sastre became more famous and more controversial. His other plays and writings, including television productions, poems, fiction, and critical material on culture and literature, continued to feed the intellect and arouse passions. Sastre has not catered to popular taste; at the same time, until the death of Franco in 1975, the playwright had been continually in trouble with the *censorship office. For his social protests, he experienced incarceration. At times, his rebelliousness manifested itself in active forms, not merely in his writings, and because of his status with a repressive government, he was forced to have his plays produced in other countries, such as France, Italy, and Greece. Nonetheless, the writer's political difficulties have enhanced his creativity by affording him opportunities to come in contact with European masters of theatrical inventiveness—Ibsen, O'Casey, Sastre, and Strindberg among them. The cultural exile has made Sastre a virtual international playwright: plays of the aforementioned authors have been rendered as Sastre's adaptations. Thus, it can be said that while Sastre recognizes his own worth, he reveres the accomplishments of those who preceded him in time and in international renown. *See also* Contemporary Spanish Theater.

BIBLIOGRAPHY

Primary Texts

Plays

Ahora no es de leil. [Produced Madrid, 1979.] Madrid: Vox, 1980.
Cargamento de sueños, Prólogo patético, Asalto nocturno. Madrid: Taurus, 1964.
La cornada. [Produced Madrid, 1960.] Madrid: Escelicer, 1965.

Cuatro dramas de la revolución. Madrid: Bullón, 1963.
En la red. [Produced Madrid, 1961.] Madrid: Escelicer, 1961.
El escenario diabólico: El cuervo, Ejercicios de terror, Las cintas magnéticas. Barcelona: Saturno, 1973.
Escuadra hacia la muerte. La mordaza. Ed. F. Anderson. Madrid: Clásicos Castalia, 1975.
El hijo único de Guillermo Tell. In *Estreno* 9 (Spring 1983).
M.S.V.; o La sangre y la ceniza. With *Crónicas romanas*. Madrid: Cátedra, 1979.
Medea. [Produced 1958.] Madrid: Escelicer, 1963.
Obras completas. Madrid: Aguilar, 1967. Plays.
Oficio de tinieblas. [Produced Madrid, 1967.] Madrid: Alfil, 1967.
El pan de todos. [Produced Barcelona, 1957.] Madrid: Escelicer, 1960.
La sangre de Dios. [Produced Valencia, 1955.] Madrid: Escelicer, 1959.
La taberna fantástica. Ed. Mariano de Paco. Murcia: U of Murcia, 1983.
Teatro. Buenos Aires: Losada, 1960. Includes *Escuadra hacia la muerte*, *Tierra roja*, *Ana Kleiber*, *Muerte en el barrio*, *Guillermo Tell tiene los ojos tristes*, *El cuervo*.
Teatro político. Donostia: Hordago, 1979. Includes *Askatasuna!*, *El camarada oscuro*, *Análisis espectral de un Comando al servicio de la Revolución Proletaria*.
Teatro selecto. Madrid: Escelicer, 1966.
Teatro de vanguardia. Madrid: Perman, 1949. Includes *Uranio 235*, *Cargamento de sueños*, and with Medardo Fraile, *Ha sonado de muerte* and *Comedia sonámbula*.
Tragedia Fantástica de la gitana Celestina. [Produced Rome, 1979.] In *Primer Acto* 192 (Jan.-Feb. 1982).

Fiction

Flores rojas para Miguel Servet. Madrid: Rivadeneyra, 1967.
El lugar del crimen-Unheimlich. Barcelona: Argas Vergara, 1982.
Lumpen, marginación, y jerigonça. Madrid: Legasa, 1980.
Las noches lúgubres. Madrid: Horizonte, 1964.
El paralelo 38. Madrid: Alfaguara, 1965.

Verse

Balada de Carabanchel y otros poemas celulares. Paris: Ruedo Ibérico, 1976.
El español al alcance de todos. Madrid: Sensemaya Chororo, 1978.
TBO. Madrid: Zero Zyx, 1978.

Literary Criticism

Anatomía del realismo. Barcelona: Seix Barral, 1965; rev. ed., 1974.
Crítica de la imaginación. Madrid: Cátedra, 1978.
Drama y sociedad. Madrid: Taurus, 1956.
Escrito en Euskadi. Madrid: Revolución, 1982.
La revolución y la crítica de la cultura. Barcelona: Grijalbo, 1970.

English Translations

Anna Kleiber. In *The New Theatre of Europe*. Ed. R. W. Corrigan. New York: Dell, 1962.
The Condemned Squad. Tr. C. de Coster. In *Players Magazine* 38 (1961): 57–68.
Death Thrust. In *Masterpieces of the Modern Spanish Theatre*. Ed. R. W. Corrigan. New York: Collier, 1967.
In the Web. Tr. L. C. Pronko. San Francisco: Literary Discoveries, 1964.

Pathetic Prologue. In *Modern International Drama* (March 1968).
Sad Are the Eyes of William Tell. In *The New Wave Spanish Drama*. Ed. G. E. Wellwarth. New York: New York UP, 1970.

Criticism

Anderson, Farris. *Sastre*. TWAS 155. New York: Twayne, 1971.
Giuliano, W. *Buero Vallejo, Sastre y el teatro de su tiempo*. New York: Las Americas, 1971.
Holt, Marion. *The Contemporary Spanish Theatre (1949–1972)*. TWAS 336. Boston: Twayne, 1975.
Naald, Anje Cornelia van der. *Sastre, dramaturgo de la revolución*. New York: Las Americas, 1973.
Ruggeri Marchetti, Magda. *Il teatro di Alfonso Sastre*. Rome: Bulzoni, 1975.

Robert Kirsner

SAU SÁNCHEZ, Victoria (1930, Barcelona–), Spanish feminist essayist, psychologist, and lecturer. A practicing psychologist and professor of psychology at the U of Barcelona, Sau has been active in the feminist movement since 1975 both as a writer and speaker who characterizes herself as a follower of Simone de Beauvoir and of Betty Friedan. She has written stories for children (*El baúl viajero* [1973; The Traveling Trunk], *La duquesa resfriada, Leyenda rusa* [The Duchess with Flu. A Russian Legend], *El globo* [1973; The Balloon], *El secreto del emperador* [1973; The Emperor's Secret]) and domestic self-help manuals for women (*La decoración del hogar* [1967; Home Decoration], and *Aprende a cocinar sin errores* [1977; Learn to Cook without Mistakes]). Somewhat more erudite are a semi-sociological study, *Sectas cristianas* (1971; Christian Sects), a lengthy investigation of folk culture; *Historia antropológica de la canción* (1972; Anthropological History of Song) and *El catalán, un bandolerismo español* (1973; Catalan, a Spanish Form of Banditry). Of greater literary and cultural interest are her feminist essays, beginning with *Manifiesto para la liberación de la mujer* (1975; Manifesto for Women's Liberation), which examines contemporary feminine stereotypes including the old maid, the witch, the devouring woman, the frigid female and the seer, and treats such themes as marriage, virginity, adultery, incest and prostitution, as well as family life and the economic exploitation of women. *Mujer: matrimonio y esclavitud* (1976; Woman: Matrimony and Slavery) expands Sau's earlier, negative considerations of marriage with a historical survey, statistics on woman's role, and a severe critique of the absence of freedom for married women. The examination of archetypes initiated in Sau's *Manifesto* is continued in *La suegra* (1976; The Mother-in-Law)—anathema by definition—and *Mujeres lesbianas* (1979; Lesbian Women), a concise historico-political analysis. More recently, Sau published *Un diccionario ideológico feminista* (1981; An Ideological Feminist Dictionary), in which she strives to redefine from the feminist stance the basic terms of family and marital relationships, sexuality and sexual politics.

BIBLIOGRAPHY

Primary Texts

Un diccionario ideológico feminista. Barcelona: Icaria, 1981.
Manifiesto para la liberación de la mujer. Barcelona: Bruguera, 1975.
Mujer: matrimonio y esclavitud. Madrid: Júcar, 1976.
Mujeres lesbianas. Madrid: Zero-Zyx, 1979.
La suegra. Barcelona: Ediciones 29, 1976.

Janet Pérez

SAWA Y MARTÍNEZ, Alejandro (1862, Málga–1909, Madrid), novelist and journalist. When he arrived in Madrid in 1885, Sawa became associated with literary anarchism, attended various literary gatherings, and contributed to so-called regenerative literature. After having lived a bohemian life in Paris from 1889, he returned to Madrid in 1896 and brought with him the new French symbolist aesthetic. Even before his stay in Paris, he had discussed Verlaine, Walt Whitman, Baudelaire, Poe, and D'Annunzio with his friends, Rubén Darío, *Azorín, Pío *Baroja, *Maeztu, *Benavente, *Unamuno, *Valle-Inclán, and others. He died in 1909, blind and poor, abandoned by everyone, and supposedly crazy. Valle-Inclán immortalized him in the character Max Estrella in *Luces de Bohemia*.

Sawa's vast and deep knowledge of the most recent theories in sociology, psychiatry, psychopathology, and especially criminal anthropology, is obvious in his works. He was up-to-date on the latest scientific investigations in Italy and France, and he played a prominent role in the vanguard of the Spanish scientific literary movement. His novels are naturalistic and, therefore, analytical.

Four of Sawa's most important novels are cornerstones in the literary presentation of psychopathological disorders: the "born criminal" in *Crimen legal* (1886; Legal Crime), suicide resulting from historical determinism in *Declaración de un vencido* (1887; Deposition of the Doomed), degeneration from the pathological to the criminal in *Noche* (1888; Night), and prostitution in *La mujer de todo el mundo* (1885; Everybody's Woman).

The posthumous work *Iluminaciones en la sombra* (1910; Light in the Shadow), which has a prologue by Rubén Darío, is a collection of articles which Sawa had originally published in magazines.

BIBLIOGRAPHY

Primary Texts

Criadero de curas. Madrid: Biblioteca de "El Motín," 1888.
Crimen legal. Madrid: Biblioteca del Renacimiento Literario, 1886.
Declaración de un vencido. Madrid: Administracion, 1887.
Iluminaciones en la sombra. Madrid: Alhambra, 1977.
La mujer de todo el mundo. Madrid: Ricardo Fe, 1885.
Noche. Madrid: Biblioteca del Renacimiento Literario, 1885.
La sima de Igúzquiza. Madrid: Biblioteca de "El Motín," 1888.

Criticism

Cansinos-Asséns, Rafael. "Alejandro Sawa, el gran Bohemio." *Indice* 15 (1961): 22–23.

Darío, Rubén. "Alejandro Sawa." In *Iluminaciones en la sombra*. Madrid: Alhambra, 1977. 69–74.

Granjel, Luis S. "Maestros y amigos del '98: Alejandro Sawa." *CH* 195 (1966): 430–44.

López Bago, Eduardo. "Apéndice: Análisis de la novela *Crimen legal*." In cited edition of *Crimen legal*. 251–80.

Paolini, Gilbert. "Tipos psicopáticos en *Declaración de un vencido* de Alejandro Sawa." *Crítica Hispánica* 1 (1979): 87–92.

Phillips, Allen W. *Alejandro Sawa. Mito y Realidad.* Madrid: Turner, 1976.

Zavala, Iris. "Estudio preliminar." In *Iluminaciones en la sombra*. Madrid: Alhambra, 1977. 3–66.

Gilbert Paolini

SBARBI Y OSUNA, José María (1834, Cádiz–1910, Madrid), priest, musicologist, literary critic. His articles, published in leading periodicals, enjoyed an enthusiastic following. He personally edited one magazine, the *Averiguador Universal* (1879–82; Universal Inquirer). He also compiled a *Diccionario de música* (n.d., Music Dictionary), other musical studies, various critical considerations of *Cervantes and the *Quijote*, and a *Refranero general español* (1847–78; General Spanish Proverb Book), a valuable source for folklorists.

BIBLIOGRAPHY

Primary Texts

Ambigú literario. Madrid: Fuentenebro, 1897.

El Averiguador Universal. Ed. J. M. Sbarbi y Osuna. 2 vols. Madrid: García, 1948.

Gran diccionario de refranes. Ed. M. J. García. Buenos Aires: Gil, 1943.

Prontuario de definiciones musicales. Badajoz: Santa María, 1861.

SEDANO, Dora (1902, Madrid–), Spanish playwright. The author of approximately fifteen plays, many composed in collaboration, Sedano also wrote some fiction and poetry, but is known primarily as the conservative author of domestic comedies and political melodramas, mostly produced during the 1940s and 1950s. Exemplifying the latter is *La diosa de arena* (1952; The Sand Goddess), in which a girl brainwashed by evil Reds is redeemed thanks to her marriage to a devout Catholic. Typical of Sedano's domestic comedies is *Nuestras chachas* (1953; Our Maids), a burlesque, farcical treatment of the servant problem. *Mercaderes de sangre* (1945; Blood Merchants) is an ideologically reactionary and melodramatic novel set in Paris during the Spanish Civil War: Franco sympathizers are uniformly good, while the Loyalists (Republicans) are deemed communists and traitors. Perhaps Sedano's chief merit is as a chronicler of the spirit of an ideology—Falangist conservatism—and an epoch, the immediate post-war Franco years. *See also* Contemporary Spanish Theater.

BIBLIOGRAPHY

Primary Texts

La diosa de arena. With Luis Fernández de Sevilla. Madrid: Artes Gráficas, 1952.
Mercaderes de sangre. Madrid: Afrodisio Aguado, 1945.
Nuestras chachas. With Luis Tejedor. Madrid: Arba, 1953.

Janet Pérez

SEGOVIA, Antonio María (1808, Madrid–1874, Madrid), journalist and satirical writer. Due to his conservative ideology, he went to Paris into exile in 1840. He became a member of the *Academia Española (1845), its secretary (1873), and secretary of the Fine Arts Academy as well. Segovia also directed the newspapers *El Estudiante*, *El Cócora*, *El Progreso*, and contributed to *La Abeja* and *Semanario Pintoresco Español*, and was a bullfight correspondent for *El Correo Nacional*. In cooperation with Santos López Pelegrín he started the magazine *Nosotros* (1838–39; We) and collected and published Mariano José de *Larra's *Artículos satíricos y festivos* (1840; Satirical and Humorous Articles). Segovia possessed classical tastes, and he wrote about *Romanticism in a satirical way. His own style was so measured and correct that it bordered on affectation. He composed a critical work titled *Del drama lírico y de la lengua castellana como elemento musical* (n.d.; On Lyrical Drama and on Castilian Language as a Musical Element); as a playwright he left *Trapisondos por bondad* (1842; Deceptions Due to Kindness) and others; he translated and adapted several French plays; and his *Composiciones . . . en prosa y en verso* (Verse and Prose Works) appeared in 1839.

BIBLIOGRAPHY

Primary Texts

Abenámar y El Estudiante. Colección de artículos satíricos y festivos. Palma: n.p., 1840.
Colección de composiciones serias y festivas . . . por 'El Estudiante.' Madrid: Repullés, 1839.
Manual del viajero español, de Madrid a París y Londres. Madrid: Gabriel Gil, 1851.
Trapisondas por bondad. Madrid: Suárez, 1842.

Criticism

González-Molleda, María Luisa. "Antonio María Segovia." *Revista de Literatura* 24 (1963): 101–24.

Salvador Garciá Castañeda

SEGUIDILLA, a type of poetry. These light, festive verses are arranged in four-line stanzas with *abab* rhyme. Sometimes only even lines rhyme. Lines alternate six- to seven-syllable length with five-syllable length. The form is derived from folk lyrics. Sixteenth- and seventeenth-c. practitioners include *Timoneda, *Horozco, and Lope de *Vega. Around the seventeenth c., the form changed to seven-line stanzas with the following rhyme scheme: free/*a*/free/*a*/*b*/free/*b*.

BIBLIOGRAPHY

Primary Text

Clarke, D. C. "The Early *seguidilla*." *HR* 12 (1944): 211–32.

SEGURA, Juan de (?–?), prose author. Under this name, in 1548, was published the first epistolary novel in any modern language. Titled *Proceso de cartas de amores (Process of Love Letters*, 1950), it narrates an ill-fated love affair with its many attendant emotions. Two other works have been attributed to Segura: *Libro de institución cristiana* (Book of Christian Instruction) and *Confesionario* (Confession); E. B. Place has disputed the attribution.

BIBLIOGRAPHY

Primary Text

Proceso de cartas de amores. Ed., tr. E. B. Place. Evanston: Northwestern UP, 1950. Spanish critical ed., English translation, and study.

English Translation
See above.

SELGAS Y CARRASCO, José (1822, Murcia–1882, Madrid), poet and novelist. Orphan of a modest postal employee, he spent his youth in obscure poverty. He studied in the Council Seminary, but had to break off his studies in order to support his family. He served in the conservative party and was a member of the *Academia Española.

Best known as a poet who imitated the German *lied*, he had a decisive influence on *Bécquer, according to Gómez de las Cortinas. The themes of his verse include the beauties of nature, flowers, innocence and religious sentiments. His poetry is characterized by a vague idealism, gentle melancholy and its minor key. He collected his poetry in volumes titled *La primavera* (1850; Spring), *El estío* (1853; Summer) and *Flores y espinas* (1884; Flowers and Thorns). He is less important as a novelist. His better known novels include *La manzana de oro* (1872; The Golden Apple) and *La mariposa blanca* (1887; *The White Butterfly*, 1898). He also wrote *cuadros de costumbres* (scenes of local color), biographical sketches and satirical essays in which he ridicules liberal attitudes of the day. His complete works were published posthumously.

BIBLIOGRAPHY

Primary Texts

Obras. 13 vols. Madrid: Pérez Dubrull, 1882–94.

English Translation

The White Butterfly. Tr. Mary J. Serrano. In *Stories by Foreign Authors*. New York: n.p., 1898.

Criticism

Gómez de las Cortinas, J. Frutos. "La formación literaria de Bécquer." *Revista Bibliográfica y Documental* 4 (1950): 77–99.

Phoebe Porter Medina

SELLÉS, Eugenio (1844, Granada–1926, Madrid), Spanish journalist, dramatist and poet. A titled nobleman (Marquis of Gerona), he was involved in politics in the period of Sagasta, writing at times under the pseudonyms E. Ugen and O'Sesell. *La política de capa y espada* (1876; Cape and Sword Politics) is a collection of articles and essays; *Narraciones* (1893; Narratives), a group of short stories. An able versifier, Sellés was best known for his dramatic works, especially *El nudo gordiano* (1878; The Gordian Knot), influenced by José *Echegaray. Of realistic cut, with some social and political preoccupations, it treats marital problems with a moralizing bent, much as in other works of this author: *Las vengadoras* (1884; The Avenging Women); *La mujer de Loth* (1896; Lot's Wife); *Icara* (1910); and *El cielo y el suelo* (1890; Sky and Soil). Other plays are of a historical nature, such as *La torre de Talavera* (1877; The Tower of Talavera), which re-creates the figure of the medieval king don Enrique de Trastamara, and *El celoso de su imagen* (1893; The Man Who Was Jealous of His Image), evoking Spain's War of Independence (i.e., the repulsion of the Napoleonic invasion). He was elected to the *Academia Española, reading a subsequently published discourse entitled *El Periodismo* (1895; Newspaper Journalism).

SEMPERE Y GUARINOS, Juan (1754, Elda, Alicante–1830, Elda), Spanish theologian, historian, and literary critic. A theologian and lawyer by training, he served in a number of political positions at a high level, including legal advocate of the Royal Council and subsequent naming by King José (Bonaparte; whom Napoleon attempted to place on the Spanish throne) as president of the Spanish Supreme Tribunal, resulting in his exile after the end of the Napoleonic wars. A highly cultured man who contributed to the history of legal institutions in Spain, he published numerous works on legal themes, some of them in French, for example, *Histoire des Cortes d'Espagne* (1815; History of the Courts in Spain). He is remembered in the literary field for his *Ensayo de una Biblioteca española de los mejores escritores del reinado de Carlos III* (1785–89, in six volumes; Essay on a Spanish Library of the Best Writers of the Reign of Charles III), the fundamental reference work for the history of Spanish literature during the period studied. His translation of Muratori, *Reflexiones sobre el buen gusto* (1782; Reflections upon Good Taste), was prefaced by an essay which formed the germ of his later six-volume history.

SEMPRÚN, Jorge (1923, Barcelona?–), Spanish novelist, essayist, memorialist. Semprún belongs chronologically to the Mid-Century Generation of writers who experienced the war as children, most of whom began writing in the late 1940s or early 1950s (*Matute, Juan *Goytisolo). The son of a Catholic jurist who was "ferociously Republican" (and continued defending the Republican cause in a series of articles 1954–66), Semprún went into exile in 1939 at the end of the war, and suffered Nazi persecution in France. He began writing somewhat later than others of his generation, and in French (his exile continued because of his clandestine affiliation with the Communist party in Spain—then the only organized opposition to Franco). Several works first published in French were rewritten or reworked by Semprún for Spanish publication, so that rather than translations, they are alternative versions. His first novel, *El gran viaje* (The Great Voyage) appeared in 1963 in French, and received the Formentor Prize but was not published in Spain until 1976. Five other novels in French appeared before Semprún's first in Spain, after the death of Franco.

La segunda muerte de Ramón Mercader (1976; The Second Death of Ramón Mercader) had appeared in French in 1969. It treats the final days of persecution of the Soviet agent Mercader (born in Spain), the assassin of Trotsky, and the death of Mercader. Semprún employs discontinuity and breaks with normal spatio-temporal laws, presenting Mercader, Jacques Mornard and Ievgueni Davidovitch, three different personifications of Trotsky's assassin, together with a number of symbolic characters, the family of Mercader and other families whose only involvement is their crossing Mercader's path, as well as members of the intelligence or security services of East Germany, Holland, and the CIA.

Semprún won the Planeta Prize with his *Autobiografía de Federico Sánchez* (1977; Autobiography of Federico Sánchez), which is a testimonial memoir, belonging to recent history and dealing with living persons, the account of Semprún's clandestine political involvement—Federico Sánchez was the name he used for his revolutionary activities when he was charged with infiltrating university and intellectual ambients in Spain during nearly a decade. In 1964, he was expelled from the Central Committee, the Political Bureau, and the PCE, or Spanish Communist party (after an inflammatory denunciation by "Pasionaria") because of his differences with the Spanish party head, Santiago Carrillo). *El desvanecimiento* (1979; The Faint) had also appeared earlier in French (1969), but is closer to fiction—despite an autobiographical substratum, doses of espionage, intrigue, persecution, conspiracy, terrorism, resistance and assassination, presented against a background of war, and a protagonist who is a Spanish exile of many aliases, a possible mask or alter ego of Semprún, but whose experiences in the narrative do not apparently coincide with those of the author.

Semprún has become an influential and prolific writer in post-war Spain, serving as minister of culture for the socialist regime of Felipe González. He continues to be especially interested in the relationship between personal experience and literature, reworking his works published earlier in French, and basing more recent fiction on his clandestine experiences.

BIBLIOGRAPHY

Primary Texts

La deuxième mort de Ramón Mercader. Paris: Gallimard, 1969.
L'évanouissement. Paris: Gallimard, 1969.
Le Grand Voyage. Paris: Gallimard, 1963.
La guerre est finie. Paris: Gallimard, 1966.

Le "Stavisky" d'Alain Resnais. Paris: Gallimard, 1974.
"Una noche de junio, no la de San Juan." *Marche* (Paris) 2 (Dec. 1966–Jan. 1967): 54–80.

English Translation

Communism in Spain in the Franco Era. The Autobiography of Federico Sanchez. Tr. Helen R. Lane. Brighton, Sussex: Harvester, 1980.

Criticism

Ortega, José. "Intriga, estructura y compromiso en *La segunda muerte de Ramón Mercader* de Jorge Semprún." *CH* 310 (April 1976): 1–16.
———. "Jorge Semprún: *Autobiografía de Federico Sánchez*." *CH* 340 (Oct. 1978): 192–98.
Valis, Noël. "Reader Exile and the Text: Jorge Semprún's *Autobiografía de Federico Sánchez*." *Monographic Review/Revista Monográfica* 2 (1986): 174–88.
Vargas Llosa, Mario. "La *Autobiografía de Federico Sánchez*." *Contra viento y marea (1962–1982)*. Barcelona: Seix Barral, 1983. 276–79.

Janet Pérez

SENA, Jorge de (1919, Lisbon–1978, Santa Barbara, California), poet, short fiction writer, novelist, playwright, critic, essayist, scholar. Jorge de Sena was a humanist, a critical observer of the human condition, and above all, a poet. Throughout his life—and in this he saw no contradiction—it had been his experience that, along with living fully immersed in the present, he could cultivate the wisdom and learning of the past. This drive led him to become pre-eminent as a scholar, cultural historian and university professor. Without becoming confessional or yet psychological, he found he could also come closer to understanding mankind by penetrating into the deepest recesses of his own being, and so became Portugal's leading contemporary man of letters: poet, playwright and fiction writer. These two avenues to human understanding—from without and within—were made all the more efficacious in him by virtue of his diverse formal training: scientific, military and literary. He received a licenciatura in civil engineering from the U of Porto in 1944, and for fifteen years exercised his profession, building roads and bridges for the National Highway Commission. He spent five years in the military: first as a cadet in the naval academy, then four years in the army. He received a Ph.D. and Livre Docencia (Brazil's highest degree) in literature from the U of São Paulo in 1964. This preparation in both the sciences and humanities made him an unconventional essayist, and he brought to Portuguese literary criticism a precision and exactness rarely seen before. In fact, his methods brought about a major re-evaluation of both the lyric and the epic poetry of Luís de *Camões.

Sena's personal experience with the world was likewise uncommonly broad. He lived on three continents and traveled extensively. He left Portugal and his engineering career in 1959 to accept a teaching position in literary theory at the U of São Paulo, Araraquara. He then accepted a professorship in Portuguese at the U of Wisconsin, Madison, in 1965, and again at the U of California, Santa

Barbara, in 1970, where from 1975 to his untimely death from cancer at the age of fifty-eight on June 4, 1978, he was concurrently chairman of the Department of Spanish and Portuguese and of the Comparative Literature Program.

Jorge de Sena's scholarly and creative production is incredibly vast and varied and includes such genres as biography, criticism, essay, literary history, short fiction, theater, the novel and poetry. He was one of the leading Camões and *Pessoa scholars and published several studies on each. His dedication to cultural history can be seen in the exhaustive study he made on Inês de Castro (See *Inés de Castro, Leyenda de*), which appears in two volumes. At home as well in Spanish literature, he brought to his Iberian studies a breadth and balance rarely seen in either Spain or Portugal, as in his study of Francisco de la *Torre, for example. Sena is the author of the standard text on English literature in Portuguese, and his output in comparative literature includes book-length essays on authors ranging from Emily Dickinson and Shakespeare to Petrarch and Mauriac. In addition to translating more than twenty volumes by major French, British and American prose writers (including Malraux, Waugh, Greene, Poe, Caldwell, Hemingway, O'Neill and Faulkner), he wrote a one-volume work on the Greek poet Constantine Cavafy, which includes ninety-four translations. In three other published volumes, he has collected and translated the major poetry of the world over the last twenty-six centuries.

Sena's own creative prose comprised four volumes of short fiction, including the classic *O Físico Prodigioso* (1977; The Prodigious Physicist), and the posthumously published novel, *Sinais de Fogo*. Sena also published seven plays, one of which, *O Indesejado* (1949; The Undesirable), is considered his masterpiece. In addition, he also was for years a music, theater and film critic, publishing his reviews in the leading periodicals of Portugal and Brazil. However, he considered himself first and foremost a poet, and during his lifetime published over a dozen volumes.

He was the recipient of numerous awards and prizes in various countries, including Italy's prestigious Etna-Taormina International Poetry Prize in 1977.

Jorge de Sena was regarded by many as not only the number one living poet of Portugal, but ranked with Camões and Pessoa. Like theirs and Eliot's, Sena's poetry is in the mainstream of Western civilization, with each passage rich in allusions to our shared cultural heritage. Yet Sena is a poet not merely of thought and culture, but also of feeling and conscience—he was especially outspoken against the repressive government of Salazar—and of love, with an incredible variety of meter and verse, rhyme and form, from the classical sonnet sequence to concretism. His first published poem appeared on March 13, 1939, in *Movimento*, a student periodical of the U of Lisbon. He became an editor of *Cadernos de Poesia*, a literary journal of great prestige in which some of the brightest members of Portugal's third Modernist generation published their work. With Sena, they sought to continue the most avant-garde tendencies of the poets in the first Modernist generation (Fernando Pessoa, *Sá-Carneiro, *Almada Negreiros), which in many ways meant reaching back over the work of many of the poets connected with *Presença*, who had become too predisposed toward poetry which only followed a prescribed philosophical, political or artistic bent. The logo for *Cadernos de Poesia* was "a poesia é só uma" or, in other words, the standard for measuring poetry should be its intrinsic quality, not the author's affiliations or predilections.

Sena began to cultivate his interest in literature early in life and on his own studied the most avant-garde European poets, particularly the surrealists. Although surrealism's official beginning in Portugal would not come until after the war (1947), Sena's early works bear the marks of its influence and although he never joined forces with the Portuguese surrealists, he is regarded as one of the movement's precursors.

Included among his major themes are culture, with myriad references to art (one of his volumes of poetry deals almost exclusively with paintings and painters, another exclusively with music), music, literature, and history of ancient and modern civilizations, Portugal, political and social satire, human dignity, love, sex, death, God and religion.

Jorge de Sena also played a major role in advancing Portuguese studies in the academic world of both Brazil and the United States. In Brazil, through his assiduous collaboration in newspapers and journals, he brought Portuguese literature to the attention of his readers and left an indelible mark in the field of literary criticism. The same impact was felt in the United States, where he brought not only Portuguese but Brazilian literature to the attention of his colleagues. Sena was also the mentor of an entire generation of American intellectuals and educators, young and old. Wherever he traveled, whenever he presented papers, wherever he taught, contributed articles or published books, he was firmly establishing the foundation for serious Luso-Brazilian studies in this nation as never before. Under his guidance, scores of Ph.D.'s were graduated who today head up Portuguese studies in numerous universities. As a tribute to the man and what he stood for, the U of California, Santa Barbara, and the U of São Paulo, Araraquara, have established Portuguese Studies Centers which bear his name.

BIBLIOGRAPHY

Primary Texts

Antigas e Novas Andaças do Demónio. Lisbon: Edições 70, 1978; 3rd ed., 1982. Short stories.

Uma Canção de Camões. Lisbon: Portugália, 1966; 2nd ed., 1984.

Dialécticas Aplicadas da Literatura. Lisbon: Edições 70, 1978.

Fernando Pessoa & Companhia Heterónima. Estudos Coligidos, 1940–1978. 2 vols. Lisbon: Edições 70, 1982.

O Físico Prodigioso. Lisbon: Edições 70, 1977; 3rd ed., 1983. Novelette.

O Indesejado, António Rei. Porto: Portucale, 1951; 2nd ed., 1974. Theater.

Poesia de 26 Séculos I, II, III. Porto: Inova, 1972–78. Translations.

Sinais de Fogo. Lisbon: Edições 70, 1979; 2nd ed., 1980. Novel.

English Translations

In Crete, with the Minotaur, and Other Poems. Bilingual ed., tr. and pref. George Monteiro. Providence: Gávea-Brown, 1980.

Over This Shore . . . Eight Meditations on the Coast of the Pacific. Tr. Jonathan Griffin. Santa Barbara: Inklings, 1979.

The Poetry of Jorge de Sena, a Bilingual Selection. Ed., intro., notes, Frederick G. Williams. Santa Barbara: Mudborn, 1980.

Criticism

Carlos, Luís Fernando Adriano. ''Jorge de Sena e a escrita dos limites, análise das estruturas paragramáticas nos *Quatro Sonetos a Afrodite Anadiómena*.'' Thesis, U of Porto, 1986.

Lisboa, Eugénio, comp. and intro. *Estudos sobre Jorge de Sena*. Lisbon: Imprensa Nacional–Casa da Moeda, 1984.

Morna, Fátima Freitas, critical presentation, sel., notes. *Poesia de Jorge de Sena*. Lisbon: Comunicação, 1985.

Picchio, Luciana Stegagno, ed. *Jorge de Sena*. Pisa: Giardini, 1985.

Sharrer, Harvey L., and Frederick G. Williams, eds. *Studies on Jorge de Sena by His Colleagues and Friends*. Santa Barbara: Jorge de Sena Center for Portuguese Studies, University of California, Santa Barbara, in association with Bandanna Books, 1981.

O Tempo e o Modo, no. 59. Lisbon: Moraes, 1968.

Torres, Alexandre Pinheiro. *O Código científico-cosmogónico-metafísico de Perseguição, 1942, de Jorge de Sena*. Lisbon: Moraes, 1980.

Frederick G. Williams

SENDER, Ramón (1902, Chalamera de Cinca, Huesca–1982, San Diego, California), novelist and journalist. Both a victim and a survivor of the Spanish Civil War, he was the most prolific and enduring writer of his generation: over forty novels, eight collections of short stories, essays, numerous newspaper articles, and theatrical pieces. After serving in the Moroccan campaign (1924), which provided the basis for his first novel, *Imán* (1930; *Earmarked for Hell*, 1934; *Pro Patria*, 1935), Sender joined the liberal newspaper *El Sol* (The Sun) in Madrid (1924–29). In the thirties, as a free-lance journalist associated with such papers as *Solidaridad Obrera* (Worker Solidarity) and *Libertad* (Freedom), he published *Seven Red Sundays* (1932), an innovative novel that chronicles the anarcho-syndicalist movement and its repression in Madrid. With the onslaught of the Civil War, he returned to military service in the Republican forces, rising to the rank of major. In 1939 he toured the United States with other government representatives seeking support for the Republican cause. Emigrating to the United States from Mexico in 1942 as a Guggenheim Fellow, he lectured at several colleges and universities. His professorship of Spanish at the U of New Mexico (1947–63) marks a period of enormous output, including such novels as *The Sphere* (1947), *The King and the Queen* (1949), *Requiem for a Spanish Peasant* (1953; also known as *Mosén Millán*), and several parts of the lengthy *Chronicle of Dawn*. He concluded his teaching career at the U of Southern

California (1965–71). Only in the last years of his life did Sender return to Spain, where many of his works were being published for the first time; he was well received.

Sender's work, much of which is autobiographical, has often been regarded as uneven, due to its extensiveness and variety. A more unified picture has emerged only from recent criticism. Francisco Carrasquer considers *Imán* to be the key to all of Sender's novels since it contains many, if not all, of the qualities attributed to his later writings: realism (objective and often crude), lyricism, symbolism, fantasy, and changing points of view in the narrative. The synthesis of these correspond to the neo-realist and magical-realist mode. Gil Casado has considered Sender's early work, especially *Seven Red Sundays*, to be perhaps the most representative of the literary current of the thirties known as the "New Romanticism" (a term taken from José *Díaz Fernández's essay *El nuevo romanticismo*, 1930) and coinciding with the appearance of a truly social novel in Spain. Another key to Sender (according to King, Peñuelas, and Eoff) is his metaphysical novel, *The Sphere*, where he seeks to reconcile life's contradictions through a monistic concept of ultimate reality. Despite his prolificness, Sender will be remembered foremost among the chroniclers, within Spain and without, of the Civil War. Most notable are two works. The very brief *Requiem for a Spanish Peasant* relates the guilt of Mosén Millán, a parish priest who is partially responsible for the murder of a villager by the fascists. The *Chronicle of Dawn* narrates the life of José Garcés, an officer in the Republican army, from his boyhood in Aragon until his death in a French concentration camp during the last days of the war.

BIBLIOGRAPHY

Note: Indispensable for any student of Sender is Charles L. King's excellent *Ramón Sender: An Annotated Bibliography, 1928–1974*. The works listed in Primary Texts are limited to those published since 1975.

Primary Texts

Adela y yo. Barcelona: Destino, 1978.
El alarido de Yaurí. Barcelona: Destino, 1977.
Arlene y la gaya ciencia. Barcelona: Destino, 1976.
La efemérides. Madrid: Sedmay, 1976.
El fugitivo. Barcelona: Destino, 1976.
El futuro comenzó ayer: lecturas mosaicas. Madrid: CVS, 1975.
La mirada inmóvil. Barcelona: Argos-Vergara, 1979.
El Mechudo y la Llorona. Barcelona: Destino, 1977.
El pez de oro. Barcelona: Destino, 1977.
Solanar y lucernario aragonés. Zaragoza: Heraldo de Aragón, 1978.
El superviviente. Barcelona: Destino, 1978.

English Translations

The Affable Hangman. Tr. Florence Hall. New York: Las Americas, 1960.
Before Noon. Tr. Willard R. Trask and Florence Hall. Albuquerque: U of New Mexico P, 1958. (Includes *Chronicle of Dawn*.)

Chronicle of Dawn. See *Before Noon*.
Counter-Attack in Spain. Boston: Houghton Mifflin, 1937. Also as *The War in Spain*. Tr. Peter Chalmers Mitchell. London: Faber and Faber, 1937.
Dark Wedding. Tr. Eleanor Clark. Garden City, NY: Doubleday, Doran, 1943; London: Grey Walls Press, 1948.
Earmarked for Hell. Tr. James Cleugh. London: Wishart, 1934. Also as *Pro Patria*. Boston: Houghton Mifflin, 1935.
The King and the Queen. Tr. Mary Low. New York: Vanguard Press, 1948; New York: Grosset and Dunlap, 1968.
A Man's Place. Tr. Oliver La Farge. New York: Duell, Sloan, and Pearce, 1940.
Mr. Witt among the Rebels. Tr. Peter Chalmers Mitchell. London: Faber and Faber, 1937; Boston: Houghton Mifflin, 1938.
Requiem for a Spanish Peasant. Tr. Elinor Randall. New York: Las Americas, 1960.
Seven Red Sundays. Tr. Peter Chalmers Mitchell. London: Faber and Faber, 1936; New York: Collier Books, 1968.
The Sphere. Tr. Felix Giovanelli. New York: Hellman, Williams, 1949.
Tales of Cibola. Tr. Florence Sender, Elinor Randall, Morse Manley, et al. New York: Las Americas, 1964.

Criticism

Bosch, Rafael. *La novela española del siglo XX*. vol. 2. New York: Las Americas, 1970–71.
Carrasquer, Francisco. *''Imán'' y la novela histórica de Sender*. London: Tamesis, 1970.
Eoff, Sherman H. *The Modern Spanish Novel*. New York: New York UP, 1961.
Gil Casado, Pablo. *La novela social española*. 2nd ed. Barcelona: Seix Barral, 1973.
King, Charles L. *Ramón J. Sender*. TWAS 307. New York: Twayne, 1974.
———. *Ramón J. Sender: An Annotated Bibliography, 1928–1974*. Metuchen, NJ: Scarecrow Press, 1976.
Norte (Amsterdam) 14. 2–4 (1973). Special issue devoted to Sender.
Peñuelas, Marcelino C. *Conversaciones con Ramón J. Sender*. Madrid: Magisterio Español, 1970.
———. *La obra narrativa de Ramón J. Sender*. Madrid: Gredos, 1971.
Rivas, Josefa. *El escritor y su senda (Estudio crítico-literario sobre Ramón J. Sender*. Mexico: Mexicanos Unidos, 1967.

Porter Conerly

SENECA, Lucius Annaeus (c. 4 B.C., Córdoba–A.D. 65, Rome), philosopher, politician, dramatist. Born to a rich, well-educated family, he was schooled in Rome, and rose to become a senator, and later tutor and adviser to Nero. He committed suicide upon Nero's command. Seneca's writings are an eclectic blend of many philosophical schools, but the Stoic and Cynic influences predominate. He advocates lofty ethical and moral standards, the supreme goal being attainment of virtue; his thought thus blends well with Christian ideals. Stylistic characteristics of his writing include a laconic, epigrammatic balance in expression, the use of paradox, antithesis, and *sententia*. His extant writings number nine tragedies, a scientific treatise—*Naturales quaestiones* (c. 62–65; *Natural Questions*,

1971), a series of dialogues on ethical topics such as Providence, the Brevity of Life, etc., and a collection of moral letters to Lucilius. *See also* Senequism.

BIBLIOGRAPHY

Primary Texts

Annaei Senecae. . . . Ed. L. D. Reynolds. 2 vols. Oxford: Clarendon, 1965.

English Translations

Seneca: Moral Epistles. Sel., ed., intro., A. L. Motto. Chico, CA: Scholars P, 1985.
Seneca, Natural Questions. Ed. T. H. Corcoran. Loeb Classical Library Series. 2 vols. Cambridge: Harvard UP, 1971.

Criticism

Bluher, K. A. *Seneca in Spanien*. . . . Munich: Francke, 1970.
González Haba, J. ''Séneca en la espiritualidad española de los siglos XVI y XVII.'' *Revista de Filosofía* 11 (1952): 287–302.
Rothe, A. *Quevedo und Seneca*. Geneva: Droz, 1965.

SENEQUISM, the philosophical and moral school of thought of Lucius Annaeus *Seneca. Similar to Stoicism, in Senequism the true end of philosophy was ethics—the attainment of virtue, justice, and ''the good.'' Man's task is self-regulation, control of *all* emotions, rejection of the physical side, and the development of reason. Other characteristics of Senequism include the rejection of vengeance, the defense of freedom for all, the obligation to help one's fellow man, the importance of friendship, and the importance of dying well. Seneca's writings formed the center of Renaissance neo-Stoicism throughout Europe; his mark on Spanish letters is particularly deep, in prose, poetry and drama. It is seen in the Marqués de *Santillana, Alonso de *Cartagena, Enrique de *Villena, *Pérez de Guzmán, Fray Luis de *Granada, and the entire body of *Ascetical literature, through the rejection of earthly possessions. Others influenced by Senequism are *Cervantes, especially in *La Numancia*, *Saavedra Fajardo, and *Quevedo.

BIBLIOGRAPHY

Criticism

González de la Calle, P. *Quevedo y los dos Sénecas*. Mexico: Colegio de México, 1965.
Griffin, M. T. *Seneca: A Philosopher in Politics*. Oxford: Clarendon, 1976.

SEPÚLVEDA, Juan Ginés de (1490?, Pozoblanco, Córdoba–1573, Pozoblanco), historian, classicist, and theologian. After receiving his education first in the humanities in Córdoba and later in philosophy in Alcalá de Henares, Sepúlveda traveled in 1517 to Bologna, where he continued his studies at the famed Colegio del Cardenal Albornoz. In Bologna he wrote Spanish translations and commentary to works of Aristotle, and the *Liber gestorum Aegidii Albornotii* (1521; The Life of Cardinal Albornoz), both of which drew praise from contemporary men of letters. He later moved to Naples, where he edited a version of the Old Testament. Upon his return to Spain, his fame spread; and in 1535 he accepted an appointment as chaplain and historian in the court of Charles V.

It is for Sepúlveda's famous polemic with Fray Bartolomé de las *Casas that he is chiefly remembered today. When Las Casas charged in his *Destruyción de las Indias* (Destruction of the Indies) that Indians were being inhumanely treated and even exterminated by their Spanish masters, Sepúlveda responded with an unauthorized ms., *Democrates alter* or *Democrates secundus; sive de justi belli causis* (The Other [or Second]; Democrates; or On the Causes of the Just War). Sepúlveda argued that war against the Indians was essential to their conversion to Christianity because they were barbarous infidels, themselves guilty of oppression and heinous deeds. Charles V was so disturbed by the controversy that in 1550 he demanded the temporary cessation of all New World conquests and summoned a Royal Council of theologians to Valladolid to debate Las Casas's allegations and Sepúlveda's rebuttal. Although Sepúlveda was absolved of charges of heresy, the case was essentially a victory for Las Casas. Shortly thereafter Sepúlveda withdrew to his native region and eventually to his hometown, where he spent the remainder of his days.

Throughout his life Sepúlveda defended the values of classical languages and literatures, a commitment he claimed to have begun in his childhood. He extolled the virtues of the Hellenic tradition and of Aristotle in particular. A remarkably prolific writer, he left many works in Latin and a substantial collection of eloquent letters. The ambivalent attitude toward him shared by many humanists of his day is exemplified by the fact that although Erasmus enthusiastically praised Sepúlveda's erudition, he had far less admiration for the ideas Sepúlveda expressed. Characteristic of Sepúlveda's thoroughness as a historian are his thirty-volume *De rebus gestis Caroli V* (1556; On the Military Achievements of Charles V) and *De rebus gestis Philippi II* (1564; On the Military Achievements of Philip II), two of his most exhaustive studies. *See also* Black Legend.

BIBLIOGRAPHY

Primary Texts

Apología [de Juan Ginés de Sepúlveda contra Fray Bartolomé de las Casas y de Fray Bartolomé de las Casas contra Juan de Sepúlveda]. Tr. from orig. Latin to Spanish and ed. Angel Losada. Madrid: Nacional, 1975.

Demócrates segundo o de las justas causas de la guerra contra los indios. Ed. Angel Losada. Madrid: CSIC, 1951.

Epistolario de Juan Ginés de Sepúlveda. Ed. Angel Losada. 2nd ed. Madrid: Cultura Hispánica, 1979.

Tratado sobre las justas causas de la guerra contra los indios. Orig. Latin text and Spanish version. Ed. Manuel García-Pelayo. Mexico City: Fondo de Cultura Económica, 1941.

Tratados políticos de Juan Ginés de Sepúlveda. Tr. to Spanish and ed. Angel Losada. Madrid: Instituto de Estudios Políticos, 1963.

Criticism

Beneyto, Juan. *Ginés de Sepúlveda, humanista y soldado*. Madrid: Nacional, 1947.

Casas, Bartolomé de las. *In Defense of the Indians*. Tr. and ed. Stafford Poole. DeKalb: Northern Illinois UP, 1974.

Hanke, Lewis. *All Mankind Is One: A Study of the Disputation between Bartolomé de las Casas and Juan Ginés de Sepúlveda in 1550 on the Intellectual and Religious Capacity of the American Indians*. DeKalb: Northern Illinois UP, 1974.

Losada, Angel. *Juan Ginés de Sepúlveda a través de su "Epistolario" y nuevos documentos*. 2nd ed. Madrid: CSIC, 1973.

———. *Juan Ginés de Sepúlveda: Estudios y su crónica indiana en el IV centenario de su muerte*. Valladolid: Seminario Americanista de la Universidad de Valladolid, 1976.

C. Maurice Cherry

SÉRGIO DE SOUSA, António (1883, Damão–1969, Lisbon), Portuguese philosopher, historian and educator, born in Damão (India), the son of the governor of this former Portuguese colony. He was a naval officer until October 5, 1910, when he resigned following the formation of the Republic and so for the next ten years he worked for an American publishing house. In 1912 he founded *A Renascença Portuguesa* (The Portuguese Renaissance) together with Jaime *Cortesão, Raul *Proença, Teixeira de *Pascoaes and others. The aim of this organization was to inject new life into a flagging Portuguese culture. Having been inspired by the climate generated by the activities of this organization he tried, unsuccessfully, to set up a "popular" university in Lisbon.

In 1914 he enrolled at the U of Geneva to study educational science. On returning to Portugal he began to criticize Republican policy, and strongly opposed the demagoguery of certain popular leaders and the lack of any basic policies of reform in education and the economy.

In 1918 he founded and directed a socio-political review entitled *Pela Grei* (For the Nation). After a period spent in Brazil he became, in 1922, assistant librarian at the National Library in Lisbon, a position which he held for five years. In 1923 he became a leading editor of *Seara Nova* (New Harvest), a review which played an important role in the political, cultural and social life of the Portuguese people. He contributed his own articles on such varied subjects as politics, pedagogy, literature, religion, philosophy and history. At the end of that year, the Seara Nova group was invited to join Alvaro de Castro's government of reform. António Sérgio was minister of education for two months, during which time he founded the Instituto de Oncologia (The Institute of Oncology) for the treatment of cancer, and the Junta de Orientação de Estudos (The Advisory Board of Studies) whose aim was to restructure the Portuguese education system. Unfortunately, Parliament did not make the necessary funds available and the attempt was abandoned.

The União Intelectual Portuguesa (The Portuguese Intellectual Union), of which António Sérgio was the leader, was founded by him in February 1924, and two years later he also founded and headed the Portuguese delegation of the Liga Propulsora da Instrução Pública (Movement for the Promotion of Public Education). Following the military coup of this same year, which established a dictatorship in Portugal, he was one of those who spoke out against the censorship which had been imposed on the media.

As delegate for Seara Nova, in January 1927, he lodged protests at embassies of some member countries of the League of Nations against the loan the government had requested from this organization. He fled under persecution to Paris, where he remained until the end of 1932. While in Paris he founded together with other exiles the Liga de Defesa da República (The League for the Defense of the Republic), which aimed to unite all those opposed to the dictatorship. In 1928 he went as spokesman to the headquarters of the League of Nations in Geneva in an extremely successful attempt to expose the fact that the loan which the Portuguese government had requested was not destined for social ends, but to satisfy growing military expenditure. Also while in Paris he wrote many articles for various periodicals on the nature of the Portuguese regime, worked for several publishing companies and was script director at Paramount Studios. He was still intensely active in the Pacifist movement, having been elected vice-president of Acção Internacional Democrática para a Paz (The International Democratic Action for Peace Movement) in 1930.

Three years later, he became reader in Portuguese at the U of Santiago de Compostela in Spain. Then, taking advantage of a general pardon bestowed by the Portuguese government shortly before the declaration of the 1933 Constitution, he returned to Portugal and continued to speak openly against the military regime. From this period date those texts in which he spoke out strongly against an interview given by Salazar for the newspaper *Diário de Notícias* (Daily News).

In 1935, he was detained without charge for eight months and expelled from Portugal. After a period of exile in Madrid, he returned to Portugal, where he continued to work for the *Enciclopédia Luso-Brasileira* (Luso-Brazilian Encyclopaedia) and to write articles of social criticism in *Seara Nova*, a review he would abandon in 1939 due to disagreements over its control.

With the promise of the fall of Nazism, the belief held in Portugal was that Salazar's regime would also crumble. In 1944, António Sérgio drafted the political program he believed should be adopted. Two years later, he protested Portugal's admission to the United Nations and campaigned widely against the despotism of the dictatorship.

From 1945 to 1959 he was extremely active in his denunciation of the regime during all the pre-electoral periods. He was one of the founder members of the Movimento de Unidade Democrática (1945; The Movement for Democratic Unity) and supported the opposing presidential campaigns of Norton de Matos (1949), Quintão de Meireles (1951) and Humberto Delgago (1958). Indeed, from 1953 onwards he was president of the Comissão Promotora do Voto, a committee formed to encourage people to register and vote.

António Sérgio was imprisoned twice more, in 1949 and in 1957, for publicly opposing Salazar's policies. He stopped writing and ceased his active involvement in politics after 1959, due to severe illness.

António Sérgio wrote essays on philosophy, history, literature, religion, pedagogy and politics. He defended the rationalist approach to philosophy, and his idealistic beliefs were given wide exposure in his polemics with the dialectic materialists and the followers of Bergson. He also believed that the principal causes of historical events should be sought in the economy of the country concerned, although the economy was only the point of departure for the historian. Other facts had then, of course, to be taken into consideration. It was this belief that led him to state, "My writing possesses none of the historical materialism of Karl Marx."

He was always fiercely active in politics, although he never belonged to any political party. For António Sérgio, politics should not be merely the struggle for power, but have as its main objective the education of the people. He vehemently opposed the First Republic's abuse of human rights, and during that period was unceasing in his criticism of the persecution of Catholics, political nepotism, the lack of a basic economic reform program and the emphasis of party interests over those of the nation.

Severely critical also of the ensuing military dictatorship which came to power in 1926, he protested strongly against the censorship which hindered both intellectual expression and the mass media. Indeed, six of his own books were considered subversive and banned as a result.

After a careful analysis of the policies upheld by the regime, he defended the alternative economic principle of cooperativism.

Much of his time was also devoted to literary criticism. He recognized the need for an intimate relationship between literature and society and strongly condemned the literati, and the sterile academism and biography which abounded in Portuguese literature. Worthy of note are his essays on Eça de Queirós, *Camões, Guerra Junquerio and António Vieira.

In his writings on pedagogy he was one of the promoters of the theories of Celestin Freinet and Maria Montessori in Portugal. In his book *Educação Cívica* (Civic Education) he endorsed the need to develop a critical spirit in the pupil and the ideal of the school as a self-governing institution. He nevertheless defended the importance of the school as an integral part of society and stressed the value of a democratic administration in the school involving the pupils, a concept which would encourage them to become responsible and socially aware as adults. He was therefore radically against a purely theoretical textbook approach to education. For António Sérgio the objective of education was to encourage creativity and emancipation in the pupil.

António Sérgio categorically defended his own points of view with regard to the Portuguese cultural movement. This led him into conflict with many intellectuals who led opposing ideas. Hence his controversial polemics with Bento de Jesus Caraça, Carlos Malheiro Dias, Abel Salazar, António José Saraiva and many others.

BIBLIOGRAPHY

Primary Texts

Cartas do Terceiro Homem [Letters from the Third Man]. 3 vols. Lisbon: Livraria Sá da Costa, 1974.

Democracia [Democracy]. Lisbon: Livraria Sá da Costa, 1974.

Educação Cívica [Civic Education]. Lisbon: Livraria Sá da Costa, 1984.
Ensaios [Essays]. 8 vols. Lisbon: Livraria Sá da Costa, 1971–80.
História de Portugal [A Sketch of the History of Portugal]. Lisbon: Seara Nova, 1928.

Criticism

''António Sérgio.'' *Revista de História das Ideias* 5 (1983). [2 vols.]
Carvalho, Montezuma de. *António Sérgio, a Obra e o Homem*. Lisbon: Arcádia, 1979.
Homenagem a António Sérgio. Lisbon: Academia das Ciências de Lisboa, 1976.
Sá, Victor de. *A Historiografia Sociológica de António Sérgio*. Lisbon: Instituto de Cultura Portuguesa, 1979.
Vilhena, Vitorino Magalhães. *António Sérgio o Idealismo Crítico e a Crise da Ideologia Burguesa*. Lisbon: Cosmos, 1975.

Daniel Pires

SERRA, Narciso (1830, Madrid–1877, Madrid), playwright. Narciso Sánz-Díez y Serra served as a cavalry officer (1845) and later as a civil servant and theatrical censor. In the last part of his life he suffered from paralysis. For many years he was the favorite of a public who enjoyed such plays as *La calle de la Montera* (1859; Montera Street), *¡Don Tomás!* (1858), *La boda de Quevedo* (1854; Quevedo's Wedding), *El loco de la guardilla* (2nd ed. 1861; The Crazy Man in the Garret—a play about *Cervantes), the dramas *El reloj de San Plácido* (1858; The Clock of San Placido), and *Con el diablo a cuchilladas* (1854; At Sword Point with the Devil), and many others. Some of his plays are comedies that criticize customs of contemporary society in the tradition of *Bretón de los Herreros; others belong to the Romantic school. Today out of favor, these works are emotional, with interesting plots and fluid verse. Serra also wrote comic one-act plays like *El último mono* (1864; Low Man on the Totem Pole) and *Nadie se muere hasta que Dios no quiere* (1860; You Die When Your Time Comes); poetry (*Poesías líricas* [1848; Lyric Poetry]); and short stories (*Leyendas, cuentos y poesías* [1877; Legends, Tales and Poems]).

BIBLIOGRAPHY

Primary Texts

La boda de Quevedo. Madrid: Rodríguez, 1854.
El loco de la guardilla. 3rd ed.? Madrid: Velasco, 1903.
Nadie se muere hasta que Dios no quiere. Madrid: Rodríguez, 1870.
Poesías líricas. Madrid: Lorente, 1848.
El último mono. Madrid: Rodríguez, 1864.

Criticism

Alonso Cortés, N. ''Narciso Serra.'' In *Revista del Ayuntamiento de Madrid* (1930): n.p.

Salvador García Castañeda

SERRAHIMA, Núria (1937, Barcelona–), novelist. After dropping out of convent school at fourteen, she studied painting intensively for five years, but later opted for literature. Her first novel, *Mala guilla* (1973; Bad Fox), a finalist for the Josep Pla Prize, was written when only a handful of women were writing in Catalan. Paralleling some events in her life (the fourteen-year-old protagonist decides to quit school), the novel portrays those formative influences which combine to repress and limit female students and abort artistic or literary interests. The title refers to the protagonist's label as ''bad'' because of innocent mischief, youthful vitality and spontaneity. *L'olor dels nostres cossos* (1982; The Odor of Our Bodies) is comprised of three novellas united by common feminist themes, the use of first-person narrative point of view and a female protagonist. In the title story, the narrator reflects, as she lies sleepless next to a snoring husband, on conjugal life. Her economic dependence rules out separation, and her love for her children causes her to reject suicide. ''Negres moments d'Emma'' (Emma's Dark Moments) is similarly disheartening, telling of the retreat into neurotic passivity of a constantly frustrated protagonist. The tone of the third story, ''Amants'' (Lovers), is completely different; it is the erotic fun-loving, lighthearted list of the protagonist's many lovers, one for each letter of the alphabet.

BIBLIOGRAPHY

Primary Texts

Mala guilla. Barcelona: Edicions 62, 1973.
L'olor dels nostres cossos. Barcelona: Edicions 62, 1982.

Kathleen McNerney

SERRAHIMA I BOFILL, Maurici (1902, Barcelona–1979, Barcelona), Catalan novelist, essayist, short story writer, critic. Serrahima studied law, and from 1926 onward, he practiced law, a traditional profession in his family. He was interested in politics from his youth, becoming involved in pro-democratic movements in Catalonia at the advent of the Second Republic. As a signer of the manifesto of the Catalan Democratic Union, he was exiled following the Civil War (subsequently, with the post-Franco transition to democracy, he was named a senator by King Juan Carlos). He was a co-founder of the daily *El Matí*, in which he was also a collaborator; and he published literary criticism and other articles in a variety of periodicals, some collected in volume form as *Assaigs sobre novel.la* (1934; Essays on the Novel), which appeared the same year as his first novel, *El principi de Felip Lafont* (The Beginning of Phillip Lafont). The short story collection *El seductor devot* (1937; The Devout Seducer) was amplified and published in successive editions with variant titles: *Petit món enfebrat* (1947; Small, Feverish World), *Contes d'aquest temps* (1955; Tales of Those Times). Among his other novels are *Després* (1951; Loose), *Estimat senyor fiscal* (1954; Dear Tax Collector), and *De Mitja nit ençà (1939–1966)* (1970; From Midnight Onward). His numerous essays include *Democracia i sufragi* (1962; Democracy and Suffrage), *El fet de creure* (1967; The Fact of Believing), *La crisi de la ficció* (1965; The Crisis of Fiction), *Sobre llegir i escriure* (1966, On Reading and Writing [Winner of the Josep Yxart Prize, 1965]), *Realitat de Catalunya* (1969; Catalan Reality), *Marcel Proust* (1971), *Dotze mestres* (1972; Twelve Masters), *Josep Maria Capdevila* (1975), and

Coneixences (1976). He is also the author of two major biographies of Joan *Maragall (1938 and 1966), and an important series of memoirs, *Del passat quan era present, Volumen I, 1940–1947* (1972; Of the Past When It Was Present), *Volumen II (1948–53)* (1974). *La frontissa* (1982; The Axis) was written in 1956, but published posthumously. The action takes place in 1930–31, culminating with the proclamation of the Republic, which suffices to explain why it was not published during the Franco regime. It is typical of Serrahima's novels in analyzing the upper bourgeoisie of Barcelona, shown here in a moment of conflict and self-doubt when their privileges and the entire social structure have been challenged. Essentially a psychological novel, *La frontissa* offers a careful dissection of the characters and their reactions. *See also* Catalan Literature.

SERRANA, a literary term. A *serrana* may refer either to a shepherdess or to a *pastoral poem, that is, a **serranilla*.

SERRANILLA, literary term. It is a short, lyrical *pastoral poem which usually narrates an encounter between a country girl and a traveler. Often they are fresh, suggestive, even lascivious. Juan del *Encina and the *Arcipreste de Hita are only two of many medieval practitioners of the *serranilla*; they were also written by *Siglo de Oro poets. *See also Pastorela*; Santillana, Iñigo López de Mendoza.

SERRANO PLAJA, Arturo (1909, San Lorenzo de El Escorial–1979, Santa Barbara, California), Spanish poet, critic and novelist. A member of the so-called *Generation of 1936 (emerging writers scattered by the war), he published *Destierro infinito* (1936; Infinite Exile), written shortly before the Civil War, in a collection directed by Manuel *Altolaguirre; the title was to prove prophetic. During the war, in the line of conflict-inspired social poetry then frequent, he published *El hombre y el trabajo* in the collection Hora de España, largely a group of propagandistic texts in favor of the Republican war effort; this particular book was praised by Antonio *Machado. The war also inspired Serrano's subsequent *Versos de guerra y paz* (1944; Verses of War and Peace). Among his novels are *Del cielo y del escombro* (1942; Of Heaven and the Trash Heap), and *Don Manuel del León* (1946). Serrano was for many years a professor of Spanish at the U of California (Santa Barbara), and in that capacity published his critical study *Realismo 'mágico' en Cervantes* (1966; ''Magic'' Realism in Cervantes). Other works include *Phokas el Americano* (1947; Phokas the American), *Galope de la suerte* (1959; The Gallop of Luck), and a final book of poems, *La mano de Dios pasa por este perro* (1965; God's Hand Passes Over This Dog).

BIBLIOGRAPHY

Primary Texts

Poetry

Los álamos oscuros. Barcelona: Plaza y Janés, 1982.
Chant a la liberté. Algiers: Charlot, 1943.

Destierro infinito. Madrid: Héroe, 1936.
Golpe de la suerte. Buenos Aires: Losada, 1958.
El hombre y el trabajo. Barcelona: Hora de España, 1938. Facs. rpt., Madrid: Ediciones de la Torre, 1978.
Les mains fertiles. Paris: not found, 1948.
Sombra indecisa. Madrid: Hoja Literaria, 1934.
Versos de guerra y paz. Buenos Aires: Nova, 1945.
Prose
El arte comprometido y el compromiso del arte y otros ensayos. Barcelona: Delos-Ayma, 1967.
Avila Camacho. Buenos Aires: Américalee, 1942.
La cacatúa atmosférica. Mexico: Mortiz, 1977.
El Creco. Buenos Aires: Poseidón, 1943.
Defensa de la Cultura. Madrid: S. Aguirre, 1936. Facs. rpt., Madrid: Ediciones de la Torre, 1981.
¿Es la religión el opio del pueblo? Madrid: José Porrúa Turanzas, 1978.
El libro de El Escorial. Buenos Aires: Poseidón, 1944.
El realismo español. Ensayo sobre la manera de ser de los españoles. Buenos Aires: Patronato Hispano Argentino de Cultura, 1944.

Criticism

Caudet, Francisco. "Arturo Serrano Plaja: Apostillas a algunos de sus ensayos." *Homenaje a Arturo Serrano Plaja*. Ed. J.L.L. Aranguren and A. Sánchez-Barbudo. Madrid: Taurus, 1984.
Fuentes, Víctor. "Serrano Plaja y el compromiso del escritor en la España de la República." In *Homenaje a Arturo Serrano Plaja*, cited above. 99–105.
Gallo, Marta. "*La cacatúa atmosférica*: novela de un poeta." In *Homenaje a Arturo Serrano Plaja*, cited above. 200–209.
Sánchez-Barbudo, Antonio. "Serrano Plaja en mi recuerdo y en sus poesías." In *Homenaje a Arturo Serrano Plaja*, cited above. 11–46.

SERRANO PONCELA, Segundo (1912, Madrid–), critic and novelist. In 1939 Serrano Poncela emigrated to America where he has taught Spanish literature in the Universities of Santo Domingo, Puerto Rico, and Venezuela (Caracas), while publishing critical essays and narrative works. Notable books of essays include *El pensamiento de Unamuno* (1953; Unamuno's Thought), *Antonio Machado, su vida y su obra* (1954; Antonio Machado, His Life and Work), *El secreto de Melibea* (1959; The Secret of Melibea), and *Formas de vida hispánica* (1963; Forms of Hispanic Life). Greatly influenced in his intellectual vision by *Unamuno and *Machado, and a self-declared cultivator of the historical essay in the mold of Américo *Castro, Serrano Poncela has from the distance of exile in America sought to reinterpret many phenomena in Spanish history. His ideological evolution, writes Marra-López, "from radical and active political positions, in the Civil War epoch, to more meditated and mature positions, transcending partisanship, is exemplary" (420).

The author's first book of narratives, *Seis relatos y uno más* (1954; Six Stories and One More), written in an intellectualized mode (reminiscent of the dehumanized literature of the twenties and early thirties in Spain), may reflect Borgian influences. It was followed by other books of short narratives: *La venda* (1956; The Bandage), *La raya oscura* (1959; The Obscure Line), *La puesta de Capricornio* (1960; The Setting of Capricorn), *Un olor a crisantemo* (1961; A Smell of Chrysanthemums), and *El hombre de la cruz verde* (1969; The Man with the Green Cross).

In Serrano Poncela's only long novel, *Habitación para hombre solo* (1963; Room for a Single Man), the police oblige the protagonist, an illegal Spanish immigrant, to flee to Mexico. The author's total narrative output is characterized by density and depth in both content and style, by an overriding concern for human values, superb use of language, and a preference for a first-person narrative point of view. Reflecting many of the same themes as his essays, much of his narrative work deals with the Spain of the author's childhood and youth.

BIBLIOGRAPHY

Primary Texts

Antonio Machado, su vida y su obra. Buenos Aires: Losada, 1954.

Habitación para hombre solo. Barcelona: Seix Barral, 1963.

El hombre de la cruz verde. Principiado de Andorra/Barcelona: Andorra, 1969.

La raya oscura. Buenos Aires: Sudamericana, 1959.

El secreto de Melibea y otros ensayos. Madrid: Taurus, 1959.

Criticism

Collard, Patrick. ''El ambiente histórico y la mirada del narrador en 'El hombre de la cruz verde' de Segundo Serrano Poncela.'' *Papeles de son Armadans* 29 (October 1975): 29–49.

De Nora, Eugenio G. *La novela española contemporánea (1939–1967)*. 2nd ed. Madrid: Gredos, 1970. 237, 39.

Domingo, José. *La novela española del siglo XX*. Barcelona: Labor, 1973. 2: 83–85.

Gimferrer, Pedro. ''En torno a la obra narrativa de Serrano Poncela.'' *Insula* 226 (Sept. 1965): 7.

Marra-López, J. R. *Narrativa española fuera de España, 1939–1961*. Madrid: Guadarrama, 1963. 413–41.

Charles King

SERVET, Miguel (1511, Villanova de Sirena, Lérida–1553, Geneva, Switzerland), physician, religious writer, heretic. Of noble birth to a pious family, he studied in Spain and abroad. As secretary to the confessor of Charles V, he accompanied the royal entourage to Italy and Germany. When the confessor died, Servet abandoned the court and settled in Germany. In 1531 he published *Trinitatis erroribus (Errors of the Trinity*, 1932), which rejected the doctrine of the Trinity, as did the subsequent publication *Dialogorum de Trinitati* (1532; *Dialogues on the Trinity,* 1932). The resulting furor forced him to move to France and change his name to Miguel de Villanueva (his birthplace). During the 1530s Servet resumed medical studies and also taught astrology. These years are further marked by his discovery of the pulmonary circulation of blood in man. Servet continued to shock and infuriate contemporaries, and underwent several confrontations with the *Inquisition. He also published sundry non-religious works during this period.

Servet's most mature work, *Christianismi Restitutio* (Restitution of Christianity), was published in 1553. It contains five books on the Trinity, two dialogues, and thirty letters he had written to Calvin. The discussions cover many other topics, and it is here that the written evidence of Servet's discovery of pulmonary circulation is found. The work contained sufficient damaging material to allow John Calvin—an enemy for years—to denounce Servet, secure his trial, and have him condemned and burned at the stake as a heretic on October 27, 1553.

BIBLIOGRAPHY

Primary Texts

Restitución de Cristianismo. Tr. A. Alcalá. N.p.: Fundación Universitaria Española, 1980.

Treinta cartas a Calvino. Tr. A. Alcalá. Madrid: Castalia, 1981.

English Translations

The Two Treatises of Servetus on the Trinity. . . . Tr. and intro. E. M. Wilbur. Cambridge: Harvard UP, 1932. Rpt. New York: Kraus, 1969.

Criticism

Bainton, R. H. *Hunted Heretic: The Life and Death of Michael Servetus*. Boston: Beacon, 1953.

Maureen Ihrie

SEVILLIAN SCHOOL. *See* Escuela Sevillana

SHEM TOV ARDUTIEL. *See* Tob, Sem

SIGEA DE VELASCO, Luisa (c. 1530?, Tarancón, Toledo–1560?, ?), humanist, scholar, writer. She was in the service of doña María de Portugal in Lisbon, and her intellectual agility and expertise in classical and Hebrew literatures made her a key figure in intellectual life at court. She wrote poetry, dialogues, and letters, in Spanish and in Latin. Most famous is her bucolic description of the town of Cintra, Portugal, replete with mythological references. In *Duarum virginum colloquium* . . . (Colloquy of Two Girls . . .), she compares at length the advantages and disadvantages of court life as compared to a rural existence. In the eighteenth c., Carolina *Coronado wrote a historical novel titled *La Sigea* which treats the difficulties faced by women in cultured society. *See also* Humanism.

BIBLIOGRAPHY

Primary Texts

Duarum virginum colloquium. . . . In BAE 270. 419–71.

Sintra descriptio poetica. In BAE 270. 403–4. Spanish tr.

Criticism

Galerstein, C., and K. McNerney. *Women Writers of Spain*. Westport, CT: Greenwood, 1986.

SIGLO DE ORO (Golden Age). The term is the most frequently used designation of the period in the sixteenth and seventeenth centuries when Spain achieved political dominance in Europe and experienced a notable flowering of arts and letters. Various problems are implicit in the term, primarily the dates of the opening and closing of the period, which range at the most inclusive from 1474, the date of the accession to power of the Catholic monarchs, to 1700, the date of the death of the last Habsburg monarch. Others (e.g., R. Trevor Davies) have chosen 1501–1621 or (e.g., Ernest Mérimée) 1517, the date of Charles V's accession to power, to 1681, the date of the death of *Calderón. Particularly when the phrase is applied to a space of two centuries it causes uneasiness and is thus sometimes replaced by *siglos de oro* (centuries of gold) or *edad de oro* (age of gold). Yet *siglo* as here used preserves its most usual Latin meaning, that is, the designation not of precisely one hundred years but of an indeterminate period of time, extending over one or more generations, marked by specific historical characteristics (Pelorson).

Although sixteenth- and seventeenth-c. Spaniards occasionally applied the term to their own age, the generalized use of the expression arose in the eighteenth c. in commentaries by historians and philologists (e.g., Antonio *Capmany and *Mayáns) as they looked back on a time more fortunate than their own when arms and letters flourished triumphantly together. It has been remarked that no such label is applied to especially glorious periods of achievement in other modern European nations. Perhaps the sense of decline from a previous "Golden Age" has not been so keenly felt elsewhere; certainly there is a conscious modeling in Spain on Greece and Rome, for the term *Siglo de Oro* is used frequently to characterize Periclean Athens and Augustan Rome.

The initial and terminal dates here selected for the Siglo de Oro are 1492 (the *annus mirabilis* of Spanish history, which saw the final victory over Spanish Islam, the achievement of apparent religious unification through the expulsion of the Jews, and Castilian expansion overseas with Columbus's first voyage of discovery) and 1681, the date of the death of Calderón. If Calderón, born in 1600 and the last of the brilliant galaxy of writers of the seventeenth c., had not enjoyed so long and continuously productive a career, the terminal date might well be 1658, the year of the death of Baltasar *Gracián. Certainly by 1659 Spanish political hegemony over Europe was wholly lost with the signing of the Peace of the Pyrenees between Spain and France.

The epoch divides into two distinct periods, the first usually classified as *Renaissance and the second as Baroque in modes of expression, though both styles are ultimately developments from classical models. Once again it is difficult to assign precise dates. If, with good reason, the Renaissance spirit is assumed to have been dissipated by the imposition of Counter-Reform orthodoxy at the end of the Council of Trent in 1563, then what is to be made of Luis de *León (d. 1591), the highest exemplar of Renaissance thought and artistic accomplishment, whose major work, *Los nombres de Cristo* (The Names of Christ), was first published in 1583? It is somewhat more satisfactory to divide the Siglo into two major segments, the first beginning in 1492 and ending in 1598 with the death of Philip II, and the second extending over the years from 1598 to 1681.

1492–1598

This is the era of Spain's maximum expansion, prosperity and power. The most significant events include Columbus's discovery of 1492, followed by the conquest of Mexico (1521) and Peru (1532) and control of American treasure; the accession to the throne of Charles I in 1517, bringing with it Spanish dominion in the Low Countries and Austria; Charles's election (as Charles V) as Holy Roman Emperor in 1519, which until his death in 1558 kept Spain in a commanding position throughout Europe and exposed her people to contacts with artists and intellectuals from the whole of Europe; the naval victory at Lepanto in 1571 over the Ottoman Empire; and Philip II's inheritance in 1580 of the throne of Portugal together with its overseas possessions. For a time everything seemed possible to the Spaniard; the world could be remade, better and brighter, under Spanish guidance. As early as 1492 Antonio de *Nebrija in the prologue of his *Gramática castellana* (Castilian Grammar), dedicated to Queen Isabel, speaks of the "unity, peace, and power" which Spain then enjoyed and predicts that Castilian will be the language of her future empire. A half century later the messianic (as well as *translatio imperii*) overtones are inescapable in a famous sonnet by Hernando de *Acuña, directed to Charles V, which announces the coming of a new glorious age in which the world will be ruled by "one monarch, one Empire, and one sword."

Intellectual life and literary expression in these years show a vigor and originality which made Spanish the second language of cultivated society in France and Italy and caused Spanish literature to be translated and read all over Europe. Fernando de *Rojas's **Celestina* (titled the *Comedia de Calisto y Melibea* on its first publication in 1499) is the first of these celebrated works. Antonio de *Guevara's *Reloj de príncipes* (1529; Dial of Princes, 1559) and *Epístolas familiares* (1539, 1541; Familiar Epistles) enjoyed wide popularity.

The poems of *Garcilaso de la Vega (pub. 1543) for the first time comfortably shaped Castilian verse in Italian meters and showed a typically Renaissance preoccupation with elegance of expression and beauty of form. Later master poets of the sixteenth c. are Fernando de *Herrera (1534–97), author of unsurpassed Petrarchan love lyrics as well as patriotic odes; Luis de León, translator of Horatian odes and biblical psalms and author of perfectly controlled, seemingly effortless lyrics singing the beauty, concert and harmony of Nature; and San *Juan de la Cruz, the incomparable lyricist of *mysticism. Among writers who cultivated the form of the classical epic the most successful is Alonso de *Ercilla, whose *Araucana* (1569, 1578, 1589) treats with dignity and nobility the wars between Spaniards and Araucans in Chile.

Prose fiction, in both its idealistic and satiric modes, is significantly developed in the sixteenth c.: the chivalric romance (*caballerías), beginning with the publication of **Amadís de Gaula* (1508); the *pastoral romance, initiated by *Montemayor's *Diana* (1559?); and the *picaresque novel, beginning with **Lazarillo de Tormes* (1554).

In the Middle Ages, if the available evidence is to be believed, the *theater had little prominence, but beginning with Juan del *Encina (1468?–1529?) this period saw an explosion of writing for the theater, culminating in the creation of a truly Spanish national drama with the work of Lope de *Vega (though most of his major plays were written in the next century). This theater, like that of Shakespeare, notably ignores the classical precepts of neo-Aristotelian critics and preserves what might be called a medieval freedom with regard to unities, the mingling of the comic and the pathetic, and the treatment of religious subject matter. Here, as in the continued popularity of folk songs and poetry, the Spanish Renaissance does not close itself off from the Middle Ages.

In many respects the period, particularly until the 1550s, is distinguished by its devotion to humanistic endeavors—the activity which gives the Renaissance its name—that is, the study of classical and biblical texts in their original languages, purified of the errors of medieval commentators and editors, as well as the development of an elegant Latin *or* vernacular style. The most original thinker among Spanish humanists is Joan Lluís *Vives, who spent most of his life outside of Spain. Antonio de Nebrija (1444–1522), though trained in Bologna and much influenced by Lorenzo Valla, returned to Spain and fought effectively to reform the ''barbaric'' Latin of his compatriots. His *Gramática castellana* is the first such analysis of a modern European language.

The ideals of Christian humanism lie behind Cardinal Francisco Jiménez de *Cisneros's foundation of Spain's Renaissance university at Alcalá de Henares (1508), designed to train an enlightened priesthood through study of the Bible directly in its original languages rather than indirectly through medieval commentaries. For this reason too he fostered at Alcalá the preparation and publication of the famed *Biblia Poliglota* (Polyglot Bible or *Bible of Alcalá), one of whose editors for a time was Nebrija.

These endeavors by Cisneros, together with reforms in the lax discipline of the old monastic orders and the creation of the new religious order of the Jesuits (1540), testify to the spiritual ferment and movement toward religious renovation which Spain shared with much of Europe, stimulated especially in Spain by the recent incorporation into the church of numerous converts from Judaism. Illuminist teachings (*Alumbrados) spread until condemned by the *Inquisition in 1525, and Erasmus's preaching of an interiorized Christianity, the *philosophia Christi*, was enthusiastically accepted by many humanists and intellectuals (*Erasmism). It is among this group especially that the dialogue or colloquy (whether based on Ciceronian, Platonic, Lucianesque, or Erasmian models) became the favorite literary form, flexible, persuasive, without open didacticism, and thus preferred over the scholastic medieval tract or sermon. Some of the best prose of the century is found in such dialogues as Alfonso de *Valdés's *Diálogo de las cosas ocurridas en Roma* (1530; Dialogue of the Events in Rome) and *Diálogo de Mercurio y Carón* (1530; Dialogue between Mercury and Charon), which attack the corruption of the church and laud the emperor; his brother Juan de *Valdés's *Diálogo de la lengua* (written 1535–36; Dialogue on the [Castilian] Language); and Luis de Léon's *Nombres de Cristo* (1583, 1585; The Names of Christ), which in elegance of expression and profundity of thought represents the culmination of the Spanish Renaissance—Christian humanism, scriptural commentary, Neoplatonic reverence for nature, beauty, order, peace, and an underlying plea for spiritual and political renovation. Although in 1559 the publication of Fernando de Valdés's Index (*Indice) of prohibited books and Inquisition prosecution of various heterodox thinkers, followed in 1564 by the Tridentine definition of Catholic orthodoxy, silenced in the final years of the century open religious debate in the Erasmian vein, the primacy of religious concerns remains evident in the explosion of Spanish orthodox mysticism, most notably in the work of Santa *Teresa de Jesús and San Juan de la Cruz.

Spanish art and architecture achieved new splendor with the work of such architects as Enrique de Egas (master of the plateresque style) and Juan de Herrera (creator of the Escorial), the sculpture of Alonso de Berruguete, and the painting of El Greco. Stimulated in good measure by the practical needs of Spanish mariners, Spain's accomplishments in science, especially cartography, astronomy, nautical inventions and mathematics (e.g., the writings on mathematics of Sánchez Ciruelo or the formulation by Martín Cortés of the concept of the magnetic pole) were as distinguished as those elsewhere in Europe.

The richness of Spanish experience at home and overseas demanded and received striking historical treatment (e.g., Diego *Hurtado de Mendoza's *Guerra de Granada* [War of Granada] or Bernal *Díaz del Castillo's *Verdadera historia . . . de la conquista de Nueva España* [True History . . . of the Conquest of New Spain]), just as the problems of imperial government led Spanish jurists to the formulation of original doctrines of politics and international relations (e.g., Francisco de *Vitoria's celebrated treatises *De indis* and *De iure bello* [1539], which set forth the doctrine of just war and laid the basis for the modern code of international law).

1598–1681

Although Spanish power and primacy in Europe continued through the 1630s, the events of the late sixteenth c.—constant wars with France and between Catholics and Protestants, the revolt of the Low Countries, the defeat of the Armada in 1588, the struggle to maintain intact the vast overseas empire, and repeated economic crises—eroded earlier optimism and led to a pervasive disenchantment (*desengaño*) with the fleeting rewards of man's earthly life. Mateo *Alemán's long and much-read picaresque novel *Guzmán de Alfarache*, published in 1599 (second part, 1604), sounds pessimistic and bitter notes which characterize much of the period. In a world increasingly felt to be unstable and untrustworthy, the emphasis now is not on renovation and change but on conformity, conservation, and reaffirmation of the necessity of spiritual salvation, all in accord with Tridentine doctrine.

Not surprisingly, scientific investigation and speculative thought are muted. This is, however, the period of maximum literary and artistic achievement: in the novel, for example, *Cervantes's *Don Quijote* (1605, 1615); *Quevedo's picaresque *Buscón* (written c. 1606); and Baltasar Gracián's allegorical romance, the *Criticón* (1651, 1653, 1657; The Book of the Critic). The most popular genre is the drama, cultivated by several scores of dramatists, among whom the most distinguished are Lope de Vega (see, e.g., *Fuenteovejuna* [The Sheep Well] or *El caballero de Olmedo* [The Knight of Olmedo]), *Tirso de Molina (author of *El burlador de Sevilla* [The Trickster of Seville]), Juan *Ruiz de Alarcón (author of *La verdad sospechosa* [Truth Suspect], adapted by an admiring Corneille in his *Le menteur*), and Pedro Calderón. Calderón's drama *La vida es sueño* (Life Is a Dream) provides in its conflictive themes, elevated style, and complicated structure an extraordinary example of the energy of Baroque drama. Calderón also perfected the form of the religious drama known as the *auto sacramental* (**auto*), a one-act allegorical play written for the feast of Corpus Christi and devoted to revealing that man's salvation depends wholly on the redemptive power of the Eucharistic sacrament.

Among the many poets of the day the greatest are the dramatist Lope de Vega, Francisco de Quevedo, and Luis de *Góngora. Especially in his *Soledades* (Solitudes) and *Polifemo* (Polyphemus) Góngora brought to its highest stage a difficult style known as **culteranismo*, marked by Latinisms in vocabulary and syntax and highly complicated metaphors and images. Quevedo is the greatest master of the style known as **conceptismo* because of its dependence on wit and the ingenious elaboration of conceits. Both Góngora and Quevedo are sometimes called Mannerists precisely because of the calculated difficulty of their poetic expression; both continued to use the forms of folk poems and ballads as well as Italianate meters; and both are formidable satirists. Quevedo especially gives voice to *desengaño* in anguished poems about the inexorable flight of time and the destruction of worldly power and beauty.

Painting rivaled poetry in its efflorescence. This is the century of Velázquez, Zurbarán, Alonso Cano, Murillo, and Ribera.

A distinguishing aspect of the period, as opposed to the sixteenth c., is the importance of the court in patronizing and employing writers and artists. Once the capital of Spain was permanently located in Madrid in 1606, aspiring literary figures and artists flocked to the city in search of support from the king and the nobility. Especially after 1621, when Philip IV ascended the throne, this support was forthcoming from the king himself or from his first minister, the Count-Duke of Olivares: Velázquez was appointed painter to the king in 1621; Calderón served frequently as superintendent of theatrical functions at the court and virtually abandoned writing for the public stage after 1651, when he became a priest. For this reason dramatists especially now responded more to the tastes of sophisticated courtiers than to those of the general populace in the public theaters, composing spectacular dramas, frequently based on classical mythology, which could, indeed, be played only with the stage settings and machinery available on palace stages. Most striking among these spectacles devised for the court is the *zarzuela*, or opera (cf. Calderón's *Eco y Narciso*, 1661), which in its combination of poetry, music, song, dance, splendid costumes, scenery, and visual effects may be considered a quintessentially Baroque genre because of its calculated appeal not only to the intellect but to the senses.

It may be argued that this royal patronage of Spanish arts and letters explains in some measure their continued vigor for some time after the sunset of the power and glory of Spanish arms. *See also* Edad Media, Literature de la; Italian Literary Influences.

BIBLIOGRAPHY

Criticism

Bataillon, Marcel. *Erasmo y España: Estudios sobre la historia espiritual del siglo XVI*. Tr. Antonio Alatorre. 2nd Span. ed. México: Fondo de Cultura Económica, 1966.

Brown, Jonathan, and J. H. Elliott. *A Palace for a King: The Buen Retiro and the Court of Philip IV*. New Haven: Yale UP, 1980.

Davies, Reginald Trevor. *The Golden Century of Spain, 1501–1621*. London: Macmillan, 1937.

Kamen, Henry. "Golden Age, Iron Age: A Conflict of Concepts in the Renaissance." *Journal of Medieval and Renaissance Studies* 4.2 (1974): 135–55.

Pfandl, Ludwig. *Cultura y costumbres del pueblo español de los siglos XVI y XVII: Introducción al estudio del Siglo de Oro*. 2nd Span. ed. Barcelona: Araluce, 1929.

Rico, Francisco, dir. *Historia y crítica de la literatura española*. Vol. 2: *Siglos de oro: Renacimiento*. Ed. Francisco López Estrada. Barcelona: Crítica, 1980. Vol. 3: *Siglos de oro: Barroco*. Ed. Bruce W. Wardropper. Barcelona: Crítica, 1983.

Río, Angel del. *Historia de la literatura española*. rev. ed. New York: Holt Rinehart and Winston, 1963. Vol. 1, Chs. 6–11.

Tuñón de Lara, Manuel, dir. *Historia de España*, vol. 5: *La frustración de un imperio (1476–1714)*. Barcelona: Labor, 1982. See especially Jean-Marc Pelorson, "La noción de 'Siglo de oro,' " 295–301.

Vossler, Karl. *Introducción a la literatura española del Siglo de Oro*. Madrid: Cruz y Raya, 1934.

Willard F. King

SIGÜENZA, José de (1544?, Sigüenza, Guadalajara–1606, El Escorial), librarian, prose author. He entered the Hieronymite order in 1567, and upon the death of *Arias Montano, became librarian of the Escorial Library. He later also assumed the position of prior of the monastery there. Sigüenza left two significant prose works, the *Vida de San Jerónimo* (1595; Life of St. Jerome) and the *Historia de la Orden de San Jerónimo* (1600 and 1605; History of the Order of St. Jerome); both boast elegant, sonorous prose. Other writings of Sigüenza include various didactic treatises, some poetry, and an *Historia de Cristo* (Story of Christ), still in ms. form.

BIBLIOGRAPHY

Primary Texts

Fundación del Monasterio de El Escorial. Ed., prol. F. C. Sáinz de Robles. Madrid: Aguilar, 1963.

Historia de la Orden de San Jerónimo. In NBAE 8 and 12.

El Padre José Sigüenza. Sus obras poéticas. Ed. L. Villalba. In *Ciudad de Dios* 99 (1914).

Criticism

Menger, M. A. *Fray José de Sigüenza, poeta e historiador.* Tr. G. Méndez Plancarte. Mexico City: n.p., 1944.

Rubio González, L. *Valores literarios del Padre Sigüenza.* Valladolid: U of Valladolid, 1976.

SILVA, Antonio de. *See* Bermúdez, Jerónimo

SILVA, Feliciano de (1492?, Ciudad Rodrigo, Salamanca–1558?, Ciudad Rodrigo), prose fiction author. Silva identified and capitalized with great success on the two most popular literary materials of the early sixteenth c., Fernando de *Rojas's **Celestina* and the **Amadís*, by writing adaptations and continuations of each. Cervantes's priest condemned to the pyre Silva's *Amadís de Grecia* for "the devilish and confused notions of its author" (*Don Quijote* I.6), whereas Don Quijote, exceedingly fond of Silva's books, heartily recommended them to Cardenio's lady (I.24). Silva's occasionally preposterous tone, artificial to the point of absurdity at times, was actually a comic distortion of the high-sounding language of decadent courtly style and is laughed at by the characters themselves. For example, from *Don Florisel de Niquea* (1532; Don Florisel of Niquea): "... con el secreto de sus secretarios que tanto con secreto para el presente secreto el suyo ha guardado" (... with his secretaries' secret which he has guarded so secretly for the sake of the present secret).

The *Segunda Comedia de Celestina* (1534; The Second Comedy of Celestina) is generally considered to be Silva's best work. Calisto is replaced by the less noble Felides, enamored of Polandria, Melibea's counterpart, in the *Segunda Celestina*, in which the author proposed to "present and depict as in real life the disillusions and deceits which usually occur with lovers and their servants." Silva's Celestina claims to have never really died, as Rojas had it, and she emerges from her close brush with death a burlesque caricature of her former self (as are most of the characters). Silva uses the basic plot of the original *tragicomedia* as a springboard to present a more diversified panorama of love stories than Rojas. Comic elements are exaggerated, and the essential lack of unity in plot may be explained as a carryover from the byzantine novel, to be expected from an author with Silva's interest in chivalric romances.

Silva's *Amadís* series includes the following, the contents of which are as disparate as their titles: *La crónica del muy valiente y esforçado príncipe y cavallero de la Ardiente Espada Amadís de Grecia* (1530; The Chronicle of the

Very Valiant and Brave Prince and Knight of the Burning Sword, Amadís of Greece); *La crónica de los muy valientes cavalleros don Florisel de Niquea y el fuerte Anaxartes* (1532; The Chronicle of the Very Valiant Knights don Florisel of Niquea and the Strong Anaxartes); *Parte tercera de la crónica de Florisel de Niquea* (1535; The Third Part of the Chronicle of Florisel of Niquea); *Cuarta parte de don Florisel de Niquea* (first book, 1551; The Fourth Part of don Florisel of Niquea); *Segundo libro de la quarta parte de la crónica de Florisel de Niquea* (1551; Second Book of the Fourth Part of the Chronicle of Florisel of Niquea).

Critical attention has focused on Silva's one significant addition to the texts he imitated, the inclusion and development of *pastoral episodes within the larger novelistic contexts, considered to be an important progression toward the pastoral romance. Although appearing in isolated sections, the scenes representing Filinides (*Segunda Celestina*) and Darinel (*Lisuarte de Grecia* and *Don Florisel* I) provide evidence of the changing sensitivities of the age from action-oriented values toward contemplative values, from sensual love toward more spiritual love.

BIBLIOGRAPHY

Primary Text

Segunda comedia de Celestina. Ed. M. I. Chamorro Fernández. Madrid: Ciencia Nueva, 1968.

Criticism

Cravens, S. "Feliciano de Silva and His Romances of Chivalry in *Don Quijote*." *Inti* 7 (1978): 28–34.

———. *Feliciano de Silva y los antecedentes de la novela pastoril en sus libros de caballerías*. Chapel Hill: Hispanófila, 1976.

López Estrada, F. *Los libros de pastores en la literatura española*. Madrid: Gredos, 1974. 272–80 and 326–39.

O'Conner, J. *Amadis de Gaule and Its Influence on Elizabethan Literature*. New Brunswick, NJ: Rutgers UP, 1970.

Elizabeth Rhodes

SILVELA, Manuel (1781, Valladolid–1832, Paris), dramatist, historian. Like his close friend Leandro Fernández de *Moratín, he cooperated with the French invaders (1808); with the departure of the French, Silvela and Moratín moved to Bordeaux and then Paris (1827). There, Silvela founded a school. Silvela's literary works include *Biblioteca selecta de literatura española* (1819; Select Library of Spanish Literature), *Una cuestión de derecho* (1829; A Matter of Law), a biography of Moratín, other biographies, and two plays, *Don Simplicio de Utrera* (Don Simplicio of Utrera) and *El reconciliador* (The Reconciler), which bear the influence of Moratín. Silvela's son collected and published his father's works under the titles *Compendio de historia antigua . . .* (1843; Compendium of Ancient History) and *Obras póstumas* (1845; Posthumous Works).

BIBLIOGRAPHY

Primary Texts

Biblioteca selecta. . . . 4 vols. Bordeaux: Lawalle, 1819.
Obras póstumas. Madrid: Mellado, 1845.
Una cuestión de derecho. Paris: Gaultier-Laguionie, 1829.

SILVELA, Manuel (1830, Paris–1892, Madrid), journalist, member of the *Academia Española, grandson of Manuel *Silvela (1781–1832). He used two pseudonyms, Velisla and Juan Fernández. Schooled in Bordeaux, he later studied law in Spain. His newspaper columns are extremely amusing, satiric comments and reactions to the foibles of contemporary society, with titles such as "La ópera y el gobierno" (Opera and Government), "El Diccionario y la gastronomía" (The Dictionary and Gastronomy), "El perfecto novelista" (The Perfect Novelist), etc. These and others were collected and published by Silvela in 1890 under the title *Obras literarias* (Literary Works). Silvela also wrote a critical analysis of his grandfather's works (1868), and completed an edition of Leandro Fernández de *Moratín's works. In several articles, he also defended the recently published Dictionary of the Spanish Academy from criticism.

BIBLIOGRAPHY

Primary Texts

Obras literarias. Madrid: Tello, 1890.

SILVESTRE, Gregorio (1520, Lisbon–1569, Granada), poet, organist. His father was João III of Portugal's physician, thus his earliest years were spent in the royal household. At age fourteen, he entered the service of the Suárez de Figueroa household, where he was exposed to the blossoming cultural life of the *Renaissance. In 1541, Silvestre became organist for the Granada cathedral, settling in that city permanently.

His early poetry employed the traditional Spanish octosyllabic line, but he gradually, gracefully adopted the new, Italianate styles: eleven-syllable lines, the sonnet, mythological themes, etc. The latter held a particular attraction, as in his "Fábula de Narciso" (Fable of Narcissus), "Fábula de Dafne y Apolo" (Fable of Daphne and Apollo), etc. Two allegorical works worthy of mention are the "Visita de amor" (Love's Visit) and "Residencia de amor" (Love's Abode), which depict the most famous "love-poets" of the day, imprisoned by their passion. Silvestre also composed fine religious poetry. His works were collected posthumously. *See also* Italian Literary Influences.

BIBLIOGRAPHY

Primary Texts

Poesías. Sel., prol., notes A. Marín Ocete. Granada: Facultad de letras, 1939.

SIMÓ, Isabel-Clara (1943, Alcoi, Valencia–), prose fiction writer, journalist, philosophy teacher, and translator. She directed the journal *Canigó* for ten years, contributing many of the articles and editing others. She teaches in an institute and has translated from Italian. In her short stories and novels, like Pablo Neruda in his poetry and for the same reason, Simó makes a deliberate and successful effort to write accessible literature—stories and novels that can be read and enjoyed by working people in a style at once simple and elegant. Hers is an agile language, sometimes brilliantly simple and always balanced, an everyday language for everyday anecdotes. Her strong social consciousness is apparent in much of her work; while never losing her artistic vigor, she skillfully sends us certain messages about the oppressed groups she is concerned with—Catalan-speaking people, women, and workers. Her first novel, *Júlia* (1983; Julia), is historical, based on the struggles of laborers in turn-of-the-century Valencia. The sudden entry into the upper class of a former factory worker underlines the protagonist's own strength of character as well as the political turbulence both within and without the household as a result of the whim of an old man who breaks the unspoken rules of class rigidity. In her collection of short stories, *Es quan miro que hi veig clar* (1979; I See Best When I Look), Simó takes a look at the problems of adolescence and old age, and the new independence of women. In this and her new collection, *Bresca* (1985; Honeycomb), she does not shy away from the problems of suicide and violence, sometimes even among children, but she never loses her sense of hope or humor. The subtlety of her pro-Catalan and profeminist stance in the novel *Idols* (1985; Idols) is masterful indeed, as she shows the strength and neglect of Catalan literature side by side with the nurturing self-sufficient woman whose ironic laugh perplexes and disturbs her husband at the close of the book. Simó's mastery of colloquial, often Valencian, speech lends great power to her narrations, and her ability and willingness to let the characters act themselves in their own way is refreshingly pervasive throughout her work. *See also* Catalan Literature.

BIBLIOGRAPHY

Primary Texts

Bresca. Barcelona: Laia, 1985.
Es quan miro que hi veig clar. Barcelona: Selecta, 1979.
Idols. Barcelona: Magrana, 1985.
Júlia. Barcelona: Magrana, 1983.
T'estimo, Marta. Barcelona: Magrana, 1986.

Kathleen McNerney

SIMÓN, Pedro (1565?, La Parrilla, Cuenca–after 1630, Bogotá?), Franciscan, New World historian. He moved to Bogotá in 1604, and served as provincial in Santafé from 1623 to 1626. Simón's chronicle, *Noticias historiales de las conquistas de Tierra Firme en las Indias occidentales* (1626; Historical Information on the Conquests of Terra Firma in the West Indies), is the best record of early events in what is now Colombia, and includes a wealth of cultural data, facts and dates, information on the earthquake of 1599, etc. He seems to have also written a *Vocabulario* (Vocabulary) and a life of Father Miguel de los Angeles, now lost.

BIBLIOGRAPHY

Primary Text

Noticias historiales. . . . Ed. M. J. Forero. 9 vols. Bogotá: Kelly, 1953.

English Translation

The Expedition of Pedro de Ursua and Lope de Aguirre in Search of El Dorado and Omagua in 1560–1. Tr. W. Bollaert. Intro. C. Markham. London: Hakluyt, 1861. (Tr. of sixth *noticia*.)

SINUÉS, María del Pilar (1835, Zaragoza–1893, Madrid), writer. She married by proxy the playwright José Marco y Sentís who, without knowing her, asked in a poem for her hand. They were later separated. She directed *El Angel del Hogar* (The Angel of the Hearth) magazine and contributed to many newspapers and magazines both in Spain and in Latin America. Her novels, directed to a public of ladies and young girls, are very sentimental, didactic and moralistic. Some titles of her works are *Memorias de una joven de la clase media* (1862; Memoirs of a Middle-Class Young Woman), *Narraciones del Hogar* (1862; Narrations from the Hearth), *Celeste* (1863), *El alma enferma* (1865; The Sick Soul), *Rosa* (3rd ed. 1864; Rose), *La dama elegante* (1880; The Elegant Lady), *Galería de mujeres célebres* (1864–69; A Gallery of Famous Women), *Hija, esposa y madre* (1863; Daughter, Wife and Mother), and *La misión de la mujer* (1886; Woman's Mission). *Cartas a mi ahijada* (1871; Letters to My Goddaughter) and *Cartas a una madre* (1888–89; Letters to a Mother) appeared in magazines.

BIBLIOGRAPHY

Primary Texts

Hija, esposa y madre. 2 vols. Madrid: Hijos de García, 1863.
La dama elegante. Madrid: S. de San Martín, 1880. Practical manual of good taste.
La misión de la mujer. Barcelona: Manero, 1886.
Rosa. 3rd ed. Madrid: J. Minuesa, 1857.
Un nido de palomas. Madrid: Correspondencia de España, 1861.

Criticism

Navales, A. M. "María del Pilar Sinués, escritora zaragozana del siglo XIX." *Heraldo de Aragón*. 12 October 1977.

Salvador García Castañeda

SOLDEVILA I ZUBIBURU, Carles (1891, Barcelona–1967, Barcelona), Catalan dramatist and novelist. Part of the *Noucentisme* movement in the early twentieth c., Soldevila helped to broaden the scope of Catalan fiction beyond the grim rural novel and, after the passing of *modernism, reincorporating the portrayal of complex human relations. Thus, certain of his novels center upon a conjugal crisis, frustration, or hedonism ending in adultery (critics have indicated that the fiction of this period is prose, but not really narrative). Soldevila's fiction did not aspire to realism, but what the author termed in his novel *Moment musical* (1936) "stylized vraisemblance." He is primarily the novelist of the middle stratum of the Barcelona bourgeoisie, which he portrayed in such works as *Fanny* (1929), *Eva* (1931), *Valentina* (1933). *Fanny*, deemed his masterpiece, was widely read in its day: this portrait of a resolute, independent woman who saves herself from her family's economic collapse by taking a job in a chorus line, depicts the confrontation between the conservative ideals of the older generation and newer values. Other novels include *El senyoret Lluís* (1926; Playboy Luis), actually a novelette published together with a dozen stories, and the later fiction *Bob a Paris* (1952; Bob in Paris) and *Papers de familia* (1960; Family Papers). One of his earliest publications was a lyric collection entitled *Lletanies profanes* (1913; Profane Litanies). His plays belong to the high comedy genre, not typical of *Noucentisme* (which favored poetry and produced relatively little drama). Other works include the drama *Civilitzats tanmateix* (1921; Civilized, Nevertheless), exemplary modernist prose highly regarded by Catalan critics.

BIBLIOGRAPHY

Primary Texts

Bola de neu. Barcelona: Millà, 1934.
Els milions de l'oncle. 2nd ed. Barcelona: Millà, 1966.
Necessitem senyoreta. Barcelona: Millà, 1935.
Obres completes. Barcelona: Selecta, 1967.

Janet Pérez

SOLDEVILA I ZUBIBURU, Ferran (1894, Barcelona–1971, Barcelona), historian, dramatist and theatrical director. Brother of Carles, Ferran tried his own hand at historical theater with *Matilde d'Anglaterra* (1923; Matilde of England) and *Guifre* (1928). A few other dramatic pieces were produced after the Civil War: *L'hostal de l'amor* (1949; Hostel of Love), *La font del Miracle* (1952; Miracle Fountain), *Albert i Francina* (1956); *Don Joan* (1960); *L'aprenent de suicida* (1961; The Apprentice Suicide), and *L'amador de la gentilesa* (1961; The Lover of Courtesy). His theater is amiable, ironic, a bit slow. *Al llarg de la meva vida* (1970; Along My Life) contains memoirs. He contributed articles and poignant chronicles to the history of Catalan exiles in France and Argentina after the Civil War, and was among the contributors to the *Revista de Catalunya*, which strove to preserve the ethnic and cultural identities of the emigrés. Ferran Soldevila collaborated with Pere Bosch i Gimpera to produce the first history of Catalonia published in exile, *Història de Catalunya* (Mexico, 1946), first received euphorically by Catalan expatriates, and then the subject of a polemic as to the historical interpretations presented.

Janet Pérez

SOLEDAD (Solitude), a lyric term. Name given to a popular Andalusian type of song, it inspired a poetry form with brief, three-line stanzas with eight-syllable lines and assonant rhyme uniting the uneven lines.

SOLER, Bartolomé (1894, Sabadell, Barcelona–1975, Palau Solitar, Barcelona), novelist, dramatist, and essayist. A self-made man, Soler, the twentieth-c. rogue, began, at age fourteen, his wanderings throughout Spain and foreign countries—France, Mexico, the United States, and South America, from the Atlantic to the Pacific coast and from the Caribbean to Tierra del Fuego.

Soler began his literary career with the publication of *Marcos Villarí* in 1927. Because of the resounding success of this novel, he was catapulted into fame both in Spain and South America. In October of the same year, his second novel, *Germán Padilla*, appeared. After dedicating a few years to writing plays, he returned in 1941 to the novel with *Almas de cristal* (Transparent Souls). In 1949 with *Patapalo* Soler received the Ciudad de Barcelona Prize, and in 1961 with *Los muertos no se cuentan* (Dead People Aren't Counted) he won the coveted Miguel de Cervantes National Prize for Literature. The main objective of Soler, like Ramón *Gómez de la Serna and Gabriel *Miró, was the continuation of the tradition of action and passion. Endowed with a powerful, creative, and descriptive force, Soler centered his primary interest on man. What makes Soler most unforgettable, however, is his style, which is rich in verbal combinations and in unusual, daring, and exploding images, reminiscent of the best of D'Annunzio and *Valle-Inclán.

BIBLIOGRAPHY

Primary Texts

Almas de cristal. Barcelona: Hispano Americana de Ediciones, 1949.
La cara y la cruz del camino. Barcelona: Alar, 1963.
Germán Padilla. Madrid: Espasa-Calpe, 1927.
Karú Kinká. 4th ed. Barcelona: Juventud, 1961.
La llanura muerta. 3rd ed. Barcelona: Planeta, 1955.
Marcos Villarí. 13th ed. Barcelona: Juventud, 1961.
Mis primeros caminos. 2nd ed. Barcelona: Juventud, 1962.
Mis últimos caminos. 3rd ed. Barcelona: Alar, 1965.
Los muertos no se cuentan. 5th ed. Barcelona: Juventud, 1962.
Occidente . . . Madrid . . . Sahara . . . Venezuela. . . . Barcelona: Juventud, 1961. A collection of selected speeches.
Patapalo. 5th ed. Barcelona: Juventud, 1962.
La selva humillada. 3rd ed. Barcelona: Planeta, 1957.
Tamara. Barcelona: Planeta, 1953.
La vida encadenada. 6th ed. Barcelona: Juventud, 1961.

English Translation

Marcos Villarí. Tr. William Stirling. London: Aldor 1948.

Criticism

Entrambasaguas, Joaquín de. "Prologue." *Las mejores novelas contemporáneas (1925–29)*. Barcelona: Planeta, 1961.
Paolini, Gilbert. *Bartolomé Soler Novelista. Procedimientos estilísticos*. Barcelona: Juventud, 1963.
Román, Antonio. *La novelística de Bartolomé Soler*. Madrid: Rocana, 1976.

Román, Antonio, and Vito di Vincenzo. *The Novels of Bartolomé Soler. Selected Excerpts. Bilingual Edition*. Madrid: Ciencias de la Educación Preescolar y Especial, 1978.

Viñas y Camps, Dolores. *Estudi sobre l'obra literaria del sabadellenc Bartomeu Soler*. Sabadell, 1978.

Gilbert Paolini

SOLÍS, Antonio de (1610, Alcalá de Henares–1686, Madrid), official chronicler of the Indies, dramatist, poet. After attending the U of Salamanca, he became secretary to the Count of Oropesa, viceroy of Valencia. Named chronicler after the death of León Pinelo, he composed the *Historia de México* . . . (1684; *History of the Conquest of Mexico by the Spaniards,* 1724), which narrates events from 1518 to 1520. Using customary sources—*Cortés, *Díaz del Castillo, *López de Gómara— Solís weaves a vigorous, dramatic tale replete with speeches, dates and facts. The figure of Cortés dominates the narrative. While nothing new is added to the record, the intelligence and artistic skill of Solís's *Historia* make it the finest, as well as the last, of the chronicles, and the work for which he is most famous. A second part was to follow, but was incomplete at his death and has never been published.

Although twentieth-c. criticism has generally neglected Solís's dramatic output, he was a leading playwright of his day. Aside from various collaborative plays (with *Calderón, *Coello, etc.), Solís wrote eleven plays. His first, *Amor y obligación* (Love and Duty), he wrote when only seventeen. Nine others were published in 1681 as *Comedias de Don Antonio de Solís* (Plays of don Antonio de Solís), and one other, *La más dichosa venganza* (The Most Fortunate Revenge) appeared in a collection in 1666. Best are *El amor al uso* (Love According to Custom) and *Un bobo hace ciento* (One Fool Makes 100), both rapid-paced, satirical works. Solís also composed several **loas*, **entremeses*, and similar short pieces, and published a volume of poetry which bears the influence of *Góngora. Solís's correspondence has been collected and published under the title *Epistolario* (Epistolary).

BIBLIOGRAPHY

Primary Texts

Comedias de Antonio de Solís. Ed., intro. M. Sánchez Regueira. 2 vols. Madrid: CSIC, 1984.

Epistolario. In BAE 13.

Historia de México. . . . In BAE 28.

Obra dramática menor. Ed. M. Sánchez Regueira. Madrid: CSIC, 1986.

Varias poesías sagradas y profanas. Ed. M. Sánchez Regueira. Madrid: CSIC, 1968.

English Translation

The history of the Conquest of Mexico by the Spaniards. Tr. T. Townsend. London: Woodward, 1724.

Criticism

Arocena, L. *Antonio de Solís, cronista indiano: estudio sobre las formas historiográficas del barroco*. Buenos Aires: Editorial Universitaria de Buenos Aires, 1963.

Serralta, F. "Nueva biografía de Antonio de Solís y Rivadeneyra." *Criticón* 34 (1986): 51–157.

———. "Las comedias de Antonio de Solís: Reflexiones sobre la edición de un texto del Siglo de Oro." *Criticón* 34 (1986): 159–74.

Frances Bell Exum

SOLÍS, Dionisio, pseudonym of Dionisio Villanueva y Ochoa (1744, Córdoba–1834, Madrid), poet and playwright. At an early age, Solís entered the theater, eventually working as a prompter, adapter, and translator as well as author of original dramas. He married the great actress María Ribera, worked with the famous actor Isidoro Máiquez, and was a friend of Leandro Fernández de *Moratín. Solís's own plays are somewhat derivative and unoriginal; for example, his *Blanca de Borbón*, concerning the unfaithful wife of Peter the Cruel, was merely one of a number of plays on the same subject, with versions by *Espronceda, and *Gil y Zárate. Nevertheless, his adaptations of Spanish *Siglo de Oro drama, including works by *Calderón, Lope de *Vega, *Tirso, *Rojas Zorrilla, and *Moreto, were influential in the Romantic re-discovery of classical Spanish drama. He published translations of works by Alfieri, Chénier, Ducis, Kotzebue, Shakespeare, and Voltaire. His poetry shows a strong personal element and traces of Romantic rebelliousness. *See also* Romanticism.

BIBLIOGRAPHY

Primary Texts

Camila. Madrid: Sancha, 1828.

Poesías. In BAE 67.

Criticism

Hartzenbusch, J. E. "Noticias sobre la vida y escritos de D. Dionisio Solís." In *Ensayos poéticos y artículos en prosa, literarios y de costumbres*. Madrid: Yenes, 1843.

McClelland, I. L. *The Origins of the Romantic Movement in Spain*. 2nd ed. Liverpool: Liverpool UP, 1975.

Peers, E. A. *A History of the Romantic Movement in Spain*. 2 vols. Cambridge: Cambridge UP, 1940.

Stoudemire, S. A. "Dionisio Solís' refundiciones of Plays, 1800–1834." *HR* 8 (1940): 305–10.

SOLÍS, Ramón (1922, Cádiz–1978, Madrid), Spanish novelist and historian. Solís obtained a doctorate in political science at the U of Madrid. He began his literary career with short stories and novelettes in various reviews and periodicals, as well as a number of historical works, turning subsequently to the novel. His first, *La bella sirena* (1954; The Beautiful Mermaid), he later disowned; his next, *Los que no tienen paz* (1957; Those Who Have No Peace), was adapted for the theater by José María *Pemán with the title *Los monos chillan al amanecer*

(The Monkeys Screech at Daybreak). This work portrays the frustrations of youth as they attempt to build a future on foundations inherited from the past while struggling against misunderstanding from their elders. *Ajena crece la yerba* (1962; Alien Grows the Grass) treats the problem—acute in Spain during the late 1950s and the 1960s—of Andalusian migrant workers forced by low wages and unemployment in Spain to travel to France and other countries of northern Europe in search of jobs in seasonal harvesting. *Un siglo llama a la puerta* (1963; A Century Is Knocking at the Door) is set in Cádiz at the end of the eighteenth c. and beginning of the nineteenth, the epoch of the famous Cortes (Constitutional Congress) in Cádiz which became the ''capital'' of the liberals in their struggle against the conservatives, and later in their defense of Spain against the Napoleonic invasion. This novel is something of a fictional rendering of a collection of historical essays, *El Cádiz de las Cortes* (1959; Cádiz during the Constitutional Congress), which won for Solís the Fastenrath Prize of the *Academia Española. From 1962 to 1968 he was secretary general of the *Ateneo of Madrid.

Janet Pérez

SOLITARIO, El. *See* Estébanez Calderón, Serafín

SOMOZA, José (1781, Piedrahita, Avila–1852, Piedrahita), essayist and poet. After some time as a student in Salamanca, Somoza went to Madrid where, through his friendship with the Duchess of Alba and the poet *Quintana, he became acquainted with personalities like *Jovellanos and Goya. He fought against the French, was persecuted for his liberal ideas, was elected governor of Avila in 1820, and a member of the Cortes in 1834 and 1836. Somoza spent most of his life secluded in his beloved Piedrahita, surrounded by his books, yet very much in contact with the latest literary currents. Endowed with a philosophical mind, Somoza was a Stoic thinker and a writer of sharp, critical wit comparable to that of Leandro Fernández de *Moratín and Mariano José de *Larra. Among his prose works are *Memorias de Piedrahita* (1837; Memoirs of Piedrahita), *Recuerdos e impresiones* (1843; Remembrances and Impressions), and the novel *El capón* (1844; The Capon). His poetry betrays the influence of *Meléndez Valdés. *See also* Essay; Romanticism.

BIBLIOGRAPHY

Primary Texts

El capón. Salamanca: Morán, 1844.
Obras en prosa y verso. Ed. J. R. Lomba y Pedraja. Madrid: RABM, 1904.
Obras poéticas. Madrid: Sancha, 1834–37.
El doctor Andrés Laguna o el tiempo de las brujas. Salamanca: n.p., 1846.

Criticism

Azorín. "José Somoza." In *Leyendo a los poetas*. Zaragoza: Librería general, 1945.
Cueto, Leopoldo A. de. "Don José Somoza." In BAE 67. 451–82.

Salvador García Castañeda

"SONETO A CRISTO CRUCIFICADO" (late sixteenth c.; Sonnet to the Christ Crucified), anonymous poem with an interesting history. This famous sonnet, which begins "No me mueve, mi Dios, para quererte" (I am not moved, my God, to love you), was included in the *Arte doctrinal y modo general para aprender la lengua matlaltzinga* (Mexico, 1638; Doctrinal Skill and General Method of Learning the Matlaltzinga Language) by the Mexican or Spanish Augustinian Miguel de *Guevara (d. 1640). The sonnet was attributed to him until it was discovered forming part of the *Libro intitulado Vida del espíritu* (Madrid, 1628; The Life of the Spirit) by fellow Augustinian Antonio de Rojas, prior to the monastery of Santiago Athatzithaquaro. The author's name was omitted from this book and as a result the poem has been attributed to St. *Teresa, St. *Juan de la Cruz, and to St. Francis Xavier, among others. Ludwig Pfandl has identified a passage from Juan de *Ávila's *Audi, filia* (ch. 50) as the inspiration for the poem.

The sonnet contains certain characteristics of sixteenth-c. ascetical and mystical literature as well as elements of the method of inner prayer and meditation called "recogimiento" (gathering in). As part of the meditative exercises called for in preparation for subsequent mystical union, writers of mystical literature recommend that the individual meditate on the humanity of Christ, and most especially, on the passion and death on the cross. Thus does the author of this poem. The piece evinces an affective (active) expression of love for Christ which is a direct result of this meditation.

In St. Theresa's *Sexta morada* (Interior Castle), ch. 7, she describes a spiritual disposition that resembles the contents of the poem. She explains that an individual who meditates on certain aspects of Christ's humanity is not as afraid of going to hell as of losing forever someone who has sacrificed so much to secure his salvation. One is moved to abandon the things of this world through meditation on Christ's passion and death on the cross. *See also* Ascetical Literature; Mysticism.

BIBLIOGRAPHY

Primary Text

Spanish Poetry from Its Beginning through the Nineteenth Century. By Willis Barnstone. New York: Oxford UP, 1970. 316.

English Translation

"Sonnet." Tr. John Bowring. In *Poets and Poetry of Europe*. Ed. H. W. Longfellow. Boston: Houghton-Mifflin, 1896.

Criticism

Bataillon, Marcel. ''El anónimo del soneto 'No me mueve, mi Dios.' '' *Príncipe de Viana* 11 (1950): 105–10.

Carreño, Alberto M. *Guevara y el célebre soneto.* Mexico: Imprenta Franco-mexicana, 1915.

López Estrada, Francisco. ''En torno al soneto 'A Cristo Crucificado.' '' *BRAE* 33 (1953): 95–106.

Rivers, Elías. ''Soneto a Cristo Crucificado, Line 12.'' *BHS* 35 (1958): 36–37.

Angelo DiSalvo

SORIA, Alonso de. *See* Alonso de Soria

SORIANO JARA, Elena (1917, Fuentidueña de Tajo, Madrid–), Spanish novelist, critic and essayist. Relatively unknown during the Franco era because of censorial prohibition of the circulation or sale of her major novels, Soriano began as a traditional realist with *Caza menor* (1951; Small Game Hunting), a novel reminiscent of nineteenth-c. regionalism. Chronicling the decadence of a family of rural gentry (an ambient Soriano would have known personally during her youth), the novel utilizes some faintly melodramatic plot elements, especially the death of a young wife fleeing the advances of her husband's two degenerate brothers. Major merits are the linguistic richness and the accurate depiction of setting and customs. Soriano's most significant fictional achievement is the novelistic trilogy, *Mujer y hombre* (1955; Woman and Man), comprising the novels *La playa de los locos* (Beach of Madmen), *Espejismos* (Mirages), and *Medea 55*. Although the parts are thematically related—all deal with the difficult and potentially tragic relationship between the sexes—the three novels are independent in having no connection in plot, setting or characters. Existential elements are strong in the trilogy, especially the themes of solitude, alienation, despair and the difficulty or impossibility of communication. Technique varies significantly between the parts of the trilogy: *Mujer y hombre* utilizes a first-person narrative perspective and is essentially a monologue or epistolary confession by the narrative consciousness/protagonist. *Espejismos* has two perspectives, the parallel monologues of husband and wife facing respective mid-life crises. *Medea 55* presents an updating of the classic drama insofar as the jealous and rejected wife or lover, driven by uncontrollable passion, destroys her/their children as part of her vengeance upon the man who has abandoned her for his new love.

In 1969, Soriano founded and (until its economic collapse in 1976) directed the cultural quarterly *El Urogallo*, one of the most important intellectual periodicals of the 1970s. Her most recent volume, *Confesión de una madre* (1986; A Mother's Confession), the result of the tragic, drug-related death of Soriano's son, contains much that is autobiographical, soul-searching and introspective. Although her production is limited, the quality of the trilogy is exceptional; reissued for sale subsequent to the late 1978 abolition of *censorship, its belated circulation has brought the author favorable critical notice and long-overdue recognition of her outstanding narrative accomplishment.

BIBLIOGRAPHY

Primary Texts

Caza menor. 2nd ed. Madrid: Prensa Española, 1976.
Mujer y hombre. 3 vols. Madrid: Calleja, 1955.

Criticism

Winecoff, Janet. "Existentialism in the Novels of Elena Soriano." *Hispania* 47.2 (May 1964): 309–15.

Janet Pérez

SOTO, Domingo de (1494, Segovia–1560, Salamanca), theologian, jurist, imperial theologian and confessor to Charles V. After attending the U of Alcalá, he attended the College of S. Barbere in Paris, receiving his bachelor's degree there. Soto then returned to Spain and secured a chair in philosophy at the U of Alcalá in 1520. Five years later, he professed in the Dominican order, teaching dialectics. In 1532, he assumed a chair at the U of Salamanca. Charles V sent him as his imperial theologian to the Council of Trent in 1545, where he discharged various responsibilities. One task was *censorship of written material for heresy and preparation of the **Indice* (Index). In 1552 he succeeded Melchor *Cano in the theology chair at the U of Salamanca. Although some critics feel his studies in physics make him a forerunner of Galileo, Soto is most famous for his *De Justitia et Jure* (1556; Concerning Justice and Law). Fray Luis de *León delivered the eulogy at Soto's funeral.

BIBLIOGRAPHY

Primary Texts

De iustitia et iure libre decem. De la justicia y del derecho. Intro. V. Diego Carro. Tr. M. González Ordóñez. 4 vols. Madrid: Instituto de Estudios Políticos, 1967–68. Latin facs. and Spanish tr.
De natura et gratia. Farnborough, England: Gregg, 1965. Rpt. of 1549 ed.
In Porphyrii Isagogen, Aristotelis Categorias. . . . Frankfurt: Minerva, 1967. Rpt. of 1587 ed.
Relección "de dominio." Ed., tr. J. Brufau Prats. Granada: U of Granada, 1964.

Criticism

Beltrán de Heredia, V. *Domingo de Soto. Estudio biográfico documentado.* Madrid: n.p., 1961.
Brufau Prats, J. *El pensamiento político de Domingo de Soto y su concepción del poder.* Salamanca: U of Salamanca, 1960.
Hamilton, B. *Political Thought in Sixteenth-Century Spain.* Oxford: Clarendon, 1963.
Tellechea Idígoras, J. I. *El obispo ideal en el siglo de la reforma.* Rome: Iglesia Nacional, 1963.

SOTO, Vicente (1919, Valencia–), Spanish novelist, short story writer and playwright. Soto had just finished his secondary studies when the Spanish Civil War erupted, and his university study was postponed until after the end of the conflict. While still a student, he wrote a play, *Rosalinda* (1942). In 1944, he received a law degree, but by then he was much more attracted by literature. He moved to Madrid, and began publishing stories in literary reviews, with a volume of the best ones collected under the title of *Vidas humildes* (1948; Humble Lives). However, recognition was slow in coming, and in 1954 he accepted a professional post in England, where he settled, teaching Spanish in various schools in Britain. He continued to write, but was not "discovered" by Spanish readers until winning the Nadal Prize in 1966 for his novel, *La zancada* (The Long Leap), a novel of awakening to life and adolescence from the viewpoint of a boy who loves, hates, and suffers intensely. A novelette or long short story, *La prueba* (1968; The Test), won the Gabriel Miró Prize, and in 1972, Soto published another novel, *Bernard, uno que volaba* (Bernard, One Who Flew), the story of a misunderstood genius, a pure spirit who continually escapes from daily reality to his own world, a modernized juvenile version of Don Quixote. Soto's third novel, *El gallo negro* (The Black Rooster) appeared the same year as another collection of stories, *Casicuentos de Londres* (1973; Almost Tales of London), which (like his somewhat Dickensian novels of post-war London) portrays his emigré experience and reflects his expatriation and sense of rootlessness. *El gallo negro* was inspired by Soto's visit to a Valencian village about to be submerged by the construction of a reservoir, which made him wonder whether no villagers had ever gone mad watching their homes, their ancestors, their lives, swallowed by the water, producing the inspiration for the character of Dimas, his unbalanced protagonist. More recent is *Una canción para un loco* (1986; Song for a Crazy Man) which received an international award.

BIBLIOGRAPHY

Primary Texts

Cuentos del tiempo de nunca acabar. Madrid: Magisterio Español, 1977.

SOTO DE ROJAS, Pedro (1584, Granada–1658, Granada), poet. He studied theology at Granada U. In Madrid he made the acquaintance of Lope de *Vega, Góngora, and Paravicino, and in 1612 he entered in the Academia Salvaje (Savage Academy) where he read his "Discurso de Poética" (Poetic Discourse). The following year he retired to his garden-house in the Albaicín of Granada.

His first poetic compositions were collected in *Desengaño de amor en rimas* (1623; Love's Disillusion in Rhymes). It consists of a repertoire of eclogues, elegies, sonnets, and madrigals plus a fable and a narrative in octaves. *Los rayos de Faetón* (1639; Phaethon Rays) is a long mythological poem in octaves divided into eight parts. In *Paraýso cerrado para muchos, jardines abiertos para pocos* (1630; Paradise Closed for Many, Gardens Opened for Few) Soto de Rojas shows himself to be a brilliant and sensual poet in the tradition of Góngora.

BIBLIOGRAPHY

Primary Texts

Desengaño de amor en rimas. Ed. M. de Zayas Alicia Yllea. Madrid: Cátedra, 1983.
Obras de don Pedro Soto de Rojas. Ed. A. Gallego Morell. Madrid: CSIC, 1950.

Paraíso cerrado para muchos, jardines abiertos para pocos. Ed. A. Egido. Madrid: Cátedra, 1981.

Los rayos de Faetón. Barcelona: Lacaballería, 1639.

Criticism

Gallego Morell, A. *El ave del vuelo. Estudio sobre la obra de Soto de Rojas*. Granada: Depto. de Literatura Española, 1984.

José Ortega

SOTO VERGES, Rafael (1936, Cádiz–), Spanish poet. He studied philosophy and letters at the U of Madrid, settling in that city after 1958. He works as a professor of business and also as a critic in various literary reviews. Soto's first significant success came when he won the important Adonais Poetry Prize in 1958 for *La agorera* (The Reader of Omens). *Epopeya sin héroe* (1967; Epic Poem without a Hero) appeared after a drama produced in 1962, *El recovero de Ulises* (1963; Ulysses's Chicken-Shed). Soto's poetry tends to be meditative and slightly ideological, tinged by the "social" (i.e., political) criticism typical of the late 1950s and early 1960s in Spain, but with careful attention to language.

SOUVIRÓN, José María (1904, Málaga–), Spanish poet and novelist. He become known through the Litoral group of poets in the Vanguard period of the years between the wars, and published his first collection of poems, *Conjunto* (The Totality), in 1928. Several other titles were published in Chile: *Fuego a bordo* (1932; Fire on Shipboard), *Plural belleza* (1936; Plural Beauty), *Romances americanos* (1937; American Ballads), etc. Several later collections appeared in Madrid (e.g., *Señal de vida* [1948; Signs of Life]), and a number of novels, including *Cristo en Torremolinos* (1963; Christ in Torremolinos); *Un hombre y unas mujeres* (1964; A Man and Various Women). One of his essays was especially successful: *El príncipe de este siglo: la literatura moderna y el demonio* (1967; The Prince of the Century: Modern Literature and the Devil).

SPANISH ACADEMY. *See* Academia Española

SPILL. *See* Roig, Jaume

STÚÑIGA, Cancionero de (2nd. half of 15th c.), poetry anthology, perhaps compiled by Lope de *Stúñiga, author of the first poem in the collection. On the basis of various historical allusions, Nicasio Salvador Miguel has posited a compilation date of 1460–1463 for the ms., and has suggested Naples as a location, through paleographic and linguistic observations. Most of the poems in the *Cancionero are by poets from the court of Alphonse V, who ruled Naples from 1443 to 1458. Forty poets are named; "Carvajal" is the most frequent author. The collection contains love songs, *decires*, **serranillas*, political poems, satire, etc. Surprisingly, *Italian literary influences are absent.

BIBLIOGRAPHY

Primary Works

Cancionero de Estúñiga. Ed., study N. Salvador Miguel. Madrid: Alhambra, 1987.

Criticism

Salvador Miguel, N. *La poesía cancioneril. El 'Cancionero de Estúñiga.'* Madrid: Alhambra, 1977. Includes biographical data for all poets represented.

STÚÑIGA, Lope de (fl. 1434, ?–?), soldier and poet. Son of Marshall Íñigo Ortiz, he participated in the Paso honroso (1434—See *Paso honroso, Libro del*), along with his cousin Suero de Quiñones, against Alvaro de Luna. His limited literary production consists of some political sayings and poems which appear in several **cancioneros*. The *Cancionero de Stúñiga,* which remained unpublished until 1872, carries his name but contains only a few of his poems; other contributors include Carvajal, Alfonso Enríquez, Juan de *Padilla, *Rodríguez del Padrón, Hugo de Urríes, and Diego de *Valera. The principal themes of Stúñiga's poems are love, friendship and politics. The collection offers valuable testimony to chivalry practiced by Spanish noblemen in the fifteenth c.

BIBLIOGRAPHY

Primary Texts

Cancionero de Estúñiga. Edición paleográfica. Ed. Manuel Alvar and Elena Alvar. Zaragoza: Institución Fernando el Católico, 1981.

La poesía cancioneril. El ''Cancionero de Estúñiga.'' Ed. N. Salvador Miguel. Madrid: Alhambra, 1977.

Lope de Stúñiga: ''Poesías.'' Ed. J. Battesti-Pelegrin. Aix-en-Provence: U de Provence, 1982.

Criticism

Battesti-Pelegrin, J. ''Lope de Stúñiga. Recherches sur la poèsie espagnole au XVeme siècle.'' Diss., U of Paris, 1978.

Veronica Sauter

SUÁREZ, Constantino (1890, Aviles, Asturias–1941, Madrid), Spanish journalist and novelist, known by his pseudonym, Españolito. He was very popular in Cuba, to which he emigrated. He published a number of novels, of which *Una sombra de mujer* (1927; A Woman's Shadow) is typical. He did linguistic studies, including *Vocabulario cubano* (1921; Cuban Vocabulary), and was very important in the local culture movements of this century for his initiating a bio-bibliographical dictionary, *Escritores y Artistas Asturianos* (1936; Artists and Writers of Asturias), of which he published the first three volumes, with four more being published by José María *Martínez Cachero (1956 and following years).

SUÁREZ, Francisco (1548, Granada–1617, Lisbon), influential Jesuit theologian, philosopher, jurist. He was initially rejected by the order, which judged him mentally and physically inferior. Ordained in 1572, he taught philosophy and theology at the leading universities in Spain, and—for five years—at the Jesuit College in Rome. His final appointment, made by Philip II, was chair of theology at the U of Coimbra, Portugal. A prolific man, Suárez was the principal exponent of Jesuit doctrinal thought. Editions of his works number twenty-three to twenty-eight volumes. Some of his most significant writings include the *Disputationes metaphysicae* (1597; Metaphysical Discussions), the first original systematic treatment of metaphysics since Aristotle. It became a standard text in seventeenth-c. Catholic and Protestant universities of Europe, exerting significant influence. Suárez's writings in politics and law are equally significant. Along with Francisco de *Vitoria, he is a founder of international law with *Ius gentium* (The Law of Peoples) and *De legibus ac Deo legistatore* (1612; On Law and God the Legislator), which contain ideas about the law of peoples and the community nature of nations. His theological writings harmonize with those of Luis de *Molina in their attempt to reconcile predestination and free will in an orthodox fashion. At the request of Pope Paul V, Suárez also composed the treatise *Defensio catholicae fidea contra anglicanae sectae errores* (1613; Defense of the Catholic Faith against Errors of the Anglican Sect), which argues against the oath of allegiance which James I required of his subjects.

BIBLIOGRAPHY

Primary Texts

Disputationes metafísicas. Ed. and tr. S. Rábade Romeo, S. Caballero Sánchez, A. Puigcerver Zanón. Madrid: Gredos, 1962. Latin and Spanish.

Guerra, intervención, paz internacional. Tr., study, notes L. Pereña Vicente. Austral 1273. Madrid: Espasa-Calpe, 1956.

Opera omnia. 26 vols. Paris: Vives, 1856–61.

Tratado de las leyes y de Dios legislador. Tr. J. Torrubiano Ripoll. 11 vols. Madrid: n.p., 1918.

English Translations

On Formal and Universal Unity; De unitate formali et universali. Tr., intro., J. F. Ross. Milwaukee: Marquette UP, 1964.

Selections from Three Works of Francisco Suárez. De legibus . . . Defensio fidei . . . De triplici virtute. Tr. G. Williams, A. Brown, J. Waldron. Oxford: Clarendon, 1944.

Criticism

Fernández, C. *Metafísica del conocimiento en Suárez*. Madrid: Colegio Máximo de Oña, 1954.

Pereña Vicente, L. *Teoría de la guerra en Francisco Suárez*. Madrid: CSIC, 1954.

Rommein, H. A. *La teoría del estado y de la comunidad internacional en Francisco Suárez*. Tr. V. García Yebra. Buenos Aires: Instituto de Derecho Internacional, 1951.

José Ortega

SUÁREZ, Gonzalo (1934, Oviedo–), Spanish novelist, short-story writer and cinematographer. His writings began appearing in the 1960s, and caused a certain consternation as they were quite unlike what was being written in Spain at that time, indeed unlike anything previously produced in Spain, being more similar to British or American writers, some of them provoking comparisons with Poe, Lovecraft, and Bierce. There is very little in Peninsular Spanish fiction to provide any antecedent for works in the Gothic vein, or tales of the fantastic and the marvelous. Among Suárez's books are *De cuerpo presente* (Lying in State), *Los once y uno* (Eleven and One), *Trece veces trece* (1972; Thirteen Times Thirteen), *El roedor de Fortimbrás* (The Rodent of Fortimbras), and *Rocabruno bate a Ditirambo* (Rocabruno Beats Ditirambo). His movie production is among the most controversial of the "New" Spanish Cinema, including "Ditirambo vela por nosotros" (Ditirambo Watches over Us), "El horrible ser nunca visto" (The Horrible Being Never Seen), "Ditirambo," "El extraño caso del doctor Fausto" (Strange Case of Dr. Faust), "Aoom," "Morbo" (Morbidity), "La loba y la paloma" (The She-Wolf and the Dove), and "La regenta" (The Governor's Wife). In addition to his tales of phantoms and terror, absurdity, anguish and hallucination, Suárez has cultivated detective fiction or the spy thriller in *Operación "Doble Dos"* (1974; Operation Double Two), based upon the visit of President Eisenhower to Spain in 1959, when the Spanish police received a tip that certain forces were planning the assassination of both heads of state. This plot—whether real or apocryphal—provides the point of departure for Suárez, who treats the complicated intrigue with subtle yet ferocious humor. Essentially ignored inside Spain, Suárez was praised and admired by Julio Cortázar, and considered one of Europe's most important writers by Max *Aub.

Janet Pérez

SUÁREZ BRAVO, Ceferino (1825, Oviedo–1896, Barcelona), journalist, dramatist and novelist. Between 1845 and 1857, Suárez composed successful plays, wrote for the newspapers *La España* and *El Contemporáneo,* and became a founder and contributor to the influential satirical weekly *El Padre Cobos* (Father Cobos). A Carlist after the 1868 revolution, he supported the cause in the daily he founded in Madrid, *El Fénix* (The Phoenix), and in his controversial novel, *Guerra sin cuartel* (1885; War without Quarter), which was awarded a prize by the *Academia Española. *Clarín condemned the work in *Nueva campaña.*

BIBLIOGRAPHY

Primary Texts

Guerra sin cuartel. Madrid: Voluntad, 1925.
El lunar de la marquesa. Madrid: Omaña, 1850.
Robespierre; crónica dramática del terror. Madrid: Tip. de los huérfanos, 1886.
Soledad, novela. Madrid: Apostolado de la Prensa, 1949.

Criticism

Clarín. *Nueva campaña 1885–86.* Madrid: Fernando Fé, 1877.

SUÁREZ DE DEZA, Enrique (1905, Buenos Aires–), Spanish playwright. Although born in Argentina, he was the son of Spanish parents, and was educated in Spain, where he obtained a degree in law and subsequently devoted himself to the theater. His first play was produced in 1925: *Ha entrado una mujer* (A Woman Has Entered). Thereafter, he added to his repertoire with *Padre* (1927; Father); *Una gran señora* (1932; A Great Lady); *El dictador* (1942; The Dictator); *Nocturno* (1946; Nocturne); *Miedo* (1946; Fear) and *El anticuario* (1948; The Antique Dealer), a work inspired by his readings of Dickens.

SUÁREZ DE FIGUEROA, Augusto (1852, Estepona, Málaga–1904, Málaga), journalist. Extremely popular in his day, his incisive columns appeared in *El Imparcial*. He also directed various papers, including *La Iberia, El Universal, El Resumen* and the *Heraldo de Madrid*, and founded the Madrid-based *Diario Universal*.

SUÁREZ DE FIGUEROA, Cristóbal (1571?, Valladolid–1644?, Italy), author and translator of didactic, satirical and *pastoral prose and poetry. The son of a lawyer from Galicia, he left home at seventeen and traveled to Italy. At Bologna or Pavia he received degrees in canon and civil law, and occupied various judicial posts in the service of the Spanish crown in Italy. In 1604, he returned to Valladolid, to seek favor at court. His irascible, backbiting and malicious temperament earned him no friends among the brilliant writers there, and he found no noble patron. After a violent altercation, he fled to Andalusía, but returned in 1605 to Madrid, where his bitter criticism of corruption at court was directed against the king's most powerful ministers. In 1609 he began serving don Juan Andrés Hurtado de Mendoza in Barajas; in 1615 he returned to Madrid, where he again engaged in satire against the idle, decadent life of the aristocracy, and in 1623 he departed for Naples to serve the new viceroy, the Duke of Alba. He was jailed in 1630 by the *Inquisition as a result of his interference in a conflict between civil and ecclesiastical authorities, and probably not freed until 1633. His refusal to overlook the serious abuses of those in power is an indication of incorruptible moral character, but his literary enmities seem based more often on envy than scruple. Figueroa opposed the overwhelmingly popular theater of Lope de *Vega on the basis of a strict reading of Horatian and Aristotelian theory, joined *Torres Rámila in ridiculing Lope's prose and poetry, made cruel allusions to *Ruiz de Alarcón's physical deformity and claims to noble ancestry, and mercilessly attacked *Cervantes only a year after his death, in *El Passagero* (1617; The Traveler). He praised only *Carrillo y Sotomayor and *Góngora among his contemporaries, although he satirized the extremes of **culteranismo*.

Figueroa's literary reputation begins with his translation of Guarini's *Il Pastor Fido* (1609; The Faithful Shepherd), which follows Guarini's rapid movement, richness of color and imagery, and varied meter more closely than did his 1602 translation, which he never acknowledged. His pastoral novel, *La constante Amarilis* (1609; The Faithful Amaryllis), is a *roman à clef* written to celebrate the marriage of Suárez's patron, don Juan Andrés Hurtado de Mendoza, to his cousin María de Cárdenas, against the wishes of her family. The work is replete with panegyric for the noble patron-protagonist. The epic poem *España defendida*

(1612; Spain Defended), dedicated to don Juan Andrés, is modeled closely on Tasso's *Gerusalemme liberata* (Jerusalem Freed), and celebrates Bernardo del Carpio's victory over Charlemagne at Roncesvalles, countering the injury to Spanish pride caused by the French version in the *Song of Roland*. Don Juan Andrés commissioned a biography of his father, Don García de Mendoza, Marquis of Cañete, governor of Chile during the 1557 rebellion of the Araucanian Indians recounted in the epic poems of Alonso de *Ercilla and Pedro de *Oña, and viceroy of Peru from 1588 to 1596.

Important for its list of contemporary actors and condemnation of Lope's theater and participation in poetic competitions is the *Plaza universal de todas ciencias y artes* (1615; Universal Forum of All Sciences and Arts), a translation of Tomasso Garzoni's encyclopedic *Piazza Universale* with the addition of material of greater interest to Spanish readers. Figueroa again attacked the *comedia* (Spanish drama) in *El passagero* (1617), a subjective and personal account of early seventeenth c. Spanish life and customs. This satirical miscellany is divided into *alivios* (rests by the wayside), a series of dialogues among four travelers on their way from Madrid to Barcelona, planning to embark for Italy. The Doctor (Figueroa), a learned theologian (Lope's enemy Torres Rámila), a soldier and a goldsmith, discuss literary, military, political, and amorous topics and tell tales of adventure, and an innkeeper narrates a *picaresque novel. Figueroa's *Varias noticias importantes a la humana comunicación* (1621; Diverse Information Important to Human Communication) is another didactic miscellany, filled with pedantic references to classical authors. *Pusilipo* (1629) is named for a hill in Naples on which a series of didactic and religious dialogues take place between four friends. Figueroa died in Italy; in an age of extravagant funerary panegyric, his death went unnoticed.

BIBLIOGRAPHY

Primary Texts

La Constante Amarilis. Prosas y versos. Valencia: Junto al molino de Rouella, 1609.

España defendida. Poema heroyco. Madrid: Juan de la Cuesta, 1612. Ed. R. Selden Rose. Madrid: n.p., 1916.

Hechos de Don García Hurtado de Mendoza, Quarto Marqués de Cañete. Madrid: Real, 1613.

Historia y Anual Relación de las cosas que hizieron los Padres de la Compañía de Jesús, por las partes de Oriente y otras. . . . Tr. of work by P. Fernão Guerreiro (1611). Madrid: Real, 1614.

El Pastor Fido, tragicomedia Pastoral. De Baptista Guarini. Tr. Suárez de Figueroa. Valencia: Mey, 1609.

El Passagero. Advertencias utilíssimas a la vida humana. Madrid: Luis Sánchez, 1617. Ed. R. Selden Rose. Madrid: Sociedad de Bibliófilos Españoles, 1914.

Plaza universal de todas Ciencias y Artes, parte traducida de Toscano, y parte compuesta por . . . Cristóbal Suárez de Figueroa. Madrid: Luis Sánchez, 1615.

Pusilipo. Ratos de conversación, en los que dura el paseo. Naples: Scoriggio, 1629.

Varias noticias importantes a la humana comunicación. Madrid: Tomás Iunti, 1621.

Criticism

Arce, Joaquín, "Un desconcertante plagio en prosa de una traducción en verso." *Filología moderna* 46–47 (1972–73): 3–29.

Crawford, J.P.W. *The Life and Works of Cristóbal Suárez de Figueroa*. Philadelphia: U of Pennsylvania, 1907.

———. "Suárez de Figueroa's *España defendida* and Tasso's *Gerusalemme Liberata*." *RR* 4 (1913): 207–20.

Wellington, Marie Z. "*La constante Amarilis* and Its Italian Pastoral Sources." *Philological Quarterly* 34 (1955): 81–87.

Emilie Bergmann

SUÁREZ DEL OTERO, Concha (1908, Luarca, Asturias–), novelist, poet, essayist, critic, short story writer. The recipient of a doctorate from the U of Madrid, Suárez del Otero also held a chair of Spanish literature at that institution. After two youthful novels in the pre-war period (*Mabel* [1928] and *Vulgaridades* [1930; Commonplaces]), she spent some two decades without publication. Both early narratives are set in her native Asturias and deal with young women's process of adjustment to life in the region. Suárez del Otero returned to literature with a collection of poems, *Vida plena* (1949; Full Life), divided in sections corresponding to three formative periods of her life, a kind of poetic journal of maturation. *La vida en un día* (1951; Life in a Day) contains a dozen short stories utilizing mainly feminine viewpoints and treating such themes as love, solitude and domesticity. *Mi amiga Andrée* (1954; My Friend Andrea), another story collection, reiterates many of the themes—and four of the stories—of the previous volume, but expands the author's exploration of the feminine existential quandary, search for happiness, and conflicting drives for self-realization and security. *Satanás no duerme* (1958; The Devil Doesn't Sleep), a medium-length novel, might be subtitled High School Reunion. It retraces the lives of six students who make a pact upon graduation from high school in 1936 to reunite in ten years. The Spanish Civil War and its ravages, the post-war hardships, and intervening careers and loves mean that the once close friends discover they now have little in common. *Me llamo Clara* (1968; My Name Is Clara) is considered by many to be the author's best novel, and belongs to the post–neo-realist vogue of metafiction, utilizing the novel-within-a-novel device. Clara, the protagonist, becomes a writer after losing her teaching job, but suspends work on her autobiographical novel in order to work as a tour guide. The remainder of the novel (which perhaps may become the end of the novel-within-the novel?) relates her travels, abortive romance, and disillusioned return to Spain. Suárez del Otero has a strong feminist bent in themes, characters and materials, without being activist or extreme.

BIBLIOGRAPHY

Primary Texts

Mabel. Madrid: Biblioteca Patria, 1928.

Me llamo Clara. Madrid: Quevedo, 1968.

Mi amiga Andrée. Madrid: Afrodisio Aguado, 1954.
Satanás no duerme. Madrid: Prensa Española, 1958.
La vida en un día. Madrid: S. Aguirre, 1951.
Vida plena. Madrid: Afrodisio Aguado, 1949.
Vulgaridades. Madrid: Mujeres Españolas, 1930.

Janet Pérez

SUEIRO, Daniel (1931, Ribasar, La Coruña–1986, Madrid), Spanish novelist, short story writer, and journalist. Sueiro belongs chronologically to the mid-century generation of "social" novelists, critical neo-realists who usually write from a posture of political *engagement*. Such socio-political criticism and denunciation of economic injustice inspires *La criba* (1961; The Sieve). *El arte de matar* (1968; The Art of Killing) and *Los verdugos españoles* (1971; The Spanish Executioners) belong to his so-called documentary works, elicited by the stereotype of Spanish fanaticism and cruelty. *Estos son tus hermanos* (1965; These are Your Brothers) treats the theme of the exile's return with a brutal twist as the former expatriate finds only the most aggressive hostility upon entering his former hometown. *La noche más caliente* (1965; The Hottest Night) is thematically related insofar as it reveals the extent to which people appear to have been brutalized by the war. Here the dramatic interest resides in the confrontation between the two authority figures who have controlled a small town since the end of the war. *Solo de moto* (1967; Motorbike Solo) is a novelette, the last of Sueiro's purely neo-realist narratives. In *Corte de corteza* (1969; Brain Transplant) he experiments with the science fiction genre, although he continues to pursue themes of social injustice and to exploit the use of cruelty and violence.

Sueiro's short stories are excellent, including the collections *Los conspiradores* (1964; The Conspirators); *Toda la semana* (1965; All Week); *El cuidado de las manos* (1974; Care of the Hands), a satirical look at courting norms; and *Servicio de navaja* (1977; Barber Service). He has also written movie scripts such as *Los golfos* (Street Urchins) for Carlos Saura and *Los farsantes* (Comics), directed by Mario Camus.

BIBLIOGRAPHY

Criticism

Navales, Ana María. *Cuatro novelistas españoles: Miguel Delibes, Ignacio Aldecoa, Daniel Sueiro, Francisco Umbral*. Madrid: Fundamentos, 1974. 151–212.

SUÑOL, Cèlia (1899, Barcelona–), novelist. The first woman writer to break the silence imposed by the Franco dictatorship, she won the first Joanot Martorell Prize for *Primera Part* (1948; First Part). The novel is a fictionalized autobiography in which she describes the atmosphere of Barcelona in the early years of the c., her contacts with the feminist movement, her illness and profound psychological crisis. Her youth was marked by tuberculosis: her own, then her husband's who died just a few years after they met, and finally, her son's. She remarried, had a daughter, and was widowed again after a few years. To support her children, she did sewing and translations and worked in a bar; this last experience resulted in a novel, ''Bar,'' which the Franco *censorship would not allow to be published because it dealt with suicide. She considered literature a pleasure rather than an occupation, and left writing to dedicate herself to her children, but in the title story of *L'home de les fires i altres contes* (1950; The Man of the Fairs and Other Stories) one hears the voice of an overworked woman who wants to write but is overwhelmed by domestic duties.

BIBLIOGRAPHY

Primary Texts

L'home de les fires i altres contes. Barcelona: Selecta, 1950.
Primera part. Barcelona: Aymà, 1948.

Isabel Segura

T

TABOADA, Luis (1848, Vigo–1906, Madrid), journalist and satirical writer. Engaged in politics, he was private secretary to Ruiz Zorrilla and Nicolás María Rivero. He was very famous for his contributions to contemporary newspapers and magazines such as *La Ilustración Española y Americana*, *Blanco y Negro*, *Pluma y Lápiz*, *ABC*, *El Imparcial*, etc. Among his prose works are *Madrid en broma* (1891; Madrid Taken Lightly), *Siga la fiesta* (1892; Let the Party Go On), *La viuda de Chaparro* (1899; Chaparro's Widow), and *Pescadero, a tus besugos* (1906; Fishmonger, To Your Sea Bream). He also left the autobiographical work *Intimidades y recuerdos* (1900; Intimacies and Memories). Taboada wrote in a light, satirical vein for a large public who wanted to be amused. He sharply depicted the customs and mores of the Madrid middle class. At times he used Juan Balduque as a pseudonym.

BIBLIOGRAPHY

Primary Texts

Intimidades y recuerdos (Páginas de la vida de un escritor). Madrid: Fortanet, 1900.

Madrid en broma. Madrid: Lasanta, 1891.

Pescadero, a tus besugos. Novela cómica. Madrid: Fortanet, 1906.

Siga la fiesta. Madrid: Lasanta, 1892.

La viuda de Chaparro. Madrid: Fortanet, 1899.

Salvador García Castañeda

TAFUR, Pero (1410?, Córdoba–1487?, Córdoba), traveler and writer of a travel book. After battling against the Moors, he took advantage of a truce to set sail from Sanlúcar to Genoa. The voyage was the beginning of a journey that lasted four years (1435–39) through the eastern Mediterranean and northern Europe. In Italy he visited numerous cities including Pisa, Florence, Rome, and Venice. He departed for the Holy Land and later went to Cypress, serving briefly as their ambassador in Cairo and then Constantinople. He traveled through Greece and Italy to Romania, Germany, and Flanders. After returning to Spain, he settled again in Córdoba, where he took a prominent part in local affairs and married doña Juana de Horozco some time before 1452.

Tafur is the author of *Las andanzas e viajes de Pero Tafur por diversas partes del mundo* (1874; *Travels and Adventures*, 1926). The journal is notable for its lively descriptions of places, peoples, cities, and even animals, mixed with traditional lore and fanciful legends. It also includes information on commerce and trade, an obvious predilection among the interests of the author.

BIBLIOGRAPHY

Primary Texts

Andanças e viajes [selected readings]. In *Libros españoles de viajes medievales*. Ed. J. Rubio Tovar. Madrid: Taurus, 1986. 189–203.

Las andanzas e viajes de Pero Tafur por diversas partes del mundo. Ed. Jiménez de la Espada. Madrid: Colección de libros raros y curiosos, 1874.

English Translation

Travels and Adventures. Ed., tr. Malcolm Letts. London: Routledge, 1926.

Criticism

LaBarge, Margaret Wade. "Pero Tafur: A Fifteenth-Century Spaniard." *Florilegium* 5 (1983): 237–47.

Helen H. Reed

TALAVERA, Hernando de (1428, Talavera de la Reina, Toledo–1507, Granada), member of the Hieronomyte order, professor, confessor to Queen Isabel, first archbishop of Granada. His illustrious career spanned one of the most optimistic moments of Spanish history. His religious writings contribute firmly to the initiation of a current of ascetic-religious literature which culminates in the works of Sta. *Teresa and San *Juan de la Cruz. *See also* Ascetical Literature; Mysticism.

BIBLIOGRAPHY

Primary Texts

Obras. Ed. Mir. In NBAE 16.

Criticism

Fernández Martínez, F. *La España imperial: Fray Hernando de Talavera, confesor de los Reyes Católicos*. Madrid: Biblioteca Nueva, 1942.

Surtz, R. "Trois 'villancicos' de Fray Hernando de Talavera." *BH* 80 (1978): 277–85.

TAMARIZ, Cristóbal de (fl. 1585, Seville?–?), poet, prose author. Little was known of the Licenciate Tamariz for many years. He was one of the first Spaniards to write Italian-inspired novellas; his stories generally rework tales by

Boccaccio, Aesop, Bandello, Pero *Alfonso, etc.; all are in verse. They remained unpublished until this c. Tamariz also wrote an *Historia de los sanctos mártires de Cartuja que padescieron en Londres* (1584; History of the Saintly Carthusian Martyrs Persecuted in London). *See also* Hagiography; Italian Literary Influences.

BIBLIOGRAPHY

Primary Texts

Historia de los sanctos mártires. . . . Seville: n.p., 1584.

Novelas en verso. Ed. D. R. McGrady. Charlottesville, VA: Biblioteca Siglo de Oro, 1974.

Novelas y cuentos en verso del Licenciado Tamariz. Ed. A. Rodríguez Moñino. Valencia: n.p., 1956.

Criticism

McGrady, D. R. "Sources and Significance of the *Novelas del Licenciado Tamariz.*" *RR* 59 (1968): 10–15.

Rodríguez-Moñino, A. "El Licenciado Tamariz, poeta del siglo XVI." In *Relieves de erudición.* Valencia: Castalia, 1959.

Maureen Ihrie

TAMAYO DE VARGAS, Tomás (1588, Madrid–1641, Madrid), historian, scholar and bibliographer. Educated at the U of Toledo, he later taught there. He acquired a fine command of classical languages, and was interested in both literary history and political events. In 1621 he was named secretary to the Spanish ambassador in Venice; later, he became a council member of the *Inquisition. When Antonio de *Herrera died in 1625, Tamayo de Vargas assumed the post of official historian of Castile. He contributed to the *Historia de Toledo* (History of Toledo) and also wrote about some of the prominent families there.

In the literary arena, Tamayo de Vargas maintained friendships with *Góngora, *Quevedo and Lope de *Vega, and he publicly defended both Lope and Góngora. In addition, he wrote the *Historia general de España del padre doctor Juan de Mariana defendida* (1616; Defense of Father Juan de Mariana's General History of Spain), in which he refuted all attacks against Father *Mariana that had been published by Pedro Mantuano. Tamayo's concern for literary history inspired his *Junta de libros la mayor que España ha visto en su lengua hasta 1624* (Greatest Collection of Spanish Books up to 1624). Although the work was never printed, it exists in three mss., one of which is in the *Biblioteca Nacional in Madrid; it has proved extremely useful to scholars of Spanish literature and established Tamayo's reputation as a bibliographer.

BIBLIOGRAPHY

Primary Texts

Descripción de la imperial ciudad de Toledo. . . . Toledo: Rodríguez, 1617.

Historia general de España del padre doctor Juan de Mariana defendida. Toledo: Rodríguez, 1616.

Toledo memorial. Madrid: n.p., 1629.

Nina Shecktor

TAMAYO Y BAUS, Manuel, pseudonym of don Joaquín Estébanez (1829, Madrid–1898, Madrid), playwright. The son of actors José Tamayo and Joaquina Baus, he always lived close to the life of the theater. This fact, combined with his skills as a dramatist, helped to perfect the technique of his dramatic works.

A conservative in politics, he occupied important offices such as that of the director of the *Biblioteca Nacional (1884) and head of the Body of Archivists; he became a member of the *Academia Española in 1858 and later served as its secretary. In his entrance speech into the academy, "De la verdad como fuente de belleza en la literatura dramática" (Truth as the Source of Beauty in Dramatic Literature), he set forth his aesthetic theories about drama.

Tamayo was a renovator of nineteenth-c. Spanish theater and his work reveals the influence of foreign writers (Schiller, Dumas, Latour de Saint Ibars, Lemercier, etc.). Some of his dramas contain sensationalist elements, yet passion motivates his characters with less rhetoric and exaggeration than in the romantics. Nevertheless, there are still romantic elements such as historical themes and figures in his dramatic works. This heritage is revealed in his first plays: *El cinco de agosto* (1849; The Fifth of August), *Angela* (1851) and *Juana de Arco* (1847; Joan of Arc), inspired by Schiller's *Maid of Orleans.* A romantic spirit impregnates his classic tragedy *Virginia* (1853). Other historical dramas include *La ricahembra* (1854; The Rich Woman), written in collaboration with Aureliano *Fernández Guerra, and *Locura de amor* (1855; Insanity of Love), a drama in prose which deals with the romantic and passionate theme of Juana la Loca's excessive love.

Tamayo also wrote a number of dramas and comedies about contemporary life which contain moral, religious or political themes: in *La bola de nieve* (1856; The Snow Ball), written in verse, he attacks unfounded jealousy; *Lo positivo* (1863; The Positive) shows virtue triumphant over selfishness and materialism; *Lances de honor* (1863; Affairs of Honor) condemns the practice of dueling, and *Hombres de bien* (1870; Good Men) criticizes contemporary society's tolerance of certain vices.

Generally considered to be his best work, *Un drama nuevo* (1867; *A New Drama*, 1915) concerns itself with aesthetic rather than ethical issues. This prose drama revives the atmosphere of Shakespearean England, and uses the device of a play in which the theatrical plot turns into reality.

Although much of his dramatic production is marred by obvious didactic intentions, Tamayo y Baus was skilled in theatrical techniques and in the creation of dramatic tension based on pure human conflict. *See also* Romanticism; Theatre in Spain.

BIBLIOGRAPHY

Primary Texts

Obras completas de Manuel Tamayo y Baus de la Real Academia Española. Prol. Alejandro Pidal y Mon. Madrid: Fax, 1947.

English Translation

A New Drama. Tr. J. D. Fitz-Gerald and T. H. Guild. New York: Hispanic Society of America, 1915.

Criticism

Alberich, José. "El papel de Shakespeare en *Un drama nuevo* de Tamayo." *Filología Moderna* 39 (1970): 301–22.

Esquer Torres, Ramón. "Tamayo y Baus: Sus proyectos literarios inacabados." *BRAE* 43 (1963): 151–64.

Flynn, Gerard C. *Manuel Tamayo y Baus*. TWAS 263. New York: Twayne, 1973.

Halsey, Martha. "Juana la Loca in Three Dramas of Tamayo y Baus, Galdós, and Martín Recuerda." *MLS* 9.1 (1978–79): 47–59.

Lassaletta, Manuel C. "*Un drama nuevo* y el realismo literario." *Hispania* 57 (1974): 856–67.

Schwartz, Egon. "Manuel Tamayo y Baus and Schiller." *Comparative Literature* 13 (1961): 123–37.

Tayler, Neale H. *Las fuentes del teatro de Tamayo y Baus; Originalidad e influencias*. Madrid: Gráficas Uguina, 1959.

Phoebe Porter Medina

TAPIA, Eugenio de (1776, Avila–1860, Madrid), playwright, historian, satirical poet. During the Spanish War of Independence Tapia was in Cádiz where, with the aid of *Quintana, he edited the *Semanario Patriotico* (The Patriotic Weekly) and directed the Government Gazette. Persecuted for his Liberal ideas, he went into exile in France (1823–34). After Ferdinand VII's death, he became, among other things, director of the *Biblioteca Nacional. A lawyer by training, he wrote many legal treatises; as a historian he left *Historia de la civilización española desde la invasión de los árabes hasta la época presente* (1840; History of Spanish Civilization from the Arab Invasion to the Present); as a playwright, he composed plays such as *Idomeneo* (1799; Idomeneus), *El preso o el parecido* (1800; The Prisoner or the Resemblance), and *El hijo predilecto* (1839; The Favorite Son). Satirical plays include *La bruja, el duende y la Inquisición* (1837; The Witch, the Goblin and the Inquisition), a famous satire against the Romantics, and *Ensayos satíricos* (1820; Satirical Essays), in which he criticizes the customs of contemporary society. *See also* Romanticism.

BIBLIOGRAPHY

Primary Texts

La bruja, el duende y la Inquisición. Madrid: Piñuela, 1837.

Ensayos satíricos en verso y en prosa. Madrid: Nacional, 1820.

El hijo predilecto. Madrid: Yenes, 1839.
Historia de la civilización española. 4 vols. Madrid: Yenes, 1840.
Idomeneo. Madrid: Villalpando, 1799.

Criticism

Cueto, Leopoldo Augusto de. "Don Eugenio de Tapia." In BAE 67: 671–76.
Moellering, W. "Eugenio de Tapia and Mesonero Romanos." *Hispania* 23 (Oct. 1940): 241–44.
Porter, M. E. "Eugenio de Tapia: A Forerunner of Mesonero Romanos." *HR* 8 (1940): 145–55.

Salvador García Castañeda

TÁRREGA, Francisco Agustín (1554, Valencia–1602, Valencia), canon of Valencia, poet and playwright. Biographical information on this important precursor of Lope de *Vega is scanty and contradictory. He was a founder of the Academia de los Nocturnos, adopting the pseudonym Miedo (Fear). *Cervantes (in the prologue to his *Comedias*) praised Tárrega's "discreción e innumerables conceptos" (discretion and countless conceits) and termed him one of the finest talents of the day. Modern criticism places him second only to Guillén de *Castro among the school of Valencian dramatists. He wrote twelve plays, ten of which survive, of religious, patriotic, historical and popular bent. Finer works include *La sangre leal de los montañeses de Navarra* (The Loyal Blood of the Mountaineers), *La duquesa constante* (The Faithful Duchess) and *El prado de Valencia* (The Meadow of Valencia). For four centuries, *Los moriscos de Hornachos* (The Moriscos of Hornachos) was attributed to him, but, in 1972, this attribution was challenged by Jean-Marc Pelorson. *See also* Academia.

BIBLIOGRAPHY

Primary Texts

Poetas dramáticos valencianos. Ed. Eduardo Juliá Martínez. 2 vols. Madrid: RAE, 1929.

Criticism

Pelorson, Jean-Marc. "Recherches sur la comedie 'Los moriscos de Hornachuelos.' " *BH* 74.1–2 (Jan.-June 1972): 5–42.
Serrano Canete, Joaquín. *El canónigo Francisco-Agustín Tárrega: Estudio biográfico-bibliográfico*. Valencia: José Ortega, 1889.
Weiger, J. G. *The Valencian Dramatists of Spain's Golden Age*. TWAS 371. Boston: Twayne, 1976.

TASIS I MARCA, Rafael (1906, Barcelona–1967, Paris), Catalan novelist, critic and historian. Tasis began writing while still a teenager, publishing his first book at the age of eighteen: *El daltabaix* (1924; The Rise and Fall). *Vint anys* (1931; Twenty Years) and *Una visió de conjunt de la novel·la catalana* (1935; An Overview of the Catalan Novel) followed, and during the war he published *La revolució en els Ajuntaments* (1937; Revolution in the City Halls), *La Literatura catalana moderna* (1937; Modern Catalan Literature), and *Les pedres parlen* (1938; The Stones Speak). Exiled in 1939 to France, he did radio work in Paris, publishing *Tot l'any* (1943; All Year), *Històries de coneguts* (1945; Stories of Acquaintances) and *L' etudiant et la sorcière* (1947; The Student and the Sorceress). Back in Barcelona, he published *Sol ponent* (1953; Setting Sun), the year in which he was awarded the Catalunya Novel Prize. He then turned to detective fiction: *La Bíblia valenciana* (1955; The Valencian Bible), *Es hora de plegar* (1956; It's Time to Fold Up), and *Un crimal Paral·lelo* (1960; Crime on the Parallel). Historical works include *Joan I, el rei caçador i músic* (1958; King John I, Huntsman and Musician), *La vida del Rei en Pere III* (1961; The Life of Peter III), and *Pere III el Ceremoniós i els seus fills* (1957; King Peter III the Ceremonious and his Sons). He worked in compiling many anthologies of Catalan fiction, and wrote such critical works as *La Renaixença catalana* (1967; The Catalan Renaissance), *El món modern i nosaltres* (1967; We and the Modern World), and *Un segle de poesia catalana* (1967; A Century of Catalan Poetry). He also wrote for the theater: *Gulliver i els gegants* (1952; Gulliver and the Giants), *Parallel 1934* (1953, in collaboration with J. M. Poblet), *Un home entre herois* (1954; One Man among Heroes)—awarded the Guimera Prize; and *La maleta* (n.d.; The Suitcase).

TENREIRO, Ramón María (1879, ?–1935, ?), Spanish lawyer. He was a collaborator of numerous literary reviews, and also wrote novels and short fiction, including *Dama pobreza* (1926; Lady Poverty), *La ley del pecado* (1930; The Law of Sin), and *Lunes antes del alba* (1918; Monday before Dawn).

TERESA DE JESÚS, Santa (1515, Avila or Gotarrendura–1582, Alba de Tormes), mystic, reformer, religious writer, commonly known as Saint Teresa of Avila in English. Born Teresa de Cepeda y Ahumada to a moderately well-placed **converso* family, she was one of eleven children, and, by her own account, was her father's favorite. Influenced by stories of the Reconquest of Spain and later by her mother's interest in the novels of chivalry (*caballeriás), she manifested an adventurous spirit when she and her brother, Rodrigo, ran away from home as children to seek martyrdom at the hands of the Moors. In 1536, with the help of the same brother, she entered the Carmelite convent of La Encarnación in Avila against her father's wishes and was professed there the following year. Her early religious life was marked by illness and lukewarm attention to the demands of the prayer life she later embraced. In 1562 she accomplished the first steps in the reform of the Carmelites with the establishment of the first convent dedicated to the primitive rule, San José in Avila. Opposition from the authorities as well as from members of her own order finally led to a division of the order, with the Discalced following Teresa's lead in observing the primitive rule. She was investigated by the *Inquisition, but the care of her confessors, especially the Dominican *Báñez, and the support of the king, Philip II, provided protection and encouragement of the reform. She helped in the establishment of seventeen convents of Discalced nuns and also encouraged the reform of the Carmelite men with the assistance of San *Juan de la Cruz. In these endeavors she traveled tirelessly and extensively throughout Spain. On her return from Burgos, she fell ill and died in Alba de Tormes in October of 1582. Beatified in 1614 and canonized in 1622, she was eventually declared a Doctor of the Church in 1970 by Pope Paul VI. Efforts by Philip III to declare her patroness of Spain in 1617 were only partially successful.

In addition to her contributions to the Counter-Reformation in Spain, she, along with San Juan de la Cruz, represents the culmination of mystical teaching in Spain. Her doctrine is spread through a number of books and other writings. Save in the case of her letters, virtually all of her writings came at the request of her confessors. The first work of note is the *Libro de la vida* (1562; *The Life of Santa Teresa*, 1960), whose original ms. is preserved in the library of the Escorial. Less an autobiography than a recounting of her spiritual experience, it represents the story of her progress in mystical prayer. A ten-chapter digression from the events of her life utilizes an extended comparison of the soul to a garden in need of water for it to flourish. The levels of prayer are likened to the means of watering the garden, first by drawing from a well and finally by rain from heaven. Assiduously examined by her confessor as well as by the Inquisition, the work finally received the approval of the bishop of Avila in 1575 although it, like all of her major works, was not published until after her death.

An early version of the *Life*, the *Relaciones* (*Relations*) was written in 1560. Other minor works such as the *Constituciones* (1563; *Constitutions*, 1979), the *Avisos espirituales* (1579; *Spiritual Counsels*, 1979), the *Avisos* (1572; *Maxims*, 1979) the *Modo de visitar los conventos* (1576; *Visitation of Convents*, 1979) and the *Vejamen* (1577; *Judgment*, 1979) deal with convent business or address specific questions raised by others. The *Conceptos del amor de Dios sobre algunas palabras de los cantares de Salomón* (1566; *Conceptions of the Love of God*, 1979), also known as *Meditaciones sobre los cantares* (Meditations on the Canticle of Canticles), provides commentary on a few verses of the Scriptural source. The *Libro de las fundaciones* (1573–77; *Foundations,* 1979) recounts the establishment of the convents of the reform and offers practical advice to superiors on the government of their nuns. The *Camino de perfección* (1562–73; *Way of Perfection*, 1964), was written for the nuns of San José as a guide to prayer and conventual living. It also includes an extended commentary on the Our Father.

Her mystical masterpiece is the *Las moradas* (1577; *Interior Castle,* 1961), a work that focuses exclusively on the means of attaining mystical union. It compares the stages in advancement to the mansions found in a walled city or interior castle. The stages are seven in number, each representing a phase of the mystical journey with which the author was familiar. The seventh and most interior mansion represents the culmination of mystical union, spiritual marriage with God. The work shows Teresa at her best both as a writer of vivacity and humanity and as an expert guide in the mystic way. Her language is vivid, direct, and compelling, while her message is both enlightening and encouraging, especially to beginners.

More than four hundred letters to a variety of people are preserved as well. They reveal added details of her life as well as the diversity of her interests and contacts. A number of poems attributed to her are of doubtful authenticity, although the gloss on "Vivo sin vivir en mí" (I live without living in myself) is probably her own. Nevertheless, the poems are far inferior in style and content to her prose works.

Her fame rests not only on her contribution to the religious history and literature of Spain but also on the naturalness of her style and the force of personality that it conveys to the reader. Her works provide a rich source of Castilian prose style of the sixteenth c., esteemed by critics such as *Menéndez Pidal for its directness and disingenuousness. It is marked by abundant use of digressions, ellipses, exclamations, incomplete sentences, and examples drawn from everyday life. It more closely resembles colloquial speech than a conscious literary style.

The saint's formal education was minimal, so that published sources of inspiration are few. She indicates that she knew no Latin and, therefore, composed entirely in Castilian. Although she cites few sources, these few are revealing, and include the *Vita Christi*, translated by Fray Ambrosio *Montesino, the *Epistles* of St. Jerome, the *Flos Sanctorum,* the *Confessions* of St. Augustine, the *Imitation of Christ*, the *Tercer abecedario* of Fray Francisco de *Osuna, and the *Subida al monte Zion por la vía contemplativa* by Bernardino de *Laredo. Her close contact with the Society of Jesus in matters of the reform suggests familiarity with Ignatian principles of spirituality, while contact with the Franciscan reformer, St. Peter of *Alcántara, proved crucial as an influence in the early stages of her own reform. Her frequent use of military allusions is often attributed to her early fondness for the chivalric romances.

Her influence on other writers and reformers is of equal importance. She was instrumental in encouraging San Juan de la Cruz to participate in the reform of the Carmelite men, and for a brief period (1572–74) the two were in close contact at La Encarnación, where she served as prioress and he as confessor. After her death, Fray Luis de *León was charged with the task of preparing her complete works for publication in 1588. The beatification and canonization celebrations within Spain produced a number of literary works dedicated to the saint, while later writers considered her contributions to prose style. Outside of Spain, she also influenced such religious writers as St. Francis de Sales and St. Thérèse de Lisieux as well as diverse literary and artistic figures such as Richard Crashaw, Bernini, George Eliot, Henri Bergson, Sarah Bernhardt, and Muriel Spark. *See also* Mysticism; Renaissance; Siglo de Oro.

BIBLIOGRAPHY

Primary Texts

Camino de perfección. Ed. José María Aguado. 2 vols. Madrid: Espasa-Calpe, 1969, 1973.

Libro de la vida. Ed. Dámaso Chicharro. Madrid: Cátedra, 1982.

Las moradas. Ed. Tomás Navarro Tomás. Madrid: Espasa-Calpe, 1968.

Obras completas. Ed. Efrén de la Madre de Dios, O.C.D. y Otger Steggink, O. Carm. 7th ed. Madrid: Católica, 1982.

English Translations

The Collected Works of Saint Teresa of Avila. Tr. and ed. Kieran Kavanaugh and Otilio Rodríguez. 2nd ed. 3 vols. Washington, DC: Institute of Carmelite Studies Publications, 1979.

The Complete Works of St. Teresa of Jesus. Tr. and ed. E. Allison Peers. 3 vols. London: Sheed and Ward, 1946.

Interior Castle. Tr. and ed. E. Allison Peers. Garden City, NY: Doubleday, 1961.

The Life of Teresa of Jesus. Tr. and ed. E. Allison Peers. Garden City, NY: Doubleday, 1960.

The Way of Perfection. Tr. and ed. E. Allison Peers. Garden City, NY: Doubleday, 1964.

Criticism

Concha, Victor G. de la. *El arte literario de Santa Teresa*. Barcelona: Ariel, 1978.

Efrén de la Madre de Dios, O.C.D. and Otger Steggink, O. Carm. *Santa Teresa y su tiempo*. 2 vols. Salamanca: Universidad Pontificia, 1982.

Hatzfeld, Helmut A. *Santa Teresa de Avila*. New York: Twayne, 1969.

Menéndez Pidal, Ramón. *La lengua de Cristóbal Colón, El estilo de Santa Teresa, y otros estudios sobre el siglo XVI*. Madrid: Espasa-Calpe, 1942.

Peers, E. Allison. *Mother of Carmel. A Portrait of St. Teresa of Jesus*. London: S.C.M., 1945.

Weber, Alison. *Teresa of Avila and the Rhetoric of Femininity*. Princeton: Princeton UP, 1990.

Elizabeth T. Howe

TERTULIA. A literary social gathering. The word first surfaces in early seventh-c. Spain, but such meetings—ranging from the institutionalized reunions of *Academias or *Ateneos to informal gatherings in cafés or private homes, have played an integral role in cultural development in Spain since the *Renaissance. The style of gathering varied through the years: the Duque de *Rivas, *Menéndez y Pelayo and *Pardo Bazán sponsored such gatherings in their homes. The nineteenth c. was a particularly fertile time for such activities—*Pérez Galdós chronicles the contemporary tertulia scene in one of his National Episodes (*La estafeta literaria*; The Literary Courier), and also in the novel *La fontana de oro*, named for the cafe in which such gatherings took place. Much remains to be written about the rich history of the tertulia.

BIBLIOGRAPHY

Criticism

Williams, E. M. *The development of the literary tertulia*. Cornell U Thesis, 1935.

THEATER IN SPAIN. The earliest extant example of drama in Spanish is a Nativity piece, the **Auto de los Reyes Magos* (Play of the Three Wise Men), which survives, probably incomplete, in a thirteenth-c. ms. copy but was written much earlier, c. 1150. In five short scenes, the work displays exceptional artistic worth and maturity (its unknown poet-author knows how to vary verse forms to suit changes in dramatic mood and situation, how to create tension through discussion and argument, and even how to convey convincingly the angry disposition of King Herod through a psychologically revealing soliloquy); so much so that it came to be regarded as proof of the existence in Castile of a particularly robust tradition of early liturgical theater. This view was modified by the discovery that the *auto*'s major sources of inspiration were French, and that its author was a Gascon or a Catalan. Nowadays critics accept that vernacular drama in Spain developed during the Middle Ages (*see* Edad Media, Literatura de la), as elsewhere in Europe, through the liturgical stimulus afforded by the church, which allowed the dramatic enactment of Gospel passages relating to the Passion and the Nativity to form part of its worship, ceremonies and festivals, in order to encourage devoutness and spiritual attentiveness in the laity. Initially such passages were enacted in Latin, within the churches, by members of the clergy; eventually they were performed partly or entirely in the vernacular, often outside the church in yards or marketplaces, frequently by the laity. And they contained increasing proportions of non-religious, popular material inserted for entertainment. Castile is no longer considered to have been the focus of liturgical dramatic activities in medieval Spain. The nature and quantity of early plays, both Latin and vernacular, which survived in Catalonia and Valencia, as opposed to the extreme scarcity of such texts in Castile, strongly indicate that liturgical theater developed more quickly and much more vigorously in those northern and eastern parts than in the Spanish center, where the social and political upheavals of the Reconquest and perhaps also the dominating influence of non-theatrically disposed Cluniac orders, doubtlessly hindered dramatic representations. Nevertheless, by the middle of the fifteenth c., liturgical drama flourished even in Castile. Recent research into the archives of the Cathedral of Toledo has revealed that plays were performed then in Toledo in celebration of the festival of Corpus Christi just as devotedly as they were in Barcelona, Gerona, Valencia and Seville. Some texts of these dramatic forerunners of the Golden Age *autos sacramentales* (**auto*) survive, notably an *Auto de la Pasión* (Passion Play) written by Alonso del Campo, for performance at Toledo between 1486 and 1497. Two anonymous works of this period deserve mention: the *Auto de la huida a Egipto* (The Flight into Egypt) and the Catalan piece, *Misteri d'Elx* (The Elche Mystery), evidently an expansion of a fourteenth-c. work dealing with the Assumption. Also important for understanding medieval theater in Spain are two plays by the courtier-soldier-poet, Gómez *Manrique (1412?–90?): *Lamentaciones hechas para Semana Santa* (Lamentations Composed for Holy Week) and *Representación del Nacimiento de Nuestro Señor* (Dramatization of the Birth of Our Lord). Neither is structurally advanced or theatrically distinguished, but both contain some outstanding lyrical passages. *Representación del Nacimiento de Nuestro Señor* (written for performance by nuns of the convent of Calabazanos where Manrique's sister was abbess) merits additional mention for its portrayal of Joseph's jealous, troubled reactions to Mary's pregnancy. Manrique's Joseph offers a first example in Spanish drama of the honor-sensitive husband, a figure destined for major roles in many serious dramatic works of Spain's *Siglo de Oro.

A primitive type of secular theater, evidently derived from degenerate forms of Low Latin amusements (spectacles, mimes, traveling shows), co-existed, indeed often cohabited, with liturgical drama in medieval Spain. **Juegos de escarnio* (Games of Mockery), as they are disapprovingly termed in the thirteenth-c. *Siete Partidas* of *Alphonse X, were regularly inserted into religious plays to provide burlesque dialogue and often obscene satirical interludes. The *Partidas* encouraged the clergy to take part in truly devout dramas, but forbade them to have anything to do with *juegos de escarnio*. The prohibition was reiterated, in Latin, two centuries later in a law promulgated by the Council of Aranda (1473) in order to oust *ludi theatrales* from church premises and activities. Such separatist, apparently restrictive measures in fact had a salutary effect upon theater in Spain. As the Middle Ages gave way to the early *Renaissance, secular drama began to distance itself from the jocular crudity of the *juegos de escarnio* and the (usually) more refined but equally superficial masques and pageantries enjoyed in courtly circles, toward more subtle and thoughtful attempts at dramatic expression. At this critical period of cultural transition, in the final decade of the fifteenth c., an extraordinary part-Medieval, part-Renaissance Spanish masterpiece was composed in dramatic form. Its originally published title, *Comedia de Calisto y Melibea* (1499), soon changed to *Tragicomedia de Calisto y Melibea*, but was then transformed into *La *Celestina*, a name rapidly determined by the popularity, in Spain and throughout Europe, of its most vigorously portrayed character: the bawd, Celestina. Its content expanded in stages until it consisted of twenty-one acts. It is now generally accepted that the **converso* Fernando de *Rojas wrote nearly the entire work, although the authorship of its lengthy first act is still unresolved. Critics also have long disputed the genre of the *Celestina*. Some stress its literary dependence on early Spanish fiction, notably the sentimental romance, or point to its ''undramatic'' length, its erudite interpolations and abundance of acts, or demonstrate that Rojas never intended it for performance but rather to be read aloud among friends. Other critics argue that its initial sources were dramatic (the late twelfth-c. Low Latin comedy **Pamphilus de Amore* and its Italian humanistic derivatives), and emphasize the realistic theatrical merits of the low-life scenes, and remind us that in the early period of the Spanish Renaissance, before the establishment of permanent theaters, many unarguably dramatic pieces were probably recited more often than they were performed. Beyond question is the fact that *La Celestina*, genuine play or not, deeply, persistently influenced the nature and development of Golden Age drama in Spain. Rojas's widely chosen sources encouraged dramatists to look for plot-material in Italian and classical as well as Spanish texts. His choice of principal theme stimulated them to concentrate on representing the predicaments and conflicts caused by love. Rojas's ability to characterize the complexities of human behavior spurred his admirers to attempt to portray convincingly self-contradictory protagonists: gallants who speak of purely spiritual love but think of sexual fulfillment, ladies who insist upon their virtue even as they relinquish it. As for Rojas's method of mixing elements of comedy into his tragedy to illuminate the "tragicomedy" of man's condition, his integration of subplot material into the main action, his development of master-servant relations, all these characteristics of *La Celestina* became standard features of Golden Age drama, from the experimental Renaissance age of Juan del *Encina and *Torres Naharro through to the Baroque epoch of Lope de *Vega and *Calderón.

The sixteenth-c. Renaissance in Spain brought in an epoch of drama characterized by persistent experiment and steady development. Classical and Italian influences understandably predominated. Some knowledge of classical authors had persisted during the Middle Ages, but only here and there, among scholars in *universities, schools or monasteries. Now, however, a new awareness of the ancients swept in from Italy, and spread throughout Spanish culture. Peninsular playwrights immersed themselves in works of Virgil, Horace, and, more importantly, the late Latin dramatists, Plautus and Terence; toward the end of the c. the tragedies of *Seneca also exercised a palpable influence. Italian works, notably humanistic comedies derived from classical originals, were read in quantity by Spanish playwrights, some of whom (Juan del Encina, Torres Naharro) spent periods of time resident in Italy, in direct contact with Italian Renaissance works and writers. More popular and improvised types of Italian plays also affected the theater in Spain, especially in the second half of the sixteenth c. when traveling troupes of Italian actors gave performances of plays in the *commedia dell'arte* tradition. Despite their interest in classical and Italian works, peninsular dramatists did not ignore native sources of inspiration and plot-material such as Spanish chivalric novels, *La Celestina*, and, later in the c., historical or legend-based ballads and chronicles. Dramatic innovation was not limited to source and subject matter. Playwrights experimented with a remarkable number of themes, conflicts and predicaments: themes of love fulfilled or frustrated, conflicts of loyalty, predicaments of honor, cases of vengeance. They tried to portray an admirable variety of character-types, some of which became key figures in the drama of Lope de Vega: the *mujer varonil* (manly woman), for instance, and the **gracioso* (witty servant), who appears to have emerged partly from the comic shepherd of Spanish medieval drama, and in part from the *zanni* (zany attendant) of the Italian *commedia dell'arte*. They were flexible in organizing dramatic structure, sometimes writing plays in five acts, sometimes in four acts, sometimes rejecting major divisions for a succession of scenes. Often they used a prologue with plot summary, or other devices, to convey necessary information to the audience. They regularly complicated their comedies of love and intrigue with subplots, not always successfully integrated into the main subject matter. They enthusiastically experimented with methods of comic relief, inserting amusing low-life scenes and characters into full-length plays, or creating entirely independent **pasos* or **entremeses* out of popular contemporary types and customs, to amuse audiences between the acts of longer works. Playwrights were equally versatile in matters of style, diction and versification, predominantly writing verse-drama, in a variety of meters, but occasionally showing a preference for prose, encouraged no doubt by the example of *La Celestina*. The new secular theater of Renaissance Spain, vigorously practiced by numerous playwrights, by no means eclipsed traditional liturgical theater. The latter also survived the Middle Ages and developed remarkably during the sixteenth c. when two special forms of religious drama were born: the one-act *autos sacramentales* (sacramental plays) and the full-length dramas of religious conversion, *comedias de santos*. Both flourished throughout the Golden Age and on into the eighteenth c. The steady artistic development of drama in Renaissance Spain was accompanied by an equally consistent growth of popular interest in attending performances. Initially the new Renaissance dramas were staged before royal and aristocratic audiences at court, in ducal palaces, or in private houses of the nobility. As the sixteenth c. progressed, however, plays began to be performed widely by itinerant troupes of professional actors and before a more general and ordinary public. These troupes were originally Italian actors who put on mainly Italian plays; but native professional troupes were soon active, traveling throughout the country performing a varied repertoire of works in Spanish. By the end of the c. so insistent was the general demand for theatrical entertainment that permanent public theaters known as **corrales* (courtyard theaters) were established in Seville, Barcelona, Valencia, Valladolid, Zaragoza, and most importantly, Madrid, which under the prodigiously fertile influence of Lope de Vega quickly became the center of Golden Age dramatic activity in Spain.

The Renaissance dramatists of Spain may be divided into two main groups: the *primitivos* (primitives), so called not because their dramatic art lacked refinement, but rather because they composed their plays in the early, most formative years of the sixteenth c.; and the *prelopistas*, who were most active as playwrights in the later part of the sixteenth c., in the period immediately preceding the dramatic emergence of Lope de Vega. Juan del Encina (1468?–1529?) stands out as the earliest of the *primitivos*, and is often described as initiator or "father of the Spanish theater." Early in his artistic career he was in the service of the Duke of Alba, and his first plays were performed in the duke's palace by himself and other courtiers. He initially wrote liturgical pieces in a mainly medieval manner, but several years in Italy brought about a markedly Renaissance development in his dramatic method, evident in his longer, more successful *églogas*: *Égloga de tres pastores* (Eclogue of the Three Shepherds), *Egloga de Cristina y Febea* (Eclogue of Cristina and Febea), and his most ambitious work, *Egloga de Plácida y Vitoriano* (Eclogue of Placida and Vitoriano), evidently performed in Rome (1513). The action of these verse-plays, as their Virgilian titles indicate, takes place within a mainly *pastoral framework, and centers on the violently unhappy conflicts of love endured by certain shepherds and their sweethearts. Encina shows an ability to create tension and suspense through quarrels, delayed arrivals, and dramatic irony. Some soliloquies also convincingly explore the emotional anguish which leads to suicide as in the *Egloga de* *tres pastores*. Plácida in the *Egloga de Plácida y Vitoriano* also kills herself, but here Encina arranges the resurrection of Plácida through the supernatural intervention of Venus. This preference for spectacle and disinclination for final tragedy become characteristic traits of many seventeenth-c. Spanish dramatists. Also worthy of mention is Encina's inclusion of traditional Spanish elements into his eclogue-plays: **villancicos* (popular songs), low-life comic scenes, low-life characters such as the Celestinesque go-between Eritea in *Plácida y Vitoriano* and the comic shepherd, with his hilarious dialect-speech, the forerunner of numerous rustic **bobos* in the Golden Age theater.

A contemporary and admirer of Encina, much less receptive to Renaissance influences, Lucas *Fernández (1474?–1542) deserves a place in any survey of early Spanish drama principally for his ambitious Easter play, *Auto de la Pasión*: its reference to the Eucharist, its careful dramatic structure, its combination of Old and New Testament characters and its musical effects make it a significant ancestor of Calderón's *autos sacramentales*. Other contemporary contributors to the development of religious drama in Spain include Diego *Sánchez de Badajoz (d. 1549) and Micael de *Carvajal (fl. 1550), both of whom dramatized the medieval Dance of Death theme. Badajoz's *Farsa de la Muerte* (Farce of Death) merits note for its allegorical complexity and its anti-clerical satire, Carvajal's *Las cortes de la Muerte* (Death's Courts of Justice) for its sophisticated use of theatrical apparatus. Carvajal also wrote the Old Testament–based *Tragedia Josefina* (1535; Tragedy of Joseph) in five acts; it and Bartolomé *Palau's *Histora de la gloriosa Santa Orosia* (1550?; Story of the Glorious Saint Orosia) constitute the first full-length dramatized characterizations in Spanish of saintly or biblical personages. But the most gifted composer of religious plays during the early sixteenth c. was undoubtedly Gil *Vicente (1465–1536?). Portugal's major Renaissance dramatist deserves a place in the history of Spanish drama because he wrote a significant number of his plays in Spanish, including the final play in his masterly series devoted to the dramatization of the "Dance of Death": *Trilogia das Barcas* (Trilogy of the Boats). Vicente both influenced and was influenced by contemporary dramatists in Spain, specifically Encina, Fernández and Torres Naharro; he has been compared to Lope de Vega because his talent likewise combined exceptional lyrical quality with extraordinary dramatic invention. He composed many different types of plays, using the most diverse sources; he was the first playwright to dramatize material from the Spanish chivalric novels. Apart from his religious plays perhaps his best pieces are his *farsas*: short, highly satirical, realistic comic plays, related to the *pasos* and *entremeses* soon to be composed in Spain by Lope de *Rueda and *Cervantes.

Though normally counted among the *primitivos*, for reasons of chronology, Bartolomé Torres Naharro (1485?–1520) displays dramatic attitudes and techniques clearly more advanced than those of his contemporaries, and even, in certain respects, more sophisticated than those of the later pre-Lopean playwrights. He was certainly the first self-consciously critical Spanish playwright, and to him is owed the first piece of Spanish theoretical writing on drama, contained in the ''Prohemio'' (Prologue) to his collected works, the *Propalladia* (1517). In it he shows an excellent knowledge of classical theory and the influence, particularly, of Horace, yet reveals also an independent artistic sensibility curiously foreshadowing that which Lope de Vega would demonstrate a c. later in his famous *Arte Nuevo de hacer comedias en este tiempo* (1609; New Art of Writing Plays in Our Time). Not the least ''Lopean'' aspect of Torres's remarks is his definition of theater: ''no es otra cosa sino un artificio ingenioso de notables y finalmente alegres acontecimientos'' (nothing other than an ingenious [ly designed] apparatus of noteworthy and eventually happy occurrences), with its emphasis on plot-intrigue and a required conciliatory ending. Torres divided his plays into two categories: *comedias a noticia* (plays of observation) and *comedias a fantasía* (plays of invention). To the first category belongs, for instance, his *Comedia Soldadesca* (Play about Soldiers), a satirical, realistic representation of soldiers' activities and conversations. Into the second category fit his most sophisticated works, his five-act verse comedies, the products of his assimilation of the characteristics and devices of Low Latin and Italian comedy during years spent in Italy, where most of his plays were written and performed. His most outstanding *comedia a fantasía* is the *Comedia Himenea* (Play about Hymen), which, with its contemporary setting in Madrid, central love-intrigue, street-scenes, swordfights and nightly confusions, and subtle parody at witty-servant level of the principal love-relationship, could almost have been written by Lope if only it had a three-act structure. Torres even introduces the theme of honor into his play, and into Spanish Golden Age drama. The heroine's brother is a truly *pundonoroso* (honor-obsessed) marquis, who almost murders his sister, with typically Golden Age dramatic words ''os doy la vida en mataros'' (in killing you I give you life) when he discovers that she has a lover. But the conflict is resolved and death averted through marriage, an outcome destined to become the conventionally favored ending of the seventeenth-c. Spanish cloak-and-sword play.

Among the *prelopistas* active in the second half of the sixteenth c. the Sevillian playwright Lope de Rueda (1510?–65) stands out as the first professional playwright in Spain, a career he combined from 1540 until his death with that of actor-manager of his own itinerant troupe of players. ''It is to Lope de Rueda rather than to anybody else that the establishment of the professional theatre in Spain is due'' (Shergold, *A History of the Spanish Stage*, 153). His main concern was to entertain his audiences, which was also one of the major acknowledged intentions of Lope de Vega, who, indeed, recognized in Rueda an influential precursor. Four of Rueda's full-length prose plays of intrigue are extant. These *comedias* rely heavily on Italian humanistic originals, but also show the influence of the *commedia dell'arte*. In them Rueda makes ingenious use of confusions of identity and shows some talent for creating dramatic suspense, but his plots are over-complicated and he lacks Torres's ability to create a structurally unified play. *Eufemia*, loosely based on a story from the *Decameron*, and depending on an interesting point of honor, is arguably his best full-length play, though

Los engañados (The Dupes), indirectly derived from Plautus's *Menaechmi*, offers the first example of a woman disguised as a man in Spanish theater. The incidental comic scenes are the most successful parts of Rueda's *comedias*, not surprisingly, for he had a special talent for portraying humorously low-life scenes and characters as his short farcical interludes, known as *pasos*, clearly demonstrate. Juan de *Timoneda (1490?–1583) was much influenced by Rueda, to the extent of composing plays in prose, a practice, however, taken up by very few Golden Age dramatists. Timoneda had little inventive talent, but his prose versions of plays by Plautus are not unsuccessful, and he contributed a good *auto sacramental* in *La oveja perdida* (The Lost Sheep). The second half of the sixteenth c. is a particularly productive period for religious plays, as is proved by a ms. of that era, *Códice de autos viejos* (Codex of Old Religious Plays), in the Madrid National Library (*Biblioteca Nacional). It contains no fewer than 96 pieces, some on biblical subjects, others dealing with saints' lives, others being rudimentary morality plays; nearly all are anonymous, but there is one by a known Valencian dramatist, Jaime Ferruz (d. 1594), an *Auto de Caín y Abel* (Cain and Abel Play). Other gifted composers of religious plays at this time were Sebastián de *Horozco (1510?–80), who wrote a *Coloquio de la Muerte con todas las edades y estados* (Dialogue of Death with All Ages and Estates of Men), and a *Representación de la famosa historia de Ruth* (Dramatization of the Famous Story of Ruth), into which he inserts a comical foolish servant to please his audience, and Luis de *Miranda, who dramatized the parable of the Prodigal Son (1554), adding some amusing *picaresque elements. Late sixteenth-c. Spanish theater stands out for playwrights' interest in experimenting with the most serious dramatic genre, tragedy. Their interest was evidently stimulated by regular and enthusiastic performances of classical tragedies in Jesuit schools and in universities. Vernacular adaptations were also staged, as were original dramas in Spanish on Spanish subjects, written in the classical form. One such work is the Jesuit school tragedy about the life of San Hermenegildo (1580). Another important stimulus was provided by a Portuguese tragedy in classical form (António Ferreira's *Dona Inêz de Castro*), dealing with a peninsular historical subject and adapted into Spanish by Jerónimo *Bermúdez as *Nise lastimosa* (Nise the Unfortunate) and *Nise laureada* (Nise Crowned) (1577). Among pre-Lopean dramatists displaying this new interest, which focused, above all, on violent tragedy in the Senecan manner, were Juan de la *Cueva in Seville, Cervantes in Madrid, and an entire group of playwrights located in Valencia. In the case of Juan de la Cueva (1550?–1610) one should not, however, overestimate the importance of classical and Senecan influences. In his *Ejemplar poético* (1606; Poetic Lesson), written years after his dramatic career had ended, he strongly defended a dramatist's right to compose plays suited to his own talent, period and country. And, indeed, though he several times chooses classical subjects (*Tragedia de la muerte de Virginia*—Tragedy on the Death of Virginia), and not infrequently writes in a sensationally Senecan manner (*Comedia del príncipe tirano*—Drama of the Tyrant Prince), he rejects the classical five-act structure in favor of four acts, and indulges, with non-classical individuality, in a variety of verse forms. Moreover, the subject matter of several of his best plays (*Tragedia de los siete infantes de Lara*—Tragedy about the Seven Princes of Lara, *Comedia de la muerte del Rey Don Sancho*—Play on the Death of Don Sancho) is Spanish history and legend. In this respect he is an extremely important precursor of Lope de Vega, as the first Spanish playwright to exploit the dramatic potentiality of national material contained in ballads and chronicles, material to be repeatedly and exhaustively utilized by Lope de Vega and his followers. Cueva's plays on national historical subjects are not well structured, and, despite some emotionally charged scenes, contain too many narrative speeches to be dramatically successful. His best drama is probably *El infamador* (The Slanderer), whose central character, the libertine and evil-tongued Leucino, is thought to have influenced *Tirso de Molina's portrayal of the most famous character in Spanish theater: *Don Juan. A *prelopista* in most of his plays, though some later works show signs of Lope's influence, Miguel de Cervantes Saavedra (1547–1616) shared Cueva's qualified interest in classical tragedy and his enthusiasm for national Spanish subject matter. In *El cerco de Numancia* (The Siege of Numantia), which treats the heroic resistance of that Spanish town to the military assaults of Scipio Africanus, Cervantes keeps to the classical unities and introduces a Greek-style chorus, but gives his drama a four-act structure. This work, though possibly the best tragedy composed in sixteenth-c. Spain, lacks a central action. Like Cueva, Cervantes achieves epic rather than dramatic effects. Cervantes also wrote some full-length comedies of intrigue, with absurdly complicated plots. His best comic plays are his satirical one-act farces, descendants of Rueda's *pasos*, which Cervantes called *entremeses*. Even in Valencia, the late sixteenth-c. "stronghold" of Senecan and other classical tendencies, playwrights by no means adhered consistently to the precepts of ancient tragedy. Cristóbal de *Virués (1550–1614?) wrote a number of tragedies in the period 1575–85 which are markedly Senecan in their treatment of monstrous crimes, horrific cases of royal tyranny and violent scenes of madness. But Virués composed only one severely classical tragedy, *Elisa Dido*, in five acts, complete with chorus and strictly conforming to the unities. Thereafter he mixed tragic and comic elements, noble and lowborn characters together into a usually three-act verse-drama. According to Lope de Vega, Virués contributed significantly to the establishment of the three-act format of Spanish drama. Virués also "gave" the Golden Age its favorite verse form, being the first playwright to use the *romance* (**romancero*) excellently employed in *La infelice Marcela* (The Unhappy Marcela). Other Valencian playwrights similarly combined national elements with classical characteristics during the transitional dramatic period of the 1580s and 1590s: Micer Andrés *Rey de Artieda (1549–1613), Francisco Agustín *Tárrega (1554–1602), Gaspar de *Aguilar (1561–1623) and many more. In 1588 Lope went to live for a period in Valencia, and greatly influenced playwrights there, but also carried back to Madrid "much of what he was able to convert into the national Spanish drama: the *comedia*" (Weiger, 132).

The long period of sixteenth-c. dramatic experiment in Spain was brought splendidly to fruition by the genius whom Cervantes called ''el monstruo de la Naturaleza'' (Nature's Monster). After several years spent in Valencia and other places, Lope Félix de Vega Carpio (1562–1635) returned, in 1594, to Madrid; there he tirelessly composed hundreds of plays, in a process by which ''he instinctively gathered together all that was promising and good in earlier drama, and by a miracle of synthesis and artistic creation fashioned out of it the Spanish comedia'' (Wilson, 39) that is, Spain's national form of drama. The age of the *comedia* endured throughout the seventeenth c. in Spain and even lived on, albeit in weakened health, into the first half of the Century of Reason. Hundreds of playwrights followed Lope's dramatic formula and attempted to match his extraordinary productivity in thousands of works, of which probably rather less than half have survived in ms. copies or early printed versions. Yet that surviving portion constitutes an enormous corpus of plays, so hugely numerous, indeed, that the entire body of works composed in England during the similar period of Elizabethan theater seems minute in quantity by comparison. Enthusiasm for writing plays in seventeenth-c. Spain was equaled only by the eagerness with which people from all classes attended performances. They flocked, in the first half of the c., above all to the Corral del Príncipe and the Corral de la Cruz, the two public courtyard-theaters. As the seventeenth c. progressed, the special interest in drama displayed by both Philip IV and his son, Charles II, led to sumptuously elaborate palace-theaters, notably the theater in the Buen Retiro Palace, known as the Coliseo (completed 1640), with a basic structure modeled on that of the *corrales*, but equipped with splendid backdrops and sophisticated stage machinery created by Italian engineers. Lope's plays were mostly put on in the *corrales*, but many of Calderón's dramas were staged in these palace-theaters, which were, with the permission of their Majesties, regularly attended by the general populace of Madrid as well as by the aristocracy.

The *comedia*, then, was written, above all, for performance on stage, by playwrights concerned to earn their living by their plays. Its main purpose, therefore, as Lope makes clear in his famous verse description of the genre, *Arte nuevo de hacer comedias en este tiempo* (1609), was to entertain its audiences. The principal characteristics of the *comedia* as set down by Lope in the *Arte nuevo*, and as practiced by him, are worth identifying. The *comedia*, a word used with the general meaning of ''play'' throughout the seventeenth c., is three-act verse-drama, of an essentially national, that is, non-classical, type. Golden Age audiences were generally unconcerned about scholarly theories and precepts of drama (e.g., the Aristotelian unities); they wanted plays that would entertain them by imitating the exciting variety and complex mixture of life. Lope and his followers gave them what they desired: a ''mixed'' drama, in which, as in life itself, serious, even tragic events frequently coincide with comic happenings; in which nobly and even royally born personages consort with servants, peasants, etc.; in which subplots intermingle with main plots; in which passages of verse-dialogue in elegant but admirably natural, rapidly pronounced Spanish are interspersed, sometimes with lengthy descriptive, elaborate, literary monologues from nobly born gallants, sometimes with coarse picaresque exchanges between servant-characters. Even the versification is mixed, to indicate changes of situation, atmosphere or mood. Lope was an extraordinarily gifted poet; but even his on the whole less lyrically accomplished poet-followers (*poeta* was the normal word for ''dramatist'' in the Golden Age) display no small degree of poetic versatility, in their employment of verse forms among which predominate the *romance* and the *redondilla* (likewise octosyllabic but in four-line verses, rhyming *abba*), the *romance* being particularly favored by dramatists writing in the second part of the seventeenth c., while Lope and his immediate followers in the period up to 1635 preferred above all the *redondilla*. Another outstanding characteristic of the *comedia* is its variety of subjects. Lope drew the material for his *comedias* from an almost incalculable number of different sources: the Bible, classical history and mythology, Spanish literature, Italian drama and *novelle*, lives of saints, ballads, folklore, the chronicles, etc.; and Lope's imitators followed his successful example as persistently in this respect as they did in many others. One notices a particular liking for violent and sensational material, involving incest, rape, regicide. . . . But gory deeds of violence are almost invariably perpetrated beyond the audience's area of witness (for the Spanish Golden Age public did not have the strong stomach of the Elizabethans for killings and mutilations onstage, though the aftermath of horrifying deeds of violence is not infrequently put on view, as at the end of Calderon's *Los cabellos de Absalón* (The Locks of Absalom), where we are treated to a tableau-like display showing Absalom dead, transfixed by spears and suspended by his treasured locks among the trees, in fullfilment of a deadly prediction. One observes also a strong predilection for dramatizing Spain's own national history, to the extent that it is scarcely possible to find a historical monarch or significant event from the Middle Ages not portrayed in works by Lope and his contemporaries. Conflicts, motives and themes treated in the *comedia* are also richly varied, though some are notably recurrent: conflicts of kings with vassals, of fathers with sons, of husbands with wives, these are often caused by love and are dependent on a point of honor. Love and honor are the two most dominant themes of Golden Age drama, figuring prominently in a remarkably elevated proportion of dramas, both comedies and serious plays, and even appearing, more modestly, in religious dramas. The popularity of love conflicts and scenes doubtless has something to do with theatrical practicalities, for in Lope's time female parts were played by actresses on the Spanish stage and no longer by boys, whose performance in women's parts in England certainly inhibited Elizabethan dramatizations of central themes of love. As for the prevalence of honor in Spanish plays, the national and social origins of that deep inward sensitivity regarding self-esteem and public reputation, which motivates so many Golden Age dramatic characters, are too complex to discuss here. But there is evidence to indicate that ''points of honor'' killings, of rivals in love or of adulterous wives, were not infrequent occurrences in seventeenth-c. Spain, though the cases of honor presented for the entertainment of seventeenth-c. Spanish audiences are, obviously, to be regarded less as reflections of contemporary reality than as the deliberately exaggerated creations of gifted dramatic artists.

The ''mixed'' nature of the *comedia* makes any rigid categorization difficult. Nevertheless, there are three broadly recognizable types of full-length play. There is first, the genre of Golden Age comedy, comedy of intrigue, which may include some critical reflections on the human condition and contemporary society, but in which lighthearted characters and humorous predicaments predominate, to achieve an amusing happy end. The *comedia de capa y espada* (the cloak and sword play) constitutes Golden Age comedy in its most widely practiced form. The action of a cloak and sword play often takes place in realistically presented contemporary Spanish surrounding, in Madrid, for example, but the plot, in amusing contrast, depends on an improbable series of adventures, coincidences, mistakes of identity, and unexpected entrances and exits, and is generally engineered by a hilariously unscrupulous *gracioso*, committed to help his noble master win the lady of his choice, or masterminded by a delightfully enterprising young lady of station, often willing to disguise herself as a man, in order to outwit the vigilance of some honor-obsessed father or brother and bring about, instead of a marriage of convenience, her union with the man she loves. Subtypes of the *comedia de capa y espada* include the *comedia palaciega*, in which the intrigue develops in a usually fictitious palace setting; the *comedia de costumbres* (comedy of manners), which satirizes contemporary Spanish society for a serious moral purpose (e.g., the comedies of Juan *Ruiz de Alarcón); and the *comedia de figurón* (comedy of caricature), a burlesque play with grotesquely ridiculous protagonists, which developed in the 1630s. An outstanding example of the *comedia de figurón* is Agustín *Moreto's *El lindo de don Diego* (Don Diego the Dandy).

An equally important second category of Golden Age theater is that of serious drama on non-religious subjects. To this category belong some of Lope's most successful works, his plays of peasant honor, for example *(Fuenteovejuna, Peribáñez)* and Calderón's three famous wife-murder dramas. In serious Golden Age drama, comic elements and characters exist, as we have indicated, but are normally kept under properly dramatic control; so that comic scenes function, as in Elizabethan drama, to bring the audience a measure of release or relief from tension; the witty figure of the *gracioso* may be used as the fool is used in Shakespeare, for serious purposes of comment on the protagonists and their predicament. Many serious dramas derive from historical material, though invented material and characters often mingle with historical personages in largely fictitious situations. As Tirso de Molina makes clear in *Los cigarrales de Toledo* (1621; The Country Houses of Toledo), Golden Age dramatists firmly believed in their artistic freedom to use and transform history in the interests of dramatic accomplishment. In the past critics have insisted on the dearth of tragedies in the Spanish Golden Age, influenced excessively by neo-Aristotelian concepts of tragedy, and partly by the infrequency with which seventeenth-c. playwrights use the word to describe their serious plays; influenced, too, by the fact that so many serious Spanish dramas have a seemingly happy or conciliatory ending. Nowadays, however, critics accept that a substantial number of Golden Age dramas are, indeed, tragedies but tragedies *al estilo español*, in the national Spanish style.

The third category, the genre of full-length religious drama, is comprised of at least as many plays as those in the categories of comedy and serious secular drama. However, in religious drama, achievement, in general, was less impressive. A few world-class plays were created, notably Tirso de Molina's *El condenado por desconfiado* (Damned for Despair) and *El burlador de Sevilla* (The Trickster of Seville); but for the most part seventeenth-c. religious *comedias*, particularly the *comedias de santos*, are superficial pieces which rely excessively on the "miraculous" properties of stage machinery. Their accomplishment in the one-act *autos sacramentales* composed for performance at Corpus Christi, in celebration of the Eucharist, was notably greater. Most playwrights at this period wrote some *autos*, but Calderón's talent for this specialized type of play excelled that of all other playwrights of the age.

Even after his death in 1635 Lope's vigorous influence determined the character of Spanish drama to such an extent that not only might all his hordes of dramatic contemporaries be legimately described as his disciples but also, without exception, the equally numerous dramatists of the next generations, from 1630 to 1700. Nevertheless, Spanish drama continued to develop as the seventeenth c. progressed and to reflect increasingly the more complex ideology and artistry of Spain's mature Baroque age. Drama in Spain became progressively influenced by a genius other than that of Lope, by Lope's most gifted follower, Pedro Calderón de la Barca (1600–1681). It is possible, therefore, to refer to two cycles of dramatic activity in seventeenth-c. Spain. The earlier cycle, with Lope at its center, exhibits extraordinary inventiveness, a notable preference for engaging characters in action rather than reflection, a careless yet often inspired improvisation in respect of structure, and poetically unforced style and diction. Dramatists of the cycle dominated by Calderón are less spontaneously creative and more self-consciously craftsmanlike; they more carefully elaborate the implications of themes and ideas, explore the conduct of principal characters, and unify plot-structure from the exposition (usually accomplished with lengthy monologues) through to the almost invariably wholly motivated denouement. They display a powerful artistic will to polish and perfect, evident in the persistence with which they recast and improve hastily composed plays by earlier authors. Another important practice of this later cycle of dramatists is their urge to write plays in collaboration (commonly three playwrights collaborate, each taking responsibility for one act). This activity is not unrelated to their reworking of old plays, for both processes involve creative exploitation of other writers. Other characteristics of Calderón and his school are their concern to dramatize sensationalist subject matter (extreme cases of honor-vengeance, for example), and to portray exaggerated character-types (for instance, the grotesquely caricatured protagonists of their *comedias de figurón*); their fondness for dramatic speeches and exchanges expressed in the elaborately cultured, richly ornate, accumulatively metaphorical poetic style, **culteranismo*; the predilection for spectacular stage effects, a fondness intensified by the fact that for the most part they wrote plays for performance at the lavishly appointed court-theaters.

Dramatists of the two schools of Lope and Calderón were so numerous and prolific in the course of the seventeenth c. that there is no space for more than a rigorously selective summary of principal names and key dramas. Exactly how many plays Lope composed during his turbulent "dramatic" life is unknown, but more than four hundred have survived to bear witness to his unique inventiveness. Even the least dramatically accomplished plays by Lope show evidence of his prodigious instinctive talent, and a high proportion of them are extremely successful dramas. Among his *capa y espada* comedies, *La dama boba* (1613; The Silly Lady), about the strangely developing effects wrought by love upon an apparently retarded young lady, deserves mention, together with *El perro del hortelano* (1613; approx. The Dog in a Manger), a palace-comedy, in which the countess-protagonist is in love with her secretary, feels she should not marry him because of his lowly status, yet is determined to prevent his marriage to anyone except herself, a truly "dog-in-a-mangerish" situation, resolved happily by means of an ingenious deception devised by the *gracioso*, Tristán. Innumerable plays by Lope dramatize Spanish national history or legend, among which are, for instance, *El bastardo Mudarra* (1612, The Bastard Mudarra), which derives from the epic legend of the seven princes of Lara; *Fuenteovejuna* (1612–14; The Sheep Well), a play with an interesting collective protagonist; *Peribáñez* (1609–12); and *El mejor alcalde, el rey* (1620–23; The King, the Best Judge). The last three form a kind of trilogy, since they are all plays of peasant honor in which a tyrant overlord is destroyed by nobly minded peasants whose conduct is ultimately approved by fair-minded Spanish monarchs. Based partially upon ballad sources, but also showing Lope's indebtedness to *La Celestina*, is *El caballero de Olmedo* (1620–25; The Knight from Olmedo), judged generally to be one of Lope's masterpieces. *El castigo sin venganza* (1631; Punishment without Vengeance), one of Lope's last plays (its source a *novella* by Bandello), is another outstanding work. It represents the merciless vengeance exacted by the Duke of Ferrara upon his son and second wife for their adultery. Tirso de Molina, Gabriel Téllez (1580?–1648), reputedly the author of three or four hundred plays, of which more than eighty survive, is Lope's most gifted disciple. Some of his comedies of intrigue, despite certain structural and technical defects, hilariously dramatize the predicaments caused by intelligent scheming ladies in male attire: *Don Gil de las calzas verdes* (1615; Don Gil with the Green Breeches); *El amor médico* (Love Turned Doctor). A more psychologically complex comedy is *El vergonzoso en palacio* (1611; The Bashful Man at Court). Tirso achieved his best work in serious dramas, in which he shows an almost Shakespearean gift for characterization in depth. Two extraordinarily strong-minded Tirsian heroines with complex personalities are Antona García in the historical drama of that name and the Queen Regent María de Molina, the heroic yet convincingly feminine embodiment of *La prudencia en la mujer* (c. 1622; Prudence in a Woman) in Tirso's dramatization of the political turmoil in Castile during the minority of Ferdinand IV. Perhaps the two best religious dramas composed during the Golden Age are generally attributed to Tirso. In *El condenado por desconfiado* Tirso creates in Paulo a tragically tormented man, condemned to hell by his own fear-ridden incapacity to trust God's mercy; in *El burlador de Sevilla* Tirso contributes to world literature the universal figure of Don Juan, not, however, the great lover that subsequent writers made of him, but rather the arch-deceiver of men as well as of women, endowed with an attractive excess of human vitality and with an extraordinary degree of spiritual courage when confronted with the monumental specter of supernatural retribution. Next to Tirso in importance among Lope's followers is Juan Ruiz de Alarcón y Mendoza (1581?–1639). His is a different talent which excels in composing bitterly amusing, socially critical comedies of manners, among them *Las paredes oyen* (1621; Walls Have Ears) and *La verdad sospechosa* (1619; The Truth Made Suspect). The moral message of the latter work is more subtle than is immediately evident, for Don García is finally punished less for lying (conduct which appears to be customary in the society depicted), than for telling lies of the exaggerated sort that lead inevitably to exposure of the truth. The Valencian dramatist Guillén de *Castro y Bellvis (1569–1631) explored the moral, social and political problems created by unjust rulers. He is remembered above all for two national historical plays dealing with Spain's medieval epic hero, the *Cid, which were to inspire Corneille's *Le Cid*. Antonio *Mira de Amescua (1574?–1644) is noteworthy for his *autos sacramentales*; for his religious play *El esclavo del demonio* (1612; The Devil's Slave), in which the protagonist makes a Faust-like pact with the devil; and for his two-part dramatization of the *Próspera y adversa fortuna de Don Alvaro de Luna* (The Rise and Fall of Don Alvaro de Luna). Other dramatists of the school of Lope worthy of mention are Andrés de *Claramonte (d. 1626); Felipe *Godínez (1585–1637); Antonio *Hurtado de Mendoza (1586–1644); Diego *Jiménez de Enciso (1585–1634?), who wrote an excellent drama dealing with Philip II of Spain's ill-fated son, *El príncipe Don Carlos* (Prince Carlos); and not least, Luis *Quiñones de Benavente (1589?–1651), the most successful and productive composer of *entremeses* of his time. A number of gifted playwrights seem to fall artistically between the two schools, writing mainly in the epoch of Lope, but continuing to compose plays into the period of Calderón and his followers with whom, indeed, they collaborated in a number of works. These transitional dramatists are Luis de *Belmonte Bermúdez (1587–1650?); Juan *Pérez de Montalbán (1602?–38), author of several highly entertaining cloak-and-sword comedies, and of an interesting series of dramas depicting Philip II at different periods of his reign; and Luis *Vélez de Guevara (1579–1644), who displayed a nearly Calderonian fondness for recasting old plays, for portraying abnormal characters and for exploiting spectacular stage effects. Curiously, Vélez's best work, *Reinar después de morir* (To Reign as

Queen after Death), is an almost classically restrained dramatization of the fatal fourteenth-c. love-relationship between Prince Pedro of Portugal and Dona Inés de Castro.

Calderón was Lope's follower, yet his equal. In a sense, he was also his dramatic opposite, for he was not a prodigiously intuitive genius like Lope, but rather an intellectual playwright and deliberately artistic craftsman. He began to write for the stage in the early 1620s and continued to compose plays until his death in 1681; his best works, however, were completed before 1651, when he entered the priesthood. After that time he wrote only *autos sacramentales* or plays for performance at court, principally on mythological subjects, with complex musical elements and elaborate stage effects, theatrically spectacular, but relatively superficial in thought-content and characterization. Some 120 of his full-length plays have survived, together with over 70 *autos sacramentales*, which represent an artistic achievement almost as outstanding as that he accomplished in other dramatic genres. His *comedias de santos* include several undeniable masterpieces: *El mágico prodigioso* (1637; The Wonder-Working Magician), for instance, a Spanish Baroque variation on the Faust theme, and *El príncipe constante* (1629; The Constant Prince), a dramatization of the fifteenth-c. martyrdom of Prince Ferdinand of Portugal. Calderón also composed many cloak-and-sword comedies, in which complications and predicaments of love, honor and jealousy are often caused or intensified by the impish, enterprising conduct of a young lady-protagonist: Angela, for instance, "the phantom lady" in the play of that name (*La dama duende*, 1629) and Marcela in *Casa con dos puertas mala es de guardar* (1629; A House with Two Doors Is Difficult to Guard). An earnest sense of life is often visible beneath the predominantly surface-wit of Calderón's comedies, indicating perhaps that his most natural talent was not, in fact, for comedy. This indication is confirmed by the quality of his serious secular dramas. Among his most outstanding works of this kind are *La vida es sueño* (1635; Life Is a Dream), which philosophically explores the theme described in the title and examines a question that much preoccupied Calderón's Baroque age, the problem of man's freedom of will; *El alcalde de Zalamea* (1644?; The Mayor of Zalamea), a case of peasant honor, involving an admirably principled yet intensely human protagonist; and Calderón's sensational trilogy of wife-murder tragedies, *El médico de su honra* (1635; The Doctor of His Honor), *A secreto agravio, secreta venganza* (1635; Secret Vengeance for Secret Insult) and *El pintor de su deshonra* (1648?; The Painter of His Own Dishonor), in which three pathologically obsessed husbands destroy their possibly foolish but still virtuous wives in order to safeguard their honor. Several dramas on which Calderón's international reputation depends (*La vida es sueño, El alcalde de Zalamea*, etc.) are derived from earlier plays so inferior artistically to Calderón's re-creations that they are largely forgotten. Calderón's two most noteworthy disciples, both first class dramatists by any standards, are Francisco de *Rojas Zorrilla (1607–48) and Agustín *Moreto y Cabaña (1618–69). Rojas Zorrilla is particularly remembered as probable author of the honor drama entitled

Del rey abajo, ninguno (None but the King), but deserves credit also for less orthodox plays, in which he explores in depth the special problems the honor code posed for women (*Lucrecia y Tarquino, Progne y Filomena*); a number of sensational neo-Senecan tragedies (*El Caín de Cataluña*—The Cain of Catalonia, *Morir pensando matar*—To Die While Intending to Kill); and for several amusing, anti-traditionalist comedies, including *Entre bobos anda el juego* (1638; Fun with Fools), arguably Spain's first *comedia de figurón*. Moreto is often compared with Alarcón because of his restrained style, his careful attention to structure and his talent for comedy. Moreto wrote several *comedias de figurón*, of which the finest is *El lindo don Diego* (Don Diego the Dandy), and some thoughtful *comedias palaciegas*, including *El desdén con el desdén* (Scorn of Scorn). Otherwise, Calderón's most gifted followers included Alvaro *Cubillo de Aragón (1596?–1661), creator of excellent comedies and a profoundly serious work, *La tragedia del duque de Verganza* (1649; The Tragedy of the Duke of Braganza); Antonio *Coello y Ochoa (1611–52), composer of a sympathetic dramatization of Elizabeth I of England's relationship with the Count of Essex (1633; *El conde de Sex*), the earliest known play about this subject; Cristóbal de *Monroy y Silva (1612–49); Antonio de *Solís (1610–86); Juan de *Matos Fragoso (1609–89); Antonio *Enríquez Gómez, also known as Fernando de Zárate (1600–1663); Juan Bautista *Diamante (1625–87); Agustín de Salazar y Torres (1642–75); and Juan Claudio de la *Hoz y Mota (1622–1714). Generally speaking, dramatists active in the last decades of the seventeenth c. are less talented than earlier Calderonian playwrights, tending to compose superficially dramatized pieces dependent on spectacular stage machinery and sensationalist protagonists. A notable exception, however, is Francisco Antonio de *Bances y López Candamo (1662–1704), a court playwright who composed dramas mainly on foreign historical or pseudo-historical subjects. Bances stands out for his persuasive portrayal of the problems and personalities of monarchs such as the Emperor Trajan (in *El esclavo en grillos de oro*—The Slave in Golden Shackles) and Queen Christina of Sweden (*Quien es quien premia al amor*—The One Who Rewards Love). Bances is an important reason why we should refer not to the decadence, but more accurately to the decline, of the *comedia* in the last years of the Golden Age. The truly decadent period of Spanish drama imitating the style of Lope and Calderón coincides with the first half of the eighteenth c.

In contrast to the Golden Age of Spanish theater, the eighteenth c. is a period of limited achievement in dramas: of innumerable bad plays and worse playwrights, of few dramas that manage to rise even to mediocrity, and of failure to produce more than the odd dramatist of full-length plays with truly outstanding genius. Nevertheless, the Age of Enlightenment is an important period in the history of drama in Spain, an epoch of transition and experiment, of recapitulation and controversy out of which the more creatively dramatic nineteenth c. emerged. Throughout the eighteenth c. the consistent powerful influence on Spanish drama was that of public taste. Despite efforts of neo-classically minded writers, despite even the legislative methods of officially constituted bodies set on theater reform, theater-goers continued to demand a popular national form of drama, after the Baroque fashion of Calderón, but with additional sensationalist elements, increased variety in style, mood and incident, greater numbers of characters, intensified use of elaborate operatic effects and a larger accumulation of spectacular stage-managed mysterious and magical occurrences. During the first half of the c., in the traditional *corrales*, then later in the theater buildings that began to replace them, audiences found their exuberantly debased "baroque" tastes repeatedly satisfied, by performances of old Golden Age favorite plays, and even more by dramatic extravaganzas composed by untalented imitators of Calderón. Predictably, these unworthy Calderonian hangers-on chose to exaggerate the already extreme forms of Baroque drama, the *comedias de figurón*, the mythological plays and **zarzuelas*, and the *comedias de santos* and their near-relations, the *comedias de magia* (plays of magic). A typical example of the popular but artistically degenerate *comedia de magia* of this period is *El mágico de Salerno* (1715; The Magician of Salerno), by Juan Salvo y Vela, an absurd series of five plays dealing with magical exploits of the wizard, Pedro Vayalarde. In truth, only two playwrights of early eighteenth-c. Spain show signs of dramatic ability: Antonio de *Zamora (1664?–1728) and José de *Cañizares (1676–1750). Both deliberately practice sensationalism and cultivate exaggeration, but they display some talent for dramatic structure and even for characterization. A number of their recasts of Golden Age originals are not unsuccessfully accomplished: Zamora's adaptation of Tirso's *El burlador de Sevilla*, entitled *No hay plazo que no se cumpla ni deuda que no se pague* (There Is No Credit That Does Not Run Out Nor Any Debt That Need Not Be Paid), offers us a less profound hero than Tirso's protagonist, but one attractively endowed with a certain vitality by virtue of his courage. Cañizares displays an intuitive historical sense, despite many distortions of fact, in his drama about Mary Queen of Scots, *Lo que va de cetro a cetro y Crueldad de Inglaterra* (From One Scepter to Another, and the Cruelty of England), and even in his spectacular *comedia de santos*, *A cual mejor, confesada y confesor, San Juan de la Cruz y Santa Teresa de Jesús* (1727; Which the Better, Confessor or Confessed, Saint John of the Cross and Saint Theresa of Jesus).

After the Treaty of Utrecht (1713), with a Bourbon dynasty securely established in Spain, interest in and respect for French culture and ideology developed steadily in court circles, at government level and among Spanish intellectuals. They were influenced by French opinions of Spanish national plays, and by French insistence that the theater should educate the masses in correct standards of behavior. They began to view with contempt the traditional *comedia*, a contempt which the lack of talent in playwrights of the period and the bad taste of the theater-going public did everything to intensify. An influential critic of the Golden Age tradition and vigorous supporter of neo-classicism was Ignacio de *Luzán Claramunt de Suelves y Guerra (1702–54). His *Poética* (1737; Poetics) emphasized the importance of the classical unities, the classically strict divisions of tragedy from comedy, the necessity for verisimilitude in drama, and the function of the theater as a medium of social and moral reform. Luzán's friend, Agustín *Montiano y Luyando (1697–1764), expressed similar ideas in *Discursos sobre las tragedias españolas* (Discourses upon Spanish Tragedies) and wrote two neo-classical tragedies, *Virginia* (1750) and *Ataulpho* (1753), neither of which was performed. After Charles III ascended the throne in 1759, a still more sympathetically French neo-classical period ensued. Charles III's chief minister, Aranda, imposed compulsory reforms of the theaters, to convert the public from their debased national ways to an appreciation of neo-classical drama. Many French plays were performed in translation or adaptation and considerable numbers of tragedies and comedies were written by neo-classically minded Spanish intellectuals, among them Nicolás Fernández de *Moratín (1737–80), who composed a tragedy entitled *Lucrecia* (1763) and a comedy called *La petimetra* (1762; The Pretentious Lady). Both rigorously conformed to the ''good'' rules of art. Despite the measures taken by Aranda and other officials to discourage plays in the national manner and to promote neo-classical works, the general Spanish public remained determined to be sensationally entertained, not morally improved, by visits to the theater. Attendances at neo-classical plays were poor, and restrictions imposed on Golden Age plays and their derivatives had to be modified. The only lasting success achieved through legislation by the neo-classicists was the permanent decree of 1765 banning the *autos sacramentales* for irreverence and lack of verisimilitude. The *comedias de santos* and *de magia*, however, although equally irreverent and fantastic to neo-classical eyes and banned by an act of 1788, were performed as before in Spanish theaters by the early 1790s. Faced by such public intransigence, more liberally minded intellectuals began to try various dramatic compromises. Golden Age dramas were recast into more restrained forms (by, for example, Tomás Sebastián y Latre and Dionisio *Solís), and theater-goers preferred to see even these pale shadows of favorite dramas to attending performances, of French-based works. Writers of tragedies began to prefer Spanish national subjects rather than material from classical history, and to adhere less rigidly to neo-Aristotelian precepts. Gaspar Melchor de *Jovellanos (1744–1811) dramatized in *Pelayo* the story of Spain's first hero of the Reconquest. Nicolás Fernández de Moratín likewise set his work *Hormesinda* (1770) in Spain during the early period of struggle against the Moors. José *Cadalso (1741–82) adhered to the unities, used rhyming couplets, organized a typically neo-classical double catastrophe but dramatized Spanish subject matter in *Don Sancho García* (1771); Ignacio *López de Ayala followed Cervantes's lead and composed the tragic history of *Numancia destruida* (1775; Numantia Destroyed), a work he supplied with detailed stage directions and an impressive stage set. Neo-classical tragedies of this more liberal type went on being composed in Spain into the nineteenth c., but attracted neither numerous nor enthusiastic audiences, with one noteworthy exception. That was *Raquel* (Rachel), first performed in Madrid in 1778. Its author, Vicente *García de la Huerta (1734–87), superficially conformed to Gallicist precepts, eliminated the *gracioso*, employed a heroic meter; but chose a traditional Golden Age three-act structure, and a national subject, the love of Alfonso VIII of Castile for a Jew. Huerta focused on the mutually intense infatuation of king and Jew, emphasizing the love scenes in almost Lopean fashion, and created the most successful dramatic tragedy of his age. In comedy some attempt was likewise made to reconcile pseudo-classical precepts and traditionally Spanish tastes. Tomás de *Iriarte (1750–91) uses rapid twists and turns of plot to illustrate the dangers of an unsuitable upbringing in *El señorito mimado* (1783; A Spoiled Young Man) and *La señorita mal criada* (1791; A Badly Brought up Young Lady). Leandro Fernández de *Moratín (1760–1828) stands out as the creator of five original comedies in which neo-classical elements, French didactic tendencies and techniques from Molière are successfully combined with characteristics derived from the Golden Age comedy of manners. His best plays are *La comedia nueva* (1792; The New Play), in which he satirically mocks degenerate forms of heroic drama, and *El sí de las niñas* (When a Girl Says Yes, first performed in 1806), a comedy that observes the unities and provides moral instruction in parenthood and guardianship, yet at the same time is an entertaining portrayal of contemporary Spanish society, with perceptively delineated characters, natural dialogue and insistent scenes of tension and suspense. Moratín the Younger was the most successful of the neo-classically inclined dramatists in comedy. Unfortunately, he left no proper school of successors; yet his work was to exercise a positive influence on the development of comedy in Spain during the first half of the nineteenth c. The biggest obstacle to widespread Gallo-classicism in late eighteenth-c. Spanish drama was the vigorous talent of Ramón de la *Cruz (1731–94). One of the few truly first-class dramatists of his century, Cruz began his career writing some neo-classical plays, but then briskly changed direction to concentrate on one-act farces (nearly five hundred) for enormously appreciative Spanish audiences. These farces were in the popular tradition of Rueda's *pasos* and Cervantes's *entremeses*, but used more sophisticated stage sets. They satirically portrayed aspects of eighteenth-c. Spanish society, depicting a variety of types from different social settings: ladies and gentlemen, priests, soldiers, gypsies, scoundrels. An entire group of **sainetes* pokes sharp fun at customs and conduct imported from France. In one such *sainete*, *El hospital de la moda* (1762; A Hospital for Fashion Disorders), a special sanatorium is created to treat people afflicted with various types of "Frenchiness" affecting their dress, social behavior, speech, etc. About thirty of Cruz's *sainetes* are connected with the world of theater (actors, rehearsals, playwrights), and for the most part criticize neo-classical tendencies, insisting on the rights of Spanish theater-audiences to decide for themselves which type of drama they prefer. Cruz composed a particularly amusing parody of overdone tragedy in *Manolo* (performed 1780), in which he uses hilariously inappropriate types from low-life Madrid society to parody the over-solemnity, lack of inevitability and final scenes heaped with corpses. Cruz also did parody eighteenth-c. imitations of Golden Age drama with their absurd flights of rhetoric and extravagant surges of emotionalism (most notably in *Los bandos de Lavapiés* (1776; The Rival Bands from Lavapiés).

During the last three decades of the eighteenth c. two new types of drama evolved which were forerunners of nineteenth-c. Romantic drama in Spain. Both types, the sentimental or domestic play, and the national heroic drama, were cultivated by many playwrights, including two of the most productive dramatists of the day: Luciano Francisco *Comella (1751–1812) and Gaspar Zavala y Zamora. The sentimental or domestic play, with its origins largely in England but reaching Spain through French adaptations, modernizes elements from neo-classical tragedy and comedy (particularly structure and a didactic emphasis on emotion), to represent problems of domestic adversity involving ordinary people who endure hardship with exemplary virtue. This type of play, of which Jovellanos's *El delincuente honrado* (1774; The Honorable Delinquent) is probably the earliest example, was well received, principally because of its melodramatic situation, use of coincidences, sudden changes of fortune, emotionally charged leave-takings and last minute reprieves. Typical examples of this genre are Comella's *Cecilia* (1786) and *Cecilia viuda* (1787; The Widow Cecilia), and Zavala y Zamora's *Las víctimas del amor: Ana y Sindham* (1789; The Victims of Love: Anne and Sindham). Some sentimental plays have militaristic elements and feature enlightened monarchs who resolve problems of their subjects (for instance, Comella's series of plays about Frederick the Great of Prussia), and thus resemble the national heroic plays by these same dramatists. However, the late eighteenth-c. heroic drama (clearly exemplified by Zavala y Zamora's trilogy devoted to Charles XII of Sweden), should be regarded as a modernized version of the Golden Age *comedia*. Scene changes are numerous; spectacular events and melodramatic incidents abound; musical and operatic effects are much used (a practice doubtless stimulated by the current vogue for Italian opera, particularly the work of Metastasio); love scenes are given emotionally charged emphasis; numerous characters, exalted and humble, are brought together; extravagantly elevated speeches are at odds with ordinary conversations. Traditional baroque elements predominate, therefore, in this revised type of heroic drama, and account for its considerable popularity onstage (equaled only by that of the *comedias de magia*. But some novel elements are also evident, certain unusual aspects of characterization, strange elements of atmosphere, macabre incidents near tombs, which carry us forward into the Age of *Romanticism.

The first thirty years of the nineteenth c. was a period of little or no change in theater; the talent of Moratín the Younger still dominated, pseudo-classical tragedies also continued to be written. On the more popular level, sentimental drama remained in vogue, while recasts of Golden Age plays and versions of Italian operas were regularly performed. Even the *comedia de magia* survived as *La pata de cabra* (1829; The Goat's Foot) well illustrates, for this spectacular adaptation of an original French popular play of magic and illusion enjoyed great success on the Spanish stage in the 1830s. But then a dramatic change came over the theater in Spain. Ferdinand VII died in 1833, political repression eased, and harsh literary censorship was relaxed. Spanish writers and intellectuals forced into exile were now able to return. They brought back with them, notably from

England and from France, turbulently different attitudes to life and art created out of the upheavals, political, social and economic, but also religious, philosophical and cultural, which violently attended the French Revolution and the Napoleonic Wars. These attitudes (of anguished skepticism toward traditional religion, of disbelief in the values of rationalism, of fatal pessimism in respect of the human condition, of fervent support for the rights and liberties of the individual, of extraordinary antagonism toward imposed rules and restrictions, whether in real life or in the imaginative world of art) had already produced the Romantic epoch elsewhere in Europe; now, belatedly, they generated Romanticism in Spain. And there the theater quickly became ''the battleground of the Romantic movement'' (Donald L. Shaw, 23), on which playwrights like the Duke of Rivas, Gutiérrez and Zorilla violently opposed neo-classical forces of rationalism and order. Influenced by Scott in England, by Hugo and Dumas in France, patriotic and nostalgic for past ages free from metaphysical uncertainties, the Spanish Romantic dramatists turned for colorful subject matter to early national history and legend. They attached much importance to the intuitions, instincts and emotions of the individual, and, therefore, liked to treat themes of love, particularly of ill-fated love, to reflect their normally pessimistic view of human destiny. Their ambivalent attitude toward God and the afterlife (skepticism mixed with a desperate longing to believe) led them to dwell on the macabre aspects of death, and to add supernatural dimension to their plot material. They profoundly admired the artistic individuality of Baroque Spanish playwrights, and consciously strove to emulate them by disregarding the classical unities, breaking down the barriers between tragedy and comedy, mixing meters and styles, incorporating changes and shifts in dramatic tone and atmosphere. In several respects the Romantics were more liberated and individualistic than their Baroque ancestors: in their manner of varying structure (sometimes their plays consist of five acts, sometimes of four acts); in their fondness for inserting barely relevant scenes and incidents; in their inclusion of numerous secondary characters; in their mingling of prose with verse; and in their predilection for supplying detailed stage directions. The ''battle'' staged in Spain for the Romantic cause did not last much more than a decade (1834–44), a period sufficient, however, to enable several playwrights to achieve a number of successes. Francisco *Martínez de la Rosa (1787–1862) is in some ways a transitional figure. He began by composing comedies in the Moratinian manner and also neo-classical tragedies, though these have certain Romantic elements (medieval settings, colorful local references, spectacular effects). His main contribution to Romanticism is *La conjuración de Venecia* (The Conspiracy in Venice). Written in France about 1830, first performed in Spain in 1834, this drama is noteworthy for its vivid fourteenth-c. Italian setting, for its treatment of fatal love and for its creation of a mysterious, love-centered and ill-destined hero. *Macías*, by Mariano José de *Larra (1809–37) was also first performed in 1834. This work dramatizes a medieval Galician legend previously used by Lope de Vega; indeed, Larra derives many techniques from Golden Age drama. The protagonist, however, is an unmistakably Romantic hero, irrationally obsessed and finally destroyed by love for Elvira, that love being his religion and sole reason for living. Like Martínez de la Rosa, Angel de Saavedra, Duque de *Rivas (1791–1865) initially composed neo-classical plays, but then went to Romantic extremes. *Don Alvaro* was first written in prose (1831), then revised in a mixture of prose and verse (1833), and finally performed in 1835. This work, with its exuberant exploitation of local color, its extraordinary coincidences, its grotesquely incongruous humor, its doom-laden atmosphere, its theme of fatal love and its mysteriously courageous hero, destroyed, as the subtitle explains, by the inevitable ''fuerza del destino'' (force of destiny), is regarded as Spain's outstanding Romantic tragedy. Well received when first performed in 1836, and enduringly popular thereafter, *El trovador* (The Troubadour) by Antonio *García Gutiérrez (1813–84), a play of unbridled love and hatred enacted in fifteenth-c. Aragon, is arguably the best constructed drama of the Spanish Romantic movement. It has a delayed climax, subtle employment of pause-scenes and a magnificent finale. Gutiérrez also composed over fifty other plays among which the most notable are *El rey monje* (1837; The King Who Was a Monk) and *Simón Bocanegra* (1843). In *Los amantes de Teruel* (1837; The Lovers of Teruel) Juan Eugenio *Hartzenbush (1806–80) emotionally represents a medieval Spanish legend to express the Romantic obsession with love as man's essential reason for living: the lovers die of anguish because their passion cannot be fulfilled. The last major author of Spanish Romantic drama is José *Zorrilla y del Moral (1817–93). He wrote a number of interesting historical plays, including *El puñal del godo* (1843; The Dagger of the Goth), a one-act work reputedly written in twenty-four hours, and *Traidor inconfeso y mártir* (1849; Traitor, Impenitent and Martyr), dramatizing the mysterious impersonation of King Sebastian of Portugal by Gabriel de Espinosa. But the play for which he is most generally remembered, his most uncompromisingly Romantic drama, is *Don Juan Tenorio* (1844), a grandiose version of the Don Juan legend in which the supernatural is spectacularly represented and the protagonist individualized by audaciously exaggerated cynicism. It differs from Tirso's original treatment in that Zorrilla's Romantic hero is saved from damnation by the redeeming power of love. Other less accomplished Romantic dramas worthy of mention are *Alfredo* (1835), written by Joaquín Francisco Pacheco (1808–65); *Elvira de Albornoz* (1836), by José María Díaz (1800–1888); *Doña María de Molina* (1837), the work of Mariano Roca de Togores (1812–89); *Bárbara de Blomberg*, by Patricio de la *Escosura (1804–78); and an extraordinary concoction of fantasy, horror and melodrama, supposedly representative of the reign of Charles II, *Carlos II el Hechizado* (1837; Charles II the Bewitched), by Antonio *Gil y Zárate (1796–1861).

Even during the most dominantly Romantic period of drama in Spain, neo-classical tragedies and comedies in the style of Moratín continued to be composed, most notably by Manuel *Bretón de los Herreros (1796–1873) and Ventura de la *Vega (1807–65). Bretón wrote more than sixty plays, including Romantic historical plays, an anti-Romantic burlesque (*Me voy de Madrid*, 1835; I'm

Leaving Madrid), classical tragedies and reconstructions of Golden Age plays. His most original works are comedies of manners, influenced by Moratín, carefully structured and amusingly ingenious. His first success in this genre was *A Madrid me vuelvo* (1823; I'm Coming Back to Madrid), followed by *Marcela o ¿a cuál de los tres?* (1831; Marcela, or Which of the Three?), a play about a young widow wooed by several suitors, in which Bretón adopts a less classical structure, uses a variety of meters and employs elements of broad comedy to satirize pretentious middle-class behavior. Other accomplished comedies written by Bretón include *Muérete y verás* (1837; You'll Find Out When You Die) and *El Pelo de la dehesa* (1840; [approx.] A Silk Purse from a Sow's Ear). Ventura de la Vega wrote a Romantic play with classical tendencies (*Don Fernando de Antequera*; written 1844, performed 1847) and *La muerte de César* (?1863; Death of Caesar), a neo-classical tragedy with certain Romantic characteristics. His most important play is a comedy of manners entitled *El hombre de mundo* (1845; Man of the World). This work conforms to the unities and moves to a morally elevating conclusion, yet is not a straightforwardly Moratinian comedy. In its earnest portrayal of a potentially disastrous marriage-conflict, *El hombre de mundo* turns into a work of transition, marking both the end of neo-classical comedy in Spain and the beginning of a more serious nineteenth-c. genre, dramatizing genuine contemporary problems of Spanish upper-class society. Another playwright whose dramas are transitional is Tomás *Rodríguez Rubí (1817–90). He criticizes contemporary behavior in the sphere of politics through several dramas: *El arte de hacer fortuna* (1845; The Art of Making One's Fortune), *El hombre feliz* (1848; A Happy Man) and *El gran filón* (1874; [approx.] The Gold Mine), in which political vindictiveness is trenchantly condemned. His dramas concerned with family (*La escala de la vida* [1857; Life's Staircase] and *Fiarse del porvenir* [1874; Trusting in the Future], in which snobbery and materialism are punished and honest diligence rewarded), are those which approach the high realism of nineteenth-c. comedy, the *alta comedia* (high comedy). The new type of play was expertly composed by Manuel *Tamayo y Baus (1829–98) and Adelardo *López de Ayala (1828–72). Tamayo's *La bola de nieve* (1856; The Snowball) begins as a satirical comedy but develops into a high drama of passion and remorse. His first authentic high comedy is *Lo positivo* (1862; Money Counts), a play of ideas intended to censure selfish business behavior and to invite us to emulate the nobly disinterested conduct of the hero, Rafael. López de Ayala's most accomplished contributions to Spanish *alta comedia* are *Consuelo* (1878), which illustrates the unhappy consequences of marrying for money and *El tanto por ciento* (1861; So Much Per Cent), which warns, through a series of rapid changes in fortune and a skillful climax of suspense, that fraudulent schemes do not pay off, whereas honesty finally brings a sure reward. Both Tamayo and López de Ayala also wrote historical dramas. Ayala composed, for instance, *Un hombre de estado* (1851; The Statesman), dealing with Philip III's unfortunate favorite, Rodrigo de Calderón. In *La locura de amor* (1855; Love's Madness), Tamayo dramatizes, in semi-Romantic fashion, the tragic Spanish history of Juana la Loca. *Un drama nuevo* (1867; A New Drama) is set in Elizabethan London and shows the effects of love, jealousy and envy upon a troupe of English actors, one of whom is Shakespeare. This play is sometimes regarded as Tamayo's masterpiece but more nearly approaches melodrama than tragedy. A dramatist of considerable success and influence in the late nineteenth c. was José *Echegaray (1832–1916), but his reputation did not long survive in the twentieth c. despite the Nobel Prize he was awarded in 1904. Echegaray was the chief perpetuator of exaggerated Romantic tendencies in Spanish drama (also called neo-romanticism) particularly during the 1870s and 1880s. He revitalized the Romantic genre of historical drama by composing a series of verse plays, rich in catastrophes, coincidences, grotesque incidents and elaborate stage effects. Plays such as *La esposa del vengador* (1874; Wife of the Avenger) and *En el puño de la espada* (1875; At the Hilt of the Sword), reminiscent in some respects of eighteenth-c. melodrama, were popular with the theater-going public, prove that Echegaray was a skillfully theatrical technician with a certain gift for communicating tragic intensity. But his characters are deficient in verisimilitude, and their predicaments neither contribute nor encourage any serious reflection upon the human condition. In a small number of dramas Echegaray, influenced evidently by the problem plays of Ibsen and Strindberg, attempts to break away from melodrama and reflect the genuine difficulties of contemporary society. *El gran galeoto* (1881; The Great Go-Between), an exaggerated but thought-provoking illustration of the tragic results of malevolent gossip, is by far the most successful work in this pseudo-realistic category. Worthy of mention among Echegaray's contemporaries and imitators are Leopoldo *Cano (1844–1934), author of various plays on social problems, Eugenio *Sellés (1844–1926), whose wife-murder drama *El nudo gordiano* (1878; The Gordian Knot) was remarkably well received, and José *Feliú y Codina (1847–97), who dramatized traditional themes of honor and vengeance in rural settings, preparing the way for *Benavente's rural dramas. The gifted Catalan dramatist Angel *Guimerà (1845–1924) wrote a number of works in the Romantic manner (for example, the historical verse-drama *Judit de Welp* [1883]), but then he turned in an almost naturalistic direction and composed two rural masterpieces: *Maria Rosa* (1894) and *Terra baixa* (1897; The Lowland). Certain works by Enrique *Gaspar (1842–1902) and Joaquín *Dicenta (1863–1917) also represent a significant advance toward social realism in the theater. In his prose dramas *Las personas decentes* (1890; Respectable People) and *La huelga de hijos* (1893; The Children's Strike), Gaspar censures the moral and sexual misconduct of the middle classes. Some of Dicenta's plays are merely products of the neo-Romantic influence of Echegaray, but others, notably *Juan José* (1895) and *El señor feudal* (1897; A Feudal Overlord), are serious dramas of social protest. The last important Spanish dramatist of the nineteenth-c. is Benito *Pérez Galdós (1843–1920). He adapted some of his realistic novels for the stage but also composed some original dramas. Among his most noteworthy plays are *Realidad* (1892; Reality), *Doña Perfecta* (1896), *Electra* (1901) and *El abuelo* (1904; The Grandfather). Galdós lacked sufficient dramatic technique to compose major works consistently. Nevertheless, he possessed a talent for creating powerfully realistic characters, for exploring the tragic depths of human problems, and for reflecting the vital realities of contemporary society. His plays of social realism prepare the theater in Spain to deal with the authentic complexity of life in the twentieth c. *See also* Contemporary Spanish Theater; *Infantes de Lara, Leyenda de los*; Italian Literary Influences.

BIBLIOGRAPHY

Primary Texts

Sáinz de Robles, Federico Carlos, ed. *El teatro español, historia y antología (desde sus orígenes hasta el siglo XIX)*. 7 vols. Madrid: Aguilar, 1942–43.

Criticism

Allen, John J. *The Reconstruction of a Spanish Golden Age Playhouse: El Corral del Príncipe 1583–1744*. Gainesville: Florida UP, 1983.

Andioc, René. *Teatro y sociedad en el Madrid del siglo XVIII*. Madrid: Fundación Juan March/Castalia, 1976.

Arróniz, Othón. *La influencia italiana en el nacimiento de la comedia española*. Madrid: Gredos, 1969.

Aubrun, Charles V. *La comedia española 1600–1680*. 2nd ed. Madrid: Taurus, 1981.

Barrera y Leirado, Cayetano Alberto de la. *Catálogo bibliográfico y biográfico del teatro antiguo español desde sus orígenes hasta mediados del siglo XVIII*. Madrid: Rivadeneyra, 1860; facs. ed., Madrid: Gredos, 1969.

Brown, Jonathan, and J. H. Elliott. *A Palace for a King. The Buen Retiro and the Court of Philip IV*. New Haven and London: Yale UP, 1980.

Casalduero, Joaquín. *Estudios sobre el teatro español*. Madrid: Gredos, 1962.

Cook, John A. *Neo-classic Drama in Spain. Theory and Practice*. Dallas: Southern Methodist UP, 1959.

Cotarelo y Mori, Emilio. *Bibliografía de las controversias sobre la licitud del teatro en España*. Madrid: RABM, 1904.

Crawford, J. P. Wickersham. *Spanish Drama before Lope de Vega*. rev. ed. Philadelphia: U of Pennsylvania P, 1967.

Deyermond, A. D. *The Middle Ages*, vol. 1 of *A Literary History of Spain*. Ed. R. O. Jones. London: Benn; New York: Barnes and Noble, 1971. See Chapter 8.

———, ed. *Edad Media*, vol. 1 of *Historia y crítica de la literatura española*. Ed. Francisco Rico. Barcelona: Crítica, 1980. See Chapter 11.

Díez Borque, José María. *Sociología de la comedia española del siglo XVII*. Madrid: Cátedra, 1976.

Donovan, Richard B. *The Liturgical Drama in Medieval Spain*. Toronto: Pontifical Institute of Medieval Studies, 1958.

Fiore, Robert L. *Drama and Ethos: Natural-Law Ethics in Spanish Golden Age Theater*. Lexington: UP of Kentucky, 1975.

Froldi, Rinaldo. *Lope de Vega y la formación de la comedia*. Madrid: Anaya, 1973.

Gilman, Stephen. "The *comedia* in the Light of Recent Criticism Including the New Criticism." *Bulletin of the Comediantes* 12 (Spring 1960): 1–5.

Glendinning, Nigel. *The Eighteenth Century*, vol. 4 of *A Literary History of Spain*. Ed.

R. O. Jones. London: Benn; New York: Barnes and Noble, 1972. See especially Chapter 4.

Goldman, Peter B. ''Plays and Their Audiences in the Eighteenth Century: Notes on the Fortunes of a *comedia* by Cañizares.'' *MLS* 14 (1984): 53–68.

Hermenegildo, Alfredo. *La tragedia en el Renacimiento español.* Barcelona: Planeta, 1973.

Jones, C. A. ''Honour in Spanish Golden-Age Drama; Its Relation to Real Life and to Morals.'' *BHS* 35 (1958): 199–210.

Kany, Charles E. *Life and Manners in Madrid 1750–1800.* Berkeley: U of California P, 1932.

McClelland, I. L. *Spanish Drama of Pathos 1750–1808.* 2 vols. Liverpool: Liverpool UP, 1970.

MacCurdy, Raymond R. *The Tragic Fall: Don Alvaro de Luna and Other Favorites in Spanish Golden Age Drama.* UNCSRLL 197. Chapel Hill: U of North Carolina P, 1978.

McKendrick, Melveena. *Woman and Society in the Spanish Drama of the Golden Age. A Study of the ''mujer varonil.''* London: Cambridge UP, 1974.

Maravall, José Antonio. *Teatro y literatura en la sociedad barroca.* Madrid: Seminarios y Ediciones, 1972.

Mérimée, Paul. *L'Art dramatique en Espagne dans la première moitié du XVIII*[e] *siècle.* Université de Toulouse-Le Mirail: France-Iberie Recherche, 1983.

Moir, Duncan. ''The Classical Tradition in Spanish Dramatic Theory and Practice in the Seventeenth Century.'' In *Classical Drama and Its Influences.* Ed. M. J. Anderson. London: Methuen, 1965. 191–228.

Parker, A. A. ''Towards a Definition of Calderonian Tragedy.'' *BHS* 39 (1962): 222–37.

Pataky Kosove, Joan Lynne. *The ''Comedia Lacrimosa'' and Spanish Romantic Drama (1773–1865).* London: Tamesis, 1977.

Peak, J. Hunter. *Social Drama in Nineteenth-century Spain.* UNCSRLL 51 Chapel Hill: U of North Carolina P, 1964.

Pörtl, Klaus, ed. *Das spanische Theater von den Anfängen bis zum Ausgang des 19. Jahrhunderts.* Darmstadt: Wissenschaftliche Buchgesellschaft, 1985.

Reichenberger, Arnold G. ''The Uniqueness of the comedia.'' *HR* 27 (1959): 303–16.

Rennert, H. A. *The Spanish Stage in the Time of Lope de Vega.* 2nd ed. New York: Dover, 1963.

Ruiz Ramón, Francisco. *Historia del teatro español (desde sus orígenes hasta 1900).* Madrid: Alianza, 1967.

Shaw, Donald L. *The Nineteenth Century*, vol. 5 of *A Literary History of Spain.* Ed. R. O. Jones. London: Benn; New York: Barnes and Noble, 1972. See especially Chapters 1, 3, 6.

Shergold, N. D. *A History of the Spanish Stage from Medieval Times until the End of the Seventeenth Century.* Oxford: Clarendon P, 1967.

Shergold, N. D. and J. E. Varey. ''Some Palace Performances of Seventeenth-century Plays.'' *BHS* 40 (1963): 212–44.

Sloman, Albert E. *The Dramatic Craftsmanship of Calderón. His Use of Earlier Plays.* Oxford: Dolphin, 1958.

Valbuena Prat, Angel. *Historia del teatro español.* Barcelona: Noguer, 1956.

Varey, J. E. *Critical Studies of Calderón's ''comedias.''* Vol 19 of *Comedias; a Facsimile*

Edition; With Textual and Critical Studies. Ed. D. W. Cruickshank and J. E. Varey. 19 vols. Farnborough, England: Gregg, 1973.
Wardropper, Bruce W., ed. *Critical Essays on the Theater of Calderón*. New York: New York UP, 1965.
——— *Siglos de Oro: Barroco*, vol. 3 of *Historia y crítica de la literatura española*. Barcelona: Crítica, 1983. See Sections 2, 3, 8, 9.
Weiger, John G. *The Valencian Dramatists of Spain's Golden Age*. TWAS 371. Boston: Twayne, 1976.
Williamsen, Vern G. *The Minor Dramatists of Seventeenth-century Spain*. TWAS 653. Boston: Twayne, 1982.
Wilson, Edward M., and Duncan Moir. *The Golden Age: Drama 1492–1700*, vol. 3 of *A Literary History of Spain*. Ed. R. O. Jones. London: Benn; New York: Barnes and Noble, 1971.
Wilson, Margaret. *Spanish Drama of the Golden Age*. Oxford: Pergamon, 1969.
Zavala, Iris M. *Romanticismo y realismo*, vol. 5 of *Historia y crítica de la literatura española*. Ed. Francisco Rico. Barcelona: Crítica, 1982. See especially Chapters 4 and 10.
Ziomek, Henryk. *A History of Spanish Golden Age Drama*. Lexington: UP of Kentucky, 1984.

Ann L. MacKenzie

THEBAIDA, HIPÓLITA Y SERAFINA, Comedias (Plays of Thebaida, Hipolita and Serafina), anonymous humanistic plays. They appeared together in 1521 (Valencia); the actual publishing history is somewhat convoluted (see Trotter and Whinnom). At one time, all were (1) attributed to Alonso de *Proaza, (2) considered imitations of the **Celestina*, and (3) censured as some of the most obscene literature in Spanish. More recent evaluation has rejected the attribution, questioned the presumption that each strove to emulate the *Celestina*, and softened the harsh censure of moral turpitude. Each is admittedly frank sexually; all depict a young man in love with a young woman, by the end he successfully possesses the object of his desires via a go-between—but here any conscious imitation of the *Celestina* ends. None is a tragedy, nor does any feature the tight chain of causality which propels the *Celestina*. *Serafina* is the best of the three; even Marcelino *Menéndez y Pelayo could not deny the power of its language. The question of authorship for each remains a mystery.

BIBLIOGRAPHY

Primary Texts

La comedia llamada Serafina. Ed., intro., G. F. Dille. Carbondale: Southern Illinois UP, 1979.
La Comedia Thebaida. Ed., intro., G. D. Trotter and K. Whinnom. London: Tamesis, 1969.
The Comedia Ypolita. Ed., intro., P. E. Douglas. Philadelphia: U of Pennsylvania, 1929.

Criticism

See introductions in Primary Texts.

THEBUSSEM, Doctor (1828, Medina–Sidonia, Cádiz–1918, Medina-Sidonia), Spanish prose writer. His real name was Mariano Pardo de Figueroa, and he was a gentleman monk, a knight of the religious Order of Santiago, restricted to the nobility. He was in many ways a fairly typical nineteenth-c. literary figure, not a professional writer but an aficionado (enthusiastic amateur) who had many avocations. He was cultured, erudite, and ingenious, eccentric and curious, and the range of his writings reflects this: he wrote books on philately (and held the title of "honorary postman of Spain"), on gastronomy, on regional themes and other topics, as well as maintaining a voluminous correspondence, treated as an art. Philatelic works include *Fruslerías postales* (1895; Trifles and Post-Cards), *Literatura filatélica* (n.d.; Philatelic Literature), *La calcografía y los sobrescritos* (n.d.; Calques [Tracings] and Write-Overs). Culinary works include *La mesa moderna: cartas sobre el comedor y la cocina cambiadas entre el Doctor Thebussem y un cocinero de S.M.* (1883; The Modern Dining-Table: Letters Exchanged Between Dr. Thebussem and His Majesty's Cook). More literary volumes were the collections of tales, *Futesas literarias* (1899; Literary Trivia), *Ristra de ajos* (1884; String of Garlic), and its sequel, *Segunda ristra de ajos* (1886; Second String of Garlic). Closer to the essay are *Señor y Don* (Baron and Squire) and *Como se acabó en Medina el rosario de la aurora* (How the Rosary of Dawn Ended in Medina).

TIERNO GALVÁN, Enrique (1918, Madrid–1986, Madrid), Spanish essayist, philosopher, politician, sociologist and political scientist, mayor of Madrid. After earning a law degree and a doctorate in philosophy, Tierro Galván taught political science at the universities of Murcia (1948–53), Salamanca (1953–65), and was a visiting professor at several foreign universities, including Puerto Rico, Bryn Mawr College, and Princeton. Although he maintained his independence of Spanish trends in philosophy, he was influenced considerably by German thinkers, including Gottlob Frege and Ludwig Wittgenstein. His first major work, *La realidad como resultado* (1959; Reality as Resultant) continues his long-standing interest in epistemology and theories of meaning, and would become the foundation for his neo-positivistic sociology as formulated in *Conocimiento y ciencias sociales* (1966; Knowledge and Social Science). Tierno Galván's long history of involvement in leftist politics had culminated in his becoming the effective leader of Spain's Social Democratic Party, although his ideology is strongly Marxist, as seen in his major theoretical treatise, *Razón mecánica y razón dialéctica* (1969; Mechanical Reason and Dialectical Reason). Tierno terms his sociological theory "operational" and he prefers to deal with the real and concrete, eschewing metaphysical preoccupations and subjectivism in favor of scientific, empirical and objective notions expressed with a dialectical rhetoric of social action. Tierno's contributions to the history of ideas include *Costa y el regeneracionismo* (1960; Costa and Regenerationism), *Tradición y modernismo* (1962; Tradition and Modernism), and *Acotaciones a la historia de la cultura universal en la edad moderna* (1964; Notes on Cultural History in the Modern

Age). He is a critic of traditional humanism, as seen in *Humanismo y sociedad* (1964; Humanism and Society), but has also written on a variety of cultural topics: *Desde el espectáculo a la trivialización* (1961; From Spectacle to Trivialization); *Diderot como pretexto* (1965; Diderot As Pretext), and several others. His personal philosophical position, including rejection of metaphysical concerns, is summarized in *¿Qué es ser agnostico?* (1975; What Does it Mean to be Agnostic?). Tierno strives to transcend long-standing dichotomies of Western thought (and in this he follows in the steps of *Unamuno and *Ortega, accepting many basic premises of atheistic existentialism, and limiting his efforts to the visible physical and social realities of the present.

BIBLIOGRAPHY

Criticism

Thomas Mermall. *The Rhetoric of Humanism: Spanish Culture After Ortega y Gasset.* New York: Bilingual P, 1976. 85–107.

TIJERAS, Eduardo (1931, Morón de la Frontera, Seville–), Spanish novelist and short story writer. He is the author of a study on narrative prose entitled *Ultimos rumbos del cuento español* (1969; Latest Paths of the Spanish Short Story), as well as of the novels *El vino del sábado* (1965; Saturday Wine) and *Jugador solitario* (1969; The Solitary Player).

TIMONEDA, Juan de (1520?, Valencia?–1583, ?), playwright, poetry and prose writer, bookseller. Both the date and place of Timoneda's birth remain unknown. Much is known of his literary activities, but little of his private life. First a tanner of hides, he later became a bookseller. This transition is not unusual, for tanned hides were used to bind books, and bookbinders often became booksellers. As a bookseller, he was in constant contact with the intellectuals of Valencia. Most documents of the time list his name as Joan Timoneda.

Timoneda's drama contributed to the increase in dramatic activity in Valencia in the mid-sixteenth c. He wrote secular and religious plays, mostly in Castilian, but with a few works in Catalan. He also helped edit and prepare other authors' works for publication; thus it is sometimes difficult to determine whether a work bearing his name is original or an edited version of another author's work. Timoneda's originality stems from the style of his writing rather than the content. In his secular theater, he attempted to combine prose as used in the **Celestina* with techniques found in the works of *Torres Naharro. His collection of plays and interludes entitled *Turiana* (1564) contains works of unknown authorship, some perhaps by him, and reflects the influence of Lope de *Rueda and the Italian theater. With his representation of *Anfitrión* (Amphitruo) and *Menemnos* (Menaechmi), Plautus is seen for the first time on the Spanish stage. While the characters and action remain those of the Latin originals, the spirit of these plays is Spanish. A major contribution of Timoneda to sacramental drama was the serious tone of his works. His two plays in Valentian, which he claims as original, are the only works of this genre in Catalan.

The fundamental characteristic of Timoneda's prose style is condensation. Few details are provided, for the author's purpose was to provide the reader with anecdotes to be retold. The reader thus could embellish the story any way he wished. Timoneda's best known work in this genre is the *Patrañuelo* (1567; Book of Stories). As Marcelino *Menéndez y Pelayo stated in 1907, this book forms "the first Spanish collection of stories written in imitation of those of Italy." In a preliminary epistle to the reader, Timoneda explains that a *patraña is a "fabricated invention, so skillfully expanded and structured that it seems to have the appearance of truth" (tr. Reynolds). He also states that stories of this type are called *novelas* in Italian and *rondalles* in Valentian. All of the tales follow the same pattern: four initial lines of verse to explain the plot, presentation of the plot, development of the plot with some sort of transgression from the norm, and final outcome proving the triumph of the norm. Two other prose collections by Timoneda are *Sobremesa* (1562; Tabletalk) and *El buen aviso y portacuentos* (1564; Good Counsel and Portable Storybook). Timoneda also published a collection of poetry called *Rosas de romances* (1573; Roses of Ballads); some poems were written by Timoneda, and some by other poets.

In general, Timoneda's style was popular rather than erudite, and his desire was to share and spread knowledge and literature rather than to create original works. He wished to teach a lesson and to entertain. *See also* Italian Literary Influences; Theater in Spain.

BIBLIOGRAPHY

Primary Texts

Cancioneros llamados: Enredo de amor, Guisadillo de amor, y El truhanesco (1573). Reimpresos. . . . Intro. A. Rodríguez-Moñino. Valencia: Castalia, 1951.

Obras. Ed. Juliá Martínez. 3 vols. Madrid: Sociedad de bibliófilos españoles, 1947–48.

El Patrañuelo. Ed. J. Romera Castillo. Madrid: Cátedra, 1978.

Turiana. Facs. Madrid: Tip. de Archivos, 1936.

English Translation

The Aucto del castillo de Emaus and the Aucto de la Iglesia of Juan Timoneda. Tr. and ed. M. E. Johnson. Iowa City: U of Iowa, 1933.

Criticism

Aróstegui, María del Pilar. "La dramaturgia de Juan Timoneda, estado actual de la cuestión." *BBMP* 48 (1972): 201–30.

Childers, J. W. *Motif index of the cuentos of Juan Timoneda*. Bloomington: Indiana U, 1948.

Reynolds, J. J. *Juan Timoneda*. TWAS 367. New York: Twayne, 1975.

Rodríguez Moñino, A. *Poesía y cancioneros (siglo XVI)*. Madrid: RAE, 1968.

Nina Shecktor

TIRANT LO BLANCH. *See* Martorell, Joanot

TIRSO DE MOLINA, pseudonym of Fray Gabriel Téllez (1580?, Madrid?–1648, Almazán, Soria), dramatist. Despite the earnest endeavors of scholars, Tirso de Molina remains a shadowy figure. It is now generally acknowledged that the name Tirso de Molina was the pseudonym of the friar Gabriel Téllez. Probably born in Madrid in 1580, he entered the Mercedarian order as a novice in 1600, and took religious vows in 1601. He studied at the U of Salamanca (1601–3), in Toledo and Guadalajara (1603–7) and at the U of Alcalá de Henares (1607–9). He lived in Toledo for periods during the years 1606–15, and may there have made the acquaintance of Lope de *Vega. Certainly his dramatic career appears to date from his Toledo days, for a contract of 1612 has survived, according to which he sold three plays to an *autor de comedias*, or manager of a troupe of actors. After a brief residence in the New World, from 1616 to 1618, Tirso returned to Spain and, in 1621, to Madrid. He claimed in that year to have written three hundred plays. Four years later he was censured by the Junta de Reformación for the evil moral effects of his plays. It was suggested to his order that he be prohibited from writing further for the theater, and that he be exiled to a remote monastery. It can be argued that the real reason for his fall from favor was political, and had its origins in his opposition to Olivares, the chief minister of the crown. Nevertheless, these years saw the publication of his miscellany, *Los cigarrales de Toledo* (1624; The Country Houses of Toledo) and the *Primera parte* (First Part) of his plays. This latter volume is dated Seville, 1627, but its publication history has given rise to much conjecture. The volume bears a license dated 1624, and the delay in its appearance may be due to the disfavor shown by the Junta de Reformación. The *Parte segunda* appeared in Madrid in 1635, but Tirso himself disowned eight of the twelve plays it contained, without disclosing the titles of the plays concerned and thus giving rise to much critical conjecture. The *Parte tercera* had appeared the year before, in Tortosa. The fourth and fifth volumes were published in Madrid in 1635 and 1636, respectively. While Tirso's plays, therefore, continued to appear in published form, he had himself been ordered in 1626 to Trujillo, as *comendador* (Knight-Commander). He was later to be nominated official historian of his order, and to write the *Historia general de la Merced*, a work which, however, remained unpublished until recently. Tirso de Molina died in Almazán in 1648.

Tirso is best known as the author of two plays, *El condenado por desconfiado* (Condemned for Lack of Faith) and *El burlador de Sevilla* (The Trickster of Seville); the paternity of both has, ironically, been disputed. *El condenado por desconfiado* reflects in part the theological controversy concerning the doctrine of predestination, but it is also, in theatrical terms, a conflation of a *comedia de santos* and a play which puts on the stage the figure of a repentant criminal. Paulo, the hermit who has spent his days praising the name of God, is at the end of the play dispatched to Hell; the brutal and licentious Enrico is received into Heaven. The outcome of the play appears, on a superficial level, to be illogical. However, Paolo, for all his apparent humility, is consumed with spiritual pride, while the depraved Enrico is less hypocritical and, through the reverence which he pays to his father, shows himself capable of repentance and worthy of salvation. Enrico reveals spiritual fortitude while Paulo is presented as a spiritual coward, doubting God because he doubts himself.

With *El burlador de Sevilla* Tirso created one of the most important figures of Western literature, that of *don Juan. The play combines the tradition of the libertine who invites a dead man to dine, and that of the statue which comes to life. Don Juan is proud of his reputation, but in a moral sense, his is an evil reputation. He confuses fame with infamy, and he is abetted in this confusion by the corruption of the society around him. He puts his trust in his own quick wits, but he can never escape divine justice, and at the end of the play he is carried off to Hell and to a deserved doom. In reality he is his own victim: in believing that he can deceive God, he is merely deceiving himself. Though Tirso's don Juan is above all a rebel, against authority human and divine, it is his ability to charm women which has inspired writers of other countries and other centuries to create their own don Juan. In nineteenth-c. Spain, José *Zorrilla created a Don Juan who, in typical Romantic fashion, is redeemed by love at the end. The trickster is also the hero of Molière's play *Don Juan*, Mozart's opera *Don Giovanni*, and part of Shaw's *Man and Superman*.

The Burlador of Sevilla also merits interest for its presentation of a corrupt city of Seville, and a corrupt court of Naples. Several of Tirso's plays deal with the relationship between the crown and its ministers, and the nature of royal authority, and it is perhaps in such plays that the true reason for the attitude of the Junta de Reformación is to be sought. Critics have endeavored to link particular plays with specific historical and political events; the imprecision of the references make such suppositions difficult to substantiate, but it is reasonable to argue that Tirso may well have been using the public theaters to comment on the elevations and falls of such figures as Lerma, Uceda, Rodrigo Calderón, and, perhaps, Olivares. Some plays, such as *Privar contra su gusto* (The Reluctant Favorite) present favorable pictures of the *privado*, but the general tone is that of *La prudencia en la mujer* (Prudence in Women) in which the Queen Mother counsels her young son not to put his trust in proud favorites. The *privado* figure appears in some of the plays of biblical inspiration, and certainly represents a general concern for the government of Spain in the early seventeenth c., even though it is difficult to date plays with precision and thus link them securely to political happenings.

In recent years a new interest has been shown by critics in Tirso's comedies, plays which delighted audiences in the early nineteenth c. and which are now again receiving their due. Once the spectator has accepted the basic premises of the plot, he witnesses a rapidly unfolding and complicated action: the speed of events is similar to that of a farce, and the playwright shows a consummate skill in his handling of characters and episodes. In many of these plays the central character is a charming and spirited young woman. In *Don Gil de las calzas verdes* (Sir Gil of the Green Breeches) the betrayed doña Juana shows herself capable of becoming her own champion and redressing the wrong done her by don Martín. She controls the actions of the other characters in the play, constructing a pseudo-reality in which they become embroiled, partly due to their own cupidity and other vices. She becomes in effect the conscience of don

Martín, and gradually manipulates events until she finds a safe haven in marriage. The comedy, like other successful pieces such as *Por el sótano y el torno* (Through Basement and Hatch) and *La villana de Vallecas* (Village Girl of Vallecas), reflects a view of Madrid as a confused society of uncertain values. If the town is corrupt, then the country, in tune with the old *Renaissance topic, is nearer to Nature, and therefore to God, even though the rustics of Tirso never reach the stature of Lope's peasant heroes in *Fuenteovejuna* or *Peribáñez*. But in *La villana de la Sagra* (Village Girl of la Sagra) and *La gallega Mari Hernández* (The Galician Mari-Hernández) Tirso created vivacious and spontaneous heroines, while his *Antona García* presents a folkloric, almost superhuman figure. Tirso excels in the creation and delineation of women characters. His approach to the theater is didactic, and he wishes both to look forward to a Spain which will be wisely and justly governed, and to correct in society those vices which he sees most commonly displayed. His characters, therefore, move always in a moral dimension.

BIBLIOGRAPHY

Primary Texts

El amor médiço y Averígüelo Vargas. Ed. A. Zamora Vicente and María J. Canellada de Zamora. Clasicos Castellanos 131. Madrid: Espasa Calpe, 1922.

Antona García. Ed. M. Wilson. Manchester: Manchester UP, 1957.

El burlador de Sevilla y El vergonzoso en palacio. Ed. A. Castro. Clásicos Castellanos 2. Madrid: Espasa-Calpe, 1922.

El condenado por desconfiado. Ed. D. Rogers. Oxford: Pergamon, 1974.

Obras dramáticas completas. Ed. Blanca de los Ríos. 3 vols. Madrid: Aguilar, 1946–58.

La venganza de Tamar. Ed. A. K. G. Paterson. Cambridge: Cambridge UP, 1969.

English Translations

Don Juan; or the Viper of Seville. Tr. J. Duckett. Medford, MA: Tufts UP, 1968.

The Double Damned. Tr. Angelita Martínez. Washington, DC: Catholic U, 1956.

The Playboy of Seville; or, Supper with a Statue. Tr. A. Schizzano and O. Mandel. In *Three Classic Don Juan Plays*. Ed. O. Mandel. Lincoln: U of Nebraska P, 1971.

The Trickster of Seville and the Guest of Stone. Tr. R. Campbell. In *World Masterpieces*. Ed. Maynard Macketal. New York: Norton, 1965.

Criticism

Agheana, I. T. *The Situational Drama of Tirso de Molina*. Madrid: Plaza Mayor, 1973.

Bushee, A. H. *Three Centuries of Tirso de Molina*. Philadelphia: U. of Pennsylvania P, 1939.

Cotarelo y Mori, E. *Tirso de Molina. Investigaciones bio-bibliográficas*. Madrid: E. Rubiños, 1893.

Darst, D. H. *The Comic Art of Tirso de Molina*. Chapel Hill: U of North Carolina P, 1974.

Dellepiane, A. B. *Presencia de América en la obra de Tirso de Molina*. Madrid: Revista Estudios, 1968.

Gijón Zapata, Esmeralda. *El humor en Tirso de Molina*. Madrid: U of Madrid, 1959.

Kennedy, Ruth Lee. *Studies in Tirso, I: The Dramatist and His Competitors 1620–26.* UNCSRLL 3. Chapel Hill: U of North Carolina P, 1974.

McClelland, I. L. *Tirso de Molina: Studies in Dramatic Realism.* Liverpool: Institute of Hispanic Studies, 1948.

Metford, J. C. J. "Tirso de Molina's Old Testament Plays." *BHS* 27 (1950): 149–63.

Poesse, Walter, and V. G. Williamsen. *An Annotated, Analytical Bibliography of Tirso de Molina Studies 1627–1977.* Columbia: U of Missouri P, 1979.

Sullivan, H. W. *Tirso de Molina and the Drama of the Counter Reformation.* Amsterdam: Rodopi, 1976.

Tirso de Molina. Ensayos sobre la biografía y obra del Padre Maestro Fray Gabriel Téllez por Revista Estudios. Madrid: Revista Estudios, 1949.

Vossler, Karl. *Lecciones sobre Tirso de Molina.* Madrid: Taurus, 1965.

Wilson, Margaret. *Tirso de Molina.* TWAS 445. Boston: Twayne, 1977.

John E. Varey

TIZÓN DE LA NOBLEZA DE ESPAÑA (Stain of the Spanish Nobility), sixteenth-c. work. Probably written by the Cardinal Archbishop Francisco de Mendoza y Bobadilla, who evidently showed it to Philip II; its theme is the paucity of "clean blood," or untainted lineage, in the sixteenth-c. Spanish aristocracy. It is a revealing document of the ideology of the day; in the nineteenth c. it underwent six editions.

BIBLIOGRAPHY

Primary Text

El tizón de la.... 3rd ed. Barcelona: Selecta, 1880.

Criticism

Foulché-Delbosc, R. "*Tizón de la nobleza de España.*" *RH* 7 (1900): n.p. Lists most editions.

Herrero García. "Ideología española del siglo XVII: la nobleza." *RFE* 14 (1927): 33–58, 161–75.

TOB, Sem; also transcribed as Santob; full name is Šem Ṭob ibn Arduṭiel b. Isaac (c. 1290, ?–c. 1369, ?), rabbi and author. Rabbi Sem Tob of Carrión is best known as the author of the *Proverbios morales* (c. 1345; Moral Proverbs), dedicated to King Peter I, the Cruel. He was also the author of a wide range of works in Hebrew, many of them unedited. The *Proverbios* (also referred to as *trobas* by the author) is written in fairly characteristic Western Hispano-Romance, much like that of the **Cancioneiros*, with Portuguese characteristics. It is made up of 686 strophes of four heptasyllabic verses each, perhaps originally being two lines of 6 plus 6 syllables each with internal rhyme, and is divided into 21 chapters. It is considered to be the introduction in Spanish poetry of moral proverbs, which was a popular genre in Arabic and Hebrew. The author's principal sources are the Bible, the Talmud, and the wide range of Arabic literature of the genre of "anthologies of wisdom." It is generally considered to be a deliberate attempt at expressing Jewish thought in Romance tongue, not through translation from the Hebrew but through adaptation of poetic techniques. The proverbs are characterized by concision and elegance, and many believe that they have not received critical attention commensurate with their importance in the development of Spanish literature. *See also* Hispano Judaic Literature.

BIBLIOGRAPHY

Primary Texts

Dom Sem Tob: Glosas de sabiduría o proverbios morales y otras rimas. Ed. Agustín García Calvo. Madrid: Alianza, 1974. Extensive intro. and notes.
Proverbios morales. BAE, 57: 331–72.
Proverbios morales. Ed. R. A. Perry. Madrid: Castalia, 1985.
Santob de Carrión, Proverbios morales. Ed. Ignacio González Llubera. Cambridge: Cambridge UP, 1947.
Sem Tob de Carrión, Proverbios morales. Ed. Guzmán Alvarez. Salamanca: Anaya, 1970. Contains intro.

English Translation

The Moral Proverbs of Santob de Carrion. Tr., study, T. A. Perry. Princeton: Princeton UP, 1987.

Criticism

See Perry, *Moral Proverbs*, above.

María Rosa Menocal

TOLEDO SCHOOL OF TRANSLATORS. *See* Escuela de Traductores de Toledo

TOMÁS, Mariano (1891, Hellín, Albacete–1957, Madrid), poet, novelist, playwright. He contributed articles to the press on a regular basis, served as the king's diplomatic courier (1926), and was editor for *Indice Cultural*—a publication of the Foreign Ministry. Tomás's poems were published in *La capa del estudiante* (1925; The Student's Cloak); his more than twenty novels include titles such as *Sinfonía incompleta* (1934; Unfinished Symphony), *Salto mortal* (1945; Mortal Leap), and *Venga Ud. a casa en primavera* (1933: Come Home in Spring); his plays, which demonstrate the influence of *Marquina, include *Isabel de España* (1934), and *La mariposa y la llama* (The Butterfly and the Flame)—which received the National Drama Guild prize in 1941.

BIBLIOGRAPHY

Primary Texts

Antología poética. Barcelona: Juventud, 1953.
La mariposa y la llama. Madrid: Nacional, 1942.
Salto mortal. Barcelona: Colección Para Todos, 1945.
Sinfonía incompleta. Barcelona: Juventud, 1934.
Venga Ud. a casa en primavera. Barcelona: Juventud, 1933.

English Translation

The Life and Misadventures of Miguel de Cervantes. Tr. W. B. Wells. Boston and New York: Houghton Mifflin, 1934.

Isabel McSpadden

TOMEO, Javier (1937?, Aragon–), Spanish novelist. Tomeo studied law and criminology at the U of Barcelona, and began his literary activity in that city as a collaborator of many periodicals. His short stories were included in various anthologies, among them *Narraciones de lo real y fantástico* (1971; Tales of the Real and the Fantastic) and *Manifiesto español o una antología de narradores* (1972; Spanish Manifesto, or, A Narrative Anthology). His first novel, *El cazador* (The Hunter) appeared in 1967 and was followed by *Ceguera al azul* (1969; Blindness to Blue); *El unicornio* (1971; The Unicorn), winner of the City of Barbastro Prize for novelettes; *Los enemigos* (The Enemies); and *El castillo de la carta cifrada* (1979; The Castle of the Coded Letter), a work very well received by Spanish critics who praised its language, its narrative interest, brilliant and seductive descriptive technique, and the combination of seriousness and humor. Translated to German, it was hailed for the mixture of melancholy and wit. *Amado monstruo* (1985; Beloved Monster) is a dialogue between two men, one a job applicant and the other a personnel manager who is interviewing him, but whose questions become progressively more personal, searching, impertinent and bizarre. As he concentrates more and more on the applicant's relationship with his mother, it becomes clear that both have serious psychological abnormalities, sordid secrets, and ulterior motives. Although the setting and style are hyper-realist, the psychological atmosphere, like that of *El castillo de la carta cifrada* is a cross between Kafka and Buñuel. Here again, the narrative zigzags between the comic and the frightening. *Amado monstruo* has been translated to German, French and Dutch. *Preparativos de viaje* (1969, 1986; Preparations for a Trip) depicts the dilemma of a salesman charged with introducing the latest model of revolving chair Benujistán—which proves to be unknown to travel agents, geographers, and every source consulted (the world presented bears unmistakable resemblances to post-war Spain). Once more Tomeo combines horror and humor most effectively.

Janet Pérez

TORDESILLAS, Seguro de (Ceasefire of Tordesillas), historical account. Published in 1611, it relates an incident in 1439 when, beset by wildly feuding nobles, King John arranged for all to meet in Tordesillas and set aside their rivalries. They did so, and then proceeded to renew their battling with even greater vigor.

BIBLIOGRAPHY

Primary Text

Haro, Pedro Fernández de Velasco, Conde de. *Seguro de Tordesillas*. Madrid: Sancha, 1969. Microfilm.

TORENO, CONDE DE, QUEIPO DE LLANO, José María (1786, Oviedo–1843, Paris), statesman and historian. During the Spanish War of Independence he was sent to England by the Asturian Junta. He later became a member of the Cádiz Courts. Subsequently he alternately occupied important government posts or lived in exile. A liberal, his political career spanned the reigns of Ferdinand VII, the Queen Regent, and Isabel II. He belonged to the Spanish Royal Academy of History. His *Historia del levantamiento, guerra y revolución de España* (1838; History of the Uprising, War and Revolution in Spain) is a clear and well-written work of historical and literary value. It was later translated into several languages. He was well known in his time as a political orator, and there is a collection of his *Discursos parlamentarios* (1872; Parliamentary Speeches). Toreno also left a *Diario de un viaje a Italia* (1882; Diary of a Voyage to Italy).

BIBLIOGRAPHY

Primary Texts

Historia del levantamiento, guerra y revolución de España. 5 vols. Madrid: Tomás Jordán, 1835–37; Madrid: Felipe González Rojas, 1910.

Discursos parlamentarios. 2 vols. Madrid: Berenguillo, 1872–81.

Diario de un viaje a Italia en 1839. Madrid: n.p., 1882.

Criticism

Cueto, Leopoldo Augusto de. Intro. to Toreno's *Historia del levantamiento*. . . . BAE 64.

Salvador García Castañeda

TORGA, Miguel, pseudonym of Adolfo Correia da Rocha since 1936 (1907, São Martinho da Anta, Trás-os-Montes–), Portuguese short story writer, novelist, diarist, poet and dramatist. Miguel Torga lives in Coimbra, where he works as a doctor. He began his career in the journal *Presença* but he broke away from the literary group associated with that magazine in 1930. With Branquinho da Fonseca (one of the founders of *Presença*) he directed the magazines *Sinal* (1930) and *Manifesto* (1938). His most important books of poetry are *O Outro Livro de Job* (1936; The Other Book of Job), *Poemas Ibéricos* (1952; Iberian Poems) and *Orfeu Rebelde* (1958; Rebel Orpheus).

Torga's poetry is filled with the despair of a humanist who faces the suffering and isolation of man in modern society. Man is, for Torga, the universal Adam who titanically ascends from mud to an earthy sense of human dignity. His poetry may be considered mystical to a certain extent, but above all, it is a poetry primarily concerned with the historical meaning of Portugal. Torga's thoughts on national and world problems are collected in his *Diário* (12 vols., 1941–77; Diary), which he started to keep in 1932 and has published every few years. *A Criação do Mundo* (5 vols., 1937–81; The Creation of the World) is an autobiographical novel which complements *Diário*.

Torga's best prose work is perhaps *Vindima* (1945; Vintage), which belongs to the tradition of realism. Published about fifty years after Eça de Queirós' *A*

Cidade e as Serras, *Vindima* offers a more modern view of Portuguese rural life and is one of the novels reminiscent of the *picaresque conception of Aquilino *Ribeiro. Highly admired among Torga's works are the animal stories collected in *Bichos* (1940; *Farrusco the Blackbird and Other Stories from the Portuguese*, 1950). In these stories the animals experience human feelings in the tradition of Aesop.

In general, hope and despair alternate in Torga's work and are presented in an epic tone with biblical echoes. Thus the poet expresses disbelief while always seeking the possibility of belief. Miguel Torga's work has an outstanding place in Portuguese literature due to its originality and stylistic qualities. It is often considered as the meeting point of traditional conventions and modern innovations.

BIBLIOGRAPHY

Primary Texts

Antologia poética. N.p.: n.p., 1981.

Bichos, contos. 4th ed. Coimbra: Atlantida, 1946.

Câmara Ardente. Coimbra: n.p., 1962.

Contos da Montanha. 4th ed. Coimbra: Grafica de Coimbra, 1969.

Diário. 12 vols. Coimbra: n.p., 1941–77.

Lamentacão. 3rd ed. Coimbra: n.p., 1970.

Novos contos da Montanha. 4th ed. Coimbra: n.p., 1959.

Orfeu Rebelde. 2nd ed., rev. Coimbra: n.p., 1970.

Pedras lavradas. Coimbra: Coimbra, 1951.

Vindima. 4th ed. Coimbra: n.p., 1971.

English Translations

The Death Penalty. No tr. Coimbra: Coimbra U, 1967.

Farrusco the Blackbird and Other Stories from the Portuguese. Tr., intro. D. Brass. London: Allen and Unwin, 1950.

Open Sesame, and Other Stories from the Portuguese. Tr. D. Brass. N.p.: n.p., 1960.

Criticism

Brass, D. "The Wisdom of the Soil." *TLS* (Oct. 7, 1977): 1168.

Clemente, A. "The Portuguese Revolution Seen through the Eyes of Three Contemporary Writers." In *Proceedings of the Fourth National Portuguese Conference: The International Year of the Child*. Providence, RI: Multilingual Multicultural Resource and Training Center, 1979. 24–51.

Lourenço, Eduardo. *O Desespero Humanista de Miguel Torga e o das Novas Gerações*. Coimbra: n.p., 1955.

Moura, Frederico de. *Vestígios de Miguel Torga*. Portugal: n.p., 1977.

Ricard, R. "Despenador et Abafador ou La Fortune d'un thème macabre de Ventura García Calderón à Miguel Torga." *Bulletin des Etudes Portugaises et de l'Institut Français au Portugal* 20 (1958): 211–19.

Rocha, Clara Crabbé. *O Espaço Autobiográfico em Miguel Torga*. Coimbra: n.p., 1977.

Leopoldo Serrão and Manuela Renata Valente de Carvalho

TORO, Arcediano de (fl. 1380, ?–?), poet. His real name is Gonzalo Rodríguez; his name appears in the *Cancionero de *Baena* as author of several poems in Castilian and in Galician.

TORÓN, Saulo (1885, Telde, Grand Canary–1974, Las Palmas, Grand Canary), poet. He shares common characteristics with other Canary Island poets such as Alonso *Quesada and Tomás *Morales, and follows post-modernism. His first work was *Las monedas de cobre* (1919; The Copper Coins). *Canciones de la orilla* (1932; Songs from the Shore) is deemed his best work. In 1963 his final volume, *Frente al muro* (1963; Facing the Wall), appeared. Torón also wrote several **sainetes* which remain unpublished.

BIBLIOGRAPHY

Primary Texts

Canciones de la orilla. Madrid: Pueyo, 1932.
El caracol encantado. Madrid: Juan Pérez, 1926.
Frente al muro. Las Palmas: Tagoro, 1963.

Isabel McSpadden

TORQUEMADA, Antonio de (?, León?–?, ?), sixteenth-c. humanist and writer of prose fiction. Torquemada dedicated his first work, the *Coloquios satíricos* (1553; Satirical Discourses) to Don Antonio Alfonso de Pimentel, Count of Benavente, whom he served as secretary. The work consists of six conversations among groups of friends on such contemporary concerns as the vices of gambling and gluttony, the merits of the rural life, absurdities of fashion, and the incompetence of pharmacists and physicians. The concluding section, the "Coloquio pastoril" (Pastoral Colloquy), is an unusual blend of dream sequence and *pastoral love story. Torquemada's novelistic technique is thought to have been derived in part from Boccaccio, and his own dialogue structure is, in turn, viewed by some as a source for *Cervantes's *Coloquio de los perros* (Colloquy of the Dogs). His *Historia del invencible caballero don Olivante de Laura* (1564; An Account of the Invincible Knight don Olivante de Laura) is a chivalric novel traditionally held in little esteem. Torquemada's most popular work by far was the *Jardín de flores curiosas* (1570; *The Garden of Curious Flowers*, 1600). Obviously influenced by popular superstitions, it contains references to supernatural, fanciful events and bizarre creatures, half-animal and half-human. The author is remembered today chiefly as a transitional figure in the development of the Spanish narrative. See also Humanism; Renaissance.

BIBLIOGRAPHY

Primary Texts

Coloquios satíricos. Selections in NBAE 7 and 21. Madrid: 1907 and 1915.
Cuentos viejos de la vieja España. Madrid: Aguilar, 1949.
Jardín de flores curiosas. Clásicos Castalia 129. Madrid: Castalia, 1982.
Manual de escribientes. Ed. María Josefa Cancellada de Zamora and A. Zamora Vicente. Anejos del *BRAE* 21. Madrid: RAE, 1970.

English Translation

The Spanish Mandevile of Myracles; or The Garden of Curious Flowers. Tr. Lewes Lewkenor. 1618 version of 1600 orig. Early English Books: 1475–1640; microfilm reel 1261. Ann Arbor, MI: University Microfilms, 1971.

Criticism

Allegra, Giovanni. ''Sobre la fábula y lo 'fabuloso' del *Jardín de flores curiosas.*'' *Thesaurus* 33 (1978): 96–110.

Elsdon, J. H. *On the Life and Work of the Spanish Humanist Antonio de Torquemada.* Berkeley: U of California P, 1937.

C. Maurice Cherry

TORRE, Alfonso de la (fl. 1430s, ?–?), author. The Bachiller Alfonso de la Torre was born in one of the villages of the Archdiocese of Burgos toward the end of the fourteenth c. Little is known of his life, not even his date of birth nor that of his death. Claims are made that he studied at the College of St. Bartholomew in Salamanca around 1437. His ticket to fame is the treatise called *Visión delectable de la vida bienaventurada* (1965; Delectable Vision of the Fortunate Life), written probably between 1430 and 1440. He may also have translated the *Ethics* of Aristotle attributed to one Bachiller de la Torre. His use of Aristotle's *Ethics* as a source for his *Visión* strongly suggests that he had firsthand knowledge of this work, a matter not repeated for some of the other sources he used. The *Visión delectable* was written at the behest of Juan de Beaumont for the education of the young prince, Charles of Viana. The work is an allegory in which the author falls asleep, has a dream in which a small child, *Entendimiento* (Understanding), ascends a mountain and is instructed in his ascent by the seven liberal arts, the maidens Grammar, Logic, Rhetoric (the trivium), Arithmetic, Geometry, Music, and Astrology (the quadrivium). In the following chapters of the first part, 8–19, the author discusses questions basic to scholastic philosophy and theology of the time. This section is based mainly on Maimonides's *Guide of the Perplexed.* Sources for his discussion of the trivium and the quadrivium are the works of Alain de Lille, Isidore of Seville, and the translations of Dominicus Gundissalinus. The second part depends less on Maimonides's *Guide* and deals primarily with ethics and politics. The work closes with an apology for its having been written in the vernacular, and requests that it not pass into the hands of a third party lest the author be unduly criticized. Finally, the author greets Prince Charles, asking that he accept the work as the first fruits of his labor.

Judging from the large number of ms. and incunabular copies of the work, there can be little doubt that it was widely read. It was published several times in Castilian, the first time about 1480. It was translated into Catalan in 1484; into Italian in 1556 by Domenico Delphini, who passed this translation off as an original work; and then was retranslated from the Italian into Spanish in 1623 by Francisco Cáceres. It appears to be one of the sources for Lope de *Vega's *Arcadia.*

BIBLIOGRAPHY

Primary Texts

"An Edition of the *Visión delectable de la vida bienaventurada* of Alfonso de la Torre." Ed. Caspar J. Morsello. Diss., Wisconsin, 1965.

Visión delectable de la filosofía y de las artes liberales." Ed. A. Castro y Rossi. BAE 36. Madrid: Rivadeneyra, 1855. 341–402 (text) and xxi (biography).

Criticism

Amador de los Ríos, José. *Historia crítica de la literatura española.* Madrid: Joaquín Muñoz, 1865. 7: 45–58.

Crawford, J. P. Wickersham. "The Seven Liberal Arts in the *Visión delectable* of Alfonso de la Torre." *RR* 4 (1913): 58–75.

———. "The Seven Liberal Arts in Lope de Vega's *Arcadia.*" *MLN* 30.1 (1915): 13–14.

———. "The *Visión delectable* of Alfonso de la Torre and Maimonides *Guide of the Perplexed.*" *PMLA* 25 (1913): 188–212.

González, G. "La *Visión delectable* de Alfonso de la Torre: Theoría de las artes liberales." *Cuadernos de Aldecu* 4.1 (1988): 31–46.

Anthony J. Cárdenas

TORRE, Claudio de la (1902, Canary Islands–1978[?], Madrid), Spanish poet, novelist and playwright. He achieved notable early success when his novel *En la vida del señor Alegre* (1924; In the Lifetime of Mr. Alegre) won the National Prize for Literature. His writings are characterized by refined humor and sensibility, with a tendency for wordplay. Outstanding plays include *Tic-tac* (n.d.), *Hotel Términus* (Railroad-Station Hotel), *Tren de madrugada* (The Early-Morning Train), and *La cortesana* (The Courtesan), which earned the City of Barcelona Prize in 1951. He aspired to an ambitious renovation of theatrical themes and techniques, not always successfully. Another novel, *El verano de Juan "el chino"* (The Summer of "Chinaman" Juan), appeared in 1971.

TORRE, Francisco de la (?–?), important transitional poet. The very existence of Torre has at times been held in doubt, although the excellence of verse attributed to this name would make Torre and Luis de *León the two finest poets of the *Escuela Salmantina. *Quevedo first published the poems in 1631; his prefatory letter states he purchased them from a bookdealer anxious to rid himself of the book, that they bore the name of Alonso de *Ercilla as official censor (Ercilla functioned as censor from 1580 to 1594), and that Francisco de la Torre was listed as author. The text Quevedo says he bought has not survived. Curious omissions and contradictions in Quevedo's remarks, plus the dearth of facts about Torre, led critics to infer biographical information from poems and a few other passing references; the resulting critical hypotheses have been summarized effectively by G. Hughes, who notes that Quevedo's decision to publish was motivated by the quality of the poetry, and its value (like the work of Fray Luis de León, which Quevedo also edited) as an example of elegant clarity of expression—an antidote to the growing popularity of **culteranismo*.

Torre wrote sixty-four sonnets, eleven odes, six *Canciones*, ten **endechas*, and eight eclogues. Primarily a *pastoral poet, his verse is marked by a sensitive, tender delicacy, themes of platonic and neo-platonic love, moods of melancholy and sadness, and recurring nocturnal themes. A restrained courtly love also surfaces in some poems. *Italian literary influences are readily apparent—some twelve sonnets are translations of Benedetto Varchi and Giambattista Amalteo. Yet, his masterful use of structural parallelism and the exquisite balance of his finest poems make him much more than a talented follower of *Garcilaso.

BIBLIOGRAPHY

Primary Texts

Poesías. Ed. A. Zamora Vicente. Clásicos Castellanos 124. Madrid: Espasa-Calpe, 1956.

Criticism

Blanco Sánchez, A. *Entre fray Luis y Quevedo: En busca de Francisco de la Torre*. Salamanca: Atlas, 1982.

Hughes, G. *The Poetry of Francisco de la Torre*. Toronto: U of Toronto P, 1982.

Rivers, E. "The Horatian Epistle and its Introduction into Spanish Literature." *HR* 22 (1954): 175–94.

Sena, Jorge de *Francisco de la Torre e D. João de Almeida*. Paris: Centro Cultural Portugués, 1974.

TORRE, Guillermo de (1900, Madrid–1971, Buenos Aires), prolific essayist, poet, translator, editor, art critic and theoretician, and one of the most well-read and knowledgeable critics with respect to the literary trends of his time. He also studied law and traveled throughout Europe. In 1920 he published the *Manifiesto vertical ultraísta* (Vertical Ultraist Manifesto), stating the goals of the *ultraísta* movement, which he defined, led, and later chronicled in *Literaturas europeas de vanguardia* (1925; European Vanguard Literatures), the most reliable guide to the understanding of the stylistic tendencies of the *postmodernista* poets. It, in turn, was re-edited, with significant changes, under a new title, *Historia de las Literaturas de Vanguardia* (1965, 2nd ed 1971; History of Vanguard Literatures).

Hélices (1923; Spirals) is a collection of his complete poetry, all of it blank and unmetered, and representative of the *ultraísta* movement, which sought to renew poetry by stripping it of rhetoric, sentimentalism, and narrative elements, leaving only metaphor and image.

In 1928, Torre published his first collection of essays, *Examen de conciencia* (Examination of Conscience). His next two books were in the field of art: *Itinerario de la nueva pintura española* (1931; Itinerary of the New Spanish Painting) and *Vida y arte de Picasso* (1936; The Life and Art of Picasso). *Menéndez Pelayo y las dos Españas* (1943; Menéndez Pelayo and the Two Spains) urges a bridgework between Spanish intellectuals in their native country and those who emigrated to Latin America. *Problemática de la literatura* (1951; Problems of Literature) is considered by many to be his most successful work.

Another theoretical opus, *Las metamorfosis de Proteo* (1956; The Metamorphoses of Proteus), states that each period has its own true style, and describes the proper role of a critic as similar to that of Proteus: with a sort of foresight, he must adapt his method with sensibility to the norms and attitudes of the individual work. The symbol of Proteus is taken up once again in *El fiel de la balanza* (1961; The Pointer on the Scales). Torre's concern with literature and its critics is re-evaluated in *El espejo y el camino* (1968, The Mirror and the Path), which decries the contemporary tendency to embrace all revolutionary new movements purely on the basis of their innovation or radicalism. In *Nuevas direcciones de la crítica literaria* (1970; New Directions in Literary Criticism), the true purpose of literary criticism is given as clarification and evaluation. The breadth of Torre's critical vision may be seen in *Del 98 al barroco* (1969; From the Generation of 1898 to the Baroque), with chapters on **Lazarillo de Tormes*, *Guzmán de Alfarache*, the Baroque in Spanish literature, *modernista* journals, memoirs and autobiography, and the writings of *Quevedo, *Pérez Galdós, *Pardo Bazán, and *Clarín.

Torre was involved with several journals of vanguard poetry as a collaborator and contributor, including *Grecia* (Seville, 1919–20), *Cervantes* (1919–20), *Ultra* (1921–22), *Tableros* (1922), and *Horizontes y Cosmópolis*. He wrote for *El Sol* and *Revista de Occidente*, and, together with Ernesto *Giménez Caballero, founded *La Gaceta Literaria* in Madrid in 1927. He engaged in polemical theorizing with Vicente Huidobro, who led the *creacionista* movement and introduced the French poetic "ismos" to Spanish poetry.

In 1928 Torre went to Argentina, where he became associated with the newspaper *La Nación* and the journal *Sur*, in which he published articles on art and literature. On his return to Spain in 1932, he worked with Pedro *Salinas to organize the contemporary literature files at the Centro de Estudios Históricos and edited the journal *Indice Literario*. He returned to Buenos Aires during the Spanish Civil War, this time permanently. There, he devoted himself to editorial work, criticism, and journalism, and became a member of the faculty of the U of Buenos Aires in 1956.

His critical focus encompasses a spectrum which includes painting, sculpture, music, the sociology of literature, Spanish literature from the Renaissance to the twentieth c., and Spanish-American writing.

BIBLIOGRAPHY

Primary Texts

Del 98 al barroco. Madrid: Gredos, 1969.
El espejo y el camino. Madrid: Prensa Española, 1968.
Hélices. Madrid: Mundo latino, 1923.
Manifiesto vertical ultraísta. Madrid: Imprenta de Hernández y Galo Saez, 1920. Re-edited as *Literaturas europeas de vanguardia*. Madrid: Carol Raggio, 1925.

Las metamorfosis de Proteo. Buenos Aires: Losada, 1956.
Problemática de la literatura. Buenos Aires: Losada, 1951.

Criticism

Doreste, Ventura. "Las metamorfosis de Guillermo de Torre." *Papeles de Son Armadans* 8 (1958): 295–306.
Gullón, Ricardo. "Guillermo de Torre o el crítico." *Ficción* 33–34 (Sept.-Dec. 1961): 144–56.
Mead, Robert G. "Guillermo de Torre y la literatura contemporánea." *RHM* 20 (1954): 224–29.
Phillips, A. N. "Guillermo de Torre y la crítica literaria." *RHM* 24 (1958): 196–201.
Zuleta, Emilia de. *Guillermo de Torre*. Buenos Aires: Culturales Argentinas, 1962.

Esther Nelson

TORRE, Josefina de la (1907, Las Palmas, Grand Canary–197?, ?), one of the few women of the *Generation of 1927. De la Torre was encouraged to write by her brother Claudio and Rafael *Alberti, as well as Pedro *Salinas, who authored the introduction to her first book, *Versos y Estampas* (1927; Verses and Vignettes). Free verse and ocean and nature themes predominate in it and in *Poemas de la Isla* (1930; Poems of the Island). She experimented with various performing arts—music, theater, and radio recitation—and wrote a novel-of-the-week, *Memorias de una estrella* (1954; Memories of a Star), about a starlet turned housewife. In later years, she returned to poetry with the retrospective and emotional *Marzo incompleto* (1968; Incomplete March). Exact dates of birth (reported as either 1907 or 1910) and death (197?) are unsubstantiated.

BIBLIOGRAPHY

Primary Texts

Marzo incompleto. Las Palmas de Gran Canaria: Lezcano, 1968.
Memorias de una estrella. Madrid: Cid, 1954.
Poemas de la Isla. Barcelona: Altés, 1930.
Versos y Estampas. Málaga: Imprenta Sur, 1927.

Criticism

Diego, Gerardo. *Poesía Española Contemporánea. 1901–1934 antología*. Madrid: Taurus, 1959. 525, 566.
Women Writers of Spain: An Annotated Bio-Bibliography. Ed. C. Galerstein and K. McNerney. Westport, CT: Greenwood, 1986.

Joy Buckles Landeira

TORRENTE BALLESTER, Gonzalo (1910, Ferrol, Galicia–), novelist, critic, and literary historian. Gonzalo Torrente Ballester has won recognition as a critic and literary historian, as well as a novelist, and has published important critical studies such as *Teatro español contemporáneo* (2nd ed., 1968; Contemporary Spanish Theater), *El 'Quijote' como juego* (1975; The *Quijote* as Play), and *Acerca del novelista y de su arte: Discurso* (1977; On the Novelist and His Art: A Discourse). The latter, delivered upon his entrance into the Real *Academia Española, is an important declaration of Torrente's own literary vision as well as a theoretical meditation on the nature of fiction, the role of language in literary discourse, and the crucial role of the reader as a producer of meaning.

It is as a novelist, however, that Torrente has moved to the forefront of Spanish letters during the post-war period. He has done so not as a member of a recognized generation of authors or as a proponent of a specific literary movement. On the contrary, he stands out for a radical independence of thought that has engendered some of the most imaginative and complex fiction of the past four decades. Even when he draws upon certain literary principles of his times, such as social realism of the 1950s or the more vanguardist techniques of the late 1960s and 1970s, he co-opts and reshapes them in unique fashion, rather than imitate what others have done before.

Torrente's first widely praised work was the trilogy *Los gozos y las sombras* (Joys and Shadows): *El señor llega* (1957; The Master Arrives); *Donde da la vuelta el aire* (1960; Where the Air Turns Around); and *La Pascua triste* (1962; The Sad Easter). Set in a small town in Torrente's native Galicia, the trilogy focuses primarily on the discord between a physician who has returned to his hometown from studying abroad, and his boyhood friend, an industrial engineer who has lived in the town all of his life. Although the conflict occurs on multiple levels, it is most powerfully played out between the spiritual authority of the doctor and the material power of his rival. It is not a Manichean world that Torrente portrays, however. Despite the apparent victory of materialism (the doctor departs), the engineer stands alone at the end of the trilogy amid emptiness and despair, while the doctor finds meaning through love and a willed escape from apathy and skepticism.

Two other novels of the 1960s also represent important steps in Torrente's novelistic evolution: *Don Juan* (1968) and *Off-Side* (1969). The former is both more intellectual and humorous than the novels of the trilogy, and is important within Torrente's fiction because it signals the growing importance of imagination in the author's narrative vision. *Off-Side*, in contrast, represents a temporary return to a more realistic framework, and focuses on reality in contemporary Madrid in the vein of *Cela or *Valle-Inclán.

Torrente's recognition as one of the most distinguished novelists of contemporary Spain stems from the publication of *La saga/fuga de J.B.* in 1972 (The Saga/Flight of J.B.). The novel represents less a break with Torrente's previous fiction than a radical development of those elements which characterize many of his previous novels: a concern for narrative theory; contrasting perspectives on reality and imagination; temporal fragmentation; parody; and the ludic joy of pure invention. The plot of the novel defies synthesis, though the thin story line in the present tense depicts the life of José Bastida and his growing awareness of his mythical status within the city of Castroforte. Torrente's vanguardist technique and play with language, at once parodic and experimental, combines with the mythic foundations of the novel to make it a masterpiece of post-war Spanish narrative.

Torrente's recent fiction (e.g., *Fragmentos de apocalipsis* [1977; Fragments of Apocalypse] and *La isla de los jacintos cortados* [1980; The Isle of Cut Hyacinths]) in large part follows the pattern of *La saga/fuga*. Less complex from a structural and linguistic point of view, these novels are more intensely theoretical and conscious of themselves as fiction and explore the nature of the literary process. *La rosa de los vientos* (1985; The Rose of the Winds) in a similar vein turns back upon itself, but in order to explore the nature of history and historiography and the way in which the real and the imaginative are enmeshed in like narrative structures.

The short story and theater also form part of Torrente's literary production, but neither has brought him the same success as his novels. The short stories (collected in *Las sombras recobradas* [1979; Shadows Recovered]) are of interest primarily for the insight they provide into Torrente's long fiction. Torrente's plays, written early in his career (primarily between 1936 and 1950), have earned scant critical attention and are best viewed as part of an apprenticeship for Torrente in the art of writing.

BIBLIOGRAPHY

Primary Texts

Don Juan. 2nd ed. Barcelona: Destino, 1981.

Fragmentos de apocalipsis. Barcelona: Destino, 1977.

La isla de los jacintos cortados. Barcelona: Destino, 1980.

La rosa de los vientos. Barcelona: Destino, 1985.

La saga/fuga de J.B. Barcelona: Destino, 1972.

Criticism

Homenaje a Gonzalo Torrente Ballester. Salamanca: Biblioteca de la Caja de Ahorros, 1981.

Miller, Stephen. "Don Juan's New Trick: Plot, Verisimilitude, Epistemology and Role Play in Torrente's *Don Juan*." *REH* 16.2 (1982): 163–80.

Pérez, Janet. *Gonzalo Torrente Ballester*. TWAS 736. Boston: Twayne, 1984.

Soldevila Durante, Ignacio. "Nueva lectura de *Javier Mariño*." *Anales de la novela de postguerra* 2 (1977): 43–53.

Spires, Robert. "El conflicto temporal/atemporal en *La Saga/fuga de J.B*." In *La novela española de postguerra*. Madrid: Planeta-Universidad, 1978. 304–37.

David K. Herzberger

TORRENTE MALVIDO, Gonzalo (1935, El Ferrol–), Galician writer of prose fiction. This son of *Torrente Ballester lives and works extensively along the shores of the Mediterranean in various countries. His novels and collections of stories reveal the moral vacuum in which his cast of contemporary international bohemians live. See his *picaresque *Hombres varados* (1964; Beached Men); *La balada de Juan Campos* (1965; The Ballad of Juan Campos); *La Raya* (1965; The Limit), winner of the Café Gijón Prize; *La muerte dormida* (1965; Sleeping Death); *Tiempo provisional* (1968; Provisional Time), awarded the Sésamo Prize; and *Cuentos de la mala vida* (1980; Stories of the Bad Life).

BIBLIOGRAPHY

Primary Texts

La balada de Juan Campos. Barcelona: Caralt, 1965.
Cuentos de la mala vida. Barcelona: La Gaya Ciencia, 1980.
Hombres varados. Barcelona: Destino, 1964.
La muerte dormida. Barcelona: Caralt, 1965.
Tiempo provisional. Madrid: Alfaguara, 1968.

Stephen Miller

TORRES FERNÁNDEZ, Xohana (1931, Santiago de Compostela–), Galician poet and prose writer. Born in Santiago, Torres studied in El Ferrol, where Ricardo *Carballo Calero was an important influence in creating her interest in literature. In 1955 she was awarded the Premio de Poesía de la Asociación de la Prensa (Press Association Prize for Poetry). At an early stage she began to publish poetry in Galician, the language of her entire work. Also in El Ferrol, Torres directed the radio program "Teresa," devoted to women. In 1963, in Vigo, she created the first totally Galician radio program, "Raíz e Tempo" (Root and Time). In the sixties she acted in the avant-garde group Teatro-Estudio. In 1972 Torres received the Pedrón de Ouro Award for her contribution to Galician culture and, particularly, for her novel *Adiós, María*. Her creative work includes poetry, theater, novel, and children's literature. She has also adapted works of other writers to Galician, has worked on albums on *Castelao and *Cunqueiro, and has written critical essays about theater and ethnography.

In Torres's early work there are frequent examples of unusual semantic combinations. Later years reveal an increase in nostalgic tone as the writer contemplates her native Galicia, but this in no manner diminishes the strength of her patriotism. Also strong is the remembrance of family and the passage of time leading to loneliness, even desolation. *See also* Galician Literature.

BIBLIOGRAPHY

Primary Texts

Adiós, María. Buenos Aires: Galicia, 1971.
Do sulco. Vigo: Galaxia (Illa Nova), 1959.
Estacións ao mar. Vigo: Galaxia, 1981.
Un hotel de primera sobre o río. Vigo: Galaxia, 1968.
Á outra banda do Íberr. Vigo: Galaxia, 1965.
Polo mar van as sardiñas. Vigo: Galaxia, 1967.
Tempo de ría. (In preparation)

Criticism

Barreira, Isaque. "*Do sulco*." *Revista Portuguesa de Filosofia* (Braga) 15.4 (1959): no pages.
Carballo Calero, Ricardo. *Libros e autores galegos. Século XX*. La Coruña: Fundación Barrié de la Maza, 1982.

Losada, Basilio. *Poetas gallegos de postguerra*. Barcelona: Ocnos, 1971.
Méndez Ferrín, Xosé Luis. *De Pondal a Novoneyra*. Vigo: Xerais de Galicia, 1984.

Kathleen March

TORRES NAHARRO, Bartolomé de (c. 1480, La Torre de Miguel Sexmero, Badajoz–c. 1525, Seville?), poet, dramatist, and dramatic theorist. Details concerning the life of Torres Naharro remain confused, primarily because much of what has been written about him is drawn from the texts of his plays under the assumption that they are in part autobiographical. He may have attended the U of Salamanca in the final decade of the fifteenth c., and there is evidence that he served in the military and later in the church. Speculations that he was of Jewish or Moorish origin and assertions that he was captured by pirates and imprisoned in Algiers need further verification. Recent studies suggest that in 1503 he arrived in Rome and was employed by Cesare Borgia and later by Giulio de Medici. In 1516 he entered the service of Cardinal Bernardino de Carvajal.

It appears clear that he composed most of his works in Rome, and the first edition of his *Propalladia* (1517; First Fruits of Pallas) was printed in Naples and included selections of poetry as well as the texts of seven of his nine plays. Subsequent editions contained one or both of the remaining dramas. Torres Naharro's death date has been posited as early as 1520 and as late as 1531, primarily because nothing concrete is known of him after 1520, one explanation being that he withdrew from society to dedicate himself exclusively to the religious life.

He is as well remembered today for the "Prohemio" or prologue to the *Propalladia* as for the plays themselves, for in these remarks he contributed Spain's first systematic dramatic formula. Like Horace, he felt that a play was best suited to a division of five acts or *jornadas*. He insisted that the actions and speech of characters be appropriate to their status; and he stated that the number of characters should range between six and twelve, though he defended his use of twenty-two in one work on the basis of plot demands. Naharro divided plays into two categories—*comedias a noticia*, which reflected events observable in the real world, and *comedias a fantasía*, fictional comedies relating imaginary or hypothetical events.

His plays present a curious blend of Italian Renaissance themes, classical allusions, Latin comedy, social and religious satire, refined and coarse language, and a spectrum of characters ranging from rustics and lackeys to aristocrats. Much of the humor in several pieces stems from the fact that many characters speak Latin and various modern languages or dialects. A convention of Naharro's drama is an opening monologue by a rustic, who delivers an *introito*, or greeting, and an *argumento*, or plot summary, usually in the *sayagués* dialect.

His earliest play and only religious drama, the *Diálogo del Nacimiento* (c. 1505; The Nativity Dialogue), is considered imitative of Juan del *Encina's early eclogues and shows little dramatic innovation. Far more typical of Naharro's theater is the *Comedia soldadesca* (c. 1510; The Military Comedy), a *comedia* *a noticia* with social protest, anti-clerical sentiment, and scenes from contemporary military life, quite possibly from the author's personal experiences in the army. The *Comedia tinelaria* (c. 1516; *The Buttery*, 1964), which derives its name from the *tinelo*, or servants' dining area, deftly satirizes the corruption among the staff in the home of a cardinal in Rome. Based on episodes from *La *Celestina*, the *Comedia Himenea* (c. 1516; *Hymen*, 1964) treats the themes of love and family honor and has been cited as Spain's first *capa y espada* drama.

Torres Naharro's poetry includes ballads, satirical verses, and love poems, most reflecting conventions of the period. He was clearly superior as a dramatist, although some of his satirical pieces have drawn praise for their boldness. The *Propalladia* was, in fact, included in the 1559 *Index* (*Indice*); however, by 1573 its republication with necessary revisions was authorized.

Torres Naharro is remembered today as a bridge between the early Spanish drama and the flourishing *comedia* at the time of Lope de *Vega and as one whose works captured both the cosmopolitan flavor of *Renaissance Europe and the modest existence of a Spanish rustic or an Italian peasant. *See also* Theater in Spain.

BIBLIOGRAPHY

Primary Texts

Comedias Soldadesca, Tinelaria, Himenea. Ed. D. W. McPheeters. Madrid: Castalia, 1973.

"Propalladia" and Other Works of Bartolomé de Torres Naharro. Ed. Joseph E. Gillet. 4 vols. vols. 1–3. Bryn Mawr, PA: G. Banta Publishing Co. of Menasha, WI, 1943–51. vol. 4. Philadelphia: U of Pennsylvania P, 1961.

Teatro selecto: Comedia Soldadesca, Ymenea, Jacinta, Calamita, Aquilana. Ed. Humberto López Morales. Madrid: Escelicer, 1970.

Tres comedias: Soldadesca, Ymenea, Aquilana. Ed. Humberto López Morales. New York: Las Américas, 1965.

English Translations

The Buttery. Tr. Jill Booty. *Early Spanish Plays*. Ed. Robert O'Brien. 2 vols. New York: Las Américas, 1964. Vol 1.

Hymen (Comedia himenea). Tr. Robert O'Brien. *Early Spanish Plays*. Ed. Robert O'Brien. 2 vols. New York: Las Américas, 1964. Vol. 1.

Criticism

Alborg, Juan Luis. *Historia de la literatura española*. 2nd ed. 4 vols. Madrid: Gredos, 1972. Vol. 1.

Crawford, James P. Wickersham. *Spanish Drama before Lope de Vega*. Rev. ed. Philadelphia: U of Pennsylvania P, 1967.

Gillet, Joseph E. *Torres Naharro and the Drama of the Renaissance*. Transcribed, ed., and completed by Otis H. Green. Vol. 4 of *"Propalladia" and Other Works of Bartolomé de Torres Naharro*. Philadelphia: U of Pennsylvania P, 1961.

Lihani, John. *Bartolomé de Torres Naharro*. TWAS 522. Boston: Twayne, 1979.

López Morales, Humberto. *Tradición y creación en los orígenes del teatro castellano.* Madrid: Alcalá, 1968.

C. Maurice Cherry

TORRES RÁMILA, Pedro (1583, Villarcayo, Burgos–1658, Alcalá de Henares), co-author, with *Mártir Rizo, of the *Spongia* (1617), a violent attack on Lope de *Vega. The two men were ardent enemies of Lope. Although the *Spongia* did not survive (Lope's friends destroyed all copies they could locate), Lope's response to it allows reconstruction of some of its content. Torres was a member of the group of Aristotelian preceptists. *See also* Aristotelianism in Spain.

BIBLIOGRAPHY

Criticism

Entrambasaguas, J. de. "Una guerra literaria del Siglo de Oro: Lope de Vega y los preceptistas aristotélicos." In his *Estudios sobre Lope de Vega.* 2nd ed. 3 vols. Madrid: CSIC, 1967. vols. 1 and 2

TORRES VILLARROEL, Diego de (1693, Salamanca–1770, Salamanca). A study of Torres Villarroel reveals the difficulty in separating his fiction from myths surrounding his person. He is one of the few eighteenth-c. writers who made a living from the publication of his works. After a period of time filled with adventure, he began to publish his famous *Almanaques y Pronósticos* (1718; Almanac and Prognostics) under the pseudonym El Piscator de Salamanca (The Forecaster from Salamanca). The annual publication brought him such fame that the first edition of his *Obras completas* (1752; Complete Works) was published by public subscription which included the royal family, the nobility, *universities, and religious orders. Torres experimented with all literary genres. Greatly influenced by *Quevedo, Torres published *Visiones y visitas de Torres con don Francisco de Quevedo por la Corte* (1727; Visions and Visits by Torres and Francisco de Quevedo through the Court), in which he brings to light the richness of his vocabulary and the ability with which he manipulates the Spanish language. Whether writing poetry, prose, theater or essay, Torres demonstrates vitality of style and literary wit. His complete works published in Madrid in fifteen volumes (1749–99) provide an insight to the character of the first half of the eighteenth c. and a fertile source for the study of aesthetics and literary style.

BIBLIOGRAPHY

Primary Texts

La Barca de Aqueronte. Madrid: Espasa-Calpe, 1969.
Los Desahuciados del Mundo y de la Gloria. Madrid: Nacional, 1979.
Sainetes. Madrid: Taurus, 1969.
Vida, Ascendencia, Nacimiento, Crianza y Aventuras. Madrid: Clásicos Castalia, 1972.
Visiones y visitas de Torres con don Francisco de Quevedo por la Corte. Madrid: Espasa-Calpe, 1976.

Criticism

Berenguer Carisomo, A. *El Doctor Diego de Torres Villarroel, o el pícaro universitario.* Buenos Aires: Esnaola, 1965.

Entrambasaguas, J. *Un Memorial autobiográfico de Don Diego de Torres y Villarroel. Estudios y ensayos de investigación y crítica.* Madrid: CSIC, 1973.

Ilie, Paul. "Grotesque Portraits in Torres Villarroel." *BHS* 45 (1968): 16–37.

———. "Franklin and Villarroel: Social Consciousness in Two Autobiographies." *Eighteenth-Century Studies* 7 (1974): 321–42.

Sebold, R. P. *Novela y autobiografía en la "Vida" de Torres Villarroel.* Barcelona: Ariel, 1975.

Zavala, Iris. *Clandestinidad y libertinaje erudito en los albores del siglo XVIII.* Barcelona: Ariel, 1978.

Carmen Chaves McClendon

TOSTADO, El. *See* Madrigal, Alfonso de

TRATADO DE LA VIDA Y ESTADO DE PERFECCIÓN (Treatise on Life and the State of Perfection). Published in 1499, it is the oldest extant Spanish text of ascetical-mystical literature. *See also* Ascetical Literature; Mysticism.

BIBLIOGRAPHY

Primary Text

Tractado de la vida y estado de perfección. Salamanca: n.p., 1499.

TRIADÚ I FONT, Joan (1921, Ribes de Freser, Catalonia–), Catalan critic and essayist. Trained as a classical philologist, Triadú has devoted his life to the cause of "threatened" languages, and most especially Catalan, together with the culture, literature and national identity of that language-speaking region. His major essays include *El collscabra* (1956); *La literatura catalana i el poble* (1961; Catalan Literature and the People); *Llegir com Viure* (1963; Reading as Living); and *Una cultura sense llibertat* (1978; A Culture without Liberty). He worked extensively as an anthologist, aiding in the diffusion and preservation of Catalan literary writings at the time of their margination by the Franco regime. *Antologia de contistes catalans 1850–1950* (1950; Anthology of Catalan Short Story Writers); *Antología de la poesía catalana* (1951; Anthology of Catalan Poetry), *Anthology of Catalan Lyric Poetry* (1953); and *Panorama de la poesía catalana* (1953; Panorama of Catalan Poetry) are examples. He also devoted attention to individual writers, doing an edition of Pindar's *Les Olimpiques* (1953), a biography of Catalonia's leading realistic novelist, Narcís *Oller, a study of *La poesia segons Carles Riba* (1954; Poetry According to Carles *Riba), and translation of Shakespeare's sonnets into Catalan. *See also* Catalan Literature.

TRIGO, Felipe (1864, Villanueva de la Serena, Badajoz–1916, Madrid), doctor, essayist and novelist. Served as a physician in the Cuerpo de Sanidad Militar (Military Medical Corps) and received a distinction for valor in the Philippines.

In addition to seventeen novels, he published a book based on his Philippine experiences and several books of social theory. Trigo is a competent, if uneven, novelist whose themes were influenced by Zola and his own personal experiences as a doctor. His frank treatment of human sexuality, prostitution, venereal disease, arranged marriages, adultery and abortion earned him the label of pornographer, but, in fact, he employs sordid situations in his novels to encourage social reform. Trigo was a utopian thinker who envisioned a social order founded on universal love, and frequently portrays a hypocritical society in which all the evil consequences of human sensuality fall on women alone. His novels of most artistic merit are listed in the bibliography.

BIBLIOGRAPHY

Primary Texts

El médico rural. Prol. José Bergamín. Madrid: Turner, 1974.
En la carrera. Buenos Aires: Araujo, 1941.
Jarrapellejos (vida arcaica, feliz e independiente de un español representativo). Prol. Rafael Conte. Madrid: Turner, 1975.
La clave. 5th ed. Madrid: Renacimiento, 1923.
No sé por qué. 3rd ed. Madrid: Renacimiento, 1920.

Roberta Johnson

TRIGUEROS, Cándido María (1736, Orgaz, Toledo–c. 1801, Seville?), dramatist, presbyter, priest, poet. Member of the Academia de Buenas Letras, his first publications, *El poeta filósofo* (1774, 1775, 1777, 1778; The Philosopher Poet) and the epic poem *La Riada* (1784; The Flood) were not successful, and in fact provoked ridicule by *Forner, Tomás de *Iriarte, Leandro Fernández de *Moratín and others. Trigueros subsequently attempted reworking Golden Age plays, with admirable results. His best adaptations, characterized by perfected construction and fine lyric moments, include *Sancho Ortiz de las Roelas* (1800), based on the *Estrella de Sevilla* sometimes attributed to Lope de *Vega; and *La Melindrosa* (The Finicky One), based on Lope's *Los melindres de Belisa*. He also wrote a four-volume continuation to *Cervantes's pastoral novel, *La Galatea*, titled *Los enamorados o Galatea y sus bodas* (1798; The Lovers, or Galatea and Their Wedding), and a book of theater criticism, the *Teatro español burlesco o Quijote de los teatros* (1802; Burlesque Spanish Theater or Quijote of the Theaters). *See also* Academia; Siglo de Oro.

BIBLIOGRAPHY

Primary Texts

Los enamorados. . . . Madrid: Imprenta Real, 1798.
Obras. Seville: Vázquez, Hidalgo, 1785.
Sancho Ortiz de las Roelas. Valencia: n.p., 1818.
Teatro español burlesco. . . . Madrid: Villalpando, 1802.

TRILLO Y FIGUEROA, Francisco de (1615 to 1620, La Coruña–1675?, ?), soldier, historian and poet. He served as a soldier in Italy and Flanders from 1640 to 1643, then returned to Granada, home to him since age eleven, and composed poetry. From 1660 to 1675 he belonged to the literary group Academia de los Nocturnos (Academy of the Nocturnal Ones), using the pseudonym Daliso.

His minor works include several epithalamiums, nuptial poems commemorating wedding feasts of noted public figures. Trillo wrote his first major work to praise the deeds of the Gran Capitán Gonzalo Fernández de Córdoba, in *Neapolisa* (1651). He garnered no literary acclaim for it, nor for his *Poesías varias, heroicas, satíricas y amorosas* (1652; Collected Heroic, Satiric and Love Poems). His lighter, satiric verse is more successful. He also left a number of unedited historical works. *See also* Academia.

BIBLIOGRAPHY

Primary Texts

Poesías In BAE 42.

Obras. Ed. A. Gallego Morell. Madrid: Biblioteca de Antiguos Libros Hispánicos, 1951.

Criticism

Gallego Morell, A. *Francisco y Juan de Trillo y Figueroa*. Granada: U of Granada, 1950.

Sabat de Rivers, G. "Trillo y Figueroa y el *Sueño* de Sor Juana." In *Actas del Quinto Congreso Internacional de Hispanistas*. Ed. Maxime Chevalier, et al. Bordeaux: P of the U of Bordeaux, 1977. 763–75.

Veronica Sauter

TRISTÁN DE LEONÍS, Libro del esforçado caballero don (Book of the Courageous Knight Tristan of Leonis), novel of chivalry. Published in 1501, it is but one of the many versions of the 1489 French narrative *Le Roman du noble et vaillant chevalier Tristan*. The Spanish text is not a faithful translation; entire sections were removed and others substituted. A continuation to the 1501 Spanish version appeared in 1534. Titled *Crónica nuevamente emendada y añadida del buen caballero don Tristán de Leonís . . . y su hijo* (Newly Corrected and Expanded Chronicle of the Fine Knight Tristan of Leonis . . . and His Son), it is entirely original, and was translated into Italian in 1555. *See also* Caballerías, Libros de.

BIBLIOGRAPHY

Primary Texts

Libro del esforzado Cavallero Don Tristán de Leonís y de sus grandes fechos en armas. Ed. Bonilla y San Martín. Madrid: Hernando, 1912. Includes various poems, subsequent versions.

Crónica nuevamente emendada y añadida del buen caballero . . . y su hijo. Seville: Domenico de Robertis, 1534.

TROBES EN LAHORS DE LA VERGE MARÍA, LES (1474; Poems in Praise of the Virgin Mary), title of the first book known to be printed in Spain. It is a collection of forty-five poems presented at a poetry competition celebrated in Valencia in 1474. One poem is in Tuscan, three are in Castilian, and the remaining forty-one are in Valencian. Jaume *Roig, Joan Roís de Corella, Jaume Gassull and Bernat Fenollar are among the forty poets represented. *See also* Printing in Spain.

BIBLIOGRAPHY

Primary Text

Les trobes en lahors de la Verge María. Prol. Luis Guarner. Valencia: Artes Gráficas Soler, 1974. Facs. edition with prol. and selected poems tr. into modern Spanish.

TROTACONVENTOS (Convent-trotter), a literary type. In the fourteenth c. there emerged from the *Arcipreste of Hita's *Libro de buen amor* (Book of Good Love), *Trotaconventos*, Juan Ruiz's outstanding characterization of the age-old figure of the old woman go-between in love intrigues. Says the aspiring lover: "I looked for a convent-trotter such as Love told me to do; . . . I found just such an old woman as I needed, wily and expert, and full of wicked wisdom" (R. Willis, tr., *Libro de buen amor* [Princeton: Princeton UP, 1972] stanzas 697–98). In the ensuing transition from generic *trotaconventos* to the individual *Trotaconventos*, the traits of her many literary precedents (from Ovid's *Amores* and her immediate source, the comedy **Pamphilus*, to the fables of Eastern literature) coalesce into an archetypal representation of the traditional panderess, aged, mercenary, crafty, and licentious. *Trotaconventos* emerges as a complex and memorable character—not merely a skillfully wrought culmination of stock figures from the past, but also an origination, the prototype for all the future go-betweens of Spanish literature.

Although the portrayal of Celestina surpasses that of *Trotaconventos* in detail and complexity, virtually all the facets of Celestina's character are found in the latter. Limited by his genre, the archpriest could only suggest those attributes of the bawd which *Rojas elaborated in his drama: her persuasiveness, her alertness and ability to improvise, her treachery and capacity for deception, her enthusiasm as a procuress, her garrulous nature and penchant for sententious proverbs and anecdotes, her guise as peddler to gain access to young ladies, her feigned religiosity, her fondness for wine, and her use of enchantment to aid in seductions. Literary counterparts have appeared in works by *Cervantes and Lope de *Vega, among others, but only these two have transcended their literary bounds to become living figures exhibiting the contradictions inherent in human nature. They are cynical yet sentimental, self-serving yet personally involved, allies of evil, sin and passion who perceive themselves as purveyors of love and happiness. *See also Celestina, La.*

BIBLIOGRAPHY

Criticism

Lida de Malkiel, María Rosa. *Two Spanish Masterpieces: the Book of Good Love and the Celestina*. Urbana: U. of Illinois, 1961.

Zahareas, A. N. "Trotaconventos: The Portrait, The Personage." *The Art of Juan Ruiz, Archpriest of Hita*. Madrid: Estudios de Literatura Española, 1965. 158–72.

Kathleen L. Kirk

TROYANA, Crónica (Trojan Chronicle), a history of the Trojan War chronicled in the spirit of medieval chivalry. This story appeared in numerous versions in the Middle Ages (*see* Edad Media, Literatura de la). Well before this period, in approximately the fourth c. A.D., several falsifications of the history of the Trojan War were written. These versions were believed at the time to have been translated from Greek and Latin versions and were quite popular during the Middle Ages. Benoit de Sainte-More, author of the lengthy poem *Le Roman de Troie* (c. 1160), found his inspiration in these stories. He added several episodes to the primitive history (e.g., the story of the Argonauts and the story of Troilus and Cressida), and his *Roman* was subsequently rewritten by Guido delle Colonne, judge of Messina, Italy, with the title *Historia troyana* (1287). No credit was given to Sainte-More; rather, the sources credited were the versions now known to be falsifications. Subsequently, several translations of the *Roman de Troie* were done in the Iberian Peninsula, and the author's name was translated as Benito de Santa María. The Marquis of *Santillana had a version in Galician in his library (the oldest extant example of Galician prose). There is also a Castilian version which was finished in 1350 (MS L-ii–16, folios 157b–180b in the Escorial). A bilingual version (Galician and Castilian) is today located in the Menéndez Pelayo Library in Santander. Guido delle Colonne's version of the *Historia troyana* was translated into Catalan (by Conesa, 1367), into Castilian (by Pedro de Chinchilla, 1443), and also into Castilian in the best known version (Chancellor Pero *López de Ayala, 1332–1407) with the title *Crónica troyana*. This version was repeatedly revised (with new episodes interpolated or added by Pedro Núñez Delgado) in the sixteenth c. A chronicle in verse form was also written and *Menéndez Pidal, on the basis of the fragments which remain, has dated it 1270, calling it *Historia troyana polimétrica*.

BIBLIOGRAPHY

Primary Texts

Crónica troyana. In Galician, Facs. of fifteenth-c. ms. in National Library in Madrid, with grammatical and lexical notes by M. R. Rodrigues. 2 vols. La Coruña: Andrés Martínez Salazar, 1900.

La Crónica Troyana. Ed. F. P. Norris. UNCSRLL 90. Chapel Hill: U of North Carolina P, 1970.

Historia troyana en prosa y verso (texto c. 1270). Ed. R. Menéndez Pidal and E. Varón Vallejo. RFE Anejo 18. Madrid: Aguirre, 1934.

Historia troyana polimétrica (fragments of version in verse). In *Tres poetas primitivos.* Ed. R. Menéndez Pidal. Buenos Aires-Mexico: Espasa-Calpe, 1948.

Criticism

Brownlee, M. S. "Towards a Reappraisal of The *Historia troyana polimétrica.*" *Corónica* 7 (1978–79): 13–17.

Burt, John R. "Courtly Love as a Destructive Force in the *Historia troyana polimétrica.*" *REH* 10 (1976): 69–84.

de Ferraresi, A. C. "Troilo y Criseida en España: Primer ensayo de poema sentimental." *Vórtice* 1.1 (1974): 59–67.

Gumbrecht, H. V. "Approaches to Medieval Romance." *YFS* 51 (1974): 205–22.

Lucy Sponsler

TROYANO, Manuel (1843, Ronda–1914, Madrid), journalist, fine political feature writer. A cautious liberal in the Spain of his day, he wrote for *La Nueva Prensa, El Imparcial* and *ABC*. In 1904 he founded and directed the daily newspaper *España*, from Madrid. His prose was correct and pointed.

Isabel McSpadden

TRUEBA, Antonio de (1819, Montella, Vizcaya–1889, Bilbao), poet, novelist and short story writer. He had little formal education and worked as a clerk in a hardware store. He is best known for his *Libro de los cantares* (1852; Book of Songs), which was a great success during his lifetime and was published in eight copious editions in twenty years. This work brought attention to folkloric themes and popular poetry. *Bécquer admired Trueba's verse and Rosalía de *Castro found poetic inspiration in it. In 1868 he published *El libro de las montañas* (The Book of the Mountains), in which all of the poems are set in the Basque region. Trueba represents a new period of Spanish poetry in his rejection of the high-flown rhetoric of the Romantics. He wrote instead a poetry of simple themes, intimate feelings and natural expression. The themes of his poetry are innocent love, the home, patriotism and Christian faith. His uncontrived verse interprets the soul of simple country people.

Apart from his poetry, Trueba is best known for his short stories, which he collected under the titles *Cuentos populares* (1853; Popular Tales), *Cuentos color de rosa* (1854; Rose-Colored Stories), *Cuentos campesinos* (1860; Rural Stories), *Cuentos de varios colores* (1866; Stories of Various Colors), *Cuentos de vivos y muertos* (1866; Stories of the Living and the Dead), etc. Like *Fernán Caballero, Trueba describes local customs and types and portrays the Basque landscape in his stories. The settings are predominantly rural and popular. He tends to idealize the life of the Basque peasants, and he extolls country virtues and traditional values. In general, his stories are characterized by their moralizing intention, sentimental Catholicism and ingenuous vision of life. Trueba also wrote a number of historical novels such as *El Cid Campeador* (1851) and *La paloma y los halcones* (1865; The Dove and the Falcons). *See also* Romanticism.

BIBLIOGRAPHY

Primary Texts

Obras. 6 vols. Madrid: A. Rubiños, 1909–25.

English Translations

Short Stories by Antonio de Trueba. Ed. John Van Horne. Chicago: B. H. Sanborn, 1922.

Criticism

Fischbach, Jacob. ''Antonio de Trueba: A Study in the Transition from Romanticism to Realism in the Spanish Tale.'' *DA* 27 (1966): 1819A–20A (Columbia).

González Blanco, A. *Antonio de Trueba: Su vida y sus obras*. Bilbao: n.p., 1914.

Montesinos, José F. ''Trueba y su realismo (Nota a un primitivo).'' *Wort und Text* 35 (1963): 434–48.

Zalba, José. ''Bibliografía de las obras de Trueba.'' *Euskalerriaren alde* (San Sebastian, Spain) no vols. 1917, 1918, 1919.

Hector Medina

TRUEBA Y COSSÍO, Joaquín Telesforo de (1799, Santander–1835, Paris), novelist and playwright. Sent by his family to study in England and in France (1812–22), he showed interest in politics and literature even as a youth. A liberal, Trueba did not remain long in his native land. He went to England by 1825 and dedicated himself to writing. Nine years later he returned to Spain and represented the province of Santander in the 1834–35 legislature. He was starting an active political and literary life when death overcame him in October 1835. His historical novels are written in English; *Gomez Arias* (1828) and *The Castilian* (1829) deal with the distant past, and *Salvador the Guerilla* (1834), with the Spanish War of Independence. Also historical are *The Romance of History. Spain* (1830), *The Life of Hernan Cortes* (1829), and *The Conquest of Peru* (1830), in which he defended the Spanish Conquista shortly after the independence of the former Spanish colonies, when anti-Spanish feeling was at its peak. He published two other novels about contemporary customs, *The Incognito* (1831) and *Paris and London* (1831). As a playwright Trueba wrote, in Spanish, several tragedies, such as *La muerte de Catón* (1821; The Death of Cato), performed in Paris, as well as comedies and farces. Among his plays for the English stage are two comedies, *The Exquisites* (1831), *The Men of Pleasure* (1832) and several comic one-act plays.

BIBLIOGRAPHY

Primary Texts

Gomez Arias or The Moors of the Alpujarras. A Spanish Historical Romance. 3 vols. London: Hurt, Chance, 1828.

The Incognito; or Sins and Peccadilloes. 3 vols. London: Whittaker, 1831.

Life of Hernan Cortes. Constable's Miscellany of Original and Selected Publications in the Various Departments of Science, Literature and the Arts, vol. 49. Edinburgh: Constable, 1829.

Paris and London. 3 vols. London: Henry Colburn and Richard Bentley, 1831.
Salvador the Guerilla. 3 vols. London: Richard Bentley, 1834.

Criticism

García Castañeda, Salvador. *Don Telesforo de Trueba y Cosío (1799–1835). Su tiempo, su vida y su obra*. Santander: Diputación Provincial Instituto de Literatura José María de Pereda, 1978.

Llorens, Vicente. *Liberales y Románticos. Una emigración española en Inglaterra (1823–1824)*. Madrid: Castalia, 1968. 267–84 *passim*.

Menéndez Pelayo, Marcelino. *Escritos críticos sobre escritores montañeses. Trueba y Cossío*. Santander: Telesforo Martínez, 1876.

Salvador García Castañeda

TUDELA, Mariano (1925, La Coruña–), Spanish novelist. Chronologically a member of the mid-century generation of social (i.e., political) critics of Spain's economic backwardness, Tudela maintained a certain distance from others of the neo-realist and objectivist schools. Among his novels are *El Torerillo de Invierno* (1951; The Little Wintertime Bullfighter), *El hombre de las tres escopetas* (1952; The Man with Three Shotguns), and *Más que moderno* (1956; More Than Modern). He also wrote a number of biographies, including those of *Valle-Inclán, the bandit Luis Candelas, and the entertainer Bella Otero. *La linterna mágica* (1948; The Magic Lantern) is a book of short stories.

TURMEDA, Anselm (c. 1352, Mallorca–c. 1430, Tunis), narrator and poet. His biography, a mixture of truth and legend, is a clear example of the spiritual crisis so prevalent at the dawn of the Middle Ages. When he was twenty years old, having studied physics and astronomy, he entered the Franciscan order. Around 1370 he went to Italy (Bologna) to study theology, and there he became adept at the rational teachings of Averroism, a heretical position within the Islamic religion. Stifled by the spiritual and social structures of medieval Europe, he converted to Islam and settled in Tunis, changing his name to Abdulla. He married and had one son. Under the protection of the sultan he held important public office several times, but at the same time was able to maintain ties with Christian Europe. Turmeda's most famous work, *Disputa de l'ase* (The Dispute of the Donkey), exemplifies his skeptical and satirical rationalism, a spirit that along with its sarcastic tone established this work as one of the precursors of the *Renaissance. The principal character is the donkey who engages himself in a dialogue against man (Fra Anselm). He points out the corruption of the church through satirical stories of incomparable wit. The individual and unconventional treatment of themes, not the material itself, is the basis of the literary merit of Turmeda's work and is reminiscent of another famous peninsular figure, the *Arcipreste de Hita, although the latter never gives vent to such extremes of scorn and heretic attitudes toward the church. Another of his works, *Present de l'home de lletres* (Gift of the Man of Letters), written in Arabic, is autobiographical, and seemingly presents a sincere profession of the Islamic faith. In the first of these works he boasts about his human qualities before a gathering of animals, who defeat him dialectically. However, he is able to convince them with the argument that God wishes to assume human form. The rest of this work presents a series of ironic and satirical anti-clerical expressions. The sources of *La Disputa* can be found in an Arabic encyclopedic work put together by an Islamic sect—Germans de la Puresa de Bàssora (Brotherhood of Purity from Basra)—but Turmeda completely turned around the original meaning of the Arabic source and utilized the apology as a vehicle for the expression of his radical skepticism. The anti-clerical diatribe is very probably inspired in Boccaccio. The Catalan original is lost but French translations from 1540, 1544, before 1548, 1548 and finally 1606 are available.

Other minor works of Turmeda are *Profecias* (1405–6; Prophecies), *Present de l'home docte en refutació dels partidaris de la Creu* (1420; Present of the Scholar in Refutation of the Followers of the Cross), and *Llibre de bons amonestaments* (1397; Book of Good Advice). *See also* Catalan Literature; Edad Media, Literatura de la.

BIBLIOGRAPHY

Primary Texts

Disputa de l'Ase (old Catalan version). Ed. by L. Deztany. Barcelona: J. Horta, 1922.

Llibre dels bons amonestaments, Cobles. Mallorca: n.p., 1972.

Obres menors. Ed. M. Olivar. Barcelona: Els Nostres Classics, 1927.

Profecies. Ed. P. M. Borday. In *Revista Ibero-Americana de Ciencias Eclesiásticas*. Madrid: n.p., 1911.

Un text català de la Profecia de l'ase, de fra Anselm Turmeda. Ed. Jordi Rubió. *Estudis Universitaris Catalans* 7 (1913).

Criticism

Asín Palacios, A. "El original árabe de la Disputa del amo contra Fray Anselmo Turmeda." *RFE* 1 (1914): 1–51.

Calvet, A. *Fray Anselmo Turmeda*. Barcelona: Casa Editorial Estudio, 1914.

Epalza, M. de. *La Tulifa, autobiografía y polémica islámica contra el cristianismo de 'Abd-dallàh al-Taryuman' (Fray Anselmo Turmeda)*. Rome: Accademia Nazionale de Lincei, 1971.

Marfany, J. L. *Ideari d'Anselm Turmeda*. Barcelona: Edicions 62, 1965.

Samsó, J. *Turmediana. Boletin. Real Academia de Buenas Letras de Barcelona* 24 (1971–72): 51–85.

Joan Gilabert

TUSQUETS, Esther (1936, Barcelona–), Spanish novelist and publisher. Director since the early 1960s of the important vanguardist publisher Editorial Lumen in Barcelona, Tusquets began her novelistic career somewhat late in life, publishing *El mismo mar de todos los veranos* (The Same Sea as Every Summer) in 1978. This first volume of her feminist trilogy made Tusquets almost immediately a force to reckon with among Spain's women narrators, and was followed in quick succession by *El amor es un juego solitario* (1979; *Love is a Solitary Game*, 1985) and *Varada tras el último naufragio* (1980; Beached after the Last Shipwreck), completing the trilogy. The woman's search for meaning and self-realization in various stages of life is an obsessive concern of Tusquets, who explores particularly the crisis provoked by awareness of aging in mid-life, but also mother-daughter relationships, the problems of marriage, female friendships and lesbian relationships. Inconstancy, solitude, and the barriers to communication and fulfillment are of special interest for Tusquets, as are other existential themes and the frustrations of heterosexual and homosexual love. In *Siete miradas en un mismo paisaje* (1981; Seven Glances at One Landscape), variously interpreted as a novel and a series of interrelated short stories, Tusquets presents seven moments of crisis or "passage" in the life of a female protagonist who, although always named Sara, is not always the same woman. The formative influences of her bourgeois Catalan background, her encounters with injustice, prejudice, and class bias, as well as her discovery of both heterosexual and lesbian love are portrayed with sensitive yet completely straightforward artistry.

BIBLIOGRAPHY

Primary Texts

El amor es un juego solitario. Barcelona: Lumen, 1979.
El mismo mar de todos los veranos. Barcelona: Lumen, 1978.
Para no volver. Barcelona: Lumen, 1985.
Siete miradas en un mismo paisaje. Barcelona: Lumen, 1981.
Varada tras el último naufragio. Barcelona: Lumen, 1980.

English Translation

Love Is a Solitary Game. Tr. B. Penman. London: Calder; New York: Riverrun, 1985.

Criticism

Bellver, Catherine. "Two New Women Writers from Spain." *Letras Femeninas* 8.2 (1982): 3–7.
Nichols, Geraldine Cleary. "The Prison-House (and Beyond): *El mismo mar de todos los veranos*." *RR* 75.3 (May 1984): 366–85.
Ordóñez, Elizabeth J. "A Quest for Matrilineal Roots and Mythopoesis: Esther Tusquets' *El mismo mar de todos los veranos*." *Crítica Hispánica* 6.1 (1984): 37–46.
———. "The Barcelona Group: The Fiction of Alós, Moix and Tusquets." *Letras Femeninas* 6.1 (1980): 38–50.
Vásquez, Mary. "Image and the Linear Progression toward Defeat in Esther Tusquets' *El mismo mar de todos los veranos*." In *LA CHISPA '83: Selected Proceedings*. Ed. Gilbert Paolini. New Orleans: Tulane UP, 1983. 307–13.

Janet Pérez

TÚY, Lucas de (?, León–1249, Túy), historian. Often referred to as El Tudense because he was canon regular of San Isidro de Túy and bishop of Túy from 1239 until his death, Lucas traveled widely in medieval Europe and the Middle East. A strong opponent of the expansion of the Albigensian heresy in Spain, he wrote a polemical book, *De altera vita fideique controversiis adversus Albigensium errores libri III* (1612), which provided moral lessons against heretical error. He is best known for his *Chronicon mundi* (Chronicle of the World), written in Latin in 1236 and translated into Spanish several decades later. Like most of his contemporary historians, Lucas follows his sources closely and exercises little critical judgment. His chronicle contains prose paraphrases of several **cantares de gesta* and is therefore important for an understanding of Castilian epic cycles.

BIBLIOGRAPHY

Primary Texts

Chronicon mundi. Ed. A. Schott. Hispaniae illustratae, 4. Frankfurt: n.p., 1608.
Crónica de España. Ed. Julio Puyol. Madrid: RABM, 1926.

Criticism

Högberg, Paul. ''La Chronique de Lucas de Tuy.'' *RH* 81 (1933): 404–20.

James Ray Green

U

UCEDA, Julia (1925, Seville–), Spanish poet and critic. Uceda received a doctorate from the U of Seville, writing her dissertation on the contemporary poet José Luis *Hidalgo. From 1966 to 1973, Uceda taught at Michigan State U. She lived briefly in Ireland, before settling in Galicia. Usually classed with the "social" poets of the mid-century generation, Uceda possesses more of an individual and intimate, personal poetic voice than do many others of the group. While the social context is always important, Uceda's poetry tends to emphasize the strange, existential and/or metaphysical. Her first collection of verse, *Mariposa en cenizas* (1959; Butterfly in Ashes), is largely love poetry, but also treats the universal theme of death and contemporary alienation and despair. *Extraña juventud* (1962; Strange Youth), dedicated to "man of my time," indicates Uceda's social and implicitly political concerns as she denounces injustice, inequality and repression. *Sin mucha esperanza* (1966; Without Much Hope) suggests the influence of Hidalgo, and introduces a newly visible interest in the poetic uses of myth and symbol. Besides the eternal themes of death and God, the volume repeatedly treats existential and patriotic concerns. *Poemas de Cherry Lane* (1968; Cherry Lane Poems) is a slim collection of free verse with a special focus upon Uceda's experiences in the United States, her sometimes hallucinatory reactions, and heightened sense of alienation and personal identity. *Campanas en Sansueña* (1977; Bells in Sansueña) was written partially in Ireland, and completed in Spain. Especially concerned with the relationship between illusion and reality, the collection also returns to several of Uceda's characteristic preoccupations: death, identity, time, and estrangement. *Viejas voces secretas de la noche* (1981; Ancient, Secret Voices of the Night) continues and intensifies the metaphysical direction already perceptible in Uceda's earlier verse, with special emphasis upon light and darkness, night and sleep or dreams as symbolic of the existential search for meaning.

BIBLIOGRAPHY

Primary Texts

Campanas en Sansueña. Madrid: Dulcinea, 1977.
La expresión/Jorge Guillén. Ferrol: Sociedad de Cultura Valle-Inclán, 1981.
Extraña juventud. Madrid: Rialp, 1962.
Poemas de Cherry Lane. Madrid: Agora, 1968.
Viejas voces secretas de la noche. Ferrol: Sociedad de Cultura Valle-Inclán, 1981.

Janet Pérez

UCETA, Acacia (1927, Madrid–), poet. Her works have appeared in numerous anthologies and have been translated into Portuguese, French, Italian and English. Her poetry has been awarded the following prizes: Contraluz, Ciudad de Cuenca, Fray Luis de León, Elisa Soriano, Amigos de la Poesía de Valencia and the Virgen del Carmen. Her short novels have also received the Sésamo and Café Gijón prizes. She has received fellowships from the Juan March Foundation and the Spanish Ministry of Culture. Her poetry collections—*El corro de las horas* (1961; The Chorus of the Hours), *Cuenca, roca viva* (1980; Cuenca, Rock Alive), *Detrás de cada noche* (1970; Behind Each Night), *Frente a un muro de cal abrasadora* (1967; Before a Wall of Burning Lime), *Intima dimensión* (1983; Intimate Dimension), and *Al sur de las estrellas* (1976; South of the Stars)—are noted for their expressions of optimism and happiness. Her novels are *Quince años* (1962; Fifteen Years) and *Una hormiga tan sólo* (1967; Only An Ant).

BIBLIOGRAPHY

Primary Texts

El corro de las horas. Madrid: Agora, 1961.
Cuenca, roca viva. Cuenca: Colección "Los Pliegos del Hocino," 1980.
Detrás de cada noche. Madrid: Nacional, 1970.
Frente a un muro de cal abrasadora. Cuenca: El Toro de Barro, 1967.
Una hormiga tan sólo. Madrid: Aguilar, 1967.
Intima dimensión. Madrid: El Toro de Barro, 1983.
Quince años. Madrid: El Español, 1962.
Al sur de las estrellas. Cuenca: Gárgola, 1976.

Criticism

Conde, Carmen. "Acacia Uceta." In *Poesía Femenina Española Contemporánea*. Barcelona: Bruguera, 1967.
Gatell, Angelina. "Acacia Uceta." In *Mis primeras lecturas poéticas*. Barcelona: Ediciones 29, 1980.
Miró, Emilio. "Poetisas Españolas Contemporáneas." In *Revista de la Universidad Complutense de Madrid* 24.95 (1975): 271–310.

Carolyn Galerstein

ULLÁN, José Miguel (1944, Villarino de los Aires, Salamanca–), poet. He lives in Paris, and has written *Amor peninsular* (1965; Peninsular Love), *Un humano poder* (1966; A Human Power), *Mortaja* (1970; Shroud), and *Manchas nombradas* (1984; Named Spots).

BIBLIOGRAPHY

Primary Texts

Amor peninsular. Barcelona: El Bardo, 1965.
Manchas nombradas. Madrid: Nacional, 1984.
Mortaja. Mexico: Era, 1970.

Isabel McSpadden

ULLOA PEREIRA, Luis de (1584, Toro, Zamora–1674, Toro), poet in the **culteranismo* tradition. He spent most of his life in his hometown, and thus did not interact with other writers of the day. At age fourteen, he married a cousin, but she died within a few months. He married two more times. He spent some time in León, serving as a magistrate, and supervising the education of John II of Austria, son of Philip IV and La Calderona. Ulloa Pereira also maintained close ties with the royal adviser, the Count-Duke of Olivares, and even provided Olivares with a place to live when the famous counselor fell from favor.

His *Obras, prosas y versos* (Works, Prose and Poetry) appeared in Madrid in 1674; it includes love sonnets, songs, eclogues and poems dedicated to Olivares. Two other collections, *Paráfrasis de los siete salmos penitenciales* (1655; Paraphrase of the Seven Penitential Psalms) and *Soliloquios* (Soliloquies) contain religious verse. Ulloa Pereira's most famous poem is *Raquel* (1643; Rachel). It narrates the love of the famous Jewish woman for Alphonse VIII and was the inspiration for *Diamante's *La judía de Toledo* and *García de la Huerta's *La Raquel*. Ulloa also wrote a prose work titled *Memorias familiares y literarias* (1925; Family and Literary Memories), in which he recounts the difficulties suffered by one of his brothers.

BIBLIOGRAPHY

Primary Texts

Memorias familiares. . . . Ed. M. Artigas. Madrid: Velasco, 1925.
Raquel. In BAE 29.

Criticism

García Aráez, J. *Don Luis de Ulloa y Pereira*. Madrid: CSIC, 1952.

Nina Shecktor

UMBRAL, Francisco (1935, Madrid–), journalist, novelist, short story writer, essayist, biographer. Eminently autobiographical with a personal-existentialist outlook, Umbral is today one of Spain's most-read authors. Blurring generic distinctions and mixing journalism and literary creation, his work reveals influences of Mariano José de *Larra (as a critic of contemporary Spanish society), of *Ortega and *Unamuno (in essayistic style and existentialist view), of Marcuse (in Marxist orientation), of *González Ruano (journalistic humor), and of Ramón *Gómez de la Serna (literature as play, cultivation of *greguerías*).

Umbral's newspaper column, "Diario de un snob" (Diary of a Snob), has appeared in Madrid's *El País* for years. Selections from it appeared in a book by the same title, *Diario de un snob* (1973). His *Diario de un español cansado* (1975; Diary of a Tired Spaniard) collects in a book and republishes articles appearing in 1974 in the Barcelona magazine *Destino*. In some later books he has continued the practice of republishing journalistic articles or columns, for example, *Spleen de Madrid, 2* (1982; Madrid's Vile Humor, 2).

The last in a series of four novels of the author's memories of his childhood and youth, *Las ninfas* (1976; The Nymphs) won the Nadal Prize for 1975. In it the private life of the narrator and the collective life or society in which he lives are woven together in concentric circles. In much the same way his critically acclaimed novel *Mortal y rosa* (1975; *A Mortal Spring*, 1980), written in the intimate, confessional nature of a private journal, becomes both individual and social, thereby acquiring value as a sociological document. Its first-person narrator dialogues (''monodialogues,'' in Unamunian terms) with his young, dying son. In successive segments of discourse graphically divided as units or untitled ''chapters,'' Umbral finds life (the ape, his own face, his son) antithetic to culture (the librarian, his mask or public image, his adult, professional self, the ''dead man'' he carries within himself). Unity derives from the narrator-protagonist and his engaging examination of his existentialist situation or ''reality'' as he sees it, a continuation of the *picaresque convention.

Umbral's first novel, *Balada de gamberros* (1965; Ballad of Street Urchins), considered by Navales to be an extended short story or a short novel, recalls the author's life as an adolescent on the streets of Valladolid. Later novels include *Travesía de Madrid* (1966; Crossing through Madrid); *Si hubiéramos sabido que el amor es eso* (1969; If We Had Known That That's Love); *Las europeas* (1970; European Women); *El Giocondo* (1970; The Giocondo), runner-up, *finalista*, for the Nadal of 1968; *Los males sagrados* (1973; Sacred Evils), and *Amar en Madrid* (1977; To Love in Madrid).

Proclaiming himself to be ''a frustrated lyrical poet,'' and a ''novelist in the essay and an essayist in the novel,'' Umbral writes books which almost defy generic classification. Umbralian essays (''intellectual autobiography'') include *Larra, anatomía de un dandy* (1965; Larra, Anatomy of a Dandy) and *Lorca, poeta maldito* (1968; Lorca, Perverse Poet). His numerous books include biographies of Lord Byron, *Valle-Inclán, Miguel *Delibes, Lola Flores, and Miguel *Mihura, and collections of short stories, for example, *Tamouré* (1965; Tamouré) and *Teoría de Lola* (1977; Lola's Theory).

Andrés Amorós regards Umbral as a leading representative ''of the new Spanish literary sensibility'' (73), a sensibility he sees manifested in the drawings of Forges or Máximo, the articles of Manuel *Vázquez Montalbán (Sixto Cámara), and the work of Juan *Marsé and Carlos Luis Alvarez (Cándido), an irreverent, playful sensibility disrespectful of traditional hierarchies and myths.

Though Umbral's definitive place in Spanish letters yet remains, of course, to be established, the importance of his accumulated work both as literature and as a chronicle of contemporary Spanish life appears to be considerable.

BIBLIOGRAPHY

Primary Texts

Larra, anatomía de un dandy. Madrid: Alfaguara, 1965.
Mortal y rosa. Barcelona: Destino, 1975.
Las ninfas. Barcelona: Destino, 1976.
La noche que llegué al Café Gijón. Barcelona: Destino, 1977.
Spleen de Madrid, 2. Barcelona: Destino, 1982.

English Translation

A Mortal Spring. Tr. Helen R. Lane. New York and London: Harcourt Brace Jovanovich, 1980.

Criticism

Amorós, Andrés. ''Perspectivas críticas: Horizontes infinitos.'' *Anales de la novela de posguerra* 2 (1977): 73–79.
Fernández Roca, José A. ''Crónica y novela en *Las ninfas*, de Umbral.'' *CH* 373 (July 1981): 109–27.
Navales, Ana M. *Cuatro novelistas españoles*. Madrid: Fundamentos, 1974. 213–95, 307–9.

Charles King

UNAMUNO, Miguel de (1864, Bilbao–1936, Salamanca), novelist, poet, dramatist, essayist. Miguel de Unamuno was born and educated in the Basque city of Bilbao. At sixteen he entered the U of Madrid, where he studied philosophy and letters. In 1891 he married his childhood sweetheart and took a teaching position at the U of Salamanca, where he taught Greek and later history of the Spanish language. He was named rector of the U in 1900 and retained the post until 1914, when he was dismissed without explanation. In the mid–1920s Unamuno publicly criticized the dictatorship of Primo de Rivera, who promptly banished the writer to the Canary Islands. Unamuno subsequently fled to France and set up a home in exile in Hendaye, from where he could see his country and address his countrymen. He returned to Spain in 1930 to the turmoil of the Spanish Republic and the outbreak of the Spanish Civil War. Initially pro-Republican, Unamuno subsequently declared his support for Franco. Shortly before his death, however, he repudiated the Franquist rebellion. Salamanca was by then in Nationalist hands, and Unamuno was placed under house arrest. He died at home on December 31, 1936.

A member of the *Generation of 1898, Unamuno shared with *Ganivet, Pío *Baroja, *Machado Ruiz and others a deep love of Spain and a desire to see her once more in the forefront of intellectual development in Europe. His rejection of the bullfight, of Catholicism (particularly as practiced in Spain), of the traditional glorification of the Hapsburgs and their role in Spanish history, all echo the regenerationist rhetoric of his contemporaries. He was the most versatile of his generation, cultivating such diverse genres as the short story, the theater, the novel, the essay, and poetry. His interests ranged from philosophy to history to art to origami. Students of Unamuno's writings have divided his work into two main categories: the agonic works, in which a strongly polemical tone seeks to awaken the reader to the anguish of his position in the world, and the contemplative works, in which Unamuno withdraws from the energetic, anguished dialogue with his contemporaries into a lyrical solitude. The two modes are generally intermixed within a single period or work, although one usually predominates.

Unamuno's most important essays examine the place of Spain in the modern world and the dilemma of modern man. *En torno al casticismo* (1902; On Authentic Tradition) seeks to identify the essence of Spain. The "true" Spain is to be found not in the history of the Hapsburg and Bourbon kings but in "intrahistory," the spirit of the Spanish people that is rooted in the medieval foundations of the country. Unamuno's desire in this first collection of essays is to fuse the intrahistorical Spanish essence with the best of the modern world. The same idea persists in subsequent works, with a changed emphasis. *La vida de don Quijote* (1905; *Our Lord Don Quijote*, 1967) stresses the Spanish over the European; Spain's heritage enables her to contribute a moral, spiritual strength that is lacking in her more progressive, technically advanced neighbors. *Del sentimiento trágico de la vida* (1913; *The Tragic Sense of Life*, 1954) continues the study of the Spanish character but in the context of the spiritual dilemma that faces the contemporary individual. Drawing from readings of Kierkegaard, William James, Carlyle, Nietzsche, and a multitude of contemporary and historical philosophers, Unamuno charts a personal metaphysics. Convinced that the most basic question facing the modern individual is the problem of mortality and life after death, Unamuno proceeds to reject the traditional solutions available to the Spanish thinker. Neither the Catholic church nor the rationalist philosophies of the preceding centuries resolve the fundamental question. The Catholics believe in life after death but are unable to base their doctrine in "rational" philosophy. It is part of dogma, appeals to the human desire to live, but is not intellectually persuasive. Conversely, the rationalists demonstrate that there is no life beyond death, but in Unamuno's view, if there is no life after death, then life on earth has no meaning. Thus, reason and will or sentiment are in constant conflict. Human beings desire eternal life, but reason demonstrates that their desire is futile. It is precisely in this conflict between reason and sentiment that Unamuno finds hope. Neither totally convinced, nor totally despairing, he calls for continual doubt, a creative uncertainty that enables life. The existentialist character of Unamuno's thought continues in his discussion of human conduct and the practical consequences of his philosophy. In the search to overcome death, he finds possible solutions in marital love, parenthood, and artistic creation. Love must be, however, an anguished, personalized experience. It requires suffering and struggle and leads to self-discovery. The problem of identity and the search for meaning is central to virtually all of Unamuno's creative works. *Niebla* (1914; *Mist*, 1928) presents the trajectory of Augusto Pérez, a characterless, disoriented man who gradually comes to self-discovery through the pain of amorous rejection and ridicule. *Abel Sánchez* (1917; *Abel Sanchez*, 1956) offers a modern version of the Cain and Abel theme, relating the struggle of Joaquín Monegro to define himself and his relationship with his friend Abel. *La tía Tula* (1921; Aunt Gertrude) offers a female protagonist who is driven by an intense maternal drive and an equally intense aversion to sex. Tula's gradual discovery of the consequences of her choices and her discovery of self parallel the experiences of Joaquín Monegro and Augusto Pérez. *San Manuel Bueno, mártir* (1933; *St. Manuel Bueno, Martyr*, 1973) presents in novelized form Unamuno's religious philosophy. The protagonist is a priest who has come to doubt the mortality of the soul but submerges his own feelings so that he can continue to provide hope and faith to his parishioners.

Unamuno's poetry examines the same themes as his novels. One of his most famous sonnets is entitled "Atheist's Prayer" and opens with the verse "Hear my plea, you God that does not exist." In other poems Unamuno expresses his grief over the loss of a son, his love for his wife—who was mother and protector to him—and his love for intrahistorical Spain.

Unamuno wrote with a severe, often polemical style. He continuously plays with words, inventing new terms and resuscitating older words. In those works which fall into the agonic mode, he utilizes paradox, exclamation, and polemical exhortation, addressing the reader directly. Unamuno experimented with new methods of presentation in virtually all of the genres he cultivated, personalizing them in the same way that he personalized his style and his characters. His theater bears the imprint of Ibsen, but is considerably starker, less theatrical, often excessively skeletal. His poetry is often considered anti-poetic, with purposely harsh sounds and unconventional metaphors. On the other hand, his *Cristo de Velázquez* (1920; *The Christ of Velazquez*, 1951) is highly visual, with a continuous succession of symbols and images. Unamuno's novel shares certain characteristics with other members of the Generation of 1898: the appearance of openness or lack of structure, the focus on a single central figure, the avoidance of realistic description of setting. It is, however, a highly personal creation, adapted to Unamuno's artistic and philosophical needs. Prolific, intriguing and often perplexing, Unamuno is, with Ortega y Gasset, one of the contemporary writers who is best known outside of Spain.

BIBLIOGRAPHY

Primary Texts

Niebla. Ed. Harriet Stevens and Ricardo Gullón. Madrid: Taurus, 1974.
Obras completas. 2nd ed. 10 vols. Madrid: Afrodisio Aguado, 1958–64.
San Manuel Bueno, mártir. Ed. Mario J. Valdés. Madrid: Cátedra, 1979.

English Translations

The Agony of Christianity. Tr. Anthony Kerrigan. Princeton: Princeton UP, 1974.
Mist. Tr. Warner Fite. New York: H. Fertig, 1928.
St. Manuel Bueno, Martyr. Tr. Mario J. Valdés and María Elena de Valdés. Chapel Hill: U of North Carolina P, 1973. Spanish and English.

Selected Works. Ed and Tr. Anthony Kerrigan and others. Princeton: Princeton UP, 1967–.

The Tragic Sense of Life. Tr. Anthony Kerrigan. Princeton: Princeton UP, 1972.

Criticism

Livingston, Leon. ''Unamuno and the Aesthetic of the Novel.'' *Hispania* 24 (1941): 442–50.

Marías, Julián. *Miguel de Unamuno*. Buenos Aires: Espasa-Calpe, 1950.

Nozick, Martin. *Miguel de Unamuno*. Boston: G. K. Hall, 1971.

Sánchez Barbudo, Antonio. *Estudios sobre Unamuno y Machado*. Madrid: Guadarrama, 1959.

———, ed. *Miguel de Unamuno*. Madrid: Taurus, 1974.

Mary Lee Bretz

UNIVERSITIES. The university world is intimately connected with the world of literature. Literary creation, especially in the Middle Ages (*see* Edad Media, Literatura de la), the *Renaissance, the *Siglo de Oro and even in later centuries, generally grows out of the university classroom. Even among the *juglares* there was a special type of wandering singer who was a cleric or ''scholar,'' as the *Arcipreste de Hita calls him in one of his songs: ''Señores, dat al escolar / Que vos viene demandar.'' (My lords, give to this scholar who is now about to beg from you.)

In addition, many authors, including Lope de *Vega, *Cervantes, *Quevedo, Mateo *Alemán, etc., described or narrated some aspect of the carefree life of the student at the time; they depicted life in cities that acquired worldwide fame as university centers. Thus, for their presence in the culture and their intimate connection with the literary world, it is essential to have an idea of what Spain's universities have represented throughout history.

In 1208 the first Spanish university was founded in Palencia; Alphonse VIII sought masters in all the arts to instruct the students, and, according to Lucas de *Túy, by the middle of the thirteenth c., the proverb ''en Palencia, armas y ciencia'' (In Palencia, arms and science) was already well known. The date of the founding of the U of Salamanca, which in the late Middle Ages could be compared with the universities of Paris, Bologna and Oxford, has been debated by many scholars; some (Gil y Zárate, for example) date it before the founding of the U of Palencia, that is, between 1180 and 1200; Gebhart fixes it in 1239, Madoz, in 1240, and still others do not consider it a university until 1250. The founder of the university center at Salamanca was Alphonse IX, but the university did not attain its full identity until 1243, under a privilege from Fernando III. It received its definitive form under the reign of Alphonse X, not only because he established thirteen chairs there (several in languages, grammar, arithmetic, rhetoric, mathematics, liturgical music, medicine, surgery, music and law), but also because he gave legal form to various aspects of university legislation, the spirit of which was to endure for several centuries.

The basis of the Fuero Académico, or Academic Law, is established in the *Partidas*:

> el rector debe castigar e apremiar a los escolares que no levanten vandos nin peleas ros los omes de los lugares do fueren los escolares ni entre si mismos. E que se guarden en todas guisas que non fagan deshonra nin tuerto a ninguno. . . . Los maestros que muestran las ciencias en los estudios pueden judgar sus escolares en las demandas que ovieren unos con otros, o en las otras que los omes les fiziesen que no fuesen sobre pleitos de sangre, e no les deven demandar ni traer a juizio delante de otro alcalde sin su placer de ellos. Pero si les quieren demandar delante de su maestro, en su escogencia e de responder a ella, o delante del obispo del lugar, o delante del juez del fuero, cual más quisiese.

(The president should reward students not to organize gangs nor fights either with men from the surrounding areas or among the students themselves. And let them take care not to dishonor or wrong anyone. . . . The teachers of sciences can judge their students in the accusations they have against each other, or in those that other men have with them, as long as they have not to do with lineage; nor should they accuse or bring to judgment before another judge without their consent. But if they want to accuse before their teacher, either in selection or in response to it, or before the local bishop, or before the legal judge, [they may do] whichever they desire.) As Vicente de la Fuente observes, the university enjoyed the privileges of the *fuero* as long as the offense was not common and did not jeopardize the order of the city. The exemptions that students enjoyed were also important: they did not have to pay tolls or other taxes, nor were sellers of textbooks subject to taxes.

There were three titles conferred by the university: *bachiller*, *licenciado* and *doctor*. For the first, a student studied for six years, and it was a title of some respect: for example, el bachiller Fernando de *Rojas. It was even used emphatically, according to literary testimony: -"Yo, señores, soy bachiller por Salamanca . . . " (Cervantes). The title of *licenciado* is mentioned in its root form (*licencia*, to have license to teach) in the *Partidas*; to obtain this teaching privilege, one had to fulfill seven tests or requirements, including five years of study and the *catar en paridat*, that is, being a person of good habits. The degree of *doctor*, which was the highest in the university hierarchy, was granted in a solemn ceremony in which the candidate had to give a lecture designed just for the occasion; it was what has come to be called the doctoral thesis. A satirical ceremony, called a *vejamen* or *gallo*, followed this lecture and consisted of a diatribe by another *doctor* against the one currently aspiring to attain this highest degree granted by the university. The *vejado*, or abused party, was defended by another student who in university slang was called *gallina*, chicken. It was said, furthermore, that the declamation was not recited but instead "crowed," and was composed in Spanish verse or macaronic Latin. The degree of *doctor* permitted one to become a professor in any university.

The university positions were: *rector* (president), *cancelario* (chancellor), *conservadores* (wardens), *consiliarios* (counselors), *primicerio* (precentor), *decano* (dean), *estacionarios* (librarians), and *bedeles* (proctors). The professorships were obtained by opposition, and the students themselves participated in the voting, which was the source of many improprieties since the votes were sold or given to the candidates who promised easier exams. For example, *Nebrija, whose *Gramática* was a textbook at Salamanca, did not get the position in his specialty in 1513; instead, the students voted in a young man who was much less capable than the famous grammarian.

The textbooks were essentially manuscripts. For this reason they were extremely expensive for the students; the *estacionarios*, or booksellers, lent the manuscripts out, which facilitated study and the possibility of making new copies, so that errors grew with alarming speed. This motivated the establishment of a *comisión de revisión de apuntes* (commission to review notes) in some universities—Lérida, Salamanca, Valladolid—to avoid the corruption of the text. *Printing changed this aspect of university education.

The courses lasted eleven months, from October 18 to September 8. Along with the rise of universities grew the *Colegios Mayores*, where the students lived and where discipline regulated both personal habits and the students' studies. In Salamanca there were as many as four of these residential colleges. There were also *Colegios Menores*, which were private institutions that were licensed to teach the humanities; among the five thousand that grew up in Spain, *López de Hoyos's *Estudio de la Villa*, where *Cervantes was educated, should be noted. The students who could not get a place in a *Colegio Mayor* lived in a guest house and were subject to certain norms dictated by the university, for example, regarding the student's diet and the locking of the residence doors. The poor student, when returning home or traveling to the university at the beginning or end of the school year, begged for alms and lodging along the roads, just as Cervantes depicts in his *La Cueva de Salamanca* (''Señoras: yo soy un pobre estudiante''); in so doing, he would recite or sing something, or, if he was traveling in a group of students, they would give a musical recital which was the origin of the university *tuna*; others invented some talent, as Cervantes depicted in the above-mentioned **entremés*.

The universities blossomed in the sixteenth c., and the most important, apart from Salamanca, which served as a model for the others, were at Alcalá and Valladolid. In 1625, the Jesuits took charge of the celebrated Estudios Reales de San Isidro, a university founded by Philip IV for the sons of Madrid nobles. In the seventeenth c., the universities began to decline and, as Ludwig Pfandl has stated, the *Colegios mayores* followed, deteriorating into centers of favoritism and partisanship, moral degeneration and spiritual and physical laziness; the decline of the *Colegios mayores* was, in turn, of great detriment to the universities for which they had provided the greatest prestige and support. The Jesuits greatly influenced education from 1564 with their method, the *Ratio studiorum*. However, there are authors who particularly fault the Society of Jesus for the decline of the universities, among them, precisely, a Jesuit father, Juan de *Mariana, who writes in *Discurso de las cosas de la Compañía*: ''No hay duda sino que hoy en España se sabe menos latín que ahora cincuenta años . . .''; ''creo yo, y aun antes lo tengo por muy cierto, que una de las causas más principales de este daño es estar encargada la Compañía destos estudios; que si la gente entendiese bien el daño que por este camino se hace, no dudo sino que por decreto público nos quitarían estas escuelas, como se ha empezado a tratar.'' (There is no doubt but that today in Spain they know less Latin than they did fifty years ago . . . ; I believe, nay, I am quite sure, that one of the principal causes of this damage is that these studies have been charged to the society; that if the people understood the danger done in this way, I have no doubt that by public decree they would take these schools away from us, as they have begun to discuss.) There were many universities in Spain in the Golden Age, but little by little they were closed down, until they were reduced to only those that still function today. Clearly, because the universities enjoyed economic autonomy, they ran the same risks as private institutions and with the general decline of the empire saw themselves pulled increasingly toward poverty. Later government measures designed to overcome this crisis resulted in the standardization of university education.

BIBLIOGRAPHY

Criticism

Ajo, C. M. *Historia de las universidades hispánicas.* 7 vols. Madrid: CSIC, 1957–68.

De la Fuente, Vicente. *Historia de la universidad, colegios y demás centros de enseñanza.* 4 vols. Frankfurt: Sauer and Auverman, 1969–75.

Mariana, Juan de. *Discurso de las enfermedades de la Compañía.* Madrid: G. Ramírez, 1768.

Pfandl, Ludwig. *Introducción al Siglo de Oro.* Barcelona: Araluce, 1929.

Andrea Warren Hamos

URABAYEN, Félix (1884, Ulzurrun, Navarra–1943, Madrid), novelist and prose writer. He resided for many years in Toledo teaching at its Escuela Normal. Considered by some critics a belated ''noventaiochista'' for his love of and identification with the Castilian landscape of Toledo, his ideology, however, is not akin to that of the *Generation of 1898. His sensibility to the quaint beauty of historic places makes him closer to *Modernism, even to the *Romanticism of *Bécquer or to Gabriel *Miró. His first book, *Toledo: Piedad* (1920; Toledo: Piety), of exquisite prose, revealed a mature writer anticipating his work to follow. His second book, a novel, *La última cigüeña* (1921; The Last Stork), confirmed the favorable judgment already given by the critics. Other subsequent novels were *El barrio maldito* (1925; Wicked District) and *Vidas difícilmente ejemplares* (1930; Hardly Exemplary Lives). Toledo and its historic cityscape appeared repeatedly in subsequent prose works: *Toledo la despojada* (1922; Toledo Despoiled); *Por los senderos del mundo creyente* (1929; Across the Path of the Believers); *Estampas del camino* (1934; Traveling Impressions); and *Serenata lírica a la vieja ciudad* (1934; Lyric Serenade to the Old City). There is a recent compilation, *Folletones en ''El Sol'' de Félix Urabayen* (1983; Feuilletons in ''El Sol'' by Félix Urabayen).

BIBLIOGRAPHY

Primary Texts

El barrio maldito. Pamplona: Pamiela, 1988.
Estampas del camino. Madrid: Calpe, 1934.
Folletones en "El Sol" de Félix Urabayen. Navarra: Diputación Foral de Navarra, 1983.
Por los senderos del mundo creyente. Madrid: Calpe, 1929.
Toledo: Piedad. Madrid: Calpe, 1920.
La última cigüeña. Madrid: n.p., 1921.
Vidas difícilmente ejemplares. Madrid: Biblioteca Atlántico, 1930.

Pilar Sáenz

URBANO, Rafael (1870, Madrid–1924, Madrid), translator, journalist. He wrote for several newspapers in northern Spain. After returning to Madrid to work in the Ministry of Public Education, he continued to write as a journalist. A regular lecturer at the *Ateneo, he also collaborated in the literary supplement *Los lunes del Imparcial*. Toward the end of his life, he studied the occult, which is the theme of *El diablo: su vida y su poder* (1922; The Devil, His Life and Power). Also his are *Tristitia seculae: Soliloquio de un alma* (1901; A Soul's Soliloquy), *El sello de Salomón* (1907; Solomon's Seal), and *Manual del perfecto enfermo* (1911; Handbook for the Perfect Patient).

BIBLIOGRAPHY

Primary Texts

El diablo: su vida y su poder. Madrid: Biblioteca del Más Alla, 1922.
Manual del perfecto enfermo. Madrid: Francisco Beltrán, 1911.
El sello de Salomón. Madrid: J. Palacios, 1907.

Isabel McSpadden

URÍA Y RÍU, Juan (1891, Oviedo–?, ?), professor, scholar. A professor of Spanish history at the U of Oviedo, his noteworthy monographical essays include *Juglares asturianos* (1940; Asturian Minstrels), *Las fundaciones hospitalarias en los caminos de la peregrinación a Oviedo* (1940; The Hospitality Lodgings on the Pilgrimage Route to Oviedo), *Notas para la historia de los judíos en Asturias* (1944; Notes on the History of Jews in Asturias), etc. His studies relate to literary history, and his most significant contribution, composed in collaboration with Vázquez de Parga y Lacarra, is *Las peregrinaciones a Santiago de Compostela* (1948–49; Pilgrimage to St. James of Compostela).

BIBLIOGRAPHY

Primary Texts

Estudios sobre la Baja Edad Media asturiana. Oviedo: Biblioteca Popular Asturiana, 1979.
Las peregrinaciones a Santiago de Compostela. 3 vols. Madrid: CSIC, 1948–49.

Isabel McSpadden

URQUIJO E IBARRA, Julio (1871, Deusto–1950, Bilbao), lawyer, historian, philologist, academician in the *Academia Española. He wrote some outstanding works about the Basque region, including *Obras vascongadas del doctor la-*

bortano Joannes d'Etcheberri (Basque Works of the Labordan [Basque town] Dr. Joannes d'Etcheberro) and *El refranero vasco* (1919; Basque Proverbs), etc. In 1925 he published a new interpretation of the "Caballeritos de Azcoitia" which disagreed with that of *Menéndez Pelayo. In 1907 he founded the *Revista internacional de estudios vascos* (International Review of Basque Studies).

BIBLIOGRAPHY

Primary Text

El refranero vasco. San Sebastián: Martín, Mena, 1919.

Isabel McSpadden

URREA, Jerónimo Jiménez de (c. 1505, Epila, Zaragoza?–before 1575, Zaragoza), soldier and writer. A descendant of the poet Pedro Manuel, he belonged to the Aranda line and followed the family tradition of loyal service to the Spanish Crown. Urrea served as a soldier under Charles V in Germany and Flanders, and aided Fernando Alvarez de Toledo, Duke of Alba, in a diplomatic capacity in Italy. Charles V named Urrea viceroy of Pulla for his noteworthy performance, and appointed him to his ministry.

Urrea's first original fictional work was a chivalric novel, *Don Clarisel de las Flores y de Austrasia* (1545; Sir Clarisel of the Flowers and of Austrasia), written in three parts. Part 1 was first published in 1879, and parts 2 and 3 only appeared in 1978. This lengthy narrative of intricately woven adventures contains many enjoyable passages and delightful poetry.

Urrea also penned a version of Ariosto's famous *Orlando furioso*, which appeared in 1550, and a translation of Olivier de la Marche's *Le chevalier délibéré*, which he titled *Discurso de la vida humana y aventuras del caballero determinado* (1555; Discourse on the Life and Adventures of the Resolved Cavalier). Neither contributed to the advancement of his literary acclaim. His nonfiction writing includes the unpublished *La famosa Epila* (The Famous Town of Epila), which praises his birthplace and ancestors, and *Diálogo de la verdadera honra militar* (1575; Dialogue of True Military Honor). The *Diálogo* is a worthy piece in which two soldiers, Altamirano and Franco, discuss contemporary military stratagems and condemn Spanish soldiers' abuse of a military privilege—the duel. It was quite popular in Spain and in France and Italy. It is possible that *Cervantes read the *Diálogo*, as it was cited by Juan de *Mal Lara in his *Filosofía vulgar*, a recognized Cervantine source.

BIBLIOGRAPHY

Primary Texts

Diálogo de la verdadera honra militar. Madrid: Sánchez, 1575.

Don Clarisel de las Flores y de Austrasia. Seville: Sociedad de Bibliófilos Andaluces, 1879. Contains part 1.

Don Clarisel de las Flores y de Austrasia. In *Le capitaine-poète aragonais Jerónimo de Urrea; sa vie et son oeuvre: ou Chevalerie et Renaissance dans l'Espagne du*

XVIe siècle. Ed. Pierre Geneste. Paris: Ed. Hispano-Americana, 1978. In Appendix C, parts 2 and 3.

Criticism

Barado y Font, J. "Gerónimo de Urrea." In *La literatura militar española*. Barcelona: Gallach, 1890. 318–25.

See also P. Geneste, in *Don Clarisel* (1978), Primary Texts.

Veronica Sauter

URRETABIZKAIA, Arantza (1947, Donostia–), poet, novelist and journalist. With a degree in modern and contemporary history from the U of Barcelona, she began her writing career as a poet, contributing a collection called "San Pedro Bezperaren Ondokoak" (What Happens after the Eve of San Pedro) to the anthology *Euskal Literatura* in 1972. Ten years later her second volume of poetry *Maitasunaren magalean* (1982; In the Lap of Love) won her the Premio Ciudad de Irún. In the meantime, she produced a lyrical narration called *Zergatik Panpox?* (1979; Why, Little One?), the interior monologue of a young mother struggling to support herself and her little son. This poignant book, translated into Catalan by Josep Daurella, brings to life the pain of abandonment and solitude felt by a still male-oriented woman. Even after several years she wishes for el Txema, wanting to believe his return would solve everything, but knowing it is not possible, and leaving the reader with the feeling that she has grown too much to return to such a relationship in any case. The first-person stream-of-consciousness format gives a look inside the mind of an unhappy woman struggling for liberation and just beginning to see and appreciate her own strength. Urretabizkaia followed with a collection of three stories called *Aspaldian espero zaitudalako, ez nago sekulan bakarrik* (1983; Since I've Waited for You so Long, I'm Never Alone Anymore), continuing the lyricism and intimate tone of her earlier novella. Her prose shows a profundity, perceptiveness and expressive tenderness not surpassed in Basque literature. With Antton Olariaga, she published the historical epic *Albaniaren Konkista* (1983; The Conquest of Albania), which was made into a film. She has written for the periodicals *Deia*, *Diario Vasco*, *Egin*, and *Ere*, and for Basque television.

BIBLIOGRAPHY

Primary Texts

Albaniaren Konkista. Donostia: not found, 1983.

Aspaldian espero zaitudalako, ez nago sekulan bakarrik. Donostia: Erein, 1983.

Maitasunaren magalean. Donostia: Caja de Ahorros Provincial de Guipúzcoa, 1982.

Zergatik Panpox. Donostia: Hordago, 1979.

Zergatik Panpox. Catalan tr. Josep Daurella. Barcelona: Mall, 1982.

Kathleen McNerney

V

VACA DE GUZMÁN, José María (1750?, Marchena–after 1801, ?), poet, attorney. He rose to the position of rector at the School of the Manriques of Alcalá and minister of crime of the Royal Court of Cataluña. He defeated each of the *Moratín brothers in competitions held by the *Academia Española. His verse was collected and published in three volumes in 1789.

His brother, Gutierre Joaquín Vaca de Guzmán (also an attorney and writer), is remembered for a novel written in English: *Travels of Henry Wanton* (1769–71). José María translated the two volumes into Spanish from an Italian version. The success of the translation prompted José María to compose his own continuation, which appeared in 1778.

BIBLIOGRAPHY

Primary Texts

Obras. Madrid: n.p., 1789.
Poemas épicos. In BAE 29 and 61.

VALBUENA PRAT, Ángel (1900, Barcelona–1977, Barcelona), literary historian, critic. Although best known for his authoritative *Historia de la literatura española* (1937; History of Spanish Literature), Valbuena Prat also authored significant studies on the Spanish theater and the *picaresque novel. His *Historia* has been revised and augmented several times, to include Latin American literature and commentaries on writings of non-Hispanic countries. Also an author of fiction and poetry, it is as a literary critic, nonetheless, that he has most distinguished himself; his books have become indispensable tools of the trade. He also taught at universities in Spain, and abroad, at Cambridge, in Wisconsin, and at various institutions in Brazil.

BIBLIOGRAPHY

Primary Texts

Alvaro Cubillo de Aragón. Las muñecas de Marcela, El Señor de noches buenas. Madrid: Compañía ibero-americana de publicaciones, 1928.

Antonio Mira de Amescua, Teatro. Madrid: Espasa-Calpe, 1926.
Autos sacramentales. Madrid: Espasa-Calpe, 1942.
Historia de la literatura española. Barcelona: Gili, 1937.
Lope de Vega. Barcelona: Argos Vergara, 1979.
Miguel de Cervantes Saavedra. Obras Completas. Madrid: Aguilar, 1965.
La novela picaresca española. Madrid: Aguilar, 1956.
Pedro Calderón de la Barca, Comedias religiosas. Madrid: Espasa-Calpe, 1930.
La poesía española contemporánea. Madrid: Compañía ibero-americana de publicaciones, 1930.
Teatro moderno español. Zaragoza: Partenón, 1944.
El teatro español en su siglo de oro. Barcelona: Planeta, 1969.

Robert Kirsner

VALBUENA Y GUTIÉRREZ, Antonio de (1844, Pedrosa del Rey, León–1929, Pedrosa del Rey), journalist. His polemical, self-assured, coarse, mocking style made him quite well known, especially as seen in his satirical articles on grammar and vocabulary corrections in writers. He often used the pen name Miguel de Escalada. His articles were compiled under such titles as *Ripios académicos* (1890; Academic Jabs), *Ripios aristocráticos* (1884; Aristocratic Jabs), *Fe de erratas del Diccionario de la Academia* (1887–1896; List of Errors of the Dictionary of the Academy), etc.

BIBLIOGRAPHY

Primary Texts

Fe de erratas del Diccionario de la Academia. 3rd ed. 4 vols. Madrid: La España, 1891–96.
Ripios académicos. 4th ed. Madrid: Asilo de huérfanos, 1912.
Ripios aristocráticos. 7th ed. Madrid: Suárez, 1906.
Ripios vulgares. 4th ed. Madrid: Tello, 1913.

Isabel McSpadden

VALDEFLORES, Marqués de. *See* Velázquez, Luis José

VALDERRAMA, Pilar (1892, Madrid–1979, Madrid), Spanish poet and dramatist who is perhaps best known at present for having been identified as the secret, Platonic love of Antonio *Machado whom the poet called Guiomar. Although married and the mother of three children, she became estranged from her husband after learning of his infidelity, seeking happiness in dreams and escape through poetry and Machado's friendship (he credited Guiomar with being an excellent critic and intellectual counsel). Her volumes of poetry include *Las piedras de Horeb* (1922; The Stones of Horeb), *Huerto cerrado* (1928; Closed Garden), *Esencias* (1930; Essences) and *Holocausto* (1941; Holocaust). In addition, Valderrama wrote a so-called dramatic poem—actually a play with two acts in prose and one in verse—entitled "El tercer mundo" (Third World), published in a collective volume entitled *Teatro de mujeres. Tres autoras españolas* (1934; Theater by Women. Three Spanish Women Writers). The play clearly has considerable autobiographical content on the psychological level, dealing as it does with a love triangle and the unhappiness of the woman, who chooses to escape to a world of illusion. Valderrama's autobiography, which remained unpublished until after her death, is entitled *Sí, soy Guiomar. Memorias de mi vida* (1981; Yes, I'm Giuomar. Memoirs of my Life).

BIBLIOGRAPHY

Primary Texts

De mar a mar. Madrid: Torremozas, 1984.
Holocausto. Madrid: Artegrafía, 1941.
Sí, soy Guiomar. Barcelona: Plaza y Janés, 1981.
"El tercer mundo." In *Teatro de mujeres*. Madrid: Aguilar, 1934.

Janet Pérez

VALDÉS, Alfonso de (1490, Cuenca–1532, Vienna), Erasmian writer. The older brother of Juan de *Valdés, Alfonso was an Erasmian reformer and also a political theorist. He became Charles V's Latin secretary and in that capacity traveled through various European areas including Germany. There he witnessed the debates between Martin Luther and representatives of the church. More importantly, he worked on some of the official letters (dispatches) between the emperor and Pope Clement VII, Henry VIII of England and Francis I of France. Alfonso was a fervent and enthusiastic follower of Erasmus and corresponded with him. As a result of this friendship he became an ardent church reformer. However, his religious fervor coincided with his firm support for the European policies of Charles V, who in his own right backed the reform movement spearheaded by Cardinal *Cisneros. Alfonso strongly believed that one of the greatest services that the emperor could render on behalf of Christendom was the reform of the church, from within, in the spirit of Evangelical Christianity proposed by Erasmus. Nonetheless, like his brother Juan, Alfonso rejected the Lutheran reformation, feeling that the church could return to a purer form of Christianity without the political and social upheavals wrought by it. It must be emphasized that Alfonso accepted and defended the principal doctrines of the church; what he objected to were the external manifestations of the religion so abused in his time.

Alfonso produced two important works (*diálogos*, dialogues) in which he developed both his political and religious ideas. The *Diálogo de Mercurio y Carón* (c. 1523; *Dialogue of Mercury and Charon*, 1986) is Erasmian in concept, content and form. The work is a political apologetic wherein Alfonso defends the emperor's position vis-à-vis the other European monarchs and at the same time supports his role in the 1527 sack of Rome. Even more important, the *Diálogo* contains elements of social satire and develops the author's stance on religious reform. The main body of the work is a dialogue between Mercury and Charon as the latter ferries the souls of the damned into the infernal regions. They interview certain condemned spirits, many of whom are members of the clergy and men of prominence. Interspersed are Mercury's discussions supporting the emperor's policies in Europe. In the second part of the work the two interlocutors converse with the saved souls at the base of the mountain as they are about to commence their ascent toward heaven. Until recent times this work had been attributed to Juan, but presently it is universally acknowledged as Alfonso's.

The dialogue *Lactancio y el Arcediano*, or *Diálogo de las cosas ocurridas en Roma* (1529; *Dialogue on the Sack of Rome*, 1590), was a defense of the emperor's part in those catastrophic events and also a harsh indictment of a good number of practices common in the church. Indeed, Alfonso avers that the destruction in Rome was God's just punishment for the rampant corruption at the papal see. Although Alfonso never mentions Erasmus by name, his ideas thoroughly imbue this work. For Alfonso, the church is a spiritual entity constantly sustained by the Scriptures, its doctrines and Christian virtues. Not once does he attack church doctrines, nor does he question the spiritual authority of the pope. He does, however, place greater emphasis on faith, the virtues and an inner spirituality. *See also* Erasmism; Renaissance; Siglo de Oro.

BIBLIOGRAPHY

Primary Texts

Diálogo de las cosas ocurridas en Rome. Clásicos Castellanos 89. Madrid: Espasa-Calpe, 1956.

Diálogo de Mercurio y Carón. Clásicos Castellanos 96. Madrid: Espasa-Calpe, 1947.

English Translations

Alfonso de Valdés and the Sack of Rome. Tr. John E. Longhurst and Raymond MacCurdy. Albuquerque: U of New Mexico P, 1952.

Dialogue of Mercury and Charon. Tr. J. V. Ricapito. Bloomington: Indiana UP, 1986.

Criticism

Bataillon, Marcel. "Alfonso de Valdés, Auteur du *Diálogo de Mercurio y Carón*." *Hommage a Menéndez Pidal* 1 (1925): 403–15.

Boehmer, E. *Bibliotheca Wifeniana. Spanish Reformers of Two Centuries from 1520*. vol. 1. Strasbourg: Trübner, 1874.

Menéndez Pelayo, Marcelino. *Historia de los heterodoxos españoles*. Santander: Aldus, 1947. 3: 123–86.

Morreale, Margherita. "¿Devoción o piedad? Apuntaciones sobre el léxico religioso de Alfonso y Juan de Valdés." *Revista Portuguesa de Filología* 7 (1956): 365–88.

Angelo DiSalvo

VALDÉS, Juan de (c. 1498, Cuenca–1541, Naples), Erasmian reformer, influenced by his older brother, Alfonso de *Valdés. Whereas Alfonso was a religious reformer and political theorist, Juan was a religious reformer and linguistic theorist. Scholars know little about his formal education other than that he studied at Alcalá. As a courtier around 1523 he served another known Erasmist, the Marquis of Villena, who sponsored gatherings of Erasmists and **alumbrados* at his castle in Escalona. At these religious gatherings Valdés apparently came into contact with other Erasmists. In his earlier years, Juan had been an avid reader of chivalric romances, but after his contact with Erasmian ideas, he abandoned them altogether and became interested in the reform of the church from the inside.

In 1528–29 Juan wrote his first important work, the *Diálogo de doctrina cristiana* (Alcalá, 1529; The Dialogue on Christian Doctrine), wherein he not only expatiates on church doctrine but also expounds on his Erasmian reforms inveighing against the abuses prevalent within the church. In the *Diálogo* he advocates an inner form of evangelical Catholicism. Throughout his adult life Juan protested the abuses in the church but did not attack doctrines like the sacraments or the Eucharist. In fact, he never expressed a desire to join Luther's reform; instead, he openly opposed it as his brother had done. A commission of theologians at Alcalá closely scrutinized the *Diálogo* and found objectionable a good portion of its material.

Soon after the commission's results were made public, Juan left Spain for good and established himself in Italy; first at the papal court of Clement VII and later in Naples around 1532–33. In that city Juan became the organizer and spiritual director of a group of religious intellectuals who met to read and discuss the Bible as well as Juan's writings. A few of these individuals were indeed declared Protestants; some left Italy altogether as a result of their ideas. In Naples Juan composed two other works for his companions and disciples. The first, titled *Alfabeto cristiano* (Naples, 1535; *The Christian Alphabet*, 1861; also called *Consideraciones divinas*—Divine Considerations), is the product of a series of conversations carried on between Juan and his favorite disciple, Julia de Gonzaga.

The second work is the *Diálogo de la lengua* (Dialogue on Language). Written between 1533 and 1535, it was not published until *Mayáns y Siscar included it in his 1737 *Orígenes de la lengua española* as an anonymous work. This dialogue between four interlocutors owes its existence to practical exigencies since Juan himself felt that his friends in Naples should perfect their knowledge of Spanish. In the work Juan studies the Castilian language by means of proverbs inasmuch as it was felt that Spain had not yet produced classics. However, Juan does mention *Mena, Jorge *Manrique, the **Celestina* and the *Cortesano* of *Castiglione among others. The book is one of the earliest examples of a theory of language text. *See also* Erasmism; Renaissance; Siglo de Oro.

BIBLIOGRAPHY

Primary Texts

Alfabeto cristiano fiel del Tratado italiano: añádese ahora dos traducciones modernas, una en castellano, otra en inglés. London: n.p., 1861.

Diálogo de doctrina cristiana. Alcalá: n.p., 1529.

Diálogo de la lengua. In *Orígenes de la lengua española*. By G. Mayáns y Siscar. vol. 2. rev. ed. Madrid: V. Suárez, 1873.

Diálogo de la lengua. Clásicos Castellanos 86. Madrid: Espasa-Calpe, 1964.

English Translations

Evangelical Catholicism as Represented by Juan de Valdés. Anonymous. In the *Library of Christian Classics*. London: SCM, 1957. Extracts from *A Dialogue on Christian Doctrine*, *One Hundred and Ten Considerations* and *The Christian Alphabet*.

Hundred and Ten Considerations. Tr. John T. Betts. In *Life and Writings of Juan de Valdés*. By Benjamin B. Wiffen. London: Quaritch, 1865.

Criticism

Boehmer, E. *Bibliotheca Wiffeniana. Spanish Reformers of Two Centuries from 1520*. vol. 1. Strasbourg: Trübner, 1874.

Hamilton, R. "Juan de Valdés and Some Renaissance Theories of Language." *BHS* 30 (1953): n. p.

Longhurst, John E. *Erasmus and the Spanish Inquisition: The Case of Juan de Valdés*. Albuquerque: U of New Mexico P, 1950.

Menéndez Pelayo, Marcelino. *Historia de los heterodoxos españoles*. Santander: Aldus, 1947. 3: 187–258.

Ricart, Domingo. *Juan de Valdés y el pensamiento religioso europeo en los siglos XVI y XVII*. Mexico: El Colegio de México, 1958.

Angelo DiSalvo

VALDIVIELSO, José de (1560, Toledo–1638, Madrid), priest, dramatist, and religious poet. Chaplain first to the Archbishop Sandoval y Rojas of Toledo and later to the Cardinal-Infante Ferdinand of Austria, Valdivielso maintained a good relationship with *Cervantes and Lope de *Vega, both of whom praised his poetry. A man of immense erudition, he was indisputably the most popular sacred poet of his age. He is best known for his *Romancero espiritual del Santísimo Sacramento* (1612; Spiritual Ballads on the Most Blessed Sacrament), a collection of brief, sentimental pieces which employed popular ballads and children's songs as the vehicle for religious subject matter. He composed longer works as well, most notably the *Vida, excelencias, y muerte del gloriosísimo patriarca San José* (1604; Life, Merits, and Death of the Most Glorious Patriarch Saint Joseph), written in octavas reales.

There is no question that his strength lay in the composition of songs, brief verses, and short dramatic pieces. Among the best known selections from his *Doce autos sacramentales y dos comedias divinas* (1622; Twelve Sacramental Autos and Two Religious Dramas) are the autos *El peregrino* (The Pilgrim), *El hijo pródigo* (The Prodigal Son), *El hospital de los locos* (The Insane Asylum), *La serrana de Plasencia* (*The Bandit Queen*, 1969), *Psiquis y Cupido* (Cupid and Psyche), and *La amistad en el peligro* (Friendship in Danger). In addition, he published at the insistence of Philip III the *Exposición parafrástica del Psalterio y cánticos del Breviario* (1623; Paraphrase and Exposition of the Psalter and Canticles from the Breviary). The name of Valdivielso is recorded in Lope's *Laurel de Apolo* and in Cervantes's *Viaje del Parnaso*. He is remembered in part for having provided comfort and spiritual nurture to Lope de Vega during the great dramatist's final years. *See also Auto; Octavas*.

BIBLIOGRAPHY

Primary Texts

"*El hospital de los locos*" *y* "*La serrana de Plasencia*." Ed. Jean Louis Flecniakoska. Salamanca: Anaya, 1971.

José de Valdivielso: Teatro completo. Ed. Ricardo Arias and Robert V. Piluso. 2 vols. Madrid: Isla, 1975–77.
Poesías. Ed. J. M. de Cossío. Poesía en la Mano 24. Barcelona: Yunque, 1941.
Psiquis y Cupido. Ed. E. Rull. *Segismundo* 2 (1966): 135–93.
El villano en su rincón. Ed. Wilbur G. Nachtigall. In ''A Critical Edition of José de Valdivielso's *El villano en su rincón* with a Study of the Play's Biblical Sources.'' Diss., U of Iowa, 1969.

English Translations

The Bandit Queen. Richard G. Barnes. In *Three Spanish Sacramental Plays*. Ed. R.G. Barnes. San Francisco: Chandler, 1969.
''Christmas Carol: On the Exposure of the Holy Sacrament'' and ''Ballad of the Epiphany: On the Exposure of the Holy Sacrament.'' Tr. J. M. Cohen. In *The Penguin Book of Spanish Verse*. Rev. ed. By J. M. Cohen. Baltimore: Penguin Books, 1960. 204–8.
''Seguidilla.'' Tr. Thomas Walsh. *Hispanic Anthology*. 1920; rpt. New York: Kraus, 1969. 265–66.

Criticism

Aguirre, J. M. *José de Valdivielso y la poesía religiosa tradicional*. Toledo: Instituto Provincial de Estudios Toledanos, 1965.
Arias, Ricardo. *The Spanish Sacramental Plays*. TWAS 572. Boston: Twayne, 1980. 111–21.
Oberlander, Barbara J. ''The *Autos Sacramentales* of José de Valdivielso: Their Dramatic Theory.'' Diss., Louisiana State U, 1969.
Piluso, Robert V. ''Honor in Valdivielso and Cervantes.'' *KRQ* 17 (1970): 67–81.
Wardropper, Bruce W. *Introducción al teatro religioso del Siglo de Oro: Evolución del auto sacramental antes de Calderón*. Salamanca: Anaya, 1967. 293–320.

C. Maurice Cherry

VALENCIA, Pedro de (1555, Zafra, Badajoz–1620, Madrid), historian and humanist. He was a doctor in law, a disciple of *Arias Montano, an eminent student of Greek and Hebrew, and royal historian for Philip III from 1607 until his death. Pedro de Valencia's multi-faceted writings have preserved the impression of an active, keen critical spirit combining the very best features of a *Renaissance humanist. His most significant work is *Academica sive de judicio erga verum* (1596; On the Criterion of Truth), so lucid a clarification of material in Cicero's *Academicae* that it was reprinted in France 150 years later. Marcelino *Menéndez y Pelayo judged Valencia to be (along with Francisco *Sánchez and Joan Luís *Vives) one of the three key representatives of sixteenth-c. critical thought in Spain.

Of interest also is the unfavorable judgment ''Censura de *Las Soledades y El Polifemo* y obras de don Luis de *Góngora, hecha a su instancia por . . . P. de V.'' (Censure of the *Solitudes* . . . of Góngora, done at his request, by P. de V.) that Valencia composed. He urged Góngora to compose a lighter, more natural poetry. *See also* Humanism.

BIBLIOGRAPHY

Primary Texts

Les Academiques ou des moyens de juger du vrai: ouvrage puise dans les sources; par Pierre Valence. In *Academiques*. By M. T. C. Cicero. (Durand edition). London: P. Vaillant, 1740.

''Censura de *Las Soledades* y *El Polifemo* y obras de don Luis de Góngora. . . .'' *RABM* 3.7 (July 1899): 391–416.

Criticism

Menéndez y Pelayo, Marcelino. ''De los orígenes del criticismo y del escepticismo y especialmente los precursores españoles de Kant.'' *Ensayos de crítica filosófica*. Ed. Enrique Sánchez Reyes. Santander: Artes Gráficas, 1948. 117–216. (See also pp. 235–276 for bio-bibliographical data.)

Popkin, Richard. *The History of Scepticism from Erasmus to Spinoza*. Berkeley: U of California P, 1979.

Maureen Ihrie

VALENTE, José Ángel (1929, Orense–), Galician poet. Although not closely associated with his native Galicia, Valente has one work in the Galician language, *Sete cántigas de alén* (1981; Seven Cantigas from Beyond), in which the compositions gain strength from the silences surrounding the words, and a nostalgic tone gives a sense of graveness to the content.

Chiefly written in Spanish, Valente's poetry seeks to create a feeling of mystery and uneasiness. The author feels form to be important in the conveying of poetic meaning, and this is observed in the manner in which poems are constructed so that a second reading reveals another entire set of interpretive signals. The ambiguities give rise to alternative—or simultaneous—decipherings which also are closely related to the identity of the poetic *I*. Valente's usage of intertextual references contributes to the connotations a poem may have, setting up an interplay that in turn creates a third text for the reader. Many of his works suggest a search for meaning and an introspection of personal experience, although the process is not necessarily expressed in first-person terms. *See also* Galician Literature.

BIBLIOGRAPHY

Primary Texts

Breve son. Madrid: Ciencia Nueva, 1968.

Ensayo sobre Miguel de Molinos. Barcelona: Barral, 1974.

Entrada en materia. Madrid: Cátedra, 1985.

El fin de la edad de plata. Barcelona: Seix Barral, 1973.

El fulgor. Madrid: Cátedra, 1984.

El inocente. Madrid: Joaquín Mortiz, 1970.

Interior con figuras. Barcelona: Barral, 1976.

Mandorla. Madrid: Cátedra, 1982.

Material memoria. Madrid: La Gaya Ciencia, 1979.

La memoria y los signos. Madrid: RO, 1966.

A modo de esperanza. Madrid: Rialp, 1955.
Noventa y nueve poemas. Madrid: Alianza, 1981.
Nueve enunciaciones. Murcia: Begar, 1984.
Las palabras de la tribu. Madrid: Siglo Veintiuno, 1971.
La piedra y el centro. Madrid: Taurus, 1982.
Poesía y poemas. N.p.: Narcea, 1983.
Presentación y memorial para un monumento. N.p.: Poesía para todos, 1970.
Punto cero: poesía 1953–1979. Barcelona: Seix Barral, 1980.
Sete cántigas de alén. La Coruña: Castro, 1981.
Siete representaciones. N.p.: El Bardo, 1967.
Sobre el lugar del canto (1953–1963). N.p.: Literaturasa, 1963.
Tres lecciones de tinieblas. Madrid: La Gaya Ciencia, 1980.

Criticism

Daydí-Tolson, Santiago. *Voces y ecos en la poesía de José Angel Valente*. Lincoln, NE: Society of Spanish and Spanish-American Studies, 1984.
Debicki, Andrew P. "Intertextuality and Reader Response in the Poetry of José Angel Valente, 1967–1970." *HR* 51.3 (Summer 1983): 251–67.
Domínguez Rey, Antonio. "Orfico descenso a los infiernos." *Nueva Estafeta* 55 (June 1983): 81–85.
González-Marín, María Carmen E. "La poesía de José Valente: *Mandorla*: Puerta, quietud, semilla." *Insula* 38.442 (Sept. 1983): 1, 11.
Ugalde, Sharon E. "José Angel Valente's *Material memoria* and the Poetic Process." *Pacific Coast Philology* 18.1–2 (Nov. 1983): 52–58.

Kathleen March

VALENTÍ, Helena (1940, Barcelona–), novelist and translator. She studied literature and became a lecturer in England, where she lived for eleven years. During that period, she was very active in the feminist movement, and did her first writing, in English, for the periodical *Shrew*. She returned to Barcelona, and began to write in Catalan and translate works of literature from English to Castilian and Catalan, including Virginia Woolf and Doris Lessing. She lived for a few years in the coastal village of Cadaqués, and now resides again in Barcelona. In her work, she explores personal relationships and alternative lifestyles with delicacy and frankness. The eleven short stories that comprise *Amor Adult* (1977; Adult Love) focus on situations women often find themselves in and must struggle with—economic dependency, unwanted pregnancies, crises of creativity, frequent separations and non-communicating marriages. She does not answer the questions she poses, but offers great insight into and analysis of the problems of self-identification and intimacy. Some of the same conflicts appear in her novel *La solitud d'Anna* (1981; The Solitude of Anna), but the emphasis is on the balance between creativity and relationships. The world portrayed is one where the difficulty of self-affirmation drives some to seek power or to abuse, while others become cruel and infantile, or retreat into solitude and hide behind facades.

BIBLIOGRAPHY

Primary Texts

Amor adult. Barcelona: Edicions 62, 1977.
La dona errant. Barcelona: n.p., 1986.
La solitud d'Anna. Barcelona: Edicions 62, 1981.

Kathleen McNerney

VALERA, Cipriano de (1532?, Seville–?, ?), scholar, monk, Protestant reformer from the monastery of San Isidro del Campo. Originally of the Hieronymite order, this monastery became a center of Protestantism during the middle of the sixteenth c. The monastery's reformist tendencies incurred the wrath of the *Inquisition, which condemned many of the clerics. Following persecution of the Inquisition, Valera fled to Geneva with eleven other friars, and he later emigrated to England. He and his fellow fugitives were burned in effigy in Seville in 1562.

Valera wrote various religious tracts, among them *Los dos tratados del Papa y de la misa* (1588; *Two treatises: the first . . .* , 1600). His most renowned work, however, was a translation of the Bible into Castilian. Based on the 1569 Spanish translation by Casiodoro de *Reina, Valera's translation was published in Antwerp in 1602 and enjoyed a wider circulation. The text has been modernized and is still distributed today. *See also* Bible in Spain.

BIBLIOGRAPHY

Primary Texts

Los dos tratados del papa, i de la misa. Madrid: L. de Usoz y Río, 1851.
Los Hechos de los apóstoles. London: Sociedad bíblica británica y extranjera, 1914.

English Translations

A full view of popery . . . & . . . A confutation of the mass. . . . London: Bernard Lintott, 1704.
Two treatises: the first, Of the lives of the popes, and their doctrine. The Second, of the masse. . . . Tr. John Golburne. London: John Harison, 1600.

Criticism

Hauben, Paul J. *Three Spanish Heretics and the Reformation*. Geneva: Droz, 1967.

Deborah Compte

VALERA, Diego de (1412, Cuenca?–1488?, Puerto de Santa María, Cádiz), historian, courtier and moralist. The son of Alonso García Chirino and Violante López, as a youth Valera was a page to John II (1427) and Prince Henry (1429). He led an active life and faithfully served and counseled the king. Valera fought at the battle of La Higuerela and was present on the expedition to the Kingdom of Granada in 1431. He traveled throughout Europe, was involved in the politics of the day, and served as castle governor for the Duke of Medinaceli in Puerto de Santa María until his death.

A prolific writer, Valera is most acclaimed for his treatise on moral, political and historical subjects which reflect in large measure the preoccupations and interests of the period. The *Epístolas* (Epistles) contains advice directed to monarchs; the *Crónica abreviada o Valeriana* (1482; Abridged or Valerian Chronicle) is a world history based on previous chronicles; and the *Memorial de diversas fazañas* (Memorial of Various Events) is a chronicle of the reign of Henry IV. Valera's major work, the *Crónica de los Reyes Católicos* (Chronicle of the Catholic Monarchs), is a continuation of the *Memorial*. It encompasses the period between 1477 and 1488 and can be divided into two sections: the war of Portugal, in which the influence of *Palencia's *Décadas* may be seen, and the war of Granada, in which Valera may have used the letters of the Marquis of Cádiz. His historical treatises often included selections from earlier writers, excerpts from contemporary documents, and personal recollections.

Other works by Valera include *Tratado de las armas o de los rieptos y desafíos* (c. 1515; Treatise on Arms or on Challenges and Duels); *Providencia contra Fortuna* (1494; Providence versus Fortune); *Espejo de verdadera nobleza* (Mirror of True Nobility); *Doctrinal de príncipes* (Catechism for Princes) and *Defensa de virtuosas mujeres* (Defense of Virtuous Women); *Arbol de las Batallas* (Tree of the Battles); and *Ceremonial de príncipes* (1462–1467?; Book of Ceremonies for Princes). Valera also wrote the following verses: *Letanía* (Litany) and *Salmos penitenciales* (Penitential Psalms).

BIBLIOGRAPHY

Primary Texts

Crónica de los Reyes Católicos. Ed. Juan de Carriazo. RFE Anejo 8. Madrid: J. Molina, 1927.

Epístolas de Mosén Diego de Valera. Ed. José A. de Balenchana. Madrid: M. Ginesta, 1878. Includes five other treatises.

Memorial de diversas fazañas. Ed. Juan de Mata Carriazo. BAE 70: 299–377.

See also BAE 116, ed. Mario Penna, for other treatises.

Criticism

Laurencin, M. de. Mosén Diego de Valera y el "Arbol de Batallas." *BRAH* 76 (1920): n.p.

Deborah Compte

VALERA, Juan (1824, Cabra, Córdoba–1905, Madrid), novelist and critic. He was the son of don José Valera and doña Dolores Alcalá-Galiano, Marquise de la Paniega, whose family hailed from the Andalusian towns of Cabra and Doña Mencía. Valera studied in Cabra and later at the seminary in Málaga (1837–40). He pursued a law degree at the Colegio del Sacro Monte in Granada and the Universities of Granada and Madrid (1841–44). During these early days, he dabbled in prose and poetry, publishing a volume of verse entitled *Ensayos poéticos* (1844; Poetic Essays), an effort subsidized by his father. No one bought it. In Madrid he joined the social whirl, exploiting his reputation as a poet and indulging in his own worldly tastes, with a display of his talents as a Don Juan (1845–46). By 1847 he had decided upon a diplomatic career, and as an attaché accompanied the Duke of *Rivas to Naples. He enjoyed himself immensely there, caught up on his reading, learned some Greek, made friends with the *costumbrista* writer *Estébanez Calderón, and fell in love with Lucía Paladi, the Marquise de Bedmar, whom Valera called ''The Lady Death'' for her extreme pallor. In 1849 he returned home and was promptly disillusioned with the pretentious vulgarity of Madrid's social and intellectual life. From 1850 to 1866 he traveled extensively as a diplomat, representing his country in Lisbon, Rio de Janeiro, Dresden, Russia, and Frankfurt. It was in Rio where he met his future wife (and cause of much unhappiness in his home life), Dolores Delavat. They married in 1867. By the 1850s he was getting serious about his writing, producing newspaper articles and criticism. His unfinished novel, *Mariquita y Antonio*, appeared as a serial in *El Contemporáneo* (1861; The Contemporary Journal), and that same year he was elected to the *Academia Española. He became active in politics, serving as a deputy to the Spanish Parliament in 1858; as subsecretary of state in 1868; and by 1881, had become a lifetime senator. From 1881 to 1895 he was back in diplomatic harness. His peripatetic career took him to Lisbon, Washington, Brussels, and Vienna. In Washington, he became involved with a young woman of society, Katherine Lee Bayard, who killed herself three days after he received his transfer orders (1886). The year before, his son Carlos had died of typhus in Madrid. The year 1873 marks Valera's first completed novel, the justly renowned *Pepita Jiménez*; he was to cultivate the novel throughout the 1870s and, later, in the 1890s. In his final years, despite blindness and the infirmities of old age, he continued to be intellectually alert, writing until his last breath.

Although Valera's poetic efforts reflect a classical formation and spirit, they are, for the most part, negligible. His criticism, though, is often delightful, ranging far and wide, from philosophical and religious essays, such as his comments in 1856 on *Donoso Cortés's *Ensayo sobre el catolicismo* (Essay on Catholicism), ''De la doctrina del progreso'' (1857–59; On the Doctrine of Progress), and ''Sobre las enseñanzas de la Filosofía en las universidades'' (1862; On the Teaching of Philosophy in Universities); historical and political studies, as for example, ''España y Portugal'' (1861–62; Spain and Portugal), ''De la revolución en Italia'' (1860; On Revolution in Italy), and ''La revolución y la libertad religiosa en España'' (1869; Revolution and Religious Liberty in Spain); to the most significant essays, his literary criticism, appearing in book form as *Estudios críticos sobre literatura, política y costumbres de nuestros días* (1864; Critical Studies on Literature, Politics, and Customs of Our Day), *Disertaciones y juicios literarios* (1878; Dissertations and Literary Judgments), *Apuntes sobre el nuevo arte de escribir novelas* (1887; Notes on the New Art of Writing Novels), *Nuevos estudios críticos* (1888; New Critical Studies), *Cartas americanas* (1889; American Letters), *Nuevas cartas americanas* (1890; New American Letters), and *Ecos argentinos* (1901; Argentine Echoes). A well-informed, genial man of letters, Valera could write persuasively on almost anything, displaying an apparently benevolent stance toward the intellectual and literary figures of his day.

His staunch defense of the Krausists, for example, is typical of his conciliatory public attitude. His private correspondence, however, reveals a much more biting, harsh attitude toward many of those same literary figures. He was a marvelous letter writer. See, for example, the *Epistolario de Valera y Menéndez Pelayo, 1877–1905*, ed. M. Artigas Ferrando y P. Sáinz Rodríguez (1946); *Correspondencia de Don Juan Valera 1859–1905*, ed. C. DeCoster (1956); and *Cartas íntimas (1853–1897)*, ed. Sáenz de Tejada Benvenuti (1974). Valera also wrote several short stories—"Parsondes" (1859), "El pájaro verde" (1860; The Green Bird), "Garuda o la cigüeña blanca" (1896; Garuda, or the White Stork), etc.; dramatic pieces, such as "Asclepigenia" and "La venganza de Atahualpa" (Atahualpa's Revenge) in *Tentativas dramáticas* (1879; Exercises in Drama); and translations, notably, of Longus's *Daphnis and Chloe* (1880). His Complete Works were issued in 53 volumes (Alemana and J. Sánchez de Ocaña, 1905–35); and later in 3 volumes (Aguilar, 1947–49).

Valera's most delightful writing is in his fiction. In his first period, 1873–79, he produced his finest novel, *Pepita Jiménez* (1874; tr. 1886, 1964; see ed. of M. Azaña, 1971), *Las ilusiones del doctor Faustino* (1875; The Illusions of Dr. Faustino; see ed. C. DeCoster, 1970), *El Comendador Mendoza* (1877; *Commander Mendoza,* 1893), *Pasarse de listo* (1878; Don Braulio, tr. 1892), and *Doña Luz* (1879; tr. 1891). *Pepita Jiménez*, as M. Azaña delicately points out, represents in Valera "an effort to recover himself, a folding into his inner garden." It is an elegantly told narrative, recounting with a very fine view to irony, the conflict between spiritual and worldly love in its hero-seminarian, Luis. His second novel, *Las ilusiones del doctor Faustino*, is an ambitious, though diffuse, effort, whose theme, the analysis of a generation (his own) and the harmful effect *Romanticism had on it, is, for the times, significant. *El Comendador Mendoza*, a charming work, centers on a favorite theme of Valera, the relationship between an old man and a young girl (also found in *Pepita Jiménez* and the major plot ingredient of *Juanita la larga*). *Pasarse de listo* is, undoubtedly, Valera's weakest novel, written mostly for the money for which he always had need. And in *Doña Luz*—for J. F. Montesinos, a *Pepita Jiménez* in reverse—the novelist takes yet another look at the power of physical love when that driving need comes into conflict with religious duty and belief. In Valera's second period of novel writing, 1895–99, he came out with the superb *Juanita la larga* (1896; Formidable Juanita), *Genio y figura* (1897; Rafaela), and *Morsamor* (1899; see ed. J. B. Avalle-Arce, 1970). Montesinos has called *Juanita la larga* "the last classical idyll of Spanish literature," though, in truth, it is less an idyll than a gently ironic, burlesque version of that universal genre, the fairy tale. *Genio y figura*, not one of Valera's best, contains his least believable heroine, Rafaela; while *Morsamor* represents an interesting attempt to create a historical allegory of Spain's past, focusing on the classic Spanish theme of *el desengaño*, or disillusionment.

For Valera the novel is a poetic genre, the child of imagination. "The only end, the sole object of poetry," he wrote, "is the attainment of the beautiful, the rare, the bewildering, the fugitive of nature in an eternal, refined and resonant art.'' Art then has its own justification. For this reason, he rejects the polemical thesis novel of his times, the realist social novel, and the experimental novel of *Naturalism. Valera isn't interested in the ''human document'' or a ''slice of life.'' In truth, he is far more of an idealist than most of his contemporary artists, *Pérez Galdós, *Clarín, *Pereda, and so on. Yet he vehemently disdains the excesses of Romanticism, seeing in it the seeds of the naturalist movement. Though his repeatedly stated aim is to entertain, and only to entertain, with his fictions, despite all this, the novelist does teach us something, albeit indirectly, for his analysis of human conduct frequently masks, and rather thinly at that, bitter truths about the duplicitous nature of man and his inner drives. As a psychological realist, Valera is unequaled in his century. And as a stylist, he reigns supreme. His prose, elegant and classical in inspiration, flows smoothly, gently ruffled by the subtle, even subversive irony of his wit and his penetrating glimpses into man's fundamental egotism, his capacity for self-deception, and his all-encompassing desire for love. As Azaña observes, ''erotic pleasure in the novels of Valera, as in the heart of the novelist himself, rises up to become the dominant theme in life. It is the necessary condition to happiness.''

BIBLIOGRAPHY

Primary Texts

Doña Luz. Madrid: Biblioteca Nueva, n.d.
Genio y figura. Ed. Cyrus C. DeCoster. Madrid: Cátedra, 1975.
Las ilusiones del doctor Faustino. Ed. Cyrus C. DeCoster. Madrid: Castalia, 1970.
Juanita la larga. 5th ed. Madrid: Aguilar, 1963.
Morsamor. Ed. Juan Bautista Avalle-Arce. Barcelona: Labor, 1970.
Obras completas. 3 vols. Madrid: Aguilar, 1947–49.
Obras desconocidas. Ed. Cyrus C. DeCoster. Madrid: Castalia, 1965.
Pepita Jiménez. Ed. Manuel Azaña. 7th ed. Madrid: Espasa-Calpe, 1971.
Pepita Jiménez. Juanita la Larga. Ed. Juana de Ontañón. 6th ed. México: Porrúa, 1975.

English Translations

Commander Mendoza. Tr. Mary J. Serrano. New York: Appleton, 1893.
Don Braulio. Tr. Clara Bell. New York: Appleton, 1892. (*Pasarse de listo*)
Doña Luz. Tr. Mary J. Serrano. New York: Appleton, 1891.
Pepita Jiménez. Tr. Harriet de Onís. Great Neck, NY: Barron's, 1964.
See also Robert S. Rudder, *The Literature of Spain in English Translation. A Bibliography* (New York: Frederick Ungar, 1975), pp. 331–32, for other translations.

Criticism

Azaña, Manuel. *Ensayos sobre Valera*. Ed. Juan Marichal. Madrid: Alianza, 1971.
Bermejo Marcos, Manuel. *Don Juan Valera, crítico literario*. Madrid: Gredos, 1968.
Bravo-Villasante, Carmen. *Vida de Juan Valera*. Madrid: Magisterio Español, 1974.
DeCoster, Cyrus C. *Juan Valera*. New York: Twayne, 1974.
Fishtine [Helman], Edith. *Don Juan Valera, the Critic*. Bryn Mawr, PA: Bryn Mawr College, 1933.

Krynen, Jean. *L'Esthétisme de Juan Valera*. Acta Salmanticensia, 2. Salamanca: Universidad de Salamanca, 1946.
Lott, Robert E. *Language and Psychology in "Pepita Jiménez."* Urbana: U of Illinois P, 1970.
Maurin, Mario. "Valera y la ficción encadenada." *Mundo Nuevo*, no. 14 (1967): 35–44; no. 15 (1967): 37–44.
Montesinos, José F. *Valera o la ficción libre*. Madrid: Castalia, 1957.
Valis, Noël M. "The Use of Deceit in Valera's *Juanita la Larga*." *HR* 49 (1981): 317–27.
Whiston, James. *Valera: Pepita Jiménez*. London: Grant and Cutler, 1977.

Noël M. Valis

VALLE, Adriano del (1895, Seville–1957, Madrid), poet. Called "el más rubeniano" (the most like Rubén Darío) of the Seville group by Guillermo de *Torre, del Valle composed poems of the *modernista* sort, but the freedom of form that is also present in his work links him with *ultraísmo*. From those avant-garde images, which share motifs with his modernist writing—the sea, stars, barbarian kings, exotic and Hellenic characters—del Valle's less audacious creation led to a neo-popularism of classical structure.

Del Valle, with Isaac del Vando-Villar, founded the Sevillian journal *Grecia* (1918–20), said to be the first to publish ultraist poems. With Fernando *Villalón and Buendía, he founded *Papel de Aleluyas* (1927) in Huelva, and directed *Santo y seña* (1940–42) in Madrid. A collaborator of *Cervantes*, *Reflector* and *Alfar*, del Valle wrote the chronicle of the first public ultraist presentation (*velada*) held May 2, 1919, in Seville by those of *Grecia*. In 1933 he received the National Prize for Literature for *Mundo sin tranvías* (1933; World without Streetcars), and in 1941, the José Antonio Primo de Rivera National Literary Prize for *Arpa Fiel* (1941; Faithful Harp), for which the following year he was also awarded the Fastenrath Prize of the *Academia Española. In November 1939 and in 1945 he was the subject of a national homage held in Madrid. He participated in the activities of the group Alforjas para la Poesía (Knapsacks of Poetry). *See also* Modernism.

BIBLIOGRAPHY

Primary Texts

Arpa Fiel. Madrid: Colección "Santo y Seña," 1941.
Egloga de Gabriel Miró y Fábula del Peñón de Ifach. Madrid: Agora, 1957.
Los gozos del río. Barcelona: Apolo, 1940.
La Innombrable. Málaga: Antonio Gutiérrez, 1954.
Lyra Sacra. Seville: Tomás Alvarez, 1939.
Misa de Alba en Fátima y Gozos de San Isidro. Madrid: Aleto, 1955.
Mundo sin tranvías. Madrid: Ministerio de Instrucción Pública, 1933.
Obra poética. Madrid: Nacional, 1977.
Obra póstuma. Barcelona: Plaza y Janés, 1971.
Oda náutica a Cádiz. Cádiz: Salvador Repeto, 1957.

Primavera portátil. Paris, Madrid, Buenos Aires: Amigos del Libro de Arte, 1934.
Sus mejores poesías. Barcelona: Bruguera, 1955.

Criticism

''Adriano del Valle.'' *Poesía Española*, new series 63 (Oct. 1957): 13–15.
Alonso, Dámaso. Prologue to *Arpa Fiel*. Madrid: Afrodisio Aguado, 1941.
Gómez de la Serna. ''Adriano del Valle.'' In *Obra poética*. Madrid: Nacional, 1977, 395–401.
Videla, Gloria. *El ultraísmo*. Madrid: Gredos, 1964.

Kathleen March

VALLE-INCLÁN, Ramón María del (1866, Villanueva de Arosa, Pontevedra–1936, Santiago de Compostela), author. Very little is known about his early life, and his autobiography, *Alma española* (1903; Spanish Soul), is filled with unlikely accounts. He studied law for a brief period at the U of Santiago de Compostela, but was forced to abandon his education upon the death of his father, who was also known for his writing. He sought employment in Madrid at the liberal newspaper *El Globo*, resided for a time in Mexico, where he collaborated on *El Correo Español* and *El Universal*, returned to his native Galicia, and appeared on the literary scene in Madrid in 1895. He was both a loner and a man who relished the attention he attracted to himself by the conspicuous, outlandish appearance he cultivated: he allowed his hair and beard to grow very long and wore tiny round spectacles and a tall hat. His wit enlivened the literary circles of the cafés, and his dramatic and outrageous behavior was a cause célèbre for forty years. His behavior gave rise to scandal when, as a result of a brawl in which one of his arms was pierced by a fragment of glass, he developed a gangrenous infection which necessitated the amputation of the arm. He served as director of the Academia de Bellas Artes de Roma during the Republic. In 1907 he married Josefina Blanco, an actress with whom he had several children. They legally separated in 1932.

Politically a Carlist in the beginning, he later moved toward the left, attacking the dictatorship of the Falange, for which he was imprisoned several times. In general, however, he remained aloof from politics, as well as from all other establishment institutions—religion, social customs, literature and art forms. He was contemptuous of bourgeois values, hypocrisy, pettiness, materialism, and conformity of any sort.

Works

Valle-Inclán wrote fictional narrative, dialogued novels, dramatic works, verse plays, poetry, essays on various subjects, and a quasi-theoretical volume on aesthetics. Because his works have been published in diverse forms and combinations and under different titles, it is difficult to classify them by date.

Valle-Inclán's production is considered to have three stages. The first is the aristocratic *modernista* period (*Modernism), of exotic, idealized settings, wherein his native Galicia is portrayed in misty shadows of past glory. The plots are romantic, the language chosen for its sound, with fresh, though not shocking, imagery. Irony, however, is never absent; his early works are a light-hearted parody of *Romanticism. The intermediate period is a transitional one, in which action becomes more intense and dramatic, displaying social commitment in its presentation of more highly developed and more varied characters, some of them from lower levels of society, especially rural types. Progressively, popular elements displace the refinement of the previous stage. Galicia now appears in its actual condition—decaying, rancid, poor. Harmony disappears. Artifice gives way to direct, popular dialogue. The final period is in one sense a return to the first: it is completely artificial—an aesthetic style in which everything is distorted, only now in a grotesque manner. In another way, it is the culmination of a trajectory away from *modernismo*: the characters are absurd, exaggerated figures, morally degraded, victims of the social order and of one another—beggars, thieves, madmen, prostitutes, the physically and mentally handicapped. Their situations are hopeless, their humanity diminished, if not totally absent. They appear as mechanized puppets or as animals. The tone is bitter, the outlook negative. Its most salient trait is the distance from which the events are presented: the fictional world and the characters are seen at a great remove, with disdain, pity and contempt by an observer who is socially, morally, and intellectually superior, and who is free of their limitations.

Narrative

Valle-Inclán's first book, *Femeninas* (1895; *Femininities*), a collection of six love stories published in Pontevedra, evinces the influence of French writers. But never absent in his early works are Galician legends and culture. *Epitalamio* (1897; Nuptial Song) and *Corte de amor* (1903; Court of Love), distinctly erotic in nature, anticipate in the style of his first series of novels, the four *Sonatas*, subtitled *Memorias del Marqués de Bradomín (The Pleasant Memoirs of the Marquis of Bradomin*, 1924). These, the most popular of his works, mark the first period of his literary greatness and are exemplary pieces of *modernista* prose. The sensuous, elaborate descriptions of exotic places rank with the best of European *décadent* authors. There is little narrative continuity in the *Sonatas*; they are episodic in structure, representing four phases in the life of the narrator—youth, plenitude, maturity, and old age. They are unified by the single perspective of the self-described "ugly, Catholic and sentimental" Marquis of Bradomín, "the most admirable of the Don Juans," and by their style—abounding in literary allusions, a nostalgic and idealized view of the past, a longing for refinement and exquisiteness, and a melancholy tone. One memoir appeared each year from 1902 to 1905: *Sonata de otoño* (Autumn Sonata), *Sonata de estío* (Summer Sonata), *Sonata de primavera* (Springtime Sonata), and *Sonata de invierno* (Winter Sonata). The eroticism of the earlier stories, overlaid with romantic sentiments, have been viewed as soft-core pornography. They are, however, interlaced with delightful irony and humor, although the characters are more than parodies of romantic archetypes: the multiplicity of perspectives from which they are presented and their inevitably metafictional qualities serve to puncture with light, witty cynicism, most of the romantic postures of the time and of our own. *Jardín Umbrío* (1903; Shady Garden) is another collection of short stories. *Flor de santidad*, subtitled *Historia milenaria* (1904; Flower of Sanctity: A Millenial Legend), is a short, lyrical novel set in rural Galicia, a mythical vision of that province. The absence of historical markers imparts a medieval aspect to this strange tale of primitive emotions, religion, exorcism, superstition, and mysterious events. A second series, three novels in dialogue form subtitled *comedias bárbaras*: *Aguila de blasón* (1907; The Emblazoned Eagle), *Romance de lobos* (1908; Ballad of the Wolves), and *Cara de plata* (1923; Silver Face), set in a semi-feudal, anachronistic world, are distinct in character, but linked by a single protagonist, don Juan Manuel Montenegro, who also appears in other works by Valle-Inclán. The best of these is *Romance de lobos*, a tale of remorse, ingratitude, vengeance, and despair that resonates with echoes of *King Lear*. A powerful social message also emerges, as a mob of beggars proclaim the dead lord as their father, while his parricide sons speculate on the likely outcome of their actions. The author's Carlism is reflected in his novels on the Carlist wars: *Los cruzados de la causa* (1908; Crusaders of the Cause), *El resplendor de la hoguera* (1909; The Glare of the Bonfire) and *Gerifaltes de antaño* (1909; Gerfalcons of Yore). His novels after 1912 are more penetrating and incisive; and there is a greater emphasis on dialogue. This trend attained its zenith in a genre he termed *esperpento*, which creates absurd and mechanical characters described in the most negative manner possible: their movements jerky, their appearance and speech are caricatures. One of them defines the *esperpento* as a view of Spain in a distorted mirror. *Esperpentos* comprise both narrative and dramatic works, such as *Luces de Bohemia* (1924; *Bohemian Lights*, 1976), *Los cuernos de don Friolera*, (1925; The Horns of the Cuckold, Don Friolera), *Retablo de la avaricia, la lujuria y la muerte* (1927; Portraits of Avarice, Lust and Death), *Las galas del difunto* (1926; The Regalia of the Deceased), and *La hija del capitán* (1927; The Captain's Daughter), which was seized by the government for its biting sarcasm aimed at the military and the government as a whole. The esperpentic vision is present in three novels: *Tirano Banderas: Novela de Tierra Caliente* (1926; *The Tyrant (Tirano Banderas): A Novel of Warm Lands*, 1929), *La corte de los milagros* (1927; The Court of Miracles) and *Viva mi dueño* (1928; Long Live My Lord), the latter two published as the series *El ruedo ibérico* (The Iberian Cycle), and his last work, ''El trueno dorado'' (Golden Thunder), published posthumously in 1936.

Drama

Valle-Inclán's theatrical works are all highly dramatic, and most were shocking to the majority of theater-goers of the time. His first play was *Cenizas* (1899; Ashes), revised under the title *El yermo de las almas* (1908; The Barrenness of Souls). *La cabeza del dragón* (1914; *The Dragon's Head*, 1919) is a humorous farce set in a fairy-tale world reminiscent of novels of chivalry, complete with magical events and anachronisms, such as references to the Indies, automobiles, and petroleum. *Divinas palabras* (1920; Divine Words), a critical, social view of Galicia, presents a cross-section of characters of the sort found in a *picaresque novel and is a masterpiece in its presentation of popular speech. His verse plays include *Farsa italiana de la enamorada del rey* (1920; Farce of the Girl Who Loved the King), about an idealistic young girl who idolizes an elderly king until, disillusioned, she marries a puppeteer. Two others, both in *modernista* tradition, are the lyrical *Cuento de abril* (1909; April Tale), marked by the frivolity and artifice of that movement—the exile of the gallant troubadour for stealing a kiss from the princess, a setting filled with peacocks, nymphs, fountains, ladies in waiting, and a Court of Love, and nymphs. *La Marquesa Rosalinda* (1913; The Marchioness Rosalinda) adds an ironic perspective to the preciosity of the setting. *Voces de gesta* (1912; Epic Voices) is a verse play set in a timeless Galicia, wherein a medieval quality is produced by the use of archaic language and the descriptions of the landscape. We are reminded of the *cantigas de serrana* of the *Arcipreste de Hita or the Marquis of *Santillana.

It is tragic in both its vision and its form: the story of a shepherdess who is raped and blinded by a captain who, ten years later, murders their child from that act. She, in turn, kills him and eventually presents his head to the king. Overlaid upon the mythified setting is the Carlist theme.

Five dramatic works dealing with the basest human passions were published in 1927 in a collection titled *Retablo de la avaricia, la lujuria y la muerte*: *El embrujado* (1913; The Bewitched); two puppet plays, *La rosa de papel* (1924; The Paper Rose); and *La cabeza del bautista* (1924; The Head of the Baptist); two *autos* for silhouettes (*Ligazón* [1926; Liaison] and *Sacrilegio* [1924; *Sacrilege*]). *Farsa y licencia de la reina castiza* (1920; Farce of the Pure-blooded Queen), a mordant attack on Queen Isabel II, portrays the queen and her court as vulgar caricatures.

In a class, each unto itself, are *La media noche: Visión estelar de un momento de guerra 1917* (1917; Midnight: A Stellar Vision of a Moment during the War) and *La lámpara maravillosa* (1916; *The Lamp of Marvels*, 1986), an esoteric work in which Valle-Inclán expounded theoretical views of language and literature, aesthetics in general; described the artist as a mystic whose three *vías* are not the familiar *purgative*, *illuminative*, and *unitive*, but painful love, joyous love, and attainment of oneness with Eternal Beauty; and confessed his interest in and practice of the occult.

Poetry

The evolution of Valle-Inclán's poetry is thematic as well as stylistic. Some of his early poems may be classified as *modernista*, while others create a simpler vision of the Spanish landscape akin to those of *Machado Ruiz. They first appeared in three collections, *Aromas de leyenda* (1907; Legendary Aromas), *La pipa de Kif* (1919; The Hashish Pipe), and *El pasajero* (1920; The Passenger), which were later published under the title *Claves líricas* (1930; Lyrical Keys). There are also loose poems. Although the influence of Darío, Baudelaire, Verlaine, and Rimbaud is evident in *Aromas de leyenda*, Valle-Inclán's Modernism is distinctly his own. Medieval motifs abound. An idealized Galicia—soft, misty, pastoral, with windmills, farm animals, fields, country estates—is created by means of sensory images—the smell of hay, the sound of church bells.

La pipa de Kif is more visual in its imagery, its verses are acrobatic, playful. Its attitude is ironic, iconoclastic, devoid of sentimentality and transcendent concerns. There is also a focus on the bizarre: caricatures, such motifs as masks, the circus, and an herbalist shop which suggests the occult; and an artistic evocation of the dream states produced by opium. A synesthetic image (''el amarillo olor del yodoformo'' [the yellow odor of chloroform]) appears in a poem describing the sensations caused by chloroform.

Animals are given human thought: in ''Fin de carnaval,'' dogs lament the sins of humans. Parody is used to demythify everything from the aesthetics of *modernismo* to the academy in general. *La pipa de Kif* may be described as a verse form of the *esperpento.*

The thematic variety of the poems in *El pasajero* would indicate that they were written at different periods. While still exhibiting many *modernista* themes and style, they are more serious and conceptual, more intimate and symbolic—more preoccupied with existential matters such as the passage of time, nostalgia for the brevity of a life that is threatened by the imminence of death. While the motif of the journey expressed in the title is reminiscent of the meditative poems of Machado, there is in *El pasajero* a sort of magical overtone, a yearning to understand the mysteries of the universe akin to the mystical and esoteric ideas expressed in *La lámpara maravillosa.* Each collection expresses a different attitude toward life.

BIBLIOGRAPHY

Primary Texts

Obras completas. 2nd ed. Madrid: Plenitud, 1952.
Obras escogidas. Madrid: Aguilar, 1974.
Teatro selecto. Intro. A. N. Zahareas. Madrid: Escelicer, 1969.
Tirano Banderas. Ed., intro. A. Zamora Vicente. Madrid: Espasa-Calpe, 1978.
El trueno dorado. Prol. G. Fabra Barreiro. Madrid: Nostromo, 1975.

English Translations

Autobiography, Aesthetics, Aphorisms. Ed., tr., intro. R. Lima. N.p.: n.p., 1966.
The Dragon's Head. Tr. M. Heywood Broun. Boston: Badger, 1919.
The Lamp of Marvels. Tr. R. Lima. West Stockbridge, MA: Lindisfarne P, 1986.
Luces de bohemia; Bohemian lights; esperpento. Tr. A. Zahareas and G. Gillespie. Intro. A. Zahareas. Austin: U of Texas P, 1976. English and Spanish.
The Pleasant Memoirs of the Marquis of Bradomin. Tr. M. Heywood Broun and T. Walsh. New York: Harcourt Brace, 1924.
The Tyrant (Tirano Banderas): A Novel of Warm Lands. Tr. M. Pavitt. New York: Hold, 1929.

Criticism

Alonso, Amado. ''Estructura de las *Sonatas* de Valle-Inclán'' and ''La musicalidad de la prosa en Valle-Inclán.'' In *Materia y forma en poesía.* Madrid: Gredos, 1955.
Díaz-Plaja, Guillermo. *Las estéticas de Valle-Inclán.* Madrid: Gredos, 1965.

Fernández Almagro, Melchor. *Vida y literatura de Valle-Inclán*. 2nd ed. Madrid: Taurus, 1966.
Gómez de la Serna, Ramón. *Don Ramón María del Valle-Inclán*. Buenos Aires: Espasa-Calpe, 1933.
Gómez-Marín, José Antonio. *La idea de sociedad en Valle-Inclán*. Madrid: Taurus, 1967.
Gullón, Ricardo, ed. *Valle-Inclán: Centennial Studies*. Austin: U of Texas P, 1968.
Homenaje a Valle-Inclán. *CH* 199–200 (1966).
Lado, Maria Dolores. *Las guerras carlistas y el reinado isabelino en las obras de Ramón del Valle-Inclán*. Gainesville: U of Florida P, 1966.
Lima, Robert. *An Annotated Bibliography of Ramón del Valle-Inclán*. University Park: Pennsylvania State UP, 1972.
Lyon, John. *The Theater of Valle-Inclán*. Cambridge and New York: Cambridge UP, 1984.
March, María Eugenia. *Forma e idea de los "esperpentos" de Valle-Inclán*. Madrid: Castalia, 1969.
Phillips, Allen W., ed., Introduction to the *Sonatas*. Mexico: Porrúa, 1969.
Risco, Antonio. *La estética de Valle-Inclán en los esperpentos y en el "Ruedo Ibérico."* Madrid: Gredos, 1966.
———. *El demiurgo y su mundo: Hacia un nuevo enfoque en la obra de Valle-Inclán*. Madrid: Gredos, 1977.
Rubia Barcia, José. *A Biobibliography and Iconography of Valle-Inclán*. Berkeley, CA: U of California P, 1960.
Saz, Agustín del. *El teatro de Valle-Inclán*. Barcelona: Gráfica, 1950.
Sender, Ramón. *Valle-Inclán y la dificultad de la tragedia*. Madrid: Gredos, 1965.
Smith, Verity. *Ramón del Valle-Inclán*. New York: Twayne, 1973.
Soriano, Ignacio. "*La lámpara maravillosa*, clave de los esperpentos." *La Torre* 62 (1962): 144–50.
Speratti-Piñero, Emma Susana. *De "Sonata de Otoño" al esperpento: Aspectos del arte de Valle-Inclán*. London: Tamesis, 1968.
Zahareas, Anthony, ed. *Ramón del Valle-Inclán, An Appraisal of His Life and Works*. New York: Las Américas, 1968.
Zamora Vicente, Alonso. *Las "Sonatas" de Ramón del Valle-Inclán*. 3rd ed. Madrid: Gredos, 1966.
———. *La realidad esperpéntica (Aproximación a Luces de Bohemia)*. Madrid: Gredos, 1967.

Esther Nelson

VALLÉS, Francisco (1524, Covarrubias, Burgos–1592, Burgos), physician, philosopher. Personal physician to Philip II, he composed various medical commentaries on works of Galenus and Hippocrates, and wrote several philosophical works, the most important of which was the *Sacra philosophia* (1587; Sacred Philosophy). *Ferrater Morá describes Vallés's thought as an eclectic blend of Aristotle, scholasticism, and some elements of skepticism. His nicknames were El divino Vallés (The Divine Vallés) and El Galeno español (The Spanish Galenus).

BIBLIOGRAPHY

Primary Text

De sacra philosophia. Lugduni: Soubron, 1622.

Criticism

Ferrater Móra, J. *Diccionario de filosofía.* 5th ed. Buenos Aires: Sudamericana, 1965.
Ortega, E., and B. Marcos. *Francisco de Vallés (el divino).* Madrid: Clásica, 1914.
Solana, M. *Historia de la filosofía española. Epoca del Renacimiento (siglo XVI).* Madrid: Real Academia de Ciencias, 1941. 3: 297–347.

VALVERDE DE AMUSCO, Juan (sixteenth c., Amusco, Palencia–?), distinguished physician and anatomist. He pursued studies in humanities and philosophy in Valladolid and studied medicine with Realdo Colombo in Padua. Valverde was also the personal physician of Cardinal Juan de Toledo, who later became Archbishop of Santiago de Compostela. His highly esteemed *Historia de la composición del cuerpo humano* (1556; History of the Composition of the Human Body) attests to a direct knowledge of human anatomy. He also wrote *De Animi et corporis sanitate tuenda* (1552; Of the Healthy Maintenance of the Soul and Body). Both books appeared in various editions in Latin, Spanish and Italian. Valverde's works are of literary value as well as scientific interest.

BIBLIOGRAPHY

Primary Texts

Historia de la composición del cuerpo humano. Rome: Salamanca y Lutrerij, 1556.
De Animi et corporis sanitate tuenda. Paris: n.p., 1552.

Catherine Larson

VARELA, Lorenzo (1917, La Habana–1978, Madrid), Galician poet. The son of Galician emigrants, Lorenzo Varela returned at a very young age to Lugo. In 1935 he went to Madrid, where he studied, wrote for the newspaper *El Sol* (The Sun) and, among other activities, participated in PAN (Poetas Andantes y Navegantes; Traveling and Sailing Poets). After taking part in the Civil War, he was forced into exile. In Mexico he founded and co-directed the journal *Romance*, and founded *Taller*. In 1941 he established residence in Buenos Aires, where he continued to be associated with literary reviews and publishers. Due to his long exile, Lorenzo Varela's work was little known in both Galicia and Spain until very late. He returned to Spain in 1977 and died shortly after.

Lorenzo Varela was a bilingual writer, and his work shows a continuous contact between literary creation and other media, specifically art and music. At the same time, his concern for social justice, his loyalty to Galicia and Republican Spain are always obvious. The political commitment which led him to compose widely recited ballads for *El mono azul* (The Blue Monkey [an antifascist literary periodical]) during the Civil War, remains afterward in his homages to poets such as Miguel Hernández and his poems to historical figures known for their valor in the struggle for freedom. There also is present an indignation at the plight of Galicians who must emigrate to find sustenance, while his love verse reveals a strong background in classical-medieval culture. The figure of the woman is often assimilated in some manner to nature.

BIBLIOGRAPHY

Primary Texts

Actualidad de la obra crítica de Baudelaire. Buenos Aires: Poseidón, 1944.
Catro poemas pra catro grabados. Buenos Aires: Resol, 1944.
Elegías españolas. Mexico: Guerra Literaria, 1942.
Homaxes. La Coruña: O Castro-Cuco rei, 1979.
Lonxe. Buenos Aires: Botella al mar, 1954.
Murillo. Buenos Aires: Poseidón, 1943.
Poesía. La Coruña: O Castro, 1979.
El Renacimiento. Buenos Aires: Atlántida, 1945.
Seoane o el arte sometido a la libertad. Buenos Aires: Ed. Esquema XX, 1966.
Torres de amor. Buenos Aires: Nova, 1942.

Criticism

Losada, Basilio. "Poesía gallega en América." *La Trinchera* 2 (April 1966).
Méndez Ferrín, X. L. and Basilio Losada. "Literatura en lengua gallega." *Cuadernos para el diálogo XIV Extraordinario* [Special Issue] (May 1969): 22–26.
March, Kathleen N. "Lorenzo Varela." *Gran Enciclopedia Gallega*. Santiago-Gijón: Silverio Canada Editor, 1974 ff.
Seoane, Luis. *Prologue to Homaxes*. La Coruña: O Castro, 1979.

Kathleen March

VARGAS PONCE, José (1760, Cádiz–1821, Madrid), scholar and creative writer. He was a naval officer who became involved in politics and was elected to Congress. Later he became a member of the Spanish, History, and Fine Arts Royal Academies (*Academia). He wrote an *Elogio de Alfonso el Sabio* (1782; In Praise of King Alphonse the Wise), which received an award from the *Academia Española, and *Declaración sobre los abusos introducidos en el castellano, presentada y no premiada en la Academia Española* (1791; Declaration on the excesses introduced into Castilian language, a work presented to, and not rewarded by, the Academia Española). He also wrote historical works, some of them related to the Spanish Navy. As a poet, he composed in a satirical and humorous way, as in *Proclama de un solterón* (1827; A Bachelor's Proclamation). His tragedy, *Abdalazis y Egilona*, 1804, reveals classical tastes.

BIBLIOGRAPHY

Primary Texts

Abdalazis y Egilona. Tragedia. Madrid: Viuda de Ibarra, 1804.
Descripciones de la Islas Pithiusas y Baleares. Madrid: Ibarra, 1787.
Diario militar o proezas de los militares españoles. Madrid: Ibarra, 1812.
Elogio de Alfonso el Sabio. Madrid: Ibarra, 1782.
Proclama de un solterón a las que aspiren a su mano. Lérida: Artes Gráficas Ilerda, 1943.

English Translation

A Voyage of Discovery to The Strait of Magellan. . . . Tr. ? London: R. Phillips, 1820?

Criticism

Cueto, L. A. de. *Poetas líricos del siglo XVIII.* In BAE 67: 601–11.
Guillén, J. ''Nuevos datos sobre Muñoz, Vargas Ponce y Navarrete.'' *Arbor* 4 (1945): 115–19.

Salvador García Castañeda

VAZ DE SOTO, José María (1938, Paymogo, Huelva–), novelist and essayist. He studied philosophy and letters in Seville and Madrid and teaches Spanish literature. Vaz de Soto has contributed to *Triunfo*, *Cambio 16*, *El Socialista*, etc. Since his first novel, *El infierno y la brisa* (1971; Hell and the Breeze), his narrative has been characterized by the autobiographical exploration of the historic conditions that traumatized those who were children during the Civil War. This novel was made into a movie by José María Gutiérrez with the title *¡Vida Hazaña!*. The dialectic analysis of a repressive Spanish society is the leitmotiv of the tetralogy *Diálogos del anochecer* (1972; Dialogues at Dusk), *Fabián and Sabas* (1982; originally two novels), and *Diálogos de la alta noche* (1982; Late Night Dialogues). Vaz de Soto is a follower of Pío *Baroja in the vitality of his dialogue, directness of approach, ironic tone, and the use of many digressions.

BIBLIOGRAPHY

Primary Texts

Diálogos de la alta noche. Barcelona: Argos-Vergara, 1982.
Diálogos del anochecer. Barcelona: Planeta, 1972.
Fabián y Sabas. Barcelona: Argos-Vergara, 1982.
El infierno y la brisa. Barcelona: EDHASA, 1971.
El precursor. Barcelona: Planeta, 1975.

Criticism

Ortega, José. ''Educación, represión y frustración en la narrativa de José María Vaz de Soto.'' *CH* 363 (n.d.): 579–89.

José Ortega

VÁZQUEZ DE MELLA, Juan (1861, Cangas de Onís, Asturias–1928, Madrid), essayist, orator, congressman. From a literary point of view, his speeches have been considered brilliant. Elected to the *Academia Española in 1904, he never composed an entrance speech. After twenty-five years as a congressman, he retired from parliamentary activities in 1916. He also wrote essays on *Pérez Galdós, *Castelar, Rosalía de *Castro, etc. Among the volumes of his posthumously collected Complete Works, most valuable are those dedicated to theological-philosophical themes, social themes, regionalism, and his epistolary. *See also* Essay.

BIBLIOGRAPHY

Primary Texts

Obras completas. 30 vols. Madrid: Junta del homenaje a Mella, 1931–47.

Isabel McSpadden

VÁZQUEZ DE PARGA IGLESIAS, Luis (1908, Madrid–), medievalist, subdirector of the National Archaeological Museum in Madrid, he was a disciple of *Sánchez Albornoz, in the group Centro de Estudios. Vázquez de Parga is the principal author of a classic work in the historiography of medieval Spain: *Las peregrinaciones a Santiago de Compostela* (3 vols., 1948–49; Pilgrimage to St. James of Compostela), written in collaboration with Lacarra and *Uría. Other works of note are ''La más antigua redacción latina de la leyenda de San Alejo?'' (1941; The Oldest Latin Edition of the Legend of St. Alejo?) and ''La poesía 'De agua de la vida' y el himno 'De gloria paradis' de San Pedro Damiano'' (The Poem ''De agua de la vida'' and the Hymn ''De gloria paradis'' of San Pedro Damiano).

BIBLIOGRAPHY

Primary Text

Las peregrinaciones a Santiago de Compostela. 3 vols. Madrid: CSIC, 1948–49.

Isabel McSpadden

VÁZQUEZ IGLESIAS, Dora (1913, Orense–), Galician poet and prose writer. After spending her early years in La Coruña, Dora Vázquez became a schoolteacher in her native Orense and subsequently taught in small villages, an experience important in her choice of a creative linguistic medium. She has published a large number of articles in newspapers and journals of Galicia, Spain, and America. Frequently her works appear in conjunction with those of her sister, Pura *Vázquez.

Dora Vázquez has given much importance to children's literature, and among her publications are plays collected in books such as *Ronseles* (Seawakes) and *Monicreques* (Toys). The purpose of such works is strongly didactic. As in the case of her poetry, Vázquez emphasizes the role of nature in her dramatic compositions. For both children and adults she maintains traditional values such as the family, love, the importance of work, and faith. *See also* Galician Literature.

BIBLIOGRAPHY

Primary Texts

Augas soltas. Orense: La Región, 1979.
Campo e mar aberto. Lugo: Ed. Celta, 1975.
Carne da terra. (in press)
Fantasías infantiles. Orense: La Región, 1980.
Irmá, poemas de ausencia. Orense: La Región, 1970.
Monicreques. Orense: La Región, 1974.

Oración junto al camino. Barcelona: Ed. Rondas, 1985.
Oriolos neneiros. Orense: La Región, 1975.
Palma y corona. Madrid: Ed. Escuela Española, 1964.
Un poema cada mes. Orense: La Región, 1969.
Ronseles. Orense: La Región, 1980.
Tres cadros de teatro galego. Orense: La Región, 1973.

Criticism

March, Kathleen N. "Dora Vázquez Iglesias." *Gran Enciclopedia Gallega*. Santiago-Gijón: Silverio Canada Editor, 1974.

Kathleen March

VÁZQUEZ IGLESIAS, Pura (1918, Orense–), Galician poet and prose writer. A very prolific writer, Pura Vázquez has been a teacher by profession. She spent a number of years in Venezuela, where she was associated with the journalism school of the Central U of Caracas. Her essays have appeared in a wide number of peninsular and American publications, and she has received several awards for literary creation, both within and outside of Galicia. Since 1949 she has been a member of the Real Academia Gallega (Royal Galician Academy).

Although the author of over twenty-five books, Pura Vázquez has two fundamental thematic orientations: children's or didactic literature, and the intimate contemplation of self and reality, often of a decidedly religious nature. She attempts to provide moral guidance for youth through her theatrical compositions, while recognizing the value of spontaneity in the human experience. In a sense, then, her child protagonists are a model for adult behavior. In the novel *Segundo Pereira*, attention is focused on family relationships and the problems that derive from a lack of communication. Some of Vázquez's poetry reveals avant-garde imagery reminiscent of *creacionismo* or Aleixandrian surrealism, while there is also an existential questioning of the meaning of life in a manner similar to Gerardo *Diego's humanistic style. *See also* Galician Literature.

BIBLIOGRAPHY

Primary Texts

Borboriños. Contos galegos. Madrid: n.p., n.d.
Columpio de Luna a Sol. Madrid: Boris Bureba, n.d.
Contacto humano del recuerdo. N.p.: n.p., 1985.
O desacougo. Vigo: Galaxia, 1971.
Desde la niebla. Segovia: Casa de Amigos de Antonio Machado, 1951.
Destinos. Caracas: Lírica Hispana, n.d.
En torno a la voz. Orense: n.p., 1948.
Íntimas. Lugo: Xistral, 1952.
Madrugada fronda. Madrid: Colección Palma, 1951.
Mañana del amor. Barcelona (Centro Gallego): Surco, 1956.
Márgenes veladas. Orense: Diputación Provincial, 1944.
Maturidade. Buenos Aires (Centro Gallego): Galicia, 1955.
Peregrino de amor. Larache, Africa: n.p., 1943.
Rondas de norte a sur. Poesía infantil. Madrid: Boris Bureba, n.d.

A saudade e outros poemas. Vigo: Galaxia (Col. Salnés), 1963.
Los sueños desandados. Bilbao: Comunicación Literaria de Autores, 1974.
Tiempo mío. Segovia: Casa Amigos de Antonio Machado, 1952.
13 Poemas a mi sombra. Caracas: Arte, n.d.
Versos pr-os menos da aldea. Orense: Caja de Ahorros Provincial, 1968.

Criticism

March, Kathleen N. "Pura Vázquez Iglesias." *Gran Enciclopedia Gallega*. Santiago-Gijón: Silverio Cañada Editor, 1974.

Kathleen March

VÁZQUEZ MONTALBÁN, Manuel (1939, Barcelona–), journalist, novelist and poet. His first book of verse, *Una educación sentimental* (1967; A Sentimental Education), established his importance as a poet, later to be identified with the *novísimo* group. He has published four additional collections: *Movimientos sin éxito* (1969; Unsuccessful Movements), *Coplas a la muerte de mi tía Daniela* (1973; Verses on the Death of My Aunt Daniela), *A la sombra de las muchachas sin flor* (1973; In the Shadow of the Flowerless Girls) and *Praga* (1982; Prague). Also a prolific fiction writer, he is the creator of a series of detective novels based on the adventures of Pepe Carvalho, initiated in 1972 with *Yo maté a Kennedy* (I Killed Kennedy). One novel in this series, *Los mares del sur* (The Southern Seas), received the Planeta Prize in 1979, and *Asesinato en el comité central* (1981; *Murder in the Central Committee*, 1985), of the same series, has been translated into English and Portuguese. Well-known as an essayist and satirist, he has published numerous articles and books on a variety of topics including politics, popular culture, social theory, the media and literature. Two important works in this category are his manifesto against rationalism, *Manifesto subnormal* (1970; Subnormal Manifesto), and a survey of popular culture in Franco Spain, *Crónica sentimental de España* (1970; Sentimental Chronicle of Spain). His *Informe sobre la información* (1963; Report on Information) is an important text for journalists.

BIBLIOGRAPHY

Primary Texts

A la sombra de las muchachas sin flor. Barcelona: El Bardo, 1973.
Coplas a la muerte de mi tía Daniela. 2nd ed. Barcelona: Laia, 1984.
Los mares del sur. Madrid: Planeta, 1980.
Movimientos sin éxito. Barcelona: El Bardo, 1969.
Una educación sentimental. 2nd ed. Barcelona: El Bardo, 1969.

English Translations

Murder in the Central Committee. Tr. Patrick Camiller. Chicago: Academy Chicago, 1985.
Recent Poetry of Spain. Tr. Louis Hammer and Sara Schyfter. Old Chatham, NY: Sachem Press, 1983. 266–83.

Criticism

Marson, Ellen Engleson. "Mae West, Superman and the Spanish Poets of the Seventies." *Literature and Popular Culture in the Hispanic World: A Symposium*. Ed. Rose S. Minc. Gaithersburg, MD: Hispanamerica, 1981. 191–98.

Miró, Emilio. "Dos poetas: Manuel Vázquez Montalbán y Tomás Segovia en una colección." *Insula* 434 (1983): 6.

Pritchett, Kay. "The Function of Irony in Vázquez Montalbán's *Coplas a la muerte de mi tía Daniela*." *Anales de Literatura Española Contemporánea* 8 (1983): 47–58.

Sunen, Luis. "Manuel Vázquez Montalbán y Fernando Quiñones." *Insula* 398 (1980): 5.

Vargas Llosa, Mario. "Un escritor numeroso: Manuel Vázquez Montalbán." *Revista de la Universidad de México* 12 (1979): 11–14.

Kay Pritchett

VÁZQUEZ RIAL, Horacio (1947). Spanish novelist, essayist and poet residing in Barcelona, Vázquez Rial obtained a degree in history at the U of Barcelona. Among his novels are *Segundas personas* (1983; Second Persons), *El viaje español* (1985; Spanish Journey), *Oscuras materias de la luz* (1986; Dark Matters of Light), *Historia del triste* (1987; History of the Sorrowful Man) and *La libertad de Italia* (1987; The Freedom of Italy). Vázquez Rial's aesthetics are comparable to expressionism, and his vision of the contemporary world is cloudy and melancholy, in spite of the presence of a gamut of colors. He portrays a world in the process of disintegration, marked by terror and impotence, fear and futility. Death and violence are less imposing than the collapse of values and the irony of relativistic ethics, the injustice of history which is written from the viewpoint of the winners.

BIBLIOGRAPHY

Primary Texts

Historia del triste. Barcelona: Destino, 1987.

La libertad de Italia. Barcelona: Destino, 1987.

Oscuras materias de la luz. Madrid: Alfaguara, 1986.

Janet Pérez

VEGA, Alonso de la (c. 1510,?–c. 1565, ?), playwright, and actor in the company of Lope de *Rueda. Very little biographical information exists about this author, although the municipal archives of Seville record that Alonso de la Vega lived there in 1560 and acted in the Corpus Christi plays that year. In 1566 in Valencia, Juan de *Timoneda published three of Vega's prose plays. The works reveal the influence of the Italian theater. The *Tragedia Serafina* (Tragedy of Serafina) is an eight-act play combining *pastoral and mythological elements with comic insertions. The work ends tragically with the suicide of the protagonists. The *Comedia Tolomea* (Play of Tolomeo) is an undistinguished piece based on the resemblance between two men, both called Tolomeo. Vega's most highly regarded work is *La duquesa de la rosa* (The Duchess of the Rose), which recalls the legendary theme of a falsely accused princess saved by the valor of a knight. The play was inspired by Bandello's *Amore de Don Giovanni di Mendozza e della Duchessa di Savoja*. *See also* Italian Literary Influences.

BIBLIOGRAPHY

Primary Texts

Tres Comedias de Alonso de la Vega. Ed. M. Menéndez y Pelayo. Dresden: Gedruckt für die Gesellschaft für romanische literatur, 1905.

Deborah Compte

VEGA, Lope de (1562, Madrid–1635, Madrid), playwright, poet, and novelist. Lope Félix de Vega Carpio, Spain's foremost dramatist and a major figure in world literature, is the most prolific playwright-poet of all time. His artistic fecundity is matched by the vitality of his life. He was born into a humble family on December 12, 1562. His father was Félix de Vega Carpio, an embroiderer, and his mother, Francisca Fernández Flores. As a child he studied at the school of the Theatins, and under the tutelage of the novelist Vicente *Espinel. According to his contemporary, the dramatist Juan *Pérez de Montalbán, Lope could read Latin and Spanish when he was five years old and at that age translated Claudianus's *De raptu Proserpinae*. Lope himself stated that he wrote his first play at the age of twelve. At fourteen he entered the service of Jerónimo Manrique de Lara, Bishop of Avila, and began to attend the U of Alcalá de Henares. Two years later his father died, and he was employed in the household of Pedro de Dávila, Marquis of Las Navas. At this time he may have attended the U of Salamanca. At the age of twenty-one he volunteered for a military expedition sent to the Azores. On his return, he began a five-year love affair with Elena Osorio, *Filis* in his poetry, daughter of the actor Jerónimo Velázquez. The affair was eventually opposed by her family, and after breaking off with Elena, Lope circulated slanderous verse about her and her relatives. Accused by the latter, he was arrested, convicted of malicious libel, and exiled from Madrid at the age of twenty-six for eight years. Elena's father pardoned him seven years later. Lope returned illegally to Madrid to marry Isabel de Urbina, *Belisa*, his first wife, on May 10, 1588. Within a few days he left to join the Invincible Armada at Lisbon, which set sail on May 29. On his return from this ill-fated venture he settled with his wife in Valencia. In 1590 he moved first to Toledo, to serve the Marquis of Malpica, and then to Alba de Torres, as the secretary of the Duke of Alba. His wife died in childbirth there in 1595, and Lope, now pardoned, returned to Madrid, site of the court. A new passion was ignited: Micaela de Luján (who is *Camila Lucinda* in his writing), who was married to the actor Diego Díaz. Lope lived with her and his new wife Juana de Guardo, whom he married in 1598, in separate households in Seville and, later, Toledo. In 1610 Lope settled definitively in Madrid; his wife Juana died there three years later in childbirth. Lope began intimate relations with Jerónima de Burgos (recreated as *Gerarda* in his writing), and a year later, in 1614, he became a priest. This did not impede his active love life. Around 1617 he met Marta de Nevares Santoya (who is *Amarilis* in his writing), wife of a businessman and the last great love of Lope's life, a love complicated by his sacrilege and her eventual blindness and insanity in 1628. Marta de Nevares died three years before Lope. His daughter Antonia Clara's abduction and other personal problems broke his health. He died on August 27, 1635, and was buried in the Church of Saint Sebastian in Madrid. Some years later his remains were cast into a common grave and their location is unknown today. During his lifetime Lope acquired an almost mythical reputation and his funeral was a national affair. A common expression for praising anything was ''Es de Lope'' (It's by Lope). But as well as supporters he had bitter enemies, including among the literati Luis de *Góngora and Juan *Ruiz de Alarcón. Lope's biography was recorded not only in documents and contemporary references, but also in his own works and letters. Then, soon after his death, his friend Pérez de Montalbán published *Fama postuma*, which includes a biography whose truth is obscured by panegyric. The first complete and documented biography is by Cayetano Alberto de la *Barrera, in the first volume of Lope's *Obras* (1890–1914; Complete Works). A far superior study of Lope's life was Hugo A. Rennert's *Life of Lope de Vega (1562–1635)* (1904). This work was translated into Spanish by Américo *Castro in 1919, with many additions and fundamental corrections (1968; 2nd ed. with additions by Castro and F. Lázaro Carreter). Though more recent biographies have appeared, that of Rennert and Castro is still classic and unsurpassed.

As an author, Lope's astonishing facility for improvisation is combined with innate lyricism. He is primarily a lyric poet—even in his drama—of sincere, emotional, melodious verse. An intuitive rather than intellectual writer, Lope captures every psychological process, every vital manifestation and expresses it with an easy delicacy and rightness. Lope's lyric outpouring represents his own experience reshaped into art. Except for the *picaresque novel, which he doesn't cultivate, there is no literary genre of the period to which Lope does not bring his lyric vision of reality. His **romancero* is an autobiography of his emotional life. Belisa, Filis, and Amarilis make appearances here and there in an ongoing process of idealization. All that remains of the facts is the harmonic nostalgia of the verse. Many youthful *romances* by Lope appear in the *Cancionero general* (1600; General Songbook), such as *De pechos sobre una torre*, Leaning from a tower; *Hortelano era Bernardo*, Bernardo was a gardener; *Mira, Zaide, que te aviso*, Look here, Zaide, I'm warning you. But his later *romances* intercalated in his works have finer expression and sentiment, especially those in *La Dorotea*. Delightful are such celebrated ballads as those which begin *Pobre barquilla mía*, Poor little boat of mine; *A mis soledades voy*, To solitude I go; and *Al son de los arroyos*, To the sound of the brooks. As sonneteer, Lope is rivaled only by Góngora and *Quevedo. His 1,800 sonnets constitute the most abundant part of his lyric production. Many of them are to be found in his plays. *Rimas humanas* (1602; Human Rhymes) was his first separate collection of sonnets. Some of them, inspired by Lucinda (Micaela de Luján), are very beautiful. An extraordinary sonnet, *Suelta mi manso, mayoral extraño* (Release my lamb, unknown shepherd), figures in *La Arcadia* (1598). Equally impressive are the religious ones of *Rimas sacras* (1614; Sacred Rhymes): *¿Qué tengo yo que mi amistad procuras*?, What do I have for you to seek my friendship?; *Pastor, que con tus silbos amorosos*, Shepherd, who with your amorous whistlings; etc. At an advanced age Lope published the *Rimas divinas y humanas de Tomé de Burguillos* (1634; Divine and Human Rhymes of Tome de Burguillos), which contains some finely ironic sonnets (*Picó atrevido un átomo viviente*, A living atom boldly bit; *Conjúrote, demonio culterano*, I beg you, euphuistic demon, and others). Some of Lope's most successful poems are his *letras para cantar* (folksongs). Lope, like Federico *García Lorca in the twentieth c., knows how to maintain the delicate, elusive nature of the popular lyric in an artistic re-elaboration. That is the secret of his art, so national in its expression of the spirit of the people. Many of his plays, and perhaps the best ones, are based on little anonymous folksongs which Lope utilizes at the opportune moment for major dramatic effect. Often the national soul appears in his work in song: harvest songs, lullabies, May songs, and so on. The fusion is total; it is impossible to know where folk stops and Lope begins. Outstanding examples are *Blanca me era yo*, I used to be white; *Como retumban los remos, madre*, How noisy the oars, mother; *Madre, unos ojuelos vi*, Mother, I saw such eyes; *Esta sí que es siega de vida*, This is indeed life's harvest; *Mariquilla me llaman*, They call me Mariquilla; *Deja las avellanicas, moro*, Leave the hazelnuts alone, moor; etc. Lope wrote numerous epistles in verse replete with autobiographical details. Notable are those directed to Gaspar de Barrionuevo and to Juan de *Arguijo. The elegies dedicated to the deaths of Baltasar Elisio de *Medinilla and to Fra Hortensio *Paravicino are famous, and particularly so, for its sorrowful tone, is the one on the death of his son Carlos Félix. Among Lope's eclogues, *Amarilis* (1633) is best, depicting his love affair with Marta de Nevares. Also noteworthy is *Filis*, which narrates the abduction of his daughter Antonia Clara.

Lope did not neglect narrative poetry. In *La hermosura de Angélica* (1602; The Beauty of Angelica), dedicated to Juan de Arguijo, he recounts the love affair of Angelica and Medora. *Jerusalén conquistada* (1609; Jerusalem Regained) depicts the world of the Crusades. It is an unsuccessful emulation of Torquato Tasso's *Gerusalemme liberata*. *La Dragontea* (1598; Drake the Pirate) sings of the adventures and death of the English corsair Sir Francis Drake. *La corona trágica* (1627; The Tragic Crown) tells the story of the tragic life of Mary Stuart, Queen of Scots. Pope Urban VIII awarded Lope the title doctor of theology and the cross of the Order of Saint John for this work, and from then on Lope signed himself *Fra* Lope de Vega. Narrative poems of mythological content are *La Circe* (1624; Circe), *La Filomena* (1621; Philomena), and *La Andromeda* (1621). *La Filomena* contains Lope's defense against *Torres Rámila, a professor at the U of Alcalá de Henares who had harshly attacked him. *La Gatomaquia* (1634; The War of the Cats) is a burlesque epic poem about the adventures of two tomcats, Marramaquiz and Micifuz, both in love with the dizzy Zapaquilda. *El Isidro* (1599; Saint Isidro) is a poem saturated with popular devotion on the life of the patron saint of Madrid, the farmer Saint Isidro. Other narrative poems are *La mañana de San Juan en Madrid* (St. John's Eve in Madrid) and *Descripción de la Tapada* (Description of the Veiled Woman). Didactic poems include *El arte nuevo de hacer comedias* (1609; "New Art of Play Writing," 1957), which contains Lope's views about the theater, and *El laurel de Apolo* (1630; The Laurel of Apollo), where the praises of more than three hundred contemporary writers are sung.

Lope also cultivated prose, though to a much lesser degree than verse. *La Arcadia* (1598) is the last important *pastoral novel to be written in Spain. Anfriso, the shepherd protagonist, represents the Duke of Alba. Beautiful poems appear throughout the work. *Los pastores de Belén* (1612; The Shepherds of Bethlehem) is a pastoral novel **a lo divino*. Like the previous work, it has many poems intercalated in the prose. The Christmas carols are especially noteworthy. *El peregrino en su patria* (1604; The Pilgrim in His Own Homeland) is a Byzantine novel, like *Cervantes's *Persiles y Segismunda*, which contains many autobiographical references. Lope appends a list of plays he had written by then. He also wrote four short novels in the courtly style, called stories for Marcia Leonarda (Marta de Nevares). Dating from 1621 and 1624, they are titled *Las fortunas de Diana* (The Fortunes of Diana), *La desdicha por la honra* (Unhappiness for Honor's Sake), *La prudente venganza* (The Prudent Revenge), and *Guzmán el Bravo* (Guzman the Brave). But Lope's best work in prose, and the masterpiece of all he wrote, is *La Dorotea* (1632; *La Dorotea*, 1984), a play written in prose and lyric poetry, not meant to be performed. In it Lope narrates the course of his youthful love affair with Elena Osorio. It is strongly influenced by *La *Celestina*; Lope's Gerarda is a reincarnation of the famous fifteenth-c. bawd. It may be poeticized autobiography, but it is also one of the most accomplished prose works of the period. *La Dorotea*, written in Lope's youth, was recast much later, and was published in 1632, three years before the author's death. The historical source is ultimately sublimated; Lope even introduces poems dedicated to Marta de Nevares, his final love. The serene conjunction of past and present sentiment makes this book one of the most human and beautiful works of the *Siglo de Oro. Lope also wrote historical works—*Triunfo de la fe en los reinos del Japón* (1618; The Triumph of Faith in the Kingdoms of Japan)—and ascetic ones—*Cuatro soliloquios* (1612; Four Soliloquies) and *Soliloquios amorosos* (1627; Loving Soliloquies).

Lope is the great founder of the Spanish national theater. He absorbs all that before him was tentative and scattered and molds it into an artistic creation of the highest worth. He establishes the definitive form of the play: three acts in polymetric verse. He is inspired mainly by the great themes of Spanish history, by folk poetry, and by national legends, which he presents without regard for *Aristotelian unities. He creates the comic sidekick, the **gracioso*, who becomes essential in almost all plays of the time. Lope's comedy offers the most comprehensive portrait of seventeenth-c. Spanish society in its most typical and most patriotic aspects. Besides the quality of his work, his astonishing production is impressive. Pérez de Montalbán spoke with awe of the speed with which Lope composed. Lope himself says that he wrote 1,800 plays, about 100 of which were composed in less than twenty-four hours. Fewer than 500 survive today. A selection of the more important or representative ones is presented below, according to the classification of *Marcelino Menéndez y Pelayo (one of many that have been proposed):

Religious plays

El cardenal de Belén (The Cardinal of Bethlehem), *Barlaam y Josefat* (Barlaam and Josaphat), *Lo fingido verdadero* (Pretended Truth), *La fianza satisfecha* (*The Outrageous Saint*, 1962); *La buena guarda* (The Good Custodian).

Mythological plays

El laberinto de Creta (The Labyrinth of Crete); *El marido más firme* (The Staunchest Husband), the story of Orpheus and Eurydice; *Adonis y Venus* (Adonis and Venus).

Pastoral plays

La Arcadia, which Lope based on his own novel *La pastoral de Jacinta* (Jacinta's Pastoral); *Belardo el furioso* (Belardo the Furious).

Historical plays

Here is where Lope is most vigorous; the best plays are those inspired by the Spanish Middle Ages. His source was often Florián de *Ocampo's edition of the *Crónica general* (1541; General Chronicle). Some of his plots are drawn from classical history: *Las grandezas de Alejandro* (The Grandeur of Alexander); *Roma abrazada* (Rome Ablaze), with Nero as a character; *Contra el valor no hay desdicha* (Valor Withstands All Misfortune), on the infancy of Cirus. *El esclavo de Roma* (The Slave of Rome) dramatizes the legend of the slave and the lion. Notable plays with plots drawn from foreign history include *La imperial de Otón* (Otocar and the Imperial Crown) and *El gran duque de Moscovia* (The Grand Duke of Moscow). But Lope is at his best, as noted, with Spanish themes. The chronicles, historical ballads, legends, and popular lyrics provide him with ample material to build a moving dramatic structure. Lope thus allies himself with the many other creators who focus on the national themes of Spanish literature. He dramatized the story of King don Rodrigo in *El último godo* (The Last of the Goths), the legend of the tribute of the hundred damsels in *Las famosas asturianas* (The Famous Women of Asturias), and the myth of Bernardo del Carpio in *El casamiento en la muerte* (Marriage after Death). The Infantes of Lara figure in *El bastardo Mudarra* (The Bastard Mudarra), and the *Cid appears in *Las almenas de Toro* (The Battlements of Toro). King Pedro the Cruel is the protagonist of *Las audiencias del rey Don Pedro* (The Audiences of King Pedro) and of *El rey Don Pedro en Madrid* (King Pedro in Madrid). This latter, also known as *El infanzón de Illescas* (The Infanzon of Illescas), is a work of great dramatic intensity. *El mejor alcalde el rey* (*The King, the*

Best Alcalde, 1936) is an accomplished presentation of royal justice prevailing over the abuses of the nobility in the time of Emperor Alfonso VII. A complete enumeration would be almost interminable: *Lo cierto por lo dudoso* (*Certainty for Doubt*, 1936); *La desdichada Estefanía* (Unfortunate Stephanie); *Las paces de los reyes y Judía de Toledo* (The Kings' Peace, or, the Jewess of Toledo); the fine play of doubtful paternity, *La Estrella de Sevilla* (*The Star of Seville*, 1955); *Porfiar hasta morir* (To Persist until Death), an episode from the life of Macías the troubadour; *El remedio en la desdicha* (Remedy in Misfortune); *El marqués de las Navas* (The Marquis of Las Navas); *Los comendadores de Córdoba* (The Commanders of Cordoba); etc. However, the most famous and notable plays of this group, and perhaps of all of Lope's theater, are *Fuente Ovejuna* (*Fuenteovejuna*, translated also as *The Sheep Well*, 1968), *Peribáñez y el comendador de Ocaña* (*Peribáñez*, 1961), and *El caballero de Olmedo* (*The Knight of Olmedo*, 1972). *Fuente Ovejuna* recounts the epic revenge of an entire town, inspired by an indestructible monarchial and national spirit, against the excesses of an irresponsible authority. The play has achieved international fame, as has *Peribáñez*, a drama with a similar background, but with the vengeance taken by one modest and honorable farmer. This play contains many beautiful popular songs, used to great dramatic effect. Songs are also important in *El caballero de Olmedo*; indeed, the plot is derived from a four-line popular lyric. Reminiscenses of *La Celestina* appear in the go-between Fabia. The little song bathes the romantic, attractive knight in a mournful, otherworldly light. The setting—Medina del Campo, Olmedo, and the pine woods between the two cities—has the intimate resonance of a geographic heartland. The knight of Olmedo, whose sad destiny is sensed from the first moments, slowly dies at the end in a scene of extraordinary beauty.

Novelistic plays

Los palacios de Galiana (The Palaces of Galiana), the legend of Mainete; *El castigo sin venganza* (Punishment without Vengeance), one of Lope's most tragic dramas; *La difunta pleiteada* (Sued after Death); *El halcón de Federico* (Federico's Falcon); *El marqués de Mantua* (The Marquis of Mantua).

Comedies of customs and manners

Some of the best are *Santiago el Verde* (Santiago the Green), *La moza de cántaro* (The Girl with a Jug), *El acero de Madrid* (The Iron Tonic of Madrid), *La hermosa fea* (The Pretty Ugly-Duckling), *El perro del hortelano* (*The Gardener's Dog*, 1948), *La dama boba* (*The Stupid Lady*, 1962), *El villano en su rincón* (*The King and the Farmer*, 1940), etc.

Lope also wrote *autos sacramentales*, one-act religious allegories meant to be performed for Corpus Christi. They contain much excellent poetry in the popular vein, far from the complicated intellectual structures to be found in the **autos* of Pedro *Calderón de la Barca. Some of Lope's *autos* are *La siega* (The Harvest), *La maya* (The May Queen), *La adúltera perdonada* (The

Forgiven Adultress), and *El hijo pródigo* (The Prodigal Son). *See also* Theater in Spain.

BIBLIOGRAPHY

Primary Texts

La Arcadia. Ed. Edwin S. Morby. Madrid: Castalia, 1975.

"Arte nuevo de hacer comedias." Ed. Federico Sánchez Escribano and Alberto Porqueras Mayo. *Preceptiva dramática española del renacimiento y el barroco*. Madrid: Gredos, 1972.

La Circe, poema. Ed. C. V. Aubrun and M. Muñoz Cortes. Paris: Centre de Recherches de l'Institut d'Etudes Hispaniques, 1962.

Colección de las obras sueltas, así en prosa como en verso, de don Frey Lope de Vega Carpio del hábito de San Juan. 21 vols. Madrid: Antonio de Sancha, 1776–79.

La Dorotea. Ed. Edwin S. Morby. 2nd ed. rev. Berkeley: U of California P; Madrid: Castalia, 1968.

La Gatomaquia. Ed. Celina Sabor de Cortázar. Madrid: Castalia, 1982.

Jerusalén conquistada. Ed. Joaquín de Entrambasaguas. 3 vols. Madrid: CSIC, 1951–54.

Novelas a Marcia Leonarda. Ed. Francisco Rico. Madrid: Alianza, 1968.

Obras de Lope de Vega. [Ed. Marcelino Menéndez y Pelayo]. *RAE*. 15 vols. Madrid: Sucesores de Rivadeneyra, 1890–1913.

Obras de Lope de Vega. [Ed. Emilio Cotarelo y Mori]. *RAE*. new ed. 13 vols. Madrid: Tipografía de la RABM, 1916–30.

Obras escogidas de Lope Félix de Vega Carpio. Ed. Federico C. Sáinz de Robles. 2nd ed. 3 vols. Madrid: Aguilar, 1958–62.

Obras poéticas. Ed. José Manuel Blecua. Barcelona: Planeta, 1983.

El peregrino en su patria. Ed. Juan Bautista Avalle-Arce. Madrid: Castalia, 1973.

Rimas de Tomé de Burguillos. Ed. José Manuel Blecua. Barcelona: Planeta, 1976.

Note: There are many editions of individual plays. See the bibliographies in Criticism. Here are editions of Lope's three best-known plays:

El caballero de Olmedo. Ed. Francisco Rico. Madrid: Cátedra, 1981.

Fuente Ovejuna. Ed. María Grazia Profeti. Madrid: Cupsa, 1978.

Peribáñez y el Comendador de Ocaña. Ed. José M. Ruano de la Haza and John E. Varey. London: Tamesis, 1980.

English Translations

La Dorotea. Tr. and ed. Alan S. Trueblood and Edwin Honig. Cambridge, MA: Harvard UP, 1985.

Five Plays. Tr. Jill Booty. London: MacGibbon and Kee; New York: Hill and Wang, 1961. (*The Knight from Olmedo*, *Justice without Revenge*, *Fuenteovejuna*, *Peribáñez*, *The Dog in the Manger*.)

Four Plays of Lope de Vega. Tr. John Garret Underhill. New York: Scribner, 1936. (*Certainty for Doubt*, *The Sheep-Well [Fuente Ovejuna]*, *The King the Greatest Alcalde*, *The Gardener's Dog*.)

Fuente ovejuna. Tr. William E. Colford. New York: Barron's, 1969.

The King and the Farmer. Tr. Cecily Radford. London: Deane, 1940. *(El villano en su rincón)*

The Knight of Olmedo. Tr. Willard F. King. Lincoln: U of Nebraska P, 1972.

The Lady Simpleton (La dama boba). Tr. Max Oppenheimer. Lawrence, KS: Coronado, 1976.

"New Art of Play Writing." Tr. James Brander Matthews. *Papers on Playmaking*. New York: Hill and Wang, 1957.

Renaissance and Baroque Poetry of Spain. Tr. Elias L. Rivers. New York: Dell, 1966.

Criticism

Amezúa, Agustín G. de. *Epistolario de Lope de Vega*. 4 vols. vol. 1. Madrid: Tipografía de Archivos, 1935. vol. 2. Madrid: Escelicer, 1940. vols. 3–4. Madrid: Artes Gráficas "Aldus," 1941, 1943.

Brown, Robert B. *Bibliografía de las comedias históricas, tradicionales y legendarias de Lope de Vega*. Mexico: Edit. Academia (State U of Iowa), 1958.

Carreño, Antonio. *El romancero lírico de Lope de Vega*. Madrid: Gredos, 1979.

Díez Borque, José María. *Sociedad y teatro en la España de Lope de Vega*. Barcelona: Antoni Bosch, 1978.

Fichter, William L. "The Present State of Lope de Vega Studies." *Hispania* 20 (1937): 327–52.

Gerstinger, Heinz. *Lope de Vega and Spanish Drama*. Tr. Samuel R. Rosenbaum. New York: Frederick Ungar, 1974.

Hayes, Francis C. *Lope de Vega*. New York: Twayne, 1967.

Larson, Donald R. *The Honor Plays of Lope de Vega*. Cambridge, MA: Harvard UP, 1977.

Menéndez y Pelayo, Marcelino. *Estudios sobre Lope de Vega*. 6 vols. Madrid: CSIC, 1949.

Morley, S. Griswold, and Courtney Bruerton. *The Chronology of Lope de Vega's "Comedias." With a Discussion of Doubtful Attributions, the Whole Based on a Study of His Strophic Versification*. New York: MLA; London: Oxford UP, 1940. Reprinted 1966.

Parker, Jack H., and Arthur M. Fox. *Lope de Vega Studies, 1937–1962. A Critical Survey and Annotated Bibliography*. Toronto: U of Toronto P; London: Oxford UP, 1964.

Pérez Pérez, María de la Cruz. *Bibliografía del teatro de Lope de Vega*. Madrid: CSIC, 1973.

Rennert, Hugo A., and Américo Castro. *Vida de Lope de Vega*. 2nd ed. with additions by Castro and Fernando Lázaro Carreter. Salamanca: Anaya, 1968.

Simón Díaz, José, and Juana de José Prades. *Ensayo de una bibliografía de las obras y artículos sobre la vida y escritos de Lope de Vega Carpio*. Madrid: Centro de Estudios sobre Lope de Vega, 1955.

———. *Nuevos estudios, adiciones al "Ensayo de una bibliografía de las obras y artículos sobre Lope de Vega Carpio."* Madrid: CSIC, 1961.

Spanish Literature, 1500–1700. A Bibliography of Golden Age Studies in Spanish and English, 1925–1980. Comp. William W. Moseley, Glenroy Emmons and Marilyn C. Emmons. Westport, CT: Greenwood, 1984. 588–662; 1,274 entries for Lope de Vega.

Trueblood, Alan S. *Experience and Artistic Expression in Lope de Vega. The Making of "La Dorotea."* Cambridge, MA: Harvard UP, 1974.

Vossler, Karl. *Lope de Vega y su tiempo*. Tr. R. de la Serna. 2nd ed. Madrid: RO, 1940.
Zamora Vicente, Alonso. *Lope de Vega: Su vida y su obra*. Madrid: Gredos, 1961.

Harold G. Jones

VEGA, Pedro de (sixteenth c., ?–?), Augustinian writer. He composed a treatise titled *Declaración de los siete salmos penitenciales* (1599; Declaration of the Seven Psalms of Penitence), characterized by a rich lexicon and elegant expression.

BIBLIOGRAPHY

Primary Text

Declaración de los siete salmos penitenciales. Zaragoza: Lauayen, 1606.

VEGA, Ricardo de la (1839, Madrid–1910, Madrid), dramatist. Son of the famous playwright Ventura de la *Vega, Ricardo wrote **zarzuelas* and comic one-act plays (**género chico*). Ricardo de la Vega's plays are among the best of their genre. Amusing, with lively dialogues, they usually depict contemporary customs, and tend to caricature. Many have a double title, thus *La verbena de la Paloma* (1894; The Festival of the Dove) is also entitled *El boticario y las chulapas* (The Pharmacist and the Maidens) or *Celos mal reprimidos* (Ill-repressed Jealousy). This famous play portrays typical characters from popular Madrid quarters. The music, by Tomás Bretón, matches Vega's lyrics perfectly. This work has become a classic in its own right and is always performed with success. Some of his other works are *El señor Luis el Tumbón o Despacho de huevos frescos* (1891; Mr. Louis the Lazy One or The Fresh Eggs Depot); *La Canción de la Lola* (1880; Lola's Song), with music by Valverde and Chueca; *Pepa la frescachona o El colegial desenvuelto* (1886: Pepa the Fresh-looking or The Easy-going Student); *De Getafe al Paraíso, o La Familia del tío Maroma* (1883; From Getafe to Paradise, or Uncle Maroma's Family); *El año pasado por agua* (1889; Last Year's Review); and *Amor engendra desdichas* (1899; Love Breeds Misfortune). Vega also wrote a drama in the style of José *Echegaray called *La Abuela* (1884; The Grandmother).

BIBLIOGRAPHY

Primary Texts

La abuela. Sainete lírico-trágico-realista. Madrid: Administración Lírico-Dramática, 1884.
El año pasado por agua. Revista general de 1889. Madrid: R. Velasco, 1890.
De Getafe al Paraíso, o La familia del tío Maroma. Madrid: Unión musical española (formerly Casa Dotesia), 1883.

El señor Luis el tumbón o Despacho de huevos frescos. Madrid: R. Velasco, 1891.
La verbena de la Paloma. Madrid: R. Velasco, 1894.

Salvador García Castañeda

VEGA, Ventura de la (1807, Buenos Aires, Argentina–1865, Madrid), poet and playwright. Born in Buenos Aires, Ventura de la Vega was sent to Spain to be educated at the age of eleven when his father died, and he never returned to his native land. He was a pupil of Alberto *Lista at the Colegio de San Mateo and there became imbued with a taste for moderate classicism. As a friend of many of the young Romantics, Vega collaborated in various literary periodicals, such as *El Artista*, *El Entreacto*, and *El Siglo*. He was jailed for a short time in a Madrid monastery for his participation in the Sociedad de Los Numantinos, a literary gathering with innocent political concerns which was nonetheless deemed dangerous by the Spanish government, but he later served as a royal tutor to Isabel II, as under-secretary of state, and as the director of the Teatro Español.

Vega was one of the major translators of the day and adapted many French plays by Delavigne, Dumas, Hugo, and Scribe for the Spanish stage. His active social life and work as a translator left little time for original work, considerably limiting his dramatic output, to which may be added a few *zarzuelas, one opera, and miscellaneous poetry and articles. In his dramas, Vega was heavily influenced by Leandro Fernández de *Moratín and is generally considered a link between neo-classical drama and the *alta comedia* of Manuel *Tamayo y Baus and Adelardo *López de Ayala, although some critics have insisted on the eclectic nature of his work and its Romantic traits; nevertheless, Vega's work proves that a current of neo-classicism persisted throughout the Romantic period.

Vega's best-known play, *El hombre de mundo* (1845; The Man of the World), is a Moratinian-style comedy concerning a reformed playboy whose marital bliss is threatened by misconceptions based on his own rakish experience and by the designs of an unrepentant philanderer. This four-act verse comedy strictly conforms to the dramatic unities and ends with a marriage; the moral that one's dissolute past may provoke future negative consequences is obvious. The popular saying "Todo Madrid lo sabía, todo Madrid menos él" (Everybody in Madrid knew about it, that is, everybody but him) comes from this play.

Vega's historical drama *Don Fernando el de Antequera* (1844, performed 1847), based on the struggle for succession to the throne of Castile after the death of Enrique III, although faithful to history as well as the dramatic unities, met with little success. Neither did his five-act tragedy *La muerte de César* (1862, performed 1863; The Death of Caesar), which was viewed as a defense of tyranny and an indirect compliment to Napoleon III.

Vega's aversion to *Romanticism is clearly visible in the short play *El plan de un drama, o la conspiración* (1835; The Outline for a Play, or the Plot), a parody of the excesses of Romanticism written in collaboration with *Bretón de los Herreros. On the other hand, his most explicit profession of faith in Moratinian principles is forcefully articulated in the one-act comedy *Crítica de El sí de las niñas* (1848; Critique of When a Girl Says "Yes"). *See also* Theater in Spain.

BIBLIOGRAPHY

Primary Texts

Don Fernando el de Antequera. Madrid: Repullés, 1847.
El hombre de mundo. Madrid: Repullés, 1845.
La muerte de César. Madrid: Rivadeneyra, 1863.
Obras escogidas de Ventura de la Vega. 2 vols. Barcelona: Montaner y Simón, 1894–95.
Obras poéticas de don Ventura de la Vega. Paris: Claye, 1866.

Criticism

Alborg, Juan Luis. *Historia de la literatura española*. vol. 4. Madrid: Gredos, 1980.
Leslie, John Kenneth. *Ventura de la Vega and the Spanish Theatre, 1820–1865*. Princeton: Princeton UP, 1940.
Montero Alonso, José. *Ventura de la Vega, su vida y su tiempo*. Madrid: Nacional, 1951.
Mundy, J. H., and E. Allison Peers. "Ventura de la Vega and the 'Justo Medio' in Drama." In *Liverpool Studies in Spanish Literature*. Ed. E. Allison Peers. Liverpool: Institute of Hispanic Studies, 1940. 202–19.
Shaw, Donald L. *A Literary History of Spain: The Nineteenth Century*. London: Benn, 1972.

Linda Maier

VEJAMEN, satiric literary composition popular in the *Siglo de Oro. Directed at contemporary authors, they criticized the literary works, appearances, habits, etc., of their subjects. Some preserve a most interesting assortment of information about certain literary figures.

BIBLIOGRAPHY

Primary Texts

Vejámenes literarios. By. J. de Cáncer and A. Pantaleón de Ribera. In BAE 42.

VELA, Fernando (1888, Oviedo–1966, Madrid), journalist, author. A journalist for many years, Vela directed both *El Sol* and *Diario de Madrid*, and was the editing secretary for *Revista de Occidente* from its founding in 1923 until his death. He translated extensively. He followed an intellectual discipline close to that of *Ortega, and was able to discuss precisely subjects ranging from art to thought, from literature to politics. His prose is quick, ingenious, and singularly clear and light, gracing the intellectual rigor of his writing. Vela published four books of essays: *El arte al cubo* (1927; Art Cubed), *El futuro imperfecto* (1934; Imperfect Future), *El grano de pimienta* (1950; The Grain of Pepper), and *Circunstancias* (1952; Circumstances). He wrote two biographies, *Mozart* (1943) and *Tallyrand* (1943), under the pen name of Hector del Valle; and a historical book, *Los Estados Unidos entran en la Historia* (1946; The United States Enters History). He also wrote abridged versions of several works, and a work on Ortega and the existentialists. *See also* Essay.

BIBLIOGRAPHY

Primary Texts

El arte al cubo y otros ensayos. Madrid: Ciudad lineal, 1927.
Los Estados Unidos entran en la Historia. Madrid: Atlas, 1946.
El futuro imperfecto. Madrid: Literatura, 1934.
El grano de pimienta. Buenos Aires: Espasa-Calpe, 1950.
Ortega y los existencialismos. Madrid: RO, 1961.

Isabel McSpadden

VELARDE, José (1849, Conil, Cádiz–1892, Madrid), minor poet. Despite his education in medicine, Velarde instead chose to dedicate himself entirely to the arts, and he moved to Madrid, where he came in contact with such authors as *Campoamor, José *Echegaray, *Núñez de Arce, and *Zorrilla. His early poetry, for example, *Teodomiro o la Cueva de Cristo* (1879; Teodomiro or the Cave of Christ), imitates Zorrilla's *leyendas*. Later, his pure lyric poetry became tinged with didacticism, resembling the realistic vein of Núñez de Arce. A selection from his works, *Voces del alma* (1884; Voices from My Soul), was quite harshly reviewed by Leopoldo Alas (*Clarín). Velarde also collaborated on the historical drama *Pedro el Bastardo* (1888; Peter the Bastard) with his friend and fellow poet Juan A. *Cavestany.

BIBLIOGRAPHY

Primary Texts

Obras poéticas. 2 vols. Madrid: F. Alvarez, 1886.
Pedro el Bastardo. With Juan A. Cavestany. Madrid: Velasco, 1888.
Teodomiro o la Cueva de Cristo. Madrid: V. Saiz, 1879.
Voces del alma. Madrid: M. Tello, 1884.

Criticism

Blanco García, Francisco. *La literatura española en el siglo XIX*. vol. 2. Madrid: Sáenz de Jubera Hermanos, 1910.

Linda Maier

VELÁZQUEZ, Luis José (1722, Málaga–1772, Málaga), historian. His title was Marquis of Valdeflores. A member of the Academia de Buen Gusto (Academy of Good Taste), he composed, by order of the king, the *Noticia del viaje en España* (1765; A Note on the Trip in Spain). He amassed a large collection of mss. in preparation of this work; they are now housed in the Academy of History. Velázquez also wrote *Orígenes de la poesía castellana* (1754; Origins of Castilian Poetry), *Anales de la nación española* (1759; Annals of the Spanish Nation), and prepared an edition of Francisco de la *Torre's poetry—attributing the poems, however, to *Quevedo. *See also* Academia.

BIBLIOGRAPHY

Primary Texts

Anales de la nación española. Málaga: Martínez de Aguilar, 1759.
Noticia del viaje en España. Madrid: Ramírez, 1765.
Orígenes de la poesía castellana. 2nd ed. Málaga: Martínez de Aguilar, 1797.

VÉLEZ DE GUEVARA, Juan (1611, Madrid–1675, Madrid), poet and playwright. Son of the more celebrated Luis *Vélez de Guevara, Juan lacked the talent and wit of his father. His best known poems include the famous sonnet that he dedicated to Velázquez and his longer poem "A la muerte de Lope de *Vega" (1636; On the Occasion of Lope de Vega's Death). His better *comedias* are *Encontráronse dos arroyuelos o la boba y el vizcaíno* (1666; The Meeting of Two Brooks or The Fool and the Biscayan) and *El mancebón de los palacios o agraviar para alcanzar* (1668?; The Daring Young Man from the Palaces or To Offend in order to Obtain a Favor). With *Cáncer y Velasco he wrote *Los siete infantes de Lara* (1651?; The Seven Princes from Lara), an excellent burlesque play. Juan Vélez also collaborated in numerous plays and **entremeses* with other poets and playwrights like *Martínez de Meneses, Juan de *Zabaleta and Bautista *Diamante. Some considered him to be a fine *entremesista*, although the authorship of some of the *entremeses* (as well of some of the plays attributed to him) is questionable. A complete bibliography of the poetic and theatrical works of Juan Vélez remains to be written. *El bodegón* (1663?; The Dive) and *El sastre* (1668? The Tailor) are probably his best *entremeses*. He also wrote a number of **loas* and dances, among them *El baile de la esgrima* (n.d.; The Dance of the Swordsmen), *Gila y Pascual* (n.d.; Gila and Pascual) and *El arquitecto* (n.d.; The Architect).

Los celos hacen estrellas (1662?; Jealousy Makes Stars), written to celebrate the birthday of Queen Mariana de Austria, is one of the first **zarzuelas* of the Spanish theater. Together with the ms. containing the *zarzuela*, five watercolors were discovered that illustrate its scenography and permit us to re-create almost in its entirety a palace theatrical performance during the time of Charles II.

BIBLIOGRAPHY

Primary Texts

El bodegón and *El sastre*. In *Antología del entremés (desde Lope de Rueda hasta Antonio de Zamora)*. Sel., intro., and notes, Felicidad Buendía. Madrid: Aguilar, 1965.
El mancebón de los palacios o agraviar para alcanzar. In *Dramáticos posteriores a Lope de Vega*. vol. 1. Sel. and intro., Ramón de Mesonero Romano. BAE 47. Madrid: Librería de los sucesores de Hernando, 1924.
Los celos hacen estrellas. Ed. and intro., J. E. Varey and N. D. Shergold. London: Tamesis, 1970.

Hector Medina

VÉLEZ DE GUEVARA, Luis (1579, Ecija, Seville–1644, Madrid), prose writer, poet and dramatist in the mode of Lope de *Vega, whose plays he mined extensively for dramatic inspiration. He was the son of a poor licentiate, Diego

Vélez de Dueñas, and Francisa Negrete de Santander. Although he traveled widely during his lifetime, he never lost his strong love for and attraction to his native Andalusian lands. After entering the U of Osuna at age seventeen, he graduated in 1596 with a degree in the arts. He then entered the service of the Archbishop of Seville, Rodrigo de Castro. He accompanied him to Madrid for the celebration of the marriage of Philip III and Margarite of Austria. A poem Vélez wrote for the occasion was published in 1599. The following year he became a soldier and joined the army of the Count of Fuentes to participate in the campaigns of Milan and Saboya. By 1603, he had returned to Spain. After brief periods of residence in Valladolid and Seville, he established himself in Madrid, where he enjoyed the favor and patronage of the nobility and royalty. Nevertheless, his life followed an irregular, disorderly course which cast him in diverse roles, some of which were most uncomfortable and embarrassing. He practiced law only intermittently, knew periods of mendicancy and was a persistent petitioner. He was married at least four times. The last wife, María López de Palacios, was a young widow of modest means, but her property and funds were consumed in the course of raising a family. Vélez declares in his will that he is sorely debt-ridden. By the time he was thirty, he had changed his name to the current version, dropping forever the Vélez de Santander under which he had previously published some of his works. To judge by the kind words of praise from Lope de Vega, *Cervantes, *Pérez de Montalbán and *Claramonte, Luis Vélez de Guevara was well esteemed for his wit and eloquence. *Quevedo praises his dramaturgy in his *Perinola* (The Teetotum). He sometimes participated in the staging of extemporaneous plays for the entertainment of the royal family. He was unable to achieve financial security, and never became the distinguished soldier that he would like to have been. His personal wish to be inducted into one of the prestigious military orders was not fulfilled, and there is reason to suspect that the decision to change his name was an effort to disassociate himself from an ill-fated namesake who had been found guilty by the *Inquisition. At the time of his death he occupied a position as royal doorkeeper. The vacant post was filled by his son, Juan *Vélez de Guevara, also an accomplished poet and playwright.

Vélez himself indicated that he had composed as many as four hundred plays, but only a small portion of that number survives. Spencer and Schevill list ninety-four works that can be attributed to him as well as others which were written in collaboration. His literary opus was not published during his lifetime, and even today there is no complete collection of his plays available.

Echoes of the turbulence of his personal life can also be seen reflected in two dissimilar currents which run through many of his compositions—an elaborate, delicate and courtly metaphorical system and a penchant for shocking conceits, parody and sharp satire. As a dramatic poet, Vélez combines a wide range of highly refined images of delicate nuance with traditional themes drawn and adapted from diverse national epic material. Still, in his poetry there prevails a refinement which is more courtly and artificial than the paradigms provided by

Lope de Vega. Vélez, too, learned to perfect the art of inserting a popular ballad or folk song at the most opportune moment in the action to enhance the scene and to highlight the fusion of word and action in a total revelation of the meaning of the work. Examples are the *fonte frida* (bathing song) included in *Los hijos de Baltasara* (Baltasara's Sons), the popular ballad "Allá en Garganta de Olla" in *La serrana de la Vera* (The Mountaingirl from la Vera), and the lines beginning "¿Dónde va el caballero?" in *Reinar después de morir* (To Rule after Dying).

Among the plays based upon national history other than Spanish are included *Atila, azote de Dios* (Attila, the Scourge of God), *Tamerlán de Persia* (Tamerlane of Persia), *El príncipe esclavo* (The Slave Prince), and *Hazañas de Escandemberg* (The Feats of Scandemberg). Vélez achieved his greatest success in the dramatization of Spanish national legends or motifs. The legend of Guzmán the Good appears in *Más pesa el rey que la Sangre* (The King Has No Peer). Pelayo's deeds at Covadonga are recalled in *La restauración de España* (The Restoration of Spain). In *El diablo está en Cantillana* (The Devil in Cantillana), a husband masquerades as a ghost to prevent Peter the Cruel from making him a cuckold. *La luna de la sierra* (The Sierra Moon) is set in the epoch of the Catholic sovereigns, and the principal character is the ill-fated Prince John. *La niña de Gómez Arias* (The Daughter of Gómez Arias) is based on a play by *Calderón which bears the same title. It dramatizes the plight of a young girl sold into slavery after being seduced. The exploits of John of Austria are heralded in *El águila del agua* (The Maritime Eagle).

Vélez's dramatic compositions include plays on biblical subjects: *La hermosura de Raquel* (Rachel's Beauty), *Santa Susana*, and *La Magdalena*. He also composed *autos sacramentales* (**autos*) and **entremeses* which include *La burla más razonada* (The Most Reasonable Prank), *La sarna de los banquetes* (The Banquet Mange), and *Auto de la mesa redonda* (The Roundtable Play). Other full-length plays include *Los hijos de la barbuda* (The Bearded Lady's Children), *El ollero de Ocaña* (The Pot Maker from Ocaña), *El embuste acreditado y el disparate creído* (The Lie Verified and the Nonsense Believed). His best-known play remains the popular *Reinar después de morir* (To Reign after Death) which recounts the tragic story of Inés de Castro and her ill-fated romance. (See *Inés de Castro, Leyenda de*) The version of Vélez de Guevara is free of many of the restrictions and limitations imposed on the material by the other interpreters. A lyrical elegance from beginning to end and an exquisite courtly atmosphere combine with the emotion of the final tragic catastrophe in a work of unusually high quality. It is generally regarded as his masterpiece. Its inclusion in most modern anthologies of Spanish Golden Age plays attests to its continued popularity.

Vélez de Guevara's major prose work, *El diablo cojuelo* (1641; The Hobbling Devil), has not enjoyed the same widespread acclaim. Literary historians have debated whether the work should be considered a novel and whether it is an example of *picaresque literature. The peculiar structural division into *trancos* (strides) and the statement by Vélez in his introduction that he tossed the work off rapidly while on vacation have led critics to classify the work erroneously. In all likelihood it was begun as many as ten years before the date of publication and was composed at intervals. The narrative framework and the brand of social criticism have a close antecedent in Rodrigo *Fernández de Ribera's *Los anteojos de mejor vista* (The Eyeglasses of Perfected Vision). Vélez also draws upon folkloric material contained in Rodrigo Caro's *Días geniales o lúdicros* (Festive Days) and on Quevedo's *Sueños* (Visions). The plan of the work is simple. A student fleeing the authorities over rooftops enters the attic workshop of an astrologer who has the devil inside a phial. Once released, the devil accompanies the student in flight over several Spanish cities, lifting roofs to spy upon the inhabitants of various buildings. The work is neither a novel nor is it picaresque literature. It belongs to a very different fictional mode which bears the closest resemblance to the tradition of Mennipean satire and the formal conventions found in the dialogues of Lucian. The work is best read not as a novel but as an anatomical vision of a corrupt society written by an embittered Jewish convert who—in his old age—resents being unable to be a complete part of the very society he ridicules. *See also* Converso; Theater in Spain.

BIBLIOGRAPHY

Primary Texts

Los celos hacen estrellas. Ed. J. E. Varey, N. G. Shergold and Jack Sage. London: Tamesis, 1970.

El diablo cojuelo. Ed. Enrique Rodríguez Cepeda and Enrique Rull. Madrid: Alcalá, 1968.

Dramáticos contemporáneos de Lope de Vega. By Ramón de Mesonero Romanos. vol. 2. In BAE 45. (Contains *Más pesa el rey que la sangre*, *Reinar después de morir*, *Los hijos de la barbuda*, *El ollero de Ocaña*, *El diablo está en Cantillana*, and *La luna de la sierra*).

El embuste acreditado. Ed. Arnold G. Reichenberger. Colección Filológica 12. Granada: U of Granada, 1956.

La serrana de la Vera. Ed. and study Enrique Rodríguez Cepeda. Madrid: Alcalá, 1967.

Criticism

Cirot, George. "Le style de Vélez de Guevara." *BH* 44 (1942): 175–80.

Hauer, Mary G. *Luis Vélez de Guevara: A Critical Bibliography*. UNCSRLL 5. Chapel Hill: U of North Carolina P, 1975.

Richard Glenn

VENEGAS DEL BUSTO, Alejo (1495?, Toledo–1554?, ?), religious and philosophical scholar. He studied with Alonso Cedillo, but married before completing a degree in theology. Nonetheless, his works attest to an impressive erudition. His principal writings are *Agonía del tránsito de la muerte* (1537; Agony of the Journey to Death), an ascetic, Senecan work in which life is viewed as preparation for death—it enjoyed numerous editions in the sixteenth c.; *De las diferencias de libros que hay en el universo* (1540: On the Different Kinds of Books There Are in the Universe); and *Tratado de orthographía y accentos en las tres lenguas* *principales* (1531; Treatise on Orthography and Accents in the Three Main Languages [Greek, Latin, and Spanish]). *See also* Humanism; Senequism.

BIBLIOGRAPHY

Primary Texts

Agonía del tránsito de la muerte. In NBAE 16.
Agonía del tránsito de la muerte. Buenos Aires: Cruz del Sur, 1948.
Primera parte de las diferencias. . . . Salamanca: Laso, 1572.
Tratado de orthografía. Toledo: Ginoves, 1531.

VENTÓS I CULLELL, Palmira, pseudonym Felip Palma (1862, Barcelona–1917, Barcelona), novelist and playwright. Publishing consistently under her pseudonym, in Catalan, Ventós lived throughout her life in Barcelona, although her works have a rural Catalan setting. She adapts a realism bordering on *Naturalism to a sentimental view of life, counter-balancing the implacability of nature with lyricism and comic scenes. The most naturalistic of her works, *Asprors de la vida* (1904; Life Is Tough), depicts the harsh human realities of village life. She treats the themes of evil, hatred, and egoism and the resultant solitude and despair of life's victims, all against the backdrop of an unresponsive natural world. Several stories are written largely in a colloquial dialogue form. *La caiguda* (1907; The Fall) combines sentimental themes and a realistic treatment of life with detailed descriptions of nature, treating the solitude of the individual and the egoism of mankind within the cycle of human life and the natural world. Her two plays, both performed at the Teatre Català (Romea) in 1909, depict relationships in small towns and include popular types and dialogue to add a humorous dimension.

BIBLIOGRAPHY

Primary Texts

Asprors de la vida. Barcelona: L'Avenç, 1904.
La bonci gent. Barcelona: L'Avenç, 1925.
La caiguda. Barcelona: L'Avenç, 1907.
L'enrenou del poble. Quadro de costums en un acte. Barcelona: Bartomeu Baxarias, 1909.
Isolats, drama de família en tres actes. Barcelona: L'Avenç, 1909.

Kathleen McNerney

VERA Y MENDOZA, Juan de (1603, Seville–?, ?), supposed author of a *Panegírico por la poesía* (1627; Poetry Eulogy). Published anonymously, it contains valuable information about contemporary poets.

BIBLIOGRAPHY

Primary Text

Panegírico por la poesía. Ed. M. Cardenal. Madrid: n.p., 1941.

VERDAGUER I SANTALÓ, Jacint [Mossen Cinto] (1845, Folgueroles–1902, Vallvidrera, Barcelona), Catalan poet, theologist and essayist. Of a very humble origin, he entered the seminary of Vic when he was only ten years old. A precocious youngster, he started writing in his teens. Around 1860, after reading Tasso and Milton, he began to write religious-epic poetry and a little later, after reading Mistral, love poetry: *Amors d'en Jordi i na Guideta* (Love between Jordi and Guideta). At the end of his life he became a defender of illuminism (**alumbrades*) and a fundamentalist evangelist. For that reason the church authorities banned him from Barcelona. In defiance of the ban, he returned to the city, and with the help of friends he began publishing, in the newspaper *El Noticiero Universal*, his own series of essays "Un sacerdot calumniat" (A Slandered Priest) taken from the letters *En defensa propia* (1895; In My Own Defense). He was immediately suspended by the bishops of Vic and Barcelona, to which Verdaguer responded with another defiant series of essays, "Un sacerdot perseguit" (1897; A Persecuted Priest). By 1899 an arrangement was reached by which he was reinstated; he devoted the last years of his life to working for Catalan magazines or founding new ones like *Lo Pensament Català* (Catalan Thought). His last official act (1902) was to deliver the necrology "in memoriam" for the poet *Rubió i Ors, "Lo Gaiter del Llobregat."

Verdaguer wrote poetry throughout his life, with a resultant enormous production. Financially backed by faithful and wealthy patrons, he traveled throughout Europe and North Africa. From northern Europe he brought back the "Sturm und Drang" of Wagnerian Germany and used it to blend his mystical love of nature with a deep Catalan nationalism. After long wanderings on foot through the mountains of Catalonia he wrote his epic poems like *Canigó* (1875–78) in honor of French Catalonia. His travels are also expressed in a memorable, though not epic, book of poems, *Excursions i viatges* (1887; Excursions and Travels). With a passionate interest in the mystical past of Catalonia and also in Catalan folklore, he produced another beautiful book of poetry, *Col·lecció de Càntics religiosos per al poble* (1882–89; Collection of Religious Songs for the People). He also wrote a great deal of poetry devoted to Montserrat (the spiritual heart of Catalonia), of which the best known piece is the "Virolai" (1889). However, Verdaguer's masterpiece is the epic-mythical poem *L'Atlàntida* (1876), in which he intermingles Christian and pagan themes in retelling the mythical legend of the sinking of a continent beneath the waters of the Atlantic Ocean. Hercules, for example, is portrayed as a hero who conquers powerful enemies, such as the traitor Gayron and the Giant Antaeus, but is, alas!, Christianized. The fabulous happenings are related by a shipwrecked old man who turns out to be Columbus, for the poem ends in praise of the discovery of the New World. It was *Milà i Fontanals who urged Verdaguer to work on this poem, and the enterprise was greatly aided by the fact that Verdaguer criss-crossed the Atlantic many times as chaplain of an ocean liner. If *L'Atlàntida* is meant to have a universal character, *Canigó* is the national epic. Less grandiloquent than the former but more emotional and penetrating, it relates the story of the French beginnings of Catalonia as a nation; regardless of its religious spirit it still appeals to the hearts of all Catalans. Unlike the pseudo-Wagnerian overtones of *L'Atlàntida*, *Canigó* alternates epic poetry with the lyric and it ends with an enchanting dialogue between the bell towers of Sant Miquel de Cuixà and Sant Martí del Canigó (both are beautiful Romanesque monasteries located in the Pyrenees in French Catalonia). On the other hand, there is still another Verdaguer: the poet of the "anyorança" (longing), less grandiloquent than the epic but perhaps the best remembered today. Poems like "Lluny de ma terra" (Far from My Homeland) or "L'emigrant" (The Emigrant) are even popular among today's pop singers: "Dolça Catalunya, / pàtria del meu cor, / quan de tu s'allunya / d'anyorança es mor." (Sweet Catalonia / land of my heart / when one is far from you / of longing one dies.) Verdaguer, very much like Wagner in Germany, wanted to be a mystic of the national spirit, but both had the unfortunate fate to live in the nineteenth c., the antithesis of true heroic spirit and, above all, of mystic passions. Only the Russia of that time might have been historically germane to an artist like him. Nonetheless, Verdaguer is one of the pivotal literary figures of the Renaixença (Catalan renaissance) not only for the intrinsic value of his poetry but especially for forging the linguistic tools that *Maragall and others would elevate to incomparable heights. Another important book of poetry is *Idil·lis i cants místics* (1879; Idyls and Mystic Songs). *See also* Catalan Literature.

BIBLIOGRAPHY

Primary Texts

L'Atlàntida. Ed. Eduardo Junyent and Martín de Riquer. Barcelona: Ayuntamiento, 1946.

La Atlántida, poema de Mossén Jacinto Verdaguer. Tr. to Castilian by Melchor de Palau. Barcelona: J. Jepús, 1878.

Epistolari. Ed. J. M. Casacuberta and Torrent i Fàbregas. Barcelona: Barcino, 1971–75.

Escrits Inèdits. Notes by J. M. Casacuberta. Barcelona: Barcino, 1958.

Obres Completes. Prologue by Marià Manent and Epilogue by Joan Bonet i Baltá. 5th ed. Barcelona: n.p., 1974.

Criticism

Condeminas, M. *La gènesi de L'Atlàntida*. Barcelona: Departamento de Filología Catalana, U of Barcelona, 1978.

Miracle, Josep. *Amb la lira. . . .* Barcelona: n.p., 1952.

Montoliu, M. de. "La Renaixença i Els Jocs Florals: Verdaguer." In vol. 8 of *Les grans personalitats de la literatura catalana*. 8 vols. Barcelona: Alpha, 1957–1962.

Riba, Carles. "Centenari de Jacint Verdaguer." In *Miscelànea Verdaguer*. Paris: E. Ragasol, 1946.

Joan Gilabert

VERDUGO Y CASTILLA, Alfonso, Count of Torrepalma (1706, Alcalá la Real, Jaén–1767, Turín), diplomat, poet, member of the Royal Academy of History and the Academy of Good Taste (*Academia). Most of his poetry has not survived. What remains is cold and characteristic of the late Baroque. The narrative poem "El juicio final" exemplifies his preference for themes of death. "El Deucalión" is a mythological translation and paraphrasing of Ovid's *Metamorphosis*. He also composed some ballads.

BIBLIOGRAPHY

Primary Texts

"Deucalión." In BAE 29.
"El juicio final." In BAE 61.

VERGARA, Francisco de (?, ?–1545, ?), humanist, professor of Greek at the U of Alcalá, and disciple of Demetrio Ducas. An admirer of Erasmus, Vergara maintained an amicable correspondence with the Dutch humanist. He did much to further the study of Hellenism at the U of Alcalá. He composed a Greek chrestomaty (*Crestomatía griega*) in 1524 to correct the lack of Greek texts at Alcalá. He also wrote an elementary Greek grammar in 1526, the first of its kind in Spanish. He was the first translator into Castilian of Heliodorus's Byzantine romance, the *Aethiopica*. Working from the only available edition of the *Aethiopica* in Europe at the time, Vergara was forced to face the textual difficulties of a defective ms. His version was never published and is now lost. The notable influence of the *Aethiopica* on *Cervantes's *Persiles y Sigismunda* (Persiles and Sigismunda) and other Byzantine romances in Spanish is due to later translations. *See also* Erasmism; Humanism.

Deborah Compte

VERGARA, Juan de (?, Toledo–1557, ?), illustrious humanist and scholar. He taught philosophy at the U of Alcalá, assisted in composition of the *Bible of Alcalá, and, at the request of Cardinal *Cisneros, completed translations of several works of Aristotle. Vergara maintained an active correspondence with his friend Erasmus, and in 1533, the *Inquisition apprehended him; he spent much of the next fourteen years in prison. Vergara also wrote the *Tratado de las Ocho Questiones del Templo*. (n.d.; Treatise on the Eight Questions of the Temple). *See also* Aristotelianism; Erasmism; Humanism.

BIBLIOGRAPHY

Primary Text

Tratado de las ocho Questiones del Templo. Toledo: n.p., 1552. Rpt. ed. by Cerdá y Rico in *Clarorum hispanorum opuscula selecta et rariora*. Madrid: n.p., 1781.

Criticism

Lasperas, J. M. "La librería del Doctor Juan de Vergara." *RABM* 79 (1976): 337–51.

VERNET I REAL, Maria Teresa (1907, Barcelona–1974, ?), poet, novelist and translator. Best known for her novel *Maria Dolors* (1926; Maria Dolors), she collaborated in several publications, where she started to publish her first short stories. Her fiction often studies feminine psychology. Half of her work is written in Castilian and half in Catalan, for she belonged to the generation of writers who encountered difficulty diffusing their books in Catalan due to the political repression of the post-war period. She translated several books from English into Spanish.

BIBLIOGRAPHY

Primary Texts

Les algues roges. Badalona: Proa, 1934.
Amor silencioso. Barcelona: Central Catalana de publicacions, 1927.
El camí reprès. Badalona: Proa, 1930.
Elisenda. Barcelona: Quaderns literaris, 1935.
Estampes de Paris. Barcelona: Quaderns literaris, 1937.
Eulàlia. Badalona: Proa, 1928.
Final i preludi. Badalona: Proa, 1933.
Maria Dolors. Barcelona: L'avenç Gràfic, 1926.
El perill. Badalona: Proa, 1930.
Poemes. Barcelona: La Revista, 1929.
Poemes II. Barcelona: La Revista, 1931.
Presó oberta. Badalona: Proa, 1931.

Kathleen McNerney

VERNEY, Luis Antonio de. *See* Barbadiño

VIANA, Antonio de (1578, La Laguna, Canary Islands–after 1650, Seville?), physician, poet. He studied medicine in Seville. Lope de *Vega and other peers praised him. His most important work is the epic poem *Antigüedades de las Islas Afortunadas de la Gran Canaria, conquista de Tenerife y aparecimiento de la Imagen de la Candelaria* (1604; Antiquities of the Fortunate Islands of Grand Canary, the Conquest of Tenerife, and Appearance of the Image of Our Lady of Candlemas). Using free verse and **octavas reales,* he weaves history and legend with a love story which finally unites the native Guanche of the islands with the Castilian people. Lope used the work as source for his drama *Los guanches de Tenerife y conquista de Canarias*. Viana also wrote a medical treatise, *Espejo de cirujía* (1631; Mirror of Surgery).

BIBLIOGRAPHY

Primary Texts

Antigüedades. In *Der Kampf um Teneriffa. Dichtung und Geschichte von Antonio de Viana*. Ed. F. von Loher. Tübingen: Literarischer verein in Stuttgart, 1883.
Conquista de Tenerife. Ed. A. Cioranescu. Sta. Cruz de Tenerife: Aula de Cultura de Tenerife, 1971.
Espejo de cirujía. Lisbon: n.p., 1631.

Criticism

Alonso, María Rosa. *El poema de Viano: estudio histórico literario de un poema épico del siglo XVII*. Madrid: CSIC, 1952.

VIANA, Carlos de (1421, Peñafiel, Valladolid–1461, Barcelona), son of John II, Prince of Aragón, writer. A friend of Ausiàs *March, Viana is credited with having written the *Crónica de los reyes de Navarra* (n.d.; Chronicle of the Kings of Navarre), which narrates events up to the reign of his grandfather, Charles III of Navarre.

BIBLIOGRAPHY

Primary Text

Crónica de los reyes de Navarra. Ed. J. Yanguas y Miranda. Pamplona: Ochoa, 1843.

Criticism

Closas, Antoni. *El primogènit Carles, Princep de Viana*. Barcelona: Dalmau, 1977.
Desdevises du Dézert, G. N. *Don Carlos d'Aragon, prince de Viana*. Paris: Colin, 1889.

VICENS, Antònia (1942, Santanyí, Majorca–), novelist. She has won literary prizes for both long and short narrations, which often depict life on the island. *La santa* (1980; The Saint) was written with a background of her own small town, depicting the streets, plaza, and people who inhabit them. With a vision that seems to come from a semi-conscious state between sleeping and waking, Vicens nonetheless gives a lucid critique of that microcosm of society which represents the universal.

BIBLIOGRAPHY

Primary Texts

Banc de fusta. Majorca: Moll, 1968.
La festa de tots els morts. Barcelona: Nova terra, 1974.
Material de fulletó. Majorca: Moll, 1971.
Primera Comunió. Majorca: Moll, 1971.
Quilòmetres de tul per a un petit cadàver. Barcelona: Laia, 1982.
La santa. Barcelona: Laia, 1980.
39 graus a l'ombre. Barcelona: Selecta, 1968.

Kathleen McNerney

VICENTE, Gil (1456?, Portugal?–1537, Portugal?), poet and dramatist. Gil Vicente is a major Portuguese and Spanish playwright bridging the medieval and *Renaissance traditions. Very little biographical information exists about his life, and even the date and place of birth are uncertain. Various towns and regions in Portugal claim to be his place of birth (Barcelos, Guimarães, Lisbon, the province of Beira Alta), yet it is almost certain that he was born in the Portuguese countryside, so readily reflected in the *pastoral nature of his plays. It is very probable that he was a goldsmith to Queen Leonor and was brought to the court at Evora for the first time in 1490 for the wedding of the Crown Prince and Isabel, daughter of the Catholic monarchs Ferdinand and Isabel of Spain. The Belem monstrance, now preserved in Lisbon's Museu Nacional da Arte Antiga, has been attributed to him. In 1509 he was appointed overseer of the gold and silver craft in Portugal, and in 1513 he became master of the royal mint until

1517. In addition, he was a musician, poet, and actor, and held a post on the Lisbon Town Council. He died sometime after the performance of his last play, *Floresta de Engaños* (Forest of Deceits), in 1536. His works were published for the first time by his son, Luis Vicente, as the *Copilaçam* (1562; Compilation).

Of the forty-four extant plays, sixteen are completely in Portuguese, eleven completely in Spanish, and seventeen combine both languages. Vicente's bilingualism has been studied extensively by Paul Teyssier, who offers various hypotheses as to why, at various intervals, Gil Vicente wrote in Spanish rather than in his native Portuguese. Literary tradition certainly exerted a strong hold upon him, and he began his dramatic career under the influence of Juan del *Encina and Lucas *Fernández. *Valbuena Prat has in fact divided Vicente's work into two groups, before and after 1520. His early works are rather simple plays built around a dialogue between shepherds and are heavily derivative of previous writers. Works written after 1520 reveal a greater originality as a definite artistic personality emerges. The later works reflect Vicente's mastery of style, language, and the stage and include chivalric, allegorical and popular plays.

Vicente's first extant play is the *Visiticão* (1502; The Visitation), or *Monólogo do vaqueiro* (Herdsman's Monologue), a panegyric in which a herdsman, played by Gil Vicente, enters Queen María's bedchamber to congratulate her on the birth of her firstborn son. The *Auto Pastoril Castelhano* (1502; Castilian Pastoral Play), the *Auto dos Reis Magos* (1503; Play of the Magi), and the *Auto de San Martinho* (1504; Play of St. Martin) constitute his first experimentation with drama and reveal his debt to Juan del Encina. Vicente continued the Salamancan tradition of Encina and Lucas Fernández in the *Auto da Sibila Cassandra* (1513 or 1514; *The Play of the Sibyl Cassandra*, 1921), the *Auto dos Quatro Tempos* (1516; The Play of the Four Seasons), and the *Auto da Mofina Mendes* (1534; Play of Mofina Mendez). The plays combine biblical and pagan elements to celebrate the Christmas theme in a more interesting and complex manner than his early works. The *Auto da Sibila Cassandra* in particular is noted for its fine lyricism. Vicente's celebrated trilogy, *Trilogía de las Barcas* (The Three Ships), and the *Auto da Feira* (Play of the Fair) illustrate his capacity for the social and anti-clerical satire of the Erasmian tradition. The theme of the *Barcas* is the medieval dance of death in which figures from diverse social stations are judged according to their deeds on Earth before their condemnation to Hell or entrance to Paradise. The *Barca do Inferno* (Ship of Hell) and the *Barca do Purgatorio* (Ship of Purgatory) were written in Portuguese, while the *Barca da Gloria* (Ship of Paradise) is in Spanish. All were composed between 1516 and 1519.

The *Comédia de Rubena* (1521; The Play of Rubena) is one of Vicente's fantastic comedies filled with lyricism and pageantry. The play includes magical elements and spells, revealing the popular and folkloric traditions behind its creation. The **villancico* "Halcón que se atreve" (Falcon That Dares) shows Vicente's adept use of musical interludes in his plays. The *Comédia do viúvo* (1521; Play of the Widower) is a sketch for *Dom Duardos* and an antecedent of his chivalric plays. The richly expressive work examines the vacillations of don

Rosvel Tenori in deciding which of two daughters to marry. Vicente's two chivalric tragicomedies, *Dom Duardos* and *Amadís de Gaula*, are both in Spanish and among his most highly developed dramatic efforts. *Dom Duardos*, Vicente's most lengthy and complex work, is based on episodes from the chivalric novel *Primaleón*, a continuation of *Palmerín de Oliva*. Disguised as a gardener, Dom Duardos woos Princess Flérida of Constantinople at her father's court. The exquisite lyrical interludes recounting the love between the two characters make the play one of Vicente's most successful.

Gil Vicente's farces make a major contribution to the development of the theatrical tradition. They combine learned and popular elements designed to entertain the audience with comic caricatures of social types and customs. The *Farsa de Inés Pereira* (Farce of Ines Pereira), one of Vicente's best plays, is built around the adage "Más quiero asno que me lleve que caballo que me derribe" (I prefer a donkey which will carry me to a horse which will throw me). The *O velho da horta* (The Old Man of the Orchard) is a farcical satire on everyday life in which an old married man pursues a young girl. *Quem tem farelos?* (1508; Who Has Bran?) ridicules a squire who serenades his lady with a lovely Castilian poem amid the accompaniment of the dogs, cats, and roosters of the neighborhood. The *Farsa dos físicos* (Farce of the Doctors) and *Farsa dos Almocreves* (*Farce of the Carriers*, 1920) present similar comic sketches of national customs.

Vicente's finest achievement is the outstanding lyrical expression of popular themes. His transformations of anonymous folkloric motifs into splendid lyrical creations are unrivaled in the theater until the time of Lope de *Vega. Songs, glosses, *villancicos* all abound in his works and constitute magnificent illustrations of Vicente's splendid poetic talents. *See also* Auto; Erasmism; *Palmerín*; Theater in Spain.

BIBLIOGRAPHY

Primary Texts

Auto da barco do Inferno. Ed. Charles David Ley. Madrid: CSIC, 1946.
Comedia del viudo. Ed. Alonso Zamora Vicente. Lisbon: Instituto de Alta Cultura, 1962.
Floresta de Engaños. Ed. Constantine Christopher Stathos. UNCSRLL 125. Chapel Hill: U of North Carolina P, 1972.
Obras completas. Lisbon: Oficinas gráficas da Biblioteca Nacional, 1928. Facs. of 1562 ed.
Obras Completas. Ed. Marqués de Braga. 6 vols. Lisbon: Sá de Costa, 1942–44.
Obras dramáticas castellanas. Ed. Thomas R. Hart. Madrid: Espasa-Calpe, 1962.
Poesías de Gil Vicente. Ed. Dámaso Alonso. Mexico: Séneca, 1940.
Tragicomedia de don Duardos. Ed. Dámaso Alonso. Madrid: CSIC, 1942.

English Translations

Four Plays of Gil Vicente. Ed. and tr. Aubrey F. G. Bell. Cambridge, Eng.: Cambridge UP, 1920. Contains *Auto da alma, Exhortação da Guerra, Farsa dos Almocreves, Tragicomedia Pastoril da Serra da Estrêla*.

Lyrics of Gil Vicente. Tr. Aubrey F. G. Bell. 3rd ed. Waterford, Eng.: Voss and Michael, 1925.
The Ship of Hell. Tr. A. F. Gerald (A.F.G. Bell). Waterford, Eng.: Voss and Michael, 1929. Re-edited by Lisbon: Agencia Geral do Ultramar Divisão de Publicacões e Biblioteca, 1954.

Criticism

Bell, Aubrey F. G. *Gil Vicente*. Oxford: Oxford UP, 1921.
Braacamp Freire, Anselmo. *Vida e obras de Gil Vicente, ''trovador, mestre da balança.''* 2nd ed. Lisbon: Ediçao da Revista Ocidente, 1944.
King, Georgiana G. *The Play of the Sibyl Cassandra*. New York: Longmans, Green, 1921.
Parker, Jack H. *Gil Vicente*. TWAS 29. Boston: Twayne, 1967.
Reckert, Steven. *Gil Vicente, espíritu y letra*. Madrid: Gredos, 1977.
Teyssier, Paul. *La langue de Gil Vicente*. Paris: C. Klincksieck, 1959.
Valbuena Prat, A. *Historia de la literatura española*. vol. 1. Barcelona: Gili, 1968.

Deborah Compte

VIDA DE SAN ILDEFONSO (Life of St. Hildephonse), anonymous late medieval poem. It is a lengthy poem (over 1,000 lines) in **mester de clerecía*, written in the second quarter of the fourteenth c. by a cleric, apparently in Toledo, who identified himself only as ''Beneficiado de Ubeda'' (Beneficiary of Ubeda). Emulating the style and form of *Berceo, the author narrates the life and miracles of a local saint (St. Hildephonse, 607–67), praises the Virgin Mary, and lauds the city of Toledo, but his poetry lacks the grace and vigor of Berceo's. The text is quite corrupt; many stanzas are incomplete or altered and the rhyme is frequently defective. The friar Martín *Sarmiento copied this poem in the eighteenth c. Manuel Alvar Ezquerra has edited a nineteenth-c. version, possibly copied from that of Sarmiento. Another poem by the Beneficiary of Ubeda, dedicated to Mary Magdalene, has been lost. *See also* Hagiography; Ildefonso de Toledo, San.

BIBLIOGRAPHY

Primary Text

Vida de San Ildefonso. Ed. Manuel Alvar Ezquerra. Bogota: Instituto Caro y Cuervo, 1975.

Kathleen L. Kirk

VIDART Y SCHUCH, Luis (1833, Madrid–1897, Madrid), career soldier, writer. He rose to the rank of lieutenant colonel. From an early age, Vidart y Schuch contributed articles to the leading magazines of Madrid. He wrote poetry, novels, and drama, but is most remembered for his philosophical investigations, as in *La filosofía española, indicaciones bibliográficas* (1866; Spanish Philosophy, Bibliographic Indications), his biographies of Vasco de Gama and *Camões, and his critical work on *Cervantes, in *Cervantes, poeta épico* (1877; Cervantes, Epic Poet), *Los biógrafos de Cervantes en el siglo XVIII* (1886;

Eighteenth-Century Cervantine Biographers), and *Un historiador francés de la vida de Cervantes* (1891; A French Historian of Cervantes's Life).

BIBLIOGRAPHY

Primary Texts

Los biógrafos de Cervantes en el siglo XVIII. Madrid: Rivadeneyra, 1886.
Camoens. Madrid: Aribau, 1880.
Cervantes, poeta épico. Madrid: Aribau, 1877.
La filosofía española. Madrid: Europea, 1866.
Un historiador francés de la vida de Cervantes. Madrid: Rivadeneyra, 1891.

VIEIRA, Afonso Lopes (1878, Leiria–1946, Lisbon), Portuguese poet, critic and historical novelist. After graduating in law from the U of Coimbra in 1900, he followed his father into the practice of law, later becoming clerk to the Chamber of Deputies. Later still, his financial circumstances allowed him to live independently and travel. He wrote poetry in the symbolist and neo-Garrettian (romantic) vein being particularly influenced by António Nobre and developing a colloquial and somewhat melancholy style.

Politically he became a passionate and somewhat strident nationalist espousing the cause of Saudosismo, becoming a member of the movement's Lisbon committee and always cleaving to the traditionalist aristocratic and conservative Catholic stance typical of his literary forerunners. As a result he despised modern times and attitudes, seeing in them the source of platitude and vulgarity. Interestingly, his opposition continued unchanged under the Salazar regime and led to his imprisonment on various occasions.

In 1911 he launched a campaign in conjunction with the actor Augusto Rosa to revive the plays of Gil *Vicente and also tried to foster an appreciation of popular poetry and song. He was one of the leading lights of the review *Lusitânia*.

The bulk of his literary production consists of volumes of poetry with the early groupings in particular being devoted to aspects of university life and to his early explorations of philosophy.

The most noteworthy of the philosophical group are *Para Quê?* (1897; Why?); *Náufrago* (1898; Shipwreck) and *O Meu Adeus* (1900; My Farewell). Other volumes bear the titles *Ar Livre* (1906; Open Air); *Rosas Bravas* (1911; Wild Roses); *Canções do Vento e do Sol* (1911; Songs of Wind and Sun); *Ilhas de Bruma* (1917; Isles of Mist) and *Onde a Terra acaba e o Mar Começa* (1940; Where the Land Ends and the Sea Begins).

His fiction consists of *Marques* (1904), the tale of a persecuted man and an example of "histoire romancée," and *A Paixão de Pedro o Cru* (1940; The Passion of Peter the Cruel).

Finally, we have his studies and attempts to re-establish Gil Vicente in Portuguese literature, as well as Jorge de *Montemayor's claim to authorship of the *Diana* and Vasco de Lobeira's of the **Amadís de Gaula*.

BIBLIOGRAPHY

Primary Texts

Diana de Jorge de Montemor. Lisbon: Libânio da Silva, 1924.
Náufrago. Lisbon: António Maria Pereira, 1898.
A Paixão de Pedro o Cru. Lisbon: Sá da Costa, 1943.
Para Quê? Coimbra: França Amado, 1897.
O Romance de Amadis. 3rd ed. Lisbon: Soc. Portugal-Brasil, 1935.

Criticism

Campos, Agostinho de. *Afonso Lopes Vieira*. Lisbon: Aillaud e Bertrand, 1925.
Ribeiro, Aquilino. "Afonso Lopes Vieira e a evolução de seu pensamento." In *Camões, Camilo, Eça e alguns mais*. Lisbon: Bertrand, 1949. 273–335.

Peter Fothergill-Payne

VIEIRA, José Luandino, pseudonym of José Vieira Mateus da Graça (1935, Lagoa do Furadouro, Portugal–), Angolan short story writer and novelist. Luandino's short stories and novels reflect his filial devotion to Angola (which gained its independence from Portugal in 1975), and his sobriquet suggests the extent of his attachment to Luanda, the city that has been his home since he arrived there at the age of three with his Portuguese settler parents. But despite their Africanness, Angolan specificity, and Luandan topophilia, Luandino's works belong unequivocally to the extended family of literature written in Portuguese.

Luuanda (1964; *Luuanda: Short Stories of Angola*, 1980), Luandino's first significant publication, won the 1965 Grand Prize for Prose Fiction awarded by the Lisbon-based Portuguese Writers Society. Ironically, at the time of the award the author was beginning a long prison term for his denunciations of Portugal's colonial empire.

Rather than the conventional *histórias* (stories) or *contos* (short stories), Luandino has called his tales *estórias* because, according to him, that Portuguese archaism best captures the spirit of the indigenous Angolan *missosso* (plural of *mussosso*), or traditional African oral fables. But in Luandino's hands the *estória* has become a unique acculturated genre blending elements of the African oral tradition, the quotidian historiography of the medieval Portuguese chronicle, and the short popular epic of the Brazilian northeast.

Luandino's experimentation with narrative genres paralles his innovative use of language. With their neologisms and syntactical stylizations, his works have elevated the black Portuguese vernacular of Luanda's *musseques* (shanty-towns) to the level of a literary language. Similarly, the compelling and non-exoticizing presence in his stories of Kimbundu phrases and syntax has lent an aura of classical dignity to that local African tongue.

Luandino wrote most of his eleven published works during several terms as a political prisoner. While serving nearly eight years in the infamous concentration camp at Tarrafal on the Cape Verdean island of Santiago, he honed his iconoclastic style and his unique anti-populist populism in the tales collected in his three most recently published volumes, all of which he wrote surreptitiously or with the indulgence of a sympathetic prison director.

Inevitably, all of Luandino's stories protest, implicitly or explicitly, against Portugal's intransigent colonial rule. Nowhere is this protest more evident than in *A Vida Verdadeira de Domingos Xavier* (1974; *The Real Life of Domingos Xavier*, 1978). Written in Lisbon, in 1961, and set in Angola on the eve of the outbreak of the armed rebellion, this novel tells the story of a young working-class African who becomes a martyred hero at the hands of the Portuguese secret police. Before its publication, nearly thirteen years after it was written, mimeographed copies of the novel circulated clandestinely in Angola and Portugal, and its story forms the basis of *Sambizanga*, a film made in 1972 by Sarah Maldoror.

Luandino is at his artistic best in the *estórias* collected in *Macandumba* (1978; a Portuguese corruption of two Kimbundu words meaning, roughly, "big doings"), *João Vêncio: Os Seus Amores* (1979; The Loves of João Vêncio), and *Lourentinho, Dona Antónia & Eu* (1981; Lourentinho, Mrs. Antónia, and I). And with *Nós, os do Makulusu* (1975; We, the Folks from Makulusu), Luandino fashioned a sensitive and haunting novel, with autobiographical overtones, around the lives of two generations of a family of Portuguese settlers and their African neighbors living in the tense atmosphere of Luanda at the outset of the war between Angolan nationalists and the colonial forces.

Following the 1974 coup that toppled Portugal's right-wing dictatorship, that country's liberal intellectual and literary establishment re-emerged triumphantly to claim Luandino as one of their own. After all, with five of his works translated into nine languages, Luandino has attained international stature as an author who has enhanced the Portuguese language. Moreover, most of his books were first published in Lisbon. The staunchly Angolan writer has indeed enriched the common language even though his literary discourse differs markedly from that of his Portuguese counterparts. Thus, besides being Angola's foremost author and among the best contemporary writers of Africa, Luandino also occupies a prominent place in the history of modern Portuguese literature.

BIBLIOGRAPHY

Primary Texts

Duas estórias. Lobito, Angola: Capricórnio, 1974.
Luuanda: estórias. 4th ed. Lisbon: Edições 70, 1972.
Macandumba. Lisbon: Edições 70, 1978.
No antigamente, na vida. Lisbon: Edições 70, 1974.
Velhas estórias. 2nd ed. Lisbon: Edições 70, 1976.
A vida verdadeira de Domingos Xavier. Lisbon: Edições 70, 1974.
Vidas novas. 3rd ed. Lisbon: Edições 70, 1976.

English Translations

Luuanda; Short Stories of Angola. Tr. T. Bender. London: Heinemann, 1980.
The Real Life of Domingos Xavier. Tr. M. Wolfers. London: Heinemann, 1978.

Criticism

Bender, Tamara. "Translator's Preface." In *Luuanda: Short Stories of Angola*. London: Heinemann, 1980.

Hamilton, Russell. "Black from White and White on Black: Contradictions of Language in the Angolan Novel." *Ideologies and Literature* (Dec. 1976-Jan. 1977): 25–58.

Laban, Michel. "Encontros com Luandino Vieira." In *Luandino: José Luandino Vieira e a Sua Obra*. Lisbon: Edições 70, 1980.

Ngwube. "On the Real Life of Domingos Xavier." *New African* (Oct. 1978): 108.

Trigo, Salvato. "O Texto de Luandino Vieira." In *Luandino: José Luandino Vieira e a Sua Obra*. Lisbon: Edições 70, 1980.

Russell G. Hamilton

VIERA Y CLAVIJO, José de (1731, Realejo Alto, Tenerife, Canary Islands–1813, Las Palmas, Canary Island), Dominican priest, historian. A prolific author of over 160 works of all types (songs, letters, sermons, pedagogy, etc.), he was also renowned for his oratorical prowess which he honed in La Laguna from 1757 to 1770. In 1770, he went to Madrid to edit one of his finest writings, the *Noticias de la Historia de Canarias* (1772–83; Historical Events of the Canary Islands). There, he also met and entered the service of the Marquis of Santa Cruz, traveling with him the next fourteen years throughout Europe. These trips yielded several travel diaries. In 1784, he returned to Las Palmas as archdeacon of the cathedral and remained there until his death.

Still valuable today is another work of Father Viera, the *Diccionario de Historia Natural de las Islas Canarias* (1866; Dictionary of Natural History of the Canary Islands). Much of his work remains in ms. form.

BIBLIOGRAPHY

Primary Texts

Noticias de la Historia de Canarias. Ed. E. Serra Ràfols. 3 vols. Sta. Cruz de Tenerife: Goya, 1950–52.

Diccionario de Historia Natural de las Islas Canarias. Sta. Cruz de Tenerife: n.p., 1942.

VIGHI, Francisco (1890, Palencia–1962, Madrid), Spanish poet and essayist. Although trained as an engineer, his vocation was poetry. Most of his work is uncollected, dispersed in various periodicals, magazines and newspapers. He tended to mix satiric verse with other compositions of sentimental themes. A familiar figure of Madrid literary cafés in the Vanguard period, he was portrayed by Ramón *Gómez de la Serna both in *Pombo* (1918)—the name of the café where their **tertulia* (literary gathering) met—and *Retratos contemporáneos* (1941; Contemporary Portraits). Some of his poems were compiled in the volume *Versos viejos* (1961; Old Lyrics) shortly before his death, illustrated with watercolors by Eduardo Vicente.

VILA-MATAS, Enrique (1948, Barcelona–), Spanish novelist, critic, journalist and short-story writer. A regular collaborator of *La Vanguardia* in its literary and cultural section, Vila-Matas is also an editor of *Trafalgar Square*, a poetry and fiction review. *Mujer en el espejo contemplando el paisaje* (1973; Woman in the Mirror Contemplating the Landscape) and *La asesina ilustrada* (1977; The Illustrated Murderess) are novelettes; *Nunca voy al cine* (1982; I Never Go to the Movies) is a collection of short stories. Full-length novels to date include *Al sur de los párpados* (1980; South of the Eyelids) and *Impostura* (1984; Imposture), based on a real incident in which a beggar arrested robbing tombs pretends to be mad and is confined to an asylum. Two women of very different social backgrounds read about the unidentified man, each believing him to be her missing husband, the upper-class, pro-Franco Dr. Bruch, an illustrious professor and writer, or a former anarchist, extortionist and petty thief. The astute madman manipulates interests and suspicions in a tale which ultimately is an inquiry into memory, identity and solitude. *Historia abreviada de la literatura portátil* (1985; Short History of Portable Literature) presents the secret "Portable Society," also known as the Shandy Conspiracy, allegedly founded in Africa in 1924 and involving writers as varied as Walter Benjamin, Duchamp, Pola Negri, Valery Larbaud, Georgia O'Keefe, Gombrowicz, *García Lorca and Scott Fitzgerald, and traces its three scandalous years of existence with "ample documentation." Highly praised by Spanish critics, the work was an international hit in translations to Italian, Swedish and German. *Una casa para siempre* (1988; A House For Always) presents the putative memoirs of a famous ventriloquist who disappears after having murdered the man who stole his beloved, undertaking a repugnant flight disguised by the narrator as beautiful, cultured and literary. An inquiry into the problem of the ventriloquist—man of many voices—who suddenly finds himself with only one voice, the nature of truth and memory, the novel also explores the inseparable presence of fiction in autobiography. Vila-Matas is considered one of the most original and disquieting of younger Spanish writers.

Janet Pérez

VILA MOURA, Bento de Oliveira Cardoso e Castro Guedes de Carvalho Lobo Visconde de (1877, Vila Moura–1935, Vila Moura), created first viscount of Vila Moura by decree on October 25, 1900, Portuguese novelist and critic. Without being inspired as a thinker nor particularly endowed as a writer he was nonetheless a representative and original member of the Decadentist movement in Portugal before moving toward an emotional conservative position similar to that of Paul Bourget in France. In his earlier years he opposed the positivist and naturalist positions and so argued against both Leonardo *Coimbra and the supporters of Zola and proclaimed himself an admirer of Ruskin, Wilde, Nietszche and d'Annunzio. His first full-length novel, *Nova Safo* (1912; The New Sapho), whose protagonist is a lesbian hypersensitive woman author, calls up all the panoply of attitudes that spans the gap between the early Huysmans's decadence and the mature Bourget's anti-intellectualism and racial theories in the ways in which Vila Moura portrays the former's opinions on neuroses and the moral and physical exhaustion of noble families combined with the latter's ideas on the ills that have beset society since its leaders abandoned an instinctive attachment to their land and tenantry for the excitement of a cosmopolitan, amoral city life. As his opinions developed, Vila Moura moved closer to the emotional conservatism of the Renascença Portuguesa and wrote a number of contributions to their review *A Águia*. He nonetheless continued the aesthetic element in his writing as witness his attempt to codify the emotions in colors in "Sonatas de Cor" (Sonatas in Color) included in his collection of short stories *Novos Mitos* (1934; New Myths), published a year before his death. His literary criticism includes studies on Camilo Castelo Branco, Fialho d'Almeida, António Nobre and Teixeira Lopes.

BIBLIOGRAPHY

Primary Texts

António Nobre. Porto: Renascença Portuguesa, 1915.
Camilo Inédito. Porto: Renascença Portuguesa, 1913.
Doentes de Beleza. 2nd ed. Rio de Janeiro: Anuário do Brasil, 1927.
"Fanny Owen e Camilo." *A Águia* 11 (1917): 5–23.
A Moral na Religião e na Arte. Coimbra: França Amado, 1906.
Nova Sapho. 2nd ed. Rio de Janeiro: Anuário do Brasil, 1921.
Novos Mitos. Porto: Imprensa Portuguesa, 1934.
A Vida Literária e Política. Porto: Magalhães e Moniz, 1911.
A Vida Mental Portuguesa. Coimbra: Imprensa da Universidade, 1908.

Criticism

Alves, João. *O Génio de Vila Moura*. Porto: Renascença Portuguesa, 1937.

Peter Fothergill-Payne

VILLAESPESA, Francisco (1877, Laujar, Almería–1936, Madrid), poet and dramatist. Preferring the literary calling over his studies, he abandoned the U of Granada in 1897 for Madrid, where his first poems were published in the literary magazine *Germinal*. The following year he returned home but not without some recognition—his first book of poetry, *Intimidades* (1898; Intimacies), had been published, and a second one, *Luchas* (1899; Struggles), was soon to appear. Back in Madrid once more, he married and attempted to supplement his income by serving on the editorial board of various journals, including some which he founded. However, poverty was to plague him throughout much of his life.

His wife's death of tuberculosis inspired *Viaje sentimental* (1909; Sentimental Journey), which recounts poetically his effort to overcome his bereavement. Villaespesa made an extensive tour of Latin America giving lectures and staging plays before returning to Spain, penniless, where he died in 1936.

Although he had several successful dramas, including *El alcázar de las perlas* (1911; The Castle of Pearls), today his theater is not highly regarded by critics. His poetry production was immense, with over fifty volumes published. Villaespesa was a neo-romantic with marked modernist tendencies. His earliest poetry shows the decided influence of *Bécquer and *Zorrilla. Later works, especially *La copa del rey de Thule* (1900; The King of Thule's Goblet), reveal his acquaintance with Rubén Darío's *Modernism, and while many of his verses are of considerable beauty and inspiration, the tone of much of his work has a plaintive quality that is sometimes viewed as superficial and belonging to another age.

BIBLIOGRAPHY

Primary Texts

La copa del rey de Thule. Madrid: Tipografía Moderna, 1900.
Intimidades. Madrid: Antonio Alvarez, 1898.
Luchas. Madrid: C. Apaolaza, 1899.
Poesías completas. Madrid: Aguilar, 1954.
Teatro escogido. Madrid: Aguilar, 1951.
Viaje sentimental. Madrid: Hispano-Americanos, 1909.

Criticism

Alvarez Sierra, J. *Francisco Villaespesa*. Madrid: Editora Nacional, 1949. Biography.
Berenguer, Angel. "El modernismo en Villaespesa: Génesis y recuperación." *CH* 349 (July 1979): 185–91.
Cortés, Eliado. *El teatro de Villaespesa (Estudio crítico)*. Madrid: Atlas, 1971.
Díaz Larios, Luis F. Prologue to *Francisco Villaespesa: Antología Poética*. Almería: Librería-Editorial Cajal, 1977.
Sánchez Trigueros, Antonio. *Francisco Villaespesa y su primera obra poética, 1897–1900*. Granada: U of Granada, 1974.

James F. Brown

VILLALÓN, Cristóbal de (?–?), name of one to four *Renaissance writers. They are as follows: (1) Cristóbal de Villalón of Valladolid, author of *Tragedia de Mirrha* (1536; Tragedy of Myrrha), inspired by Ovid's *Metamorphosis*, and of *El escolástico* (The Scholastic), a delineation of qualities inherent in the ideal professor and the ideal student. (2) Cristóbal de Villalón, author of *El crotalón* (pub. 1871; Cymbals), a clever, negative social satire in which a cock and shoemaker engage in Erasmist dialogue, and of the *Diálogo de las transformaciones de Pitágoras* (Pub. 1907; Dialogue on the Transformations of Pythagoras). A very famous work, the *Viaje de Turquía* (1919; Turkish Trip), was also attributed to him; the attribution was questioned by M. Bataillon, who offered evidence for composition by Andrés *Laguna. Bataillon's arguments have been challenged by recent scholarship (see Kincaid and Portuondo, ed.). (3) Cristóbal de Villalón, author of *La ingeniosa comparación entre lo antiguo y lo presente* (1539; Clever Comparison between Antiquity and the Present) and *El provechoso tratado de cambios y contrataciones de mercaderes y reprobación de usura* (1541; Profitable Treatise on Premiums and Commerce among Merchants and the Censure of Usury). (4) Cristóbal de Villalón, author of the *Gramática castellana* (Antwerp, 1558; Castilian Grammar), which criticizes the

Grammar of Antonio de *Nebrija. Some critics have argued that there is only one Villalón. *See* J.J. Kincaid, criticism, for futher dicussion.

BIBLIOGRAPHY

Primary Texts

El crotalón. In NBAE 7.

El crotalón. Madrid: Cátedra, 1982.

Diálogo de las transformaciones. In NBAE 7.

Gramática castellana. Antwerp: Simon, 1558. Rpt. Madrid: CSIC, 1971. Facs., study by C. García.

Ingeniosa comparación. . . . Madrid: Tello, 1898.

Provechoso tratado de cambios. . . . Valladolid: n.p., 1546. Rpt. Valladolid: Castellana, 1945.

"El provechoso tratado de cambios of Cristóbal de Villalón: A Critical Edition." Ed. A. E. Szymkowiak. *DAI* 37 (1977): 5876A (Catholic U of America).

El scholástico. Ed. R. J. A. Kerr. Madrid: CSIC, 1967.

Tragedia de Mirrha. Madrid: Suárez, 1926.

"Viaje de Turquía de Christóbal de Villalón: Edición y estudio." A. Tamayo Portuondo. *DAI* 36 (1975): 2246A (Catholic U of America).

Viaje de Turquía: (la odisea de Pedro de Urdemalas). Ed. F. G. Salinero. Madrid: Cátedra, 1980.

Criticism

Kiger, J. M. "The Extent and Nature of the Use of Classical Sources in Villalón's *El scholástico.*" *Romance Quarterly* 36.3 (1983): 368–98.

Kincaid, J. J. "Cristóbal de Villalón: The Authorship of the Anonymous Works and the Problem of Identity." *DAI* 31 (1970): 1282A–82A (Vanderbilt U).

López-Vázquez, A. R. "Ideología y mito en el Siglo de Oro: De Cristóbal de Villalón a Calderón de la Barca." In *Hommage des hispanistes français a Noël Salomon.* Intro. H. Bonneville. Barcelona: Laia, 1979. 527–41.

Meregalli, F. "Partes inéditas y partes perdidas del *Viaje de Turquía.*" *BRAE* 54 (1974): 193–201.

Ortolá, Marie Sol. *Un estudio del* Viaje de Turquia: *autobiografía o ficción.* London: Tamesis, 1983.

Salinero, F. "El *Viaje de Turquía* y la Orden de Malta: Revisión de una interpretación de la obra y su autor." *REH* (University, AL) 14 (1980): 19–30.

Maureen Ihrie

VILLALÓN, Fernando (1881, Arcos de la Frontera, Seville–1930, Madrid), count of Miraflores, breeder of *toros de lidia* (fighting bulls), and poet. With the family title, he inherited the Andalusian ranch where he lived all his life in close contact with nature and the world of bullfighting. As a child he studied in Puerto de Santa María, where his stay coincided with that of Juan Ramón *Jiménez. This friendship with the poet from Moguer, and his later acquaintance with the younger poets of the *Generation of 1927, saw his poetry evolve from his early interest in popular themes, through the discovery of *Góngora, to the more refined approach, akin to surrealism, of his last compositions. He published three books of poetry which show these three modalities: *Andalucía, la Baja* (1926; Lower Andalusia), *La Toriada* (1928), and *Romances del ochocientos* (Ballads of the 1800s). In 1944 his *Poesías completas* (Complete Poems) were published with an introduction by J. M. *Cossío, and in 1956 Gerardo *Diego and Adriano del Valle published his *Taurofilia racial*. Despite these posthumous efforts, most of Villalón's works remain dispersed in various publications.

BIBLIOGRAPHY

Primary Texts

Poesías completas. Madrid: Hispánica, 1944.

Criticism

Cano, José Luis. *La poesía de la Generación del 27*. Madrid: Guadarrama, 1973. 47–51.

Cortines, Jacobo, and Alberto González Troyano, eds. *Escritos sobre Fernando Villalón*. Seville: Ayuntamiento de Sevilla, 1982.

Halcón, Manuel. *Recuerdos de Fernando Villalón*. 3rd ed. Madrid: Sucesores de Rivadeneyra, 1941.

Murciano, Carlos. "Recuerdo y sombra de un poeta." *La Estafeta Literaria* 5 (1973): 523.

María A. Salgado

VILLALONGA, Llorenç (1897, Palma de Mallorca–1980, Palma de Mallorca), novelist and playwright. He studied medicine in Barcelona and Zaragoza, finishing his studies in psychiatry in Paris during the twenties. From 1932 to 1967 he was the associate director of the state mental hospital at Palma de Mallorca. At the beginning of the Spanish Civil War he was active in politics as a member of the Phalangist party (1936–37), but he soon became disappointed and retired from public life. After 1919 he was a contributor to several publications, and in 1934 he started directing the journal *Brisas*. His literary career started in 1931 with the publication in Catalan of his first novel, *Mort de dama* (Death of a Lady). His most important novel, *Bearn*, was first published in 1956 in a Castilian translation, and in its original language, Catalan, in 1961, receiving the Premio de la Crítica (Critics' Award) in 1962. Some critics have seen the influence of Lampedusa's *Il Gatopardo* (The Leopard) in this novel. As a matter of fact, Villalonga translated *Il Gatopardo* into Catalan in 1962. Most of his literary production was first published in Catalan and later appeared in Castilian translations. Among his novels, of special interest are *La novel.la de Palmira* (1952; The Novel of Palmira), *L'àngel rebel* (1960; The Rebel Angel), *Desenllaç de Montlleó* (1963; Ending at Montlleó), *Les fures* (1967; The Furies), *La Lulú* (1970; Loulou) and *Andrea Victrix* (1974; Victorious Andrea), which was awarded the Josep Pla Prize in 1973. He was also the author of several plays, among others *Aquil.les o l'impossible* (1964; Achilles or the Impossible) and *Silvia Ocampo* (1966). For many years Villalonga was underestimated as an author, due to non-literary circumstances. His conservatism and brief but intensive political activity have caused his work not to be recognized nowadays as much as it should be.

BIBLIOGRAPHY

Primary Texts

Aquil.les o l'impossible; Alta i benemerita senyora. Palma de Mallorca: Moll, 1964.
Bearn, o la sala de las muñecas. Madrid: Cátedra, 1985.
Desbarats. Palma de Mallorca: Daedalus, 1965. Plays.
L'hereva de donya Obdulia. Barcelona: Club Editor, 1964.

English Translation

The Dolls' Room. Tr. anon. London: Deutsch, 1988.

Criticism

Martínez Cachero, José María. *La novela española entre 1936 y 1980*. Madrid: Castalia, 1985.

Samuel Amell

VILLAMEDIANA, Don Juan de Tassis y Peralta, Conde de (1582, Lisbon–1622, Madrid), poet in the tradition of both Petrarch and *Góngora. His early love poetry reflects the Italian influence which was brought to Spain by *Boscán and *Garcilaso de la Vega, while much of his later work consists of political satire. In a separate category is his play, *La gloria de Niquea* (The Glory of Niquea).

He was born in Lisbon while his father was there with the Spanish royal family, and the son was soon to follow in the father's footsteps with court appointments. In 1599, his literary career began with a poem published by Vargas Machuca, and in the same year he accompanied the king, Philip III, to Valencia to receive Doña Margarita of Austria, thus commencing his political career. The prospect of such a promising future was soon to change, as the count's life became more and more filled with disaster. When he decided to get married in 1601, he was turned down by those women who were his first choices, or perhaps by their families, and when he finally married Doña Ana de Mendoza, his own family refused the dowry. Although he was made a count and chief courier of the court, he was forced into exile several times because of both the political satire he was writing and the scandalous life he was leading. His children died at an early age, leaving the family with no successors, and around 1618, his wife also died. The count's own death was the tragic culmination of an ill-fated life, when on August 21, 1622, he was assassinated as he left the palace, probably because of one of his scandalous love affairs.

Villamediana's works were recently edited by Juan Manuel Rozas, who states that during the count's own lifetime, only about a half dozen of his poems were published, while the rest of his works appeared posthumously in 1629. Rozas divides Villamediana's poetry into four categories: (1) love poetry in the style of Spanish poets who were followers of Petrarch; (2) aesthetic poetry in the tradition of Góngora and having as its theme external beauty; (3) poems based on Ovidian mythology and also in the style of Góngora; and (4) poems that present a moral message and those whose purpose is to satirize, on a political or a personal level. Additionally, there is the play, *La gloria de Niquea*, written as a favor to the queen to celebrate the birthday of King Philip IV in 1622. Here too, in the play's excessive visual symbolism and contrast of darkness and light, ugliness and beauty, the influence of Góngora is reflected. According to Rozas, Villamediana is considered one of Góngora's most important disciples. For his unforgettable life as well as for his historically important literary production, the Conde de Villamediana is one of the most impressive figures of Golden Age Spain. *See also* Italian Literary Influences; Siglo de Oro.

BIBLIOGRAPHY

Primary Texts

Obras. Ed. Juan Manuel Rozas. Madrid: Clásicos Castalia, 1969. Contains introductory study.

Nina Shecktor

VILLANCICO, a type of simple, popular verse, usually meant to be sung. Derived from the *zéjel, its first verse is one to four lines long, and it is then glossed wholly or in part as the refrain in subsequent stanzas. The line lengths may vary. Many *villancicos* celebrate Christ's birth or other religious events, other *villancicos* revolved around traveling (**serranillas)*, the bucolic, etc. The form was also popular among court poets of the Renaissance. Juan del *Encina, *Valdivielso, and Lope de *Vega are but a few of the practitioners of this verse form.

BIBLIOGRAPHY

Criticism

Sánchez Romeralo, A. *El villancico*. Madrid: Gredos, 1968.

VILLANUEVA, Santo Tomás de (1488, Fuenllana, Ciudad Real–1555, Valencia), Augustinian monk, religious writer and saint. He founded one of the first schools to instruct future priests which was not affiliated with a university (El Colegio Mayor de la Presentación, Valencia). He also served as prior of the monastery of San Agustín in Salamanca, provincial of the order in Andalusia, archbishop of Valencia and preacher to Charles V. A church reformer, he composed religious tracts and vibrant sermons. A large proportion of his literary output was written in Latin, but he also enriched devotional literature in the vernacular. He was one of a distinguished group of Augustinian preachers which included *Malón de Chaide, *Orozco, Villavicencio and Valderrama. These men were instrumental in the reform of the Spanish pulpit. Villanueva wrote down his sermons in Latin and later translated them into Spanish. The sermons have been collected and published in both languages.

Referred to as Father of the Poor, Villanueva was a humble and saintly man who consistently aspired to live a purely ascetical life of spiritual retreat in spite of his secular duties. He wrote a short ascetical manual called *Modo breve de servir a Nuestro Señor en diez reglas* (Madrid, 1763; Short Method of Serving Our Lord in Ten Rules). With these ten rules or precepts, Villanueva proposed to lead the individual away from a sinful life to the practice of the Christian virtues and to the active love of God and neighbor. In Rule 4 Villanueva advocates an inner spirituality which will lead the reader to discover *deleites interiores* (spiritual delights of the soul). Physically unable to be present at the Council of Trent because of his frail health, nonetheless, Villanueva's input into the proceedings have made him an important church reformer. He was important enough in his day to have had *Quevedo compose a work dealing with his life and deeds. *See also* Ascetical Literature.

BIBLIOGRAPHY

Primary Texts

Obras: sermones de la Virgen y obras castellanas. Biblioteca de Autores Cristianos 96. Madrid: Católica, 1952.

Criticism

Capánaga, Victoriano. *Santo Tomás de Villanueva. Vidas de santos españoles*. Madrid: n.p., 1942.

Escrivá, Vicente. *Tomás de Villanueva, Arzobispo del Imperio: Estampas singulares sobre una vida ejemplar*. Valencia: Tipográfica Moderna, 1941.

Quevedo Villegas, Francisco de. *Epítome a la Historia de la vida ejemplar y gloriosa muerte del bienaventurado Fr. Tomás de Villanueva, religioso de la Orden de San Agustín y arzobispo de Valencia*. BAE 2. Madrid: Atlas, 1929.

Rodríguez, Tomás. *Estudio sobre los escritos de Santo Tomás de Villanueva de la Orden de San Agustín*. 2nd ed. Salamanca: Calatrava, 1896.

Salón, Miguel. *Vida de Santo Tomás de Villanueva, arzobispo de Valencia, ejemplar y norma de obispos y prelados*. New ed. El Escorial: Real Monasterio, 1925.

Angelo DiSalvo

VILLAR JANEIRO, Helena (1940, Becerreá, Lugo–), Galician poet and prose writer. Helena Villar is most frequently mentioned along with her husband, Xesús Rábade Paredes, with whom she has published several books (poetry and one novel), although she has written children's literature singly and her *Rosalía no espello* (1985; Rosalía in the Mirror) is a sign of her return to individual creativity in the area of intimate poetry.

The principal theme of Villar and Rábade's poetic work is love, love in telluric terms and with a sense of the passing of time that is yet eternal. The fatalism they portray is not, however, negative defeatism, but rather a following of natural processes. Through quotes and style one finds clear evidence of the author's multiple readings, setting up an intertextuality that makes no effort to defy identification. The novel *Morrer en Vilaquinte* (1980; To Die in Vilaquinte) is reminiscent of a modern Latin American narrative motif, with Vilaquinte as microcosmos of Galician society. *Rosalía no espello* is a self-study of the author as woman and writer, her link to the Galician land through natural elements such as stone, water, and time.

BIBLIOGRAPHY

Primary Texts

Alalás. Lugo: n.p., 1972.
No aló de nós. Santiago: n.p. 1981. (with X. Rábade Paredes)
Contos de nós e da xente. Madrid: n.p., 1983.
O libro de María. Santiago: n.p., 1984.
O libro que non se quería pechar. Madrid: n.p., 1984.
Morrer en Vilaquinte. Santiago: n.p., 1980. (with X. Rábede Paredes)
Rosalía no espello. Santiago: n.p., 1985.
O sangue na paisaxe. Santiago: n.p., 1980. (with X. Rábade Paredes)

Criticism

March, Kathleen N. "Helena Villar Janeiro." *Gran Enciclopedia Gallega*. Santiago-Gijón: Silverio Cañada, 1974 ff.

Kathleen March

VILLARTA TUÑÓN, Ángeles (1921, Belmonte, Asturias–), Spanish novelist, journalist, poet and essayist. Educated in Switzerland, Villarta brings the advantages of a cosmopolitan upbringing to her fiction and editorial work (she edited the second series of *La novela corta* as well as the comic magazine *Don Venerando*). Most of her activity seems to have been concentrated during the first quarter century following the Civil War; since then, her publication has diminished. Villarta's novels include the following titles: *Un pleno de amor* (1942; a play on words, meaning variously Full Moon of Love, Love Dance, and Complete Love), *Por encima de las nieblas* (1943; Above the Fog), *Muchachas que trabajan* (1944; Working Girls), *Ahora que soy estraperlista* (1949; Now That I'm a Black Marketeer), and *Con derecho a cocina* (1950; With Cooking Privileges). The latter two titles belong to the post-war literature of social criticism and economic preoccupation which predominates in the 1950s and early 1960s. Villarta progresses from beginnings closer to the *novela rosa* (pulp romance) to growing feminist concerns and politico-social *engagement*. With *Una mujer fea* (1954; An Ugly Woman) she won the Premio Femina Prize for 1953, and began to connect more specifically her early Asturian background with her increasing interest in feminist issues.

Villarta has also written short stories, and in 1953 published *La taberna de Laura—Poemas del mar* (Laura's Tavern: Poems of the Sea). Unfortunately, most of her works are of difficult access, and given her writing before the present critical interest in women's fiction, there is almost no secondary bibliography.

BIBLIOGRAPHY

Primary Text

Una mujer fea. Madrid: Calenda, 1954.

Janet Pérez

VILLAVICIOSA, José de (1589, Sigüenza–1658, Cuenca), poet. Doctor of law, he became Inquisitor in Murcia and Cuenca. In this latter city, Villaviciosa was canon until his death.

His only work is the burlesque heroic poem *La Mosquea* (1615; The City of the Flies). It is based on Teófilo Folengo's poem *Moschaea*, written in macaronic Latin. The influence of Dante, Homer, Virgil and Ovid is also apparent in Villaviciosa's poem. *La Mosquea* relates the war between the flies, commanded by their King Sanguilión who is allied with the horseflies and mosquitos, against the ants, fleas, lice and spiders. At the end, victory goes to the ants. Although *La Mosquea* never reaches the heights of *La Gatomaquia* by Lope de *Vega, Villaviciosa's poem stands out as the first manifestation of the burlesque epic in Spain.

BIBLIOGRAPHY

Primary Text

La Mosquea. In *Poemas épicos*. vol. 1. Ed., intro., notes by Cayetano Rosell. BAE 17.

Criticism

González Palencia, Angel. "José de Villaviciosa y 'La Mosquea.' " In *Historias y Leyendas*. Madrid: CSIC, 1942.

Hector Medina

VILLAYZÁN, Jerónimo de (1604, Madrid–1633, ?), lawyer, poet and playwright. A premature death, and the overwhelming star of Lope de *Vega, which eclipsed so many fine dramatists, unfortunately cut short Villayzán's most promising dramatic efforts and curtailed subsequent appreciation of them. In 1630, he became a doctor of law, returned to Madrid, and only then threw himself into literary activities. He met with immediate success, becoming the instant favorite of Philip IV. As many as eight plays have been attributed to Villayzán; Inserni accepts four of them. All are divided into three acts, and betray Lope's influence and the grace of a talented young poet.

BIBLIOGRAPHY

Primary Texts

A gran daño, gran remedio. In *Vida y obra de Jerónimo de Villaizán*. Ed. Frank M. Inserni. Barcelona: Rumbo, 1960.

Ofender con las finezas and *Sufrir más por querer más*. In BAE 45.

Criticism

See Inserni, in *Vida y obra*, above.

VILLEGAS, Antonio de (fl. 1565, ?–?), poet and prose writer. Little is known of this talented *Renaissance author who in 1565 published a work titled *Inventario* (Inventory), a collection of prose and poetry works. The most famous is the charming Moorish tale **Abencerraje y la hermosa Jarifa*. (Abencerraje and the Beautiful Jarifa).

BIBLIOGRAPHY

Primary Texts

Ausencia y soledad de amor. Ed. López Estrada. In *BRAE* 24 (1949): n.p.

Inventario. Ed. F. López Estrada. Colección Joyas Bibliográficas 13, 15. 2 vols. Madrid: n.p., 1955–56.

English Translation

Antonio de Villegas' "El Abencerraje." Tr. J. E. Keller and F. López Estrada. Chapel Hill: U of North Carolina P, 1964. Spanish and English texts.

Criticism

Bataillon, M. "¿Melancolía renacentista o melancolía judía?" In *Homenaje a Archer M. Huntington*. Wellesley: Wellesley College, 1952. 39–50.

VILLEGAS, Esteban Manuel de (1589, Matute, Logroño–1669, Nájera, Logroño), poet and translator. He studied in Madrid and Salamanca, and was royal treasurer in Nájera. Although Villegas came from a well-off family, he had economic difficulties most of his life. According to his biographers, Villegas was undisciplined, contemptuous, vain, and wasteful. In 1625, when he was thirty-six years old, he married doña Antonia de Leiva, a very young woman (fifteen years old) from a distinguished family. At age sixty-one, Villegas became involved in an Inquisitional prosecution. Among the twenty-two counts, he was accused of expressing himself too freely on religious matters. For example, he stated that God gave free will to men only in order for them to behave virtuously; he declared that he understood certain religious points better than Saint Augustine and other saints. He was also accused of having a notebook full of satirical pieces, one of which was against religious communities. Villegas was put under arrest and exiled from Nájera, Logroño and Madrid. He was later allowed to return to Nájera, where he died at age eighty.

Villegas's most important work is a collection of poetry entitled *Eróticas o Amatorias* (1618; Erotic and Amatory Poems). The book includes odes, elegies, idylls, sonnets and Anacreontic poems that would be imitated by Juan *Meléndez Valdés and other neo-classic poets of the eighteenth c. His poetry is uncompromisingly classical and contains many imitations of Horace, Anacreon, Tibullus and others. Villegas successfully adapted certain Latin meters to Spanish. He also translated *De Consolatione* by Boethius, but chastened by the *Inquisition, he left in its original Latin the section of the book that deals with the problem of human free will. He also wrote two volumes of dissertations in which he studied classical poetry. These have been lost.

BIBLIOGRAPHY

Primary Texts

Eróticas o Amatorias. Ed., notes, Narciso Alonso Cortés. Madrid: Espasa-Calpe, 1956.

Criticism

Bocchetta, Vittore. *Horacio en Villegas y en Fray Luis de León*. Madrid: Gredos, 1970.
Colombi Monguió, Alicia de. "La Oda XII de Esteban Manuel de Villegas y su tradición poética." *MLS* 12 (Spring 1982): 31–40.

Hector Medina

VILLEGAS SELVAGO, Alonso de (1534, Toledo–1615, Toledo), playwright and hagiographer. Villegas studied at the U of Toledo and later became chaplain of the Toledan Mozarabs. His most acclaimed work is the five-act *Comedia Selvagia* (1554; Play of Selvago). Written when the author was twenty years old and still a student, the play is one of the finest imitations of the **Celestina.* While evidently imitating Fernando de *Rojas, Villegas was also influenced by Feliciano de *Silva. The work is one of the shortest continuations of the *Celestina*, and its plot prefigures some of the later cloak-and-sword plays. Once a priest, Villegas abandoned secular themes and dedicated himself to hagiography. His five-volume *Flos Sanctorum* (1580–1603; *The lives of Saints, written in Spanishe*, 1636) enjoyed deserved acclaim, and was translated into Italian and English in the early seventeenth c. He also published various works on the lives of individual saints, the *Vida de San Isidro* (1592) and *Vida de San Tirso* (1595), among others. *See also* Hagiography.

BIBLIOGRAPHY

Primary Texts

Comedia llamada Selvagia. In *Colección de libros españoles raros o curiosos*. Vol. 5. Madrid: Rivadeneyra, 1879.
Flos sanctorum. Gerona: N. Oliva, 1794.

English Translation

The lives of Saints, written in Spanishe. Tr. W. and E. Kinsman. Rouen: J. Cousturier, 1636.

Deborah Compte

VILLENA, Enrique de (1384?, Castile–1434, ?), autodidact author of varied prose works written in a heavily Latinate style, forerunner of the Spanish *Renaissance. Enrique de Villena was a descendant of the royal house of Aragón on his mother's side and of the royal house of Castile on his father's. Bits of information from *Pérez de Guzmán's *Generaciones y semblanzas*, the *Crónica del Halconero de Juan II*, and Villena's own dedication in his translation of the *Aeneid* reveal that he was fifty years old when he died, that he died on December 15, 1434, and that his maternal language was Castilian. Until recently his entire biography was shrouded in legends depicting him as a wizard and sorcerer in league with the devil. Pérez de Guzmán portrays him in a less than complimentary light—perhaps because Villena was more inclined to study than to the chivalrous arts. Certainly it is easy to take exception to the less fortunate, and such is exactly what Villena's lot turned out to be. Because of circumstance and the impetuosity of his grandfather, don Alfonso de Aragón, the latter was stripped of all his Castilian titles and holdings, which is what don Enrique would have inherited. Although he was elected to head the Order of Calatrava (1404), the election demanded his renunciation of title as Count of Cangas and Tineo as well as his divorce from his wife, María de Albornoz, who, because of her heritage, brought to the marriage some of the estate which had formerly belonged to Enrique's grandfather, don Alfonso. The divorce was granted based on Villena's supposed impotence and dona María's decision to enter the convent, which she never did. In 1414, however, the Order of Calatrava, which had never been satisfied with Villena's mastership, declared his election to head of the Order as null and void. Villena was now without inheritance, without title, and without marriage. In 1414 King Ferdinand wrote doña María asking for a conjugal reconciliation so desired by her husband. Pope Benedict annulled the divorce. Economically curtailed, Villena remained politically active until 1422, when he retired entirely from politics and turned all his energy to scholarship.

Only two of his works predate this retirement: *Los doze trabajos de Hércules* (1417; The Twelve Labors of Hercules) and the *Tratado de lepra* (1417–40?; Treatise on Leprosy). He is considered a writer of secondary importance, but there is still considerable work to be done in order to assess accurately his influence on Spanish letters. Works attributed to him are *Arte Cisoria* (1423; Art of Meat Carving), *Tratado de consolación* (1424; Treatise on Consolation), *Esposición del salmo ''Quoniam videbo''* (1424; Exposition of the Psalm ''Quoniam videbo''), *Tratado de la fascinación (aojamiento)* (1425; Treatise on the Evil Eye), translations of the *Aeniad* (1428) and the *Divine Comedy* (1428), the *Arte de trobar* (1433; Art of Poetry), and the *Epístola a Suero de Quiñones* (1430–34?; Letter to Suero de Quiñones). Apocryphally attributed to him are *Las fazañas de Hércules* (The Feats of Hercules) and the *Libro de Guerra* (Book of War). Of doubtful authorship is the *Tratado de astrología* (Astrology Treatise). There are other minor attributions. *See also Paso Honroso, Libro del.*

BIBLIOGRAPHY

Primary Texts

''Arte de trobar.'' Ed. F. J. Sánchez Cantón. *RFE* 6 (1919): 158–80.

Los doze trabajos de Hércules. Ed. Margherita Morreale. Madrid: Biblioteca Selecta de Clásicos Españoles, 1958.

Enrique de Villena: ''Tratado de consolación.'' Ed. D. C. Carr. Clásicos Castellanos 208. Madrid: Espasa-Calpe, 1976.

''Enrique de Villena's *Arte Cisoria*: A Critical Study and Edition.'' Ed., study R. V. Brown. Diss. Wisconsin—Madison 1974. (Last published edition: F. C. Sáinz de Robles. Madrid: Espasa-Calpe ''edición fuera de comercio,'' 1967.)

La *Epístola que enbió Don Enrique de Villena a Suero de Quiñones* y la fecha de la

Crónica Sarracina de Pedro de Corral.'' Ed. D. C. Carr. In *University of British Columbia Hispanic Studies*. Ed. H. Livermore. London: Tamesis, 1974. 1–18.

''Tratado de la lepra.'' Ed. J. Soler. [Pseudonym of R. Foulché-Delbosc.] *RH* 41 (1917): 198–214.

''Tratado del aojamiento.'' Ed. J. Soler [Pseudonym of R. Foulché-Delbosc.] *RH* 41 (1917): 182–97.

Criticism

Arjona, D. K. ''Enrique de Villena and the *Arte Cisoria.*'' *Hispania* 43 (1960): 209–13.

Cátedra García, P.M. ''Enrique de Villena y algunos humanistas.'' *Elio Antonio de Nebrija*. Salamanca: U of Salamanca, 1983. 187–203.

Keightley, R. G. ''Enrique de Villena's *Los doze trabajos de Hércules*: A Reappraisal.'' *Journal of Hispanic Philology* 3 (1978): 49–68.

Macdonald, Inez. ''A Cornation Service, 1414.'' *MLR* 36 (1941): 351–68.

Sachs, Leonie F. ''Enrique de Villena: Portrait of the Magician as an Outsider.'' *Studies in Philology* 64 (1967): 109–31.

———. Sobre la vida y la obra de don Enrique de Villena. Barcelona: Universidad Autónoma, 1981.

Anthony J. Cárdenas

VILLENA, Isabel de, born Elionor Manuel de Villena (1430, Valencia–1490, ?), abbess and religious writer. The illegitimate daughter of the Castilian writer Enrique de *Villena, she was educated in Valencia at the court of Queen Mary of Castile. At the age of fifteen, she became a nun in the convent of the Holy Trinity and assumed the position of superior in 1463. Villena is the only female writer of note from the Catalan classical literary period, but she was very famous and widely known in her time. Her intellectual background was dominated by her extensive knowledge of theology and the Holy Scriptures. She wrote only one book we know of, *Vita Christi* (1497; The Life of Christ), which has a basically pedagogical purpose. Its simple and candid realism is one of the most remarkable charms of the work. The book is essentially biographical and contemplative; the narration is a series of theological and ascetic reflections on sentences or incidents of the Bible on an allegorical level. On the other hand, the episodes that narrate daily life are full of color and realism, and the style is equally contrastive. The first part of the book is based directly or indirectly on the Apocryphal Scriptures. The most important thematic feature of the *Vita Christi* is perhaps that Villena shows a woman in direct spiritual communication with Jesus and the Virgin Mary, something truly revolutionary in feminist terms of the late Middle Ages. The *Vita Christi* was edited in Valencia in 1497 by the mother superior of the convent of the Holy Trinity at the request of Queen Isabel of Castile. The main literary influences are the books of chivalry, Ramon *Llull and Francesc *Eiximenís. *See also* Catalan Literature; Edad Media, Literatura de la.

BIBLIOGRAPHY

Primary Text

Llibre anomenat Vita Christi, compost per Sor Isabel de Villena. Ed. Miquel i Planas. 3 vols. Barcelona: Biblioteca Catalana, 1916.

Criticism

Barrera, Jaume. "La escriptora mística Sor Isabel de Villena, abadessa de la Trinitad de València." *El Correo Catalán*, July 14, 1913.
Fuster, J. *Obres Completes*. vol. 1. Barcelona: Ediciones 63, 1968.

Kathleen McNerney

VINYES, Cèlia (1915, Lleida–1954, Majorca), poet. She wrote in both Catalan and Castilian, and is considered one of the writers who renovated poetry in Majorca of the post-war period.

BIBLIOGRAPHY

Primary Texts

Antología lírica. Madrid: Rialp, 1976.
Canción tonta del sur. Almería: Peláez, 1948.
Del foc a la cendra. Palma de Mallorca: Moll, 1953.
Estampes de la vida de Cervantes. Madrid: Gredos, 1949.
Trigo del corazón. Almería: La Independencia, 1946.

Kathleen McNerney

VIRUÉS, Cristóbal de (1550?, Valencia–1614?, ?), soldier, epic poet and playwright. He was the son of a prominent physician and a friend of Joan Lluís *Vives. Virués's talent was lauded by both *Cervantes (in the book-burning scene of *Don Quijote* I.6) and Lope de *Vega (in the *Arte nuevo de hacer comedias*). As a poet, his most famous work is *Monserrate* (1587). Written in **octavas reales*, this lengthy, intricate, anti-Reformist epic treats the legend of the hermit Juan Garin. It was quite popular, re-edited in 1588 and 1601, and given a sequel in 1602 (*El Monserrate segundo*, The Second Monserrat).

Five tragedies comprise Virués's dramatic output: *La gran Semiramis* (The Great Semiramis); *La cruel Casandra* (Cruel Cassandra); *Atila furioso* (Attila Enraged); *La infelice Marcela* (Unfortunate Marcela); *Elisa Dido* (Elisa Dido). They follow the tradition of *Seneca, with shocking, brutal dialogue, violent deaths, etc. Apparently written between 1570 and 1590, they nonetheless were not published until 1609. *Elisa Dido*, generally considered the best, is also the most traditional—written in five acts, with a chorus, within the unities of time, place and action. Virués is classified as a precursor of Lope.

BIBLIOGRAPHY

Primary Texts

Obras trágicas y líricas del Capitán Cristóbal de Virués. Madrid: Esteban Bogia, 1609.
Poetas dramáticos valencianos. Ed. Eduardo Juliá Martínez. 2 vols. Madrid: RAE, 1929.
Historia del Monserrate. BAE 17.

Criticism

Sargent, C. V. *A Study of the Dramatic Works of Cristóbal de Virués*. New York: Instituto de las Españas, 1930.

Weiger, John C. *The Valencian Dramatists of Spain's Golden Age*. TWAS 371. Boston: Twayne, 1976.

VITORIA, Francisco de (1492, Burgos–1546, Salamanca), Dominican theologian, professor, scholar. Critic C. Noreña ranks Vitoria with *Vives among sixteenth-c. intellectuals. Of **converso* origins, he entered the order in 1504, and around 1509 went to Paris, then strongly humanistic, to study. He stayed through 1522, lecturing in theology from 1516 on. In 1523 the Dominican order recalled him to Spain where, for the next twenty-four years, he lectured in theology, first at the College of San Gregorio in Valladolid (1524–26), and then at the U of Salamanca (1526–46). He was extraordinarily popular. Vitoria published nothing, but his thought is preserved for us in student notes on lectures. He is best known for his attacks on the atrocities committed during the conquest of the New World, and the complex moral issues of reconquest. These lectures delivered in 1539, titled *De Indis* (On the Indians) and *De jure belli* (On a Just War), examine the rights of all participants; Charles V was extremely provoked, but Vitoria did not alter his stance. Other lectures on civil power have given Vitoria, along with Francisco *Suárez, the distinction of being a founder of international law.

BIBLIOGRAPHY

Primary Texts

Comentarios a la Secunda Secundae de Santo Tomás. Ed. Beltrán de Heredia. 2 vols. Salamanca: n.p., 1932.
De Indis et de iure belli relectiones. Ed. E. Nyes. Washington: Carnegi, 1917.
De Justitia. Ed. Beltrán de Heredia. 3 vols. Madrid: Asociación Francisco de Vitoria, 1928.
Relecciones teológicas. Tr. J. Torrubiano. Madrid: Hernández, 1917.
Relecciones teológicas. . . . Ed. L. G. Alonso Getino. 3 vols. Madrid: La Rafa, 1933–35.
Relectio de indis o libertad de los indios. Ed., notes L. Pereña and J. M. Pérez Prendes. Study V. Beltrán de Heredia et al. Madrid: CSIC, 1967. Latin and Spanish.
Relectio de Indis; o, Libertad de los Indios. Ed. L. Pereña and J. M. Pérez Prendes. Intro. V. Beltrán de Heredia. Madrid: CSIC, 1967. Latin and Spanish.

English Translations

The Principles of Political and International Law in the Work of Francisco de Vitoria. Sel., intro., notes A. Truyol Serra. Madrid: Cultura Hispánica, 1946.
See also Noreña, in Criticism.

Criticism

Brown Scott, T. *The Spanish Origin of International Law. Francisco de Vitoria and His Law of Nations*. Oxford: n.p., 1934.
Hamilton, B. *Political Thought in Sixteenth-C. Spain*. Oxford: Clarendon, 1963.

Noreña, C. *Studies in Spanish Renaissance Thought*. Hague: Nijhoff, 1975. 36–149.
Ramos Pérez, D. *La ética en la conquista de América*. Madrid: CSIC, 1984.

Maureen Ihrie

VIVANCO, Luis Felipe (1907, El Escorial–1975, ?), poet, scholar and literary critic. While not exactly under-rated as a poet, Vivanco has not achieved the distinction due him. Without a doubt, he deserves to be included among the finest Spanish poets of the twentieth c. His artistic sensitivity has extended to his appreciation of other poets and prose writers; he has tirelessly expressed his admiration for the achievements of his contemporaries as well as for those authors who preceded him. Much of his own poetry since 1939—and this is corroborated by his daughter, who edited his "Diary" after his death—projects his feeling of culpability for having fought in the Spanish Civil War on the side of Franco. (It is to his credit that he took pride in not having fired a shot.) His *Tiempo de dolor* (Time of Pain), published after the Spanish Civil War, captures his experience of a period of collective fratricide. Vivanco, who was trained as an architect, practiced that profession even after he became a renowned poet.

BIBLIOGRAPHY

Primary Texts

Antología poética. Intro., sel. José María Valverde. Madrid: Alianza, 1976.
Los caminos, Continuación de la vida, El descampado y Lugares vividos: 1945–1965. Madrid: Cultura Hispánica, 1974.
Cantos de primavera. Madrid: Cruz y Raya, 1936.
Felipe Vivanco, Diario 1946–75. Ed. Soledad Vivanco. Madrid: Taurus, 1983.
Moratín y la ilustración magica. Madrid: Taurus, 1972.
Los ojos de Toledo, leyenda autobiográfica. Barcelona: Barna, 1953.
Poemas en prosa (1923–32). Santander: Bedia, 1972.

Robert Kirsner

VIVES, Joan Lluís (1493, Valencia–1540, Bruges), humanist, pedagogue and writer. He was scion of a converted Jewish family persecuted by the *Inquisition. He studied in Valencia (1503) and Paris (1509). Between 1512 and 1523 he resided in Bruges, Louvain and Antwerp, teaching and pursuing scholarly endeavors. He was offered a chair, succeeding *Nebrija, by the then enlightened U of Alcalá, but refused to accept it probably because he feared persecution by the Inquisition and also considered that institution to be too conservative. Together with Erasmus and Budé, he is generally thought to be one of the most influential humanists of the *Renaissance. From 1523 to 1528 he was a professor in the prestigious Corpus Christi College of Oxford U, where he cemented a close friendship with his spiritual friend Sir Thomas More. At the height of his prestige he became a close adviser of Queen Catherine of England and was the preceptor of her daughters but lost royal favor after her divorce from Henry VIII. He died broken and poor in the Low Countries. Vives, like Erasmus, More and others, typifies the misery and glory of the great Renaissance intellectual locked between the free spirit of the times and the political and religious revolution whose result would be the rekindling of fanaticism and dogmatism. Vives is, without a doubt, the greatest figure of Renaissance critical thought to come from the Iberian Peninsula. The major part of the voluminous *Opera* is devoted to refuting the teachings of scholasticism with their obvious political and social implications. A truly modern champion of social and moral reformation, he was also a strong advocate of world peace. His perhaps best known apology, *De veritate fidei christianae* (On The Truth of Christian Faith), magnificently shows his eclectic philosophical mind, great tolerance, and, above all, vital message of spiritual introspection. Vives always wrote in Latin. *See also* Converso; Erasmism; Humanism; Siglo de Oro.

BIBLIOGRAPHY

Primary Texts

De anima et vita. Photocopied reproduction with introductory note by Mario Sancipriano. Torino: Bottega d'Erasmo, 1963.

Diálogos. Tr. Cristóbal Coret y Peris. Valencia: Prometeo, 1921.

Introducción a la sabiduría. Tr. Diego de Astudillo. Valencia: B. Montfort, 1765.

Libro llamado Instrucción de la mujer cristiana. Tr. Juan Justiniano. Madrid: Signo, 1936.

Obras completas; primera translación castellana íntegra y directa, comentarios, notas y un ensayo bibliográfico por Lorenzo Riber. Madrid: Aguilar, 1947–48.

Tratado del alma. Tr. José Ontañón. Madrid: Lectura, 1923.

English Translations

In Pseudodialecticos: a critical edition / Juan Luis Vives. Intro., tr., commentary by Charles Fantazzi. Leiden: Brill, 1979.

Instruction of a Christian Woman. Tr. Ruth Kuschmiérz. London: Thomas Berthelet, 1984.

Introduction to Wisdom: A Renaissance Textbook. Tr. Marian Leona Tobrines. New York: Teachers College P, 1968.

Juan Luis Vives against the Pseudodialecticians: A Humanist Attack on Medieval Logic: The Attack on the Pseudodialecticians and on Dialectic, books 3, 5, 6, 7, from *The Causes of the Corruption of the Arts*. Tr. Rita Guerlac. Boston: D. Reidel, 1979.

Tudor School-boy Life: The Dialogues of Juan Luis Vives. Tr. Foster Watson. London: F. Cass, 1970.

Vives: On Education; A Translation of the "De tratendis disciplinis" of Juan Vives. Totowa, NJ: Rowman and Littlefield, 1971.

Vives: On Education. . . . Tr. Foster Watson. Cambridge: Cambridge UP, 1913.

Criticism

Bonilla Sanmartín, A. *Luis Vives y la filosofía del Renacimiento*. Madrid: Asilo de huérfanos del S.C. de Jesús, 1903.

Guy, A. *Vivès ou l'humanisme engagé*. Paris: Seghers, 1972.

Noreña, C. G. *Juan Luis Vives*. The Hague: M. Nijhoff, 1970.

Ventura, J. ''El 'cas' de Joan Luis Vives.'' In *Inquisició espanyola i cultura renaixentista al País Valencià*. Valencia: Eliseo Climent, 1978.

Joan Gilabert

XÉRICA, Pablo de (1781, Vitoria-Cagnot–1841, Landes, France), poet, fabulist. He attended the U of Oñate but soon left the study of law to write poetry. In 1804 in Cádiz he joined local militia against the French invaders and collaborated on the newspaper *El Duende* (The Goblin). Persecuted by Ferdinand VII for his liberal ideas, Xérica went to France at the end of the war and stayed there until 1820, when the Constitutionals came to power. Difficulties in Spain with the absolutist government and *censorship proved so serious, however, that Xérica returned to France permanently, marrying there in 1826. Xérica was a product of the Enlightenment: broad-minded and open to progress, liberal in politics, of neo-classical inclination in literature. His *Poesías* (1814; Poems), which enjoyed several editions, includes numerous fables which bristle with ironic wit and a critical sense of contemporary society.

BIBLIOGRAPHY

Primary Texts

Ensayos poéticos. Valencia: n.p., 1814.

Poesías. 5th ed. Vitoria: Norte de España, 1869.

Criticism

Cueto, Leopoldo Augusto de. In *Poetas líricos del siglo XVII*. BAE 67.

Ochoa, Eugenio de. *Apuntes para una biblioteca de autores contemporáneos en prosa y verso*. Paris: n.p., 1840.

XIMÉNEZ DE RADA, Rodrigo (1170/1180, Navarre–1247, Ródano), primate of Spain, chancellor of Castile, chronicler. After initiating his studies in Navarre, he went abroad as a deacon in 1195 studying philosophy and law in Bologna, and theology in Paris (1204). His background, travels, and studies made him one of the outstanding polyglots of his age; his biographer, Father Gorosterratzu, documents his knowledge of Basque, Castilian, Latin, French, Italian, German, English, and thorough understanding of Arabic, which would come to fruition in his *Historia Arabum*. He embarked on an illustrious diplomatic career in the service of Sancho the Strong, passing later into the court of Alphonse VIII of Castile, who rewarded him with the bishopric of Osma (1208). The founding of the U of Palencia by Alphonse is owed to the influence of Don Rodrigo. As archbishop of Toledo (1209) he established the primacy of his see and founded the cathedral. Rodrigo was the principal organizer of the crusade of Spanish, French, Italian, and German forces which culminated in the decisive and key victory at Las Navas de Tolosa (1212). His greatest work, commissioned by Ferdinand III el Santo, was the *De rebus Hispaniae*, or *Historia Gothica*. It epitomizes the neo-gothic perspective of earlier chronicles, yet, as Derek Lomax has noted, it also responds to the new conditions of the monarchy created by the military and political successes of Ferdinand III. It was a source and model for *Alphonse X the Learned's *History of Spain*. *See also* Crónicas.

BIBLIOGRAPHY

Primary Texts

Crońica latina de los reyes de Castilla. Ed. María D. Cabanes Pecourt. Valencia: Textos Medievales, 1964.

Historia Arabum. Ed. José Lozano Sánchez. Seville: Universidad de Sevilla, 1974.

Opera. Madrid, 1793. Rpt. Valencia: Textos Medievales, 1968.

Criticism

Gorosterratzu, Javier. *Don Rodrigo Jiménez de Rada. Gran estadista, escritor y prelado*. Pamplona: Bescansa, 1925.

Linehan, Peter. *The Spanish Church and the Papacy in the 13th Century*. Cambridge: Cambridge UP, 1971.

Lomax, Derek. "Rodrigo Jiménez de Rada como historiador." *Actas del Quinto Congreso Internacional de Hispanistas*. Bordeaux: Presse Universitaire, 1977. 587–92.

Porter Conerly

XIRINACS I DÍAZ, Olga (1936, Tarragona–), poet and novelist. Very active in the cultural life of her native city, she began writing as a child but didn't become known in literary circles until 1971. Since then she has won numerous prizes for both prose and poetry. She believes writers have an obligation to get closer to the public, broadening cultural fields as much as possible, and that the money spent on war preparations should be spent on cultural life. Some of her favorite writers are Proust, Simenon, de Beauvoir and Woolf, about whose suicide she wrote the novel *Al meu cap una llosa* (1985; A Gravestone at My Head). In it, she re-creates wartime England, contrasting the suffering of ordinary people with the crisp, official version of the progress of the war heard on the BBC. Woolf's presence is that of a shadow during the period after her drowning but before her body was found, and her thoughts in this state are interwoven with the reactions to her of the townspeople, whom she barely knew. Much of her poetry is love poetry; *Botons de tiges grises* (1977; Gray Stem Buttons) tells of an adolescent girl, with lyricism and intimacy in stark contrast with the background of the violence of the 1940s. The author describes *Música de cambra* (1982; Chamber Music) as a book of memories into which are woven a series of strange adventures. In 1980 she formed the group El nus with several other writers and artists to collaborate on a work called *Tramada*, published by the Institut d'Estudis Tarrconenses.

BIBLIOGRAPHY

Primary Texts

Al meu cap una llosa. Barcelona: Proa, 1985.
Botons de tiges grises. Barcelona: Proa, 1977.
Clau de blau. Tarragona: Institut d'Estudis Tarrconenses, 1978.
Interior amb difunts. Barcelona: Destino, 1983.
Llençol de noces. Barcelona: Proa, 1979.
Música de cambra. Barcelona: Destino, 1982.
Preparo el té sota palmeres roges. Barcelona: Vosgos, 1981.
Zona marítima. Barcelona: Planeta, 1986.

Kathleen McNerney

Y

YOÇEF, Coplas de (Poetry of Joseph), a fourteenth-c. Judeo-Spanish poem on the story of the patriarch Joseph. It is based on Genesis, possibly in vernacular translations, with borrowings from Josephus, the Midrashim, and the *Sefer ha-Yashar*, a collection of Jewish legends. The surviving fifty stanzas, which are contained in the same ms. as the *Proverbs* of Santob de Carrión (*Tob), narrate the last part of the life of Joseph. Its **cuaderna vía* form is noteworthy for the introduction of internal rhyme. The poem has been carefully edited, translated, and studied by González Llubera. *See also* Hispano-Judaic Literature.

BIBLIOGRAPHY

Primary Text

Coplas de Yoçef. A Medieval Spanish Poem in Hebrew Characters. Ed. Ignacio González Llubera. Cambridge: Cambridge UP, 1935.

Porter Conerly

YÚÇUF, Poema de (Poem of Joseph). A principal survivor of the *aljamiado* tradition (Spanish works written in Arabic or Hebrew characters), this anonymous fourteenth- or fifteenth-c. poem is written in an irregular **cuaderna vía*. The poem, whose dialect features are clearly Aragonese, is preserved in two incomplete mss., the longest containing 312 strophes. It narrates the story of the patriarch Joseph from the jealousy of his brothers to their return from Egypt. The poem's immediate sources are unknown. It differs from two other Hispano-Arabic versions: one by the Muslim geographer Abu 'Ubayd al-Bakri which was incorporated into *Alphonse X the Learned's *History of the World*; the other, an *aljamiado Legend of Joseph* in prose. The ultimate source of the poem is not Genesis, but the Koran. An additional source is the *Sefer ha-Yashar*, the rabbinical *Book of Yashar*, a widely circulated collection of Jewish legends. *See also* Hispano-Judaic Literature.

BIBLIOGRAPHY

Primary Texts

Leyendas de José, hijo de Jacob, y de Alejandro Magno, sacadas de dos manuscritos moriscos de la Biblioteca Nacional de Madrid. Ed. Francisco Guillén Robles. Zaragoza: n.p., 1888.

Poema de Yúçuf. Materiales para su estudio. Ed., study Ramón Menéndez Pidal. Granada: Universidad de Granada, 1952.

The "Poema de José." A Transcription and Comparison of the Extant Manuscripts. Ed. William W. Johnson. University, AL: Romance Monographs, 1974.

Criticism

Nykl, A. R. "A Compendium of Aljamiado Literature." *RH* 77 (1929): 409–611.

Porter Conerly

Z

ZABALETA, Juan de (1610, Madrid?–1670?, Madrid?), prose writer in the *costumbrista* tradition, dramatist, chronicler for Philip IV. Little is known of his personal life. A man of exemplary virtue, he expected others to set the same high standards for themselves and was intolerant of any flaws he saw. Zabaleta was also known for his extreme ugliness. Contemporaries commented on it, and he himself was very conscious of it. Yet, he always had friends, including *Calderón de la Barca, Juan *Vélez de Guevara and *Cáncer y Velasco. His education is not known with certainty, but references in his own works to the classics indicate familiarity with them and a knowledge of Latin. He also appears to have studied the humanities, history, law, philosophy and theology.

In December of 1664, Zabaleta suddenly became blind. This terrifying event prompted a stronger turn to religion. He reviewed all his writings with the intent of destroying any he considered too mundane. The exact date of his death is unknown.

Zabaleta is best known for a didactic prose work written in two parts, called *Día de la fiesta por la mañana y por la tarde* (1654; Holidays in the Morning and in the Afternoon). The second part was not completed until 1660. The work demonstrated how days designated for holy celebration were currently being profaned. In part one, the *Día de la fiesta por la mañana*, the author studies twenty different character types and describes how each one devotes the holy days to enjoyment instead of solemn contemplation. *Día de la fiesta por la tarde* focuses on places where people go for diversion on those days, rather than on the people themselves. Both parts enjoyed such success that the author considered adding yet another part, which would have been called "Día de la fiesta por la noche" (Holidays in the Evening).

Zabaleta was also fond of the theater. Although he met with less success on the stage, he did complete several plays, some of which were written in collaboration with other playwrights. Among his own works are the full-length plays *El ermitaño galán* (The Gallant Hermit) and *El hijo de Marco Aurelio* (The Son of Marcus Aurelius). *See also* Romanticism.

BIBLIOGRAPHY

Primary Text

El día de fiesta por la mañana y por la tarde. Ed. Cristóbal Cuevas García. Madrid: Castalia, 1983.

Criticism

Simón Díaz, J. "Juan de Zabaleta." In *Cien escritores madrileños del Siglo de Oro*. Madrid: Instituto de Estudios Madrileños, 1975. 138–41. Bibliography.

Stevens, James R. "The Costumbrismo and Ideas of Juan de Zabaleta." *PMLA* 81 (1966): 512–20.

Nina Shecktor

ZAHONERO, José (1853, Ávila–1931, Madrid), lawyer, doctor, fiction author. An activist in the 1874 revolutionary movement, he went into exile in France. He was greatly influenced by Zola, especially in his novel *La carnaza* (1885; The Bait). Also worthy of mention are *El señor obispo* (1887; The Bishop), *Barrabás* (1891), and *La vengadora* (The Avenger). He also wrote short stories of merit.

BIBLIOGRAPHY

Primary Texts

La carnaza. Madrid: Bueno, 1885.

La vengadora. Madrid: Muñoz Sánchez, n.d.

Cuentos pequeñitos. Madrid: Fortanet, 1887.

Isabel McSpadden

ZAMÁCOLA, Juan Antonio de Iza. *See* Iza Zamácola, Juan Antonio de

ZAMBRANO, María (1904, Vélez-Málaga–), philosopher, essayist and professor. She studied philosophy at the U of Madrid with *Ortega and *Zubiri, and while she is considered one of the most important disciples of the former, she has many affinities with the latter, especially his expansion of Ortega's notion of vital reason. She was in Chile in 1936–37 when the Civil War erupted, and upon returning to Spain in 1937 worked actively in Barcelona for the defense of the Republic. In 1939 she sought refuge in Paris, then in Mexico, Havana and Puerto Rico, where she taught philosophy. In 1953 Zambrano took up residence in Rome, Italy, devoting herself to journalism, and before returning to Spain in 1984, she resided in Geneva, Switzerland. Like Ortega, her inspiration derives from a German phenomenology that is more Heideggerian than Husserlian. Her books have treated themes as diverse as liberalism, the thought of *Seneca, knowledge of the soul, man and the Divine, democracy, *Pérez Galdós's Spain, love, and time in dreams. But her most enduring subject of study has been the phenomenological investigation of what she calls "poetic reason" (poetic intuition as a philosophical method).

BIBLIOGRAPHY

Primary Texts

Claros del bosque. Barcelona: Seix Barral, 1978.

La confesión: género literario y método. Mexico: Ediciones ''Luminar,'' 1943.

Filosofía y Poesía. Morelia, Mexico: Universidad de Morelia, 1939.

Pensamiento y poesía en la vida española. Mexico: Fondo de Cultura Económica, 1939.

El sueño creador. Mexico: Universidad Veracruzana, 1965.

Roberta Johnson

ZAMORA, Antonio de (1670?, Madrid–1728, Madrid), dramatist. A royal servant of the Bourbons, Zamora was an official in the office of New Spain. As a playwright, he was a transition figure who imitated *Calderón and rewrote many of the latter's works to suit eighteenth-c. Spanish theater taste. In 1722, he published his *Comedias nuevas* (New Plays), a collection which included such original works as *Judas Iscariote*, *Todo vence el amor* (Love Conquers All), *Ser fino y no parecerlo* (Elegant and Not Looking It), *El Hechizado por Fuerza* (Bewitched in Spite of Himself), *Don Bruno de Calahorra o el indiano perseguido* (Don Bruno of Calahorra, or the Persecuted Indian) and many *refundiciones* (rewritings) of Baroque plays. Among the latter is the play which has earned Zamora some degree of notoriety—*No hay plazo que no se pague, y Convidado de Piedra* (Deadlines Arrive and Debts Must Be Paid, and the Stone Guest)—which is based on *Tirso's *El burlador de Sevilla*. Zamora also wrote some **entremeses* published in the 1722 work which foreshadowed the *costumbrismo* of later years. *See also* Romanticism; Theater in Spain.

BIBLIOGRAPHY

Primary Texts

Comedias nuevas con los mismos saynetes con que se executaron. New York: Olms, 1975.

Criticism

Barlow, J. W. ''Zorrilla's Indebtedness to Zamora.'' *RR* 17 (1926): 303–18.

Dowling, John C. ''Capricho as Style in Life, Literature and Art from Zamora to Goya.'' *Eighteenth-Century Studies* 10 (1977): 413–33.

McClendon, Carmen Chaves. ''Zamora's Treatment of Fatalism in 'Judas Iscariote.' '' *Crítica Hispánica* 4 (1982): 51–56.

Trijilo, S. S. ''Influencias calderonianas en el drama de Zamora y de Cañizares.'' *Hispanófila* 4 (1961): 39–46.

Carmen Chaves McClendon

ZAPATA, Luis (1526, Extremadura–1595, Extremadura), page at the court of Philip II, translator and writer. Zapata distinguished himself as a courtier and swordsman and accompanied Philip II to Flanders and Italy. He dedicated thirteen years to writing a panegyric history in verse to Charles V, entitled *El Carlos Famoso* (1566; The Renowned Charles). Although the chronicle follows in detail the history of the period, it is largely acknowledged to be an unsuccessful work lacking in unity. Zapata included various burlesque episodes and intercalated tales which are not, however, well integrated into the narrative. He also produced a translation of Horace's *Ars Poetica* in 1592. His most acclaimed work is the *Miscelánea* (c. 1590; Miscellany), a collection of court anecdotes and sayings which record the literary, social and political histories of the period. It is an excellent document of the customs of the time and offers entertaining reading.

BIBLIOGRAPHY

Primary Texts

El arte poético de Horacio. Tr. Don Luis Zapata. Madrid: RAE, 1954.
El Carlos Famoso. Valencia: Mey, 1566.
Miscelánea. Ed. A. Rodríguez Moñino. Madrid: Compañía Iberoamericana de Publicaciones, 1931.
Varia historia (Miscelánea). Ed. Isidoro Montiel. 2 vols. Madrid: Castilla, 1949.

Deborah Compte

ZAPATA, Marcos (1845, Zaragoza–1913, Madrid), poet, playwright. His *Poesías* (Poems) appeared in 1902 with a foreword by Santiago *Ramón y Cajal. His plays include *La capilla de Lanuza* (1871; The Chapel at Lanuza), *El castillo de Simancas* (1878; The Castle of Simancas), *El solitario de Yuste* (1877; The Lonely Man at Yuste) and *La piedad de una reina* (1887; The Pity of a Queen), which was inspired by the insurrection of Villacampa (1886). The government banned production of the last work; it still became very popular, and was read in the *Ateneo. Its historical setting is not very accurate, as Zapata evokes the past but interpolates political allusions of his day, with a polemical intent. He also wrote some scripts for **zarzuelas*, such as *El anillo de hierro* (1878; The Iron Ring), and *El reloj de Lucerna* (1884; Lucerna's Clock). Marqués wrote the music for both zarzuelas.

BIBLIOGRAPHY

Primary Texts

La piedad de una reina. 1887. Rpt. Louisville, KY: Falls City Microcards, 1964.
Poesías. Madrid: Fe, 1902.
Un regalo de boda. 1885. Louisville, KY: Falls City Microcards, 1963.
El reloj de Lucerna. 1884. Louisville, KY: Falls City Microcards, 1964.
El solitario de Yuste. 1887. Rpt. Louisville, KY: Falls City Microcards, 1964.

Isabel McSpadden

ZARAGÜETA, Juan (1883, Guipúzcoa–1974, San Sebastián), priest, philosopher, professor. A disciple of Cardinal Mercier in Belgium, he was a professor of pedagogy at the U of Madrid, and in 1947, assumed a chair in metaphysics. In 1953 he retired. His philosophical thought follows an eclectic system derived from the neo-Thomism and the vitalist intuitionism of Bergson. Among his publications are *El cristianismo como doctrina de vida y como vida* (1939; Christianity as a Doctrine of Life and Way of Life), *La finalidad en la filosofía* *de Santo Tomás* (1923; The Aim or End in St. Thomas's Philosophy), *Filosofía y vida* (1950; Philosophy and Life), etc. *Cuarenta años de periodismo* (1971; Forty Years of Journalism) contains articles published between 1930 and 1970, and was awarded the Francisco Franco Literature Prize.

BIBLIOGRAPHY

Primary Texts

El cristianismo como doctrina de vida y como vida. Madrid: Espasa-Calpe, 1939.
Cuarenta años de periodismo. Madrid: Prensa Española, 1971.
Filosofía y vida. 2nd ed. Madrid: CSIC, 1957.
El lenguaje y la filosofía. Madrid: CSIC, 1945.
La pedagogía, ciencia social. Madrid: Aguado, 1944.
Vocabulario filosófico. Madrid: Espasa-Calpe, 1955.

Isabel McSpadden

ZÁRATE, Agustín de (c. 1506, ?–c. 1565, ?), New World historian, secretary to the Royal Council of Castile. He was sent in 1543 by Charles I to Peru to audit the Treasury there. When he returned to Europe he composed the *Historia de la conquista del Perú* (1555; *The Discovery and Conquest of Peru,* 1968). In elegant, literary prose, he recounts the discovery and conquest by Pizarro (1532–33) and narrates events up to Pizarro's insurrection against the king, which Zárate witnessed. He also wrote a *Censura de la obra de "Varones ilustres de Indias" de Juan de Castellanos* (n.d.; Censure of the Work *Illustrious Men of the Indies* by Juan de *Castellanos).

BIBLIOGRAPHY

Primary Texts

Censura de la obra de "Varones ilustres de Indias" de Juan de Castellanos. In BAE 4.
Historia de la conquista del Perú. In BAE 26.
Historia del descubrimiento y conquista del Perú. Buenos Aires: U of Buenos Aires, 1965.

English Translation

The Discovery and Conquest of Peru. Tr., intro., J. M. Cohen. Baltimore: Penguin, 1968.

Hector Medína

ZÁRATE, Fernando de. *See* Enríquez Gómez, Antonio

ZÁRATE, Hernando de (?, Madrid–before 1597, ?), Augustinian father, preacher and professor. Much admired for his sermons, Father Hernando wrote *El discurso de la paciencia cristiana* (1592; Discourse on Christian Patience). In clear language, with copious examples, he demonstrates that man's troubles and misfortunes are trials of God designed to temper and test him. He also taught theology at the U of Osuna.

BIBLIOGRAPHY

Primary Text

Discursos. . . . In BAE 27.

ZARDOYA, Concha, pseudonym (used 1946 to present) of María de la Concepción Zardoya González (1914, Valparaiso, Chile–). Pre–1946 pseudonym: Concha de Salamanca. Prolific poet and critic. Born in Chile of Spanish parents, she returned to Spain in 1932, wrote history readers for adolescents and obtained an undergraduate degree at the U of Madrid. Zardoya then moved to the United States in 1948, received a doctorate in 1952 at the U of Illinois, and taught Spanish literature in various U.S. universities until her retirement in Madrid in 1977. Although she has published extensive literary criticism—*Poesía española contemporánea* (1961; Contemporary Spanish Poetry) and *Poesía española del '98 y del '27* (1968; Spanish Poetry of the 1898 and 1927 Generations)—and numerous essays and translations, Zardoya is principally a poet, having published eighteen volumes of poetry and received various prizes: Premio Accésit Adonais in 1947 for *Dominio del llanto* (Domain of the Mournful Cry), Accésit del Ifach de Poesía in 1952 for *Los Signos* (The Signs), Premio Boscán in 1955 for *Debajo de la luz* (Beneath the Light—not published until 1959), Premio Fémina de Poesía in 1975 for *El corazón y la sombra* (Heart and Shadow), and Premio Esquío de Poesía in 1983 for *Manhattan y otras latitudes* (Manhattan and Other Latitudes), her most recent prize. Typical poetry themes include illumination of art and poetry, Spain, the Negro, social awareness, and solitude. Attentive to technical crafting, Zardoya continues to write and participate in literary events.

BIBLIOGRAPHY

Primary Texts

Corral de vivos y muertos. Buenos Aires: Losada, 1965.

Debajo de la luz. Barcelona: Instituto de Estudios Hispánicos, 1959.

Los Engaños de Tremont. Colección Agora. Madrid: Alfaguara, 1971.

Hondo Sur. Colección El Bardo. Madrid: Editorial Ciencia Nueva, 1968.

Pájaros del nuevo mundo. Adonais 27. Madrid: Hispánica Adonais, 1946.

Criticism

Sin Nombre 9.3 (n.d.): 32–113. Essays on Zardoya by Ciplijauskaité, Paraíso de Leal, and Manuel Durán.

Women Writers of Spain: An Annotated Bio-Bibliography. Westport, CT: Greenwood Press, 1986.

Joy Buckles Landeira

ZARZUELA, a type of theatrical work alternating music with spoken parts. The name derives from the location where they first were presented for Philip IV—the Real Sitio de la Zarzuela (Royal Site of Zarzuela). With antecedents in the sixteenth-c. **entremés*, **égloga*, and **jácara* (which all included music as an essential feature), the genre flourished under *Calderón, its creator. In a desire to surprise a king fully familiar with four decades of theater, Calderón reduced the customary number of acts from three to two, and alternated music with recitative (thereby greatly increasing the importance of music to the work). The first work was probably *El jardín de Falerina* (1648; Falerina's Garden); it met with great enthusiasm and so was followed with ones such as the two-act *El laurel de Apolo* (1658; Apollo's Laurel) and the one-act *La púrpura de la rosa* (1660; The Purple of Rose). Often performed outdoors, the *zarzuela* was stylized, allegorical, elaborate and thus expensive, occasional in nature, and tailored more to an aristocratic audience.

The *zarzuela* flourished in the eighteenth c.—many were written between 1700 and 1757—still following the precepts of Calderón. Around 1730 an Italian influence appears, as "comedias de música" (music plays) begin to compete with and squeeze out the *zarzuela*. French influences also surface.

In the nineteenth c. the *zarzuela* enjoyed a second flowering. Two types of *zarzuela* developed: (1) a longer, three-act composition, dubbed the *zarzuela grande*, and (2) a one-act piece, called the **género chico*. Dance became an integral feature as well. Some outstanding practitioners after Calderón include *Bances Candamo, Ramón de la *Cruz, José *Picón, *Bretón de los Herreros, and, in the twentieth c., Manuel de Falla.

BIBLIOGRAPHY

Criticism

Bussey, W. *French and Italian Influence on the zarzuela; 1700–1770.* Ann Arbor, MI: UMI Research P, 1982.

Cotareli y Mori, A. "Ensayo histórico sobre la zarzuela." *BRAE* 19 (1932): 625 and ss.; 20 (1933): 97 and ss.; 21 (1934) ss.

James, B. *Manuel de Falla and the Spanish Musical Renaissance.* London: Golancz, 1979.

Maureen Ihrie

ZAYAS, Antonio de (1871, Madrid–1941, Madrid). A titled nobleman (Duke of Amalfi) with literary inclinations, he was associated with Antonio *Machado in turn-of-the-century intellectual and literary circles. He experimented with modernist poetry, but without really abandoning the traditional tone and methods of Spanish poetry. Among his books are *Joyeles bizantinos* (1902; Byzantine Jewelry-Boxes) and *Reliquias* (Relics). He also published a volume of essays, *Ensayos de crítica histórica y literaria* (1907; Essays of Historical and Literary Criticism).

ZAYAS Y SOTOMAYOR, María de (1590, Madrid–1661?, Madrid?), writer. The first Spanish woman novelist, she is also one of the few in her day who did not belong to a religious order. Very little biographical information exists other than her date and place of birth. Her family belonged to the upper class, which allowed doña María to pursue her career in literature. No documents indicate whether she ever married, or exactly when she died.

She wrote one play, *La traición en la amistad* (Treachery in Friendship), but is primarily known for two novels: *Novelas amorosas y ejemplares* (1637; Amorous and Exemplary Tales) and *Desengaños amorosos* (1647; Disillusion in Love). Both works employ the same structure as Boccaccio's *Decameron*; several men and women have gathered together to tell stories, both for entertainment and to convey a message. Most characters from the first novel reappear in the second, with a few new characters. While the theme of the first work is love and that of the second is disillusion, continuity is achieved through the protagonist, Lisis, who hosts both novels and develops her own situation involving two suitors.

Novelas amorosas takes place on five nights during the Christmas season, and both men and women tell stories. Lisis has been courted by don Juan, but he has recently rejected her for another woman in the group. To satisfy her need for revenge, Lisis accepts don Diego as her fiance, and they announce their engagement. *Desengaños* occurs during the days.

As critics note, Zayas is unique for her time in her presentation of a woman's point of view of many circumstances. For instance, the convent is seen as a refuge in many stories because there women can take charge and perform useful tasks. Critics have debated whether Zayas can be considered a feminist; there is no doubt that the protagonist of the prose works is a militant feminist, stating that women should not be deprived of education in the arts and in weapons. While it has been argued that Lisis does not necessarily speak for the author, it cannot be denied that María de Zayas was an educated woman in an age when most women were not, and that she wrote and published two novels in an era when literature was dominated by men. That in itself is an act of feminism, giving María de Zayas y Sotomayor a place of supreme importance not only in Spanish literature but in the history of women's studies as well.

BIBLIOGRAPHY

Primary Texts

Novelas amorosas y ejemplares. Ed. and prol. A. de Amezúa. Madrid: RAE, 1948.

Parte segunda del Sarao y entretenimiento honesto: desengaños amorosos. Madrid: Cátedra, 1983.

English Translation

A Shameful Revenge and Other Stories. Tr. J. Starrock. London: Folio, 1963.

Criticism

Foa, S. "María de Zayas y Sotomayor: Sibyl of Madrid (Spanish, 1590–1661?)." In *Female Scholars: A Tradition of Learned Women before 1800*. Ed. J. R. Brink. Montreal: Eden, 1980. 54–67.

Stackhouse, K. "Verisimilitude, Magic and the Supernatural in the Novels of María de Sayas y Sotomayor." *Hispanófila* 62 (1978): 65–76.

Vasileski, I. V. *María de Zayas y Sotomayor: Su época y su obra*. Madrid: Playor, 1973.

Nina Shecktor

ZEA, Francisco (1825, Madrid–1857, Madrid), poet. Zea's father, a master of arms in the royal court, inculcated in his son a taste for the poetry of *Garcilaso de la Vega, Fernando de *Herrera, and Fray Luis de *León. Reduced to poverty by his father's death, Zea was forced to give fencing lessons to make a living, and he later received a minor government job. Nevertheless, he died at the age of thirty-two due to poor health. During his short lifetime, Zea edited the newspapers *El Observador* (The Observer), *El Orden* (Order), and *El Panorama* (The Panorama) and contributed to the *Semanario Pintoresco Español* (Picturesque Spanish Weekly), using the pseudonyms El Lazarillo de Tormes and El bachiller Sansón Carrasco (a character from *Cervantes's *Quijote*). His literary works were posthumously arranged and edited by his friends as *Obras en verso y prosa* (1858; Works in Prose and Poetry). Zea also produced several works for the theater, among them *La batalla de Clavijo* (1847; The Battle of Clavijo) and *Noche y día de aventuras, o Los galanes duendes* (1848; Night and Day of Adventures, or The Ghostly Gallants).

BIBLIOGRAPHY

Primary Texts

La batalla de Clavijo. Madrid: Luneta, 1847.
Noche y día de aventuras, o Los galanes duendes. Madrid: n.p., 1848.
Obras en verso y prosa. Madrid: Nacional, 1858.

Criticism

Cejador y Frauca, Julio. *Historia de la lengua y literatura castellana*. vol. 7. Madrid: RABM, 1917.

Linda Maier

ZÉJEL. The *zéjel*, like the *muwashshaḥ* to which it bears a strong resemblance, is a strophic poem which originated in Islamic Spain and flourished there during the Almoravid period. An essential difference between the *zéjel* and the *muwashshaḥ* is linguistic: the *zéjel* is written in colloquial rather than classical Arabic. The notion that its inventor was the blind poet Muqaddam of Cabra is no longer accepted. In any case, it was Ibn Quzmán (?1078–1160?) who perfected the form. Samuel Stern distinguished between two types of *zéjel*: the "*muwashshaḥ*-like *zéjel*" and the *zéjel* proper. The *zéjel* proper has three components: (1) a prelude, usually of two verses (Spanish = *estribillo*; Arabic = *maṭla'*); (2) a rhyming tercet (Spanish = *mudanza*; Arabic = aghsān); and (3) a refrain or *volta* (Spanish = *vuelta*; Arabic = *simṭ*), which repeats only half of the prelude. The general scheme of the typical *zéjel* is therefore: *AA bbbA cccA dddA*, etc., or *AB bbbA cccA dddA*, etc. There were several variations of this form. The *zéjel*, unlike the *muwashshaḥ*, was not limited by a traditional number of strophes (five or six). The origins and influence of the *zéjel* are considered to be intimately related to early Romance lyric poetry; variations of the *zéjel* are found in the French *virelais*, the Italian *ballate* and *laude*, and the Galician *cantigas* of *Alphonse X the Learned. The popularity and expansion of the *zéjel* made it subject to modifications, as seen, for example, in the *Libro de Buen Amor* by the *Arcipreste de Hita.

BIBLIOGRAPHY

Primary Text

Libro de Buen Amor. By Juan Ruiz. Ed., intro., and English paraphrase by R. S. Willis. Princeton: Princeton UP, 1972.

Criticism

Menéndez Pidal, Ramón. *Poesía arabe y poesía europea*. 5th ed. Madrid: Espasa-Calpe, 1963.

Nykl, A. R. *Hispano-Arabic Poetry and Its Relations with the Old Provençal Troubadours*. Baltimore: J. H. Furst, 1946.

Stern, Samuel. *Hispano-Arabic Strophic Poetry*. Ed. L. P. Harvey. Oxford: Oxford UP, 1974.

Porter Conerly

ZORRILLA, José (1817, Valladolid–1893, Madrid), Romantic poet and dramatist. José Zorrilla was a complete unknown in February 1837, when he stepped out in front of a gathering of Madrid's leading intellectuals to read his poem ''Ese vago clamor'' (That Errant Plaint) commemorating the recent suicide of Mariano José de *Larra. The listeners were stunned by the poem's depth of feeling, beauty and sensitivity. Zorrilla left the funeral a famous man. He became—and was to remain—the most popular writer of his time.

Zorrilla's fame as a Romantic dramatist rests primarily on *Don Juan Tenorio* (1844; *Don Juan Tenorio*, 1944), but his *Romanticism is radically different from that of Larra or *Espronceda. It is the heroic Romanticism of *Durán and *Rivas, who longed for the return to the chivalric, Christian and monarchical ways of the past. Zorrilla's flirtations with the despairingly rebellious brand of Romanticism was brief.

Born in Valladolid in 1817, Zorrilla was the only child of an exceedingly conservative family. His father worked enthusiastically for Ferdinand VII, rising to become the chief of police of the state, and ending up supporting Larra's abhorred Carlist faction. Zorrilla studied in Madrid at the Real Semanario de Nobles from 1827 to 1833, and then spent two years studying law at the Universities of Toledo and Valladolid, where he met several of the youths who would be his friends for life—Miguel de los Santos *Alvarez, Pedro de Madrazo and Enrique *Gil y Carrasco. But the adolescent Zorrilla found life under the eye of his domineering father too difficult, so in the summer of 1836 he escaped to Madrid, leaving his family and his studies behind. His stunning entrance into Madrid's literary world in 1837 gained him immediate access to writers and publishers: he was befriended by *Hartzenbusch, Espronceda, Ventura de la *Vega, *García Gutiérrez, and others; he published his first volume, *Poesías* (1837; Poetry); and he began to write for newspapers. Within two years, three more volumes of poetry reached the public to general acclaim.

His marriage in 1839 to a woman sixteen years his senior was sudden and only briefly happy. Florentina O'Reilly's jealousy and inability to adjust to

Zorrilla's artistic world turned their relationship sour. Zorrilla later claimed that his frequent trips out of the capital were pretexts to get away from her.

Zorrilla's first staged drama, *Juan Dándolo* (1839; John Dandolo), written in collaboration with García Gutiérrez, was awarded a tepid reception, but more plays followed. *Cada cual con su razón* (1839; Everyone Has His Reasons) and *Lealtad de una mujer aventuras de una noche* (1840; A Woman's Loyalty and a Night's Adventure) received equally indifferent attention. When *El zapatero y el rey* (1840; The Cobbler and the King) appeared, however, it caused a mild sensation, and gave Zorrilla, heretofore acclaimed solely as a poet, renown as a dramatist. Two years later, he wrote a second part to *El zapatero y el rey* (1842), earning himself a handsome sum of money along with fame; and his writing activities increased. His prolific pen produced more narrative and lyric verses, rewrites of Golden Age plays, circumstantial one-acters, and several original dramas, including *El eco del torrente* (1842; The Echo of the Torrent); *Los dos virreyes* (1842; The Two Viceroys); *Un año y un día* (1842; A Year and a Day); *Sancho García* (1842); *El puñal del godo* (1843; *The Dagger of the Goth*, 1929); *El molino de Guadalajara* (1843; The Windmill of Guadalajara); and *El caballo del rey don Sancho* (1843, King Sancho's Horse). He received the Cross of Charles III, a prestigious honor granted by the queen in 1843.

Most of Zorrilla's fame rests on the play produced on March 28, 1844. Even though *Don Juan Tenorio* enjoyed only a modest reception, and even though Zorrilla had harsh words to say about it later in his life, it is the play most closely associated with him. It is a work of astonishing lyrical beauty which strikes resonant chords in the religious, middle-class audiences which still flock to it. Zorrilla claims to have written it in three weeks, basing it vaguely on *Tirso de Molina's *El burlador de Sevilla*. When it was finished he sold the rights quickly and very cheaply, a mistake which he came to regret. This "religious-fantastic drama" (as the subtitle describes it) deals with Don Juan Tenorio's cynical seduction and abandonment of Doña Inés, who returns from the grave to intercede with Don Juan and help him gain God's eternal love. Juan, having witnessed a sample of Hell's horrors during his dinner with the statue of Don Gonzalo (Inés's father, whom he had murdered), accepts God's grace and earns eternal life. Zorrilla creates a rebellious Romantic character in the play's first part, only to change him into the very embodiment of bourgeois conformity in the second. Therein lies *Don Juan Tenorio's* greatest strengths—the universality of the theme, the mythical hero—and its greatest weakness—the rejection of Romantic ideals.

Soon after the debut of *Don Juan Tenorio*, Zorrilla traveled to Granada to collect material for his narrative poem, *Granada* (published in 1852), and to visit with Rivas. *La copa de marfil* (1844; The Ivory Chalice) was staged in Madrid, and another collection of poems, *Recuerdos y fantasías* (1844; Memories and Fantasies), appeared. One year later, two more books of poems came out, and additional dramas were staged in Madrid. In that year, 1845, he took his first trip to France and became acquainted in Paris with George Sand, Musset and Gautier, only to be called back to Spain in early 1846 by his mother's death. This tragedy solidified the relationship between Zorrilla and his father, who since the 1830s had actively disdained his son's literary career, causing a near-total estrangement. Many more plays followed: *El rey loco* (1847; The Crazy King); *La reina y los favoritos* (1847; The Queen and Her Favorites); *La calentura* (1847; The Fever, the second part of *El puñal del godo*); *El excomulgado* (1848; The Excommunicant), etc. He was elected to the *Academia Española in 1848.

One of Zorrilla's best dramas, *Traidor, inconfeso y mártir* (1849; Traitor, Unconfessed, and Martyr), was successfully produced in Madrid in 1849. This play, the author's own favorite, deals with the historical-legendary exploits of the Portuguese King Sebastian, whose mysterious death caused a number of impostors to come forward to claim his throne. In Zorrilla's version, Gabriel de Espinosa, a pastry cook from Madrigal, is the king, who had not died but had gone into seclusion after Spain's annexation of Portugal. He is not believed, of course, and is executed as an impostor. Zorrilla's treatment of the story, with his original perspective and dramatic portrayal of a humane, sensitive and valiant hero, is excellent.

Notwithstanding Zorrilla's prolific production and tremendous popular success, he was often short of cash. Even the great reception accorded the publication of *Granada* did little to alleviate his financial troubles. He had returned to Paris in 1850, but by 1854 he had decided to emigrate to Mexico, where he took up residence for twelve years. His fame, the generosity of the company he kept, and a few publications kept him relatively satisfied. The arrival of Emperor Maximilian in 1864 heightened Zorrilla's fortunes, for he was named to several government posts. The new Palace Theater was innaugurated in 1864 with a presentation of *Don Juan Tenorio*.

By 1866 he had little left to do in Mexico, and he decided to go back to Spain. His return was a cause for national jubilation, and everywhere he went he was heaped with praise and honors. He wrote an autobiographical poem, *Album de un loco* (1867; A Crazy Man's Album), followed by *El drama del alma* (1867; The Soul's Play), a poetic history of the Mexican Empire of Maximilian, stimulated by the news of Maximilian's execution. A widower since 1865, in 1869 Zorrilla married a girl of twenty, Juana Pacheco. Other plays followed, but still in economic difficulty, the author soon accepted Juan *Valera's suggestion that he go to Italy to do some research for the Spanish government. He disliked the work but needed the pension, so he and his new wife spent three years in Italy, moving to France in 1874, and finally returning to Madrid in 1876. The pension stopped. A religious drama, *Pilatos* (1877; Pilate), increased his already considerable fame, as did the new musical version of *Don Juan Tenorio* he produced that same year (1877), but his need for money forced from him constant entreaties to the government. When the newspaper *El Imparcial* (The Impartial) offered him a good price for his memoirs, he began to publish the interesting and valuable *Recuerdos del tiempo viejo* (collected in book form in 1880–82; Memories of Old Times). He began to travel around Spain, giving poetry readings and seeing to the publication of new works, tasks which were both disagreeable to him and exhausting. Finally, he settled down in Valladolid in 1885. There, the city inaugurated a theater in his name and opened it with a production of his beloved *Traidor, inconfeso y mártir*. The Spanish Royal Academy invited him to deliver the formal acceptance speech he had never given; his discourse in verse was well received. Zorrilla's last public honor was the triumphant celebration staged for him in Granada in 1889—he was crowned as a national poet.

That year, claiming that he was already on government pension (he was, but it was a paltry sum), Valladolid revoked the small pension it had granted him. He moved back to Madrid, where he spent his last four years. Old and worn out from his constant financial difficulties, he died in January 1893. His funeral was a national event, attended by every political and literary celebrity in the capital. His remains were moved to his hometown, Valladolid.

Zorrilla's ever-present threat of poverty forced him to write perhaps too much and too fast, dissipating his considerable poetic skills. But his tremendous energy and kind nature earned him numerous friendships. His best works are beautiful evocations of the Spanish soul, tempered with a deeply felt Christian vision which he captured with delicate artistry. His complete works were not published during his lifetime, due in part to their sheer abundance. *See also* Don Juan, Legend of.

BIBLIOGRAPHY

Primary Texts

Don Juan Tenorio. Ed. S. García Castañeda. Barcelona: Labor, 1975.

Don Juan Tenorio. Ed. Jorge Campos. Madrid: Alianza, 1985.

Don Juan Tenorio. Ed. Aniano Peña. Madrid: Cátedra, 1986.

Don Juan Tenorio. Ed. Francisco Nieva. Madrid: Espasa-Calpe, 1990.

Obras completas. 2 vols. Ed. N. Alonso Cortés. Valladolid: Santarén, 1943.

El zapatero y el rey. Ed. Jean-Louis Picoche. Madrid: Castalia, 1980.

English Translations

The Daggar of the Goth. Tr. W. K. Jones. In *Spanish One Act Plays in English*. Dallas: Tardy, 1934.

Don Juan Tenorio. Tr. W. I. Oliver. In *Spanish Plays of the Nineteenth Century*. New York: Las Americas, 1964.

Criticism

Abrams, F. "The Death of Zorrilla's Don Juan and the Problem of Catholic Orthodoxy." *RN* 6 (1964): 42–46.

Alonso Cortés, N. *Zorrilla. Su vida y sus obras*. Valladolid: Santarén, 1943.

Feal, C. "Conflicting Names, Conflicting Laws: Zorrilla's *Don Juan Tenorio*." *PMLA* 96 (1981): 375–87.

Gies, D. T. "José Zorrilla and the Betrayal of Spanish Romanticism." *Romanistische Jahrbuch* 31 (1980): 339–46.

Leslie, J. K. "Towards the Vindication of Zorrilla: The Dumas-Zorrilla Question Again." *HR* 13 (1945): 288–93.

Pérez Firmat, G. "Carnaval in *Don Juan Tenorio*." *HR* 51 (1983): 269–81.
Sánchez, R. "Between Macías and Don Juan: Spanish Romantic Drama and the Mythology of Love." *HR* 44 (1976): 27–44.
Singer, A. E. *The Don Juan Theme. Versions and Criticism. A Bibliography*. Morgantown: West Virginia U, 1965.
ter Horst, R. "Ritual Time Regained in Zorrilla's *Don Juan Tenorio*." *RR* 70 (1979): 80–93.

David Thatcher Gies

ZOZAYA, Antonio (1859, Madrid–1940, Madrid), Spanish journalist, playwright and novelist. Dramatic works include *Cuando los hijos lloran* (n.d.; When Children Cry), while novels are *La noche grande* (The Big Night), *La bala fría* (The Cold Bullet), *La maldita culpa* (1915; The Damnable Guilt), etc. He also attempted poetry in *Poemas de humildad y de ensueños* (1914; Poems of Humility and Daydreams), and brief fiction in *Cuentos y escenas que no son de amores* (1919; Stories but not of Love). As a thinker influenced by *Krausism and *Sanz del Río, he wrote the philosophical essay *La crisis religiosa* (1891; Religious Crisis) and the tangentially related essay, *La guerra de las ideas* (1915; The War of Ideas). He was the founder of the publishing series Biblioteca Económica Filosófica (Economical Philosophical Library) in 1980.

ZUBIRI APALÁTEGUI, Xavier (1898, San Sebastián–1983, Madrid) philosopher, lecturer and teacher. The influence that Zubiri has exerted on writers and intellectuals cannot be overstated. Even when he ceased teaching at the U of Madrid, he held court, as it were, and eminent thinkers, Pedro *Laín Entralgo and Luis Felipe *Vivanco among them, subscribed to the lecture series that featured the philosophical teaching of Zubiri. Thus, it can be said that Zubiri attracted disciples in and out of the classroom. The master, himself, was a brilliant student of *Ortega and Heidegger. A doctor of philosophy by the time he was twenty-one, his dissertation on phenomenology caused a sensation in Spain. His first major work as an already recognized philosopher, *Naturaleza, Historia, Dios* (1944; Nature, History, God), still reigns as a supreme reference for the material in question.

BIBLIOGRAPHY

Primary Texts

Inteligencia sentiente. Madrid: Alianza, Sociedad de Estudios y Publicaciones, 1980.
Naturaleza, Historia, Dios. Madrid: Nacional, 1944.
Sobre la esencia. Madrid: Alianza, Sociedad de Estudios y Publicaciones, 1980.

English Translations

On essence. Tr. and intro A. Robert Caponigri. Washington: Catholic U of America P, 1980.

Criticism

Aranguren, José Luis, and others. *Homenaje a Xavier Zubiri*. Madrid: Revista Alcalá, 1953.

Garagorri, Paulino. *Unamuno, Ortega, Zubiri en la filosofía española*. Madrid: Plenitud, 1968.

Santamarta, Ceferino Martínez. *El hombre y Dios en Xavier Zubiri*. Salamanca: Biblioteca de la Caja de Ahorros y Monte de Piedad, Edición Universidad, 1981.

Robert Kirsner

ZULUETA, Luis de (1878, Barcelona–1964, New York), Catalan professor, politician and essayist. He belonged to that small but significant group of Spaniards of the period formed in their early years by the Jesuits, and then by foreign universities (Berlin and Paris). Following terms in the Spanish parliament between 1910 and the beginning of the dictatorship of Primo de Rivera in 1923, he was very active in the formation and government of the Republic; he was secretary of state (1931–33) and ambassador to Berlin and Rome. In 1937 he went into exile to Colombia where he helped found the U of the Andes, and lived his last years in New York and Geneva. Active in contributing to magazines such as *Ortega's *Revista de Occidente*, he also wrote the following: *La edad heroica* (1916; The Heroic Age), *La Oración del incrédulo* (1920; The Prayer of the Unbeliever), and *El rapto de América* (1952; The Kidnapping of America).

BIBLIOGRAPHY

Primary Texts

La edad heroica. 4th ed. Madrid: Fortanet, 1916.

El rapto de America. Buenos Aires: Sudamérica, 1952.

Stephen Miller

ZÚÑIGA, Francesillo de (1490?, Béjar–1532, Navarredonda), court jester to Charles V, author of a scandalous chronicle. It is thought that Zúñiga, originally a poor tailor, served the Duke of Béjar. He incurred the favor of Charles V with his sardonic wit and was brought to court as his jester. Zúñiga's *Corónica istoria* (1527; Historical Chronicle) contrasts with the heroic and solemn accounts of official chroniclers. The work begins with the death of Ferdinand and presents a highly selective burlesque catalog of the figures in the court of Charles V. He satirizes even the most eminent courtiers, occasionally comparing them to animals. The *picaresque tone of the work is most entertaining, and attests to Zúñiga's striking talent. The popularity of the chronicle is demonstrated by the existence of more than twenty surviving mss.—but the work was not published until 1855 by the *Biblioteca de Autores Españoles. Zúñiga later fell into disfavor in 1529 and retired to Navarredonda, where he was killed by an assassin, probably hired by one of the courtiers portrayed in the chronicle. Melchor de *Santa Cruz recounts an amusing anecdote about Zúñiga's death in the *Floresta española de apotegmas y sentencias*.

BIBLIOGRAPHY

Primary Texts

Crónica burlesca del emperador Carlos V. Ed., intro., notes, Diane Pamp de Avalle-Arce. Barcelona: Crítica, 1981.

Don Francesillo de Zúñiga: Cartas inéditas. Ed. J. Menéndez Pidal. RABM 20 (1909): 182–99 and 21 (1909): 72–95. Includes study.

Criticism

González Palencia, A. "El Mayorazgo de Don Francesillo de Zúñiga." In *Del "Lazarillo" a Quevedo, estudios histórico-literarios.* Madrid: CSIC, 1946.

Deborah Compte

ZÚÑIGA, Juan Eduardo (1919, Madrid–), Spanish novelist and short story writer. He began as a story writer for various magazines, later collecting a selection of them in volume form in *Inútiles totales* (Totally Useless). His novel *El Coral y las Aguas* (1962; The Coral and the Waters) is set in the Greece of Alexander the Great, but is not a historical novel; instead, through parallels and suggested analogy, it treats a contemporary problem.

ZÚÑIGA Y ÁVILA, Luis de (1510?, Plasencia–1573, Plasencia), courtier and chronicler. Son of the Count of Risco, Zúñiga was a close friend of Charles V, and accompanied him on military campaigns to Tunis (1535) and Germany (1546–47). Appointed ambassador to Rome in 1539, he maintained friendships with Italian and Spanish writers of the period (Tasso, Aretino, *Hurtado de Mendoza). From his experiences in Germany he wrote the historical work *Comentario de la guerra de Alemania* (1548; Commentary on the German War). When Charles retired to Yuste, Zúñiga returned to Plasencia, although he accompanied the king at the time of his death. Zúñiga also served Philip II as a negotiator in Rome for the prosecution of the Tridentine Council.

BIBLIOGRAPHY

Primary Text

Comentario de la guerra de Alemania. BAE 21.

Criticism

González Palencia, A. *Don Luis de Zúñiga y Avila Gentilhombre de Carlos V.* Madrid: Maestre, 1932.

Deborah Compte

ZUNZUNEGUI, Juan Antonio de (1901, Portugalete-Vizcaya–), Basque novelist and short story writer. At age twenty-five Zunzunegui, the son of wealthy parents, privately published his first book, *Vida y paisaje de Bilbao* (1926; Life and Landscape of Bilbao), a collection of tales of local customs and manners, a harbinger of his later extensive narrative production. His first long novel, *Chiripi* (1931; alias of the principal character, Jose Gómez, a football player), effectively re-creates the atmosphere, life and customs of Bilbao as they relate to football but essentially fails as a novel. His second long novel, *El chiplichandle* (1940; popular corruption of "The Ship-Chandler") portrays life among the sailors of Bilbao and is a vast improvement over the earlier novel. Alborg calls it one of the best Spanish novels ever written "of marine environment"

(150). Though subtitled ''Picaresque Action,'' the work's links to the Spanish *picaresque tradition are, according to Valbuena Prat (13), limited to its social background presented as ''realism of customs,'' and as the objective product of the author's social observation.

In *La quiebra* (1947; The Bankruptcy) Zunzunegui has depicted the business and industrial world of Bilbao, an environment which he knew intimately through his family and through a stint of work in business circles. Alborg appraises it as ''a real 'human comedy' of all of a society during some significant years, not only for the Bilbaoan region but for the Spanish nation'' (164). Another long novel in a similar vein, *La úlcera* (1947; The Ulcer), won for the author Spain's National Literary Prize awarded in 1948.

Having moved to Madrid, Zunzunegui published *El supremo bien* (1951; The Supreme Good), the first of a series of long novels which have the Spanish capital rather than Bilbao as their social context. Thus his novelistic production falls into two divisions: novels set in or near Bilbao and those which portray life in Madrid, much as do the novels of Pío *Baroja. Belonging to the Madrid series and generally regarded as Zunzunegui's very best novel to date is *Una mujer sobre la tierra* (1959; A Woman on Earth). Its action revolving around a peasant woman, Matildona, a *portera* or doorkeeper to a government apartment building, mirrors the society of post–Civil War Madrid somewhat like *Cela's *The Hive*. It was followed by other novels: *El mundo sigue* (1960; Life Goes On), *El premio* (1961; The Prize), *El camino alegre* (1962; The Happy Way), *Don Isidoro . . . y sus límites* (1963; Don Isidoro . . . and His Limits), *La hija malograda* (1973; The Wasted Daughter), and others. All the titles just given are of long novels, or as Zunzunegui insists on calling them, ships of ''great tonnage,'' as opposed to his shorter books of ''pequeño tonelaje'' (little tonnage). Most noteworthy of the books of little tonnage are the five ''ships'' launched in his series *Cuentos y patrañas de mi ría* (Stories and Fakes from My Estuary), which he began in 1935 with *Tres en una o la dichosa honra* (Three in One or Lucky Honor).

Not in number of titles but in sheer number of pages or extent, Zunzunegui is the most prolific Spanish novelist of the post–Civil War period. Possessing his own style, he has largely ignored the latest literary fashions and followed in the long tradition of the realistic novel in Spain—*Cervantes, the picaresque novel, the novel of customs, *Pérez Galdós, and Baroja. Exceptions to this stance of objective realism are found occasionally in his longer novels but most notably in some of his shorter works in which he has experimented with an amalgamation of realism and fantasy, for example, in the series, Stories and Fakes from My Estuary. In April of 1957, about six months after Baroja's death, Zunzunegui was elected to occupy the seat in the *Academia Española formerly held by Baroja. ''For me,'' he wrote in 1958, ''the best writer, narrative writer, I do not mean novelist, of Spanish literature today, is don Pío Baroja'' (*Mis páginas preferidas* [Madrid: Gredos, 1958], 9). Using the technique of personal biography, Zunzunegui's novels follow a linear, somewhat episodic, structure around which revolve numerous secondary characters or types, each with the drama of his or her own life. The whole becomes a "world," which in turn generates its own moral climate, a climate which mirrors grave defects in Spanish life, much as do the novels of Baroja. Noteworthy in Zunzunegui's style are his imaginative use of metaphors, his neologisms and playful use of language, and his heavy dependence upon dialogue. A defect is excessive repetition, a failure to economize. Prominent themes are the isolation or loneliness of the individual in today's society, the moral failure or ineffectiveness of much of Spanish Catholicism, the conflict of generations, sex, the dehumanization of the individual, and the superiority of country life over life in the city.

As a youth Zunzunegui studied at a *lycée* in Tours, France. Later he attended the U of Deusto in Bilbao, the U of Perugia in Italy, and the U of Salamanca. At the last institution he studied under *Unamuno, who inspired him to a lasting admiration for Portuguese literature, especially the works of Camilo Castello Branco, Guerra Junqueior, and Eça de Queiroz.

BIBLIOGRAPHY

Primary Texts

Obras completas de Juan Antonio de Zunzunegui. 7 vols. Barcelona: Noguer, 1969–75.

Criticism

Alborg, Juan Luis. *Hora actual de la novela española*. Madrid: Taurus, 1962. 2: 137–85.

Carbonell Basset, Delfín. *La novelística de Juan Antonio de Zunzunegui*. Madrid: "Dos Continentes," 1965.

Ilie, Paul. "Zunzunegui y la nueva moral española." *Cuadernos Americanos* 16 (n.d.): 217–34.

[Pérez], Janet Winecoff. "The Twentieth-Century Picaresque Novel and Zunzunegui's *La vida como es*." *Romance Notes* 7.2 (1966): 108–13.

Tamayo, Juan A. "Prólogo" to *Obras completas de Juan Antonio de Zunzunegui*. Barcelona: Noguer, 1971. 3: 7–43.

Valbuena Prat, Angel. "Prólogo" to *Obras Completas de Juan Antonio de Zunzunegui*. Barcelona: Noguer, 1969. 1: 7–68.

Charles King

ZURITA, Jerónimo de (c. 1512, Béjar–1580, Navarredonda), historian. Zurita is considered one of the founders of modern Spanish historiography. Son of a physician at the courts of Ferdinand and Charles V, he was educated at the U of Alcalá. In 1548 he was appointed first chronicler of Aragón and also served as secretary to Philip II. In his travels to Germany and Italy, he conducted extensive research in the archives, and also compiled a splendid private library, which is now in the Escorial Library.

Zurita dedicated himself to the conscientious collection and critical examination of data, and it is this task which distinguished him from previous historians. His six-volume *Anales de la Corona de Aragón* (1562–80; Annals of the Crown of Aragon) is the culmination of nearly thirty years of investigative effort.

With scientific vigor, he records data culled from his extensive research of contemporary documents. The *Anales* recount Aragon's history from the Arab invasion in 711 to the death of Ferdinand in 1516 with exacting meticulousness. Although criticized by Alonso de *Santa Cruz, the *Anales* was defended by Juan Pérez de Castro and Ambrosio de *Morales, the chronicler of Castile. Zurita's successor was the poet Bartolomé Leonardo de *Argensola, who narrated the events of 1516–20.

BIBLIOGRAPHY

Primary Texts

Anales de la Corona de Aragón. In *Las Glorias Nacionales*. Barcelona: L. Tasso, 1852–54. 4:1–908.

Anales de la Corona de Aragón. Ed. A. Canellas López. 8 vols. Zaragoza: Fernando el Católico, 1967–77.

Progresos de la historia en Aragón y vidas de sus cronistas. By J. F. Uztarroz. Zaragoza: Hospicio, 1878 (rpt. of 1680 ed.).

Criticism

Canellas López, Angel. *Fuentes de Zurita, documentos de la alacena del cronista, relativos a los años 1302–1478*. Zaragoza: Fernando el Católico, 1974.

Deborah Compte

ZURITA, Marciano (1887, Palencia–1929, Madrid), Spanish journalist and essayist. An assiduous collaborator of such major Madrid dailies as *ABC* and the weekly *Blanco y negro*, he dabbled in poetry, writing modernist verse in which the influence of Antonio *Machado has been perceived, together with that of the early Juan Ramón *Jiménez. Among his books are *El tiempo del silencio* (Time of Silence), *La musa campesina* (The Country Muse), *Castilla*, and the critical-bibliographical study, *Historia anecdótica del género chico* (1920; Anecdotal History of the One-Act Play).

ZURITA Y HARO, Fernando Jacinto (seventeenth c., ?–?), novelist. Following the lead of *Alcalá y Herrera, he authored a novel in which one vowel, here the letter *a*, is suppressed throughout.

BIBLIOGRAPHY

Primary Text

Méritos disponen premios. Madrid: Díaz de la Carrera, 1654.

Index